# A-Z SUPER SCA

# GREAT BRITAIN NORTHERN IRELAND

GW01393032

## Journey Route Planning maps

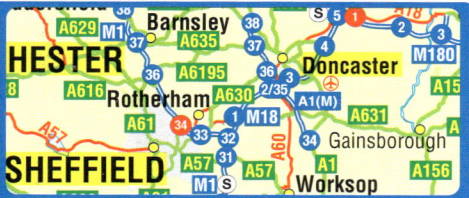

## Britain & Northern Ireland Road maps

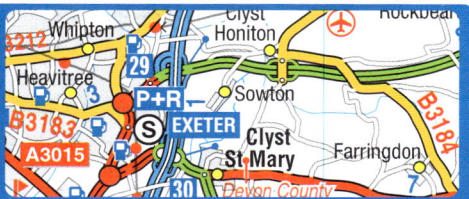

## Detailed Main Route maps

## City and Town centre maps

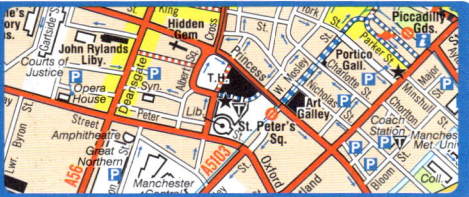

## Sea Port & Channel Tunnel plans

## Airport plans

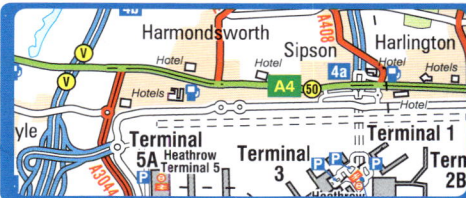

## Over 32,000 Index References

| A | |
|---|---|
| Abbas Combe. *Som* ..........4C 22 | Abersoch. *Gwyn* ..........3C |
| Abberley. *Worc* ..........4B 60 | Abersychan. *Torf* ..........5F |
| Abberley Common. *Worc* ..4B 60 | **Abertawe**. *Swan* |
| Abberton. *Essx* ..........4D 54 | ..........3F 31 & Swansea 2 |
| Abberton. *Worc* ..........5D 61 | Aberteifi. *Cdgn* ..........1B |
| Abberwick. *Nmbd* ..........3F 121 | Aberthin. *V Glam* ..........4D |
| Abbess Roding. *Essx* ......4F 53 | **Abertillery**. *Blae* ..........5F |
| Abbey. *Devn* ..........1E 13 | Abertridwr. *Cphy* ..........3E |
| | Abertridwr. *Powy* ..........4C |
| | **Abertyleri**. *Blae* ..........5F |
| | Abertysswg. *Cphy* ..........5F |

Including cities, towns, villages, hamlets and locations..........206-238

## Index to Places of Interest

| L | | |
|---|---|---|
| Lacock Abbey (SN15 2LG) ..........5E 35 | Marwood |
| Lady Lever Art Gallery (CH62 5EQ) ..........2F 83 | Mary Ard |
| Lady of the North (NE23 8AU) ..........2F 115 | Mary, Qu |
| Laing Art Gallery (NE1 8AG) ..........Newcastle 197 | Mary Ros |
| Lake District Nat. Pk. (LA9 7RL) ..........3E 103 | Max Gate |
| Lakeside & Haverthwaite Railway (LA12 3AL) ..1C 96 | Megginch |
| Lamb House (TN31 7ES) ..........3D 28 | Melbourn |
| Lamphey Bishop's Palace (SA71 5NT) ..........4E 43 | Melford H |
| | Mellersta |
| | Melrose A |
| | Manai S |

Full postcodes to easily locate popular places of interest on your SatNav ..........239-242

## Motorway Junctions

| Junction | M1 | |
|---|---|---|
| 2 | Northbound | No exit, access from A1 only |
| | Southbound | No access, exit to A1 only |
| 4 | Northbound | No exit, access from A41 only |
| | Southbound | No access, exit to A41 only |
| 6a | Northbound | No exit, access from M25 only |
| | Southbound | No access, exit to M25 only |

Details of motorway junctions with limited interchange..........243

## Safety Camera Information

Details of Safety Camera symbols used on the maps, and the responsible use of Camera information ..........Inside back cover

EDITION 26 2017

Copyright © Geographers' A-Z Map Company Ltd.

Telephone: 01732 781000 (Enquiries & Trade Sales)
01732 783422 (Retail Sales)

A-Z A-Z AtoZ
registered trade marks of Geographers' A-Z Map Company Ltd

www.az.co.uk

*Map of the Irish Sea region, Wales, south-west England and eastern Ireland*

IRISH SEA

ISLE OF MAN

REPUBLIC OF IRELAND

WALES (CYMRU)

CARDIGAN BAY

BRISTOL CHANNEL

LUNDY

ISLES OF SCILLY

LAND'S END

ENG

Major towns and cities: Monaghan, Newry, Warrenpoint, Newcastle, Carrick..., Dundalk, Kells, Navan, Drogheda, Dublin, Dun Laoghaire, Bray, Kildare, Naas, Wicklow, Carlow, Gorey, Enniscorthy, New Ross, Wexford, Rosslare Harbour, Arklow

Ramsey, Peel, Douglas, Castletown

Ravenglass, Coniston, Kendal, Kirkby Lonsdale, Settle, Barrow-in-Furness, Morecambe, Heysham, Lancaster, Fleetwood, Blackpool, Clitheroe, Colne, Preston, Blackburn, Burnley, Southport, Chorley, Darwen, Rochdale, Formby, Ormskirk, Bolton, Bury, Oldham, Wigan, St Helens, Liverpool, Wallasey, Birkenhead, Runcorn, Warrington, Stockport, Macclesfield, Northwich, Congleton

Holyhead (Caergybi), Amlwch, Llandudno, Colwyn Bay, Rhyl, Llangefni, Beaumaris, Conwy, Bangor, Caernarfon, Denbigh (Dinbych), Flint (Y Fflint), Ellesmere Port, Queensferry, Chester, Mold (Yr Wyddgrug), Ruthin (Rhuthun), Wrexham (Wrecsam), Whitchurch, Newcastle-under-Lyme, Stoke-on-Trent

Betws-y-Coed, Llan Ffestiniog, Bala (Y Bala), Llangollen, Oswestry (Croesoswallt), Ellesmere, Market Drayton, Stafford, Pwllheli, Porthmadog, Dolgellau, Barmouth (Abermaw), Welshpool (Y Trallwng), Shrewsbury, Telford, Wolverhampton, Bridgnorth, Dudley, Stourbridge, Kidderminster, Bromsgrove

Machynlleth, Newtown (Y Drenewydd), Montgomery (Trefaldwyn), Llangurig, Aberystwyth, Rhayader (Rhaeadr Gwy), Llandrindod Wells, Ludlow, Leominster, Worcester, Great Malvern, New Quay (Ceinewydd), Cardigan (Aberteifi), Lampeter (Llanbedr Pont Steffan), Llandovery (Llanymddyfri), Builth Wells (Llanfair-ym-Muallt), Brecon (Aberhonddu), Hereford, Tewkesbury, Gloucester

Fishguard (Abergwaun), St David's (Tyddewi), Carmarthen (Caerfyrddin), Llandeilo, Abergavenny (Y Fenni), Ross-on-Wye, Haverfordwest (Hwlffordd), St Clears, Merthyr Tydfil (Merthyr Tudful), Monmouth (Trefynwy), Chepstow (Cas-gwent), Stroud, Milford Haven (Aberdaugleddau), Pembroke (Penfro), Tenby (Dinbych-y-Pysgod), Llanelli, Aberdare (Aberdar), Neath (Castell-nedd), Abertillery, Pontypool (Pontypwl), Cwmbran, Swansea (Abertawe), Port Talbot, Pontypridd, Caerphilly, Newport (Casnewydd), Bristol, Malmesbury, Chippenham, Porthcawl, Bridgend (Pen-y-Bont Ar Ogwr), Cardiff (Caerdydd), Barry (Barri), Weston-super-Mare, Bath, Wells, Trowbridge, Warminster

Ilfracombe, Lynton, Minehead, Burnham-on-Sea, Glastonbury, Shepton Mallet, Frome, Barnstaple, Bideford, Bridgwater, Taunton, Yeovil, Shaftesbury, Bude, Tiverton, Chard, Blandford Forum, Okehampton, Honiton, Bridport, Dorchester, Launceston, Exeter, Sidmouth, Lyme Regis, Weymouth, Fortuneswell, Padstow, Wadebridge, Tavistock, Buckfastleigh, Newton Abbot, Newquay, Bodmin, Liskeard, Torquay, Paignton, Brixham, Dartmouth, St Austell, Looe, Saltash, Plymouth, Kingsbridge, Salcombe, St Ives, Redruth, Truro, St Just, Penzance, Helston, Falmouth

Cherbourg (proposed), Roscoff / St Malo / Santander

## REFERENCE

| | |
|---|---|
| MOTORWAY WITH NUMBER | M4 — s Service Area |
| MOTORWAY (Under Construction / Proposed) | |
| MOTORWAY JUNCTIONS | 5 — 7 Limited |
| PRIMARY ROUTE | A5 |
| A ROAD | A272 |
| NATIONAL BOUNDARY | |
| TOWNS SHOWN IN THE MILEAGE CHART | NORWICH |

SCALE

0  10  20  30 Miles

0  10  20  30  40 Kilometres

**IV**

**SCOTLAND**

NORTH SEA

Stromness
Scrabster
Thurso
John o'Groats
Tongue
Wick
Helmsdale
Scourie
Lochinver
Lairg
Bonar Bridge
Tain
Ullapool
Moray Firth
Cromarty
Lossiemouth
Banff
Fraserburgh
Poolewe
Kinlochewe
Achnasheen
Dingwall
Nairn
Elgin
Keith
Shieldaig
Strathcarron
Inverness
Dufftown
Huntly
Peterhead
Kyle of Lochalsh (Caol Loch Ailse)
Loch Ness
Grantown-on-Spey
Oldmeldrum
Inverurie
Invermoriston
Aviemore
Petercuiter
ABERDEEN
Invergarry
Newtonmore
Spean Bridge
Braemar
Ballater
Banchory
Stonehaven
Fort William
S C O T L A N D
Glencoe
Pitlochry
Brechin
Montrose
Oban
Blairgowrie
Forfar
Arbroath
Crianlarich
Dunkeld
Dundee
Carnoustie
Inveraray
Crieff
Perth
St Andrews
Lochgilphead
Doune
Dunblane
Kinross
Glenrothes
Pittenweem
Loch Lomond
Stirling
Dunfermline
Kirkcaldy
Cowdenbeath
North Berwick
Dunoon
Greenock
Clydebank
Falkirk
Firth of Forth
Dunbar
Rothesay
Paisley
GLASGOW
Airdrie
EDINBURGH
Musselburgh
Eyemouth
Largs
Hamilton
Motherwell
Livingston
Dalkeith
ISLE OF BUTE
Ardrossan
East Kilbride
Penicuik
Duns
Berwick-upon-Tweed
Irvine
Kilmarnock
Lauder
Coldstream
Prestwick
Biggar
Peebles
Galashiels
Selkirk
Kelso
Troon
Ayr
Cumnock
Hawick
Jedburgh
Wooler
ISLE OF ARRAN
Sanquhar
Moffat
Alnwick
Brodick
Girvan
New Galloway
Amble
Newton Stewart
Lockerbie
Langholm
Ashington
Morpeth
Blyth
Whitley Bay
Amsterdam
Stranraer
Dumfries
Annan
Brampton
NEWCASTLE UPON TYNE
Tynemouth
South Shields
Castle Douglas
Dalbeattie
Carlisle
Hexham
Corbridge
Gateshead
Washington
SUNDERLAND
Kirkcudbright
Consett
Seaham
Whithorn
Solway Firth
Alston
Durham
Peterlee
HARTLEPOOL
Workington
Cockermouth
Penrith
Bishop Auckland
STOCKTON-ON-TEES
Whitehaven
Keswick
Brough
Barnard Castle
Darlington
MIDDLESBROUGH
Whitby
Egremont
Ambleside
Richmond
Catterick
Ravenglass
Coniston
Windermere
Kendal
Leyburn
Northallerton

NORTH SEA

This chart shows the distance in miles and journey time between two cities or towns in Great Britain. Each route has been calculated using a combination of motorways, primary routes and other major roads. This is normally the quickest, though not always the shortest route.

Average journey times are calculated whilst driving at the maximum speed limit. These times are approximate and do not include traffic congestion or convenience breaks.

To find the distance and journey time between two cities or towns, follow a horizontal line and vertical column until they meet each other.

For example, the 285 mile journey from London to Penzance is approximately 4 hours and 59 minutes.

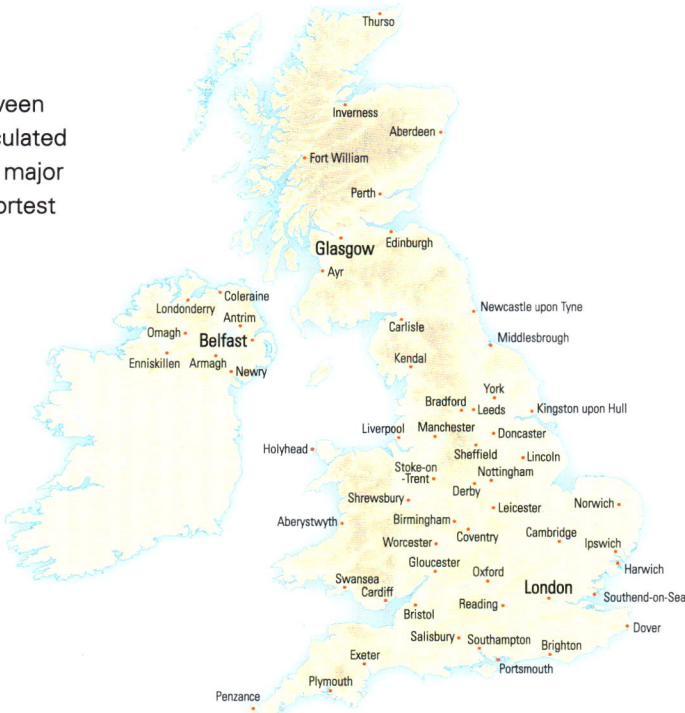

## Northern Ireland

Journey times

| | | | | | | | |
|---|---|---|---|---|---|---|---|
| Antrim | 1:01 | 0:53 | 1:41 | 1:14 | 1:07 | 1:13 | 0:30 |
| | Armagh | 1:32 | 1:06 | 1:39 | 0:31 | 0:46 | 0:57 |
| | | Coleraine | 2:09 | 0:52 | 2:00 | 1:43 | 1:11 |
| 43 | | | Enniskillen | 1:29 | 1:37 | 0:39 | 1:38 |
| 40 | 61 | | | Londonderry | 2:09 | 0:54 | 1:33 |
| 86 | 49 | 94 | | | Newry | 1:15 | 0:51 |
| 55 | 69 | 31 | 60 | | | Omagh | 1:16 |
| 53 | 19 | 92 | 69 | 88 | | | Belfast |
| 54 | 35 | 65 | 27 | 34 | 54 | | |
| 22 | 41 | 56 | 84 | 72 | 37 | 68 | |

Distance in miles

Belfast to London = 440m / 9:46h (excluding ferry)
Belfast to Glasgow = 104m / 4:46h (excluding ferry)

## Britain

Journey times

Distance in miles

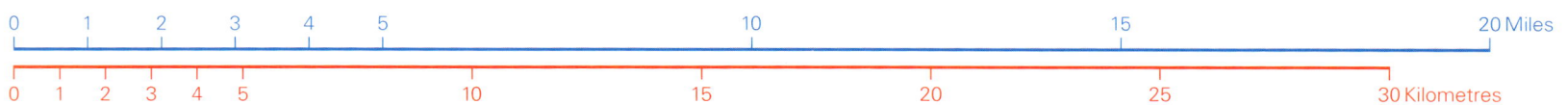

## Motorway
Autoroute
Autobahn

**M1**

## Motorway Under Construction
Autoroute en construction
Autobahn im Bau

## Motorway Proposed
Autoroute prévue
Geplante Autobahn

## Motorway Junctions with Numbers
Unlimited Interchange **4**
Limited Interchange **5**

Autoroute échangeur numéroté
Echangeur complet
Echangeur partiel

Autobahnanschlußstelle mit Nummer
Unbeschränkter Fahrtrichtungswechsel
Beschränkter Fahrtrichtungswechsel

## Motorway Service Area (with fuel station)
with access from one carriageway only

Aire de services d'autoroute (avec station service)
accessible d'un seul côté
Rastplatz oder Raststätte (mit tankstelle)
Einbahn

## Major Road Service Area (with fuel station) with 24 hour facilities
Primary Route **(S)** Class A Road **(S)**
Aire de services sur route prioritaire (avec station service) Ouverte 24h sur 24
Route à grande circulation Route de type A
Raststätte (mit tankstelle) Durchgehend geöffnet
Hauptverkehrsstraße A- Straße

## Major Road Junctions
Jonctions grands routiers
Hauptverkehrsstraße Kreuzungen

Detailed
Détaillé
Ausführlich **4**

Other Autre Andere

## Truckstop (selection of)
Sélection d'aire pour poids lourds
Auswahl von Fernfahrerrastplatz **(T)**

## Primary Route
Route à grande circulation
Hauptverkehrsstraße **A41**

## Primary Route Junction with Number
Echangeur numéroté
Hauptverkehrsstraßenkreuzung mit Nummer **5**

## Primary Route Destination
Route prioritaire, direction
Hauptverkehrsstraße Richtung **DOVER**

## Dual Carriageways (A & B roads)
Route à double chaussées séparées (route A & B)
Zweispurige Schnellstraße (A- und B- Straßen)

## Class A Road
Route de type A
A-Straße **A129**

## Class B Road
Route de type B
B-Straße **B177**

## Narrow Major Road (passing places)
Route prioritaire étroite (possibilité de dépassement)
Schmale Hauptverkehrsstraße (mit Überholmöglichkeit)

## Major Roads Under Construction
Route prioritaire en construction
Hauptverkehrsstraße im Bau

## Major Roads Proposed
Route prioritaire prévue
Geplante Hauptverkehrsstraße

## Safety Cameras with Speed Limits
Single Camera **30**
Multiple Cameras located along road **50**
Single & Multiple Variable Speed Cameras **V** **V**

Radars de contrôle de vitesse
Radar simple
Radars multiples situés le long de la route
Radars simples et multiples de contrôle de vitesse variable

Sicherheitskameras mit Tempolimit
Einzelne Kamera
Mehrere Kameras entlang der Straße
Einzelne und mehrere Kameras für variables Tempolimit

## Fuel Station
Station service
Tankstelle

## Gradient 1:7 (14%) & steeper
(descent in direction of arrow)
Pente égale ou supérieure à 14% (dans le sens de la descente)
14% Steigung und steiler (in Pfeilrichtung)

## Toll
Barrière de péage
Gebührenpflichtig *Toll*

## Dart Charge
www.gov.uk/pay-dartford-crossing-charge **C**

## Park & Ride
Parking avec Service Navette
Parken und Reisen **P+R**

## Mileage between markers
Distence en miles entre les flèches
Strecke zwischen Markierungen in Meilen **8**

## Airport
Aéroport
Flughafen

## Airfield
Terrain d'aviation
Flugplatz

## Heliport
Héliport
Hubschrauberlandeplatz **(H)**

## Ferry
(vehicular, sea) Bac (véhicules, mer) Fähre (auto, meer)
(vehicular, river) (véhicules, rivière) (auto, fluß)
(foot only) (piétons) (nur für Personen)

## Railway and Station
Voie ferrée et gare
Eisenbahnlinie und Bahnhof

## Level Crossing and Tunnel
Passage à niveau et tunnel
Bahnübergang und Tunnel

## River or Canal
Rivière ou canal
Fluß oder Kanal

## County or Unitary Authority Boundary
Limite de comté ou de division administrative
Grafschafts- oder Verwaltungsbezirksgrenze

## National Boundary
Frontière nationale
Landesgrenze

## Built-up Area
Agglomération
Geschlossene Ortschaft

## Town, Village or Hamlet
Ville, Village ou hameau
Stadt, Dorf oder Weiler

## Wooded Area
Zone boisée
Waldgebiet

## Spot Height in Feet
Altitude (en pieds)
Höhe in Fuß · *813*

## Relief above 400' (122m)
Relief par estompage au-dessus de 400' (122m)
Reliefschattierung über 400' (122m)

## National Grid Reference (kilometres)
Coordonnées géographiques nationales (Kilomètres)
Nationale geographische Koordinaten (Kilometer) ¹00

## Page Continuation
Suite à la page indiquée
Seitenfortsetzung **48**

## Area covered by Main Route map
Repartition des cartes des principaux axes routiers
Von Karten mit Hauptverkehrsstrecken **MAIN ROUTE 180**

## Area covered by Town Plan
Ville ayant un plan à la page indiquée
Von Karten mit Stadtplänen erfaßter Bereich **PAGE 194**

---

# Information
## Touristeninformationen

# Tourist Information

**i**

## Abbey, Church, Friary, Priory
Abbaye, église, monastère, prieuré
Abtei, Kirche, Mönchskloster, Kloster **†**

## Animal Collection
Ménagerie
Tiersammlung

## Aquarium
Aquarium
Aquarium

## Arboretum, Botanical Garden
Jardin Botanique
Botanischer Garten

## Aviary, Bird Garden
Volière
Voliere

## Battle Site and Date
Champ de bataille et date
Schlachtfeld und Datum *1066*

## Blue Flag Beach
Plage Pavillon Bleu
Blaue Flagge Strand

## Bridge
Pont
Brücke

## Castle (open to public)
Château (ouvert au public)
Schloß / Burg (für die Öffentlichkeit zugänglich)

## Castle with Garden (open to public)
Château avec parc (ouvert au public)
Schloß mit Garten (für die Öffentlichkeit zugänglich)

## Cathedral
Cathédrale
Kathedrale **†**

## Cidermaker
Cidrerie (fabrication)
Apfelwein Hersteller

## Country Park
Parc régional
Landschaftspark

## Distillery
Distillerie
Brennerei

## Farm Park, Open Farm
Park Animalier
Bauernhof Park

## Fortress, Hill Fort
Château Fort
Festung

## Garden (open to public)
Jardin (ouvert au public)
Garten (für die Öffentlichkeit zugänglich)

## Golf Course
Terrain de golf
Golfplatz

## Historic Building (open to public)
Monument historique (ouvert au public)
Historisches Gebäude (für die Öffentlichkeit zugänglich)

## Historic Building with Garden (open to public)
Monument historique avec jardin (ouvert au public)
Historisches Gebäude mit Garten (für die Öffentlichkeit zugänglich)

## Horse Racecourse
Hippodrome
Pferderennbahn

## Industrial Monument
Monument Industrielle
Industriedenkmal

## Leisure Park, Leisure Pool
Parc d'Attraction, Loisirs Piscine
Freizeitpark, Freizeit pool

## Lighthouse
Phare
Leuchtturm

## Mine, Cave
Mine, Grotte
Bergwerk, Höhle

## Monument
Monument
Denkmal

## Motor Racing Circuit
Circuit Automobile
Automobilrennbahn

## Museum, Art Gallery
Musée
Museum, Galerie **M**

## National Park
Parc national
Nationalpark

## National Trust Property
National Trust Property
National Trust- Eigentum

## Nature Reserve or Bird Sanctuary
Réserve naturelle botanique ou ornithologique
Natur- oder Vogelschutzgebiet

## Nature Trail or Forest Walk
Chemin forestier, piste verte
Naturpfad oder Waldweg

## Picnic Site
Lieu pour pique-nique
Picknickplatz

## Place of Interest
Site, curiosité
Sehenswürdigkeit *Craft Centre* •

## Prehistoric Monument
Monument Préhistorique
Prähistorische Denkmal

## Railway, Steam or Narrow Gauge
Chemin de fer, à vapeur ou à voie étroite
Eisenbahn, Dampf- oder Schmalspurbahn

## Roman Remains
Vestiges Romains
Römischen Ruinen

## Theme Park
Centre de loisirs
Vergnügungspark

## Tourist Information Centre
Office de Tourisme
Touristeninformationen

(All year)
(ouvert toute l'année)
(ganzjährig geöffnet) **i**

(Summer season only)
(été seulement)
(nur im Sommer geöffnet) **i**

## Viewpoint
Vue panoramique
Aussichtspunkt

(360 degrees)
(360 degrés)
(360 Grade)

(180 degrees)
(180 degrés)
(180 Grade)

## Vineyard
Vignoble
Weinberg

## Visitor Information Centre
Centre d'information touristique
Besucherzentrum **V**

## Wildlife Park
Réserve de faune
Wildpark

## Windmill
Moulin à vent
Windmühle

## Zoo or Safari Park
Parc ou réserve zoologique
Zoo oder Safari-Park

**4**

80   90   100   60

**20**

**A**   **B**   **C**   **D**

# ISLES OF SCILLY

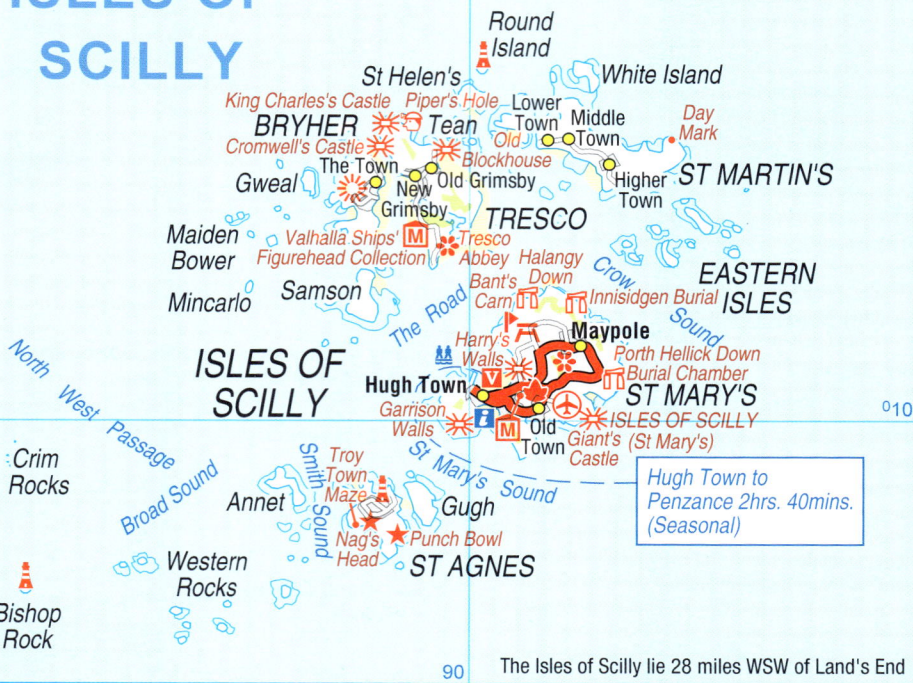

**1**

Round Island
St Helen's   White Island
King Charles's Castle   Piper's Hole   Lower   Day
**BRYHER**   Tean   Town   Old   Mark
Cromwell's Castle   Blockhouse   Middle Town
Gweal   The Town   New   Old Grimsby   Higher   **ST MARTIN'S**
Grimsby   Town
Maiden   Valhalla Ships'   Tresco   **TRESCO**
Bower   Figurehead Collection   Abbey   Halangy   **EASTERN**
Mincarlo   Samson   Bant's   Down   **ISLES**
Carn   Innisidgen Burial

North West Passage   The Road   Crow   Sound

Crim Rocks   **Maypole**
Harry's   Porth Hellick Down
**ISLES OF**   Walls   Burial Chamber
**SCILLY**   **Hugh Town**   **ST MARY'S**
Garrison   Old   Giant's   **ISLES OF SCILLY**
Walls   Town   Castle   (St Mary's)

Broad Sound   St Mary's Sound   **0**10   **0**50

Hugh Town to
Penzance 2hrs. 40mins.
(Seasonal)

Smith Sound   Troy Town
Annet   Maze
Gugh
**2**   Nag's   Punch Bowl
Bishop   Western   Head   **ST AGNES**
Rock   Rocks

90   The Isles of Scilly lie 28 miles WSW of Land's End

30   40   150

**40**

**C O R N W A L L**

The Carracks   Navax Point   Crane
Godrevy   Hell's   Islands   Portreath
Island   Mouth   **B3301**   Illogan
**3**   Barbara   Tate   Lifeboat   Tehidy   Park
Hepworth   Station   **A30**   Tuckingmill   Bottom
Gurnard's   Hellesveor   **St Ives**   **St Ives Bay**   Gwithian   Treswithian   Pool   Brea
Head   Carbis   Kehelland   Roseworthy Penponds   **CAMBORNE**
Penbeagle   Bay   The   Phillack   Connor Downs   Trevithick   Shire Horse
Carn Galver   Wayside   Towans   Angarrack   Farm
Engine House   Folk   Halsetown   Knill's   **Hayle**   Barripper   Troon
Zennor   Towednack   Cripplesease   **Copperhouse**   Gwinear   Carnhell   Wall
Zennor   Trencrom   Lelant   Canonstown   **St Erth**   Green   Praze-an-Beeble   **Crowan**
Treen   Quoit   Hill   Downs   **A30**   Praze   Fraddam
Porthmeor   9 Maidens   Mulfra   Nancledra   **A30**   Releath
**Pendeen**   828   Stone Circle   Quoit   St Erth   Leedstown   Dryw   Townshend
**Watch**   Higher   Morvah   Men-an-Tol   Chysauster   Ludgvan   Praze   Drym
Levant Mine &   Bojewyan   Ancient Village   R. Hayle   **B3302**
Beam Engine   Chun   Ding Dong   New   Crowlas   Paradise   Relubbus   Nancegollan
Geevor   Castle   Engine House   Mill   Park   Trescowe
Tin Mine   **Pendeen**   Great   Lanyon   Boswarthen   Godolphin   Godolphin   Crowntown
Trewellard   Bosullow   Quoit   Holy Well   **Madron**   St Hilary   Goldsithney   Cross   Helston
Carnyorth   Standing Stone   Trevarrack   Gulval   Longrock   Rosudgeon
Botallack   **A3071**   Tregeseal   Heamoor   **Marazion**   **A394**   Carleen   Trew   Lowertown
Count House   **8**   Chyandour   Perranuthnoe   Kenneggy   Trescowe   Germoe   Ashton   Sithney
**Cape Cornwall**   Newbridge   Trengwainton   Downs   Pengersick   **Breage**   **Helston**
The   **St Just**   Trereife   **PENZANCE**   St Michael's   Praa   Rinsey
Brisons   Ballowall   **A30**   Trewidden   **Newlyn**   Mount   Sands
Barrow   Sancreed   Drift   Cudden   Wheal Prosper   Wheal Trewavas
Kelynack   736   Resr.   Point   Engine House   Engine Houses   **Porthleven**
Carn Euny   Tredavoe   Paul   Trewavas
Escalls   Ancient Village   Brane   Crows-an-wra   Kerris   Mousehole   Head   The Loe
**LAND'S END**   **10**   Drift   Loe Bar
Longships   (St Just)   Boscawen-un   Pipers   St Clement's   Loe Pool
Maen Castle   **A30**   Stone Circle   Standing   Isle   & Bar   Berepper
**4**   Sennen   Lifeboat   **St Buryan**   Stones   Bird
Cove   Station   Trewoofe   Hospital
Land's   **Sennen**   Lamorna   **M O U N T ' S   B A Y**
**LAND'S END**   End   Trevescan   Merry Maidens   Poldhu Point
Trevilley   Stone Circle
Telegraph   Tregiffian   Marconi
Burial Chamber   Monument
Porthcurno   Treen   Penberth   Penzance to   Mullion Cove
**Gwennap**   Minack   Logan   Hugh Town 2hrs. 40mins.   Mullion
**Head**   Porthgwarra   St   Theatre   Rock   (Seasonal)   Island   Mullion
Levan   Cribba Head   Cove

Runnel
Stone

**5**   Vellan Head

Wolf Rock
**Wolf Rock**   Kynance

30   40   150   60

**A**   **B**   **C**   **D**

Watergate Bay
Towan Head
NEWQUAY
Newquay Bay
Fistral Bay
B3276
NEWQUAY CORNWALL
Gluvian
Mawgan
St Columb Minor
Trebarber
Trevenning
B3274
Tregonetha
St Columb Major
Lamorick
Lanivet
Retire
Demelza
Tregullon
Trebyan
Lanhy
A30
Kelsey Head
West Pentire
Pentire
Blue Reef Aquarium
Huer's Hut
Porth
Colan
Mountjoy
A3059
Porth Resr.
Trebudannon
Trekenning
703
Belowda
Victoria
CORNWALL
744
A391
Bokiddick
Lockenga
Sweetshouse
5
60
Holywell Bay
E
Holywell
Crantock
Trencreek
Lane
A392
Quintrell Downs
Black Cross
Castle-an-Dinas
Springfields
Ruthvoes
Trevarren
Roche
Tregoss
G
Screech Owl Sanctuary
Enniscaven
Roche Rock
Bilberry
H
Bugle
Rosevean
Lanlivery
Luxulyan
Penhale Point
Penhale Camp
Holywell Bay Fun Park
Cubert
Kestle Mill
Trence
St Columb Road
St Enoder
Penhale
Fraddon
Indian Queens
St Dennis
Hendra
Whitemoor
Hensbarrow Downs 1025
Stenalees
Nanpean
Carthew
Wheal Martyn
Penwithick
Trethurgy
A390
Penpillick
Hidden Valley
Ligger or Perran Bay
Perranporth
Rejerrah
St Newlyn East
Newlyn Downs 490
Mitchell
Chapel Town
Brighton
Menna
A30
Summercourt
Treviscoe
Goonabarn
Foxhole
Nanpean
Trethosa
Carpalla
Eden Project
St Blazey Gate
Tregrehan Mills
Tywardreath Highway
Marsh Vill
Tywar
St Piran's Oratory
Mount
Lappa Valley Steam Railway
A3076
A3075
A3058
St Stephen
High Street
St Austell
Brewery
Boscoppa
Holmbush
Tregrehan
Pat
Perranzabuloe
Bolingey
Carnkief
Zelah
Carland Cross
Trelassick
Trendeal
New Mills
Lanjeth
Trewoon
Lanjeth
Carlyon Bay
Polkerris
St Agnes Head
St Agnes
Wheal Coates Engine House
Goonvrea
Perranzabuloe
Penhallow
Callestick
Healey's Cyder Farm
St Allen
Trispen
Tregear
Ladock
Grampound Road
A3058
Coombe
Downderry
St Mewan
A390
Hewas Water
Polgooth
Sticker
Tregorrick
Higher
Charlestown
London Apprentice
Porthpean
St Austell Bay
Gribbin
Head
Blackwater
Three Burrows
Greenbottom
B3284
Shortlanesend
Idless
Kenwyn
Bosvigo
Tresillian
Merther
Probus
Creed
Grampound
Trewithen
St Ewe
Rescorla
Lost Gardens of Heligan
B3273
Trenarren
Pentewan
Black Head
Redruth
St Day
Carharrack
Gwennap
Chacewater
Scorrier
Wheal Busy Engine House
Hugus
Highertown
Royal Cornwall
Skinner's Brewery
TRURO
St Clement
Tregony
A390
A3078
Polmassick Vineyard
Polmassick
Kestle
Gorran High Lanes
Mevagissey
Mevagissey Bay
World of Model Railways
Chapel Point
Carnon Downs
Devoran
Perranwell
Penpol
Trelissick
Feock
Old Kea
Playing Place
Coombe
Penelewey
Philleigh
Treworthal
St Michael Penkevil
Lamorran
Ruan Lanihorne
Ruan High Lanes
St Michael Caerhays
Melinsey Mill
Veryan Green
Portloe
St Michael Caerhays
Portholland
Caerhays Castle
Boswinger
Gorran Churchtown
Gorran Haven
Veryan Bay
Penare
Cliff Castle
Dodman Point
Stithians
Stithians Lake
Stithians Reservoir
Perranarworthal
Harcourt
Mylor Bridge
Enys
Lanterns
Mylor Churchtown
St Just in Roseland
Trewithian
Trist House
Veryan
Carne
Gerrans Bay
Nare Head
Gull Rock
Nare Point
Penmarth
Carnkie
Rame
Longdowns
Mabe Burnthouse
St Gluvias
Penryn
Flushing
Lamorran
A3078
Gerrans
Portscatho
Heritage Centre
St Mawes
Greeb Point
3
Burras
Porkellis
Poldark Mine
Wendron
Seworgan
Treverva
Budock Water
FALMOUTH
Pendennis
St Mawes
St Anthony
Bohortha
Penjerrick
Pendennis Point
St Anthony Battery
Zone Point
Falmouth Bay
Trewennack
Brill
Potager
Carlidnack
Maenporth
Mawnan Smith
Carwinion
Constantine
Glendurgan
Trebah
Mawnan
Rosemullion Head
Gweek
Seal Sanctuary
Flambards
Porth Navas
Helford
Bosahan
Helford River
St Anthony-in-Meneage
Gillan
Nare Point
RNAS Culdrose Viewing Enclosure
Mawgan
St Martin
Manaccan
Newtown-in-St Martin
Tregarne
Roskorwell
Porthallow
4
Garras
Halliggye Fogou
Tregowris
St Keverne
Giant's Quoits
Porthoustock
Manacle Point
White Cross
Cross Lanes
Cury
Bonython Estate
Goonhilly Downs 369
Traboe
Lanarth
Roskilly's Organic Farm
The Manacles
20
Mullion
A3083
B3296
Penhale
Trelan
Ponsongath
Raised Beach
Coverack
Ruan Major
Gwenter
Kuggar
Predannack
St Ruan
Poltesco
Ruan Minor
Cadgwith
Black Head
5
Toll Cove
Devil's Frying Pan
Lizard
Lifeboat Station
Hot Point
LIZARD POINT
E
F
G
H
10
70
80
90
200

*Map of Cornwall (southwest England) — grid reference page*

Grid columns: A, B, C, D — Row labels: 6, 1, 2, 3, 4, 5

**Coastal / sea features:**
Port Isaac Bay, The Mouls, Rumps Point, Port Quin Bay, Pentire Point, Padstow Bay, Gunver Head, Gulland Rock, TREVOSE HEAD, Quies, Constantine Bay, Park Head, Berryl's Point, Watergate Bay, Towan Head, Newquay Bay, Fistral Bay, Kelsey Head, Holywell Bay, Penhale Point, Ligger or Perran Bay, Bawden Rocks, St Agnes Head, Crane Islands, Falmouth Bay, Rosemullion Head, Gerrans Bay, Nare Head, Gull Rock, Greeb Point, Veryan Bay, Dodman Point, Zone Point

**Towns and villages:**
Port Isaac, Port Gaverne, Trelights, Trewetha, St Endellion, St Minver, St Kew, Lower Amble, Chapel Amble, Polzeath, New Polzeath, Rock, Stoptide, Trebetherick, Trevone, Padstow, Wadebridge, Egloshayle, Sladesbridge, Burlawn, Polbrock, St Issey, Little Petherick, Trevance, Edmonton, Whitecross, St Breock Downs, Rosenannon, St Wenn, Withiel, Tremore, Retire, Demelza, St Columb Major, Victoria, Roche, Bugle, Stenalees, Nanpean, Foxhole, Carthew, ST AUSTELL, Trewoon, Polgooth, Mevagissey, Gorran Haven, Gorran Churchtown, Gorran High Lanes, Caerhays, Veryan, Portloe, Portholland, Boswinger

NEWQUAY CORNWALL, St Columb Minor, Trebarber, Colan, Mountjoy, Quintrell Downs, St Columb Road, Fraddon, Indian Queens, St Dennis, St Stephen, Summercourt, Mitchell, Brighton, Ladock, Probus, Grampound, Grampound Road, Tresillian, TRURO, St Clement, Malpas, Old Kea, Kea, Kenwyn, Highertown, Threemilestone, Chacewater, Scorrier, REDRUTH, CAMBORNE, Pool, Illogan, Portreath, Porthtowan, St Agnes, Perranporth, Goonhavern, St Newlyn East, Cubert, Crantock, Pentire, Holywell, Penhale Camp

Falmouth, Penryn, Flushing, Mylor Churchtown, Mylor Bridge, St Just in Roseland, St Mawes, St Anthony, Gerrans, Portscatho, Feock, Devoran, Carnon Downs, Perranwell, Perranarworthal, Ponsanooth, Stithians, Stithians Reservoir, Longdowns, Mabe Burnthouse, Budock Water, Treverva, Mawnan Smith, Mawnan, Constantine, Helford, St Anthony-in-Meneage, Helston, Porthleven, Crowan, Leedstown, Praze-an-Beeble, Nancegollan, Crowntown

**Road numbers:**
A389, A39, A30, A392, A3059, A3058, A3076, A3075, A390, A393, A394, A3078, A3277, A3284, A3285, B3276, B3274, B3275, B3279, B3277, B3287, B3289, B3292, B3297, B3300, B3301, B3303, B3304, B3314, B3261

**Points of interest:**
National Lobster Hatchery, Prideaux Place, Royal Cornwall Showground, Japanese Garden, Cornish Birds of Prey Centre, Nine Maidens Stone Row, St Breock Downs Monolith, Pawton Quoit, Castle-an-Dinas, Screech Owl Sanctuary, Roche Rock, Hensbarrow Downs, Lost Gardens of Heligan, Caerhays Castle, Cliff Castle, Trelissick, Trewithen, Lappa Valley Steam Railway, Dairyland Farm World, Blue Reef Aquarium, Huer's Hut, St Piran's Oratory, St Piran's Round, Wheal Coates Engine House, Healey's Cyder Farm, Polmassick Vineyard, Tehidy, Cornish Engines, Carn Brea, Shire Horse Farm, Poldark Mine, Flambards, RNAS Culdrose Viewing Enclosure, Seal Sanctuary, Trebah, Glendurgan, Old MacDonald's Farm, Bedruthan Steps, Mellingey Mill

CORNWALL

Delabole · Rockhead · Pipers Pool · Tregadillett · **Launceston** · Lifton · Dippertown

Treligga · Slate Quarry · Trevia · Tregoodwell · Crowdy Resr. · St Clether Holy Well · Laneast · Trewen · Trethorne · A30 · Marystow

Westdowns · Pengelly · Valley Truckle · Camelford · Bowithick · St Clether · Daw's House · Lawrence House · Lawhitton · 40 · Meadwell

B3311 · Pencarrow · Tresinney · Treween · Tredaule · **South Petherwin** · Tregada · B3362 · River Tamar · Bradstone · Kelly · Meadwell

St Teath · Helstone · Truck · Altarnun · Wesley Cottage · Fivelanes · 70 · **Polyphant** · Lewannick · Trewarlett · Lezant · Dunterton · **7** · Milton Abbot

Treveighan · Charlotte Dymond Monument · 10 · Hut Circles · Rough Tor · 1377 · Brown Willy · Codda · A30 · B3254 · Trebartha · Trewarlett · **H** · A388 · Hotel Endsleigh · Sydenham Damerel

Michaelstow · St Breward · Stannon Stone Circle Stone Circle · Fernacre Stone Circle · Brown Willy · 1209 · Trevadlock · Illand · Newtown Coad's Green · Trebullett · Trekenner · Rezare · Bealsmill · **1** · Horsebridge

St Tudy · Row · Lank · King Arthur's Hall · Garrow Tor · BODMIN · Trebartha · North Hill · Bathpool · Middlewood · Rilla Mill · Treburley · Tutwell · Chilsworthy

St Kew Highway · Penpont · Wenfordbridge · Daphne Du Maurier's Smugglers · Bolventor · Jamaica Inn · 22 · Henwood · 1280 Kilmar Tor · South Hill · Stoke Climsland · Old Mill · Downgate · Luckett · Latchley · St Ann's Chapel

St Mabyn · Blisland · Jubilee Rock · Waterloo · Temple · Stripple Stones Henge & Circle · Dozmary Pool · 1109 Brown Gelly Barrows · Cheesewring The Hurlers Stone Circles · Upton · Upton Cross · Plushabridge · Kelly Bray · 1096 Kit Hill · Golberdon · Ginnisla

Croanford · Pencarrow · A30 · Hellandbridge · Helland · DANGER AREA · Millpool · Maidenwell · 10 · Siblyback Lake · King Doniert's Stone · Minions · Caradon Hill · Caradon Town · Haye · Harrowbarrow · Metherell · Cal

Washaway · **Bodmin** · Bodmin & Wenford Railway · Cardinham · Churchyard Cross · Warleggan · 924 · Redgate · Golitha Falls · Darite · **Pensilva** · Trevigro · Frogwell · **Callington** · Dupath Well · St Dominick · Cotehele

Laveddon · Tregullon · Lanhydrock · Bodmin Jail · Cardinham · Fawton · Mount · St Neot Holy Well · Tremar · St Cleer's Well · Merrymeet · St Ive · Keason · Gang · Ken-Caro · Cadson Bury Fort · Callington · Bere Alston

A389 · A30 · Trebyan · Maudlin · Tredinnick · Ley · St Neot · Carnglaze Caverns · Golitha Falls · St Cleer · A390 · St Ive · Parkfield · Cotehele Mill

A389 · Lanivet · B3268 · Cutmadoc · Middle Taphouse · Doublebois · **Liskeard** · Pengover Green · Quethiock · Pillaton · Ellbridge · Cargreen

Lockengate · Sweetshouse · Restormel · West Taphouse · East Taphouse · **Dobwalls** · A38 · Menheniot · Trehunist · Blunts · Cuttivett · Hatt · Botus Fleming · Landulph

A391 · Bokiddick · Pinsla · Bodrane · Lamellion · St Keyne · Trehunist · Tideford Cross · Landrake · Trematon · Saltash

A390 · Lanlivery · Luxulyan · Milltown · Lostwithiel · Couch's Mill · Herodsfoot · Trewidland · Duloe Stone Circle · Tideford · Budge's Shop · Port Eliot · St Erney · Markwell · **Saltash** · Burraton

Rescorla · Trethurgy · Hidden Valley · Penpillick · St Winnow · Lerryn · Muchlarnick · Sandplace · Widegates · Hessenford · Trerulefoot · Priory Church · St Germans · Trehan · St Stephens · Budea

Eden Project · Tywardreath Highway · Golant · Lanreath · Pelynt · Morval · A387 · Seaton Valley · Narkurs · Polbathic · St Winnolls · A374 · Antony · Maryfield · Wilcov · Devo

St Blazey · St Blazey Gate · Marsh Villa · Castle Dore · Penpoll · St Veep · Trenewan · A387 · Looe · Seaton · Downderry · Sheviock · Antony Woodland · Torpoint

A391 · Tregrehan · Boscoppa · Par · Tywardreath · Bodinnick · Lanteglos Highway · Lansallos · East Looe · West Looe · Old Guildhall · Portwrinkle · Crafthole · A374 · Antony · St John · Millbrook · Kings

A3082 · Holmbush · Carlyon Bay · Polkerris · Fowey · Readymoney · Model Village · Polperro · Talland Bay · Looe Bay · St George's or Looe Island · Sharrow Grotto · Freathy · Tregonhawke · Caws

Charlestown · Higher Porthpean · Menabilly · Gribbin Daymark · Porthallow · Smuggling & Fishing · Monkey Sanctuary · Whitsand Bay · **8** · Rame

St Austell Bay · Black Head · 35 mins. (Seasonal) · Gribbin Head · Pencarrow Head · Whitsand Bay · Rame Head · Per Po

Trenarren · World of Model Railways · Mevagissey Bay · **4** · Eddystone Rocks

Chapel Point · **5** · 40 · 30

E · F · G · H

10 · 20 · 30 · 40

**DARTMOOR NATIONAL PARK**

DARTMOOR FOREST

**PLYMOUTH**

DEVON

TAVISTOCK

Princetown

Dartmoor Prison Dartmoor National Park

Ashburton

Buckfast

Buckfastleigh

South Brent

Ivybridge

Ugborough

Modbury

Kingsbridge

Salcombe

Bolt Head

Bolt Tail

Prawle Point

Rame Head

Penlee Point

Eddystone Rocks

The Sound

Bigbury Bay

Stoke Point

Great Mew Stone

Wembury Bay

Plymouth to:
Roscoff 6hrs.
(Seasonal)
St Malo 8hrs. 30mins.
(Seasonal)
Santander 20hrs.
(Seasonal)

Lifton  Lydford  North Bovey  Manaton  Haytor Vale

Milton Abbot  Mary Tavy  Peter Tavy  Postbridge  Bellever  Widecombe in the Moor

Lamerton  Merrivale  Rundlestone  Two Bridges  Dartmeet  Poundsgate

Gunnislake  Calstock  Horrabridge  Walkhampton  Yelverton  Dousland

Bere Alston  Buckland Monachorum  Crapstone  Meavy  Sheepstor

St Mellion  Pillaton  Bere Ferrers  Milton Combe  Clearbrook  Shaugh Prior

Botus Fleming  Roborough  Woolwell  Bickleigh  Lee Moor  Wotter

Saltash  Landrake  St Germans  St Stephens  Devonport  Plympton

Torpoint  Antony  Millbrook  Kingsand  Cawsand  Rame

Crafthole  Sheviock  Freathy  Tregonhawke

Plymstock  Hooe  Goosewell  Staddiscombe  Down Thomas  Wembury

Brixton  Yealmpton  Newton Ferrers  Noss Mayo  Netton

Torr  Dunstone  Ford  Holbeton  Battisborough Cross  Mothecombe

Luson  Westlake  Ermington  Penquit

Cornwood  Sparkwell  Lee Mill  Bittaford

Modbury  Ringmore  Kingston  Challaborough  Bigbury-on-Sea  Burgh Island  Bantham

Aveton Gifford  Loddiswell  Churchstow  West Alvington

Thurlestone  Outer Hope  Inner Hope  Malborough  Bolberry  Rew

Woodleigh  East Allington  Buckland-tout-Saints  Dodbrooke  Frogmore

Goveton  Ledstone  Woolston  South Milton  South Huish  West Buckland  East Buckland

Galmpton  Collaton  Batson  East Portlemouth  Rickham  South Pool  East Charleton  West Charleton

Bigbury Bay

River Tamar  River Tavy  River Plym  River Yealm  River Erme  River Avon  River Dart

A30  A38  A374  A379  A381  A382  A384  A385  A386  A388  A390  A3121  A3196

B3257  B3362  B3212  B3357  B3335  B3417  B3416  B3413  B3214  B3186  B3392  B3380  B3352  B3387

Dartmoor National Park

Lustleigh · Wreyland · Lower Ashton · Ashton · Christow · Bennah · Powderham · East Budleigh

Trenchford Resr · Tottiford Resr · Canonteign Falls · Hennock · Trusham · Exeter · A38 · A380 · Kenton · South Town · Starcross · Lympstone · A la Ronde · Bystock · Hulham · Withycombe Raleigh · Knowle · Kersbrook · B3179

East Dartmoor Woods and Heaths · Heritage Centre · Bovey Tracey · Chudleigh Knighton · Coburg · Chudleigh · Waddon · Ashcombe · Milton Hill · A379 · Dawlish Warren · EXMOUTH · World of Country Life · Littleham · Budleigh Salterton · Fairlynch

Brimley · Ilsington · House of Marbles · Bovey Heath · Heathfield · Coldeast · Ideford · Luton · Holcombe · Little Haldon · Dawlish

Lewthorn Cross · Liverton · Sigford · A38 · Trago Mills · Orchid Paradise · Stover · B3195 · Sandygate · Humber · Rural Life · Coombe · Teignmouth · Teign Heritage Centre

Caton · South Knighton · Bickington · A382 · Teigngrace · Kingsteignton · Highweek · A383 · Bishopsteignton · R. Teign · Ringmore · Shaldon

Goodstone · A383 · West Ogwell · NEWTON ABBOT · East Ogwell · Netherton · Combeinteignhead · Stokeinteignhead · Lower Gabwell · Higher Gabwell · Maidencombe

Woodland · Forder Green · Denbury · Abbotskerswell · Plant World · Devon Wildlife Centre · Coffinswell · Watcombe · Babbacombe Bay · Bygones · Model Village

Hill House · Woolston Green · Torbryan · Ipplepen · Two Mile Oak · North Whilborough · A3022 · Kingskerswell · Barton · Hele · St Marychurch · Cliff Railway · Babbacombe

Broadhempston · Staverton · Dartington Hall · A381 · Littlehempston · Combe Fishacre · Compton · Shiphay · Torre · Cockington · Torre Abbey · TORQUAY · Kents Cavern · Hope's Nose

Week · Shinner's Bridge · Dartington · Cott · Totnes · A385 · Marldon · Berry Pomeroy · Blagdon · Ayreville · Round Hill · Shorton · A3022 · Oldway · Kirkham House · Wellswood · Living Coasts

Harberton · Bridgetown · Collaton St Mary · Higher Yalberton · St Michaels · B3201 · PAIGNTON · TORBAY · Tor Bay

Harbertonford · Sharpham Wines & Cheeses · Aish · Stoke Gabriel · Waddeton · A3022 · Galmpton Warborough · Goodrington · Seashore Cen. · Splashdown Waterpark

Washbourne · Tuckenhay · Cornworthy · East Cornworthy · Dittisham · Galmpton · Churston Ferrers · Lifeboat Sta. · Berry Head

Allaleigh · Greenway · Dartmouth Steam Railway · A379 · Hillhead · Woodhuish · Brixham · A3022 · Sharkham Point

Halwell · Capton · Newcomen Engine · A3122 · Woodlands · Norton · Coleton Fishacre · Start Bay

Woodford · Hutcherleigh · Blackawton · Ash · Bowden · A379 · Dartmouth · Warfleet · Kingswear · Mew Stone

Burlestone · Fast Rabbit Farm · Blackpool · Stoke Fleming · B3205 · Strete

Harleston · Start · A379 · Slapton · Monument · Slapton Ley · Start Bay

Sherford · Frittiscombe · Chillington · Stokenham · Torcross · Sherman Tank Memorial

Ford · Beeson · Beesands · Kellaton · Chivelstone · Hallsands · South Allington · East Prawle · Start Point

**Grid numbers:** 200 · 10 · 20 · 20 · 10 · 100 · 90 · 80 · 70 · 200 · 10

**CORNWALL**

**BODMIN MOOR**

Hartland Quay · Hartland · Stoke · Velly · B3248 · B3237 · Clovelly · Donkeys · Higher Clovelly · Buck's Cross · Buck's Mills
Milford · Philham · Natcott · 24 · 30 · Milky Way Adventure Park · 710
Elmscott · Edistone · Welsford · Woolfardisworthy or Woolsery
Docton Mill · South Hole · Parkham · Alminstone Cross · Ash

Knaps Longpeak · Welcombe · A39 · Meddon · R. Torridge · Ashmansworthy
Mead · Gooseham · East Youlstone · 771
Higher Sharpnose Point · Hawker's Hut · Morwenstow · Shop · West Youlstone · Dinworthy · Bradworthy · Gnome Reserve & Wild Flower Garden · West Putford · East Putford · Colscott
Lower Sharpnose Point · Woodford

Kilkhampton · Upper Tamar Lake · Sutcombe
Coombe · Tamar Lakes · Alfardisworthy · Soldon Cross · Waldon
Stibb · B3254 · Lower Tamar Lake · Dexbeer · A388
Poughill · Bush · Hersham · Grimscott · Dunsdon Farm · Holsworthy Beacon
Flexbury · Stratton 1643 · Stratton · Lana · Chilsworthy
Castle Heritage Centre · Launcells · Red Post · A3072 · Derril · Derriton · Whimble · Anvil Corner
Bude · Lynstone · Pancrasweek · Holsworthy · Chasty · Staddon
Bude Bay · Upton · Hobbacott Inclined Plane · Bridgerule · Pyworthy · Leworthy
Marhamchurch · Titson · Whitstone · North Tamerton · Clawton · Tetcott
A39 · Box's Shop · Coppathorne · Week St Mary · Street · B3254 · R. Claw · Lana · A388
Widemouth Bay · Poundstock · Bangors · Treskinnick Cross · Penhallam Manor · Week Green · West Curry · North Petherwin · Luffincott · Chapmans Well
Dizzard Point · Dizzard · Tregole · Trewint · Higher Whiteleigh · South Wheatley · Maxworthy · Bennacott · Northcott · Henford
St Gennys · CORNWALL · Hele · East Panson · A388
Cambeak · Crackington Haven · Wainhouse Corner · Jacobstow · Langdon · Boyton · West Panson
Fire Beacon Point · High Cliff · Tresparrett Posts · Trengune · Warbstow Bury · Canworthy Water · Brazacott · North Petherwin · Langdon Cross · St Giles on the Heath
Beeny · B3263 · Tresparrett · Marshgate · Trelash · Warbstow · Tremaine · Petherwin Gate · Tamar Otter & Wildlife Centre · Ladycross · Werrington
Witchcraft · Boscastle · Lesnewth · Otterham · Hallworthy · Splatt · Tregeare · Egloskerry · Yeolmbridge · Dutson
Rocky Valley · Halgabron · B3266 · Treneglos · Tresmeer · Tregaire · Badgall · Langore · Launceston Steam Railway · St Stephens · Newport · Liftondown
Tintagel Head · King Arthur's Great Halls · Trevalga · B3262 · Davidstow · Tremail · Cold Northcott · Hidden Valley · Trethorne · Launceston · Tregadillett · Lawrence House
Tintagel · Old Post Office · Bossiney · Trewarmett · Trewassa · Trevivian · St Clether Holy Well · St Clether · A395 · Pipers Pool · Daw's House
Treknow · 1009 · B3263 · Slaughterbridge · Trewen · South Petherwin · Tregada
Gull Rock · Trebarwith · Prince of Wales Quarry · 6 · Trefrew · Treween · Polyphant · Lewannick · B3254 · Trewarlett
Delabole · Rockhead · Trevia · Tregoodwell · Crowdy Resr. · St Clether · Laneast · 70 · A30 · Lezant · A388
Slate Quarry · Camelford · Pencarrow · Charlotte Dymond Monument · Bowithick · Altarnun · Tredaule · Polyphant · Congdon's Shop · Illand · Trebullett · Trekenner · Rezare
Treligga · Westdowns · Pengelly · Valley Truckle · Tresinney · Hut Circles · Rough Tor · Treween · Fivelanes · Trevadlock · Newton Coad's Green · Bray Shop · Bealsmill
Port Isaac Bay · Helstone · Trewalder · B3314 · 1377 · Brown Willy · 1209 · Wesley Cottage · Trebartha · North Hill · Middlewood · Venterdon · Old Mill
Port Quin · Port Isaac · Trewetha · Treore · Stannon Stone Circle · Fernacre Stone Circle · Garrow Tor · 1082 · Kilmar Tor · Linkinhorne · South Hill · Stoke Climsland
Lifeboat Station · Long Cross Victorian · Treligga · Michaelstow · Fentonadle · St Breward · Codda · 22 · 1280 · Bathpool · Downgate
Trelights · Pendoggett · Trelill · King Arthur's Hall · Row · Lank · Garrow Tor · Henwood · Rilla Mill · Plushabridge · Kelly Bray · 1096 · Kit Hill
B3267 · St Endellion · A39 · R. Allen · St Tudy · Wenfordbridge · Daphne Du Maurier's Smugglers · Jamaica Inn · Bolventor · Upton Cross · The Hurlers Stone Circles · Heritage Centre · Golberdon · Downgate
St Minver · St Kew · Penpont · Stripple Stones Henge & Circle · Jubilee Rock · 1109 · Dozmary Pool · River Fowey · Middlewood · Caradon Town · Pensilva
Lower Amble · St Kew Highway · Blisland · Waterloo · Temple · Brown Gelly Barrows · Cheesewring · Darite · Tremar · Ken Caro · Trevigro · Ca
Trevanson · Chapel Amble · Bodieve · St Mabyn · Hellandbridge · A30 · Colliford Lake · Maidenwell · Golitha Falls · Minions · 1216 · Caradon Hill · Tremar · Keason
Wadebridge · Egloshayle · Helland · DANGER AREA · Millpool · Siblyback Lake · St Neot · Redgate · St Cleer · St Ive · Parkfield · Frogwell
Burlawn · Croanford · Pencarrow · Sladesbridge · Cardinham · Bury Castle · Bleggan · Mount · Fawton · King Doniert's · Tretheny Quoit · St Cleer's Well · Merrymeet · Cadson Bury Fort
Royal Cornwall Showground · Culverhouse · Berry Tower · Bodmin · Churchyard Cross · St Neot Holy Well · 924 · Golitha Falls · St Neot · Tremar · A390 · Cardinham · Pawton Quoit · Polbrock · A389 · Bodmin · St Lawrence · Cardinham · Carnglaze Caverns · St Ive
Nanstallon · Ruthernbridge · Bodmin & Wenford · Tredinnick · Ley · Doublebois · Liskeard · A38 · Merrymeet · 8
St Wenn · Tremore · A389 · Pinsla · Withiel · Rosenannon

Port Isaac Bay · Quin Bay · Gull Rock · Bude Bay

South Molton
Bishop's Nympton
George Nympton
Mariansleigh
Alswear
Meshaw
Venha

Horns Cross
Fairy Cross
Ford
Woodtown
Littleham
Adventure Park
Landcross
Hallspill
Gammaton Cross
Huntshaw
Yarnscombe
Atherington
Umberleigh
Eastacott
Warkleigh
Satterleigh
Clapworthy
Bish Mill
Newtown

Alwington
Goldworthy
Parkham
Buckland Brewer
Monkleigh
Frithelstock
Langridgeford
High Bullen
Stevenstone
Sherwood Green
High Bickington
King's Nympton
Chittlehamholt
Chulmleigh
Romansleigh
Lutworthy

A386
Weare Giffard
B3232
B3227
B3217
R. Mole
B3226
B3137
B3096
21

Tythecott
Thornehillhead
Southcott
Taddiport
Great Torrington
St Giles in the Wood
Ebberley Hill
Roborough
Burrington
Elstone
Week
West Worlington
East Worlington
Thelbridge Barton
Filleigh
Chawleigh
Cheldon
L. Dart River
Drayf

Langtree
Stibb Cross
Berry Cross
Peters Marland
Winswell
Little Torrington
Beaford
Riddlecombe
Ashreigney
Bridge Reeve
East Ashley
Eggesford
B3042
Lapford
Eastington
Brown

Haytown
Bulkworthy
Abbots Bickington
Shop
Newton St Petrock
Shebbear
Thornbury
Buckland Filleigh
Folly Cross
Bradford
North Town
Petrockstowe
Meeth
Merton
Huish
Dolton
A3124
Hollocombe
Wembworthy
Brushford
Coldridge
Nymet Rowland
Eggesford
Lapford Cross
Morchard Bishop
Oldborough
Weeke

Milton Damerel
Gratton
Woodacott
Cookbury Wick
Brandis Corner
Holemoor
Cookbury
Black Torrington
Sheepwash
R. Torridge
Dowland
Upcott
Winkleigh
Ingleigh Green
Broadwoodkelly
Bondleigh
Lowton
West Leigh
East Leigh
Zeal Monachorum
Down St Mary
Burston
Newbuildings
Copplestone
Els

Hollacombe
Chilla
Graddon Moor
Highampton
Hannaborough
Hatherleigh
Morris Monument
Monkokehampton
Honeychurch
Sampford Courtenay
North Tawton
Bow
Nymet Tracey
Colebrooke
Coleford
Knowle

Ashwater
Ashmill
Quoditch
Virginstow
Halwill Forest
Halwill Junction
Winsford Walled
Whiddon
Beaworthy
Crowden
Patchacott
Ashbury
Northlew
Cruft
Inwardleigh
Jacobstowe
A386
A3072
Exbourne
Sampford Courtenay
Trecott
Week
Itton
A3072
Nymet Tracey
Hillerton
Hittisleigh
Barton
Yeof

Broadbury
Germansweek
Eworthy
Boasley Cross
Grindhill
Southcott
Thorndon Cross
Folly Gate
Padson
Brightley
Chichacott
Belstone Corner
Rowden
Taw Green
Spreyton
Heath Cross
A3124
Hittisleigh
Woodl
Hea

A3079
Roadford Lake (Reservoir)
Bratton Clovelly
Okehampton
Belstone
Sticklepath
Finch Foundry
South Tawton
South Zeal
Ramsley
Whiddon Down
A30
Cheriton Bishop
Cheriton Cross
Crockernwell

Cross Green
Grinacombe Moor
Broadwoodwidger
Kellacott
Rexon
Stowford
Lewdown
Lobhillcross
Combebow
Bridestowe
Southerly
Shortacombe
A386
Meldon
Dartmoor Railway
Okehampton Camp
Cosdon Hill
East Week
Throwleigh
Wonson
Gidleigh
Murchington
Teigncombe
Chagford
Middlecott
Sloncombe
Moretonhampstead
A382
Drewsteignton
Castle Drogo
Easton
Cranbrook Castle
R. Teign
B3206
Doccom

Lifton
Tinhay
Dingles Fairground Heritage Centre
Portgate
Lewtrenchard
Dippertown
A386
Lydford
Lydford Gorge
Black Down
Bridestowe and Sourton Common
Black-a-Tor Copse
Yes Tor 2030
DANGER AREA
2038 High Willhays
Okement Hill
Cranmere Pool
Scorhill Stone Circle
DANGER AREA
Shovel Down Stone Rows
Frenchbeer
Fernworthy Resr.
Lettaford
Miniature Pony Centre
North Bovey
A382
Lustleigh
Wreyla

Stowford
Marystow
Coryton
Liddaton
Chillaton
Kelly
Meadwell
Bradstone
Dunterton
Sydenham Damerel
Milton Abbot
Chaddlehanger
Lamerton
Rushford
Horsebridge
Brentor
North Brentor
Mary Tavy
Horndon
Cudlipptown
Peter Tavy
Wheal Betsy
Tavy Cleave
DANGER AREA 1919
Amicombe Hill
1938
1980 Cut Hill
1763 Sittaford Tor
DARTMOOR
Grey Wethers Stone Circles
Grimspound
Hameldown Tor
Bowerman's Nose
Manaton
Water
Hound Tor Medieval Village
Lustleigh
Becky Falls
Haytor Granite Tramway
Haytor Rocks
Haytor Vale
Lewthorn Cross
Sigford
Bickingto
Caton

Tutwell
Luckett
Chilsworthy
St Ann's Chapel
Gunnislake
Albaston
Morwellham Quay
Calstock
Bere Alston
St Mellion
Harrowbarrow
Metherell
Cotehele
Tamar Valley Donkey Park
A390
TAVISTOCK
Middlemoor
Whitchurch
Sampford Spiney
Merrivale
Prehistoric Settlement
Dartmoor National Park
Rundlestone
Two Bridges
Crockern Tor
Bellever
Postbridge
East Dart R.
Church House
Widecombe in the Moor
Bonehill
Higher Dunstone
Leusdon
Ponsworthy
Buckland in the Moor
Dartmeet
Dartmoor Otters & Buckfast Butterflies
Buckfast
Buckfastleigh
A38
A3380

Horrabridge
Walkhampton
Dousland
Yelverton
Burrator Resr.
Sheepstor
Meavy
Buckland Monachorum
The Garden House
Buckland Abbey
Crapstone
Cater's Beam
1491
William Crossing Memorial
Ryder's Hill 1691
Michelcombe
Holne
Scorriton
Combe
Hembury Castle
Ashburton
Buckfast Abbey
Landscove
Woolst
Goods

A386
PRINCETOWN
Hexworthy
Poundsgate
Venford Resr.
Whiteworks
1461
DARTMOOR FOREST NATIONAL PARK
Wistman's Wood
Crockern Tor
Two Bridges
B3357
B3212
Great Mis Tor 1768
DANGER AREA
West Dart R.
Upper Plym Valley Prehistoric Sites
Stall Moor
Avon Dam Resr.
Avon

Grid references: E F G H
11 1 2 3 12 4 5 8

A3065 · Henlade · Ham · Knapp · Helland · Sutton · Knole · Northover · A372 · B3151

Bradford-on-Tone · Hillfarrance · Thornfalcon · Lillesdon · Newport · Swell · Isle · Muchelney · Long · Load · Ilchester · Yeovil

TAUNTON · Rumwell · Haydon · Stoke St Mary · Meare Green · Wrantage · Fivehead · Isle Brewers · Midelney · Thorney · Milton · A303 · A37

A38 · Shepp's Cider · TAUNTON DEANE · Shoreditch · Orchard Portman · West Hatch · Curry Mallet · Isle Abbotts · Hambridge · Kingsbury Episcopi · Stapleton · M

Wellington · Poole · Ham · Trull · Staplehay · Thurlbear · Hatch Beauchamp · Beercrocombe · Westport · Barrington Court · Lambrook · Bower Hinton · Martock · Tintinhull · 13

Rockwell Green · Corfe · Angersleigh · Howleigh · Blagdon Hill · Staple Fitzpaine · Hatch Green · Puckington · Ilford · Barrington · Stocklinch · Shepton Beauchamp · South Petherton · A3088

Blackdown Hills · Churchstanton · Blackwater · Buckland St Mary · Broadway · Horton Cross · Seavington St Michael · Seavington St Mary · Over Stratton · Lopen · A303 · Montacute

Hemyock · Clayhidon · Birchwood · Bishopswood · Newtown · Street Ash · Ilminster · Kingstone · Dinnington · Hinton St George · Merriott · Chiselborough · West Chinnock · East Chinnock · West Coker · A30

SOMERSET · Combe St Nicholas · Peasmarsh · Knowle St Giles · Chillington · Cricket Malherbie · Cudworth · Broadshard · Crewkerne · North Perrott · Haselbury Plucknett · Hardington Mandeville

Dunkeswell · Upottery · Yarcombe · Chard · Winsham · Clapton · Misterton · South Perrott · Corscombe · Weston

Stockland · Chardstock · South Chard · Thorncombe · Broadwindsor · Beaminster · Toller Whelme

Honiton · Wilmington · Axminster · Hawkchurch · DORSET · Stoke Abbott · Mapperton · Powerstock

Seaton · Colyton · Uplyme · Lyme Regis · Charmouth · Morcombelake · Bridport · Bradpole · Shipton Gorge

SIDMOUTH · Beer · Branscombe · Seaton Bay · Beer Head · LYME BAY · West Bay · Burton Bradstock · West Bexington

YEOVIL
SHERBORNE
DORCHESTER
WEYMOUTH
ISLE OF PORTLAND
BILL OF PORTLAND

Chesil Beach
Weymouth Bay
Ringstead Bay
Lulworth Cove
Worbarrow Bay
Durdle Door
Portland Harbour
West Bay

DANGER AREA
Weymouth to Cherbourg (Proposed)
Portland Bill Lighthouse
Tout Quarry Sculpture Park
Sandsfoot Castle
Nothe Fort
Sea Life

BLACKMOOR VALE
DORSET

A30 A303 A37 A359 A357 A3030 A350 A352 A354 A35 A356 A37 A31 A353 A352
B3151 B3145 B3148 B3143 B3146 B3157 B3159 B3163 B3066 B3081 B3092 B3091 B3093 B3142 B3390 B3070 B3071

Ilchester, Yeovilton, Fleet Air Arm, Marston Magna, Queen Camel, West Camel, Cadbury, Cheriton, Kington Magna, West Stour, East Stour, Sherborne Causeway, Abbas Combe, Henstridge, Stalbridge, Marnhull, Sturminster Newton, Child Okeford, Okeford Fitzpaine, Shillingstone, Stourpaine, Durweston, Iwerne Minster, Fontmell Magna, Sutton Waldron, Manston, Hinton St Mary, Fifehead Magdalen, Stour Provost, Stour Row, Todber, Moorside, Hammoon, Fiddleford, Newton, Lydlinch, Bishop's Caundle, Purse Caundle, Stourton Caundle, Haydon, North Wootton, Alweston, Folke, Longburton, Holwell, Pulham, Mappowder, Pidney, Droop, Ibberton, Turnworth, Winterborne Stickland, Winterborne Houghton, Winterborne Clenston, Winterborne Whitechurch, Winterborne Kingston, Milton Abbas, Dewlish, Cheselbourne, Milborne St Andrew, Bere Regis, Tolpuddle, Puddletown, Athelhampton, Burleston, Affpuddle, Briantspuddle, Bovington Camp, Wool, Moreton, Crossways, Woodsford, Stokeford, East Stoke, East Lulworth, West Lulworth, Coombe Keynes, Winfrith Newburgh, Owermoigne, Osmington, Warmwell, Galton, Broadmayne, West Stafford, West Knighton, East Knighton, Watercombe, Preston, Overcombe, Chaldon Herring, Holworth, Ringstead, Upton, Sutton Poyntz, White Horse, Bincombe, Broadway, Upwey, Nottington, Radipole, Chickerell, Fleet, Charlestown, Westham, Melcombe Regis, Rodwell, Wyke Regis, Chiswell, Fortuneswell, Castletown, Grove, Easton, Weston, Southwell, Portland, Abbotsbury, Portesham, Langton Herring, West Bexington, Swyre, Puncknowle, Litton Cheney, Burton Bradstock, Shipton Gorge, Chilcombe, Long Bredy, Littlebredy, Kingston Russell, Winterbourne Abbas, Winterbourne Steepleton, Martinstown, Winterborne St Martin, Winterborne Monkton, Winterborne Herringston, Maiden Castle, Poundbury, Charminster, Stratton, Grimstone, Frampton, Maiden Newton, Cattistock, Chilfrome, Toller Porcorum, Toller Fratrum, Hooke, Beaminster, Netherbury, Powerstock, Nettlecombe, West Milton, Loders, Bradpole, Waditch, Askerswell, Compton Valence, Bradford Peverell, Charlton Down, Forston, Godmanstone, Nether Cerne, Charminster, Piddletrenthide, Piddlehinton, White Lackington, Plush, Alton Pancras, Cerne Abbas, Minterne Magna, Minterne Parva, Up Cerne, Buckland Newton, Duntish, Sharnhill Green, Lyon's Gate, Middlemarsh, Glanvilles Wootton, Hilfield, Hermitage, Batcombe, Leigh, Totnell, Chetnole, Melbury Bubb, Melbury Osmond, Melbury Sampford, East Chelborough, West Chelborough, Evershot, Holywell, Frome St Quintin, Rampisham, Higher Kingcombe, Lower Kingcombe, Higher Wraxall, Lower Wraxall, Uphall, Benville, Corscombe, Halstock, Closworth, Chetnole, Yetminster, Ryme Intrinseca, Knighton, Beer Hackett, Thornford, Bradford Abbas, Barwick, Stoford, East Coker, West Coker, North Coker, Hardington Moor, Sutton Bingham, Pendomer, Closworth, Chiselborough, West Chinnock, East Chinnock, North Perrott, South Perrott, Haselbury Plucknett, Middle Chinnock, Odcombe, Montacute, Stoke sub Hamdon, Norton sub Hamdon, Tintinhull, Chilthorne Domer, Mudford, Trent, Nether Compton, Over Compton, Stallen, Oborne, Milborne Port, Goathill, Stowell, Templecombe, Henstridge Marsh, Yenston, Upper Nyland, Lower Nyland, Gartell, Milborne Wick, Poyntington, Sandford Orcas, Corton Denham, Charlton Horethorne, Sutton Montis, Rimpton, Adber, Chilton Cantelo, Draycott, Limington, Bridgehampton, Podimore, Northover, Long Load, Milton, Stapleton, Ash, Knole, Coat, Thorncombe, Bryanston, Belchalwell, Belchalwell Street, Woolland, Stoke Wake, King's Stag, Woodbridge, Bishop's Down, Boys Hill, Crouch Hill, Sandhills, Packers Hill, Woodrow, Kingston, Fifehead Neville, Hazelbury Bryan, Wonston, Westfields, Higher Ansty, Lower Ansty, Hilton, Higher Melcombe, Lower Melcombe, Melcombe Bingham, Bingham's Melcombe, Higher Whatcombe, Lower Whatcombe, Bulbarrow Hill, Woodrow, Pidney

Hardy's Cottage, Higher Bockhampton, Lower Bockhampton, Kingston Maurward, Stinsford, Ilsington, Tincleton, Pallington, Clouds Hill, Monkey World, Tank, Dorset Collection of Clocks, Mill House Cider, Roman Temple, Maumbury Rings, Max Gate, Dinosaur, Military, Wolfeton Ho., Burton, Stinsford, Blacknoll

PAGE 192

Poole to:
Cherbourg 4hrs. 30mins.
Guernsey 3hrs.
(Fast Ferry, Seasonal)
Jersey 4hrs. 30mins.
(Fast Ferry, Seasonal)
St Malo 6hrs.
(Fast Ferry, Seasonal)

HAMPSHIRE

NEW FOREST

NATIONAL PARK

NEW FOREST New Pa

BOURNEMOUTH

POOLE

Poole Harbour

POOLE BAY

ISLE OF PURBECK

PURBECK HILLS

The Foreland or Handfast Point

Swanage Bay

Durlston Bay

DURLSTON HEAD

ST ALDHELM'S OR ST ALBAN'S HEAD

ENGLISH CHANNEL

Christchurch Bay

HENGISTBURY HEAD

THE NEEDLE

CRANBORNE CHASE

A B C D

**NEW FOREST NATIONAL PARK**

**SOUTHAMPTON**

EASTLEIGH

TOTTON

Romsey

HYTHE

FAREHAM

Portchester

GOSPOR T

Lee-on-the-Solent

Lymington

New Milton

Highcliffe

Barton on Sea

Milford on Sea

Lyndhurst

Brockenhurst

Beaulieu

Fawley

Calshot

THE NEEDLES

Freshwater

Totland

Yarmouth

COWES

East Cowes

NEWPORT

RYDE

Wootton Bridge

Havenstreet

Brading

SANDOWN

SHANKLIN

VENTNOR

Niton

St Catherine's Point

Brighstone

Shorwell

Godshill

Wroxall

**ISLE OF WIGHT**

**THE SOLENT**

Cowes Roads

Ryde Roads

Gurnard Bay

Thorness Bay

Newtown Bay

Colwell Bay

Totland Bay

Alum Bay

Compton Bay

Brighstone Bay

Chale Bay

Atherfield Point

Christchurch Bay

Stokes Bay

Gilkicker Point

**Southampton Water**

**E N G L I S H**

Bramshaw

Nomansland

Landford

Whiteparish

Redlynch

Hamptworth

Lover

Minstead

Cadnam

Copythorne

Brook

Bartley

Netley Marsh

Woodlands

Ashurst

Marchwood

Dibden

Dibden Purlieu

Hardley

Holbury

Blackfield

Langley

Exbury

Lepe

Sway

Boldre

Pilley

Bull Hill

East End

Keyhaven

Hamstead

Newtown

Shalfleet

Ningwood

Calbourne

Carisbrooke

Gatcombe

Chillerton

Rookley

Kingston

Chale Green

Blackgang

St Lawrence

Whitwell

Niton

Bonchurch

DUNNOSE

Bembridge

Arreton

Newchurch

Winford

Lake

Apse Heath

Sandford

Branstone

Wootton Common

Fishbourne

Whippingham

Northwood

Gurnard

Eastleigh

West End

Hedge End

Botley

Bursledon

Swanwick

Locks Heath

Warsash

Titchfield

Stubbington

Bridgemary

Portsmouth Harbour

Wickham

Shedfield

Swanmore

Bishop's Waltham

Droxford

Corhampton

Meonstoke

Exton

Upham

Durley

Fair Oak

Bishopstoke

Chandler's Ford

Otterbourne

Colden Common

Owslebury

Baybridge

Romsey

North Baddesley

Chilworth

Nursling

Rownhams

Maybush

Shirley

Bitterne

Sholing

Woolston

Netley Abbey

Hamble-le-Rice

Hound

M27 M271 M3 A27 A31 A33 A35 A36 A337 A326 A334 A3051 A3024 A3025 A32 A3090 A3057 A335 A336 A3055 A3056 A3020 A3021 A3054

B3054 B3055 B3058 B3078 B3079 B3080 B3084 B3035 B3037 B3342 B3054 B3053 B3401 B3399 B3323 B3333 B3335 B2177

NEW FOREST

## Map — South Downs / West Sussex / Portsmouth region

West Meon, Lower Bordean, Green Stroud, Sheet, Rogate, Fyning, Bexleyhill, Lodsworth, River, Upperton, Petworth House & Park

A272, Langrish, Ramsdean, Weston, PETERSFIELD, Trotton, Dumpford, Chithurst, Iping, Woolbeding, Easebourne, Tillington, Petworth

East Meon, Butser Hill, Nyewood, Stedham, Minsted, Midhurst, South Ambersham, Selham, Byworth, A283, Pulborough

Coombe, Nursted, West Harting, East Harting, Elsted, Marsh, West Lavington, Upper Norwood, Fittleworth, Stopham, Lower Hornecroft, Coldwal

Old Winchester Hill Fort, Queen Elizabeth, South Harting, Elsted, Cocking Causeway, Hoyle, Graffham, Duncton, Coates, B2138

Chidden, Hambledon Cricket Club Memorial, Clanfield, Chalton, Uppark, North Marden, Didling, Bepton, Cocking, Heyshott, East Lavington, Barlavington, Sutton, Watersfield

SOUTH DOWNS NATIONAL PARK, Bevis's Thumb, Devil's Jumps Barrows, Treyford, Graffham, Bignor, Amberley

Hambledon, Hoe Gate, Anthill Common, HORNDEAN, Blendworth, West Marden, Compton, Up Marden, Chilgrove, West Dean, Singleton, Charlton, East Dean, Upwaltham, Bury, Houghton

WEST SUSSEX, Forestside, Stoughton, Kingley Vale, The Trundle, Goodwood, Cass Sculpture Park, Stane Street, Madehurst, North Stoke, Offham

Denmead, Lovedean, Rowland's Castle, Deanlane End, Walderton, Woodend, Mid Lavant, Weald & Downland Open Air, Goodwood House, Eartham, Slindon, Arundel Park

Worlds End, Furzeley Corner, Cowplain, Stansted Park, Lordington, Aldsworth, Funtington, West Stoke, East Lavant, Waterbeach, Halnaker Priory, Denmans, Fontwell, A29, Arundel

WATERLOOVILLE, Southwick, Purbrook, Staunton, Leigh Park, New, Brighton, Westbourne, Woodmancote, West Ashling, East Ashling, Summersdale, Boxgrove, Norton, Nyton, Fontwell Park, Walberton, Binsted, A27

A3, Stakes, Bedhampton, HAVANT, Hermitage, Breach, Southbourne, CHICHESTER, Oving, Aldingbourne, Westgate, Eastergate, Yapton, LITTLEHAMPTON

Ports Down, Drayton, Cosham, Warblington, Emsworth, Prinsted, Nutbourne, Chidham, A259, Fishbourne, Donnington, Merston, Runcton, Colworth, Shripney, Barnham, Flansham, Clymping, Ford, Wick

Port Solent, Hilsea, Langstone, Northney, North Hayling, Bosham, Apuldram, Planetarium, Hunston Mundham, North Bersted, Middleton-on-Sea

M275, Whale Island, Stoke, Fleet, Tye, Thorney Island, West Thorney, Chichester Harbour, Rookwood, Shipton Birdham Green, Street End, South Mundham, Lagness, South Bersted, Felpham

PORTSEA ISLAND, Langstone Harbour, South Town, West Town, SOUTH HAYLING, Lifeboat Station, West Wittering, Itchenor, Somerley, Highleigh, Almodington, Sidlesham, Aldwick, Butlin's, BOGNOR REGIS

PORTSMOUTH, North End, Landport, Milton, Eastney, Royal Marines, HAYLING ISLAND, Hayling Bay, East Wittering, Bracklesham, Earnley, Norton, Pagham Harbour, St Wilfrid's Chapel, Pagham

City, Southsea, A288, Spitbank Fort, Bracklesham Bay, Selsey, East Beach, St Wilfrid's Chapel, Church Norton, East Beach

SPITHEAD, Horse Sand Fort, No Man's Land Fort, SELSEY BILL, Selsey Lifeboat Station

Nettlestone Point, Seaview, Nettlestone, St Helen's Fort, St Helens, Bembridge Point, Bembridge, FORELAND, Lane End, Lifeboat Station, Whitecliff Bay, Culver Cliff

Portsmouth to:
Bilbao 24hrs.
Caen 6hrs. (Seasonal)
Cherbourg 6hrs. (Seasonal)
Cherbourg 3hrs. (Fast Ferry, Seasonal)
Guernsey 7hrs.
Jersey 8hrs.
Le Havre 5hrs. 30mins.
St Malo 9hrs.
Santander 24hrs.

Nab Tower

CHANNEL

B R I S T O L

North West
Point

LUNDY

*Lundy Marine
Conservation Zone*

Lundy to:
*Bideford 2hrs. (Seasonal)
Ilfracombe 2hrs. (Seasonal)*

*Rat Island*

South West
Point

*BARNSTAPLE*

*OR*

*BIDEFORD BAY*

HARTLAND POINT

Windbury
Point

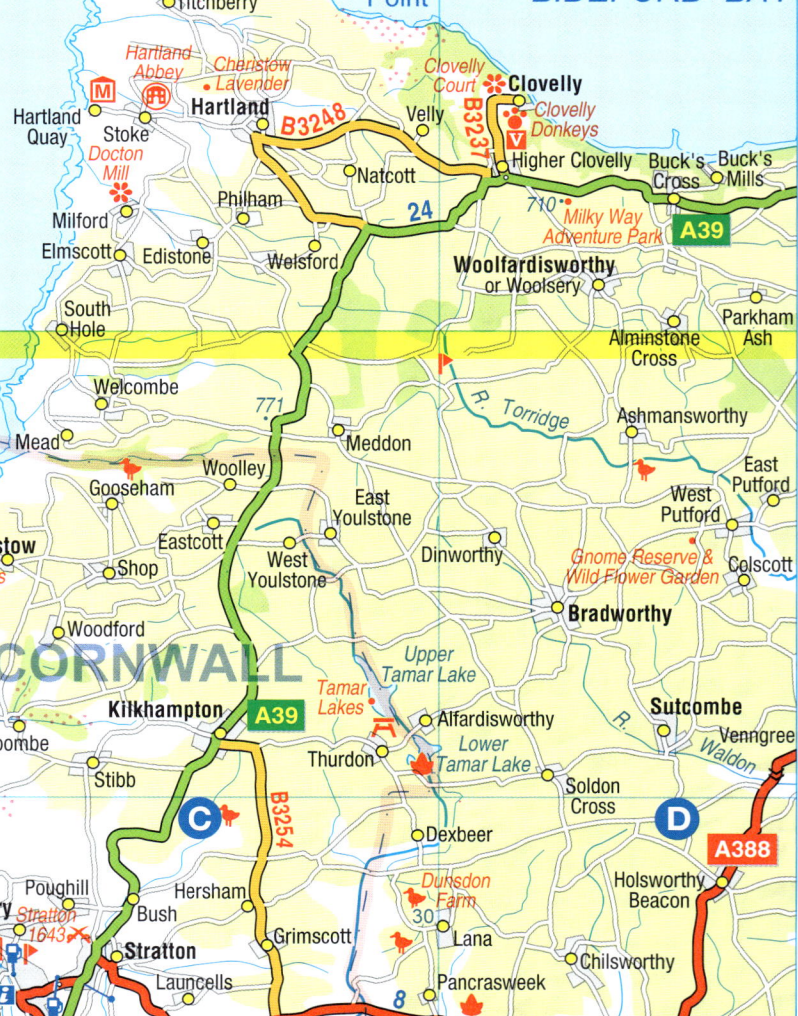

Titchberry

*Hartland
Abbey*          *Cheristow
Lavender*       *Clovelly
Court*      Clovelly

Hartland          Velly          *Clovelly
Quay       Hartland          B3248          Donkeys*

Stoke          Higher Clovelly     Buck's    Buck's
Docton          Natcott          Cross     Mills
Mill          B3237
710  *Milky Way
Milford          Philham          Welsford     Adventure Park*   A39

Elmscott          Edistone          Woolfardisworthy
or Woolsery
South          Alminstone     Parkham
Hole          Cross

Welcombe          R. Torridge          Ashmansworthy

771

Mead          Meddon          West     East
Putford    Putford

Gooseham          Woolley          East
Youlstone
West          Colscott
Morwenstow          Eastcott          Youlstone    *Gnome Reserve &
Wild Flower Garden*
Higher Sharpnose          *Hawker's          Shop          Dinworthy
Point     Hut*

Woodford          *Upper          Bradworthy
Tamar Lake*
CORNWALL
Lower Sharpnose          *Tamar          Sutcombe
Point     Lakes*

Kilkhampton          A39          Alfardisworthy          Venngree

Coombe          *Lower          Soldon
Tamar Lake*    Thurdon          Cross

Stibb          B3254

Dexbeer     A388

Poughill          Hersham          *Dunsdon          Holsworthy
Farm*     Beacon

Flexbury     *Stratton          Bush          Grimscott          Lana     Chilsworthy
1643*
*Castle Heritage
Centre*          Pancrasweek
Stratton     Launcells
Bude          Lynstone     Holsworthy

## BRISTOL CHANNEL

C H A N N E L

Foreland Point

Ilfracombe to Lundy 2hrs. (Seasonal)

Bideford to Lundy 2hrs. (Seasonal)

Bull Point
Rockham Bay
Morte Point
Morte Bay
Baggy Point
Croyde Bay

ILFRACOMBE
Aquarium
Tunnels Beaches
Lee
Higher Slade
Mullacott
Lower Slade
Hele
Berrynarbor
Chambercombe Manor
Watermouth Castle
Combe Martin Bay
Combe Martin
Pack o' Cards
Wildlife & Dinosaur Park
Corn Mill

Trentishoe
Martinhoe
Woody Bay
Heddon Valley
Heale
Dean
Lynton & Barnstaple Railway
Martinhoe Cross
Parracombe
Churchtown
Shallowford

Cliff Railway
Countisbury Cliffs
Lynton
Lynmouth
Countisbury
Lynbridge
Barbrook
Watersmeet
Brendon
Malmsmead
Tippacott
Doone Valley

Beacon Roman Fortlet
Cheriton
Furzehill
Brendon Common
Col. R.H. Maclean Memorial
Hoar Oak Tree

EXMOOR NATIONAL PARK
EXMOOR FOREST

Woolacombe
Mortehoe
Morte Point
North Buckland
Pickwell
Putsborough
Georgeham
Croyde
Forda
Darracott
Knowle
Nethercott
Winsham
Halsinger
Lobb
Saunton
Braunton
Heanton Punchardon
Wrafton
Chivenor
Ashford
Marwood
Prixford
Kingsheanton
Pippacott
Middle Marwood
Milltown
Muddiford
Shirwell
Guineaford
Broomhill Sculpture
Bradiford

West Down
Dean Cross
Cheglinch
Bittadon
Berry Down Cross
Patchole
East Down
Clifton
Churchill
Kentisbury
Kentisbury Ford
Arlington Beccott
Arlington
Arlington Court
Loxhore
Lower Loxhore
Knightacott
Stowford
Challacombe
Barton Town
Shoulsbarrow Common
Shoulsbury Castle
Fortescue Memorial
Simonsbath
Wistlandpound Resr.
Blackmoor Gate

Bratton Fleming
Stoke Rivers
Lower Loxhore
Leworthy
Lydcott
Brayford
High Bray
North Radworthy
North Heasley
South Radworthy
Heasley Mill
North Molton

BARNSTAPLE
Newport
Jungleland
Landkey
Landkey Newland
Bishop's Tawton
Swimbridge Newland
Swimbridge
Hannaford
Heddon
Cobbaton
Castle Hill
Stag's Head
Filleigh
Quince Honey Farm
SOUTH MOLTON
Bishop's Nympton
George Nympton
Marianslegh
Alswear
Romansleigh
Meshaw

Fremington
Fremington Quay
Yelland
Instow
Bickleton
Westleigh
Eastleigh
Horwood
Holmacott
Lake
Bickington
Tawstock
St John's Chapel
Eastacombe
Harracott
Week
Newton Tracey
Hiscott
Ensis
Chapelton
Herner
Combat Collection
Chittlehampton
East Stowford
Clapworthy

Appledore
Northam Burrows
Lifeboat Station
Signal Box
Northam
Westward Ho!
Buckleigh
Big Sheep
Abbotsham
Orchard Hill
BIDEFORD
East-the-Water
Burton Art Gallery
Railway
Atlantis Adventure Park
Landcross
Huntshaw
Weare Giffard
Hallspill
Saltrens
Littleham
Monkleigh
Buckland Brewer
Frithelstock
Frithelstock Stone
Southcott
Taddiport
GREAT TORRINGTON
RHS Rosemoor
Dartington Crystal
Priory
Little Torrington
St Giles in the Wood
Kingscott
Stevenstone
Cranford
Huish
Stony Cross
Gammaton
Woodtown
Lower Lovacott
Alverdiscott
Yarnscombe
Atherington
Umberleigh
Eastacott
Warkleigh
Satterleigh
Chittlehamholt

High Bullen
Sherwood Green
Langridgeford
High Bickington
King's Nympton

Parkham
Fairy Cross
Ford
Woodtown
Alwington
Goldworthy
Littleham
Tythecott
Thornehillhead
Langtree
Stibb Cross
Berry Cross
Peters Marland
Winswell
Merton
Barometer World
Dolton
Dowland
Upcott
Iddesleigh
Winkleigh
Ashreigney
Riddlecombe
Burrington
Roborough
Beaford
Elstone
Aylescott
Eberley Hill
Bulkworthy
Abbots Bickington
Haytown
Newton St Petrock
Gratton
Caute
Shop
Milton Damerel
Thornbury
Shebbear
Buckland Filleigh
Folly Cross
North Town
Petrockstowe
Meeth
Woodacott
Bradford
Cookbury Wick
Cookbury
Holemoor
Sheepwash
Black Torrington
Monkokehampton
Broadwoodkelly
Ingleigh Green

Chulmleigh
Cheldon
West Worlington
East Worlington
Thelbridge Barton
Chawleigh
Eggesford
East Ashley
Hollocombe
Bridge Reeve
Coldridge
Nymet Rowland
Lapford
Lapford Cross
Morchard Bishop
Eastington
Filleigh
Nymet Rowland
West Worthy
West Leigh
East Leigh
Weeke
Oldborough

Rivers: R. Yeo, R. Taw, R. Mole, R. Bray, River Torridge, R. Torridge, River Taw, L. Dart River, R. Yeo

Roads: A39, A361, A377, A386, A388, A399, A3123, A3124, B3343, B3230, B3231, B3232, B3233, B3234, B3226, B3227, B3229, B3358, B3226, B3137, B3096, B3042, B3220, B3042

DEVON

A    B    32    C    D

**B R I S T O L  C H A N N E L**

Point

1

Foreland Point

Cliff Railway
Countisbury Cliffs
nton Lynmouth Countisbury
A39  1135
Glenthorne Pinetum
xmoor
3234
Lynbridge
Watersmeet
Barbrook
Brendon  Malmsmead
Cheriton  Tippacott  Oare
Oareford
Furzehill
hallowed  West Lyn
Doone Valley
Brendon Common
Culbone Hill  Toll
Culbone
Whit Stones
Toll  Greencombe
Porlock Weir
West Porlock
Lynch
Porlock  Brandish Street
Dovery Manor
Horner
Dunkery & Horner Wood
Luccombe
Huntscott

Porlock Bay
Bossington  1012
Selworthy Beacon  Chapel  North Hill
Woodcombe Higher Town
Selworthy  Bratton  Peri ton
Allerford
Tivington  Alcombe
**MINEHEAD**
Butlin's
Exmoor National Park
Marsh Street
Blue Anchor
Dunster
Carhampton
Withycombe

**Blue Anchor Bay**
Blue Anchor Railway
Chapel Cleeve  Old Cleeve
Watchet  Doniford
West Quantoxhead
Five Bells
Williton
B3191
B3190
Sampford Brett  Bicknoller
A358
Newton
Kingswood
Stogumber

2

Hoar Oak Tree
Pinkworthy Pond  1598
E X M O O R
Col. R.H. Maclaren Memorial
Alderman's Barrow  1527
Stoke Pero
Dunkery Beacon  1704
Dunkery Hill  1403
1456

sbarrow mon
mmon
F O R E S T
Dure Down
isbury stle
19

**EXMOOR**
River Exe
Burrow
Timbercombe

Croydon Hill
Rodhuish
Bilbrook  Hungerford
Torre  Beggearn Huish
Golsoncott  Roadwater
Yarde  Stream  Capton
Monksilver  951  Chidgley
Vellow
Higher Vexford  Lower Vexford
Willett
Combe Sydenham
Elworthy  Elworthy Cottage
B3188
B3224

3

North Radworthy
North Heasley
South Radworthy  1427
Heasley Mill
Simonsbath
B3223
Fortescue Memorial  1618
Newland
Edgcott  17  B3224
Exford  1265
Withypool
Withypool Common
Winsford Hill  1405
Wambarrows
Liscombe
Caratacus Stone
Tarr Steps
Week
Dane's Brook
Molland Brook  Common
Hawkridge

**NATIONAL**  **PARK**
R. Barle  1454
Winsford
B3223
R. Exe
20
Wheddon Cross
Cutcombe
Luckwell Bridge  17
Exton  Bridgetown
A396

B R E N D O N  H I L L S
1252
Kingsbridge
Luxborough  Treborough
Leighland Chapel
B3224  17
Gupworthy
Brompton Regis
Withiel Florey
Woolcotts
Wimbleball Lake Country Park
Hartford  1039
Upton
Clatworthy Reservoir
Huish Champflower
Langley Marsh  Whitefield
Langley  Ford
Pitsford Hill  Tarr
Brompton Ralph  Tolland
Rook's Nest
Willett
B3188
B3224

4

Twitchen
Molland
North Molton
R. Mole
Mill  Newtown
Bishop's Nympton
Mariansleigh
Alswear
B3137
Romansleigh
B3227  60
South Molton
Lee
West Anstey
East Anstey
Bottreaux Mill  Yeo Mill
Ash Mill
Knowstone  13
Roachill
Oakfordbridge
Dulverton
Guildhall Heritage & Arts Cen.
Battleton  Brushford
Nightcott  Oldways End
B3222
Exebridge
Bury
Morebath
Skilgate
Blackwell
Waterrow
Petton
Shillingford
Clayhanger
B3227
Hartswell
Milverton
B3187
Wiveliscombe
Croford
Fitzhead
Heydon Hill
Chipstable
Bathealton
Chipley
Langford Budville  Runnington
Ashbrittle  Appley  Thorne St Margaret  Payton
Cothay Manor
Greenham  Holywell  Westford

E X E  V A L E
Staple Cross
Huntsham
Hockworthy
Cove
Grand Western Canal

D E V O N

5

Meshaw
Venhay  Rackenford
Bradford Barton
Queen Dart
Mogworthy
Week  Lutworthy
West Worlington  Drayton
East Worlington
Thelbridge Barton
Washford Pyne
Creacombe
Stoodleigh Beacon  987
Ford Barton
Stoodleigh
12
A396
Cheldon  Nomansland
Witheridge
North Coombe
Loxbeare  60
Washfield
Lurley  Calverleigh
Chettiscombe
Templeton
Withleigh
B3137
Pennymoor
Cruwys Morchard
Way Village
Mid Devon Life
Cotteylands
Cowleymoor
**TIVERTON**
Knightshayes Court  Chevithorne
Bolham
Uplowman
Whitnage
Ayshford
Fair Oak
Holcombe Rogus
Westleigh  A38
Burlescombe
Sampford Arundel
M5
Appledore  Nicholashayne
Prescott  Whitehall
**TIVERTON**
Uffculme  Culmstock
Coldharbour Mill
Craddock  Northcott  845  Hackpen Hill
Ashill

Chawleigh
Dart River
eigh
Filleigh
Lapford
A377
Morchard Bishop
Eastington
Black Dog
Oldborough
Kennerleigh
East Village
Cheriton Fitzpaine
Poughill
Upham
Hayne
Puddington
Woolfardisworthy
Littleborough
Cadeleigh
Devon Railway Centre
Bickleigh
Butterleigh
East Butterleigh
**CULLOMPTON**
Cullompton
Willand
Digg
Stoneyford
Sampford Peverell
Smithincott
Ash Thomas
Halberton
Willand
B3440
Kentisbeare
Blackborough
Sheldon
Saint Hill
Kerswell
Mutterton  Dulford
Colebrook
Broadhembury
A361
A396
12
28
M5

B3042
ymet  nton
A377
Morchard Cross
Lapford Cross
gh
Weeke
B327

Flat Holm

Sand Bay

Kewstoke

St George's

Bourton

Hewish

West Hewish

Congresbury

Redhill

A38

Worle

Puxton

Wrington

Cowslip Green

A370

BRISTOL

Steep Holm

Weston Bay

WESTON-SUPER-MARE

SeaQuarium

Milton

West Wick

NORTH SOMERSET

Lower Langford

Butcombe

Nempnet Thrubwell

Regil

33

M5

B3440

G

A371

Stoneridge

Banwell

A368

Sandford

Churchill

Upper Langford

Burrington

Blagdon Lake

Blagdon

21

A368

Ubley

Compton Martin

Uphill

Locking

Hutton

Knightcott

Winscombe

Sidcot

Shipham

Rowberrow

Rock of Ages

Combe

MENDIP HILLS

Brean Down Fort

Tropical Bird Garden

Brean Down

Oldmixon

Bleadon

Christon

Barton

Compton Bishop

Cross

King John's Hunting Lodge

Charterhouse

Mendip Forest

B3134

Brean

A370

M5

Loxton

Lower Weare

Axbridge

Cheddar Resr

Cheddar

Cheddar Gorge

Bradley Cross

Draycott

Rodney Stoke

DANGER AREA

Priddy

Animal Farm Adventure Park

Brean Leisure Park

Lympsham

Wick

Eastertown

Edingworth

Biddisham

Badgworth

Weare

Brinscombe

Alston Sutton

Clewer

Crickham

Nyland Hill

Westbury-sub-Mendip

Easton

Wookey Hole

Burcott

Berrow

B3140

East Brent

Rooks Bridge

Tarnock

Stone Allerton

Chapel Allerton

Cocklake

Bagley

Bleadney

Henton

Wookey

Haybridge

BURNHAM-ON-SEA

Brent Knoll

Battleborough

Edithmead

Vole

Mark

B3139

West Stoughton

Middle Stoughton

Wedmore

Sand

Heath House

Theale

Panborough

B3139

Highbridge

B3140

Apex

Northwick

Mark Causeway

Yarrow

Westham

Blackford

Bleadney

Mudgley

Lilstock

Kilton

Knighton

Burton

Shurton

Wick

Stockland Bristol

Steart

Otterhampton

Stretcholt

West Huntspill

Huntspill

Bason Bridge

East Huntspill

Burtle

Westhay

Meare

Oxenpill

Stileway

B3151

East Quantoxhead

Kilve

Stringston

Stogursey

Combwich

Pawlett

A38

Dunball

Woolavington

Cossington

Chilton Polden

Edington

Catcott

Shapwick

Westhay

Lower Godney

Upper Godney

Polsham

Coxley

Southway

Holford

Dodington

Nether Stowey

Fiddington

A39

Rodway

Cannington

Chilton Trinity

Puriton

A39

Horsey

Bawdrip

Stawell

Moorlinch

Greinton

Ashcott

Walton

A39

Street

GLASTONBURY

Glastonbury Tor

Northover

Edgarley

Havyatt

Halsway

QUANTOCK HILLS

Over Stowey

Coleridge Cottage

Walled

Charlynch

Bradley Green

Wembdon

Northfield

Blake

Sydenham

Chedzoy

Sutton Mallet

Pedwell

POLDEN HILLS

Baltonsborough

Butleigh Wootton

Crowcombe

Triscombe

Wills Neck

Aisholt

Plainsfield

Four Forks

Pightley

Enmore

BRIDGWATER

Bussex

Westonzoyland

Greylake

Henley

Dundon

Compton Dundon

Butleigh

Flaxpool

Heathfield

Bagborough

Terhill

Merridge

Goathurst

Durleigh

Huntworth

A372

Middlezoy

Thorngrove

Othery

Beer

High Ham

Littleton

Kingweston

Combe Florey

Cothelstone

Broomfield

Huntstile

M5

Northmoor Green or Moorland

A361

King's Sedge Moor

Stembridge

Somerton

Charlton Mackrell

Ash Priors

Bishops Lydeard

Courtway

Ash

Kingston St Mary

Thurloxton

North Newton

Bankland

Pathe

Burrow Mump

Aller

Bowdens

Low Ham

Pitney

B3153

Charlton Adam

Lydeard St Lawrence

East Combe

Fulford

Adsborough

West Monkton

West Newton

West Lyng

East Lyng

Athelney

Stathe

DANGER AREA

Wearne

Pict's Hill

Langport

Huish Episcopi

Upton

Kingsdon

TAUNTON DEANE

Nailsbourne

Cheddon Fitzpaine

Monkton Heathfield

Bathpool

Creech St Michael

Charlton

North Curry

Stoke St Gregory

Curry Rivel

Portfield

Long Sutton

Catsgore

A372

Preston Bowyer

Norton Fitzwarren

Staplegrove

A3259

Durston

Meare Green

Huntham

West Sedge Moor

Wick

Drayton

Muchelney

Knole

Northover

B3151

Ilchester

Halse

West Somerset Railway

A358

Staplehay

Bishop's Hull

Ruishton

Ham

Knapp

Helland

Burton Pynsent

Priest's House

Pibsbury

Midelney

Long Load

Milton

A303

TAUNTON

Trull

Stoke St Mary

Thornfalcon

Lilleston

Newport

Swell

A378

Midelney

Muchelney Ham

Thorney

Kingsbury Episcopi

Stapleton

A37

Wellington

Rockwell Green

West Buckland

M5

Haydon

Shoreditch

Orchard Portman

Thurlbear

Wrantage

Hatch Green

West Hatch

Curry Mallet

Beercrocombe

Fivehead

Isle Brewers

Hambridge

Somerset Distillery

Coat

Stembridge

Chilthorne Domer

Tonedale

A38

Nynehead

Chelston

Poole

Galmington

Rumwell

Trull

Sheppy's Cider

Fulwood

Sellick's Green

Corfe

Pitminster

Fivehead

Hatch Beauchamp

Slough Green

Hatch Green

Westport

New Cross

East Lambrook

Barrington Court

Tintinhull

Martock

A3088

Ford Street

Angersleigh

Howleigh

Blagdon Hill

Staple Fitzpaine

Bickenhall

Curland

Ashill

Ilton

Ilford

Puckington

Lambrook

South Petherton

Stoke sub Hamdon

Montacute House

BLACKDOWN HILLS

Clayhidon

Rosemary Lane

Otterford

Churchstanton

Blackwater

Blindmoor

Buckland St Mary

Staple Hill

Curland Common

Hare

Windmill Hill

Broadway

Horton

Horton Cross

Shepton Beauchamp

Barrington

Hurcott

Seavington St Michael

Wigborough

Odcombe

Norton sub Hamdon

Chiselborough

Brympton D'Evercy

Montacute

Hemyock

Clayhidon

Culm Davy

Rosemary Lane

Stapley

Birchwood

Buckland St Mary

Newtown

Ham

A303

Horton

Donyatt

Ilminster

Kingstone

Seavington St Mary

Allowenshay

Over Stratton

Lopen

A356

West Chinnock

Chiselborough

West Coker

Abbey

Dunkeswell

Madford

Bolham Water

Smeatharpe

Churchinford

Royston Water

Bishopswood

Beetham

Ashill

Marsh

Whitestaunton

Northay

Combe St Nicholas

Wadeford

Nimmer

Knowle St Giles

Cricket Malherbie

Dowlish Wake

Perry's Cider

Dinnington

Hinton St George

Chillington

Merriott

Lower Severalls

Crewkerne

Haselbury Plucknett

North Perrott

Hardington Mandeville

Upottery

Newcott

Yarcombe

Wambrook

Chard

B3162

Chaffcombe

Tatworth

Knowle St Giles

Cudworth

Chard Junction

Roundham

Heritage Centre

Hewish

Haselbury Plucknett

Misterton

North Perrott

South Perrott

A3066

Luppitt

Rawridge

Beacon

Upottery

Crawley

Burridge

B3167

Forton

Holy City

Whatley

Winsham

Perry Street

Wayford

Clapton

Seaborough

Mosterton

Drimpton

Corscombe

Bromham
St Edith's Marsh
Millennium White Horse
Bishops Cannings
Allington
Stanton St Bernard
Alton Priors
Huish
Oare
Wootton Rivers
Ram Alley
Durley
Great Bedwyn
Crofton
Stibb Green
Beam Engines
Wilton

MELKSHAM
A342
Rowde
Roundway
Dunkirk
Coate
Horton
Alton Barnes
Honey Street
West Stowell
New Mill
Milton
Easton Royal
Burbage
Eastcourt
23

A365
B3101
Sells Green
Seend Cleeve
Wiltshire
Broadleas
DEVIZES
Nursteed
Etchilhampton
Woodborough
Wilcot
Pewsey
Southcott
Easton
Grafton
Wexcombe
Tidcombe

B3107
Bowerhill
Kennet & Avon Canal
A361
Stert
Patney
Wedhampton
Chirton
Marden
Wilsford
Manningford Bruce
North Newnton
Charlton
Rushall
Manningford Bohune
White Horse Pewsey Hill
Aughton
Brunton

Hilperton
Poulshot
Potterne
A360
Worton
Marston
Conock
A342
Everleigh
East Everleigh
Collingbourne Kingston
Sunton
Cadley
Collingbourne Ducis
A346
Ludgershall

A350
Keevil
Bulkington
Urchfont
Eastcott
Easterton
West Chisenbury
East Chisenbury
Lower Everleigh
A342
A338
West Grafton

Steeple Ashton
Great Hinton
Coulston
DANGER AREA
Littleton Pannell
Market Lavington
Compton
Enford
Littlecott
Longstreet
Coombe
Haxton Down
North Tidworth
Tidworth
A3026
Great Shoddesden
Perham Down
Little Shoddesden

West Ashton
Edington
Bratton
B3098
Erlestoke
Little Cheverell
West Lavington
Fifield
Fittleton
Netheravon
Dovecote
Figheldean
Brigmerston
Milston
Shipton Bellinger
Tidworth Camp
South Tidworth
A338
Kimpton
Fyf
Thruxton

White Horse
Bratton Camp
Summer Down
Imber
West Down
Black Heath
DANGER AREA
Enford Down
Ablington
DANGER AREA
Knighton Down
A345
Larkhill
Durrington
Bulford
Kiwi
Bulford Camp
Beacon Hill
2
A303
Quarley

WARMINSTER
Boreham
Heytesbury
Knook
SALISBURY
Tilshead
Orcheston Down
Orcheston
Elston
B3086
Maddington
Shrewton
Woodhenge
The Cursus
Stonehenge
Countess
Amesbury
Charlie's Farm
Cholderton
B3084
Newton Tony or Newton Toney
Grateley
Over Wallop

Norton Bavant
Bishopstrow
Sutton Veny
Tytherington
Corton
Codford
Upton Lovell
Boyton
Fisherton de la Mere
Deptford
Berwick St James
Over Street
Stapleford
Winterbourne Stoke
A360
West Amesbury
Wilsford
Lake
Great Durnford
A345
Allington
Boscombe Down
Boscombe
Idmiston
Porton
Gomeldon
Idmiston
A303
A343
Lopcombe Corner
Middle Winterslow
East Winterslow
A30

A36
PLAIN
Sherrington
Stockton
Bapton
Wylye
Hanging Langford
Little Langford
Steeple Langford
Wylye Valley
Stoford
Middle Woodford
Upper Woodford
Heale
Salterton
Netton
Winterbourne Dauntsey
Winterbourne Gunner
A338
Winterbourne Earls
Firsdown
West Winterslow
The Common

A350
Pertwood
Great Ridge
A303
Chicklade
Berwick St Leonard
Hindon
B3089
Great Wishford
South Newton
A36
Chilhampton
Lower Woodford
Stratford sub Castle
Hurdcott
Ford
Bishopdown
A30
Laverstock
Pitton
Farley
West Tytherley

East Knoyle
Fonthill Bishop
Ridge
Chilmark
Teffont Magna
Philipps Ho.
Little Clarendon
Baverstock
Barford St Martin
Ditchampton
Fugglestone
St Peter
Quidhampton
Old Sarum
P+R
Bemerton
SALISBURY
PAGE 201
Petersfinger
Farley
East Grimstead
West Dean
Lockerle

Fonthill Gifford
Lower Chicksgrove
Teffont Evias
B3089
Dinton
Compton Chamberlayne
Burcombe
Ugford
Wilton
Wilton House
Netherhampton
Harnham
Mompesson
A3094
P+R
Britford
Alderbury
Whaddon
West Grimstead
East Dean
Dean Hill

Tisbury
Upper Chicksgrove
Sutton Mandeville
Fovant
Badges
Chiselbury Hillfort
Stratford Tony
Coombe Bissett
Odstock
Homington
Nunton
Bodenham
The Pepperbox
4
Whiteparish

Newtown
East Hatch
Swallowcliffe
Ansty
West End
Fifield Bavant
Bishopstone
Stoke Farthing
Croucheston
R. Ebble
Odstock Down
Charlton All Saints
A36
Newton

Pythouse Kitchen
Old Wardour
St Bartholomew's Hill
Donhead St Andrew
A30
Ebbesbourne Wake
Broad Chalke
Alvediston
Bowerchalke
Woodminton
A354
Rockbourne Down
Wick Down
Wick
Downton
Morgan's Vale
Redlynch
Lover
Hamptworth
Landford
West Wellow

Donhead St Mary
Milkwell
Ludwell
Berwick St John
Winkelbury Camp
Win Green
Martin Drove End
Woodyates
Martin
15
Tidpit
Whitsbury
Upper Street
North Charford
Woodfalls
Breamore House
Platford

Gold Hill
Cann Common
B3081
Charlton
Melbury Abbas
Compton Abbas
Ashmore
Well Bottom
Tollard Royal
Larmer Tree
Tollard Farnham
Woodcutts
Deanland
New Town
Martin Down
Pentridge
607 Pentridge Hill
Rockbourne
Rockbourne Villa
Sir Eyre Coote's Monument
Outwick
Breamore
Woodgreen
Castle Hill
Nomansland
Bramshaw
5

Ashmore
Stubhampton
Dean
Gussage St Andrew
Minchington
Sixpenny Handley
Boveridge
Damerham
Sandleheath
Alderholt Mill
Lower Burgate
Upper Burgate
Godshill
Fritham
Upper Canterton
Brook
Copy

Tarrant Gunville
Chettle
Chettle House
Cashmoor
Monkton Up Wimborne
Cranborne Manor
Cranborne
Crendell
Daggons
Fordingbridge
Stuckton
Bickton
Blissford
Frogham
Hungerford
North Gorley
Hyde
Stoney Cross
Reptile Cen

SOUTH
Tarrant Hinton
A354
Gussage St Michael
Gussage All Saints
Wimborne St Giles
Knowlton Church & Earthworks
Edmondsham
B3081
Dorset Heavy Horse Centre
Alderholt
A338
South Gorley
Mockbeckgar
HAMPSHIRE
NEW FOREST
Pimperne
Long Crichel
Moor Crichel
Manswood
Woodlands
Whitmore
Verwood
Ebblake
Ellingham
Linwood
Rockford
A31
NATIONAL PARK
Deer Sanctuary
Bolderwood
Knightwood Oak
Emery Down

Blandford Camp
Royal Signals
Blandford Forum
Tarrant Monkton
Tarrant Rawston
Witchampton
Hogstock
Chalbury Common
Chalbury
Horton
Wigbeth
Crab Orchard
Moors Valley
B3081
Verwood
Blashford
Hangersley
Linford
Poulner
Picket Post
Burley
Rhinefield Ornamental Drive
Bolderwood Ornamental Drive
Minstea

Langton Long Blandford
Tarrant Rushton
Hemsworth
Hinton Martell
Gaunt's Common
Mannington
Three Legged Cross
Ashley Heath
Ringwood
Hangersley
Pikes
Newtow

**WILTSHIRE**

**HAMPSHIRE**

**BASINGSTOKE**

**ANDOVER**

**WINCHESTER**

**SOUTHAMPTON**

**EASTLEIGH**

**FAREHAM**

**HYTHE**

**TOTTON**

**NEW FOREST NATIONAL PARK**

Major roads: A338, A339, A340, A343, A34, A303, A30, A31, A33, A35, A36, A27, A272, A32, A326, A337, A3090, A3057, A342, A346, A3026, M3, M27, M271, B3400, B3048, B3420, B3049, B3046, B3047, B3084, B3079, B3078, B3060, B3035, B2177, B3354, A3024, A3025, A3051, A334, A336, A331

Towns and villages: Burbage, East Grafton, Great Bedwyn, Shalbourne, Ham, Combe, Inkpen, Woolton Hill, Highclere, Burghclere, Kingsclere, Overton, Whitchurch, Ludgershall, Tidworth, Andover, Appleshaw, Weyhill, Thruxton, Over Wallop, Middle Wallop, Stockbridge, Broughton, Houghton, King's Somborne, Sparsholt, Winchester, Romsey, Mottisfont, Michelmersh, Braishfield, Ampfield, Chandler's Ford, North Baddesley, Rownhams, Nursling, Totton, Southampton, Eastleigh, West End, Hedge End, Botley, Bishop's Waltham, Swanmore, Shedfield, Wickham, Fareham, Titchfield, Locks Heath, Park Gate, Swanwick, Bursledon, Netley Abbey, Hythe, Dibden, Marchwood, Ashurst, Lyndhurst, Minstead, Cadnam, Winsor, Copythorne, Bramshaw, Landford, Whiteparish, West Dean, Mottisfont, Lockerley, Broadlands, Basingstoke, Oakley, Overton, Preston Candover, Old Alresford, New Alresford, Cheriton, Bramdean, Twyford, Colden Common, Owslebury, Upham, Corhampton, Meonstoke, Droxford, Waltham Chase, Curdridge, Warsash, Sarisbury Green

MAIN ROUTE 184    38    MAIN ROUTE 185

NORTH DOWNS    SURREY    WEST SUSSEX    SOUTH DOWNS NATIONAL PARK    ST LEONARDS FOREST

**GUILDFORD** PAGE 195    **DORKING**    **REIGATE**    **CRAWLING / CRAWLEY**    **HORSHAM**    **GODALMING**    **HASLEMERE**    **MIDHURST**    **PETWORTH**    **PULBOROUGH**    **BILLINGSHURST**    **STORRINGTON**    **HENFIELD**    **ARUNDEL**    **LITTLEHAMPTON**    **WORTHING**    **SHOREHAM-BY-SEA**    **PORTSLADE-by-Sea**    **SOUTHWICK**    **BOGNOR REGIS**    **Middleton-on-Sea**

A322 A324 A323 A331 A323 A31 A3 A247 A246 A25 A24 A246 A248 A281 A25 A29 A24 A23 A264 A281 A272 A283 A286 A287 A29 A283 A284 A285 A27 A259 A280 A259 A2037 A281 A2044 A217

South Downs    West Dean    Goodwood    Bognor Harbour    Pagham Harbour

E N G L I S H

CATERHAM
M25
SEVENOAKS
Kent Street
Mereworth
Nettlestead

Westerham
Plaxtol
West Peckham
Nettlestead Green

REDHILL
Oxted
Limpsfield
Knole
Ightham Mote
East Peckham

A25
Godstone
Ide Hill
Shipbourne
Hadlow
Barnes Street
A228

M23
Bletchingley
Crockham Hill
Sevenoaks Weald
Hildenborough
Golden Green
East Peckham

A23
Redhill
A22
Edenbridge
Chiddingstone Causeway
Leigh
TONBRIDGE
River Medway
Hop Farm Family Park
Paddock Wood

Outwood
Crowhurst
Hever
Chiddingstone
Penshurst
Southborough
A228

HORLEY
Lingfield
Dormansland
Cowden
Markbeech
Speldhurst
High Brooms
PEMBURY
Brenchley
Horsmonden

Smallfield
Dormans Park
Hammerwood
Ashurst
Fordcombe
Rusthall
ROYAL TUNBRIDGE WELLS
Matfield

Copthorne
Crawley Down
EAST GRINSTEAD
Forest Row
Groombridge
Frant
Lamberhurst

M23
Turners Hill
Ashurst Wood
Hartfield
Withyham
Eridge Green
Cousley Wood
Wadhurst

Balcombe
West Hoathly
Sharpthorne
ASHDOWN FOREST
Crowborough
Mark Cross
Durgates
Three Leg Cross

HAYWARDS HEATH
Horsted Keynes
Chelwood Gate
Nutley
Poundfield
Rotherfield
Mayfield
Stonegate
King John's Lodge

Cuckfield
Danehill
Chelwood Common
Duddleswell
Heron's Ghyll
Jarvis Brook
Witherenden Hill
Burwash

Lindfield
Scaynes Hill
Fletching
Maresfield
Five Ash Down
Hadlow Down
Five Ashes
Burwash Common

Hurstpierpoint
BURGESS HILL
Newick
Piltdown
Buxted
Broad Oak
Heathfield
Burwash Weald

Wivelsfield
North Chailey
Ridgewood
UCKFIELD
Framfield
Blackboys
Cross in Hand
Punnett's Town
Three Cups Corner

Hassocks
Ditchling
Chailey
Isfield
Little Horsted
Waldron
Little London
Old Heathfield

Keymer
Westmeston
Plumpton
Barcombe Cross
Halland
East Hoathly
Horam
Herstmonceux

Clayton
Plumpton Green
Barcombe
Shortgate
Chiddingly
Gun Hill
Magham Down
Windmill Hill

A23
Offham
Broyle Side
Laughton
Whitesmith
Hellingly
Herstmonceux
Boreham Street

SOUTH DOWNS
Hamsey
Ringmer
Golden Cross
Lower Dicker
HAILSHAM
Pevensey Levels

Falmer
LEWES
Glyndebourne
Ripe
Upper Dicker
Polegate
Pevensey

BRIGHTON
Kingston near Lewes
Iford
Glynde
Chalvington
Wilmington
Stone Cross
Westham

HOVE
Woodingdean
Rodmell
Firle
Selmeston
Alfriston
Willingdon
Pevensey Bay

Saltdean
Telscombe
South Heighton
Berwick
Folkington
EASTBOURNE

Rottingdean
Peacehaven
Denton
Litlington
Jevington
Ratton Village

NEWHAVEN
SEAFORD
Exceat
Friston
East Dean
BEACHY HEAD

CHANNEL
Seven Sisters

MAIDSTONE

NORTH

HIGH WEALD

LOW WEALD

WEALD

EAST SUSSEX

ROYAL TUNBRIDGE WELLS

ASHFORD

Mereworth · Wateringbury · Barming · Shepway · Leeds · Harrietsham · Lenham · Charing · Challock

Kent Street · Pound · Nettlestead · Teston · East Farleigh · Loose · Langley · Broomfield · Sandway · Leadingcross Green · Charing Heath · Westwell · Boughton Lees

Golden Green · East Peckham · Yalding · Coxheath · Linton · Boughton Monchelsea · Chart Corner · Langley Heath · Kingswood · Lenham Heath · Hothfield · Great Chart · Kingsnorth

Five Oak Green · Paddock Wood · Laddingford · Collier Street · Marden · Staplehurst · Headcorn · Pluckley · Chilmington Green · Stubb's Cross

Pembury · Matfield · Brenchley · Horsmonden · Goudhurst · Sissinghurst · Biddenden · High Halden · Bethersden · Shadoxhurst · Woodchurch

Lamberhurst · Kilndown · Cranbrook · Benenden · Tenterden · St Michaels · Brissenden Green · Hamstreet · Orlestone

Wadhurst · Flimwell · Hawkhurst · The Moor · Sandhurst · Rolvenden · Rolvenden Layne · Wittersham · Appledore · Brookland

Ticehurst · Stonegate · Hurst Green · Bodiam · Northiam · Beckley · Peasmarsh · Iden · Playden · Rye · Camber

Burwash · Etchingham · Robertsbridge · Ewhurst Green · Mill Corner · Clayhill · Rye Foreign · East Guldeford · Winchelsea · Rye Harbour

Punnett's Town · Brightling · Mountfield · Netherfield · Cripp's Corner · Broad Oak · Udimore · Icklesham · Winchelsea Beach

Herstmonceux · Windmill Hill · Ninfield · Battle · Whatlington · Sedlescombe · Westfield · Three Oaks · Guestling Green · Pett · Cliff End

Wartling · Hooe · Crowhurst · Catsfield · Baldslow · Ore · Fairlight · Fairlight Cove

Stone Cross · Westham · Pevensey · Pevensey Bay · Bexhill · St Leonards · HASTINGS

EASTBOURNE · PAGE 194

ENGLISH CHANNEL

Pevensey Bay · Rye Bay

A20 · A21 · A26 · A28 · A228 · A229 · A259 · A262 · A268 · A271 · M20

# CHANNEL TUNNEL

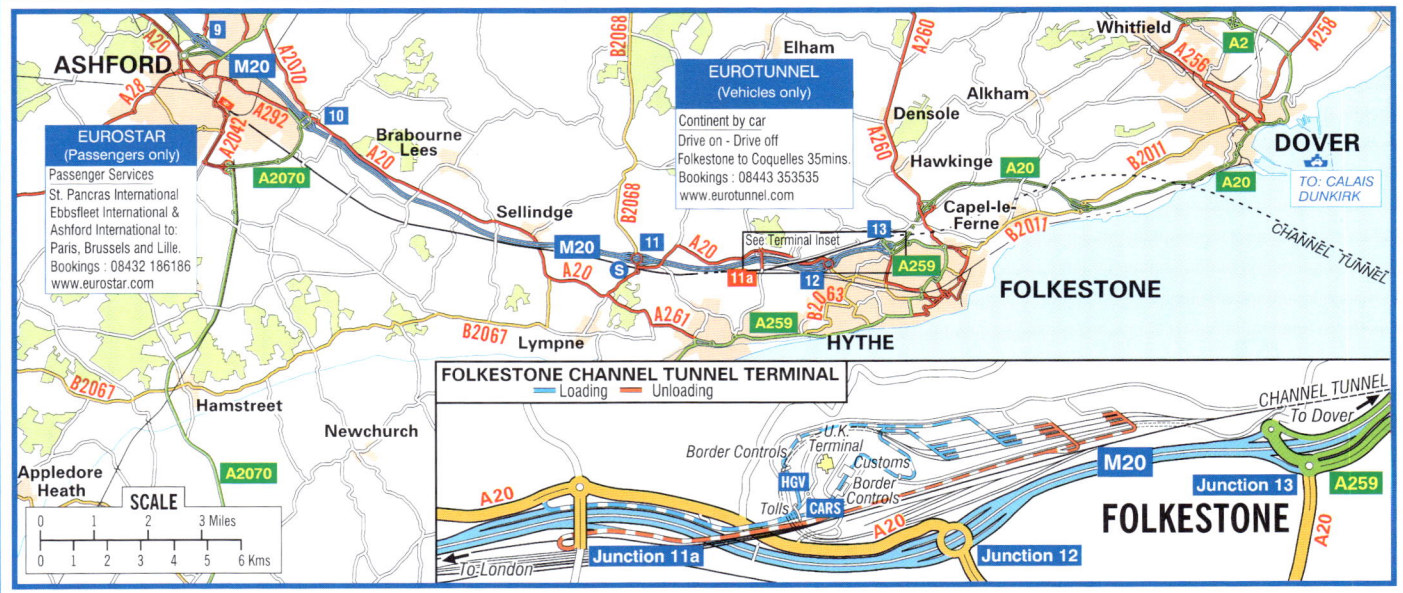

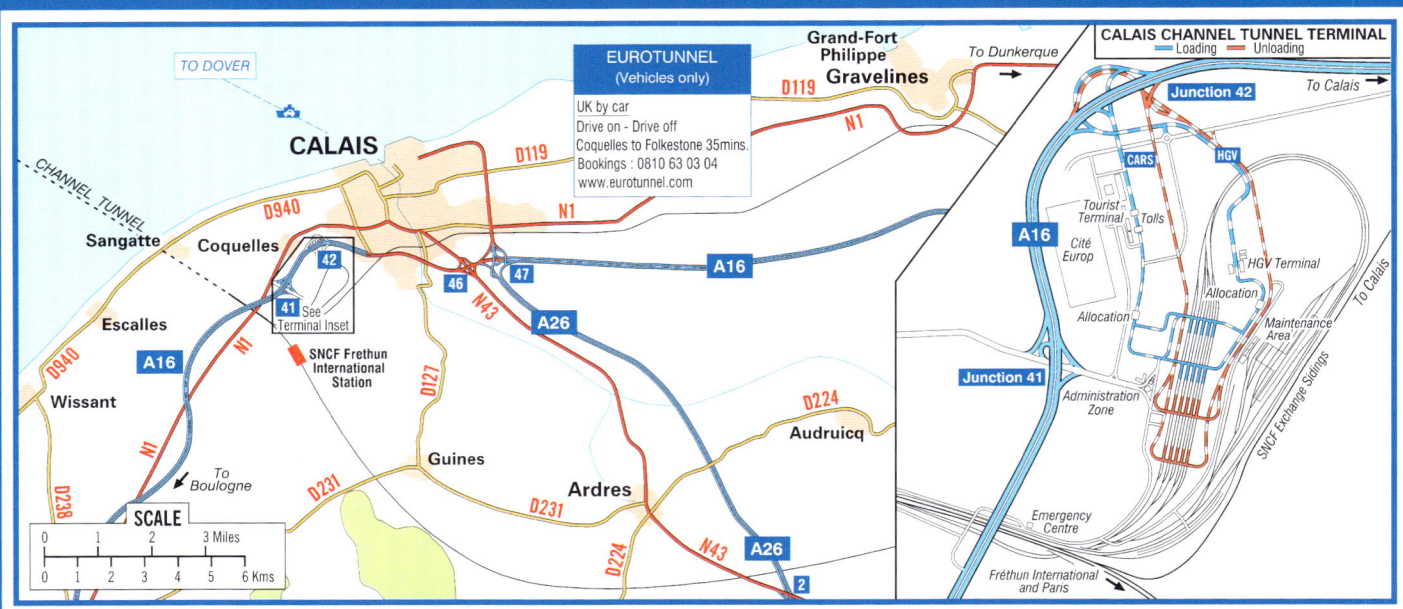

The Downs

**DEAL**

SOUTH FORELAND

STRAIT OF DOVER

**DOVER** PAGE 194

**FOLKESTONE** PAGE 195

Dover to:
Calais 1hr. 30mins.
Dunkirk 2hrs.

CHANNEL TUNNEL
Folkestone to
Calais 35mins.

East Wear Bay

ROMNEY MARSH

DOWNS

---

**EUROSTAR**
(Passengers only)
Passenger Services
St. Pancras International
Ebbsfleet International &
Ashford International to:
Paris, Brussels and Lille.
Bookings : 08432 186186
www.eurostar.com

**EUROTUNNEL**
(Vehicles only)
Continent by car
Drive on - Drive off
Folkestone to Coquelles 35mins.
Bookings : 08443 353535
www.eurotunnel.com

**ASHFORD**

**DOVER**

TO: CALAIS
DUNKIRK

**FOLKESTONE**

See Terminal Inset

**FOLKESTONE CHANNEL TUNNEL TERMINAL**
Loading    Unloading

CHANNEL TUNNEL
To Dover

U.K. Terminal
Customs
Border Controls
Border Controls
Tolls
HGV
CARS

**FOLKESTONE**

Junction 11a    Junction 12    Junction 13

To London

SCALE
0    1    2    3 Miles
0    1    2    3    4    5    6 Kms

---

**EUROTUNNEL**
(Vehicles only)
UK by car
Drive on - Drive off
Coquelles to Folkestone 35mins.
Bookings : 0810 63 03 04
www.eurotunnel.com

**CALAIS**

TO DOVER

**CALAIS CHANNEL TUNNEL TERMINAL**
Loading    Unloading

Grand-Fort
Philippe
Gravelines

To Dunkerque

Junction 42    To Calais

CARS    HGV

Tourist
Tolls
Cité
Europ

HGV Terminal

Allocation

Allocation

Maintenance
Area

A16

Junction 41

Administration
Zone

SNCF Exchange Sidings    To Calais

Emergency
Centre

Fréthun International
and Paris

Sangatte

Coquelles

SNCF Fréthun
International
Station

See Terminal Inset

Escalles

Wissant

To Boulogne

Guines

Ardres

Audruicq

SCALE
0    1    2    3 Miles
0    1    2    3    4    5    6 Kms

## Map labels

Moat
fran
Pennfford
Penfford
Bletherston
Gelli
Caraston Bridge
Bethesda
aden
Robeston Wathen
B4313
Narberth (Arberth)
Robeston Back
B4314
Crinow
Cold Blow
Princes Gate
A4075
A4115
Templeton
B4315
PEMBROKESHIRE
Ludchurch
A478
Thomas Chapel
Loveston
Reynalton
Folly Farm
B4586
Kilgetty (Cilgeti)
Jeffreyston
Begelly
Cresselly
Broadmoor
geston
Redberth
East Williamston
A4075
Pentlepoir
Sardis
B431
Stepaside
Heatherton World of Activities
Control Tower
Manor House
B4318
The Dinosaur Park
A478
St Florence
Gumfreston
New Hedges
Silent World
Monkstone Point
Broadfield
Saundersfoot
Broadfield
rbeston
Penally (Penalum)
Tenby (Dinbych-y-Pysgod)
Tudor Merchant's House
National Park Centre
swell
Old House
Lydstep
on
Giltar Point
B45
Caldey Sound
St Margaret's Island
Caldey Priory
Old Abbey
Caldey Island
norbier
DANGER AREA
Old Castle Head
Chapel Point

Llanycefn
A478
Login
Cwm-miles
Cr 20hands
Llanboidy
Mynach
Llandissilio
Hiraeth
Henllan Amgoed
Cwmfelin Boeth
eg
Clunderwen
Llanfallteg West
Llanddewi Velfrey
Lampeter
Whitland
Marlais
Trevaughan
Lampeter Velfrey
Llwyn-y-brain
B4328
Llan-mill
Tavernspite
Llanteg
B4314
Red Roses
Marros
Llanmiloe
Pendine (Pentywyn)
Museum of Speed
DANGER AREA
Colby Woodland
Summerhill
Amroth
Stepaside Ironworks

CARMARTHEN BAY
(BAE CAERFYRDDIN)

Llangynin
Meidrim
Esgair
Drefach
B4299
Backe
St Clears
A477
Llanddowror
A4066
Halfpenny Furze
Llandawke
Llansadurnen
Broadway
Brook
Laugharne
Dylan Thomas Boathouse
DANGER AREA

Gellywen
Caerlleon
Gwyn
Afon
B4298
Pwlltrap
Grove Land Adventure World
Glyn-Coch Craft Centre
Hywel Dda Centre
B4299
Bancyfelin
Langynog
Cywyn
Morfa Bach
Llanybri
Llansteffan
Llanmiloe

Talog
Bwlchnewydd
Newchurch
Abernant
Dyffryn
Merthyr
Ffynnon-dofan
Trevaughan
Henallt
CARMARTHEN (Caerfyrddin)
P+R
Llanllwch
Johnstown
Pen-sarn
Pibwrlwyd
Cwmffrwd
A40
A40
Llangain
Croesyceiliog
Idole
Morfa Bach
Ferryside
Broadlay
Broadway
St Ishmael
Ginst Point
DANGER AREA
Gwendraeth
DANGER AREA
DANGER AREA
Pembrey
Pembrey Forest
DANGER AREA
Pembrey
Burry Port (Porth Tywyn)

Bronwydd Arms
Merlin's Hill Centre
White Mill
Abergwili
Llangunnor
B4300
Tanerdy
Pen-sarn
CARMAR
A48
A484
Bancycapel
Llangyndeirne
B4306
Pontantwn
B4309
Llandyfaelog
Four Roads
Pontyates (Pont-iets)
Mynyddygarreg
Llangadog
Llansaint
Kidwelly (Cydweli)
Pinged
Mynydd Pen-bre
Graig
Cwm Capel
A484
Pembrey
Trimsaran
Waun y Clyn
Pen
Crwbin
Meinciau
Carway
Ffos Las
B4317

Whiteford Point
Whiteford
Burry Holms
Llanmadoc
Cheriton
Landimore
Llangennith
Samson's Jack Standing Stone
Burry Green
Burry
G O
Hillend
Rhossili Bay
Llanddewi
Reynoldston
Rhossili
B42
Knelston
WORMS HEAD (Penrhyn-gwyr)
Middleton
Gower Coast
Pitton
Scurlage
Pilton Green
Mewslade Bay
A4118
Horton
Overton
The Salt House
Port-Eynon Point

B R I S T O L

POWYS

FFOREST FAWR

BRECON BEACONS NATIONAL PARK

BLACK MOUNTAIN

NEATH PORT TALBOT

SWANSEA

CARMARTHENSHIRE

Llandeilo
Ffairfach
Nantgaredig
Llanegwad
Llanddarog
Cwmisfael
Porthyrhyd
Llanfihangel-uwch-Gwili
Llanllwch
Bancffosfelen
Pontyberem
Pont-Henri
Five Roads
Heol
Horeb
Pwll
Llanelli
Millennium Coastal Park
Discovery Centre
Llwynhendy
Bynea
Loughor
Gorseinon
Penllergaer
Gowerton
Pen-clawdd
Crofty
Llanmorlais
Three Crosses
Waunarlwydd
Dunvant
Sketty
Killay
Upper Killay
Lower Sketty
Brynmill
Mayals
Blackpill
West Cross
Norton
Oystermouth
Mumbles (Mwmbwls)
Mumbles Head
Newton
Caswell
Langland
Bishopston
Southgate
Pennard
Parkmill
Murton
Penmaen
Nicholaston
Oxwich
Oxwich Bay
Oxwich Point
Port-Eynon
Port-Eynon Bay
Horton
Rhossili
Reynoldston
Cefn Bryn
Llanrhidian
Oldwalls
Llanmadoc
Weobley
Landimore

BRISTOL CHANNEL

Ammanford (Rhydaman)
Garnant
Glanaman
Brynamman
Gwaun-Cae-Gurwen
Cwmgors
Cwmllynfell
Ystalyfera
Ystradgynlais
Gurnos
Abercraf
Seven Sisters (Blaendulais)
Resolven (Resolfen)
Glyn-neath
Neath (Castell-Nedd)
Briton Ferry (Llansawel)
Skewen
Birchgrove
Tonna (Tonnau)
Cadoxton-juxta-Neath
Cwmgwrach
Blaengwrach
Clyne (Y Clun)
Cymmer (Cymer)
Caerau
Croeserw
Nantyffyllon
Maesteg
Pontycymer
Garth
Cwmfelin
Baglan
Cwmafan
Brynbryddan
Port Talbot
Aberavon (Aberafan)
Sandfields
Margam
Margam Abbey
Taibach
Kenfig Hill
Cefn Cribwr
North Cornelly
South Cornelly
Pyle
Kenfig
Mawdlam
Sker Point
Porthcawl
Porthcawl Point
Nottage
Newton
Newcastle
Laleston (Trelales)
Tythegston
Merthyr Mawr
Candleston
Ogmore
Ogmore-by-Sea
Southerndown
Tusker Rock

M4

A40  A48  A465  A474  A476  A483  A4067  A4069  A4109  A4118  A4138  A4216  A4221  A4240  A4241  A4067  A4063  A4106  A4107

B4297  B4300  B4310  B4436

National Botanic Garden of Wales
Paxton's Tower
Dinefwr Park
Gelli Aur Arboretum
Carreg Cennen
Black Mountain Centre
Henrhyd Waterfall
Dan-yr-Ogof National Showcaves Centre for Wales
Wales Ape & Monkey Sanctuary
Melincourt Waterfall
Afan Forest Park
South Wales Miners Museum
Bedford Park
Kenfig Pool
National Wetland Centre Wales
National Waterfront Swansea Centre
Egypt Centre
Dylan Thomas Centre
Crymlyn Bog
Swansea Bay (Bae Abertawe)
Pwlldu Head
Glamorgan Heritage Coast

POWYS

NEATH PORT TALBOT

BRIDGEND

RHONDDA CYNON TAFF

MERTHYR TYDFIL

THE VALE OF GLAMORGAN

BRISTOL CHANNEL

Rhosaman
Cefn-bryn-brain
Cwmllynfell
Ystradowen
Lower Brynamman
Tairgwaith
A4068
Cwmgors
Cwmgiedd
Abercraf
Ynyswen
Pen-y-cae
A4067
Cae'r-gont
Caehopkin
Penrhos
Coelbren
A4221
Onllwyn
Ystradgynlais
Cwm-twrch Isaf
Cwm Gwrelych
Glan-rhyd
B4599
Mynydd y Drum
Seven Sisters (Blaendulais)
Dyffryn Cellwen
A4109
Pontneddfechan
Penderyn
Distillery
Cader Fawr
Garnant
Garwnant Forest
A4059
Pontsticill Reservoir
Pontsarn
Trefil

Cilmaengwyn
A4067
Godre'r-graig
Glais
A4067
Crynant
Abergarwed
Resolven (Resolfen)
Melincourt Waterfall
Clyne (Y Clun)
Rhigos
Hirwaun
A4059
Penywaun
Cwmdare
Aberdare (Aberdâr)
Llwydcoed
Robertstown
Cefn-coed-y-cymmer
Gethin Woodland Park
Dowlais
MERTHYR TYDFIL (Merthyr Tudful)
Pentrebach
RHYMNEY (Rhymni)
Pontlottyn
A469
Bedlinog
Troedyrhiw
A4054
Aberfan
Merthyr Vale

NEATH (Castell-Nedd)
Cadoxton-juxta-Neath
Tonna (Tonnau)
Rhydding
Cilfrew
Aberdulais
AFAN FOREST PARK
Glyncorrwg
Blaengwynfi
Blaenrhondda
Blaencwm
Tynewydd
Treherbert
Maerdy
Blaenllechau
MOUNTAIN ASH (Aberpennar)
Penrhiwceiber
Abercwmboi
Aberaman
Cwmbach
Aberaman
Edwardsville
Treharris

Briton Ferry (Llansawel)
A48
Baglan
Aberavon (Aberafan)
PORT TALBOT
Cwmafan
A4107
Pontrhydyfen
Cynonville
Caerau
Duffryn
South Wales Miners
A4063
Nantyffyllon
Blaengarw
Nant-y-moel
Price Town
Tonypandy
Trealaw
Penygraig
Gilfach Goch
Porth
Trehafod
PONTYPRIDD
Treforest
Abercynon
Ynysybwl
Ynyshir
A4054
Ton Pentre
Treorchy (Treorci)
Cwmparc
Pentre
Ystrad
Ferndale
Ynys-wen
RHONDDA

Margam
Groes
A4241
Margam Stones
Margam Abbey
Mynydd Margam
MAESTEG
Garth
Cwmfelin
Llangynwyd
Pontycymer
Garw Fach Woodland Park
A4064
Bettws
Llangeinor
Blackmill
A4061
Ogmore Vale
Gilfach Goch
Evanstown
Hendreforgan
Thomastown
Coedely
Tonyrefail
A4119
Beddau
Llantwit Fardre
Church Village
Upper Church Village
Efail Isaf
Llantrisant
A4119
Pentyrch
Creigiau
Morganstown

Pyle
North Cornelly
South Cornelly
Kenfig
B4283
Mawdlan
A48
Laleston (Trelales)
Newcastle
BRIDGEND (Pen-y-bont Ar Ogwr)
Brackla
Coity
Coychurch
Pencoed
SARN PK.
Penprysg
Bryncethin
Tondu
Sarn
Aberkenfig
Cefn Cribwr
Cefn Cribwr Ironworks
Bedford Park
Kenfig Hill
A4281
B4281
Coytrahen
Abergarw
Brynmenyn
Bryncae
Dolau
Llanharan
Talbot Green
Cross Inn
Pontyclun
Miskin
Brynsadler
A473
Llanharry
Groes-faen
A4119
Capel Llanilltern
A4232
CARDIFF WEST
M4

PORTHCAWL
Porthcawl Point
Nottage
A4229
Tythegston
Merthyr Mawr
Candleston
Newton
A4106
Ogmore
Ewenny
Corntown
St Brides Major (Tregolwyn)
Ogmore-by-Sea
Southerndown
Glamorgan Heritage Coast
Wick
B1270
Broughton
Monknash
Marcross
St Donat's (Sain Dunwyd)
Llantwit Major (Llanilltud Fawr)
Nash Point
St Donat's Art Centre
Boverton
Gileston
West Aberthaw
East Aberthaw
Rhoose (Y Rhws)
Porthkerry (Porthceri)
Pleasure Beach
Breaksea Point

Tusker Rock
Sker Point

Colwinston
Pentre Meyrick
Llandow (Llandw)
Llysworney
Llanmihangel
Llandough
St Mary Church
COWBRIDGE (Y Bont-Faen)
Llanblethian (Llanfleidian)
Llandow
Sigingstone (Tresigin)
St Hilary
Old Beaupre Castle
Llanmaes
St Athan (Sain Tathan)
Flemingston
Eglwys-Brewis (Llancatal)
Llancadle (Llancatal)
Llancarfan
Moulton
Penmark (Pen-marc)
Font-y-gary (Ffont-y-gari)
Fonmon
Tredogan
Nurston

THE VALE OF GLAMORGAN
Aberthin
Maendy
Llansannor
Ystradowen
Penllyn
Graig Penllyn
St Mary Hill
Treoes
St Mary Hill
Llangan
Llanharry
Welsh St Donats
Pendoylan
Peterston-super-Ely
St George's
A48
Bonvilston (Tresimwn)
St Nicholas
Dyffryn
St Lythans
Wenvoe
St Andrews
A4050
Penmark
A4226
Tinkinswood
Walterston
Welsh Hawking Centre
Llancarfan
BARRY (Y Barri)
CARDIFF
Dyffryn
National History Museum
Greenway

Llanbethery (Llanbydderi)
Llantrithyd
Llancarfan

ABERGAVENNY (Y-Fenni)

A465 A4047 Beaufort EBBW VALE (Glyn Ebwy) Brynmawr Nantyglo Blaenavon MONMOUTH (Trefynwy) Wyesham Redbrook

TREDEGAR BLAENAU GWENT New Tredegar Blaina Blackwood Oakdale Crumlin Newbridge (Cefn Bychan)

TORFAEN New Inn PONTYPOOL (Pontypwl) Griffithstown Cwmbran CWMBRAN

MONMOUTHSHIRE Raglan Usk Llangwm Devauden St Arvans Chepstow Tintern

CAERPHILLY Abercarn Crosskeys Risca Machine Rogerstone CAERPHILLY (Caerffili) Thornhill

Caerleon (Caerllion) Malpas Bettws Bishton Magor (Magwyr) Caerwent Caldicot Portskewett Severn Tunnel

NEWPORT (Casnewydd) NEWPORT M4 A48 A4810

Marshfield Blacktown St Mellons Rumney

CARDIFF (Caerdydd) Penarth Dinas Powys Sully

MOUTH OF THE SEVERN

Second Severn Crossing Avonmouth Portishead Point Portishead Portbury GORDANO Easton-in-Gordano BRISTOL

Clevedon NORTH SOMERSET Nailsea Backwell West Town Long Ashton Failand

Sand Point Sand Bay Kewstoke St George's Worle Milton West Wick Congresbury Yatton Wrington

WESTON-SUPER-MARE Uphill Bleadon Banwell Sandford Churchill Blagdon

Flat Holm Steep Holm

M5 M4 M48 A40 A449 A466 A48 A38 A370 A371 A368

MONMOUTH (Trefynwy)

A466  A40  A4136

FOREST OF DEAN

GLOUCESTER
P+R

A48  A4151

STROUD

CHEPSTOW (Cas-gwent)

M48  SEVERN VIEW  Severn Bridge

M4  Second Severn Crossing

MOUTH OF THE SEVERN

Avonmouth

Portishead Point  Portishead

GORDANO

SOUTH GLOUCESTERSHIRE

M5

BRISTOL
PAGE 193
P+R

Yate  Chipping Sodbury

Kingswood

KEYNSHAM

Mangotsfield

BATH & N.E. SOMERSET

BATH
PAGE 192
P+R

Bradford on-Avon

TROWBRIDGE

Dursley  Wotton-under-Edge  Nailsworth

Thornbury  Berkeley  Cambridge

Stonehouse  Woodchester

Lydney  Tintern  Chepstow

Caldicot  M48  M4

A38  A46  A420  A4  A37  A39  A368  A369  A370  A431  A4174

Map page — Cotswolds / Wiltshire region (Cirencester, Swindon, Chippenham, Marlborough, Devizes area).

Major places: CIRENCESTER, SWINDON, CHIPPENHAM, MELKSHAM, DEVIZES, MARLBOROUGH, Malmesbury, Tetbury, Calne, Fairford, Lechlade on Thames, Faringdon, Highworth, Cricklade, Royal Wootton Bassett, Wroughton, Pewsey, Burford.

Key roads: A46, A435, A417, A419, A429, A433, A4040, A350, A342, A361, A360, A365, A4, A3102, A345, A346, A338, A420, A361, A4361, A4198, A4311, A4259, A4553, A4587, B4425, B4070, B4425, B4696, B4040, B4042, B4122, B4014, B4528, B4069, B4019, B4000, B4508, B4507, B4006, B4005, B4003, B4192, B4507, B4192, B3107, B3101, M4.

Grid references: 35, 1, 2, 3, 4, 5 (right margin); E, F, G, H (margins); 49, 23, 16, 15, 36.

PAGE 203

Numerous village names including: Sheepscombe, Cranham, Brimpsfield, Elkstone, Colesbourne, Chedworth, Northleach, Great Barrington, Burford, Bisley, Miserden, North Cerney, Bibury, Eastleach Turville, Barnsley, Ampney Crucis, Poulton, Fairford, Lechlade, Kelmscott, Coates, South Cerney, Down Ampney, Kempsford, Highworth, Watchfield, Shrivenham, Kemble, Ashton Keynes, Cricklade, Purton, Broad Blunsdon, Hannington, Bishopstone, Tetbury, Oaksey, Minety, Charlton, Lydiard Millicent, Haydon Wick, Stratton St Margaret, Swindon, Wanborough, Aldbourne, Malmesbury, Brinkworth, Wootton Bassett, Wroughton, Chiseldon, Ramsbury, Hullavington, Lyneham, Broad Town, Clyffe Pypard, Barbury Castle, Ogbourne St George, Ogbourne St Andrew, Mildenhall, Chippenham, Calne, Cherhill, Avebury, Winterbourne Monkton, Marlborough, Savernake Forest, Great Bedwyn, Lacock, Bromham, Rowde, Devizes, All Cannings, Stanton St Bernard, Alton Barnes, Woodborough, Wilcot, Pewsey, Burbage, Melksham, Seend, Potterne, Urchfont, Collingbourne Kingston.

10    20    30    40

**NORTH**

Holliwell Point

Foulnes
Sands

Foulness
Point

Courtsend

Maplin Sands

**SEA**

90

80

1

2

3

...arden Point

South Channel

Turner
Contemporary
Lifeboat
Station    Walpole
Bay Hotel    Foreness Point

Leysdown-on-Sea    Westgate
on Sea    **MARGATE**    B2051    Kingsgate    70    **NORTH
FORELAND**

Shell
Ness    Herne Bay    Reculver    Reculver Towers    Minnis Bay    Westbrook    Cliftonville
Drapers    B2052

Harty    **HERNE BAY**    Hampton    Reculver Roman Fort    Birchington    40    6    30    **ISLE OF THANET**    St
Peter's    B2052    **BROADSTAIRS**

Swalecliffe    Beltinge    Hillborough    A299    **A28**    Acol    B2050    Spitfire &    Lydden    A255    Northwood    Tower    **Dickens House**

**WHITSTABLE**    Tankerton    Greenhill    Hunters    Broomfield    Marshside    Hurricane    B2190    Manston    A256    A254    **RAMSGATE**

Whitstable Bay    Chestfield    West    Herne    Forstal    St Nicholas    Sarre    A299    Maritime    4

Seasalter    South Street    End    Herne    Maypole    at Wade    Boyden    A28    Minster    Cliffsend

A299    Radfall    Herne    Hoath    Gate    Chislet    A253    **Monkton**    Abbey    Richborough Port    Pegwell
Bay

Graveney    Yorkletts    Denstroude    Honey Hill    Tyler    Calcott    Upstreet    Grove    West    Plucks    Richborough    A256    60

Fleur    Goodnestone    Dargate    Druidstone    Hill    Broad Oak    Hersden    Stourmouth    Gutter    Fort    Sandwich

de Lis    Hernhill    Park    Sturry    Westbere    Stodmarsh    East Stourmouth    Westmarsh    Cooper    Bay

Preston    Blean    A290    Fordwich    Preston    Paramour    Street    Great Stonar

Mount    Rough    Westbre    Wickhambreaux    Ware    Goldstone    A256    Sandwich

Hogben's    Ephraim    Common    Harbledown    **CANTERBURY**    Ickham    Wingham    Elmstone    Amphitheatre    Guildhall

Hill    Boughton under    A2050    PAGE 193    Ash    Marshborough    Secret    Toll    The Small

Selling    Blean    Dunkirk    Littlebourne    A257    Staple    Nash    White    Sandwich    Downs    5

Oversland    A2    Thanington    Howletts    Wingham    Barnsole    Woodnesborough    Worth    A258    Sandown

Old Wives    Without    Bekesbourne    Bramling    Goodnestone    Eastry    Ham    Castle

Lees    A28    Chartham    Bridge    Patrixbourne    Goodnestone    Chillenden    Finglesham    Fowlmead    Sholden

Perrywood    Chartham    Street    Park    Hammill    Heronden    Betteshanger    **DEAL**

Chilham    Shalmsford    Hatch    Nackington    Adisham    Nonington    Knowlton    Northbourne    Timeball    Lifeboat Station

Shottenden    Street    Street    Bishopsbourne    A2    Womenswold    A256    Tower    Walmer

A252    Mountain    Garlinge    End    Upper    Frogham    Great Mongeham

Molash    Street    Green    Lower    Hardres    Kingston    Aylesham    Tilmanstone    East    The Downs

Godmersham    Petham    Hardres    Pett    Bottom    Barham    Elvington    Studdal    Ri    150

A28    Bilting    Sole    Bosham    Woolage Village    Barfrestone    Eythorne    Ashley    Sutton    Kingsdown

Boughton    Crundale    Street    Denstone    Woolage    East Kent    Shepherdswell    West    Ringwould

Aluph    Waltham    North Leigh    Green    Railway    or Sibertswold    Langdon    Martin    A258

Wye    Wye    Stelling    Wingmore    Denton    A2    Coldred    East    Martin Mill

Kempe's    Crown    Minnis    Stelling    Lydden    Langdon    DANGER

Corner    Hassell    Bodsham    Minnis    A260    Hill    Wootton    Lydden    Whitfield    AREA    40

Hastingleigh    Maxted    Guston

STRUMBLE HEAD

*Fishguard to Rosslare 3hrs. 30mins.*

Carregwastad Point

Pen Brush

Fishguar (Bae Ab

Penbwchdy

Llanwnda

Trefasser

Goodwick (Wdig)

Ocean Lab

Dyffryn

Manorowen

Lower Town

St Nicholas

Fishguard (Abergwaun)

*Melin Tregwynt*

A487

A4219

A40

Granston

Scleddau

Abercastle

Jordanston

Trecwn

Penclegyr

*Blue Lagoon*

Porthgain

Mathry

Llangloffan

Newbridge

Trefin

Llanrhian

Castlemorris

B4331

Carreg-gwylan-fach

Abereiddy

Croes-Goch

Letterston

Penclegyr

A487

Treffynnon

Welsh Hook

*Wolfscastle Pottery*

ST DAVIDS HEAD

Penllechwen

Tretio

6

R. Solva

Hayscastle Cross

Wolf's Castle

Treleddyd-fawr

Rhodiad-y-Brenin

Carnhedryn

Caerfarchell

Llandeloy

Brimaston

B4583

*Whitesands Bay (Porth Mawr)*

R. Alun

St Davids

*Solva Woollen Mill*

Hayscastle

Mountain Water

Treffgarne

P E M B R O K E

*Bishop's Palace*

St Davids (Tyddewi)

Whitchurch

Gignog

14

Leweston

Rhosson

Oriel y Parc

Solva

Wolfsdale

Ramsey Island

*Ramsey Sound*

St Non's Chapel

Penycwm

Camrose

A40

Rudbaxton

Ynys Bery

Green Scar

Newgale

Wood

16

Roch

Dudwells

Cuttybridge

*Haverford west*

Crundale

Rickets Head

A487

Simpson Cross

Keeston

Pelcomb Cross

Tangiers

Pelcomb Bridge

ST BRIDES BAY

Nolton Haven

Simpson

*Pembrokeshire Motor*

Lambston

HAVERFORDWEST (Hwlffordd)

Prendergast

Nolton

Druidston

Sutton

Portfield Gate

Albert Town

Merlin's Bridge

Boulston

Haroldston West

7

Dreenhill

Stack Rocks

B4341

Broadway

B4327

*Hangstone Davey*

Broad Haven

Little Haven

Walton West

Talbenny

12

A4076

Pope Hill

Freystrop

Tower Point

Walwyn's Castle

Tiers Cross

Skomer Island

Wooltack Point

St Brides

Hasguard

Robeston West

Johnston

Sardis

Grassholm Island

*Harold Stone*

Midland Isle

Marloes

Thornton

Rosemarket

A477

BROAD SOUND

Gateholm Island

St Ishmael's

Sandy Haven

Herbrandston

*Priory*

Steynton

5

Skokholm Island

Dale

B43 2.7

Dale Point

Hubberston

Hakin

B4325

Honeyborough

*Pembroke to Rosslare 4hrs.*

Thorn Island

*Milford*

MILFORD HAVEN (Aberdaugleddau)

Waterston

Llanstadwell

Neyland

St Ann's Head

*Gun Tower*

Haven

Angle

*DANGER AREA*

Angle Bay

Pembroke Dock (Doc Penfro)

Pennar

Sheep Island

Rhoscrowther

Pwllcrochan

Wallaston Green

Monkton

Hundleton

Freshwater West

B4320

B4319

Maiden Wells

Castlemartin

*DANGER AREA*

13

Warren

St Twynnells

St Petrox

Linney Head

*DANGER AREA*

Merrion

Crow Rock

Toes

*Elegug Stacks*

*The Wash*

Bosherston

*DANGER AREA*

*St Govan's Chapel*

St Govan's Head

PEMBROKESHIRE COAST NATIONAL PARK (PARC CENEDLAETHOL ARFORDIR PENFRO)

DINAS HEAD
Trwyn-y-bwa

Newport Bay (Bae Trefdraeth)
Pembrokeshire Coast National Park

Dinas Cross
Newport (Trefdraeth)
Nevern (Nanhyfer)
Berry Hill
Bryn-henllan
Parrog
Felindre Farchog
Eglwyswrw
Monington
Glanrhyd
Pen-y-bryn
Bridell
Llantood
Cilgerran
Cwm Plysgog
Cnwcau
A487
A484
Llechryd
Llandygwydd
Brongwyn
Coed-y-bryn
Llyn
Croes-
National Coracle Centre
A475
Aber-banc
Horeb
Cenarth
Teifi Falls
Cwm-cou
Adpar
Penrhiw-llan
Pentrecagal
Waungilwen
Llandyfriog
Henl
Teifi Valley
A484
A475

Castell Henllys Iron Age Fort
Pengelli Forest
Newchapel (Capel Newydd)
Abercych
Newcastle Emlyn (Castell Newydd Emlyn)
Aberarad
Cilwendeg Shell House
Penrhiw
Penrherber
Cwmhiraeth
Llangeler Drefach
Felindre
Saron
Glynteg

Rhos-hill
Llanfair-Nant-Gwyn
Boncath
Blaenffos
Whitchurch
Penygroes
Bro Meigan
Bwlch-y-groes
Cwmcych
Capel Iwan
1100 Moelfre

PEMBROKESHIRE COAST NATIONAL PARK
(PARC CENEDLAETHOL ARFORDIR PENFRO)
MYNYDD PRESELI

Crymych
Star
Clydey
Cilrhedyn
Cwmorgan
Cwmduad
Hermon

Ty Canol
Pentre Ifan Burial Chamber
Pontyglazier
Crosswell
Penygroes
Frenni Fawr 1295
Tegryn

Tafarn-y-bwlch
Brynberian
Foel-cwmcerwyn 1759
Glan-rhyd
Pentre Galar
Hermon
Henfeddau Fawr
Dinas
Trelech

Foeleryr 1535
Greenway
Rosebush
Mynachlog-ddu
Foeldrych
Glandwr
Blaenwaun
Pen-y-bont
Esgair
Cynwyl Elfed

CARMARTHENSHIRE

Puncheston (Cas-Mael)
Morvil
Rosebush
Gors Fawr Stone Circle
Llanglydwen
Cwmfelin Mynach
Cwmbach
Talog
Bwlchnewydd
Newchu

Little Newcastle
Castlebythe
Henry's Moat (Castell Hendre)
Maenclochog
Llandilo
Llangolman
Glandy Cross
Pant-y-Caws
Efailwen
Cefn-y-pant
Welsh Chocolate Farm
Cwmfelin Boeth
Llanwinio
Gellywen
Caerlleon
Dyffryn
Abernant

AMBLESTON
Wallis
Gwastad
Woodstock Slop
Llys-y-fran Reservoir
Llys-y-fran
New Moat
Llanycefn
Login
Cwm-miles
Crosshands
Llanboidy
Meidrim
Esgair
Drefach

Golden Hill
Spittal
Penffordd
A478
Llandissilio
Hiraeth
Henllan Amgoed
Langynin
Merthyr
CARMARTHEN (Caerfyrddin)

Manor
Scolton
Pembrokeshire Virtual
Clarbeston
Clarbeston Road
Bletherston
Clunderwen
Llanfallteg
Llanfallteg West
Cwmfelin Boeth
Grove Land Adventure World
Glyn-Coch Craft Centre
Pwlltrap
Bancyfelin
A40
Llangynog
Llangain

Leachpool
Rudbaxton Rath Hillfort
Wiston
Gelli
Bethesda
Llanddewi Velfrey
A40
Whitland
Backe
St Clears
Llanllwch
Llanilwch

Plain Dealings
Llawhaden
Robeston Wathen
B4313
Lampeter Velfrey
Trevaughan
Hywel Dda Centre
A477
Llanddowror
Halfpenny Furze
Llandawke
Llansadurnen
Broadway
A40
Morfa Bach
Llangynog

Clerkenhill Adventure Farm
Canaston Bridge
Narberth (Arberth)
Crinow
Llan-mill
Lampeter Vale
Llwyn-y-brain
Llansadurnen
Laugharne
Dylan Thomas Boathouse
Llansteffan
Llanybri

The Rhos
Picton
Minwear
Blackpool Mill
Narberth Bridge
Cold Blow
Princes Gate
Tavernspite
B4314
Red Roses
Marros
Llanmiloe
Brook
Broadway
Ginst Point
Ferryside
St Ishmael

Hook
Landshipping
Bluestone
Oakwood
A4075
Templeton
A4115
Ludchurch
Lanteg
B4314
DANGER AREA
Pendine (Pentywyn)
Museum of Speed
DANGER AREA
Broadlay

Black Tar
Martletwy
Yerbeston
Reynalton
Thomas Chapel
Loveston
A478
Folly Farm
A477
Colby Woodland
Summerhill
Amroth
DANGER AREA

Llangwm
Port Lion
Houghton
Lawrenny
Cresswell R.
Cresswell Quay
Jeffreyston
Broadmoor
Begelly
Kilgetty (Cilgeti)
Stepaside
Stepaside Ironworks
Sardis
Saundersfoot

Burton
West Williamston
Carew Newton
Upton
Sageston
Redberth
Pentlepoir
East Williamston
Broadfield

Cosheston
Upton Castle
Carew
Milton
A477
A4075
Control Tower
Carew Cheriton
Manor House
B4318
Gumfreston
Heatherton World of Activities
The Dinosaur Park
New Hedges
Silent World
Monkstone Point

Pembroke Ferry
Toll Pembroke Ferry
Waterloo
A477
Pembroke (Penfro)
Upper Nash
Bishop's Palace
Cheriton
St Florence
Manorbier Newton
Carswell Old House
Penally (Penalun)
Tenby (Dinbych-y-Pysgod)
Tudor Merchant's House
National Park Centre

Lamphey
Hodgeston
Manorbier Newton
Jameston
Gumfreston
CARMARTHEN BAY (BAE CAERFYRDDIN)

Cheriton or Stackpole Elidor
Freshwater East
A4139
Lydstep
Manorbier
B45
DANGER AREA
Giltar Point
Caldey Sound

Trewent Point
Old Castle Head
St Margaret's Island
Caldey Old Priory
Abbey
Caldey Island
Chapel Point

Stackpole
Stackpole Head
Burry Holms

WORMS HEAD (Penrhyn-gwyr)
Gower

250 | 200 | A | B | 10 | C | 20 | D

Cardigan Island
Cemaes Head
Cardigan Island Coastal Farm Park
Rainforest Centre
Parcllyn
Aberporth
West Wales (Aberporth)
Internal Fire
56
Llangranog
Penllyn
Morfa
Pontgarreg
Blaen Celyn
Tresaith
Brynhoffnant
Pentregat
Plwmp

Pwllygranant
Gwbert
Allt-y-goed
Y Ferwig
Felinwynt
Blaenannerch
Tan-y-groes
CERE
Glynarthen

Cippyn
St Dogmaels (Llandudoch)
Cardigan (Aberteifi)
Penparc
Tremain
Blaenporth
Noyadd Trefawr
Glynarthen
Felin Wnda
Brithdir
Ffostrasol
Rhydlewis

Moylgrove (Trewyddel)
Abbey Watermill
Castle
Monington
Llangoedmor
Pantgwyn
Ponthirwaun
Beulah
Bettws Ifan
Curlew Weavers Woollen Mill
Penrhiw-pal
Hawen
Coed-y-bryn
Maes Llyn

Trwyn-y-bwa
Dinas Head
Dinas Island
Newport Bay (Bae Trefdraeth)
Nevern (Nanhyfer)
Berry Hill
Felindre Farchog
Pengelli Forest
Pen-y-bryn
Bridell
Cilgerran
National Coracle Centre
Cenarth
Cwm-cou
Cenarth Falls
Adpar
Aberarad
Newcastle Emlyn (Castell Newydd Emlyn)
Llandyfriog
Henllan
A475
Aber-banc
A484

DINAS HEAD
Fishguard Bay (Bae Abergwaun)
Dinas Cross
Parrog
Newport (Trefdraeth)
Castle
Eglwyswrw
Llanfair-Nant-Gwyn
Rhos-hill
43
Newchapel (Capel Newydd)
Penrhiw
Penrherber
Caws Cenarth Cheese
Cwmhiraeth
Glynteg
Drefach
Langeler

Lower Town
Fishguard (Abergwaun)
Llanychaer
Pontfaen
PEMBROKESHIRE COAST NATIONAL PARK
PARC CENEDLAETHOL ARFORDIR PENFRO
Pembrokeshire Candle Centre
Pentre Ifan Burial Chamber
Ty Canol
Dyfed Shire Horse Farm
Whitchurch
Boncath
Cilwendeg Shell House
Bwlch-y-groes
Capel Iwan
Cwmpengraig

MYNYDD PRESELI
Foeleryr 1535
Foel-cwmcerwyn 1759
Crymych
Glan-rhyd
Pentre Galar
Hermon
Tegryn
Cilrhedyn
Cwmmorgan
1100 Moelfre

Punceston (Cas-Mael)
Castlebythe
Tufton
Greenway
Rosebush
Mynachlog-ddu
Foel-drych
Glandwr
Llanfyrnach
Henfeddau Fawr
Dinas
Trelech

Little Newcastle
Ambleston
Wallis
Woodstock Slop
Gwastad
Henry's Moat (Castell Hendre)
Llandilo
Maenclochog
Llangolman
Glandy Cross
Hebron
Blaenwaun
Pen-y-bont
Blaen-y-coed
Cynwyl Elfed

Wolf's Castle
Golden Hill
Spittal
Walton East
New Moat
Llys-y-fran Reservoir
Llanycefn
Efailwen
Pant-y-Caws
Cefn-y-pant
Welsh Chocolate Farm
Llanglydwen
Cwmfelin Mynach
Cwmbach
Llanwinio
Talog
Bwlchnewydd

Western Cleddau
Rudbaxton
Pembrokeshire Virtual Manor
Scolton
Clarbeston
Clarbeston Road
Penffordd
Bletherston
A478
Llandissilio
Llanfallteg
Login
Cwm-miles
Crosshands
Llanboidy
Caerllleon
Gellywen
Abernant
Dyffryn
Nant Cynnen
Merthyr

43
Haverfordwest
Leachpoll
Crundale
Wiston
Plain Dealings
Bethesda
Llawhaden
Canaston Bridge
Llanddewi Velfrey
Henllan Amgoed
Cwmfelin Boeth
A40
Meidrim
Llangynin
Esgair
Drefach
Grove Land Adventure World
Glyn-Coch Craft Centre
Bancyfelin
Llangynog
A40

Prendergast
A40
Uzmaston
Clerkenhill Adventure Farm
Gelli
Clunderwen
Llanfallteg West
Whitland
Hywel Dda Centre
10
Pwlltrap
St Clears
A477
Backe
Llanddowror
A4066
Laugharne
Llansteffan

HAVERFORDWEST (Hwlffordd)
4
The Rhos
Picton Castle
Minwear
Oakwood
Bluestone
Blackpool Mill
Robeston Wathen
Narberth (Arberth)
Crinow
Narberth Bridge
Llan-mill
Cold Blow
Lampeter Velfrey
Princes Gate
Tavernspite
Red Roses
Llansadurnen
Halfpenny Furze
Llandawke
Broadway
Dylan Thomas Boathouse
Llanybri
Morfa Bach

Boulston
Hook
Landshipping
Martletwy
Yerbeston
Reynalton
Templeton
Ludchurch
Llanteg
Marros
Llanmiloe
Brook
DANGER AREA
Ginst Point
St Ishmael
Ferryside

Llangwm
Sardis
Port Lion
Houghton
Lawrenny
Cresswell R
Jeffreyston
Begelly
Kilgetty (Cilgeti)
Stepaside
Colby Woodland
Summerhill
Amroth
Pendine (Pentywyn)
Museum of Speed
DANGER AREA

Burton
Honeyborough
West Williamston
Cresswell Quay
Carew Newton
Broadmoor
Pentlepoir
Sardis
Stepaside Ironworks
Saundersfoot
Broadfield
New Hedges
Silent World
Monkstone Point
CARMARTHEN BAY (BAE CAERFYRDDIN)

Neyland
A477
Cosheston
Milton
Carew
Redberth
Sageston
East Williamston
Heatherton World of Activities
The Dinosaur Park
A478
Tenby (Dinbych-y-Pysgod)

Pembroke Dock
Waterloo
Pembroke (Penfro)
Lamphey
Upper Nash
Carew Cheriton
Control Tower
Manor House
St Florence
Gumfreston
Penally (Penalun)
Merchant's House
National Park Centre
43

Monkton
Maiden Wells
St Petrox
Hodgeston
Lydstep
Manorbier
Newton
Manorbier Old House
Carswell
Trewent Point
A4139
Freshwater East
Stackpole
Elidor
DANGER AREA
Old Castle
St Margaret's Island
Caldey Sound
Giltar Point
Caldey Island
St Margaret's Island
Caldey Old Priory
Abbey
Chapel Point

# Map — Carmarthenshire / Brecon Beacons area

**CAMBRIAN MOUNTAINS**

**BRECON BEACONS NATIONAL PARK**

**FOREST OF BRECHFA**

**CEREDIGION** · **CARMARTHENSHIRE** · **SWANSEA**

## Towns and villages

Mydroilyn, Ffynnon-oer, Bettws Bledrws, Llangybi, Llanfair Clydogau, Pen y Rhiw, Talgarreg, Gorsgoch, Cribyn, Silian, Cellan, Pentrefelin, Craig Twrch, Pen y urnos, Nant-y-bai, Bwlch-y-fadfa, Cwrtnewydd, Maestir, Lampeter (Llanbedr Pont Steffan), Aber, Llanwnnen, Pentre-bach, Cwmann, Mynydd Mallaen, Ystra, Rhand, Pont-Sian, Cwmsychpant, Drefach, Alltyblacca, Pencarreg, Ffaldybrenin, Ffarmers, Cwrt-y-Cadno, Cilycwm, Cyng, Rhydowen, Llanwenog, Glan Duar, Rhuddlan, Pumsaint, Calo, Aberbowlan, Porthyrhyd, Llandysul, Capel Dewi, Llanybydder, Rhuddlan, Llanllwni, Rhydcymerau, Llidiad-Nenog, Llansawel, Edwinsford, Crugybar, Dolaucothi Gold Mines, Llandovery (Llanymddyfri), Croes-lan, Pontwelly, Llanfihangel-ar-Arth, Maesycrugiau, Aber-Giâr, Llanwrda, Pren-gwyn, Banc-y-ffordd, New Inn, Gwernogle, Abergorlech, Mynydd Figyn, Talley, Llansadwrn, Llanwrda, Heritage Centre, Pencader, Gwyddgrug, Dol-gran, Brechfa, Cwmdu, Halfway, Felindre, Cilgwyn, Myddfai, Talsarn, Cwmduad, Alltwalis, Llanllawddog, Horeb, Soar, Maerdy, Hermon, Llangadog, Esgair, Llanpumsaint, Pontarsais, Capel Isaac, Salem, Cwmifor, Manordeilo, Twynllanan, Newchurch, Bronwydd Arms, Rhydargaeau, Sarnau, Peniel, Llanfihangel-uwch-Gwili, Pentrefelin, Pen-y-banc, Bethlehem, Dyffryn Ceidrych, Pontarllechau, Llanddeusant, Ffynnon-ddrain, Trevaughan, Henallt, Felingwmuchaf, Felingwmisaf, Court Henry, Broad Oak, Cilsan, Dinefwr Park, Llandeilo, Rhosmaen, Y Garn Goch Hill Forts, Capel Gwynfe, Carmarthen (Caerfyrddin), Abergwili, Capel Dewi, Nantgaredig, Llanegwad, Felindre, Dryslwyn, Llangathen, Gelli Aur Arboretum, Ffairfach, Trapp, Carreg Cennen, Black Mountain Centre, Pen-sarn, Llangunnor, Llanarthne, Golden Grove, Llandyfan, Foel Fraith, Johnstown, Pibwrlwyd, Paxton's Tower, National Botanic Garden of Wales, Temple Bar, Carmel, Pant-y-llyn, Bylchau Rhos-faen, Cefn Carn Fadog, Cwmffrwd, Llanddarog, Cwmisfael, Porthyrhyd, Maesybont, Pentre Gwenlais, Llandybie, Upper Brynamman, Rhosaman, Llangain, Idole, Bancycapel, Llangendeirne, Crwbin, Capel Seion, Cwm-mawr, Cae'r-bryn, Ammanford (Rhydaman), Glanaman, Brynamman, Cwmllynfell, Ystradowen, Cwmgiedd, Croesyceiliog, Pontantwn, Bancffosfelen, Pontyberem, Meinciau, Cefneithin, Gorslas, Pen-y-groes, Drefach Cross Hands, Saron, Tir-y-dail, Garnant, Gwaun-Cae-Gurwen, Cefn-bryn-brain, Gurnos, Kidwelly (Cydweli), Llandyfaelog, Four Roads, Pontyates (Pont-iets), Pont-Henri, Tumble (Y Tymbl), Cwmgwili, Penybanc, Pantyffynnon, Pontamman, Tairgwaith, Cwm-twrch Uchaf, Cwmgors, Ystalyfera, Broadway, Llansaint, Mynyddygarreg, Llangadog, Llannon, Llwyn-têg, Pont Abraham, Capel Hendre, Tycroes, Betws, Pantyffynnon, Banc Cwmhelen, Pen Rhiw-fawr, Cwm-twrch Isaf, Carway, Five Roads, Horeb, Cynheidre, Sylen, Sardis, Pentrebach Drum, Garnswllt, Cwmcerdinen, Carn Llechart Burial Chamber, Cwmgiedd, Trimsaran, Pen-y-Mynydd, Pinged, Waun y Clyn, Cwm Capel, Graig, Felinfoel, Llannon, Pontarddulais, Hendy, Tyn-y-cwm, Cwm Dulais, Cwm-twrch, Craig-Cefn-Parc, Clydach, Pontardawe, Trebanos, Rhos, Cadoxton juxta-Neath, Pembrey, Pwll, Llanelli, Llwynhendy, Gorseinon, Pontlliw, Tircoed Forest Village, Ynystawe, Allt-wen, Glais, Bryncoch, Pembrey Forest, Burry Port (Porth Tywyn), Cefncaeau, Bynea, Loughor, Penyrheol, Penllergaer, Llangyfelach, Morriston, Birchgrove, Neath Abbey, Rhydding, Tonna (Tonnau), Whiteford Point, Millennium Coastal Park Discovery Centre, Llwynhendy, Gowerton, Penclawdd, National Wetland Centre Wales, Garden Village, Gorseinon, Llangennech, Loughor, Cadle, Portmead, Fforest-fach, Winsh-wen, Skewen, NEATH (Castell-Nedd)

## Roads

A485, A482, A475, A486, A484, A40, A482, A4069, A483, A474, A476, A48, A474, A4068, A4067, A4138, A4240, A4217, B4338, B4337, B4459, B4476, B4336, B4335, B4310, B4302, B4300, B4297, B4309, B4306, B4308, B4317, B4556, B4620, B4296, M4

## Physical features / Rivers

Afon Teifi, Afon Cothi, Afon Gwenlais, Afon Tywi, Afon Bran, Afon Sawdde, Afon Llwchwr, Afon Loughor, Afon Gwili, Gwendraeth Fawr, Gwendraeth Fach, Llyn Llech Owain, Black Mountain, Foel Fraith 1982, Garreg Las 2076, Mynydd Llanllwni 1339, Mynydd Pencarreg 1360, Llyn Brianne, Red Kite Feeding Station

Grid reference numbers: 45, 46, 1, 2, 3, 4, 5, 44, 43

CAMBRIAN MOUNTAINS

A B C D

BRECON BEACONS
NATIONAL PARK
(PARC CENEDLAETHOL
BANNAU BRYCHEINIOG)

BRECON BEACONS

PEN Y FAN
2906

**Towns and villages:**

Builth Road, Builth Wells (Llanfair-ym-Muallt), Llanelwedd, Llanfaredd, Cilmery (Cilmeri), Cregrina, Llandewi'r Cwm, Aberedw, Llanbadarn-y-garreg, Llandeilo Graban, Erwood, Crickadarn, Gwenddwr, Llanstephan, Maesmynis, Garth, Llanafan-fechan, Llangammarch Wells, Cefngorwydd, Llanwrtyd Wells (Llanwrtyd), Abergwesyn, Beulah, Troedrhiwdalar, Pentre-llwyn-llwyd, Llanwrthwl

Pentre Dolau Honddu, Upper Chapel, Lower Chapel, Merthyr Cynog, Pentre-bach, Pont-faen, Llanfihangel Nant Bran, Llandeilo Fan, Battle, Cradoc, Brecon (Aberhonddu), Llanddew, Llanhamlach, Llanfrynach, Pencelli, Talybont-on-Usk, Cross Oak, Groesffordd, Llanfihangel Tal-y-llyn, Talyllyn

Ystradffin, Rhandirmwyn, Nant-y-bai, Bryn Nicol, Tirabad, Cynghordy, Cilycwm, Llandovery (Llanymddyfri), Babel, Pentre-ty-gwyn, Pentrebach, Halfway, Myddfai, Llanwrda, Llanddeusant, Twynllanan, Talsarn, Llangadog, Myddfai, Trecastle, Llywel, Pentre'r-felin, Sennybridge, Defynnog, Penpont, Aberbran, Trallong, Aberyscir, Libanus

Cwmwysg, Pont ar Hydfer, Crai, Heol Senni, Penderyn, Hirwaun, Ystradfellte, Pontsticill, Cefn-coed-y-cymmer, Merthyr Tydfil (Merthyr Tudful), Dowlais, Rhymney (Rhymni), Pontlottyn, Bedlinog, Troedyrhiw, Aberfan, Mountain Ash (Aberpennar), Abercynon, Treharris, Quakers Yard

Glyntawe, Penwyllt, Craig-y-nos, Pen-y-cae, Abercraf, Ynyswen, Caehopkin, Coelbren, Onllwyn, Dyffryn Cellwen, Seven Sisters (Blaendulais), Glyn-neath, Morfa Glas, Blaengwrach, Cwmgwrach, Resolven (Resolfen), Clyne (Y Clun), Cilfrew, Melincourt, Blaenrhondda, Treherbert, Treorchy (Treorci), Ystrad, Pentre, Ton Pentre, Cwmparc

Brynamman, Cwmllynfell, Cefn-bryn-brain, Rhosaman, Gurnos, Ystalyfera, Ystradgynlais, Penrhos, Cae'r-bont, Cwm-twrch Isaf, Cwm-twrch Uchaf, Pantyffynnon, Glanrhyd, Glan-rhyd, Cwmgiedd, Cwmgors, Cwmllynfell, Cilmaengwyn, Godre'r-graig, Cilybebyll, Gellinudd, Rhos, Alltwen, Pontardawe, Trebanos, Clydach, Crynant, Cadoxton-juxta-Neath, Tonna (Tonnau), Neath (Castell-Nedd), Skewen, Birchgrove

A483, A481, A470, A40, A4069, A4068, A4109, A4067, A474, A4221, A4215, A4059, A4061, A4233, A4054, A4058, A4107, A4060, A4069, A465, A469, A470, B4520, B4519, B4518, B4594, B4560, B4561, B4602, B4599, B4434, B4221, B4242, B4287, B4310

PORT TALBOT
NEATH
RHONDDA
RHONDDA CYNON TAF
MERTHYR
POWYS
CARMARTHENSHIRE

BLACK MOUNTAIN
FOREST FAWR
MYNYDD BWLCH-Y-GROES
DANGER AREA
Tywi Forest
Crychan Forest
Cambrian Woollen Mill
Caerau Roman Fort
Brecon Gaer Roman Fort
Pen-y-Crug Hillfort
National Showcaves Centre for Wales
Dan-yr-Ogof
Henrhyd Waterfall
Nedd Fechan Waterfalls
Sgwd yr Eira
Afon Pyrddin Waterfalls
Melincourt Waterfall
Afan Forest Park

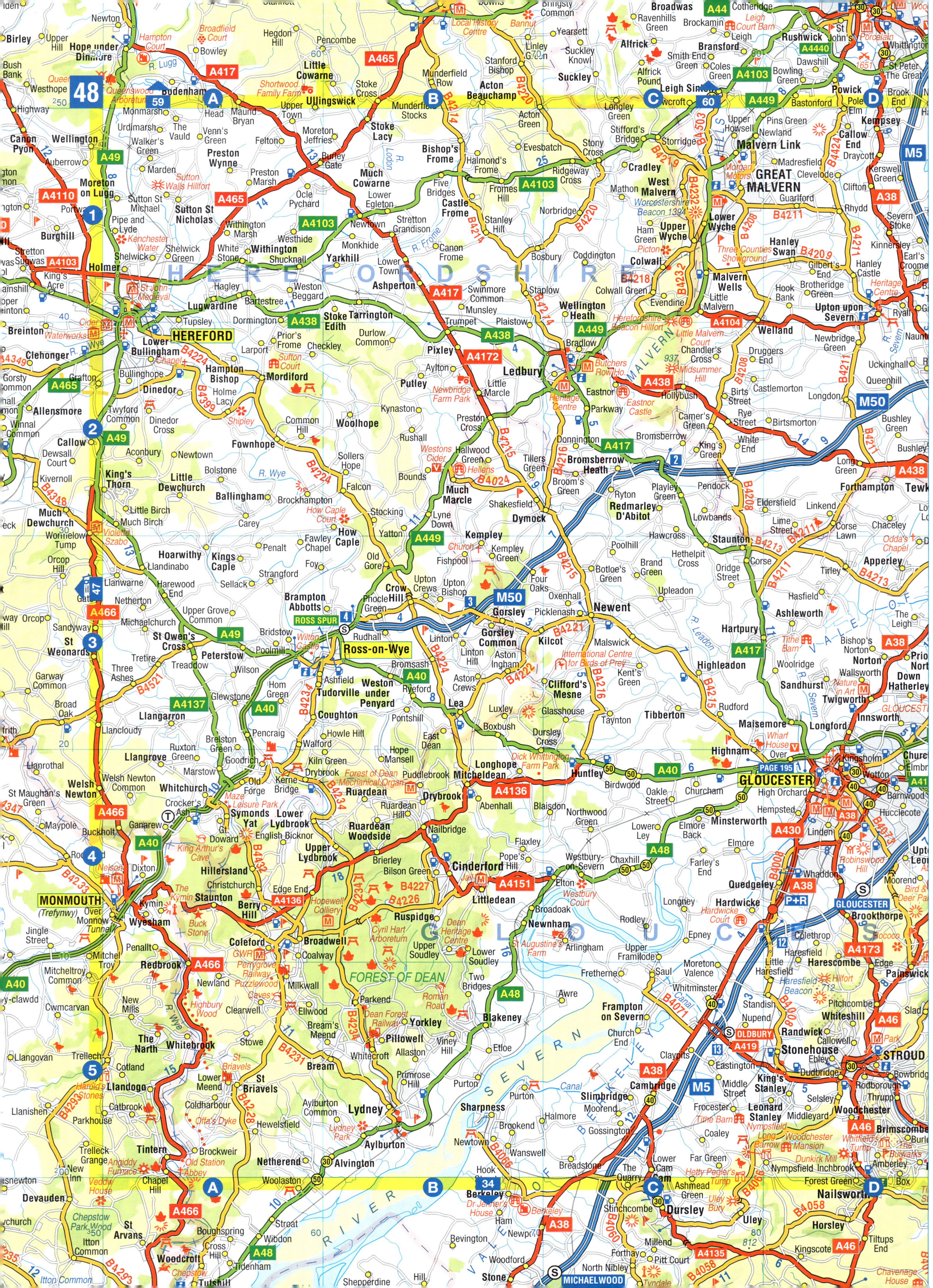

A422 · A3400 · A429

**WARWICKSHIRE**

-UPON-AVON · Bridge Town · Loxley · Wellesbourne Mountford · Watermill · Motor Centre · Gaydon · Knightcote · Upper Boddington · Westhorp · Byfield · Woodford Halse · Capel · Farthingstone · Little Preston · Maidford · Adstone

Wimpstone · Crimscote · Aldermister · Ettington · Pillerton Hersey · Butlers Marston · Kineton · Chadshunt · Compton Verney · Northend · Fenny Compton · Wormleighton · Wormleighton Resr. · Lower Boddington · Aston le Walls · West Farndon · Canons by House · Canons Ashby · Blak

A3400 · A429 · Armscote · Newbold on Stour · Halford · Idlicote · Pillerton Priors · Little Kineton · Stone · B4086 · Radway · Arlescote · Farnborough · Cropredy · Chipping Warden · Appletree · Eydon · Moreton Pinkney · Plumpton · Woodend

Blackwell · Tredington · Honington · Oxhill · Middle Tysoe · Edgehill · Alkerton · Shotteswell · Horley · Great Bourton · Wardington · Culworth · Thorpe Mandeville · Sulgrave · Weston · Weedon Lois · Milthorpe

Shipston-on-Stour · Upper Tysoe · Winderton · Shenington · Balscote · Wroxton · Drayton · **BANBURY** · Grimsbury · Middleton Cheney · Thenford · Greatworth · Crowfield · Radstone

A4035 · Lower Bra02 · Barcheston · Willington · Burmington · Upper Brailes · Lower Brailes · Sibford Gower · Swalcliffe · Broughton · Bodicote · Kings Sutton · Astrop · Charlton · Evenley · Westbury

Stretton-on-Fosse · Tidmington · Sutton-under-Brailes · Sibford Ferris · Burdrop · Tadmarton · Bloxham · Adderbury · Aynho · Croughton · Brackley

A429 · Todenham · Little Wolford · Cherington · Stourton · Milcombe · Milton · Barford St John · Barford St Michael · Clifton · Deddington · Souldern · Cottisford · Newton Purcell

Lower Lemington · Great Wolford · Whichford · Scotland End · South Newington · Hempton · Nether Worton · Over Worton · North Aston · Fritwell · Baynard's Green · Stoke Lyne · Fringford · Hardwick · Hethe

Moreton-in-Marsh · Barton-on-the-Heath · Long Compton · Hook Norton · Wigginton · Duns Tew · Middle Aston · Somerton · Fewcott · Ardley · Bucknell · Caversfield · Stratton Audley

A44 · Little Compton · Great Rollright · Swerford · Great Tew · Ledwell · Lower Heyford · Upper Heyford · **CHERWELL VALLEY** · Bicester · Launton

Chastleton · Little Rollright · Over Norton · Heythrop · Little Tew · Sandford St Martin · Middle Barton · Steeple Aston · Caulcott · Woodfield · Caversfield

Salford · **Chipping Norton** · Church Enstone · Cleveley · Radford · Steeple Barton · Rousham · Middleton Stoney · Chesterton · A4421

Cornwell · Churchill · Lidstone · Enstone · Gagingwell · Kiddington · Glympton · Northbrook · Bletchingdon · Wendlebury · Ambrosden

Kingham · Sarsden · Chadlington · Dean · Taston · Spelsbury · Over Kiddington · Nethercott · Kirtlington · Weston-on-the-Green · Merton · Upper Arncott

Bledington · Foscot · Lyneham · Shorthampton · Charlbury · Wootton · Tackley · Hampton Poyle · Islip · Charlton-on-Otmoor · Oddington · Murcott

**OXFORDSHIRE**

Milton-under-Wychwood · Ascott-under-Wychwood · Stonesfield · Combe · Woodstock · Old Woodstock · Shipton-on-Cherwell · Thrupp · Noke · Horton-cum-Studley

Shipton-under-Wychwood · Leafield · Finstock · Ramsden · Combe · Blenheim Palace · Bladon · Begbroke · Gosford · **DANGER AREA OT MOOR**

Fulbrook · Swinbrook · Asthall · Field Assarts · Fordwells · Whiteoak Green · Delly End · North Leigh · Long Hanborough · Kidlington · Woodeaton · Beckley

**Burford** · Asthall Leigh · Minster Lovell · Hailey · New Yatt · East End · Freeland · Church Hanborough · Yarnton · Marston · **OXFORD** · Stanton St John · Forest Hill

Westwell · Holwell · Crawley · Poffley End · Woodgreen · Barnard Gate · Cassington · Wolvercote · Sunnymead · Elsfield · Sandhills

Shilton · Charterville Allotments · Curbridge · **WITNEY** · Cogges · High Cogges · Eynsham · Wytham · Park Town · Headington · Barton · Holton

Cotswold Wildlife Park · Brize Norton · Ducklington · South Leigh · Toll House · Godstow Nunnery · Botley · Ashmolean · Shotover · Wheatley

Carterton · **BRIZE NORTON** · Lew · Hardwick · Farmoor · Farmoor Reservoir · Grandpont · Cowley · Horspath

Alvescot · Black Bourton · Yelford · Brighthampton · Stanton Harcourt · Blackditch · Bablock Hythe · Cumnor · Chawley · South Hinksey · Iffley · Littlemore · Garsington · Denton · Cuddesdon

Kencot · Broadwell · Bampton · Aston · Cote · Standlake · Northmoor · Eaton · Boars Hill · Kennington · Toot Baldon · Little Milton

Langford · Little Faringdon · Little Clanfield · Clanfield · Chimney · B4449 · Appleton · Bessels Leigh · Bayworth · Sunningwell · Sandford-on-Thames · Marsh Baldon · Chiselhampton

Lechlade on Thames · Kelmscott · Grafton · Duxford · Longworth · Fyfield · Cothill · Dry Sandford · Radley · Nuneham Courtenay · Stadhampton

Buscot · Eaton Hastings · Buckland · Hinton Waldrist · Southmoor · Kingston Bagpuize · Frilford · Garford · Marcham · **ABINGDON-ON-THAMES** · Clifton Hampden · Drayton St Leonard

Faringdon · Badbury Hill · Pusey · Charney Bassett · Kingston Bagpuize House · A415 · A34 · County Hall · Northcourt · Culham · Burcot

Road numbers visible: A422, A3400, A429, A436, A424, A361, A4095, A415, A420, A417, A40, A44, A34, A41, A4421, A4260, A423, A4525, A43, A421, A422, A4031, A4074, A4183, A4142, A4044, A4020, A4047, A4035, A4026, A4450, A4437, A4022, A4030, A4027, A430, A4100, B4100, M40

Grid references: A · B · C · D · 50 · 61 · 62 · 1 · 2 · 3 · 4 · 5 · 49 · 36

BEDFORD

ONSHIRE

B U C K I N G H A M S H I R E

CHILTERN HILLS OF AYLESBURY

THREE HUNDREDS

**Major towns:** NEWPORT PAGNELL, MILTON KEYNES, BLETCHLEY, AYLESBURY, DUNSTABLE, LEIGHTON BUZZARD, Linslade, Houghton Regis, Toddington, BERKHAMSTED, CHESHAM, AMERSHAM, CHORLEYWOOD, Tring, Princes Risborough, Great Missenden, Thame, Buckingham, Towcester, Silverstone, Winslow, Waddesdon, Wendover, Kempston, Flitwick

**A-roads:** A43, A5, A413, A508, A509, A422, A421, A428, A6, A507, A5130, A4146, A418, A41, A505, A4012, A5120, A512, A404, A4251, A416, A4010, A4128, A40, M1, M40, A329, A4129, B4033, B4034, B4032

Silverstone, Whittlebury, Whittlewood Forest, Stowe Landscape, Buckingham, Stony Stratford, Old Stratford, Wolverton, Woburn, Woburn Sands, Woburn Safari Park, Woburn Abbey, Aspley Guise, Cranfield, Husborne Crawley, Ridgmont, Steppingley, Flitwick, Ampthill, Millbrook, Lidlington, Marston Moretaine, Stewartby, Wootton, Kempston, Bromham, Biddenham, Clapham, Oakley

Whitchurch, Oving, Quainton, Waddesdon, Westcott, Ashendon, Dorton, Brill, Long Crendon, Haddenham, Thame, Chinnor, Stokenchurch, Radnage, Bradenham, Naphill, Hughenden Valley, Downley, Coleshill, Penn, Holmer Green, Amersham, Chesham, Bovingdon, Berkhamsted, Tring, Wendover, Princes Risborough, Great Missenden, Prestwood, Wigginton, Cholesbury, The Lee, Chartridge, Ballinger Common, Ashley Green, Whelpley Hill, Ley Hill, Bellingdon, Lye Green

Aylesbury, Stone, Weston Turville, Aston Clinton, Wilstone, Marsworth, Ivinghoe, Pitstone, Cheddington, Edlesborough, Eaton Bray, Totternhoe, Dunstable, Houghton Regis, Leighton Buzzard, Linslade, Stanbridge, Tilsworth, Billington, Slapton, Wing, Wingrave, Rowsham, Weedon, Hardwick, Watermead, Bierton, Hulcott, Buckland, Drayton Beauchamp, New Mill, Bulbourne, Dagnall, Ringshall, Little Gaddesden, Great Gaddesden, Studham, Whipsnade, Kensworth, Markyate

Milton Keynes Village, Walton, Woughton, Simpson, Fenny Stratford, Bletchley, Bow Brickhill, Great Brickhill, Little Brickhill, Stoke Hammond, Soulbury, Stewkley, Hollingdon, Burcott, Newton Longville, Stoke Mandeville, Halton, RAF Halton, Weston Turville

Grand Union Canal, River Great Ouse, River Thame, River Tove, River Ouzel, Claydon Brook

Leighton Buzzard, Stanbridge, Eggington, Hockliffe, Tebworth, Chalton, Toddington, Harlington, Westoning, Flitwick, Clophill

Grebe Lake, Claydon, Middle Claydon, East Claydon, Botolph Claydon, Steeple Claydon, Granborough, Hoggeston, Dunton, Littlecote, North Marston, Edgcott, Grendon Underwood, Marsh Gibbon, Twyford, Poundon, Charndon, Calvert, Kingswood, Ludgershall, Wotton Underwood, Piddington, Brill, Boarstall

52
A
B
C
D
1
2
3
4
5
BEDFORD
Kempston
Oakley
Clapham
Bromham
Biddenham
Goldington
Renhold
Ravensden
Salph End
West End
Stevington
Stagsden
Box End
Green End
Kempston Hardwick
Wootton
Elstow
Cardington
Cople
Harrowden
Shortstown
Cotton End
Willington
Moggerhanger
Great Barford
Blunham
Tempsford
Roxton
Sandy
Everton
Potton
Gamlingay
Gamlingay Cinques
Gamlingay Great Heath
Waresley
Little Gransden
Hatley St George
East Hatley
Cockayne Hatley
Wrestlingworth
Tadlow
Croydon
Arrington
Wimpole
Orwell
Kingston
Great Eversden
Wendy
Shingay
Meldreth
Whaddon
Kneesworth
Bassingbourn
Litlington
Royston
Abington Pigotts
North Brook End
Steeple Morden
Guilden Morden
Eyeworth
Dunton
Millow
Biggleswade
Sutton
Beeston
Upper Caldecote
Northill
Ickwell
Thorncote Green
Hatch
Old Warden
Southill
Broom
Stanford
Langford
Edworth
Hinxworth
Ashwell
Caldecote
Astwick
Newnham
Bygrave
BALDOCK
Stotfold
Radwell
Henlow
Clifton
Shefford
Church End
Arlesey
LETCHWORTH GARDEN CITY
Norton
Willian
Cadwell
Ickleford
Walsworth
Pirton
HITCHIN
Great Wymondley
Little Wymondley
Graveley
Charlton
Gosmore
St Ippolyts
Preston
Langley
Great Offley
Offley Hoo
Lilley
Ley Green
King's Walden
St Paul's Walden
Breachwood Green
Cockernhoe
Stopsley
LUTON
New Town
Caddington
Kensworth
Whipsnade
Studham
Markyate
Flamstead
Trowley Bottom
Redbourn
Harpenden
Wheathampstead
Kimpton
Codicote
Ayot St Lawrence
Ayot St Peter
Welwyn
WELWYN GARDEN CITY
Digswell
Tewin
Datchworth
Knebworth
Old Knebworth
STEVENAGE
Shephall
Aston
Walkern
Benington
Weston
Clothall
Wallington
Redhill
Rushden
Sandon
Kelshall
Therfield
Reed
Buckland
Chipping
Wyddial
Buntingford
Cottered
Ardeley
Westmill
Cherry Green
Great Munden
Haultwick
Dane End
Sacombe
Watton at Stone
Stapleford
Waterford
HERTFORD
Hertingfordbury
Hertford Heath
WARE
HODDESDON
Essendon
HATFIELD
Welham Green
Brookmans Park
POTTERS BAR
Northaw
Cuffley
CHESHUNT
Waltham Cross
ENFIELD
Hadley Wood
Cockfosters
Monken Hadley
BARNET
SOUTH MIMMS
Ridge
Shenley
London Colney
Colney Heath
ST ALBANS
Park Street
Frogmore
Bricket Wood
RADLETT
Aldenham
Letchmore Heath
BOREHAMWOOD
Elstree
BUSHEY
WATFORD
Abbots Langley
Kings Langley
HEMEL HEMPSTEAD
Chipperfield
Bovingdon
Flaunden
Sarratt
Croxley Green
Chandler's Cross
CHORLEYWOOD
Chenies
Latimer
Chesham Bois
Little Chalfont
Ashley Green
BERKHAMSTED
Potten End
Great Gaddesden
Little Gaddesden
Aldbury
Ringshall
Dagnall
DUNSTABLE
Houghton Regis
Totternhoe
Eaton Bray
Stanbridge
Tilsworth
Wingfield
Chalton
Toddington
Harlington
Westoning
Flitwick
Flitton
Silsoe
Ampthill
Maulden
Clophill
Haynes
Wilstead
Houghton Conquest
Marston Moretaine
Lidlington
Brogborough
Cranfield
Steppingley
Tingrith
Barton-le-Clay
Hexton
Pegsdon
Shillington
Meppershall
Campton
Chicksands
Gravenhurst
CENTRAL BEDFORDSHIRE
HERTFORDSHIRE
CAMB
A1
A1(M)
A6
A41
A428
A421
A4280
A603
A600
A507
A505
A5120
A5
A4012
A4146
A5183
A1081
A414
A4147
A4251
A416
A404
A411
A405
A1057
A1000
A602
A1155
A1072
A119
A10
A1198
A6001
A1170
M1
M25
B1042
B1040
B1046
B658
B659
B655
B656
B651
B652
B653
B1000
B158
B197
B4540
B4506
B4505
B487
B556
B5378
B462
B156
B157
B198
DANGER AREA

A1301 Trumpington P+R · Gog Magog Hills · Wandlebury · Fleam Dyke · Brinkley · East Green · Cowlinge · Wickhambrook · Clopton Green · Hawkedon

Haslingfield · Great Shelford · A1307 · Weston Colville · Willingham Green · Carlton · Great Bradley · Little Bradley · Hobbles Green · Pound Green · Farley Green · Denston · Stradishall · Stansfield

R I D G E S H I R E · A11 · E · Stapleford · Little Shelford · F · West Wratting · Balsham · 65 · G · Great Thurlow · Little Thurlow · H · Chimney Street · Barnardiston · 53 · Hundon · B1063 · Poslingford

Harston · Hauxton · Sawston · Babraham · Little Abington · West Wickham · Burton End · Streetly End · Withersfield · Great Wratting · Brockley Green · Chilton Street · Clare · A1092

Barrington · Newton · A1307 · FOURWENTWAYS · Pampisford · Great Abington · Hildersham · Horseheath · Little Wratting · A143 · Haverhill · Calford Green · Boyton End · Stoke by Clare · Ancient House · Castle Priory · 1 · M

Shepreth · Foxton · A505 · Whittlesford · A505 · Chilford Hall Vineyard · Linton · A1307 · Cardinal's Green · A143 · A1017 · Sturmer · New England · Wixoe · Ashen · Belchamp St Paul · Castle Hedingham

A10 · Fowlmere · Heathfield · A1301 · Duxford · A11 · Hinxton · Ickleton · Hadstock · Bartlow · Bartlow Hills · Shudy Camps · Steventon End · Castle Camps · Wiggens Green · A1017 · Tilbury Green · Kedington · Ovington · Castl

Melbourn · A505 · Imperial War Museum Duxford · M11 · 9A · Great Chesterford · Little Chesterford · Little Walden · Church End · Ashdon · Camps End · Castle Camps · Helions Bumpstead · Steeple Bumpstead · Birdbrook · Ridgewell Airfield · Ridgewell · Great Yeldham · North End

B1039 · B1368 · Heydon · Great Chishill · Elmdon · Crawley End · Strethall · Littlebury · B184 · Bridge End · Fry Art Gallery · Castle Turf Maze · Sewards End · Stocking Green · Radwinter · Hempstead · B1054 · Stambourne · Toppesfield · Pool Street · Colne Valley Railway

Barley · Little Chishill · Chrishall · Langley · Pond Street · Duddenhoe End · Bridge Green · Littlebury Green · Audley End · Saffron Walden · B1053 · B1055 · Great Sampford · Cornish Hall End · Robinhood End · Gainsford End · Delvin End · 2 · Highfield Green · Sible Hedingham · Castle Hedingham

Barkway · Nuthampstead · Lower Green · Upper Green · Arkesden · Wendens Ambo · Newport · Wimbish Green · Tye Green · Wimbish · Howe Street · B1053 · Little Sampford · Finchingfield · School Green · Southey Green · A1017 · Gosfield

Anstey · Meesden · Brent Pelham · Starling's Green · Clavering · Hill Green · Rickling · Debden · Elder Street · Howlett End · Boyton End · B1057 · Great Bardfield · Shalford · Morris Green · A1017 · A131

Hare Street · Great Hormead · Furneux Pelham · Berden · Quendon · Rickling Green · Widdington · Hamperden End · Debden Green · Thaxted · Cutlers Green · Guildhall John Webb's · Bardfield End Green · Oxen End · Wethersfield · Shalford Green · Blackmore End · Panfield · Bocking Churchstreet · High Garrett

B1038 · Dassels · Hay Street · Patmore Heath · Mallows Green · Manuden · Ugley Green · Henham · Woodend Green · Monk Street · Duton Hill · Lindsell · Bran End · Duck End · Bardfield Saling · Jasper's Green · Great Saling · Stebbing Green · 54 · Bocking · BRAINTREE · B1256 · M

Braughing · Standon · Little Hadham · A120 · Stansted Mountfitchet · Farnham · Elsenham · Molehill Green · Pledgdon Green · Broxted · Great Easton · Stebbing · Church End · Andrewsfield · Great Saling · 3 · Rayne · Great Notley · A131 · Tye Green · White Notley

Wellpond Green · Hadham Ford · Bury Green · Bishop's Stortford · Birchanger · Burton End · Tye Green · Little Easton · Bamber's Green · Easton Lodge · Little Dunmow · Felsted · Bartholomew Green · Pelstar Brewery · Black Notley

Puckeridge · Bromley · Latchford · Clapgate · Upwick Green · Farnham Green · A120 · Birchanger · 8 · 8A · LONDON STANSTED · Takeley · B1256 · Great Canfield · Barnston · North End · B1417 · Cock Green · Willows Green · Rank's Green · Fairstead · Faulkbourne

Barwick · Hopleys Forge · Much Hadham · Thorley Street · BIRCHANGER GREEN · Great Hallingbury · Start Hill · Takeley Street · Smith's Green · Puttock's End · Bacon End · Onslow Green · Hartford End · Littley Green · Great Leighs · Chatham Green · Fuller Street · Terling · Dor Sayer

Babbs Green · Hadham Cross · Perry Green · Green Tye · Little Hallingbury · A1184 · Hatfield Forest · Bedlar's Green · Taverners Green · High Roding · Bishop's Green · Ford End · Great Waltham · Little Leighs · 4 · Flack's Green

Wareside · Widford · Hunsdon · High Wych · Sawbridgeworth · Wright's Green · Hatfield Broad Oak · Hatfield Heath · The Rodings · Bishop's Green · Pleshey · Great Waltham · Howe Street · Little Waltham · P+R · A130 · A12 · Hatfield Peverel

A414 · St Margarets · Eastwick · Sheering · A1060 · White Roding · Leaden Roding · Good Easter · Chignal Smealy · Fanner's Green · Broomfield · B1008 · A130 · 20A · A12 · Boreham · Little Baddow

Stanstead Abbotts · Harlow · Mark Hall · Church Langley · Matching Green · Abbess Roding · Nether Street · Margaret Roding · High Easter · Stagden Cross · Mashbury · Chignal St James · Broad's Green · Parsonage Green · A1016 · Widford · CHELMSFORD · A138 · Little Baddow

Hoddesdon · Roydon · Harlow · A1025 · Potter Street · High Laver · Matching Tye · Birds Green · Beauchamp Roding · Shellow Bowells · Roxwell · Cooksmill Green · Great Oxney Green · Writtle · 30 · P+R · Great Baddow · A414 · Danbury · 5

A1170 · Roydon Hamlet · Lower Nazeing · A1169 · Foster Street · Magdalen Laver · Moreton · Fyfield · Willingale · Beggar Hill · Mill Green · A414 · Hylands House · Galleywood · A12 · Sandon · Butt's Green · Gay Bower

Nazeing Common · B1393 · Epping Green · Thornwood Common · Bovinger · Bobbingworth · Norton Mandeville · High Ongar · Norton Heath · Loves Green · Edney Common · Margaretting · Great Baddow · Galleywood · Howe Green · Bicknacre

Holyfield · Hayes Hill Farm · Epping · Epping Upland · North Weald Airfield · North Weald Bassett · Greensted · Toot Hill · Chipping Ongar · Nine Ashes · Elkins Green · Margaretting Tye · 14 · 15 · A12 · West Hanningfield · B1418

Harold's Park Farm · Coopersale · Coopersale Street · Fiddlers Hamlet · Saxon Wooden Church · Stanford Rivers · A113 · Blackmore · Wyatt's Green · Fryerning · 16 · A130 · South Hanningfield · RHS Hyde Hall

WALTHAM ABBEY · Copthall Green · Theydon Bois · 39 · Stapleford Tawney · Little End · A128 · Stondon Massey · Doddinghurst · Ingatestone · 40 · G · Stock · H · A130 · Rettendon · A132

A121 · A104 · M11 · A113 · Hobbs Cross · Stapleford Abbotts · Kelvedon Hatch · Secret Nuclear Bunker · Mountnessing · Heybridge · Queen's Park · Ramsden Heath · Downham

High Beech · Epping Forest · Debden Green · Abridge · Passingford Bridge · Navestock · Crow Green · A12 · Hutton · Havering's Grove · Runwell

A112 · LOUGHTON · M25 · Lambourne · Stapleford Abbotts · Old MacDonald's Farm · Navestock Side · Pilgrims Hatch · BILLERICAY · Ramsden Bellhouse

A143 · B1063 · A1092 · A1017 · A134 · A131 · A1124 · A1071 · A1141 · A12 · A137 · A133 · A1232 · A1341 · A133 · A120 · B1029 · B1027 · A130 · A132 · A138 · A414 · A130 · A1016 · B1137 · A1124 · B1053 · B1256

**Suffolk** · **Essex**

Wickhambrook · Clopton Green · Lawshall · Windsor Green · Thorpe Green · Brettenham · Battisford · Needham Market · Barking · Baylham

Pound Green · Farley Green · Hawkedon · Somerton · Smithwood Green · Thorpe Morieux · Hitcham · Wattisham · Charles Tye · Ringshall Stocks · Great Blakenham

Stradishall · Assington Green · Hartest · Shimpling Street · Rooksey Green · Preston · Bildeston · Nedging Tye · Somersham · Little Blakenham

Chimney Street · Hundon · Thurston End · Boxted · Shimpling · Lavenham · Little Hall · Guildhall · Brent Eleigh · Monks Eleigh · Chelsworth · Naughton · Offton · Blakenham Woodland

Stoke by Clare · Clare · Castle Priory · Cavendish · Glemsford · Long Melford · Bridge Street · Milden · Lindsey Tye · Lindsey · Kersey · Hadleigh · Hintlesham

Kedington · Ovington · Foxearth · Borley · Acton · Great Waldingfield · Little Waldingfield · Rose Green · Chapel · Wicker Street Green · Grotton · Calais Street · Upper Layham · Copdock

Stambourne · Ridgewell · Tilbury Juxta Clare · Great Yeldham · Sudbury · Gainsborough's Ho · Ballingdon · Bulmer · Great Cornard · Newton · Boxford · Hadleigh Heath · Lower Layham · Holton St Mary · Capel St Mary · Bentley

Toppesfield · Castle Hedingham · Sible Hedingham · Gosfield · Halstead · Little Maplestead · Pebmarsh · Bures · Nayland · Stoke-by-Nayland · Thorington Street · Higham · Stratford St Mary · East Bergholt · Brantham · Mistley

Greenstead Green · Earls Colne · Wakes Colne · White Colne · Chappel · Fordham · West Bergholt · Great Horkesley · Boxted · Langham · Dedham · Manningtree · Lawford · New Mistley

Braintree · Bocking · Coggeshall · Marks Tey · Stanway · Copford · Colchester · Elmstead Market · Wivenhoe · Alresford · Great Bentley

Rayne · Great Notley · Black Notley · Cressing · Feering · Kelvedon · Messing · Layer Marney · Birch · Layer-de-la-Haye · Abberton · Rowhedge · Fingringhoe · Thorrington · Brightlingsea · St Osyth

Great Leighs · Fairstead · Terling · Silver End · Witham · Rivenhall · Tiptree · Tolleshunt Knights · Great Wigborough · Salcott · Langenhoe · Peldon · South Green · West Mersea · **Mersea Island** · East Mersea · Point Clear

Little Waltham · White Notley · Faulkbourne · Wickham Bishops · Great Totham North · Tolleshunt Major · Tolleshunt D'Arcy · Tollesbury · Blue Row · **Colne Point**

Chelmsford · Boreham · Hatfield Peverel · Nounsley · Langford · Heybridge · Heybridge Basin · Goldhanger · **Virley Channel** · **Sales Point**

Great Baddow · Sandon · Danbury · Little Baddow · Woodham Walter · Maldon · Northey Island · Osea Island · **River Blackwater** · Bradwell Waterside · Bradwell-on-Sea · St Peter's Chapel

Galleyend · Bicknacre · Woodham Mortimer · Hazeleigh · Rudley Green · Mundon · Maylandsea · Mayland · Ramsey Island · St Lawrence · Tillingham · **Holliwell Point**

West Hanningfield · East Hanningfield · Cock Clarks · Purleigh · Howegreen · Latchingdon · Asheldham · Dengie · **Foulness Sands**

Hanningfield Reservoir · South Hanningfield · Rettendon · Woodham Ferrers · Cold Norton · Stow Maries · North Fambridge · Althorne · Southminster · Stoneyhills · Ostend · Burnham-on-Crouch · **Foulnes Sands**

South Woodham Ferrers · Marsh Farm · South Fambridge · Mangapps Railway · **RIVER CROUCH** · **Foulness Point**

NORTH SEA

Bay
Orford Ness
Hollesley Bay

Harwich to:
Hook of Holland 6hrs. 15mins.

Tunstall
Sudbourne
Bentwaters Cold War
Rendlesham
Chillesford
A1152
Butley
Capel Green
Butley High Corner
Capel St Andrew
Dunwich Underwater Exploration
Orford
Orford Ness
R. Aide
Butley R.
B1084
B1078
Debach
Pettistree
Bredfield
Gibraltar
493rd Bomb Group
Corner
Ashbocking
Hemingstone
Ilham House Breeds Farm
Bell's Cross
Barham
Henley
Claydon
Akenham
Westerfield
Castle Hill
Rushmere St Andrew
Witnesham
Grundisburgh
Swinland
Burgh
Hasketon
Great Bealings
Little Bealings
Playford
Tuddenham St Martin
Woodbridge
Melton
Bromeswell
Eyke
B1438
B1084
A12
Martlesham
Martlesham Heath
Martlesham Heath Control Tower
Suffolk Showground
Kesgrave
California
Ipswich
Chantry
Gainsborough
Orwell
A1156
A1214
A1189
A12
A1156
A14
Sutton
Shottisham
Hollesley
Shingle Street
Alderton
Martello Tower
Bawdsey
Martello Tower
Boyton
Newbourne
Hemley
Waldringfield
Brightwell
Bucklesham
Kirton
Falkenham
Trimley St Martin
River Deben
Felixstowe Ferry
Martello Towers
Walton
Old Felixstowe
Felixstowe
Trimley St Mary
Trimley Lower Street
Thorpe Common
Levington
Nacton
Woolverstone
Freston
Wherstead
Belstead
A14
A137
B1456
B1456
Chelmondiston
Pinmill
Shotley
Erwarton
Shotley Gate
HMS Ganges
Harkstead
Stutton
Lower Holbrook
Holbrook
Alton Water
Wonder Upper Street
Tattingstone White Horse
Tattingstone
B1080
RIVER STOUR
Maritime
Guildhall
Harwich Harbour
Redoubt
Landguard Fort
Harwich
Dovercourt
Parkeston
Ramsey
Upper Dovercourt
Wrabness
Bradfield
Mistley Heath
Bradfield Heath
A120
B1352
Wix
Great Oakley
Stones Green
Little Oakley
B1414
Tendring Green
Beaumont
Horsey Island
Hamford Water
The Naze
Maritime
B1035
Tendring
Thorpe Green
Weeley
B1033
Kirby-le-Soken
B1034
Walton-on-the-Naze
Thorpe-le-Soken
Weeley Heath
B1414
Kirby Cross
B1033
Great Holland
Frinton-on-Sea
A133
Little Clacton
Row Heath
St Osyth Heath
B1442
B1032
Holland Haven
Holland-on-Sea
Great Clacton
B1027
Clacton-on-Sea
Jaywick
Seawick
Martello Tower

Martello Tower
Tower

Orford Ness

Martello Tower

P+R
PAGE 196
DANGER AREA
Tide Mill
Sutton Hoo

N O R T H   S E A

650
250
40
30
20
10
200
650
41

10     20     30     40

**A**    **B**   68    **C**     **D**

300

1

90

2

80

C A R D I G A N    B A Y

( B A E    C E R E D I G I O N )

3

70

4

Aberaeron

Ffos-y-ffin   A482

60

New Quay    Marine Wildlife Centre

(Ceinewydd)    Llwyncelyn

Maen-y-groes    Gilfachreda

Cwmtudu    Llanarth   Oakford

Cross    (Derwen Gam)

Inn    New Quay   Geneva

Nanternis    Honey Farm   Pen-cae

Caerwedros    A486

Ynys-Lochtyn    Blaen   Synod Inn   Mydroilyn

5    Celyn   Llwyndafydd   (Post-Mawr)

Cardigan    Llangranog   Morfa   Pontgarreg

Island    Penbryn   A487   Plwmp

Rainforest   Tresaith   Pentregat

Centre   Aberporth   Brynhoffnant

Cemaes Head   Cardigan Island   Parcllyn   Talgarreg

Coastal Farm Park   West Wales   Sarnau

250   Felinwynt   (Aberporth)   B4338

Allt-y-goed   **A**   44   **B**   Internal Fire   Capel   **C**   **D**

Pwllygranant   enannerch   Tan-y-groes   Cynon   Bwlch-y-fadfa

Cippyn   Tremain   15   A486   B4459

10   Blaenporth   Glynarthen   40

St   B4548   Penparc   Felin   Brithdir

Dogmaels   Y Ferwig   Wnda   Rhydlewis   Ffostrasol   Pont-Sian

(Llandudoch)   Cardigan   20   Bettws   Hawen   B4571   A475

Moylgrove   (Aberteifi)   A487   Noyadd   Ifan   Curlew Weavers   12 Cwm

(Trewyddel)   Abbey   Castle   Pantgwyn   Trefawr   Beulah   Woollen Mill   11

Watermill   B4570   Troedyraur   Penrhiw-

llangoedmor   Ponthirwaun   pal Maes

Tonfanau
Bryncrug
Pandy
Broad Water
Aber Dysynni
Rhyd-yr-onen
Dolgoch Falls
Trum Gelli
Torrenhendre
Railway
Pantperthog
Centre for Alternative Technology
Llanwrin
Road
A470
A487
B4404
Abercegir
Darowen
Commins Coch
Tafolwern
Llan

250
Tywyn
Narrow Gauge Railway
A493
Pennal
A487
Dyffryn Dyfi
Machynlleth
Penegoes
A489
Forge
Tal-y-Wern
Pennant
Moelfre 1537

POWYS

Penhelig
Aberdovey (Aberdyfi)
Snowdonia National Park
Glandyfi
Derwenlas
Dyfi Furnace
Eglwys Fach
Furnace
Melinbyrhedyn
Aberhosan
Dylife

Ynyslas
B4353
Llancynfelyn
Tre'r-ddol
Tre Taliesin
A487
Pencarreggopa 1467
Moel y Llyn 1708
Llyn Dwfn
Llyn Conach
Bugeilyn
Glaslyn
Llwynygog
Afon Lwy

Borth
Station
Animalarum
Upper Borth
Tal-y-bont
Afon Leri
Llyn Craigypistyll
Drosgol 1806
Nant-y-moch Reservoir
Pen Pumlumon Arwystli 2431
Source of R. Severn
Hafren Forest
Esgair y Maesnant
R. Severn
Llyn Clywedog (Reservoir)
Llaniwa

Rhyd-meirionydd
Llandre
Pen-y-garn
Bow Street
B4353
Dol-y-Bont
Bontgoch
Salem
Cwmsymlog
PLYNLIMON (PUMLUMON FAWR)
Drum Peithnant
Source of R. Wye (Afon Gwy)
Y Foel
A44
Wye Valley
R Wye (Afon Gwy)
Afon Bidno

Llangorwen
Camera Obscura
Cliff Railway
National Library
A487
Penrhyn-coch
Garth
Cefn Llwyd
Pen-bont Rhydybeddau
Cwmerfyn
Bwlch Nant yr Arian Forest
Dinas Resr.
Llyn Syfydrin
Afon Rheidol
Esgair y Maesnant
1849
Esgair Ychion

ABERYSTWYTH
The Bar
Llanbadarn Fawr
A4159
Comins Coch
Capel Dewi
Blaen-geufordd
Dollwen
Goginan
Rheidol Power Station
Ponterwyd
B4343
Dyffryn Castell
58
Banc Nant Rhys

Penparcau
Southgate
A44
Capel Bangor
Cwmbrwyno
Llywernog
Llywernog Silver-Lead Mine
Ystumtuen
Ysbyty Cynfyn
Bryn Garw

Rhydyfelin
Moriah
Capel Seion
Aberffrwd
Vale of Rheidol
Rheidol Falls
Mynach Falls
Yr Allt

Chancery
Llanfarian
Gors
New Cross
Llanfihangel-y-Creuddyn
Three Bridges
Devil's Bridge (Pontarfynach)
Jubilee Arch
B4574
Elan Valley

Blaenplwyf
Llanilar
B4340
Cnwch Coch
Trisant
New Row
Cwmystwyth
B4574
Geifas 1878
Llyn Fyrddon Fawr

Carreg Ti-pw
Llanddeiniol
A487
B4576
Rhos-y-garth
Crosswood (Trawsgoed)
Llanafan
Afon Ystwyth
Ysbyty Ystwyth
Pont-rhyd-y-groes
Llyn Fyrddon Fach 1944
Llyn Du
Llyn Cerrigllwydion Isaf
Llyn Cerrigllwydion Uchaf
Trumau

Llangwyryfon
Lledrod
B4575
Wenallt
Mynydd Bach 1092
Tynygraig
Marchnant
Trawsallt 1944
Llyn Hir
Drygarn Fawr 2104

Llanrhystud
A485
Trefenter 1183
Bronnant
Ffair Rhos
Ystradmeurig
B4340
Pontrhydfendigaid
Llyn Teifi
Llyn y Gorlan
Claerwen Reservoir
Esgair Garthen

Llansantffraed
Llan-non
A487
Rhyd-Rosser
Rhydfudr
Swyddffynnon
Corsgoch Gran Teifi
Strata Florida
Abbey
Dibyn Du
Pen-y-bwlch

Aberarth
Pennant
B4577
Nebo
Rhos Haminiog
Cross Inn
Bethania
Bontnewydd
Blaenpennal
Afon Teifi
1738
Pen-y-bwlch
Bryn Garw 1827

Monachty
Ciliau
Newbridge
Cilcennin
B4337
Bwlch-Llan
Penuwch
B4571
Ty'n-yr-eithin
Cors Caron
Y Drum 1668
Esgair Ambor
Bryn Crwn 1732

Llanaeron
Llanerchaeron
Trefilan
Ystrad Aeron
Abermeurig
Capel Betws Lleucu
Llangeitho
B4578
A485
Tregaron
Tregaron Red Kite Centre & Museum
Esgair Fraith 1592
LlynBerwyn
Esgair Cerrig 1588
Gamallt
1641 Cefn-Coch
Nant Irfon

Diheuyd
B4342
Felinfach
Talsarn
Gartheli
Llundain-fach
Llwyn-y-groes
Olmarch
A485
Llanddewi Brefi
Esgair Llethr 1543
Bryn Brawd 1589
Drygarn Fawr
Cefn Fannog 1476
Abergwesyn

Cribyn
Silian
Bettws Bledrws
Llangybi
Llanfair Clydogau
Pen Rhiw-clochdy
Pen y Gurnos
1497
Llyn Brianne
Tywi Forest

Gorsgoch
A482
Cellan
Craig Twrch
46
Mynydd Trawsnant 1695
Llanwrtyd
Cambrian Woollen Mill

Cwrtnewydd
Maes
45
Lampeter (Llanbedr Pont Steffan)
Pentrefelin
A475
Cwmann
Ystradffin
Llanwrtyd Wells (Llanwrtyd)

Llanwnnen
Pentre-bach
Alltyblacca
CARMARTHENSHIRE
1515

A  B  70 C  D

1

2

57

3

4

5

A  B  46  C  D

**CAMBRIAN MOUNTAINS**

**P O W Y S**

**RADNOR FOREST**

Road
Pandy
Llanbrynmair
Commins Coch
Tafolwern
Dol-fâch
Talerddig
Cefn Coch
Llanllugan
Llanwyddelan
New Mills (Felin Newydd)
Manafon
Rhiw
B4390
Pant-y-ffridd
B4385
Berriew (Aberriw)
A483

Melinbyrhedyn
Llan
Bont Dolgadfan
B4518
Ffridd
300
Mynydd Clogau
Gwgla
Tregynon
Brooks
Pentre Llifior
Fron
Garthmyl
Hendomen
Old Bell

Pennant
Afon Twymyn
Brynamlwg 1602
Carno
Bwlch y Garreg
Llyn y Tarw
Bwlch-y-ffridd
Highgate
Aberbechan
Dolforwyn
Abermule (Aber-miwl)
B4386
B4385
Montgomery (Trefaldwyn)
A489

Aberhosan
Moelfre 1537
Moel y Golfa
Trannon
Llyn Mawr
Esgair Cwnowen
Llanwnog
B4568
Aberhafesp
Robert Owen Textile
Llanllwchaiarn
Llanmerwig
Cefn-y-coed
Llandyssil
A489

Dylife
Afon Biga
Staylittle (Penffordd-Lâs)
Clatter
Pontdolgoch
Caersws
Milford
Newtown (Y Drenewydd)
Hodley
Gwern-y-go
Sarn
City

Glaslyn
Bugeilyn
Y Foel
Llwynygog
Llawryglyn
Gleiniant
Waen
A489
Maesyrhandir
Garth Owen
A489
Kerry (Ceri)
Glanmule
Brynllywarch
Pentre
A489

Source of R. Severn
en Pumlumon Arwystli 2431
Hâfren Forest
Esgair y Maesnant
R. Severn
Esgair Ychion
Trefeglwys
A470
Little London
Mochdre
Dolfor
Kerry Hill Cross Dyke 1732
Cilfaesty Hill
Anchor
Black Mountain 1469
R. Clun
Clun Forest
B4368

Y Foel
Afon Bidno
Glan-y-nant
Bryn y Fan 1583
B4569
Van
Cerist
Llandinam
R. Severn
Pentre
Quabbs

Llyn Clywedog (Reservoir)
Bryntail Lead Mine
Afon Clywedog
Oakley Park
Llyn Ebyr
Llaithddu
David's Well
Beguildy
Dutlas

Esgair Ychion
Glynbrochan
Llanidloes
B4518
Newchapel
Dethenydd
Red Lion Hill 1618
Llanbadarn Fynydd
Gors Lydan 1736
Black Mountain 1584
Beacon Hill 1796

A44
A470
Llangurig
Llaniwared
Cwmbelan
Afon Dulas
1921
Rhydnwll
Ddyle
Llananno
Pool Hill 1690
Llanllwest

Esgair Garthen
Bryn Titli
Dolfach
Tylwch
Sychnant
Nantgwyn
Bwlch-y-sarnau
B4356
Llanbister
Crug
Llangunllo
R. Lugg

Geifas 1878
Llyn Cerrigoydion Isaf
Craig Goch Reservoir
Dolhelfa
R. Wye
Pant-y-dwr
Afon Marteg
St Harmon
Moel Hywel
Cefngin
Abbey-cwm-hir
Abbey
Camlo Hill 1670
A483
Heartsease
Fishpools
Bleddfa

Llyn Cerrigllwydion Uchaf
Trumau
Penygarreg Resr.
Gamallt
B4518
A470
Maelienydd
Llanddewi Ystradenni
Dolau
Little Hill
Llanfihangel Rhydithon
A488

Claerwen Reservoir
Garreg-ddu Resr.
Lower Llanfadog
Rhayader (Rhaeadr Gwy)
Gaufron
Welsh Royal Crystal
Red Kite Feeding Cen.
Gwastedyn Hill 1566
Nantmel
Coedglasson
Gwystre
Fron
Crossgates
Penybont
Llandegley
RADNOR FOREST
2166
DANGER AREA
Bache Hill

Esgair Garthen
Elan Village
Elan Valley
Llansantffraed Cwmdeuddwr
Llanwrthwl
Nant Glas
A44
Llanyre
Penybont
A44
Llandegley Rhos
New Radnor

Bryn Garw 1827
Caban Coch Reservoir
Afon Claerwen
Gorllwyn 2010
Drygarn Fawr 2104
Argoed Mill
Castell Collen Roman Fort
Radnorshire
Llandrindod Wells (Llandrindod)
Cefnllys Castle
Ridgebourne
Frank's Bridge
Gilwern Hill 1440
Bryn-y-maen Gwaunceste Hill 1777
Yardro

Bryn Crwn 1732
Gravel 1761
A470
Newbridge on Wye
Disserth
Howey
Crossway
Llansantffraed-in-Elwel
Glascwm
1718
Glascwm Hill
Hundred House
A481
R. Arrow
Newchurch

Cefn-Coch 1641
Nant Irfon
Llanafan-fawr
Bryn 1572
A483
Cwmbach Llechrhyd
Llanelwedd
Cregrina
Red Hill
Clyro Hill 1276
Rhosgoch

Cefn Fannog 1476
Abergwesyn
Pentre-llwyn-llwyd
B4358
Builth Road
R. Wye (Afon Gwy)
Cilmery (Cilmeri)
Llywelyn the Last Monument
Royal Welsh Showground
Builth Wells (Llanfair-ym-Muallt)
Oaklands
Llanfaredd
Llanbedr Hill
Painscastle

Cambrian Woollen Mill
A483
Beulah
Garth
Llanafan-fechan
A483
Aberedw
Aberedw Rocks
Llandeilo Graban

Llanwrtyd Wells (Llanwrtud)
Mynydd Trawsnant 1695
Cefngorwydd
Llangammarch Wells
DANGER AREA
Maesmynis
Llanddewi'r Cwm
A470
Alltmawr
Llanbadarn-y-garreg
Llanbedr

Map of Shropshire and Herefordshire border region (road atlas).

Grid references: **59**

SHROPSHIRE — HEREFORDSHIRE — WALES / ENGLAND

**Towns and villages:**
Fron, Kingswood, Stockton, Marton, Meadowtown, Bentlawnt, Rorrington, Wotherton, Chirbury, Dudston, Priest Weston, Shelve, The Marsh, The Bog, Pennerley, Stiperstones, Snailbeach, Habberley, Pulverbatch, Church Pulverbatch, Picklescott, Woolstaston, Leebotwood, Longnor, Netley, Dorrington, Stapleton, Longden Common, Wrentnall, Oaks, Pitchford, Frodesley, Ruckley, Kenley, Golding, Harnage, Cound, Upper Cound, Cressage, Harley, Much Wenlock, Buildwas, Sheinton

Mitchell's Fold Stone Circle, Corndon Hill, Hyssington, Llanerch, Church Stoke, Alport, Hurdley, Shead, Owlbury, Lydham, Norbury, Wentnor, Whitcot, More, Linley, Asterton, Medlicott, Ratlinghope, All Stretton, Ashbrook, Worldsend, Caer Caradoc, Cardington, Gretton, Longville in the Dale, Easthope, Shipton, Stanton Long, Derrington, Middleton Priors, Ditton Priors, Cleobury North, Burwarton

Church Stretton, Hope Bowdler, Wall under Heywood, Rushbury, Hungerford, Holdgate, Ashfield, Abdon, Clee St Margaret, Stoke St Milborough, Cleedownton, Cleestanton, Bitterley, Clee Hill, Titterstone Clee Hill, Doddington, Cleehill, Angelbank, Knowbury, Hope Bagot, Nash

Bishop's Castle, Lydbury North, Edgton, Plowden, Horderley, Cheney Longville, Sibdon Carwood, Hopesay, Aston on Clun, Clungunford, Clunbury, Clun, Clunton, Purslow, Hopton Castle, Bedstone, Bucknell, Leintwardine, Brampton Bryan, Walford, Buckton, Adforton, Wigmore, Leinthall Starkes, Leinthall Earls, Lingen, Presteigne (Llanandras), Knighton (Tref-y-Clawdd), Bryn, Colebatch, Mainstone, Reilth, Newcastle, Whitcott Keysett, Bettws-y-crwyn, Mardu, Bicton, Guilden Down, Kempton, Broome, Rowton, Twitchen, Hoptonheath, Hopton Heath, Coxall, Marlow, Todding, Kinton, Downton on the Rock, Burrington, Pipe Aston, Elton

Craven Arms, Stokesay, Norton Camp, Shropshire Hills Discovery Centre, Wistanstow, Strefford, Halford, Seifton, Culmington, Stanton Lacy, Bromfield, Ludlow, Ludford, Overton, Ashford Carbonel, Ashford Bowdler, Richards Castle, Orleton, Comberton, Wooferton, Middleton, Little Hereford, Brimfield, Tenbury Wells, Burford, Greete, Whatmore, Knighton Common, Boraston

Acton Scott, Hatton, Ticklerton, Eaton, Broadstone, Munslow, Diddlebury, Corfton, Peaton, Great Sutton, Tugford, Baucott, Cockshutford

Knucklas, Knighton, Milebrook, Stowe, Weston, Lloyney, Skyborry Green, Bailey Hill, Garth, Llan-wen Hill, Beguildy

Llanfair Waterdine, Purlogue, New Invention, Chapel Lawn, Caer Caradoc, Stanage

WALES / ENGLAND, Offa's Dyke

Presteigne, Rhos-y-meirch, Discoed, Norton, Dolley Green, Whitton, Kinnerton, Evenjobb, Walton, Old Radnor, Dolyhir, Gladestry, Kington, Hergest, Lower Hergest, Upper Hergest, Huntington Castle, Kingswood, Chickward, Lyonshall, Titley, Staunton on Arrow, Kinnersley, Eardisley, Almeley, Woonton, Logaston, Newchurch, Michaelchurch-on-Arrow

Lucton, Mortimer's Cross, Yatton, Aymestrey, Shobdon, Pembridge, Marston, Eardisland, Monkland, Dilwyn, Weobley, Sarnesfield, King's Pyon, Birley, Canon Pyon

Kingsland, Luston, Eye, The Hundred, Yarpole, Bicton, Croft Ambrey, Cock Gate, Bircher, Berrington, Moreton, Ashton, Middleton on the Hill, Stoke Prior, Leominster, Ivington, Brierley, Stoke Prior, Docklow, Steen's Bridge, Hatfield, Pudleston, Whyle, Stockton, Grafton, Kimbolton, Bredenbury, Edwyn Ralph, Thornbury, Bromyard

Risbury, Humber, Buckland, Wharton, Newton, Hope under Dinmore, Bodenham, Maund Bryan, Marston Stannett, Pencombe, Ullingswick, Little Cowarne, Stoke Lacy, Much Cowarne, Lower Egleton, Ocle Pychard, Moreton on Lugg, Sutton St Michael, Sutton St Nicholas, Wellington, Marden, Preston Wynne, Felton, The Vauld, Venn's Green, Moreton Jeffries

Dorstone, Bredwardine, Brobury, Clifford, Whitney-on-Wye, Winforton, Willersley, Letton, Staunton on Wye, Monnington on Wye, Byford, Mansel Lacy, Yazor, Tillington, Canon Bridge

**Road numbers:** A49, A488, A489, A490, A458, A459, A4169, A4168, A4371, A4117, A4364, A4113, A4361, A4362, A4363, A456, A4112, A4110, A44, A465, A417, A480, A4111, A438, A4355, A4356, A4357, A4372, B4499, B4386, B4385, B4383, B4368, B4370, B4371, B4318, B4364, B4365, B4360, B4529, B4362, B4352, B4530, B4355, B4357

WOLVERHAMPTON

WORCESTER

KIDDERMINSTER

STOURBRIDGE

DUDLEY

BILSTON

WILLENHALL

WEDNESFIELD

COSELEY

SEDGLEY

TIPTON

BRIERLEY HILL

HALESOWEN

BROMSGROVE

DROITWICH SPA

Bridgnorth

Much Wenlock

Ironbridge

Madeley

Albrighton

Codsall

Tettenhall

Kinver

Stourbridge

Bewdley

Stourport-on-Severn

Tenbury Wells

Bromyard

GREAT MALVERN

West Malvern

Malvern Link

SHROPSHIRE

WORCESTERSHIRE

WYRE FOREST

Cleobury Mortimer

Cleehill

Burford

Clifton upon Teme

Great Witley

Abberley

Martley

Wichenford

Ombersley

Hartlebury

Chaddesley Corbett

Hagley

Clent

Wombourne

Seisdon

Claverley

Worfield

Pattingham

Penn

Lower Penn

Wightwick

A4169  A458  A442  A454  A449  A41  A451  A456  A491  A450  A448  A442  A443  A44  A449  A4103  A38  A4440  A456  A4117  A44  A465  A4169  B4176  B4363  B4194  B4555  B4189  B4190  B4373  B4368  B4364  B4201  B4202  B4203  B4204  B4220  B4197  M5

**BIRMINGHAM**

**COVENTRY**

**TAMWORTH**

**WALSALL**

**WEST BROMWICH**

**WEDNESBURY**

**SMETHWICK**

**ATHERSTONE**

**NUNEATON**

**BEDWORTH**

**ROYAL SUTTON COLDFIELD**

**SOLIHULL**

**REDDITCH**

**ROYAL LEAMINGTON SPA**

**WARWICK**

**KENILWORTH**

**STRATFORD-UPON-AVON**

**FRANKLEY**

**HOPWOOD PARK**

LEICESTER
PAGE 196

LEICESTER FOREST EAST

COVENTRY
PAGE 194

RUGBY

NUNEATON

HINCKLEY

BEDWORTH

ROYAL LEAMINGTON SPA

WARWICK

DAVENTRY

NORTHAMPTON

ATHERSTONE

WIGSTON

Braunstone Town

Oadby

Hartshill

WARWICKSHIRE

NORTHA

LEICESTERS

Towcester

Naseby

Husbands Bosworth

Lutterworth

Market Bosworth

Southam

Gaydon

Watford Gap

River Chater

Lyndon • Weston • North Luffenham • Ketton • Aldgate • the Hill • Barnack • Ufford • Clare Cottage
Manton • Wing • Pilton • A6121 • Priest's House • Geeston • A43 • Collyweston • A1 • Southorpe
A6003 • Ridlington • Preston • South Luffenham • Wakerley • White Water Resr. • Wittering • Wittering
Belton-in-Rutland • Ayston • Glaston • Morcott • A47 • 75 • Bainden • Tixover • Duddington • A47 • Thornhaugh • Sacrewell Farm
Skeffington • Loddington • Eye Brook • Uppingham • Bisbrooke • Seaton • Harringworth • King's Cliffe • Apethorpe • Nassington • Wansford • Stibbington • Sutton • Ailsworth
Tugby • East Norton • Allexton • Wardley • A47 • F • G • Duddington • H • Yarwell • Water Newton • Peterborough (Sibson) • Castor
Rolleston • Noseley • Goadby • Stockerston • Lyddington • Thorpe by Water • Laxton • Woodnewton • Prebendal Manor House • Sibson • Nene Valley Railway • Over End • Esterton
HIRE • Horninghold • Stoke Dry • Lyddington Bede House • Blatherwycke Lake • Apethorpe • Fotheringhay • Elton • Alwalton
Hallaton • Blaston • Caldecott • Viaduct • Blatherwycke • FOREST • Southwick Hall • Elton Hall • A1
Stonton Wyville • Glooston • A6003 • Gretton • Deene • Deenethorpe • Southwick • Warmington • Haddon
Church Langton • Slawston • Great Easton • Kirby Hall • Deene Park • Glapthorn • Cotterstock • A605 • Morborne • Folksworth
Thorpe Langton • Medbourne • Bringhurst • Rockingham • Deenethorpe • Oundle • Ashton • Polebrook • Tansor • Eaglethorpe
East Langton • Welham • Weston by Welland • Drayton • B670 • Upper Benefield • Lower Benefield • Stoke Doyle • Barnwell • Hemington • Luddington in the Brook
A6 • Sutton Bassett • Cottingham • Middleton • East Carlton • CORBY • A427 • Weldon • Oundle • Armston • Barnwell • B660
Great Bowden • Ashley • Wilbarston • A427 • Stanion • Woodland Park • Brigstock • Fermynwoods Contemporary Art • Wadenhoe • Pilton • Great Gidding
Harborough • Little Bowden • Stoke Albany • Dingley • A6014 • Great Oakley • Little Oakley • A4300 • Fermyn Woods • Lyveden New Bield • Achurch • Wigsthorpe • Thurning • Little Gidding
MARKET HARBOROUGH • Brampton Ash • Pipewell • Newton • Geddington • A6116 • Sudborough • Aldwincle • Thorpe Waterville • Clopton • Steeple Gidding
Braybrooke • Desborough • Rushton • Eleanor Cross • Boughton • Lowick • Islip • Titchmarsh • Winwick • Ham
Great Oxendon • Arthingworth • Rothwell • Triangular Lodge • Weekley • 384th Bombardment Group Memorial • Grafton Underwood • Slipton • Thrapston • Old Weston • B662
Kelmarsh • Harrington • A43 • A4300 • Warkton • Twywell • Denford • A14 • Bythorn • Molesworth • Buckworth
A14 • Loddington • Orton • Thorpe Malsor Resr. • KETTERING • Barton Seagrave • Cranford St John • Woodford • Keyston • Brington • Leighton Bromswold • Barham
Maidwell • Draughton • Cransley Resr. • A6030 • Cranford St Andrew • A14 • Ringstead • A14 • Catworth • Spaldwick
Lamport • Hanging Houghton • Broughton • A14 • Burton Latimer • A6 • Great Addington • Raunds • Three Shire Stone • Covington • Little Catworth • Easton
Scaldwell • Walgrave • Pytchley • Isham • A509 • Little Addington • Stanwick • Hargrave • Shelton • Lower Dean • Tilbrook • Newtown
Brixworth • Holcot • Orlingbury • Finedon • A45 • Chelveston • Caldecott • Upper Dean • Kimbolton • Stow Lo.
Pitsford Resr. • Hannington • Little Harrowden • Great Harrowden • A510 • Irthlingborough • Chichele College • Wood End • Stonely • Great Staughton
Boughton • Pitsford • Sywell • Mears Ashby • Wilby • WELLINGBOROUGH • Transport • Higham Ferrers • Yielden • Swineshead • Pertenhall • Keysoe
Moulton • Overstone • Sywell Aviation • A509 • Little Irchester • A45 • RUSHDEN • A6 • Newton Bromswold • Melchbourne • Keysoe Row • Little Staughton
A5076 • Boothville • Earls Barton • Railway • Irchester • A5028 • Farndish • Riseley • Bourne End • Bushmead
Kingsthorpe • A5123 • Cottarville • Little Billing • Ecton • Great Doddington • Wymington • Knotting • Bolnhurst • Colmworth
NORTHAMPTON • Weston Favell • Great Billing • B573 • Wollaston • Strixton • Podington • Knotting Green • Milton Ernest • Rootham's Green
Far Cotton • Delapre Abbey • Little Houghton • Lower End • Hinwick • Souldrop • 306th Bombardment Group • Thurleigh • Channel's End
St James' End • Great Houghton • Cogenhoe • Whiston • Castle Ashby • Grendon • Santa Pod Raceway • Sharnbrook • Thurleigh Farm Centre • Wilden
Hardingstone • Brafield-on-the-Green • Denton • Chadstone • Easton Maudit • Bozeat • Odell • Harrold-Odell • Radwell • Milton Ernest • Ravensden
Milton Malsor • Wootton • Hackleton • Horton • YARDLEY CHASE • Yardley Hastings • Harrold • Carlton • Pavenham • Glenn Miller • Oakley • Salph End • Colesden
Collingtree • Piddington • Warrington • Lavendon • Cold Brayfield • Chellington • Felmersham • Bromham • Clapham • Renhold
M1 • Quinton • Salcey Forest • Olney • Turvey • A428 • West End • Stevington • BEDFORD • John Bunyan • Great Barford
Blisworth • Courteenhall • Roade • Hartwell • Eakley Lanes • Weston Underwood • Clifton Reynes • Newton Blossomville • Bridge End • Kempston • A4280 • Cople
A508 • Stoke Bruerne • Ashton • Ravenstone • Emberton • Petsoe End • A509 • Biddenham • Kempston • Moot Hall • Moggerhanger
Stoke Goldington • Filgrave • Hardmead • A422 • Box End • Elstow • Cardington • A603
A5 • Yardley • Castlethorpe • Hanslope • Tyringham • Sherington • Astwood • Chicheley • Little Crawley • Wavendon • Keeley Green • Shortstown • Airship Hangars • Cotton End

Outwell · Barroway Drove · Broomhill · Stradsett · Shingham · South Pickenham · Cockley Cley
Downham Market · A1122 · Crimplesham · Eastmoor · Coughton · Gooderstone Water · Iceni Village & Museum · Great Cressingham · Saham Tone

Upwell · Stow Bardolph Fen · Salters Lode · Bexwell · Oxborough · Oxburgh Hall · Gooderstone · A1065 · Hilborough

Fens 550 · B1094 · Nordelph · Denver · A1122 · Fordham · West Dereham · Wretton · Stoke Ferry · Whittington · Foulden · Beckett End · Bodney · The Arms · Cressingham 300

Three Holes · E · F · 77 · G · Oxburgh · H · B1108 · 65

Iron Bridge · B1098 · Christchurch · Lakesend · Wetland Centre · Hilgay · R. Wissey · Northwold · Little London · Cranwich · Ickburgh · 1

Tipps End · A1101 · Welney · Ten Mile Bank · A10 · Southery · Brookville · Methwold Hythe · Methwold · Lynford Arboretum · West Tofts · DANGER AREA · THETFORD FOREST PARK 90

Manea · Gold Hill · Little London · Southery Fens · Methwold Fens · Queen's Ground · Feltwell · B1112 · Mundford · A134 · Grimes Graves · Santon Downham · Croxton

Purl's Bridge · Pymoor · Oxlode · Black Bank · Brandon Creek · Little Ouse · Brandon Bank · Feltwell Anchor · Hockwold cum Wilton · Weeting · A1065 · Weeting Castle (remains of) · Brandon · High Lodge Forest Centre · 2 · Thetford

Way Head · California · Littleport · Sandhill · Burnt Fen · Hockwold Fens · Weeting Heath · Town Street · Heritage Centre · Brandon · Thetford Warren Lodge · B1106 · Ancient House · A134

Little Downham · Chettisham · Prickwillow · Mile End · A1101 · Lakenheath · Wangford Fen · Wangford · Brandon Park · Thetford Warren DANGER AREA · Elveden · A11

Coveney · Queen Adelaide · Prickwillow Engine · B1382 · Undley · The Delph · Wangford Warren · Croxton

BEDFORD (SOUTH) · Oliver Cromwell's House · Ely · Babylon · LEVEL (LEVEL) · Kennyhill · Wilde Street · B1112 · Lakenheath Warren · Elveden War Memorial · 99

Wentworth · Witchford · Stained Glass · Middle Fen · Weston Ditch · Holywell Row · RAF Lakenheath · 11 · RAF Honington

A142 · RAF Witchford Display of Memorabilia · Stuntney · A142 · Great Fen · Thistley Green · RAF Mildenhall · Beck Row · Eriswell · Mildenhall · A11 · B1106

Wilburton · Little Thetford · Barway · Broad Hill · Isleham Fen · Waterside · West Row · Worlington · Barton Mills · A1101 · Icklingham · Anglo-Saxon Village · West Stow · Brockley Corner · Ingham

Stretham · Soham Cotes · Priory Church · Isleham · B1102 · Freckenham · Tuddenham · Cavenham Heath · Lackford · Flempton · Timworth Green · Conyer's Green

A1123 · Stretham Old Engine · Soham · Down Field · Fordham · B1102 · Chippenham · Red Lodge · Herringswell · Cavenham · SUFFOLK · A1101 · Hengrave · Fornham All Saints · Fornham St Martin

Elford Closes · Wicken · Wicken Fen · Little Fen · B1102 · Chippenham Fen · A11 · B1085 · Kennett · A1101 · B1106

Chittering · Upware · River Bank · Burwell · A142 · Snailwell · A14 · 38 · Kentford · 39 · A14 · 40 · Risby · 41 · Westley · BURY ST EDMUNDS · 4 · Blackthorpe

Farmland Museum & Denny Abbey · Reach · Stevens · Exning · 37 · A1304 · B1506 · Moulton · Packhorse Bridge · Needham Street · Higham · Burthorpe · Suffolk Regiment · Nowton Park

Waterbeach · Clayhithe · Fosters · Swaffham Prior · Devil's Dyke · Newmarket Heath · NEWMARKET · National Horseracing · Cheveley · Gazeley · Barrow · Great Saxham · Horringer · Ickworth · B1066 · Sicklesmere

Milton · Horningsea · Lode · Anglesey Abbey · Long Meadow · Commercial End · National Stud · B1063 · Ashley · Dalham · Dunstall Green · Denham · A143

A10 · Stow cum Quy · Swaffham Bulbeck · A14 · Saxon Street · Broad Green · Upend · Barrow · Great Saxham · Chevington · Whepstead · Bradfield Combust · Hoggard's Green

Fen Ditton · Bottisham · A1303 · Stetchworth · Ditton Green · Wooditton · Back Street · Baxter's Green · Tan Office Green · Pinford End · Great Whelnetham

CAMBRIDGE PAGE 193 · A1134 · A1303 · Teversham · Little Wilbraham · Great Wilbraham · Dullingham · Westley Waterless · Dullingham Ley · Kirtling · Meeting Green · Depden Green · Depden · Rede · Hawstead · A143

Cherry Hinton · Church End · Fulbourn · A11 · Six Mile Bottom · Burrough End · Burrough Green · Kirtling Green · Mill End · Lidgate · Boyden End · Thorns · Clopton Green · Brockley Green · Mickley Green · Gulling Green

Gog Magog Hills · Wandlebury · Fleam Dyke · Weston Colville · Brinkley · Carlton · East Green · Cowlinge · Denston · Hawkedon · Somerton · Lawshall

Stapleford · A1307 · Weston Green · Willingham Green · Great Bradley · Little Bradley · Hobbles Green · Wickhambrook · Pound Green · Farley Green · Stradishall · Stanfield · Hartest · Shimpling Street

Sawston · FOURWENTWAYS · E · 53 · West Wickham · Burton End · Withersfield · Streetly End · Great Wratting · Little Wratting · F · Chimney Street · Barnardiston · Hundon · G · Boxted · H · Stanstead · Shimpling

Pampisford · A505 · Balsham · West Wratting · B1052 · Horseheath · Little Thurlow · Great Thurlow · Sowley Green · Chilton Street · Assington Green · Thurston End · Glemsford · 54

Great Abington · Linton · A1307 · Horseheath · Cardinal's Green · Little Wratting · Brockley Green · Chilton Green · A143 · Cavendish · Clare · A1092 · Long Melford · Melford Hall

Duxford · A1301 · Linton · Bartlow · Haverhill · Calford · A1017 · Kedington · Ancient House · R. Stour · Liston · Bridge Street · A134

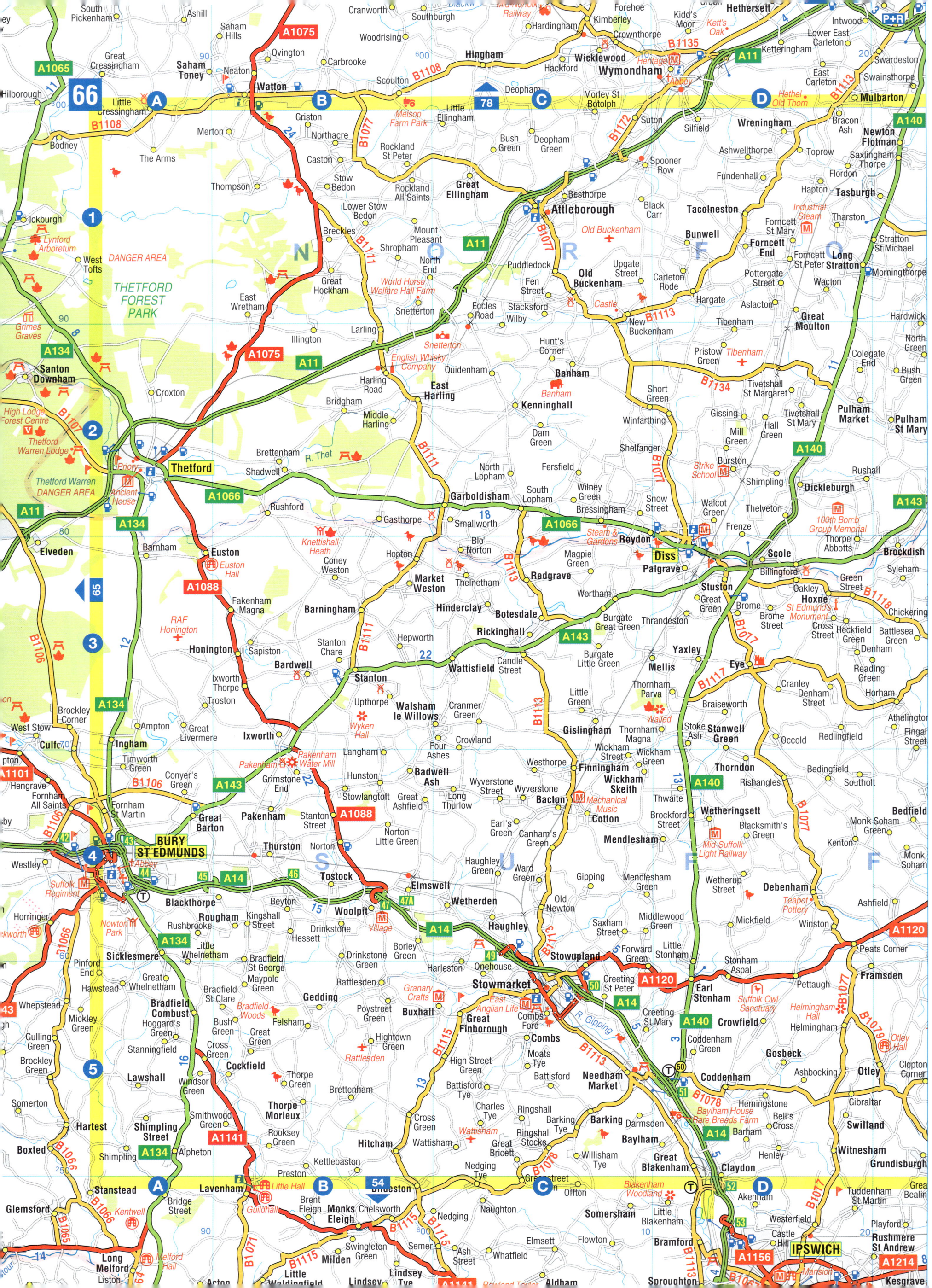

South Pickenham  Ashill  Cranworth  Southburgh  Midnorfolk Railway  Forehoe  Kidd's Moor  Hethersett  Intwood  P+R

Saham Hills  A1075  Woodrising  Hardingham  Kimberley  Crownthorpe  Kett's Oak  Lower East Carleton

Great Cressingham  Saham Toney  Ovington  Carbrooke  Hingham  Wicklewood  Wymondham  Heritage  Abbey  A11  Ketteringham

A1065  Neaton  Scoulton  B1108  Hackford  Deopham  B1135  East Carleton  Swardeston

Little Cressingham  Watton  B  Hethel Old Thorn  D  Mulbarton  B1113  Swainsthorpe

66  B1108  Griston  Northacre  Little Ellingham  Deopham Green  Morley St Botolph  Silfield  Wreningham  Bracon Ash  A140  Newton Flotman

Hilborough  Merton  Caston  78  Suton  Spooner Row  Ashwellthorpe  Toprow  Saxlingham Thorpe

Bodney  The Arms  Stow Bedon  Rockland St Peter  Bush Green  Besthorpe  Hapton  Tasburgh

1  Thompson  Lower Stow Bedon  Rockland All Saints  Great Ellingham  Attleborough  Black Carr  Tacolneston  Forncett St Mary  Industrial Steam  Tharston

Ickburgh  Breckles  Mount Pleasant  Old Buckenham  Bunwell  Forncett End  Long Stratton  Stratton St Michael

Lynford Arboretum  West Tofts  East Wretham  Shropham  North End  Puddledock  Upgate Street  Carleton Rode  Pottergate Street  Wacton  Morningthorpe

DANGER AREA  Great Hockham  Snetterton  Fen Street  Old Buckenham  Castle  Hargate  Aslacton  Great Moulton  Hardwick

THETFORD FOREST PARK  A1075  Illington  Larling  Eccles Road  Stacksford  Wilby  New Buckenham  B1113  Tibenham  North Green

Grimes Graves  A134  Croxton  Bridgham  Snetterton  English Whisky Company  Quidenham  Hunt's Corner  Banham  Tibenham  Gissing  Pristow Green  Colegate End  Bush Green

Santon Downham  B1107  Middle Harling  Harling Road  East Harling  Banham  Short Green  Tivetshall St Margaret  Mill Green  Great Moulton  North Green

High Lodge Forest Centre  Thetford Warren Lodge  Brettenham  R. Thet  Shadwell  Kenninghall  Winfarthing  Shelfanger  Hall Green  Tivetshall St Mary  Pulham Market  Rushall

2  Priory  Thetford  A1066  Rushford  Gasthorpe  Smallworth  North Lopham  Dam Green  Fersfield  Burston  Shimpling  Dickleburgh  A143

Thetford Warren DANGER AREA  Ancient House  Garboldisham  South Lopham  Wilney Green  Snow Street  Walcot Green  Thelveton  Pulham St Mary

A11  A134  Barnham  Knettishall Heath  Hopton  Blo' Norton  Bressingham  Frenze  Strike School  Thorpe Abbotts  Brockdish

Elveden  65  Euston  Coney Weston  Market Weston  Thelnetham  Steam & Gardens  Roydon  Scole  Syleham

Euston Hall  A1088  Barningham  Magpie Green  Diss  Billingford  Green Street  B1118

3  RAF Honington  Fakenham Magna  Hinderclay  Botesdale  Redgrave  Wortham  Palgrave  Stuston  Oakley  Hoxne  Chickering

B1106  Honington  Sapiston  Stanton Chare  Rickinghall  Wattisfield  A143  Burgate Great Green  Thrandeston  Brome  St Edmund's Monument  Heckfield Green  Battlesea Green

Brockley Corner  A134  Bardwell  Hepworth  Candle Street  Burgate Little Green  Great Green  Brome Street  Cross Street  Denham

West Stow  Ampton  Ixworth Thorpe  Stanton  Upthorpe  Crowland  Little Green  Yaxley  Eye  Reading Green  Horham

Culford  Troston  Ixworth  Walsham le Willows  Cranmer Green  Gislingham  Thornham Parva  Walled  Cranley  Denham Street  Athelington

A1101  Ingham  Timworth Green  Wyken Hall  Four Ashes  Thornham Magna  Stanwell Green  Occold  Redlingfield  Fingal Street

Hengrave  Great Livermere  Pakenham  Pakenham Water Mill  Langham  Westhorpe  Wickham Street  Stanwell Green  Thorndon  Bedingfield  Southolt

Fornham All Saints  B1106  Conyer's Green  Grimstone End  Hunston  Badwell Ash  Wyverstone Street  Finningham  Wickham Skeith  A140  Rishangles  Monk Soham

Fornham St Martin  Great Barton  Stowlangtoft  Great Ashfield  Long Thurlow  Wyverstone  Bacton  Mechanical Music  Cotton  Thwaite  Kenton  Bedfield

4  BURY ST EDMUNDS  A143  Pakenham  Stanton Street  Norton  Norton Little Green  Earl's Green  Canham's Green  Mendlesham  Brockford Street  Mid-Suffolk Light Railway  Monk Soham

42  Abbey  Thurston  Norton  A1088  Haughley Green  Old Newton  Blacksmith's Green  Debenham  Ashfield

43  Suffolk Regiment  Blackthorpe  Tostock  Elmswell  Wetherden  Ward Green  Saxham Street  Wetheringsett  Teapot Pottery  Winston  A1120

44  45  A14  46  Beyton  47  47A  Wetherden  Haughley  A14  Gipping  Mendlesham Green  Wetherup Street  Mickfield  Peats Corner

Horringer  Nowton Park  Rougham  Kingshall Street  Woolpit  Village  Middlewood Green  Stonham Aspal  Framsden

5  A134  Rushbrooke  Hessett  Drinkstone  Borley Green  Haughley  Stowupland  Forward Green  Little Stonham  Pettaugh  A1120

Westley  Sicklesmere  Little Whelnetham  Drinkstone Green  Harleston  A14  A1120  Earl Stonham  Suffolk Owl Sanctuary  Otley Hall

43  Bradfield Combust  Bradfield St George  Maypole Green  Gedding  Poystreet Green  Hightown Green  49  Stowmarket  Creeting St Peter  Helmingham Hall  B1079

Whepstead  Hoggard's Green  Bradfield St Clare  Bush Green  Felsham  Rattlesden  Buxhall  Granary Crafts  East Anglian Life  50  A14  Creeting St Mary  A140  Crowfield  Helmingham

Gulling Green  Stanningfield  Great Green  Rattlesden  Great Finborough  Combs Ford  Coddenham Green  Gosbeck

Brockley Green  5  Lawshall  Cockfield  Thorpe Green  Brettenham  High Street Green  Combs  Moats Tye  Coddenham  Ashbocking  Otley  Clopton Corner

Somerton  Windsor Green  Battisford  Battisford Tye  Needham Market  B1078  Hemingstone  Bell's Cross  Swilland

Hartest  Smithwood Green  Thorpe Morieux  Cross Green  Charles Tye  Ringshall  50  Baylham  Gibraltar

Shimpling Street  A1141  Rooksey Green  Wattisham  Ringshall Tye  Barking  Baylham House Rare Breeds Farm  A14  Witnesham  Grundisburgh

Boxted  A134  Shimpling  Alpheton  Preston  Hitcham  Wattisham Stocks  Great Bricett  Darmsden  A1156

Stanstead  Lavenham  Kettlebaston  Nedging Tye  Willisham Tye  Great Blakenham  Claydon  Tuddenham St Martin

A  Bridge Street  Little Hall  Brent Eleigh  Monks Eleigh  54  Bildeston  Nedging  Naughton  Offton  Somersham  Little Blakenham  52  Great Bealings

Glemsford  Guildhall  Chelsworth  B1115  Semer  Ash Street  Whatfield  Flowton  Blakenham Woodland  53  A1156  Westerfield  B1077  Playford

B1066  Kentwell  Swingleton Green  Milden  Lindsey  Elmsett  Bramford  Castle  Mansion  Rushmere St Andrew

Long Melford  Melford Hall  Little Waldingfield  Lindsey Tye  Aldham  IPSWICH  A1214  Kesgrave

Liston  Acton  A1141  B1071  A1156

NORTH SEA

LOWESTOFT

Gorleston-on-Sea
Hopton on Sea
Corton
Oulton
Oulton Broad
Kirkley
Pakefield
Carlton Colville
Kessingland
Kessingland Beach
Benacre
Covehithe
Wrentham
South Cove
Reydon
Southwold
Walberswick
Dunwich
Westleton
Minsmere Haven
Thorpeness
Aldeburgh
Aldeburgh Bay
Orford Ness

Burgh Castle
Bradwell
Lifeboat Station
Belton
Browston Green
Bunker's Hill
Fritton
The Dell
St Olaves
Herringfleet
Somerleyton
Blundeston
Haddiscoe
Aldeby
Burgh St Peter
Wheatacre
Toft Monks
Maypole Green
Barnby
North Cove
Mutford
Gisleham
Rushmere
Black Street
Henstead
Ellough
Hulver Street
Sotterley
Shadingfield
Weston
Ringsfield
Ringsfield Corner
Beccles
Barsham
Shipmeadow
Worlingham
Mettingham
Ilketshall St Andrew
Ilketshall St Lawrence
Ilketshall St Margaret
High Street
Stone Street
Redisham
Cox Common
Brampton
Stoven
Clay Common
Church Corner
Benacre
Wangford
Henham
Uggeshall
Westhall
Holton
Blyford
Wenhaston
Blackheath
Blythburgh
Thorington
Bramfield
Darsham
High Street
Middleton
Theberton
East Bridge
Minsmere
Leiston Abbey
Sizewell
Leiston
Aldringham
Knodishall
Coldfair Green
Friston
Snape
Iken
Sudbourne
Orford

Reedham
Cantley
Langley Green
Limpenhoe
Freethorpe
St Mary
Claxton
Carleton St Peter
Ashby St Mary
Hellington
Langley Street
Hardley Street
Nogdam End
Norton Subcourse
Lower Thurlton
Thurlton
Thorpe
Hales
Chedgrave
Loddon
Sisland
Mundham
Seething
Kirstead Green
Stubbs Green
Raveningham
Raveningham
Brundish
Thwaite St Mary
Kirby Green
Stockton
Ellingham
Kirby Cane
Geldeston
Gillingham
Broome
Ditchingham
Bungay
Earsham
Mettingham
Flixton
Homersfield
Wortwell
St Cross South Elmham
St Margaret South Elmham
St Michael South Elmham
All Saints South Elmham
St Nicholas South Elmham
St James South Elmham
Rumburgh
Spexhall
Wissett
Chediston Green
Chediston
Broadway
Halesworth
Holton
Cookley
Huntingfield
Walpole
Bramfield
Laxfield
Ubbeston Green
Brundish
Wilby
Stradbroke
Fressingfield
Wingfield
Weybread
Metfield
Needham
Harleston
Starston
Alburgh
Denton
Homersfield

Framingham Pigot
Poringland
Stoke Holy Cross
Brooke
Shotesham
Saxlingham Nethergate
Hempnall
Topcroft
Woodton
Bedingham Green
Hedenham
Alpington
Bergh Apton
Thurton
Chedgrave
Loddon

Saxtead Green
Earl Soham
Framlingham
Brandeston
Cretingham
Easton
Monewden
Charsfield
Wickham Market
Pettistree
Bredfield
Ufford
Melton
Bromeswell
Woodbridge
Martlesham
Hasketon
Burgh
Dennington
Badingham
Peasenhall
Yoxford
Sibton
Rendham
Saxmundham
Sternfield
Benhall Green
Stratford St Andrew
Farnham
Gromford
Blaxhall
Tunstall
Rendlesham
Chillesford
Butley
Capel Green
Boyton

North Sea roads

A143
A146
A12
A1117
A1145
A146
A144
A145
A12
A1095
A1094
A1152
A1120
A12
B1062
B1332
B1136
B1074
B1531
B1127
B1437
B1126
B1387
B1125
B1122
B1069
B1353
B1078
B1084
B1438
B1079
B1116
B1117
B1118
B1119
B1120
B1121
B1123
B1124
B1125
B1527
B1332

CAERNARFON BAY
(BAE CAERNARFON)

CARDIGAN
(BAE CEREDIGION)

Inigo Jones Slate Works
Penygroes
Pontllyfni
Llanllyfni
Aberdesach
Capel Uchaf
Tai'n Lon
Nasareth
Clynnog-fawr
A499
St Beuno
St Beuno's Well
Pant Glas
A487
Trefor
Gyrn Ddu 1712
Bwlch Mawr
Bwlchderwin
Trwyn y Gorlech
Yr Eifl
Tre'r Ceiri Hill Fort
Llanaelhaearn
PENINSULA
Cenin
Carreg Ddu
Porth Dinllaen
Pistyll
B4417
Lliithfaen
St Cybi's Well
Morfa Nefyn
Nefyn
Lleyn Historical & Maritime
Fron
B4354
Rhos-fawr
Y Ffor
Pencaenewydd
Llangybi
Groesffordd
Edern
Garn Boduan
A497
Pentre-uchaf
14
Llanarmon
Llanystumdwy
Porth Ysglaig
Rhos-y-llan
B4417
Glanrhyd
Boduan
L L Y N
Llannor
A499
B4354
Chwilog
A497
Dwyfor Ranch
Tudweiliog
Dinas
Garn Fadryn Fort
Efailnewydd
Penarth Fawr Medieval House
Abererch
9
Rhos-ddu
Denio
Penllech
Garnfadryn
Llaniestyn
Rhyd-y-clafdy
Penrhos
Pwllheli
Llangwnnadl
Bryn-mawr
Marian-y-de
Carreg yr Imbill
Pen-y-graig
14
Sarn Meyllteyrn
B4415
16
Marian-y-mor
Pen-ychain
Penrhyn Mawr
Y Gamlas
Porth Colmon
Y Gamlas
7
Porth Oer
Bryncroes
Botwnnog
B4413
Mynytho
Llanbedrog
Trwyn Llanbedrog
Rhydlios
St Tudwal's Road
Rhoshirwaun
Plas yn Rhiw
Llawr Dref
Llangian
A499
Braich Anelog
Rhiw
Anelog
Penycaerau
Abersoch
B4413
Porth Neigwl or Hell's Mouth
Llanengan
Sarn Bach
Machroes
Braich y Pwll
Aberdaron
Llanfaelrhys
Bwlchtocyn
St Tudwal's Islands
Uwchmynydd
Aberdaron Bay
Cilan Uchaf
Trwyn yr Wylfa
BARDSEY SOUND
(SWNT ENLLI)
Pen y Cil
Ynys Gwylan-fawr
Trwyn Cilan
Abbey
Bardsey Island
(Ynys Enlli)

Talysarn • Nantlle
B4418
Rhyd-Ddu
A4085
Nebo
250
Craig Cwm Silyn 2299 •2408 Garnedd-goch

Llyn Cwellyn
Llanau Diwaunyddyn
Hafod Eryri
SNOWDON (YR WYDDFA) 3560
Llyn Llydaw
Y Cribau
Llyn Gwynant
Bethania Waterfalls
Bethania
A498
Castell Dinas Emrys

Llyn y Foel 2661
Pont-y-pant
Cribau
Dolwyddelan
Pentre-bont
Blaenau Dolwyddelan
Moel Penamnen 1978
A470
81
Yr Arddu
Moelwyn Mawr 2527

Fairy Glen
Capel Garmon Burial Chamber
Conwy Falls
Machno Falls
Pont Rhyd-y-Gynnen
Ty'n-y-Coed Uchaf
Penmachno
A5
Rhydlanfair
Glan-Conwy
Pentrefoelas
Pentrefoelas Castle
Rhydly...

Beddgelert
Snowdonia National Park
Sygun Copper Mine
Gelert's Grave
2566 Moel Hebog
Pass of Aberglaslyn
Nantmor
Croesor
Cnicht 2265

Tal-y-waenydd
Llechwedd Slate Caverns
Blaenau Ffestiniog
Rhiwbryfdir
Tanygrisiau
Llyn Conglog
Llyn Newydd
Cwm Penmachno
Llyn Bowydd
CONWY

Llyn Conwy
13 Afon Conwy
Carrog
Ysbyty Ifan
Garn Prys 1751
Arenig Fach 2259

Bryncir
Garndolbenmaen
Llanfihangel-y-pennant
Moel-ddu 1814

A498
Moel Gerrig
Tan-lan
Plas Brondanw
Ffestiniog Railway
Rhyd
Maentwrog
Moelwyn Mawr
Tanygrisiau Resr.
Congl-y-wal
Bethania
Llyn y Manod
Llyn Morwynion
Rhyd-y-sarn
Llan Ffestiniog
B4391
Bont Newydd
Rhaeadr Cynfal
Rhaeadr Y Cwm
B4391
Migneint
Arenig Fach

Glan-Dwyfach • Dolbenmaen
Rhoslan
18
Golan
Afon Dwyfor
Penmorfa
Tremadog
Pentrefelin
A487
Welsh Highland Heritage Railway
Penrhyndeudraeth
Minffordd
A497
Garreg
Llanfrothen
Tan-y-bwlch
A4085

Maentwrog
Gellilydan
Craig Gyfynys
Tomen y Mur
Castell Prysor
A470
18
Graig Wen 1824
Craig yr Hyrddod
Arenig Fawr 2801
Llyn Arenig fawr
Llidiardau
Rhyd...
Fron...
Ciltalga...

Porthmadog
Lloyd George
Cricieth
Y Dref
Morfa Bychan
Garth
Borth-y-Gest
Portmeirion
A496
Llandecwyn
Traeth Bach

Talsarnau
Soar
Llanfihangel-y-traethau
Glan-y-wern
Eisingrug
Morfa Harlech

Llyn Trawsfynydd
A4212
A470
Trawsfynydd
Fronoleu
Cwm Prysol
Bronaber
Moel Llyfnant 2461
Moel y Feidiog
Mynydd Bryn-llech

Llanuwchllyn
A494
Bala Lake Railway
Pandy
30
Castell Carndochan
Rhosdylluan
Dyrysgol
Cwm Cynllwyd
Aran Benllyn 2901

TREMADOG BAY (BAE TREMADOG)
Harlech
Snowdonia National Park
B4573
Moel Goedog Hillfort
Roman Steps
Rhinog Fawr 2362
Rhinog
Llyn Cwm Bychan
Craig Ddrwg
G W Y N E D D
SNOWDONIA NATIONAL PARK
(PARC CENEDLAETHOL ERYRI)
CAMBRIAN MOUNTAINS

Llanfair
Llanfair Slate Caverns
Pen-sarn
Llandanwg
Pentre Gwynfryn
Llanbedr
Llanbedr Morfa Dyffryn
Moelfre 1932

Bryn Eden
13
Llech Idris Standing Stone
Rhaeadr Mawddach
Coed y Brenin
Pistyll Cain
COED Y BRENIN FOREST PARK
Rhobell Fawr 2408
Afon Mawddach
Afon Eden
18

Coed Ystumgwern
Llanenddwyn
Dyffryn Ardudwy
Dyffryn Ardudwy Burial Chamber
Llanddwywe
Tal-y-bont
11

Llyn Hywel
Y Llethr 2475
Llyn Bodlyn
Diffwys 2462
Llyn Cwm-Mynach
Y Garn 2063
Craig-y-cae

Rhaeadr Ddu
Ganllwyd
Glasdir Forest Garden
Llanfachreth
A470
Rhydymain
Cymer Abbey
A494
A470
11

MOUNTAINS
20
Cywarch
Aran Fawddwy 2971
Aber-Cywarch
Dinas Mawddwy 2111
Minllyn
Pont Minllyn
Cwm-Cewydd
Mallwyd
Clipiau
Esgair Afon Ddu 1523

A496
Llanaber
Caerdeon
Cutiau
Bontddu
Toll
Wildlife Centre
Penmaenpool
Llanelltyd
Dolgellau
Snowdonia National Park
Brithdir
B4416
Cross Foxes
Waun-oer 2197
Cribin Fawr 2111
Cae Afon
Foel-y-ffridd
Mynydd Dolgoed

Barmouth (Abermaw)
Lifeboat
FB (Toll)
The Bar
Barmouth Bay (Bae Bermo)
Fairbourne Steam Railway
Arthog
Waterfalls
A493
Friog
Fairbourne Nature Centre
20
Esgair Berfa

B A Y

CADAIR IDRIS 2040
Cadair Idris 2928
Llyn Cau
Mary Jones Monument (Tyn-y-ddol)
Llanfihangel-y-pennant
Tal-y-llyn Lake
Tal-y-llyn
Graig Goch 1882
Aberllefenni
Corris Uchaf
Corris
King Arthur's Labyrinth
Bards Quest
Railway
Esgairgeiliog

A487
DYFI FOREST
Aberangell
A470
Cemmaes
POWYS
Cwm-Llinau
Cemmaes Road
A470

Llwyngwril
Mynydd Pennant
Abergynolwyn
Dolgoch
Talyllyn Railway
Dolgoch Falls
Torrenhendre 2076
Pantperthog
Centre for Alternative Technology
Llanwrin
A489
Abercegir
Darowen
Commins Coch
Tafolwern

Llangelynin
Rhoslefain
Peniarth
Llanegryn
Bryncrug
Llanfendigaid
Tonfanau
Pandy
Rhyd-yr-onen
Trum Gelli
B4405
B4404
Abercegir
Penegoes
Machynlleth
Dyfi Valley
A489

Aber Dysynni
Broad Water
Tywyn
Narrow Gauge Railway
57
Pennal
Cwrt
11
A493
Pennal
Derwenlas
Machynlleth
Forge
Melinbyrhedyn
Moelfre 1537
B4518

Penhelig
Aberdovey (Aberdyfi)
Snowdonia National Park
Dyfi Furnace
A487
Eglwys Fach
Glandyfi
Glaspwll
River Dovey
Afon Dulas
Aberhosan
Pennant

A  B  C  D

**GWYNEDD**

**BERWYN**

**DENBIGHSHIRE**

**POWYS**

**CAMBRIAN MOUNTAINS**

CYRN

Capel Garmon Burial Chamber
Glen
Pentrefoelas Castle
Rhydlanfair
Glan-Conwy
Ty'n-y-Coed Uchaf
Pentrefoelas
Ysbyty Ifan
Rhydlydan
Glasfryn
Cefn-brith
A5
Cerrigydrudion
Llanfihangel Glyn Myfyr
Garn Prys 1751
Afon Conwy
Afon Ceirw
B4501
Ewe-phoria Sheepdog Centre
Llangwm
Ty-nant
Dinmael
Maerdy
Bettws Gwerfil Goch
Gylchedd 2196
Carnedd y Filiast
Foel Goch 2004
Wenallt
Glan-yr-afon
Druid
Glassblobbery
Glan-yr-afon
Llangar Church
A5
Corwen
Cynwyd
Cynwyd Forest
Arenig Fach
Llyn Arenig Fach 2259
A4212
Ciltalgarth
Llyn Celyn
Afon Tryweryn
Frongoch
Llidiardau
Rhyd-uchaf
Rhiwlas
Llanfor
Llandderfel
B4402
Bethel
Sarnau
Cefn-ddwysarn
River Dee
B4401
Llandrillo
Cadwst
Pennant
Cefn Coch
Arenig Fawr 2801
Bala (Y Bala)
Llanycil
B4391
Rhos-y-gwaliau
Pale
B4403
Llangower
Llyn Tegid or Bala Lake
Bala Lake Railway
A494
Parc
Pentre-piod
Penllyn Forest
Moel Fferna
Ceiriog Forest
Glyn Ceiriog
Llyfnant 461
Mynydd yn-llech
Llanuwchllyn
Castell Carndochan
Pandy
Rhosdylluan
Talardd
Foel Figenau
Foel y Geifr 2054
1848 Bryn Du
Pentre
Llanarmon Dyffryn Ceiriog
B4500
Tregeiriog
Foel Rhiwlas 1490
Rhiwlas
Llangadwaladr
Ty Issa
Ty
Dyrysgol
Aran Benllyn 2901
Cwm Cynllwyd
Foel Rhudd
Bwlch y Groes
Pennant
Aran Fawddwy 2971
Pistyll Rhaeadr
Y Clogydd
Tan-y-pistyll
Tyn-y-wern
Commins
Cefn-coch
2265 Foel Wen
Mynydd Tarw
Tyn-y-ffridd
Moelfre
Llansilin
Felin Newydd
Tai-bach
B4580
Llanrhaeadr-ym-Mochnant
Efail-rhyd
Mynydd-y-briw
Sycharth Castle
Sycharth
Golfa
Llangynog
Penybontfawr
Pennant Melangell
Afon Tanat
Tanat Valley
Pedair-ffordd
B4580
Rhos-y-brithdir
Llangedwyn
B4396
Pen-y-bont
Llanfyllin
Llanfechain
Afon Cain
Llansantffraid-ym-Mechain
Hirnant
Penygarnedd
B4391
B4396
Bwlchyddar
Llyn Efyrnwy (Lake Vyrnwy)
B4393
Llanwddyn
Lake Vyrnwy
Abertridwr
Tycrwyn
A490
Bwlch-y-cibau
Waen Fach
Aran
Llanymawddwy
Pen y Ffridd Cownwy
Dyfnant Forest
Ddol Cownwy
Llanfihangel-yng-Ngwynfa
Nant-y-meichiaid
A495
Pentre'r-beirdd
Geuffordd
Cwm Croes
Cywarch
Aber-Cywarch
Tir Rhiwiog 1787
Afon Dyfi
Pont Llogel
Mynydd y Gadfa
B4395
Afon Efyrnwy (R. Vyrnwy)
Dyffryn Meifod Efyrnwy (R. Vyrnwy)
Meifod
Broniarth Hill
A490
Guilsfield (Cegidfa)
Fawr 2111
Cae Afon
A470
Dinas Mawddwy
Minllyn
Pont Minllyn
Cwm-Cewydd
Nant-y-dugoed
A458
Wern
Foel
B4382
Dolanog
Pontrobert
A495
Heniarth
Afon Banwy neu
Cloddiau
Frochas
Powysland
Welshpool (Y Trallwng)
Powis Castle
Mallwyd
Clipiau
Esgair Afon Ddu 1523
Dugoed
Llyn Coch-hwyad
Llangadfan
Llanerfyl
Tyn-y-rhyd
Afon Efyrnwy (R. Vyrnwy)
A495
Neuadd
Melin-y-ddol
B4389
Einion
A458
Sylfaen
Castle Caereinion
Aberangell
Cwm-Llinau
Pen Coed
Four Crosses
Llanfair Caereinion
Welshpool & Llanfair Light Railway
Pwll
A470
Cemmaes
Cemmaes Road
Pandy
Nant yr Eira
Bryn y Castell
Llyn Hir
Cefn Coch
Sychtyn
Llanllugan
Llanwyddelan
New Mills (Felin Newydd)
Manafon
B4390
Pant-y-ffridd
Rhiw
B4385
Llwynderw
A483
Abercegir
Darowen
Commins Coch
Tafolwern
Llanbrynmair
Dol-fach
A470
Talerddig
Esgair Cwmowen
Glan-yr-afon
Adfa
Tregynon
Bettws Cedewain
Berriew (Aberriw)
Fron
Garthmyl
Hendomen
Melinbyrhedyn
Tal-y-Wern
Llan
Bont Dolgadfan
Moelfre 1537
Brynamlwg 1602
Carno
Llyn Mawr
Bwlch y Garreg
Bwlch-y-ffridd
Pentre Llifior
Sculpture
Montgomery (Trefaldwyn)
Aberhosan
Pennant
Trannon
Afon Twrch
Llyn y Tarw
Gwgia
A483
Old Bell

A  B  C  D

Map of the Shropshire / Wrexham / Cheshire East border region.

Grid references: E · F · G · H (top); 1 · 2 · 3 · 4 · 5 (right); E · F · G · H (bottom)

**Major places:** WREXHAM (Wrecsam), OSWESTRY (Croesoswallt), SHREWSBURY, NANTWICH, Whitchurch, Malpas, Ellesmere, Wem, Chirk (Y Waun), Ruabon (Rhiwabon), Much Wenlock, Pontesbury, Minsterley, Westbury, Worthen, Bishop's Castle area.

CHESHIRE EAST

WALES / ENGLAND border

**Roads (selection):** A525, A541, A534, A483, A5152, A5156, A5125, A528, A539, A5069, B5426, B5130, A495, A41, A49, A530, A53, A442, A5, A458, A488, A490, A489, A4169, A5112, A5064, A5124, B4396, B4398, B4393, B4391, B4386, B4387, B4499, B4385, B4380, B5063, B5062, B5065, B5061, B5476, B5395, B5069, B5070, B5068, B5009, B5097, B4579, B5605.

**Selected settlements:** Holt, Farndon, Crewe-by-Farndon, Tilston, Shocklach, Threapwood, Tallarn Green, Bangor-is-y-coed, Overton (Owrtyn), Penley, Hanmer, Bettisfield, Welshampton, Breaden Heath, Bronington, Grindley Brook, Broughall, Ash Magna, Ash Parva, Wilkesley, Burleydam, Newhall, Aston, Wrenbury, Marbury, Norbury, Whixall, Prees, Darliston, Fauls, Moreton Say, Bletchley, Hodnet, Marchamley, Stanton upon Hine Heath, High Hatton, Shawbury, Hadnall, Astley, Preston Brockhurst, Clive, Grinshill, Myddle, Newton on the Hill, Baschurch, Ruyton-XI-Towns, Knockin, Kinnerley, Llanymynech, Pant, Llanyblodwel, Four Crosses, Llandrinio, Melverley, Shrawardine, Montford, Bicton, Battlefield, Harlescott, Atcham, Cross Houses, Condover, Dorrington, Longnor, Acton Burnell, Cardington, Church Stretton area, Leebotwood, Woolstaston, Pulverbatch, Stiperstones, Snailbeach, Bentlawnt, Chirbury, Middletown, Buttington, Wollaston, Westbury, Yockleton, Hanwood, Bayston Hill, Bomere Heath, Shrawardine.

Offa's Dyke, Wat's Dyke, Montgomery Canal, Shropshire Union Canal, Llangollen Canal, R. Dee (Afon Dyfrdwy), R. Severn, R. Roden, R. Perry, R. Tern.

The Wrekin, Breidden Hill, Corndon Hill, The Long Mynd, Caer Caradoc.

**STOKE-ON-TRENT**

**NEWCASTLE-UNDER-LYME**

**WOLVERHAMPTON**

**TELFORD**

**STAFFORD**

NANTWICH

CHESHIRE EAST

SHROPSHIRE

MARKET DRAYTON

Newport

Wellington

Oakengates

Ironbridge

Much Wenlock

Shifnal

Albrighton

Codsall

Penkridge

Stone

Eccleshall

Gnosall

Burslem

Hanley

Fenton

Longton

Tunstall

Silverdale

Keele

Trentham

Blythe Bridge

Madeley

Woore

Audlem

Wrenbury

Whitchurch

Prees

Hodnet

Hinstock

Cheswardine

Loggerheads

Ashley

Maer

Swynnerton

Yarnfield

Great Bridgeford

Seighford

Haughton

Bishops Wood

Brewood

Coven

Featherstone

Wednesfield

Bilston

Donnington

Lilleshall

Newport

Edgmond

High Ercall

Crudgington

Waters Upton

Coalbrookdale

Madeley

Broseley

Cressage

Buildwas

Dawley

Stirchley

Coven

Shareshill

Essington

Bushbury

Wightwick

Tettenhall

PAGE 202

PAGE 203

M6

M54

A41

A49

A51

A53

A500

A525

A529

A442

A5

A518

A519

A449

A460

A454

A464

A458

A5011

LINCOLNSHIRE

RUTLAND

NEWARK-ON-TRENT

GRANTHAM

MELTON MOWBRAY

Sleaford

Bourne

Oakham

STAMFORD

Uppingham

Wansford

A1 · A46 · A52 · A153 · A17 · A15 · A607 · A151 · A606 · A43 · A47 · A1175 · A6121 · A6003

Upper, Averham, Staythorpe, Coddington, New Balderton, Beckingham, Brant Broughton, Welbourn, Temple Bruer Tower, Ashby de la Launde, Digby, Billing, Rolleston, Farndon, Balderton, Barnby in the Willows, Stragglethorpe, Leadenham, Cranwell, Bloxholm, Dorrington, Ruskin, Fiskerton, East Stoke, Hawton, Thorpe, Fenton, Fulbeck, Caythorpe, Frieston, Normanton, North Rauceby, Leasingham, Holdingham, Evedon, Ewerby, Kirkby la Thorpe, Asgarby, Howel, Elston, Syerston, Cotham, Brandon, Hough-on-the-Hill, Gelston, Carlton Scroop, Sudbrook, South Rauceby, Cranwell Aviation Heritage Centre, Quarrington, Silk Willoughby, Heckington, Burton Pedwardine, Flintham, Sibthorpe, Shelton, Westborough, Hougham, Marston, Honington, Barkston, Syston, Belton, Ancaster, West Willoughby, Wilsford, Kelby, Heydour, Culverthorpe, Swarby, Aswarby, Osbournby, Northbeck, Scredington, Aslockton, Orston, Normanton, Allington, Great Gonerby, Manthorpe, Londonthorpe, Welby, Oasby, Alsby, Aunsby, Spanby, Swato, Whatton, Elton, Bottesford, Eastthorpe, Sedgebrook, Belton House, Dembleby, Haceby, Horbling, Brid, Sutton, Granby, Barnstone, Barkestone-le-Vale, Muston, GRANTHAM NORTH, Gonerby Hill Foot, Grantham House, Earlesfield, Old Somerby, Ropsley, Braceby, Sapperton, Pickworth, Newton, Walcot, Threekingham, Stow, Billingborough, Sempringham, Redmile, Stenwith, Barrowby, Belvoir, Woolsthorpe By Belvoir, Denton Resr., Woodnook, Boothby Pagnell, Humby, Hanby, Folkingham, Birthorpe, Pointon, Little Wisbeach, Harby, Stathern, Plungar, Castle, Harlaxton, Little Ponton, Norman Manor House, Ingoldsby, Lenton, Laughton, Aslackby, Graby, Dowsby, Hose, Eastwell, Eaton, Branston, Harston, Great Ponton, Bassingthorpe, Westby, Bitchfield, Keisby, Hawthorpe, Kirkby Underwood, Rippingale, Water Spout, Wyville, Stroxton, Stoke Rochford, Easton, Irnham, Dunsby, A607, Bescaby, Saltby, Skillington, Woolsthorpe-by-Colsterworth, Colsterworth, Burton Coggles, Corby Glen, Willoughby Memorial Trust, Grimsthorpe Castle, Elsthorpe, Hanthorpe, Haconby, Morton, Waltham on the Wolds, Goadby Marwood, Chadwell, Sproxton, Buckminster, Stainby, Birkholme, Swayfield, Grimsthorpe, Cawthorpe, Dyke, Scalford, Stonesby, Coston, Gunby, North Witham, Creeton, Swinstead, Edenham, Scottlethorpe, Bourne, Abbey Church, Holwell, Potter Hill, Twinlakes Theme Park, Melton, Thorpe Arnold, Freeby, Garthorpe, Saxby, Sewstern, South Witham, Castle Bytham, Little Bytham, Careby, Lound, Witham on the Hill, Toft, Northorpe, Thurlby, Asfordby Hill, Brentingby, Wyfordby, Wymondham, Edmondthorpe, Thistleton, Clipsham, Aunby, Carlby, Manthorpe, Obthorpe, Thetford, Baston, Langtoft, Burton Lazars, Stapleford, Teigh, Market Overton, Barrow, Stretton, Lime Kiln, Pickworth, Essendine, Greatford, Wilsthorpe, Braceborough, Great Dalby, Little Dalby, Whissendine, Ashwell, Cottesmore, Rutland Railway, Greetham, Ryhall, Barholm, Market Deeping, Thorpe Satchville, Pickwell, Somerby, Langham, Barleythorpe, Oakham Castle, Burley, Barnsdale, Exton, Great Casterton, Little Casterton, Belmesthorpe, Tinwell, West Deeping, Knossington, Cold Overton, Egleton, Whitwell, Empingham, Ingthorpe, Browne's Hospital, Priory, STAMFORD, Pilsgate, Bainton, Etton, Braunston-in-Rutland, Rutland County, Brooke, Manton, Lyndon, Tickencote, Great Casterton, Burghley, Barnack, Helpston, Tilton on the Hill, Halstead, Knossington, Loddington, Ridlington, Wing, Pilton, North Luffenham, Ketton, Aldgate, Easton on the Hill, Wothorpe, Geeston, Collyweston, Wittering, Southorpe, Clare Cottage, Skeffington, Tugby, Rolleston, Belton-in-Rutland, Ayston, Glaston, Morcott, Barrowden, Tixover, Duddington, King's Cliffe, Wittering, Thornhaugh, Nassington, Noseley, Goadby, Stockerston, Wardley, Allexton, Bisbrooke, Seaton, Wakerley, Apethorpe, Prebendal, Castor, Stonton Wyville, Hallaton, Horninghold, Blaston, Lyddington, Stoke Dry, Harringworth, Viaduct, Lyddington Bede House, Thorpe by Water, Laxton, Blatherwycke Lake, Blatherwycke, Woodnewton, Peterborough (Sibson), Nene Valley Railway, Gloosten, Horninghold, Stonton, Eyebrook

THE

LINCOLNSHIRE

BEDFORD LEVEL (NORTH LEVEL)

PETERBOROUGH PAGE 201

WISBECH

BOSTON

SPALDING

BOURNE

Sleaford

Market Deeping

Deeping St James

Deeping St Nicholas

Crowland

Thorney

Whittlesey

March

Donington

Gosberton

Pinchbeck

Holbeach

Long Sutton

Sutton Bridge

Sutton St James

Tydd St Mary

Tydd St Giles

Newton

Wisbech St Mary

Leverington

Gorefield

Kirton

Sutterton

Swineshead

Heckington

Great Hale

Helpringham

Billingborough

Horbling

Rippingale

Dunsby

Morton

Thurlby

Baston

Langtoft

Deeping Gate

West Deeping

Tallington

Barnack

Glinton

Peakirk

Newborough

Eye

Gunthorpe

Werrington

Bretton

Orton

Old Fletton

Stanground

Eastrea

Coates

Thorney Toll

Guyhirn

Ring's End

Coldham

Elm

Friday Bridge

Begdale

Three Holes

Digby

Dorrington

Billinghay

North Kyme

South Kyme

Chapel Hill

York

Sibsey

Old Leake

Wrangle

Leake Common Side

Frithville

Leverton

Benington

Butterwick

Freiston

Skirbeck

Wyberton

Frampton

Kirton End

Kirton Holme

Algarkirk

Fosdyke

Sutterton Dowdyke

Moulton Seas End

Moulton

Whaplode

Holbeach Bank

Gedney

Lutton

Sutton Crosses

Four Gotes

Tydd St Giles Fen

Gedney Drove End

Gedney Marsh

Holbeach Marsh

A153 A17 A52 A16 A15 A151 A152 A1121 A1175 A1101 A605 A47 A1139 A141 A1 A1175

B1188 B1209 B1395 B1394 B1177 B1397 B1181 B1180 B1356 B1173 B1172 B1165 B1166 B1167 B1168 B1357 B1515 B1391 B1392 B1397 B1359 B1393 B1390 B1169 B1443 B1040 B1187 B1099 B1101 B1525 B1443

Bicker

Bicker Bar

Quadring

Risegate

Surfleet

Weston

Whaplode Drove

Holbeach Drove

Gedney Hill

Sutton St Edmund

Parson Drove

Murrow

Thorney

Dowsdale

Cowbit

Moulton Chapel

Pode Hole

Little London

Fen End

Weston Hills

Crowland

Eye Green

Newark

Dogsthorpe

Peterborough

Castor

Ailsworth

Wansford

The Deepings

Boston Deeps

Scolt Head Island

Brancaster Bay

Holkham Ba

WASH

Holme Dunes
Titchwell Marsh
Holme next the Sea
Lifeboat Station
Cliffs
Sea Life Sanctuary
B1161
Old Hunstanton
Hunstanton
Thornham
A149
Titchwell
Brancaster
Marsh Side
Brancaster Staithe
Burnham Deepdale
17
Burnham Norton
Burnham Overy Staithe
Burnham Overy Town
1
Friary
Burnham Market
B1155
Holkham
W
Ringstead
Burnham Thorpe
40
New Holkham
Heacham
Norfolk Lavender
B1454
Docking
Stanhoe
Muckleton
North Creake
Creake Abbey
M Forge
South Creake
B1355
Eaton
Sedgeford
Burntstalk
B1153
B1155
Fring
Bircham Newton
Bircham
Great Bircham
Bircham Tofts
Bagthorpe
B1155
Syderstone
Barmer
Wicken Green Village
Sculthorp
2
Southgate
19
Shepherd's Port
Snettisham
Snettisham Park
Ingoldisthorpe
B1440
Shernborne
B1454
Tattersett
Dunton Patch
Dunton
Shereford
H
Dersingham
Doddshill
Anmer
B1153
Houghton Hall
New Houghton
East Rudham
Coxford
Priory
78
Tatterford
Helhoughton
Toftrees
A10
Wolferton
16
Sandringham
Babingley
West Newton
B1440
Flitcham
Harpley
West Rudham
3
West Raynham
South Raynham
Ray
Babingley River
B1439
Hillington
22
A148
NORFOLK
North Wootton
Castle Rising
A149
Congham
Roydon
Congham Hall Herb
Grimston
Pott Row
Little Massingham
Great Massingham
Great Massingham
Weasenham St Peter
Wellingham
South Wootton
A148
A1078
A1076
A148
Gaywood
30
Fairstead
Bawsey
Ashwicken
B1145
Rougham
Weasenham All Saints
Tittles
Terrington St Clement
Bellmount
Clenchwarton
True's Yard Fisherfolk
West Lynn
African Violet Centre
KING'S LYNN
Caithness Crystal
A149
Leziate
Gayton
Gayton Thorpe
B1145
B1153
West Lexham
Litcham
Walpole Cross Keys
A17
16
Shepherd's Gate
Hay Green
Tilney All Saints
Tilney High End
Fair Green
Tower End
East Winch
West Bilney
West Acre
South Acre
Newton
East Lexham
4
Great Dunham
Walpole Marsh
Walpole St Andrew
Walpole Water
Church End
Walpole St Peter
Ingleborough
Walton Highway
A47
Terrington St John
Walpole Highway
Tilney St Lawrence
Saddle Bow
Eau Brink
West Winch
West Bow
North Runcton
Middleton
Blackborough End
Blackborough
Pentney
East Walton
West Acre
Castle Acre
Priory
South Acre
A1065
Sporle
Little Dunham
A4
Great Fransham
B198
M Fenland & West Norfolk Aviation
Emneth
Gaultree
The Smeeth
Chequers Corner
Emneth Hungate
Walpole Gate
St John's Fen End
Tilney Fen End
Wiggenhall St Mary the Virgin
Wiggenhall St Germans
A10
Wiggenhall St Peter
Wiggenhall St Mary Magdalen
Setchey
Runcton Holme
Tottenhill Row
Watlington
West Briggs
Wormegay
Priory
R. Nar
Narborough
Marham
RAF Marham
Shouldham
Green Britain Centre
A1065
Necton
T
R. Wis
Holly End
Outwell
A1101
Barroway Drove
Stowbridge
A10
West Head
Tottenhill
South Runcton
Thorpland
Shouldham Thorpe
A1122
14
Fincham
Barton Bendish
Beachamwell
Beachamwell Warren
DANGER AREA
Iceni Village & Museums
Swaffham
i M
North Pickenham
13
Stow Bardolph Fen
A1122
Wimbotsham
Broomhill
Stow Bardolph
Church Farm
A1122
Crimplesham
Bexwell
Stradsett
A134
Shingham
Eastmoor
Cockley Cley
Gooderstone Water
South Pickenham
5
Great Cressingham
Upwell
A1101
Nordelph
A1122
Denver
Salters Lode
Downham Market
Wereham
West Dereham
A134
Boughton
Oxborough
Oxburgh Hall
Gooderstone
Hilborough
A1065
Little Cressingham
Saha Tone
Three Holes
B1094
Iron Bridge
B1094
16
Fordham
Stoke Ferry
Whittington
Foulden
B1108
Christchurch
20
Lakesend
Hilgay
B1160
West Dereham
Northwold
80
Beckett End
Bodney
The Arms
Tipps End
A10
Ten Mile Bank
R. Wissey
Brookville
Little London
Cranwic
Southery

90 600 10 20

Head Island
Holkham Bay
Blakeney Point

Burnham Norton
Overy Staithe
Lifeboat Station
Wells Harbour Railway
Salt Marshes
Blakeney
Cley next the Sea
Cley Marshes
Muckleburgh Military
North Norfolk Railway
Sheringham
West Runton
East Runton
Lifeboat Station

17 Friary
Burnham Market
Burnham Overy Town
Holkham
B1105
Wells-next-the-Sea
Stiffkey
Cockthorpe
Morston
Guildhall
Salthouse
Newgate
Priory
Weybourne
Gazebo
Priory Maze
Beeston Regis
Shire Horse Sanctuary
A1082
A149
A148

B1155
Burnham Thorpe
New Holkham
Warham
Warham Camp Hillfort
Wighton
Wells and Walsingham Light Railway
Priory
Langham
Glandford
Shell
Natural Surroundings
Upper Sheringham
High Kelling
Bodham
West Beckham
Aylmerton
Felbrigg
Felbrigg Hall
Crossdale Street
B1436

Muckleton
North Creake
Forge
Copy's Green
Great Walsingham
Little Walsingham
Binham
Westgate
Saxlingham
Field Dalling
Lower Green
Bale
Sharrington
Thornage
Brinton
Letheringsett
Little Thornage
Watermill
Holt
Hempstead
B1149
B1110
Metton
Gresham
Bessingham
Sustead
Roughton

South Creake
B1355
Southgate
Ruined Church
Egmere
Shrine
Abbey
Slipper Chapel
Shirehall
North Barsham
Houghton St Giles
Great Snoring
Hindringham
Thursford Green
Thursford Collection
Gunthorpe
Brinningham
Stody
Edgefield
Baconsthorpe
Plumstead
Matlaske
Little Barningham
Wickmere
Wolterton
Alby Hill
Erpingham
Strawberry
A140
Alby
Colby

19 Barmer
Syderstone
Wicken Green Village
Dunton Patch
West Barsham
East Barsham
Little Snoring
A148
Barney
Croxton
Kettlestone
Swanton Novers
Fulmodestone
Melton Constable
Briston
B1354
Edgefield Street
Craymere Beck
Nethergate
Thurning
Norton Corner
Tyby
Crabgate
Heydon
Little London
Corpusty
Saxthorpe
Itteringham
Itteringham Common
Blickling Estate
Blickling
Silvergate
Oulton
Oulton Street
Drabblegate
Banningham
Ingworth
B1149
Aylsham
Burgh next Aylsham
Brampton

B1454
Tattersett
East Rudham
West Rudham
Coxford
Priory
77
Tatterford
Toftrees
Sculthorpe
Dunton
Shereford
Hempton
Fakenham
Glass
The Heath
Pensthorpe
Gas & Local History
Fakenham
Little Ryburgh
Stibbard
Wood Norton
Guestwick
Guestwick Green
Wood Dalling
Salle
Southgate
Reepham
Cawston
B1145
Eastgate
Marsham
The Heath
Hevingham
Stratton Strawless

Great Massingham
Weasenham St Peter
Wellingham
West Raynham
East Raynham
South Raynham
Oxwick
Hamrow
Horningtoft
Colkirk
A1065
B1146
Great Ryburgh
Gateley
Broom Green
Twyford
Bintree
Guist
Bexfield
Themelthorpe
Pettywell
Bawdeswell
Sparham
Booton
Brandiston
Great Witchingham
Swannington
Upgate
Alderford
Felthorpe
Newton St Faith
Horsford
Horsham St Faith
Aviation
Waterloo
New Hainford

Rougham
Weasenham All Saints
Tittleshall
Whissonsett
Godwick Deserted Village
Potthorpe
Stanfield
Brisley
B1145
North Elmham
County School Station
Saxon Cath. (ruins)
Foxley
Fousham
Jordan Green
A1067
Whitwell & Reepham Station
Dinosaur Adventure
Morton
Attlebridge
Weston Longville
Weston Green
Ringland
Taverham
Thorpe Marriott
Drayton

Castle Acre
Priory
Newton
West Lexham
East Lexham
Litcham
Castle
Mileham
East Bilney
Bittering
Farm & Workhouse
Beetley
Gressenhall
Longham
Beeston
Great Dunham
Drury Square
Sparrow Green
Crane's Corner
Bushy Common
Bishop Bonner's Cottage
Worthing
Billingford
Mill Street
Hoe
Swanton Morley
Greengate
Woodgate
North Tuddenham
Peaseland Green
Easthaugh
Primrose Green
Lyng
Lenwade
Hockering
Hockering Heath
Weston Green
A47
Greensgate
B1535
R. Wensum
Costessey
R. Tud
Hellesdon
A1067
A140
New Costessey
A1074

A1065
Little Dunham
Great Fransham
Wendling
Scarning
Little Fransham
Sporle
A47
Dereham
Toftwood
Clippings Green
Mattishall Burgh
Rotten Row
Honingham
East Tuddenham
Colton
Mattishall
Welborne
Brandon Parva
Barnham Broom
Marlingford
Barford
Easton
Norfolk Showground
Bowthorpe
Bawburgh
B1108
Earlham
A140
Eaton
A47

Swaffham
Necton
R. Wissey
Ivy Todd
Bradenham
Daffy Green
Yaxham
Westfield
Whinburgh
Clint Green
Brakefield Green
Runhall
Kimberley
Crownthorpe
Carleton Forehoe
Kidd's Moor
Great Melton
Little Melton
Lynch Green
High Green
Hethersett
B1172
Colney
Samson's Cen
Intwood
Lower East Carleton
Keswick
A11
Cringleford

A1075
Shipdham
Shipdham
Holme Hale
Ashill
North Pickenham
Cranworth
Southburgh
Hardingham
Garvestone
High Common
Reymerston
Thuxton
Low Street
Coston
Blackwater
Mid-Norfolk Railway
Wicklewood
Hackford
Morley St Botolph
Wymondham
Abbey
Heritage
B1135
Kett's Oak
Ketteringham
Swardeston
East Carleton
Swainsthorpe
B1172
Mulbarton
A140

Pickenham
Great Cressingham
Saham Hills
Saham Toney
Neaton
Ovington
Carbrooke
Scoulton
B1108
Hingham
Deopham
Woodrising
Little Ellingham
Bush Green
Deopham Green
Silfield
Hethel Old Thorn
Wreningham
Bracon Ash
New Flotman
A140

A1065
Hilborough
Little Cressingham
Bodney
The Arms
Merton
Watton
Griston
Northacre
B1077
Melsop Farm Park
66
Caston
Stow Bedon
Rockland St Peter
Rockland All Saints
Lower Stow Bedon
Great Ellingham
Besthorpe
Black Carr
Tacolneston
Spooner Row
Ashwellthorpe
Toprow
Fundenhall
Flordon
Hapton
Tasburgh
Attleborough
Wrenningham
Saxlingham Thorpe
Industrial

B1108
A1075
Thompson
Great Ellingham

Navigation markers: 1 2 3 4 5 A B C D

NORTH

SEA

**CROMER**
RNLI
A149
Overstrand
Foulness
Northrepps
Sidestrand
Frogshall
Trimingham
A149
Southrepps
Gimingham
Cliftonville
Mundesley
Maritime
Stow
Paston
B1436
Thorpe Market
Lower Street
Trunch
Bradfield
Knapton
Old Hall Street
Bacton Green
Bacton
Keswick
Antingham
Swafield
Lyngate
Broomholm
Edingthorpe
Pollard Street
Witton Bridge
Walcott
Ostend
Gunton Sawmill
Suffield
Little London
Spa Common
Priory
Happisburgh
Whimpwell Green
Happisburgh Lifeboat Station
B1145
Felmingham
Tungate
North Walsham
White Horse Common
Ridlington
Crostwight
Happisburgh Common
Eccles on Sea
Norfolk Motorcycle
Meeting House Hill
Honing
Old Vicarage
Lessingham
Hempstead
Skeyton Corner
Westwick
Withergate
Bengate
Briggate
East Ruston
Ingham Corner
Sea Palling
Tuttington
Swanton Abbott
Lyngate
Worstead
Dilham
Ingham
Waxham
B1150
Skeyton
Sco Ruston
Smallburgh
Stalham
Stalham Green
Calthorpe Street
RAF Coltishall
Little Hautbois
Sloley
Frankfort
Anchor Street
Sutton
Hickling
Buxton
The Heath
Scottow
Tunstead
Pennygate
Barton Turf
Wood Street
Hickling Heath
Hickling Green
Horsey
Lamas
Bure Valley Railway
A1151
Neatishead
Irstead
Catfield
Sharp Street
Catfield Common
Hickling Broad
Horsey Mere
Horstead
Coltishall
Ashmanhaugh
Cangate
Threehammer Common
How Hill
Ludham
Potter Heigham
West Somerton
East Somerton
Hainford
Frettenham
Belaugh
Wroxham Barns
Hoveton Hall
Radar
BeWILDerwood
Ludham
Damgate
Winterton-on-Sea
Wroxham
Hoveton
Upper Street
Horning
A1062
Toad Hole Cott.
Johnson Street
Bastwick
Cess
Martham
Hemsby Hole
Spixworth
Crostwick
A1151
Upper Street
Woodbastwick
Ranworth
R. Bure
St Benet's Abbey
Thurne
Repps
Rollesby
Hemsby
Newport
Scratby
California
Salhouse
B1140
Pilson Green
Cargate Green
Clippesby
Fleggburgh (Burgh St Margaret)
Ormesby St Michael
Ormesby St Margaret
NORWICH INTERNATIONAL
Old Catton
P+R
PAGE 200
New Rackheath
Little Plumstead
Great Plumstead
Pedham
South Walsham
Upton
Fishley
Billockby
Thrigby
Mautby
Caister Roman Site
Motor
Caister
Caister-on-Sea
A1042
NORWICH
Sprowston
Thorpe End
Blofield Heath
Hemblington
North Burlingham
Acle
Stokesby
Thrigby Hall
Runham
West End
West Caister
A149
Great Yarmouth
Sprowston
Thorpe St Andrew
Witton
A47
Blofield
Damgate
Stracey Arms
R. Bure
A47
THE
Thorpe Hamlet
Broads
Brundall
Beighton
Moulton St Mary
Tunstall
GREAT YARMOUTH
Lakenham
Newton
A47
Postwick
Surlingham
Lingwood
Strumpshaw
Strumpshaw Steam
Buckenham
South Burlingham
Halvergate Marshes
Halvergate
BROADS
Breydon Water
Sea Life Model Village
Kirby Bedon
Southwood
Wickhampton
Berney Arms
Burgh Castle
Southtown
A1243
Bramerton
Rockland St Mary
Hassingham
Freethorpe
Burgh Castle
Gorleston-on-Sea
B1332
A146
Claxton
Langley Green
Limpenhoe
Belton
Bradwell
Lifeboat Station
Hellington
Ashby St Mary
Carleton St Peter
Langley Street
Hardley Street
Nogdam End
Reedham
A143
B1534
Hopton on Sea
Stoke Holy Cross
Poringland
Yelverton
Alpington
Bergh Apton
Thurton
Redwings Horse Sanctuary
Fritton
The Dell
Bunker's Hill
Browston Green
Hawes Green
West Poringland
Howe
R. Chet
Chedgrave
Norton Subcourse
67
St Olaves
Fritton Lake
A12
Shotesham
Brooke
Mundham
Sisland
Loddon
Thorpe
Lound
Blundeston
Corton
Saxlingham Nethergate
Seething
Hales
Thurlton
Herringfleet
Somerleyton
B1074
A146
Kirstead Green
Stubbs Green
Ravingham
Haddiscoe
Pleasurewood Hills
B1375
B1385
Seething Control Tower
Maypole Green
Brundish
Thwaite

10 20 30 40

A B C D

400

1

Middle Mouse
(Ynys Badrig)

West Mouse
(Maen y Bugael)

The Skerries
(Ynysoedd y Moelrhoniaid)

Carmel Head
(Trwyn y Gader)

90

Cemaes
Bay

Porth
Wen

Bull Bay
(Porthllechog)

Bull Bay
(Porth Llechog)

East Mouse
(Ynys Amlwch)

Cemlyn
Bay

Penrhyn

Llanbadrig

Burwen

Llaneilian

Wylfa

A5025

Amlwch
Port

Pengorffwysfa

Cemaes

B5111

Amlwch

Tregele

Llanfechell

Penysarn

Llanfairynghornwy

Bodewyrd

Parys
Mountain

Gadfa

Nebo

Thomas
Mon.

Mynydd
Mechell

Rhosgoch

Rhosybol

Penygraigwen

A5025

Church Bay
(Porth Swtan)

Llanrhyddlad

Rhydwyn

Llyn
Llygeirian

Llanfflewyn

Carreglefn

City Dulas

Llar

Swtan

Llanddeusant

A N G L E S E Y

Llandyfrydog

Brynr

Llanfaethlu

Llanbabo

Llyn Alaw

Gwredog

An

HOLYHEAD BAY
(BAE CAERGYBI)

Llanfwrog

Llynnon

Melin
Hywel

Llyn Alaw

Magaddwyn

Holyhead to:
Dublin 3hrs. 15mins.
Dublin 1hr. 50mins.
(Fast Ferry)

Llanddeusant

Pen-llyn

Carmel

( Y N Y S

Llanerchymedd

Bachau

M Ô N )

Maenaddwyn

Capel
Coch

2

Breakwater

Salt Island

Tregwehelydd
Standing Stone

Llanerchymedd
Station

Gogarth
Bay

Caer Y
Twr Hillfort

Porth-y-
felin

HOLYHEAD
(Caergybi)

Llanfachraeth

Tryfil

M

B5112

ISLE O

Ellins Tower

Llaingoch

Fort

A5

Penrhos

Presaddfed
Burial
Chambers

Llangwyllog

Rhosmeir

Strydd

Newlands
Park

Llanynghenedl

Llyn
Llywenan

Trefor

Llynfaes

B5111

Holyhead Mountain
Hut Circles

Kingsland

HOLY

T

Valley
(Y Fali)

Bodedern

B5109

Cefni Res

Oriel

80

Penrhos Feilw
Standing Stones

Ty Mawr
Standing Stone

Trefignath
Burial Chamber

A5

B5109

Mona

A5

Bodffordd

Ynys Môn

A N G L E S E

Porth
Dafarch Ancient Huts

Trearddur

B4545

A55

Caergeiliog

4

A5

Gwalchmai

Heneglwys

M

Four Mile
Bridge

3

Llyn
Penrhyn

Bryngwran

Rhostrenwfa

Llangefni

ISLAND

Llanfihangel
yn Nhowyn

3

A5

A55

3

Llyn Dinam

(YNYS
GYBI)

Llanfairy-
neubwll

Llyn Traffwll

Capel
Gwyn

5

Cerrigceinwen

Llangristiolus

6

St Gwenfaen's
Well

Valley

Ty Newydd
Burial Chamber

A4080

Dotham

Cymyran
Bay

Rhoscolyn

Llanfaelog

Pencarnisiog

Din Dryfol
Chambered Tomb

Capel
Mawr

Pentre Berw

Llyn
Maelog

Bryn Du

Soar

B4422

3

Rhosneigr

Bethel

Llyn
Coron

Trefdraeth

Afon Cefni
Malltraeth Marsh
(Cors Ddyga)

B4419

70

Barclodiad Y
Gawres Grave

Langwyfan-isaf

Llangadwaladr

Malltraeth

B4421

Bodowyr Burial
Chamber

Anglesey

Aberffraw

Hermon

Llangaffo

Castell
Bryn Gwyn

St Cwyfan's
'The Church in the Sea'

Bodorgan

A4080

Tacla Taid

B4419

Aberffraw
Bay

Malltraeth Sands

Newborough
(Niwbwrch)

M

Dwyran

Foel Farm
Park

4

Anglesey
Model Village

Malltraeth
Bay

Newborough
Forest

Abermenai
Point

Llanddwyn Island
(Ynys Llanddwyn)

Llanddwyn
Bay

Llanfaglan

60

Foryd
Bay

Llanfaglan

Saron

CAERNARFON BAY

Caernarfon

(BAE    CAERNARFON)

M

Airworld

Dinas Dinlle

5

Llandwrog

A499

Glynllifon

350

Inigo Jones
Slate Works

Penygroes

Pontllyfni

Llanllyfni

Aberdesach

Capel
Uchaf

Tai'n Lon

Na

A B

68

C

D

Clynnog-fawr

St Beuno

A487

St Beuno's
Well    1671
Bwlch Mawr

10

20 30

Trefor

40

Gyrn Ddu
1712

Pant Glas

Trwyn y
Gorlech

Yr Eifl

Tre'r Ceiri

Bwlchderwin

250  60  70  80  90  400

E  F  G  H  1

**Point Lynas**
*(Trwyn Eilian)*

*Ynys Dulas*

Dulas

*Dulas Bay*

*Lligwy Bay*
Rhôs Lligwy
Capel Lligwy
**Moelfre**
Seawatch Centre
Din Lligwy Ancient Village
Lligwy Burial Chamber
Llanallgo
Marian-glas

**Great Ormes Head**
*(Pen-y-Gogarth)*
Cable Cars
Happy Valley & Tramway
Great Orme Toll
Ormes Bay or Llandudno Bay
Haulfre Toll
Penrhyn-side
Penrhyn Bay *(Bae Penrhyn)*
St Trillo's
Rhôs-on-Sea *(Llandrillo-yn-Rhos)*
*Colwy*

*Puffin Island (Ynys Seiriol)*

**Brynteg**
Tynygongl
**Benllech**
B5108
B5110
Llanbedrgoch
Llanddyfnan
B5109
**Pentraeth**
Stone Science
Talwrn
Rhoscefnhir
Penmynydd
B5420
**Llanfair Pwllgwyngyll**
Gaerwen
A5
**Llanddaniel Fab**
Bryn Celli Ddu Burial Chamber
Plas Newydd
A4080

**Red Wharf Bay** *(Traeth-coch)*
Red Wharf Bay
Pentrellwyn
**Llanddona**
**Llangoed**
Llanfaes
Castell Aberlleiniog
Haufre Stables
Mariandyrys
Caim  Penmon
Glan-yr-afon
Penmon Priory
**Beaumaris**
Courthouse
Bulkeley Mon.
Gaol
Llansadwrn
Llandegfan
Pen-y-garnedd
Llyn Bodgylched
**Menai Bridge** *(Porthaethwy)*
Pili Palas
Penrhyn Castle
Upper Bangor
Llandygai
Tal-y-bont
A545
A5
Britannia Bri.
Menai Bri.
Lord Nelson Statue
**BANGOR**
Penrhos Garnedd
A55
BANGOR
Glasinfryn

*Penmaen Swatch*

*CONWY BAY*
Conwy Sands
Conwy Castle
Llanrhos
**LLANDUDNO**
Oriel Mostyn Gallery
**Deganwy**
A546
**Tywyn**
Llandudno Junction
Mochdre
**Conwy**
Gyffin
A547
Welsh Mountain
Old Colwyn
**COLWYN BAY** *(Bae Colwyn)*
Penmaen Rhos
A55
Llanelian-yn-Rhos
B5383
Bryn-y-maen
Llansanffraid Glan Conwy
Pentrefelin
B5113
Dawn
Bodnant
Graig
Brymbo
Eglwysbach
Mwdwl Eithin 1277
Gell
Llangernyw

*Lavan Sands (Traeth Lafan)*
**Llanfairfechan**
Nant-y-felin
Nant-y-pandy
Cefn Coch Stone Circle
**Penmaenmawr**
Dwygyfylchi
A55
Abergwyngregyn
Aber Falls
Maen y bardd Burial Chamber
Tal y fan 2000
Rowen
Henryd
Ty'n-y-groes
Pontwgan
Canovium Roman Fort
Tal-y-cafn
B5106

**CAMBRIAN MOUNTAINS**
*C O N W Y*
Moel Wnion 1902
Llyn Anafon
Drosgl 2484
Drum 2526
Llyn Eigiau Resr.
Afon Dulyn
Dulyn Resr.
Melynllyn
Castell
Llanbedr-y-cennin
Pen-y-Gaer Hillfort
Tal-y-Bont
Vale of Conwy
**Dolgarrog**
A470
Llanddoged

**FOEL-FRAS** 3091
**CARNEDD LLEWELYN**
3485
**CARNEDD DAFYDD**
3425
Mynydd Perfedd 2665
Llanllechid
Rachub
Gerlan
Bethesda
Bryn Eglwys
Braichmelyn
A5
Marchlyn Mawr Resr.
Afon Llugwy
Tryfan 3002
Llyn Ogwen
Pont Pen-y-benglog
Pen Llithrig y Wrach 2620
Llyn Cowlyd Resr.
Llyn Crafnant Resr.
Tan-lan
Trefriw
Woollen Mills
**Llanrwst**
Grey Mare's Tail
Gwydir Castle
Gwydir Uchaf Chapel
Melin-y-coed
Gwytherin

Brynsiencyn
Sea Zoo
Segontium Roman Fort
A4080
A487
Y Felinheli
Greenwood Forest Park
Tregarth
Mynydd Llandegai
Rhiwlas
Penisa'r Waun
A4244
B4366
Pont-Rhythallt
Deiniolen
Clwt-y-bont
Brynrefail
Dinorwig
A4086
Llanrug
Pont-rug
**CAERNARFON**
Caeathro
Bontnewydd
Waunfawr
Croesywaun
Bryn Pistyll
A4085
Rhostryfan
Dinas
Llanwnda
Rhosgadfan
Penyffridd
Carmel
Y Fron
Nantlle
B4418
Talysarn
Nebo
Clynnog-goch
Nantmor

*MENAI STRAIT*

**G W Y N E D D**
Cwm-y-glo
Llanberis
Llanberis Lake Railway
Llyn Padarn
Dinorwig Power Station
National Slate
Electric Mountain
Dolbadarn
Llyn Peris
Nant Peris *(Old Llanberis)*
Pass of Llanberis
**GLYDER FAWR** 3279
Cwm Idwal
Llyn Idwal
Capel Curig
A4086
A5
Ty Hyll
Pont-Cyfyng
Llynnau Mymbyr
Swallow Falls
Llyn y Parc
**GWYDYR FOREST PARK**
Llyn Geirionydd
Snowdonia National Park
**Betws-y-Coed**
Conwy Valley Railway
A470
Nebo
B5113
Moel Seisiog 1514

**SNOWDON** *(YR WYDDFA)* 3560
Snowdon Mountain Railway
Betws Garmon
Welsh Highland Railway
Llyn Cwellyn
Rhyd-Ddu
Beddgelert
Sygun Copper Mine
Gelert's Grave
Snowdonia National Park
Yr Aran 2451
Bethania Waterfalls
Moel Hebog 2566
Craig Cwm Silyn 2408
Glaslyn
Hafod Eryri
Llyn Llydaw
Llyn Gwynant
Castell Dinas Emrys
Llyn Dinas
A498
Bethania
Nantmor
Pass of Aberglaslyn
Cnicht 2265

Carnedd Moel-Siabod 2861
Llynau Diwaunydd
Y Cribau
Mynydd Cribau
Llyn Elsi Resr.
Fairy Glen
Pont-y-pant
Conwy Falls
Machno Falls
Pont Rhyd-y-Gynnen
**Dolwyddelan**
Pentre-bont
Ty Mawr Wybrnant
Penmachno
Moel Penamnen 1978
Carrog
Afon Machno
Conwy Falls
Capel Garmon
Capel Garmon Burial Chamber
Ty'n-y-Coed Uchaf
Rhydlanfair
Glan-Conwy
A5
Pentrefoelas
Pentrefoelas Castle
Rhyd

**SNOWDONIA NATIONAL PARK**
**(PARC CENEDLAETHOL ERYRI)**

Garnedd-goch 2408

69  A470

E  F  G  H

**Blaenau Ffestiniog**
Llechwedd Slate Caverns
Tal-y-waenydd
Tanygrisiau
Llyn Conglog
Rhiwbryfdir
Llyn Cwmorthin
Llyn Newydd
Cwm Penmachno
Ysbyty Ifan
B4407
Gylchedd 2196
Garn Pry 1751
A548
Pandy Tudur
Gwytherin
B5113
Llanddoged
A470

L I V E R P O

B A Y

HOYLAKE
Lifeboat
A540
Hilbre Islands
WEST KIRBY
Lifeboat Sta.

Point of Ayr

Little Ormes Head
Penrhyn Bay (Bae Penrhyn)
St Trillo's
Rhôs-on-Sea (Llandrillo-yn-Rhos)
Colwyn Bay
COLWYN BAY (Bae Colwyn)
Mochdre
Welsh Mountain
Penmaen-Rhos
A55
Llanddulas
Abergele Roads
Belgrano
Towyn
Kinmel Bay (Bae Cinmel)
SeaQuarium
Sky Tower
RHYL
Prestatyn
A548
A547
Talacre
Llawndy
Gronant
Gwespyr
Efynnongroyw
Bryn-llwyn
Gwaenysgor
Meliden (Gallt Melyd)
Tan-yr-allt
Mostyn Quay
Pen-y-ffordd
Trelogan
A548
Mostyn
Glan-y-don
A547
Dyserth
Bodrhyddan Hall
Trelawnyd
Rhewl-Mostyn
Berthengam
Whitford (Chwitffordd)
Maen Achwyfan Cross
Greenfield (Maes-glas)
Basingwerk Abbey (remains)
Whelston

Old Colwyn
Llanddulas
Terfyn
A547
Abergele
Llanfair-yn-Rhos
Glyn
Llysfaen
Rhyd-y-foel
A547
Rhuddlan
Pengwern
A525
B5429
Cwm
Marian Cwm
A5151
Offa's Dyke
Llyn Helyg
A55
Lloc
A5026
Gorsedd
Pantasaph
Carmel
Holywell (Treffynnon)
Dolphin

Llansanffraid Glan Conwy
Bryn-y-maen
B5381
Dolwen
A548
Moelfre
St George
KIMMEL PARK
Bodelwyddan
Marble Church
Glascoed
St Asaph (Llan-Elwy)
Waen Goleugoed
Graig
Sodom
Rhuallt
Pen-y-cefn
Tremeirchion
A541
Ysceifiog
Afon-wen
Ddol
Brynford
Caerwys
Babell
Wacco
Pant-y-
B5122
Pentre Halkyn
Halkyn Mountains
Halkyn (Helygain)
Rhosesmor
Nannerch
B5123

Bodnant
Graig
Brymbo
Eglwysbach
Mwdwl Eithin
Betws-yn-Rhos
Moelfre Uchaf
Mynydd Bodrochwyn
Llannefydd
Bont-newydd
Cefn Berain
Plas yn Cefn
Trefnant
Bodfari
Aberwheeler (Aberchwiler)
Castell
B5429
Llangwyfan
Moel Llys-y-Coed
Cilcain
Cefn-bychan
Pont-newydd
Gwernaffield
Gwernymynydd
Cadole

Llanfair Talhaiarn
A544
Llangernyw
B5382
Llansannan
Groes
Henllan
Gwaenynog Bach
Denbigh (Dinbych)
Friary (remains)
A543
Town Walls
Waen
Llandyrnog
Gellifor
Moel Famau
Jubilee Tower
Tafarn-y-Gelyn
Maeshafn

Pandy Tudur
Gwytherin
B5384
Tan-y-fron
Bylchau
Waen
Nantglyn
Prion
Pant-pastynog
Pentre-Llanrhaeadr
Llanrhaeadr
A525
Llanynys
Rhewl
Bachymbyd Fawr
Hirwaen
Moel Famau 1818

Pentre-tafarn-y-fedw
B5113
Cwydir Castle
Melin-y-c
B5427
B5113
A470
Conwy Valley Railway
Waterloo Br.
Nebo
Capel Garmon
Capel Garmon Burial Chamber
Glen
Rhydlanfair
Glan-Conwy
A5
Pentrefoelas
Pentrefoelas Castle
Rhydlydan
Glasfryn
Cefn-brith
Rhydlydan

C O N W Y
Aled Isaf Resr.
Moel Llyn 1528
Bryn Trillyn 1627
Llyn Bran
Moel Seisiog 1514
Llyn Aled
A543
Mynydd Hiraethog
Llyn Brenig
Alwen Resr.
Pentre-llyn-cymmer
B4501
Cyffylliog
Clocaenog
CLOCAENOG FOREST
Cefn Du
B5105
Clawdd-newydd
Churchyard Cross
Derwen
Melin-y-wig
Bryn-Saith Marchog

D E N B I G H S H I R E
Llanfwrog
Ruthin (Rhuthun)
Nantclwyd y Dre
Ruthin Gaol
Efenechtyd
Llanfair Dyffryn Clwyd
Pwll-glas
Graig-fechan
Pentre-celyn
Llanelidan
Rhyd-y-meudwy
A525
Llandegla
Pen-y-stryt
A5104

A494
Bontuchel
Pen-Y-Ffrith Bird Gardens
Llanbedr-Dyffryn-Clwyd
B4430
Eryrys
Graianrhyd
Llanarmon-yn-Ial
A5104
A5431

Ysbyty Ifan
Garn Prys 1751
A5
Cerrigydrudion
Llanfihangel Glyn Myfyr
Afon Alwen
A494
Gwyddelwern
Bettws Gwerfil Goch
Dinmael
Bryneglwys
Horseshoe Pass
A542
Ewe-phoria Sheepdog Centre
Eliseg's

A547
B5115
B5381
A55
A548
A544
A543
A525
A541
A494
A5104
A5

Butterwick
Messingham
Epworth
Old Rectory
Low Burnham
Susworth
Scotterthorpe
Manton
Howsham
Owmby
Clixby
Pelham Pillar

Epworth Turbary
A161
Kelfield
Scotter
Hibaldstow
500
Cadney
North Kelsey Moor

Scotton
Kirton in Lindsey
94
Redbourne
North Kelsey
87
Caistor

Owston Ferry
East Ferry
A15
B1206
South Kelsey
Moortown
Nettleton

Haxey
East Lound
Mount Pleasant
Northorpe
Kirton in Lindsey
Waddingham
Holton le Moor
A46

Graiselound
Laughton
B1205
Grayingham
Brandy Wharf
Thornton le Moor
Glebby
Normanby le Wold

West Stockwith
Heckdyke
Blyton
Pilham
Aisby
Blyborough
Snitterby
Atterby
North Owersby
South Owersby
Usselby
Kirkby
Osgodby
Horse World
Otby
Walesby

Misterton
East Stockwith
Walkerith
Morton
A159
Willoughton
Bishop Norton
Bishopbridge
Kingerby
Middle Rasen
Market Rasen

Walkeringham
Beckingham
A161
Hemswell
Harpswell
Glentham
A1103
West Rasen
Market Rasen

Gringley on the Hill
A631
GAINSBOROUGH
Old Hall
B1433
Springthorpe
Sturgate
Hemswell Cliff
Caenby
Normanby-by-Spital
Owmby-by-Spital
Toft next Newton
Newton by Toft
Buslingthorpe
Legsby

Clayworth
Saundby
Heapham
Glentworth
Saxby
Faldingworth
Linwood
Bleasby Moor

North Wheatley
Bole
Lea
Knaith Park
Upton
Fillingham
Spridlington
Cold Hanworth
Snarford
Friesthorpe
Lissington
West Torrington

A620
Hayton
South Wheatley
Knaith
Kexby
Willingham by Stow
Coates
Ingham
Hackthorn
A46
Wickenby
Holton cum Beckering

Clarborough
Fenton
Gate Burton
Cammeringham
Brattleby
Welton
Reasby
Snelland
B1399

Welham
North Leverton
Habblesthorpe
Littleborough
Marton
Stow
Thorpe in the Fallows
Aisthorpe
Scampton
Welton Hill
Dunholme
Stainton by Langworth

Grove
Treswell
A156
Sturton by Stow
A1500
Scampton
Lincolnshire Showground
B1202

South Leverton
Cottam
Torksey
Brampton
Bransby
Home of Rest for Horses
Broxholme
North Carlton
South Carlton
Langworth
Barlings
Apley
Kingthorpe

Headon
Stokeham
Rampton
Saxilby
Burton-by-Lincoln
Riseholme
Nettleham
Sudbrooke
Reepham
Low Barlings
Stainfield

Upton
Laneham
Church Laneham
A1133
Fenton
Broadholme
Ermine
North Greetwell
Cherry Willingham
Fiskerton
Young Wood

Askham
East Drayton
A57
Dunham-on-Trent
Newton on Trent
Kettlethorpe
Laughterton
Skellingthorpe
LINCOLN
PAGE 197
Washingborough
A158
Bardney

East Markham
A6075
Darlton
Ragnall
North Clifton
Thorney
Harby
Doddington
A46
New Boultham
B1308
B1190
Branston Booths
B1190

Tuxford
Castle
Fledborough
High Marnham
Wigsley
Doddington Hall
Birchwood
Swanpools
Boultham
Canwick
Heighington
Potterhanworth

A1
Skegby
Low Marnham
South Clifton
Spalford
Eagle Moor
Whisby
A1192
Bracebridge
Bracebridge Heath
Branston
B1202
Potterhanworth Booths
Southrey

Moorhouse
Normanton on Trent
Weston
Grassthorpe
Eagle
Natural World Centre
Road Transport
Swallow Beck
North Hykeham
Nocton
Wasps Nest
Dunston

Ossington
Sutton on Trent
Weecar
North Scarle
A1133
Morton
A1434
North Hykeham
Waddington
A15
Metheringham

Norwell Woodhouse
Besthorpe
Girton
South Scarle
Eagle Barnsdale
Thorpe on the Hill
South Hykeham
Haddington
RAF Waddington
B1178
B1202
B1189

A616
Norwell
Carlton-on-Trent
Morton
Witham St Hughs
Harmston
Blankney

Caunton
Bathley
Holme
Langford
Swinderby
A46
Thurlby
Coleby
B1178
Metheringham Airfield
Timberland

Little Carlton
North Muskham
Brough
Stapleford
Norton Disney
Bassingham
A607
Boothby Graffoe
Scopwick
Kirkby Green
Thorpe Tilney
Walcott

A617
Kelham
South Muskham
Winthorpe
Carlton-le-Moorland
Wellingore
Navenby
B1191
Ashby de la Launde
Digby
Billing

NEWARK-ON-TRENT
Newark Showground
Newark Air
A17
Coddington
Brant Broughton
Welbourn
A15
Bloxholm
Dorrington
North Ings Farm

A612
Averham
Staythorpe
New Balderton
Beckingham
Stragglethorpe
Leadenham
Temple Bruer Tower
Cranwell
Ruskington
A153

Rolleston
Farndon
Balderton
A1
Barnby in the Willows
Fenton
Fulbeck
Cranwell
Leasingham
Anwick

A46
Thorpe
Claypole
Stubton
Caythorpe
Frieston
A607
Cranwell Aviation Heritage Centre
North Rauceby
Sleaford
A17
Kirkby la Thorpe

Elston
Syerston
Flintham
Sibthorpe
Claypole
Brandon
Dry Doddington
Hough-on-the-Hill
Normanton
Carlton Scroop
Gelston
Westborough
Holdingham
South Rauceby
Evedon
Ewerby
Asgarby

LINCOLNSHIRE

Caistor · Nettleton · North Kelsey Moor · Moortown · Holton le Moor · South Owersby · Usselby · Osgodby · Kirkby · Middle Rasen · Market Rasen · Tealby · Walesby · Normanby le Wold · Claxby · Linwood · Legsby · Bleasby · Buslingthorpe · Friesthorpe · Lissington · Wickenby · Holton cum Beckering · Snelland · Fulnetby · Rand · Wragby · Langworth · Apley · Kingthorpe · Barlings · Low Barlings · Stainfield · Bardney · Southrey · Bucknall · Horsington · Martin · Woodhall Spa · Kirkby on Bain · Tattershall · Coningsby · Billinghay · Digby · Dorrington · Ruskington · Anwick · South Kyme · North Kyme · Walcott · Thorpe Tilney · Kirkby Green · Scopwick · Blankney · Metheringham · Nocton · Dunston · Potterhanworth · Branston Booths · Sleaford · Kirkby la Thorpe · Evedon · Ewerby · Howell · Asgarby · Anwick

Rothwell · Cabourne · Swallow · Cuxwold · Beelsby · Hatcliffe · Croxby · Thorganby · Swinhope · Brookenby · Binbrook · Kirmond le Mire · Stainton le Vale · Thoresway · Otby · Sixhills · North Willingham · Hainton · East Torrington · West Torrington · West Barkwith · East Barkwith · Benniworth · South Willingham · Market Stainton · Sotby · Panton · Hatton · Great Sturton · Baumber · Minting · Gautby · Wispington · Edlington · Thimbleby · Langton · Woodhall · Thornton · Horncastle · Martin · Roughton · Haltham · Dalderby · Wood Enderby · Wilksby · Moorby

Irby upon Humber · Waltham · New Waltham · Barnoldby le Beck · Brigsley · Ashby cum Fenby · Grainsby · Holton le Clay · Tetney · North Cotes · Marshchapel · Eskham · Grainthorpe · North Somercotes · South Somercotes · Conisholme · Saltfleet · Skidbrooke · Saltfleetby · Theddlethorpe All Saints · Three Bridges · Manby · Great Carlton · Little Carlton · Legbourne · Louth · Keddington · South Cockerington · North Cockerington · Grimoldby · Stewton · Raithby · Hallington · Welton le Wold · South Elkington · North Elkington · Ludborough · North Thoresby · Fulstow · Covenham St Bartholomew · Covenham St Mary · Fotherby · Utterby · North Ormsby · Yarburgh · Alvingham · Little Grimsby

West Ravendale · East Ravendale · Wold Newton · Great Tows · Kelstern · Gayton le Wold · Donington on Bain · Stenigot · Asterby · Cawkwell · Scamblesby · Goulceby · Ranby · Belchford · Fulletby · Tetford · Salmonby · Somersby · Brinkhill · Oxcombe · Ruckland · Farforth · Maidenwell · Withcall · Tathwell · Haugham · Muckton · Burwell · White Pit · Swaby · South Thoresby · Belleau · Aby · Claythorpe · Woodthorpe · Strubby · Withern · Tothill · Gayton le Marsh · Authorpe · Reston · Saleby · Bilsby · Alford · Well · Ulceby · Mawthorpe · Skendleby · Candlesby · Welton le Marsh

Hemingby · Farthorpe · Low Toynton · High Toynton · Greetham · Ashby Puerorum · Mareham on the Hill · Scrafield · Winceby · Lusby · Asgarby · Hagworthingham · Harrington · Aswardby · Sausthorpe · Langton · Partney · Spilsby · Halton Holegate · Great Steeping · Little Steeping · Firsby · Monksthorpe · Bratoft · Hundleby · Mavis Enderby · Raithby by Spilsby · Old Bolingbroke · New Bolingbroke · Hareby · Hameringham · Low Hameringham · Miningsby · Revesby · East Keal · West Keal · Hagnaby · Keal Cotes · Toynton All Saints · Toynton St Peter · Toynton Fenside · Stickford · Stickney · Midville · Eastville · New Leake · Thorpe Fendike · Wainfleet Bank

Scrivelsby · Moorby · Mareham le Fen · Tumby · Wood Enderby · Carrington · Medlam · New York · Sandy Bank · Bunkers Hill · Moorhouses · Reedham · Hawthorn Hill · Scrub Hill · Dogdyke · Chapel Hill · Haven Bank · Langrick · Holland Fen · Frith Bank · Fishtoft Drove · Frithville · Sibsey · Sibsey Fen Side · Northlands · Leake Common Side · Leake Fold Hill · Old Leake · Wrangle · Wrangle Lowgate · Friskney · Friskney Eaudyke · Lade Bank · Leverton · Leverton Outgate · Benington · Butterwick · Haltoft End · Brothertoft · Amber Hill · Gipsey Bridge · Dudgeon · Hilldyke · Burton Corner

Roads: A1084 · A1173 · A46 · A18 · A16 · A1031 · A1103 · A631 · A157 · A158 · A153 · A155 · A1200 · A1104 · A1028 · A1196 · A52 · A17 · B1225 · B1203 · B1434 · B1202 · B1399 · B1190 · B1189 · B1191 · B1188 · B1192 · B1183 · B1184 · B1195 · B1196 · B1373 · B1201 · B1520 · B1395 · B1209

THE WOLDS · LINCOLNSHIRE

N O R T H

S E A

Theddlethorpe
St Helen

Seal Sanctuary
& Wildlife Centre

Meers
Bridge

Lifeboat
Station

**Mablethorpe**

Ye Olde
Curiosity

**Trusthorpe**

**A1104**

Thorpe

**Sutton on Sea**

altby
Marsh

Sandilands

**A1111**

Hannah

**A52**

Markby

Anderby
Creek

Thurlby

**Huttoft**

**B1449**

Anderby

Drainage

Farlesthorpe

**Mumby**

Cumberworth

Authorpe
Row

Bonthorpe

Helsey

**Chapel St
Leonards**

Willoughby

**Hogsthorpe**

Sloothby

**A52**

Hasthorpe

Slackholme
End

Hardys
Animal Farm

Addlethorpe

**Ingoldmells**

Orby

Ingoldmells
Point

Skegness
(Ingoldmells)

Butlin's

Orby   Marsh

Water
Leisure Park

**A158**

**Seathorne**

Winthorpe

Burgh le
Marsh

Natureland
Seal Sanctuary

Church
Farm

Bottons
Pleasure
Beach

**SKEGNESS**

Croft

Model
Village

**A52**

Thorpe
St Peter

Croft Marsh

Seacroft

Batemans
Brewery

Magdalen

**Wainfleet
All Saints**

Wainfleet
St Mary

Gibraltar

Key's Toft

Gibraltar
Point

DANGER AREA

Deeps

Boston

Sc   Head Island

Holme
Dunes

Brancaster Bay

Holkham Ba

**BLACKPOOL** PAGE 192

**SOUTHPORT**

**FORMBY**

**LIVERPOOL BAY**

**CROSBY**
**LITHERLAND**
**BOOTLE**
**WALLASEY**
**HOYLAKE**
**BIRKENHEAD**

**LIVERPOOL** PAGE 197

**PRESTON** PAGE 201

**FULWOOD**
**LEYLAND**
**CHORLEY**
**SKELMERSDALE**
**ORMSKIRK**
**MAGHULL**
**KIRKBY**
**ST HELENS**
**PRESCOT**
**HUYTON**
**WIGAN**
**STANDISH**
**ASHTON-IN-MAKERFIELD**
**GOLBORNE**
**NEWTON-LE-WILLOWS**
**WARRINGTON**

Liverpool to Dublin 8hrs.

Liverpool to Douglas 2hrs. 30mins. (Fast Ferry, Seasonal)

Birkenhead to: Belfast 8hrs. Douglas 4hrs. 15mins. (Seasonal)

MANCHESTER

BLACKBURN
BOLTON
BURNLEY
ACCRINGTON
NELSON
Colne
Clitheroe
RAWTENSTALL
RAMSBOTTOM
BURY
ROCHDALE
OLDHAM
MIDDLETON
ASHTON-UNDER-LYNE
STOCKPORT
ALTRINCHAM
SALE
STRETFORD
ECCLES
SALFORD
SWINTON
WORSLEY
WALKDEN
FARNWORTH
RADCLIFFE
WHITEFIELD
PRESTWICH
HEYWOOD
MOSSLEY
STALYBRIDGE
DUKINFIELD
HYDE
DENTON
DROYLSDEN
FAILSWORTH
CHADDERTON
ROYTON
SHAW
LITTLEBOROUGH
Todmorden
Hebden Bridge
Mytholmroyd
Ripponden
Rishworth
Bacup
Whitworth
Littleborough
Milnrow
Uppermill
Greenfield
Delph
Diggle
Dobcross
Grasscroft
Leigh
Atherton
Tyldesley
Westhoughton
Horwich
Darwen
Haslingden
Edenfield
Stubbins
Cheadle
Cheadle Hulme
Hazel Grove
Romiley
Marple
New Mills
Glossop
Hollingworth
Tintwistle
Mottram in Longdendale

THE FOREST OF TRAWDEN
THE FOREST OF ROSSENDALE
ROSSENDALE
KEIGHLEY MOOR
Haworth Moor
Keighley & Worth Valley Railway
Brontë Parsonage
East Lancs Railway

M65 M66 M60 M61 M62 M602 M67 M6

A59 A56 A682 A6068 A6114 A671 A646 A681 A6066 A6033 A58 A672 A640 A62 A627 A670 A635 A628 A626 A627 A6 A34 A560 A5145 A57 A6010 A560 A662 A663 A664 A665 A666 A667 A576 A6044 A6045 A6046 A6053 A572 A580 A577 A578 A579 A582 A5082 A673 A676 A675 A666 A680 A677 A679 A678 A6068 A6119 A6062 A673 A5081 A5103 A5102 A5149 A5143 A538 A5144 A5145 A534

NORTH YORKSHIRE

Major towns: Tadcaster, Selby, Goole, Howden, Castleford, Pontefract, Knottingley, Ferrybridge, Featherstone, Doncaster, Rotherham, Mexborough, Wath upon Dearne, Swinton, Conisbrough, Rawmarsh, Greasbrough, Wombwell, Maltby, Thorne, Stainforth, Hatfield, Bentley, Armthorpe, Bawtry, Harworth, Crowle, Epworth, Haxey, Westwoodside, Finningley, Thurcroft

ISLE OF AXHOLME

DEARNE VALLEY

ROBIN HOOD DONCASTER SHEFFIELD

Motorways: M1, M62, M18, M180, M62, A1(M)

Road numbers: A64, A659, A162, A1246, A656, A642, A63, A163, A614, A19, A1238, A1041, A645, A161, A634, A631, A638, A630, A618, A633, A60, A18, A6182, A6021, A6023, A6022, A6195, A6109, A6123, A629, A635, A639, A57, B1222, B1223, B1217, B1228, B1396, B1403, B6091, B6090, B6089, B6422, B6273, B6428, B6463

EAST RIDING OF YORKSHIRE

NORTH LINCOLNSHIRE

LINCOLN

Melbourne
Bielby
Kiplingcotes
South Dalton
Arram
Leven
Leconfield
H Leconfield
A1035
A165

Thorpe le Street
Goodmanham
Shiptonthorpe
Market Weighton
Arras
Gardham
Cherry Burton
Molescroft
Grovehill
Weel
Meaux
Everingham
A1079
A1035
BEVERLEY
Minster
A164
Woodmansey
Wawne

Seaton Ross
Harswell
Sancton
Bishop Burton
A1079
Walkington
Bentley
Risby
Skidby
Rural Life
COTTINGHAM
New Village
Inglemire
Stoneferry
Sutton
Bransholme on Hull
Sutton Ings

Laytham
Holme-on-Spalding-Moor
A163
Moor End
North Cliffe
South Cliffe
A1034
North Newbald
South Newbald
High Hunsley
Rowley
Little Weighton
A164
Eppleworth
Willerby
Kirk Ella
Anlaby Park
East Ella
A1079
Sculcoates
Newland

Harlthorpe
Highfield
Foggathorpe
Water End
Sand Hole
Rascal Moor
Hotham
A614
Wauldby
West Ella
Swanland
B1231
Anlaby
B1231
Northfield

Breighton
Gribthorpe
Spaldington
Bursea
Hive
Sandholme
North Cave
Everthorpe
West End
South Cave
Brantingham
Riplingham
A1105
HESSLE
KINGSTON UPON HULL
PAGE 196

Willitoft
Wressle
Brind
Portington
M62
Scalby
Newport
Ellerker
Elloughton
A63
Welton
Melton
Brough
North Ferriby
South Field
A63
The Deep

Newsholme
Eastrington
Gilberdyke
Staddlethorpe
Broomfleet
Humber Bridge
Barton Waterside
New Holland
Goxhill Haven

Howden
Knedlington
Balkholme
Blacktoft
Yokefleet
Faxfleet
Whitton
Read's Island
Redcliff Channel
Barton-upon-Humber
Barrow Haven
New Holland
Barrow upon Humber
Goxhill

Airmyn
Hook
Kilpin Pike
Kilpin
Skelton
Laxton
Saltmarshe
Reedness
Ousefleet
Whitton
Winteringham
A1077
Ferriby Sluice
South Ferriby
Horkstow
Bridge
A15
Baysgarth House
Kingsforth
The Hallands
South End

GOOLE
Swinefleet
Whitgift
Alkborough
Turf Maze
Walcot
West Halton
Horkstow
Saxby All Saints
Deepdale
Burnham
A1077
Thornton Curtis
Wootton
Ulceby Skitter

A161
Goole Fields
Garthorpe
Fockerby
Burton Stather
Coleby
Winterton
A1077
Thealby
Roxby
Appleby
Bonby
Worlaby
B1206
B1211
Ulceby

THORNE WASTE or MOORS
Eastoft
Luddington
Burton upon Stather
Flixborough
Normanby
Normanby Hall
Dragonby
Risby
B1207
Elsham
Elsham Hall
A15
A180
Croxton
Kirmington

Crowle
Keadby
Amcotts
A1077
Gunness
Crosby
SCUNTHORPE
Frodingham
Wressle
M180
Wrawby
Melton Ross
New Barnetby
HUMBERSIDE

A18
M180
Althorpe
M181
A18
Old Brumby
A1029
Broughton
Brigg
Barnetby le Wold
Bigby

Ealand
Derrythorpe
Burringham
B1450
Ashby
Holme
A18
Island
Scawby Brook
Wrawby Post Mill
Somerby
A1084
Grasby

Sandtoft
Westgate
Grey Green
Bracon
Belton
Church Town
Beltoft
Yaddlethorpe
Bottesford
Pink Pig Farm
B1501
Scawby
Sturton
B1206
Howsham
Searby
Clixby

West Carr
Carrhouse
ISLE OF AXHOLME
Epworth
Old Rectory
East Butterwick
West Butterwick
A159
Messingham
Manton
B1398
B1207
Hibaldstow
North Kelsey Moor
Caistor

Wroot
Epworth Turbary
A161
Low Burnham
Kelfield
Susworth
Scotterthorpe
Scotter
B1400
Gainsthorpe Medieval Village
A15
Redbourne
North Kelsey
B1205
Nettleton

Westwoodside
Upperthorpe
East Lound
Owston Ferry
East Ferry
Scotton
Kirton in Lindsey
B1206
South Kelsey
Moortown
A46

Haxey
Graiselound
Gunthorpe
Heckdyke
Wildsworth
Northorpe
Laughton
B1205
Grayingham
Waddingham
Brandy Wharf
Thornton le Moor
Holton le Moor
B1434

West Stockwith
East Stockwith
Blyton
Pilham
Aisby
Blyborough
Snitterby
Bishop Norton
Atterby
North Owersby
South Owersby
Usselby
Claxby

Walkeringham
Morton
A159
Walkerith
GAINSBOROUGH
Springthorpe
Willoughton
Hemswell
York Model Railway
Spital in the Street
Glentham
Caenby
Normanby-by-Spital
Owmby-by-Spital
A1103
Market Rasen

Gringley on the Hill
A631
Beckingham
Old Hall
B1433
Heapham
Sturgate
Blyborough
A631
Spital
A15
West Rasen
Middle Rasen
A631

Clayworth
Saundby
Springthorpe
Cleatham
Corringham
Bishop Norton
Hemswell
Glentworth
Caenby
Toft next Newton
Newton by Toft
A46

North Wheatley
A620
Lea
Knaith Park
Kexby
Fillingham
Saxby
Buslingthorpe
Linwood

NORTH SEA

River Humber

THE WOLDS

NORTH EAST LINCOLNSHIRE

SHIRE

95

89

88

101

**Grid references (top):** E 101, F, G, H · 30, 40, 550

**Places (reading across the map):**

little twick · Long Riston · Arnold · Skirlaugh · New Ellerby · Marton · Rise · Little Hatfield · Great Hatfield · Rolston · Mappleton · Great Cowden · Withernwick · DANGER AREA

Swine · Coniston · Ganstead · Old Ellerby · Burton Constable Hall · Flinton · Aldbrough · East Newton · Thirtleby · Wyton · Sproatley · Humbleton · Garton · Grimston · West Newton · Fitling · Hilston · Tunstall

Bilton · Lelley · Elstronwick · Owstwick · North End · Roos · Waxholme

West End · Preston · Burton Pidsea · Rimswell · Owthorne · Withernsea

Marfleet · Hedon · Burstwick · B1362 · Halsham · East End · Winestead · Hollym · Holmpton

Paull · Fort Paull · Thorngumbald · Camerton · Ryehill · Keyingham · Ottringham · Patrington · Welwick · RAF Holmpton · Out Newton

Paull Holme Sands · Foulholme Sands · Patrington Haven · Weeton · Skeffling · Easington

East Halton · Sunk Island · Sunk Island Sands · Kilnsea · Spurn Heritage Coast

North Killingholme · South Killingholme · Immingham Dock · Immingham · Habrough · Grimsby Roads · Trinity Sands · Spurn · SPURN HEAD

Brocklesby · Stallingborough · Healing · Great Coates · Pyewipe · West Marsh · GRIMSBY

Keelby · Pelham Mausoleum · Wybers Wood · Little Coates · Old Clee · CLEETHORPES · Discovery Centre · Jungle · Cleethorpes Coast Light Railway

Great Limber · Aylesby · Nunsthorpe · Humberston · Pleasure Island

Riby · Laceby · Bradley · Scartho · Pelham's Pillar · Irby upon Humber · Waltham · New Waltham · Holton le Clay · Tetney High Sands

Swallow · Rural Lincolnshire Life · Barnoldby le Beck · Brigsley · Waithe · Tetney · North Cotes · Tetney Lock · DANGER AREA · North Cotes

Cabourne · Beelsby · Hatcliffe · Ashby cum Fenby · Grainsby · Marshchapel · Donna Nook · Eskham

Rothwell · Croxby · Thorganby · West Ravendale · East Ravendale · North Thoresby · Fulstow · Grainthorpe · North Somercotes · DANGER AREA

Thoresway · Swinhope · Brookenby · Wold Newton · Lincolnshire Wolds Railway · Grainthorpe Fen · Conisholme · Church End · Skidbrooke North End

Stainton le Vale · Ludborough · Covenham Resr. · Covenham St Bartholomew · Austin Fen · South Somercotes · Saltfleet

Otby · Kirmond le Mire · Walesby · Binbrook · North Ormsby · Utterby · Covenham St Mary · Yarburgh · North Cockerington · Skidbrooke · Saltfleetby St Clements

Tealby · Great Tows · Kelstern · North Elkington · Fotherby · Little Grimsby · Alvingham · Keddington Corner · Saltfleetby St Peter · Saltfleetby St Helen · Saltfleetby All Saints

Market Rasen · North Willingham · Ludford · Welton le Wold · South Elkington · Keddington · South Cockerington · Grimoldby · Theddlethorpe St Helen · Seal Sanctuary & Wildlife Centre

Legsby · Sixhills · Burgh on Bain · Gayton le Wold · LOUTH · Stewton · Manby · Three Bridges · Theddlethorpe All Saints · Lifeboat Station

Hallington · Manby · Great Carlton · Meers Bridge · Mablethorpe

**Roads:** B1243 · B1242 · B1238 · B1240 · B1239 · B1237 · A165 · A1033 · A160 · A1173 · A180 · A1136 · A46 · A1098 · A1243 · B1203 · B1219 · A1031 · A18 · B1210 · B1225 · B1200 · A631 · A157 · A16 · B1201 · A1031 · B1520

**Ferry note:** Hull to: Rotterdam (Europoort) 10hrs. Zeebrugge 12hrs. 30mins.

LAKE DISTRICT NATIONAL PARK

FURNESS

Selker Bay

DANGER AREA

Broad Oak
Newbiggin
Waberthwaite
Ulpha
Stainton Fell
Caw 1735
Torver
Grizedale
Top
Far Sawrey
Blackwell
Crook
Storrs
B5360
Winster
R. Gilpin
Underb

Whitfell 1880
Corney Fell
Stickle Pike
R. Duddon
1231
Broughton Mills
A593
Sunny Bank
A5084
Grizedale
Cunsey
Beck Forge
Winster
A592
Crosthwaite

Hycemoor
Corney
96
Stoneside Hill
Bootle Fell
Swinside Stone Circle
Duddon Bridge
Lower Hawthwaite
Broughton in Furness
A595
B
Beacon 836
High Nibthwaite
Water Yeat
A5084
Force Mills
Force Falls
Force Forge
Satterthwaite
Graythwaite Hall
C
Ludderburn
Bowland Bridge
Row
A5074

Bootle
Beckfoot
A595
Blawith
Ickenthwaite
Crosslands
Rusland
Finsthwaite
Tannery
Stott Park Bobbin Mill
The Howe
Cartmel Fell

Annaside
Whitbeck
Broadgate
Lady Hall
Foxfield
Hallthwaites
Grizebeck
A5092
Lowick Bridge
Colton
Lakeside & Haverthwaite Railway
Lakes Aquarium
Lakeside
Fell Foot Park
Staveley-in-Cartmel
Mill Side
Witherslack
A590

Duddon Ironworks
Duddon Bridge
The Green
The Hill
Kirkby-in-Furness
Beck Side
Soutergate
Chapels
Netherhouses
Broughton Beck
Lowick
Lowick Green
Spark Bridge
Booth
Lakeland Motor
Newby Bridge
Backbarrow
A590
Seatle
Ayside
High Newton
Town End
A590

A5093
Lacra Stone Circles
Wall End
Beck Side
1088 Shooting House Hill
Mansriggs
Penny Bridge
Arrad Foot
Greenodd
Haverthwaite
Low Wood
Barber Green
Field Broughton
Beck Side
Hampsfell Hospice
Lindale
Meathop
Kent Viaduct

Silecroft
Giant's Grave
Kirksanton
Millom
B5281
Barrow Mon.
Laurel & Hardy
Cumbria Crystal
Leven Viaduct
Holker Hall
Cark
Flookburgh
Priory Gatehouse
Cartmel
Ornamental
Grange-over-Sands
Allithwaite
Holme Island
Arnside
Arnside Tower

Haverigg
Discovery
Askam in Furness
Ireleth
Marton
Lindal in Furness
Ulverston
Pennington
Swarthmoor
Sandside
Conishead Priory
Chapel Island
Ravenstown
Miniature Village
Kents Bank
B5277
Humphrey Head Point
Silverdale
Silverdale Green

Barrow (Walney)
Walney Island
North Scale
Dalton-in-Furness
Furness Abbey
Hawcoat
Ormsgill
Newton
Great Urswick
Stainton with Adgarley
Little Urswick
Scales
Castle
Bardsea
Birkrigg Stone Circle
Baycliff

MORECAMBE BAY

North Walney
Vickerstown
Dock
BARROW-IN-FURNESS
A590
Dendron
Gleaston
Water Mill
Leece
Roosecote
Newbiggin
A5087
Roosebeck
Aldingham

Lancaster Sound

Hest Bank
A5105
Bare
Torrisholme
MORECAMBE
Sandylands
West End
Heysham
Higher Heysham
Lower Heysham
A589
B5273
Heaton
LANCASTER
A683
Aldcliffe

Biggar
Rampside
Roa Island
Lifeboat Station
Piel
Piel Island
Foulney Island
South End
Hilpsford Scar
Piel Bar

Heysham to Douglas 3hrs. 30mins.
Power Station
Middleton
Overton
Sunderland
Glasson
Conder Green
Lower Thurnham
Upper Thurnham
A588
Sunderland Point
Cockerham
Braides

Wyre
Pilling Lane
Knott End-on-Sea
FLEETWOOD
Rossall Point
Preesall
A585
A587
B5268
B5270
Pilling
Smallwood Hey
Scronkey
Stalmine
Preesall Park
Fisher's Row
Stake Pool
Winmarleigh
Ford Gr

Burn Naze
Staynall
Cold Row
Sower Carr
Eagland Hill
Nateby

CLEVELEYS
Little Bispham
Norbreck
Bispham
Thornton
Anchorsholme
Trunnah
Stanah
Little Thornton
Hambleton
Whin Lane End
Out Rawcliffe
A588
Ratten Row
Skitham
St Michael's on Wyre
Great Eccleston
A586

North Shore
Hoohill
Warbreck
A584
Carleton
Poulton-le-Fylde
Singleton
Thistleton
90
Elswick
Crossmoor
Inskip
B5269

BLACKPOOL
PAGE 192
Queenstown
Marton
Newton
Normoss
A587
A586
B5260
THE FYLDE
Roseacre
Greenhalgh
Corner Row
Wharles
Staining

A595  A590  A5092  A5093  A5087  A585  A586  A587  A588  A589  A683

YORKSHIRE DALES
NATIONAL PARK

NORTH YORKSHIRE

LANCASHIRE

FOREST OF BOWLAND

KENDAL
LANCASTER

Kentrigg · Plumgarths · Fisher Tarn Resr. · Cautley · Abboside Common · Cotterdale · High Shaw · High Shaw
Barrow · Oxenhol · New Hutton · Millholme · Marthwaite · Sedbergh · Fairfield Mill · Garsdale Head · Cotter Force · Hardraw Force · Hardraw · Sedb
Brigsteer · Natland · Middlewshaw · KILLINGTON LAKE · Killington · Millthrop · Hallbank · Garsdale · Wensleydale Creamery · Hawes · Gayle · Burters
Sizergh Castle · Cotes · Barrows Green · Halfpenny · Old Hutton · Beckside · Lenacre · Rise Hill 1825 · Gawthrop · Dent · Cowgill · Lea Yeat · Stone House · Wether
Levens · Sedgwick · Force Falls · Stainton · Gatebeck · Goose Green · Middleton · Deepdale · Wold Fell 1829 · Dodd Fell 2192 · Deep
Leasgill · Heversham · Ackenthwaite · Crooklands · Milton · Scout Hill 935 · Mansergh · Barbon · Crag Hill 2250 · WHERNSIDE 2414 · Gayle Moor · Blea Moor · LANGSTROTHDALE CHASE · Foxup · Halton Gill
Milnthorpe · Whasset · Nook · Farleton · Lupton · Kearstwick · Casterton · Leck Fell 2057 · Ribblehead Viaduct · Ribblehead Station · High Birkwith · Oughershaw
Heron Corn Mill · Storth · Beetham · Holme · Hutton Roof · Whittington · KIRKBY LONSDALE · Cowan Bridge · Leck · Ireby · Masongill · Thornton Force · White Scar Cave · Ingleborough 2376 · Selside · Simon Fell · Horton Moor · New Houses · New Inn · Pen-y-ghent Side · Pen-y-ghent 2277 · Fountains Fell 2191
Slack Head · Hale · Lakeland Wildlife Oasis · Burton-in-Kendal · Newton · Overtown · Nether Burrow · Westhouse · Thornton in Lonsdale · Skirwith · Ingleborough Common · Gaping Gill · Ingleborough Cave · Horton in Ribblesdale · Wharfe · Helwith Bridge
Yealand Storrs · Yealand Redmayne · Leighton Hall · Yealand Conyers · Priest Hutton · Docker Park Farm · Tunstall · Cantsfield · Ingleton · Cold Cotes · Newby Cote · Newby · Clapham · Austwick · Feizor · Little Stainforth · Stainforth
Crag Foot · Warton · Millhead · Borwick · Arkholme · Wrayton · Burton in Lonsdale · Low Bentham · High Bentham · Keasden · Lawkland · Eldroth · Stainforth Force · Stackhouse · Langcliffe
Carnforth · Over Kellet · Capernwray · Melling · Wennington · Tatham · Giggleswick · Settle · Scaleber Force · Kirkby Fell 1815 · Malha
Bolton-le-Sands · Nether Kellet · Hornby · Farleton · Butt Yeats · Wray · Aughton · Claughton · Great Stone of Fourstones · Yorkshire Dales Falconry Centre · Mearbeck · Kirkby Malham
Bolton Town End · Slyne · Halton · Caton · Brookhouse · Whit Moor · Caton Moor · Lowgill · Salter · Lowgill · Tatham Fells 1318 · Burn Moor Fell · Rathmell · Long Preston · Otterburn · Bell B
Skerton · Crossgill · Blanch Fell · Haylot Fell · Goodber Common · Thrushgill · Botton Head · Catlow Fell 1595 · Black Hill · Wigglesworth · Hellifield · Nappa
Scotforth · Quernmore · Clougha Pike · White Hill 1786 · White Hill · Halton West · Newsholme · West Marton
Bailrigg · Ward's Stone 1839 · Lee Fell · Tarnbrook · Croasdale Fell · Stocks Resr. · Tosside · Tosside Beck · Ellel · Lee · Abbeystead · Marshaw · Whins Brow 1561 · Paythorne · Horton
Galgate · Four Lane Ends · Dolphinholme · Trough of Bowland · Hawthornthwaite Fell Top 1572 · Sykes · Dunsop Bridge · Slaidburn · Holden · Bolton-by-Bowland · Gisburn · Bracewell
Potters Brook · Forton · Street · Calder Fell · Hareden · Newton · Lane Ends · Sawley · Rimington · Barnoldswick · Salter
Scorton · Calder Vale · Fair Snape Fell · Whitewell · Easington Fell 1300 · Grindleton · West Bradford · Chatburn · Downham · Twiston · Bancroft Mill Engine · Weets Hill · Blacko
Garstang · Cabus · Bonds · Bowgreave · Catterall · Oakenclough · Beacon Fell 873 · Bowland · Bowland Wild Boar Park · Browsholme Hall · Bashall Eaves · Bashall Town · Waddington · Horrocksford · Worston · Pendle Hill 1827 · Barley · Roughlee · Higherford · Blackcod
Churchtown · Claughton · Whitechapel · Chipping · Walker Fold · Low Moor · Clitheroe · Wiswell · Sabden · Fence · Higham · Nelson
Bilsborrow · Inglewhite · Hesketh Lane · Longridge Fell · Knowle Green · Woodfields · Mitton · Pendleton · Newchurch in Pendle · Wheatley Lane · Barrowford · Brierfield
Myerscough · Longridge · Ward Green Cross · Cromwell's Bridge · Whalley · Billington · Ribchester · Gawthorpe

A684 · A685 · A683 · A65 · A6 · A591 · A590 · A6070 · A683 · A687 · A59 · A65 · A682 · A671 · A6068 · M6 · M65 · B6257 · B6256 · B6254 · B6255 · B6479 · B6480 · B6478 · B6243 · B6245 · B6247 · B6251 · B6252 · B5272 · B6385 · A6071

97

YORKSHIRE DALES

NATIONAL PARK

LANGSTROTHDALE CHASE

NORTH YORKSHIRE

THE PENNINE WAY

LANCASHIRE

THE FOREST OF TRAWDEN

KEIGHLEY MOOR

**Places and features (selection):**

Cotterdale, Abbotside Common, Askrigg Common, Redmire Moor, Barden, West Appleby, East Hauxwell, Arrathorne, Hutton, Patrick Brompton

Cotter Force, Hardraw Force, Hardraw, High Shaw, Sedbusk, Askrigg, Newbiggin, Woodhall, Carperby, Castle Bolton, Bellerby, Garriston, West Witton, Bellerby Camp, Leyburn, Constable Burton Hall, A6108, A684

Hawes, Mossdale, Gayle, Burtersett, Bainbridge, Worton, Aysgarth, Thoralby, Redmire, Preston-under-Scar, Wensley, Harmby, Middleham, East Witton, Constable Burton, Finghall, Spennithorne, Newton-le-Willows

Wensleydale Creamery, Wether, Countersett, Semer Water, Marsett, Stalling Busk, Thornton Rust, West Burton, Penhill 1792, Agglethorpe, Coverham, Melmerby, Carlton, St Simon's Chapel, Caldbergh, Braithwaite Hall, Jervaulx Abbey, Thornton Steward, Thirn, Low Ellington, High Ellington

Dodd Fell 2192, Oughtershaw, Deepdale, Kidstones, Walden, Newbiggin, Harland Hill, Carlton Moor, Gammersgill, West Scrafton, Colsterdale Moor, Colsterdale, Gollinglith Foot, Ellingstring, Fearby, Healey, Black Sheep Brewery, Theakston Brewery, Swinton, Warthermarske

Cam Beck, Yockenthwaite, Hubberholme, Cray, Buckden, Walden Head, Woodale, Bradley, Great Haw 1786, Horsehouse, Hindlethwaite Moor, Masham Moor, Leighton, Druid's Temple, Ilton

High Birkwith, Halton Gill, Foxup, Litton, Starbotton, Buckden Pike 2302, Cover Head Bents, Little Whernside 1984, Angram Reservoir, Scar House Reservoir, Brown Ridge 1407, Middlesmoor, Stean, How Stean Gorge, Lofthouse, Hambleton Hill 1331, Carlesmoor, Swetton, Greygarth

Horton Moor, Hull Pot, Pen-y-ghent 2277, New Houses, New Inn, Dambrook Fell, Fountains Fell 2191, Arncliffe, Hawkswick, Kettlewell, Great Whernside 2308, Riggs Moor, How Stean Beck, Stean Moor, Bouthwaite, Ramsgill, Gouthwaite Reservoir, Heathfield Moor, Wath, Pateley Moor

Stainforth, Stainforth Force, Malham Tarn, Arncliffe Cote, Kilnsey Crag, Kilnsey, Kilnsey Park, Conistone, Conistone Moor, Grimwith Reservoir, Greenhow Hill, Pateley Bridge, Nidderdale, Brimham Rocks, Wilsill, Dacre Banks, Summer Bridge

Langcliff, Settle, Craven Lime, Scaleber Force, Malham Cove, Janet's Foss, Gordale Scar, Bordley, Grassington, Yorkshire Dales National Park, Threshfield, Hebden, Stump Cross Caverns, Bewerley, Glasshouses, Dacre, Darley

Mearbeck, Malham, Hanlith, Calton, Linton, Thorpe, Burnsall, Appletreewick, Parcevall Hall, Pock Stones Moor, Padside, Darley Head, Low Green, Thornthwaite

Kirkby Fell 1815, Kirkby Malham, Airton, Winterburn Reservoir, Boss Moor, Threapland, Drebley, Howgill, Barden Fell, Thruscross Reservoir

Long Preston, Hellifield, Bell Busk, Eshton, Hetton, Rylstone, Cracoe, Winterburn, Flasby, Barden Reservoirs, Barden Tower, Earl Seat, Brown Bank Head 1344, Bramley Head, West End, Kettlesing, Bland Hill

Otterburn, Coniston Cold, Gargrave, Stirton, Thorlby, Broughton, Embsay Moor, Barden Scale, The Strid, Barden Priory, Barden 1341, Round Hill, Timble, Swinsty Reservoir, Fewston, Blubberhouses, Jack Hill

Payanthorne, Newsholme, Bank Newton, Embsay & Bolton Abbey Steam Railway, Embsay, Eastby, Halton East, Hesketh Farm Park, Bolton Abbey, Bolton Priory, Hill End, Beamsley, Langbar, March Ghyll Reservoir, Farnley, Askwith, Clifton

Gisburn, Thornton-in-Craven, Elslack, Carleton, Low Bradley, Draughton, Chelker Reservoir, Addingham, Nesfield, Middleton, Manor House, Ilkley, Denton, Skipton, A6069, A6131, Craven

Barnoldswick, Bancroft Mill Engine, Earby, Yorkshire Dales Mining, Salterforth, Cononley, Lothersdale, Silsden, Swartha, Brunthwaite, White Wells Spa Cottage, Cow & Calf Rocks, Ilkley Moor 1320, Burley in Wharfedale, Newall, Otley

Howgill, Weets Hill, Kelbrook, Glusburn, Kildwick, Eastburn, Farnhill, Steeton, Sutton-in-Craven, Cowling, Beechcliffe, Cliffe Castle, Riddlesden, East Morton, Stockbridge, Micklethwaite, Burley Woodhead, Menston, Guiseley, Yeadon

Twiston, Blacko, Foulridge, Laneshaw Bridge, Laneshaw Reservoir, Cross Hills, Cowling, Braithwaite, Thwaites, Hawksworth, East Carlton, Leeds Helipoint, Bingley, Baildon, Shipley

Barrowford, Newchurch in Pendle, Higherford, Roughlee, Barley, Wheatley Lane, Fence, Colne, Trawden, Wycoller, Oakworth, Hainworth, Harden, Ingrow, Keighley, Eldwick, Saltaire, Salts Mill, Baildon Green

Nelson, Brierfield, Lane Bottom, Water Sheddles Reservoir, The Forest of Trawden, Boulsworth Hill 1696, Walshaw Dean, Ponden Reservoir, Stanbury, Brontë Parsonage, Haworth, Lees, Keighley & Worth Valley Railway, Oxenhope, Cullingworth, Wilsden, Frizinghall, Heaton, Eccleshill, Idle, Calverley, Shipley

Pendle, M65, Burnley

**Road numbers:** A684, A6108, A6160, B6160, B6479, A65, A682, A59, A56, A6068, A629, A6034, A650, A657, A658, A659, A660, A6038, A6037, A6144, A6120, B6265, B6160, B6265, B6160, B6382, B6429, B6451, B6165, B6251, B6252, B6383

**Grid references:** 98, 104, 105, 19, 20, 91, 92, 97, 16, 25, 11, 15, 21, 8, 9, 13, 30, 40, 60

NORTH YORK MOORS NATIONAL PARK

Beck · East Moors · River Seph · Hodge Beck · Rudland Rigg · Ridge · River Seven · Chimney Ironworks · Toll · Dudley Cross · Blakey Topping · Cross · Silpho

Helmsley Moor · Rievaulx Moor · B1257 · Old Byland · awton · Rievaulx · Terrace & Abbey · Duncombe Park · Helmsley · A170 · B1257

Fadmoor · Hutton-le-Hole · Spaunton Moor · Hartoft End · Stape · Skelton Tower · A169 · Newton Dale · Levisham · Lockton · Stain Dale · Bridestones · Toll · Langdale End · Broxa · Hackness

Lastingham · Spaunton · Ryedale Folk · M · Cropton Brewery · Cropton · Cawthorne · Cawthorne Camps · Newton-on-Rawcliffe · North Yorkshire Moors Railway · Dalby Forest Drive · Dalby Forest · Wykeham Forest · Everley

Carlton · Pockley · Beadlam · Nawton · Wombleton · Kirkbymoorside · Kirkdale Cave · Kirby Mills · Keldholme · Sinnington · Aislaby · Middleton · Beck Isle Rural Life · Newbridge · Pickering · Low Dalby · Ellerburn · Sawdon · North Moor · Hutton Buscel · Wykeham · Ruston · Forge Valley Wood

Wytherstone Gardens · Helmsley · Harome · Sproxton · Welburn · Great Edstone · Marton · Normanby · Costa Beck · Pickering · Thornton-le-Dale · Allerston · A170 · Wilton · Ebberston · B1415 · B1258 · Snainton · Brompton

Ampleforth · Ampleforth College · Oswaldkirk · East Newton · Nunnington · Nunnington Hall · Muscoates · Salton · West Ness · East Ness · Stonegrave · Butterwick · South Holme · Brawby · Little Habton · Great Habton · Ryton · Flamingo Land · Kirby Misperton · High Marishes · Low Marishes · Wykeham · Yedingham · East Heslerton · THE · West Heslerton · Sherburn

Thorpe Hall · Yearsley · Gilling East · B1363 · Cawton · Hovingham Hall · Hovingham · Fryton · Slingsby · Barton-le-Street · B1257 · Amotherby · Broughton · Swinton · Eden Camp · Scampston · Rillington · Scampston Hall · West Knapton · East Knapton · A64 · Wintringham · Thorpe Bassett · Place Newton · Weaverthorpe

Brandsby · 24 · Stearsby · Skewsby · Coulton · Terrington · Yorkshire Lavender · Ganthorpe · Coneysthorpe · Castle Howard · Malton · B1248 · Norton-on-Derwent · Settrington · Helperthorpe

Crayke · Marton Abbey · Whenby · Farlington · Bulmer · Welburn · High Hutton · Whitewall Corner · Menethorpe · Huttons Ambo · North Grimston · Weaverthorpe · West Lutton · East Lutton · Kirby Grindalythe · Duggleby · B1253 · Cowlam · Sledmere

Stillington · 66 · Sheriff Hutton · Castle · West Lilling · Whitwell-on-the-Hill · Foston · Crambeck · Kirkham · Firby · Westow · Langton · Kennythorpe · Birdsall · Wharram-le-Street · Towthorpe · B1251 · Sledmere House · B1252

Huby · Sutton-on-the-Forest · Sutton Park · Thornton-le-Clay · Crambe · Priory · Barton Hill · Howsham · Burythorpe · Wharram Percy Deserted Medieval Village · Burdale · Thixendale · B1251 · Fimber · B1248 · Sir Tatton Sykes's Monument

Flaxton · Barton-le-Willows · Leavening · Acklam · Waggoners Memorials

Strensall · Harton · Bossall · Leppington · Painsthorpe · Fridaythorpe · Wetwang · B1248

Strensall Camp · DANGER AREA · Scrayingham · Kirby Underdale · Bugthorpe · A166 · Huggate · The Wolds · Tibthorpe

Shipton · A19 · Wigginton · B1363 · Haxby · Earswick · A1237 · Towthorpe · A64 · Claxton · Sand Hutton · Buttercrambe · Skirpenbeck · Youlthorpe · Bishop Wilton · Great Givendale · North Dalton · Bainton

Skelton · A1237 · Huntington · New Earswick · Stockton-on-the-Forest · Brockfield Hall · Warthill · Gate Helmsley · Upper Helmsley · Full Sutton · Gowthorpe · Fangfoss · Meltonby · B1246 · Middleton-on-the-Wolds

Netherpleton · Rawcliffe · A19 · A1036 · Heworth · Holtby · Murton · A166 · Holtby · Stamford Bridge · Stamford Bridge 1066 · Full Sutton · Low Catton · High Catton · Bolton · Yapham · Millington · Warter

Clifton · Knapton · Acomb · PAGE 203 · YORK · A1036 · M · Osbaldwick · Tang Hall · A1079 · Grimston · Dunnington · Kexby · Wilberfoss · Barmby Moor · B1246 · Pocklington · Burnby Hall · Nunburnholme · A614

Woodthorpe · Nunthorpe · Heslington · A19 · Fulford · A64 · Crockey Hill · Elvington · Yorkshire Air · Brickyard Windpump · Sutton upon Derwent · Newton upon Derwent · Thornton · Allerthorpe · Hayton · Burnby · Londesborough · A1079

Bishopthorpe · Naburn · Deighton · Wheldrake · B1228 · Storwood · Melbourne · Melbourne · Bielby · Thorpe le Street · A1079 · Shiptonthorpe · Kiplingcotes · South Dalton · Lund

Acaster Malbis · 5 · Escrick · Thorganby · East Cottingwith · Seaton Ross · Everingham · Goodmanham · Market Weighton · Gardham · Arras · A1079

Acaster Selby · B1222 · Stillingfleet · A19 · Skipwith · Aughton · North Duffield · Harlthorpe · Bubwith · Highfield · Gribthorpe · A614 · Holme-on-Spalding-Moor · Harswell · Sancton · North Cliffe · South Cliffe · North Newbald · A1034

Kelfield · Cawood · Riccall · Wistow · Ellerton · Laytham · A163 · Water End · Sand Hole · Moor End · Rascal Moor · South Newbald

NORTH SEA

Cayton Bay
The Wyke
FLAMBOROUGH HEAD
Bridlington Bay

**SCARBOROUGH**
**BRIDLINGTON**
**DRIFFIELD**
**BEVERLEY**

Cloughton
Burniston
Suffield
Scalby
Scalby Mills
Sea Life
North ... Railway
Rotunda
Throxenby
Newby
Barrowcliff
Falsgrave
Art Gallery
East Ayton
West Ayton
Irton
Seamer
Crossgates
Eastfield
Cayton
Osgodby
Betton Farm
Lebberston
Gristhorpe
Newbiggin
Filey
Lifeboat Station
Flixton
Folkton
Muston
Staxton
Ganton
Potter Brompton
Fordon
Foxholes
Butterwick
Octon
Thwing
Cottam
Langtoft
Royal Oak
Primrose Valley
Hunmanby Sands
Hunmanby
Reighton
Speeton
Wold Newton
Burton Fleming
Grindale
Buckton
Bempton
Danes Dyke
Flamborough
Marton
Sewerby Hall
Sewerby
Bondville Miniature Village
Lifeboat Station
Boynton
Rudston
Monolith
Gypsey Race
West Hill
Bayle
Carnaby
John Bull World of Rock
Bessingby
Hilderthorpe
Kilham
West End
Norman Manor House
Hall
Haisthorpe
Thornholme
Burton Agnes
Park Rose Birds of Prey
Wilsthorpe
Ruston Parva
Harpham
Fraisthorpe
Great Kendale
Lowthorpe
Little Kelk
Gransmoor
Barmston
Nafferton
Great Kelk
Gembling
Lissett
East End
Ulrome
West End
Skipsea
Wansford
Foston on the Wolds
Beeford
Dringhoe
Upton
Skipsea Brough
Garton-on-the-Wolds
Elmswell
Little Driffield
Kirkburn
Southburn
Skerne
Hutton
Brigham
Church End
North Frodingham
Rotsea
Dunnington
Atwick
Bewholme
Watton
Kilnwick
Hempholme
Burshill
Little Burton
Brandesburton
Hornsea
Hornsea Burton
Hornsea Mere
Beswick
Lockington
Thorpe
Aike
Little Leven
Leven
Seaton
Sigglesthorne
Goxhill
Rolston
Mappleton
Scorborough
Arram
Catwick
Little Catwick
Leconfield
Leconfield
Etton
Cherry Burton
Routh
Tickton
Arnold
Long Riston
Rise
Little Hatfield
Great Hatfield
Great Cowden
Withernwick
Bishop Burton
Molescroft
Grovehill
Meaux
Weel
Woodmansey
Walkingt...
Bentley
Thearne
Wawne
New Ellerby
Marton
West Newton
Old Ellerby
Burton Constable
Hall
Flinton
Aldbrough
East Newton
Garton
Grimston
Swine
Coniston
Dunswell
Bishy...

DANGER AREA

A — B — 112 — C — D

Cowper Yearngill Low Row Bolton Low Houses Bolton Westward
Westnewton Heathfield Crookdale Fletchertown Bolton New Wood Lane
Allonby Aspatria B301 A596 Watchhill Bolton Houses
Allonby Bay B5300 Hayton B5299 Blennerhasset Mealsgate A595
Salt Pans Mileforthot Prospect Waterside Harriston Kirkland Guards Howk-Bobbin Mill
Crosscanonby Westmoor End Threapland Boltongate The Howk
Senhouse Roman Parsonby Plumbland Bothel B5299 Dundale Whelpo
Alauna Roman Fort Crosby Villa Gilcrux Plumbland Torpenhow Ireby Upton
Maritime Birkby Crosby Greengill Whitrigg High Aughertree Fell Side
Maryport Dearham Ireby Ruthwaite Branthwaite
Netherton Townhead Moota Hill Sunderland Binsey 1467 Uldale Longlands High Pike 2159
Ellenborough Tallentire Blindcrake Over Water Orthwaite Knott 2329
Fothergill Little Redmann Bewaldeth North Row Great Calva 2265
Flimby Broughton Broughton Isel Hall River Derwent Lake Bassenthwaite Whitewater Dash
St Helens Moor Papcastle Elva Plain Stone Circle District Chapel SKIDDAW FOREST
Siddick Seaton Camerton Broughton Brigham Wordsworth House Embleton High Side SKIDDAW 3054
North Side Great Clifton Cross Cockermouth Kilnhill A591
Stainburn A66 A66 Wythop Mill Mirehouse Little Crosthwaite Millbeck Applethwaite Threlkeld
WORKINGTON A66 Bridgefoot Greysouthen A5086 Whinlatter Forest Park Thornthwaite Ormathwaite Castlerigg Stone Circle
Jane Pit Helena Thompson Little Clifton Eaglesfield Low Lorton Whinlatter Forest A66 Keswick Castlerigg
Moss Bay Westfield Winscales Deanscales High Lorton Lord's Seat 1811 Whinlatter Pass Braithwaite Portinscale Dale Bottom
A597 High Harrington A595 Dean Lorton Yew B5292 Stair Castlerigg
Harrington Grayson Green Branthwaite Ullock Pardshaw Lorton Vale Grisedale Pike 2595 Centenary Stone Walla
Distington Gilgarran Mockerkin Loweswater Fell Brandelhow Derwent Barrow Falls Legburthwaite
Lowca Common End Pica Kidburngill Asby Lamplugh Loweswater Grasmoor 2795 Causey Pike Little Town Memorial Water High Seat 1996
Parton Moresby Parks Arlecdon Rowrah Loweswater Crummock Water Moss Force Grange Lodore Falls High Seat
Branksty High Leys Kirkland Murton Fell 1880 Scale Force Derwent Fells Jaws of Borrowdale Bowder Stone Launchy Gill Force
The Beacon Frizington Great Borne 2021 Sour Milk Gill Buttermere Dale Head Watendlath
WHITEHAVEN Rum Story Cleator Moor A5086 Kirkland Ennerdale Water Red Pike 2648 Buttermere Fell 2470 Rosthwaite Blea Tarn Wythburn Fells
Saltom Pit Kells Wath Brow Ennerdale Bridge Buttermere Hassness Gatesgarth Honister Seatoller Stonethwaite Borrowdale Fells Ullscarf 2382
Saltom Bay Hensingham Keekle Moor Row Blakeley Raise Kinniside Ennerdale Fell High Stile Hay Stacks Honister Slate Mine Borrowdale Yews Galleny Force Dunmail Raise
St Bees Head Mirehouse Sandwith Bigrigg Cleator Lourdes Grotto Stone Circle Kinniside Common R. Liza Pillar 2927 Seathwaite Taylorgill Force Greatend
Sandwith Lowes Court Gallery Egremont Wilton Black Sail Pass Glaramara 2569 Stake Pass Easedale Tarn
Rottington Priory Wilton Kinniside Common 2100 Scoat Fell Great Gable 2949 High Raise 2500 Langdale Pikes 2415 B5343
St Bees Coulderton Carleton Thornhill Haile Caw Fell 1998 Haycock Black Sail Pass Great End Seathwaite Fell Sour Milk Gill Dungeon Ghyll Force
Middletown Haile Monks Bridge Wasdale Head SCAFELL PIKE 3209 Bow Fell 2960 Great Langdale Chapel Stile
Nethertown B5345 Calder Bridge R. Calder Seatallan 2270 Packhorse Bridge Lingmell 3162 Lingcove Packhorse Bridge Little Langdale
Beckermet Calder Abbey COPELAND FOREST St Olaf's Church SCAFELL Three Shire Stone
Braystones Cross FOREST Nether Wasdale Wast Water The Screes 1998 Burnmoor Tarn CUMBRIAN Hardknott Roman Fort Hardknott Pass Wrynose Pass Tilberthwaite
Wellington Gosforth Santon Wast Water Eskdale Moor Stone Circles Hardknott Cockley FURNESS FELLS Gill
Seascale Grey Croft Stone Circle Santon Bridge Giggle Alley Japanese Eskdale Mill Beck THE OLD MAN OF CONISTON
Hallsenna Moor Stubble Green Irton Cross Eskdale Green Boot Beckfoot Eskdale Birker Force Harter Fell 2142 Levers Water Levers Waterfall 2635 Ruskin Coniston
Holmrook R. Mile Stanley Ghyll Force Birks Bridge Rapids Seathwaite Tarn Bowmanstead Brantwood
Drigg DANGER AREA R. Irt R. Esk Devoke Water Woodend Hall Dunnerdale Seathwaite Torver Coniston Water
Saltcoats Ravenglass & Eskdale Railway Broad Oak Ulpha Park Caw 1735 Sunny Bank
Ravenglass Muncaster Castle Waberthwaite Stainton Fell Whitfell 1880 Ulpha R. Duddon 1231 Stickle Pike Bridge End A593 A5084
Roman Bath House Hall Waberthwaite Newbiggin Corney Fell Ulpha Park FURNESS Woodland Fell 96 Water Yeat Ickenthwaite
Selker Bay Hycemoor Stone Hill Swinside Stone Circle Duddon Bridge Lower Hawthwaite Blawith Oxen Park
Bootle Bootle Fell Beckfoot Duddon Ironworks Broughton in Furness High Nibthwaite Lowick Bridge
Hyton Black Combe 1969 Broadgate Lady Hall A595 A5092 Lowick Grizebeck Lowick Green
Annaside Foxfield Hallthwaites Nibthwaite

A596 A595 B5301 A594 A5086 A591 A597 B5306 B5294 B5295 B5345 B5289 B5292 B5299

**PENRITH**

**KENDAL**

**Windermere**

**Bowness-on-Windermere**

**Ambleside**

**Grasmere**

**DISTRICT**

**PARK**

**HELVELLYN** 3117

**YORKSHIRE DALES NATIONAL PARK**

**HOWGILL FELLS**

**Appleby-in-Westmorland**

**GILDERDALE FOREST**

**MILBURN FOREST**

**GREYSTOKE FOREST**

**GRIZEDALE FOREST**

Caldbeck, Newlands, Hesket Newmarket, Millhouse, Calebreck, High Row, Haltcliff Bridge, Mosedale, Bowscale, Mungrisdale, Scales, Troutbeck, Berrier, Motherby, Penruddock, Greystoke, Newbiggin, Greystoke Gill, Hutton, Dacre, Soulby, Sparket, Bennethead, Matterdale End, Thornythwaite, Dockray, Ulcat Row, Knotts, High Force, Watermillock, Longthwaite, Wreay, Pooley Bridge, Sandwick, Martindale, Yew Tree, St Martin's Church, Glenridding, Patterdale, Rooking, Dale Head, Beda Fell, Bridgend, Hartsop, Brothers Water, Grisedale Tarn, Fairfield 2864, High Street 2717, Hayeswater, Haweswater Reservoir, Mardale Common, Harter Fell 2552, Gatescarth Pass, Shap Fells, Kentmere Reservoir, Sadgill, Kentmere, Staveley, Ings, Troutbeck, Elterwater, Skelwith Bridge, Clappersgate, Rydal, Hawkshead, Colthouse, Roger Ground, Near Sawrey, Far Sawrey, Satterthwaite, Grizedale, Lakeside, Newby Bridge, Bouth, Finsthwaite, Rusland, Crosthwaite, Underbarrow, Crook, Winster, Bowland Bridge, Cartmel Fell, Levens, Sedgwick, Natland, Oxenholme, Brigsteer, Stainton, Sizergh Castle

Kirkoswald, Lazonby, Great Salkeld, Glassonby, Gamblesby, Melmerby, Hunsonby, Langwathby, Edenhall, Winskill, Ousby, Skirwith, Kirkland, Blencarn, Culgaith, Milburn, Newbiggin, Temple Sowerby, Kirkby Thore, Knock, Dufton, Keisley, Long Marton, Brampton, Crackenthorpe, Colby, Murton, Hilton, Bolton, King's Meaburn, Newby, Morland, Great Strickland, Little Strickland, Sleagill, Reagill, Maulds Meaburn, Hoff, Drybeck, Great Asby, Crosby Ravensworth, Orton, Raisbeck, Gaisgill, Kelleth, Tebay, Old Tebay, Newbiggin-on-Lune, Ravenstonedale, Sedbergh, Marthwaite, Middleton, Dent, Gawthrop, Cautley, Cross Fell 2930, Moor House, Melmerby Fell 2331

A686, A66, A6, M6, A591, A592, A593, A5091, A5074, A683, A684, A685, A65, B5305, B5288, B5320, B5284, B5285, B5360, B6412, B6413, B6260, B6261, B6542, B6257, B6256

Long Meg & Her Daughters Stone Circle, Gamelands Stone Circle, Oddendale Stone Circle, Gunnerkeld Stone Circle, The Cockpit Stone Circle, Shap Abbey, Brougham Hall, Lowther Castle, Rheged Centre, Dunmallard Hillfort, Aira Force, Dove Cottage, Rydal Mount, World of Beatrix Potter, Sizergh Castle, Killington Lake

ILDERDALE FOREST
A686
Leadgate
Garrigill
Nenthead
10
A689
B6277
B6295
Killhope Lead Mining
Killhope Lead Mining
Lanehead
Cornriggs
Copthill
Middlehope Moor
Rookhope
Lintzgarth
Stanhope Common
B6278
1694 Collier Law
Waskerley
Waskerley Reservoir

104
A Force
Cowshill
B
114
West Blackdene
Weardale
C
Crawley Side
Dales
Stanhope
V
D
Durham Dales
Wolsingham

Wearhead
Ireshopeburn
Westgate 10
Eastgate
A689
Wolsingham
A689

St John's Chapel
Daddry Shield
Brotherlee
Frosterley
Hill End
White Kirkley
Weardale Railway

Alston Moor
Round Hill 2249
Cross 2930
1
Moor House
MILBURN FOREST
Milburn
Knock
Dufton Fell 2518
Viewing Hill 2099
Harwood
B6277
Langdon Beck
Widdybank Fell
Ettersgill
Forest-in-Teesdale
Summerhill Force
Gibson's Cave
Newbiggin
Chapelfell Top 2284
Snowhope Hill
Newbiggin Common
1599 Pawlaw Pike
1511
Pikeston Fell
HAMSTERLEY FOREST
Hamsterley Forest Drive
Woodland

2
Dufton
Keisley
Cronkley Fell
High Force
Bowlees
Low Force
Holwick
Wynch Suspension Bridge
Skears Limekilns
Middleton-in-Teesdale
B6282
Bowbank
Laithkirk
Mickleton
Eggleston Hall
Eggleston
Woodland Fell
Hill Top
B6282
Woodland

Brampton
Crackenthorpe
High Cup Nick
Mickle Fell 2591
Murton Fell 2207
Lune Moor
Thringarth
Laithkirk
Romaldkirk
Hunderthwaite
B6276
B6279
B6281
Kinninvie

Appleby-in-Westmorland
Murton
Hilton
LUNE FOREST
Warcop Fell
River Lune
Grassholme
Grassholme Reservoir
Selset Reservoir
Hury
Hury Reservoir
East Briscoe
Lartington
Cotherstone
Stainton

B6542
Burrells
Hoff
Great Ormside
Coupland
A66
Eden Valley
Dow Crag 1843
Stainmore Common
Hunderthwaite Moor
River Balder
Balderhead Reservoir
Blackton Reservoir
Cotherstone Moor
DANGER AREA
Deep Dale
BARNARD CASTLE
Startforth
Bowes
Westwick
Eggleston Abbey
B6277

Drybeck
Rutter Force
103
Little Ormside
Sandford
Warcop
Hillbeck
North Stainmore
Brough
DANGER AREA
10
Bowes Moor
A66
God's Gridge
Lavatrae Roman Fort
A67
Boldron
Cross Lanes
Stainton

Great Asby
Town Head
Little Musgrave
Great Musgrave
Church Brough
Brough Sowerby
South Stainmore
13
Old Spital
Stainmore Forest
Bowes
Gilmonby
A66
Thwaite
Brignall
Scargill

Little Asby
Soulby
Kaber
Rookby
A685
Winton
Moudy Mea
Sleightholme
1674 Cleasby Hill

Crosby Garrett
Kirkby Stephen
Hartley
Winton Fell
Sleightholme Moor
Nettle Hill 1253
Smardale
Waitby
Nateby
Tan Hill Inn
Tan Hill
Arkengarthdale Moor
Whaw
Washfold
Hurst

Newbiggin-on-Lune
Smardale Gill
4
A685
Ash Fell 1264
B6259
B6270
Stonesdale Moor
Ravenseat
West Stonesdale
2203 Rogan's Seat
1914 Great Pinseat
Langthwaite
Arkle Town
Booze
Wath
Bowderdale
Weasdale
Ravenstonedale
Pendragon
Shoregill
Outhgill
10
Keld
Angram
YORKSHIRE DALES
Melbecks Moor
Old Working Smithy
Gunnerside
Feetham
Kearton
Healaugh
Reeth
Grinton
Fremington

West Fell
A683
Northwaite
Fell End 2324
Mallerstang Common
2349 Great Shunner Fell
Thwaite
Muker
Ivelet
Satron
Gunnerside 23
Crackpot
Low Row
Hazel Brow Farm
Maiden Castle
Harkerside Moor
Gibbon Hill

GILL FELLS
The Calf 2219
Cautley Spout
Garsdale Head
The Buttertubs
SWALEDALE
NATIONAL PARK
Whitaside Moor
Redmire Moor

5
Sedbergh
Fairfield Mill
Hallbank
Millthrop
Lenacre
A684
Rise Hill 1825
Garsdale
A
97
Mossdale Moor
Cotter Force
Hardraw Force
Hardraw
High Shaw
Sedbusk
Askrigg
Newbiggin
Carperby
Bolton
Castle Bolton
Redmire
Preston-under-Scar

Cotterdale
Abbotside Common
Cotter Force
High Shaw
Dales Countryside
Yorkshire Dales National Park
A684
Worton
Woodhall
B6160
Swinithwaite
D
A684
West Witton

Gawthrop
Dent
Cowgill
Lea Yeat
Stone House
2205
Wether
Widdale Fell
B6255
Appersett
Hawes
Gayle
Burtersett
Wensleydale Creamery
B
Countersett
Semer Water
Thornton Rust
Bainbridge
C
WENSLEYDALE
Aysgarth
Thoralby
West Burton
Penhill 1792
98
A684
Melmerby

DURHAM

Langley Park · HillTop · Quebec · Framwellgate Moor · Aykley Heads · Carrville · Pittington · Littletown · Haswell · High Haswell · Easington Colliery

West Butsfield · Satley · Cornsay · Cornsay Colliery · Esh · Ushaw Moor · Bearpark · DURHAM · Gilesgate Moor · Sherburn · Sherburn Hill · Haswell Plough · Easington · Horden Point

A68 · B6302 · B6301 · Esh Winning · New Brancepeth · Broompark · Langley Moor · Shincliffe · High Shincliffe · Ludworth · Shotton Colliery · PETERLEE · Horden

High Stoop · East Hedleyhope · Waterhouses · Brandon · Meadowfield · University Botanic Garden · Bowburn · Cassop · Old Cassop · Old Quarrington · Thornley · Wheatley Hill · Shotton · Castle Eden Dene · Blackhall Rocks

Tow Law · Thornley · Dan's Castle · Sunniside · Stanley Crook · Brancepeth · Croxdale · Sunderland Bridge · Quarrington Hill · Town Kelloe · Wingate · Castle Eden · Eden Vale · Crimdon Park

Billy Row · Roddymoor · Helmington Row · Oakenshaw · Page Bank · Hett · Tursdale · Coxhoe · Kelloe · Trimdon Grange · Station Town · Hutton Henry · Sheraton · Hart · Hart Station

Crook · Fir Tree · Willington · Byers Green · Tudhoe · Tudhoe Grange · Cornforth · Trimdon Colliery · Trimdon · A1086 · A179

Howden-le-Wear · North Bitchburn · Spennymoor · Middlestone Moor · North Close · Dean Bank · Ferryhill · West Cornforth · Fishburn · Elwick · West Park · Dalton Piercy

Witton-le-Wear · High Grange · Binchester · Middlestone · Kirk Merrington · Leasingthorne · Ferryhill Station · Mainsforth · Bishop Middleham · Sedgefield · Butterwick · Embleton · Summerhill · Owton Manor

Hamsterley Forest · Bedburn · Hamsterley · BISHOP AUCKLAND · Toronto · Etherley Dene · Westerton · Chilton Lane · Great Chilton · Hardwick Hall · Sedgefield · Newton Bewley · Wolviston · BILLINGHAM

Morley · High Etherley · St Helen Auckland · Coundon · Coundon Grange · Old Eldon · Rushyford · Chilton · Mordon · Bradbury · Thorpe Larches · Wynyard Village · Wynyard Woodland Park · Cowpen Bewley

Butterknowle · High Lands · West Auckland · Shildon · Middridge · Eldon · Shotton · Foxton · Stillington · Thorpe Thewles · Carlton · Norton · Roseworth · STOCKTON-ON-TEES

Copley · Evenwood · Cockfield · Bildersdale · Royal Oak · NEWTON AYCLIFFE · School Aycliffe · Aycliffe Village · Preston-le-Skerne · Elstob · Whitton · Bishopton · Redmarshall · Hardwick · Thornaby-on-Tees · MIDDLESBROUGH

Staindrop · Ingleton · Killerby · Redworth · Houghton Bank · Heighington · Houghton-le-Side · Walworth Gate · Denton · Coatham Mundeville · Newton Ketton · Great Stainton · Little Stainton · Whinney Hill · Elton · Eaglescliffe · Ingleby Barwick

Cleatlam · South Cleatlam · Langton · Headlam · Summerhouse · Archdeacon Newton · Harrowgate Hill · Beaumont Hill · Barmpton · Great Burdon · Sadberge · Long Newton · Urlay Nook · Yarm

Little Newsham · Winston · Gainford · Piercebridge · Carlbury · High Coniscliffe · Faverdale · Haughton-le-Skerne · DARLINGTON · Middleton St George · Oak Tree · DURHAM TEES VALLEY · Aislaby · Egglescliffe · Maltby

East Shaws · Whorlton · Ovington · Wycliffe · Cliffe · Merrybent · Manfield · Mowden · Low Coniscliffe · Cleasby · Blackwell · Eastbourne · Middleton One Row · High Leven · Middleton-on-Leven

Rokeby Park · Hutton Magna · Caldwell · Forcett · Eppleby · Stanwick Fortifications · Stapleton · Croft-on-Tees · Hurworth-on-Tees · Low Dinsdale · Neasham · Low Worsall · High Worsall · Kirklevington · Crathorne

Barningham · Newsham · Dalton · Ravensworth · Melsonby · Barton · Newton Morrell · Hurworth Place · Eryholme · Dalton-on-Tees · Girsby · Sockburn · Picton · Rudby · Hutton Rudby

Helwith · Kirby Hill · Whashton · Gilling West · Moulton · Middleton Tyas · Scotch Corner · North Cowton · Appleton Wiske · Hornby · West Rounton · East Rounton · Potto · Ingleby Arncliffe · Swainby

A1(M) Due Open Spring 2017 · Skeeby · Uckerby · Pepper Arden · Birkby · Hutton Bonville · Deighton · East Harlsey · Harlsey Castle · Mount Grace Priory · Osmotherley

Richmond · Scorton · Bolton-on-Swale · Forest · East Cowton · Danby Wiske · Brompton · Ellerbeck · Foxton · Thimbleby

Skelton · Marske · Hudswell · Holly Hill · Easby Abbey · Colburn · Hipswell · Catterick Bridge · Catterick · Ellerton-on-Swale · Kiplin Hall · Streetlam · Battle of the Standard 1138 · Northallerton · Over Silton · Nether Silton

Marrick · Downholme · Catterick Garrison · Walkerville · Brompton-on-Swale · East Appleton · Kirkby Fleetham · Great Langton · Yafforth · Romanby · Borrowby

B6270 · Stainton · Hipswell Moor · Scotton · Tunstall · Ellerton-on-Swale · Kirkby Fleetham · Scruton · Ainderby Steeple · Crosby Court · Leake · Knayton · Upsall

Bellerby · East Hauxwell · Barden · Garriston · Hunton · Arrathorne · Langthorne · Little Fencote · Great Fencote · Thrintoft · Warlaby · Thornton-le-Moor · Thornton-le-Beans · Borrowby

Leyburn · Bellerby Camp · Constable Burton Hall · Patrick Brompton · Little Crakehall · Kirkbridge · Leeming Bar · Ainderby · Morton-on-Swale · North Otterington · Knayton · Kirby Knowle

Wensley · Harmby · Spennithorne · Finghall · Great Crakehall · Aiskew · Leeming · Londonderry · Newby Wiske · South Otterington · Kirby Knowle

Middleham · White Rose Candle Workshop · Newton-le-Willows · Wensleydale Railway · BEDALE · LEEMING BAR · Leeming · Gatenby · Maunby · North Kilvington · Kirby Wiske · Thornton-le-Street · Felixkirk

A6108 · Coverham · East Witton · Braithwaite · Jervaulx Abbey · Thornton Steward · Thornton Watlass · Burrill · Cowling · Firby · Exelby · Thirn · Thorp Perrow Arboretum · Theakston · Kirklington · A1(M)

**NORTH SEA**

E  F  G  H

70  80  90  500

40

30

20

10

500

90

1

2

3

4

5

Brotton
Skinningrove
Boulby Cliffs
Cleveland Ironstone Mining
Boulby
Cowbar
Lifeboat Station
Captain Cook & Staithes Heritage
Carlin How
Loftus
A174
Staithes
North Skelton
Kilton Thorpe
Liverton Mines
Easington
Dalehouse
Port Mulgrave
Stanghow
Liverton
Roxby
Hinderwell
Borrowby
Runswick
Runswick Bay

R & L A N D

Moorsholm
B1366
Scaling Dam
Scaling
B1266
Ellerby
Newton Mulgrave
Kettleness
Goldsborough
14  A174  Lythe
Sandsend
East Row
Moorsholm Moor
A171
21
Scaling Dam Reservoir
Mickleby
West Barnby
East Barnby
Raithwaite
Dunsley
Dracula Experience
WHITBY
Abbey
Roxby High Moor
Ugthorpe
Newholm
Castle Park
Captain Cook Memorial
Saltwick Bay
Danby Low Moor
Lealholm Moor
Danby Beacon 981
Stonegate
Hutton Mulgrave
Ruswarp
Golden Grove
Long Lease
Danby
Moors Centre
Houlsyke
A171
Briggswath
B1416
Stainsacre
High Hawsker
Castleton
Ainthorpe
Lealholm
Aislaby
Iburndale
Sneaton
Low Hawsker
Ness Point or North Cheek
Danby Botton
Duck Bridge
Sleights
Ugglebarnby
B1447
Raw
Robin Hood's Bay
Street
Victorian Science
Egton
Egton Bridge
Sneatonthorpe
Fylingthorpe
Old Coastguard Station
Botton
Glaisdale
Lease Rigg
Grosmont
A169
B1416
A171
Boggle Hole
Glaisdale Rigg
Key Green
Esk Valley
Green End
The Hermitage
Robin Hood's Bay & Fylingdales
Coastal Centre
Old Peak or South Cheek

NORTH YORK MOORS

Beck Hole
Thomason Foss Waterfall
Falling Foss (Waterfall)
Peak Alum Works
Ravenscar
Loose Howe
Rosedale Moor
Mallyan Spout
Goathland
Fylingdales Moor

NATIONAL PARK

Pike Hill Moor
Nelly Ayre Foss Waterfall
Staintondale
Crowdon
Staintondale Shire Horse Farm

Y O R K    M O O R S

Low Bell End
Rosedale Abbey
Wheeldale Moor
Wheeldale Roman Road
North Yorkshire Moors Railway
959
Lilla Cross
Burn Howe Rigg
LANGDALE FOREST
Goathland Moor
Harwood Dale Forest
Cloughton Newlands
Thorgill
Rosedale Chimney Ironworks
Newton Dale Spring
Saltergate
Malo Cross
Harwood Dale
Cloughton
Spaunton Moor
Stape
Hole of Horcum
Blakey Topping
Burniston
Gillamoor
Ryedale Folk
Lastingham
Hartoft End
Skelton Tower
Bridestones
Toll
Bickley
Langdale End
Broxa
Silpho
Suffield
A171
A165
Scalby Mills
Sea Life
North Bay Railway
Cawthorne Camps
Levisham
Newton Dale
Dalby Forest Drive
Hackness
Scalby
Kirkbymoorside
Keldholme
Hutton-le-Hole
Spaunton
E
100
Cropton
Cawthorne
Newton-on-Rawcliffe
Lockton
F
Low Dalby
Dalby Forest
G
Wykeham Forest
Everley
Three...
101
H
Barrowcliff
Rotunda
Art Gallery
Kirkby Mills
Cropton Brewery
Appleton-le-Moors
Wrelton
Aislaby
North Yorkshire Moors Railway
Trouts Dale
North Moor
Falsgrave
SCARBOROUGH
Sinnington
Middleton
Newbridge
Beck Isle Rural Life
A170
East Ayton
A170
Forge Valley Woods
Hutton
Betton Farm
Osgodby
P+R
P+R

POINT OF AYRE

Rue Point
The Ayres
The Ayres
A16
A10
Cranstal
The Lhen
B6
B2
B13 A19
B3
Dhowin
Bride
A17
Shellag Point
A10
Jurby Head
Jurby West
Jurby East
A10
B5
B4
Jurby
Andreas
Crosses
A9
Ramsey Bay
Ballasalla
Sandygate
Civil War Fort
B7
Regaby
The Cronk
A13
A14
St Judes
Dhoor
A13
Grove
Ramsey
Orrisdale Head
Orrisdale
A3
Ballaugh
A17
Sulby
B14
A3
Manx Electric Railway
Port e Vullen
Churchtown
Lhergy Frissel
Ravensdale
B9
T.T. Course
Curraghs
B8
6
Glen Auldyn
Elfin Glen
Lewaigue
A15
Crosses
Maughold
Bishopscourt Glen
Glen Wyllin
A14
Tholt-y-Will Glen
1854
North Barrule
B16
B19
Ballajora
Maughold Head
Kirk Michael
Glen Mooar
Ballaleigh
SNAEFELL
2036
T.T. Course
14
Clagh Ouyr
Corrany
A2
Cornaa
Cashtal Yn Ard
Port Mooar
Ballacarnane Beg
Barregarrow
Slieau Dhoo 1601
Snaefell 2036
Snaefell Mountain
Glen Mona
Port Cornaa
Gob y Deigan
A4
T.T. Course
B10
B10
Sulby Resr.
21
Laxey Wheel
Laxey Glen
Great Laxey Mine
Dhoon
Dhoon Glen
Bulgham Bay
Knocksharry
A3
Cronk-y-Voddy
Rhenass Waterfall
Colden 1599
A18
Laxey
Minorca
Old Laxey
Ballacannell
St Patrick's Isle
Leece
Ballagyr
Lambfell Moar
Glen Helen
ISLE OF MAN
B22
B12
B12
Laxey Head
House of Manannan
A20
Injebreck Resr.
Ballaheannagh
B20
A18
B12
Contrary Head
Peel
A1
Ballig
St John's
Greeba Castle
Baldwin
B21
A2
Baldrine
Laxey Bay
Patrick
Tynwald Hill
Slieau Ruy 1570
A1
A23
Hillberry
A2
Clay Head
Glen Maye
A30
Lower Foxdale
Crosby
Glen Vine
Strang
Willaston
Onchan
Groudle Glen Railway
Dalby Point
A27
Glen Maye
A3
Foxdale
Eairy
A24
Garth
A22
A6
Groudle Glen
Port Groudle
Niarbyl
Dalby
B35
Union Mills
A1
Onchan Head
Niarbyl Bay
A36
South Barrule Hill 1586 Fort
B36
12
B35
Braaid
A24
Cooil
Spring Valley
DOUGLAS
A11
Stroin Vuigh
A36
B39
13
Close Clark
B30
St Mark's
B37
A5
Quine's Hill
Kewaigue
Manx
Douglas Bay
Fleshwick Bay
A27
Ballamodha
B29
Newtown
A26
Home for Old Horses
Keristal
B80
Douglas Head
Lingague
B41
Ronague
Grenaby
A3
B25
Port Soderick
Little Ness
Bradda Head
Bradda
Surby
B44
B42
B40
Ballabeg
Isle of Man Steam
10
Bradda Glen
A41
Colby
A5
Rushen Abbey
Santon Head
Port Erin
Railway
A7
5
Ballasalla
Chambered Cairn
The Howe
A5
Four Roads
A12
Derby Fort
Cregneash
Port St Mary
Castletown
ISLE OF MAN
Derbyhaven
St Michael's Island
Kitterland
A31
National Folk
B18
Nautical Scarlett
Rushen
Keys
The Sound
SPANISH HEAD
Dreswick Point
Calf of Man

Douglas to:
Belfast 2hrs.45mins.
(Fast Ferry, Seasonal)
Birkenhead 4hrs. 15mins.
(Seasonal)
Heysham 3hrs. 30mins.
Dublin 2hrs. 45mins.
(Fast Ferry, Seasonal)
Liverpool 2hrs. 30mins.
(Fast Ferry, Seasonal)

PAGE NOT CONTINUED

**SOUTH AYRSHIRE**

**DUMFRIES & GALLOWAY**

**MULL OF GALLOWAY**

Tormitchell
Barr
CHANGUE FOREST
Grey Hill 975
Pinmore
A714
A77
River Stinchar
Merkland
Cairn Hill 1572
Knockinlochie
Polmaddie Hill 1854
David Memo.
116
B734
Lendalfoot
Strai
G
853
Knockdaw Hill
Poundland
Pindonnan Craigs 1098
R. Cree
Standard
1
Bennane Head
Ballantrae Bay
Colmonell
Knockdolian
B734
Pinwherry
Pinwherry Hill
Dusk River
Bellamore
Black Clauchrie
Knockdolian
Heronsford
Knockdhu 756
Water of Tig
752 Shiel Hill
Barrhill
Corwar House
A714
GLENTR
Ballantrae
Garleffin
Downan Point
1041
Strawarren Fell
B7027
Drumlamford Loch
Drumlamford House
Loch Dornal
2
Cairnryan (Loch Ryan Port) to Belfast 2hrs. 15mins. (Fast Ferry, Seasonal)
Currarie Port
Low Ballochdowan
1046 Carlock Hill
Beneraird 1439
1321 Milljoan Hill
Chirmorie
High Murdonochee
Loch Maberry
Loch Ochiltree
Polbae
Milleur Point
Cairnryan to Larne 2hrs.
Finnarts Bay
Penderry Hill
A77
Glen App
844 Mid Moile
725 Stab Hill
Glenwhilly
Quarter Fell
605 Urrall Fell
742 Eldrig Fell
Knowe
70
Corsewall Point
Portencalzie
Barnhills
B738
Knockcoid
Loch Connell
Kirkcolm
The Wig
Main Water of Luce
Braid Fell
Loch Doon Hill 780
888 Artfield Fell
Carseriggan
110
Dounan Bay
Ervie
Airies
B798
A718
Penwhirn Resr.
Balmurrie
Black Loch
Tarf Bridge
Loch Heron
West Culvennan
3
Portobello
Slouchnawen Bay
Leswalt
Galdenoch Castle
Glenstockadale
B7043
Loch Ryan
Innermessan
Cairnscarrow
New Luce
Bught Fell 672
Gleniron Fell
Loch Ronald
Shennanton
A751
Lochinch Castle
Craig Fell 538
Water of Luce
Dernaglar Loch
B733
Kirkcow
Stranraer
B737
A77
White Loch
Castle Kennedy
Carscreugh Castle
Carscreugh
A75
60
Broadsea Bay
B738
Craigenlee Fell
St John
Aird
Castle Kennedy
Challoch Hill
Glenwhan
Glenluce Abbey
Glenluce
Motor
Knock Moss
Black Head
Dunskey Estate
Cairn Pat 596
Lochans
Mark
A75
Dunragit 484
Whitefield Loch
Castle Loch
4
Portpatrick
Lifeboat Station
Dunskey Castle
A77
Bean Hill
B7077
West Freugh
B7084
Torrs Warren
Kilfillan
Milton
Stairhaven
A747
Auchenmalg
Craignarget Hill
B7005
Port of Spittal Bay
A716
Stoneykirk
B7042
Kildonan
B7084
DANGER AREA
Auchenmalg Bay
Mochrum Loch
Kirklauchline
Sandhead
LUCE BAY
Garheugh Port
Chapel
Mochrum Fell
646
Loch Head
Cairngarroch Bay
Cairngarroch
Kirkmadrine Stones
Money Head
Float Bay
Low Ardwell
Ardwell
Chapel Rossan Bay
Milton Point
A747
Moch
Ardwell Point
Ardwell
Balgowan Point
Port William
Logan House
Barsalloch Point
Mor
Mull of Logan
Logan Botanic Garden
Logan Fish Pond
Port Logan
A716
Terally Point
Port Logan Bay
B7065
Cairnywellan Head
INSET
G
H

**Inset:**
Clanyard Bay
B7065
A716
Kilstay Bay
Kirkmaiden
Drummore
Cailiness Point
Maryport
B7041
Maryport Bay
Crammag Head
E
Port Kemin
MULL OF GALLOWAY
Laggantalluch Head
Clanyard Bay
Kirkmaiden

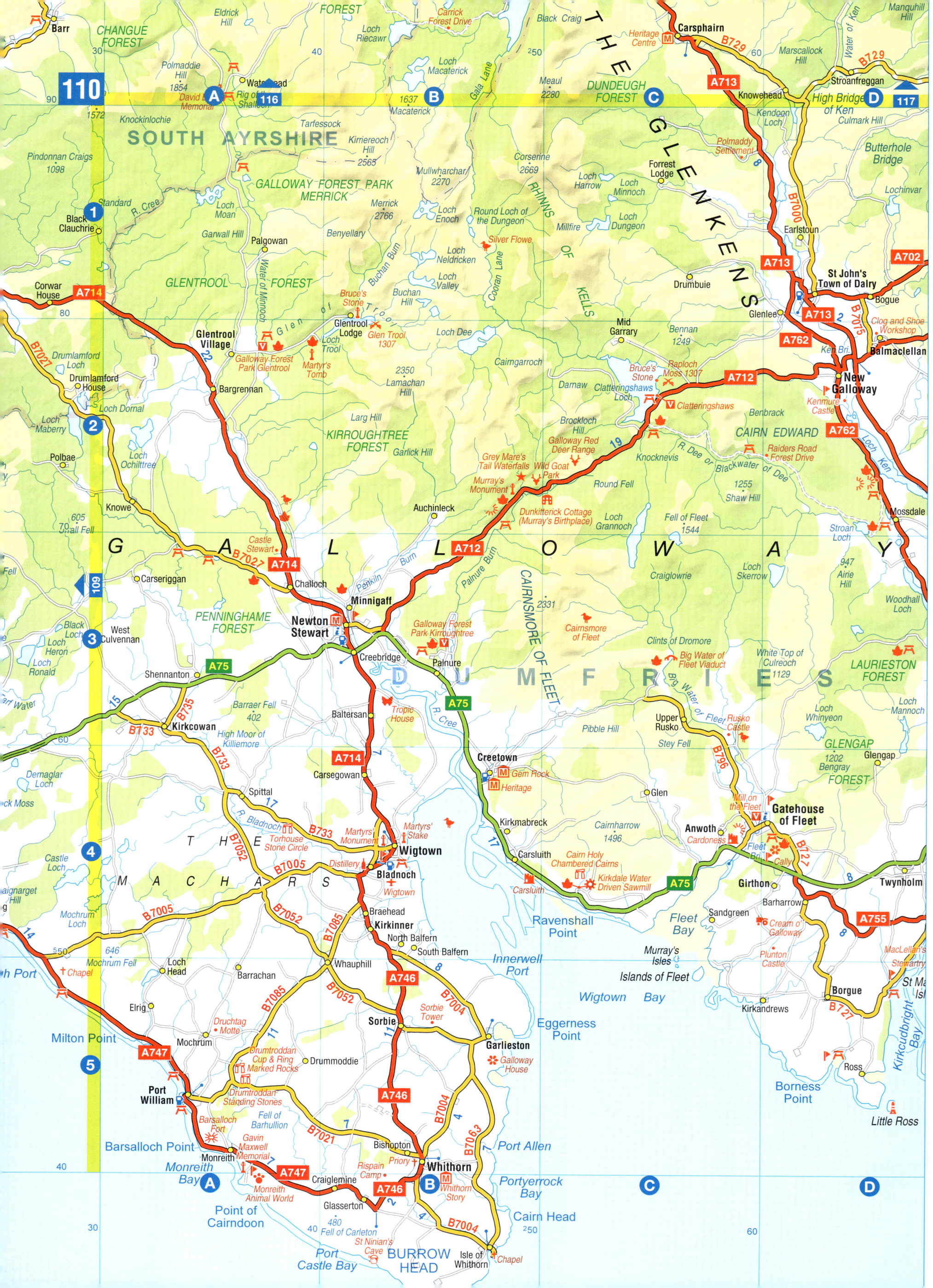

Barr

CHANGUE FOREST

Eldrick Hill

FOREST

Black Craig

Carrick Forest Drive

Loch Riecawr

Loch Macaterick

Meaul 2280

THE GLENKENS

Carsphairn

Heritage Centre

B729

Marscalloch Hill

Water of Ken

Manquhill Hill

B729

Stroanfreggan

High Bridge of Ken

Culmark Hill

A713

Knowehead

Kendoon Loch

Polmaddie Hill 1854

David Bell Memorial

Waterhead

Rig of the Shalloch

116

Gala Lane

Loch Macaterick 1637

Macaterick

DUNDEUGH FOREST

A713

117

Polmaddy Settlement

Knockinlochie 1572

Tarfessock

Kirriereoch Hill 2565

Mullwharchar 2270

Corserine 2669

Loch Harrow

Forrest Lodge

SOUTH AYRSHIRE

Pindonnan Craigs 1098

GALLOWAY FOREST PARK MERRICK

Benyellary

Merrick 2766

Loch Enoch

Round Loch of the Dungeon

Loch Minnoch

Loch Dungeon

Earlstoun

B7000

Standard

Black Clauchrie

R. Cree

Loch Moan

Garwall Hill

Palgowan

Silver Flowe

RHINNS OF KELLS

Millfire

Drumbuie

St John's Town of Dalry

A702

A713

A713 2

Corwar House

A714

80

Glen Trool

Loch Neldricken

Loch Valley

Mid Garrary

Bennan 1249

Glenlee

Ken Bri

Clog and Shoe Workshop

Balmaclellan

B7021

Drumlamford Loch

Glentrool Village

22

Galloway Forest Park Glentrool

Martyr's Tomb

Glentrool Lodge

Glen Trool 1307

Loch Dee

Bruce's Stone

Raploch Moss 1307

A712

New Galloway

Kenmure Castle

A762

Drumlamford House

Loch Dornal

Bargrennan

2350

Lamachan Hill

Cairngarroch

Darnaw

Clatteringshaws Loch

Clatteringshaws

Benbrack

CAIRN EDWARD

Loch Maberry

2

Polbae

Loch Ochiltree

KIRROUGHTREE FOREST

Larg Hill

Garlick Hill

Brockloch Hill

Galloway Red Deer Range

Knocknevis

R. Dee or Blackwater of Dee

Raiders Road Forest Drive

1255

Shaw Hill

Mossdale

Knowe

605

Urall Fell 70

Auchinleck

Grey Mare's Tail Waterfalls

Wild Goat Park

Round Fell

Fell of Fleet 1544

Stroan Loch

G A L L O W A Y

Murray's Monument

Dunkitterick Cottage (Murray's Birthplace)

Loch Grannoch

Craiglowrie

L'och Skerrow

947 Airie Hill

Woodhall Loch

Castle Stewart

B7027

A714

Challoch

Penkiln Burn

Palnure Burn

CAIRNSMORE OF FLEET

2331

Cairnsmore of Fleet

Clints of Dromore

White Top of Culreoch 1129

LAURIESTON FOREST

109

Carseriggan

Minnigaff

Galloway Forest Park Kirroughtree

Cairnsmore of Fleet

Big Water of Fleet Viaduct

Loch Whinyeon

Loch Mannoch

PENNINGHAME FOREST

Newton Stewart

Creebridge

Palnure

Big Water of Fleet

GLENGAP FOREST

West Culvennan

3

Black Loch

Loch Heron

Loch Ronald

A75

Shennanton

DUMFRIES

Upper Rusko

Rusko Castle

B796

1202 Bengray

Glengap

Glenglap

arf Water

B735

Barraer Fell 402

Baltersan

Tropic House

A75

Pibble Hill

Stey Fell

Loch Mannoch

15

B733

Kirkcowan

High Moor of Killiemore

R. Cree

Mill on the Fleet

Gatehouse of Fleet

Dernaglar Loch

60

A714

Carsegowan

Creetown

Gem Rock

Heritage

Glen

Anwoth

Cardoness

Fleet Bri

Cally

k Moss

THE MACHARS

Spittal

17

R. Bladnoch

B733

Martyrs' Monument

Martyrs' Stake

Kirkmabreck

Cairnharrow 1496

Girthon

A755

Twynholm

Castle Loch

4

Torhouse Stone Circle

Distillery

Wigtown

Bladnoch

Cairn Holy Chambered Cairns

Kirkdale Water Driven Sawmill

Sandgreen

Barharrow

aignarget Hill

Mochrum Loch

B7052

B7005

B7005

Wigtown

Carsluith

Carsluith

Cream o' Galloway

A75

B727

Mochrum Fell

646

Loch Head

Barrachan

Braehead

Kirkinner

North Balfern

South Balfern

Ravenshall Point

Fleet Bay

Murray's Isles

Plunton Castle

MacLellan's Stewartry

St Ma Isl

14

550

Chapel

Elrig

Mochrum

Whauphill

A746

Innerwell Port

Islands of Fleet

Borgue

Kirkandrews

B727

Milton Point

A747

Druchtag Motte

B7085

B7052

Sorbie

Sorbie Tower

B7004

Eggerness Point

Wigtown Bay

Kirkcudbright Bay

5

Port William

Drumtroddan Cup & Ring Marked Rocks

Drummoddie

A746

Garlieston

Galloway House

Borness Point

Ross

Barsalloch Fort

Drumtroddan Standing Stones

Fell of Barhullion

B7021

7

Bishopton

B7004

B7063

Port Allen

Little Ross

Barsalloch Point

Gavin Maxwell Memorial

Monreith

Craiglemine

A747

Rispain Camp

Priory

Whithorn

Whithorn Story

Port Allen

Portyerrock Bay

Monreith Bay

A

Monreith Animal World

Glasserton

A746

B

Whithorn

Cairn Head

C

D

Point of Cairndoon

480

Fell of Carleton

St Ninian's Cave

B7004

250

Port Castle Bay

BURROW HEAD

Isle of Whithorn

Chapel

# Map — Dumfries & Galloway

**Grid references:** E, F, G, H (top and bottom); 1, 2, 3, 4, 5 (right side)

## Place names and features

Penpont
Tynron
James Renwick Monument
A702
Keir Mill
Closeburn
Cample
NITHSDALE
FOREST OF AE
1157 Great Hill
St Ann's
Whitetauld Hill
Johnstonebridge
Hill 1747
Dalwhat Water
B729
Moniaive
Kirkland
Keir Hills 1172
A76
Park
118 Kirkpatrick
Brownmoor Hill
300
Courance
B7020
Loch
A702
Craigmuie
B729
Wallaceton
Blackwood
Glenmidge
Auldgirth
High Auldgirth
Glenmaid Moor
Ae
Parkgate
Nethermill
Templand
Marjoriebanks
Milli
Bogrie Hill 1471
Dunscore
Throughgate
Ellisland Farm
A76
Dalswinton
Auchencairn
Shieldhill
A701
A709
Castle Loch
B7020
Craigenputtock
Glenesslin
Stepford
Morrington
Steilston Hill 787
B729
Holywood
Kirkton
Duncow
Amisfield
Tinwald
Barr Hill
Brockloch Hill
Newtonairds
Locharbriggs
Loch Urr
A712
Glenkiln Resr.
Glenkiln
Shawhead
Twelve Apostles Stone Circle
New Bridge
Lincluden Church
Heathhall
Dalscone Farm Fun
The Grove
Dumfries & Galloway Aviation
Cruck Cottage
Torthorwald
Torthorwald Castle
Mossburn Animal Centre
Garcrogo Forest
Corsock
Lochenkit Loch
Crofts
Maxwelltown
Robert Burns House
Collin
Greenlea
Woodside
Craig
A712
Crocketford or Ninemile Bar
Milton Loch
Lochaber Loch
A711
Cargenbridge
Troqueer
DUMFRIES
PAGE 194
Crichton Grounds
Elizafield
Racks
A75
Mouswald
Knockvennie
Auchenreoch Loch
Milton
Lochrutton Loch
Drumsleet
Islesteps
Mabie Farm Park
A710
Kingholm Quay
Kelton
Bankend
Clarencefield
B7
A713
Parton
B794
Kirkpatrick Durham
Springholm
Beeswing
Loch Arthur
Mabie Forest
Kirkconnell
Glencaple
Shearington
Brow Well
Ruth
Loch Roan
Old Bridge of Urr
Hardgate
Kirkgunzeon
Drumcoltran Tower
Lotus Hill
Mabie
B725
Blackshaw
112
Crossmichael
Ernactoglo Loch
Clarebrand
Corra
Long Fell 1256
Corn Mill
Waterloo Monument
New Abbey
Sweetheart Abbey
Loch Kindar
Caerlaverock
Caerlaverock Wetland Centre
Laurieston
Dornell Loch
Glenlochar
Townhead of Greenlaw
Haugh of Urr
Leaths
Meikle Hard Hill
B795
Mote of Urr
B794
1032 Maidenpap
Criffel 1868
Drumburn
A762
Glentoo Loch
Castle Douglas
GALLOWAY
Old Buittle Tower
B793
Boreland Hill
Carsethorn
A713
Kelton Mains Open Farm
Sulwath Brewery
Carlingwark Loch
A745
Dalbeattie
Kirkbean
A710
Bargatton Loch
Threave
B736
Craignair
B727
DALBEATTIE FOREST
John Paul Jones Birthplace
Bridge of Dee
Rhonehouse or Kelton Hill
Gelston
Barnbarroch
Prestonmill
A75
Ringford
Palnackie
Orchardton Tower
A711
Caulkerbush
Mainsriddle
Loaningfoot
Southerness
A711
A762
R. Dee
Kippford or Scaur
Colvend
Sandyhills
Southerness Point
1283 Bengairn
Screel Hill
Mote of Mark
Portling
Tongland
Tongland Bridge
Galloway
Barcloy Hill
Rockcliffe
Rough Island
Castlehill Point
FIRTH
Kirkcudbright
Broughton House
Auchencairn
Hestan Island
Auchencairn Bay
Balcary Point
Beckfoot
550
Mutehill
A711
Dundrennan
Rascarrel
Abbey
Rascarrel Bay
Dubmill Point
Mawb
Salta
Townhead
Netherlaw
Port Mary
SOLWAY
5
Allonby
Allonby Bay
DANGER AREA
Abbey Head
B5300
Salt Pans
Mileforth
Allerby
Crosby
Villa
A596
Crosby
Senhouse Roman Alauna Roman Fort
Maryport
Maritime
Netherton
Dearham
Townhead
Ellenborough

A   B   118   C   D

**DUMFRIES & GALL**

FOREST OF AE

St Ann's
Whitefauld Hill
1157 Great Hill
Brownmoor Hill
Glenmaid Moor
High Auldgirth
Kirkpatrick
Park
Auldgirth
Dalswinton
Auchencairn
Ae
Parkgate
Nethermill
Shieldhill
Courance
Johnstonebridge
ANNANDALE WATER
Broomhillbank
Bankshill
Boreland
Berscaur
CASTLE O'ER FOREST
Castle O'er
Bentpath
Telford Memorial
The Shin
Hart Fell 1087
Calkin Rig 1478
Raes Knowes
Glentenmont Height

NITHSDALE

Ellisland Farm
Duncow
Amisfield
Kirkton
Holywood
Locharbriggs
Tinwald
Twelve Apostles Stone Circle
New Bridge
Dalscone Farm Fun
Heathhall
The Grove
Dumfries & Galloway Aviation
Cruck Cottage
Torthorwald
Torthorwald Castle
Linclomen
Maxwelltown
Robert Burns House
Troqueer
**DUMFRIES PAGE 194**
Collin
Greenlea
Elizafield
Racks
Woodside
Mossburn Animal Centre
Hightae
Smallholm
Kettleholm
Dalton
Carrutherstown
Dalton Pottery
Hoddom Castle
Hoddomcross
Carlyle's Birthplace
Ecclefechan
Eaglesfield
Middlebie
Kirkconnel
Waterbeck
Craigs
Kirtleton
Howat's Hill
1047 Grange Fell
Paddockhole
Chapelknowe
Merkland Cross
Moorend
Newton
Kirkpatrick Fleming
King Robert the Bruce's Cave

Templand
Millhousebridge
Applegarthtown
Marjoriebanks
**A709** Lochmaben
Castle Loch
Heck
Greenhill
**A74(M)**
Lockerbie
Dryfesdale Lodge
Sibbaldie
Claydaubing Bridge
Corrie Common
Burnswark
Brydekirk
Charlesfield
Warmanbie
Creca
Gretna Green
Gretna
Old Graitney
Rigg
Dornock
Eastriggs
Annan
Welldale
Howes
Cummertrees
Powfoot
Newbie
Ruthwell
Savings Banks
Brow Well
Ruthwell Cross
Clarencefield
Bankend
Shearington
Blackshaw
Caerlaverock
Caerlaverock Wetland Centre
Glencaple
Kirkconnell
Kelton
Kingholm Quay
Islesteps
Cargenbridge
Drumsleet
Mabie Farm Park
Lochaber Loch
Mabie
Mabie Forest
Meikle Hard Hill
Criffel 1868
Boreland Hill
Waterloo Monument
Corn Mill
New Abbey
Sweetheart Abbey
Loch Kindar
Drumburn
Carsethorn
Kirkbean
John Paul Jones Birthplace
Prestonmill
Mainsriddle
Loaningfoot
Southerness
Southerness Point

**SOLWAY FIRTH**

SCOTLAND
ENGLAND
Barnkirk Point
Bowness-on-Solway
Port Carlisle
Torduff Point
Redkirk Point
King Edward I Monument
Glasson
Drumburgh
Easton
Boustead Hill
Longburgh
Dykesfield
Cardurnock
Anthorn
Longcroft
Whitrigg
Angerton
Newton Arlosh
Kirkbride
Little Bampton
Oughterby
Wampool
Biglands
Gamelsby
Aikton
Wiggonby
Thornby
Knoxwood Wildlife Rescue Trust
Thornby Moor Dairy
Low Whinnow
Crofton
West Woodside
Skinburness
Calvo
Seaville
Moss Side
Raby
Kelsick
Dundraw
Lessonhall
Oulton
Moorhouse
Parton
Micklethwaite
Silloth
Lifeboat Station
Greenrow
Blitterlees
Blackdyke
Highlaws
Abbeytown
Moor Row
Waverbridge
Aikhead
Standingstone
Kirkland
Waverton
Wigton
Highmoor
Old Carlisle Roman Fort
Carwath
Brackenthwaite
Beckfoot
The Gincase
Wolsty
Newtown
Pelutho
Tarns
Aldoth
Southerfield
Blencogo
Bromfield
Langrigg
High Scales
Parkgate
Waterside
Woodrow
Low Row
Watchhill
Low Whitrigg
Bolton Low Houses
Bolton
Westward
Rosley
Mawbray
Salta
Holme St Cuthbert
Mealrigg
Edderside
New Cowper
Yearngill
Westnewton
Heathfield
Crookdake
Fletchertown
Bolton New Houses
Bolton Wood Lane
Allonby
Allonby Bay
Dubmill Point
Hayton
Prospect
Aspatria
Oughterside
Blennerhasset
Mealsgate
Harriston
Kirkland Guards
Boltongate
Sandale
Howk Bobbin Mill
The Howk
Salt Pans
Mawbray
Crosscanonby
Allerby
Westmoor
Arsonby
Threapland
Plumbland
Bothel
Ireby
High Ireby
Whitrigg
Aughertree
Fell Side
Ruthwaite
Uldale
Longlands
Branthwaite
Senhouse Roman
Alauna Roman Fort
Crosby
Crosby Villa
Bullgill
Gilcrux
Greengill
Birkby
Maritime
Maryport
Netherton
Dearham
Townhead
Tallentire
Moota Hill
Sunderland
Binsey 1204
Upton
Ellenborough

NORTHUMBERLAND

DUMFRIES & GALLOWAY — DALEWAY

KIELDER FOREST

KIELDER WATER & FOREST PARK

Kielder Castle
Kielder Viaduct
Butteryhaugh
Kielder
Toll
Steele Road
Foulmire Heights
Earl's Seat 1303
Dinmont Lairs
Leaplish Waterside Park
Kielder Water
Birds of Prey Centre
Tower Knowe
Yarrow
Falstone
Stannersburn

The Rigg
Reeker Pike
Black Knowe 1615
Paddaburn Moor
Churnsike Lodge

Broad Head 1614
Pike Fell
Watch Hill 119
North Birny Fell 902
Lamiston Fells
Wilson's Pike
Black Knowe

Crumpton Hill 1575
Hog Fell
Black Edge 1464
Newcastleton or Copshaw Holm
Newcastleton Forest
Lewis Burn
Rough Pike

Kirkstile or Ewes
Tarras Water
Millholm Cross
Liddesdale Heritage Centre
Kershope Burn
Glendhu Hill 1685

Clan Armstrong
MacDiarmid Memorial
Malcolm Moriument
Tinnis Hill 1326
Kershope Bri.
Kershopefoot

New Langholm
Langholm
Skipper's Bridge
Bruntshiel Hill
Kershopefoot
KERSHOPE FOREST
Bewcastle Fells

Earshaw Hill 921
Caulside
Nook
Blackpool Gate
The Flatt
Sighty Crag
Black Knowe 1701

Gilnockie Tower
Claygate
Harelaw
B6318
Crossings
Oakshaw Ford
Roughsike
Bewcastle
DANGER AREA
Butterburn
Gowk Bank
Black Fell

Hollows
Rowanburn
Catlowdy
Kinkry Hill
Roadhead
Bew Castle
Cross Shopford
Middle Shield Park

Canonbie
Evertown
Scuggate
Moat
Haggbeck
Lyneholmeford
Wiley Sike
Whiteside

Milltown
Glenzierfoot
Scot's Dyke
Carwinley
Easton
Netherby
Stapleton
R. Lyne
Thirlwall Common
Gilsland Spa

Scotsdike
Netherby
Kirkcambeck
West Hall
Thirlwall Castle
Cawfields Roman Wall
Walltown Crags
Aesica Roman Fort
Hadrian's Wall

Old Blacksmith's Shop
Oakbank
Longtown
Kirklinton Hall
Boltonfellend
Mossedge
Hethersgill
B6318
King Water
Piper Sike Turret
Gilsland
Greenhead
Roman Army
Haltwhistle

Springfield
Solway Moss 1542
Kirklinton
Hetherside
Skitby
Walton
Banks
Hadrian's Wall
Birdoswald Roman Fort
Alston Arches
Melkridge

Rockcliffe Cross
Westlinton
Smithfield
A6071
Burtholme
Lanercost
Pike Hill Signal Tower
Low Row
A69
Park Village
Plenmeller

Todhills
Scaleby Hill
Scaleby
Laversdale
Newtown
Priory
A69
Denton Fell
Rowfoot

Rockcliffe
Todhills
Blackford
Barclose
Oldwall
Solway Aviation
Irthington
Brampton
Milton
Featherstone Castle
Coanwood

Burgh by Sands
Harker
Longpark
Newtown
Carlisle
Warwick Bridge
Farlam
Hallbankgate
Tindale
Midgeholme
Lambley
Stonehouse

Beaumont
Cargo
Houghton
Low Crosby
High Crosby
Newby East
A689
Talkin Tarn
Forest Head
Tindale Tarn
Halton Lea Gate
Viaduct

Monkhill
Grinsdale
Linstock
Aglionby
Hayton
Talkin
Tindale Fells
Eals

Kirkandrews-on-Eden
Knowefield
Rickerby
Warwick-on-Eden
How Fenton
Greenwell
Cold Fell 2037
Glendue Fell
Knarsdale

Moorhouse
Stainton
Carlisle
A69
Heads Nook
Faugh
King's Forest of Geltsdale
Whitfield Moor 1723

Great Orton
Little Orton
Morton
Scotby
Wetheral
Broadwath
Castle Carrock
River Gelt
Knarsdale

Newby West
Harraby
Priory Gatehouse
Great Corby
Cumwhinton
1678
Geltsdale Middle
Slaggyford

Baldwinholme
Cummersdale
Carleton
Cumwhitton
Albyfield
Geltsdale Middle
A686

Thursby
Dalston
Brisco
Cotehill
Hornsbygate
Cumrew
Newbiggin
Whitley Castle
South Tynedale Railway
The Hub
Alston

Cumdivock
Buckabank
Durdar
Wreay
Hornsby
Croglin
Ayle
Raise

West Curthwaite
Bridge End
Hawksdale
Foulbridge
Holmwrangle
Croglin Water
Scale Houses
Bay
Leadgate

Nether Welton
Raughton
Gaitsgill
Low Hesket
Aiketgate
Lockhills
Towngate
Ainstable
Watch Hill 1999
GILDERDALE FOREST
A686

Grassgarth
Raughton Head
Skiprigg
Mellguards
High Hesket
Nunclose
Longdales
Renwick
Harescheugh
B6294

Sebergham
Churchtown
Middlesceugh
Stockdalewath
Southwaite
Old Town
Dale
Ruckcroft
Busk
Unthank

Parkhead
Welton
Thethwaite
Highbridge
Ivegill
Calthwaite
Staffield
High Bankhill
Gamblesby

Caldbeck
Newlands
Sour Nook
Sowerby Row
Thomas Close
Morton
Fieldhead
Plumpton Foot
Kirkoswald
Glassonby
Glassonby
Glassonby

Hesket Newmarket
Hutton End
Brockleymoor
Kirkoswald Castle
Lacy's Caves
Long Meg & Her Daughters Stone Circle
Melmerby

Millhouse
Haltcliff Bridge
New Rent
Hutton-in-the-Forest
Lazonby
Townhead
Glassonby
Melmerby Fell

Calebrack
High Row
Lamonby
Plumpton
Great Salkeld
Salkeld Dykes
Little Salkeld
Hunsonby
Shire
Melmerby Fell 2331

M6
A7
A595
A689
A6
A66
M6

A B C D

**KIELDER WATER & FOREST PARK**

Leaplish Waterside Park
Kielder Water
Birds of Prey Centre
Tower Knowe
Yarrow
Falstone
Stannersburn
North Tyne
Charlton
Lanehead
Greenhaugh
Highgreen Manor
Black Middens Bastle House
Gatehouse
Bower
Hesleyside
Chirdon Burn
Trough Common
Padon Hill 1240
Blackburn Common
Earl's Seat 1303
HARWOOD FOREST
Fontburn Reservoir
Otterburn 1388
Otterburn Hall
Castle
B6341
Elsdon
Raylees
Old Town
A696
Winter's Gibbet
B6342
Herterton House
Rothley
Scot's Gap
Middleton
B6343
Cambo
Kirkwhelpington
Wallington
River Wansbeck
Capheaton
Sir Edward's Lake
Ingoe
Fenwick
Kirkheaton
Ryal
Hallington
Great Whittington
Matfen
Ouston
Halton Shields
High House Farm Brewery
A68
Halton
B6321
Aydon Castle
Newton Hall
Newton
A69
Ovington
Eltringham
Cherryburn
Branch End
Bywell
B6530
Broomhaugh
Riding Mill
Stocksfield
Painshawfield
Broomley
Hindley
New Ridley
Apperley Dene
Whittonstall
A68
B6309

NORTHUMBERLAND

DANGER AREA

West Woodburn
East Woodburn
Chesterhope
Ridsdale
Knowesgate
Great Bavington
Little Bavington
Thockrington
Sweethope Loughs
Colt Crag Reservoir
Hallington Reservoirs
A68
Little Swinburne
Great Swinburne
Colwell
Barrasford
A6079
Chollerton
Bingfield
Gunnerton
Nunwick
Simonburn
Uppertown
Humshaugh
Chollerford
Cocklaw
Walwick
Chesters Roman Fort
Low Brunton
Heavenfield 635
Brunton Turret
Planetrees Roman Wall
B6318
Wall
Acomb
Anick
Sandhoe
Aydon
Fourstones
Warden
A6079
B6531
Abbey
Tyne Green
Roman Town
A695
Corbridge
Dilston Castle & Chapel
Dilston
B6530
B6037

NORTHUMBERLAND NATIONAL PARK

Haughton Common
Brocolitia Roman Fort
Temple of Mithras (Mithraeum)
Black Carts Turret
B6320
Black Fell
Butterburn
Gowk Bank
Wark
Birtley
Park End
Chipchase Castle
Whygate
Stonehaugh
Warks Burn

WARK FOREST

Churnside Lodge

Broomlee Lough
Sewingshields Wall
Greenlee Lough
Housesteads Roman Fort
Winshields Wall
Crag Lough
Cawfields Roman Wall
Northumberland National Park Once Brewed
Roman Vindolanda
Thorngrafton
Newbrough
B6319
Chesterwood
Haydon Bridge
Low Gate
B6305
B6306
HEXHAM
Old Gaol
Hexham
Hexham 1464
Ordley
Juniper
Dalton
Steel
Slaley
Slaley Forest
Strothers Dale
Colpitts Grange
Minsteracres
Kiln Pit Hill
Shotleyfield
Carterway Heads
Snods Edge
Mosswood
Allensford

Whiteside
Thirlwall Common
Walltown Crags
113
Hadrian's Wall
Aesica Roman Fort
Thirlwall Castle
Roman Army
Greenhead
B6318
Haltwhistle
Aesica
Alston Arches
Melkridge
Redburn
Henshaw
Bardon Mill
Ridley
Featherstone Castle
Rowfoot
Coanwood
Park Village
Plenmeller
Plenmeller Common
Whitfield Moor 1723
Whitfield
Bearsbridge
Catton
Thornley Gate
Allendale Chimneys & Allen Smeltmill Flues
Allendale Town
A686
The Garden Station
Stublick Chimney & Flue
Langley
B6305
B6295
B6303
Hexhamshire Common
Broadwell House
Whitley Chapel
Dukesfield
Rawgreen
Healey
1345
Blanchland Moor
Blanchland
Newbiggin
Baybridge
Edmundbyers
Derwent Resr.
Pow Hill
Muggleswick
Muggleswick Common
Healeyfield
Horsleyhope Reservoir
Smiddy Shaw Reservoir
Hisehope Reservoir
Waskerley Reservoir
Waskerley

Lambley
Viaduct
Eals
Knarsdale
Slaggyford
South Tyne
Whitley Castle
A689
Ayle
B6292
The Hub
Raise
Alston
Blagill
Nenthall
Bayles
Middle Fell
Leadgate
B6277
Nenthead
Nenthead Mines Heritage Centre
Killhope Lead Mining
A689
Garrigill
Ashgill Force
Coalcleugh
Lanehead
Cornriggs
Cowshill
104
Wearfield
Ireshopeburn
High House Chapel
Ireshope Moor
St John's Chapel
Daddry Shield
Brotherlee
Westgate
A689
Eastgate
Crawley Side
Dales
Stanhope
Durham Dales
Wolsingham
Frosterley
White Kirkley
Weardale Railway
A689
Hill End

Gilderdale Forest
A686
Whitfield Moor
Keirsleywell Row
Limestone Brae
Carr Shield
Sinderhope
Allendale Common 1640
Spartylea
Green Hill
Dirt Pot
Allenheads
Heritage Centre
B6295
Middlehope Moor
Nookton Fell
1567
Bolt's Law 1773
Hunstanworth
Townfield
Ramshaw
Rookhope
Lintzgarth
Stanhope Common
B6278
1694 Collier Law
1345 Blanchland Moor
Burnhope Reservoir
Burnhope Seat 2448
Round Hill 2249
Alston Moor
Black Burn
Tunstall Reservoir
Wolsingham Park Moor

NORTH SEA

Newcastle to: Amsterdam (IJmuiden) 15 hrs.

**NEWCASTLE UPON TYNE**

**MORPETH**

**ASHINGTON**

**BEDLINGTON**

**BLYTH**

Newbiggin-by-the-Sea

**WHITLEY BAY**

**TYNEMOUTH**

**SOUTH SHIELDS**

**JARROW**

**HEBBURN**

**GATESHEAD**

**WALLSEND**

**LONGBENTON**

**GOSFORTH**

**SUNDERLAND**

**WASHINGTON**

**CHESTER-LE-STREET**

**HOUGHTON-LE-SPRING**

**SEAHAM**

**CONSETT**

**STANLEY**

**DURHAM**

**PETERLEE**

Marsden Bay

Beacon Point

Souter Lizard Point

Horden Point

Dene Mouth

Newbiggin

Cresswell

Ellington

Lynemouth

Woodhorn

North Seaton

Hirst

Guide Post

Choppington

Bebside

Cowpen

Cramlington

Dudley

Seaton Delaval

Seaton Sluice

Holywell

St Mary's or Bait Island

Monkseaton

Shiremoor

New York

Cullercoats

North Shields

Westoe

Marsden

Harton

Whitburn

South Bents

Seaburn

Roker

Monkwearmouth

Penshaw

Shiney Row

Bournmoor

Philadelphia

Newbottle

Seaton

Ryhope

Murton

Dalton-le-Dale

Cold Hesledon

Dawdon

Easington Colliery

Horden

Blackhall Colliery

Crimdon Park

Hart

Hartlepool Rd

d Point

Ardrossan to Brodick 55mins

126

40

10

A  B  C  D

Ardrossan
Stevenson
Saltcoats
Horse Isle
North Ayrshire

Kilwinning
Torranyard
Montgreenan
A738
A736
A735
Eglinton
Doura
Cunninghamhead
Rowallan Castle
B751
A77
Fen
Laigh Fenwick

Clauchlands Point
Holy Island
Kingscross Point
gscross
Whiting Bay
Largybeg Point
pin Head

Campbeltown to Brodick 2hrs 20mins. (Seasonal)
Ardrossan to Campbeltown 2hrs. 40mins. (Seasonal)

20

123

3

4

5

Lady Isle

Irvine Bay

Scottish Maritime
IRVINE
Irvine Mains
Dreghorn
Stanecastle
Springside
Perceton
A737
Beach Park
Crosshouse
Gatehead
Laigh Milton Viaduct
Drybridge
A759
B730
Dundonald
A78
Barassie
Loans
Troon
A759
Symington
Monktonhill
B749
A77
Monkton
GLASGOW PRESTWICK
New Prestwick
St Quivox
Whitletts
Prestwick
A79
Newton upon Ayr
AYR
Ayr
Wallacetown
Seafield
Cunning Park
Greenan Castle
Doonfoot
Heads of Ayr
Heads of Ayr Farm Park
Belleisle Estate
Robert Burns Birthplace
Alloway
Brig o' Doon
Doonholm
A719
Fisherton
943
Brown Carrick Hill
Dunure
Culroy
Knockdon
Knoweside
Electric Brae
17

Kilmaurs
Onthank
Knockentiber
Altonhill
A735
B7081
Knockinlaw
KILMARNOCK
Dean Castle
Crookedholm
A77
PAGE 196
A71
Grange
Riccarton
Hurlford
B7073
Earlston
A76
Crossroads
Craigie
Bogend
A719
Carnell
B730
Fail
Tarbolton
B744
Failford
Mossblown
Annbank
B743
Milton
Stair
Yett
B742
Gadgirth
Trabboch
Dalmilling
Belston
Joppa
Coalhall
Coylton
Hillhead
Belmont
A70
Low Coylton
Drongan
Barbieston
Sinclairston
Martnaham Loch
A713
Carcluie
Dalrymple
Minishant
Hollybush
Knockshinnoch
Rankinston
Polnessan
Kilmein Hill 1408
Patna
Lethanhill
Burnfoot
Waterside
Scottish Industrial Railway Centre
River Doon
B741

Culzean Bay
Culzean Castle
Maidenhead Bay
Maidens
A719
Turnberry Castle
Turnberry Bay
Turnberry
Matthew's Port
Dipple
60
A77
Kilgrammie
B741
Woodland Bay
Byne Hill
Glendoune
Girvan
McKechnie Institute
A714
Grey Hill 975
Tormitchell
Pinmore
River Stinchar
Barr
CHANGE FOREST
A77
Lendalfoot
Straid
Knockdaw Hill
853
109
A  B
Bennane Head
Colmonell
Knockdolian
B734
Pinwherry
Pinwherry Hill
Poundland
Bellamore
Pindonnan Craigs 1098

B7024
Maybole
A77
Whitefaulds
Church
B7023
Kirkoswald
Crossraguel Abbey
Souter Johnnie's Cottage
Kirkmichael
Kilkerran
Ruglen
Wallacetown
Dalquharran Castle
Daily
Bargany
Old Daily
Penkill
B734
Hadyard Hill 1060
Penwhapple Reservoir
Mull of Miljoan 1165
Dalquhairn
1395 Glenalla Field
Garleffin Fell 1408
Crosshill
Blairquhan Castle
Straiton
B741
16
Loch Spallander Reservoir
B7045
Dersalloch Hill
Bogton Loch
Big Hill of Glenmount 1252
Derclach Loch
Loch Finlas
Tairlaw Ring
Tairlaw Plantation
Tallaminnock
Linfern Loch
Loch Bradan Resr.
Craiglee
Stinchar Falls
Black Hill
CARRICK FOREST
Carrick Forest Drive
Loch Riecawr
Loch Macaterick
Kirriereoch Hill 2565
GALLOWAY FOREST PARK
MERRICK
Merrick 2770
Mullwharchar 2270

SOUTH
CARRICK
AYRSHIRE

Polmaddie Hill David Bell Memorial 1854
Waterhead
Rig of the Shalloch
Cairn Hill 1572
Knockinlochie
C
Tarfessock
D
1637 Macaterick

Waterside
A719
Whitelee Forest
Whitelee Hill 927
Strathaven
Blackwood
Kirkfieldbank
LANARK
New Lanark
Kirkmuirhill
Auchenheath
Stonebyres Holdings
New Lanark World Heritage Site
Falls of Clyde
127  E
A71  F
128  G
H

Moscow
Loudoun Castle
Newmilns  Darvel
Greenholm
Galston
Priestland
A71
Drumclog
B743
Hawkwood Hill
Kype Muir
Kype Reservoir
Kype
Logan Water
Sandford
Caldermill
B7086
Boghead
Lesmahagow
Turfholm
Brocketsbrae
SOUTH
Douglas Water
A70
B744
Sornhill
Loudoun Hill 1036
Mill Rig 1099
Glengavel Resr.
Dunside Resr.
Logan Reservoir
Nutberry Hill 1712
Tod Law
R. Nethan
Coalburn
Bellfield
Braehead
Rigside
HAPPENDON
Douglas Water
Uddington
Douglas
M74
A70

Crosshands
Auchmillan
Montgarswood
B7037
Little Hartmidden
Twopenny Knowe
Bibblon Hill
1530
Middlefield Law
Greenock Bridge
Black Hill
Glenbuck
1532
Glenbuck Loch
Glespin
Hareshaw Hill
Hagshaw Hill
St Bride's Church
Pagie Hill
LANARKSHIRE
M74

Cessnock Water
Blackside
Sorn
B743
River Ayr
Greenock Mains
Smallburn
Muirkirk
Kames
Urit Hill
13
Douglas
Heritage
M74

Mauchline
Ballochmyle
Catrine
Haugh
Shawwood
B713
B705
Airds Moss
A70
Wardlaw Hill 1631
Cairn Table 1945
Mount Stuart 1568
Common Hill
Dungeaton Water
White Hill
20
B797

Roddenloft
Crosshill
KYLE
Lugar Water
A76
B7036
Auchinleck
Lugar
Holmhead
Logan
Cronberry
Dalblair
Auchtitench Hill 1527
Kirkland Hill 1675
Fingland
Cairn Kinny
Spango Hill 1392
Spango Bridge
B740
LOW
Crawfordjohn
Rake Law 1621
118
Leadhills
Wanlockhead

Ochiltree
A70
Dumfries House
Terringzean Castle
Baird Institute
Cumnock
Craigens
Netherthird
Garrallan
Skares
B7046
AYRSHIRE
Carsgailoch Hill
Pathhead
Mansfield
Kirkland
Wedder Dod 1460
Conrig Hill 1591
Stood Hill 1926
Beam Engine
Lead Mining
Wanloc

Stannery Knowe 1192
Waterhead
Bankglen
New Cumnock
Connel Park
R. Nith
A76
Kirkconnel
Kelloholm
Crawick
Sanquhar
SOUTHERN
UPLANDS
NITHSDALE
Thirstane Hill
1912

Kyle Forest
Benbeoch 1522
Burnton
Pennyvenie
Dalmellington
Bellsbank
Burnside
Dalleagles
B741
Enoch Hill 1866
Milray Hill
Craignane 1646
Prickeny Hill
The Knipe 1886
Hare Hill
Quintin Knowe 2298
Blackcraig Hill
Afton Water
Afton Resr.
Craigdarroch
Kello Water
Mid Hill
Euchan Water
Barr
Tolbooth
Sanquhar Castle
Post Office
Mennock
B797
Shiel Hill 1567
Cairn Hill 1473
Enterkinfoot
A76
Enoch

A713
Campbell's Hill 1485
Windy Standard
Brockloch Rig
Waterhead Hill 1768
Cairnsmore of Carsphairn 2614
Dodd Hill
Benbrack
Windy Standard
Alhang
Craiglorg Hill 2232
Corse Hill
Polskeoch
Countam
Ox Hill 1657
Blackcraig Hill 1639
Cairnkinna Hill 1817
Chanlockfoot
Drumlanrig Castle
Holm of Drumlanrig
Tibbers Castle
Burnhead
Carronbridge
B732
Thornhill

Loch Muck
Loch Doon
Craigmalloch
Black Craig
Meaul 2280
Corserine 2669
THE GLENKENS
DUNDEUGH FOREST
Carsphairn
Heritage Centre
B729
A713
Knowehead
Kendoon Loch
Polmaddy Settlement
Forrest Lodge
Loch Harrow
Loch Minnoch
Lamford Hill
Water of Deugh
Carsphairn Forest
Beninner
Cairnsmore of Carsphairn
DUMFRIES
&
GALLOWAY
Corlae
Benbrack 1906
Benbuie
Manquhill Hill
Wether Hill 1747
Dalwhat Water
Shinnel Water
Auchenbrack
Bennan
Tynron
Keir Mill
A702
Penpont
Keir Hills 1172
Closeburn

Stroanfreggan
B729
High Bridge of Ken
Culmark
Lochinvar
Butterhole Bridge
Craigmuie
Craiginn
Moniaive
A702
Kirkland
B729
Wallaceton
Glenmidge
Bogrie Hill 1471

110  E
F
G
111
A702
H

A713

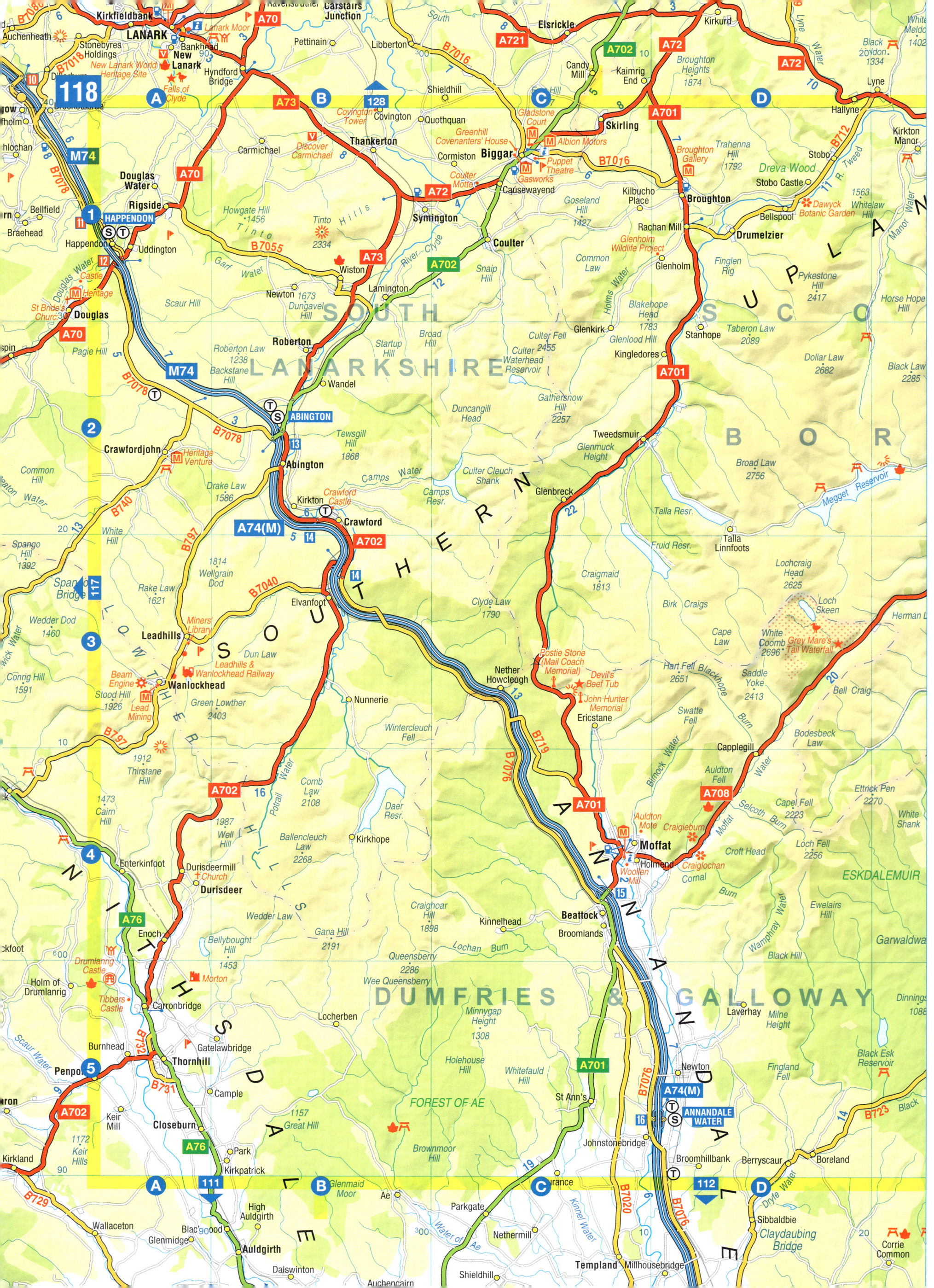

Auchenheath
Kirkfieldbank
LANARK
Stonebyres Holdings
New Lanark
New Lanark World Heritage Site
Lanark Moor
Ravenstruther
Carstairs Junction
Elsrickle
Kirkurd
Lyne
White Meldo
Black Meldon 1334

A70 A721 A702 A72 A72
Bankhead
Hyndford Bridge
Falls of Clyde
Douglas Water
Rigside
Happendon
Uddingston
Douglas
St Bride's Church
Heritage

South Lanarkshire

Pettinain
Libberton
B7016
Covington Tower
Covington
Quothquan
Candy Mill
Kaimrig End
Broughton Heights 1874
Broughton Gallery
Trahenna Hill 1792
Stobo
Stobo Castle
R. Tweed
Kirkton Manor

Carmichael
Discover Carmichael
Thankerton
Greenhill Covenanters' House
Gladstone Court
Skirling
Albion Motors
A701
Kilbucho Place
Dreva Wood

Cormiston
Biggar
Puppet Theatre
Gasworks
Causewayend
Broughton
Bellspool
Dawyck Botanic Garden
Whitelaw Hill

Symington
Coulter
A702
Coulter Motte
Snaip Hill
Goseland Hill 1427
Rachan Mill
Glenholm Wildlife Project
Glenholm
Drumelzier
Pykestone Hill 2417
Horse Hope Hill

Newton
Dungavel Hill 1673
Lamington
Startup Hill
Broad Hill
Culter Fell 2455
Culter Waterhead Reservoir
Glenkirk
Glenwood Hill
Common Law
Finglen Rig
Stanhope
Taberon Law 2089
Dollar Law 2682
Black Law 2285

Roberton
Roberton Law 1238
Backstane Hill
Wandel
Gathersnow Hill 2257
Kingledores
A701
Broad Law 2756
Megget Reservoir

Abington
Duncangill Head
Tewsgill Hill 1868
Culter Cleuch Shank
Tweedsmuir
Glenmuck Height
Lochcraig Head 2625
Loch Skeen
Herman

Crawfordjohn
Heritage Venture
Drake Law 1586
Kirkton
Crawford Castle
Crawford
Camps Water
Camps Resr.
Glenbreck
Craigmaid 1813
Talla Resr.
Fruid Resr.
Talla Linnfoots
White Coomb 2696
Grey Mare's Tail Waterfall

A74(M)
A702
Elvanfoot
White Hill
B797
Wellgrain Dod
B7040
Clyde Law 1790
Craigmaid
Birk Craigs
Cape Law
Saddle Yoke 2413
Bell Craig

Leadhills
Miners' Library
Leadhills & Wanlockhead Railway
Dun Law
Nunnerie
Nether Howcleugh
Hart Fell 2651
Blackhope
Bodesbeck Law

Wanlockhead
Beam Engine
Stood Hill 1926
Lead Mining
Green Lowther 2403
Wintercleuch Fell
Bostie Stone (Mail Coach Memorial)
Devil's Beef Tub
John Hunter Memorial
Ericstane
Swatte Fell
Capplegill
Auldton Fell
A708
Ettrick Pen 2270
White Shank

Thirstane Hill 1473
Cairn Hills
A702
Comb Law 2108
Daer Resr.
Kirkhope
B7076
A701
Auldton Mote
Craigieburn
Moffat
Croft Head
Loch Fell 2256

Enterkinfoot
Durisdeermill
Durisdeer Church
Durisdeer
Well Hill 1987
Ballencleuch Law 2268
Craighoar Hill 1898
Kinnelhead
Beattock
Broomlands
Holmend
Woollen Mill
Craiglochan
Cornal
ESKDALEMUIR

A76
Enoch
Drumlanrig Castle
Tibbers Castle
Morton
Carronbridge
Wedder Law
Gana Hill 2191
Queensberry 2286
Wee Queensberry
Lochan Burn
Laverhay
Milne Height
Ewelairs Hill
Garwaldwa
Black Hill
Dinnings 1085

Penpo
Thornhill
Gatelawbridge
Cample
Locherben
DUMFRIES & GALLOWAY
Minnygap Height 1308
Holehouse Hill
Whitefauld Hill
FOREST OF AE
St Ann's
A701
Wamphray Water
Newton
A74(M)
Fingland Fell
Black Esk Reservoir

Keir Mill
Closeburn
A76
Park
Kirkpatrick
Great Hill 1157
Brownmoor Hill
Johnstonebridge
Broomhillbank
ANNANDALE WATER
Berryscaur
Boreland
B723
Black

Kirkland
Keir Hills 1172
Wallaceton
Glenmidge
Blac
Auldgirth
High Auldgirth
Glenmaid Moor
Ae
Parkgate
rance
Nethermill
Water of Ae
Shieldhill
Templand
Millhousebridge
Broomhillbank
Sibbaldie
Claydaubing Bridge
Corrie Common
Dalswinton
Auchencairn
Kinnel Water
Dryfe Water

M74
A73
A70
A76
A702
B7078

A703
A7
A68
A6105
119

Peebles
Glentress Forest
Dunslair Heights 1975
Whitethope Law
Windlestraw Law 2163
Black Law 1764
Great Law 1666
William Law 1314
Legerwood
Huntlywood
Greenknowe Tower
Nether Blainslie
LAUDERDALE
B6397
B6400

Cross Kirk
Kings Muir
John Buchan Story
Cademuir Hill
Kailzie
Glentress
Horsbrugh Ford
Lee Pen 1648
Priesthorpe Hill 1802
Pirn Hill Fort
St Ronan's Wells
Knowes Hill 1222
Buckholm
Langshaw
Earlston
Redpath
Smailholm Tower
129
130
A72
B709
B710
B6356
1

Cardrona Forest
Preston Law
Hundleshope Heights 2218
Wallace's Hill 1507
Traquair House
Innerleithen
Walkerburn
Robert Smail's Printing Works
Clovenfords
Caddonfoot
Meigle Hill 1389
Old Gala House
Lowood
Tweedbank
Gattonside
Newstead
Leaderfoot
GALASHIELS
Melrose Roman
Clintmains
Bemersyde
A72
B7062
A707
A7
B6360
B6374
B6360
B6374

Traquair
Kirkhouse
Glen House
Elibank and Traquair Forest
Ashiestiel Hill
Peel
Boleside
Abbotsford
Darnick
Dingleton
Eildon
Newtown St Boswells
Abbey
Dryburgh
Mertoun Bridge
Mertoun House
St Boswells
Deuchar Law 1779
Blake Muir
Minch Moor 1859
Broomy Law
Yair Hill Forest
Lindean Mill Glass
Cauldshiels Hill
Eildon Hills
Bowden
Maxton
A699
B709
B7060
B6359
B6360
B6398
B6399

Dun Rig 2441
Yarrow Ford
Linglie Hill
Lindean
Sir Walter Scott's Courtroom
A708
A699

Deer Law
Yarrow
Yarrow Water 1645
Newark Castle
Bowhill House & Country Estate
Bowhill
Philiphaugh
Lochcarron Mill
Selkirk
Hallwell's House
Longnewton
Sandystones
Ancrum
A68
Ancrum Moor 1545

Cappercleuch
St Mary's Loch
The Wiss 1933
Loch of the Lowes
A708
Mountbenger
Yarrow Feus
Fastheugh Hill
Brockhill
Ettrickbridge
FOREST
Ashkirk
Midlem
Lilliesleaf
Bloomfield
Lanton
Castle Jail
Newton
A698
B709
B6400
B6453
B6359
B6405

Black Knowe Head 1805
Gilmanscleuch
Caver's Hill 1209
Essenside Loch
Akermoor Loch
Shaws Under Loch
Hassendean
Minto Hills 905
Minto
Spittal-on-Rule
Fatlips Castle
Dunion Hill
A7
B709
B6399

Tushielaw
Dun Knowe
Hellmoor Loch
Redfordgreen
Alemoor Loch
Drinkstone Hill
Appletreehall
Horsleyhill
Clarilaw
Leyden Monument
Denholm
Bedrule
Rubers Law 1391
120
B711
B6359
B6405

James Hogg Monument
Ettrick
Ramsey Knowe
Law Kneis 1634
Buccleuch
Smasha Hill
Scottish Borders Art Glass
Burnfoot
Wilton
Cauldmill
3
B711
A698
A6088

Black Knowe 1804
Glenkerry
Sauchie Law
Redcleuch Edge 1278
Roberton
Burnfoot
Deanburnhaugh
Newmill
Branxholme
HAWICK
Borders Textile Towerhouse
Kirkton
Leyden Obelisk
Hobkirk
Bonchester Bridge
Chesters
B709
B711
B6399
A6088
B6357

CRAIK FOREST
Craik
Hott Hill
White Hill 987
Southdean
Green Law

Cross Hill
Craik Cross Hill
Pike Hill 1369
Dryden Fell
Allan Water
Stobs Castle
WAUCHOPE FOREST
Carlin Tooth
B709
TEVIOTDALE

FOREST
Davington
Blaeberry Hill
Eweslees Knowe
Teviothead
River Teviot
Skelfhill
Skelfhill Pen 1746
The Pike 1516
Langburnshiels
Wyndburgh Hill
Fanna Hill 1688
Lamblair Hill
Needs Law
Hartshorn Pike
A7
600

Kagyu Samye Ling
Eskdalemuir
Jamestown
Causeway Grain Head
Comb Hill
Millstone Edge
Maiden Paps
Cauldcleuch Head 1996
Greatmoor Hill 1966
Leap Hill
Sandy Edge
Saughtree Fell
Deadwater
4

Hog Hill
White Hope Edge
Mosspaul
Tudhope Hill 1965
Wisp Hill 1953
Geordie's Hill
Din Fell 1737
Hermitage Castle
Hermitage Chapel
Hermitage
Amton Fell 1464
Saughtree
Foulmire Heights
Kielder
Butt
Kielder Viaduct
Toll
V
5
B709
B6357
B6399

CASTLE O'ER FOREST
Castle O'er
Broad Head 1614
Faw Side 1722
Crumpton Hill 1575
Roan Fell 1862
North Birny Fell 902
Wilson's Pike
SCOTLAND
ENGLAND
Black Knowe
KIELDER FOREST

Hart Fell 1087
The Shin
Calkin Rig 1478
Bentpath
Telford Memorial
Kirkstile or Ewes
Watch Hill
Black Edge 1464
Newcastleton
Copshaw Holm
LIDDESDALE
Newcastleton Forest
Lewis
Rough Pike
E
F
A7
G
113
H
B709

Glentenmont Height
Clan Armstrong
MacDiarmid Memorial
Tinnis Hill 1326
Millholm Cross
Liddesdale Heritage Centre
Glendhu Hill
KIELDER WA

SCOTTISH BORDERS

Legerwood · Huntlywood · Gordon · Fans · Leitholm · Lambden · Eccles · Birgham · Coldstream · Cornhill-on-Tweed · Etal · Ford · Duddo · Castle Heaton · Felkington

A68 · A6105 · A6089 · A697 · A698 · A6112 · A6437

Earlston · Nenthorn · Stichill · Ednam · Kelso · Carham · Wark · West Learmouth · East Learmouth · Pressen · Crookham · Branxton · Flodden · Kimmerston · Milfield

Greenknowe Tower · Mellerstain House · Smailholm · Hume · Hume Castle · Sweethope Hill 730 · James Thomson Obelisk · Wark Castle · Flodden Field Monument · Flodden Field 1513 · Heatherslaw Light Railway · Heatherslaw Mill · Lady Waterford Hall

Redpath · Newstead · Leaderfoot · Melrose · Bemersyde · Clintmains · Dryburgh · Newtown St Boswells · St Boswells · Maxton · Roxburgh · Heiton · Maxwellheugh · Hadden · Sprouston · Lempitlaw · Mindrum · Pawston · Kilham · Lanton · Kirknewton · Coupland · Akeld · Yeavering · Humbleton

B6397 · B6404 · B6360 · B6398 · A699 · B6352 · B6350 · B6396 · B6357

Smailholm Tower · Floors · Abbey · Mertoun Bridge · Mertoun House · Eildon · Abbey · Roman · Hoselaw Loch · Houseden Hill 877 · Maelmin Heritage Trail

Longnewton · Sandystones · Bloomfield · Ancrum · Crailing · Eckford · Morebattle · Town Yetholm · Kirk Yetholm · Linton · Primsidemill · Hethpool · Westnewton · Yeavering Bell · Langleeford

Longnewton Forest · Ancrum Moor 1545 · Waterloo Monument · Peniel Heugh · Teviot Game Fare Smokery & Water Gardens · Bowmount Forest · Linton Hill 926 · Kale Water · Bowmount Water · Goldsmouth Hill · White Law · Steer Rig · Newton Tors 1761 · Preston Hill · Cold Law 1485 · Fredden Hill

A698 · B6400 · B6401 · B6436 · A68 · B6405 · B6358

Minto · Spittal-on-Rule · Denholm · Bedrule · Newton · Lanton · Jedburgh · Nisbet · Bonjedward · Crailinghall · Cessford · Whitton · Hownam · Mowhaugh · Sourhope · Craik Moor 1496 · The Curr · The Schil 1985

Fatlips Castle · Minto Hills 905 · Mary, Queen of Scots' · Castle Jail · Abbey · Monteviot House · Harestanes Countryside · Whitton Loch · Hownam Law 1472 · Crookedshaws Hill · SCOTLAND · ENGLAND

Rubers Law 1391 · Dunion Hill · Ferniehirst · Mossburnford · Oxnam · Swinside Hall · Capehope Burn · Mozie Law · Windy Gyle 2032 · Cock Law · THE CHEVIOT 2674

Leyden Obelisk · A6088 · Bonchester Bridge · Hobkirk · Chesters · Camptown · Jedforest Deer & Farm Park · Woden Law 1388 · Whitestone Hill · Beefstand Hill 1842 · Loft Hill · Bell Hill · Shillmoor

Southdean · Jed Water · Oxnam Water · Upper Hindhope · Blindburn · Barrowburn · Kidland Forest · Wether Cairn · High Knowes · Biddlestone

WAUCHOPE FOREST · Green Law · Carlin Tooth · Needs Law · Deerlee Knowe · Leithope Forest · Redeswire Fray 1575 · Carter Bar · Hungry Law 1644 · Leap Hill · Grindstone Law · Clennell · Alwinton · Castle Ruins · Harbottle · Sharperton

Fanna Hill 1688 · Lamblair Hill · Hartshorn Pike · Kielderhead Moor · Girdle Fell · Ellis Crag · Catcleugh · Byrness · Catcleugh Resr. · Dour Hill · R. Coquet · Shillmoor · Linshiels · DANGER AREA · Lady's Well · Holystone

Peel Fell 1975 · Deadwater · Saughtree · Foulmire Heights · REDESDALE FOREST · Hindhope Law · Sills · Redesdale Camp · Brigantium · Rochester · North Yardhope · Rushy Knowe 1065 · NORTHUMBERLAND NATIONAL PARK

Kielder · Butteryhaugh · Kielder Castle · Kielder Viaduct · Toll · Emblehope Moor · Rooken Edge · Blackburn Common · Horsley · Elishaw · Otterburn Hall · Otterburn · Blakeman's Law · Blakehope Fell · Padon Hill 1240 · Otterburn Camp · Otterburn 1388 · Elsdon · Castle

KIELDER FOREST · Earl's Seat 1303 · Highgreen Manor · Troughend Common · Old Town · A696 · Rayleees · Winter's Gibbet

Dinmont Lairs · Leaplish Waterside Park · Kielder Water · Black Middens Bastle House · Gatehouse · Greenhaugh · West Woodburn · East Woodburn

KIELDER WATER & FOREST PARK · Rough Pike · Birds of Prey Centre · Tower Knowe · Yarrow · Falstone · Stannersburn · North Tyne · Lanehead · B6320 · DANGER AREA · A68 · B6341

HOLY ISLAND
LINDISFARNE

Berrington Law
B6525
Goswick
Haggerston
Beal
Holy Island
Keel Head
Lindisfarne Centre
Lindisfarne Priory
Castle Point
Burrows Hole

Bowsden
Berrington
12 60 A1 131
Fenham
Fenwick
West Kyloe East Kyloe
Kyloe Hills

Lowick
B6353
Barmoor
B6353
B6525
Buckton
Elwick
Ross
Budle Bay
Waren Mill
Budle
Bamburgh
B1342
B1340

Nesbit
Doddington
Hetton Steads
Holburn
St Cuthbert's Cave
North Hazelrigg
Detchant
Middleton
Easington
Bradford
Spindlestone
Burton
Grace Darling
New Shoreston
Staple Sound
FARNE ISLANDS
Chapel
Longstone
Inner Sound

West Horton East Horton
South Hazelrigg
Lyham
Belford
Bellshill
Warenton
Adderstone
Lucker
Elford
North Sunderland
Seahouses
Heritage
Carr End
Lifeboat Station

Weetwood Hall
Homildon Hill 1402
Wooler
B6349
Greendykes
Chatton
B6348
Warenford
Newham
Swinhoe
West Fleetham
Chathill
Beadnell
Lime Kilns
Beadnell Bay
Snook Point

Earle
North Middleton
South Middleton
Haugh Head
A697
Chillingham
Wild Cattle
Ros Castle
Hepburn
Newtown
Lilburn Tower
East Lilburn
876 Cateran Hill
Middle Moor
North Charlton
Ellingham
Preston
Tower
Brunton
Doxford
Tughall
High Newton-by-the-Sea
Low Newton-by-the-Sea
Embleton Bay

Langlee Crags
Ilderton
Roseden
Roddam
Old Bewick
Harehope
South Charlton
Armstrong's Household & Farming
Rock
Christon Bank
Embleton
Dunstanburgh
NORTH SEA

Greensidehill
Wooperton
Hedgeley Moor 1464
New Bewick
Percy's Cross
Beanley
Eglingham
B6346
East Bolton
Shipley
B6347
Rennington
Stamford
Dunstan
Craster
Ingram
Northumberland National Park
Brandon
Branton
Powburn
Glanton Pyke
Titlington
Heiferlaw Tower
Littlemill
Howick
Howick Hall

Prendwick
Alnham
Little Ryle
Great Ryle
Eslington Hall
Yetlington
Glanton
Bolton
Abberwick
Hulne Priory
Hulne Park
B6341
B6346
Littlehoughton
Longhoughton
Boulmer

Scrainwood
Whittingham
Thrunton
Callaly
ALNWICK
Abbey Bailiffgate
1093
Denwick
House of Hardy
B6341
Boulmer
B1339

Netherton
Burradon
High Trewhitt
Lorbottle
A697
Edlingham
Newton-on-the-Moor
Shilbottle Grange
High Buston
Lesbury
Hipsburn
Bilton
Alnmouth
B1338
Alnmouth Bay

UMBERLAND
Cartington
Snitter
Northumberland National Park
Cragside
FOREST
Warton
B6341
Rothbury
Thropton
Newtown
Whitton
Cragside
B6342
ROTHBURY
Longframlington
Shilbottle
Hazon
Swarland
Old Swarland
Morwick
Guyzance
Eastfield Hall
Hermitage
Birling
Warkworth
Gloster Hill
Amble
Coquet Island
Hauxley Haven

Hepple
Caistron
Flotterton
Great Tosson
Swindon
Bickerton
1444 Tosson Hill
B6344
Pauperhaugh
Weldon
Brinkburn Priory
Low Hesleyhurst
Longframlington
R. Coquet
Felton
West Thirston
East Thirston
Acklington
B6345
North Broomhill
South Broomhill
Togston
Radcliffe
Hadston
Druridge Bay
Red Row

HARWOOD FOREST
Fallowlees
Fontburn Reservoir
Forestburn Gate
Wingates
Longhorsley
Rayburn Lake
Causey Park
Eshott
West Chevington
Widdrington
A1068
Druridge Bay

Nunnykirk
Ewesley
Netherwitton
Stanton
Bide-a-Wee Cottage
Fenrother
Tritlington
Stobswood
Widdrington Station
Cresswell
Ellington
Tower
Lynemouth
A1068

B6342
Herterton House
Longwitton
Pigdon
Hebron
B115
Longhirst
Ulgham
Linton Colliery
Sanctuary Wildlife Care Centre
B1337
A1068
A189
Woodhorn
Beacon Point

Rothley
Scot's Gap
B6343
Cambo
Hartburn
Throphill
Mitford
A192
MORPETH
A196
High Church
A197
Pegswood
ASHINGTON
Heritage
Woodhorn
Wansbeck Riverside
Bothal
Sheepwash
Hirst
North Seaton
Newbiggin-by-the-Sea
Queen Elizabeth
B1334
Stakeford
North Seaton Colliery

ISLE OF GIGHA

West Tarbert Bay
East Tarbert Bay
Eilean Garbh
Gamhna Gigha
Point
Druimyeon Bay
Mill Loch
Ardminish
Ardminish Bay
Achamore
Craro Island
Gigalum Island
Cara Island
Mull of Cara
A' Chleit
Sound of Gigha

Ballochroy
Rhunahaorine
Tayinloan
Killean
Muasdale
Cnoc Donn 660
Loch Ciaran
Loch Garasdale
Loch a' Ghatha
Cruach Mhic Fhiugain 813
Loch an Fhraoich
Loch Dirigadale Cnoc nan Craobh 1058
Loch Ulagadale
Uillt
Leth
Clachaig Water
Barr Water

Fraoich
Fuar Larach
Loch Romain
Crossaig Glen
Loch nam Breac 791
Beinn Bhreac
Loch Tana
Carradale Water

Clachaig Bay
Eascairt Point
Crossaig
Cour Bay
Cour
Rubha Airigh Bheirg
Grogport

B842
13
E 80
BUTE
KINTYRE

Glenacardoch Point
Port a' Bhorrain
Glenbarr
Glenbarr Abbey
Arnicle
Barr Glen
Blary Hill 930
Beinn an Tuirc 1490
Beinn Bhreac 1398
Cnoc nan Gabhar
Diollaid Mhor

Network Carradale Heritage Centre
Carradale
Dippen
Port Righ
Torrisdale
Torrisdale Castle Organic Tannery
Carradale Bay
Carradale Point
Rubha nan Sgarbh

Dougarie Point
B879

Bellochantuy Bay
Bellochantuy
Meall Buidhe 1228
Bordadubh Water
A'Chruach 1120
Saddell Water
Saddell Glen
Saddell Abbey
Saddell
Saddell Bay

Port Corbert
Cnoc Buidhe 1023
Lussa Loch
Sgreadan Hill 1302
Tangy Loch
Skeroblingarry
Ugadale
Ugadale Point
Black Bay

19
B842

Machrihanish Bay
Kilchenzie
Ranachan Hill 696
Glen Lussa Water
Glenlussa
Peninver
Aucha Lochy
Ardnacross Bay

A83
KNAPDALE
13

Machrihanish
CAMPBELTOWN
Campbeltown
Springbank Distillery
Mill Knowe
Drumlemble
Stewarton
Heritage Centre
Cross
Island Davaar

Campbeltown to Ballycastle 1hr. 30 mins. (Seasonal)

B843
B842
6

Earadale Point
Rubha Dùin Bhàin
Rubha' a' Mharaiche
A' Chruach
Cnoc Moy 1465
The Slate 1263
Killypole Loch
Tirfergus Hill 854
Killellan
Beinn Ghuilean 1155
Achinhoan Head

Dalsmirren
Cnoc Odhar 908
Conie Glen
Tod Hill
Kerran Hill 788
Feochaig
Johnston's Point

Remuil Hill
Glen Breackerie Water
Conieglen Water
Chiscan Water
Balnabraid Glen

ARGYLL
B842
10

Beinn na Lice 1404
Glemanuilt Hill
766
Lephenstrath
Carskiey
Feorlan
High Keil
Southend
Brunerican Bay
Macharioch
Polliwilline Bay
Cove Point

MULL OF KINTYRE
Rubha Chlachan
Port Mean
Black Point
Sheep Island
Sanda Island

175

KILBRANNAN SOUND

Tarbert to (Seas)
Rubha Creagan Dubha
South Newton
Torr Meadhonach 1089
Lochranza
Catacol
Arran Distillery
Torr Nead an Eoin
A841
1057

Lenimore
Thundergay
Pirnmill
Alltgobhlach
Coire Fhionn Lochan
Whitefarland Point
Whitefarland
Imachar
Mullach Buidhe 2366
Loch Tanna
Caisteal Abhail 2817
Cir M 262
Beinn Tarsuinn 2710
Sail Chalmadale

ISLE OF A
NO AYRS

Dougarie
Beinn Lochain 749
Iorsa Water
Auchencar
An Tunna 1184
Garbh Thorr
Garbh Allt

Auchagallon Stone Circle
Machrie
Machrie Bay
Machrie Moor Stone Circles
Tormore
Moss Farm Road Stone Circle
A' Chruach 1686
Beinn Bhreac 1649
Cnoc a' Chapuill 1371

Drumadoon Point
Torbeg
Shedog
Shiskine
Birchburn
Ballymichael
Blackwaterfoot
North Feorline
Drumadoon Bay
Kilpatrick
Kilpatrick Dun
South Feorline
The Torr
Loch Cnoc an Loch

Brown Head
Cnoc Reamhar 737
Glenree
Corriecravie
Bennecarrigan
Torr A'chaisteal Fort
Sliddery
Torrylin Creamery
Lagg
Torrylin Cairn
Kilmory
Sliddery Water

B880

A841
A83
90 80 70 60
60 50 40 30 20 10 600

Bay
St Blane's
Dunagoil Bay
Dunagoil
Mid Kirkton
Robertson Museum & Aquarium
Fairlie Road
Castle
Southannan
Kaim Hill 1271
Resr.
Loch
Beith
Glengarnock
Gateside
Hessilhead
B777
B784
B780
Longbar
B737
Highgat
B706
B7
Highfield
Knockendon Resr.
Baidland Hill 1102
Rye Water
Auldmuir Resr.
G
Crosbie
Drakemyre
The Den
Dalry
H
123
A78
Power Station
Campbelton
Portencross
Craft Town
West Kilbride
NORTH AYRSHIRE
CUNNINGHAME
Auchenmade
Auchenbiber
A736
The Tan
Little Cumbrae Island
Gull Point
F
Farland Head
Ardneil Bay
Seamill
B7048
B7047
B782
B781
B780
Mill Glen Resr.
Ashgrove Loch
B714
Dalgarven
Ayrshire Country Life & Costume
A737
Lylestone
B778
Torranyard
Montgreenan
Kilwinning
Doura
A736
B785
B769
Cunninghamhe
B7080
Eglinton
Abbey
Girdle Toll
Perce
A738
A78
B779
Stanecastle
Stanecastle
Springside
Knocke
Millstone Point
126
E
Firth of Clyde
Ardrossan
Stevenston
Saltcoats
Horse Isle
North Ayrshire
Scottish Maritime
Irvine Mains
Dreghorn
Crossho
IRVINE
A737
A71
Irvine
Crossh
Gate
North Sannox
Sannox
Corrie
Glen Sannox
Sannox Bay
Goatfell 2866
126
Merkland Point
Ardrossan to Brodick 55mins.
Beach Park
Drybridge
B730
Laigh Milton Viaduct
Irvine Bay
Dundonald
A759
B730
B751
Brodick Castle
Isle of Arran Brewery
A841
Glenrosa
Isle of Arran Heritage
Brodick Bay
Brodick
Strathwhillan
B880
Corrygills
Clauchlands Point
Campbeltown to Brodick 2hrs. 20mins. (Seasonal)
Barassie
B746
A78
Loans
Troon
A759
Symington
A77
Margnaheglish
10mins.
Lamlash
Holy Island
Lamlash Bay
Monamore Bri.
Cordon
Urie Loch
A841
Kingscross Point
Kingscross
Knockenkelly
Whiting Bay
Lady Isle
B749
Monktonhill
Ardrossan to Campbeltown 2hrs. 40mins. (Seasonal)
Tighvein 1503
Carn Ban
Glenashdale Falls
Largymore
Largymeanoch
Largybeg
Largybeg Point
Monkton
GLASGOW PRESTWICK
New Prestwick
B74
St Quivox
Ann
Kilmory Water
Shannochie
East Bennan
Levencorroch
Dippin
Kildonan
Dippin Head
Sound of Pladda
Prestwick
A79
Newton upon Ayr
Whitletts
B743
West Bennan
Bennan Head
Pladda
AYR
Ayr
Dalmilling
A70
Seafield
Cunning Park
Belmont
Bels
A70
116
Greenan Castle
Heads of Ayr Farm Park
Belleisle Estate
Rozelle House
Robert Burns Birthplace
Alloway
Brig o'Doon
Doonholm
A742
Heads of Ayr
Doonfoot
Doonholm
A713
Ailsa Craig 1109
E
Dunure
Fisherton
943 Brown Carrick Hill
A719
Culroy
Carclure
SOUTH
A713
B7034
Dunure
Knockdon
Knoweside
Dalrymple
Minishant
4
B742
Electric Brae
Culzean Bay
Culzean Castle
B7023
Maybole
Kirkmichael
Maidenhead Bay
Maidens
A77
Whitefaulds
B7023
Turnberry Castle
A719
Crossraguel Abbey
Kirkoswald
Souter Johnnie's Cottage
AYRSHIRE
Crosshill
Blairquhan Castle
B741
B7045
Turnberry Bay
Turnberry
Matthew's Port
Dipple
Kilkerran
Ruglen
Straiton
1395 Glenalla Field
Wallacetown
Kilgrammie
Dalquharran Castle
Dailly
B7035
A77
B741
Bargany
B734
Old Dailly
G
Hadyard Hill 1060
Penwhapple Reservoir
H
Garleffin Fell 1408
Woodland Bay
F
Girvan
McKechnie Institute
Glendoune
Penkill
B734
Saugh Hill 971
1165 Mull of Miljoan
B703
Byne
Tallaminnoc
Linfern Loch
Dalquhairn
Black Hill
Stinchar Falls

20 30 150

90 A B C D
132

Corpach Bay

COLONSAY

Eilean a' Chladaich

Scalasaig

Aird

Colonsay

Loch Staosnaig
40

Rubha Dubh

Garvard

Eilean Leathann

Colonsay to Port Askaig 1hr. 10mins. (Seasonal)

Allt an Tairbh
Rainberg Mór
1487

Shian Bay

Dubh Eilean

Priory
Oronsay

ORONSAY

Eilean Ghaoideamal

Eilean nan Ron

Caolas Mór

Ceann Riobha

Loch an Tuim Uaine

Loch Righ Mor

Cruib
1036

Shian River

Loch Righ Beag

Loch Lùbanach

Rubh'an t-Sailein

80

JURA

Lochan Maol an t-sornaich

Post Rocks

RUBHA A'MHAIL

Rubh' a' chrois-aoinidh

Loch Tarbert

Cnoc

Rubha Bholsa

Glen Batrick

Allt na Gile

Loch an Aircill

Beinn Bhreac
1439

Loch Lesgamaill

Nave Island

Sgarbh Breac
1195

ARGYLL

Beinn an Oir
2576

Loch an Oir

Eilean Beag

Sgarbh Dubh
965

Loch Smigeadail

1037

JURA FOREST

PAPS OF JURA

Beinn a' Chaolais
2477

Loch a' Chnuic Bhric

Corran

Ardnave Point

Gortantaoid

Beinn Bhreac
940

Bunnahabhain

Distillery

Ardnahoe Loch

Lochan Gleann Astaile

Gleann Astaile

Glas Bheinn
1839

Gleann Iubharnadeal

Knockrome

70

Tòn Mhór

Loch Laingeadail

Kilnave

Loch an Fhir Mhór

Loch Staoisha

Caol Ila

Distillery

Leargybreck

Ardfernal

Jura

Braigo

Sanaigmore

B8018

Loch Còrr

Rubha Lamanais

Grulinbeg

Leckgruinart

Loch Gruinart

Keills

Port Askaig
(Port Asgaig)

Feolin Ferry

Keils

Loch na Mile

Small Isles

Saligo Bay

Gruinart

B8017

Loch Allan

Sound of Islay

Isle of Jura Distillery

Craighouse

Coul Point

Saligo

Loch Gorm

Castle

ISLAY

B8018

Loch Sibhinn

Loch Drolsay

Abhainn Ghlas

R. Sorn

Ballygrant

8

Loch Ballygrant

Loch Lossit

Loch a' Bhaile-Mhargaidh

Ullibh

Brat Bheinn
1123

Cabrach

A846

Port na Birlinne

Machir Bay

Kilchoman

Distillery

Cnoc Dubh

Blackrock

A847

Carnain

Islay Ales Brewery

Fallabus

Kilmeny

Esknish

Glas Eilean

Ardfin

Na Cùiltean

Kilchiaran Bay

Conisby

Carraigo Dhubh

Distillery

Bruichladdich

Redhouses

Islay Woolen Mill

Bridgend
(Beul an Atha)

Beinn Dubh
875

Am Fraoch Eilean

Rubha na Tràille

Kilchiaran

Loch Gearach

Octomore

Loch Indaal

Distillery

Bowmore

Church

Dun Nosebridge Hillfort

Brosdale Island

Cultoon Stone Circle

Beinn Tart a' Mhill
760

Port Charlotte

Natural History Centre

Islay Life

RHINNS OF ISLAY

Lossit

Neribus

Laggan

Laggan Point

B8016

Mulindry

Laggan Bri.

River Laggan

River Duich

Glas Bheinn
1544

Loch Allallaidh

McArthur's Head

Kennacraig to Port Askaig 2hrs.

Octofad

A847

Port Gleann na Gaoidh

Kilennan

Beinn Bhàn
1544

Loch nan Breac

Beinn Bheigeir
1612

Claggain River

Carraig Mhór

Ardtalla

Lossit Bay

Portnahaven

Port Wemyss

Orsay

RHINNS POINT

650

Laggan Bay

Torra

Glenegedale Lots

Glenegedale

ISLAY

Beinn Uraraidh
1490

Loch Beinn Uraraidh

Beinn Sholum
1138

Leora River

Cnoc Mór na Claigin
354

Claggain Bay

Aros Bay

Kintour

Ardmore Point

Slugaide Glas

Dùn Mór Ghil

Glenastle Loch

Maol Buidhe
541

Loch Muchairt

Port Alsaig

Kintra

Loch nan Gabhar

A846

Leorin Lochs

Lochan Sholum

Loch Uigeadail

Loch Carn a' Mhaoil

Loch Leathann an Sgorra

Loch Iarnan

Kildalton Cross

Eilean Craobhach

Eilean a' Chuirn

THE OA

Cragabus

Risabus

A846

Port Ellen

Laphroaig

Distillery

Lagavulin

Ardbeg

Distillery

Dunyvaig Castle

Eilean Imersay

Eilean Bhride

Rubha na Gainmhich

MULL OF OA

Lower Killeyan

American Monument

Loch Kinnabus

Beinn Mhór
661

Rubha na Meise Bàine

Texa

50

40

20 30 40 150

A B C D

Port Ellen to Ballycastle 1hr. (Seasonal)

Kennacraig to Port Ellen 2hrs. 20mins.

Bay

Lochanan Tana

Loch Fada Cul na Beinne 60

Garbhsdale 1198

a' Gheoidh

Lochan Tana

Loch Crinan

Ardnoe Point

Crinan

Kilmahumaig

B8025

River

Cup & Ring Marks

Dunadd

Kilmichael Glassary

Loch Glashan

Gleann

River Add

Beinn Bhreac 1106 1532

Cruach a' Uillt Fhearna

Dubh Bheinn

Maol nam Damh 887

Loch Cathar nan Eun

Fishing Loch

Ardlussa

Inverlussa

Lussaginen

Lussa Point

Port Laogh

Lealt

Ruadh Sgeir

Rubha nam Bàrr

Cnoc Reamhar 870

Kilmartin

B841

Islandadd Bri.

Bellanoch

B84

Achnabreck Cup & Ring Marks

A816

Bridgend

Scotston Hill 698

90

A83 16

Lochgair

Loch Gair

H

Lussa River

1701

KNAPDALE

133

Cairnbaan

G

Lochgilphead

Crinan Canal

B8000

Lochan Chuilceacha

Cruach Chuilceachan 1428

Lussa Point

Gob Dubh

622 Beinn Sgaillinish

JURA

Tayvallich

B8025

Achnamara

FOREST

Loch Coille-Bharr

Cam Loch

Loch an Add

Gleann an Loch

KILMORY WOODLAND PARK

Port Ann

Largiemore

679 Tom an h-Iolaire

1

Loch Fyne

Eilean Dubh

Carsaig Bay

Eilean nan Coinean

Eilean Loain

Kilmichael of Inverlussa

Loch nam Breac Buidhe

Loch Clachaig 1071

Cruach nam Fiadh

Ardrishaig

A83

Castleton

Otter Ferry

Kilmodan Sculptured Stones

16

A846

927

Lagg

Barrahormid

Taynish

Loch Sween

Daltot

Loch na Craige Grainde

Cruach Lusach 1530

Cruach Brenfield 1044

Inverneil House

Eilean Mór

Liath Eilean

507 Barr Ganuisg

1144 Cruach nan Tarbh

Tarbert

Keills Chapel

B8025

Keillmore

Dunrostan

An Stuchd

1247

Loch Arail

Bàgh an Tailleir

Kilfinan Bay

Kilfinan

Cruach nan Caonra 1503

80

Port Doir' a' Chrorain

An Dunan

Island of Danna

Sween

Loch na h-Earrainn

Achahoish

Loch Fuar-Bheinne

Cruach a' Phubuill 1564

B8024

Loch Melldalloch

Melldalloch

A8003

Skervuile

Bàgh na Doide

Eilean Mor

Chapel

Kilmory

St Columba's Cave

Cnoc Stighseir 792

Abhainn Mhór

Ellary

Clachbreck

Sliabh Gaoil 1843

Erines

Port Leathan

River Meldda

872 Creag Mhór

A8003

Auchalick Bay

Tighnabruaich

Dris

M

Point of Knap

Loch Caolisport

B U T E

Baile Boidheach

Cruach a' Chaoruinn

Coire Thomag

Meall Mhór Loch

Loch Chaorunn Resr.

Ardmarnock Bay

Asgog Loch

Kames

Millho 70e

Ormsary

Ormsary Water

Dubh Chreag 1574

Meall Reamhar 1079

Barmore Island

25 mins.

Portavadie

680 Cnoc na Carraige

Miller's Bay

Cruach an Tailleir 1000

KNAPDALE FOREST

Loch a' Chaoruinn

Loch nan Torran

Loch Chaorunn Beag

Tarbert

i

A8015

East Loch Tarbert

West Tarbert

Eilean Aoidhe

Fionn Phort

Eilean na Leac

Kilbride Bay

Ardlamont House

3

Ardlamont Bay

Crear Burn

Cruach Lagain 867

Loch Racadal 1035

Cruach an Locha

Achaglachgach Forest

Kilberry Head

Sculptured Stones

Kilberry

Abhainn Learg an Uinnsinn

Loch a' Bhaillidh

Torinturk

B8024

7

6

Choc a' Bhaile-Shios 1383

Rubha Leathan

834

Camas na Ceardaich

Ardlan Poi

60

Port Mór

Carse House

Loch Stonoway

7

Dunmore

Ardpatrick

Kennacraig

Whitehouse

B8001

5

Skipness River

1 hr. 25 mins.

Inch

Ardpatrick Point

West

Loch

Portachoillan

Loch nan Gad

Loch Freasdail

Loch Crainn 882

Cruach nam Fiadh

Claonaig Water

Loch Romain

Claonaig

Skipness

Skipness

Chapel

Skipness Point

SOUND

An Dubh-sgeir

Dunskeig Bay

Clachan

A83

13

Cnoc Donn 660

Cruach Mhic-Gougain 813

886 Lochan Fraoich

704 Cnoc Creagach

Fuar Larach

B842

Claonaig Bay

30 mins.

Tarbert to Lochranza (Seasonal)

Rubha Creagan Dubha

4

SOUND

Eilean Garbh

West Tarbert Bay

East Tarbert Bay

Gamhna Gigha

Ballochroy

Loch Ciaran

Loch Garasdale

Loch a' Ghatha

Crossaig Glen

Crossaig

Eascairt Point

Loch Ranza

South Newton

Torr Meadhonach 1089

Torr Nead an Eoin

A841

Sound of Gigha

Leth

Uillt

Carradale Water

Cour Bay

Cour

Rubha Airigh Bheirg

Lochranza

Catacol

Arran Distillery

650

Cock of Ar

M

ISLE OF GIGHA

331 Creag Bhan

Druimyeon Bay

Mill Loch

Drumyeon Bay

Loch an Fhraoich

Loch Ulagadale

791 Beinn Bhreac

Loch Tana

Lenimore

Thundergay

Coire Fhionn Lochan

Gle

Ardminish

Ardminish Bay

20 mins.

Rhunahaorine

Loch Dirigadale 1058

Cnoc nan Craobh

Pirnmill

Alltgobhlach

2366 Mullach Buidhe

Loch Tanna

ISLE OF

ARRAN

Craro Island

Achamore

Tayinloan

Killean

Grogport

Whitefarland Point

Whitefarland

2710 Beinn Tarsuinn

GOATFEL

Gigalum Island

Cara Island

A83

Cruach nan Gabhar 1161

Imachar

Sail Chalmadale

40

Caisteal Abhail 2817

Cir Mhòr 2621

Mull of Cara

A' Chleit

Clachaig Water

A83

Cnoc nan Gabhar

Network Carradale Heritage Centre

B879

Carradale

Port Righ

Dougarie Point

Dougarie

Beinn 901 Lochain 749

An Tunna 1184

B88

Port a' Bhorrain

Glenbarr

Arnicle

Beinn Bhreac 1398

Barr Water

B842

Dippen

Carradale Point

Torrisdale Castle Organic Tannery

G

Imachar

B901

Garbh Allt

10

Glenbarr Abbey

Blary Hill 930

Beinn an Tuirc 1490

Torrisdale

Glenacardoch Point

60

E

F

122

Muasdale

Loch nan Breac

Coire Fhionn Lochan

Auchencar Burn

Auchagallon

Auchagallon Burn

A83

LOCH FYNE

Lochgair
Largiemore
Otter Ferry
Kilfinan Bay
Kilfinan
Melldalloch
Portavadie
Eilean Aoidhe
Kilbride Bay
Ardlamont Bay
Camas na Ceardaich
Rubha Leathan
Skipness Point
Chapel
Skipness Bay

B8000
B8003
B8000
B836
B886

Kilmodan Sculptured Stones
Clachan of Glendaruel
Glendaruel Forest
Cruach nan Cuilean 1416
Balliemore
Auchenbreck
Craig Lodge
Dun Mór 1329
Tighnabruaich
Tighnabruaich Gallery
Port Driseach
Rhubodach
Auchenlochan
Kames
Millhouse
Asgog Loch
Cnoc na Carraige
Glecknabae
Ardlamont House
Ardlamont Point

Beinn Bhraec 1488
Cruach nan Caorach 1503
Cruach nan Tarbh
Creag Mhór

Leprinmore
Garv
Conchra
Glenmassan
Glenlean
Clachaig
Inverchaolain Glen
Iverchaolain
Colintraive
Altgaltraig
Torran Tùrach 746
Windy Hill 913

A886
A885
A815
A880

Benmore Forest
Beinn Mhór 2432
Meall Dubh 2103
Beinn Ruadh 2178
Sgorach Mór 1972
Loch Tarsan
Benmore Botanic
Rashfield
Ardbeg
Inverech
Kilmun Arboretum
Blairmore
Kilmun
Holy Loch
Sandbank
Adam's Grave
Ardnadam
Kirn
Hunter's Quay

DUNOON
Castle House
Morag's Fairy Glen
Bullwood
Corlarach
Beinn Ruadh 1057 Forest
Innellan
Toward
Toward Point

Bernice
Loch Eck
Glenfinart Forest
Creachan Mór 2156
Cnoc na h-Airighe
Ardentinny
Stronchullin Hill 1798
Gairletter
Coulport
Peaton
Clynder
Rosneath
Cove
Kilcreggan
Strone Point
Strone

Carrick Castle
Portincaple
Cruach a' Bhuic 2084
Beinn Chaorach 2339
DANGER AREA
Garelochhead
Greenfield
Auchenvennel
Shandon
Rhu
Hill House
HELENSBURGH
Craigendoran
Rosneath Point
Gourock
Fort Matilda
Ashton
McLean
Midton
GREENOCK
Larkfield
Braeside
Inverkip
Wemyss Bay
Lunderston Bay
Upper Skelmorlie
Skelmorlie

A817
A814
A818
A770
A78
A8
B7054
B788
B833
B872

INVERCLYDE
Creuch Hill 1448
Daff Resr.
Crawhin Resr.
Leap Moor
Garvock
Gryfe Resrs.
Loch Thom
Greenock Cut
Harelaw Resr.
North Burnt Hill 1408
Duchal Moor
Queenside Muir
Hill of Stake 1712
Waterhead Moor
Muirshiel
Heathfield
Calder Dam
CLYDE MUIRSHIEL REGIONAL PARK
Ladyland Moor
Mistylaw Muir
Burnt Hill 1084
Glengarnock Castle
Kilbirnie
Glengarnock

A78
A760
B780
B784
B781

ISLE OF BUTE
Kames Bay
Port Bannatyne
Rothesay Bay
Ettrick Bay
Ardbeg
Ballochgoy
ROTHESAY
Discovery
Bogany Point
Craigmore
Ardencraig
Montford
Ascog
Ascog Hall
Castle Gallery
Kirk Dam
Straad
Loch Fad
Loch Dhu
Lake Quien
Kerrycroy
Scoulag Point
Mount Stuart
Meikle
Kilchattan Butts
Kingarth
Kilchattan
Kilchattan Bay
St Blane's
Dunagoil
Dunagoil Bay
Garroch Head
Ardscalpsie Point
Scalpsie Bay
Stravanan Bay

A844
A875
B878
B881
B881

Inchmarnock
St Colmac

SOUND OF BUTE

GREAT CUMBRAE ISLAND
Upper Kirkton
Mid Kirkton
Millport
Robertson Museum & Aquarium
Cumbraes
Little Cumbrae Island
Gull Point
The Tan
Fairlie Roads
Largs Bay
Largs
Vikingar
Skelmorlie Aisle
Kelburn Castle & Country Centre
Whitehill
Fairlie
Fairlie Castle
Southannan
Kaim Hill 1271
Camphill Resr.
Muirhead Resr.
Kilburn
Knockendon Resr.
Baidland Hill 1102
Auldmuir Resr.
Drakemyre
Highfield
Caaf Resr.
Ashgrove Loch
Kilwinning
Eglinton

B896
B899
B906
B784
B780

FIRTH OF CLYDE

Quarter
Girtley Hill 1254
Noddsdale Water
Irish Law 1586

NORTH AYRSHIRE

Power Station
Campbeltown
Portencross
Farland Head
Ardneil Bay
WEST KILBRIDE
Seamill
Horse Isle
Ardrossan
Saltcoats
Stevenston
Ardrossan Castle
North Ayrshire Maritime
IRVINE
Irvine Bay
Scottish Maritime

A737
A738
A78
B7048
B7047
B780
B714
B752

ISLE OF ARRAN
South Newton
Lochranza
Catacol
Arran Distillery
Torr Nead an Eoin 1057
Cock of Arran
Rubha Creagan Dubha
Loch Ranza
Millstone Point
North Sannox
Sannox
Sannox Bay
Corrie
Glen Sannox
Caisteal Abhail 2817
Cir Mhòr 2621
Goatfell 2866
Beinn Tarsuinn 2710
An Tunna 1184
Brodick Castle
Isle of Arran Brewery
Isle of Arran Heritage
BRODICK
Brodick Bay
Merkland Point
Strathwhillan

A841
B880

Tarbert to Lochranza (Seasonal)
Ardrossan to Brodick 55mins

**GLASGOW**

STIRLING

WEST DUNBARTONSHIRE

EAST DUNBARTONSHIRE

RENFREWSHIRE

EAST RENFREWSHIRE

SOUTH LANARKSHIRE

EAST AYRSHIRE

Luss · Inchlonaig · Inchfad · Balmaha · Drymen · Buchlyvie · Kippen · Cauldhame · Gargunnock · Arnprior

Aldochlay · Inchcailloch · Inchmurrin · Gartocharn · Killearn · Balfron · Fintry · Kilsyth · Balmalloch

Dumfin · Arden · Auchendennan · Balloch · Alexandria · Jamestown · Bonhill · Renton · Dumbarton

Cardross · Port Glasgow · Bishopton · Erskine · Clydebank · Bearsden · Milngavie · Bishopbriggs

Kilmacolm · Bridge of Weir · Johnstone · Paisley · Renfrew · GLASGOW · Rutherglen · Coatbridge

Lochwinnoch · Beith · Barrhead · Neilston · Newton Mearns · Busby · East Kilbride · Hamilton · Bothwell

Dunlop · Stewarton · Fenwick · Waterside · Eaglesham · Strathaven

Kilmaurs · Kilmarnock · Crosshouse · Galston · Newmilns · Darvel · Drumclog

Whitelee Forest · Whitelee Wind Farm · Carron Valley Forest · Campsie Fells · Kilpatrick Hills

STIRLING
FALKIRK
NORTH LANARKSHIRE
SOUTH LANARKSHIRE
CLYDESDALE
WEST LOTHIAN
DUNFERMLINE

A811 · M9 · A907 · A905 · A977 · A985 · A994 · B903 · B904 · B905 · B913 · B914 · B9080 · B9037

Gargunnock · Kippen · Touch Hills · Cambusbarron · St Ninians · Borestone Brae · Bannockburn · Cowie · Plean · Airth · Letham · Dunmore · Kincardine · Clackmannan · Alloa · New Sauchie · Keilarsbrae · Forest Mill · Saline · Oakley · Carnock · Comrie · Blairhall · Culross · Torryburn · Low Torry · Cairneyhill · Crombie · Charlestown

STIRLING PAGE 202

Milnholm · West Plean · Torwood · Stenhousemuir · Carronshore · Skinflats · Grangemouth · Bo'ness · Grangepans · Bridgeness · Carriden · Blackness · Muirhouses

M80 · M876 · A872 · A88 · A9 · Denny · Dunipace · Larbert · Carron · Bainsford · Camelon · FALKIRK · Laurieston · Polmont · Brightons · Rumford · Whitecross · Maddiston · Linlithgow · Linlithgow Bridge · Philpstoun

KILSYTH · Banknock · Longcroft · Bonnybridge · High Bonnybridge · Greenhill · Shieldhill · California · Standburn · Avonbridge · Torphichen · Bathgate · Broxburn · Uphall · Livingston

Queenzieburn · Twechar · Croy · Balloch · CUMBERNAULD · Condorrat · Luggiebank · Greengairs · Wattston · Slamannan · Binniehill · Limerigg · Armadale · Blackridge · Harthill · Whitburn · Blackburn · West Calder · Addiewell · Polbeth · Murieston

KIRKINTILLOCH · Waterside · Moodiesburn · Chryston · Muirhead · Glenboig · Glenmavis · Plains · Caldercruix · Hillend · Forrestfield · Westrigg · Bathville · Stoneyburn · Loganlea · Breich

COATBRIDGE · AIRDRIE · Craigneuk · Chapelhall · Calderbank · Salsburgh · Newhouse · Hareshaw · Kirk o' Shotts · Shotts · Stane · Dykehead · Fauldhouse · Longridge · Bents · Stoneyburn

Viewpark · Uddingston · Bellshill · Mossend · Holytown · Newarthill · Yett · Stevenston · Carfin · Cleekhimin · Newmains · Morningside · Bowhousebog · Allanton · Wilsontown · Forth · Haywood

Bothwell · Blantyre · HAMILTON · MOTHERWELL · WISHAW · Craigneuk · Shieldmuir · Coltness · Cambusnethan · Newmains · Overtown · Waterloo · Wildmanbridge · Hare Hill · Rootpark

Strathaven · Stonehouse · Glassford · Larkhall · Millheugh · Machan · Ashgill · Netherburn · Law · Carluke · Braidwood · Yieldshields · Kilncadzow · Carnwath · Newbigging

Quarter · Swinhill · Rosebank · Crossford · Hazelbank · Nemphlar · Cartland · Carstairs · Carstairs Junction · Ravensruther · Kaimend

Kirkmuirhill · Blackwood · Auchenheath · Kirkfieldbank · LANARK · New Lanark · Bankhead · Pettinan · Libberton · Elsrickle · Walston

Lesmahagow · Turfholm · Brocketsbrae · Boghead · Dillarburn · Hyndford Bridge · Thankerton · Covington · Quothquan · Biggar · Carmichael · Cormiston

A73 · A70 · A71 · A721 · A724 · A726 · A72 · A706 · A801 · A89 · A800 · A779 · A705 · A704 · A702 · M74 · M73 · M8 · B7016 · B7018 · B7078 · B7086 · B7066 · B7010 · B7011 · B717 · B743

Carron Valley Forest · Carron Valley Reservoir · Loch Coulter Reservoir · Black Loch · Hillend Reservoir · Roughrigg Reservoir · Gair Reservoir · Springfield Reservoir · Hendreys Course · Cobbinshaw Reservoir · Crosswood Reservoir · Dunside Reservoir · Logan Reservoir · Kype Reservoir

HEART OF SCOTLAND · Falkirk Wheel · Antonine Wall · Bannockburn · New Lanark World Heritage Site · Falls of Clyde

**EDINBURGH** PAGE 195

FIRTH OF FORTH

SCOTTISH BORDERS

SOUTHERN UPLANDS

MIDLOTHIAN

MOORFOOT HILLS

Kirkcaldy · Kinghorn · Burntisland · Aberdour · Dalgety Bay · Inverkeithing · North Queensferry · South Queensferry · Dalmeny · Cramond · Leith · Portobello · Joppa · Musselburgh · Prestonpans · Cockenzie and Port Seton · Longniddry · Aberlady · Gullane

Cowdenbeath · Lumphinnans · Lochgelly · Kelty · Crossgates · Halbeath · Rosyth · Kirkliston · Newbridge · Ratho · Currie · Balerno · Kirknewton · East Calder · Mid Calder

Dalkeith · Bonnyrigg · Loanhead · Lasswade · Newtongrange · Gorebridge · Pathhead · Penicuik · Roslin · Rosewell · Arniston · Temple · Middleton · Heriot · Fountainhall · Stow · Gilston

West Linton · Carlops · Romannobridge · Leadburn · Howgate · Dolphinton · Broughton · Peebles · Eddleston · Innerleithen · Walkerburn · Clovenfords

Tranent · Macmerry · Ormiston · Pencaitland · Gladsmuir · Elphinstone · Whitecraig

Pen,keland routes: A90 · A92 · A823 · A921 · A909 · A907 · A71 · A70 · A720 · A702 · A701 · A703 · A766 · A768 · A772 · A6093 · A6094 · A6106 · A6124 · A68 · A7 · A1 · A198 · A6137 · A199 · A6093 · A72

Firth of Forth · Inchcolm · Inchkeith · Inchmickery · Cramond Island · Eyebroughy · Gullane Bay · Aberlady Bay · Gosford Bay

Pentland Hills · Moorfoot Hills · Southern Uplands · Scottish Borders · Midlothian

Blackhope Scar 2137 · Dun Law 1691 · Windlestraw Law 2163 · Blackhope · Great Law 1666 · Collie Law 1254 · Ladyside Height · Torfichen Hill 1510 · William Law 1314 · Knowes Hill 1222 · Meigle Hill 1389

White Meldon 1402 · Black Meldon 1334 · Dunslair Heights 1975 · Black Law 1764 · Whitehope Law 2038 · Priesthorpe Hill · Cardrona Forest · Glentress Forest

Scald Law 1898 · Black Hill 1636 · Castlelaw Hill Fort · Rullion Green 1666 · Loganlea Resr. · Glencorse Resr. · Threipmuir Reservoir · Harlaw Resr. · Malleny Mills · Bonaly · Boghall

Broughton Heights 1874 · Trahenna Hill 1792 · Dreva Wood · Stobo · Lyne · Kailzie · Cademuir Hill · Wallace's Hill 1507 · Traquair

West Water Resr. · Baddinsgill Resr. · Mendick Hill 1481 · Cairns Castle · White Craig · Byrehope Mount 1752 · The Mount 1763 · Nine Mile Burn · Eight Mile Burn

Portmore Loch · Gladhouse Resr. · Hirendean Castle · Rosebery Reservoir · Edgelaw Resr. · Mount Lothian · Carrington · Borthwick · Crichton · Tynehead · Fala · Fala Moor · Fala Dam · Crichton

Dere Street Roman Road · Soutra Aisle · Gilston · Killochyett · Pirn Hill Fort · St Ronan's Wells · Robert Smail's Printing Works · John Buchan Story · Tweeddale · Cross Kirk

Glenkinchie Distillery · National Mining [Museum] · Rosslyn Chapel · Dalhousie · Newbattle · Mayfield · Easthouses · Dewartown · Edgehead · Peaston · Peastonbank · Gilchriston · West Saltoun · East Saltoun · Humbie · Samuelston · New Winton · New Town

Forth Bridge · Forth Road Bridge · Queensferry Crossing (Open 2017) · Deep Sea World · Hopetoun House · Dalmeny House · Lauriston · Royal Botanic [Garden] · Britannia · Arthur's Seat 822 · Royal Observatory · Craiglockhart

Haddington · Macmerry · Penston · Meadowmill · Prestongrange · Cuthill · Wallyford · Levenhall · Fisherrow · Newcraighall · Inveresk · Whitecraig · Millerhill · Sheriffhall · Cousland · Crossgatehall

90 350 60 70 80

A 137 B C D

1

Bass Rock

Fidra Lamb Craigleith
Eyebroughy

North Berwick
Scottish Seabird Centre
A198
Tantallon
Gullane Bay Dirleton B1347
North Berwick Law 613
Saltcoats Castle Kingston
Gullane B1345
Aberlady Bay Fenton Barns Whitekirk
Myreton Motor M Drem
Aberlady Chesters Hill Fort National Flag Heritage Centre
Craigielaw Ballencrieff Camptoun East Fortune 22 Preston
Gosford Bay A198 Spittal Flight
Longniddry A6137 Huntington B1343 Athelstaneford Barnes Castle Garleton Hills 610
ockenzie and Port Seton B1371 Elvingston Hopetoun Monument
Church Meadowmill A1 Haddington St Martin's Kirk
Tranent Macmerry Gladsmuir A199 B6471 St Mary's Pleasance
New Winton Penston B6363 Samuelston Lennoxlove House
New Town A6093 Bolton Colstoun House
Cross Pencaitland B6355 Morham
iston Peastonbank East Saltoun Gifford Yester Castle
Peaston B6368 West Saltoun
Gilchriston Longyester
thhead Humbie
Fala Dam B6457 Fala
Fala Moor Soutra Aisle A68 Dere Street Roman Road Gilston
Carfrae
Oxton Addinston Cleekhimin Bridge
Collie Law 1254 A697 Edgarhope Wood
Fountainhall SOUTHERN
A7 Thirlestane
Killochyett B6362 Lauder Flat Cat Gallery B6362
Stow Nether Blainslie
Old Kirk & Bishop's House A68
Pack Bridge Legerwood

East Linton A199 Hailes R. Tyne
Stenton
Luggate Burn Pitcox
Papple
Garvald B6370
Whitelaw Hill
Nunraw Abbey White Castle Hillfort Clints Dod 1307 Dunbar Common
Branxly Hill 1301
B6355 Sparleton Edge
HILLS
Whiteadder Resr. 19 Cranshaws Hill 1245 Cranshaws
Lammer Law 1734 Hopes Resr. Meikle Says Law 1755
Stobshiel Resr. Crib Law 1670 Hunt Law 1625 Mutiny Stones Dye Water
1593 Blythe Edge Watch Water Resr.
Hogs Law 1470 SCOTTISH Longformacus
Scoured Rig Dirrington Great Law 1307
UPLANDS Dirrington Little Law
B6456 Westruther Polwarth
BORDERS Halliburton A6105
Thirlestane Houndslow Greenlaw
B6362 A6089 Bassendean
Leader Water Eden Water Gordon
Greenknowe Tower
A6105 Fans Huntlywood Hume
Hume Castle
Sweethope Hill 730

E A S T
L O T H I A N
Tyne Mouth John Muir East Links Family Pk. West Barns
Dunbar Castle Town House Dunbar A1087
Belhaven Broxburn Barns Ness
A1 Doon Hill Homestead Dunbar 1650 East Barns
Spott Brunt Hill 737 Pinkerton Power Station
Innerwick Skateraw Thorntonloch
Dry Burn 8
Reed Point
Cocklaw Hill 1046 Dunglass Collegiate Church Cove
Oldhamstocks Cockburnspath Siccar
803 Meikle Black Law
Monynut Edge 1283 Heart Law
Blackburn Rig A1
Grantshouse
A6112
Ellemford Abbey St Bathans
Edin's Hall Broch
Whitchester B6355 Preston
M E R Cumledge Mill
Millburn Bridge B6365
Jim Clark Room Manderston
Duns
Gavinton Nisbet Hill
A6112
Fogo
A6105 Fogorig B6460
Charterhall M E R S
Blackadder Water Leitholm
A697 Lambden
Hume Eccles
Ednam

A Buckholm 314 William Law 119 B Langshaw C A6089 D 120
Knowes Hill 1222 B710 Earlston Mellerstain House A6089 Stichill A698 rgham
Clovenfords A72 A7 GALASHIELS B6374 Redpath Smailholm Nenthorn Wark Castle
Meigle Hill 1389 Lowood Gattonside B6360 Smailholm Ednam Carham
Great Law 1666 40 Tweedbank Kelso James Thomson Obelisk R. Tweed B6350 Hadden

90  400  10  20

E  F  G  H

1

80

N O R T H    S E A

70

Point

Fast Castle Head

Fast Castle

Telegraph Hill  Lumsdaine

Cross Law 744

Coldingham Moor

ST ABB'S HEAD

St Abbs

Lifeboat Staion

A1107

Coldingham  Priory

Coldingham Bay  Lifeboat Station

Houndwood

B6438

Eyemouth

Gunsgreen House

Gunsgreenhill

3

Eye

859 Water

Horseley Hill

Reston

B6355

A1107

60

60

60

Auchencrow

18

Ayton

60

Burnmouth  Ross

B6438

B6437

A1

60

Lintlaw

B6355

Lamberton

70

Marshall Meadows

Chirnside

12

B6355

Tithe Barn

Clappers

Halidon Hill 1333

Conundrum Farm

60

Chirnsidebridge

Whiteadder  Water

Foulden

Bell Tower

Cell Block

4

Arch

Edrom

A6105

A6105

Castle

BERWICK-UPON-TWEED

Allanton

Hutton

Paxton

B6461

60

Main Guard

B6437

Tweedmouth

B6460

B6460

B6461

Tweed

Lifeboat Station

Spittal

A1167

Whitsome

B6461

Union Bridge

Loanend

East Ord

Pora-Doodle-Do

Redshin Cove

Chain Bridge Honey Farm

A698

2

Fishwick

Horncliffe

Horndean

Murton

Scremerston

650

Ladykirk

Thornton

B6525

Swinton

Norham

B6470

West Allerdean

Cheswick

12

B6470

Norham Station

Shoreswood  Shoresdean

Ancroft

Goswick

5

E

Simprim

Upsettlington

Grindon

Felkington

B6354

Berrington Law

Haggerston

LINDISFARNE

HOLY ISLAND

A6112

Twizel Bridge

Duddo Stone Circle

Duddo

Berrington

Beal

Keel Head

B6437

Castle Heaton

Bowsden

12

60

Holy Island

Lindisfarne Centre

Lindisfarne Priory

Castle Point

Hirsel

Lennel

Melkington

A698

NORTHUMBERLAND

B6353

West Kyloe

A1

Fenham

Burrows Hole

40

dstream

A698

Cornhill-on-Tweed

Heatherslaw Light Railway

Etal

Waterford Hall

Barmoor

Lowick

G

East Kyloe

121

H

60

Bareless

A697

Heatherslaw Mill

B6353

Buckton

Staple Sound

FAR ISLA

West Learmouth

Crookham

Ford

Kyloe Hills

10

20

Pressen

East Learmouth

Flodden Field Monument

90

Cranxton

12

B6354

400

Holburn

Elwick

Ross

Budle Bay

Inner

Flodden  Flodden Field 1513

St Cuthbert's Cave

Detchant

B13

Bamburgh

Easington  Waren

Middleton

132

ISLE OF MULL

Fingal's Cave
Erisgeir
Gribun
Derryguaig
BEN MORE 3171
Glen
Beinn Talaidh 2502
Sgurr Dearg 2429
Lochan an Doire Dharaich
over Mull
Oakbank
A849

A  B  139  B8035  C  D
Glen
Loch
Strathcoil
Carn Bàn 812

Coirc Bheinn 1837
Corra-bheinn 2311
60
Lussa River
14

Creach Bheinn 1613
Rubha na h Uamha
MacCulloch's Fossil Tree
Tavool House
ARDMEANACH
Tiroran
Port na Croise
Kilfinichen Bay
Scridain
Coladoir River
Loch Sguabain
Loch Airdeglais
Creach Beinn 2290
Ben Buie 2354
Kinlochspelve
Croggan
Loch Spelve

Rubha an Cearc
Garbh Phort
Kintra
Creich
Columba Centre
Aridhglas
nnphort
Loch Poit na h-I
ROSS
Knockvologan 20
369 Ross of Mull Historical Centre
Bunessan
Loch Assopol
OF
Ardchrishnish
Eorabus
Knockan
Loch na Làthaich
MULL
Bun an Leoib
A849
12
Torrans
Pennyghael
Leidle
Beinn na Croise 1649
River
Beinn Chreagach 1235
Carsaig
BROLASS
Beinn Mheadhon
Lochbuie
Standing Stone Circle
Moy Castle
Loch Uisg
Loch an t-sithein
Druim Fada 1329

Ardalanish
Uisken
Ardchiavaig
Beinn a' Chaol-Airigh 411
Ardalanish Bay
Rubha nam Bràithrean
Cruachan Min 1232
Beach River
Aoineadh
Carsaig Bay
Frank Lockwood's Island
Scottish Slate Heritage C
Easd

Rubh' Ardalanish
Carsaig Arches
Malcolm's Point
FIRTH
Dubh-fheith
SL
ISLA
Belnahua
Fladda

INSET
Eilean Annraidh
130
Rubha nan Cearc
Garbh Phort
Réidh Eilean
IONA
Maclean's Cross
Abbey & Nunnery
Kintra
Creich
Columba Centre
Aridhglas
A849
Garbh Eileach
Garvellachs
Eilean Dubh Mòr

Iona Heritage
Baile Mòr
Fionnphort
Loch Poit na h-I
10
Eileach an Naoimh
Lunga
Sound of Luing

Stac an Aoineidh
Eilean nah-Aon Chaorach
Greave
Fidden
Erraid
Knockvologan
720
Guirasdeal

Soa Island
Eilean nam Muc
Eilean a' Chalmain
5

Rubha nam Faoilean
Cruach Scarba 1474
SCARBA
Kilmory Lodge

700
Port na Cuilce
Balnahard
Glengarrisdale Bay
619 An Cruachan

Kiloran Bay
469 Carnan Eoin
Port Ceann a' Gharraidh
Cruach na Seilcheig 971
Loch na Conaire
Rubh' a' Bhacain

Uragaig
Loch an Sgoltaire
Kiloran
B8086
Colonsay House
COLONSAY
Port a' Bhàta
Corryvreckan Whirlpool
Gulf
of
Corryvreckan

Sgreadan
Kilchattan
B8086
Loch Fada
B8086
4
Glas Aird
Loch Doire na h-Achlaise
Ben Garrisdale 1198
Loch a' Bhurra
Loch a' Gheoidh

Eilean a' Chladaich
Colonsay
3
Scalasaig
Loch Staosnaig
Glendebadel Bay
Lochanan Tana
Cruach Ionnastail 967

Eilean Leatham
Garvard
B8085
Rubha Dubh
Corpach Bay
Loch Fada Cul na Beinne
Lussa River
Port nan Laogh
Ruadh Sgeir

Dubh Eilean
Priory
Oronsay
ORONSAY
Beinn Bhreac 1532
Cruach an Uillt Fhearna
Lealt
Lealt

Eilean Ron
5
Eilean Ghaoideamal
Ceann Riobha
Caolas Mòr
124
Shian Bay
Allt an Tairbh
Rainberg Mòr 1487
Shian River
Dubh Bheinn
Maol nam Damh 887
Loch Cathar nan Eun
Ardlussa
Ardlussa Bay
Eilean Dubh
Carsaig Bay
Eilean nan Coinean

Rubh'an t-Sailein
Loch an Tuim Uaine
Loch Righ Mor
Loch Righ Beag
Loch Lùbanach
Cruib 1036
Gleann
Inverlussa
Lussagiven
Lussa Point
Gob Dubh

Oban to Colonsay 2hrs 20mins.
Colonsay to Port Askaig 1hr. 10mins. (Seasonal)

80
Post Rocks
RUBHA A'MHAIL
124
Rubh' a' chrois-aoinidh
JURA
A846
Cnoc an Ime 927
Tarbert
622 Beinn Sgaillinish
Barrahormid

A  B  C  D
Loch
Tarbert
Maol an Tarraich
16
Lagg
Keills Chapel
Keillmore
Loch na Cille
B8025
Sween

Rubha Bholsa
Allt na Gile
150
Loch an Aircill
Glen Batrick
1439 Beinn Bhreac
Loch Lesgamaill
60
Port Doir' a' Chrorain
SOUND
Island of Danna
Cnoc Stighseir 792

Sgarbh Breac 1195
Loch an Oir
Loch na Fudarlaich
Beinn an Oir
Bàgh na Dojde
Eilean Mor

# Map — Argyll (Oban, Inveraray, Lochgilphead area), Page 133

Musdile · Duart · Oban to Craignure 45mins · Dunstaffnage · Oban · Connel · Glennoe · Lochdon

Lochdon · Oban to Craignure · Achnacloich · Stonefield · Bonawe · Glen Noe · Beinn Eunaich 3242

**A85** · Ganavan · Dunbeg · 90 · Black Lochs · A85 · Airds Bay · Bonawe Historic Iron Furnace · Inverawe Smokery

E 140 · Eilean nan Gramhna · McCaig's Tower · War · Dunollie · Fearnoch Forest · Taynuilt · G · Ichr 141 · CRUACHAN · H · B8077 · 133

Grass Point · KERRERA · Balliemore · **OBAN PAGE 201** · Distillery · Pulpit Hill · Dalintart · Deadh Croimhead 1257 · Angus's · Bridge of Awe · Cruachan Reservoir · Beinn a' Bhuiridh 2941 · Lochawe · Falls of Cruachan · Kilchurn · Str

Bach Island · Carn Breugach · Loch Seil · Loch Nell · Glen Lonan · Beinn Ghlas 1691 · River Awe · Pass of Brander · Cruachan Power Station · 12 · St Conan's Kirk · Kinch

Dubh Sgeir · Gylen Castle · Kilmore · Cleigh · Kilbride · Glen Feochan · A'Chruach 1208 · Beinn Chapull 1690 · A85 · 3695 · Eilean Castle · A819 · 1

Rubha Seanach · Minard Point · Eilean Dùin · 689 Beinn Mhòr · Kilninver · **A816** · Euchar · Loch Scammadale · Allt a' Chromraig · Kilchrenan · North Port · Upper Sonachan · Cladich · Cladich River · Allt Fearna · Tea

Insh Island · Bridge over the Atlantic **B844** · Clachan-Seil · Braes of Lorn · Loch Tralaig · Meall Odhar 1255 · Abhainn Fionan · Inverinan · Portsonachan · South Port · B840 · Beinn Ghlas 1804 · 20

SEIL · Ellenabeich · An Cala · Folk · Balvicar · Ardmaddy Castle · Pass of Melfort · Loch a' Phearsain · Loch Dubh-mor 1239 · Cruach Maolachy · Tom an t-Saighdeir 993 · Lochan Dubh · 1932 Cruach Mhòr · A819 · 2 · Scardan 1599

Cuan · An Coire · Dun Crutagain 895 · Melfort · Kilmelford · Lochavich · Dalavich · Ardchonnell · Loch an Eilean Dubh · Three Bridges · 837 Barr Mor · Dubh Loch

Cullipool · Torsa · Loch Melfort · Loch an Losgainn Mór · Carn Duchara 1610 · Lochan a' Bhruic · Portinnisherrich · Loch nan Car · Beinn Bhreac 1726 · Carloonan · 10

LUING · Rubh' a' Chnaip · Arduaine **A816** · Tom Soilleir 1199 · Inverliever Forest · Eredine · Lochan Long · Malt Lane · **INVERARAY** · 134 · A83

Shuna · ARGYLL · Barbreck River · Inverliever Lodge · Durran · Braevallich · Am Buachaille 1060 · Bell Tower · Inveraray Jail · St Catherines

Toberonochy · Craobh Haven · Barravullin · Cruach an Eachlaich 1148 · Eredine Forest · Douglas Water · Beinn Dearg 1583 · Achnagoul · Argyll

Eilean Ona · Soroba Hill 549 · Kintraw · Ardfern **B8002** · Ford · **B840** · Fincharn · Loch Leachd · Loch Geoidh 1503 · Auchindrain · Dun Leacainn · A83 · Creggans · Creagan an Eich 1070 · **A815** · 3 · Strachur Smiddy

Rèisa Mhic Phaidean · Eilean Mhic Chrion 745 · Creag Mhòr · Loch Ederline · Loch nan Ceard Mor · Cruach Mhic Fhionnlaidh · 1179 · Beinn Ghlas 1378 · FYNE · Strachur Bay · Clachan Strachur

Aird · Island Mcaskin · Eilean Righ · Carnasserie · Loch Gaineamhach 1339 · Sidh Mór · Furnace · Leachd · Newton · Tombuidhe · A815 · 700

Rèisa an t-Sruith · Garbh Rèisa · Kilmartin House · **Kilmartin** · Lochan Leathan · KILMICHAEL FOREST · Minard Forest · Crarae · Castle Lachlan · **B8000** · Cruach nan Capull 1577 · Glensluain · **A886** · Glenbranter · 4

Rubha Garbh-ard · Slockavullin · Kilmartin Glen Prehistoric Sites · Killinochonoch · Lochan Add · Dùn Dubh 758 · Blackmill Loch · Minard · Tullochgorm · Lachan Bay · Crauch an Lochain 1666 · Beinn Bheag 2029 · Cr

Ardnoe Point · Loch Crinan · **A816** · Kilmichael Glassary · Bridgend · Gleann Airigh · Loch Glashan · A83 · Lephinmore · Caol · Meall Dubh 2103 · Beinn Mhòr 2432 · Bernice

Rubha nam Bàrr · Crinan · Kilmahumaig · Islandadd Bri. · Cup & Ring Marks · Achnabreck Cup & Ring Marks · Scotston Hill 698 · 16 · Loch Gair · Lephinchapel · Garvie · 90

KNAPDALE · Bellanoch · **B841** · Cairnbaan · Cnoc Reamhar 870 · Loch Linne · Daill Loch · Lochgair · Lochan Chuilceachan · Cruach Chuilceachan 1428 · An Socach 1345 · Glenmassan

125 · FOREST · Coille-Bharr · Gleann Loch · Cam Loch · **Lochgilphead** · Kilmory Woodland Park · Port Ann · Largiemore · **A886** · Conchra · Glendaruel Forest · Cruach nan Cuilean 1416 · Ballimore · Sgorach Mòr 1972 · 5 · Benmore Botanic

Taynish · Taryallich · **B8025** · Achnamara · Loch an Add · Loch nam Breac Buidhe · Ardrishaig · Castleton · Otter Ferry · 679 Tom na h-Iolaire · Kilmodan Sculptured Stones · Clachan of Glendaruel · Loch Tarsan · Glenlean · Inbhir · Clachaig · B836

Eilean Loain · Kilmichael of Inverlussa · Cruach nam Fiadh 1071 · Cruach Brenfield 1044 · Inverneil House · Eilean Mór · Liath Eilean · 507 Barr Ganuisg · 1144 Cruach nan Tarbh · Cruach nan Caorach 1503 · Dun Mòr 1329 · Cruach nan Capull 2005 · Sa

Daltot · Loch na Craige Gràinte · Loch Arail · Bàgh an Tailleir · Kilfinan Bay · Beinn Bhraec 1488 · Auchenbreck · Benmore Forest

Dunrostan · An Stucha 1247 · E · 125 · B8024 · F · Kilfinan · G · Craig Lodge · 126 · H · Lochan na Lèirg · Glenstriven

St Columba's Cave · Achahoish · Loch Fuar-Bheinne · Cruach a' Phubuill 1564 · Port Leathan · Beinn Bhraec 1662 · A886 · Iverchaolain

Ellary · Clachbreck · Erines · River · Loch Melldalloch · B836

A B C D

**Grid references (left margin):** 11, 10, 12, 1, 20, 2, 133, 3, 4, 5, 13

GLEN CRUACHAN

Beinn Eunaich 3242
Allt Mhoille
Glen Noe
Beinn a' Bhuiridh 2941
Cruachan Reservoir
Falls of Cruachan
Cruachan Power Station
Pass of Brander
A85
Lochawe
Lochawe
Kilchurn
St Conan's Kirk
Kinchrackine
Fraoch Eilean Castle
Duncan Ban MacIntyre Monument
B8017
Stronmilchan
Edendonich
Dalmally
A85
Achnafanich
River Orchy
River Strae
Beinn Donachain 2127
Beinn na Sròine
B8074
141
Beinn Udlaidh 2759
Beinn Bhreac-liath 2633
Beinn Odhar 2948
Clifton
Tyndrum
A82
A85
Ben Challum 3354
Beinn nan Imirean 2769
Beinn Cheathaich 3076
Meall a' Churain
Lochdochart House
Loch Lubhair
A85
Ben More 3852
Stob Binnein 3821
Beinn Tulaichean 3099
Monachyle
Beinn Bhreac 2254

Ben Lui 3708
Beinn Dubhchraig 3204
Cononish
Fiarach 2132
Loch Dochart
Crianlarich
A82
Strath Fillan
Glen

Upper Sonachan
Cladich
A819
B840
Allt Fearna
Cladich River
Teatle Water
Beinn Bhalgairean 2085
Meall nan Tighearn 2423
Glen Lochy
Allt Fhoinn Ghlinne
Falls of Falloch
A82
River Falloch
Ben Glas
Troisgeach 2407
Inverarnan
Beinn Chroin 3084
Inverlochlarig
Loch Doine

LOCH LOMOND & THE TROSSACHS NATIONAL PARK

Tullich
Stuc Scardan 1599
A819
Three Bridges
Kilblaan Burn
Barr Mor
Glen Shira
Lochan Shira
Beinn Ghlas 1804
Lochan Sròn Mòr
Beinn Bhuidhe 3112
Rob Roy's House
Clachan Hill 2159
Brannie Burn
River Shira
Glenfyne Lodge
Eagle's Fall
Loch Sloy
Ardlui
Ben Vorlich 3093
Stob a' Choin 2839
Cruinn Bheinn 1787
Strath

Carlonan
Malt Land
Inveraray
Bell Tower
Inveraray Jail
Loch Shira
133
Dubh Loch
Clachan Farm
A83
Cairndow
Ardkinglas Woodland
A815
Binnein an Fhidhleir
BEINN IME 3318
Beinn an Lochain
Glen Kinglas
Rest and be thankful
Ben Vane 3004
Inveruglas Water
Inveruglas
Rob Roy's Cave
Inversnaid
Inversnaid Waterfall
Cruachan 1762
Stronachlachar
Loch Katrine
Frenich
Loch Chon
Loch Tinker
Loch Ard Forest

LOCH FYNE
St Catherines
Laglingarten
Cruach nan Capull 1854
Stob an Eas 2401
B828
B839
Ben Arthur 2891
Succoth
Cruach Tairbeirt 1362
Tarbet
LOCH LOMOND
A82
Cruinn a' Bheinn 2077
Gleann Dubh
Loch Dub 1675
Kinlochard

A815
Creagan an Eich 1070
Creggans
Strachur Smiddy
Clachan Strachur
Mullach Coire a' Chuir 2098
Beinn Lochain 2306
Lochgoilhead
Ardgartan
Glen Croe
Glen Croe Forest
Ben Donich 2777
The Brack
A83
Arrochar
Ardmay
B838
Ardgartan
A814
Beinn Bheac 2233
Ben Lomond 3194
Rowardennan
Beinn Uird 1957
QUEEN ELIZABETH FOREST PARK
LOCH ARD

A886
Tobuidhe
Glensluain
ARGYLL FOREST PARK
Beinn Bheula 2556
Lochain nan Cnaimh
The Saddle 1704
Ardgoil & Estate
Cnoc Coinnich 2497
Ardgoil Forest
Douglas Water
Doune Hill 2408
Inverbeg
Ben Lomond National Memorial Park
Rowardennan Forest
Cruach nan Capull 1577
Glenbranter
Craigbrack
Beinn Bheag 2029
Cruach a' Bhuic 2084
Carrick Castle
Clach Beinn 1435
Beinn a' Mhanaich 2328
Beinn Eich 2302
Edentaggart
Glen Luss
Luss
Inchlonaig
Gualann 1514
Garadhba

Benmore Forest
Bernice
Creachan Mór 2156
Portincaple
Cnoc na h-Airighe
Beinn Chaorach 2339
Beinn Ruisg 1946
Luss Water
Inchfad
Conic Hill 1175
National Park
Inchcailloch
Balmaha
Milton
B837

Meall Dubh 2103
Glenmassan
A815
Stronchullin Hill 1798
Ardentinny
Coulport
B833
Lochan Ghlas Laoigh
126
Garelochhead
Greenfield
DANGER AREA
Glen Fruin
Shandon
Auchenvennel
A817
Callendoun
Dumfin
Arden
Lennox Castle
Inchmurrin
Gartocharn
Croftamie
Buchanan Smithy
Kilmaronock Castle

Glenmore
Loch Tarsan
Benmore Botanic
Benmore Forest
Gairletter
Peaton
Clynder
Rosneath
Rhu
Shandon
A814
Glenarn
Hill House
HELENSGORGH
A818
Craigendoran
B832
Auchendennan
Balloch Castle
Bird of Prey Centre
Caldarvan Loch
A811
Blairquhan
Mill of Haldane
Auchencarroch

Sgorach Mor
Glenlean
Rashfield
Ardbeg
Inverнеck
Clachaig
B836
Kilmun
A880
Kilmun Arboretum
Blairmore
Cove Bay
Linn Botanic
Cove
Kilcreggan
Rosneath Point
A82
Sea Life
Balloch
Jamestown
Alexandria
DANGER AREA
Motoring Heritage Centre

Sandbank
A885
A815
Ardnadam
Strone
Holy Loch
Stone Point
Hunter's Quay
126
12mins
30mins
Robert the Bruce Heritage Centre
Geilston
Cardross
Castlehill
Renton
A813
Bonhill
A82
A857
Dumbarton

DUNOON
Castle House
Morag's Fairy Glen
Kirn
Ashton
Gourock
Midton
Fort Matilda
McLean
Coves Res
Larkfield
Braeside
GREENOCK
PORT GLASGOW
Cardross
Silverton
Townend
DUMBARTON

# PERTH & KINROSS

Creag Mhòr 2359
Falls of Lochay
Longhouse
Breadalbane Folklore!
Falls of Dochart
Finlarig Castle
Killin
Auchnafree
Meall Reamhar 2188
Meall Tarsuinn 2126

A827
250
R. Dochart
Luib
Ardchyle
Beinn Lebhain 2312
Glen Ogle
Lochan Breaclaich
Creag Gharbh 2090
Creag Uchdag 2883
Finglen Burn
River Almond
Bridge

Auchnafree Hill
142
A85
Glen
Loch Lednock Reservoir
Ben Chonzie 2589
143
Loch Turret Reservoir
Meall Reamhar 2188

R. Dochart
Meall an t-Seallaidh 2794
Kirton Glen
Meall a' Mhadaidh
Lochearnhead
A85 11
St Fillans
Loch Earn
Ardvorlich
Spout Rolla
Invergeldie
Carn Chois
Glen Turret

Rob Roy's Grave
Balquhidder
Auchtubh
Kingshouse
A84
Falls of Edinample
Meall Reamhar 2225
Ben Halton 2033
Water of Ruchill
Deil's Cauldron
Comrie
Melville Monument
Dunira
Fordie
Clathick
Ochtertyre
Hosh
Famous Grouse Experience
Monzie Castle
Gilmerton

Balquhidder
Bygones
STRATHYRE FOREST
BEN VORLICH 3231
FOREST OF GLENARTNEY
Dalchruin
Arlney
Culloch
Cultybraggan Camp
Earthquake House
Ross
Dalginross
A85
Crieff
Tomaknock
B8062
Monzievaird
Lochlane
Balloch
Dargill
A822

QUEEN ELIZABETH FOREST PARK
Ballimore
Strathyre
Lochan a' Chroin
Beinn Each 2660
Meall Odhar 2066
DANGER AREA
Ben Clach 1748
Glen
Finchu Glen
KINROSS
Ochtermuthill
Machany Water
Torlum Wood
Drummond
Muthill
Old Church Tower
Bishop's Bridge
Innerpeffray Chapel
A822

TROSSACHS
Meall Cala 2212
Benvane 2685
Ardchullarie
BEN LEDI 2882
Glen Finglas Reservoir
Loch Lubnaig
Uamh Bheag 2181
Creag Beinn nan Eun
Glenlichorn
River Knaik
Cromlet
Braco Castle
Blackhall Camps
Ardoch Roman Fort
A822
136
Risebreck
Loch
Blackford
70

BEN A'N
The Trossachs
1851 Meall Gainmheich
Brig o' Turk
Lendrick
Pass of Leny
Falls of Leny
Kilmahog
Hamilton Toy Collection
Bracklinn Falls
Callander
Braes of Doune
Argaty Red Kites
Ardoch Burn
Kinbuck
A9
Sheriffmuir
Coire Odhar
Slymaback
Braco
Greenloaning
Muckle Burn
Bullie
Allan
Blackford
70

BEN VENUE 2386
A821
Loch Achray
Loch Drunkie
Loch Venachar
Lochan Balloch 1396
Beinn Dearg
A81
Torrie Forest
Drumvaich
Burn of Cambus
Buchany
Doune
A820
Dunblane
Pisgah
B8033
Sheriffmuir 1715
Blairdenon Hill 2073
700

ACHRAY FOREST
Achray Forest Drive
Milton
Aberfoyle
B829
Menteith Hills
Port of Menteith
Ruskie
A873
B822
Loch Rusky
Muir Dam
B8032
Deanston
Distillery
Buchany
Doune
Kilmadock Heritage Centre
A824
Leighton Library
Dunblane
A9
Sunnylaw
B998
Menstrie
Wallace Monument
King o' Muirs
Alva Glen
A91
Alva
Mill Trail
Alloa

FOREST 560
Drum of Clashmore
Gartmore
Scottish Wool Centre
Cunninghame Graham Memorial
Trossachs Discovery Centre
Braeval
Inchmahome Priory
Lake of Menteith
Flanders Moss
Thornhill
B826
Loch Watston
Blair Drummond
Blair Drummond Safari & Adventure Park
Bridge of Allan
Drip Moss
A84
Causewayhead
Craigmill
Menstrie Castle
A907
Tullibody
Cambus
ALLOA
Alloa Tower

A81
B835
Arnprior
B8037
Kippen
Cauldhame
Gargunnock
Gargunnock House
A811
Blairdrummond Moss
Forth
Drip Moss
A811
M9
Raploch
STIRLING
Cambuskenneth
Fallin
South Alloa
Throsk

A811
Buchlyvie
A875
B822
Loch Laggan
Mill Dam
Carleatheran 1592
Gargunnock Hills
Touch Hills
Gillies Hill
Cambusbarron
St Ninians
Borestone
Robert the Bruce
Bannockburn
A905
Cowie
Dunmore
90

Drymen
127
Endrick Bridge
Balfron
Stronend 1678
128
Earl's Hill 1442
North Third Resr.
Milnholm
West Plean
Plean
Bruce's Castle
Pineapple
B9124
Air

Killearn Bridge
Drymen Bridge
A81
Boquhan
Gartness
Killearn
Fintry Hills
Fintry
Loup of Fintry
Loch Walton
Easter Buckieburn
Loch Coulter Resr.
A872
Torwood
Torwood Castle
M80
M876
Denny
Dunipace
Larbert
Stenhousemuir
5
A88

A809
B834
Buchanan
A875
Dumgoyne
Glengoyne Distillery
Earl's Seat 1897
CAMPSIE FELLS
B822
Endrick Water
Carron Valley Resr.
Carron Valley Forest
Tomtain 1487
High Banton
Fankerton
Head of Muir
Denny
M80
Bonnybridge
Antonine Wall
FALKIRK

The Whangie 1172
Auchineden Hill
127
Blanefield
Strathblane
Netherton
A81
EAST DUNBARTONSHIRE
Clachan of Campsie
Birkenburn Resr.
Colzium Walled
Banton
Kilsyth
Kilsyth Hills
Castlecary
Longcroft
Greenhill
Bonnybridge
Falkirk Wheel
Glen Village

Burncrooks Resr.
Craigallian Loch
Mugdock Castle
Lillie Gallery
A81
Lennoxtown
Milton of Campsie
Queenzieburn
Twechar
KILSYTH
Balmalloch
A803
Auchinstarry
Dullatur
Cumbernauld
M80
A803
Croy
Birdston
R. Kelvin
Bar Hill
Canal
Abronhill

STRATHORD FOREST

A822  B8063  143  B8060  Luncarty  A93  A94  Scone  PERTH PAGE 201

Newton Bridge  Glen Almond  Chapelhill  Moneydie  Stormontfield  Stanley  Guildtown  Newmiln  St Martins  Balbeggie  Wolfhill  Saucher  Kinrossie  Collace  Kirkton of Collace  Dunsinan Hill

Meall Reamhar 2188  Meall nan Caorach 2045  Little Glenshee  Milton Burn  Shochie Burn  Buchanty  Tulchan  Harrietfield  Glenalmond  Busby  Pitcairngreen  Almondbank  Perth  Scone Palace Pinetum  Huntingtower  Old Scone  Pole Hill 945  Kilspindie  Pitroddie  Nether Durdie  Glendoick

Auchnafree  Auchnafree Hill 2589  Meall Tarsuinn 2126  Sma' Glen  Monzie  Castle  Gilmerton  Fowlis Wester  Sculptured Stone  Keillour  Braegrum  Methven  Tibbermore  Tibbermore 1644  Hillyland  Tulloch  Huntingtower  Muirton  Gannochy  Bridgend  Kinnoull Hill Woodland Park  Kinfauns  Glencarse  Leetown  Chapelhill  St Madoes  Inchyra

Loch Turret Reservoir  Loch Meallbrodden  KEILLOUR FOREST  Madderty  Inchaffray Abbey  STRATH EARN  Dupplin Lake  Craigie  Cherrybank  Barnhill  Craigend  M90  A90  Walnut Grove  Moncreiffe Hill 725  Rhynd  Elcho  Easter Rhynd  A913

Ochtertyre  Clathick  Hosh  Loch Monzievaird  Crieff  Crieff  Milton of Cultoquhey  St David's  Mayfield  Clathy  Findo Gask  Dalreoch Bridge  A9  Forgandenny  A912  Kintillo  Bridge of Earn  Dron  Aberargie  Pitversie  Abernethy 923  PITMEDDEN FOREST

Lochlane  Balloch  Dargill  Tomaknock  A85  Muir o' Fauld Roman Signal Station  Ardunie Roman Signal Station  Millearn  Kinkell Bridge  Dalreoch  Dupplin Moor 1332  Aberdalgie  Milltown of Aberdalgie  Forteviot  B934  A9  Glenfoot  Balvaird  Balvaird  Strathmiglo

Torlum 1291  A822  Innerpeffray Library  Innerpeffray Chapel  Old Church & Tower  Caerlaverock  Aberuthven  Tullibardine  A824  Maggie Wall's Memorial  Dunning  Newton of Pitcairns  church & Dupplin Cross  Pathstruie  Path of Condie  Balmanno Hill 751  Glenfarg  Newton of Balcanquhal  A912  Gateside  A91  Upper Urquhart  Kilgour  Cash Feus

Torwood  Drummond  Muthill  Ochtermuthill  Bishop's Bridge  A823  Chapel  West Castleton  Mains  Muirton  Auchterarder  A9  Heritage Centre  Craig Rossie 1346  Marcassie Bridge  B8062  Thorter Bridge  Glen Farg Reservoir  Glenfarg  Duncrievie  M90  Nether Urquhart  West Lomond 1713  Lomond

Coire Odhar  Machany Water  B827  Blackhall Camps  Braco Castle  A822  Braco  135  Ardoch Roman Fort  Carsebreck Loch  Blackford  Gleneagles  Tullibardine Distillery  Castle  Braes of Ogilvie  Common of Dunning  Corb Bridge  Water of May  Stronachie  Dochrie Hill 1198  Middleton  Upper Tillyrie  Burnside  Bishop Hill  Harperleas Resr.  Ballo Resr.  Lomond

B827  River Knaik  B8081  Greenloaning  Allan Water  Gleneagles  Glen Eagles  Wether Hill 1647  Steele's Knowe 1592  Sim's Hill 1583  Innerdouny Hill 1630  Glenfarg Reservoir  Glenvale  M90  B919  Scotlandwell  Arnot Resr.  Kinnesswood

STRATHALLAN  A9  Sheriff Muir  Sheriffmuir 1715  Blairdenon Hill 2073  Ben Cleuch 2364  A823  Glendevon  Glendevon Forest  Glen Devon  Burnfoot  Lendrick Hill 1496  South Queich  Dalqueich  Carnbo  A91  Milnathort  Orwell Stones  Michael Bruce  Easter Balgedie  Wester Balgedie  Loch Leven  R. Leven

King's Seat Hill 2126  Castle Campbell  Glensherup Reservoir  Glenquey Reservoir 1549  Commonedge Hill  Pool o' Muckhart  Yetts o' Muckhart  A823  A91  Drum  Coldrain  KINROSS  A922  Kinross  Portmoak  New Gullet Bridge  Auchmuirbridge

CLACKMANNANSHIRE  Blairlogie  Menstrie  Mill Trail  A91  King o' Muirs  Alva  Ochil Hills  Glen Woodland Park  Tillicoultry  Dollar  Dollar Glen  Vicar's Bridge  Rumbling Bridge  Gorge  Cauldron Linn  Crook of Devon  B9097  Gairney Bank  Benarty Hill 1168  Ballingry  Lochore  Auchterderran

Alva  Sauchie Tower  A908  Devonside  B913  Blairingone  Powmill  Cult Hill  Hill End  Cleish Hills  Cleish  Dowhill Castle  Blairadam Forest  Loch Glow  Loch Ore  Lochore Meadows Castle  Crosshill  Glencraig  B921

Causewayhead  A907  Wallace Monument  Menstrie Castle  Tullibody  A91  Coalsnaughton  New Sauchie  Keilarsbrae  A977  Forest Mill  Black Devon  Balgonar  Knock Hill-Knockhill 1194  Killernie Castle  Scottish Vintage Bus  Kelty  Lower Oakfield  Lumphinnans  Lochgelly  A92

Craigmill  Cambuskenneth Abbey  A907  4  Gartmorn Dam  ALLOA  Alloa Tower  South Alloa  Cambus  Fallin  A910  Clackmannan  Clackmannan Tower  Kennet  Saline  Steelend  Cowstrandburn  Craigluscar Hill  Craigluscar Resrs.  Loch Fitty  Cantsdam  Kingseat  B981  Cowdenbeath  A92  Auchtertool

STIRLING  Bannockburn  A905  Throsk  Clackmannanshire Bridge  Kilbagie  A907  A823  Gowkhall  Townhill  Bowershall  Hill of Beath  Cowdenend  Crossgates  B925  A909

Ninians  St Ninians  Cowie  Dunmore  A876  Kincardine  Peppermill Dam  128  Blairhall  Comrie  Oakley  Carnock  Milesmark  Wellwood  Pitfirrane Palace  Halbeath  M90  Fordell  Cullaloe Resr.

Plean  West Plean  Bruce's Castle  Pineapple  B9124  Airth  Letham  A985  Shires Mill  Newmills  High Valleyfield  Low Torry  Crossford  DUNFERMLINE  A994  Cairneyhill  A823  Crossgates  2A  A921  Aberdour

M9  A872  Torwood  Torwood Castle  A88  A905  Kincardine Bridge  Kincardine  Culross  Culross Palace  Low Valleyfield  Torryburn  A985  Pattiesmuir  A823(M)  Hillend  Dalgety Bay  St Bridget's Kirk

Dunipace  Stenhousemuir  Carronshore  Skinflats  Longannet Point  Scottish Railway  Torry Bay  Charlestown  Limekilns  Rosyth  Inverkeithing  Inverkeithing Bay  Inchcolm  Inchcolm Abbey  Mortimer's Deep

Denny  Larbert  Carron  Bainsford  GRANGEMOUTH  BO'NESS  Grangepans  Bridgeness  Carriden  House of The Binns  Blackness  Blackness Castle  Hopetoun  Queensferry Crossing (Open 2017)  North Queensferry  Deep Sea World  Jamestown  P+R  South Queensferry  Dalmeny  Cramond Island  Inchmickery

Bonnybridge  M876  B902  FALKIRK  Laurieston  Polmont  A904  Newtown  Borrowstoun  Muirhouses  Champany  Champany  A904  Blackness  B903  Society  Abercorn  Midhope Castle  A904  Forth Bridge  Forth Road Bridge  South Queensferry  Dalmeny House  Eagle Rock  Cramond

Antonine Wall  Camelon  Glen Village  Falkirk Wheel  High Bonnybridge  Greenhill  Shieldhill  California  Maddiston  B825  Brightons  Rumford  Whitecross  Linlithgow  Linlithgow Palace  Union Canal  Kingscavil  Old Philpstoun  Philpstoun  Newbigging  Craigie  Craighall  M90  A90

FIRTH OF TAY

Osprey Centre
A923
Woodland
Clatto Resr.
Whitfield
Murroes
Ardestie Earth House
Barry
A930
Carnoustie
Fowlis
Muirhead
Birkhill
Downfield
Fintry
A961
Monifieth
DANGER AREA
11
Knapp
St Marnoch's Church
Lift
A90
Lochee
Camperdown
Craigie
A92
Claypotts Castle
Barnhill
Broughty Ferry
A930
Abernyte
Castlehill
Benvie
Mills Observatory
DUNDEE
A930
Broughty Castle
Broughty
Invergowrie
Longforgan
Kingoodie
A85
A930
HMS Frigate Unicorn
60
144
E
F
G
145
H
30
BUDDON NESS
Kinnaird
Craigdallie
Inchture
Tay Road Bridge
Discovery Point
DUNDEE
Tay Bridge
B946
Newport-on-Tay
Tayport
Tentsmuir
Rait
Westown
19
Woodhaven
B945
TENTSMUIR FOREST
1
Grange
Seaside
Wormit
A92
Pickletillem
Tentsmuir Sands
Cairn o' Mohr Winery
Inchmichael
Balmerino
Kirkton
Bottomcraig
A914
B946
Megginch Castle
North Muir
Errol Station
Gauldry
4
Muiredge
Errol
A90
Balmerino Abbey
Moray Water
A919
Deep Laing
Creich
Hazelton Walls
Kilmany
Lucklawhill
Leuchars
ST ANDREWS BAY
South Deep
936 Norman's Law
Brunton
Rathillet
571 Forret Hill
Logie
Leuchars
Eden Mouth
20
Newburgh
Glenduckie
Luthrie
Kedlock Feus
A914
Inner Bridge
Eden Estuary Centre
Castle
Den of Lindores
Dunbog
Moonzie
Lordscairnie Castle
Kilmaron
Foodieash
Dairsie or Osnaburgh
Guardbridge
A91
Aquarium
British Golf
St Andrews
Lindores
Lindores Loch
726 Mount Hill
A913
Kincaple
Grange of Lindores
A92
Letham
Cupar
Kemback
Strathkinness
Newpark
Blackfriars Chapel
Botanic Garden
Monimail
A91
Cupar Muir
Blebocraigs
B939
Craigtoun
Buddo Ness
2
Auchtermuchty
Collessie
Bow of Fife
B940
Pitscottie
Denhead
A915
Prior Muir
Boarhills
B9131
10
A917
Kingsbarns
Giffordtown
Innerleith
Scottish Deer Centre
Springfield
Bridgend
B939
Ceres
Baldinnie
Cameron Reservoir
Bonnytown
Stravithie
Cambo
FIFE NESS
Dunshalt
Ladybank
Chance Inn
Fife Folk
Peat Inn
Radernie
Dunino
Craighead
A912
HOWE OF FIFE
A914
Pitlessie
Cults
Scotstarvit Tower
Struthers Castle
Craigrothie
West Lingo
Kingsmuir
Lochty
B940
Scotland's Secret Bunker
10
Crail
Falkland Palace
Kingskettle
Balmalcolm
Clatto Resr.
Backmuir of New Gilston
Pittarthie Castle
Tolbooth
Crail
Falkland
Freuchie
Kettlebridge
Montrave
Woodside
B941
Lathones
Largoward
Kellie Law 603
Carnbee
East Pitcorthie
West Pitcorthie
A917
Hills
Muirhead
Langdyke
Carlhurlie Resr.
Largo Law 952
A915
B941
Arncroach
Kellie Castle
B9171
Kilrenny
Holl Resr.
Newton of Falkland
Kirkforthar Feus
Baintown
Standing Stones
Kirkton of Largo or Upper Largo
Drumeldrie
B942
Colinsburgh
B941
Abercrombie
Anstruther Wester
Cellardyke
Scottish Fisheries
Collydean
Star
Bonnybank
B927
A915
Lower Largo
Alexander Selkirk Memorial
A917
Kilconquhar
St Monans
Anstruther Easter
Pittenweem
St Fillan's Cave
Leslie
Cadham
Balbirnie Stone Circle
Kennoway
Lundin Links
Newark Castle
Heritage Collection
A911
Markinch
Balcurvie
Broom
Scoonie
Silverburn
Kilconquhar Loch
13
Walkerton
Fife
A911
Leven
Largo Bay
Ruddons Point
Earlsferry
Elie
Sauchar Point
700
GLENROTHES
Milton of Windygates
Innerleven
Chapel Ness
Kinglassie
Thornton
Methilhill
Methil
Heritage Centre
Coaltown of Balgonie
Denbeath
Buckhaven
Macduff's Castle
A915
East Wemyss
Wemyss Caves
FORTH
4
Cluny
A92
Ore Bridge
Coaltown of Wemyss
Wemyss Castle
denden
B981
Gallatown
A955
West Wemyss
Chapel
Sinclairtown
Dysart
Templehall
Pathhead
Harbourmaster's House Coastal Centre
A910
Ravenscraig
KIRKCALDY
Linktown
90
129
130
Pitteadie Castle
A921
Seafield Tower
Bass Rock
B9157
Kinghorn
Craigleith
B923
Pettycur
Craigleith
Lamb
Fidra
Scottish Seabird Centre
Tantallon
tisland
Alexander III Monument
Eyebroughy
North Berwick
A198
5
Communication
Inchkeith
Gullane Bay
Dirleton
North Berwick Law 613
Whitekirk
FIRTH
Gullane
B1345
Kingston
Saltcoats Castle
B1347
Aberlady Bay
Fenton Barns
EAST LOTHIAN
80
Aberlady
Myreton Motor
Drem
130
22
H
Tyninghame
East Fortune
B1407
E
129
F
Craigie
G
A198
Gosford Bay
Ballencrieff
Chesters Hill Fort National
Preston
Knowes
30
40
Spittal
B1377
Athelstaneford
B1343
B1347
A199
EDINBURGH
Cockenzie and Port Seton
Longniddry
A6137
East Linton
A901
Newhaven
Trinity
Britannia
A199
Hopetoun Monument 610
Leith
PAGE 195
B1348
Huntington
Hailes

80     100     10     20     30

A    B    C    D

**1**

Oban to Lochboisdale 5hrs. 20mins. (Seasonal)

**2**

70

Oban to Castlebay 5hrs.

Cairns of Coll

Eag na Maoile

Rubha Mór

Eilean Mór

Bousd

Rubh'a' Bhinnein

Cornaigmore

Sorisdale

B8072

Loch Fada

**COLL**

60

Cliad Bay

Grishipoll

B8071

7

Rubha Hogh

Clabhach

Bagh Feisdlum

Loch Cliad

B8011

Hogh Bay

340

Loch nan Cinneachan

**Arinagour**

Ben Nogh

Stables

Loch Anlaimh

V

Loch Eathar

**3**

Tiree to Barra 2hrs. 45mins. (Seasonal)

Totronald

Acha

Coll

Eilean Ornsay

Feall Bay

Uig

5

B8010

Calgary Point

Loch Breachacha

Port na h-Eathar

Oban to Tiree 3hrs. 20mins. (Seasonal)

Gunna

Friesland Bay

Crossapol Bay

Soa

Treshnish

750

Caolas Bàn

Port a' Mhurain

Gunna Sound

Rubha Dubh

Coll to Tiree 55mins.

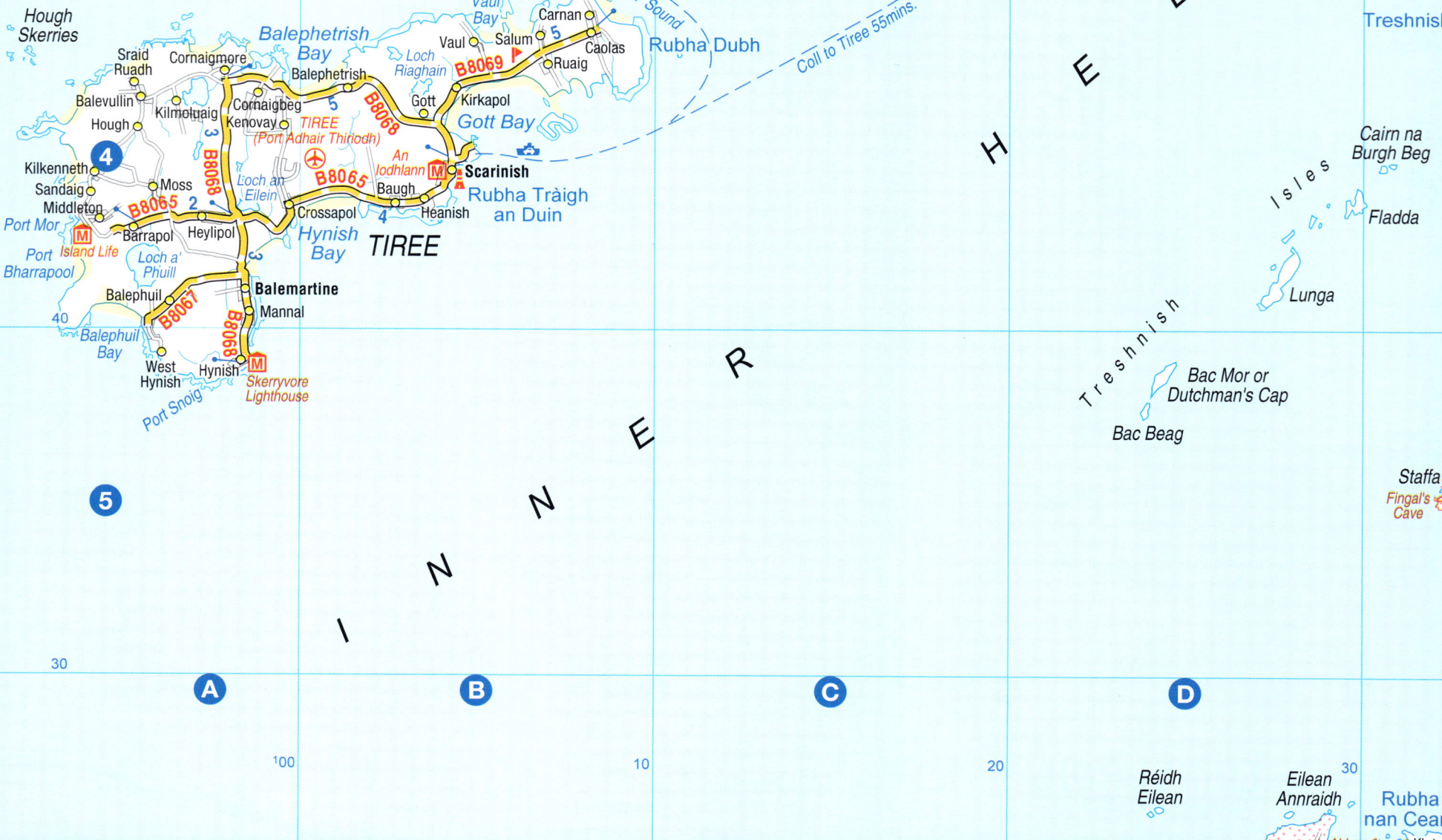

Hough Skerries

Vaul Bay

Miodar

Carnan

H

Sraid Ruadh

Cornaigmore

Balephetrish Bay

Vaul

Salum

5

E

Loch Riaghain

Caolas

Balevullin

Balephetrish

Ruaig

B8069

B

Hough

Kilmoluaig

Cornaigbeg

Gott

Kirkapol

5

B8068

Kenovay

**TIREE** (Port Adhair Thiriodh)

An Iodhlann

Gott Bay

R

**4**

Kilkenneth

3

B8068

Loch an Eilein

B8065

M

**Scarinish**

Sandaig

Moss

2

Baugh

Rubha Tràigh an Duin

I

Middleton

Crossapol

4

Heanish

Port Mor

B8065

Barrapol

Heylipol

**Hynish Bay**

Cairn na Burgh Beg

Port Bharrapool

Island Life

M

Loch a' Phuill

**TIREE**

Fladda

Balephuil

Mannal

**Balemartine**

B8067

West Hynish

Hynish

Balephuil Bay

B8068

M

Lunga

Port Snoig

Skerryvore Lighthouse

N

Bac Mor or Dutchman's Cap

E

Bac Beag

Treshnish Isles

**Staffa**
Fingal's Cave

**5**

30

A    B    C    D

100     10     20

Réidh Eilean

Eilean Annraidh

30

Rubha nan Cearc

E  146  F  G  H

MUCK

Eilean nan Each
Gòdag
Port Mor
Dubh Sgeir

Sound of Eigg
Sgeir Eskernish
Galmisdale
An Ogan 1292
Rubha na' Crannaig
Eilean Chathastail

Mallaig to Muck 35mins
Eigg to Muck 35mins
150

Islands Centre  Glen Cottage  Druimindarroch
Prince's Cairn
Rubh' Arisaig
Eilean a' Ghaill
Camas Ghaoideil
Loch nan Uamh
Loch Doire
A861
Roshven
Loch Ailt
80
Eilean nan Gobhar
Sound of Arisaig
Glenuig Bay
Glenuig (Gleann Uige)
Samalaman Island
Samalaman
Smirisary
Lochan na Cloiche Sgoilte
Loch nam Paitean
M O I
1
17
Loch na Bairness
Rubh' Aird an Fheidh
Baramore
Arean
Eilean Shona
Loch Moidart
Castle Tioram
Kinlochmoidart
(Ceann Loch Muideirt)
Ardmolich
Brunery
Newton of Ardtoe
Ardtoe
Shielfoot
Blain
Dalnabreck
Langal
Dalelia
70
Mingarrypark
Moss
B8044
Kentra Bay
Kentra
Arivegaig
Acharacle (Ath-Tharracail)
Ardshealach
Gorteneorn
A861
Salen (An Sailean)
2
Resipole

Sanna Point
Sanna Bay
Ardnamurchan Lighthouse
Point of Ardnamurchan
Achosnich
Portuairk
Sanna
Achnaha
Fascadale
Kilmory
Achateny
Branault
Ockle Point
Ockle
Port Bàn
Rubha Aird Druimnich
Gortenfern
A R D N A M U R C H A N
An R 1433
Beinn Bhraec 1171
Beinn Na Seilg 1123
Kilchoan
Ormsaigmore
Ormsaigbeg
B8007
An Acairseid
Kilchoan Bay
Mingary
Mingary Castle
Loch Mudle
B800
1026 Beinn nan Losgann
Ben Hiant 1731
16
Maclean's Nose
35mins
Cladh Chiaran Burial Ground
Ardslignish
Glenmore
Glenbeg
Ardnamurchan Natural History Centre
Glenborrodale
Laga
B8007
Leac Shoilleir
Lochan nam Fiann
Meall nan Each 1607
Ben Laga 1679
Oronsay
Risga
Carna
Loch Sunart
Glencripesdale Burn
Meall an Damhain 1693
60
Meall an

E S E S

Coll to Oban 2hrs. 45mins.

Ardmore Bay
Ardmore Point
Rubha nan Gall
Auliston Point
140
H I G H L A N D
Beinn Iadain 1873
Kinloch
3

Quinish Point
Glengorm Castle
Meall an Inbhire 865
An Tobar
Mull
Tobermory
Hebridean Whale and Dolphin Trust
Isle of Mull Cheese
Tobermory Distillery
Calve Island
Drimnin
M O R V E R N
Beinn Bhuidhe 1481
Loch Doire nam Mart
1806
Lochanan Dubha
Beinn na h-Uamha
An t-Aoineadh Mor Deserted Village
Caliach Point
Croig
Calgary
Calgary Bay
Point
Ensay
Haunn
B8073
Dervaig
'S Airde Beinn 959
Loch an Torr
Loch a' Chumhainn
Old Byre Heritage Centre
7
B8073
Loch Peallach
A R O S
Cruachan Druim na Croise 866
Speinne Mór 1458
Ardnacross
Lettermore
Salen Forest
9
A848
Sound of Mull
Rhemore
Killundine
Fiunary
Fiunary Forest
10
B849
Caisteal nan Con
Sithean na Raplaich
Loch Arienas
Claggan
A884
Larachbeg
Ardtornish
Achranich
Rannoch
10
50

Rubh a' Chaoil
Burg
Kilninian
Achleck
Fanmore
Cnoc an da Chinn 1280
Ballygown
Eas Fors Waterfall
A R G Y L L
Kengharair
Crannich
Tenga
Aros
River Bellart
Beinn na Drise 1392
Aros Mains
Aros Castle
Rubha Mor
Mull
Salen
13
A849
Fishnish Bay
Fishnish
Ardtornish Castle
Inninmore Bay
Lochaline
4
Glais Bheinn 1570
Lochan a' Chulla
40

Eilean Dioghlum
Loch Tuath
Gometra
Gometra House
Mâisgeir
Eilean na Creiche
Little Colonsay
Inch Kenneth
Laggan Bay
Laganulva
Oskamull
Isle of Ulva Heritage Centre
Ulva House
U L V A
Beinn Creagach 1026
Samalan Island
Chapel
13
B8073
Sound of Ulva
Eorsa
Loch na Keal
Killiechronan
Kellan
Gruline
Macquarie Mausoleum
Knock
Loch na Dairidh
Beinn Bhuidhe 1352
B8035
Tomsléibhe
Beinn Creagach Mhòr 1903
Bailemeonach
Garmony
Scallastle Bay
Craignure Bay
Craignure
Wings Over Mull
Dùn da Ghaoithe 2512
5
Loch Beàrnach
Duart Bay
15mins
R U AN F

Erisgeir
Rubha na h Uamha
MacCulloch's Fossil Tree
Tavool House
Creach Bheinn 1613
A R D M E A N A C H
132
Tiroran
Derryguaig
Gribun
Coirc Bheinn 1837
B E N M O R E
Ben More 3171
B U T E
Corra-bheinn 2311
Glen
Loch Ba
Loch Scridain
Beinn a' Ghràig 1939
Bein na Srèine 1704
B8035
17
Gleann
Seilisdeir
Kilfinichen Bay
150
Garbh Phort
Creach Bheinn
Port na Croise
Coladoir River
A849
Loch Fuaran
Beinn na Croise
I S L E O F M U L L
Beinn Talaidh 2502
Sgurr Dearg 2429
Loch Airdeglais
Lussa River
Beinn Talaidh
Loch Sguabain
Glen More
Strathcoil
Carn Bàn 812
30
A849
Oakbank
Loch
Glen Cannel
Ben Buie 2354
Kinlochspelve
Lochbuie
Loch Spelve
Croggan
Loch Uisg
Moy
14
G
H
60
70
40

# 140

## A  147  B  C  Glenfinnan  D

Rubh' Arisaig — Islands Centre — Glen Cottage — Druimindarroch — Loch na Creige Duibhe — Druim 1675 — Slios Garbh — Sgurr an Utha 2610 — Glas-charn 2076 — Beoraid — Gleann Du

Eilean a' Ghaill — Polnish — Prince's Cairn — A830 — Lochailort (Ceann Loch Ailleart) — Ranochan — Loch Eilt — 90 — Station — 14 — M — The Jacobite — V — Viaduct — Glenfinnan — Glen Finnan — Callop River — Glen Garvan — Dubh Lighe — Gleann Fion...

Eilean an t-Snidhe — 60 — 80 — Sound of Arisaig — 70 — Loch nan Uamh — Inverailort — Loch Doire a' Ghearrain — Eilean nan Gobhar — Glenfinnan Monument

## 1

Glenuig Bay — Roshven — A861 — ROIS-BHEINN 2895 — Druim Fiaclach 2852 — Croit Bheinn 2175 — Beinn Odhar Bheag 2895 — Sgorr Craobh a' Chaorainn — Glen Garvan

Samalaman Island — Samalaman — Glenuig (Gleann Uige) — MOIDART — Sgurr Dhomhuill Mór — Beinn Gàire 2179 — Loch Shiel — Meall nan Creag Leac

Smirisary — Rubh' Aird an Fheidh — Baramore — Loch na Bairness — Lochan na Cloiche Sgoilte — Loch nam Paitean — River Moidart — Gaskan — Scamodale — Sgorr an Tarmachain 2474

Eilean Shona — Arean — Loch Moidart — Kinlochmoidart (Ceann Loch Muideirt) — Ardmolich — Brunery — Lochan Dubh — Beinn Mheadhoin 2579 — Cona Glen — Cona River — Druim Leathad nam Fias 1893

Farquhar's Point — Ardtoe — Newton of Ardtoe — Castle Tioram — Shielfoot — Dalnabreck — Langal — Dalelia — Glenhurich — Sgurr Dhomhnuill 2915 — Glen Scaddle — Scaddle

17 — Blain — Mingarrypark — Moss — Pollach — Loch Doilet — River Hurich — Glen Hurich

## 2

Leac Shoilleir — Kentra Bay — B8044 — Shiel Br. — Acharacle (Ath-Tharracail) — Ardshealach — SUNART 2775 — Beinn Resipol — Ariundle — Scotstown — Strontian River — ARDGOUR — Lochan na Beinne Báine

Rubha Aird Druimnich — Gortenfern — Kentra — Arivegaig — Gorteneorn — Resipole — Ardery — Anaheilt — Strontian (Sron an t-Sithein) — Glen Tarbert — Glen Gour — Glen Gour

Lochan Sligneach — Meall nan Each 1607 — Loch Laga — Ben Laga 1679 — Salen (An Sailean) — A861 — 11 — Ardnastang — A861 — River Tarbert — Garbh Bheinn 2903 — 6

Lochan nam Fiann — Ardslignish — Glenborrodale — Ardnamurchan Natural History Centre — B8007 — Laga — Loch Sunart — Inversanda — Inversanda Bay

## 3

Glenmore — Glenbeg — Glencripesdale Burn — Meall an Damhain 1693 — Laudale House — Beinn nam Beathrach 1911 — A884 — Creach Bheinn 2798 — Kilmalieu — B8043 — Camas Chil-Mhalieu

Drimnin — B849 — Oronsay — Risga — Carna — Kinloch — Beinn Iadain 1873 — Dubh — Lochuisge — Loch Uisge — B8043 — Fuar Bheinn 2511 — Camus Chil-Mhalieu

Beinn Bhuidhe 1481 — Lochanan Dubha — Beinn Chlaonleud 1569 — Loch Uisge — Bheinn na Cille 2136 — Kingairloch — LOCH LINNHE — Eilean Bainagowan — Rubha Mor

MORVERN — An t-Aoineadh Mor Deserted Village 1806 — Sithean na Raplaich — Claggan — 10 — Loch Arienas — Beitheach — Beinn Mheadhoin 2423 — Camasnacroise — Loch a' Choire — Dalnatrat

## 4

Rhemore 750 — Fiunary Forest — Larachbeg — A884 — Ardtornish — Achranich — Rannoch River — Loch Tearnait — Loch nan Clach — Glensanda — Glensanda Castle — Port a' Chaisteil — Creag Shuna — Shuna Island — Castle Shuna — Glen Stockdale — Beinn Donn 1553 — Portnacroish

Killundine — Caisteal nan Con — Fiunary — 10 — B849 — Lochaline — Loch Aline — Beinn a' Chaisil 1431 — Camas Airigh Shamhraidh — Eilean nan Caorach — Port Ramsay — Eilean Loch Oscair — Kinlochlaich — Appin

Sound Of Mull — Aros Mains — Aros Castle — Ardtornish Castle — Inninmore Bay — Glais Bheinn 1570 — Lochan Mam a' Chullaich 1684 — An Sleaghach — Eignaig — Glensanda — Port Appin — B8045 — Druimneil House — North Shian — Eriska

Salen — Rubha Mor — Mull — 13 — Fishnish Bay — Fishnish — 15mins. — Camas Gorn — RUBHA AN RIDIRE — Isle of Lismore Gaelic Heritage — Clachan — Tirefour Castle Broch — Scottish Sea Life Sanctuary

## 5

ISLE — B8035 — Loch na Daindidh — Tomsléibhe — Dùn da Ghaoithe 2512 — Craignure — Bailemeonach — Garmony — A849 — Salen Forest — Scallastle Bay — Craignure Bay — Wings over Mull — Duart Bay — Duart — Duart Point — Achadun Castle — Achinduin — Kilcheran — Eilean Dubh — Balliveolan — Killandrist — Achnacroish — LISMORE — Bernera Island — Barr Mor — BENDERLOCH — Ledaig — A828

OF — Macquarie Mausoleum — Beinn Creagach Mhór 1903 — Beinn Talaidh 2502 — Sgurr Dearg 2429 — Lochan an Doire Dharaich — Lochdon — Oakbank — Loch Bearnach — Eilean Musdile — Creag Island — Pladda Island — Rubha Garbh-àird — South Ledaig — Dunstaffnage — Connel — Ardmucknish Bay — Kiel Crofts — Baravullin — Barcaldine — A85

MULL — Beinn Talaidh 2502 — Mòre — Loch Don — A849 — Grass Point — Oban to Craignure 45mins. — Oban to Lismore 50mins. — Dunbeg — Ganavan — Dunollie — War & Peace — McCaig's Tower — OBAN — A85 — Lusragan Burn — Achaleven — Stonefield — Loch — Black Lochs

Corra-bheinn 2311 — Beinn Talaidh — Coladoir River — 30 — Loch Sguabain — Strathcoil — Carn Bàn 812 — KERRERA — Balliemore — Carn Breugach — Pulpit Hill — Distillery — Dalintart — 5 — ARGYLL — Beinn Ghlas 1691 — Beinn Lora — Falls of Lora — Black Crofts — Ardchattan Priory — Beinn Ghlas

Ben Buie 2354 — Creach Beinn 2290 — Kinlochspelve — Croggan — 14 — Loch Spelve — 70 — Bach Island — Gylen Castle — Eilean nan Gramhna — Dubh — RUBHA SEANACH — Sound of Kerrera — Loch Seil — Kilbride — Cleigh — Kilmore — Croimhead 1257 — Beinn Ghlas 1691

Loch Fuaran — Beinn na Croise — Lochbuie — Moy — Lussa River — Loch Airdeglais — Creach Beinn — Loch Uisg — Loch Spelve — Ballimore — Bach Island — Rubha Seanach — Loch Nell — Fearnoch Forest

## A  132  B  C  OBAN PAGE 201  133  D

PAGE 201
139

Gairlochy  B8004  Stronenaba  Creag Dhubh 3437

Allt Glas Dho...

River Loy

Gleann Suileag  An t-Suileag  200  Stob a' Ghrianain  Brackletter  Spean Bridge  A86  Inverroy  Roybridge  Bohenie 30  Creag Dhubh

Druim Fada  Commando Memorial  Alltour  Achluachrach  GLEN  SPEAN

Muirshearlich  Highbridge  Commando  Monessie Falls  Invervar Falls

Beinn an t-Sneachda  148  E  F  B8004  A86  Spean  G  Bunroy  149  H  Loch  Braes o' Lochaber

Kinlocheil  Corribeg  Fassfern  Achdalieu  Tor Castle  A82  Leanachan Forest  Beinn Chlianaig 2343  Fersit  80

A830  Treasures of the Earth  FORT WILLIAM  Crofting  70

Loch  Eil  South Garvan  Duisky  Blaich  A861  The Jacobite  Banavie  Corpach  Caol  Camaghael  Torlundy  Creag Aoil  Nevis Range Gondola  Allt Laire  Chno Dearg 3433

Achaphubuil  20  Lochyside  Ben Nevis Distillery  Inverlochy  1  Allt Feith Thuill

Camusnagaul  Trislaig  Inverlochy  Victoria Bridge  Claggan  Inverlochy 1645  Killiechonate Forest  Stob Choire Claurigh 3858  Stob Coire Easain 3658  Stob Coire Easain  Beinn na Lap

Stob Coire a' Chearcaill 2528  West Highland  Bridge of Nevis  Glen Nevis  AONACH BEAG 4048  Laing Leabach  Stob Coire  Loch Treig

Stronchreggan  Lime Tree Gallery  Lochan Meall an t-Suidhe  BEN NEVIS 4411  Abhainn Rath  Loch na Lap

Ach an Todhair  Rocking Stone  Glen Nevis Waterslide  Uamh Shomhairle  Steall Falls  Beinn na Lap

Druimarbin  Nevis Forest  Water of Nevis  Creaguaineach Lodge

Blarmachfoldach  Achriabhach  Glen Nevis Lower Falls  MAMORE FOREST  Loch Eilde Mór  Leum Uilleim 2971  Loch na Sgeallaig

Conaglen  A82  Achriabhach Falls  Nevis  Sgurr a' Mhàim 3601  Binnein Mór 3700  Loch Eilde Beag  2

Inverscaddle Bay  Mullach nan Coirean  Mam na Gualainn 2611  Grey Mare's Tail  Kinlochmore  Ciaran Water  Black

Sgurr na h-Eanchainne 2395  A861  Beinn na Gucaig 2022  Lochan Lùnn Dà-Bhrà  Leven  Aluminium Story  Kinlochleven  River  Leven  Blackwater Reservoir  60  Black Wa...

Ardgour  Narrows  Inchree  Inchree Falls  Garbh Bheinn 2844  Meall nan Ruadhag 2120

Clovullin  Corran  Bunree  A82  North Ballachulish  B863  Loch  B863  142 2423

Sallachan  Onich  Sallachan Point  Glencoe & North Lorn Folk  Leven  Pap of Glencoe 2430  3173  3118  A' CHRUACH  3

Bridge of Coe  Glencoe  M  Aonach Eagach  Stob a' Bhruaiche 2423

South Ballachulish  Monument  Glencoe  Clachaig  The Three Sisters  Altnafeadh  Beinn a' Chrùlaiste 2811  Black Corries

Kentallen  Ballachulish  Meall Mór  Ossian's Cave  Glencoe Gorge  Kingshouse  Lochan Coir na Mèinne

A828  Beinn a' Bheithir  Bidean nam Bian 3766  Buachaille Etive Beag  River Coupall  Buachaille Etive Mór  23  A82  RANNOCH

Duror  Achindarroch  Glenduror Forest  Royal Forest  Dalness  White Corries  Lochan Gaineamhach  Loch Bà 750

Fraochaidh 2883  Creran Forest  Sgùrr na h-Ulaidh 3258  Beinn Maol Chaluim 2774  Etive  Clach Leathad 3602  BLACK  MOUNT

Salachan Glen  Beinn Fhionnlaidh 3145  Invercharnan  Stob Dubh 2897  Allt Coire a' Chaolain  Stob Ghabhar 3565  Achallader

Elleric  An Iola  Glen Ure  Aonach Mór  River  Bà  Lochan na h-Achlaise  Beinn a' Chreachain 3540

Fasnacloich  Loch Baile Mhic Chailein  Loch Dochard  Black Mount  Loch Tulla  Beinn Achaladair 3404

Invercreran  Gualachulain  Stob Coir an Albannach 3425  4  Beinn an Dòthaidh 3267

Beinn Churalain 1792  3059  Beinn Sgulaird 2807  Beinn Trilleachan 2752  Victoria Bri.  Beinn Mhanach 3125

South Creagan  Ben Starav 3541  Beinn nan Aighenan 3141  Loch Dochard  Beinn Suidhe 2215  Beinn Inverveigh 2087  Beinn Dorain 3524  Bridge of Orchy

Creach Bheinn 2656  Dail  Glenkinglass Lodge  Allt  Tolaghan  Allt Chonoghlais

LOCH  B845  River Esragan  Beinn Mheadhonach 2344  2327  Beinn nan Lus  2283  Meall Garbh  Beinn Mhic-Mhonaidh 2602  Beinn Udlaidh 2759  Beinn Breac-liath 2633  A82  5  Beinn Odhar 2948

Inveresragan  Craig  Inverliver  Glen Liver  Beinn Eunaich 3242  Kinglass  River Strae  B8074  Clifton

Bonawe  Glennoe  Bealm Mhoille  BUTE  Beinn Donachain 2127  A85  Lochan na Bì  Tyndrum

A85  Airds Bay  Bonawe Historic Iron Furnace  BEN CRUACHAN  Orchy  134  River Lochy  A82

Taynuilt  Inverawe Smokery  3695  E  F  G  H  30

Ichrachan  Bridge of Awe  Cruachan Reservoir  Beinn a' Bhuiridh 2941  Stronmilchan  Edendonich  Achnafalnich  River  Cononish  Ben Lui 3708

Angus's  Airdeny  A85  Falls of Cruachan  Lochawe  Kilchurn  Kinchrackine  Dalmally  A85 26  Beinn na Sròine  Eas a' Ghaill  Fiarach 2132

Cruachan Power Station  St Conan's Kirk  Duncan Ban MacIntyre Monument  Ben Dubhchraig 3204

# Map labels

Moy Forest
Creag Dhubh 2160
Beinn a' Chaorainn 3437
Ardverikie Forest
Moy Lodge
A86
Loch Laggan Resr.
Binnein Shuas
Lochan na h-Earba
Geal Charn 3443
River Pattack
Meall Cruaidh 2941
Creagan Mór 2522
Carn na Caim 3087
Loch an Duin

Falls
Falls
Fersit
Tulloch
A
Lochan an Turic
B
149
Loch a'
Loch Pattack
C
A9
D

Meall Luidh Mór
Beinn a' Chlachair 3569
Allt a' Chaoil rèidhe
A' Bhuidheanach Bhéag 3072
Sronphadruig Lodge

HIGHLAND

Creag Dhubh
Allt Lòraich
Allt Laire
Loch Treig
Meall Luidh Mór
Loch Ghuilbinn
Aonach Beag 3647
Loch An Sgòir
An Lairig 3391
Càrn Dearg
Ben Alder Lodge
Gealm Charn 3005
Glas Mheall Mór 3037

Luachrach
1
Chno Dearg 3433
River Ossian
Uisge Labhair
Ben Alder 3765
Loch a' Bhealaich Bheithe
Loch Ericht
Corrievarkie Lodge
An Torc or Boar of Badenoch 3174
The Sow of Atholl
Dalnaspidal Lodge
Dalnacardoch Lodge

Loch Na Lap
Allt Feith Thuill
FOREST
Dalnacardoch Forest
GLEN
Edendon Water
Loch Con
Dalnacardoch Lodge 3037

Beinn na Lap
Corrour Shooting Lodge
Sgor Gaibhre 3124
Stob an Aonaich Mhóir 2805
Beinn Ùdlamain 3306
Ar Cearcall
Loch Garry
Meall na Lèitreach 2544

uaineach odge
Loch Ossian
Corrour Forest
Carn Dearg 3080
Talla Bheith Forest
Beinn Mholach 2759
Allt Sleibh
Allt Con
Loch Errochty
Trinafour
B817

2
Leum Uilleim 2971
Allt na Caim
Rannoch Forest
Sròn Bheag 1631
Loch Mheugaidh
Craiganour Forest
Aullich Burn
Allt Ruighe nan Saorach
Loch na Caillich 2927
Beinn a' Chuallaich

Reservoir
Black Water
Allt Eigheach
River Ericht
Killichonan Burn

141
Stob na Cruaiche 2423
Lochan Lòin nan Donnlaich
River Ericht
Bridge of Ericht
Killichonan
16
Loch Rannoch
Carie
Kinloch Rannoch
Dunalastair
B846
Tempar
Dunalastair Water

A' CHRUACH
Lochan Sròn Smeur
B846
Rannoch Station
Loch Eigheach
River Gaur
Bridge of Gaur
Finnart
Camghouran
Dall House
Allt na Bogair
Schiehallion 3554

3
Lochan Coire na Mèinne
Abhainn Duibhe
Gleann Dubh
Gleann Chomraidh
Loch Finnart
Loch Monaghan
Dall Burn
TAY FOREST PARK

RANNOCH MOOR
R A N N O C H
Meall a' Mhuic 2444
Carn Gorm 3377
Carn Mairg 3419
P

RANNOCH
L750 Ba'
Meall Buidhe 3054
Cam Chreag 2823
Bridge of Balgie
Innerwick
Camusvrachan
Invervar
Carnbane Castle

Water of Tulla
Meall Cruinn 2717
Meall Luaidhe 2558
Lyon River

MOUNT
Achallader 4
Beinn a' Chreachain 3540
Eas Daimh
Stuchd an Lochain 3144
Gallin
Allt Conait
Lairig a Mhuic
Gleann Da Eig
Meall Garbh 3661
Lochan nan Cat
Lawers Burn
Fearnan
Bridge of Lyon
Gleann Da-ghob

Beinn Achaladair 3404
Meall Buidhe
River Lyon
Cashlie
Stronuich Reservoir
Allt Bail a' Mhuilinn
Meall Ghaordie 3410
3421
Meall nan Tarmachan
BEN LAWERS 3984
Lochan na Lairige
Ben Lawers
Meall Odhar
Lawers
Ardtalnaig

Beinn an Dòthaidh 3267
Beinn Mhanach 3125
Beinn Heasgarnich 3530
Sgiath Bhuidhe
Meall Taurnie
Carie
Tullich Hill

ridge Orchy
Loch Lyon
Kenknock
Glen Lochay
River Lochay
Laira Breisleich
Morenish
Milton Morenish
Loch Tay
Ardeonaig
Finglen Burn

Beinn Dorain 3524
Creag Mhòr 3387
Forest of Mamlorn
BREADALBANE
Creag Mhòr 2359
Moirlanich Longhouse
A827
Finlarig Castle
Creag Gharbh 2090
Creag Uchdag 2883

A82
5
Beinn Odhar 2948
Ben Challum 3354
Beinn Cheathaich 3076
3007
Meall a' Churain
Allt Riobain
Falls of Lochay
Breadalbane Folklore
Killin
Falls of Dochart
Lochan Breaclaich

Clifton
Tyndrum
Beinn nan Imirean 2769
STIRLING
Glen Dochart
R. Dochart
Beinn Lebhrain 2312
Loch Breaclaich

A82
A
134
B
Lochdochart House
Luib
Ardchyle
C
A85
Auchlyne West Burn
Glen Ogle
D
135

A85
Fiarach 2132
Strath Fillan
Loch Lubhair
Glen Dochart
Loch Dochart
Meall a' Mhadaidh
Creag Each 2205
Loch Boltachan

BEN MORE

# CAIRNGORMS NATIONAL PARK

Gaick Lodge

Loch Bhrodainn
Gaick Forest

Uchd a' Chlarsair 2587

Beinn Bhreac 2992

An Sgarsoch 3276

An Sgarsoch 3300

Carn Bhac 3014

Baddoch
Sgor Mór

Beinn Iutharn Mhór 3424

Carn a' Gheòidh 3194
3059 The Cairnwell

Loch nan Eun

E 150    F    G 151    H    1

MOUNTAINS

BEINN DEARG 3307

Braigh Sròn Ghorm 2882

Bruar Lodge

Carn an Righ 3377

Glas Tulaichean 3449

Glenlochsie Lodge

2641 Ben Gulabin

2470 Carn an Daimh

Dalnamein Forest

Sròn a' Chleirich 2678

Gleann Diridh

Beinn a' Ghlo 3673

Meall a' Choire Bhuidhe 2846

Spittal of Glenshee
70    A93

Edendon Bridge

Forest Lodge

Carn Liath 3197

Loch Valligan

Ben Vuirich 2962

Ben Earb 2627

2600 Meall Uaine

Dalnamein Lodge    A9

Falls of Bruar

Tirinie

Loch Moraig

Creag an-t Sithein 2075

Straloch    Dirnanean

Lamh Dearg 1879

Calvine Struan    Pitagowan

Clan Donnachaidh    Blair    B8079

Old Blair

Old Bridge of Tilt

Blair Atholl

Ballentoul

Enochdhu

Whitefield Castle

Errochty    B847

Atholl Country Life

Tulach Hill 1542

Aldclune

1689    Claverhouse Stone

Ben Vrackie 2760

A924

Glen Brerachan

Creag Dhubh 2092

Kirkmichael    60    B950

25    144

Tummel Forest

Craig nan Caisean 1566

Lochan nan Nighean

Killiecrankie

Tenandry

Pass of Killiecrankie

Craigower Hill

Loch Curran

River Ardle    STRATHARDLE

Tummel Bridge    20    Tressait    B8019

Linn of Tummel

Moulin

Loch Broom

Meall Reamhar 1751

Knock of Balmyle 1458    Ballintuim

River Tummel Aqueduct    B846

Foss    Queen's View Centre

Loch Faskally    Pitlochry    Caisteal Dubh

Edradour Distillery    A924

Ballintuim    3    A924

TAY FOREST PARK

Loch Kinardochy

Meall Tairneachan 2583

2559 Farragon Hill

Loch Derculich

Explorers Pitlochry Hydro Electric    A9

Dunfallandy Stone

Lochan Oisinneach Mór

Creag nam Mial 1842

Blackcraig Hill 1573

White Bridge

Loch Farleyer

Weem Hill

Loch Glassie

Strathtay    Pitnacree    9

Haugh of Ballechin

A827    Ballinluig    Tulliemet

Forest of Clunie

Loch Benachally

Bridge of Cally

Blackcraig Forest

Cluny House

Derculich    Grandtully    Little Ballinluig

Balnaguard    Logierait    60    Kindallachan

Riemore Lodge    1594 Benachally

Cochrage Muir

Castle Menzies    Boltachan    Pitcairn

Dewar's World of Whisky

Guay    Deuchary Hill 1676

Camserney    Weem    Aberfeldy

Dull    Black Watch Memorial

Kincraigie    Dowally

Keltneyburn    B846 DULL

Bolfracks    Grandtully Hill 1747

Loch Scoly    Dalguise

A9

Butterstone    Forneth    4    72    A92

Fortingall    Yew Tree    Comrie Castle

Falls of Moness    Loch na Cragie

Loch Skiach    Craigvinean Forest

Loch of Butterstone    Clunie    Castle    Loch Drumel

Fortingall Standing Stones    Drummond Hill

Craig Hill 1857    Uilar Burn

Loch Kennard    Ossian's Hall

Snaigow House    Kirkton of Lethendy

A827    Kenmore

Scottish Crannog Centre    A826

Loch Hoil    Meall Dearg 2264

Ossian's Cave    Trochry    Dunkeld    Little Dunkeld    Birnam

Beatrix Potter Centre    Spittalfield    A984

Acharn    Falls of Acharn

Beinn Bhreac

Wester Shian    Garrow

Loch Fender    Cochill Burn    Ballinloan Burn

Inver    Newtyle Hill 1041

Kingswood    Caputh

A923    Murthly

Beinn Chonzie 3048

Auchnafree Hill 2589

Croftmill    Amulree    Strathbraan

Obney Hills    Stare Dam

Gellyburn    Ardoch    A9    B867    Mill Dam

River Tay    Me

Gleann a' Chilleine

Meall nam Fuaran 2641

Lochan a' Mhuilinn

Tullybeagles Lodge    Waterloo    A9

Bankfoot    Airntully    5    14    B8099

Auchnafree

Meall Reamhar 2188

Glen Quaich    Glen Shee    Milton Burn

Little Glenshee    Ordie Burn    Stanley    Gui

Newmiln

River Almond    Newton Bridge    A822

Meall Tarsuinn 2126    Shaggie Burn    B8063    Logiealmond    136    Harrietfield    B8063    H    Moneydie    Stormontfield    A93

Carn Chrois    Loch Turret Reservoir    Buchanty    Tulchan    Chapelhill    Luncarty 30

Invergeldie    Glenalmond    River Almond    Pitcairngreen

Bertha Loch    Scone Palace Pinetum

Busby    Pitcairngreen    Perth    Old Scone

Monzie    Keillour    Braegrum    Almondbank    A85    Huntingtower    Scone Palace    Muirton    Pi

**CAIRNGORMS**

**NATIONAL PARK**

PERTH & KINROSS

ANGUS

SIDLAW HILLS

STRATHARDLE

GLENSHEE

Key place names (north to south, west to east):

Baddoch · Creag nan Gabhar · Sgor Mór · Loch Vrotachan · Carn an Tuirc · Tolmount · Broad Cairn · Black Hill of Mark · Easter Balloch · Monawee · Kirkton · Invermark Castle

Glas Maol · The Cairnwell · Devil's Elbow · Caenlochan Forest · Creag Leacach · Finalty Hill · Mayar · Driesh · Cairn Inks · Cairn Baddoch · Glendoll Forest · Acharn · Clova · White Hill · Ben Tirran · Hunthill Lodge

Spittal of Glenshee · Ben Gulabin · Carn an Daimh · Monamenach · Auchavan · Runtaleave · Balnaboth · Hill of Couternach · Glenprosen Village · Glenmoy · Auld Darkney · Hill of Garbet · Pinderachy · Auchnacree · Glenogil · Easter Ogil · Noranside

Meall Uaine · Mealna Letter or Duchray Hill · Badandum Hill · Eskielawn · Glen Prosen · Easter Lednathie · Captain Scott & Dr Wilson Cairn · Dykehead · Cortachy · Memus · Shielhill · Oathlaw

Enochdhu · Whitefield Castle · Kirkmichael · Lamh Dearg · Cray · Mount Blair · Folda · Auchintaple Loch · Glenhead Farm · Loch Shandra · Backwater Reservoir · Brewlands Bridge · Kirkton of Glenisla · Blacklunans · Cairn Gibbs · Cairn Drumderg · Baldruff Hill · Dykend · Braes of Coul · Cat Law · Balintore · Creigh Hill · Mile Hill · Kirkton of Kingoldrum · Kinnordy · Camera Obscura · Northmuir · Bogindollo

Knock of Balmyle · Ballintuim · Blackcraig Hill · Netherton · Stone Bridge · Tullymurdoch · Bridge of Craigisla · Milnacraig · Reekie Linn · Loch of Lintrathen · Bridgend of Lintrathen · Kirkton of Airlie · Craigton · Kirriemuir · J M Barrie's Birthplace · Gateway to the Glens · Westmuir · Maryton · Padanaram · Whitehills · Forfar

Forest of Alyth · Blackcraig Forest · Bridge of Cally · Cochrage Muir · Hill of Alyth · Alyth · Ruthven · Roundyhill · Drumgley · Meffan · FORFAR

Butterstone · Loch of Butterstone · Blairgowrie · Kinloch · Rattray · Westfields of Rattray · New Alyth · Leitfie · Eassie · Bridgend · Glamis · St Orland's Stone · Glamis Folk · Douglastown · Fothringham Hill

Clunie · Loch of Drumellie · Craigie · Muirton of Ardblair · Rosemount · Arthurstone · Newbigging · Meigle · Sculptured Stone · Balkeerie · Eassie and Nevay · Charleston · Thornton · Kirkton · Foffarty · Carterhaugh · Inverarity

Snaigow House · Kirkton of Lethendy · Coupar Angus · Monk Myre · Ardler · Kinchin · Keillor · Newtyle · Kinpurney Hill · Ark Hill · Milton · Gallowfauld · Over Finlarg · Happas

Caputh · Spittalfield · Meikleour · Beech Hedge · Kinclaven Castle · Bridge of Isla · Markethill · Kettins · Leys · Hill of Keillor · Long Loch · Bonnyton · Kirkton of Auchterhouse · Hillside of Prieston · Tealing · Carrot Hill

Kingswood · Murthly · Ardoch · Gellyburn · Woodside · Burrelton · Campmuir · Pitcur · Lundie · Auchterhouse · North Dronley · Dronley · Bridgefoot · Newbigging · Westhall Terrace · Wellbank · Kellas · Murroes

Airntully · Wolfhill · Saucher · Gallowhill · Cargill · Laird's Loch · Piperdam Osprey Centre · Muirhead · Birkhill · Woodland · Clatto · Downfield · Fintry · Whitfield · Claypotts Castle · Broughty Ferry

Stanley · Guildtown · Kinrossie · Collace · Dunsinane Hill · Kirkton of Collace · Abernyte · Knapp · Benvie · Liff · Lochee · St Marnoch's Church · Camperdown · Mills Observatory · DUNDEE

Luncarty · Moneydie · Newmiln · St Martins · Castlehill · Invergowrie · Longforgan · Kingoodie · Discovery Point · Tay Road Bridge · Newport-on-Tay · Tayport

Stormontfield · Scone · Scone Palace Pinetum · Old Scone · Perth · Kinnaird · Craigdallie · Inchture · Kilspindie · Rait · Pole Hill · Cairn o' Mohr Winery · Wormit · Woodhaven · Tay Bridge

Old Scone · Muirton · Pitcairngreen · Huntingtower · **PERTH**

Road numbers: A93 · A924 · A984 · A923 · A926 · A928 · A932 · A94 · A9 · A85 · A90 · A930 · A92 · A914 · B951 · B950 · B954 · B952 · B953 · B955 · B957 · B9127 · B9128 · B960 · B961 · B946 · B9999 · B947

Grid references: A · B · C · D (top and bottom); 1 · 2 · 3 · 4 · 5 (sides)

PAGE 194 · 137 · 136 · 143 · 151

NORTH SEA

ABERDEENSHIRE

HOWE OF THE MEARNS

BUDDON NESS

Mount Battock 2552
Edendocher
Brae of Glenbervie
Tolbooth Cas
Dunnot
A92
Thorny Bay
Glen Dye
Spital Burn
Drumtochty Forest
Burnes Memorial
70
Glenbervie
Drumlithie
Bruxie
153
711
Roadside of Catterline
Crawton
Crawton Bay
Catterline
Braidon Bay
Todhead Point

Tarfside
Cairncross
Millden Lodge
Colmeallie Stone Circle
152
Glenesk Folk
Glensaugh
Drumtochty Castle
Strath Finella
Auchenblae
Bridge of Mondynes
Milton of Barras
Roadside of Kinneff
Kinneff
Little John's Haven

Hill of Fingray 1593
1725 Meluncart
1526 Goyle Hill
Glenfarquhar Lodge
Herscha Hill 723
A90
Parkneuk
Inverbervie
Bervie Bay

1492 Cairn o' Mount
Deer Dyke
Fordoun
Bridge of Kair
Grassic Gibbon Centre
Arbuthnott House
Arbuthnott
Knox Hill
Gourdon
Maggie Law Lifeboat

1785 Sturdy Hill
Auchmull
Arch Distillery
B974
B966
Bent
Laurencekirk
West Burnside
Garvock
Easter Tulloch
Benholm
Mill
Inverbervie

2224 Hill of Wirren
Fettercairn
B9120
A90
50
A937
Johnshaven

Gannochy
Luthermuir
Luther Water
Marykirk
Craigo
Lochside
St Cyrus
B9120

Bridgend
Balfield
Edzell
Dalhousie Memorial Arch
Inglismaldie Forest
Capo Long Barrow
North Water Bridge
Logie Pert
North Craigo
Logie
Pathhead

1578 Peat Hill
Brown Caterthuns
Dunlappie
Inchbare
Hillside
Kirkhill

Hill of Menmuir
White Caterthuns
Trinity
River North Esk
Dun
House of Dun
A935
Montrose Air Station
William Lamb Sculpture Studio

1031 Tullo Hill
Kirkton of Menmuir
Tigerton
Belliehill
Little Brechin
Caledonian Railway
Montrose Basin
MONTROSE

Fern
West Muir
Careston
Brechin Castle Centre
Maison Dieu
Town House
BRECHIN
Castle Centre Round Tower
Bridge of Dun
Barnhead
Montrose Basin
Inchbraoch
Ferryden

Vayne Castle
Nether Careston
River South Esk
A933
9
Maryton
Kirkton of Craig
Usan

Tannadice
A90
13
Netherton
Middle Drums
A934
Farnell
Westerton
Rossie Moor 503
Dunninald
Boddin Point

Finavon Doocot
Finavon
B9134
Montreathmont Forest
Braehead

Milton of Finavon
Crosston
Sculptured Stones
Aberlemno
Montreathmont Moor
Bolshan
A92
Lunan
Red Castle
Lunan Bay

Hill of Finavon 751
826 Turin Hill
Pitkennedy
Dubton
Glasterlaw
Braikie Castle
Inverkeilor
Ethie Haven

Lunanhead
Restenneth Priory
Rescobie
B9113
Rescobie Loch
Balgavies Loch
Guthrie
Kinnell
Lunan Water
12
Red Head

Burnside
A932
Milldens
Letham
Pitmuies
Friockheim
Chapelton
Drunkendub

Kingsmuir
Dunnichen
Memorial Cairn
Middleton
15
B965
Leysmill
Marywell
Auchmithie

Lownie Moor
B9128
Bowriefauld
Craichie
Cononsyth
Redford
Colliston
RM Condor
Sculptured Stones

Whigstreet
Greystone
Carmyllie
B961
A933
St Vigeans

Kirkbuddo
B978
Kirkton of Monikie
B9127
B9127
Hayshead
Cliffburn

Crombie
Arbirlot
Bonnington
Balcathie
ARBROATH
Arbroath Signal Tower

Monikie
Monikie Reservoir
Monikie
Craigton
Salmond's Muir
Elliot
A92

Newbigging
Drumsturdy
Carlungie Earth House
Muirdrum
Panbride
East Haven

B962
Ardestie Earth House
Barry
Clayholes
A930
Carnoustie

Barnhill
Broughty Castle
Monifieth
DANGER AREA

BUDDON NESS

Tentsmuir
350
Tentsmuir Sands
Bell Rock

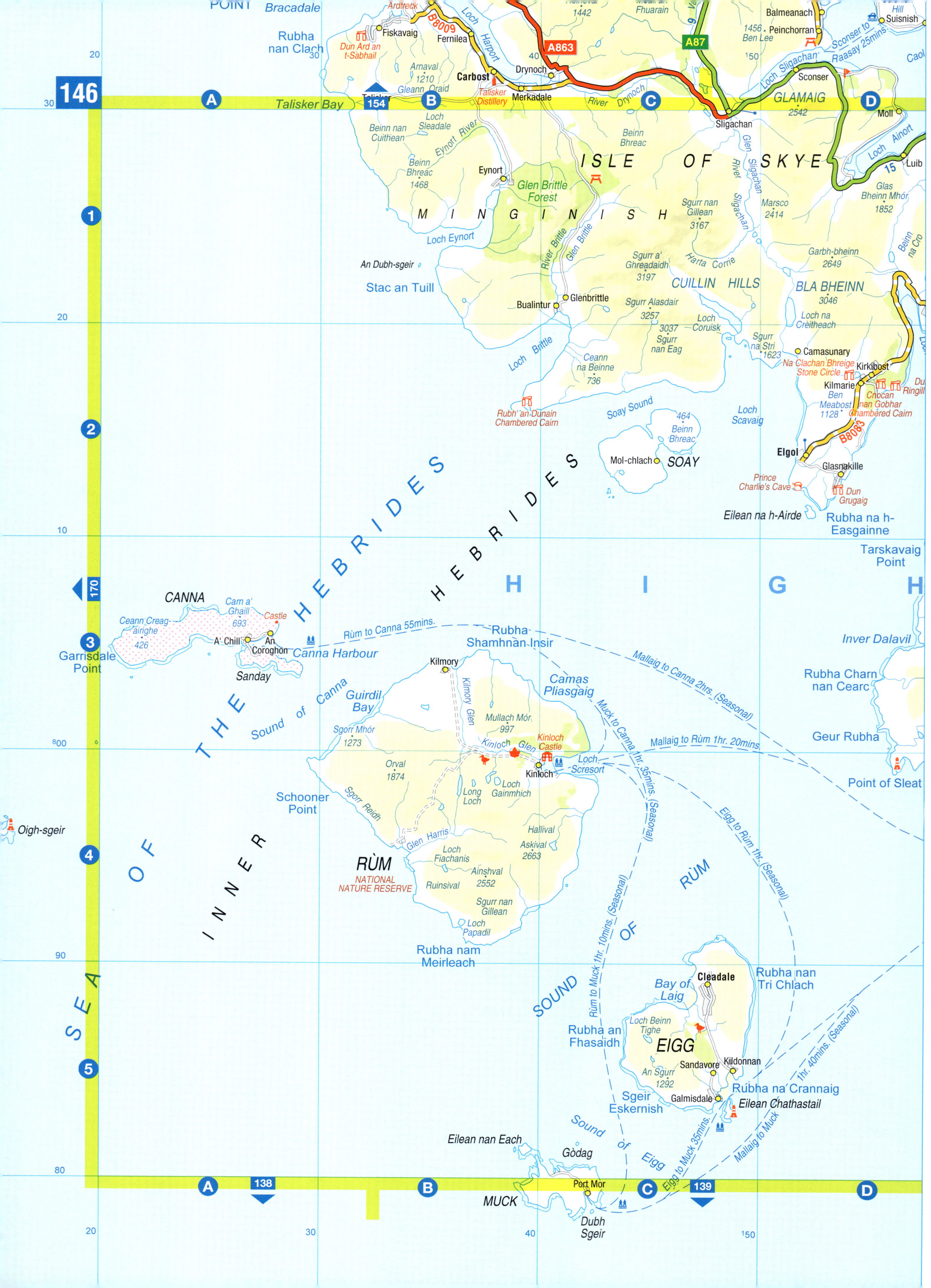

POINT Bracadale

Rubha nan Clach 30

Ardtreck
B8009
Fiskavaig
Fernilea
Dun Ard an t-Sabhail
Carbost
Talisker
154
Talisker Bay
A

Loch Harport
Drynoch
40
A863
Talisker Distillery
Merkadale
River Drynoch
C

Balmeanach
1456 Peinchorran
Ben Lee
Hill Suisnish
Sconser to Raasay 25mins
A87
150
Sconser
Loch Sligachan
GLAMAIG 2542
D
Moll
Caol

Arnaval 1210
Gleann Oraid
Beinn nan Cuithean
Loch Sleadale
Eynort River
Sligachan
Loch Sligachan
Glen Sligachan
River Sligachan
Loch Ainort
Luib
15

Beinn Bhreac 1468
Eynort
Loch Eynort
Glen Brittle Forest
MINGINISH
Sgurr nan Gillean 3167
Beinn Bhreac
Marsco 2414
Glas Bheinn Mhòr 1852
Beinn na Cro

An Dubh-sgeir
Stac an Tuill
River Brittle
Glen Brittle
Sgurr a' Ghreadaidh 3197
Harta Corrie
Garbh-bheinn 2649

Bualintur
Glenbrittle
Sgurr Alasdair 3257
CUILLIN HILLS
Sgurr nan Eag
3037
Loch Coruisk
Sgurr na Stri 1623
BLA BHEINN 3046
Loch na Crèitheach

Loch Brittle
Ceann na Beinne 736
Soay Sound
464 Beinn Bhreac
Loch Scavaig
Na Clachan Bhreige Stone Circle
Camasunary
Kirkibost
Kilmarie
Ben Meabost 1128
Chocan Inan Gobhar Chambered Cairn
Dun Ringill

Rubh' an Dunain Chambered Cairn
Mol-chlach
SOAY
Elgol
B8003
Glasnakille

THE HEBRIDES
HEBRIDES
HEBRIDES
HIGH
H

Prince Charlie's Cave
Dun Grugaig
Eilean na h-Airde
Rubha na h-Easgainne

Tarskavaig Point

CANNA
Carn a' Ghaill 693
Castle
Ceann Creag-airighe 426
A' Chill
An Coroghon
Sanday
Canna Harbour
Rùm to Canna 55mins.
Rubha Shamhnàn Insir
Mallaig to Canna 2hrs. (Seasonal)
Inver Dalavil

170
Garrisdale Point

Sound of Canna
Guirdil Bay
Sgorr Mhór 1273
Kilmory
Kilmory Glen
Camas Pliasgaig
Mullach Mór 997
Kinloch Glen
Kinloch Castle
Loch Scresort
Mallaig to Rùm 1hr. 20mins
Rubha Charn nan Cearc

800
Oigh-sgeir
Schooner Point
Sgorr Reidh
Orval 1874
Long Loch
Kinloch
Loch Gainmhich
Muck to Canna 1hr. 35mins. (Seasonal)
Eigg to Rùm 1hr. (Seasonal)
Geur Rubha

Point of Sleat

SEA OF
INNER
RÙM
NATIONAL NATURE RESERVE
Glen Harris
Loch Fiachanis
Hallival
Askival 2663
Ainshval 2552
Ruinsival

Rùm to Muck 1hr. 10mins. (Seasonal)
SOUND OF RÙM

Sgurr nan Gillean
Loch Papadil
Rubha nam Meirleach

Rubha nan Tri Chlach
Cleadale
Bay of Laig
Rubha an Fhasaidh
Loch Beinn Tighe
EIGG
An Sgurr 1292
Sandavore
Kildonnan
Rubha na' Crannaig

Sgeir Eskernish
Sound of Eigg
Galmisdale
Eilean Chathastail
Eigg to Muck 35mins. (Seasonal)
Mallaig to Muck 1hr. 40mins. (Seasonal)

Eilean nan Each
Gòdag
A
138
B
MUCK
Port Mor
C
139
D

Dubh Sgeir

20
30
40
150

CROWLIN ISLANDS

Eyre
Eyre Point
Sgeir Dhearg
Eilean Mòr
Longay
Loch an Leòid
Mullach na Càrn 1298
Scalpay House
E 155 SCALPAY
Guillamon Island
Pabay
Black Islands
F

Stromeferry
Plockton
Highland Farm
Achmore
Loch na Gillean
Loch na Leitire
Loch Lundie
Loch Achaidh na h-Inich
Loch Scalpaidh
Balmacara Square
Auchtertyre Hill
G A890
Loch Beinn a' Mheadhoin
Loch na h-Onaich
Sallachy
Killilan
gùman bìnntich 2003
H

Dunan (An Dúnan)
Scalpay House
Broadford Bay
Corry
Lower Breakish
Waterloo (Achadh a' Chuirn)
Isle of Skye
A87
Kyle of Lochalsh (Caol Loch Ailse)
Kyle Railway
Kyle Railway
Balmacara
Auchtertyre
A87
Conchra
Camas-luinie
Loch nan Eun
Sgurr an Airgid 2759
Inverinate
1

Liveras Chambered Cairn
Broadford (An t Ath Leathann)
Harrapool (Harrapul)
Skulamus (Sculamus)
Breakish (Brecais Ard)
Bright Water
Kyleakin
Casteal Maol
Donald Murchison's Monument
Lochalsh Woodland
Kirkton
Nostie
Ardelve
Dornie
Carndu
Bundalloch
Keppoch
Loch Bhuic Mhóir
Sgurr an Airgid 2759
Inverinate

2403 Beinn na Caillich
Serpentarium
Suardal Chambered Cairn
Lochain Dubha
Glen Arroch
Allt Mòr
Kylerhea Otter Haven
Kyle Rhea
Loch Alsh
Ardintoul Point
Glas Eilean
Caisteal Grugaig Broch
Eilean Donan
Letterfearn
Loch Duich
Ruarach
Morvich
Carr
Lienassie
Countryside Centre
Ault a' chruinn
FIVE SISTERS
DR

Torrin
Loch Cill Chriosd
Kilbride
B8083 14
Clach na h'Annait
Dun Kearstack Hillfort
Beinn nan Càrn 983
Heaste
Ben Aslak 1984
Bernera
Galltair
Glenelg Bay
Glenelg
Beinn a' Chuirn 1977
Beinn a' Chaoinich
Sgurr Mhic Bharraich 2553
Shiel Bridge
A87
Sgurr Fhuaran 3505

Rubha Suisnish
Ord (An t-Órd)
Sgòrach Breac 981
Lochan Fada
Duisdalemore (Duisdeil Mòr)
Gallery an Talla Dearg
Ornsay
Eilanreach
Dun Troddan Broch
Dun Telve Broch
Chambered Cairn
Balvraid
Beinn a' 2434 Chapuill
Dun Grugaig Broch
BEINN SGRITHEALL 3194
Beinn nan Caorach 2539
The Saddle 3319
Sgurr na Sgine 3098
Glenshiel Forest
2

Dunscaith Castle
Tokavaig (Tocabhaig)
Loch an Iasgaich
Isleornsay (Eilean Iarmain)
Camuscross (Camus Croise)
Sandaig Islands
Upper Sandaig
Màm na Staing
Arnisdale
Eilean Ràrsaidh
Loch Hourn
Corran
Dubh Lochain
Glen Arnisdale 2327
Druim Fada
Buidhe Bheinn 2884
Sgurr a' Mhaoraich 3365
3

Tarskavaig (Tarscabhaig)
Achnacloich (Ach na Cloiche)
Loch Dhùghaill
Teangue (An Teanga)
Knock Castle
Saasaig
Camas Baravaig
Camas Garbh
Inverguseran
Beinn na Caillich 2573
Ladhar Bheinn 3343
Barrisdale Bay
Kinloch Hourn
148

Kilmore
Ferindonald (Fearann Dhomhnaill)
Kilbeg
Isles
A851
Knock Bay
Airor
Sandaig
Scottas
Inverie
Sgurr Coire Choinnichean 2612
Loch an Dubh-Lochain
Gleann an Dubh-Lochain
Luinne Bheinn 3083
Glen Barrisdale
River Barrisdale
Abhainn Chosaidh
Sgurr a' Choire-bheithe 2994
Gleann Còsaidh

Gleann Meadhonach
Armadale Castle
Clan Donald
Bay Pottery
Armadale (Armadail)
Ardvasar (Àird a Bhasair)
An Fhaochag
Sandaig Bay
Inverie Bay
Kilchoan
Beinn Bhuidhe 2805
Sgurr Coire nan Gobhar
Meall Buidhe 3107
Lochan nam Breac
Sgurr Mòr 3290
4

Sgurr nan Caorach 920
Calligarry
Tormore
Aird (An Àird)
Ard Thurinish
Mallaig to Lochboisdale 3hrs. 30mins. (Seasonal)
Mallaig 25mins.
Mallaig to Eigg 1hr. 10mins.
Malaig Bheag
Courteachan
Sgurr an Eilein Ghiubhais 1713
2hrs.
Loch Nevis
Stoul
Finiskaig
Sgurr na Ciche 3412
Lochan a' Mhàim

Mallaig (Malaig)
Heritage Centre
Glasnacardoch (Glas na Cardaich)
A830
Loch Eireagoraidh
Loch an Nostarie
Ardnamurach
Kylesmorar
Sgurr Breac 2387
Carn Mòr 2718
Sgurr nan Coireachan 3136
River Dessarry
Glen Dessarry
Strathan
5

Beoraidbeg
Morar
Bracara
Lochan Stole
Tarbet
NORTH MORAR
MORAR
Sgurr Thuilm 3164
Allt Cuirnean

Glenancross
Camusdarach (An Camus Darach)
Lòn Liath
The Jacobite
SOUTH MORAR
Loch Morar
An Stac 2356
Meith Bheinn 2328
Lochan a' Bhrodainn
Sgurr an Utha 2610
River Pean
Glen Pean

Portnaluchaig
Bunacaimb
Kinlòid (Ceann an Leothaid)
Back of Keppoch (Cul na Caepaich)
ARISAIG
Burn Sidhean Mòr
Beinn nan Cabar 1888
Glen Beasdale
Loch Tain Mhic Dhughaill
Lochan a' Bhrodainn
Loch Beoraid
Glas-charn 2076
River Finnan
Glen Finnan

Eilean Ighe
Luinga Bheag
Luinga Mhòr
Arisaig (Arasaig)
Land, Sea and Islands Centre
Glen Cottage
Loch nan Eala
Druimindarroch
17
Loch na Creige Duibhe
Creag Bhàn 1675
Slios Garbh

Rubh' Arisaig
Eilean a' Ghaill
Eilean an t-Snidhe
Prince's Cairn
Polnish
Loch nan Uamh
Lochailort (Ceann Loch Àilleart)
Inverailort
Ranochan
A830
Loch Eilt
Station
Viaduct
Glenfinnan
Glenfinnan Monument
The Jacobite
A830
Kinlocheil

Sound of Arisaig
Samalaman Island
Eilean nan Gobhar
E 140 F
ROIS-BHEINN 2895
Druim Fiaclach 2852
Croit Bheinn 2175
Beinn Odhar Bheag 2895
G
Shiel H A830
Sgurr Dhomhuill Mòr
Meall nan Creag Leac

Roshven
A861
Glenuig Bay
Smirisary
Samálaman
Glenuig (Gleann Uige)
Lochan na Cloiche Sgoilte
Sgurr na Bàirness
Beinn Gàire
Loch nan Moidart
Sgorr Craobh a' Chaorainn
Glen Garvan

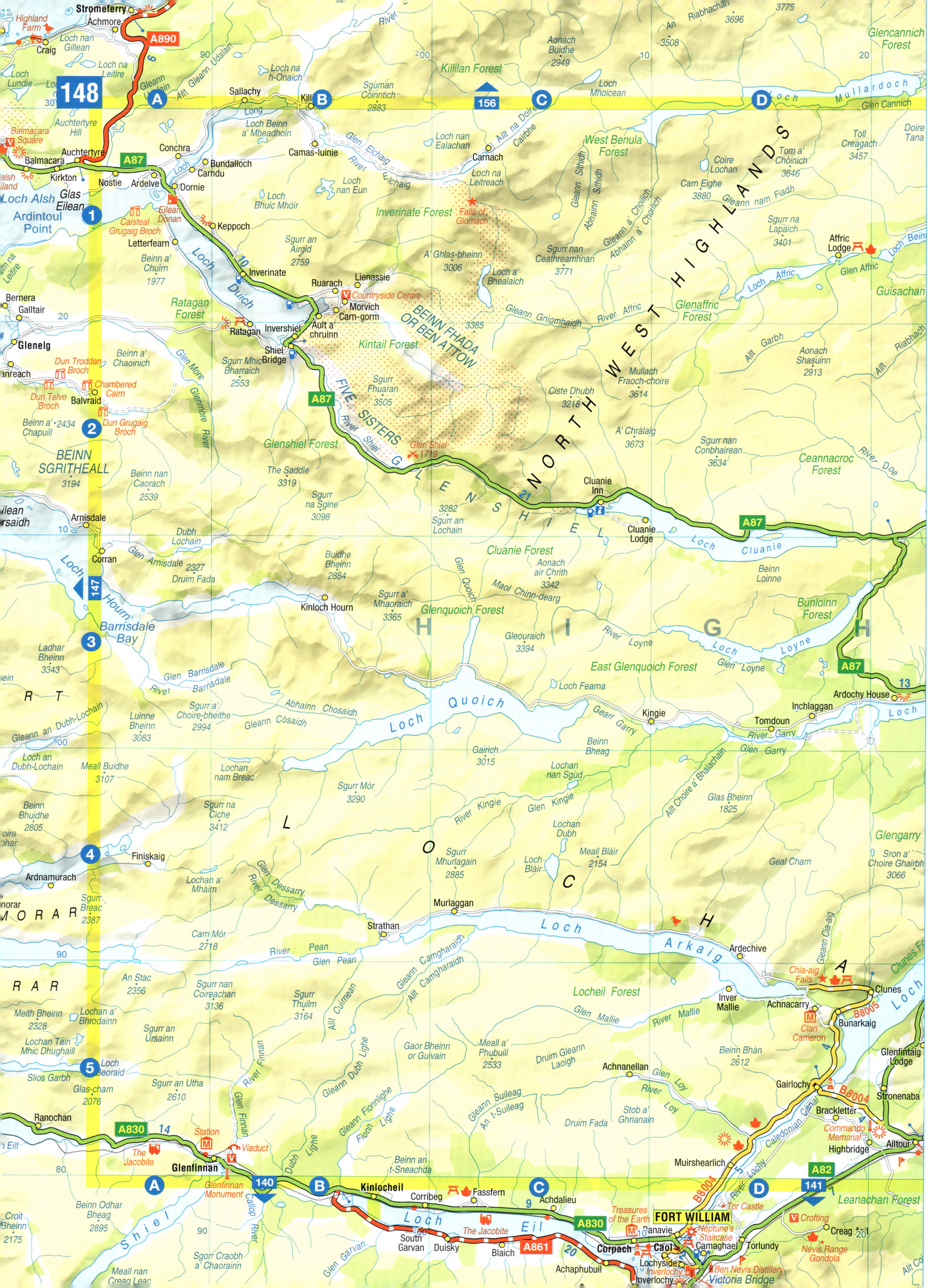

A890
Stromeferry
Highland Farm
Achmore
Loch nan Gillean
Craig
Loch Lundie
Loch na Leitire

Sallachy
Kill
A
Long
Loch Beinn a' Mheadhoin
Glen Elchaig
River Elchaig
Camas-luinie
156
Killilan Forest
Sgùman Còinntich 2883
Loch nan Ealachan
B
Carnach
C
Aonach Buidhe 2949
Loch Mhoicein
D
Loch Mullardoch
Glen Cannich
An 3508
Riabhachan 3696
3775
Glencannich Forest

Auchtertyre Hill
Balmacara Square
Auchtertyre
A87
Conchra
Bundalloch
Carndu
Camas-luinie
Dornie
West Benula Forest
Gleann Sìdh
Gleann Sìdhh
Coire Lochan
Carn Eighe 3880
Tom a' Chòinich 3457
Toll Creagach
Doire Tana

Balmacara
Kirkton
Nostie
Ardelve
Loch Duich
Keppoch
Eilean Donan
Caisteal Grugaig Broch
Loch Bhuic Mhóir
Sgurr an Àirgid 2759
Falls of Glomach
Inverinate Forest
A' Ghlas-bheinn 3006
Sgurr nan Ceathreamhnan 3771
Abhainn a' Chonaig
Abhainn a' Chòilich
Mullach Fraoch-choire 3614
Carn nam Fiadh
Sgurr na Lapaich 3401
Affric Lodge
Glen Affric

Glas Eilean
Ardintoul Point
Letterfearn
Inverinate
Ruarach
Lienassie
Countryside Centre
Morvich
Carn-gorm
BEINN FHADA OR BEN ATTOW
Loch a' Bhealaich
Loch Affric
Guisachan

Bernera
Galltair
Ratagan Forest
Invershiel
Ault a' chruinn
Shiel Bridge
Kintail Forest
3385
Gleann Gniomhaidh
River Affric
A' Chràlaig 3673
Glenaffric Forest
Allt Garbh
Aonach Shasuinn 2913
Allt Riabhach

Glenelg
Ratagan
Sgurr Mhic Bharraich 2553
Sgurr Fhuaran 3505
FIVE SISTERS
Ciste Dhubh 3218
Sgurr nan Conbhairean 3634
Ceannacroc Forest
River Doe

Dun Troddan Broch
Beinn a' Chaoinich
Chambered Cairn
A87
Glenshiel Forest
River Shiel
Glen Shiel 1719
NORTH WEST HIGHLANDS

Dun Telve Broch
Balvraid
Dun Grugaig Broch
The Saddle 3319
Sgurr na Sgine 3098
GLEN SHIEL
Cluanie Inn
A87

Beinn a' Chapuill 2434
BEINN SGRITHEALL 3194
Beinn nan Caorach 2539
Sgurr an Lochain
3282
Cluanie Lodge
Loch Cluanie
Beinn Loinne

Arnisdale
Loch Hourn
147
Dubh Lochain
Glen Arnisdale
Druim Fada 2327
Buidhe Bheinn 2884
Sgurr a' Mhaoraich 3365
Cluanie Forest
Aonach air Chrith 3342
Maol Chinn-dearg
Glenquoich Forest
River Loyne
Glen Loyne
Loch Loyne
Bunloinn Forest
A87
13

Corran
Barrisdale Bay
Kinloch Hourn
HIGHLAND
Gleouraich 3394
River Loyne
Ardochy House
Inchlaggan

Ladhar Bheinn 3343
Glen Barrisdale
River Barrisdale
Gleann Còsaidh
Abhainn Chosaidh
Sgurr a' Choire-bheithe 2994
Luinne Bheinn 3083
Gairich 3015
Loch Quoich
Beinn Bheag
East Glenquoich Forest
Loch Fearna
Kingie
Tomdoun
River Garry
Glen Garry
Loch Garry

Loch an Dubh-Lochain
Meall Buidhe 3107
Sgurr na Ciche 3412
Sgurr Mór 3290
Lochan nam Breac
Glen Kingie
River Kingie
Lochan nam Sgud
Lochan Dubh
Glas Bheinn 1825
Glengarry

Beinn Bhuidhe 2805
Finiskaig
Lochan a' Mhàim
Glen Dessarry
River Dessarry
Sgurr Mhurlagain 2885
Loch Blàir
Meall Blàir 2154
Geal Charn
Sron a' Choire Ghairbh 3066

Ardnamurach
Sgurr Breac 2387
Carn Mór 2718
Murlaggan
LOCH ARKAIG
Ardechive
Glen Garry
Chia-aig Falls
A
Clunes

MORAR
River Pean
Glen Pean
Strathan
Loch Arkaig
Locheil Forest
Inver Mallie
Achnacarry
Clan Cameron
Bunarkaig
Glenfintaig Lodge

An Stac 2356
Sgurr nan Coireachan 3136
Sgurr Thuilm 3164
Allt Cuirnean
Gleann Camgharaidh
Allt Camgharaidh
Gaor Bheinn or Gulvain 2533
Meall a' Phubuill 2533
Druim Gleann Laoigh
Achnanellan
Glen Loy
River Loy
Beinn Bhàn 2612
Gairlochy
B8005
Stronaba

Meith Bheinn 2328
Lochan a' Bhrodainn
Sgurr an Ursainn
Lochan Tàin Mhic Dhughaill
Gleann Fionnlighe
Fìon Lighe
An t-Suileag
Stob a' Ghrianain
Brackletter
Commando Memorial
Highbridge
Alltour

Ranochan
A830
14
Station
The Jacobite
Viaduct
Sgurr an Utha 2610
Glas-charn 2076
Loch Beoraid
Slios Garbh
Glen Finnan
Dubh Lighe
Beinn an t-Sneachda
Muirshearlich
River Lochy
A82
141
Leanachan Forest

Croit Bheinn 2175
Beinn Odhar Bheag 2895
Glenfinnan
Glenfinnan Monument
A
140
B
Kinlocheil
Corribeg
Fassfern
C
Achdalieu
9
A830
Treasures of the Earth
FORT WILLIAM
Caledonian Canal
Tor Castle
Crofting
Creag 361
Victoria Bridge

Meall nan Creag Leac
Sgorr Craobh a' Chaorainn
Loch Shiel
South Garvan
Duisky
Blaich
A861
20
Corpach
Banavie
The Jacobite
Caol
Camaghael
Neptune's Staircase
Inverlochy
Ben Nevis Distillery
Torlundy
Nevis Range Gondola
Lochyside
Achaphubuil

Muchrachd
Glassburn
Balmore Forest
Carn Mòr 1497
Loch an Tairt
Loch Gorm
A833
Meall na h-Eilrig 1526
Abriachan
Dores
A82
B857
B862
Liatrie
River Cannich
A831
12
40
Cannich
F
Balnaglaic
Balbeg
Balnagrantach
Achmony
Loch Ness Exhibition
Drumnadrochit
Tom Bailgeann
H
Stac na Cathaig 1463
30

Loch Sealbhanach
Corrimony
Buntait
Braefield
Glen
Rychraggan
Polmaily
A82
157
G
Urquhart
Milton
Nessieland
1522

E
Fasnakyle Forest
Kerrow
Corrimony Chambered Cairn
Loch Meiklie
Balnain
River
Enrick
Drum Farm Centre
Lewiston
Strone
Urquhart Bay
Borlum
13
Loch a' Choire
1

River Affric
Tomich
Loch a' Mhuilinn
Suidhe Ghuirmain 1896
Balmacaan Forest
Loch Aslaich
Loch nam Breac Dearga
Coiltie
Divach
Falls of Divach
Upper Lenie
Lower Lenie
John Cobb Memorial
Torness
Loch Ruthven
Aberarder

Abhainn Deabhag
River Glass
Meall a' Chràthaich 2226
Loch nam Meur
Bunloit
Balbeg
Inverfarigaig
Dun Dearduil
Errogie
Farraline
Dunmaglass Lodge
B857

Loch nan Sean-each
Forest
Carn a' Chaochain 2314
Loch ma Stac
Loch na Ruighe Duibhe
Loch a' Chràthaich
Alltsigh
Levishie Forest
Loch nan Eun
Achnaconeran
A82
Foyers
Falls of Foyers
Lyne of Gorthleck
Wester Aberchalder
Farigaig Forest
Loch Conagleann
20

Loch na Beinne Bàine
Levishie
Invermoriston
Invermoriston Falls
Portclair Forest
River Moriston
Whitebridge
Lochgarthside
Carn Odhar 2618
Càrn na Làraiche Maoile 2658

Dundreggan Forest
Glen
A887
Dundreggan Reservoir
Burach 1986
Loch nan Lann
Loch Knockie
Upper Knockchoillum
Bunkegivie
Càrn Saobhaidhe 2658
2

Allt na Muic
15
Dundreggan
Inverwick Forest
Knockie Lodge
Glenbrein Lodge
Garrogie Lodge
Carn na Làraiche Maoile 2658
Coignafe
10

Dalchreichart
Torgyle
Loch Tarff
Loch Killin
Burrach Mòr 2686
Glen Markie

Ceannacroc Lodge
A887
Allt Phocaichain
Bunoich
Caledonian Canal
Jenkins Park
Fort Augustus
Glendoebeg
Loch nan Eun
Killin Lodge
Coire Odhar
Allt Càm Ban
Carn Coire na Creiche 2702
MON

Ceannacroc Bridge
Beinneun Forest
Inchnacardoch Forest
Auchteraw
Clansman Centre
Culachy Falls
River Oich
Allt Doe
Glen Brein
Glendoe Forest
Càrn Easgann Bàna
2554
Càrn Ban 3087
Càrn Dearg

Meall Dubh 2581
Bridge of Oich
Newtown
A82
Glen Tarff
Carn a' Chuilinn 2677
Lochan Dearg Uillt
Loch Carn a' Chuillin Resr.
Loch na Lairige
Loch Dubh
800

L
Loch a' Bhainne
Bridge of Oich
Aberchalder
River Tarff
Lochan na Stairne
Càrn Odhar
Crom Allt
Allt Odhar
Geal Charn 3036
Abhainn Cró Chlach
150

GARRY
Munerigie
Loch Lundie
Faichem
Invergarry
Heritage Centre
Invergarry Castle
Corrieyairack Pass
Meall na h-Aisre 2828
Felt Talagain
Allt Coire Iain Og
Marg na Craige 2731
Allt Madagain
3

Allt na Cailliche Falls
Wester Mandally
Well of Seven Heads
Laggan Swing Bridge
Caledonian Canal
Loch an Aonaich Odhair Gairbeinn 2929
Creag Mhòr 2498
Garva Bridge
Crathie
4
Laggan
Balgowan

Ben Tee 2957
Forest
Laggan
Kilfinnan
Carn Dearg 2677
Carn Leac 2889
Corrieyairack Forest
Melgarve
Drummin
Garvamore
Glenshero Lodge
River Spey
Drumgask
Catlodge
A889

South Laggan Forest
A82
15
River Gloy
Brae Roy Lodge
Burn of Agie
Loch Crunachdan
Allt Crunachdain
Feagour
Strathmashie House
Loch Caoldair
90

Lochy
Altrua
Glen Gloy
Beinn Iaruinn 2636
River Roy
Carn Dearg 2736
Càrn Liath 3298
Coille Coire Chrannaig
Kinloch Laggan
Cromra
River Mashie
Strath Mashie
A86

New Bridge
B
Upper Glenfintaig
Parallel Roads
Coire Ceirsle Hill
Beinn Teallach 2994
Lochan a'Choire
Creag Meagaidh 3700
Lochan Coire Choille-rais
Loch Laggan
Ardverikie Forest
Beinn Eilde 2207
Lochan na Doire-uaine
Distillery
5
Dalwhinnie

Glen
Bohenie
Creag Dhubh 2160
Beinn a' Chaorainn 3437
Moy Forest
28
Moy Lodge
Binnein Shuas
Lochan na h-Earba
Geal Charn 3443
Beinn a' Chlachair
Meall Cruaidh 2941
Creagan Mòr 2780
A9

Spean Bridge
Inverroy
Roybridge
Achluachrach
SPEAN
A86
Loch Laggan Resr.
Loch na Turic
Loch a' Bhealaich Leamhain
Loch Pattack
A9

E
Commando
A86
Bunroy
Monessie Falls
Tulloch
Inverlair Falls
River Spean
Braes o' Lochaber
F
Meall Luidh Mòr
Beinn a' Chlachair 3569
G
142
H
Meall Cruaidh
Gealan Charn 3005
60

Beinn Chlianaig 2343
Fersit
Allt Laire
40
Allt Cam
An Lairig 3391
Càrn Dearg
Loch Pattack
Ben Alder Lodge
R. Truim
60
An Torc or Boar of Badenoch
2422
Pass of Drumochter

A    B    158    C    D

Dores
Inverarnie
Moy Castle
Ruthven
Carn an t-Sean-liathanaich 2076
Creag a' Chlachain 1196
Dunlichity Lodge
Farr 70
Carn na h-Easgainn 2022
Balvraid Lodge
Strathnairn Forest
Carn Glas-choire 2162
Corrybrough
Raigbeg 2057
Carn a' Choire Mhóir
Loch an t-Sidhein

Stac na Cà 1463
Loch Farr
Distillery
Tomatin
60
Loch Ceo Glais
Brin Herb Nursery
Beinn Bhreac 1969
Findhorn Bridge
A9
Carn nam Bain-tighearna 2082
Carrbridge
A938
Duthil
River Dulnain
B9007
9
Speyside Heather Centre

1
Torness
Loch Ruthven
East Croachy
13
Strathnairn
Glen Kyllachy
Clune
Slochd
60
3
Ellan
Landmark Forest Adventure Park
B9153
Drumuillie
Boat of Garten
Abern

Dunmaglass Lodge
Farraline
Aberarder
B851
Carn na Saobhaidh 2321
Glenmazeran Lodge
Corrievorrie
Carn Phris Mhóir 2021
Sluggan
Chapelton
Kinveachy
Beinn Ghuilbin 1895
Loch Garten

Loch Conagleann 20
Wester Lairchalder
Carn Ghriogair 2637
Beinn Bhreac Mhór 2647
Dalmigavie
Carn Dubh'Ic an Deòir 2461
Carn Sleamhuinn 2217
Allt Lorgy
Avielochan
A9
A95
60
Granish
Cairngorm Brewery
Strathspey Railway
West Croftmore

2
na Saobhaidhe 2658
Abarchalder Burn
Carn Odhar 2618
Coignafearn Lodge
River Findhorn
H I G H L
Cnoc Fraing 2444
Geal-charn Mór 2703
River Dulnain
Loch Pityoulish
Aviemore
Rothiemurchus Centre
GLENMORE
Glenmore

Carn na Làraiche Maoile 2658
Coignafearn Forest
River Eskin
Carn Coire na h-Easgainn 2591
Doune
Lynwilg
Loch Alvie
Inverdruie
Coylumbridge

Burrach Mór 2686
Calpa Mór 2668
149
Càm Ban
Abhainn Cro Chlach
Carn Coire na Creiche 2702
MONADHLIATH MOUNTAINS
Carn Sgùlain 2665
Carn an Fhreiceadain 2879
An Suidhe 1775
Delfour
Alvie
Duke of Gordon's Monument
Duchess of Gordon's Monument
Polchar
Castle
Loch an Eilein
Loch Gamhna
Loch an Eilein
Carn Eilrig 2435
Castle Hill 2366
Reindeer

3
A Chailleach 3045
Carn Ban 3087
Carn Dearg
Loch Dubh
Allt Madagain
Raitts Burn
Leault Working Sheepdogs
Highland
Speybank
Kincraig
Feshiebridge
Lagganlia
Feshiebridge
Inshriach Nursery
Inshriach Forest
Loch Mhic Ghille-chaoil
Sgoran Dubh Mór 3635
CAIRNGORMS
Sgòr Gaoith 3658
Loch Einich
BRAERIACH (Braigh Riabhach) 4248

Loch Gynack
Creag an Lòin 1788
Clan Macpherson
Strone
Kingussie
Lynchat
Ruthven Barracks
Farr
Loch Insh
B970
Insh
Sgòran Dubh Mór
Carn Bàn Mór 3443
CAIRN TOUL (Carn an t-Sabhail) 4236

4
Crathie
Laggan
Balgowan
Newtonmore
A86
Balavil
Creag Dhubh
Glen Banchor
River Calder
Ruthven
Drumguish
Glentromie Lodge
Creag nam Bodach 1610
Lynaberack Lodge
Meall Buidhe 2058
Allt Mór
Glen Feshie
Glenfeshie Lodge
Mullach Clach a' Bhlèir 3338
Monadh Mór 3651
Beinn Bhrotain 3795

Feagour
Strathmashie House
Drumgask
Catlodge
Glentruim House
Cruban Beag 1935
Crubenbeg
Etteridge
Falls of Truim
Garbh-mheall Mór 1944
River Tromie
Glen Tromie
Carn Dearg Mór 2813
GLENFESHIE FOREST
River Eidart

Cromra
Loch Mashie
A889
Crubenmore Lodge
Méalloch Mhór 2521
Allt Bhran
Beinn Bhrotain

Loch Caoldair
60
A9
Loch Cuaich
Cuaich
Glen Truim
Loch an t-Seilich
River Feshie

5
Distillery
Dalwhinnie
Lochan na Doire-uaine
Gaick Lodge
Carn an Fhidhleir or Carn Ealar 3276
An Sgarsoch 3300

Ben Alder Lodge
Gealm Charn 3005
Creagan Mór 2522
R. Truim
Carn na Caim 3087
Loch an Duin
Loch Bhrodainn
Allt Garbh Ghaig
Loch Mhairc
Beinn Bhreac 2992
Uchd a' Chlarsair 2587
Carn an Fhidhleir
Braigh 90
Braigh Ghorm 2882

A9
A
142
B
C
143
D

Meall Cruaidh 2941
A' Bhuidheanach Bheag 3072
Glas Mheall Mór 3037
Sronphadruig Lodge
Dalnamein Forest
Sròn a' Chleirich 2678
Bruar Water
BEINN DEARG 3307
Water
PERTH & KINROSS

An Tòrc or Boar of Badenoch 2422
Pass of Drumochter
Gaick Forest
Mullinn
Bruar Lodge
Gleann
FOREST

**HILLS OF CROMDALE**
**LADDER HILLS**
**GRAMPIAN MOUNTAINS**
**NATIONAL PARK**
**CAIRNGORM MOUNTAINS**
**FOREST PARK**
**ABERDEENSHIRE**
**BRAEMAR**
**FOREST OF MAR**
**LOCHNAGAR**

Chronach 1587
Upper Derraid
Auchnagallin
Advie
Tormore Distillery
B900
Glen Fiddich Lodge
Bridgend
Inver
A941
Creag Liath 1473
Glaschoil
Delliefure
Dalvey
Tomnacay 1605
B9009
Fiddich Lodge
19
Ballieward
Cottartown
A95
Dufftown
F
159
Drumin Castle
Packhorse Bridge
G
Corryhabbie Hill 2561
H
River Fiddich
Glenlivet 1872 Round Hill
Ca
Grantown-on-Spey
B9102
Cromdale
Glenlivet
Shenval
Glenlivet 1594
Glenfiddich Forest
Blackwater Forest
1
Achnahannet
Speybridge
Haughs of Cromdale
Knock Earth House
Glenlivet Distillery
Castleton
Auchbreck
Cairn Muldonich 1857
Carn an t-Suidhe 2401
Cairnbrallan 2029
Hill of Three Stones 2073
Craggan
A938 Dulnain Bridge
A95
Revack Highland Estate & Adventure Park
Carn Liath 1795
Tomnavoulin
Carn Daimh 1866
Strath Avon
River Livet
Geal Charn
Glenbuchat Lodge
Creag an Eunan 2073
Skye of Curr
B970
Broomhill
Explora Abernethy
Sgòr Gaoithe
Creagan a' Chaise 2369
Knockandhu
Clashnoir
Braes of Glenlivet
Chapelton
College of Scalan
Carn Mór 2639
Moss Hill 2159
Belnacraig
Nethy Bridge
A939
Bridge of Brown 1742
Milton
Tom an t-Suidhe Mhòr
Congies
Tomintoul
Carn Liath 2598
Carn Mór 2639
Ladylea Hill 1998
Kirkton of Glenbuchat
2
Nethy Forest
Osprey Centre
Tore Hill 1087
Clachaig
Dorback Lodge
Cam Meadhonach 1928
Lecht Mine
Well of the Lecht
A939
Ernan Water
Breagach Hill 1825
Doune of Invernochty
Bellabeg
Forbestown
Strathdon
Tulloch
Braes of Abernethy
Carn na Farraidh 2257
Water of Ailnack
11
Carn Ealasaid 2600
Glen Ernan
A944
Heugh-head
Tornashean Forest 1742
Meall a' Bhuachaille 2654
Geal Charm 2692
Carn Bheadhair 2636
Allnack Gorge
Cnap Chaochan Aitinn 2337
Burn of Loin
Craig Veann 2332
Milltown
Corgarff
8
Craig of Bunzeach
Cairngorm Funicular Railway
Mountain Exhibition
Mam Suim 2435
Carn na Feannaige
Big Garvoun 2431
Allt Tuileach
Cock Bridge
Corgarff
Carn Leac Saighaeir 2294
River Don
6
Cairn Mona Gowan 2456
152
CAIRN GORM 4085
Bynack More
The Bruach 2338
Forest of Glenavon
Brown Cow Hill 2721
3
Morven 2861
CAIRNGORM
NATIONAL PARK
Loch Avon
Beinn a' Chaorainn 3553
Stob an t-Sluichd 3843
BEN AVON
Loch Buidh
MOUNTAINS
Gairnshiel Lodge
A939
Peter's Hill 1863
Lary
Culc
Loch Etchachan
3924
Carn Eas 3556
River Gairn
Glen Fenzie
8
BEN MACDUI (Beinn MacDuibh) 3788
Derry Cairngorm 3788
Beinn Bhreac 3051
Beinn a' Bhuird
2953 Culardoch
2830 Creag an Dail Bheag
B976
2438 Geallaig Hill
A939
McEwan Gallery
Milton of Tullich
ABERDEENSHIRE
Devil's Point 3303
Carn a' Mhaim 3329
Derry Burn
Dubh Gleann
Meall Gorm 2029
Feardar Burn
5
A93
River Dee
Bridge of Gairn
B912
Pannanich Wells
BRAEMAR
Lui Water
Glen Lui
2681 Carn na Drochaide
1969 Creag nan Gall
Inver
Crathie
Balmoral Castle
Balnacroft
Littlemill
Ballater
Pannanich Hill
Knock Castle
4
Sgòr Mòr 2666
FOREST OF MAR
Creag Bhalg
Linn of Quoich
Braemar
Highland Heritage Centre
Castleton
Keiloch
Easter Balmoral
Royal Lochnagar Distillery
Birkhall
The Coyles of Muick 1956
Aucholzie
2293 Cairn Leuchan
Cairn Geldie 2039
River Dee
Linn of Dee
Mar Lodge
Inverey
Invercauld Bridge
Ballochbuie Forest
Gelder Shiel
Balmoral Forest
Glen Muick
2365 Fasheilach
Carn Liath 2676
The Colonel's Bed
Morrone or Morven
Sandy Beag
Cac Carn Beag 3789
Conachcraig 2827
Lochnagar
5
Carn Geldie
Glen Ey
Clunie Water
Callater Burn
Loch Phadruig
Loch nan Eun
White Mounth
Dubh Loch
Spittal of Glenmuick
Glen Mark
Easter Balloch
Carn Bhac 3014
Carn Liath
Glen Ey Burn
A93
2736 Creag nan Gabhar
Glen Callater
Loch Callater
3314 Calm Bannoch
Glas-allt Shiel
Loch Muick
Glen Lee
Allt Garbh Buidhe
Beinn Iutharn Mhòr 3424
AN SOCACH 3073
Baddoch 886
Sgor Mór
Loch Vrotachan
F
144
3340 Carn an Tuirc
3143 Tolmount
G
3268 Broad Cairn
Black Hill of Mark 2731
H
Carn an Righ 3377
Loch nan Eun
Carn a' Gheòidh 3194
3059 The Cairnwell
Devil's Elbow
GLAS MAOL
Caenlochan Forest
20
Glen Doll
Loch Esk
30
Lair of Aldararie
Water of Unich
2726
2699 Muckle Cairn
Gleann Mòr
Glas Tulaichean 3449
3504
2954
Glendoll Forest
Acharn
Loch Brandy
Loch Wharral

A  B  C  D

Glen Fiddich
Glenfiddich Forest
Coynachie
Clashindarroch Forest
Clashindarroch
Kirkney
River Bogie
Gartly
Cults
Glens of Foudland
Auchenhove
Hill of Foudland 1531
Glenfiddich Forest
Bridgend
Inverharroch
Ardwell
Kirkney Water
Knockandy Hill 1425
Wardhouse
Lenchie
Largie
Upper Boddam
Picardy Symbol Stone
Colpy
A920
Cairnhill
Tocher
Kirkton of Culsalmond
Newseat
Meikle Wartle

Glenfiddich Forest
Black Water
Round Hill 1872
Cabrach
Mount of Haddoch 1708
A941
Milton of Lesmore
Tap o' Noth
Tap O'Noth 1848
A97
Leith Hall
160
Kennethmont
B9002
Knockenbaird
Knockandy
B992
Insch
Pitmachie
Dunnideer Castle
Durno
Old Rayne
Whiteford
Pitcaple
A96
Chapel of Garioch

Moss Hill 2159
Geal Charn
Glenbuchat Lodge
Creag an Eunan 2073
The Buck 2366
Belhinnie
Rhynie
Elrick
B9002
Craw Stane
St Mary's Kirk
Clova
Clatt
Duncanston
MORAY
Cairnbralian 2029
Hill of Three Stones 2073
Lumsden
CORREEN HILLS 1599
Coldwells Croft
Whitehaugh Forest
Leslie
Kirkton
Old Westhall
B9002
River Urie
Oyne
Kirkton of Oyne
Maiden Stone
GARIOCH

Ladylea Hill 1998
Water of Buchat
Belnacraig
Rinmore
Mossatt
A97
Lord Arthur's Cairn 1699
Tullynessie
Syllavethy Gallery
Montgarrie
Keig
Glenton
Bennachie Forest 1733
Bennachie Hill 1340
Donview
Bennachie Centre
Bogragie
Ramstone

Breagach Hill 1825
Doune of Invernochty
Bellabeg
Forbestown
Strathdon
A944
Kildrummy
Milltown
Glenbuchat
A97
Glenkindie
Towie
Bridge of Alford
Muir of Alford
Howe of Alford
Grampian Transport
Haughton
Alford
Alford Valley Railway
Heritage Centre
Whitehouse
A944
Kirkton
PITFICHIE FOREST
Rorandie
River Don
Arts Centre
Monymusk
Craigearn
B993
Pitfichie 1468
Cairn William
Grantlodge

Heugh-head
Tornashean Forest 1742
Craig of Bunzeach
Sinnahard
Milltown of Towie
Frosty Hill
Milton of Cushnie
Leochel Cushnie
Muir of Fowlis
Craigievar
Craigievar Castle
Mill of Craigievar
A980
Benaquhallie 1621
Corrennie Moor
Corrennie Forest
Tillyfourie
Ordhead
Sauchen
Black Hill 608
Kinnernie
Old Kinnernie
Castle Fraser

ABERDEENSHIRE
Deskry Water
Cairn Mona Gowan 2456
151
Migvie
Pressendye 2031
Corse Castle
Tornaveen
Bankhead
Comers
Tillybirloch
Midmar Kirk Stone Circle
Sunhoney Stone Circle
Barmekin
Drumlasie
HILL OF FARE 1545
Midmar Forest

Morven 2861
Coynach
B9119
Craiglich 1562
Culsh Earth-house
Milton of Auchinhove
Peel Ring of Lumphanan
Lumphanan
B9119
B993

Logie Coldstone
A97
Tarland
Tomnaverie Stone Circle
Coull Castle
Scar Hill 984
Mortlich 1248
Milton Auchlossan
Torphins
Kincardine O'Neil
Mid Beltie
Milltown of Campfield
A980
Cluny Crichton Castle
Craigton

Peter's Hill 1863
Culblean Hill 1983
Ordie
Loch Davan
New Kinord Settlement
Loch Kinord
Loch of Aboyne
A93
Aboyne
Belwade Farm
B993
Potarch
B976
Brathens
East Mains
Upper Lochton
Silverbank

A939
Glen Fenzie
Lary
Burn o' Vat
Cambus o' May
B9119
Dinnet
Oakwood
A93
Aboyne
B97.6
River Dee
Birsemore
Birse
Marywell
Burn of Cattie
Bridge of Canny
Arbeadie
Banchory
Deebank
Scolty Woodland Park
Blackhall Forest
Scolty Tower 1017
Auchattie
Belts of Collonach
Bridge of Feugh

McEwan Gallery
Milton of Tullich
A93
Pannanich
Bridge of Gairn
Ballater
Littlemill
B976
Pannanich Wells
Muir of Dinnet
Millfield
Glen Tanar House
24
Black Craig 1742
Glen Tanar
Forest of Glen Tanar
Tom's Cairn
Whitestone
Strachan
Waulkmill
B974
Nine Stanes Stone Circle

Knock Castle
Birkhall
Pannanich Hill
Pollagach Burn
Water of Tanar
Carnferg 1724
Glencat 1325
Lamahip
Forest of Birse
Finzean
B976
Water of Feugh
Craig of Dalfro 1042
Kerloch 1754

The Coyles of Muick 1956
Aucholzie
Cairn Leuchan 2293
Clachan Yell 2054
Craigmahandle 1878
Ballochan
White Hill
Peter Hill 2025
Mount Shade 1662
Bridge of Dye
Tipperweir 1440

Fasheilach 2365
CAIRNGORMS NATIONAL PARK
Mount Keen 3080
Cock Cairn 2387
Hill of Cat 2433
Mudlee Bracks 2259
Hill of Cammie 2028
Mount Battock 2552
Hill of Edendocher 1944
Meluncart 1725
Glen Dye
Goyle Hill 1526
Drumtochty Forest
Glenfarquhar Lodge

The Coyles
2731
Glen Muick
Black Hill of 80rk
Easter Balloch
Monawee 2276
Kirkton
Invermark Castle
River North Esk
Glen Effock
Tarfside
Cairncross
Millden Lodge
Colmeallie Stone Circle
Glenesk Folk
145
Glensaugh
Auchenblae
Drumtochty Castle

2726
Lair of Aldararie
Muckle Cairn 2699
Cruys 2424
West Knock 2267
Bulg 1986
Sturdy Hill 1785
Deer Dyke
Strath
Finella
ANGUS
144

A  B  C  D

**ABERDEEN** PAGE 192

FORMARTINE

NORTH SEA

Aberdeen to:
Kirkwall (Hatston) 6hrs.
Lerwick (Holmsgarth)
12hrs. 30mins.

Bay of Cruden
Whinnyfold
Old Slains Castle
Kirktown of Slains
Collieston
Meikle Loch
Denhead
Kirkton of Logie Buchan
Tipperty
Meikle Tarty
Knockhall Castle
Forvie
Hackley Head or Forvie Ness
Newburgh
Foveran
Newburgh Bar
Drums
Foveran Burn

St Katherines
Barthol Chapel
Earlsford
Ythanbank
Inverebrie
Broomfield
Yonderton
Haddo House
Medieval Tomb
Prop of Ythsie
Tarves
Kinharrachie
Ellon
P+R
Folla Rule
Core Hill 804
Cross of Jackston
Tulloch
Wedderlairs
Thornroan
Craigdam
South Ythsie Stone Circle
Esslemont Castle
Heritage
Tolquhon Castle
Tolquhon Gallery
Pitmedden
Daviot
Glen Garioch Distillery
Oldmeldrum
Loanhead Stone Circle
Hill of Barra 634
Kirkton of Bourtie
Hattoncrook
Whiterashes
Affleck
Udny Green
Udny Station
Hill of Fiddes
Tillery
Balhalgardy
Inveramsay
Harlaw 1411
Brandsbutt Symbol Stone
Carnegie
Inverurie
Easter Aquhorthies Stone Circle
Port Elphinstone
Kinmuck
Reisque
Newmachar
Tillery
Craigie
Whitecairns
Belhelvie
Balmedie
Burnhervie
Broomend
Little Treasures
Clovenstone
Kemnay
Burgh Muir
Hallforest Castle
Kintore
River Don
Mill of Fintray
Hatton of Fintray
Cothal
Potterton
Blackdog
DANGER AREA
Leylodge
Letter
Lyne of Skene
Blackburn
Tyrebagger Hill 821
Aiky Brae Stone Circle
ABERDEEN INTERNATIONAL
Overton
Fowlershill
Corby Loch
Bridge of Don
Dyce Symbol Stones
Dyce
Stoneywood
Danestone
Hayton
Cruickshank Botanic
Old Aberdeen
Kings Museum
Zoology
Dunecht
Loch of Skene
Gairloch
Masons Lodge
Elrick
Garlogie
Kirkton of Skene
Westhill
Kingswells
Sheddocksley
Mastrick
Kittybrewster
Bankhead
Bucksburn
Northfield
Woodside
Brimmond & Elrick
Brimmond Hill 874
Echt
South Kirkton
Landerberry
Redhill
Cullerlie Farm Park
Cullerlie Stone Circle
Easter Ord
Blacktop
Cults
Summerhill
Mannofield
Gordon Highlanders
Ferryhill
Torry
Maritime
Nigg Bay
West Cullerlie
Hardgate
Mains of Drum
Drum Castle
Craigton
Milltimber
Bieldside
Ruthrieston
Kincorth
Loirston
Nigg
David Welch Winter
Doonies Farm
Souter Head
Peterculter
Coalford
Drumoak
Park
Kirkton of Maryculter
Blairs
Banchory-Devenick
Crossroads
Charlestown
Cove Bay
Hirn
Myrebird
The Neuk
Crathes
Royal Deeside Railway Preservation Society
Kirkton of Durris
Denside
Woodlands
Netherley
Cookney
Windyedge
Hillside
Findon
Portlethen
Portlethen Village
Cammachmore
Downies
Newtonhill
Cammachmore Bay
Durris Forest
Cairn-mon-earn 1241
Meikle Carewe Hill 872
Berry Top 558
Raedykes Roman Camp
Bridge of Muchalls
Muchalls
Doonie Point
Crossroads
Damford
Lochton
Rickarton
New Mains of Ury
Cowie
Garron Point
Burn of Sheeoch
Mongour 1232
Hill of Trusta 1052
Fetteresso Forest
Leachie Hill 1289
Brae of Glenbervie
Kirktown of Fetteresso
Tewel
Stonehaven
Tolbooth
Dunnottar
Castle Haven
Burnes Memorial
Bervie Water
Glenbervie
Drumlithie
Bruxie Hill 711
Thornyhive Bay
Herscha Hill 723
Bridge of Mondynes
Milton of Barras
Crawton
Crawton Bay
Braidon Bay
Fordoun
Parkneuk
Arbuthnott
Grassic Gibbon Centre
Roadside of Catterline
Catterline
Fernieflatt
Roadside of Kinneff
Todhead Point

THE LITTLE MINCH

Fladda-chùain  Sgeir nam Maol

171

Eilean Trodday

Rubha Hunish  Rubha na h-Aiseig

Loch Hunish  The Aird  Kilmaluag Bay

An t-Iasgair  Tulm Bay  Shulista  Balmacqueen

Duntulm  Kilmaluag

Duntulm Castle  Connista

Lùb Score  15

Skye Island Life  Clachan  Flodigarry

Camas Mór  Flora Macdonald Monument

Hungladder  Heribusta  1781 Meall na Suiramach  Quiraing  Digg

Bornesketaig (Borgh na Sgiotaig)  Kilmuir  Kilvaxter (Cille a' Bhacstair)  Glashvin

Dùn Liath  Balgown  Hut Circles  Brogaig

Carn Liath  Loch Sneosdal  Stens

Linicro (Lionacro)  Bioda Buidhe 1523  Loch Cleap

Totscore

Uig to Tarbert 1hr. 40mins.

Uig to Lochmaddy 1hr. 40mins.

WATERNISH POINT

Eilean Iosal  Eilean Creagach

Dun Gearymore Broch  Healaval

Dun Borrafiach Broch

Ascrib Islands

Dun Skudiburgh  Uig

Idrigill

Uig Bay

River Rha

The Trial Stone  Church  931 Ben Geary

Ardmore Point  Trumpan

LOCH SNIZORT

Standing Stone  Balnaknock

Beinn Edra 2006

Halistra  Knockbreck

Hallin  Gillen  Loch Losait

DUNVEGAN HEAD  170

Mingay  Dun Hallin

Isay  Sgeir nam Biast  Score Horan

Skyeskyns  Beinn Charnach Bhéag

Stein  Lusta

Eilean Mór  Greshornish Point

Lyndale Point

Earlish (Earlais)

A87  Hinnisdal Hut Circle  Peinlich

Loch Mor

Hinnisdal Bridge  River Hinnisdal

Beinn a' Sgà

Creag a' Lain 1995

Galtrigill  Claigan  Bay  Beinn Bhreac  Beinn Chreagach  Annait  Fairy Bridge

Kingsburgh

Greshornish  Knott  TROTTERNISH

Flashader  Kildonan  Clachamish  Romesdal  Eyre

Dun Flashader Broch  Treaslane  River Romesdal

A850  Edinbane (An t-Aodann Ban)  The Aird  Carn Liath  Kensaleyre

Blackhill  Edinbane Pottery  Bernisdale  Rhenetra  River Haultin

Borreraig  Dun Borreraig

Ben Ettow  Uig

Borreraig Park

Lower Milovaig  Feriniquarrie  Totaig

An Ceannaich

Upper Milovaig  Glendale

Oisgill Bay  Lephin  Colbost

Waterstein  Borrodale  Holmisdale  Toy  Colbost Croft  Skinidin

Moonen Bay

Loch Mór

Ramasaig

HEALABHAL MHOR 1538

HEALABHAL BHEAG 1600

Hoe Rape

The Hoe 759

Hoe Point

Am Bì-bogha Mór

An Dubh-sgeir

Hoe Point

Dun Osdale Broch  Kilmuir  Lonmore

Dunvegan  Giant Angus Macaskill

Suardal Hut Circle

Dun Fiadhairt

Loch Dunvegan

A863  10

Ben Uigshader 806

Glen Bernisdale  St Columba's Isle

Loch Niarsco  Skeabost  Tote  Crepkill

Clach Ard  Borve

Borve Standing Stones

Carbost  A87  Drumuie

Roskhill  Vatten  Cruachan Beinn a' Chearcaill

Roag  Ardroag  Chambered Cairns

Orbost  Orbost Gallery

Harlosh  Loch Caroy

Loch Bharcasaig  Balmore  Ose

Beinn na Boineid 1207

Ben Connan 799

Ben Idrigill

Harlosh Point

Colbost Point

Tarner Island

Harlosh Island

Loch Bracadale

Wiay

Oronsay

Macleod's Maidens

IDRIGILL POINT

Rubha nan Clach

Ben Uigshader  Uigshader

Loch Ravag 682

Beinn a' Ghlinne Bhig 682

ISLE OF SKYE

B885  Glengrasco

Loch Connan  9  Shulishadermor (Sùlaisiadar Mòr)  Aros 1376

Beinn na Greine

B885  Glenmore  Stroc-bheinn 1300

Tungadal Souterrain  Ben Duagrich  Mugeary

Dun Mor  Dun Beag  Totardor

Bracadale  Coillore

Cnoc Ullinish Chambered Cairn  Ullinish  Struan  Struanmore

Carn Liath Chambered Cairn

Roineval 1442  Meall an Fhuarain

A863  9

Dun Ardtreck  Portnalong

B8009  Loch Harport

Fiskavaig  Fernilea

Dun Ard an t-Sabhail

Arnaval 1210  Gleann Oraid

Carbost  Talisker Distillery  Drynoch  River Drynoch

Talisker  Merkadale

Talisker Bay

146

Beinn nan Cuithean

Glendale River

Eynort River

Beinn Bhreac 1468

Eynort  Glen Brittle Forest

MINGINISH

Beinn Bhreac

Sgurr Gillean

**WESTER ROSS**

Seana Chamas
Peterburn
Cnoc Breac 962
Brae
Loch Ewe
Naast
Inverewe
Poolewe
Loch Mhic Riabh
ndubh
Loch Ghiurag

Port Erradale
North Erradale
162
Big Sand
Caolas Beag
River Sand
Loch nan Liagh
Loch Bad a' Crimh
A832
Loch na Curra
Loch Tollaidh
Tollie Farm
Loch Kernsary
River Ewe

Longa Island
B8021
Lonemore
Mial
Strath
Heritage
A832
Loch Airigh a' Puill
Meall an Doirein 381

Smithstown
Gairloch
Loch Gairloch
Eilean Horrisdale
Gairloch Marine Life Centre
Aird
Charlestown
1
A832

Port Henderson
B8056
Badachro
Loch Shieldaig
Opinan
Loch nan Eun
South Erradale
Loch Clàir
Shieldaig
River Kerry
Loch Bad an Sgalaig

Sgeir Eirin
Eilean Flodigarry
River Erradale
Allt a' Ghiubhais
Meall na h-Uamha

Staffin Bay
Staffin Island
Redpoint
Sgeir Ghlas
Sgeir na Trian
Loch Gaineamhach
Shieldaig Forest
Baosbheinn 2869
2

Carn Ban
Garafad
Staffin (Stafainn)
Kilt Rock
Mealt Falls
choll
Clachan
Ellishadder
Dun Grianan
Maligar
Loch Mealt
Valtos
Craig
Craig River
Beinn Bhreac 2031
Loch a' Bhealaich
Beinn Alligin 3232
60

Marishader
Garros
Grealin
A855
Rubha nam Brathairean
Culnacnoc
Loch a' Bhràige
Rubha na Fearn
Fearnmore
Fearnbeg
Lower Diabaig
Upper Diabaig
Loch na h-Uamhaig
Alligin Shuas
156

Lealt River
Lealt
Lealt Falls
Port an Fhearainn
RONA
Rubha Chuaig
Arinacrinachd
Loch Torridon
Loch Diabaigas Airde
Inveralligin

Loch Liuravay
THE STORR
S H
Old Man of Storr 2358
Leac Tressirnish
Eilean Garbh
Caol Rona
Cuaig
Kenmore
Loch a' Chracaich
Loch Shieldaig
Upper Loch Torridon
Torrido
Deer

Bearreraig Bay
Eilean Tigh
Garbh Eilean
Callakille
Ardheslaig
Shieldaig Island
3

Loch Leathan
Holm Island
Eilean Fladday
Loch a' Squirr
Lonbain
Abhainn Chuaig
Allt an t-Strathain
Allt na h-Eirigh
Loch Gaineamhach
Shieldaig
Balgy
1692
Falls of Balgy
Ben-damph Fores

Loch Fada
Manish Point
Loch Arnish
Torran
Arnish
Croic-bheinn 1619
An Dubh-loch
Ben Shieldaig
Abhainn
Loch Damh

Achachork
Dun Gerashader
Torvaig
Brochel
Brochel Castle
Loch nan Eun
Heritage Centre
River Applecross
Loch Lundie
Glenshieldaig Forest
Beinn Da 2957

A855
Portree (Port Righ)
Loch Portree
Penifiler 1355
Heatherfield
Ben Tianavaig 1355
RAASAY
Applecross Bay
Applecross
Milton
Applecross Forest
Loch Coire Attadale
Beinn Bhan 2938
Loch Gaineamhach
A896
Loch Coultrie
Sgurr a' Gharaidh 2396

Camastianavaig
Conordan
Lower Ollach
B883
Upper Ollach
Gedintailor
Balmeanach
Peinchorran
Ben Lee 1456
Glame
Balachuirn
Dun Caan 1455
Rubha ná Leac
Camusteel
Camusterrach
Ard-dhubh
Culduie
Sgurr a' Chaorachain 2539
Bealach na Bà
Meall Gorm
Loch Coire nan Arr
Rassal Ashwood
Sm Heritag
4

Glen Varragill
Holoman Bay
Tianavaig Bay
Oskaig
St Moluag's Chapel
Clachan
Inverarish
North Fearns
Eilean na Bà
Toscaig
River Toscaig
Loch Braigh an Achaidh
Loch Maol Fharochag
Kishorn
Ardarroch
Achintraid
Bad a' Chreamha
Lochcarron Weavers
Stromemore
Lochc

Glam Burn
Suisnish Hill
Suisnish
Eyre
Eyre Point
Eilean Beag
Uags
CROWLIN ISLANDS
Eilean Mòr
Caolas Mòr
Meall Loch Airigh Alasdair
Kishorn Island
Ardaneaskan
Stromeferry
Strome
5
A890

Loch Sligachan
Sconser
Sconser to Raasay 25mins
Narrows of Raasay
Sgeir Dhearg
Longay
Plockton
Plockton
Highland Farm
Achmore
Craig
Loch nan Gillean
Loch na Leitire
Gleann Udalain
Allt Glea

GLAMAIG 2542
Sligachan
Moll
E
147
Mullach na Càrn 1298
Loch an Leòid
SCALPAY
Black Island
G
Port Cam
Drumbuie
Duirinish
Loch Lundie
Loch Achaidh na h-Inich
A890

Glen Sligachan
Luib
Dunan (An Dùnan)
Scalpay House
F
Guillamon Island
Pabay
Erbusaig
Badicaul
Loch Scalpaidh
Kyle of Lochalsh (Caol Loch Ailse)
Kyle Railway
Balmacara Square
Balmacara
Auchtertyre Hill
Auchtertyre
H
A87

River Sligachan
Glas Bheinn Mhór 1852
A87
Caolas Scalpay
Broadford
Black Island
Plock of Kyle
Bright Water
Kyleakin
Donald Murchison's Monument
Lochalsh Woodland
Kirkton
Nostie
Ardelve
Conchra

Marsco 2414
Glen Sligachan
15
Dunan
C60
Lower Isle
Caisteal Maol
Kyle Akin
Loch Alsh
Glas Eilean
Loch Alsh
Dorni

Loch Ewe

Brae
Naast
Loch Mhic'ille Riabhaich
Loch na Mòine Buige
Inverewe
Londubh
Loch Ghiuragarstidh
Aird Dubh
Bad Pen
Beinn a'Chàisgein Beag 2230
Loch na Sealga
Loch Toll an Lochain
Loch Coire Chaorachain
Carn a'Bhiorain 1665
Loch Allt Eigin
Loch an Airceil
Auchlunachan

Strathnasheallag Forest

Meall na Mèine 820
Fisherfield Forest
Beinn Dearg Mòr 2974
Dundonnell Forest
Lochan Fada
Loch a'Bhraoin

River Broom
Lael Forest

162 **B**  **C**  Loch t-Sidhein  **D** 163 A835

A832

Heritage
Loch Tollaidh
Tollie Farm
Loch Kernsary
Loch na Moine
Fionn Loch
Loch Beinn Dearg
Beinn a'Chlaidheimh
Dundonnell River
Meall an t-Sithe 1971
1270 Carn Breac Beag
Abhainn Cuileig
Braemore
Corrieshalloch Gorge
Falls of Measach
Braemore Forest

Charlestown
Loch Airigh a'Phuill
Meall an Doirein 1381
2595 Beinn Airigh Charr
Dubh Loch
Lochan Feith Mhic'illean
Fuar Loch Mòr
Loch a'Bhrisidh
Mullach Coire Mhic Fhearchair
Groban 2424
A'Chailleach 3276
Loch Toll an Lochain
Meall a'Chrasgaidh 3062
Loch a'Mhadaidh
Sgurr Mòr 3637

Loch Maree Islands
Eilean Sùbhainn
Letterewe
Letterewe Forest
Beinn Làir 2817
Loch Garbhaig
Loch an Sgeireach
Gorm Loch Mòr
Gleann Tanagaidh
Abhainn a'Chadh'Bhuidhe
Beinn nan Ramh 2333
Fannich Forest
Fannich Lodge

Shieldaig
Loch Bad an'togalaig
Talladale
Victoria Falls
A832 16

SLIOCH 3215

WESTER ROSS

Heights of Kinlochewe
Fionn Bheinn 3062
Loch na Mòine Mòr
Loch na Mòine Beag
Lochrosque

Shieldaig
Baosbheinn 2869
Loch na h-Oidhche 2805
Beinn an Eòin
Strath Lungard
Bridge of Grudie
River Grudie
Glen Grudie
Beinn a'Mhùinidh
Kinlochewe Forest
Carn a'Ghlinne 1769
2313 Meall a'Chaorainn
River Bran
Strath

Shieldaig Forest
Beinn Bhreac 2031
Loch a'Bhealaich
Ruadh-stac Mòr 3313
Beinn Eighe
Beinn Eighe
Kinlochewe
Incheril
Glen Docherty
Badavanich
Loch a'Chroisg
Achnasheen
A832

Upper Diabaig
Beinn Alligin 3232
BEINN EIGHE
LIATHACH 3456
A896 17
Loch Bharranch
Coulin Lodge
Loch Clair
Abhainn Dubh
Loch an Fhiarlaid
Carn Beag 1804
Ledgowan
Loch Gowan
A890
1765 Carn Mhartuin
WEST

Alligin Shuas
Torridon Forest
Rechullin
Inveralligin
Fasag
Countryside Centre
Torridon
Deer
Annat
Glen Torridon
River Torridon
Sgorr Dubh 2566
Lochan Neimhe
Loch Coulin
Coulin Forest
Ledgowan Forest
Scardroy
Loch Coire a'Bhuic

Upper Loch Torridon
Balgy
Falls of Balgy
Ben-damph Forest
Abhainn Thràil
Lochan Uaine
H
2223 Carn Breac
I
Glen Carron
Loch Sgamhain
Moruisg 3026
G
Carn Gorm
Glencarron & Glenuig Forest
Creag na h-Iolaire

Idaig
1692
Loch Damh
Beinn Damh 2957
Maol Chean-dearg 3060
Sgorr Ruadh 3142
River Lair
Loch Coire Làir
Glencarron Lodge
Craig
18
Allt a'Chonais
Gleann Fhiodhaig
River Meig
Loch na Caoidhe 3304
Loch na Caoidhe

Glenshieldaig Forest
Loch Coire an Ruadh-stic
Achnashellach
Achnashellach Forest
Eagan
Creag a'Chaorainn
Sgurr na Feartaig
Beinn Tharsuinn
West Monar Forest
Maoile Lunndaidh 3304
An Gorm-loch

A896
Loch Gaineamhach
An Gorm-loch
Loch a'Mhuilinn
Coulags
Balnacra
A890
Loch Dùghaill
Sgurr a'Chaorachain 3455

Loch Coire nan Arr
Rassal Ashwood
Sgurr a'Gharaidh 2396
Glas Bheinn 2332
Tullich
New Kelso
Strathcarron
River Carron
Beinn Dronaig
Loch Calavie
Loch an Laoigh
Loch Mhuilich
Loch Monar
Monar Lodge

Kishorn
Ardarroch
Smithy Heritage Centre
Kirkton
A896
Achintee
Lochcarron
Attadale
Loch nan Creadha
Carn Geuradainn 1950
Bendronaig Lodge
An Gead Loch
Loch an Tachdaich
Meallan Buidhe

Achintraid
Lochcarron Weavers
Bad a'Chreamha 1296
Stromemore
Ardaneaskan
Strome
Ardnarff
Attadale Forest
R. Attadale
River Ling
Loch Calavie
Loch Gobhlach
An Cruachan 2312
Sgurr na Lapaich 3775

5 Stromeferry
A890
Highland Farm
Craig
Achmore
Loch nan Gillean
Carn nan Iomairean
Loch an Iasaich
Loch Ling
Loch Cruoshie
An 3508
An Riabhachan 3696
Glencannich Forest

Loch Lundie
Loch Achaidh na h-Inich
Gleann Udalain
Allt Gleann Udalain
Loch na h-Onaich
Sgùman Còinntich 2883
Aonach Buidhe 2949
Killilan Forest
Coire Lochan
Toll Creagach 3457
Doire Tana

Balmacara Square
Auchtertyre
Conchra
Sallachy
Long
Loch Beinn a'Mheadhoin
Killilan
148
Loch nan Ealachan
Carnach
West Benula Forest
Loch Mhoicean
Loch Mullardoch
Coire Lochan 3646
Carn Eighe 3880
Glen Cannich

A **B** **C** **D**

Kirkton
Nostie
Ardelve
Dornie
Bundalloch
Carndu
Loch Bhuic Mhòr
Loch nan Eun
Inverinate Forest
Falls of
Gleann nam Fiadh
Tom a'Chòinich 3646
Carn Eighe

Balmacara
Auchtertyre Hill
A87
Glas Eilean
Loch Alsh
Ardintoul
Camas-luinie
River Elchaig
Loch Long
Gleann Sithidh
Coire Lochan

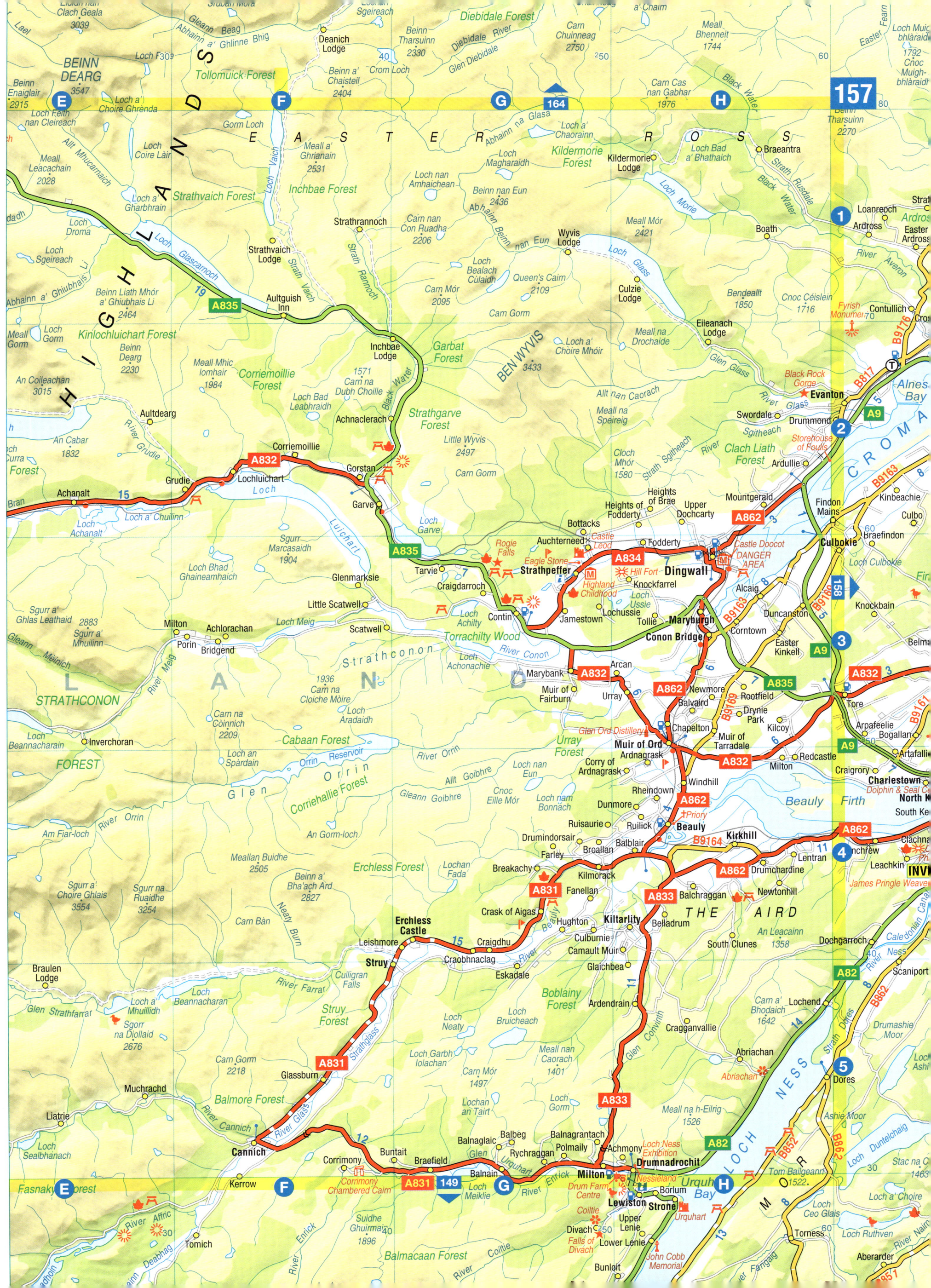

E F G 164 H

BEINN DEARG 3547
Beinn Enaiglair 2915
Meall Leacachain 2028

Tollomuick Forest
Diebidale Forest
Diebidale River
Glen Diebidale
Carn Chuinneag 2750
Meall Bhenneit 1744
Carn Cas nan Gabhar 1976
Braeantra

Deanich Lodge
Beinn a' Chaisteil 2404
Beinn Tharsuinn 2330
Crom Loch

Loch Vaich
Strathvaich Forest
Inchbae Forest
Strathrannoch
Strathvaich Lodge
Meall a' Ghrianain 2531
Kildermorie Forest
Kildermorie Lodge
Loch Morie
Loanreoch
Ardross
Easter Ardross

A835
Aultguish Inn
Inchbae Lodge
Garbat Forest
BEN WYVIS 3433
Wyvis Lodge
Meall Mór 2421
Loch Glass
Boath
Culzie Lodge
Eileanach Lodge
Bendeallt 1850
Cnoc Céislein 1716
Fyrish Monument
Evanton
Alness Bay

Kinlochluichart Forest
Beinn Dearg 2230
Corriemoillie Forest
Carn na Dubh Choille
Strathgarve Forest
Little Wyvis 2497
Carn Gorm
Meall na Speireig
Cloch Mhór 1580
Clach Liath Forest
Ardullie
Black Rock Gorge
Swordale
Drummond
Storehouse of Foulis
CROMARTY

A832 Corriemoillie
Grudie
Lochluichart
Gorstan
Garve
Loch Luichart
Loch Garve
Achnaclerach
Rogie Falls
Eagle Stone
Strathpeffer
Castle Leod
Hill Fort
DANGER AREA
Castle Doocot
Mountgerald
Findon Mains
Kinbeachie
Culbo
Braefindon
Culbokie
Loch Culbokie
Knockbain

Achanalt
Achnalt
Loch Achanalt
Loch a' Chuilinn
A835
Tarvie
Craigdarroch
Auchterneed
Heights of Fodderty
Heights of Brae
Upper Dochcarty
Foddity
Knockfarrel
Dingwall
Alcaig
Duncanston
Easter Kinkell
A9

Milton
Achlorachan
Porin
Bridgend
Glenmarksie
Little Scatwell
Scatwell
Loch Achilty
Contin
Jamestown
Lochussie
Tollie
Maryburgh
Conon Bridge
Corntown
A835
Tore
Arpafeelie
Bogallan
A832

STRATHCONON
Inverchoran
Carn na Coinnich 2209
Loch Meig
Torrachilty Wood
River Conon
Marybank
Muir of Fairburn
Arcan
Urray
Newmore
Rootfield
Drynie Park
Kilcoy
Redcastle
Milton
Craigrory
Charlestown

Cabaan Forest
Loch Aradaidh
Loch Achonachie
A832
Balvaird
A862
Muir of Ord
Ardnagrask
Chapelton
Muir of Tarradale
A832

Glen Ord Distillery
Urray Forest
Corry of Ardnagrask
Rheindown
Dunmore
Windhill
Beauly Firth
North K

Erchless Forest
Lochan Fada
Breakachy
Farley
Broallan
Kilmorack
Ruisaurie
Drumindorsair
Ruilick
Balblair
Beauly
Kirkhill
Drumchardine
Clachna
Leachkin
INV

A831
Fanellan
Crask of Aigas
Hughton
Kiltarlity
Belladrum
Newtonhill
Balchraggan
A862

Erchless Castle
Leishmore
Struy
Craigdhu
Craobhnaclag
Culburnie
Camault Muir
Glaichbea
Eskadale
South Clunes
An Leacainn 1358
Dochgarroch
A82

Braulen Lodge
Glen Strathfarrar
Loch a' Mhuillidh
Sgurr na Diollaid 2676
Culligran Falls
River Farrar
Struy Forest
Boblainy Forest
Ardendrain
Glen Convinth
Cragganvallie
Carn a' Bhodaich 1642
Abriachan
Lochend
Drumashie Moor

Muchrachd
Carn Gorm 2218
Glassburn
A831
Strathglass
Loch Neaty
Loch Bruicheach
Meall nan Caorach 1401
Loch Gorm
A833
Meall na h-Eirlig 1526
Dores
Ashie Moor
A82

Liatrie
Loch Sealbhanach
Cannich
Corrimony
Buntait
Braefield
Balnaglaic
Glen
Balbeg
Rychraggan
Balnagrantach
Polmaily
Achmony
Drumnadrochit
A82
LOCH NESS

Fasnakyle Forest
Kerrow
Corrimony Chambered Cairn
A831 149
Balnain
Loch Meiklie
Glen Urquhart
Milton
Drum Farm Centre
Loch Ness Exhibition
Nessieland
Lewiston
Strone
Urquhart Bay
Borlum
River Affric
Tomich
Suidhe Ghuirmain 1896
Coille
Divach
Upper Lenie
Lower Lenie
Falls of Divach
John Cobb Memorial
Bunloit
Urquhart
Loch Ceo Glais
Torness
Aberarder

Balmacaan Forest

A  164  B  165  C  D

Edderton
A836
Glenmorangie Distillery
Morangie
Tarlogie
DANGER AREA
Portmahomack
Bindal
Tarbat Discovery Centre
Seafield
Rockfield
B9174
Tain
Tain Through Time
Inver
Lower Arboll
Toulvaddie
Tarrel

Easter Fearn
B9176
1218
Loch Muigh-bhlàraidh
1792 Cnoc Muigh-bhlàraidh
Aultnamain Inn
Morangie Forest
Hilton
Lochslin
Lower Pitkerrie
Geanies
B9165

Beinn Tharsuinn 2270
Loch Sheilah
Cnoc an t-Sabhail 1243
Glen Aldie
Hartmount Holdings
A9
Hill of Fearn
Fearn
B9166
Hilton of Cadboll Chapel
Tullich
Hilton of Cadboll
Balintore
Shandwick

O  S  S
Braeantra
Loanreoch
Ardross
Strathy
Easter Ardross
Stittenham
Dalnavie
Cnoc Corr Guinie
Kinrive Hill 1056
Kinhrive
Scotsburn
Lamington
Brenachie
Marybank
Pitmaduthy
Kildary
Milton
Arabella
Ankerville
Wester Rarichie
Clach a' Charridh
Port an Righ

Ardross Forest 1301
Badachonacher
Newmore
Coillemore
Kilmuir
Delny
Polio
Barbaraville
Nigg Bay
Pitcalnie
Nigg
Bayfield Loch
Hill of Nigg 665
Castlecraig

Contullich
Fyrish Monument
Crosshills
Obsdale
Achnagarron
Tomich
Broomhill
Balintraid
Balnabruaich
Nigg Ferry (Seasonal)
Hugh Miller

Alness
A9
Dalmore
Distillery
Invergordon
Saltburn
Balnapaling
Cromarty
Courthouse
Blue Head
Sutors of Cromarty

Evanton
Black Rock Gorge
Drummond
Alness Bay
Balblair
Ferryton
Udale Bay
Cromarty Bay
Newton
A832
McFarquhar's Cave

Swordale
Ardullie
Storehouse of Foulis
CROMARTY
Alnessferry
Resolis
Jemimaville
B9163
Davidston
Muirton

Mountgerald
Findon Mains
Kinbeachie
Culbo
Wester Brae
Easter Brae
Mount High Forest
Whitebog

A862
Culbokie
Braefindon
Mount Eagle
Loch Culbokie
Millbuie Forest
B9160

Alcaig
A9 157
Duncanston
Knockbain
BLACK ISLE
Killen
Findon Forest
Rosemarkie Bay
DANGER AREA
Whiteness Head

Corntown
Easter Kinkell
Belmaduthy
Easter Suddie
Rosemarkie
Fortrose
Groam House
Fort George
Chanonry Point
Avoch Bay

A835
Rootfield
Tore
Munlochy
A832
Avoch
Chanonry Point
Ardersier
Connage Highland Dairy
NAIRN
Tradespark
Kingsteps
Druim
Loch Loy
A96

Drynie Park
Kilcoy
A832
Arpafeelie
Bogallan
Black Isle Wildlife Park
Drumsmittal
Kilmuir
Munlochy Bay
Fisherton
INVERNESS
B9039
Milton of Gollanfield
Gollanfield
Lochside
Loch Flemington
B9006
Clephanton
B9091
Brackla
Piperhill
Regoul
Geddes
Laikel Forest
Auldearn
Blackhills

Redcastle
Milton
Craigrory
Charlestown
Dolphin & Seal Centre
North Kessock
Kilravock Castle
Cawdor
Culcharry
Urchany
A939
Littlemill

Beauly Firth
South Kessock
A82
Clachnaharry
Drumossie
Tornagrain
Newton
Dalcross
Croy
Cantray
Easter Galcantray
Wester Galcantray
Clunas

rkhill
A862
Bunchrew
Leachkin
Craig Phadraig
James Pringle Weavers
PAGE 196
INVERNESS
Culcabock
Culloden
A96
Balloch
Cantraywood
Cantraybruich
Assich Forest
Alt Dearg
Clunas Reservoir
Newlands of Fleenas Wood
Redburn
Loch Belivat
Ardclach Bell Tower

AIRD
An Leacainn 1358
Dochgarroch
Scaniport
Essich
Westhill
Smithton
Newlands Memorial Cairn
Culloden
1746 Well of the Dead
Clava Cairns
Saddle Hill 1227
Carn a' Chrasgie
Glenferness Mains

Lochend
Drumashie Moor
Loch Ashie
Milton of Leys
Lochardil
B851
Saddle Hill
Carn Sgumain 1370
Drynachan Lodge
Loch Kirkaldy

Abriachan
Dores
Creag a' Chlachain 1196
Inverarnie
Daviot
Craggiemore
B9154
Beinn Bhreac 1675
Moy Burn
Meall a' Bhreacraibh 1809
Carn an t-Sean-liathanaich 2076
Lochindorb Lodge

Carn a' Bhodaich 1642
Dunlichity Lodge
Farr
Strathnairn Forest
Stac na Cathaig 1463
Meall Mòr 1611
Moy
Loch Moy
Moy Castle
Ruthven
Balvraid Lodge
B9007

Torness
Loch Ruthven
River Nairn
Carn na h-Easgainn 2022
Findhorn
Funtack Burn
Rhilean Burn
Leonach Burn
Tomlachlan Burn
Duthil Burn

A  150  B  C  D
Brin Herb Nursery
Beinn Bhreac 1969
Tomatin
Findhorn Bridge
Corrybrough
Raigbeg
Carn a' Choire Mhóir
Carn Glas-choire 2162
A9

300 10 20 30 80

E F G H

70

1

2

Spey Bay

Caves
Fisheries & Community
Stotfield
Branderburgh
Covesea
Seatown
Hopeman
Duffus
Lossiemouth
Well
Lossiemouth
B9040
A941
Burghead
B9040
Cummingstown
St Peter's Kirk
Roseisle
Duffus
Loch Spynie
Lossie Forest
Burghead Bay
Roseisle Forest
B9012
College of Roseisle
Spynie Palace
WDCS Wildlife Centre
DANGER AREA
Tugnet Ice House
Kingston
B9089
B9013
Quarrywood
Moray Motor
Lochhill
Spey Bay
Porttannachy
Nether Dallachy
Findhorn
Heritage Centre
Newton
Moray
Elgin
Castle
Bishopmill
Urquhart Stone Circle
Garmouth
Lower Dallachy
Findhorn Foundation
Kinloss
Coltfield
Alves
Old Mills
Elgin
Ashgrove
Urquhart
B9015
Bogmoor
Auchenhalrig
Newlands of Tynet
Upper Dallachy
Culbin Forest
Findhorn Bay
A96
12
17
Glen Moray Distillery
New Elgin
Linkwood
Sheriffston
Lhanbryde
Cowfords
Mosstodloch
Baxters
Folk
A98
Cloddymoss
Kintessack
B9011
Sueno's Stone
Kinloss Abbey
Miltonduff
Distillery
Glassgreen
Moss of Barmuckity
Coxton Tower
Scotsburn
7
Crofts of Dipple
A96
Whiteash Hill Wood
Benromach Distillery
Broom of Moy
Nelson Tower
Lochaber
Muir of Miltonduff
Foresterseat
B9010
Loch na Bo
Cranloch
Fochabers
Speymouth Forest
A96
B9016
Dyke
Brodie
FORRES
Falconer
Calific
Monaughty Forest
Heldon Hill
Pluscarden Abbey
Barnhill
Thomshill
Longmorn
Whitewreath
Millbuies
Coleburn
Ordiquish
Inchberry
Wood of Ordiequish
3
Brodie
Balnageith
Whiterow
Dallas Dhu Historic Distillery
Rafford
Moor of Granary
Black Burn
Pluscarden
Kellas
Upper Bogside
B9013
Longmorn
22
B9015
11
Orton
B9015
Auchroisk Distillery
Malcolmburn
1019 Hill of Mulderie
River Findhorn
A940
Loch of Blairs
Damhead
Dallas Forest
Hill of the Wangie 1046
Glenlattererach Reservoir
Pikey Hill 1164
13
Glen of Rothes
Orton
B9015
B9013
Mulben 850
A95
Whitemire
Conicaval
Altyre Woods
Romach Loch
Branchill
Dallas
Meikle Hill 932
Cairn Uish 1197
Leanoch Burn
Glen Grant Distillery
Rothes
Ben Aigan 1546
Mount Pleasant
1111 Hill of Towie
Forest
Logie
Drumine Forest
Newtyle Forest
Hill of Tomechole 1129
Mill Buie 1218
M O R A Y
Cairn Cattoch 1210
Burn of Rothes
Rothes
A941
B9014
Logie Steading
Randolph's Leap
Carnach
Dunphail
Loch Dallas
Loch Noir
Carn na Cailliche 1324
Elchies Forest
Braehead
Craigellachie Bridge
Speyside Way
Maggieknockater
4
& Dufftown Keith & Dufftown (Whisky Line)
Drumm
Relugas
B9007
Glenernie
14
River Divie
Larig Hill 1783
Carn Kitty 1712
Cardhu Distillery
Cardow
Archiestown
B9102
Robertstown
Macallan Distillery
Speyside Cooperage
Craigellachie
Tullich
Lock Park
11
Knock of Braemoray 1495
Dorback Burn
Upper Knockando
Knockando
Dalmunach
Speyview
Carron
Charlestown of Aberlour
Balvenie
Glenfiddich Distillery
Milltown of Auchindoun
A940
A939
Dava
Carn na Loine 1800
Alla t Gheallaidh
Scotmore Forest
Birchview
B9138
A95
Marypark
Glenfarclas Distillery
Milltown of Edinvillie
Glenallachie Distillery
Dufftown
Balvenie
Distillery
A920
Knock of Braemoray
B9102
Belleheiglash
Ballindalloch Castle
Kirktown of Mortlach
Giant's Chair
Auchindoun
1599 The Scalp
Carn Ruigh Chorrach 1587
Upper Derraid
Auchnagallin
Cragganmore Distillery
Bridge of Avon
B9137
Inveravon Stones
Ben Rinnes 2759
Meikle Conval 1867
Laggan
Glaschoil
A95
13
Advie
Tormore Distillery
1605 Cairnacay
B9008
Glen Rinnes
Dullan Water
Glenfiddich Lodge
19
Carn Ruigh Chorrach
A940
A939
Dalvey
Drumin Castle
Packhorse Bridge
Glen Fiddich
A941
Bridgend
Glenfiddich Forest
Creag Liath 1473
Ballieward
Cottartown
Delliefure
Drumin
B9009
11
Glenfiddich Lodge
Grantown-on-Spey
E
B9102
Cromdale
F
151
Glenlivet
Glenlivet Distillery
Castleton
Shenval
Auchbreck
G
Corryhabbie Hill 2561
River Fiddich
H
Ca
Beinn Mhor 1545 300
Craggan
Speybridge
A939
Granton
Haugh of Cromdale
HILLS OF CROMDALE
Knock Earth House
Avon
Glen Livet
1594
30
1872 Round Hill
A938
Dulnain Bridge
A95
B9136
Tomnavoulin
Carn Liath
20
Carn Muldonich 1857
Carn an t-Suidhe 2401
Blackwater Forest
Carn Daimh

N O R T H

Spey Bay

Kingston
Garmouth
Tugnet
Ice House
WDCS Wildlife Centre
Spey Bay
Nether Dallachy
Lower Dallachy
Upper Dallachy
Porttannachy
Buckpool
Portgordon
Auchenhalrig
Newlands of Tynet
Slackhead
Broadley
Clochan
Drybridge
Slackhead

B9021 Portknockie
B9020 Findochty
A942 Portessie
Bauds of Cullen
Findochty Castle
Seatown
Cullen Bay Logie Head
Cullen
Sandend Bay
Findlater Castle
Sandend
Mercat Cross
Lintmill
Bin of Cullen 1051
Milton
Joiner's Workshop
Dum Hill 653
Fordyce
Kirktown of Deskford
Deskford Church
Berryhillock
Brodiesord

Redhythe Point
Portsoy
Salmon Bothy
Boyne Castle
Seatown
Boyne Bay
Knock Head
Whitehills
Boyndie Bay
Boyndie
Wester Culbeuchly
Macduff Marine Aquarium
Inverboyndie
Newtown
Banff
Macduff
Duff House Country Gallery
Kirktown of Alvah
Itlaw
King Edward
Eden Castle
Newton of Mountblairy
Muirden

Buckie
A990
A942 Rathven
A98

DANGER AREA
Spey Viaduct
Bogmoor
B9014
B9015
Cowfords
Crofts of Dipple
Mosstodloch
A98
Baxters
Folk
Fochabers
159
Speymouth Forest
Whiteash Hill Wood
Ordiquish
Inchberry
Wood of Ordiequish
Forgie
Broadrashes
Aultmore
Auchroisk Distillery
Malcolmburn
Mulben
Hill of Mulderie 1019
B9013
Newmill
B9017
Keith
Fife Keith
Mains of Auchindachy
Strathisla Distillery
A96
A95

M O R A Y

Millstone Hill 987
Deerhill
Grange Crossroads
Shiel Muir
Aultmore
Burn of Aultmore
Crannoch
Sillyearn
Bracobrae
Lurg Hill 1028
Mains of Edingight
Knock Hill 1412
Drums of Park
Gordonstown
Finnygaud
Knowes of Elrick
Cornhill
A95
B9022
B9023
B9025
B9121
Aberchirder
A97
Bogton
B9025

Knock
Drumnagorrach
Farmtown
Nethermills
Ramsburn
Marnoch
Dubiton
Turtory
Hillbrae
Milltown of Rothiemay
Yonder Bognie
Bogniebrae
Inverkeithny
Auchininna
Fortrie
B9024
A95
B9117

A B E R D E E N

Thomastown
Kirktown of Auchterless
Balgaveny
Aucharnie
New Mill
B992

Drummuir
Keith & Dufftown Railway (Whisky Line)
Towiemore
Pitlurg Castle
B9115
Upper Cuttlehill
Glen of Coachford
Ruthven
Cairnie
The Bin 1027
The Bin Forest
Corse of Kinnoir
Fourman Hill
Largue
Corse
Drumblade
Brideswell
Aucharnie

Maggieknockater
Mount Pleasant
Hill of Towie 1111
A95
B9014

Tullich
Lock Park
B9014
Glenfiddich Distillery
Milltown of Auchindoun
Invermarkie
Blairmore
Daugh of Invermarkie
Daugh of Cairnborrow
A96
T
A920
Haugh of Glass
Dean's Shortbread
Clashmach Hill
Brander
Huntly
Drumblade
Bridgend

S T R A T H B O G I E

Dufftown
Kirktown of Mortlach
Giant's Chair
Auchindoun
Laggan
The Scalp 1599
Bailiesward
Tillathrowie
Succoth
Coynachie
Clashindarroch Forest
Kirkney
Kirkney Water
Cults
Knockandy Hill 1425
Wardhouse
Picardy Symbol Stone
Hillhead
Bainshole
Glens of Foudland
Hill of Foudland 1531
Lenchie
Largie
Upper Boddam
Colpy
Fisherford
Hill of Tillymorgan 1249
Kirkton of Culsalmond
Newseat
Rothienorman
B992
B9001

A941
Glen Fiddich
Bridgend
Inverharroch
Ardwell
Mount of Haddoch 1708
Milton of Lesmore
Tap o' Noth
Tap O'Noth 1848
152
Kennethmont
B9002
Duncanston
Dunnideer Castle
Insch
Pitmachie
Old Rayne
A920
Cairnhill
Tocher
Meikle Wartle
Kirkton of Rayne
A96
Oyne

Cabrach
Belhinnie
Rhynie
Craw Stane
B9002
Elrick
Clatt
Leslie
Kirkton
Old Westhall
Pitcaple
Whitefo

Black Water
Round Hill 1872
Mount of Haddoch

A941
A97

80 · 90 · 400 · 10

1

70

S E A

Troup Head
Pennan Head
Quarry Head
Rosehearty
Kinnaird Head
Scottish Lighthouses
Heritage Centre
Broadsea
**Fraserburgh**
Cairnbulg Point
Pittulie
Sandhaven
B9031
Head of Garness
Gamrie Bay
Fort Fiddes
Crovie
Pennan
Peathill
Pitsligo Castle
Percyhorner
A98
Kirktown
Fraserburgh Bay
Cairnbulg
Maggie's Hoosie
Inverallochy
Silverhillocks
Gardenstown
B9123
Dubford
B9031
New Aberdour
Upper Boyndlie
Mid Ardlaw
Cardno
A981
B9033
Cairnbulg Castle
Charlestown
Inzie Head
Longmanhill
Netherbrae
22
Tyrie
Woodhead
B9032
Memsie
A90
Moss-side of Cairness
Inverallochy Castle
Gowanhill
St Combs
A98
Hill of Overbrae
Ladysford
Blackhills
60
Rathen
B9033
Cairness
Loch of Strathbeg
60
Clochforbie
Hill of Fishrie 745
Craigmaud
Corsehill
Hillhead of Auchentumb
Memsie Cairn
60
Crimonmogate
Rattray Head
Crudie
Cauldwells
A950
Middlemuir
Waughton Hill 768
White Stag
A952
Dartfield
Crimond
Plaidy
B9105
Craigston
Fintry
Litterty
New Byth
Balnamoon
New Pitsligo
B9093
Willows Animal Sanctuary
White Horse
Strichen
Cockmuir
New Leeds
Belfatton
Longhill
Keyhead
Rattray
A90
60
17
Garmond
B9027
Whitestones
Bonnykelly
Strichen Stone Circle
15
Adziel
North Ugie Water
B9093
Rowanhill
St Fergus Moss
Middle Essie
St Fergus
Muiryfold
Balthangie
Oldwhat
A981
Denhead
Hythie
Backfolds
Rora Moss
Shielhill
Kirktown
60
Turriff
Delgatie
B9170
5
618 · Hill of Corseight
Brucklay
11
Forest of Deer
Fetterangus
Dunshillock
Backhill
Cuttyhill
Rora
Ravenscraig Castle
River Ugie
Old Salmon Fish House
Cuminestown
Fedderate Castle
Owl & Pussycat Centre
Loudon Wood Stone Circle
Drinnie's Wood Observatory
Mintlaw
Longside
Inverugie
B9170
North Commonty
A981
Maud
B9029
Deer Abbey
Old Deer
Aberdeenshire Farming
Aden
Flushing
Peterhead (H)
A950
Buchanhaven
Darra
Howe of Teuchar
Culsh Monument
Railway (M)
Backhill of Clackriach
Quartalehouse
South Ugie Water
8
Peterhead
Keith Inch
Delgaty Forest
Birkenhills
Deer's Hill 584
New Deer
Auchreddie
Drymuir
Bulwark
Stuartfield
Inverquhomery
Millbreck
Little Dens
Cocklaw
A982
Burnhaven
Invernettie
A947
Greens
Slacks of Cairnbanno
B9170
7
A948
B9030
Kinnadie
Clola
Nether Kinmundy
Boddam
Steinmanhill
Kirkton
Middlemuir
Knaven
Cairnorrie
Auchnagatt
Mains of Auchnagatt
Kinnockie
Blackhill
Stirling
Sandfordhill
Boddam Castle
Seggat
Inverythan
Tifty
Reemshill
Monkshill
Backhill
Lethenty
Cottown
Little Ardo
578 · Hill of Skilmafilly
13
Milton Coldwells
Muirtack
Hatton
Coldwells
A90
Long Haven
Fyvie
Parkburn
Gight Castle
River Ythan
Braeside
Quilquox
Hill of Dudwick 570
A952
12
Bridgend
Bullers of Buchan
North Haven
A975
Twa Havens
Woodhead
Upper Kirkton
Haddo
Methlick
Drumwhindle
Arthrath
Bogbrae Croft
Chapel Hill
Cruden Bay
Slains Castle
Port Erroll
Folla Rule
St Katherines
Hillbrae
Barthol Chapel
Earlsford
Haddo House
Haddo
B9005
Ythanbank
16
Whinnyfold
Core Hill 804
Cross of Jackston
Tulloch
Wedderlairs
Thornroan
Medieval Tomb
Prop of Ythsie Stone Circle
Inverebrie
Yonderton
Broomfield
10
Old Slains Castle
Tarves
Craigdam
B999
Kinharrachie
Esslemont Castle
Ellon
P+R
A90
Denhead
Meikle Loch
**FORMARTINE**
Loanhead Stone Circle
A947
Heritage
**153**
G
B9005
Kirkton of Logie Buchan
Collieston
B9003
Kirktown of Slains
Daviot
A920
Tolquhon Castle
Tolquhon Gallery
A920
5
Tipperty
Meikle Tarty
31
Forvie
A975
Oldmeldrum
Pitmedden
B9000
Udny Green
Hill of
Knockhall Castle
B9000
Hackley Head or Forvie Ness

2

3

8 · 50

4

5

30

10

E F G H

A    B    C    D

60   70   80   90

30

1

20

2

10

171

3

900

4

90

5

80

A     B     C     D

60   70   80   90

Seisiadar

Camas Eilean Ghlais

Reiff

Eilean Mullagrach

Isle Ristol

Glas-leac Mór

Tanera Beg

Ullapool to Stornoway 2hrs. 40mins.

Summer

Glas-leac Beag

Eilean Dubh

Priest Island

Bottle Island

Greenstone Point

Rubha Beag

Loch na Doire Duinne

Opinan

Mellon Udrigle

Gruinard Island

Stattic Point

Loch nan Clachan Geala

Loch a' Choire

Loch an t-Slagain

Achgarve

Gruinard Bay

Mungasdale

Eilean Furadh Mór

Slaggan Bay

Beinn Dearg Nhór 513

Mellon Charles

Laide

Gruinard House

Rubha Reidh

Camas Mór

Cove

Rubha nan Sasan

Ormiscaig

A832

Sand

Second Coast

First Coast

Loch an Draing

Mellangaun

Aultbea

Loch na Bà

An Cuaidh 972

Loch Airigh an Eilein

Isle of Ewe

Drumchork

Beinn Dearg Bad Chailleach 897

Melvaig

Aultgrishan

Loch Sguod

Loch a' Bhaid-luachraich

Little Gruinard River

Uisge Toll

B8021

Midtown

Loch Ewe

Loch Mhic' ille Riabhaich

Loch na Mòine Buige

Aird Dubh

Beinn a' Chàisgein Beag 2230

Brae

Seana Chamas

Cnoc Breac 962

Naast

Loch nan Liagh

Inverewe

Loch Fada

Loch na Mèine 820

Bad Bog

Peterburn

Port Erradale

Londubh

Loch Ghiuragarstidh

Meall na Mèine 820

North Erradale

155

River Sand

Poolewe

A832

River Ewe

Loch na Moine

Big Sand

Loch na Curra

Loch Kernsary

Fionn Loch

Longa Island

Caolas Beag

Lonemore

Mial

Strath

Heritage M

Loch Bad a' Chreamh

Tollie Farm

Loch na Beannach Mór

B8021

Smithstown

Gairloch

Loch Tollaidh

Loch Airigh a' Phuill

Meall an Doirein 1381

2595 Beinn Airigh Charr

Loch Gairloch

Eilean

Beinn Airigh Charr

Kinloch
A838
Loch Merkland
Merkla Lodge

Kylestrome
Kylesku
Glendhu Forest
Beinn a' Bhuta
Loch a' Chàirn Bhàin
Maryck Memories of Childhood
Unapool
Newton
Glendhu
Beinn Aird da Loch 1722
Dubh a' Chuail
Loch Merkland 30

Cluas Deas
Loch Cùl Fraioch
Culkein
Eilean Chrona
Oldany Island
Culkein Drumbeg
200
Rhubha Stoer
Achnacarnin
Oldany
Clashnessie Bay
Drumbeg
Loch Nedd
Nedd
Glenleraig
B869
Loch Poll 16
Loch an Leothaid
166
A894
QUINAG 2651
Loch na Gainmhich
Beinn Leoid 2599
H
A837
Loch an Eircill
Loch nan Caorach
Gorm Loch Mór
Loch a' Ghriama
Corriekinloch
1

Clashmore
Balchladich
Clashnessie
E
B869
Loch nan Lub
Loch an Loinne
Gorm Loch Mór
Lochassynt Lodge
Glas Bheinn 2541
Eas a' Chual Aluinn (Waterfall)
Inchnadamph Forest
BEN MORE ASSYNT 3273
Maovally 1673

Stoer
Clachtoll
Clachtoll Broch
Loch Beannach
Loch Cròcach
A837 10
River Tràighaich
Allt an Tiaghaich
Loch Assynt
Ardvreck Castle
Beinn Uidhe 2410
Gleann Dubh
River Traligill
Benmore Forest
Inchnadamph
2338
Fionn Loch Mór
Duchally

Bay of Stoer
Achmelvich Bay
Rhicarn
Brackloch
Baddidarach
Lochinver
Assynt
Loch Inver
River Inver
Beinn Gharbh 1769
Loch Féith an Leòthaid
Inchnadamph
River Loanan
Loch Awe
Inchnadamph Bone Caves
2670
Breabag
Beabag
Loch Carn nan Conbhairean
Meall an Aonaich 2344

Rubha Rodha
Achmelvich
B869
Soyea Island
A' Chleit
Kirkaig Point
Badnaban
Strathan
Loch Culag
Loch Kirkaig
Glencanisp Forest
River Abhainn
Clach Airigh
SUILVEN 2399
CANISP 2779
Lochan Fada
Ledbeg River
Benmore Lodge
Loch Meall a' Bhuirich

Rubha Coigeach
Eilean Mór
Inverkirkaig
Fionn Loch
Loch a' Ghille
Falls of Kirkaig
Loch na Gainimh
Cam Loch
Ledmore
A837
Loch Ailsh
An Stùc 1195
Beinn an Fh 1786

Enard Bay
Inverpolly Lodge
Loch Buine Moire
River Polly
Loch Doire na h-Airbhe
Loch Veyatie
River
Ledmore
Altnacealgach
Loch Borralan
Cnoc na Glas Choille 1006
Glen Oykel River Oykel
Beinn an
164

Rubha Mór
Brae of Achnahaird
Altandhu
Loch Raa
Loch Vatachan
Badentarbat
Camas Coille
Aird of Coigach
Stac Pollaidh 2009
Inverpolly Forest
CUL MOR 2787
Elphin
A835
Knockan
Drumrunie Forest
Lochan an Ais
Knockan Crag
Loch Urigill
Crom Allt
1692
Meall an Fhuarain 1895
Eileag
A837
Loch Craggie
Coire a' Chonachair
18
Fionn Bheinn Mhór 1084
3

Badentarbat Bay
Achiltibuie
Polglass
Badenscallie
Achiltibuie
Polbain
Linneraineach
Cùl Beag 2523
Lochan Dearg
Clar Loch Mór
CROMALT HILLS
Loch a' Chroisg
Allt a' Chaoruinn
Allt
An Stùc
Lubcroy
900
Oykel Bridge

Tanera Mór Isles
Horse Island
Culnacraig
Achduart
COIGACH
Ben More Coigach (Beinn Mhòr na Còigich) 2438
Lochan Tuath
Lochanan Dubha
Drumrunie
18
Strath Canaird
Loch Eadar dha Bheinn
Na Dromannan 1337
Lochan nan Sàilean Móra
Rappach
Allt
Meall an Fhuarain
River Oykel 18

Carn nan Sgeir
Camas Mór
Isle Martin
Strathcanaird
River Runie
River Canaird
Strath Canaird
Loch Dubh
Loch na Maoile
Lochan nan Sàilean Móra
Beinn Donuill
Rappach Water
River Glen Einig
Creag Loisgte 1353

Cailleach Head
Leac Dhonn
Annat Bay
A835
Loch Kanaird
Ardmair
Rhue
947 Creag na h-Iolaire
Loch ob an Lochain
Loch a' Choire Bhuig
Rhidorroch Forest
Meall Liath Choire 1798
Corriemulzie River
4

Scoraig
Achmore
Carnach
Rireavach
Beinn Ghobhlach 2082
Morefield
Village Clock
Ullapool
M
Ullapool River
Rhidorroch
Glen Achall
Loch Achall
Clar Lochan
Loch an Daimh
East Rhidorroch Lodge
Strath Mulzie
Sidhean Raireag 1769
Glas'a Burn

Badluarach
Little Loch Broom
Durnamuck
Badcaul
Badrallach
A835
Loch na h-Uidhe
Allt na h' Airbhe
A835
Leckmelm
Beinn Eilideach 1830
Glen Douchary
Meall nam Bràgham 2221
River Douchary
Meall a' Choire Mhóir
Loch a' Choire Mhóir
Freevater Forest
90

Badluarach
38
Ardessie
Camusnagaul
A832
Sàil Mhór 2508
Dun Ruigh Ruaidh
Blarnalearoch
Dun Lagaidh
Rhiroy
Loch Lagaidh
Ardindrean
Loggie
Ardcharnich
Meall Dubh 2105
Loch Reidh Creagain
Carn Mór 2122
Seana Bhraigh 3040
Eididh nan Clach Geala 3039
Càrn Bàn 2772

Carn nam Buailean 1283
Ardessie Falls
Lochan Gaineamhaich
Dundonnell
Loch Mór 'Bad an Ducharaich
AN TEALLACH 3484
Strath Beag
Strathnasheallag Forest
Letters
River Broom
Loch a' Chairn Mor
Inverlael
Lael Forest
Inverlael Forest
Carn a' Bhiorain 1665
Auchlunachan
River Lael
BEINN DEARG 3547
Loch Prille
Abhainn a' Ghlinne Bhig
Deanich Lodge

Fisherfield Forest
Beinn Dearg Mór 974
156
E
Dundonnell Forest
Loch Coire Chaorachain
Loch Toll an Lochain
Loch Allt an Eigin
Lochan Fada
Loch an Airceil
Dundonnell River
F
Carn Breac Beag 1270
Braemore
A835
Corrieshalloch Gorge
Meall Leacachain 2028
157
G
Strathvaich Forest

Beinn a' Chlaidheimh
Beinn a' Mhadaidh 2802
Loch Beinn Dearg
Loch Beinn a' Chlaidheimh
A832
Meall an t-Sithe 1971
Loch an t-Sidhein
Falls of Measach
Braemore Forest
Loch Vaich
Inchbae Forest
Beinn a' Chaisteil 2404
Meall a' Ghrianain 2531
H

NORTH WEST HIGHLANDS
HIGHLAND

Kinloch

A **166**
B
C **A836**
D

Beinn Leoid
2599

Loch a' Chuail

Merkland Lodge
**A838**
38

Ben Hee
2863

Loch a' Ghorm-choire

River Mu

Ath

Loch Ben Harrald

250

BEN KLIBRECK
2367

60

Loch Choire

Creag na h-Iolaire
2278

Loch nan orach

Gorm Loch Mór

Loch a' Ghriama

Cnoc a' Ghriama
1221

Fiag Lodge

Loch Fiag

An Glas-loch

Meall an Fhuarain
1549

3157

A836
21

Meall nan Con

Loch Choire Forest
Loch Choire

Ben Armine Beag

Gòrm-Loch Beag

Ben Armine Forest
2311

Corriekinloch

Abhainn a' Choire

Loch Merklan

Overscaig

Cnoc an Alaskie
1024

Crask

Cnoc a' Ghiubhais
1135

Loch nan Uan

Meall a' Bhata
1907

Ben Armine Lodge

Dubh a' Chuail

1

Fionn Loch Mór

BEN MORE ASSYNT
3273

20

Loch Carn nan Conbhairean

Maovally
1673

River Flag

Glen Flag

Fiag Bridge

Loch an Ulbhaidh

Strath Tirry

River Tirry

Rhian

Rhian Bridge

Abhainn Sgeamhaid

Féith a' Chaorainn

Rhian

Dalnessie

Creag Riabhach na Greighe
1506

Sidhean Achadh nan Eun
1040

Meallan Liath Mór
1407

Coirefrois Burn
1230

Meall a' Phiobaire

Meall an Aonaich
2344

Benmore Forest

2

Loch Sgeireach

Beinn Sgeireach
1561

Allt a' Bhunn

Strath an Lòin

Allt Car

HIGHLA

Beinn Sgreamhaidh
1428

Arscaig

Shinness

A838

Achnairn

Achfrish

Tirryside

A836

Loch Beannach

Loch na Gaineimh

River Brora

978

West Langwell

Grumby Rock

Benmore Lodge

ilsh

10

Loch Meall a' Bhuirich

River Cassley

Loch an Ràsail

Loch na Caillich

Dalchork

Loch Tigh na Creige

Loch na Luibe

Loch Craggie

Torbreck Burn

East Langwell

An Stùc
1195

163

Glen Oykel

River Oykel

Elleag

Glencassley Castle

Loch na Faic

Beinn an Eòin
1786

Glen Cassley

Loch na Claise Mòire

Loch na Fuaralaich

River Cassley

Cnoc a' Choire
1318

Guidie Burn

Colaboll

Sallachy

A836

Saval

Lairg Muir

Lairg

Allt Chaiseagail

Loch Craggie

An Stoc-bheinn
1104

Loch Cracail Mór

Creagan Glas
1028

3

Loch Craggie

Coire a' Chonachair

18

Lubcroy

Fionn Bheinn Mhór
1084

Strath Oykel

Oykel Bridge

Invercassley

Achness Waterfall

Ferrycroft Countryside Centre
The Ord

Gruids

A839

Chambered Cairn

Ballan

Tomich

Rhian Breck

Torroble

A836

Achany Glen

A839

Muie

Ardachu

Strath Fleet

River Fleet

14

Tressady

Dalmore

Pittentrail

Loch an Lagain

Lochan na Gaoithe

Abhainn an t-Stratha

Meall Moraig
1090

Achvaich

River Evelix

Doune

Oape

Rosehall

A837

Einig

River Oykel

Altass

Achany

Cnoc Ceann nam Bad
881

Achinduich

Loch Laro

Sròn Ach a' Bhacaidh
928

Loch Buidhe

Beinn Domhnaill
1144

River Glen Einig

Meòir Langwell

Beinn Ulbhaidh
1616

Linsidemore

A837

Kyle of Sutherland

Shin Forest

Falls of Shin

4

Creag Loisgte
1353

Corriemulzie River

Strath Culleannach

Abhainn an t-Strath Chuileannach

Carn a' Choin Deirg
2301

Loch an Tuill Riabhaich

Meall Dheirgidh
1659

Loch Meall Dheirgidh

Achnahanat

Torroy

Inveran

B864

Inveran

1650 Carbisdale

Culrain

Balblair

A836

Airdens

Tulloch

Migdale

Loch a' Ghobhair

Glasha Burn

Sidhean Raireag
1769

90

Amat Forest

Croich

The Craigs

Amatnatua

Glencalvie Lodge

Alladale Lodge

Alladale River

Strathcarron

Carn Caol

Wester Gruinards

Culeave

Soyal

Cornhill

Lower Gledfield

Dounie

Bonar Bridge

A949

Ardgay

Kincardine

Little Creich

Loch Migdale

Bardnabeinne

Spinningdale

Ospisdale

Whiteface

Loch a' Choire Mhòir

Freevater Forest

Glencalvie Forest

Carn Bhrain
2117

Oldtown

Ardchronie

A836

Dun Creich

Easter Fearn

Ardmore

Dounie

Clach Biorach

Edderton

Loch Sruban Móra

Càrn Bàn
2772

Lòchan Sgeireach

Deanich Lodge

Diebidale Forest

Diebidale River

Glen Diebidale

Loch Chuinneag

Lochan a' Chairn

Carn Chuinneag
2750

Meall Bhenneit
1744

Black Water

Wester Fearn

Wester Fearn Burn

Easter Fearn Burn

Struie
1218

Loch Muigh-bhlàraidh

B9176

1792 Cnoc Muigh-bhlàraidh

Aultnamain Inn

Strath Rory

Loch Sheilah

Tollomuick Forest

Gleann Beag

Abhainn a' Ghlinne Bhig

Inchbae Forest

Beinn a' Chaistell
2404

Crom Loch

80

EASTER

Beinn Tharsuinn
2330

Diebidale Forest

Carn Cas nan Gabhar
1976

Loch More

ROSS

Beinn Tharsuinn
2270

Cnoc Corr Guinie
1243

Kinrive Hill
1056

A
B **157**
C
D **19**

Gorm Loch

Meall a' Ghrianain
2531

Abhainn na Chaorainn

Kildermorie Forest

250

Loch Magharaidh

Loch nan Amhaichean

Beinn nan Eun
2436

Kildermorie Lodge

Loch Bad a' Bhathaich

Braeantra

Loch Morie

Black Water

Strath Rusdale

Loanreoch

Strathy

Scotsburn

Ardross Forest

E | F | A897 | 168 | G | H

**N O R T H   S E A**

**Lothbeg Point**

**Ord Point**

Boch-ailean

**DORNOCH FIRTH**

**TARBAT NESS**

**DANGER AREA**

B871
A897
B871
A9
A839
A949
A836
B9168
B9165
B9174
B9166

Loch Badanloch
Loch Arichlinie
Dunbeath Water
Loch an Alltan Fheàrna
Loch na Gaineimh
Badanloch Lod
Achentoul
Féith Gaineimh Mhór
Cnoc Loch Mhadadh 1000
Braemore
Balnabr
Knockally
Kinbrace
River Helmsdale
Gobernuisgeach
Bennie Water 1587
Maiden Pap
Cnoc an Liath-bhaid Mhóir 1423
Cnoc Coire na Feàrna 1434
Morven 2313
Scaraben 2055
Meall na Caorach 1301
Ramscraigs
Borgue
Newport
Altanduin
Borrobol Forest
Cnoc an Breun-choille 1194
Loch Ascaig
Borrobol Lodge
Creag nam Fiadh 1271
Cnoc an Eireannaich 1699
Wag
Langwell Forest
Aultibea
Langwell Water
Berriedale
Berriedale Castle
Allt an Eàlaidh
Kildonan
River Helmsdale
Beinn Dubhain 1365
Cnoc na Maoile 1315
Ousdale
Badbea Clearance Village
Ousdale Broch
Garvary
Loch na Gaineimh
Craggie
Tuarie Burn
Strath of Kildonan
Torrish
Strath Ullie
Eldrable Hill 1338
Marrel
Navidale
East Helmsdale
Loch Bad an t-Sean-tighe
Cnoc Meadhonach 1134
Craggie Water
Meallan Liath Beag 1512
Beinn Dhorain 2060
West Helmsdale
Helmsdale
Cnoc Leamhnachd 961
Balnacoil
Gordonbush
Col-bheinn 1765
Glen Sletdale
Glen Loth
Gartymore
Portgower
Timespan
River Brora
Lothmore
Kilmote
Dalreavoch
Rhilochan
Knockarthur
Achvoan
Ben Horn 1706
Loch Horn
Loch an Tubairnaich
Lothbeg
Crackaig
Scottarie Burn
Kilbraur Hill 1063
Achrimsdale
A9
East Clyne
West Clyne
Clynelish
Dalchalm
Distillery
Badnellan
Heritage Centre
Brora
Cagar Feosaig 1239
Uppat
Doll
Little Rogart
Rogart
Beinn Lunndaidh 1463
Beinn a' Bhragaidh 1293
Backies
Orcadian Stone Company
Carn Liath
Morvich
Duke of Sutherland Monument
Dunrobin
Mound Rock
Golspie
Kirkton
Little Torboll
Loch Fleet
Loch Laoigh
Skelbo
Littleferry
Badninish
Skelbo Street
Embo
Lednabirichen
Birichen
Poles
Embo Street
Rearquhar
Astle
Fleuchary
Evelix
Pitgrudy
Dornoch
Littletown
Camore
Historylinks
Clashmore
Loch Evelix
Lonemore
Dornoch
Wilkhaven
Bindal
Portmahomack
Tarbat Discovery Centre
Seafield
Rockfield
Glenmorangie Distillery
Morangie
Tarlogie
Inver
Tain
Tain Through Time
Lochslin
Lower Arboll
Toulvaddie
Tarrel
Geanies
rangie Forest
Hartmount Holdings
Glen
Lamington
Brenachie
Pitmaduthy
Marybank
Hill of Fearn
Fearn
Lower Pitkerrie
Loch Eye
Hilton of Cadboll Chapel
Tullich
Hilton of Cadboll
Balintore
Arabella
Kildary

158 | 159 | E | F | G | H

80
10    20    30    40

A    B    C    D

1

*Duslic*
**CAPE WRATH**
Stack Clò Kearvaig
*Clo Mor Cliffs*
Kearvaig
*A' Ghoil*
**Faraid Head**

70

Cnoc a' Ghiubhais 976
Sgribhis-bheinn 1216
*DANGER AREA*
Inshore
Loch Inshore
Achiemore
*Balnakeil Bay*
Balnakeil
Durness
*Craft Village*
Smoo Cave
Sangomore
Leirinmore

Bay of Keisgaig
Loch Keisgaig
Loch a' Gheodha Ruaidh
Fashven 1498
Loch Borralie
Keoldale
Loch na Gainmhich
Beinn an Amair 911
Loch Caladail
Loch Meadaidh
Bein Ceannab 1257

2

Sandwood Loch
Creag Riabhach 1592
An Grianan 1527
Abhainn an t-Strathain
Strath Shinary
Grudie River
Ghlas-bheinn 1085
Meall Meadhonach 1387

60

Sheigra
Balchrick
Blairmore
Droman
Oldshore Beg
Oldshoremore
Loch Aisir Mor
An Socach 1165
Farrmheall 1709
**A838**
Gualin House
Beinn Spionnaidh 2534
Laid
*Eilean Choraidh*

Eilean an Ròin Mór
Loch Clash
**Kinlochbervie**
Badcall
Inshegra
Loch Innis na Ba Buidhe
Loch na Gainimh
Lochan Sgeireach
Cranstackie 2630
Polla
**A838**
An Leanachm 1705

3

Bàgh Loch an Ròin
**B801**
Loch Inchard
**Achriesgill**
Rhuvoult
Achlyness
Rhiconich
Loch na Claise Carnaich
River Dionard
Strath Dionard

Loch Dughaill
Loch Crocach
Ardmore
Skerricha
Loch na Thull
Ganu Mór 2980
Mathair a' Gharbh Uillt
Loch Dionard
Loch Staonsaid

Ardmore Point
Fanagmore
**A838**
Loch a' Gharbh-bhaid Mór
**FOINAVEN**

50

Tarbet
Foindle
Handa Island
Sound of Handa
Laxford Bridge
River Laxford
Loch a' Bhadaidh Dàraich
Arkle 2580
Loch an Easain Uaine
Lochan Sgéireach
Glen

Scourie Bay
**Scourie**
Scourie More
**A894**
Badnabay
Lochstack Lodge
Loch an Nighe Leathaid
Loch na Seilge
Sàbhal Beag 2393

4

Rubh' Aird an t-Sionnaich
Upper Badcall
Lower Badcall
Loch a' Mhuilinn
Gorm Loch
Ben Stack 2356
**A838**
Loch Stack
Lone
Abhainn an Loin
Glen

40

Badcall Bay
Eilean a Bhreitheimh
Meall Mór
Ben Auskaird 1265
Clàr Loch
Cnoc Thormaid
Reay Forest
Achfary
Loch na Mucnaich
Meallan Liath Coire Mhic Dhughaill 2627
Coire Loch

Point of Stoer
Sgeir nan Gall
Oldany Island
*Eddrachillis Bay*
Calbha Beag
Calbha Mór
Duartmore Bridge
Loch Crocach
Allt nan Ramh
Ben Strome 1374
Loch an Leathaid Bhuain 1777
Loch Ulbhach Coire

5

Eilean Chrona
Culkein
Rhubha Stoer
Achnacarnin
Clashmore
Balchladic
Clashnessie
*Clashnessie Bay*
**B869**
Culkein Drumbeg
Oldany
Loch Nedd
Drumbeg
Nedd
Glenleraig
**B869**
Loch an Leothaid
Kylestrome
Kylesku
Unapool
*Maryck Memories of Childhood*
Loch Glendhu
Glendhu Forest
Beinn Aird da Loch 1722
Gleann Dubh
Kinloch
Loch Merkland

Bay of Stoer
Stoer
Clachtoll
*Clachtoll Broch*
Loch nan Lub
**B869**
Loch Poll
Gorm Loch
Loch an Leothaid
Newton
**A894**
Loch Glencoul
**163**
**QUINAG** 2651
*Loch na Gainmhich*
Glen Coul
Beinn Leoid 2599
Dubh a' Chuail
Merkland Lodge
**A838**

Achmelvich Bay
Loch Crocach
**A837**
Eas a' Chual Aluinn (Waterfall)
Glas Bheinn 2541
Loch an Eircill
Loch nan Caorach
Loch a' Ghriama
Corriekinloch
Cnoc a' Ghriama 1221

50    40

E F G H

250 60 70 80

2
1

70 STRATHY POINT

Eilean Hoan

Sangobeg
Rispond

Eilean Clùimhrig

Whiten Head or An Ceann Geal

Port Allt a' Mhuilinn
Totegan
Aultivullin
Ardmore Point
Brawl
Kirtomy Point
Armadale Bay
Aultiphurst
Strat
Strat Ba

Ben Hutig 1338

Achininver
Midfield
Lubinvullin
Strathan
West Strathan
Achinahuagh
Talmine

Port Vasgo
Tongue Bay
Rabbit Islands

Caol Raineach
Eilean nan Ron

Neave or Coombe Island

Farr Point
Bay of Swordly
Clasheddy
Strathan Skerray
Skerray
Achtoty
Torrisdale Bay
Clachan
Farr
Swordly
Kirtomy
Armadale
Lednagullin
18
Strathy Forest

Portnancon
Hope
756 Ben Arnaboll

Loch Eriboll

30
A838
Loch Maovally

Skinnet
Midtown
Loch a' Mhuilinn

Coldbackie
Rhitongue
Blandy
Skullomie

Modsarie
Torrisdale
Clerkhill
M Strathnaver
Bettyhill
Achina
Invernaver
Leckfurin
Coille na Borgie Chambered Tomb
A836

Loch Gaineimh
Loch Meadie
Loch Buidhe Beag
Beinn nam Bò 751
Loch Buidhe Mór

168
Strathy Forest

3

Eriboll

Loch Hope

Loch Fhionnaich
Achuvoldrach
Tongue
Caisteal Bharraich
Braetongue
Ribigill
Dalcharn
A836
Loch Cormaic
10
Borgie
Na Caol Lochan
Skelpick
Archargary
B871
River Naver

Loch Mór na Caorach
Loch nan Clach
Cnoc Ba na Ga
950

Kyle of Tongue

Kinloch Lodge
Kinloch River
Lochan Hakel
Cnoc Craggie 1043
Beinn Bhreac 1018
Loch Craggie
Borgie Forest
Lochan nan Carn
Loch nan Ealachan
Loch Stephan
Carnachy
Rhifail
Skelpick Burn
Dunviden Lochs
Loch Strathy

Cashel Dhu
Loch Cròcach
BEN HOPE
3040

Meallan Liath 1962

Ben Loyal 2509
Loch Loyal
Beinn Stumanadh 1728
Loch nam Breac
Loch Meleag
6
Rough Haugh
963 Beinn Rifa-gil
Loch Strathy
Loch nam Breac
Loch na Saobhaidhe

1519 Feinne-bheinn Mhór
Alltnacaillich
Dun Dornaigil

Loch an Dherue
Loch Haluim
1828 Loch Loyal Lodge
Cnoc nan Cuilean
17
B871
Skail Chambered Cairn
Skail
Strathnaver
1133 Cnoc nan Tri-chlach
Caol-loch Mór
Loch Cròcach
Loch Druim a' Chliabhain 1902 Ben Griam Beg

Strathmore River
Loch nan Ealachan
Loch Coulside
Loch Bad na Gallaig
Pole Hill 965
Loch Syre
Syre
Rosal Clearance Village
Rhifail Loch
Alt Lon a' Chul
Rimsdale
Garbh-allt
40

Gobernuisgach Lodge
Allt a' Chraois
Loch Meadie
Loch Elleanach
B873
Navar Forest
B871
16
Garvault
Ben Griam Mór 1938
Ach

Loch Coire na Saidhe Duibhe
Allt Coire na Saidhe Duibhe
Meadie Burn
Mudale
Altnaharra
B873
Grummore
Loch Naver
Grumbeg Settlement
11
Loch Rimsdale
Loch nan Clàr
Loch an Alltan Fheàrna
Loch Truderscaig
Badanloch Forest
Badanloch Lodge
5
Loch Achnamoine
River Hel
B871
30

Hee 863
Loch a' Ghorm-choire
River Mudale
Klibreck Burn
Loch Ben Harrald
Meall an Fhuarain 1549
An Glas-loch
BEN KLIBRECK 2367
Mallart River
Loch Choire Lodge
Loch Choire
Creag na h-Iolaire 2278
Loch na Gaineimh
Cnoc an Liath Mhór 1423
165

Loch Fiag
Fiag Lodge
164
F
Vagastie
A836
Loch nan Uan
Meall nan Con 3157
Loch Choire Forest
G
Gorm-Loch Beag
Allt nan

21
60
Cnoc an Alaskie 1024
Meall a' Bhata 1907
Loch a' Bhealaich
Ben A'one 2311
Gorm-Loch Beag
Borrobol Forest
Altanduin
Abha
Allt an Ealaidh
Allt an Aisc

A B C D

Stromness 1hr. 30mins.

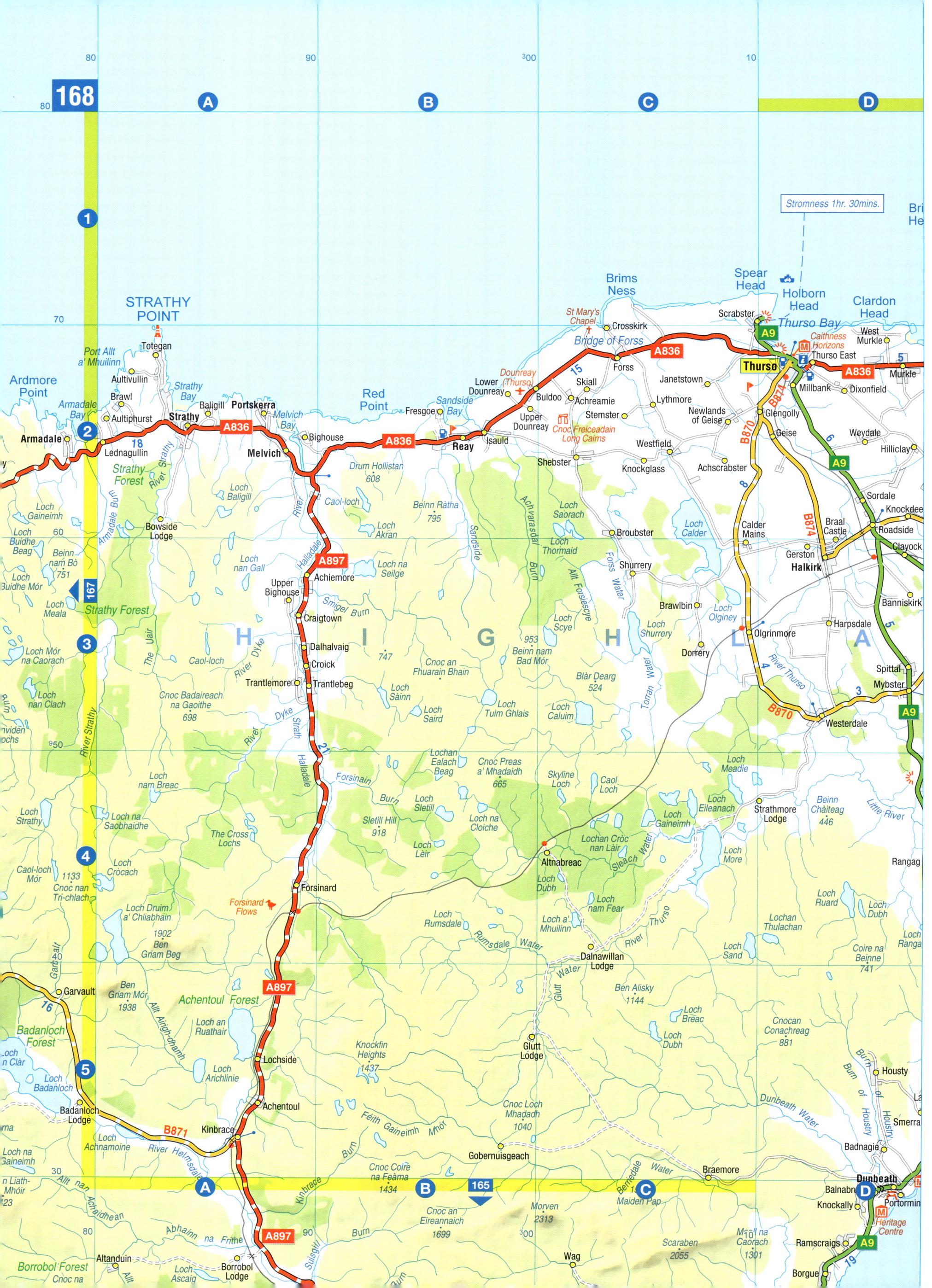

STRATHY POINT

Brims Ness

Spear Head

Holborn Head

Clardon Head

St Mary's Chapel

Crosskirk

Scrabster

Thurso Bay

West Murkle

Ardmore Point

Port Allt a' Mhuilinn

Totegan

Aultivullin

Brawl

Strathy Bay

Bridge of Forss

Dounreay (Thurso)

Forss

A836

Caithness Horizons

Thurso

Thurso East

Murkle

5

Armadale Bay

Baligill

Portskerra

Red Point

Lower Dounreay

Buldoo

Skiall

Achreamie

Janetstown

Millbank

Dixonfield

Armadale

Aultiphurst

Strathy

Melvich Bay

Fresgoe

Sandside Bay

Upper Dounreay

Stemster

Lythmore

Newlands of Geise

Glengolly

Geise

Weydale

Hilliclay

Lednagullin

A836

Bighouse

A836

Reay

Isauld

Cnoc Freiceadain Long Cairns

Westfield

Knockglass

Achscrabster

Calder Mains

Sordale

Knockdee

Strathy Forest

River Strathy

18

Melvich

Shebster

Broubster

Loch Calder

Gerston

Braal Castle

Roadside

Clayock

Drum Hollistan 608

Beinn Ràtha 795

Loch Saorach

Loch Thormaid

Shurrery

Brawlbin

Loch Olginey

Olgrinmore

Halkirk

Banniskirk

Loch Gaineimh

Loch Buidhe Beag

Bowside Lodge

Loch Baligill

Caol-loch

Loch Akran

A897

Achiemore

Loch na Seilge

Loch Scye

Loch Shurrery

River Thurso

Harpsdale

Loch Buidhe Mór

Strathy Forest

167

Loch Meala

Upper Bighouse

Smigel Burn

Dorrery

Spittal

Mybster

Loch Mór na Caorach

Craigtown

Cnoc an Fhuarain Bhain

953

Beinn nam Bad Mór

Blàr Dearg 524

A9

Loch nan Clach

Dalhalvaig

747

Loch Sàinn

Loch Tuim Ghlais

Loch Caluim

Westerdale

B870

Croick

Loch Saird

Trantlemore

Trantlebeg

Loch Meadie

Beinn Chàiteag 446

Little River

Loch Strathy

Caol-loch Mór

1133

Cnoc nan Tri-chlach

Loch na Saobhaidhe

Loch nam Breac

River Dyke

Dyke Strath

21

Forsinain Burn

Lochan Ealach Beag

Cnoc Preas a' Mhadaidh 665

Skyline Loch

Caol Loch

Loch Eileanach

Strathmore Lodge

Loch More

Rangag

Loch Dubh

Loch Crocach

Loch Druim a' Chliabhain

1902

Ben Griam Beg

The Cross Lochs

Forsinard

Sletill Hill 918

Loch Sletill

Loch Lèir

Loch na Cloiche

Altnabreac

Loch Dubh

Lochan Croc nan Làir

Sleach Water

Loch nam Fear

River Thurso

Loch Sand

Lochan Thulachan

Loch Ruard

Coire na Beinne 741

Loch Ranga

Garvault

16

Ben Griam Mór 1938

Forsinard Flows

Achentoul Forest

Loch Rumsdale

Rumsdale Water

Loch a' Mhuilinn

Dalnawillan Lodge

Ben Alisky 1144

Loch Breac

Loch Dubh

Cnocan Conachreag 881

Badanloch Forest

Loch an Ruathair

A897

Loch Arichlinie

Lochside

Knockfin Heights 1437

Glutt Lodge

Glutt Water

Loch Dubh

Housty

Badanloch Lodge

Achentoul

Cnoc Loch Mhadadh 1040

Dunbeath Water

Badnagie

Loch Badanloch

Kinbrace

B871

River Helmsdale

Gobernuisgeach

Bernedale Water

Braemore

Maiden Pap

Dunbeath

Balnabruich

Knockally

Portormin

Loch Achnamoine

A897

Cnoc Coire na Feàrna 1434

165

Cnoc an Eireannaich 1699

Morven 2313

Heritage Centre

Ramscraigs

Borrobol Forest

Altanduin

Borrobol Lodge

Wag

Scaraben 2055

Maoi na Caorach 1301

A9

19

Borgue

20 30 40 350

E F G H

Swona

Burwick B9041 Tomb of the Eagles

Brough Liddle

172

Nethertown

Island of Stroma

Uppertown

St John's Point

Pentland Skerries

DUNNET HEAD

374 Burifa Hill

Long Loch

B855

Dunnet Hill 398

Brough

Loch of Bushta

Hunspow

West Dunnet

Mary-Ann's Cottage

Dunnet Bay

Seadrift-Dunnet

Castletown

Scarfskerry

Tang Head

Castle of Mey

Ham

Rattar

St John's Loch

Corsback

A836

Dunnet

B876

Olrig

Tain

Greenland

Greenland Mains

Durran

Stemster

Corsback

Gillock

Loch Scarmclate

Larel

A882

Oldhall

B870

B874

Loch Watten

Watten

N D

Loch of Toftingall

Acharole

Burn of Acharole

Strath

Badlipster

Camster Burn

Hill of Rangag 623

Loch Stemster

Achavanich

Standing Stones

Stemster Hill

Sheppardstown

A9

Crofts of Benachielt

Rumster Forest

Achow

Reisgill Burn

Osclay

Upper Lybster

A99

Achow

Swiney

Lybster

Upper Latheron

Standing Stones

Burrigill

Forse

Forse Castle

Waterlines

Inyershore

andhallow

Latheron

Clan Gunn Heritage Centre

Latheronwheel

Knockinnon

Laidhay Croft

Barrock

Inkstack

Greenland

Lochend

Slickly

Reaster

Alterwall

Bowermadden

Sortat

Lyth Arts Centre

Lyth

Howe

Halcro

Bowertower

Hastigrow

North Watten

Kirk

Mireland

Burn of Lyth

Myrelandhorn

Killimster

Knapperfield

B870

B874

B876

Winless

Bilbster

Sibster

Wick River

Milton

Haster

Janetstown

A882

Newton

Whiterow

Loch Hempriggs

Tannach

Hill of Oliclett 462

Raggra

Gansclet

Loch of Yarrows

South Yarrows North Long Cairn

South Yarrows Broch

Grey Cairns of Camster

Cnoc an Earrannaiche 692

Camster

South Yarrows South Long Cairn

Cairn o'Get

Roster

East Clyth

Bruan

Hill o' Many Stanes

Mid Clyth

Clyth

Overton

Halberry Head

East Mey

Mey

Upper Gills

Gills

Kirkstyle

Warse

Brabster

Kirk Burn

Gills Bay

Huna

Seater

Canisbay

Gill Burn

Warth Hill 406

Boars of Duncansby

Last House

M

John o' Groats

Duncansby Stacks

Stacks of Duncansby

DUNCANSBY HEAD

A99

Skirza

Skirza Head

Tofts

Freswick

Freswick Bay

Ness Head

Caithness Broch Centre

M

Auckengill

Nybster

Brough Head

Keiss

Keiss Castle

Tang Head

A99

Westerloch

Sinclair's Bay

Sinclair Girnigoe

Noss Head

Reiss

Ackergillshore

Ackergill

Sealky Head

WICK Heritage

Staxigoe

Papigoe

A99

M

Broadhaven

Wick

Wick Bay

Pulteney Distillery

South Head

Castle of Old Wick

Gote o' Tram

Hempriggs

Helman Head

Thrumster

Borrowston

Sarclet

Sarclet Head

Ulbster

1 2 3 4 5

950

70 60 40 30

E F G H

20 30 40 350

**WESTERN ISLES (NA H-EILEANAN AN IAR)**

**NORTH UIST** (Uibhist a Tuath)

**BENBECULA** (Beinn na Faoghla)

**SOUTH UIST** (Uibhist a Deas)

**BARRA** (Barraigh)

**VATERSAY** (Bhatarsaigh)

**ERISKAY** (Eiriosgaigh)

THE LITTLE MINCH

SOUND OF HARRIS

SOUND OF MONACH (Caolas Mhonach)

SOUND OF BARRA (An Caolas Barrach)

SEA OF THE HEBRIDES

OUTER HEBRIDES

THE WESTERN ISLES

PABBAY (Pabaigh)

BERNERAY (Bearnaraigh)

Leverburgh (An t-Ob)

RENNISH POINT (Rubha Reinis)

WATERNISH POINT

DUNVEGAN HEAD

HEALABHAL MHOR 1538

HEALABHAL BHEAG 40

CANNA

Garrisdale Point

Haskeir Eagach

Haskeir Island (Eilean Hasgeir)

Heisker or Monach Islands (Theisgeir no na H-Eileanan Monach)

Ceann Iar

Ceann Ear

Siolaigh

Stocaidh

Huskeiran

Deasker

Kirkibost Island (Eilean Chircebost)

Baleshare (Baile Sear)

Causamul

Aird an Runair

Rubha Mhanais

Griminis

Scolpaig

Valley (Bhalaigh)

Rubha Bheilis

Rubha Ghriminis

Hosta

Hogha Gearraidh

Baile Mhartainn

Taigh a Ghearraidh

Rubha Port Scolpaig

Paibeil

Baile Mor

Paiblesgearraidh

Baile Raghaill

Balranald

Ceann a Bhaigh

Cladach a Chaolais

Cladach Iolaraigh

Cladach Chirceboist

Clachan na Luib

Teanna Machair

Samhla

Cairinis

Bail Iochdrach

Baile Glas

Cladach Chairinis

Carinish

Knockline

Locheport

Eaval (Eabhal) 1139

Claddach Baleshare

Ceathramh Meadhanach

Solas

Grenetobht

Malacleit

Clachan Shannda

Port nan Long

Baile MhicPhail

Orasaigh

Aird a' Mhorain

Lingeigh

Sollas

Crogearraidh Mor 588

Barpa Langass Chambered Cairn

Hebridean Smokehouse

Maireabhal 756

Blashaval 332

Lochmaddy

Rubha nam Pleac

Rubha an Fhigheadair

Rubha an Duine

Li a Tuath 824

Rubha an Duine

Loch Portain

Loch Eport

Eigneig Mhor

An t-Aigeach

BENBECULA (Port Adhair Bheinn na Faoghla)

Gramasdail

Uachdar

Balivanich (Baile a Mhanaich)

Aird

Griminis

Torlum

Creag Ghoraidh

Liniclate

Nan Eilean

Borgh

Baile nan Cailleach

Lionacleit

Haclait

Carnan

Gramsay (Griomasaigh)

Grimsay

Ronay (Ronaigh)

Maragaidh Mor

Rubha Cam nan Gall

Wiay (Fuidhaigh)

Loch Bagh nam Faoileann

Flodaigh Beag

Flodaigh Mor

Roisinis

Iochdar

Ard Mhor

Aird a' Mhachair

Cill Amhlaidh

Loch a Charnain

Geirinis

Groigearraidh

Stadhlaigearraidh

Dreumasdal

Tobha Mor

Tobha Beag

Eilean Bheirean

Sniseabhal

Staoinebrig

Ormaclete

Bornais

Cill Donnain

Kildonan

Calbhaigh

Taobh a Tuath Loch Aineort

Taobh a Deas Loch Aineort

Gearraidh Bhailteas

Mingearraidh

Frobost

Aisgernis

Dalabrog

Daliburgh

Lochboisdale (Loch Baghasdail)

Ceann a Tuath Loch Baghasdail

Cille Pheadair

Baghasdal

Orasaigh

An Leth Meadhanach

Gearraidh ma Monadh

Smeircleit

Cille Bhrighde

Ludag

Fiaraigh

Gob Sgurabhal

Eolaigearraidh

Orosaigh

Fuday (Fuideigh)

Hellisay (Theileisaigh)

Gighay (Gioghaigh)

Eriskay (Eiriosgaigh)

Haun

Bun a' Mhuillinn

Am Baile

Acairseid

Na Stacan Dubha

Ceann Aird Ghrein

Cliaid

Grein

Eoligarry

Aird Mhor

Aird

Cuidhir

Bagh Shiarabhagh

Mhdhinis

Bruairnis

Buaile nam Bodach

Flodaigh

Bruernish Point

Earsairidh

Gob Bhuirgh

Rubha na Doirlinn

Tangasdal

Borgh

Gallanach

Breibhig

Uidh

BARRA (Barraigh)

Kisimul

Castlebay (Bagh a' Chaistell)

Rubha Mor

Caolas

Bioruaslum

Bhatarsaigh

Flodaigh

Greanamul

Lingeigh

Sandray (Sanndraigh)

Pabbay (Pabaigh)

An Tobha

Mingulay (Miughlaigh)

Berneray (Bearnaraigh)

Bagh Mhiughlaigh

MINGULAY

A865  A867  A859  A888  A879

Scale 5 miles to 1 inch 1:316,800

Lochmaddy to Uig 1hr. 40mins.

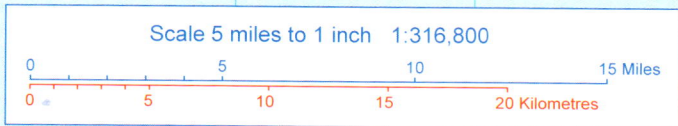

Lochboisdale to: Mallaig 3hrs. 30 mins. (Seasonal) Oban 5hrs. 20mins. (Seasonal)

Castlebay to: Oban 5hrs. Tiree 2hrs. 45mins. (Seasonal)

# WESTERN ISLES (NA H-EILEANAN AN IAR)

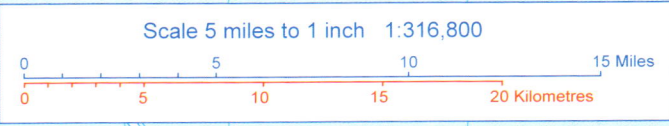

OUTER HEBRIDES

ISLE OF LEWIS (Eilean Leòdhais)

NIS

BUTT OF LEWIS (Rubha Robhanais)

TOLSTA HEAD (Ceann or Rubha Tholastaidh)

TIUMPAN HEAD (Rubha an T-Siumpain)

EYE PENINSULA (An Rubha)

STORNOWAY (Steòrnabhagh)

GREAT BERNERA (Bearnaraigh)

PARK (Pairc)

NORTH HARRIS (Ceanna Tuath na Hearadh)

HARRIS (Na Hearadh)

SOUTH HARRIS (Ceann a Deas na Hearadh)

TARANSAY (Tarasaigh)

SCARP

Tarbert (Tairbeart)

Leverburgh (An t-Ob)

RENNISH POINT (Rubha Reinis)

PABBAY (Pabaigh)

BERNERAY (Beàrnaraigh)

SOUND OF HARRIS

THE LITTLE MINCH

WESTERN ISLES

SOUND OF SHIANT (Caolas Nan Eilean)

Shiant Islands (Na H-Eileanan Mora)

SCALPAY (Scalpaigh)

WATERNISH POINT

Kilmaluag Bay

Staffin Bay

Staffin (Stafainn)

Kilt Rock

Uig

Uig Bay

Scale 5 miles to 1 inch  1:316,800

0      5      10      15 Miles

0    5    10    15    20 Kilometres

Stornoway to Ullapool 2hrs. 40mins.

Tarbert to Uig 1hr. 40mins.

Lochmaddy to Uig 1hr. 40mins.

Uig to Tarbert 1hr. 40mins.

Uig to Lochmaddy 1hr. 40mins.

ORKNEY ISLANDS

MAINLAND

HOY

WESTRAY

ROUSAY

EDAY

SANDAY

NORTH RONALDSAY

STRONSAY

SHAPINSAY

SOUTH RONALDSAY

BURRAY

Kirkwall

Stromness

St Margaret's Hope

PENTLAND FIRST

DUNNET HEAD

DUNCANSBY HEAD

Thurso

Castletown

169

Stromness to Scrabster 1hr. 30mins.

Kirkwall (Hatston) to:
Aberdeen 7hrs. 15mins.
Lerwick (Holmsgarth) 7hrs. 45mins.

Fair Isle to:
Lerwick 5hrs. (Seasonal)
Sumburgh 2hrs. 30mins.

Fair Isle lies approx. 27 miles
ENE of North Ronaldsay

Scale 5 miles to 1 inch 1:316,800

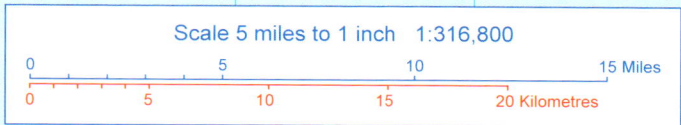

PAGE NOT CONTINUED

**SHETLAND ISLANDS**

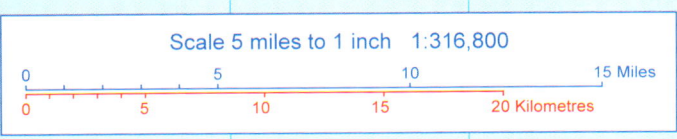

ST MAGNUS BAY

MAINLAND

SHETLAND ISLANDS

PAGE NOT CONTINUED

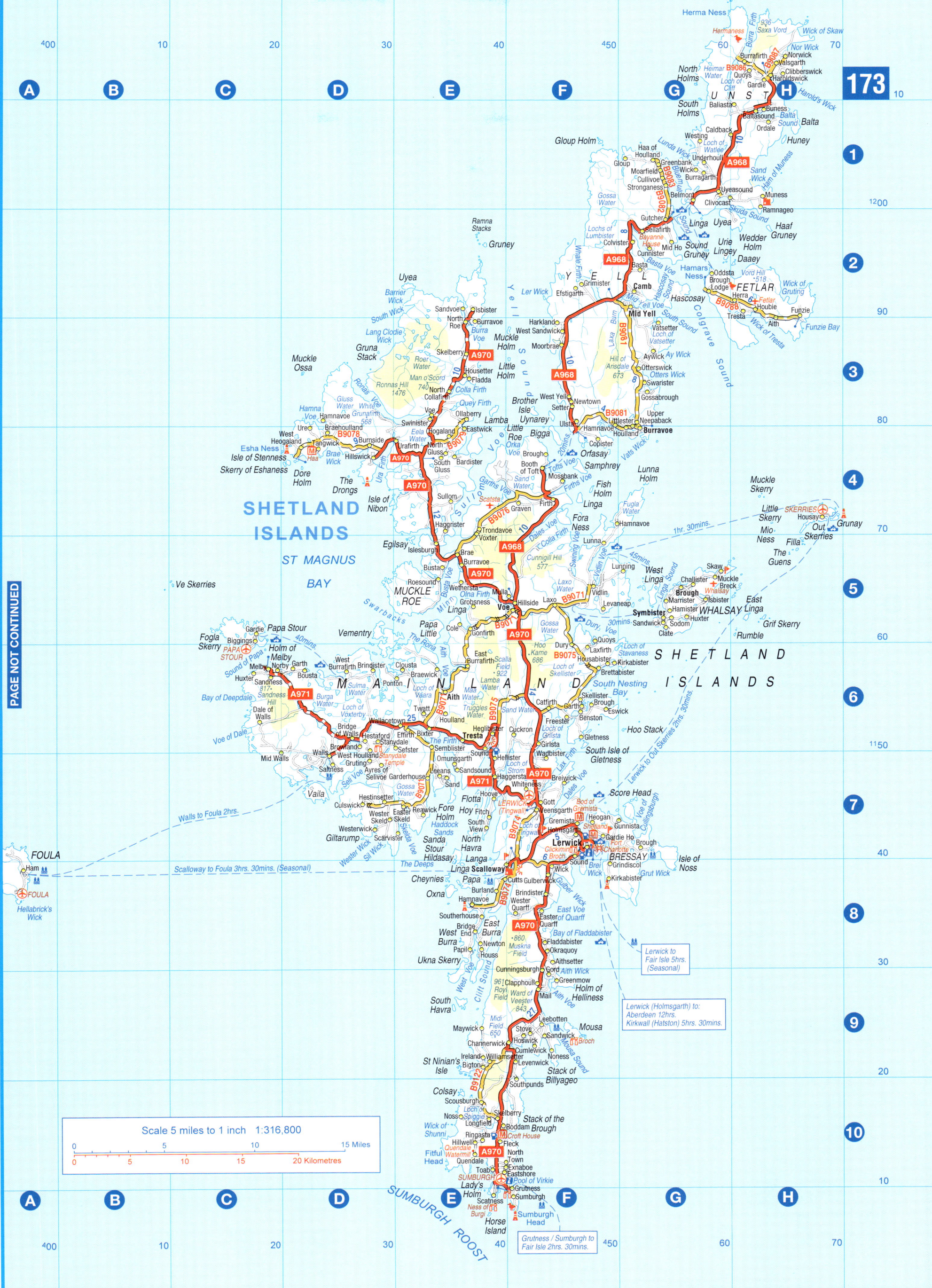

Scale 5 miles to 1 inch   1:316,800

0   5   10   15 Miles

0   5   10   15   20 Kilometres

UNST

Herma Ness
Hermaness
Saxa Vord 936
Wick of Skaw
Burrafirth
Norwick
Nor Wick
Valsgarth
Quoys
Clibberswick
Gardie
Haroldswick
North Holms
Heimar Water
Loch of Cliff
Baliasta
Buness
South Holms
Westing
Caldback
Baltasound
Ordale
Balta
Balta Sound
Sand Wick
Haa of Houlland
Gloup
Underhoull
Huney
Moarfield
Cullivoe
Greenbank
Burragarth
Stronganess
Uyeasound
Muness
Ham of Muness
Belmont
Uyeasound
Clivocast
Ramnageo
Gutcher
Skuda Sound

YELL

Sellafirth
Colvister
Bayanne House
Linga
Uyea
Haaf Gruney
Cunnister
Mid Ho
Sound Gruney
Wedder Holm
Basta
Hamars Ness
Daaey
Grimister
Vord Hill 518
Oddsta
Brough Lodge
FETLAR
Wick of Gruting
Efstigarth
Harkland
West Sandwick
Herra
Houbie
Tresta
Aith
Funzie
Funzie Bay
Camb
Mid Yell
Vatsetter
Loch of Vatsetter
Hill of Arisdale 673
Aywick
Ay Wick
Hascosay
Otterswick
Otters Wick
Swarister
Newtown
West Yell
Setter
Gossabrough
Brother Isle
Ulsta
Hamnavoe
Houlland
Upper Neepaback
Littlester
Copister
Burravoe

Ramna Stacks
Gruney
Gloup Holm
Uyea
Gruting
Muckle Skerry
Little Skerry
SKERRIES
Housay
Out Skerries
Grunay
Mio Ness
Filla
The Guens
Grif Skerry
Rumble

Muckle Ossa
Uyea
Barrier Wick
South Wick
Sandvoe
Isbister
Burravoe
North Roe
Skelberry
Gruna Stack
Lang Clodie Wick
Man o'Scord
Roer Water
Housetter
Fladda
Little Holm
Muckle Holm
Ronas Hill 1476
North Collafirth
Colla Firth
Gluss Water
White Grunafirth 568
Quey Firth
Voe
Ollaberry
Lamba
Eela Water
Swinister
Hamnavoe
Braehoulland
Burnside
North Roe
Hogaland
Eastwick
Gluss
Bigga
Little Roe
Orka Voe
Brough
West Heogaland
Ureo
Tangwick
Urafirth
South Gluss
Bardister
Booth of Toft
Samphrey
Esha Ness
Isle of Stenness
Haa
Hillswick
Sullom
Mossbank
Orfasay
Skerry of Eshaness
Dore Holm
Isle of Nibon
Haggrister
Firth
Fish Holm
Lunna Holm
The Drongs
Sullom
Graven
Fora Ness
Linga
Scatsta
Dales Voe
Hamnavoe
Lunna
Muckle Skerry
Egilsay
Islesburgh
Brae
Burravoe
Voxter
Trondavoe
Toft Firth
Fugla Water
Little Skerry
Ve Skerries
MUCKLE ROE
Roesound
Wethersta
Mulla
Laxo Water
Laxo
West Linga
Skaw
Whalsay
Busta
Grobsness
Hillside
Cunnigill Hill 577
Lunning
Challister
Muckle Breck
East Linga
Fogla Skerry
Papa Stour
Gardie
Biggings
Holm of Melby
Vementry
Papa Little
Cole
Hoo
Dury
Hoo Kame 686
Gossa Water
Brough
Marrister
Isbister
PAPA STOUR
Norby
Garth
Huxter
Melby
Sandness
The Rona
East Burrafirth
Scalla Field 922
Loch of Skellister
South Nesting Bay
Symbister
Hamister
Huxter
Clate
Sodom
Sandwick
Sound of Papa
Bousta
Sandness Hill 817
Aith
Mat Water
Brettabister
Quoys
Loch of Stavaness
Sandness
Burga Water
Loch of Voxterby
Twatt
Loch of Girlsta
Laxfirth
Housabister
Kirkabister
Bay of Deepdale
Dale of Walls
Mid Walls
Wallacetown
Bridge of Walls
Bixter
Catfirth
Heglibister
Skellister
Brough
Heogan
West Burrafirth
Brindister
Clousta
Braewick
Truggles Water
Cuxroon
Freester
Eswick
Gunnista
Brough
MAINLAND
Ponton
Houlland
Tresta
Sound
Wadbister
Girlsta
Gletness
Isle of Noss
Hestaford
Stanydale
Effirth
Hellister
Breiwick
Gletness
Walls
West Houlland
Stanydale Temple
Semblister
Omunsgarth
Haggersta
Whiteness
South Isle of Gletness
Score Head
Browland
Gruting
Sefster
Sandsound
Veensgarth
Hoo Stack
Saltness
Ayres of Selivoe
Garderhouse
Leeans
Gott
Gremista
Scarvister
Sand
Weisdale
Holmsgarth
Gardie Ho
Brough
Vaila
Hestinsetter
Flotta
Hoy
Fitch
Hoove
Tingwall
Gremista
Culswick
Wester Skeld
Reawick
Fore Holm
Stour
North Havra
LERWICK
Tingwall
Clickimin Broch
BRESSAY
Westerwick
Easter Skeld
Skeld
Sanda
Hildasay
Langa
Sound
Brei Wick
Giltarump
Linga
Scalloway
Wick
Grindiscol
Grut Wick
Cheynies
Papa
Burland
Cutts
Gulberwick
Oxna
Hamnavoe
Burland
Brindister
Wester Quarff
Kirkabister
Southerhouse
East Burra
West Burra
Bridge End
Newton
Houss
Easter Quarff
East Voe of Quarff
Bay of Fladdabister
Papil
Fladdabister
Ukna Skerry
Cunningsburgh
Gord
Aith Wick
Greenmow
Okraquoy
Aithsetter
South Havra
Clapphoull
961 Royl Field
Ward of Veester 843
Mail
Holm of Helliness
Maywick
Midi Field 650
Leebotten
Mousa
Ireland
Bigton
Channerwick
Hoswick
Sandwick
Noness
Broch
St Ninian's Isle
Williamsetter
Cumlewick
Levenwick
Stack of Billyageo
Colsay
Scousburgh
Skelberry
Stack of the Brough
Noss
Longfield
Boddam
Wick of Shunni
Ringasta
Fleck
North Town
Hillwell
Quendale
Watermill
Virkie
Exnaboe
Eastshore
Fitful Head
Lady's Holm
Quendale
Toab
Grutness
Scatness
Sumburgh
Ness of Burgi
Horse Island
SUMBURGH
Sumburgh Head

SUMBURGH ROOST

FOULA
Ham
FOULA
Hellabrick's Wick

Walls to Foula 2hrs.
Scalloway to Foula 3hrs. 30mins. (Seasonal)

1hr. 30mins.
45mins
30mins
Lerwick to Out Skerries 2hrs 30mins.

Lerwick to Fair Isle 5hrs. (Seasonal)

Lerwick (Holmsgarth) to:
Aberdeen 12hrs.
Kirkwall (Hatston) 5hrs. 30mins.

Grutness / Sumburgh to Fair Isle 2hrs. 30mins.

A968   A970   A971   B9071   B9072   B9074   B9075   B9076   B9078   B9081   B9082   B9083   B9084   B9086   B9088

1200   1150

# NORTHERN IRELAND

Scale: 3.5 miles to 1 inch    1:221,760

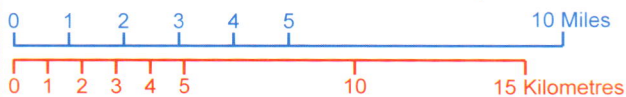

0 1 2 3 4 5 ... 10 Miles
0 1 2 3 4 5 ... 10 ... 15 Kilometres

LOUGH FOYLE

Carndonagh
Slieve Snaght 2017
Moville
Culmore
Ballynagard
Lishahawley
Maydown
Campsey
EGLINTON
GREYSTEEL
BALLYKELLY
LIMAVADY
Drumraighland
Glenhead
Moys
Lackagh
Baranailt
Bovevagh
Bonnanaboigh
Gortnahey
LONDONDERRY (DERRY)
Lettershendoney
Drumahoe
Ervey Cross Roads
Gortilea Cross Roads
Ness Wood
Burntollet
NEW BUILDINGS
Magheramason
Bready
Cloghcor
Dunnamanagh
Liscloon
Ballynamallaght
Lough Ash
Moor Lough
Craig
Mullaghdoo 1847
Mullaghclogher 1876
Mullaghclogha
SPERRIN
Dart Mountain 2224
Sawel Mountain 2083 2030
MOUNTAINS
Mullaghaneany 2057 1866
Oughtmore
Cranagh
Sperrin
Sawelabeg Forest
Goles Forest
Glenlark Forest
Plumbridge
Douglas Bridge
NEWTOWNSTEWART
Gortin
Rousky
Glenhull
Owenkillew River
Greencastle
Mullaghcarn 1778
Gortin Glen

FERMANAGH & OMAGH
DERRY & STRABANE

Foreglen
CLAUDY
Craigdarragh
Feeny
DUNGIVEN
Altnaheglish Reservoir
Banagher Forest
White Mountain 1762
Mullagmore 1804
Glenshane Forest
Moydamlaght Forest
Crockbrack Rock Hill 1725
Davagh Forest
Tintagh Mountain 1732
Mobuy Wood
Lough Fea
Beaghmore Stone Circles
Cashel Wood
The Six Towns
MONEYMORE

Magilligan
Ballyscullion
CASTLEROCK
Downhill
Milltown
Ballywildrick
Bolea
Artikelly
Crindle
Carrowclare
Downhill Demesne & Mussenden Temple
Hazlett House
Binevenagh Forest
Ballyhanna Forest
COLERAINE
Giant's Sconce
Ballinrees Reservoir
Macosquin
Articlave
Blagh
Cloyfin
Ballyrashane
Ballybogy
Crossgare
Ballylintagh
Letterloan
Springwell Forest
Ringsend
Cam Forest
Drumsurn
Gortnamoyagh Forest
Brockaghboy
GARVAGH
Bovedy
Craigavole
Moran's Cross Roads
Swatragh
Tamlaght O'Crilly
Upperlands
Culnady
Grillagh
KILREA
Inishrush
Killelagh Lough
Knockcloghrim
Gulladuff
MAGHERA
Tobermore
Curran
DRAPERSTOWN
Straw
Desertmartin
CASTLEDAWSON
MAGHERAFELT
Moneystaghan Wood
MID ULSTER

PORTRUSH
PORTSTEWART
PORTBALLINTRAE
BUSHMILLS
Dunluce
Giant's Causeway
Causeway School
The Skerries
Ramore Head
Dunmull Hill
Revallagh
BALLYMONEY
Balnamore
Bendoragh
Agivey
Mullan
Cullycapple
Killykergan
Moneydig
Aghadowey
McLaughlins Corner
CAUSEWAY COAST
Castleroe

A2  A29  A37  A26  A54  A6  A5  A40  A31  A42
B192  B68  B64  B66  B190  B70  B201  B69  B510  B202  B186

Earadale Point 40
Rubha Dùin Bhàin
Rubha a' Mharaiche

MULL OF KINTYRE

122

K I N T Y R E

Killypole Loch   854 Tirfergus Hill
1263 The Slate   Killellan
1465 Cnoc Moy   786
Dalsmirren   908 Cnoc Odhar   Tod Loch
Remuil Hill
A' Chruach   766 Lephenstrath
Beinn na Lice *1404   Glemanuilt Hill   Carskiey   High Keil
Feorlan   Port Mean   Southend   Brunerican Bay
Rubha Chlachan   Black Point 50   Cov

Bull Point   Doonmore   Bruce's
Rathlin Island   Ushet Lough

RATHLIN SOUND

Ballycastle to Campbeltown 1hr. 30mins. (Seasonal) Port Ellen 1hr. (Seasonal)

NORTH CHANNEL

Benbane Head   Dunseverick
White Park Bay   Sheep Island
B146   Dunseverick   Ballintoy   Carrick-a-rede Island   Carrick-a-Rede Rope Bridge   Kinbane
B17   A2   B15   Carnduff   Clare Wood   BALLYCASTLE   Ballyvoy
Castlecat   Liscolman   Cape Castle   Ballycastle Forest   1686 Knocklayd
B66   Cloonty Wood   Capecastle Wood   Mazes Wood   A44   B15   Ballypatrick Forest   A2
B67   Moss-Side   B147   Breen Forest   Owencam River   Cushendun   Knocknacarry
Derrykeighan   Dervock   Stranocum   Kirkhills   The Drones   Pharis   Loughguile   Slieveanorra 1666   Slieveanorra Forest   Glendun River
B66   A26   Dunaghy   Killyrammer   Kilraghts   Loughguile   Altnahinch Dam   Trostan 1804   CUSHENDALL   Glenariff or Waterfoot   A2   Cloghastucan   Garron Point
B16   B16   Lough-Guile   A N T R I M   Corkey   B14   A43   Glenariff Forest Park   Hunters Point
Mullan Head   Finvoy   DUNLOY   Newtown-Crommelin   Cargan   Dungonnell Reservoir   Cranny Falls   CARNLOUGH   Straidkilly Point
Craigs Wood   A26   CLOGHMILLS   B64   Clogh   Martinstown   Cleggan Forest   Glenarm Bay   Whitebay Point
RASHARKIN   Glenvale   Glarryford   A43   McGregor's Corner   M O U R N E   Cleggan River   A42   Glenarm   A2
B93   B64   Craigs   Correen   Quarrytown   A42   14 The Sheddings   Great Deer Park   B97
Arthur Cottage   CULLYBACKEY   M2   BROUGHSHANE   Buckna   Slemish   Carnalbanagh Sheddings   Ballygally
PORTGLENONE   AHOGHILL   Gracehill   BALLYMENA   The Eccos Centre   A36   Slemish   Shillanavogy Wood   Capanagh Wood   Carncastle   Carnfunnock Country Park   Drains Bay
Glenone Forest   A54   B52   Galgorm   Moorfields   Glenwhirry River   Killylane Reservoir   Ballyboley Forest   Killyglen   A2
Clady   B62   A42   B53   Kells   A36   Kilwaughter   LARNE   Island Magee   Portmuck   Mullaghboy
BELLAGHY   Grange Corner   Whitesides Corner   Connor   KELLS   B98   Millbrook   A8   Glynn   Swan Island   Millbay
Lough Beg   Moneyglass   Roxhill   Peters Bridge   A26   Tardree Forest   Ballyeaston   Strad Dam   Glenoe   Beltoy   Ballycarry   Ballystrudder
Milltown   B18   Randalstown Forest   Five Corners   Burnside   BALLYCLARE   Woodburn Forest   Whitehead   Black Head
Toome   A6   RANDALSTOWN   M22   Mill Town   Potterswalls Reservoir   Doagh   South Woodburn Reservoirs   B90   CARRICKFERGUS   Eden
Traad Point   A6   ANTRIM   Antrim Castle   Muckamore   A6   Parkgate   Ballyrobert   County Antrim War Memorial   Carrickfergus
Rea's Wood   Walled Gar. at Green   Dunadry   Roughfort   Mallusk   Monkstown   Greenisland
178   G   H   J   Clady Water   TEMPLEPATRICK   A8(M)   Carnmoney   NEWTOWNABBEY   179   Grey Point   BANGOR
LOUGH NEAGH   Antrim   Ballywonar   Hyde Park   Boghill   M2   M5   Glengormley   Whiteabbey   Ulster Folk & Transport Mus.   Helen's Bay   Crawfordsburn

Larne to: Cairnryan 2hrs.

Belfast to: Birkenhead 8hrs. Douglas 2hrs. 45mins. (Fast Ferry, Seasonal) Cairnryan (Loch Ryan Port) 2hrs. 15mins. (Fast Ferry, Seasonal)

1   2   3   4   5   6   7   8

MID & EAST ANTRIM
EAST & GLENS
ANTRIM & NEWTOWNABBEY

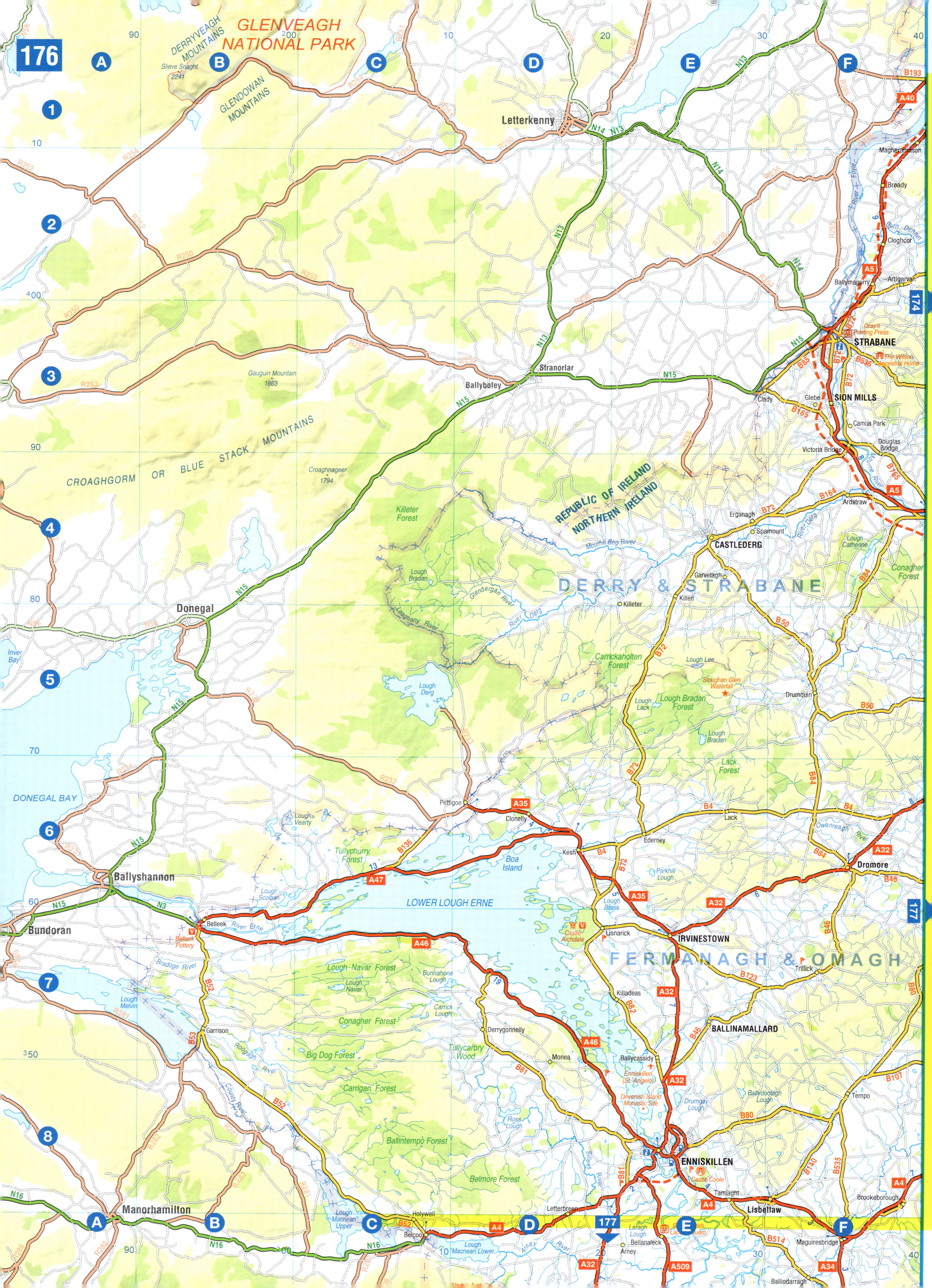

GLENVEAGH
NATIONAL PARK

A    B    C    D    E    F

DERRYVEAGH MOUNTAINS
Slieve Snaght 2241
GLENDOWAN MOUNTAINS

Letterkenny

Magheramason
Bready
Cloghcor
Ballymagorry
Artigarvan

STRABANE
Gray's Printing Press
The Wilson Ancestral Home

Stranorlar
Clady
Glebe
SION MILLS
Camus Park
Douglas Bridge

Ballybofey

Gauguin Mountain 1863

Victoria Bridge

CROAGHGORM OR BLUE STACK MOUNTAINS

Croaghnageer 1794

Killeter Forest

Erganagh
Spamount
Lough Catherine
Ardstraw

REPUBLIC OF IRELAND
NORTHERN IRELAND

Mourne Beg River
CASTLEDERG

DERRY & STRABANE

Garvetagh
Killen
Killeter

Conagher Forest

Lough Bradan

Glendergan River

River Derg

Carrickaholten Forest
Lough Lee
Sloughan Glen Waterfall

Drumquin

Donegal

Leaghany River

Lough Derg

Lough Lack
Lough Bradan Forest
Lough Bradan
Lack Forest

Inver Bay

DONEGAL BAY

Pettigoe
Clonelly
A35
Kesh
Ederney
Lack

Dromore
A32

Ballyshannon

Tullychurry Forest
B136
13

Boa Island

LOWER LOUGH ERNE

Parkhill Lough
Lough Bresk
A35
Usnarick
IRVINESTOWN

Bundoran

Lough Scolban
Lough Vearty

Belleek
River Erne
Belleek Pottery
A46

Castle Archdale

Killadeas
A32

FERMANAGH & OMAGH

Trillick

Bradoge River
B52
Garrison

Lough Navar Forest
Lough Navar
Bunnahone Lough

Carrick Lough
Derrygonnelly

BALLINAMALLARD

Lough Melvin
B53
Rooguin River

Big Dog Forest

Tullycarby Wood
B81
Monea

Ballycassidy
Enniskillen (St. Angelo)
A32

Tempo

Conagher Forest

Carrigan Forest
Ross Lough

A46
Devenish Island Monastic Site

Drumgay Lough
Ballydoolagh Lough
B80

Ballintempo Forest

Belmore Forest

ENNISKILLEN
Castle Coole

Tamlaght
Lisbellaw

Brookeborough

Manorhamilton

A    B    Holywell    C    A4    D    177    E    Laragh Lough    F
Belcoo
Lough Macnean Upper
Lough Macnean Lower
Letterbreen
Bellanaleck
Arney
Maguiresbridge

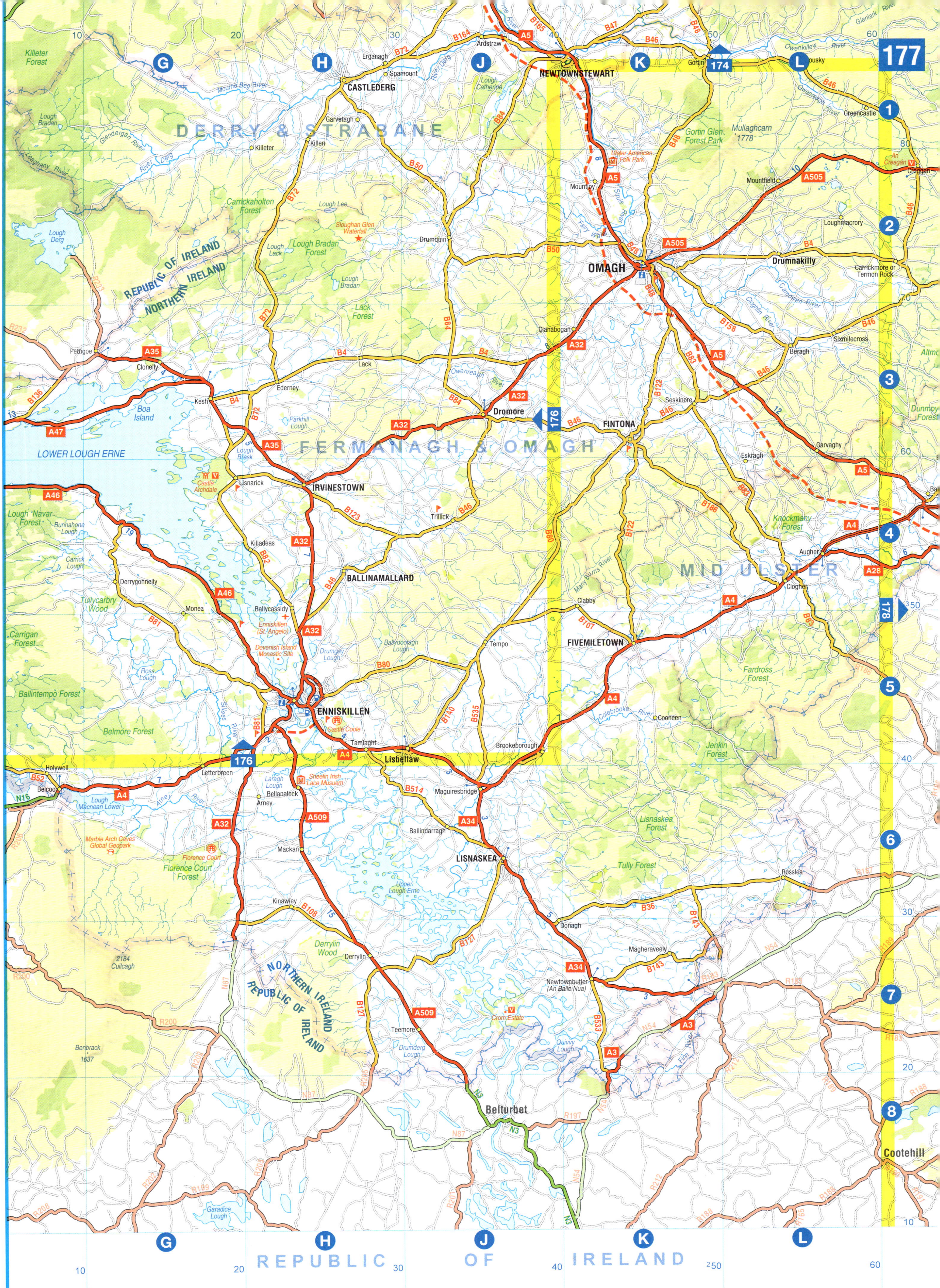

G  H  J  K  L

**DERRY & STRABANE**

REPUBLIC OF IRELAND
NORTHERN IRELAND

Killeter Forest
Lough Bradan
Leaghany River
Glenderg River
Mourne Beg River
Erganagh
Spamount
CASTLEDERG
Garvetagh
Killen
Killeter
Carrickaholten Forest
Sloughan Glen Waterfall
Lough Lack
Lough Bradan Forest
Drumquin
Lough Bradan
Ardstraw
Lough Catherine
NEWTOWNSTEWART
174
Gortin
Owenkillew River
Glenlark River
Greencastle
Plumbridge
Mountjoy
Ulster American Folk Park
Gortin Glen Forest Park
Mullaghcarn 1778
Mountfield
A505
Ari Creagan
Creagan
Loughmacrory
Carrickmore or Termon Rock
Drumnakilly
Clanabogan
**OMAGH**
A505
Beragh
Sixmilecross
Altmo
Dunmore Forest

REPUBLIC OF IRELAND
NORTHERN IRELAND
Pettigoe
A35
Clonelly
Boa Island
LOWER LOUGH ERNE
Kesh
Ederney
Lack
Drumdran
Owenreagh River
Dromore
176
Fintona
Eskragh
Garvaghy
A5
Knockmany Forest
Augher
A4
A28
178
Lisnarick
Castle Archdale
IRVINESTOWN
Trillick
Killadeas
**FERMANAGH & OMAGH**
Clabby
**MID ULSTER**
Clogher
Lough Navar Forest
Bunnahone Lough
Carrick Lough
Derrygonnelly
A46
Monea
Ballycassidy
BALLINAMALLARD
Tempo
FIVEMILETOWN
Fardross Forest
Carrigan Forest
Tullycarbry Wood
Ballintempo Forest
Ross Lough
Belmore Forest
Enniskillen (St Angelo)
Devenish Island Monastic Site
A32
Drumgay Lough
Ballydoolagh Lough
B107
A4
A4
Holywell
N16
Belcoo
B52
A4
Lough Macnean Lower
Letterbreen
Laragh Lough
Bellanaleck
Arney
**ENNISKILLEN**
Castle Coole
Tamlaght
176
LISBELLAW
Sheelin Irish Lace Museum
Maguiresbridge
Brookeborough
Cooneen
Colebrooke River
Jenkin Forest
Marble Arch Caves Global Geopark
Florence Court
Florence Court Forest
Mackan
A32
A509
Ballindarragh
A34
LISNASKEA
Lisnaskea Forest
Tully Forest
Rosslea
2184 Cuilcagh
Kinawley
B108
Derrylin Wood
Derrylin
B127
Donagh
Magheraveely
B36
Benbrack 1637
NORTHERN IRELAND
REPUBLIC OF IRELAND
A509
Teemore
Drumerg Lough
Crom Estate
Newtownbutler (An Baile Nua)
A34
Quivvy Lough
A3
Finn River
N54
Belturbet
N87
N3
Cootehill

R E P U B L I C   O F   I R E L A N D

G  H  J  K  L

ANTRIM

LOUGH NEAGH

MID ULSTER

ARMAGH, BANBRIDGE & CRAIGAVON

NORTHERN IRELAND
REPUBLIC OF IRELAND

MONEYMORE
COOKSTOWN
COALISLAND
DUNGANNON
Moygashel
MOY
ARMAGH
RICHHILL
MARKETHILL
KEADY
CROSSMAGLEN
Castleblayney
Monaghan
Cootehill

LURGAN
MAGHERALIN
DOLLINGSTOWN
CRAIGAVON
PORTADOWN
WARINGSTOWN
BLEARY
TANDRAGEE
GILFORD
BANBRIDGE
BESSBROOK
NEWRY
WARRENPOINT
MOIRA

REPUBLIC OF IRELAND

179

Belfast to:
Birkenhead 8hrs.
Douglas 2hrs. 45mins.
(Fast Ferry, Seasonal)
Cairnryan (Loch Ryan Port)
2hrs. 15mins.
(Fast Ferry, Seasonal)

CARRICKFERGUS

ANTRIM & NEWTOWNABBEY

NEWTOWNABBEY

BELFAST
Divis - 1562
Black - 1275
Mountain

HOLYWOOD

DUNDONALD

NEWTOWNARDS

NORTH DOWN ARDS

BANGOR

DONAGHADEE

MILLISLE

BALLYWATER

COMBER

Greyabbey

A R D S   P E N I N S U L A

Ballyhalbert

Burr Point

PORTAVOGIE

Ringboy Point

CRUMLIN

Glenavy

DUNMURRY

LISBURN

CARRYDUFF

BALLYGOWAN

SAINTFIELD

S T R A N G F O R D   L O U G H

KILLYLEAGH

PORTAFERRY

Mahee Island

HILLSBOROUGH

ANNAHILT

BALLYNAHINCH

CROSSGAR

DROMORE

DRUMANESS

DOWNPATRICK

ARDGLASS

Killard Point

NEWRY MOURNE & DOWN

DUNDRUM

CASTLEWELLAN

RATHFRILAND

NEWCASTLE

DUNDRUM BAY

M O U R N E   M O U N T A I N S
Slieve Donard
853 m (2798 ft)

Silent Valley Reservoir

ROSTREVOR

ANNALONG

IRISH SEA

KILKEEL

CARLINGFORD LOUGH

TEMPLEPATRICK

## REFERENCE

| | |
|---|---|
| MOTORWAY | M25 |
| MOTORWAY JUNCTION NUMBERS — Unlimited interchange 18, Limited interchange 19 | |
| MILEAGES BETWEEN MOTORWAY JUNCTIONS | 6 |
| MOTORWAY SERVICE AREA | Heston S |
| PRIMARY ROUTE DESTINATION | WATFORD |
| JUNCTION NAMES | HYDE PARK CORNER |
| PRIMARY ROUTE | A1 |
| PRIMARY ROUTE JUNCTION NUMBERS | 12 |
| A ROAD | A5 |
| B ROAD | B450 |
| NORTH & SOUTH CIRCULAR ROADS and INNER RING ROAD | |
| TRANSPORT FOR LONDON ROAD NETWORK and WEST MIDLANDS RED ROUTE | |
| SAFETY CAMERA WITH SPEED LIMIT | 30 |
| CONGESTION CHARGING ZONE — For more information visit www.tfl.gov.uk/modes/driving/ | C |
| DART CHARGE Dartford-Thurrock River Crossing — For more information www.gov.uk/pay-dartford-crossing-charge | C |
| LOW EMISSION ZONE — For more information visit www.tfl.gov.uk/modes/driving/ | LEZ |

**SCALE: approx. 1¼ Miles to 1 Inch**

0   1   2 Miles
0   1   2   3   4 Kilometres

### KEY TO LONDON MAIN ROUTES MAPS

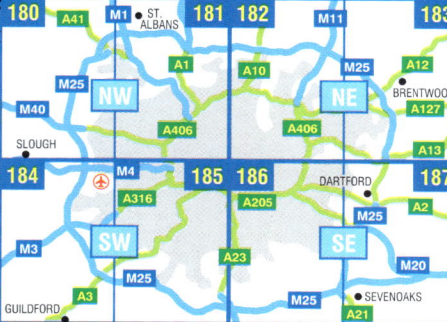

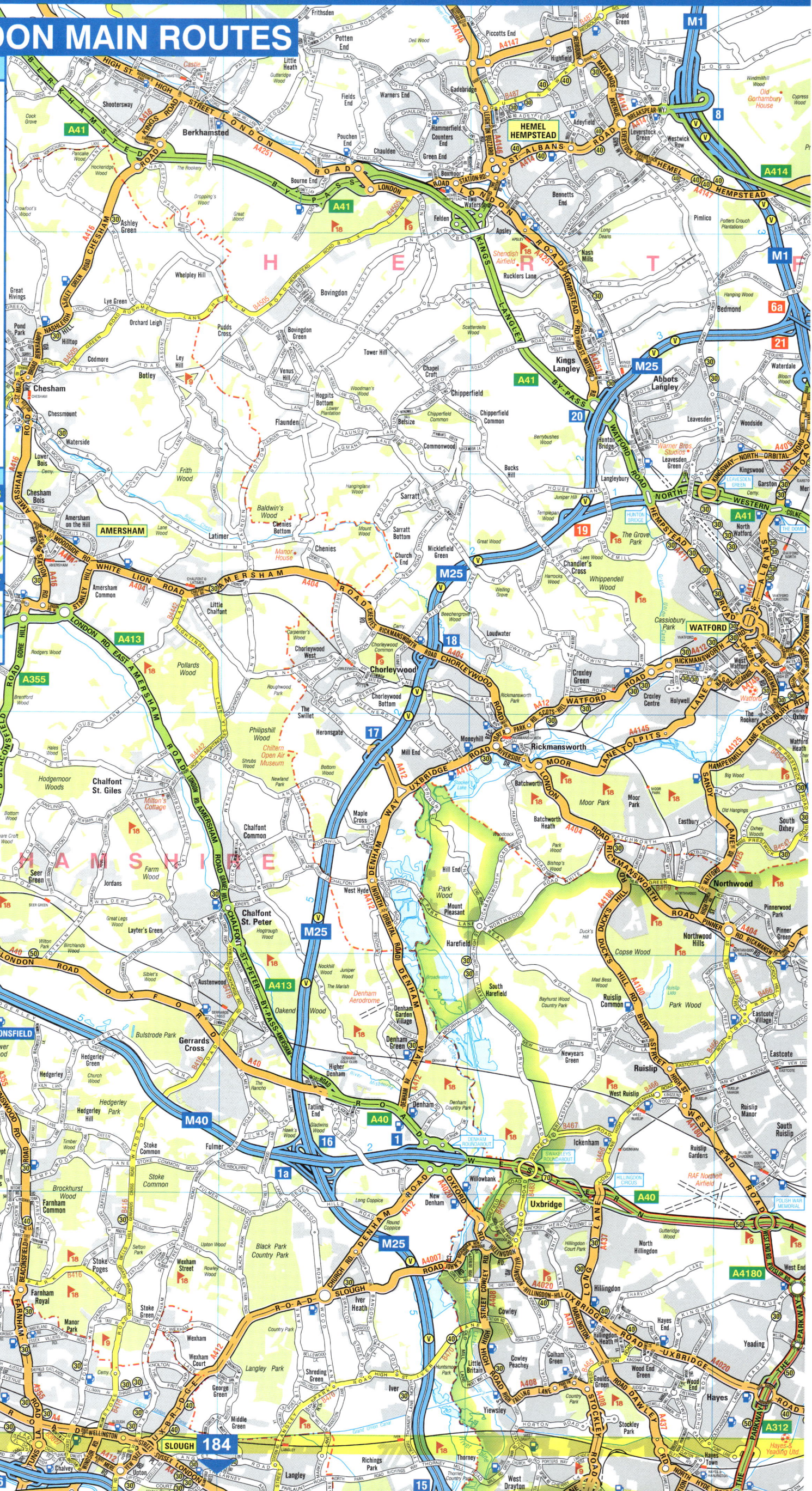

| 180 | 181 | 182 | 183 |
|---|---|---|---|
| NW | | NE | |
| 184 | 185 | 186 | 187 |
| SW | | SE | |

Map references: 180 A41 M1 ST. ALBANS · A1 · A10 · A12 BRENTWOOD A127 · A13 · A406 · M40 SLOUGH · M4 · A316 · M3 · A23 · A205 DARTFORD M25 A2 · A21 · M20 · GUILDFORD A3 SEVENOAKS

*Place names on map include:* Berkhamsted, Hemel Hempstead, Kings Langley, Abbots Langley, Watford, Rickmansworth, Chorleywood, Amersham, Chesham, Chesham Bois, Beaconsfield, Gerrards Cross, Chalfont St. Giles, Chalfont St. Peter, Uxbridge, Ruislip, Northwood, Eastcote, Harefield, Denham, Iver, Slough, Langley, Wooburn Green, Burnham Beeches, Stoke Poges, Fulmer, Taplow, HERTFORDSHIRE, BUCKINGHAMSHIRE

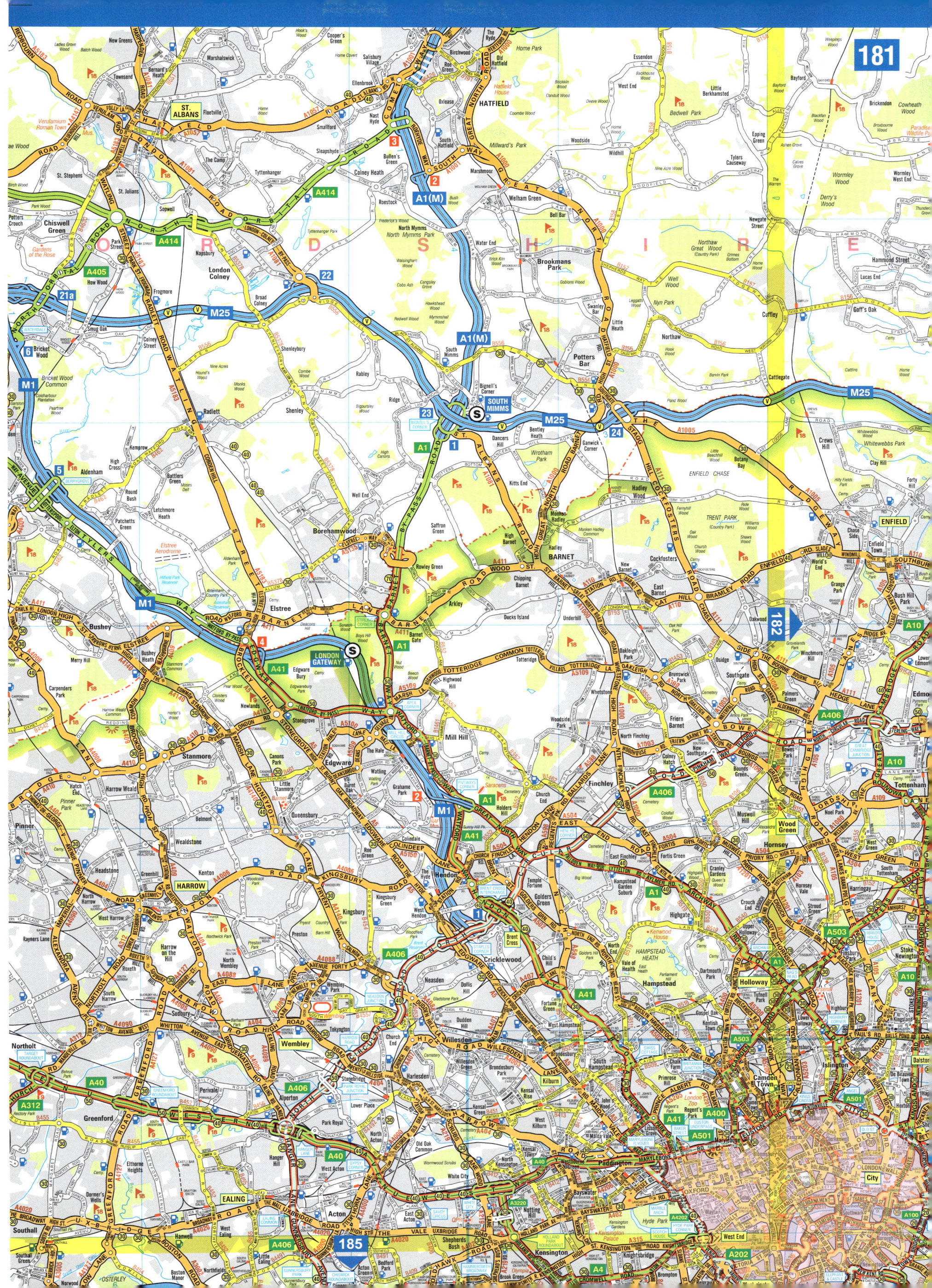

ST. ALBANS
HATFIELD
BROOKMANS PARK
POTTERS BAR
ENFIELD
SOUTH MIMMS
BARNET
BOREHAMWOOD
ELSTREE
STANMORE
EDGWARE
MILL HILL
FINCHLEY
WOOD GREEN
HARROW
WEMBLEY
HENDON
CRICKLEWOOD
HAMPSTEAD
HOLLOWAY
ISLINGTON
CAMDEN TOWN
GREENFORD
EALING
ACTON
PADDINGTON
WEST END
CITY

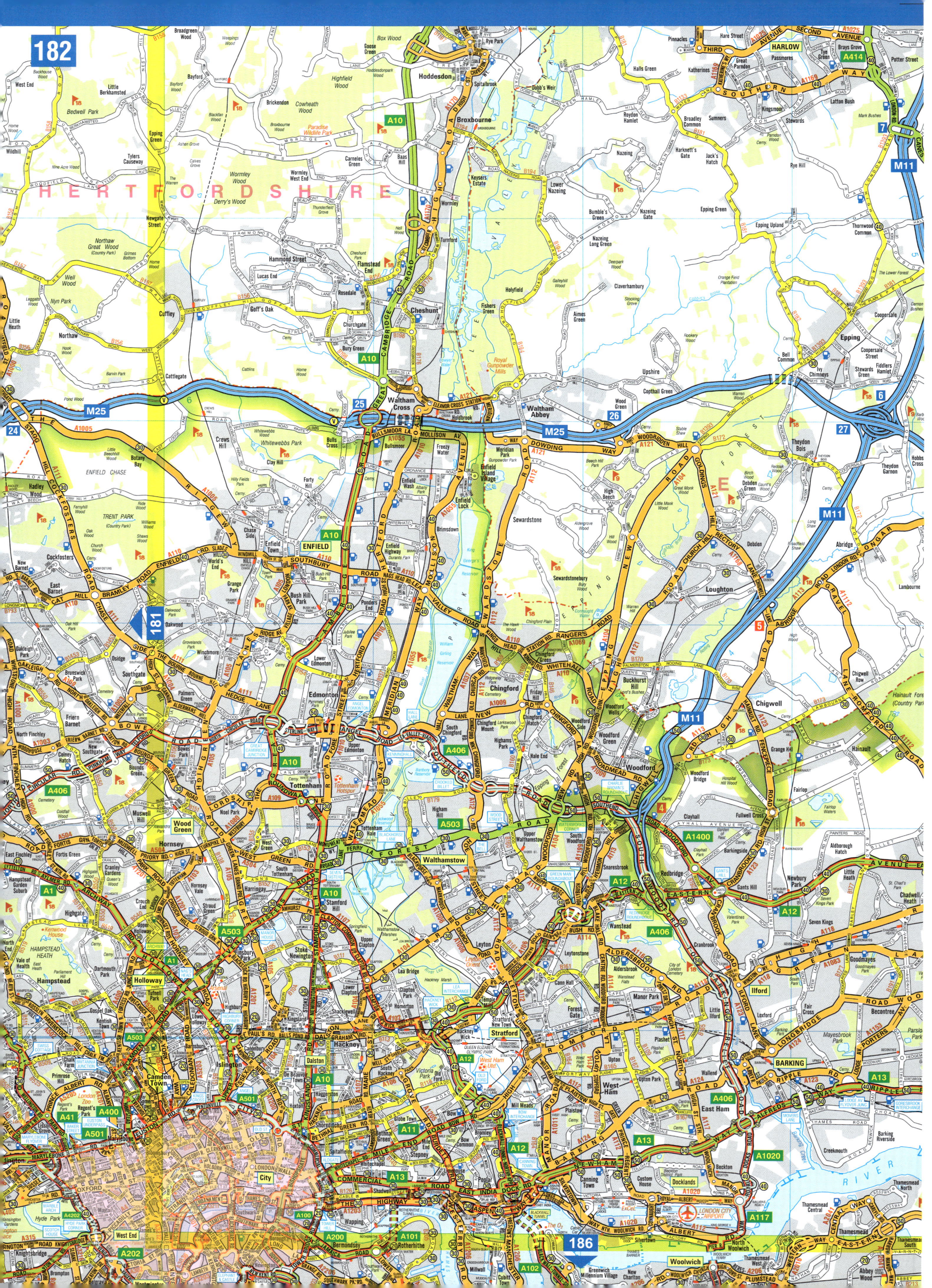

HERTFORDSHIRE

HARLOW

A10

Hoddesdon

Broxbourne

Cheshunt

Waltham Cross

Waltham Abbey

Epping

M25

M11

ENFIELD

Southbury

Loughton

Chingford

Edmonton

Chigwell

Woodford

Tottenham

Wood Green

Walthamstow

Buckhurst Hill

Muswell Hill

Hornsey

Leyton

Wanstead

Redbridge

Ilford

Highgate

Stamford Hill

Leytonstone

Seven Kings

Goodmayes

Hampstead

Holloway

Stoke Newington

Manor Park

BARKING

Camden Town

Islington

Hackney

Dalston

Stratford

West Ham

East Ham

City

West End

London City Airport

Docklands

Woolwich

RIVER

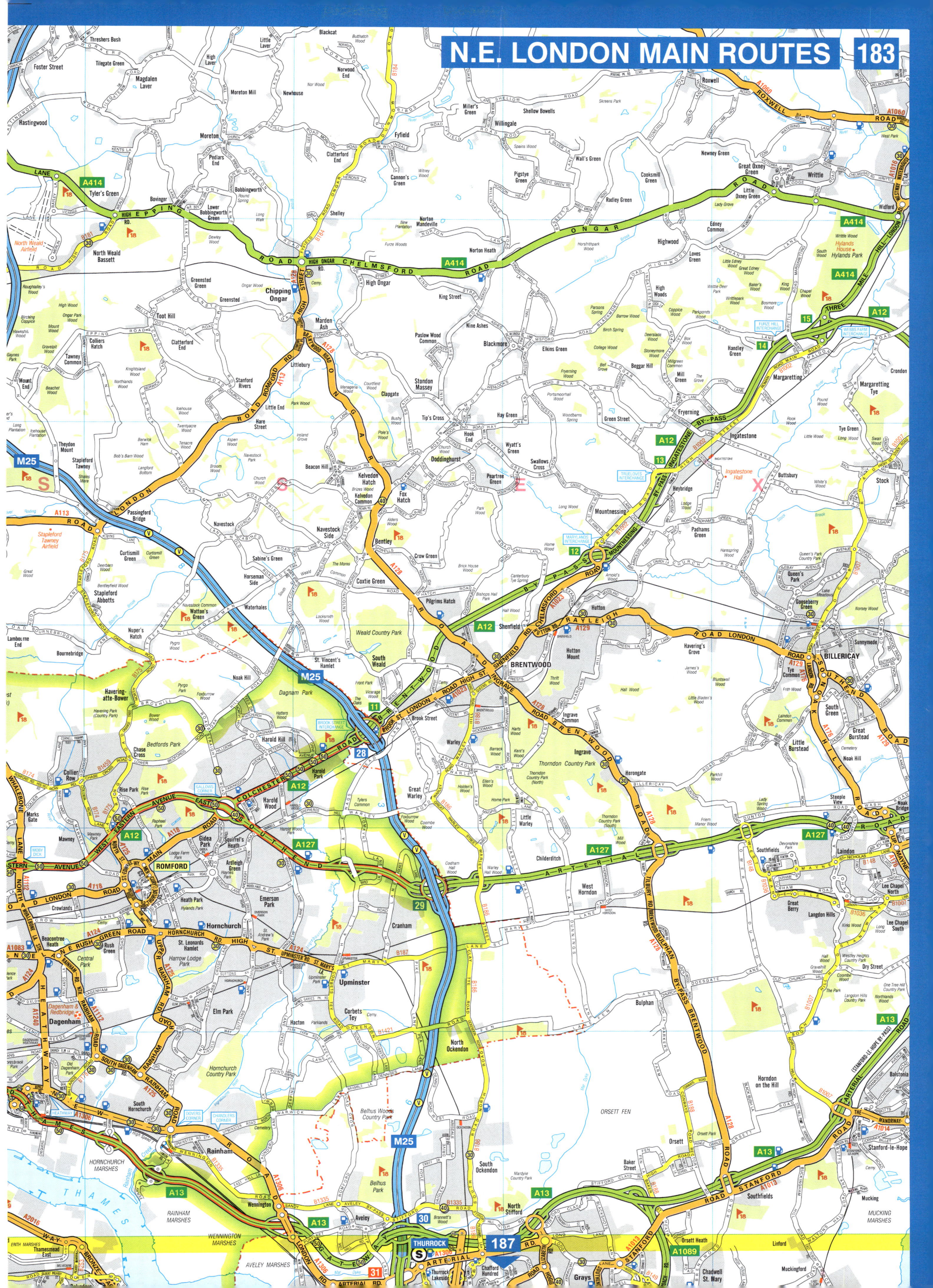

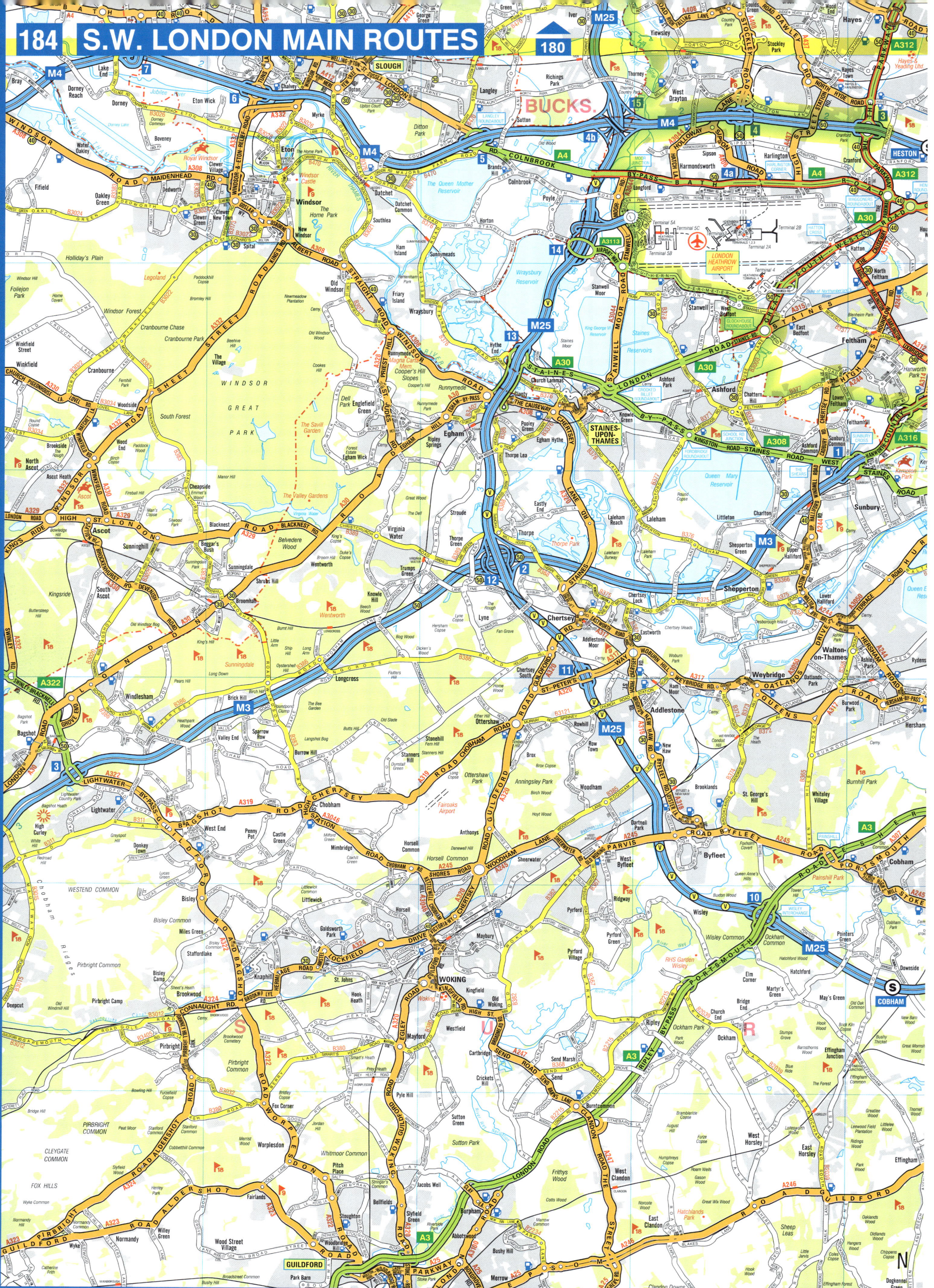

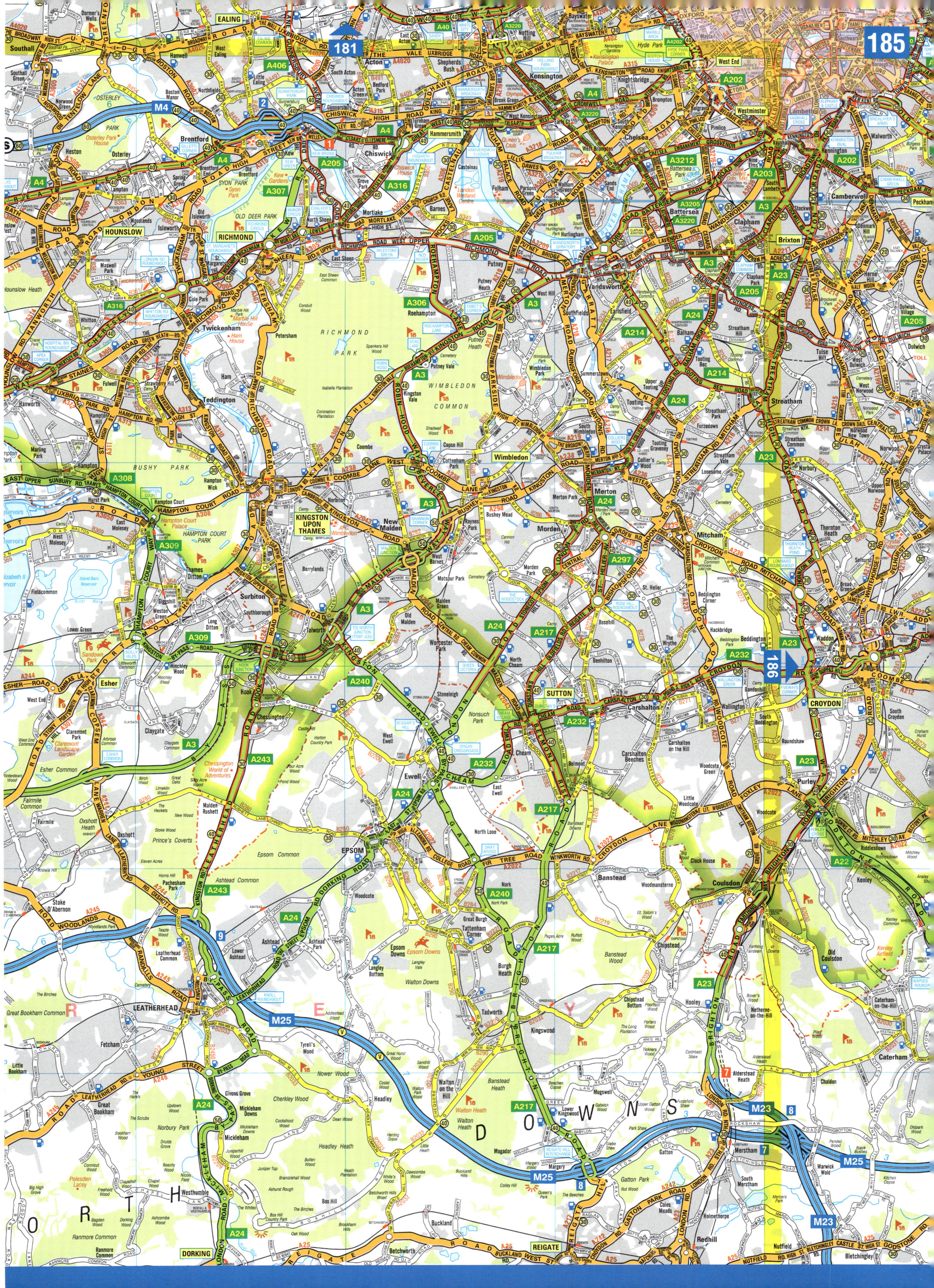

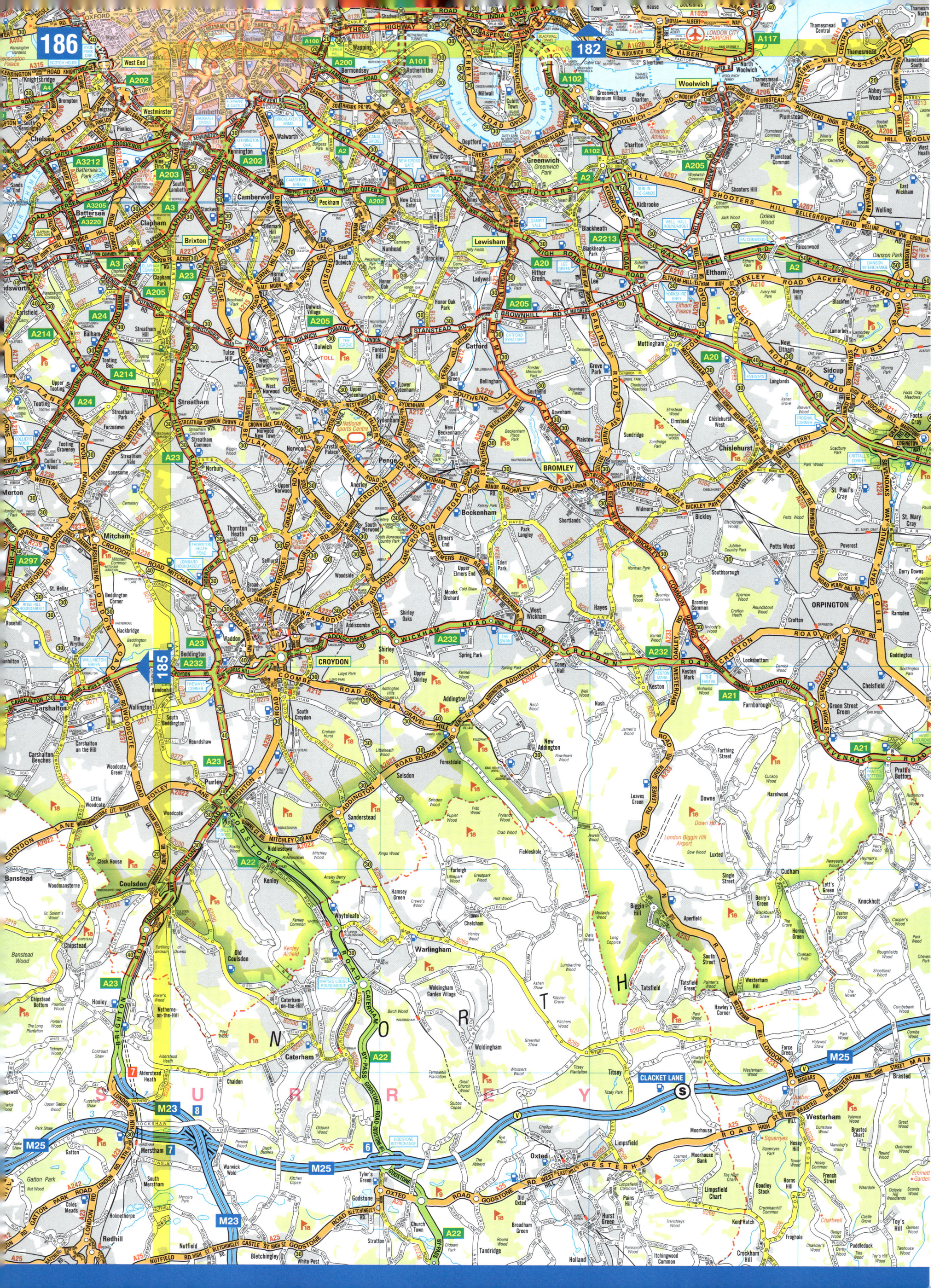

West End
Westminster
Chelsea
Pimlico
Battersea
Clapham
Brixton
Camberwell
Peckham
Walworth
Bermondsey
Rotherhithe
Wapping
Deptford
Greenwich
Greenwich Park
New Cross
Blackheath
Lewisham
Charlton
Woolwich
W. Woolwich
Silvertown
North Woolwich
Thamesmead
Thamesmead Central
Thamesmead South
Abbey Wood
Plumstead
Plumstead Common
Shooters Hill
East Wickham
Welling
Bostall Hill
Falconwood
Eltham
Mottingham
Sidcup
Blackfen
Lamorbey
New Eltham
Longlands
Chislehurst
Chislehurst West
Elmstead
Grove Park
Hither Green
Catford
Brownhill
Stansted
Forest Hill
Honor Oak
Dulwich
Tulse Hill
Streatham
Streatham Hill
Tooting Bec
Tooting
Balham
Wandsworth
Earlsfield
Merton
Mitcham
St. Helier
Carshalton
Carshalton Beeches
Carshalton on the Hill
Wallington
Beddington
Hackbridge
Woodcote Green
South Beddington
Roundshaw
Waddon
Croydon
South Croydon
Purley
Coulsdon
Kenley
Whyteleafe
Old Coulsdon
Caterham-on-the-Hill
Caterham
Chaldon
Warlingham
Woldingham
Woldingham Garden Village
Sanderstead
Riddlesdown
Selsdon
Forestdale
New Addington
Addington
Shirley
Upper Shirley
Spring Park
West Wickham
Hayes
Coney Hall
Keston
Keston Mark
Farnborough
Green Street Green
Orpington
Locksbottom
Petts Wood
Poverest
Derry Downs
St. Mary Cray
St. Paul's Cray
Bickley
Bromley
Bromley Common
Shortlands
Widmore
Beckenham
Elmers End
Eden Park
Park Langley
Penge
Anerley
Norwood
Thornton Heath
Norbury
Streatham Common
Crystal Palace
Upper Norwood
South Norwood
Selhurst
Woodside
Addiscombe
Shirley Oaks
Monks Orchard
Biggin Hill
London Biggin Hill Airport
Aperfield
Tatsfield
Westerham Hill
Cudham
Knockholt
Pratt's Bottom
Chelsfield
Goddington
Ramsden
Downe
Luxted
Farleigh
Chelsham
Hamsey Green
Leaves Green
Titsey
Limpsfield
Oxted
Godstone
Merstham
South Merstham
Redhill
Nutfield
Bletchingley
Godstone
Tandridge
Holland
Crockham Hill
Westerham
Brasted
Chipstead
Sundridge
Knockholt
Halstead
Pratts Bottom

SURREY
NORTH DOWNS
KENT

CLACKET LANE

M25
M23
A22
A23
A21
A20
A2
A232
A212
A205
A24
A25

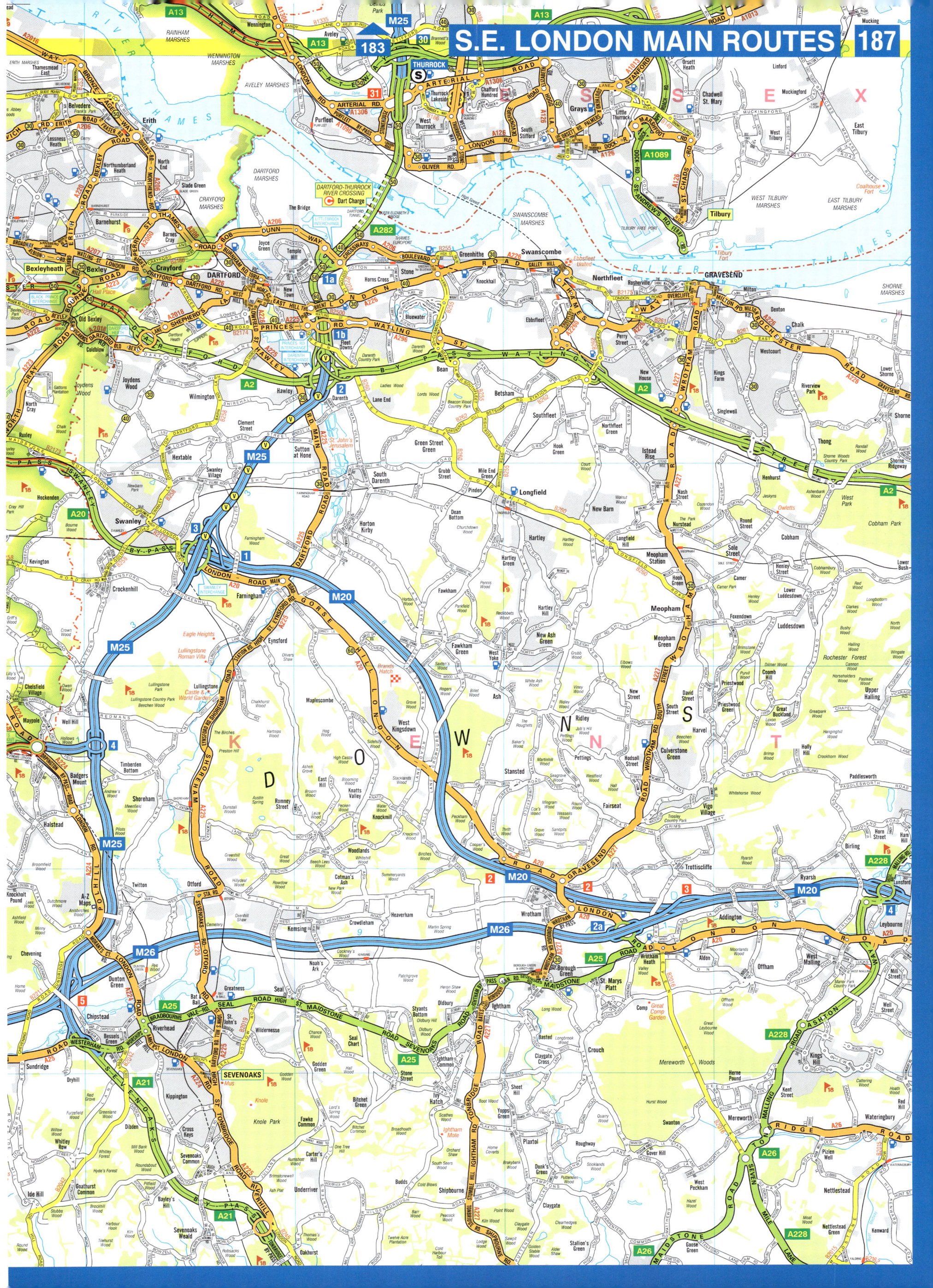

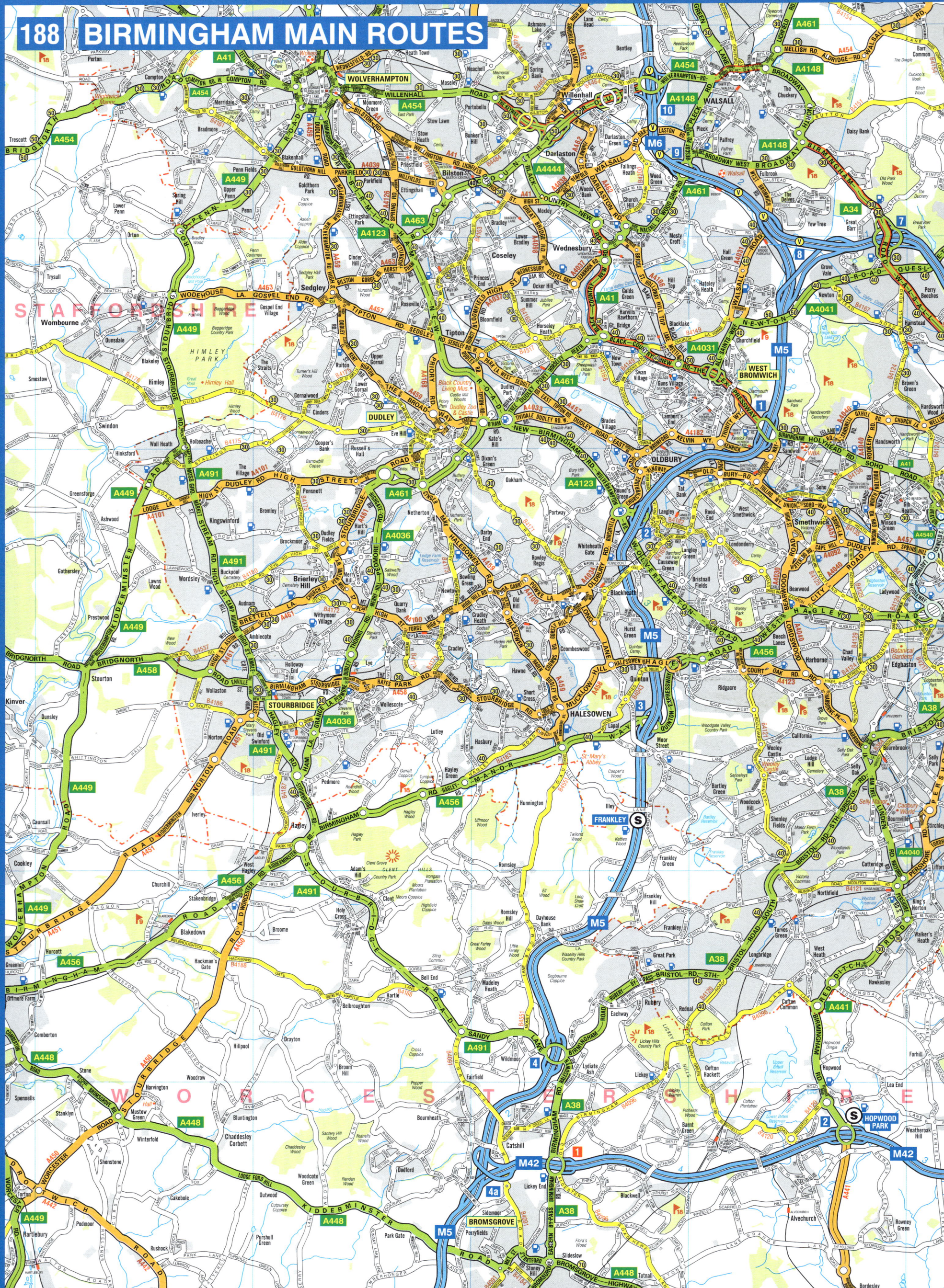

BIRMINGHAM
SOLIHULL
Sutton Coldfield
SUTTON PARK
WARWICKSHIRE
W A R W I C K S H I R E
BIRMINGHAM AIRPORT
NATIONAL EXHIBITION CENTRE
National Motorcycle Museum
Packington Park
Forest of Arden
Maxstoke Castle
Kingsbury
Coleshill
Shustoke
Maxstoke
Castle Bromwich
Chelmsley Wood
Marston Green
Sheldon
Elmdon
Hampton in Arden
Meriden
Berkswell
Balsall Common
Knowle
Dorridge
Shirley
Hockley Heath
Lapworth
Packwood House
Baddesley Clinton
Wroxall
Honiley
Erdington
Aston
Small Heath
Acock's Green
Yardley
Stechford
Water Orton
Minworth
Curdworth
Middleton
Drayton Bassett
Dosthill
Hockley
Dordon
Whateley
Lea Marston
Marston
Nether Whitacre
Whitacre Heath
Furnace End
Little Packington
Stonebridge
Four Oaks
New Oscott
Kingstanding
Perry Barr
Handsworth Wood
Hall Green
Billesley
Moseley
Yardley Wood
Solihull Lodge
Hollywood
Wythall
Earlswood
Tanworth-in-Arden
Portway
Umberslade
Nuthurst
Cheswick Green
Monkspath
Bentley Heath
Catherine-de-Barnes
Bickenhill
Barston
Temple Balsall
Chadwick End
Kingswood
M6
M6 TOLL
M42
M40
A446
A452
A38
A34
A45
A41
A435
A4177
A5
A47
A4040
T1
T2
T3
4a
7a
3a
10
16

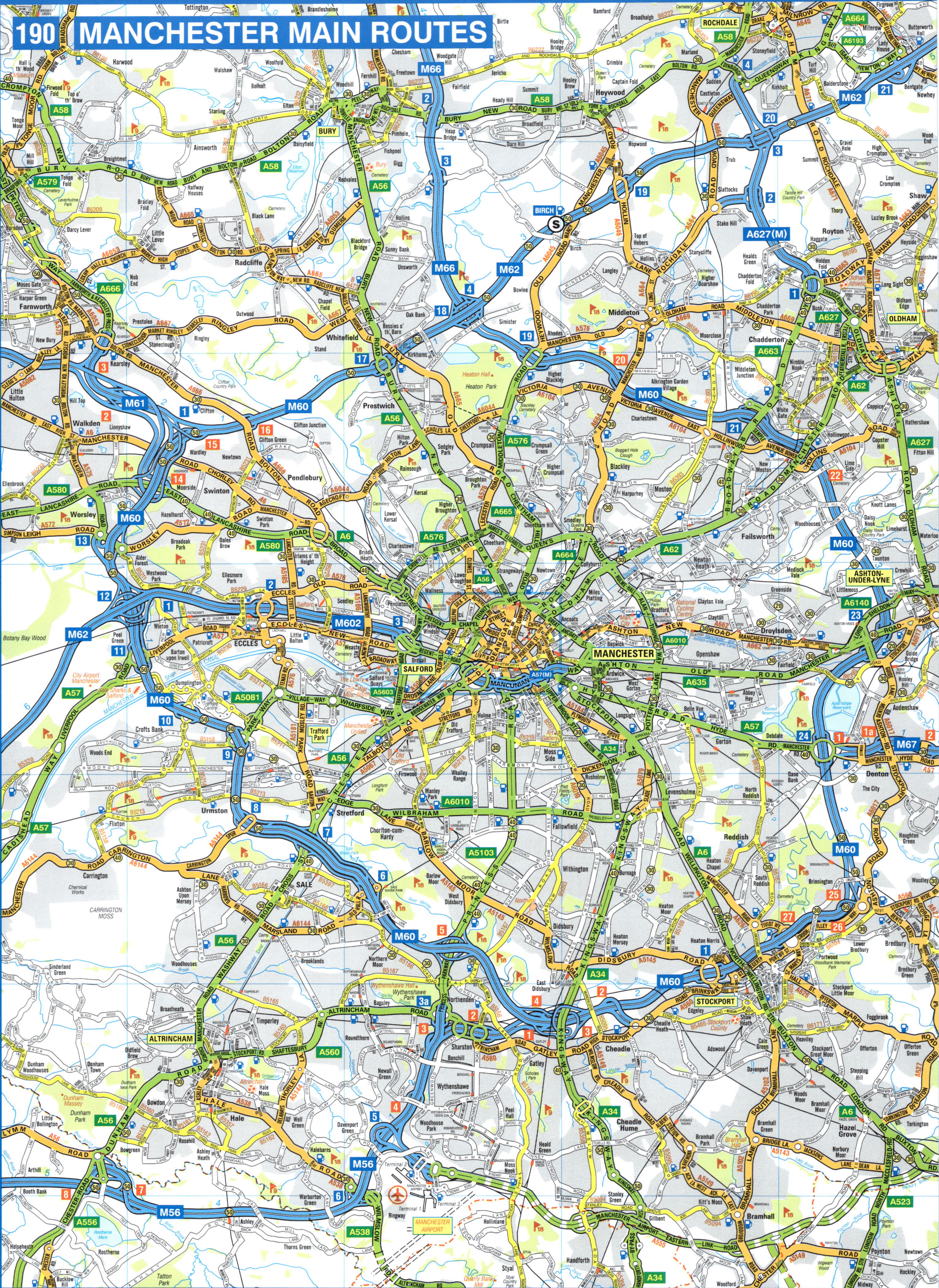

## City & Town Centre Plans

## Port Plans 🚢

## Airport Plans ✈

## Reference to City & Town Plans　Légende　Zeichenerklärung

| Symbol | English | Français | Deutsch |
|---|---|---|---|
| **M1** | Motorway | Autoroute | Autobahn |
| | Motorway Under Construction | Autoroute en construction | Autobahn im Bau |
| | Motorway Proposed | Autoroute prévue | Geplante Autobahn |
| **4** **5** | Motorway Junctions with Numbers — Unlimited Interchange 4, Limited Interchange 5 | Autoroute échangeur numéroté — Echangeur complet, Echangeur partiel | Autobahnanschlußstelle mit Nummer — Unbeschränkter Fahrtrichtungswechsel, Beschränkter Fahrtrichtungswechsel |
| **A41** | Primary Route | Route à grande circulation | Hauptverkehrsstraße |
| | Dual Carriageways (A & B roads) | Route à double chaussées séparées (route A & B) | Zweispurige Schnellstraße (A- und B- Straßen) |
| **A129** | Class A Road | Route de type A | A-Straße |
| **B177** | Class B Road | Route de type B | B-Straße |
| | Major Roads Under Construction | Route prioritaire en construction | Hauptverkehrsstraße im Bau |
| | Major Roads Proposed | Route prioritaire prévue | Geplante Hauptverkehrsstraße |
| | Minor Roads | Route secondaire | Nebenstraße |
| 30 | Safety Camera | Radars de contrôle de vitesse | Sicherheitskamera |
| | Restricted Access | Accès réglementé | Beschränkte Zufahrt |
| | Pedestrianized Road & Main Footway | Rue piétonne et chemin réservé aux piétons | Fußgängerstraße und Fußweg |
| | One Way Streets | Sens unique | Einbahnstraße |
| ⛽ | Fuel Station | Station service | Tankstelle |
| TOLL | Toll | Barrière de péage | Gebührenpflichtig |
| | Railway & Station | Voie ferrée et gare | Eisenbahnlinie und Bahnhof |
| DLR | Underground / Metro & DLR Station | Station de métro et DLR | U-Bahnstation und DLR-Station |
| | Level Crossing & Tunnel | Passage à niveau et tunnel | Bahnübergang und Tunnel |
| | Tram Stop & One Way Tram Stop | Arrêt de tramway | Straßenbahnhaltestelle |
| | Built-up Area | Agglomération | Geschlossene Ortschaft |
| † | Abbey, Cathedral, Priory etc | Abbaye, cathédrale, prieuré etc | Abtei, Kathedrale, Kloster usw |
| ✈ | Airport | Aéroport | Flughafen |
| | Bus Station | Gare routière | Bushaltestelle |
| P | Car Park (selection of) | Sélection de parkings | Auswahl von Parkplatz |
| † | Church | Eglise | Kirche |
| | City Wall | Murs d'enceinte | Stadtmauer |
| | Congestion Charging Zone | Zone de péage urbain | City-Maut Zone |
| | Ferry (vehicular) (foot only) | Bac (véhicules) (piétons) | Fähre (autos) (nur für Personen) |
| | Golf Course | Terrain de golf | Golfplatz |
| 🚁 | Heliport | Héliport | Hubschrauberlandeplatz |
| H | Hospital | Hôpital | Krankenhaus |
| | Lighthouse | Phare | Leuchtturm |
| | Market | Marché | Markt |
| NT / NT / NTS | National Trust Property (open) (restricted opening) (National Trust for Scotland) | National Trust Property (ouvert) (heures d'ouverture) (National Trust for Scotland) | National Trust- Eigentum (geöffnet) (beschränkte Öffnungszeit) (National Trust for Scotland) |
| P+🚌 | Park & Ride | Parking relais | Auswahl von Parkplatz |
| ■ | Place of Interest | Curiosité | Sehenswürdigkeit |
| ▲ | Police Station | Commissariat de police | Polizeirevier |
| ★ | Post Office | Bureau de poste | Postamt |
| | Shopping Area (main street & precinct) | Quartier commerçant (rue et zone principales) | Einkaufsviertel (hauptgeschäftsstraße, fußgängerzone) |
| | Shopmobility | Shopmobility | Shopmobility |
| ▽ | Toilet | Toilettes | Toilette |
| i | Tourist Information Centre | Syndicat d'initiative Information | |
| | Viewpoint | Vue panoramique | Aussichtspunkt |
| V | Visitor Information Centre | Centre d'information touristique | Besucherzentrum |

## ABERDEEN
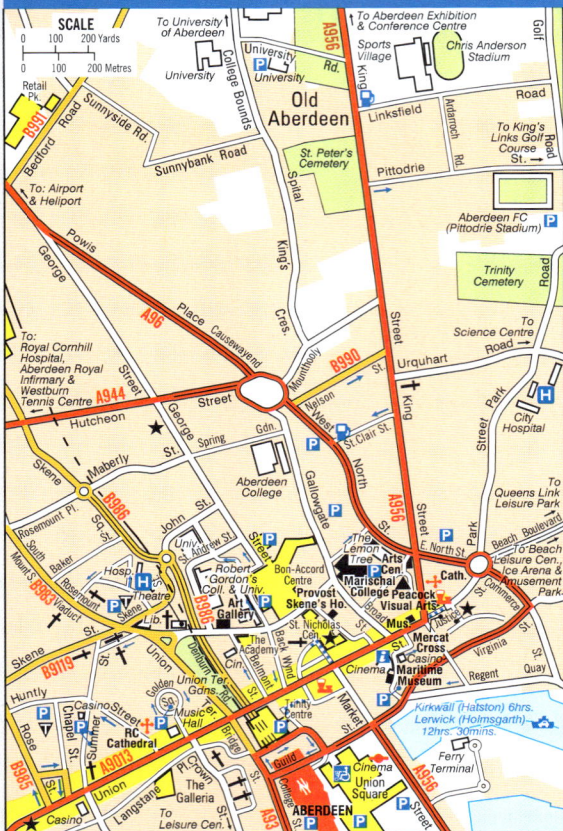

## BATH
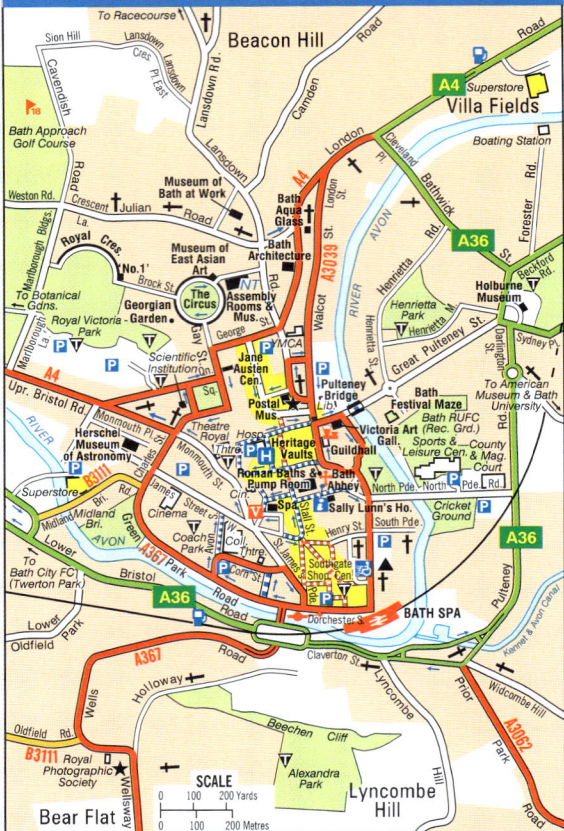

## BLACKPOOL
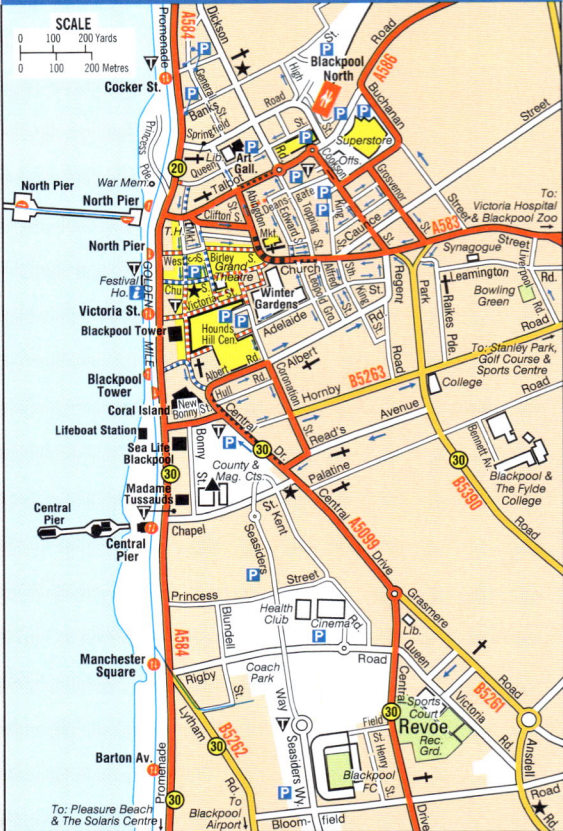

## BIRMINGHAM (CITY CENTRE)

## BOURNEMOUTH
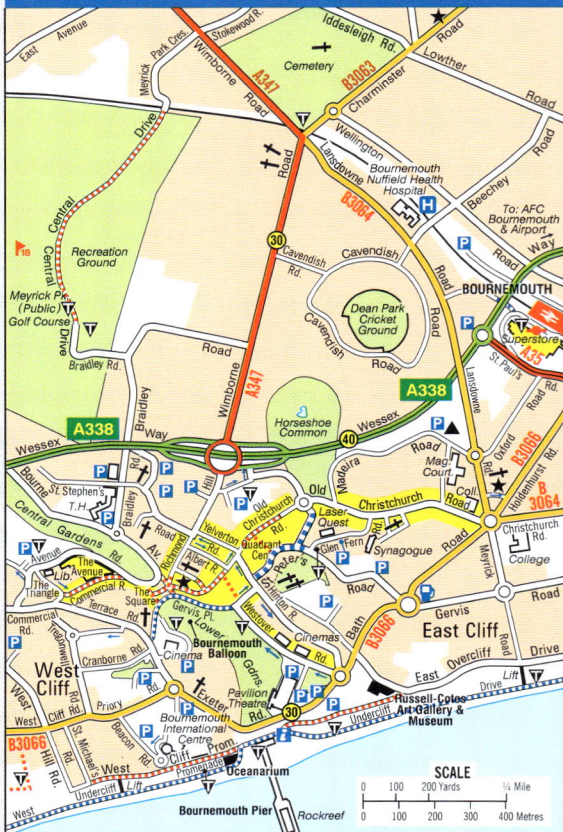

## BRADFORD
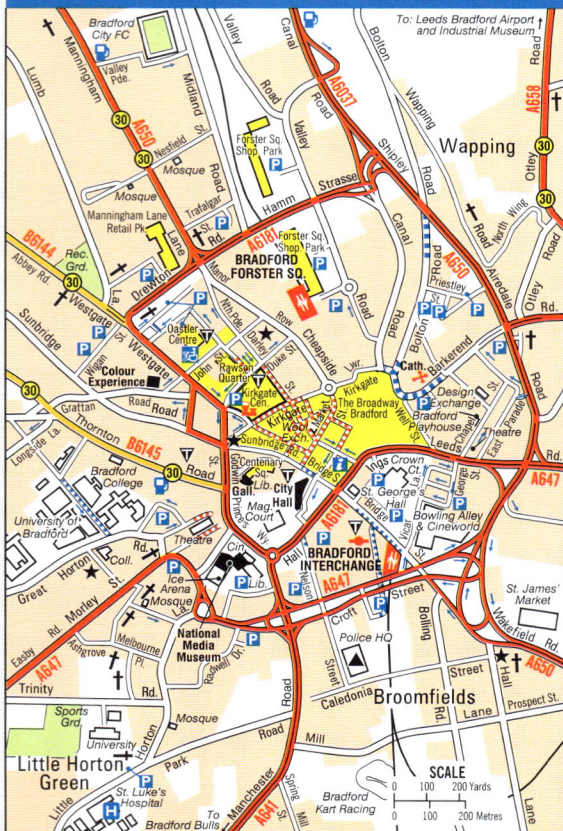

## BRIGHTON and HOVE

## BRISTOL

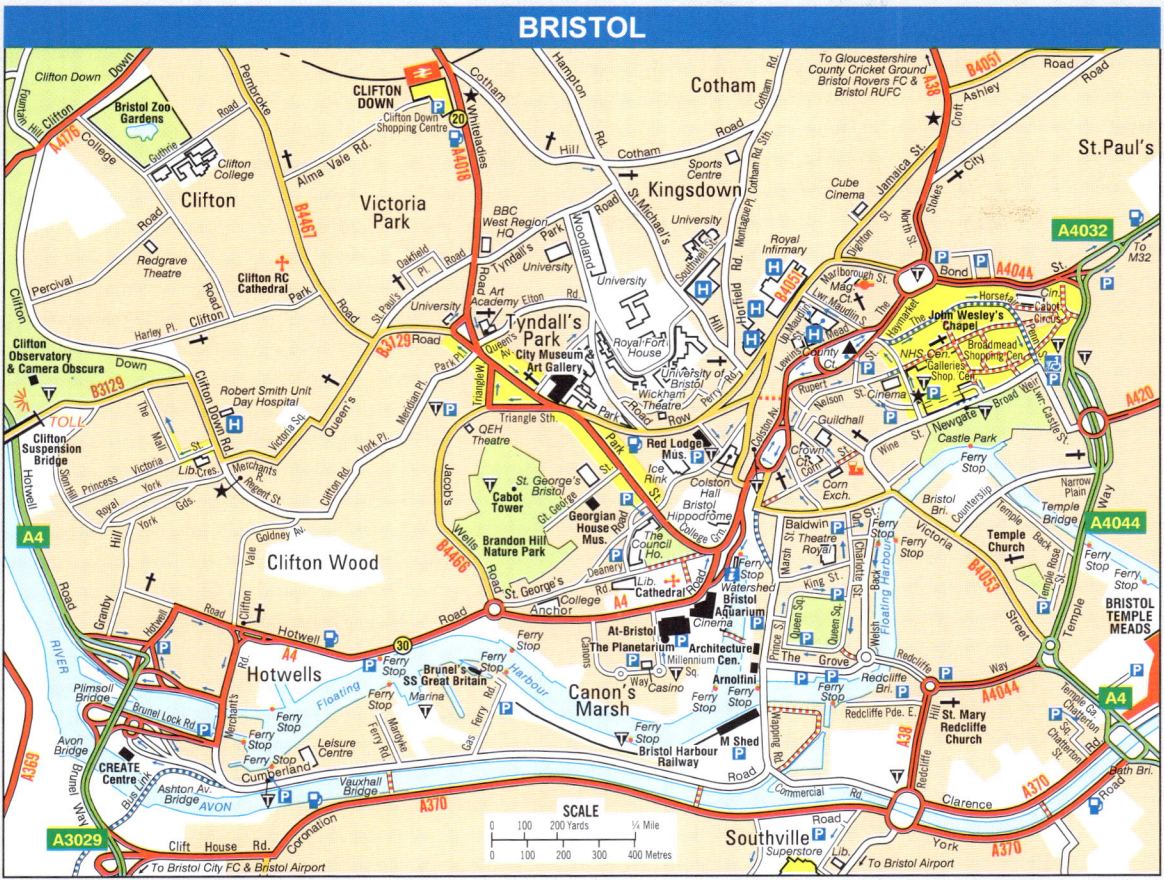

## CANTERBURY

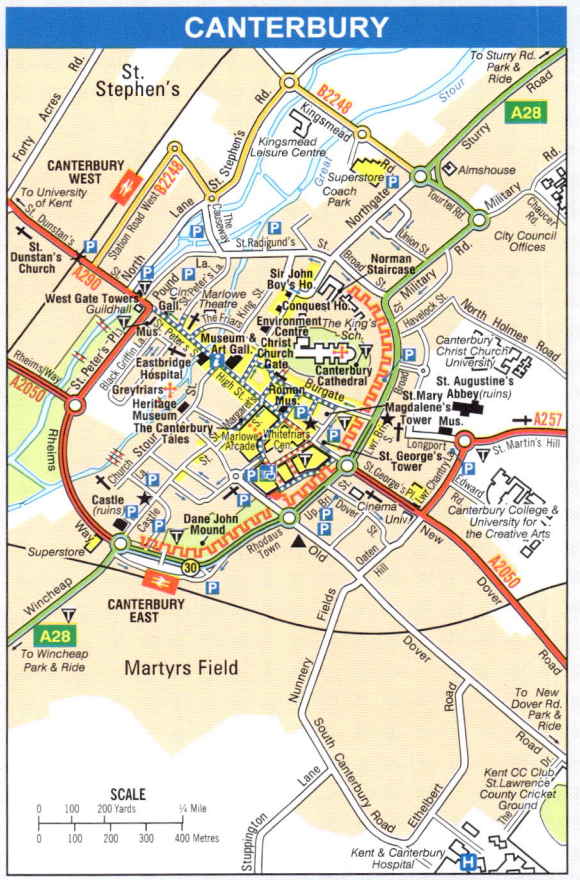

## CAMBRIDGE

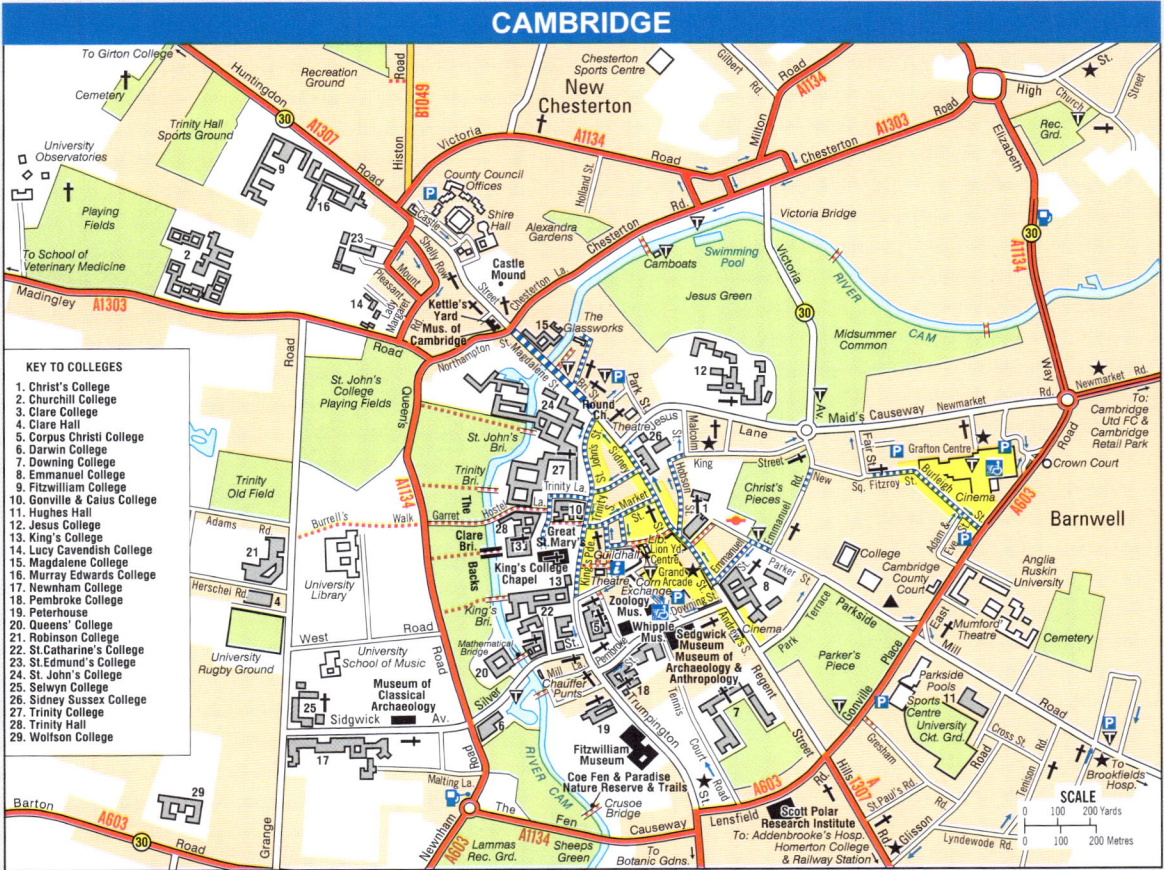

**KEY TO COLLEGES**
1. Christ's College
2. Churchill College
3. Clare College
4. Clare Hall
5. Corpus Christi College
6. Darwin College
7. Downing College
8. Emmanuel College
9. Fitzwilliam College
10. Gonville & Caius College
11. Hughes Hall
12. Jesus College
13. King's College
14. Lucy Cavendish College
15. Magdalene College
16. Murray Edwards College
17. Newnham College
18. Pembroke College
19. Peterhouse
20. Queens' College
21. Robinson College
22. St Catharine's College
23. St Edmund's College
24. St John's College
25. Selwyn College
26. Sidney Sussex College
27. Trinity College
28. Trinity Hall
29. Wolfson College

## CARLISLE

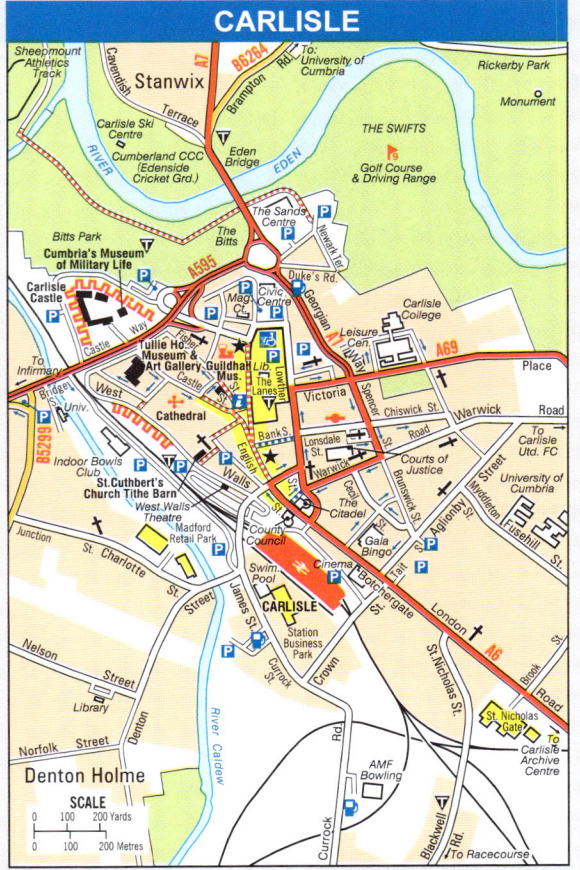

## CARDIFF (CAERDYDD)

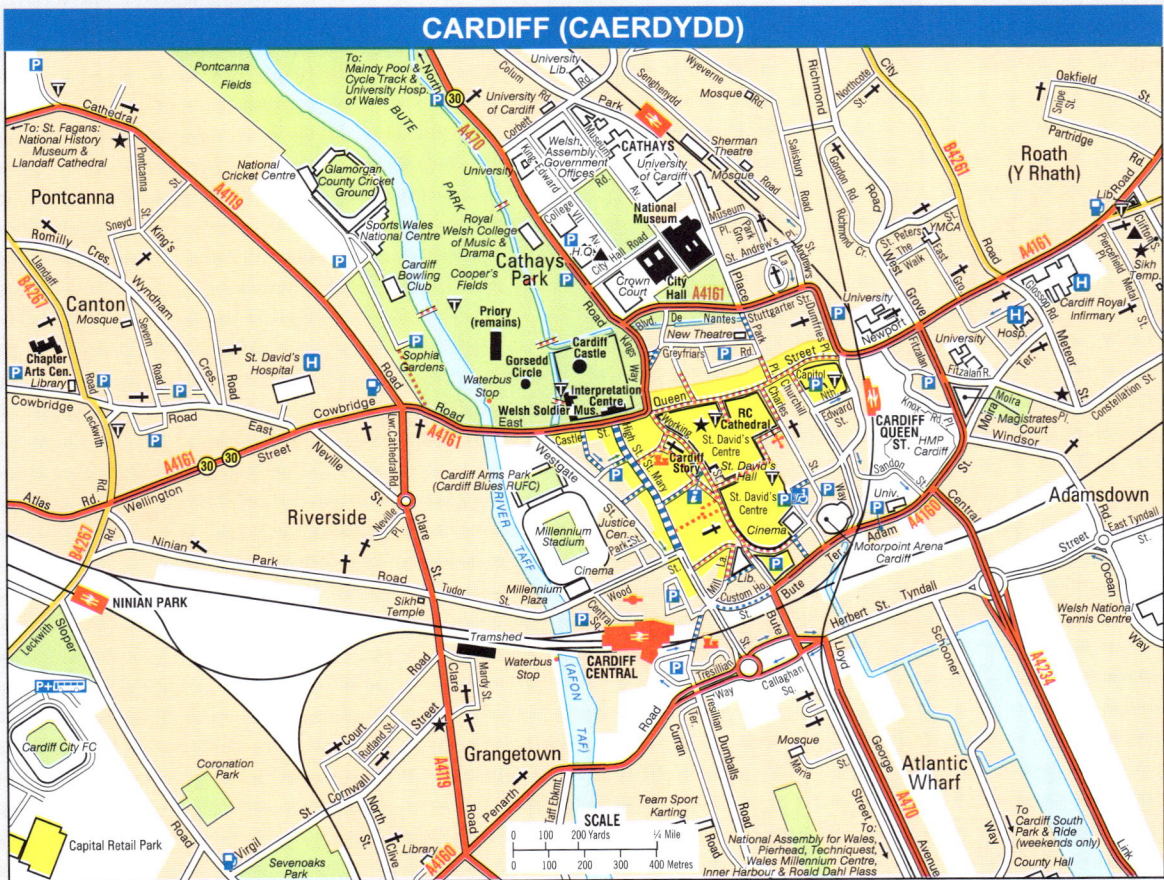

## CHELTENHAM

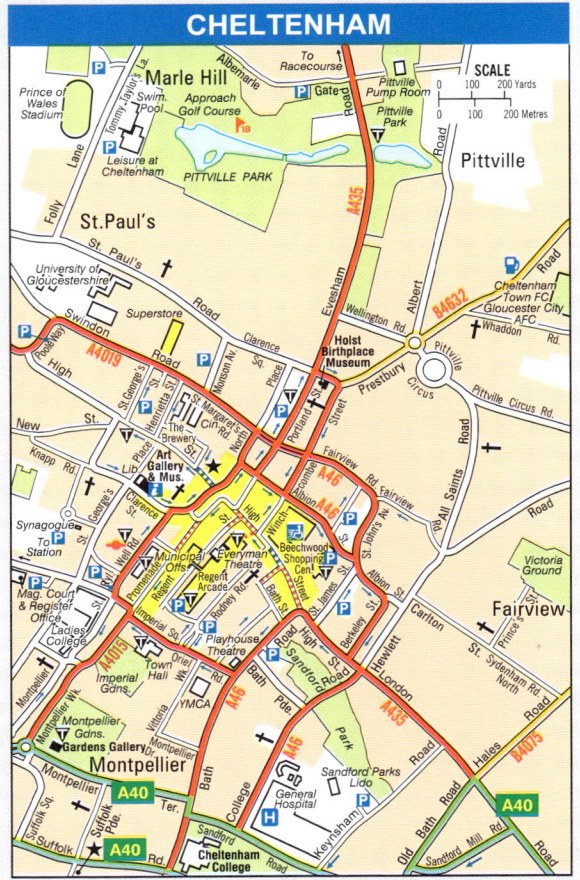

## CHESTER

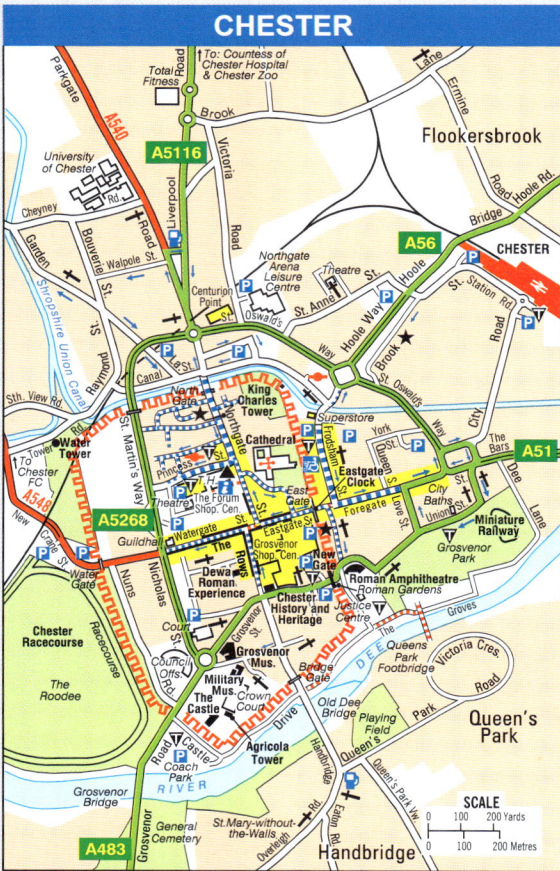

## COVENTRY

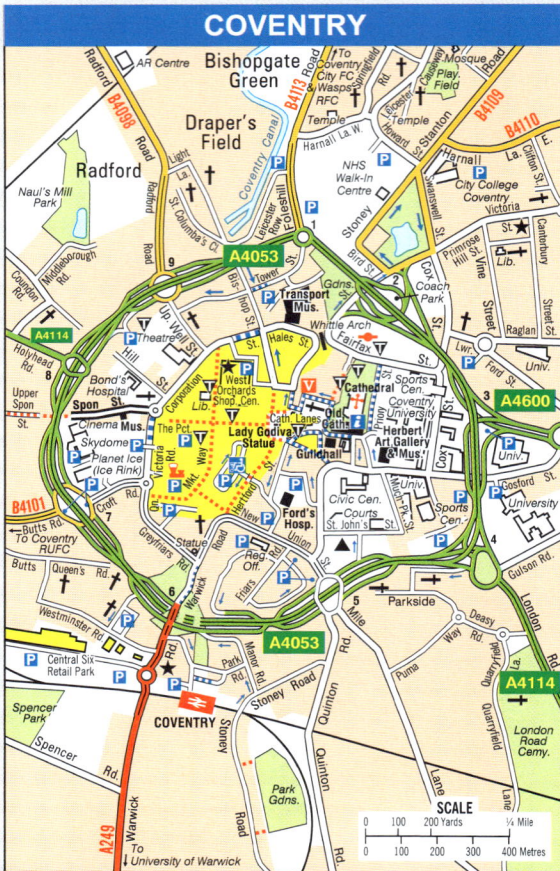

## DERBY

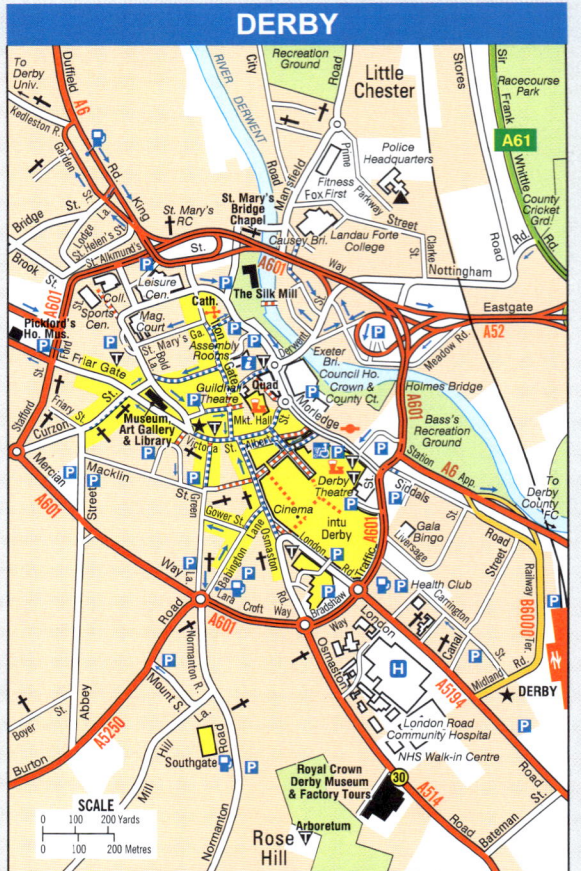

## DOVER

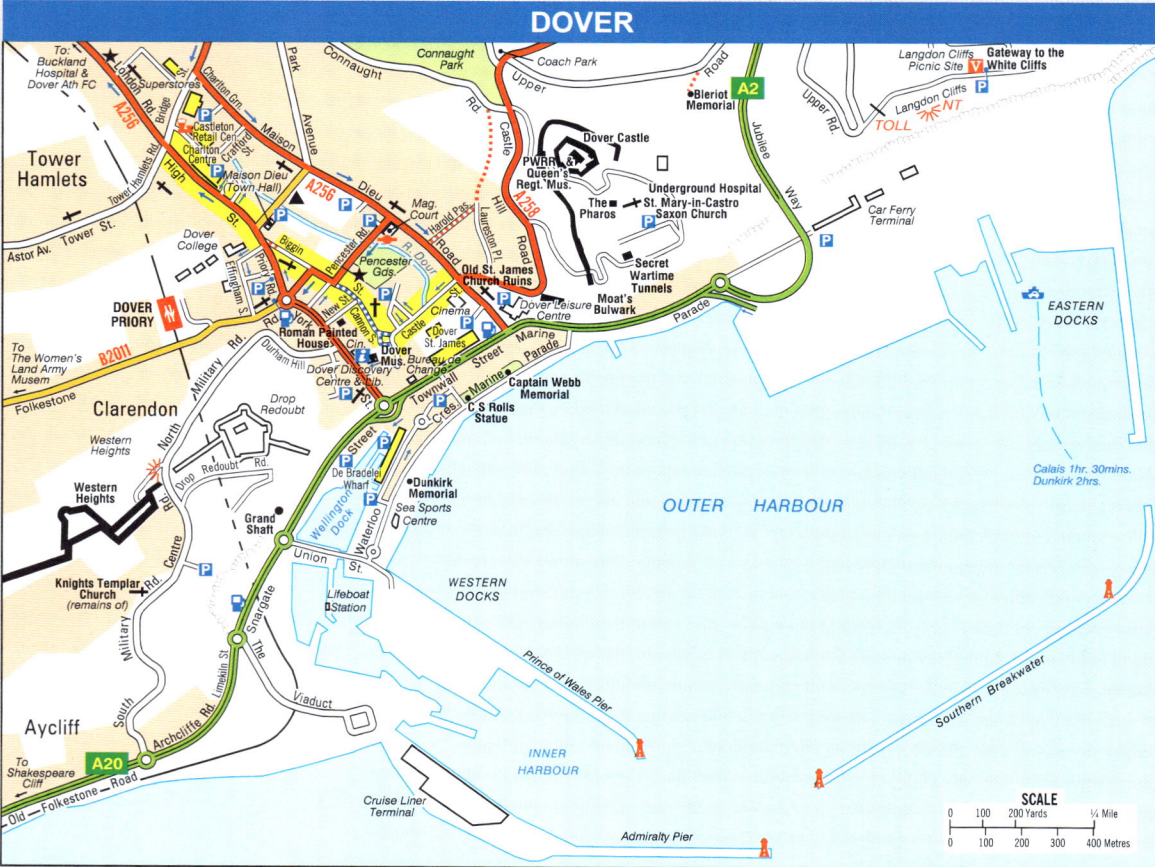

## DUMFRIES

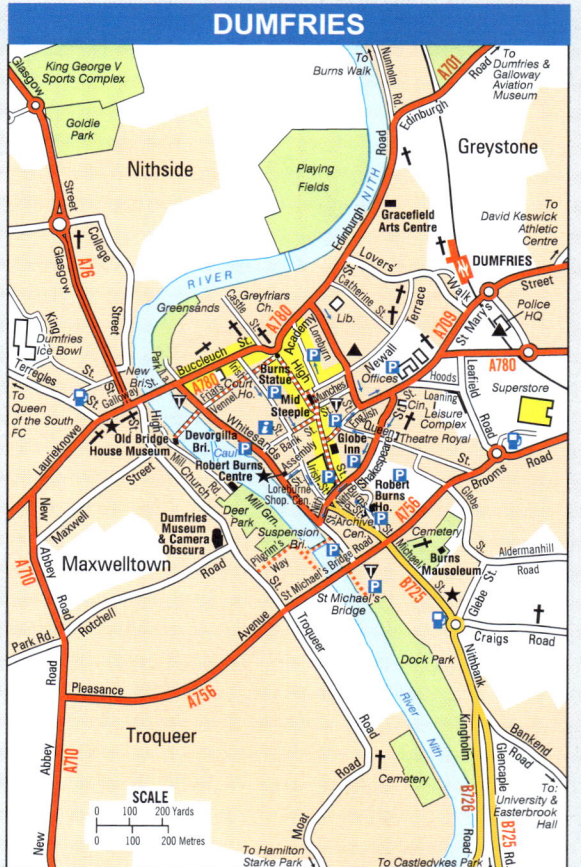

## DUNDEE

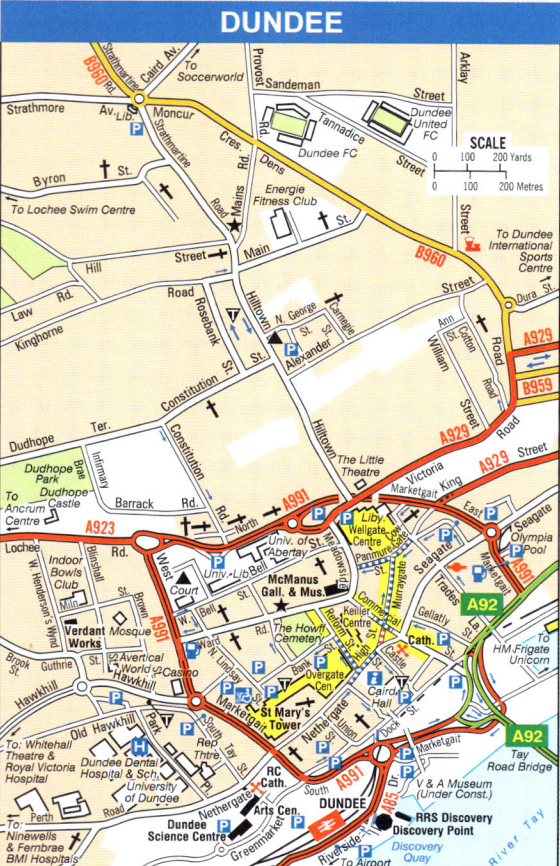

## DURHAM

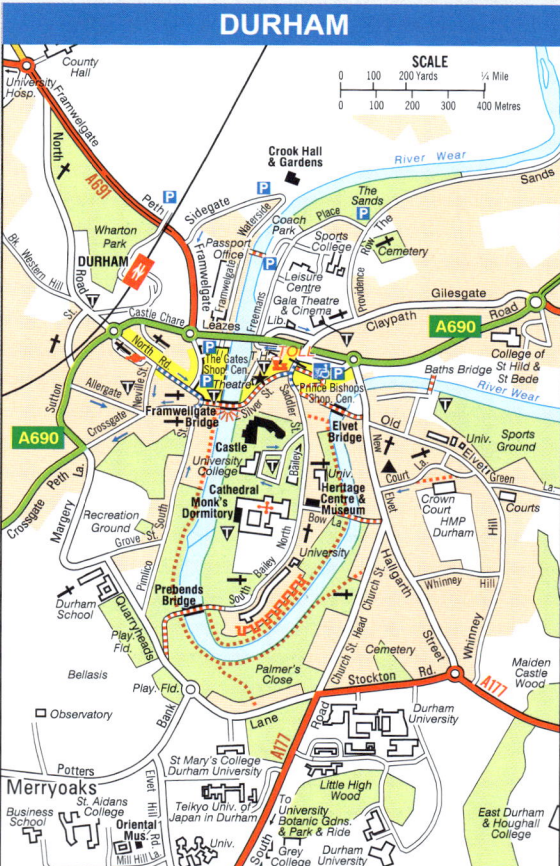

## EASTBOURNE

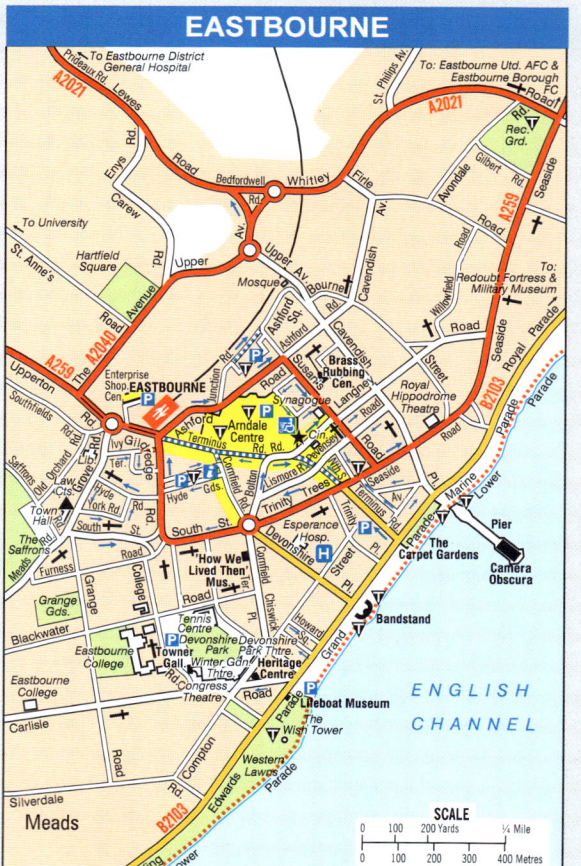

## EDINBURGH

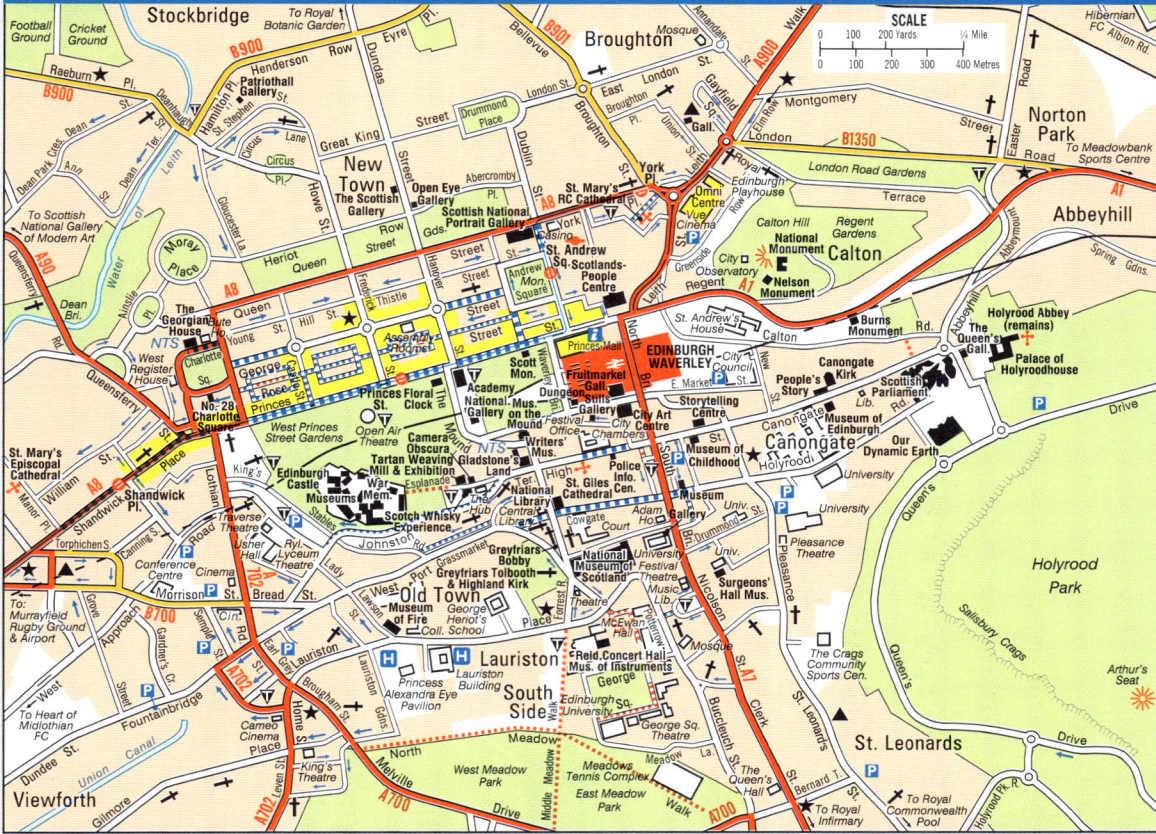

## FOLKESTONE

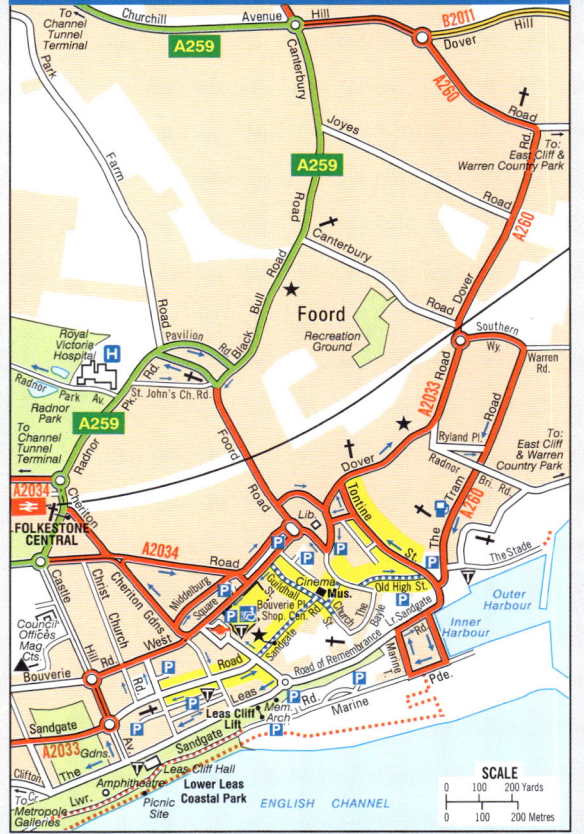

## EXETER

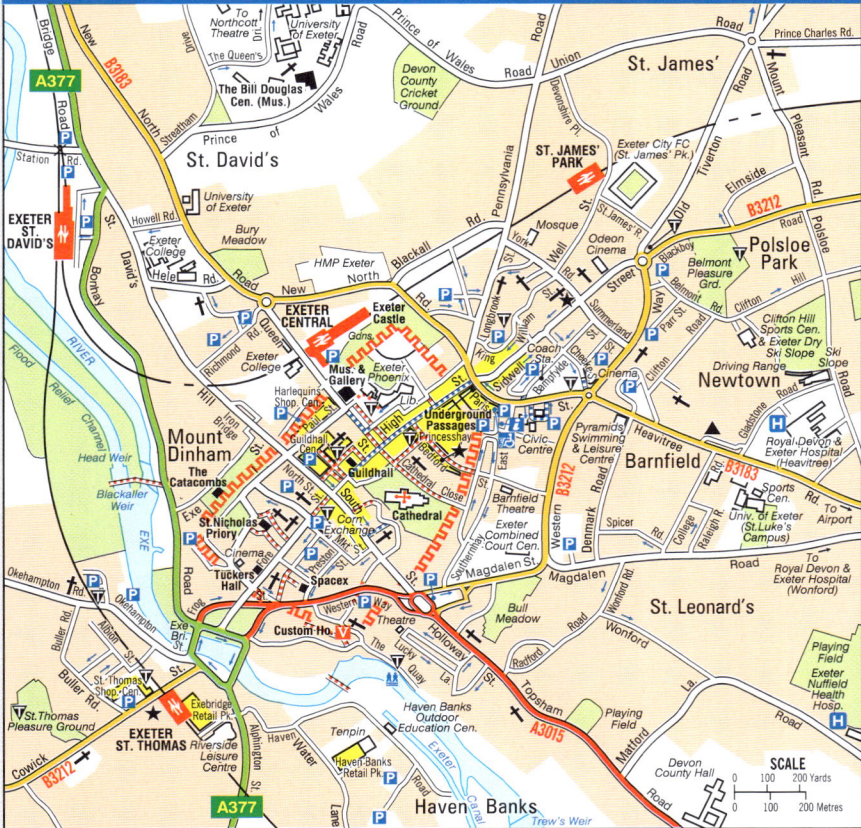

## GUILDFORD

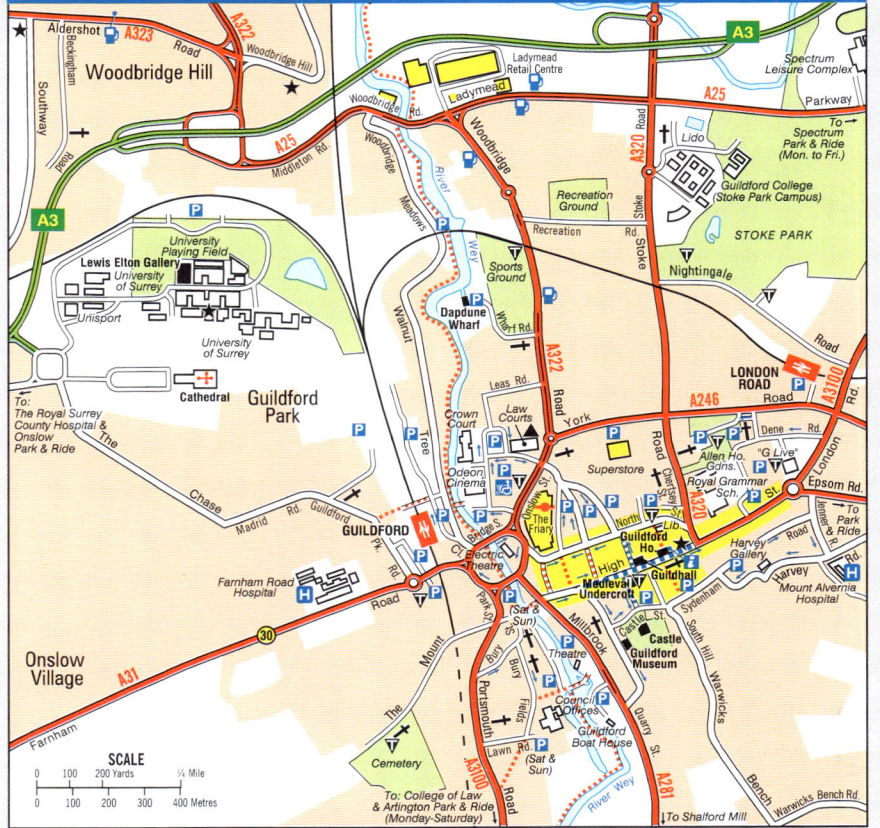

## GLASGOW

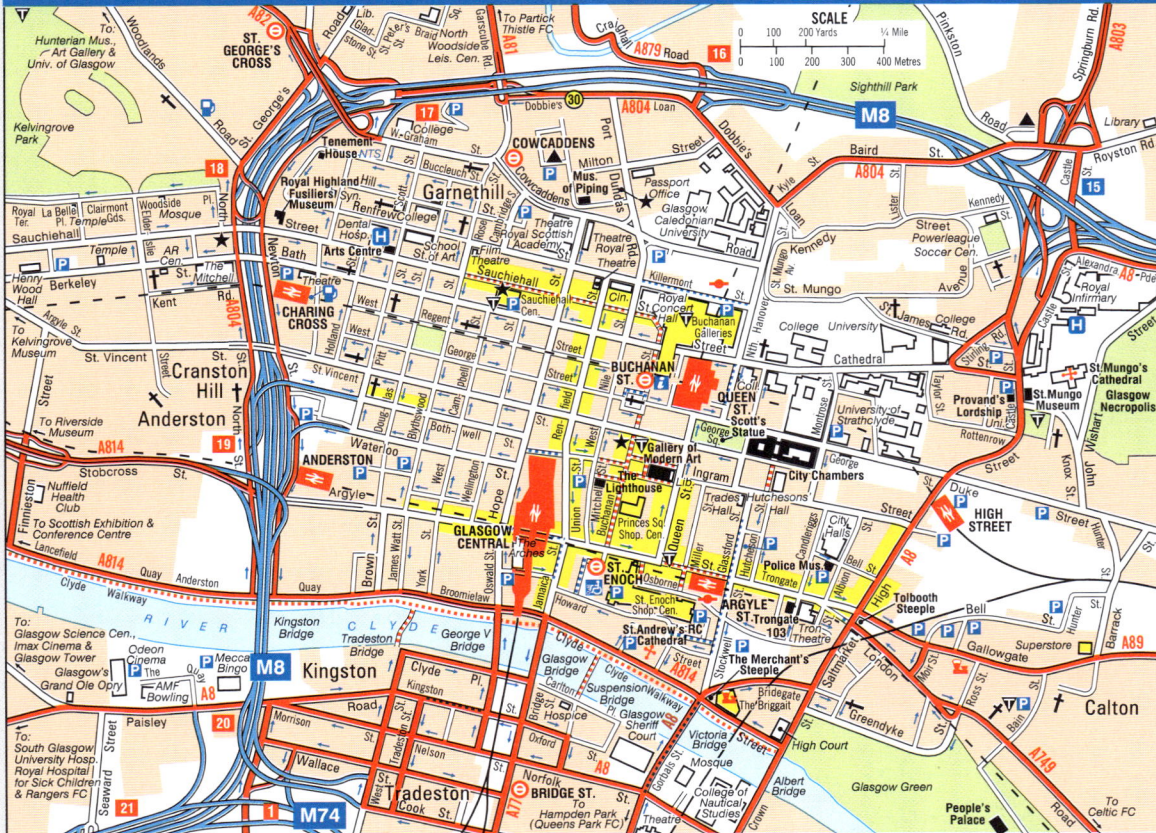

## GLOUCESTER

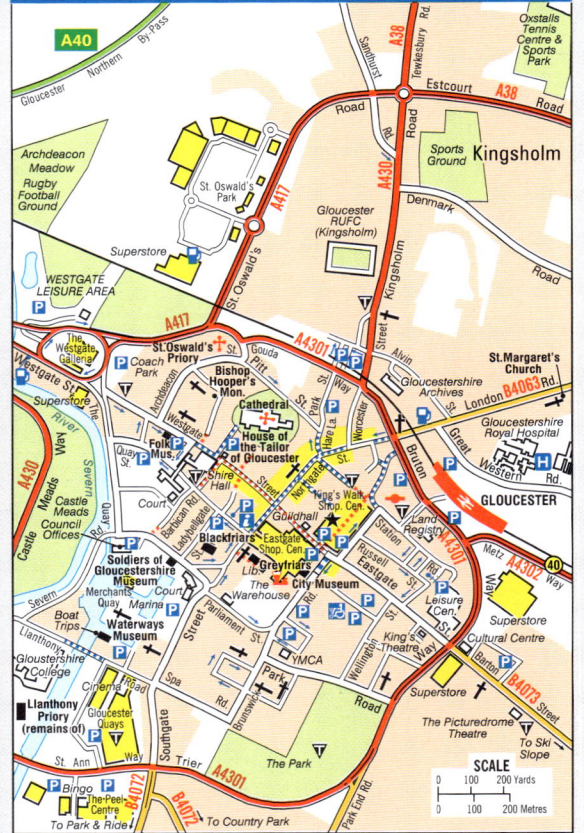

## HARROGATE

## INVERNESS

## IPSWICH

## KILMARNOCK

## LEEDS

## KINGSTON UPON HULL

## LEICESTER

## LINCOLN

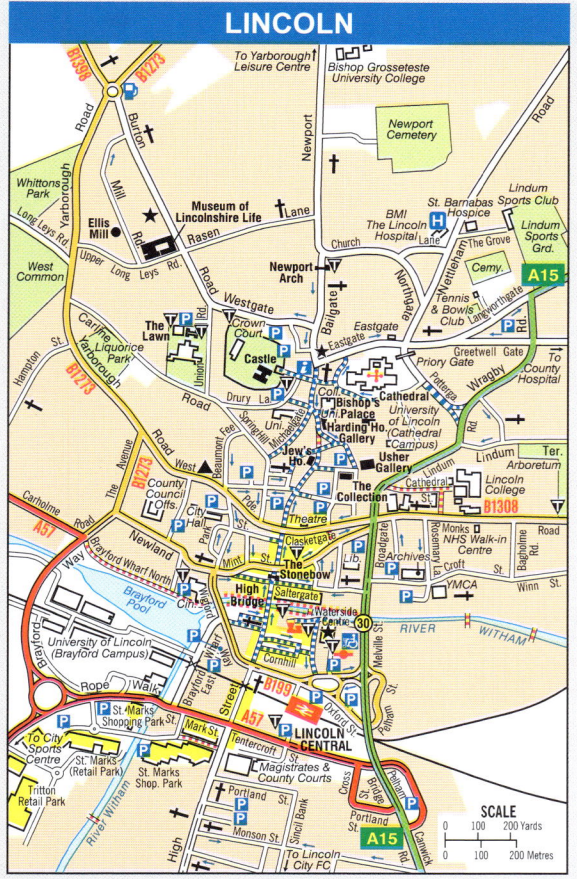

## LIVERPOOL

## MANCHESTER (CITY CENTRE)

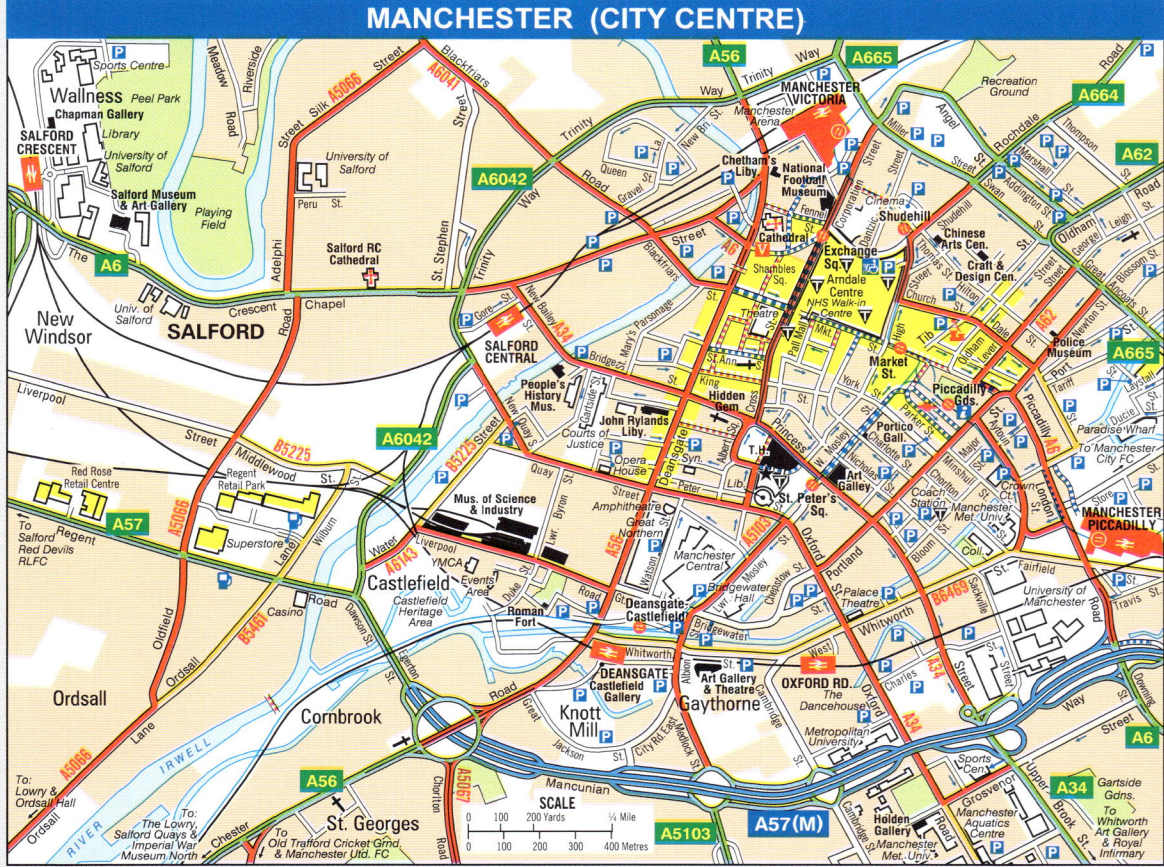

## MIDDLESBROUGH

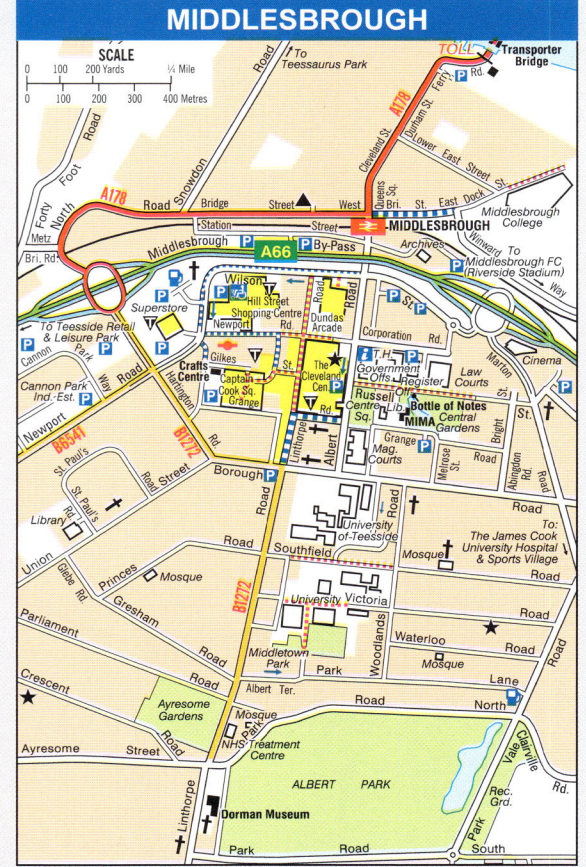

## MEDWAY TOWNS

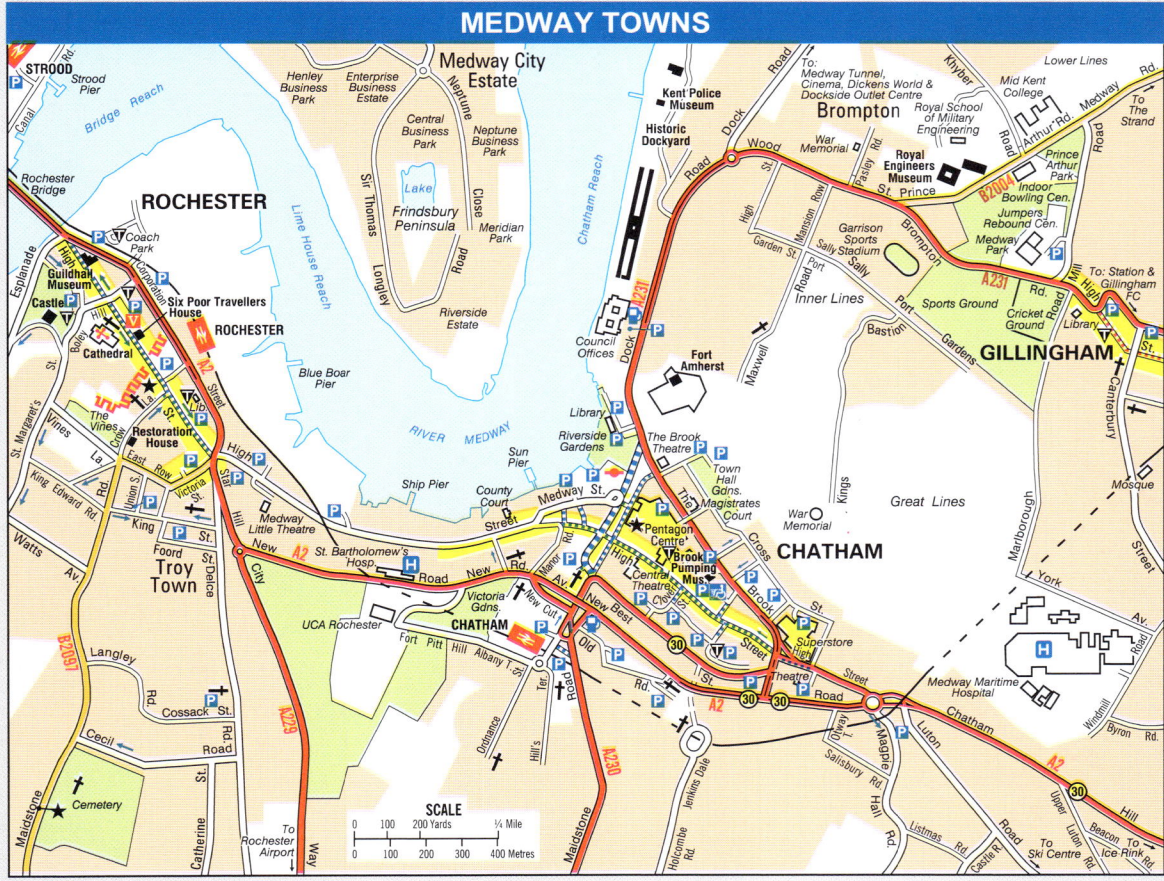

## NEWCASTLE UPON TYNE

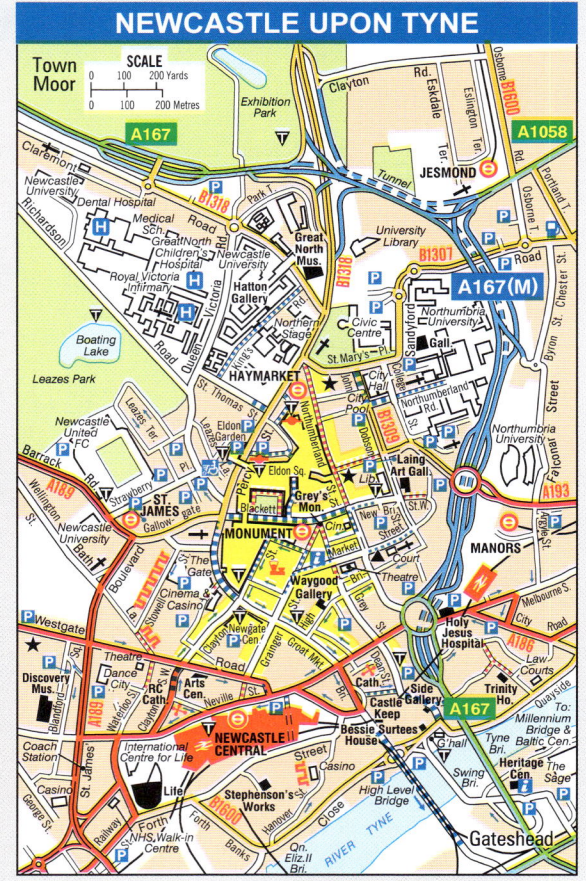

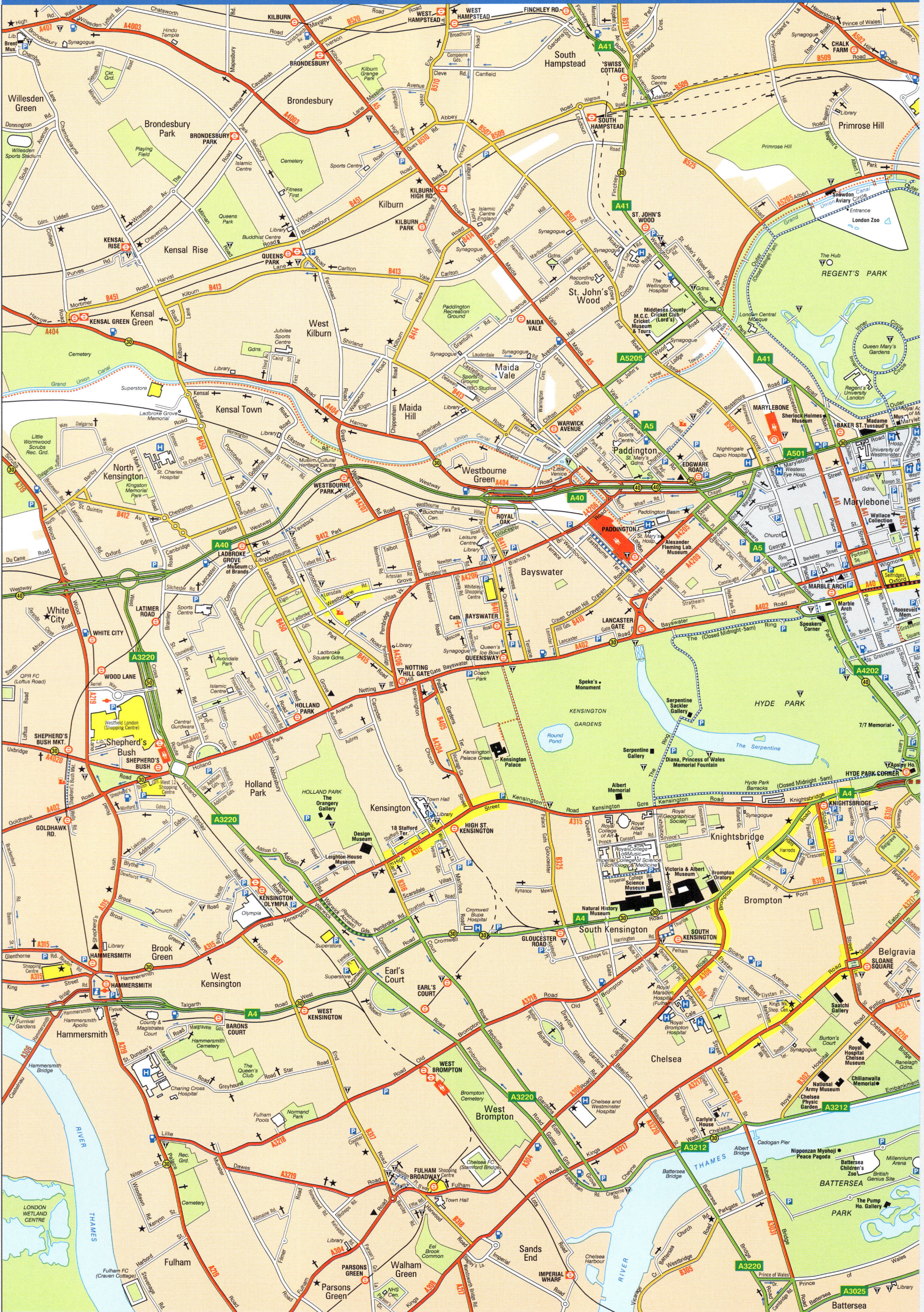

Willesden Green

Brondesbury Park

Brondesbury

Kilburn

Kensal Rise

Kensal Green

West Kilburn

Kensal Town

Maida Hill

Maida Vale

St. John's Wood

South Hampstead

Swiss Cottage

Primrose Hill

REGENT'S PARK

London Zoo

Marylebone

North Kensington

Westbourne Green

Westbourne Park

Paddington

Edgware Road

Marble Arch

White City

Ladbroke Grove

Latimer Road

Bayswater

Lancaster Gate

Queensway

Notting Hill Gate

HYDE PARK

Speaker's Corner

Shepherd's Bush

Holland Park

KENSINGTON GARDENS

The Serpentine

Knightsbridge

Kensington

South Kensington

Brompton

Belgravia

Sloane Square

Hammersmith

Brook Green

West Kensington

Barons Court

Earl's Court

West Brompton

Chelsea

Fulham

West Brompton

Parsons Green

Walham Green

Sands End

Imperial Wharf

Battersea

BATTERSEA PARK

RIVER THAMES

LONDON WETLAND CENTRE

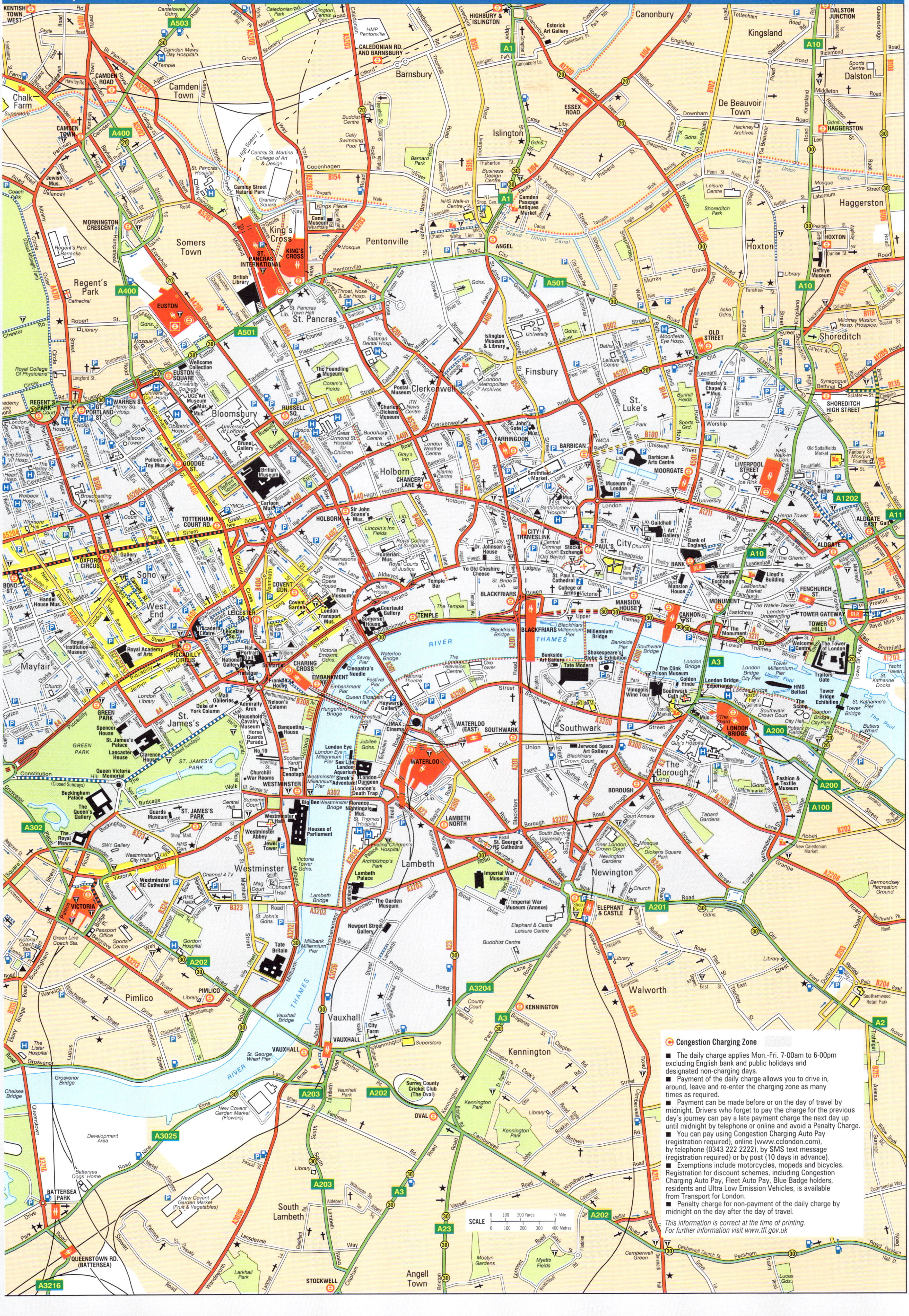

**Congestion Charging Zone**

■ The daily charge applies Mon.–Fri. 7·00am to 6·00pm excluding English bank and public holidays and designated non-charging days.

■ Payment of the daily charge allows you to drive in, around, leave and re-enter the charging zone as many times as required.

■ Payment can be made before or on the day of travel by midnight. Drivers who forget to pay the charge for the previous day's journey can pay a late payment charge the next day up until midnight by telephone or online and avoid a Penalty Charge.

■ You can pay using Congestion Charging Auto Pay (registration required), online (www.cclondon.com), by telephone (0343 222 2222), by SMS text message (registration required) or by post (10 days in advance).

■ Exemptions include motorcycles, mopeds and bicycles. Registration for discount schemes, including Congestion Charging Auto Pay, Fleet Auto Pay, Blue Badge holders, residents and Ultra Low Emission Vehicles, is available from Transport for London.

■ Penalty charge for non-payment of the daily charge by midnight on the day after the day of travel.

This information is correct at the time of printing. For further information visit www.tfl.gov.uk

SCALE

0    100    200 yards

0    200    400    600 Metres

## MILTON KEYNES

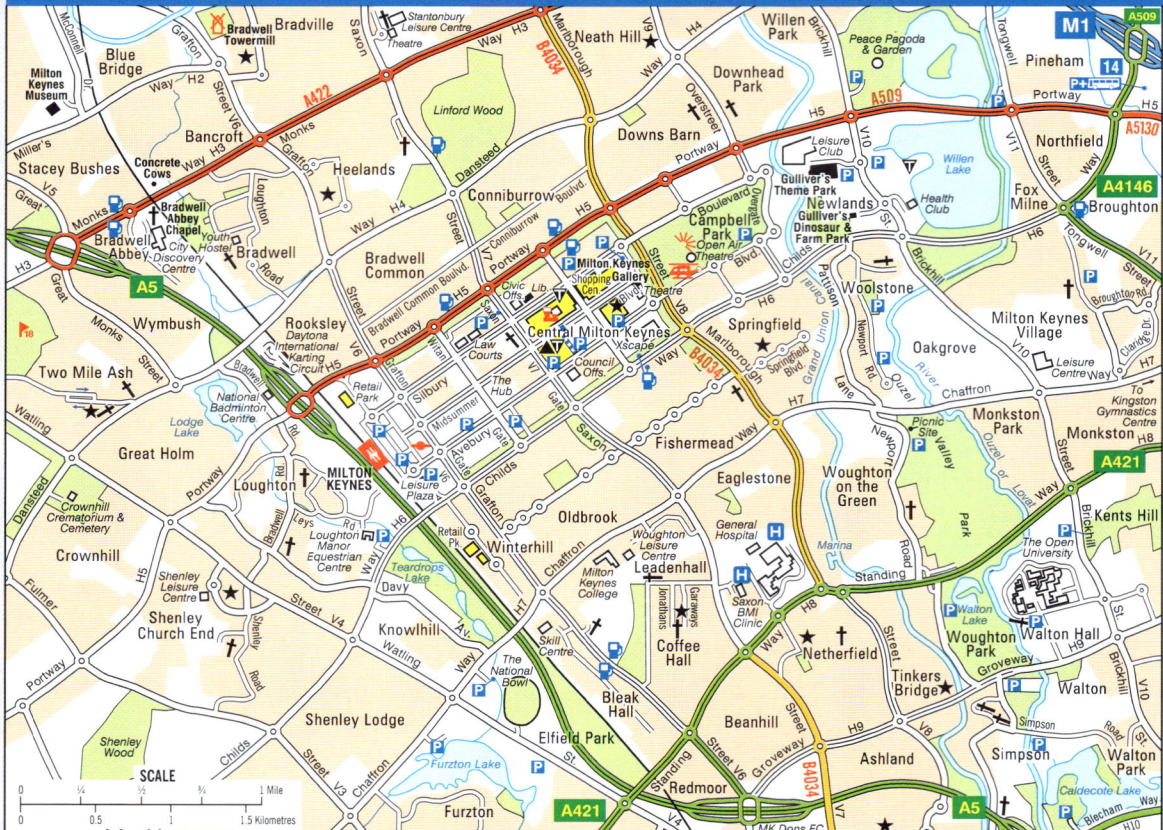

## NEWPORT (CASNEWYDD)

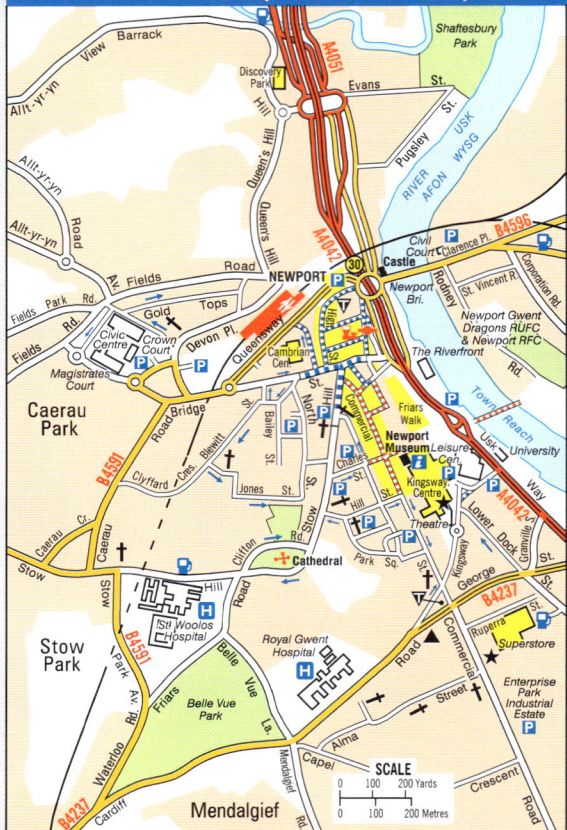

## NORWICH

## NOTTINGHAM

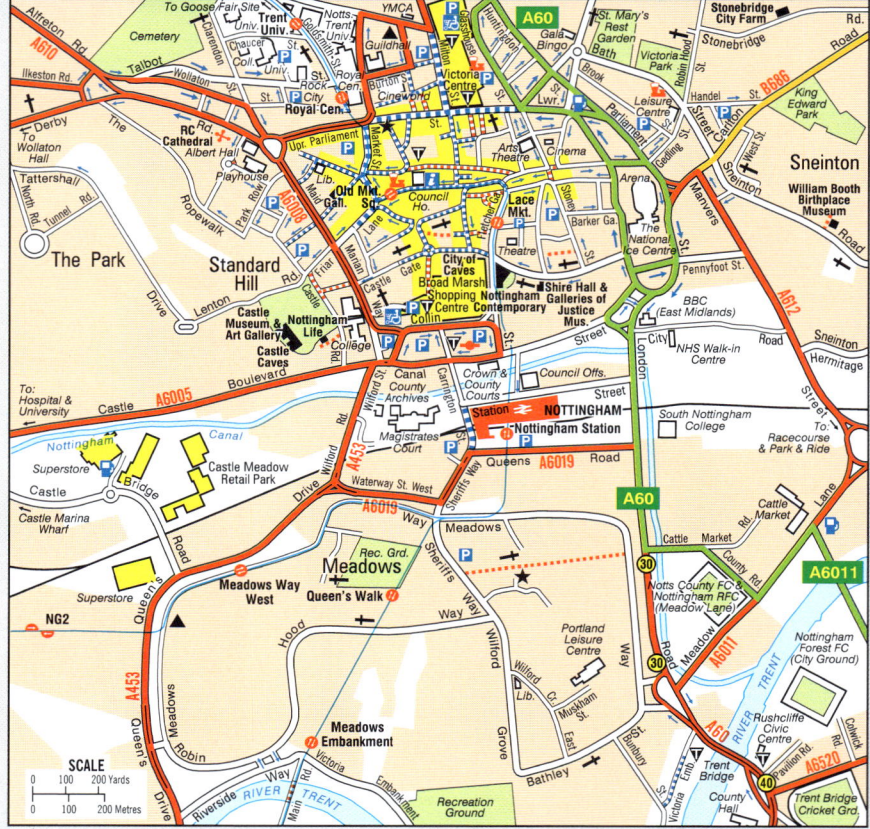

## NORTHAMPTON

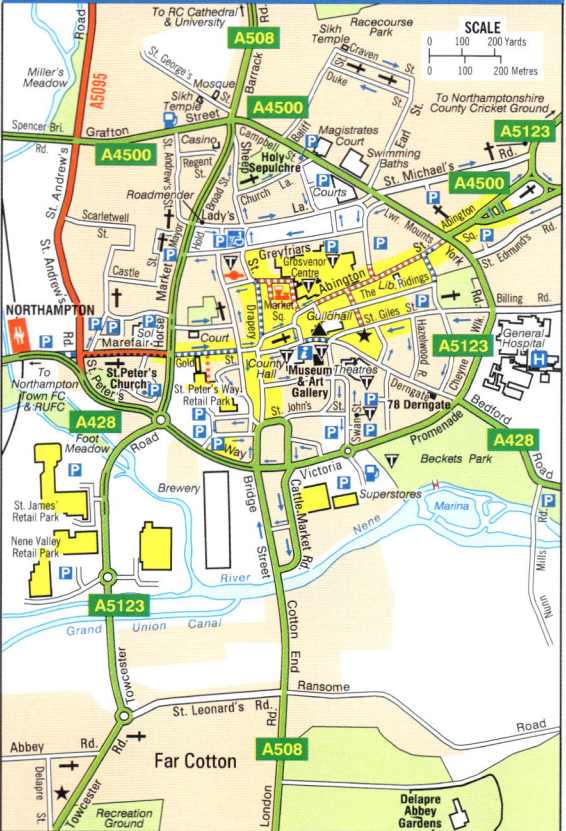

## OXFORD

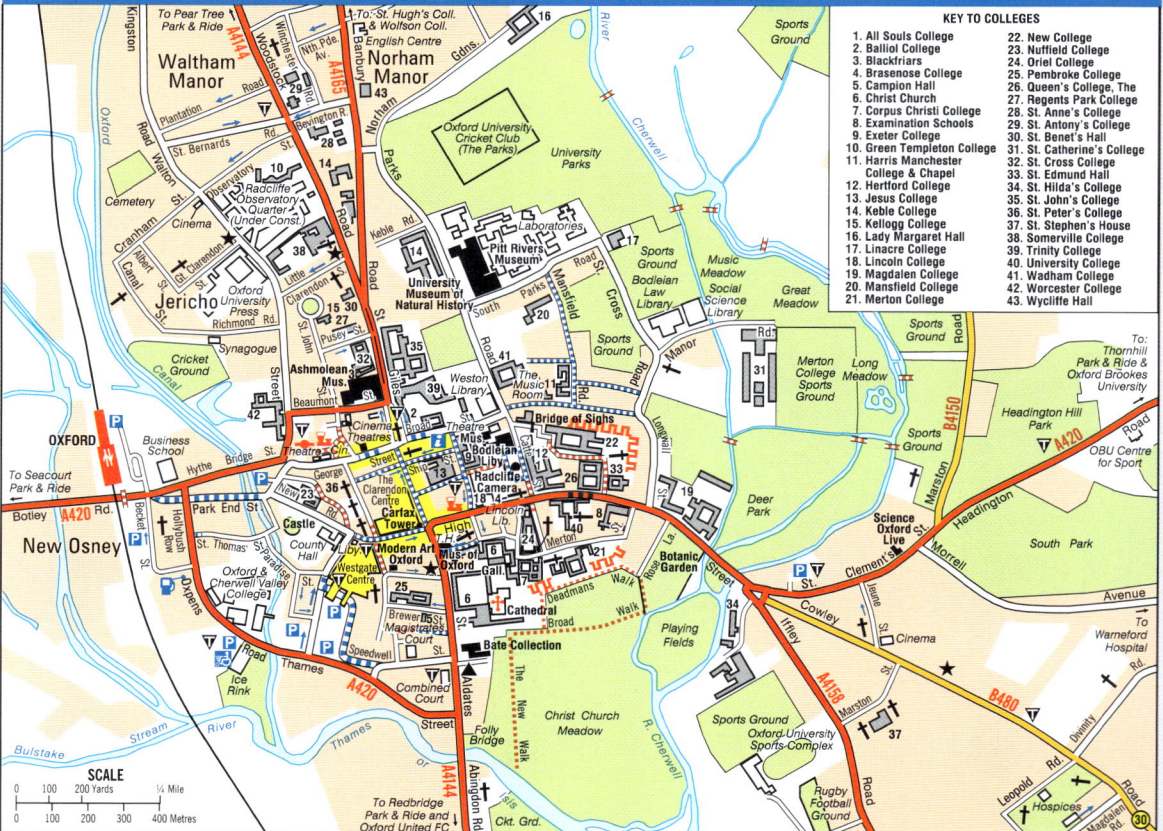

KEY TO COLLEGES
1. All Souls College
2. Balliol College
3. Blackfriars
4. Brasenose College
5. Campion Hall
6. Christ Church
7. Corpus Christi College
8. Examination Schools
9. Exeter College
10. Green Templeton College
11. Harris Manchester College & Chapel
12. Hertford College
13. Jesus College
14. Keble College
15. Kellogg College
16. Lady Margaret Hall
17. Linacre College
18. Lincoln College
19. Magdalen College
20. Mansfield College
21. Merton College
22. New College
23. Nuffield College
24. Oriel College
25. Pembroke College
26. Queen's College, The
27. Regents Park College
28. St. Anne's College
29. St. Antony's College
30. St. Benet's Hall
31. St. Catherine's College
32. St. Cross College
33. St. Edmund Hall
34. St. Hilda's College
35. St. John's College
36. St. Peter's College
37. St. Stephen's House
38. Somerville College
39. Trinity College
40. University College
41. Wadham College
42. Worcester College
43. Wycliffe Hall

## OBAN
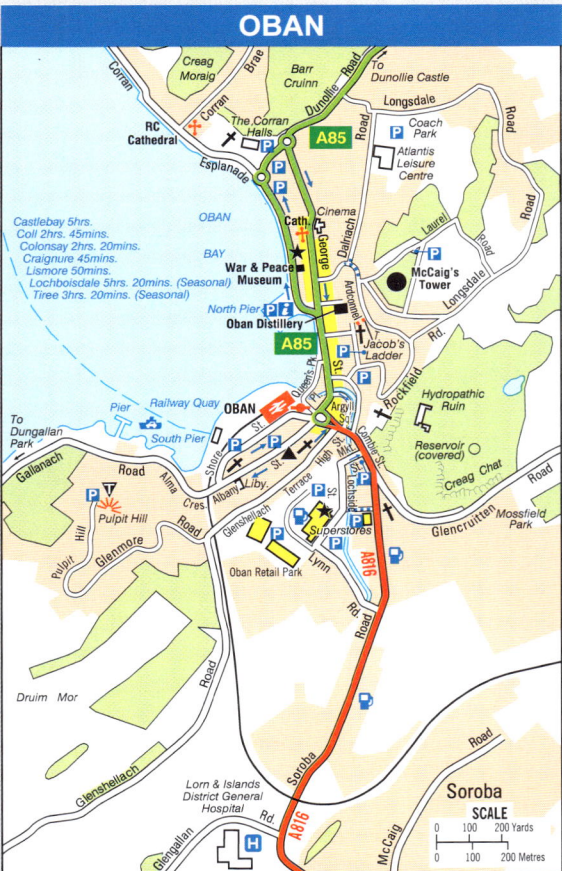

## PERTH
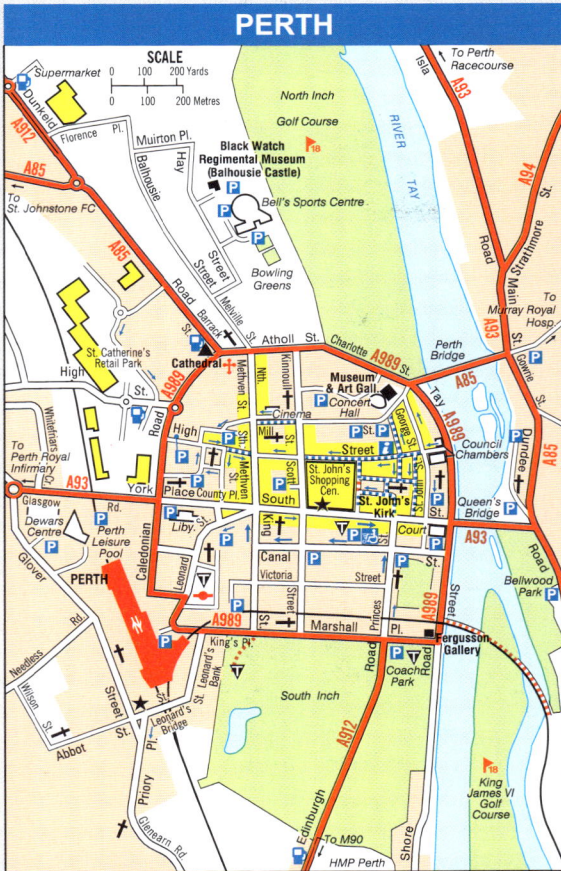

## PETERBOROUGH
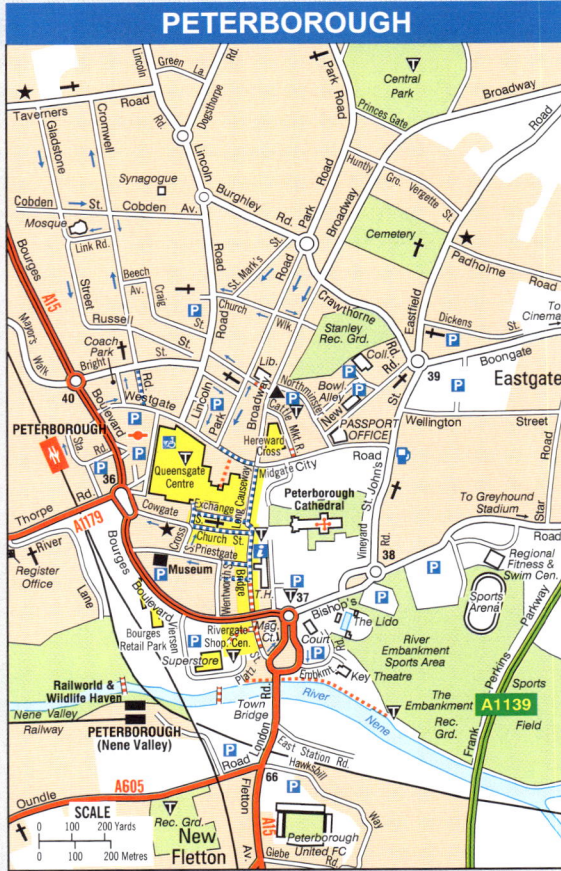

## PLYMOUTH
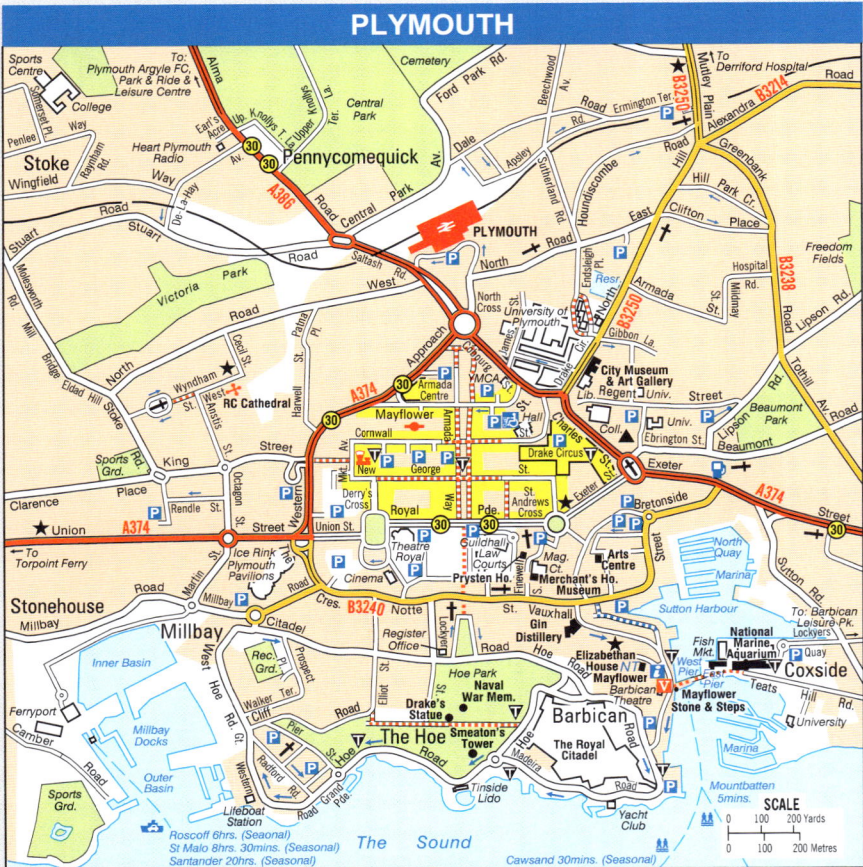

## PORTSMOUTH
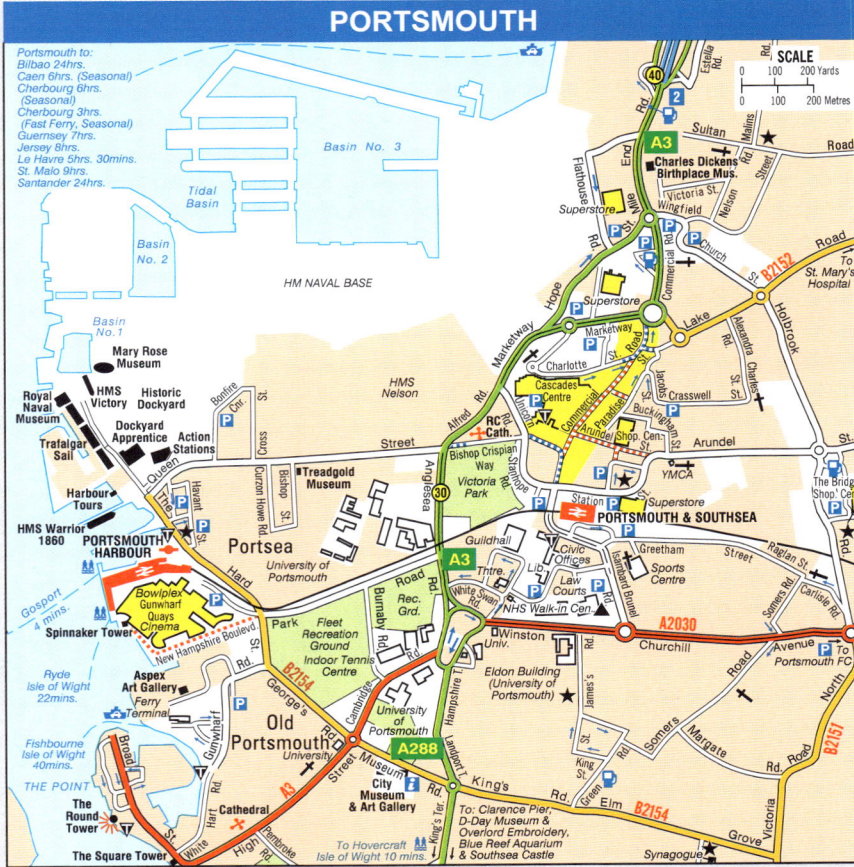

## PRESTON

## READING
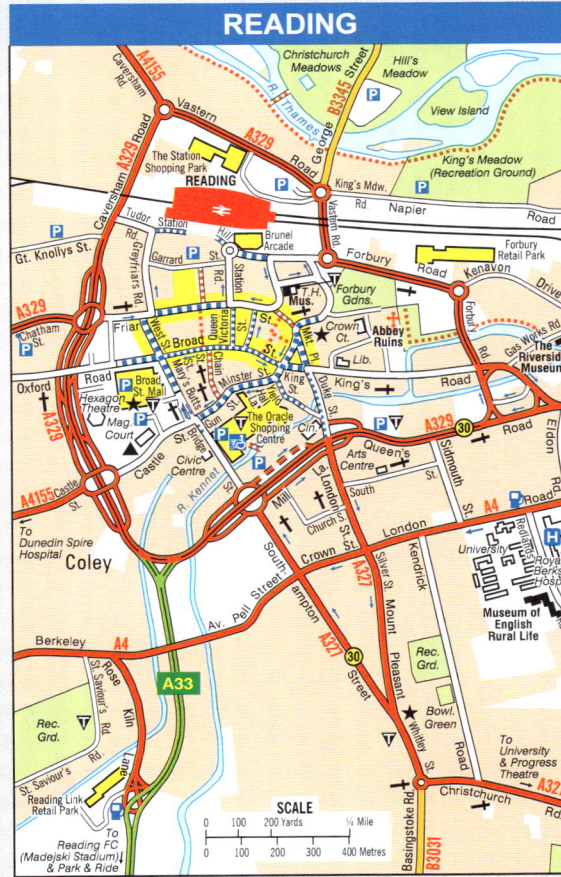

## SALISBURY
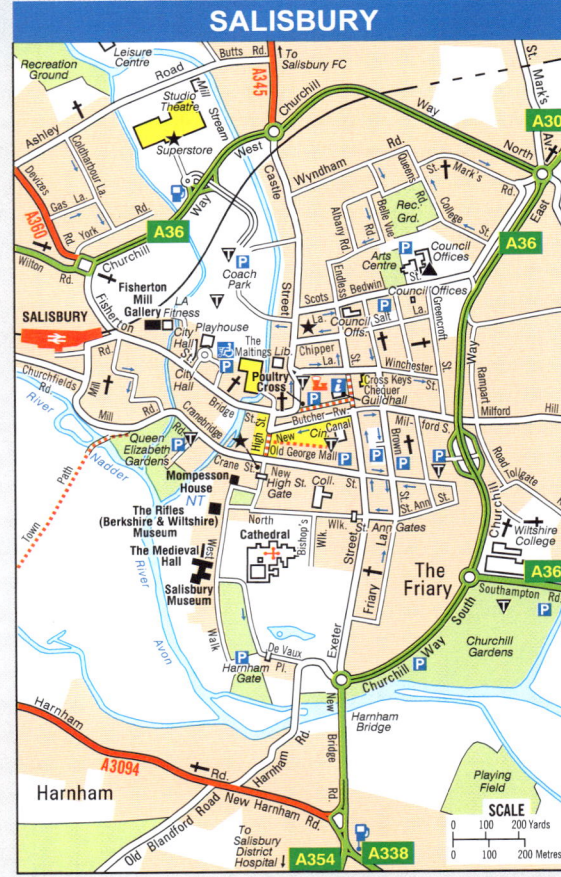

# SHEFFIELD

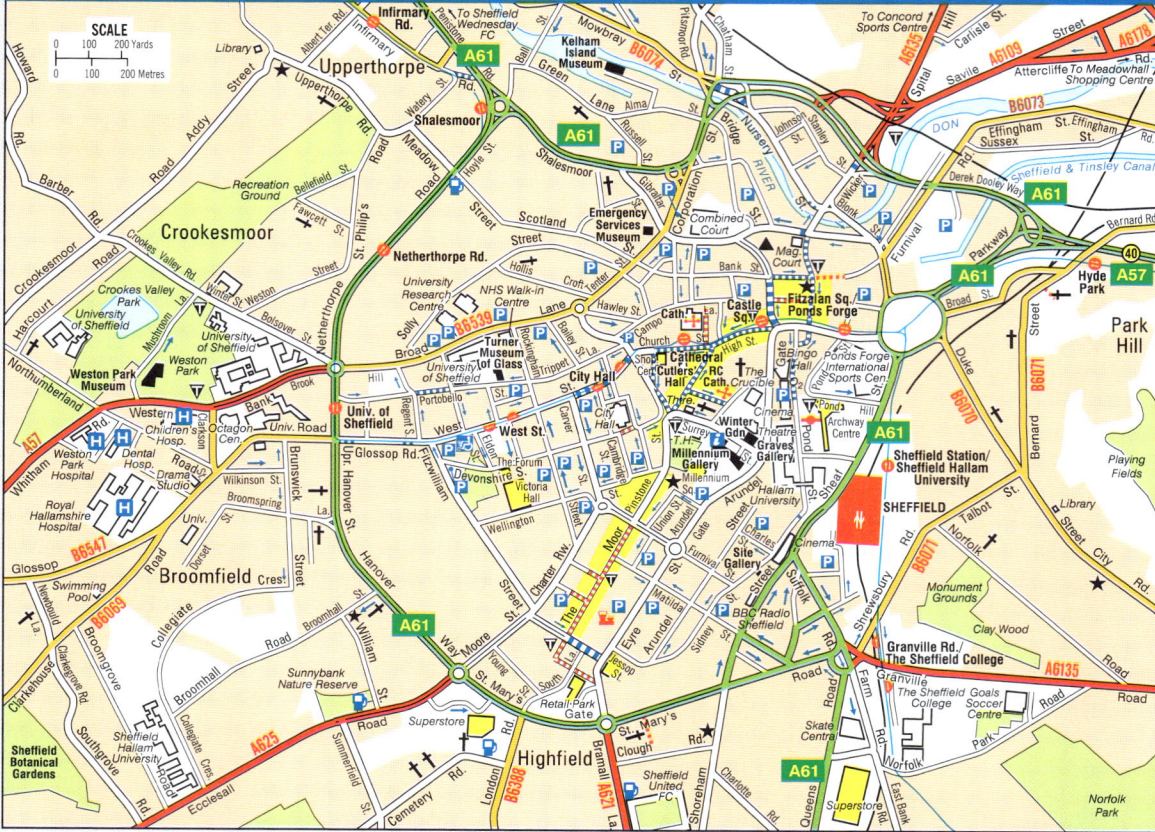

# SHREWSBURY

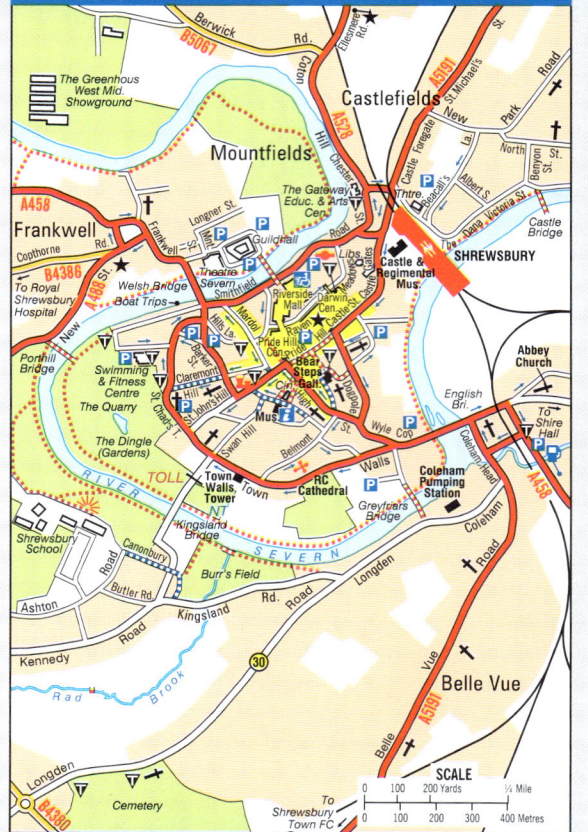

# SOUTHAMPTON

# STIRLING

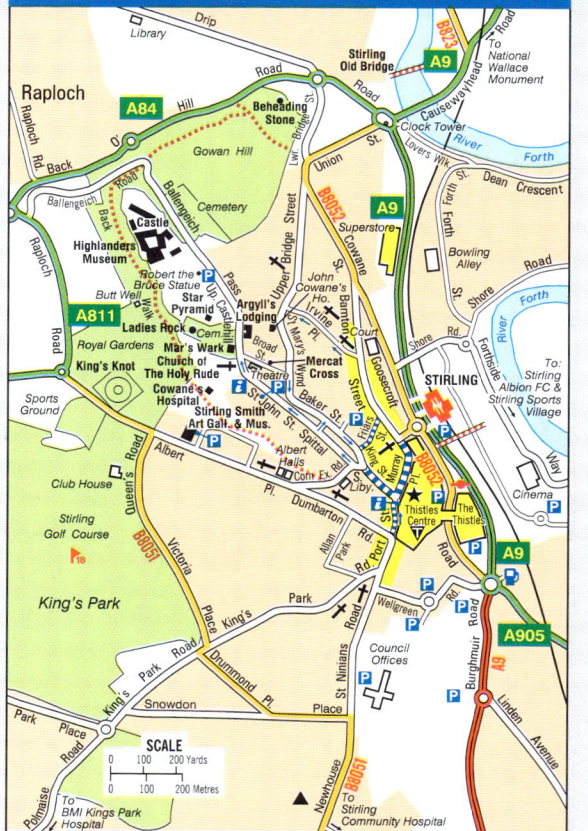

# STOKE-ON-TRENT

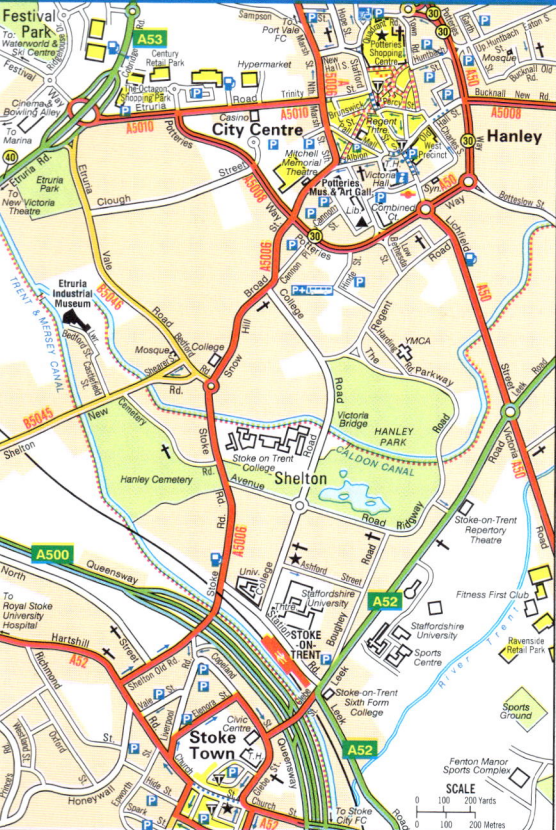

# STRATFORD UPON AVON

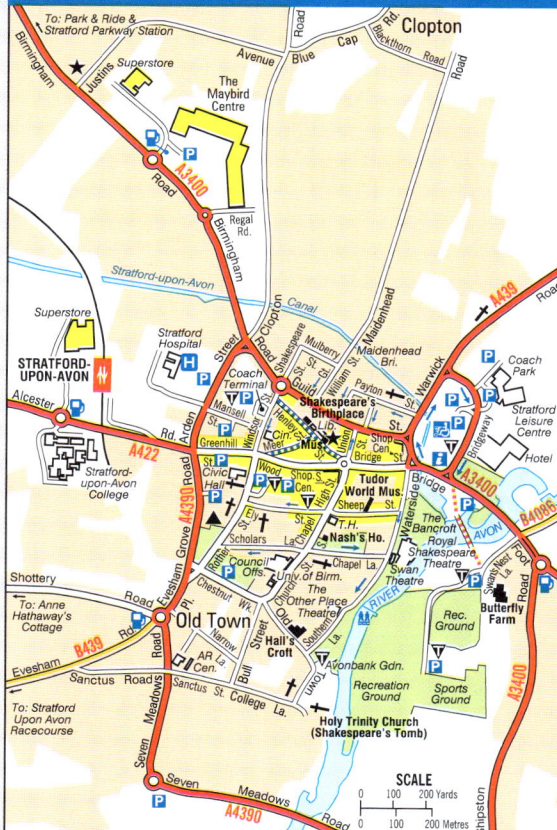

# SUNDERLAND

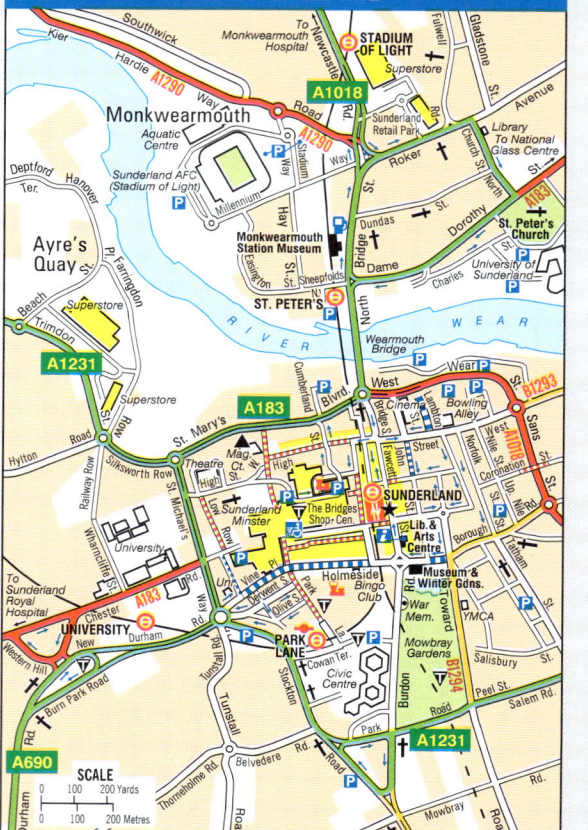

## SWANSEA (ABERTAWE)

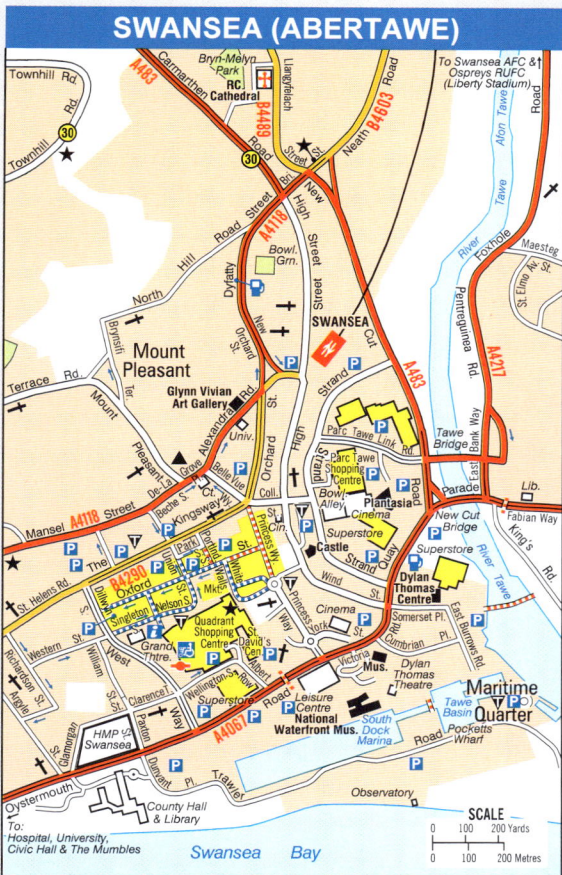

## SWINDON

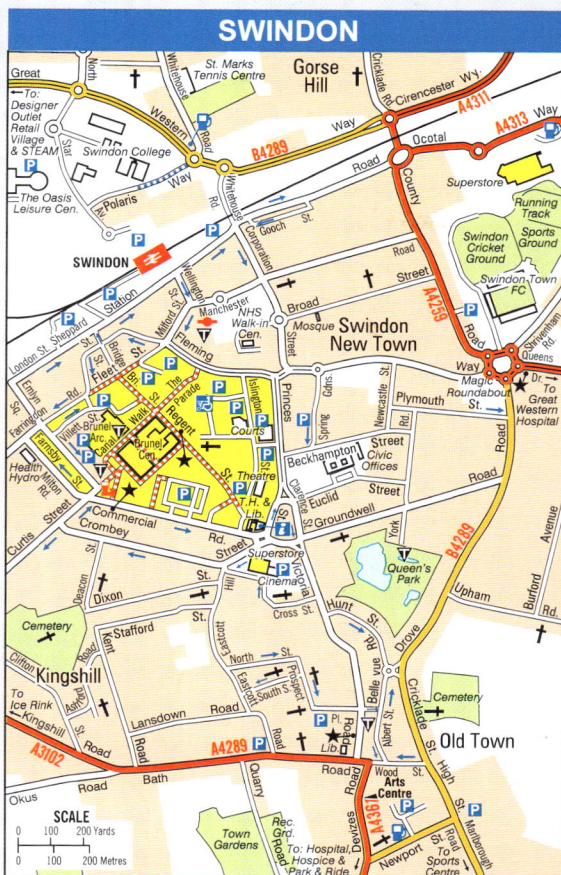

## TAUNTON

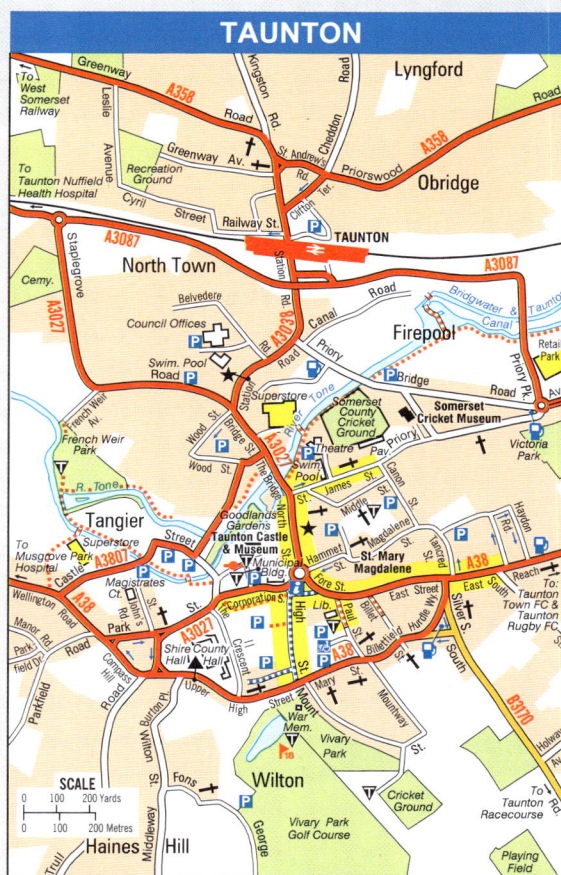

## WINCHESTER

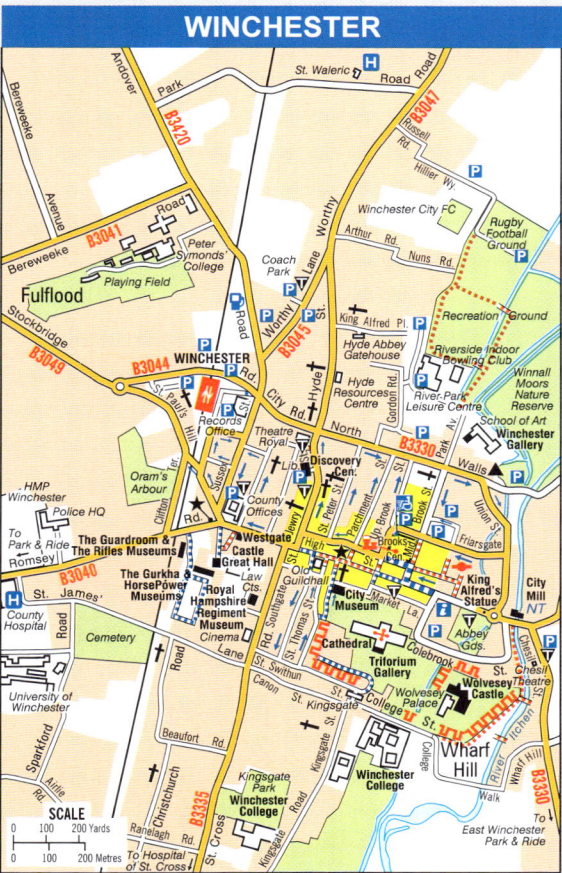

## WINDSOR

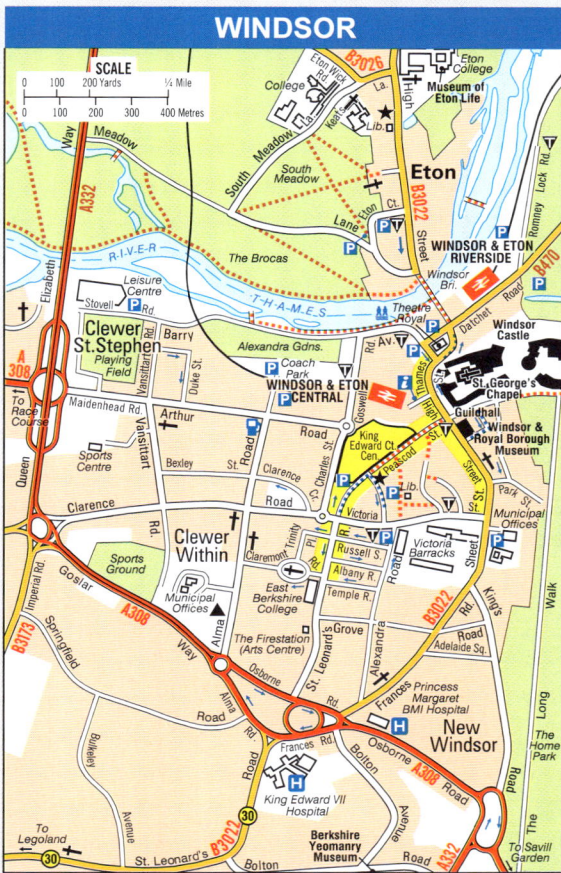

## WOLVERHAMPTON

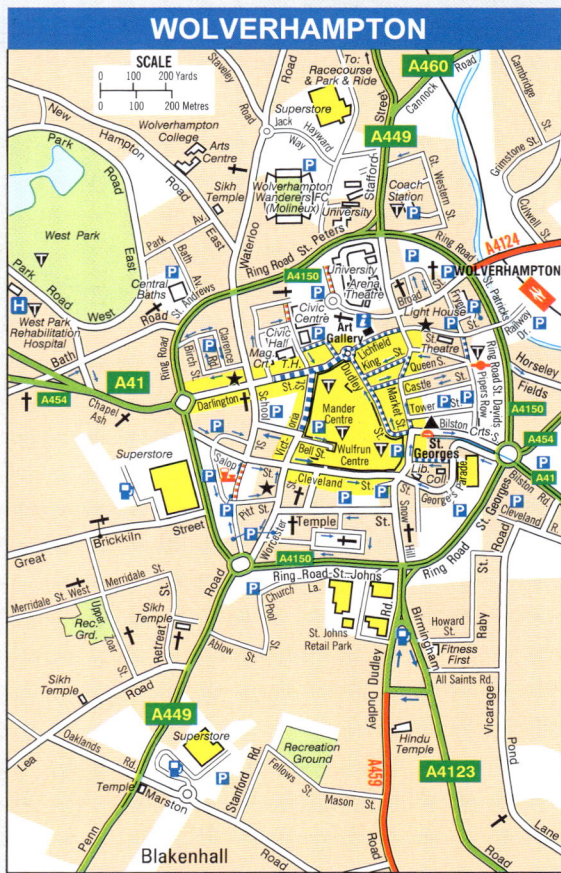

## WORCESTER

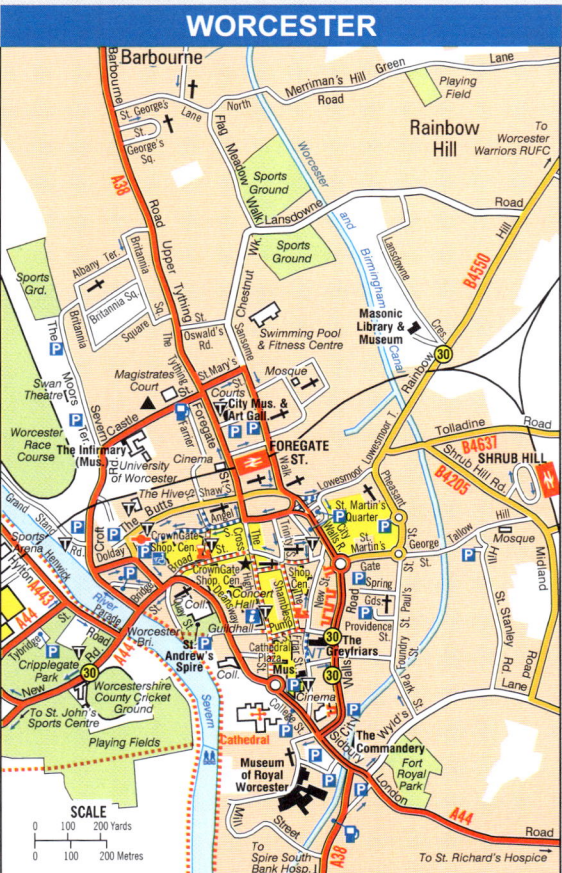

## YORK

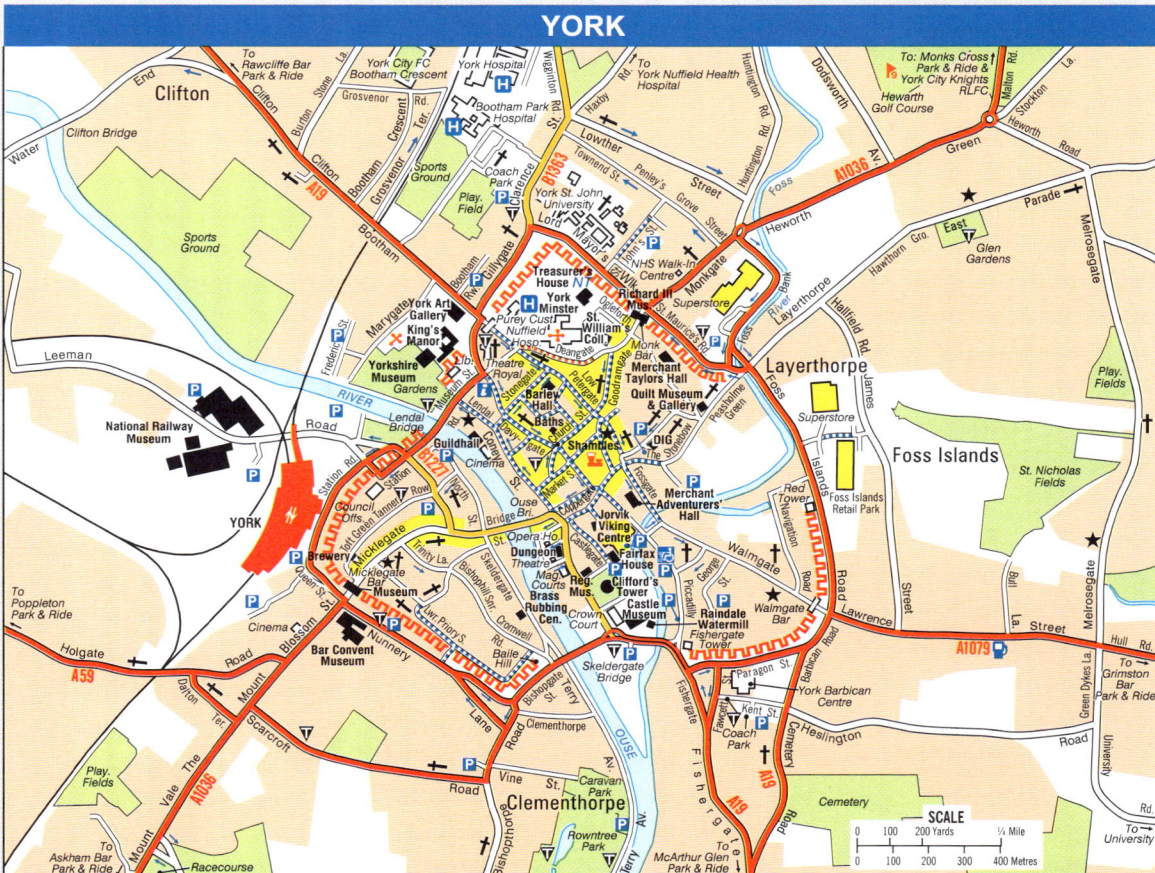

## HARWICH

## KINGSTON UPON HULL

## NEWCASTLE UPON TYNE

## NEWHAVEN

## PEMBROKE DOCK (DOC PENFRO)

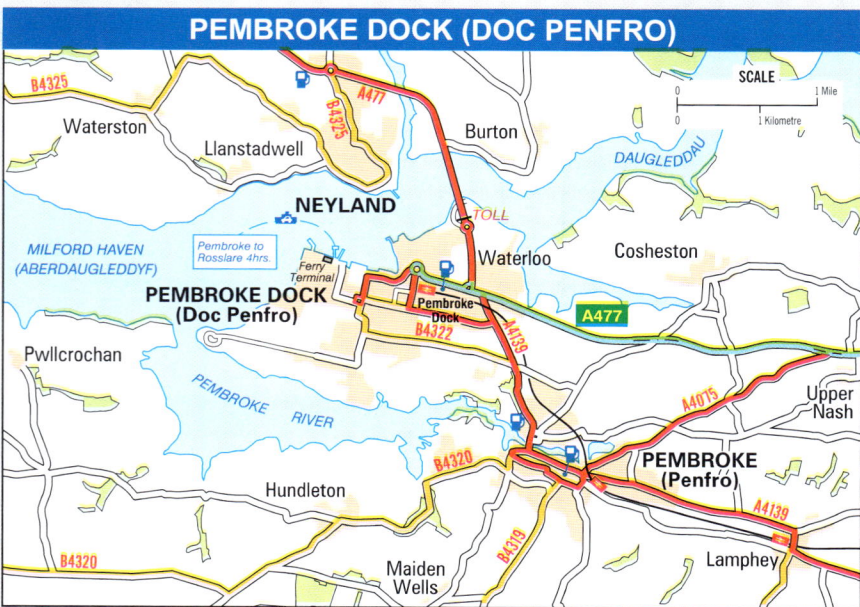

## POOLE

## PORTSMOUTH

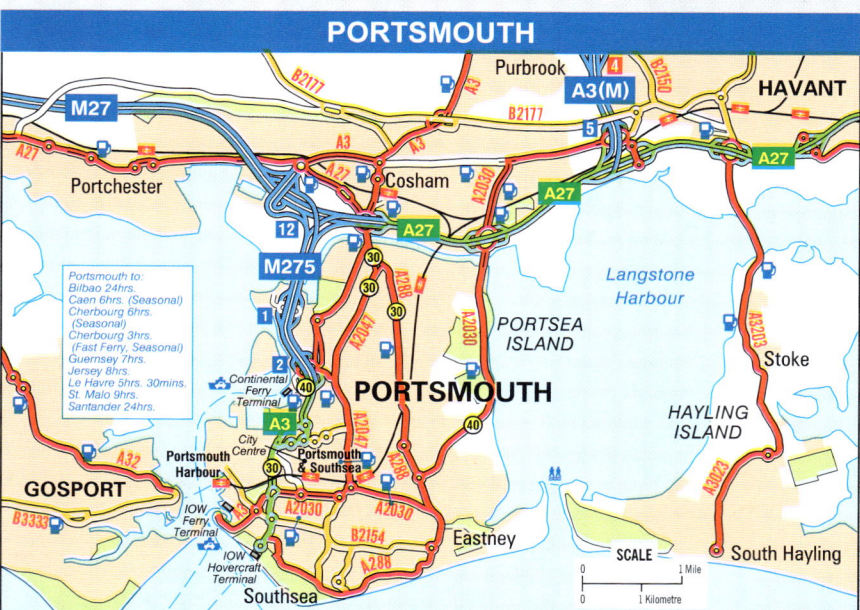

## WEYMOUTH

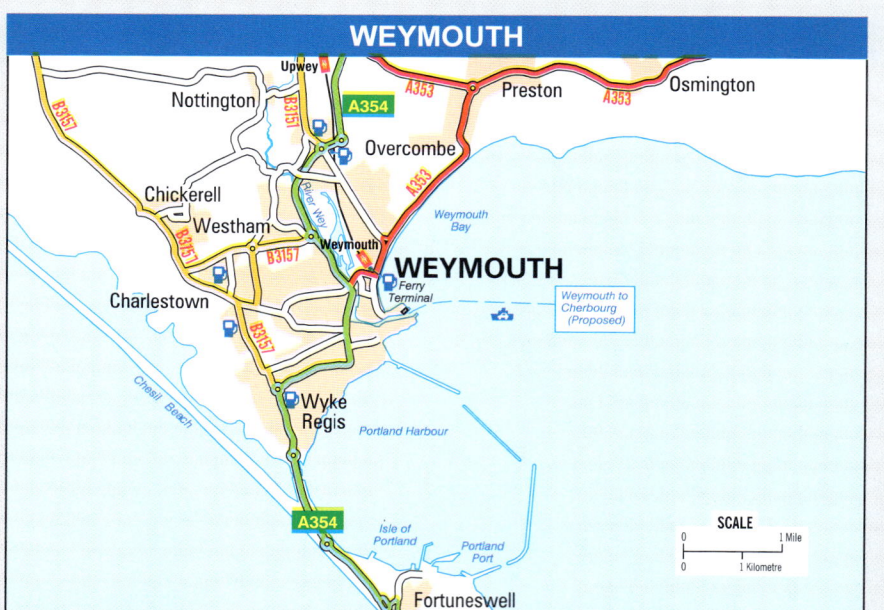

## BIRMINGHAM

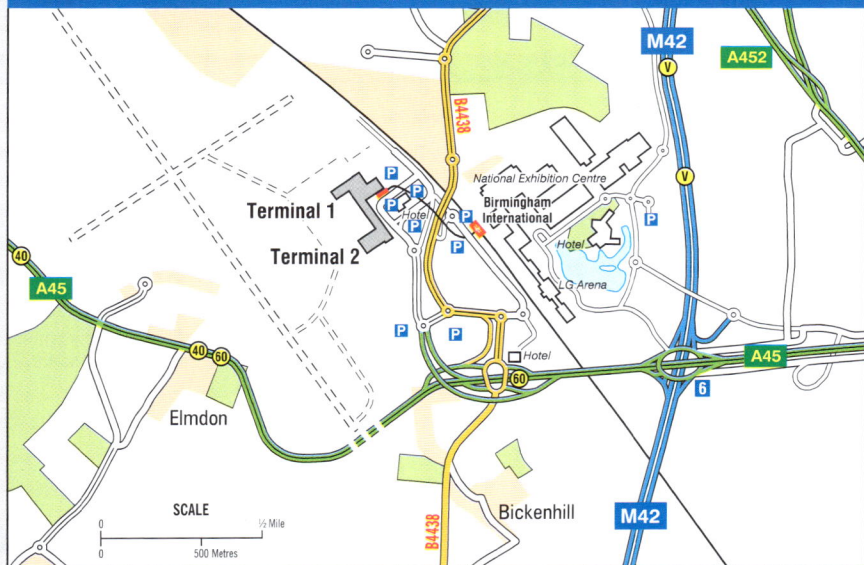

## EAST MIDLANDS

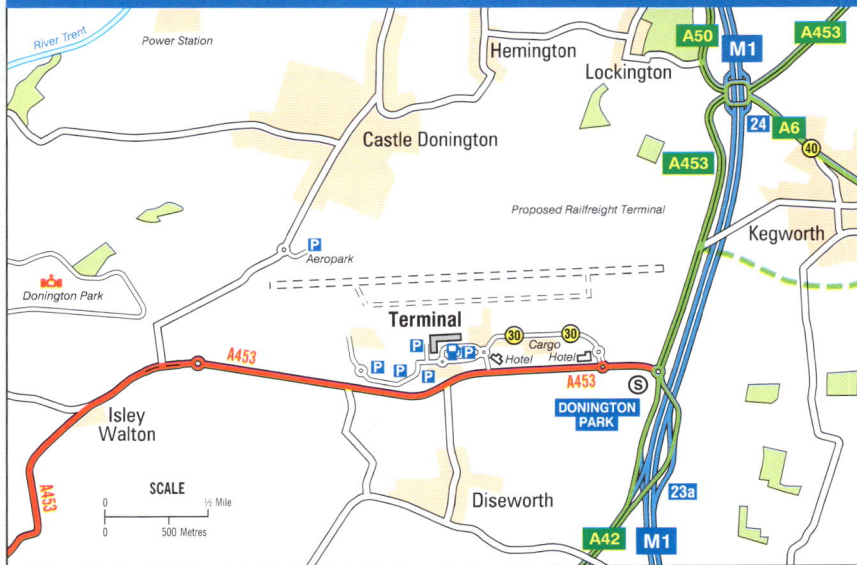

## GLASGOW

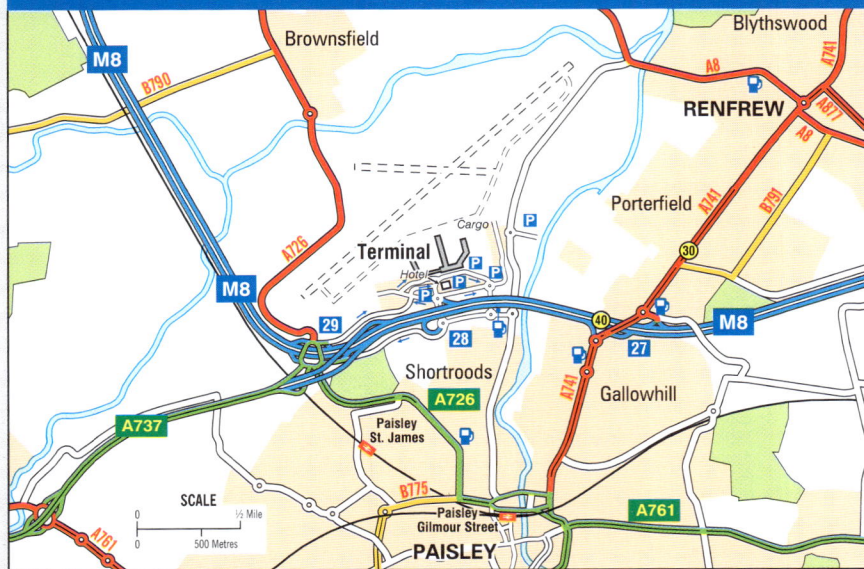

## LONDON GATWICK

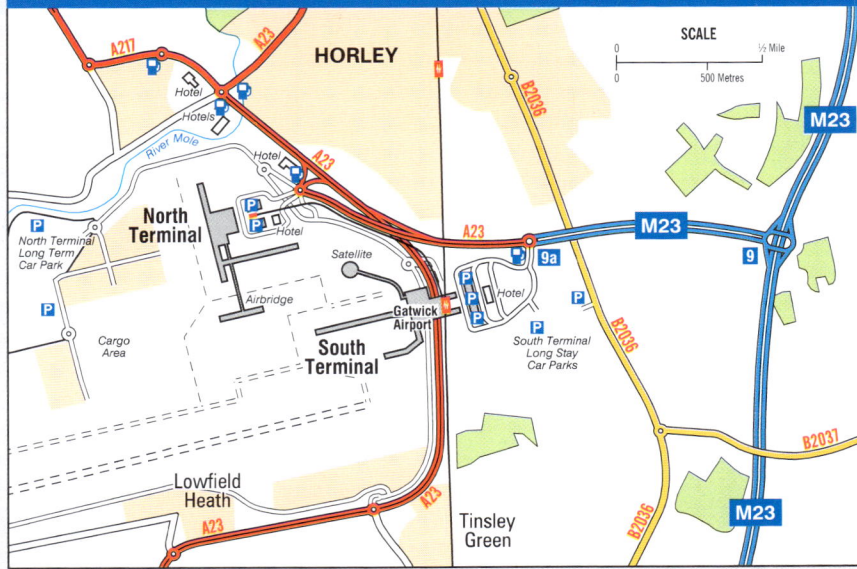

## LONDON HEATHROW

## LONDON LUTON

## LONDON STANSTED

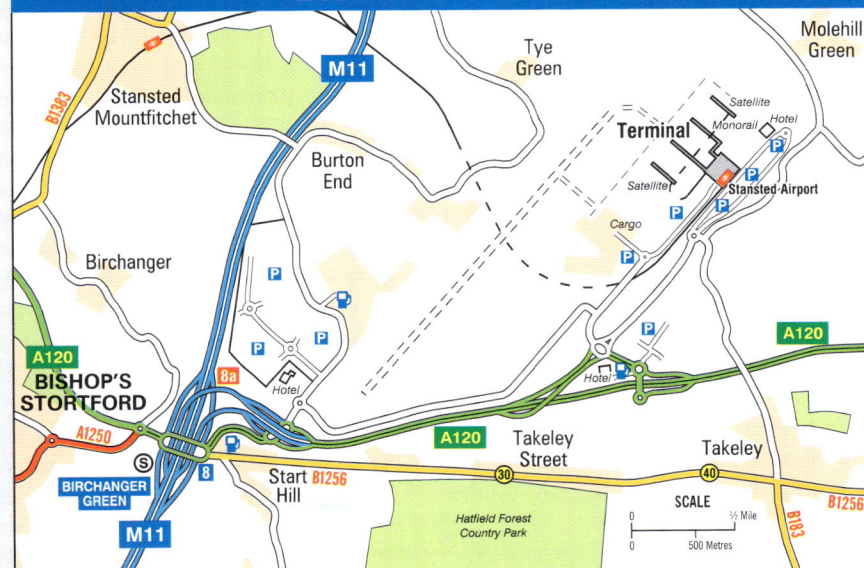

## MANCHESTER

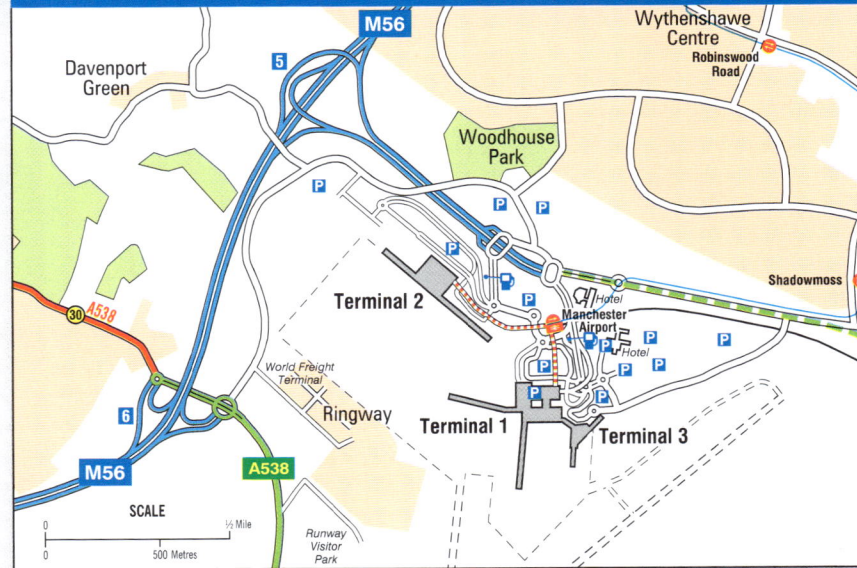

# INDEX TO CITIES, TOWNS, VILLAGES, HAMLETS, LOCATIONS, AIRPORTS & PORTS

(1) A strict alphabetical order is used e.g. An Dùnan follows Andreas but precedes Andwell.

(2) The map reference given refers to the actual map square in which the town spot or built-up area is located and not to the place name.

(3) Major towns and destinations are shown in bold, i.e. **Aberdeen**. *Aber* . . . .3G **153** & **192** Where they appear on a Town Plan a second page reference is given.

(4) Where two or more places of the same name occur in the same County or Unitary Authority, the nearest large town is also given; e.g. Achiemore. *High* . . . .2D **166** (nr. Durness) indicates that Achiemore is located in square 2D on page **166** and is situated near Durness in the Unitary Authority of Highland.

(5) Only one reference is given although due to page overlaps the place may appear on more than one page.

## COUNTIES and UNITARY AUTHORITIES with the abbreviations used in this index

Aberdeen : *Aber*
Aberdeenshire : *Abers*
Angus : *Ang*
Antrim & Newtownabbey : *Ant*
Argyll & Bute : *Arg*
Armagh, Banbridge & Craigavon : *Arm*
Bath & N E Somerset : *Bath*
Bedford : *Bed*
Belfast : *Bel*
Blackburn with Darwen : *Bkbn*
Blackpool : *Bkpl*
Blaenau Gwent : *Blae*
Bournemouth : *Bour*
Bracknell Forest : *Brac*
Bridgend : *B'end*
Brighton & Hove : *Brig*
Bristol : *Bris*
Buckinghamshire : *Buck*
Caerphilly : *Cphy*
Cambridgeshire : *Cambs*
Cardiff : *Card*
Carmarthenshire : *Carm*
Causeway Coast & Glens : *Caus*
Central Bedfordshire : *C Beds*
Ceredigion : *Cdgn*
Cheshire East : *Ches E*
Cheshire West & Chester : *Ches W*
Clackmannanshire : *Clac*
Conwy : *Cnwy*
Cornwall : *Corn*
Cumbria : *Cumb*
Darlington : *Darl*
Denbighshire : *Den*
Derby : *Derb*
Derbyshire : *Derbs*
Derry & Strabane : *Derr*
Devon : *Devn*
Dorset : *Dors*
Dumfries & Galloway : *Dum*
Dundee : *D'dee*
Durham : *Dur*
East Ayrshire : *E Ayr*
East Dunbartonshire : *E Dun*
East Lothian : *E Lot*
East Renfrewshire : *E Ren*
East Riding of Yorkshire : *E Yor*
East Sussex : *E Sus*
Edinburgh : *Edin*
Essex : *Essx*
Falkirk : *Falk*
Fermanagh & Omagh : *Ferm*
Fife : *Fife*
Flintshire : *Flin*
Glasgow : *Glas*
Gloucestershire : *Glos*
Greater London : *G Lon*
Greater Manchester : *G Man*
Gwynedd : *Gwyn*
Halton : *Hal*
Hampshire : *Hants*
Hartlepool : *Hart*
Herefordshire : *Here*
Hertfordshire : *Herts*
Highland : *High*
Inverclyde : *Inv*
Isle of Anglesey : *IOA*
Isle of Man : *IOM*
Isle of Wight : *IOW*
Isles of Scilly : *IOS*
Kent : *Kent*
Kingston upon Hull : *Hull*
Lancashire : *Lanc*
Leicester : *Leic*
Leicestershire : *Leics*
Lincolnshire : *Linc*
Lisburn & Castlereagh : *Lis*
Luton : *Lutn*
Medway : *Medw*
Merseyside : *Mers*
Merthyr Tydfil : *Mer T*
Mid & East Antrim : *ME Ant*
Middlesbrough : *Midd*
Midlothian : *Midl*
Mid Ulster : *M Ulst*
Milton Keynes : *Mil*
Monmouthshire : *Mon*
Moray : *Mor*
Neath Port Talbot : *Neat*
Newport : *Newp*
Newry, Mourne & Down : *New M*
Norfolk : *Norf*
Northamptonshire : *Nptn*
North Ayrshire : *N Ayr*
North Down & Ards : *N Dwn*
North East Lincolnshire : *NE Lin*
North Lanarkshire : *N Lan*
North Lincolnshire : *N Lin*
North Somerset : *N Som*
Northumberland : *Nmbd*
North Yorkshire : *N Yor*
Nottingham : *Nott*
Nottinghamshire : *Notts*
Orkney : *Orkn*
Oxfordshire : *Oxon*
Pembrokeshire : *Pemb*
Perth & Kinross : *Per*
Peterborough : *Pet*
Plymouth : *Plym*
Poole : *Pool*
Portsmouth : *Port*
Powys : *Powy*
Reading : *Read*
Redcar & Cleveland : *Red C*
Renfrewshire : *Ren*
Rhondda Cynon Taff : *Rhon*
Rutland : *Rut*
Scottish Borders : *Bord*
Shetland : *Shet*
Shropshire : *Shrp*
Slough : *Slo*
Somerset : *Som*
Southampton : *Sotn*
South Ayrshire : *S Ayr*
Southend-on-Sea : *S'end*
South Gloucestershire : *S Glo*
South Lanarkshire : *S Lan*
South Yorkshire : *S Yor*
Staffordshire : *Staf*
Stirling : *Stir*
Stockton-on-Tees : *Stoc T*
Stoke-on-Trent : *Stoke*
Suffolk : *Suff*
Surrey : *Surr*
Swansea : *Swan*
Swindon : *Swin*
Telford & Wrekin : *Telf*
Thurrock : *Thur*
Torbay : *Torb*
Torfaen : *Torf*
Tyne & Wear : *Tyne*
Vale of Glamorgan, The : *V Glam*
Warrington : *Warr*
Warwickshire : *Warw*
West Berkshire : *W Ber*
West Dunbartonshire : *W Dun*
Western Isles : *W Isl*
West Lothian : *W Lot*
West Midlands : *W Mid*
West Sussex : *W Sus*
West Yorkshire : *W Yor*
Wiltshire : *Wilts*
Windsor & Maidenhead : *Wind*
Wokingham : *Wok*
Worcestershire : *Worc*
Wrexham : *Wrex*
York : *York*

## INDEX

### A


Abbas Combe. *Som* 4C **22**
Abberley. *Worc* 4B **60**
Abberley Common. *Worc* 4B **60**
Abberton. *Essx* 4D **54**
Abberton. *Worc* 5D **61**
Abberwick. *Nmbd* 3F **121**
Abbess Roding. *Essx* 4F **53**
Abbey. *Devn* 1E **13**
Abbey-cwm-hir. *Powy* 3C **58**
Abbeydale. *S Yor* 2H **85**
Abbeydale Park. *S Yor* 2H **85**
Abbey Dore. *Here* 2G **47**
Abbey Gate. *Devn* 3F **13**
Abbey Hulton. *Stoke* 1D **72**
Abbey St Bathans. *Bord* 3D **130**
Abbeystead. *Lanc* 4E **97**
Abbeytown. *Cumb* 4C **112**
Abbey Village. *Lanc* 2E **91**
Abbey Wood. *G Lon* 3F **39**
Abbots Bickington. *Devn* 1D **11**
Abbots Bromley. *Staf* 3E **73**
Abbotsbury. *Dors* 4A **14**
Abbotsham. *Devn* 4E **19**
Abbotskerswell. *Devn* 2E **9**
Abbots Langley. *Herts* 5A **52**
Abbots Leigh. *N Som* 4A **34**
Abbotsley. *Cambs* 5B **64**
Abbots Morton. *Worc* 5E **61**
Abbots Ripton. *Cambs* 3B **64**
Abbot's Salford. *Warw* 5E **61**
Abbotstone. *Hants* 3D **24**
Abbots Worthy. *Hants* 3C **24**
Abbotts Ann. *Hants* 2B **24**
Abcott. *Shrp* 3F **59**
Abdon. *Shrp* 2H **59**
Abenhall. *Glos* 4B **48**
Aber. *Cdgn* 1E **45**
Aberaeron. *Cdgn* 4D **56**
Aberafan. *Neat* 3G **31**
Aberaman. *Rhon* 5D **46**
Aberangell. *Powy* 4H **69**
Aberarad. *Carm* 1H **43**
Aberarder. *High* 1A **150**
Aberargie. *Per* 2D **136**
Aberarth. *Cdgn* 4D **57**
Aberavon. *Neat* 3G **31**
Aber-banc. *Cdgn* 1D **44**
Aberbargoed. *Cphy* 2E **33**
Aberbechan. *Powy* 1D **58**
Aberbeeg. *Blae* 5F **47**
Aberbowlan. *Carm* 2G **45**
Aberbran. *Powy* 3C **46**
Abercanaid. *Mer T* 5D **46**
Abercarn. *Cphy* 2F **33**
Abercastle. *Pemb* 1C **42**
Abercegir. *Powy* 5H **69**
Aberchalder. *High* 3F **149**
Aberchirder. *Abers* 3D **160**
Aberchwiler. *Den* 4C **82**
Abercorn. *W Lot* 2D **129**
Abercraf. *Powy* 4B **46**
Abercregan. *Neat* 2B **32**
Abercrombie. *Fife* 3H **137**
Abercwmboi. *Rhon* 2D **32**
Abercych. *Pemb* 1C **44**
**Abercynon**. *Rhon* 2D **32**
Aber-Cywarch. *Gwyn* 4A **70**
Aberdalgie. *Per* 1C **136**
**Aberdar**. *Rhon* 5C **46**
**Aberdare**. *Rhon* 5C **46**
Aberdaron. *Gwyn* 3A **68**
**Aberdaugleddau**. *Pemb* 4D **42**
**Aberdeen**. *Aber* 3G **153** & **192**
Aberdeen International Airport. *Aber* 2F **153**
Aberdesach. *Gwyn* 5D **80**
Aberdour. *Fife* 1E **129**
Aberdovey. *Gwyn* 1F **57**
Aberdulais. *Neat* 5A **46**
Aberdyfi. *Gwyn* 1F **57**
Aberedw. *Powy* 1D **46**
Abereiddy. *Pemb* 1B **42**
Abererch. *Gwyn* 2C **68**
Aberfan. *Mer T* 5D **46**
Aberfeldy. *Per* 4F **143**
Aberffraw. *IOA* 4C **80**
Aberffrwd. *Cdgn* 3F **57**
Aberford. *W Yor* 1E **93**
Aberfoyle. *Stir* 3E **135**
Abergarw. *B'end* 3C **32**
Abergarwed. *Neat* 5B **46**
**Abergavenny**. *Mon* 4G **47**
Abergele. *Cnwy* 3B **82**
Aber-Giâr. *Carm* 1F **45**
Abergorlech. *Carm* 2F **45**
Abergwaun. *Pemb* 1D **42**
Abergwesyn. *Powy* 5A **58**
Abergwili. *Carm* 3E **45**
Abergwynfi. *Neat* 2B **32**
Abergwyngregyn. *Gwyn* 3F **81**
Abergynolwyn. *Gwyn* 5F **69**
Aberhafesp. *Powy* 1C **58**
Aberhonddu. *Powy* 3D **46**
Aberhosan. *Powy* 1H **57**
Aberkenfig. *B'end* 3B **32**
Aberlady. *E Lot* 1A **130**
Aberlemno. *Ang* 3E **145**
Aberllefenni. *Gwyn* 5G **69**
Abermaw. *Gwyn* 4F **69**
Abermeurig. *Cdgn* 5E **57**
Aber-miwl. *Powy* 1D **58**
Abermule. *Powy* 1D **58**
Abernant. *Carm* 2H **43**
Abernant. *Rhon* 5D **46**
Abernethy. *Per* 2D **136**
Abernyte. *Per* 5B **144**
Aber-oer. *Wrex* 1E **71**
**Aberpennar**. *Rhon* 2D **32**
Aberporth. *Cdgn* 5B **56**
Aberriw. *Powy* 5D **70**
Abersoch. *Gwyn* 3C **68**
Abersychan. *Torf* 5F **47**
**Abertawe**. *Swan* 3F **31** & **Swansea 203**
Aberteifi. *Cdgn* 1B **44**
Aberthin. *V Glam* 4D **32**
**Abertillery**. *Blae* 5F **47**
Abertridwr. *Cphy* 3E **32**
Abertridwr. *Powy* 4C **70**
**Abertyleri**. *Blae* 5F **47**
Abertysswg. *Cphy* 5E **47**
Aberuthven. *Per* 2B **136**
Aber Village. *Powy* 3E **46**
Aberwheeler. *Den* 4C **82**
Aberyscir. *Powy* 3C **46**
**Aberystwyth**. *Cdgn* 2E **57**
Abhainn Suidhe. *W Isl* 7C **171**
**Abingdon-on-Thames**. *Oxon* 2C **36**
Abinger Common. *Surr* 1C **26**
Abinger Hammer. *Surr* 1B **26**
Abington. *S Lan* 2B **118**
Abington Pigotts. *Cambs* 1D **52**
Ab Kettleby. *Leics* 3E **74**
Ab Lench. *Worc* 5E **61**
Ablington. *Glos* 5G **49**
Ablington. *Wilts* 2G **23**
Abney. *Derbs* 3F **85**
Aboyne. *Abers* 4C **152**
**Abram**. *G Man* 4E **90**
Abriachan. *High* 5H **157**
Abridge. *Essx* 1F **39**
Abronhill. *N Lan* 2A **128**
Abson. *S Glo* 4C **34**
Abthorpe. *Nptn* 1E **51**
Abune-the-Hill. *Orkn* 5B **172**
Aby. *Linc* 3D **88**
Acairseid. *W Isl* 8C **170**
Acaster Malbis. *York* 5H **99**
Acaster Selby. *N Yor* 5H **99**
Accott. *Devn* 3G **19**
**Accrington**. *Lanc* 2F **91**
Acha. *Arg* 3C **138**
Achachork. *High* 4D **155**
Achadh a' Chuirn. *High* 1E **147**
Achahoish. *Arg* 2F **125**
Achaleven. *Arg* 5D **140**
Achallader. *Arg* 4H **141**
Acha Mor. *W Isl* 5F **171**
Achanalt. *High* 2E **157**
Achandunie. *High* 1A **158**
Ach' an Todhair. *High* 1E **141**
Achany. *High* 3C **164**
Achaphubuil. *High* 1E **141**
Acharacle. *High* 2A **140**
Acharn. *Ang* 1B **144**
Acharn. *Per* 4E **143**
Acharole. *High* 3E **169**
Achateny. *High* 2G **139**
Achavanich. *High* 4D **169**
Achdalieu. *High* 1E **141**
Achduart. *High* 3E **163**
Achentoul. *High* 5A **168**
Achfary. *High* 5C **166**
Achfrish. *High* 2C **164**
Achgarve. *High* 4C **162**
Achiemore. *High* 2D **166** (nr. Durness)
Achiemore. *High* 3A **168** (nr. Thurso)
A' Chill. *High* 3A **146**
Achiltibuie. *High* 3E **163**
Achina. *High* 2H **167**
Achinahuagh. *High* 2F **167**
Achindarroch. *High* 3E **141**
Achinduich. *High* 3C **164**
Achinduin. *Arg* 5C **140**
Achininver. *High* 2F **167**
Achintee. *High* 4B **156**
Achintraid. *High* 5H **155**
Achleck. *Arg* 4F **139**
Achlorachan. *High* 3F **157**
Achluachrach. *High* 5E **149**
Achlyness. *High* 3C **166**
Achmelvich. *High* 1E **163**
Achmony. *High* 5H **157**
Achmore. *High* 5A **156** (nr. Stromeferry)
Achmore. *High* 4E **163** (nr. Ullapool)
Achnacarnin. *High* 1E **163**
Achnacarry. *High* 5D **148**
Achnaclerach. *High* 2G **157**
Achnacloich. *High* 3D **147**
Ach na Cloiche. *High* 3D **147**
Achnaconeran. *High* 2G **149**
Achnacroish. *Arg* 4C **140**
Achnafalnich. *Arg* 1B **134**
Achnagarron. *High* 1A **158**
Achnagoul. *Arg* 3H **133**
Achnaha. *High* 2F **139**
Achnahanat. *High* 4C **164**
Achnahannet. *High* 1D **151**
Achnairn. *High* 2C **164**
Achnamara. *Arg* 1F **125**
Achnanellan. *High* 5C **148**
Achnasheen. *High* 3D **156**
Achnashellach. *High* 4C **156**
Achosnich. *High* 2F **139**
Achow. *High* 5E **169**
Achranich. *High* 4B **140**
Achreamie. *High* 2C **168**
Achriabhach. *High* 2F **141**
Achriesgill. *High* 3C **166**
Achrimsdale. *High* 3G **165**
Achscrabster. *High* 2C **168**
Achtoty. *High* 2G **167**
Achurch. *Nptn* 2H **63**
Achuvoldrach. *High* 3F **167**
Achvaich. *High* 4E **164**
Achvoan. *High* 3E **165**
Ackenthwaite. *Cumb* 1E **97**
Ackergill. *High* 3F **169**
Ackergillshore. *High* 3F **169**
Acklam. *Midd* 3B **106**
Acklam. *N Yor* 3B **100**
Ackleton. *Shrp* 1B **60**
Acklington. *Nmbd* 4G **121**
Ackton. *W Yor* 2E **93**
Ackworth Moor Top. *W Yor* 3E **93**
Acle. *Norf* 4G **79**
Acocks Green. *W Mid* 2F **61**
Acol. *Kent* 4H **41**
Acomb. *Nmbd* 3C **114**
Acomb. *York* 4H **99**
Aconbury. *Here* 2A **48**
Acre. *G Man* 4H **91**
Acre. *Lanc* 2F **91**
Acrefair. *Wrex* 1E **71**
Acrise. *Kent* 1F **29**
Acton. *Arm* 5E **178**
Acton. *Ches E* 5A **84**
Acton. *Dors* 5E **15**
**Acton**. *G Lon* 2C **38**
Acton. *Shrp* 2F **59**
Acton. *Staf* 1C **72**
Acton. *Suff* 1B **54**
Acton. *Worc* 4C **60**
Acton. *Wrex* 5F **83**
Acton Beauchamp. *Here* 5A **60**
Acton Bridge. *Ches W* 3H **83**
Acton Burnell. *Shrp* 5H **71**
Acton Green. *Here* 5A **60**
Acton Pigott. *Shrp* 5H **71**
Acton Round. *Shrp* 1A **60**
Acton Scott. *Shrp* 2G **59**
Acton Trussell. *Staf* 4D **72**
Acton Turville. *S Glo* 3D **34**
Adabroc. *W Isl* 1H **171**
Adam's Hill. *Worc* 3D **60**
Adbaston. *Staf* 3B **72**
Adber. *Dors* 4B **22**
Adderbury. *Oxon* 2C **50**
Adderley. *Shrp* 2A **72**
Adderstone. *Nmbd* 1F **121**
Addiewell. *W Lot* 3C **128**
Addingham. *W Yor* 5C **98**
Addington. *Buck* 3F **51**
Addington. *G Lon* 4E **39**
Addington. *Kent* 5A **40**
Addinston. *Bord* 4B **130**
Addiscombe. *G Lon* 4E **39**
**Addlestone**. *Surr* 4B **38**
Addlethorpe. *Linc* 4E **89**
Adeney. *Telf* 4B **72**
Adfa. *Powy* 5C **70**
Adforton. *Here* 3G **59**
Adgestone. *IOW* 4D **16**
Adisham. *Kent* 5G **41**
Adlestrop. *Glos* 3H **49**
Adlingfleet. *E Yor* 2B **94**
Adlington. *Ches E* 2D **84**
Adlington. *Lanc* 3E **90**
Admaston. *Staf* 3E **73**
Admaston. *Telf* 4A **72**
Admington. *Warw* 1H **49**
Adpar. *Cdgn* 1D **44**
Adsborough. *Som* 4F **21**
Adstock. *Buck* 2F **51**
Adstone. *Nptn* 5C **62**
Adversane. *W Sus* 3B **26**
Advie. *High* 5F **159**
Adwalton. *W Yor* 2C **92**
Adwell. *Oxon* 2E **37**
**Adwick le Street**. *S Yor* 4F **93**
Adwick upon Dearne. *S Yor* 4E **93**
Adziel. *Abers* 3G **161**
Ae. *Dum* 1A **112**
Affleck. *Abers* 1F **153**
Affpuddle. *Dors* 3D **14**
Affric Lodge. *High* 1D **148**
Afon-wen. *Flin* 3D **82**
Agglethorpe. *N Yor* 1C **98**
Aghagallon. *Arm* 3F **178**
Aghalee. *Lis* 3F **178**
Aglionby. *Cumb* 4F **113**
Ahoghill. *ME Ant* 6G **175**
Aigburth. *Mers* 2F **83**
Aiginis. *W Isl* 4G **171**
Aike. *E Yor* 5E **101**
Aikers. *Orkn* 8D **172**
Aiketgate. *Cumb* 5F **113**
Aikhead. *Cumb* 5D **112**
Aikton. *Cumb* 4D **112**
Ailey. *Here* 1G **47**
Ailsworth. *Pet* 1A **64**
Ainderby Quernhow. *N Yor* 1F **99**
Ainderby Steeple. *N Yor* 5A **106**
Aingers Green. *Essx* 3E **54**
Ainsdale. *Mers* 3B **90**
Ainsdale-on-Sea. *Mers* 3B **90**
Ainstable. *Cumb* 5G **113**
Ainsworth. *G Man* 3F **91**
Ainthorpe. *N Yor* 4E **107**
Aintree. *Mers* 1F **83**
Aird. *Arg* 3E **133**
Aird. *Dum* 3F **109**
Aird. *High* 1G **155** (nr. Port Henderson)
Aird. *High* 3D **147** (nr. Tarskavaig)
Aird. *W Isl* 3C **170** (on Benbecula)
Aird. *W Isl* 4H **171** (on Isle of Lewis)
Àird a Bhasair. *High* 3E **147**
Aird a Mhachair. *W Isl* 4C **170**
Aird a Mhulaidh. *W Isl* 6D **171**
Aird Asaig. *W Isl* 7D **171**
Aird Dhail. *W Isl* 1G **171**
Airdens. *High* 4D **164**
Airdeny. *Arg* 1G **133**
Aird Mhidhinis. *W Isl* 8C **170**
Aird Mhighe. *W Isl* 8D **171** (nr. Ceann a Bhaigh)
Aird Mhighe. *W Isl* 9C **171** (nr. Fionnsabhagh)
Aird Mhor. *W Isl* 8C **170** (on Barra)
Aird Mhor. *W Isl* 4D **170** (on South Uist)
**Airdrie**. *N Lan* 3A **128**
Aird Shleibhe. *W Isl* 9D **171**
Aird, The. *High* 3D **154**
Aird Thunga. *W Isl* 4G **171**
Aird Uig. *W Isl* 4C **171**
Airedale. *W Yor* 2E **93**
Airidh a Bhruaich. *W Isl* 6E **171**
Airies. *Dum* 3E **109**
Airmyn. *E Yor* 2H **93**
Airntully. *Per* 5H **143**
Airor. *High* 3F **147**
Airth. *Falk* 1C **128**
Airton. *N Yor* 4B **98**
Aisby. *Linc* 1F **87** (nr. Gainsborough)
Aisby. *Linc* 2H **75** (nr. Grantham)
Aisgernis. *W Isl* 6C **170**
Aish. *Devn* 2C **8** (nr. Buckfastleigh)
Aish. *Devn* 3E **9** (nr. Totnes)
Aisholt. *Som* 3E **21**
Aiskew. *N Yor* 1E **99**
Aislaby. *N Yor* 1B **100** (nr. Pickering)
Aislaby. *N Yor* 4F **107** (nr. Whitby)
Aislaby. *Stoc T* 3B **106**
Aisthorpe. *Linc* 2G **87**
Aith. *Shet* 3H **173** (on Fetlar)
Aith. *Shet* 6E **173** (on Mainland)
Aithsetter. *Shet* 8F **173**
Akeld. *Nmbd* 2D **120**
Akeley. *Buck* 2F **51**
Akenham. *Suff* 1E **55**
Albaston. *Corn* 5E **11**
Alberbury. *Shrp* 4F **71**
Albert Town. *Pemb* 3D **42**
Albert Village. *Leics* 4H **73**
Albourne. *W Sus* 4D **26**
Albrighton. *Shrp* 4G **71** (nr. Shrewsbury)
Albrighton. *Shrp* 5C **72** (nr. Telford)
Alburgh. *Norf* 2E **67**
Albury. *Herts* 3E **53**
Albury. *Surr* 1B **26**
Albyfield. *Cumb* 4G **113**
Alby Hill. *Norf* 2D **78**
Alcaig. *High* 3H **157**
Alcaston. *Shrp* 2G **59**
Alcester. *Warw* 5E **61**
Alciston. *E Sus* 5G **27**
Alcombe. *Som* 2C **20**
Alconbury. *Cambs* 3A **64**
Alconbury Weston. *Cambs* 3A **64**
Aldborough. *Norf* 2D **78**
Aldborough. *N Yor* 3G **99**
Aldbourne. *Wilts* 4A **36**
Aldbrough. *E Yor* 1F **95**
Aldbrough St John. *N Yor* 3F **105**
Aldbury. *Herts* 4H **51**
Aldcliffe. *Lanc* 3D **96**
Aldclune. *Per* 2G **143**
Aldeburgh. *Suff* 5G **67**
Aldeby. *Norf* 1G **67**
Aldenham. *Herts* 1C **38**
Alderbury. *Wilts* 4G **23**
Aldercar. *Derbs* 1B **74**
Alderford. *Norf* 4D **78**
Alderholt. *Dors* 1G **15**
Alderley. *Glos* 2C **34**
Alderley Edge. *Ches E* 3C **84**
Aldermaston. *W Ber* 5D **36**
Aldermaston Soke. *W Ber* 5E **36**
Aldermaston Wharf. *W Ber* 5E **36**
Alderminster. *Warw* 1H **49**
Alder Moor. *Staf* 3G **73**
Aldersey Green. *Ches W* 5G **83**
**Aldershot**. *Hants* 1G **25**
Alderton. *Glos* 2F **49**
Alderton. *Nptn* 1F **51**
Alderton. *Shrp* 3G **71**
Alderton. *Suff* 1G **55**
Alderton. *Wilts* 3D **34**
Alderton Fields. *Glos* 2F **49**
Alderwasley. *Derbs* 5H **85**
Aldfield. *N Yor* 3E **99**
Aldford. *Ches W* 5G **83**
Aldgate. *Rut* 5G **75**
Aldham. *Essx* 3C **54**
Aldham. *Suff* 1D **54**
Aldingbourne. *W Sus* 5A **26**
Aldingham. *Cumb* 2B **96**
Aldington. *Kent* 2E **29**
Aldington. *Worc* 1F **49**
Aldington Frith. *Kent* 2E **29**
Aldochlay. *Arg* 4C **134**
Aldon. *Shrp* 3G **59**
Aldoth. *Cumb* 5C **112**
Aldreth. *Cambs* 3D **64**
**Aldridge**. *W Mid* 5E **73**
Aldringham. *Suff* 4G **67**
Aldsworth. *Glos* 4G **49**
Aldsworth. *W Sus* 2F **17**
Aldwark. *Derbs* 5G **85**
Aldwark. *N Yor* 3G **99**
Aldwick. *W Sus* 3H **17**
Aldwincle. *Nptn* 2H **63**
Aldworth. *W Ber* 4D **36**
Alexandria. *W Dun* 1E **127**
Aley. *Som* 3E **21**
Aley Green. *C Beds* 4A **52**
Alfardisworthy. *Devn* 1C **10**
Alfington. *Devn* 3E **12**
Alfold. *Surr* 2B **26**
Alfold Bars. *W Sus* 2B **26**
Alfold Crossways. *Surr* 2B **26**
Alford. *Abers* 2C **152**
Alford. *Linc* 3D **88**
Alford. *Som* 3B **22**
**Alfreton**. *Derbs* 5B **86**
Alfrick. *Worc* 5B **60**
Alfrick Pound. *Worc* 5B **60**
Alfriston. *E Sus* 5G **27**
Algarkirk. *Linc* 2B **76**
Alhampton. *Som* 3B **22**
Aline Lodge. *W Isl* 6D **171**
Alkborough. *N Lin* 2B **94**
Alkerton. *Oxon* 1B **50**
Alkham. *Kent* 1G **29**
Alkington. *Shrp* 2H **71**
Alkmonton. *Derbs* 2F **73**
Alladale Lodge. *High* 5B **164**
Allaleigh. *Devn* 3E **9**
Allanbank. *N Lan* 4B **128**
Allanton. *N Lan* 4B **128**
Allanton. *Bord* 4E **131**
Allaston. *Glos* 5B **48**
Allbrook. *Hants* 4C **24**
All Cannings. *Wilts* 5F **35**
Allendale Town. *Nmbd* 4B **114**
Allen End. *Warw* 1F **61**
Allenheads. *Nmbd* 5B **114**
Allensford. *Dur* 5D **115**
Allen's Green. *Herts* 4E **53**
Allensmore. *Here* 2H **47**
Allenton. *Derb* 2A **74**
Aller. *Som* 4H **21**
Allerby. *Cumb* 1B **102**
Allercombe. *Devn* 3D **12**
Allerford. *Som* 2C **20**
Allerston. *N Yor* 1C **100**
Allerthorpe. *E Yor* 5B **100**
Allerton. *Mers* 2G **83**
Allerton. *W Yor* 1B **92**
Allerton Bywater. *W Yor* 2E **93**
Allerton Mauleverer. *N Yor* 4G **99**
Allesley. *W Mid* 2G **61**
Allestree. *Derb* 2H **73**
Allet. *Corn* 4B **6**
Allexton. *Leics* 5F **75**
Allgreave. *Ches E* 4D **84**
Allhallows. *Medw* 3C **40**
Allhallows-on-Sea. *Medw* 3C **40**
Alligin Shuas. *High* 3H **155**
Allimore Green. *Staf* 4C **72**
Allington. *Kent* 5B **40**
Allington. *Linc* 1F **75**
Allington. *Wilts* 3H **23** (nr. Amesbury)
Allington. *Wilts* 5F **35** (nr. Devizes)
Allithwaite. *Cumb* 2C **96**
**Alloa**. *Clac* 4A **136**
Allonby. *Cumb* 5B **112**
Allostock. *Ches W* 3B **84**
Alloway. *S Ayr* 3C **116**
Allowenshay. *Som* 1G **13**
All Saints South Elmham. *Suff* 2F **67**
Allscott. *Shrp* 1B **60**
Allscott. *Telf* 4A **72**
All Stretton. *Shrp* 1G **59**
Allt. *Carm* 5F **45**
Alltami. *Flin* 4E **83**
Alltgobhlach. *N Ayr* 5G **125**
Alltmawr. *Powy* 1D **46**
Alltnacaillich. *High* 4E **167**
Allt na h' Airbhe. *High* 4F **163**
Alltour. *High* 5E **148**
Alltsigh. *High* 2G **149**
Alltwalis. *Carm* 2E **45**
Alltwen. *Neat* 5H **45**
Alltyblacca. *Cdgn* 1F **45**
Allt-y-goed. *Pemb* 1B **44**
Almeley. *Here* 5F **59**
Almeley Wooton. *Here* 5F **59**
Almer. *Dors* 3E **15**
Almholme. *S Yor* 4F **93**
Almington. *Staf* 2B **72**
Alminstone Cross. *Devn* 4D **18**
Almodington. *W Sus* 3G **17**
Almondbank. *Per* 1C **136**
Almondbury. *W Yor* 3B **92**
Almondsbury. *S Glo* 3B **34**
Alne. *N Yor* 3G **99**
Alness. *High* 2A **158**
Alnessferry. *High* 2A **158**
Alnham. *Nmbd* 3D **121**
Alnmouth. *Nmbd* 3G **121**
Alnwick. *Nmbd* 3F **121**
Alphamstone. *Essx* 2B **54**
Alpheton. *Suff* 5A **66**
Alphington. *Devn* 3C **12**
Alpington. *Norf* 5E **79**
Alport. *Derbs* 4G **85**
Alport. *Powy* 1E **59**
Alpraham. *Ches E* 5H **83**
Alresford. *Essx* 3D **54**
Alrewas. *Staf* 4F **73**
**Alsager**. *Ches E* 5B **84**
Alsagers Bank. *Staf* 1C **72**
Alsop en le Dale. *Derbs* 5F **85**
Alston. *Cumb* 5A **114**
Alston. *Devn* 2G **13**
Alstone. *Glos* 2E **49**
Alstone. *Som* 2G **21**
Alstonefield. *Staf* 5F **85**
Alston Sutton. *Som* 1H **21**
Alswear. *Devn* 4H **19**
Altandhu. *High* 2D **163**
Altanduin. *High* 1F **165**
Altarnun. *Corn* 4C **10**
Altass. *High* 3B **164**
Alterwall. *High* 2E **169**
Altgaltraig. *Arg* 2B **126**
Altham. *Lanc* 1F **91**
Althorne. *Essx* 1D **40**
Althorpe. *N Lin* 4B **94**
Altnabreac. *High* 4C **168**
Altnacealgach. *High* 2G **163**
Altnafeadh. *High* 3G **141**
Altnaharra. *High* 5F **167**
Altofts. *W Yor* 2D **93**
Alton. *Derbs* 4A **86**
**Alton**. *Hants* 3F **25**
Alton. *Staf* 1E **73**
Alton Barnes. *Wilts* 5G **35**
Altonhill. *E Ayr* 1D **116**
Alton Pancras. *Dors* 2C **14**
Alton Priors. *Wilts* 5G **35**
**Altrincham**. *G Man* 2B **84**
Altrua. *High* 4E **149**
Alva. *Clac* 4A **136**
Alvanley. *Ches W* 3G **83**
Alvaston. *Derb* 2A **74**
Alvechurch. *Worc* 3E **61**
Alvecote. *Warw* 5G **73**
Alvediston. *Wilts* 4E **23**
Alveley. *Shrp* 2B **60**
Alverdiscott. *Devn* 4F **19**
Alverstoke. *Hants* 3D **16**
Alverstone. *IOW* 4D **16**
Alverthorpe. *W Yor* 2D **92**
Alverton. *Notts* 1E **75**
Alves. *Mor* 2F **159**
Alvescot. *Oxon* 5A **50**
Alveston. *S Glo* 3B **34**
Alveston. *Warw* 5G **61**
Alvie. *High* 3C **150**
Alvingham. *Linc* 1C **88**
Alvington. *Glos* 5B **48**
Alwalton. *Cambs* 1A **64**
Alweston. *Dors* 1B **14**
Alwington. *Devn* 4E **19**
Alwinton. *Nmbd* 4D **120**
Alwoodley. *W Yor* 5E **99**
Alyth. *Per* 4B **144**
Amatnatua. *High* 4B **164**
Am Baile. *W Isl* 7C **170**
Ambaston. *Derbs* 2B **74**
Ambergate. *Derbs* 5H **85**
Amber Hill. *Linc* 1B **76**
Amberley. *Glos* 5D **48**
Amberley. *W Sus* 4B **26**
Amble. *Nmbd* 4G **121**
Amblecote. *W Mid* 2C **60**
Ambler Thorn. *W Yor* 2A **92**
Ambleside. *Cumb* 4E **103**
Ambleston. *Pemb* 2E **43**
Ambrosden. *Oxon* 4E **50**
Amcotts. *N Lin* 3B **94**
**Amersham**. *Buck* 1A **38**
Amerton. *Staf* 3D **73**
Amesbury. *Wilts* 2G **23**
Amisfield. *Dum* 1B **112**
Amlwch. *IOA* 1D **80**
Amlwch Port. *IOA* 1D **80**
**Ammanford**. *Carm* 4G **45**
Amotherby. *N Yor* 2B **100**
Ampfield. *Hants* 4B **24**
Ampleforth. *N Yor* 2H **99**
Ampleforth College. *N Yor* 2H **99**
Ampney Crucis. *Glos* 5F **49**
Ampney St Mary. *Glos* 5F **49**
Ampney St Peter. *Glos* 5F **49**
Amport. *Hants* 2A **24**
Ampthill. *C Beds* 2A **52**
Ampton. *Suff* 3A **66**
Amroth. *Pemb* 4F **43**
Amulree. *Per* 5G **143**
Amwell. *Herts* 4B **52**
Anaheilt. *High* 2C **140**
An Àird. *High* 3D **147**
An Baile Nua. *Ferm* 7K **177**
An Camus Darach. *High* 4E **147**
Ancaster. *Linc* 1G **75**
Anchor. *Shrp* 2D **58**
Anchorsholme. *Lanc* 5C **96**
Anchor Street. *Norf* 3F **79**
An Cnoc. *W Isl* 4G **171**
An Cnoc Ard. *W Isl* 1H **171**
An Coroghon. *High* 3A **146**
Ancroft. *Nmbd* 5G **131**
Ancrum. *Bord* 2A **120**
Ancton. *W Sus* 5A **26**
Anderby. *Linc* 3E **89**
Anderby Creek. *Linc* 3E **89**
Anderson. *Dors* 3D **15**
Anderton. *Ches W* 3A **84**
Andertons Mill. *Lanc* 3D **90**
**Andover**. *Hants* 2B **24**
Andover Down. *Hants* 2B **24**
Andoversford. *Glos* 4F **49**
Andreas. *IOM* 2D **108**
An Dùnan. *High* 1D **147**
Andwell. *Hants* 1E **25**
Anelog. *Gwyn* 3A **68**
Anfield. *Mers* 1F **83**
Angarrack. *Corn* 3C **4**
Angelbank. *Shrp* 3H **59**
Angersleigh. *Som* 1E **13**
Angerton. *Cumb* 4D **112**
Angle. *Pemb* 4C **42**
An Gleann Ur. *W Isl* 4G **171**
Angmering. *W Sus* 5B **26**
Angmering-on-Sea. *W Sus* 5B **26**
Angram. *N Yor* 5B **104** (nr. Keld)
Angram. *N Yor* 5H **99** (nr. York)
Anick. *Nmbd* 3C **114**
Ankerbold. *Derbs* 4A **86**
Ankerville. *High* 1C **158**
Anlaby. *E Yor* 2D **94**
Anlaby Park. *Hull* 2D **94**
An Leth Meadhanach. *W Isl* 7C **170**
Anmer. *Norf* 3G **77**
Anmore. *Hants* 1E **17**
Annacloy. *New M* 5J **179**
Annadorn. *New M* 5J **179**
Annaghmore. *Arm* 4D **178**
Annaghugh. *Arm* 4D **178**
Annahilt. *Lis* 4G **179**
Annalong. *New M* 8H **179**
Annan. *Dum* 3D **112**
Annaside. *Cumb* 1A **96**
Annat. *Arg* 1H **133**
Annat. *High* 3A **156**
Annathill. *N Lan* 2A **128**
Anna Valley. *Hants* 2B **24**
Annbank. *S Ayr* 2D **116**
Annesley. *Notts* 5C **86**
Annesley Woodhouse. *Notts* 5C **86**
**Annfield Plain**. *Dur* 4E **115**
Annsborough. *New M* 6H **179**
Annscroft. *Shrp* 5G **71**
An Sailean. *High* 2A **140**
Ansdell. *Lanc* 2B **90**
Ansford. *Som* 3B **22**
Ansley. *Warw* 1G **61**
Anslow. *Staf* 3G **73**
Anslow Gate. *Staf* 3F **73**

Ansteadbrook—Banbury


Ansteadbrook. Surr 2A **26**
Anstey. Herts 2E **53**
Anstey. Leics 5C **74**
Anston. S Lan 5D **128**
Anstruther Easter. Fife 3H **137**
Anstruther Wester. Fife 3H **137**
Ansty. Warw 2A **62**
Ansty. W Sus 3D **27**
Ansty. Wilts 4E **23**
An Taobh Tuath. W Isl 9B **171**
An t-Aodann Ban. High 3C **154**
An t Ath Leathann. High 1E **147**
An Teanga. High 3E **147**
Anthill Common. Hants 1E **17**
Anthorn. Cumb 4C **112**
Antingham. Norf 2E **79**
An t-Ob. W Isl 9C **171**
Anton's Gowt. Linc 1B **76**
Antony. Corn 3A **8**
An t-Ord. High 2E **147**
**Antrim**. Ant 8H **175**
Antrobus. Ches W 3A **84**
Anvil Corner. Devn 2D **10**
Anwick. Linc 5A **88**
Anwoth. Dum 4C **110**
Apethorpe. Nptn 1H **63**
Apeton. Staf 4C **72**
Apley. Linc 3A **88**
Apperknowle. Derbs 3A **86**
Apperley. Glos 3D **48**
Apperley Dene. Nmbd 4D **114**
Appersett. N Yor 5B **104**
Appin. Arg 4D **140**
Appleby. N Lin 3C **94**
Appleby-in-Westmorland. Cumb 2H **103**
Appleby Magna. Leics 5H **73**
Appleby Parva. Leics 5H **73**
Applecross. High 4G **155**
Appledore. Devn 3E **19** (nr. Bideford)
Appledore. Devn 1D **12** (nr. Tiverton)
Appledore. Kent 3D **28**
Appledore Heath. Kent 2D **28**
Appleford. Oxon 2D **36**
Applegarthtown. Dum 1C **112**
Applemore. Hants 2B **16**
Appleshaw. Hants 2B **24**
Applethwaite. Cumb 2D **102**
Appleton. Hal 2H **83**
Appleton. Oxon 5C **50**
Appleton-le-Moors. N Yor 1B **100**
Appleton-le-Street. N Yor 2B **100**
Appleton Roebuck. N Yor 5H **99**
Appleton Thorn. Warr 2A **84**
Appleton Wiske. N Yor 4A **106**
Appletree. Nptn 1C **50**
Appletreehall. Bord 3H **119**
Appletreewick. N Yor 3C **98**
Appley. Som 4D **20**
Appley Bridge. Lanc 3D **90**
Apse Heath. IOW 4D **16**
Apsley End. C Beds 2B **52**
Apuldram. W Sus 2G **17**
Arabella. High 1C **158**
Arasaig. High 5E **147**
Arbeadie. Abers 4D **152**
Arberth. Pemb 3F **43**
Arbirlot. Ang 4F **145**
Arborfield. Wok 5F **37**
Arborfield Cross. Wok 5F **37**
Arborfield Garrison. Wok 5F **37**
Arbourthorne. S Yor 2A **86**
**Arbroath**. Ang 4F **145**
Arbuthnott. Abers 1H **145**
Arcan. High 3H **157**
Archargary. High 3H **167**
Archdeacon Newton. Darl 3F **105**
Archiestown. Mor 4G **159**
Arclid. Ches E 4B **84**
Arclid Green. Ches E 4B **84**
Ardachu. High 3D **164**
Ardalanish. Arg 2A **132**
Ardaneaskan. High 5H **155**
Ardarroch. High 5H **155**
Ardbeg. Arg 1C **126** (nr. Dunoon)
Ardbeg. Arg 5C **124** (on Islay)
Ardbeg. Arg 3B **126** (on Isle of Bute)
Ardboe. M Ulst 2D **178**
Ardcharnich. High 5F **163**
Ardchiavaig. Arg 2A **132**
Ardchonnell. Arg 2G **133**
Ardchrishnish. Arg 1B **132**
Ardchronie. High 5D **164**
Ardchullarie. Stir 2E **135**
Ardchyle. Stir 1E **135**
Ard-dhubh. High 4G **155**
Arddleen. Powy 4E **71**
Arddlîn. Powy 4E **71**
Ardechive. High 4D **148**
Ardeley. Herts 3D **52**
Ardelve. High 1A **148**
Arden. Arg 1E **127**
Ardendrain. High 5H **157**
Arden Hall. N Yor 5C **106**
Ardens Grafton. Warw 5F **61**
Ardentinny. Arg 1C **126**
Ardeonaig. Stir 5D **142**
Ardersier. High 3B **158**
Ardery. High 2B **140**
Ardessie. High 5E **163**
Ardfern. Arg 3F **133**
Ardfernal. Arg 2D **124**
Ardfin. Arg 3C **124**
Ardgartan. Arg 3B **134**
Ardgay. High 4D **164**
Ardglass. New M 6K **179**
Ardgour. High 2E **141**
Ardheslaig. High 3G **155**
Ardindrean. High 5F **163**
Ardingly. W Sus 3E **27**
Ardington. Oxon 3C **36**
Ardlamont House. Arg 3A **126**
Ardleigh. Essx 3D **54**
Ardler. Per 4B **144**
Ardley. Oxon 3D **50**
Ardlui. Arg 2C **134**
Ardlussa. Arg 1E **125**
Ardmair. High 4F **163**
Ardmay. Arg 3B **134**
Ardmillan. N Dwn 3K **179**
Ardminish. Arg 5E **125**
Ardmolich. High 1B **140**
Ardmore. High 3C **166** (nr. Kinlochbervie)
Ardmore. High 5E **164** (nr. Tain)
Ardnacross. Arg 4G **139**
Ardnadam. Arg 1C **126**
Ardnagrask. High 4H **157**
Ardnamurach. High 4G **147**
Ardnarff. High 5A **156**
Ardnastang. High 2C **140**
Ardoch. Per 5H **143**
Ardochy House. High 3E **148**
Ardpatrick. Arg 3F **125**
Ardrishaig. Arg 1G **125**
Ardroag. High 4B **154**
Ardross. High 1A **158**
**Ardrossan**. N Ayr 5D **126**
Ardshealach. High 2A **140**
Ardsley. S Yor 4D **93**
Ardslignish. High 2G **139**
Ardstraw. Derr 4F **176**
Ardtalla. Arg 4C **124**
Ardtalnaig. Per 5E **142**
Ardtoe. High 1A **140**
Arduaine. Arg 2E **133**
Ardullie. High 2H **157**
Ardvasar. High 3E **147**
Ardvorlich. Per 1F **135**
Ardwell. Dum 5G **109**
Ardwell. Mor 5A **160**
Arean. High 1A **140**
Areley Common. Worc 3C **60**
Areley Kings. Worc 3C **60**
Arford. Hants 3G **25**
Argoed. Cphy 2E **33**
Argoed Mill. Powy 4B **58**
Aridhglas. Arg 2B **132**
Arinacrinachd. High 3G **155**
Arinagour. Arg 3D **138**
Arisaig. High 5E **147**
Ariundle. High 2C **140**
Arivegaig. High 2A **140**
Arkendale. N Yor 3F **99**
Arkesden. Essx 2E **53**
Arkholme. Lanc 2E **97**
Arkle Town. N Yor 4D **104**
Arkley. G Lon 1D **38**
Arksey. S Yor 4F **93**
Arkwright Town. Derbs 3B **86**
Arlecdon. Cumb 3B **102**
Arlescote. Warw 1B **50**
Arlesey. C Beds 2B **52**
Arleston. Telf 4A **72**
Arley. Ches E 2A **84**
Arlingham. Glos 4C **48**
Arlington. Devn 2G **19**
Arlington. E Sus 5G **27**
Arlington. Glos 5G **49**
Arlington Beccott. Devn 2G **19**
Armadail. High 3E **147**
Armadale. High 3E **147** (nr. Isleornsay)
Armadale. High 2H **167** (nr. Strathy)
Armadale. W Lot 3C **128**
**Armagh**. Arm 5C **178**
Armathwaite. Cumb 5G **113**
Arminghall. Norf 5E **79**
Armitage. Staf 4E **73**
Armitage Bridge. W Yor 3B **92**
Armley. W Yor 1C **92**
Armoy. Caus 3G **175**
Armscote. Warw 1H **49**
Arms, The. Norf 1A **66**
Armston. Nptn 2H **63**
**Armthorpe**. S Yor 4G **93**
Arncliffe. N Yor 2B **98**
Arncliffe Cote. N Yor 2B **98**
Arncroach. Fife 3H **137**
Arne. Dors 4E **15**
Arnesby. Leics 1D **62**
Arnicle. Arg 2B **122**
Arnisdale. High 2G **147**
Arnish. High 4E **155**
Arniston. Midl 3G **129**
Arnol. W Isl 3F **171**
Arnold. E Yor 5F **101**
**Arnold**. Notts 1C **74**
Arnprior. Stir 4F **135**
Arnside. Cumb 2D **96**
Aros Mains. Arg 4G **139**
Arpafeelie. High 3A **158**
Arrad Foot. Cumb 1C **96**
Arram. E Yor 5E **101**
Arras. E Yor 5D **100**
Arrathorne. N Yor 5E **105**
Arreton. IOW 4D **16**
Arrington. Cambs 5C **64**
Arrochar. Arg 3B **134**
Arrow. Warw 5E **61**
Arscaig. High 2C **164**
Artafallie. High 4A **158**
Arthington. W Yor 5E **99**
Arthingworth. Nptn 2E **63**
Arthog. Gwyn 4F **69**
Arthrath. Abers 5G **161**
Arthurstone. Per 4B **144**
Articlave. Caus 3D **174**
Artigarvan. Derr 2F **176**
Artikelly. Caus 4C **174**
Artington. Surr 1A **26**
Arundel. W Sus 5B **26**
Asby. Cumb 2B **102**
Ascog. Arg 3C **126**
**Ascot**. Wind 4A **38**
Ascott-under-Wychwood. Oxon 4B **50**
Asenby. N Yor 2F **99**
Asfordby. Leics 4E **74**
Asfordby Hill. Leics 4E **74**
Asgarby. Linc 4C **88** (nr. Horncastle)
Asgarby. Linc 1A **76** (nr. Sleaford)
Ash. Devn 4E **9**
Ash. Dors 1D **14**
Ash. Kent 5G **41** (nr. Sandwich)
Ash. Kent 4H **39** (nr. Swanley)
Ash. Som 4H **21**
Ash. Surr 1G **25**
Ashampstead. W Ber 4D **36**
Ashbocking. Suff 5D **66**
Ashbourne. Derbs 1F **73**
Ashbrittle. Som 4D **20**
Ashbrook. Shrp 1G **59**
Ashburton. Devn 2D **8**
Ashbury. Devn 3F **11**
Ashbury. Oxon 3A **36**
Ashby. N Lin 4B **94**
Ashby by Partney. Linc 4D **88**
Ashby cum Fenby. NE Lin 4F **95**
Ashby de la Launde. Linc 5H **87**
**Ashby-de-la-Zouch**. Leics 4A **74**
Ashby Folville. Leics 4E **74**
Ashby Magna. Leics 1C **62**
Ashby Parva. Leics 2C **62**
Ashby Puerorum. Linc 3C **88**
Ashby St Ledgars. Nptn 4C **62**
Ashby St Mary. Norf 5F **79**
Ashchurch. Glos 2E **49**
Ashcombe. Devn 5C **12**
Ashcott. Som 3H **21**
Ashdon. Essx 1F **53**
Ashe. Hants 2D **24**
Asheldham. Essx 5C **54**
Ashen. Essx 1H **53**
Ashendon. Buck 4F **51**
Ashey. IOW 4D **16**
Ashfield. Hants 1B **16**
Ashfield. Here 3A **48**
Ashfield. Shrp 2H **59**
Ashfield. Stir 3G **135**
Ashfield. Suff 4E **66**
Ashfield Green. Suff 3E **67**
Ashfold Crossways. W Sus 3D **26**
Ashford. Devn 3F **19** (nr. Barnstaple)
Ashford. Devn 4C **8** (nr. Kingsbridge)
Ashford. Hants 1G **15**
**Ashford**. Kent 1E **28**
Ashford. Surr 3B **38**
Ashford Bowdler. Shrp 3H **59**
Ashford Carbonel. Shrp 3H **59**
Ashford Hill. Hants 5D **36**
Ashford in the Water. Derbs 4F **85**
Ashgill. S Lan 5A **128**
Ash Green. Warw 2H **61**
Ashgrove. Mor 2G **159**
Ashill. Devn 1D **12**
Ashill. Norf 5A **78**
Ashill. Som 1G **13**
Ashingdon. Essx 1C **40**
**Ashington**. Nmbd 1F **115**
Ashington. W Sus 4C **26**
Ashkirk. Bord 2G **119**
Ashleworth. Glos 3D **48**
Ashley. Cambs 4F **65**
Ashley. Ches E 2B **84**
Ashley. Dors 2G **15**
Ashley. Glos 2E **35**
Ashley. Hants 3A **16** (nr. New Milton)
Ashley. Hants 3B **24** (nr. Winchester)
Ashley. Kent 1H **29**
Ashley. Nptn 1E **63**
Ashley. Staf 2B **72**
Ashley. Wilts 5D **34**
Ashley Green. Buck 5H **51**
Ashley Heath. Dors 2G **15**
Ashley Heath. Staf 2B **72**
Ashley Moor. Here 4G **59**
Ash Magna. Shrp 2H **71**
Ashmanhaugh. Norf 3F **79**
Ashmansworth. Hants 1C **24**
Ashmansworthy. Devn 1D **10**
Ashmead Green. Glos 2C **34**
Ashmill. Devn 3D **11** (nr. Holsworthy)
Ash Mill. Devn 4A **20** (nr. South Molton)
Ashmore. Dors 1E **15**
Ashmore Green. W Ber 5D **36**
Ashorne. Warw 5H **61**
Ashover. Derbs 4A **86**
Ashow. Warw 3H **61**
Ash Parva. Shrp 2H **71**
Ashperton. Here 1B **48**
Ashprington. Devn 3E **9**
Ash Priors. Som 4E **21**
Ashreigney. Devn 1G **11**
Ash Street. Suff 1D **54**
Ashtead. Surr 5C **38**
Ash Thomas. Devn 1D **12**
Ashton. Corn 4D **4**
Ashton. Here 4H **59**
Ashton. Inv 2D **126**
Ashton. Nptn 2H **63** (nr. Oundle)
Ashton. Nptn 1F **51** (nr. Roade)
Ashton. Pet 5A **76**
Ashton Common. Wilts 1D **23**
Ashton Hayes. Ches W 4H **83**
**Ashton-in-Makerfield**. G Man 1H **83**
Ashton Keynes. Wilts 2F **35**
Ashton under Hill. Worc 2E **49**
**Ashton-under-Lyne**. G Man 1D **84**
Ashton upon Mersey. G Man 1B **84**
Ashurst. Hants 1B **16**
Ashurst. Kent 2G **27**
Ashurst. Lanc 4C **90**
Ashurst. W Sus 4C **26**
Ashurst Wood. W Sus 2F **27**
Ash Vale. Surr 1G **25**
Ashwater. Devn 3D **11**
Ashwell. Herts 2C **52**
Ashwell. Rut 4F **75**
Ashwellthorpe. Norf 1D **66**
Ashwick. Som 2B **22**
Ashwicken. Norf 4G **77**
Ashwood. Staf 2C **60**
Askam in Furness. Cumb 2B **96**
Askern. S Yor 3F **93**
Askerswell. Dors 3A **14**
Askett. Buck 5G **51**
Askham. Cumb 2G **103**
Askham. Notts 3E **87**
Askham Bryan. York 5H **99**
Askham Richard. York 5H **99**
Askrigg. N Yor 5C **104**
Askwith. N Yor 5D **98**
Aslackby. Linc 2H **75**
Aslacton. Norf 1D **66**
Aslockton. Notts 1E **75**
Aspatria. Cumb 5C **112**
Aspenden. Herts 3D **52**
Asperton. Linc 2B **76**
Aspley Guise. C Beds 2H **51**
Aspley Heath. C Beds 2H **51**
Aspull. G Man 4E **90**
Asselby. E Yor 2H **93**
Assington. Suff 2C **54**
Assington Green. Suff 5G **65**
Astbury. Ches E 4C **84**
Astcote. Nptn 5D **62**
Asterby. Linc 3B **88**
Asterley. Shrp 5F **71**
Asterton. Shrp 1F **59**
Asthall. Oxon 4A **50**
Asthall Leigh. Oxon 4B **50**
Astle. High 4E **165**
Astley. G Man 4F **91**
Astley. Shrp 4H **71**
Astley. Warw 2H **61**
Astley. Worc 4B **60**
Astley Abbotts. Shrp 1B **60**
Astley Bridge. G Man 3F **91**
Astley Cross. Worc 4C **60**
Aston. Ches E 1A **72**
Aston. Ches W 3H **83**
Aston. Derbs 2F **85** (nr. Hope)
Aston. Derbs 2F **73** (nr. Sudbury)
Aston. Flin 4F **83**
Aston. Here 4G **59**
Aston. Herts 3C **52**
Aston. Oxon 5B **50**
Aston. Shrp 1C **60** (nr. Bridgnorth)
Aston. Shrp 3H **71** (nr. Wem)
Aston. S Yor 2B **86**
Aston. Staf 1B **72**
Aston. Telf 5A **72**
Aston. W Mid 1E **61**
Aston. Wok 3F **37**
Aston Abbotts. Buck 3G **51**
Aston Botterell. Shrp 2A **60**
Aston-by-Stone. Staf 2D **72**
Aston Cantlow. Warw 5F **61**
Aston Clinton. Buck 4G **51**
Aston Crews. Here 3B **48**
Aston Cross. Glos 2E **49**
Aston End. Herts 3C **52**
Aston Eyre. Shrp 1A **60**
Aston Fields. Worc 4D **60**
Aston Flamville. Leics 1B **62**
Aston Ingham. Here 3B **48**
Aston juxta Mondrum. Ches E 5A **84**
Astonlane. Shrp 1A **60**
Aston le Walls. Nptn 5B **62**
Aston Magna. Glos 2G **49**
Aston Munslow. Shrp 2H **59**
Aston on Carrant. Glos 2E **49**
Aston on Clun. Shrp 2F **59**
Aston-on-Trent. Derbs 3B **74**
Aston Pigott. Shrp 5F **71**
Aston Rogers. Shrp 5F **71**
Aston Rowant. Oxon 2F **37**
Aston Sandford. Buck 5F **51**
Aston Somerville. Worc 2F **49**
Aston Subedge. Glos 1G **49**
Aston Tirrold. Oxon 3D **36**
Aston Upthorpe. Oxon 3D **36**
Astrop. Nptn 2D **50**
Astwick. C Beds 2C **52**
Astwood. Mil 1H **51**
Astwood Bank. Worc 4E **61**
Aswarby. Linc 2H **75**
Aswardby. Linc 3C **88**
Atcham. Shrp 5H **71**
Atch Lench. Worc 5E **61**
Athelhampton. Dors 3C **14**
Athelington. Suff 3E **66**
Athelney. Som 4G **21**
Athelstaneford. E Lot 2B **130**
Atherfield Green. IOW 5C **16**
Atherington. Devn 4F **19**
Atherington. W Sus 5B **26**
Athersley. S Yor 4D **92**
**Atherstone**. Warw 1H **61**
Atherstone on Stour. Warw 5G **61**
**Atherton**. G Man 4E **91**
Ath-Tharracail. High 2A **140**
Atlow. Derbs 1G **73**
Attadale. High 5B **156**
Attenborough. Notts 2C **74**
Atterby. Linc 1G **87**
Atterley. Shrp 1A **60**
Atterton. Leics 1A **62**
Attical. New M 8G **179**
Attleborough. Norf 1C **66**
Attleborough. Warw 1A **62**
Attlebridge. Norf 4D **78**
Atwick. E Yor 4F **101**
Atworth. Wilts 5D **34**
Auberrow. Here 1H **47**
Aubourn. Linc 4G **87**
Aucharnie. Abers 4D **160**
Auchattie. Abers 4D **152**
Auchavan. Ang 2A **144**
Auchbreck. Mor 1G **151**
Auchenback. E Ren 4G **127**
Auchenblae. Abers 1G **145**
Auchenbrack. Dum 5G **117**
Auchenbreck. Arg 1B **126**
Auchencairn. Dum 4E **111** (nr. Dalbeattie)
Auchencairn. Dum 1A **112** (nr. Dumfries)
Auchencarroch. W Dun 1F **127**
Auchencrow. Bord 3E **131**
Auchendennan. W Dun 1E **127**
Auchendinny. Midl 3F **129**
Auchengray. S Lan 4C **128**
Auchenhalrig. Mor 2A **160**
Auchenheath. S Lan 5B **128**
Auchenlochan. Arg 2A **126**
Auchenmade. N Ayr 5E **127**
Auchenmalg. Dum 4H **109**
Auchentiber. N Ayr 5E **127**
Auchenvennel. Arg 1D **126**
Auchindrain. Arg 3H **133**
Auchininna. Abers 4D **160**
Auchinleck. Dum 2B **110**
Auchinleck. E Ayr 2E **117**
Auchinloch. N Lan 2H **127**
Auchinstarry. N Lan 2A **128**
Auchleven. Abers 1D **152**
Auchlochan. S Lan 1H **117**
Auchlunachan. High 5F **163**
Auchmillan. E Ayr 2E **117**
Auchmithie. Ang 4F **145**
Auchmuirbridge. Per 3E **136**
Auchmull. Ang 1E **145**
Auchnacree. Ang 2D **144**
Auchnafree. Per 5F **143**
Auchnagallin. High 5E **159**
Auchnagatt. Abers 4G **161**
Aucholzie. Abers 4H **151**
Auchreddie. Abers 4F **161**
Auchterarder. Per 2B **136**
Auchteraw. High 3F **149**
Auchterderran. Fife 4E **136**
Auchterhouse. Ang 5C **144**
Auchtermuchty. Fife 2E **137**
Auchterneed. High 3G **157**
Auchtertool. Fife 4E **136**
Auchtertyre. High 1G **147**
Auchtubh. Stir 1E **135**
Auckengill. High 2F **169**
Auckley. S Yor 4G **93**
**Audenshaw**. G Man 1D **84**
Audlem. Ches E 1A **72**
Audley. Staf 5B **84**
Audley End. Essx 2F **53**
Audmore. Staf 3C **72**
Auds. Abers 2D **160**
Augher. M Ulst 4L **177**
Aughertree. Cumb 1D **102**
Aughnacloy. M Ulst 4A **178**
Aughton. E Yor 1H **93**
Aughton. Lanc 3E **97** (nr. Lancaster)
Aughton. Lanc 4B **90** (nr. Ormskirk)
**Aughton**. S Yor 2B **86**
Aughton. Wilts 1H **23**
Aughton Park. Lanc 4C **90**
Auldearn. High 3D **158**
Aulden. Here 5G **59**
Auldgirth. Dum 1G **111**
Auldhouse. S Lan 4H **127**
Ault a' chruinn. High 1B **148**
Aultbea. High 5C **162**
Aultdearg. High 2E **157**
Aultgrishan. High 5B **162**
Aultguish Inn. High 1F **157**
Ault Hucknall. Derbs 4B **86**
Aultibea. High 1H **165**
Aultiphurst. High 2A **168**
Aultivullin. High 2A **168**
Aultmore. Mor 3B **160**
Aultnamain Inn. High 5D **164**
Aunby. Linc 4H **75**
Aunsby. Linc 2H **75**
Aust. S Glo 3A **34**
Austerfield. S Yor 1D **86**
Austin Fen. Linc 1C **88**
Austrey. Warw 5G **73**
Austwick. N Yor 3G **97**
Authorpe. Linc 2D **88**
Authorpe Row. Linc 3E **89**
Avebury. Wilts 5G **35**
Avebury Trusloe. Wilts 5F **35**
Aveley. Thur 2G **39**
Avening. Glos 2D **35**
Averham. Notts 5E **87**
Aveton Gifford. Devn 4C **8**
Avielochan. High 2D **150**
Aviemore. High 2C **150**
Avington. Hants 3D **24**
Avoch. High 3B **158**
Avon. Hants 3G **15**
Avonbridge. Falk 2C **128**
Avon Dassett. Warw 5B **62**
Avonmouth. Bris 4A **34**
Avonwick. Devn 3D **8**
Awbridge. Hants 4B **24**
Awliscombe. Devn 2E **13**
Awre. Glos 5C **48**
Awsworth. Notts 1B **74**
Axbridge. Som 1H **21**
Axford. Hants 2E **24**
Axford. Wilts 5H **35**
Axminster. Devn 3G **13**
Axmouth. Devn 3F **13**
Aycliffe Village. Dur 2F **105**
Aydon. Nmbd 3D **114**
Aykley Heads. Dur 5F **115**
Aylburton. Glos 5B **48**
Aylburton Common. Glos 5B **48**
Ayle. Nmbd 5A **114**
Aylesbeare. Devn 3D **12**
**Aylesbury**. Buck 4G **51**
Aylesby. NE Lin 4F **95**
Aylescott. Devn 1G **11**
**Aylesford**. Kent 5B **40**
Aylesham. Kent 5G **41**
Aylestone. Leic 5C **74**
Aylmerton. Norf 2D **78**
Aylsham. Norf 3D **78**
Aylton. Here 2B **48**
Aylworth. Glos 3G **49**
Aymestrey. Here 4G **59**
Aynho. Nptn 2D **50**
Ayot Green. Herts 4C **52**
Ayot St Lawrence. Herts 4B **52**
Ayot St Peter. Herts 4C **52**
**Ayr**. S Ayr 2C **116**
Ayres of Selivoe. Shet 7D **173**
Ayreville. Torb 2E **9**
Aysgarth. N Yor 1C **98**
Ayshford. Devn 1D **12**
Ayside. Cumb 1C **96**
Ayston. Rut 5F **75**
Ayton. Bord 3F **131**
Aywick. Shet 3G **173**
Azerley. N Yor 2E **99**


## B


Babbacombe. Torb 2F **9**
Babbinswood. Shrp 2F **71**
Babbs Green. Herts 4D **53**
Babcary. Som 4A **22**
Babel. Carm 2B **46**
Babell. Flin 3D **82**
Babingley. Norf 3F **77**
Bablock Hythe. Oxon 5C **50**
Babraham. Cambs 5E **65**
Babworth. Notts 2D **86**
Bac. W Isl 3G **171**
Bachau. IOA 2D **80**
Bacheldre. Powy 1E **59**
Bachymbyd Fawr. Den 4C **82**
Backaland. Orkn 4E **172**
Backaskaill. Orkn 2D **172**
Backbarrow. Cumb 1C **96**
Backe. Carm 3G **43**
Backfolds. Abers 3H **161**
Backford. Ches W 3G **83**
Backhill. Abers 5E **161**
Backhill of Clackriach. Abers 4G **161**
Backies. High 3F **165**
Backmuir of New Gilston. Fife 3G **137**
Back of Keppoch. High 5E **147**
Back Street. Suff 5G **65**
Backwell. N Som 5H **33**
Backworth. Tyne 2G **115**
Bacon End. Essx 4G **53**
Baconsthorpe. Norf 2D **78**
Bacton. Here 2G **47**
Bacton. Norf 2F **79**
Bacton. Suff 4C **66**
Bacton Green. Norf 2F **79**
**Bacup**. Lanc 2G **91**
Badachonacher. High 1A **158**
Badachro. High 1G **155**
Badanloch Lodge. High 5H **167**
Badavanich. High 3D **156**
Badbury. Swin 3G **35**
Badby. Nptn 5C **62**
Badcall. High 3C **166**
Badcaul. High 4E **163**
Baddeley Green. Stoke 5D **84**
Baddesley Clinton. W Mid 3G **61**
Baddesley Ensor. Warw 1G **61**
Baddidarach. High 1E **163**
Baddoch. Abers 5F **151**
Badenscallie. High 3E **163**
Badenscoth. Abers 5E **160**
Badentarbat. High 2E **163**
Badgall. Corn 4C **10**
Badgers Mount. Kent 4F **39**
Badgeworth. Glos 4E **49**
Badgworth. Som 1G **21**
Badicaul. High 1F **147**
Badingham. Suff 4F **67**
Badlesmere. Kent 5E **40**
Badlipster. High 4E **169**
Badluarach. High 4D **163**
Badminton. S Glo 3D **34**
Badnaban. High 1E **163**
Badnabay. High 4C **166**
Badnagie. High 5D **168**
Badnellan. High 3F **165**
Badninish. High 4E **165**
Badrallach. High 4E **163**
Badsey. Worc 1F **49**
Badshot Lea. Surr 2G **25**
Badsworth. W Yor 3E **93**
Badwell Ash. Suff 4B **66**
Bae Cinmel. Cnwy 2B **82**
**Bae Colwyn**. Cnwy 3A **82**
Bae Penrhyn. Cnwy 2H **81**
Bagby. N Yor 1G **99**
Bag Enderby. Linc 3C **88**
Bagendon. Glos 5F **49**
Bagginswood. Shrp 2A **60**
Bàgh a Chàise. W Isl 1E **170**
Bàgh a' Chaisteil. W Isl 9B **170**
Bagham. Kent 5E **41**
Baghasdal. W Isl 7C **170**
Bagh Mor. W Isl 3D **170**
Bagh Shiarabhagh. W Isl 8C **170**
Bagillt. Flin 3E **82**
Baginton. Warw 3H **61**
Baglan. Neat 2A **32**
Bagley. Shrp 3G **71**
Bagley. Som 2H **21**
Bagnall. Staf 5D **84**
Bagnor. W Ber 5C **36**
Bagshot. Surr 4A **38**
Bagshot. Wilts 5B **36**
Bagstone. S Glo 3B **34**
Bagthorpe. Norf 2G **77**
Bagthorpe. Notts 5B **86**
Bagworth. Leics 5B **74**
Bagwy Llydiart. Here 3H **47**
**Baildon**. W Yor 1B **92**
Baildon Green. W Yor 1B **92**
Baile. W Isl 1E **170**
Baile Ailein. W Isl 5E **171**
Baile an Truiseil. W Isl 2F **171**
Baile Boidheach. Arg 2F **125**
Baile Glas. W Isl 3D **170**
Bailemeonach. Arg 4A **140**
Baile Mhanaich. W Isl 3C **170**
Baile Mhartainn. W Isl 1C **170**
Baile MhicPhail. W Isl 1D **170**
Baile Mór. Arg 2A **132**
Baile Mor. W Isl 2C **170**
Baile nan Cailleach. W Isl 3C **170**
Baile Raghaill. W Isl 2C **170**
Bailey Green. Hants 4E **25**
Baileyhead. Cumb 1G **113**
Baileysmill. Lis 4H **179**
Bailiesward. Abers 5B **160**
Bail' Iochdrach. W Isl 3D **170**
Baillieston. Glas 3H **127**
Bailrigg. Lanc 4D **97**
Bail Uachdraich. W Isl 2D **170**
Bail' Ur Tholastaidh. W Isl 3H **171**
Bainbridge. N Yor 5C **104**
Bainsford. Falk 1B **128**
Bainshole. Abers 5D **160**
Bainton. E Yor 4D **100**
Bainton. Oxon 3D **50**
Bainton. Pet 5H **75**
Baintown. Fife 3F **137**
Baker Street. Thur 2H **39**
Bakewell. Derbs 4G **85**
Bala. Gwyn 2B **70**
Balachuirn. High 4E **155**
Balbeg. High 5G **157** (nr. Cannich)
Balbeg. High 1G **149** (nr. Loch Ness)
Balbeggie. Per 1D **136**
Balblair. High 4C **164** (nr. Bonar Bridge)
Balblair. High 2B **158** (nr. Invergordon)
Balblair. High 4H **157** (nr. Inverness)
Balby. S Yor 4F **93**
Balcathie. Ang 5F **145**
Balchladich. High 1E **163**
Balchraggan. High 4H **157**
Balchrick. High 3B **166**
Balcombe. W Sus 2E **27**
Balcombe Lane. W Sus 2E **27**
Balcurvie. Fife 3F **137**
Baldersby. N Yor 2F **99**
Baldersby St James. N Yor 2F **99**
Balderstone. Lanc 1E **91**
Balderton. Ches W 4F **83**
Balderton. Notts 5F **87**
Baldinnie. Fife 2G **137**
Baldock. Herts 2C **52**
Baldrine. IOM 3D **108**
Baldslow. E Sus 4C **28**
Baldwin. IOM 3C **108**
Baldwinholme. Cumb 4E **113**
Baldwin's Gate. Staf 2B **72**
Bale. Norf 2C **78**
Balearn. Abers 3H **161**
Balemartine. Arg 4A **138**
Balephetrish. Arg 4B **138**
Balephuil. Arg 4A **138**
Balerno. Edin 3E **129**
Balevullin. Arg 4A **138**
Balfield. Ang 2E **145**
Balfour. Orkn 6D **172**
Balfron. Stir 1G **127**
Balgaveny. Abers 4D **160**
Balgonar. Fife 4C **136**
Balgowan. High 4A **150**
Balgown. High 2C **154**
Balgrochan. E Dun 2H **127**
Balgy. High 3H **155**
Balhalgardy. Abers 1E **153**
Baliasta. Shet 1H **173**
Baligill. High 2A **168**
Balintore. Ang 3B **144**
Balintore. High 1C **158**
Balintraid. High 1B **158**
Balk. N Yor 1G **99**
Balkeerie. Ang 4C **144**
Balkholme. E Yor 2A **94**
Ball. Shrp 3F **71**
Ballabeg. IOM 4B **108**
Ballacannell. IOM 3D **108**
Ballacarnane Beg. IOM 3C **108**
Ballachulish. High 3E **141**
Ballagyr. IOM 3B **108**
Ballajora. IOM 2D **108**
Ballaleigh. IOM 3C **108**
Ballamodha. IOM 4B **108**
Ballantrae. S Ayr 1F **109**
Ballards Gore. Essx 1D **40**
Ballasalla. IOM 4B **108** (nr. Castletown)
Ballasalla. IOM 2C **108** (nr. Kirk Michael)
Ballater. Abers 4A **152**
Ballaugh. IOM 2C **108**
Ballencrieff. E Lot 2A **130**
Ballencrieff Toll. W Lot 2C **128**
Ballentoul. Per 2F **143**
Ball Hill. Hants 5C **36**
Ballidon. Derbs 5G **85**
Balliemore. Arg 1B **126** (nr. Dunoon)
Balliemore. Arg 1F **133** (nr. Oban)
Ballieward. High 5E **159**
Ballig. IOM 3B **108**
Ballimore. Stir 2E **135**
Ballinamallard. Ferm 7E **176**
Ballindarragh. Ferm 6J **177**
Ballingdon. Suff 1B **54**
Ballinger Common. Buck 5H **51**
Ballingham. Here 2A **48**
Ballingry. Fife 4D **136**
Ballinluig. Per 3G **143**
Ballintoy. Caus 2G **175**
Ballintuim. Per 3A **144**
Balliveolan. Arg 4C **140**
Balloan. High 3C **164**
Balloch. High 4B **158**
Balloch. N Lan 2A **128**
Balloch. Per 2H **135**
Balloch. W Dun 1E **127**
Ballochan. Abers 4C **152**
Ballochgoy. Arg 3B **126**
Ballochmyle. E Ayr 2E **117**
Ballochroy. Arg 4F **125**
Balloo. N Dwn 3J **179**
Balls Cross. W Sus 3A **26**
Ball's Green. E Sus 2F **27**
Ballsmill. New M 8D **178**
Ballyalton. New M 5K **179**
Ballybogy. Caus 3F **174**
Ballycarry. ME Ant 7L **175**
Ballycassidy. Ferm 7E **176**
Ballycastle. Caus 2H **175**
Ballyclare. Ant 7J **175**
Ballyeaston. Ant 7J **175**
Ballygally. ME Ant 6K **175**
Ballygawley. M Ulst 4A **178**
Ballygowan. N Dwn 3J **179**
Ballygown. Arg 4F **139**
Ballygrant. Arg 3B **124**
Ballyhalbert. N Dwn 3L **179**
Ballyholland. New M 7F **178**
Ballyhornan. New M 5K **179**
Ballykelly. Caus 4C **174**
Ballykinler. New M 6J **179**
Ballylesson. Lis 3H **179**
Ballymagorry. Derr 2F **176**
Ballymartin. New M 8H **179**
**Ballymena**. ME Ant 6H **175**
Ballymichael. N Ayr 2D **122**
Ballymoney. Caus 4F **174**
Ballynagard. Derr 4A **174**
Ballynahinch. New M 4H **179**
Ballynakilly. M Ulst 3C **178**
Ballynoe. New M 5J **179**
Ballynure. Ant 7K **175**
Ballyrashane. Caus 3E **174**
Ballyrobert. Ant 8J **175**
Ballyronan. M Ulst 8F **174**
Ballyroney. Arm 6G **179**
Ballyscullion. Caus 3C **174**
Ballystrudder. ME Ant 7L **175**
Ballyvoy. Caus 2H **175**
Ballyward. New M 6G **179**
Ballywater. N Dwn 3L **179**
Ballywonard. Ant 1G **179**
Balmacara. High 1G **147**
Balmaclellan. Dum 2D **110**
Balmacqueen. High 1D **154**
Balmaha. Stir 4D **134**
Balmalcolm. Fife 3F **137**
Balmalloch. N Lan 2A **128**
Balmeanach. High 5E **155**
Balmedie. Abers 2G **153**
Balmerino. Fife 1F **137**
Balmerlawn. Hants 2B **16**
Balmore. E Dun 2H **127**
Balmore. High 4B **154**
Balmullo. Fife 1G **137**
Balmurrie. Dum 3H **109**
Balnaboth. Ang 2C **144**
Balnabruaich. High 1B **158**
Balnabruich. High 5D **168**
Balnacoil. High 2F **165**
Balnacra. High 4B **156**
Balnacroft. Abers 4G **151**
Balnageith. Mor 3E **159**
Balnaglaic. High 5G **157**
Balnagrantach. High 5G **157**
Balnaguard. Per 3G **143**
Balnahard. Arg 4B **132**
Balnain. High 5G **157**
Balnakeil. High 2D **166**
Balnaknock. High 2D **154**
Balnamoon. Abers 3G **161**
Balnamoon. Ang 2E **145**
Balnamore. Caus 4F **174**
Balnapaling. High 2B **158**
Balornock. Glas 3H **127**
Balquhidder. Stir 1E **135**
Balsall. W Mid 3G **61**
Balsall Common. W Mid 3G **61**
Balscote. Oxon 1B **50**
Balsham. Cambs 5E **65**
Balstonia. Thur 2A **40**
Baltasound. Shet 1H **173**
Balterley. Staf 5B **84**
Baltersan. Dum 3B **110**
Balthangie. Abers 3F **161**
Baltonsborough. Som 3A **22**
Balvaird. High 3H **157**
Balvaird. Per 2D **136**
Balvenie. Mor 4H **159**
Balvicar. Arg 2E **133**
Balvraid. High 2G **147**
Balvraid Lodge. High 5C **158**
Bamber Bridge. Lanc 2D **90**
Bamber's Green. Essx 3F **53**
Bamburgh. Nmbd 1F **121**
Bamford. Derbs 2G **85**
Bamfurlong. G Man 4D **90**
Bampton. Cumb 3G **103**
Bampton. Devn 4C **20**
Bampton. Oxon 5B **50**
Bampton Grange. Cumb 3G **103**
Banavie. High 1F **141**
**Banbridge**. Arm 5F **178**
**Banbury**. Oxon 1C **50**

Brechin—Burton-in-Kendal

Brechin. Ang . . . 3F 145
Breckles. Norf . . . 1B 66
Brecon. Powy . . . 3D 46
**Brecon Beacons**. Powy . . . 3C 46
**Bredbury**. G Man . . . 1D 84
Brede. E Sus . . . 4C 28
Bredenbury. Here . . . 5A 60
Bredfield. Suff . . . 5E 67
Bredgar. Kent . . . 4C 40
Bredhurst. Kent . . . 4B 40
Bredicot. Worc . . . 5D 60
Bredon. Worc . . . 2E 49
Bredon's Norton. Worc . . . 2E 49
Bredwardine. Here . . . 1G 47
Breedon on the Hill. Leics . . . 3B 74
Breibhig. W Isl . . . 9B 170 (on Barra)
Breibhig. W Isl . . . 4G 171 (on Isle of Lewis)
Breich. W Lot . . . 3C 128
Breightmet. G Man . . . 4F 91
Breighton. E Yor . . . 1H 93
Breinton. Here . . . 2H 47
Breinton Common. Here . . . 2H 47
Breiwick. Shet . . . 7F 173
Brelston Green. Here . . . 3A 48
Bremhill. Wilts . . . 4E 35
Brenachie. High . . . 1B 158
Brenchley. Kent . . . 1A 28
Brendon. Devn . . . 2A 20
**Brent Cross**. G Lon . . . 2D 38
Brent Eleigh. Suff . . . 1C 54
**Brentford**. G Lon . . . 3C 38
Brentingby. Leics . . . 4E 75
Brent Knoll. Som . . . 1G 21
Brent Pelham. Herts . . . 2E 53
**Brentwood**. Essx . . . 1G 39
Brenzett. Kent . . . 3E 28
Brereton. Staf . . . 4E 73
Brereton Cross. Staf . . . 4E 73
Brereton Green. Ches E . . . 4B 84
Brereton Heath. Ches E . . . 4C 84
Bressingham. Norf . . . 2C 66
Bretby. Derbs . . . 3G 73
Bretford. Warw . . . 3B 62
Bretforton. Worc . . . 1F 49
Bretherdale Head. Cumb . . . 4G 103
Bretherton. Lanc . . . 2C 90
Brettabister. Shet . . . 6F 173
Brettenham. Norf . . . 2B 66
Brettenham. Suff . . . 5B 66
Bretton. Flin . . . 4F 83
Bretton. Pet . . . 5A 76
Brewlands Bridge. Ang . . . 2A 144
Brewood. Staf . . . 5C 72
Briantspuddle. Dors . . . 3D 14
Bricket Wood. Herts . . . 5B 52
Bricklehampton. Worc . . . 1E 49
Bride. IOM . . . 1D 108
Bridekirk. Cumb . . . 1C 102
Bridell. Pemb . . . 1B 44
Bridestowe. Devn . . . 4F 11
Brideswell. Abers . . . 5C 160
Bridford. Devn . . . 4B 12
Bridge. Corn . . . 4A 6
Bridge. Kent . . . 5F 41
Bridge. Som . . . 2G 13
Bridge End. Bed . . . 5H 63
Bridge End. Cumb . . . 5D 102 (nr. Broughton in Furness)
Bridge End. Cumb . . . 5E 113 (nr. Dalston)
Bridge End. Linc . . . 2A 76
Bridge End. Shet . . . 8E 173
Bridgefoot. Ang . . . 5C 144
Bridgefoot. Cumb . . . 2B 102
Bridge Green. Essx . . . 2E 53
Bridgehampton. Som . . . 4A 22
Bridge Hewick. N Yor . . . 2F 99
Bridgehill. Dur . . . 4D 115
Bridgemary. Hants . . . 2D 16
Bridgemere. Ches E . . . 1B 72
Bridgemont. Derbs . . . 2E 85
Bridgend. Abers . . . 5C 160 (nr. Huntly)
Bridgend. Abers . . . 5H 161 (nr. Peterhead)
Bridgend. Ang . . . 2E 145 (nr. Brechin)
Bridgend. Ang . . . 4C 144 (nr. Kirriemuir)
Bridgend. Arg . . . 4F 133 (nr. Lochgilphead)
Bridgend. Arg . . . 3B 124 (on Islay)
**Bridgend**. B'end . . . 3C 32
Bridgend. Cumb . . . 3E 103
Bridgend. Devn . . . 4B 8
Bridgend. Fife . . . 2F 137
Bridgend. High . . . 3F 157
Bridgend. Mor . . . 5A 160
Bridgend. Per . . . 1D 136
Bridgend. W Lot . . . 2D 128
Bridgend of Lintrathen. Ang . . . 3B 144
Bridgeness. Falk . . . 1D 128
Bridge of Alford. Abers . . . 2C 152
Bridge of Allan. Stir . . . 4G 135
Bridge of Avon. Mor . . . 5F 159
Bridge of Awe. Arg . . . 1H 133
Bridge of Balgie. Per . . . 4C 142
Bridge of Brown. High . . . 1F 151
Bridge of Cally. Per . . . 3A 144
Bridge of Canny. Abers . . . 4D 152
Bridge of Dee. Dum . . . 3E 111
Bridge of Don. Aber . . . 2G 153
Bridge of Dun. Ang . . . 3F 145
Bridge of Dye. Abers . . . 5D 152
Bridge of Earn. Per . . . 2D 136
Bridge of Ericht. Per . . . 3C 142
Bridge of Feugh. Abers . . . 4E 152
Bridge of Gairn. Abers . . . 4A 152
Bridge of Gaur. Per . . . 3C 142
Bridge of Muchalls. Abers . . . 4F 153
Bridge of Oich. High . . . 3F 149
Bridge of Orchy. Arg . . . 5H 141
Bridge of Walls. Shet . . . 6D 173
Bridge of Weir. Ren . . . 3E 127
Bridge Reeve. Devn . . . 1G 11
Bridgerule. Devn . . . 2C 10
Bridge Sollers. Here . . . 1H 47
Bridge Street. Suff . . . 1B 54
Bridgetown. Devn . . . 2E 9
Bridgetown. Som . . . 3C 20
Bridge Town. Warw . . . 5G 61
Bridge Trafford. Ches W . . . 3G 83
Bridgeyate. S Glo . . . 4B 34
Bridgham. Norf . . . 2B 66
**Bridgnorth**. Shrp . . . 1B 60
Bridgtown. Staf . . . 5D 73
**Bridgwater**. Som . . . 3G 21
**Bridlington**. E Yor . . . 3F 101
**Bridport**. Dors . . . 3H 13
Bridstow. Here . . . 3A 48
**Brierfield**. Lanc . . . 1G 91
Brierley. Glos . . . 4B 48
Brierley. Here . . . 5G 59
Brierley. S Yor . . . 3E 93
Brierley Hill. W Mid . . . 2D 60
Brierton. Hart . . . 1B 106
Briestfield. W Yor . . . 3C 92
Brigg. N Lin . . . 4D 94
Briggate. Norf . . . 3F 79
Briggswath. N Yor . . . 4F 107
Brigham. Cumb . . . 1B 102
Brigham. E Yor . . . 4E 101
**Brighouse**. W Yor . . . 2B 92
Brighstone. IOW . . . 4C 16
Brightgate. Derbs . . . 5G 85
Brighthampton. Oxon . . . 5B 50
Brightholmlee. S Yor . . . 1G 85
Brightley. Devn . . . 3G 11
Brightling. E Sus . . . 3A 28
Brightlingsea. Essx . . . 4D 54
**Brighton**. Brig . . . 5E 27 & 192
Brighton. Corn . . . 3D 6
Brighton Hill. Hants . . . 2E 24
Brightons. Falk . . . 2C 128
Brightwalton. W Ber . . . 4C 36
Brightwalton Green. W Ber . . . 4C 36
Brightwell. Suff . . . 1F 55
Brightwell Baldwin. Oxon . . . 2E 37
Brightwell-cum-Sotwell. Oxon . . . 2D 36
Brigmerston. Wilts . . . 2G 23
Brignall. Dur . . . 3D 104
Brig o' Turk. Stir . . . 3E 135
Brigsley. NE Lin . . . 4F 95
Brigsteer. Cumb . . . 1D 97
Brigstock. Nptn . . . 2G 63
Brill. Buck . . . 4E 51
Brill. Corn . . . 4E 5
Brilley. Here . . . 1F 47
Brimaston. Pemb . . . 2D 42
Brimfield. Here . . . 4H 59
Brimington. Derbs . . . 3B 86
Brimley. Devn . . . 5B 12
Brimpsfield. Glos . . . 4E 49
Brimpton. W Ber . . . 5D 36
Brims. Orkn . . . 9B 172
Brimscombe. Glos . . . 5D 48
Brimstage. Mers . . . 2F 83
Brincliffe. S Yor . . . 2H 85
Brind. E Yor . . . 1H 93
Brindister. Shet . . . 6D 173 (nr. West Burrafirth)
Brindister. Shet . . . 8F 173 (nr. West Lerwick)
Brindle. Lanc . . . 2D 90
Brindley. Ches E . . . 5H 83
Brindley Ford. Stoke . . . 5C 84
Brineton. Staf . . . 4C 72
Bringhurst. Leics . . . 1F 63
Bringsty Common. Here . . . 5A 60
Brington. Cambs . . . 3H 63
Brinian. Orkn . . . 5D 172
Briningham. Norf . . . 2C 78
Brinkhill. Linc . . . 3C 88
Brinkley. Cambs . . . 5F 65
Brinklow. Warw . . . 3B 62
Brinkworth. Wilts . . . 3F 35
Brinscall. Lanc . . . 2E 91
Brinscombe. Som . . . 1H 21
Brinsley. Notts . . . 1B 74
Brinsworth. S Yor . . . 2B 86
Brinton. Norf . . . 2C 78
Brisco. Cumb . . . 4F 113
Brisley. Norf . . . 3B 78
Brislington. Bris . . . 4B 34
Brissenden Green. Kent . . . 2D 28
**Bristol**. Bris . . . 4A 34 & 193
Bristol Airport. N Som . . . 5A 34
Briston. Norf . . . 2C 78
Britannia. Lanc . . . 2G 91
Britford. Wilts . . . 4G 23
Brithdir. Cphy . . . 5E 47
Brithdir. Cdgn . . . 1D 44
Brithdir. Gwyn . . . 4G 69
Briton Ferry. Neat . . . 3G 31
Britwell Salome. Oxon . . . 2E 37
**Brixham**. Torb . . . 3F 9
Brixton. Devn . . . 3B 8
**Brixton**. G Lon . . . 3E 39
Brixton Deverill. Wilts . . . 3D 22
Brixworth. Nptn . . . 3E 63
Brize Norton. Oxon . . . 5B 50
Broad Alley. Worc . . . 4C 60
Broad Blunsdon. Swin . . . 2G 35
Broadbottom. G Man . . . 1D 85
Broadbridge. W Sus . . . 2G 17
Broadbridge Heath. W Sus . . . 2C 26
Broad Campden. Glos . . . 2G 49
Broad Chalke. Wilts . . . 4F 23
Broadclyst. Devn . . . 3C 12
Broadfield. Inv . . . 2E 127
Broadfield. Pemb . . . 4F 43
Broadfield. W Sus . . . 2D 26
Broadford. High . . . 1E 147
Broadford Bridge. W Sus . . . 3B 26
Broadgate. Cumb . . . 1A 96
Broad Green. Cambs . . . 5F 65
Broad Green. C Beds . . . 1H 51
Broad Green. Worc . . . 3D 61 (nr. Bromsgrove)
Broad Green. Worc . . . 5B 60 (nr. Worcester)
Broadhaven. High . . . 3F 169
Broad Haven. Pemb . . . 3C 42
Broadheath. G Man . . . 2B 84
Broad Heath. Staf . . . 3C 72
Broadheath. Worc . . . 4A 60
Broadheath Common. Worc . . . 5C 60
Broadhembury. Devn . . . 2E 12
Broadhempston. Devn . . . 2E 9
Broad Hill. Cambs . . . 3E 65
Broad Hinton. Wilts . . . 4G 35
Broadholme. Derbs . . . 1A 74
Broadholme. Linc . . . 3F 87
Broadlay. Carm . . . 5D 44
Broad Laying. Hants . . . 5C 36
Broadley. Lanc . . . 3G 91
Broadley. Mor . . . 2A 160
Broadley Common. Essx . . . 5E 53
Broad Marston. Worc . . . 1G 49
Broadmayne. Dors . . . 4C 14
Broadmere. Hants . . . 2E 24
Broadmoor. Pemb . . . 4E 43
Broad Oak. Carm . . . 3F 45
Broad Oak. Cumb . . . 5C 102
Broad Oak. Devn . . . 3D 12
Broadoak. Dors . . . 3H 13 (nr. Bridport)
Broad Oak. Dors . . . 1C 14 (nr. Sturminster Newton)
Broad Oak. E Sus . . . 4C 28 (nr. Hastings)
Broad Oak. E Sus . . . 3H 27 (nr. Heathfield)
Broadoak. Glos . . . 4B 48
Broadoak. Hants . . . 1D 16
Broad Oak. Here . . . 3H 47
Broad Oak. Kent . . . 4F 41
Broadrashes. Mor . . . 3B 160
Broadsea. Abers . . . 2G 161
Broad's Green. Essx . . . 4G 53
Broadshard. Som . . . 1H 13
**Broadstairs**. Kent . . . 4H 41
**Broads, The**. Norf . . . 5G 79
Broadstone. Pool . . . 3F 15
Broadstone. Shrp . . . 2H 59
Broad Street. E Sus . . . 4C 28
Broad Street. Kent . . . 1F 29 (nr. Ashford)
Broad Street. Kent . . . 5C 40 (nr. Maidstone)
Broad Street Green. Essx . . . 5B 54
Broad, The. Here . . . 4G 59
Broad Town. Wilts . . . 4F 35
Broadwas. Worc . . . 5B 60
Broadwath. Cumb . . . 4F 113
Broadway. Carm . . . 5D 45 (nr. Kidwelly)
Broadway. Carm . . . 4G 43 (nr. Laugharne)
Broadway. Pemb . . . 3C 42
Broadway. Som . . . 1G 13
Broadway. Suff . . . 3F 67
Broadway. Worc . . . 2F 49
Broadwell. Glos . . . 4A 48 (nr. Cinderford)
Broadwell. Glos . . . 3H 49 (nr. Stow-on-the-Wold)
Broadwell. Oxon . . . 5A 50
Broadwell. Warw . . . 4B 62
Broadwell House. Nmbd . . . 4C 114
Broadwey. Dors . . . 4B 14
Broadwindsor. Dors . . . 2H 13
Broadwoodkelly. Devn . . . 2G 11
Broadwoodwidger. Devn . . . 4E 11
Broallan. High . . . 4G 157
Brobury. Here . . . 1G 47
Brochel. High . . . 4E 155
Brockaghboy. Caus . . . 5E 174
Brockamin. Worc . . . 5B 60
Brockbridge. Hants . . . 1E 16
Brockdish. Norf . . . 3E 66
Brockencote. Worc . . . 3C 60
Brockenhurst. Hants . . . 2A 16
Brocketsbrae. S Lan . . . 1H 117
Brockford Street. Suff . . . 4D 66
Brockhall. Nptn . . . 4D 62
Brockham. Surr . . . 1C 26
Brockhampton. Glos . . . 3E 49 (nr. Bishop's Cleeve)
Brockhampton. Glos . . . 3F 49 (nr. Sevenhampton)
Brockhampton. Here . . . 2A 48
Brockhill. Bord . . . 2F 119
Brockholes. W Yor . . . 3B 92
Brockhurst. Hants . . . 2D 16
Brocklesby. Linc . . . 3E 95
Brockley. N Som . . . 5H 33
Brockley Corner. Suff . . . 3H 65
Brockley Green. Suff . . . 1H 53 (nr. Bury St Edmunds)
Brockley Green. Suff . . . 5H 65 (nr. Haverhill)
Brockleymoor. Cumb . . . 1F 103
Brockmoor. W Mid . . . 2D 60
Brockton. Shrp . . . 2F 59 (nr. Bishop's Castle)
Brockton. Shrp . . . 5B 72 (nr. Madeley)
Brockton. Shrp . . . 1H 59 (nr. Much Wenlock)
Brockton. Shrp . . . 5F 71 (nr. Pontesbury)
Brockton. Staf . . . 2C 72
Brockton. Telf . . . 4B 72
Brockweir. Glos . . . 5A 48
Brockworth. Glos . . . 4D 49
Brocton. Staf . . . 4D 72
Brodick. N Ayr . . . 2E 123
Brodie. Mor . . . 3D 159
Brodiesord. Abers . . . 3C 160
Brodsworth. S Yor . . . 4F 93
Brogaig. High . . . 2D 154
Brogborough. C Beds . . . 2H 51
Brokenborough. Wilts . . . 3E 35
Broken Cross. Ches E . . . 3C 84
Bromborough. Mers . . . 2F 83
Bromdon. Shrp . . . 2A 60
Brome. Suff . . . 3D 66
Brome Street. Suff . . . 3D 66
Bromeswell. Suff . . . 5F 67
Bromfield. Cumb . . . 5C 112
Bromfield. Shrp . . . 3G 59
Bromford. W Mid . . . 1F 61
Bromham. Bed . . . 5H 63
Bromham. Wilts . . . 5E 35
**Bromley**. G Lon . . . 4F 39
Bromley. Herts . . . 3E 53
Bromley. Shrp . . . 1B 60
Bromley Cross. G Man . . . 3F 91
Bromley Green. Kent . . . 2D 28
Bromley Wood. Staf . . . 3F 73
Brompton. Medw . . . 4B 40
Brompton. N Yor . . . 5A 106 (nr. Northallerton)
Brompton. N Yor . . . 1D 100 (nr. Scarborough)
Brompton. Shrp . . . 5H 71
Brompton-on-Swale. N Yor . . . 5F 105
Brompton Ralph. Som . . . 3D 20
Brompton Regis. Som . . . 3C 20
Bromsash. Here . . . 3B 48
Bromsberrow. Glos . . . 2C 48
Bromsberrow Heath. Glos . . . 2C 48
**Bromsgrove**. Worc . . . 3D 60
Bromstead Heath. Staf . . . 4B 72
Bromyard. Here . . . 5A 60
Bromyard Downs. Here . . . 5A 60
Bronaber. Gwyn . . . 2G 69
Broncroft. Shrp . . . 2H 59
Brongest. Cdgn . . . 1D 44
Brongwyn. Cdgn . . . 1C 44
Bronington. Wrex . . . 2G 71
Bronllys. Powy . . . 2E 47
Bronnant. Cdgn . . . 4F 57
Bronwydd Arms. Carm . . . 3E 45
Bronydd. Powy . . . 1F 47
Bronygarth. Shrp . . . 2E 71
Brook. Carm . . . 4G 43
Brook. Hants . . . 1A 16 (nr. Cadnam)
Brook. Hants . . . 4B 24 (nr. Romsey)
Brook. IOW . . . 4B 16
Brook. Kent . . . 1E 29
Brook. Surr . . . 1B 26 (nr. Guildford)
Brook. Surr . . . 2A 26 (nr. Haslemere)
Brooke. Norf . . . 1E 67
Brooke. Rut . . . 5F 75
Brookeborough. Ferm . . . 8F 176
Brookenby. Linc . . . 1B 88
Brookend. Glos . . . 5B 48
Brook End. Worc . . . 1D 48
Brookfield. Lanc . . . 1D 90
Brookfield. Ren . . . 3F 127
Brookhouse. Lanc . . . 3E 97
Brookhouse. S Yor . . . 2C 86
Brookhouse Green. Ches E . . . 4C 84
Brookhouses. Staf . . . 1D 73
Brookhurst. Mers . . . 2F 83
Brookland. Kent . . . 3D 28
Brooklands. G Man . . . 1B 84
Brooklands. Shrp . . . 1H 71
Brookmans Park. Herts . . . 5C 52
Brooks. Powy . . . 1D 58
Brooksby. Leics . . . 4D 74
Brooks Green. W Sus . . . 3C 26
Brook Street. Essx . . . 1G 39
Brook Street. Kent . . . 2D 28
Brook Street. W Sus . . . 3E 27
Brookthorpe. Glos . . . 4D 48
Brookville. Norf . . . 1G 65
Brookwood. Surr . . . 5A 38
Broom. C Beds . . . 1B 52
Broom. Fife . . . 3F 137
Broom. Warw . . . 5E 61
Broome. Norf . . . 1F 67
Broome. Shrp . . . 1H 59 (nr. Cardington)
Broome. Shrp . . . 2G 59 (nr. Craven Arms)
Broome. Worc . . . 3D 60
Broomedge. Warr . . . 2B 84
Broomend. Abers . . . 2E 153
Broomer's Corner. W Sus . . . 3C 26
Broomfield. Abers . . . 5G 161
Broomfield. Essx . . . 4H 53
Broomfield. Kent . . . 4F 41 (nr. Herne Bay)
Broomfield. Kent . . . 5C 40 (nr. Maidstone)
Broomfield. Som . . . 3F 21
Broomfleet. E Yor . . . 2B 94
Broom Green. Norf . . . 3B 78
Broomhall. Ches E . . . 1A 72
Broomhall. Wind . . . 4A 38
Broomhaugh. Nmbd . . . 3D 114
Broom Hill. Dors . . . 2F 15
Broomhill. High . . . 1D 151 (nr. Grantown-on-Spey)
Broomhill. High . . . 1B 158 (nr. Invergordon)
Broomhill. Norf . . . 5F 77
Broomhill. S Yor . . . 4E 93
Broom Hill. Worc . . . 3D 60
Broomhillbank. Dum . . . 5D 118
Broomholm. Norf . . . 2F 79
Broomlands. Dum . . . 4C 118
Broomley. Nmbd . . . 3D 114
Broom of Moy. Mor . . . 3E 159
Broompark. Dur . . . 5F 115
Broom's Green. Glos . . . 2C 48
Brora. High . . . 3G 165
Broseley. Shrp . . . 5A 72
Brotherhouse Bar. Linc . . . 4B 76
Brotheridge Green. Worc . . . 1D 48
Brotherlee. Dur . . . 1C 104
Brothertoft. Linc . . . 1B 76
Brotherton. N Yor . . . 2E 93
Brotton. Red C . . . 3D 107
Broubster. High . . . 2C 168
Brough. Cumb . . . 3A 104
Brough. Derbs . . . 2F 85
Brough. E Yor . . . 2C 94
Brough. High . . . 1E 169
Brough. Notts . . . 5F 87
Brough. Orkn . . . 6C 172 (nr. Finstown)
Brough. Orkn . . . 9D 172 (nr. St Margaret's Hope)
Brough. Shet . . . 6F 173 (nr. Benston)
Brough. Shet . . . 4F 173 (nr. Booth of Toft)
Brough. Shet . . . 7G 173 (on Bressay)
Brough. Shet . . . 5G 173 (on Whalsay)
Broughall. Shrp . . . 1H 71
Brougham. Cumb . . . 2G 103
Brough Lodge. Shet . . . 2G 173
Broughshane. ME Ant . . . 6H 175
Brough Sowerby. Cumb . . . 3A 104
Broughton. Cambs . . . 3B 64
Broughton. Flin . . . 4F 83
Broughton. Hants . . . 3B 24
Broughton. Lanc . . . 1D 90
Broughton. Mil . . . 2G 51
Broughton. Nptn . . . 3F 63
Broughton. N Lin . . . 4C 94
Broughton. N Yor . . . 2B 100 (nr. Malton)
Broughton. N Yor . . . 4B 98 (nr. Skipton)
Broughton. Orkn . . . 3D 172
Broughton. Oxon . . . 2C 50
Broughton. Bord . . . 1D 118
Broughton. Staf . . . 2B 72
Broughton. V Glam . . . 4C 32
Broughton Astley. Leics . . . 1C 62
Broughton Beck. Cumb . . . 1B 96
Broughton Cross. Cumb . . . 1B 102
Broughton Gifford. Wilts . . . 5D 35
Broughton Green. Worc . . . 4D 60
Broughton Hackett. Worc . . . 5D 60
Broughton in Furness. Cumb . . . 1B 96
Broughton Mills. Cumb . . . 5D 102
Broughton Moor. Cumb . . . 1B 102
Broughton Park. G Man . . . 4G 91
Broughton Poggs. Oxon . . . 5H 49
Broughtown. Orkn . . . 3F 172
Broughty Ferry. D'dee . . . 5D 144
Browland. Shet . . . 6D 173
Brownbread Street. E Sus . . . 4A 28
Brown Candover. Hants . . . 3D 24
Brown Edge. Lanc . . . 3B 90
Brown Edge. Staf . . . 5D 84
Brownhill. Bkbn . . . 1E 91
Brownhill. Shrp . . . 3G 71
Brownhills. Shrp . . . 2A 72
**Brownhills**. W Mid . . . 5E 73
Brown Knowl. Ches W . . . 5G 83
Brownlow. Ches E . . . 4C 84
Brownlow Heath. Ches E . . . 4C 84
Brown's Green. W Mid . . . 1E 61
Brownshill. Glos . . . 5D 49
Brownston. Devn . . . 3C 8
Brownstone. Devn . . . 2A 12
Browston Green. Norf . . . 5G 79
Broxa. N Yor . . . 5G 107
Broxbourne. Herts . . . 5D 52
Broxburn. E Lot . . . 2C 130
**Broxburn**. W Lot . . . 2D 128
Broxholme. Linc . . . 3G 87
Broxted. Essx . . . 3F 53
Broxton. Ches W . . . 5G 83
Broxwood. Here . . . 5F 59
Broyle Side. E Sus . . . 4F 27
Brù. W Isl . . . 3F 171
Bruach Mairi. W Isl . . . 4G 171
Bruairnis. W Isl . . . 8C 170
Bruan. High . . . 5F 169
Bruar Lodge. Per . . . 1F 143
Brucehill. W Dun . . . 2E 127
Brucklay. Abers . . . 3G 161
Bruera. Ches W . . . 4G 83
Bruern Abbey. Oxon . . . 3A 50
Bruichladdich. Arg . . . 3A 124
Bruisyard. Suff . . . 4F 67
Bruisyard Street. Suff . . . 4F 67
Brund. Staf . . . 4F 85
Brundall. Norf . . . 5F 79
Brundish. Norf . . . 1F 67
Brundish. Suff . . . 4E 67
Brundish Street. Suff . . . 3E 67
Brunery. High . . . 1B 140
Brunswick Village. Tyne . . . 2F 115
Brunthwaite. W Yor . . . 5C 98
Bruntingthorpe. Leics . . . 1D 62
Brunton. Fife . . . 1F 137
Brunton. Nmbd . . . 2G 121
Brunton. Wilts . . . 1H 23
Brushford. Devn . . . 2G 11
Brushford. Som . . . 4C 20
Brusta. W Isl . . . 1E 170
Bruton. Som . . . 3B 22
Bryansford. New M . . . 6H 179
Bryanston. Dors . . . 2D 14
Bryant's Bottom. Buck . . . 2G 37
Brydekirk. Dum . . . 2C 112
Brymbo. Cnwy . . . 3H 81
**Brymbo**. Wrex . . . 5E 83
Brympton D'Evercy. Som . . . 1A 14
Bryn. Carm . . . 5F 45
Bryn. G Man . . . 4D 90
Bryn. Neat . . . 2B 32
Bryn. Shrp . . . 2E 59
Brynamman. Carm . . . 4H 45
Brynberian. Pemb . . . 1F 43
Brynbryddan. Neat . . . 2A 32
Bryncae. Rhon . . . 3C 32
Bryncethin. B'end . . . 3C 32
Bryncir. Gwyn . . . 1D 69
Bryncoch. Neat . . . 3G 31
Bryncroes. Gwyn . . . 2B 68
Bryncrug. Gwyn . . . 5F 69
Bryn Du. IOA . . . 3C 80
Bryn Eden. Gwyn . . . 3G 69
Bryneglwys. Den . . . 1D 70
Bryn Eglwys. Gwyn . . . 4F 81
Brynford. Flin . . . 3D 82
Bryn Gates. G Man . . . 4D 90
Bryn Golau. Rhon . . . 3D 32
Bryngwran. IOA . . . 3C 80
Bryngwyn. Mon . . . 5G 47
Bryngwyn. Powy . . . 1E 47
Bryn-henllan. Pemb . . . 1E 43
Brynhoffnant. Cdgn . . . 5C 56
Bryn-llwyn. Flin . . . 2C 82
Brynllywarch. Powy . . . 2D 58
**Brynmawr**. Blae . . . 4E 47
Bryn-mawr. Gwyn . . . 2B 68
Brynmenyn. B'end . . . 3C 32
Brynmill. Swan . . . 3F 31
Brynna. Rhon . . . 3C 32
Brynrefail. Gwyn . . . 4E 81
Brynrefail. IOA . . . 2D 81
Brynsadler. Rhon . . . 3D 32
Bryn-Saith Marchog. Den . . . 5C 82
Brynsiencyn. IOA . . . 4D 81
Brynteg. IOA . . . 2D 81
Brynteg. Wrex . . . 5F 83
Brynygwenyn. Mon . . . 4G 47
Bryn-y-maen. Cnwy . . . 3H 81
Buaile nam Bodach. W Isl . . . 8C 170
Bualintur. High . . . 1C 146
Bubbenhall. Warw . . . 3A 62
Bubwith. E Yor . . . 1H 93
Buccleuch. Bord . . . 3F 119
Buchanan Smithy. Stir . . . 1F 127
Buchanhaven. Abers . . . 4H 161
Buchanty. Per . . . 1B 136
Buchany. Stir . . . 3G 135
Buchley. E Dun . . . 2G 127
Buchlyvie. Stir . . . 4E 135
Buckabank. Cumb . . . 5E 113
Buckden. Cambs . . . 4A 64
Buckden. N Yor . . . 2B 98
Buckenham. Norf . . . 5F 79
Buckerell. Devn . . . 2E 12
Buckfast. Devn . . . 2D 8
Buckfastleigh. Devn . . . 2D 8
**Buckhaven**. Fife . . . 4F 137
Buckholm. Bord . . . 1G 119
Buckholt. Here . . . 4A 48
Buckhorn Weston. Dors . . . 4C 22
Buckhurst Hill. Essx . . . 1F 39
Buckie. Mor . . . 2B 160
**Buckingham**. Buck . . . 2E 51
Buckland. Buck . . . 4G 51
Buckland. Glos . . . 2F 49
Buckland. Here . . . 5H 59
Buckland. Herts . . . 2D 52
Buckland. Kent . . . 1H 29
Buckland. Oxon . . . 2B 36
Buckland. Surr . . . 5D 38
Buckland Brewer. Devn . . . 4E 19
Buckland Common. Buck . . . 5H 51
Buckland Dinham. Som . . . 1C 22
Buckland Filleigh. Devn . . . 2E 11
Buckland in the Moor. Devn . . . 5H 11
Buckland Monachorum. Devn . . . 2A 8
Buckland Newton. Dors . . . 2B 14
Buckland Ripers. Dors . . . 4B 14
Buckland St Mary. Som . . . 1F 13
Buckland-tout-Saints. Devn . . . 4D 8
Bucklebury. W Ber . . . 4D 36
Bucklegate. Linc . . . 2C 76
Buckleigh. Devn . . . 4E 19
Buckler's Hard. Hants . . . 3C 16
Bucklesham. Suff . . . 1F 55
**Buckley**. Flin . . . 4E 83
Buckley Green. Warw . . . 4F 61
Buckley Hill. Mers . . . 1F 83
Bucklow Hill. Ches E . . . 2B 84
Buckminster. Leics . . . 3F 75
Bucknall. Linc . . . 4A 88
Bucknall. Stoke . . . 1D 72
Bucknell. Oxon . . . 3D 50
Bucknell. Shrp . . . 3F 59
Buckpool. Mor . . . 2B 160
Bucksburn. Aber . . . 3F 153
Buck's Cross. Devn . . . 4D 18
Bucks Green. W Sus . . . 2B 26
Buckshaw Village. Lanc . . . 2D 90
Bucks Hill. Herts . . . 5A 52
Bucks Horn Oak. Hants . . . 2G 25
Buck's Mills. Devn . . . 4D 18
Buckton. E Yor . . . 2F 101
Buckton. Here . . . 3F 59
Buckton. Nmbd . . . 1E 121
Buckton Vale. G Man . . . 4H 91
Buckworth. Cambs . . . 3A 64
Budby. Notts . . . 4D 86
Bude. Corn . . . 2C 10
Budge's Shop. Corn . . . 3H 7
Budlake. Devn . . . 2C 12
Budle. Nmbd . . . 1F 121
Budleigh Salterton. Devn . . . 4D 12
Budock Water. Corn . . . 5B 6
Buerton. Ches E . . . 1A 72
Buffler's Holt. Buck . . . 2E 51
Bugbrooke. Nptn . . . 5D 62
Buglawton. Ches E . . . 4C 84
Bugle. Corn . . . 3E 6
Bugthorpe. E Yor . . . 4B 100
Buildwas. Shrp . . . 5A 72
Builth Road. Powy . . . 5C 58
Builth Wells. Powy . . . 5C 58
Bulbourne. Buck . . . 4H 51
Bulby. Linc . . . 3H 75
Bulcote. Notts . . . 1D 74
Buldoo. High . . . 2B 168
Bulford. Wilts . . . 2G 23
Bulford Camp. Wilts . . . 2G 23
Bulkeley. Ches E . . . 5H 83
Bulkington. Warw . . . 2A 62
Bulkington. Wilts . . . 1E 23
Bulkworthy. Devn . . . 1D 11
Bullamoor. N Yor . . . 5A 106
Bull Bay. IOA . . . 1D 80
Bullbridge. Derbs . . . 5A 86
Bullgill. Cumb . . . 1B 102
Bull Hill. Hants . . . 3B 16
Bullinghope. Here . . . 2A 48
Bull's Green. Herts . . . 4C 52
Bullwood. Arg . . . 2C 126
Bulmer. Essx . . . 1B 54
Bulmer. N Yor . . . 3A 100
Bulmer Tye. Essx . . . 2B 54
Bulphan. Thur . . . 2H 39
Bulverhythe. E Sus . . . 5B 28
Bulwark. Abers . . . 4G 161
Bulwell. Nott . . . 1C 74
Bulwick. Nptn . . . 1G 63
Bumble's Green. Essx . . . 5E 53
Bun Abhainn Eadarra. W Isl . . . 7D 171
Bunacaimb. High . . . 5E 147
Bun a' Mhuillinn. W Isl . . . 7C 170
Bunarkaig. High . . . 5D 148
Bunbury. Ches E . . . 5H 83
Bunchrew. High . . . 4A 158
Bundalloch. High . . . 1A 148
Buness. Shet . . . 1H 173
Bunessan. Arg . . . 1A 132
Bungay. Suff . . . 2F 67
Bunkegivie. High . . . 2H 149
Bunker's Hill. Cambs . . . 5D 76
Bunkers Hill. Linc . . . 5B 88
Bunker's Hill. Suff . . . 5H 79
Bunloit. High . . . 1H 149
Bunnahabhain. Arg . . . 2C 124
Bunny. Notts . . . 3C 74
Bunoich. High . . . 3F 149
Bunree. High . . . 2E 141
Bunroy. High . . . 5E 149
Buntait. High . . . 5G 157
Buntingford. Herts . . . 3D 52
Bunting's Green. Essx . . . 2B 54
Bunwell. Norf . . . 1D 66
Burbage. Derbs . . . 3E 85
Burbage. Leics . . . 1B 62
Burbage. Wilts . . . 5H 35
Burcher. Here . . . 4F 59
Burchett's Green. Wind . . . 3G 37
Burcombe. Wilts . . . 3F 23
Burcot. Oxon . . . 2D 36
Burcot. Worc . . . 3D 61
Burcote. Shrp . . . 1B 60
Burcott. Buck . . . 3G 51
Burcott. Som . . . 2A 22
Burdale. N Yor . . . 3C 100
Burdrop. Oxon . . . 2B 50
Bures. Suff . . . 2C 54
Burford. Oxon . . . 4A 50
Burford. Shrp . . . 4H 59
Burf, The. Worc . . . 4C 60
Burg. Arg . . . 4E 139
Burgate Great Green. Suff . . . 3C 66
Burgate Little Green. Suff . . . 3C 66
**Burgess Hill**. W Sus . . . 4E 27
Burgh. Suff . . . 5E 67
Burgh by Sands. Cumb . . . 4E 113
Burgh Castle. Norf . . . 5G 79
Burghclere. Hants . . . 5C 36
Burghead. Mor . . . 2F 159
Burghfield. W Ber . . . 5E 37
Burghfield Common. W Ber . . . 5E 37
Burghfield Hill. W Ber . . . 5E 37
Burgh Heath. Surr . . . 5D 38
Burghill. Here . . . 1H 47
Burgh le Marsh. Linc . . . 4E 89
Burgh Muir. Abers . . . 2E 153
Burgh next Aylsham. Norf . . . 3E 78
Burgh on Bain. Linc . . . 2B 88
Burgh St Margaret. Norf . . . 4G 79
Burgh St Peter. Norf . . . 1G 67
Burghwallis. S Yor . . . 3F 93
Burham. Kent . . . 4B 40
Buriton. Hants . . . 4F 25
Burland. Ches E . . . 5A 84
Burland. Shet . . . 8E 173
Burlawn. Corn . . . 2D 6
Burleigh. Brac . . . 4G 37
Burleigh. Glos . . . 5D 48
Burlescombe. Devn . . . 1D 12
Burleston. Dors . . . 3C 14
Burlestone. Devn . . . 4E 9
Burley. Hants . . . 2H 15
Burley. Rut . . . 4F 75
Burley. W Yor . . . 1C 92
Burleydam. Ches E . . . 1A 72
Burley Gate. Here . . . 1A 48
Burley in Wharfedale. W Yor . . . 5D 98
Burley Street. Hants . . . 2H 15
Burley Woodhead. W Yor . . . 5D 98
Burlingjobb. Powy . . . 5E 59
Burlington. Shrp . . . 4B 72
Burlton. Shrp . . . 3G 71
Burmantofts. W Yor . . . 1D 92
Burmarsh. Kent . . . 2F 29
Burmington. Warw . . . 2A 50
Burn. N Yor . . . 2F 93
Burnage. G Man . . . 1C 84
Burnaston. Derbs . . . 2G 73
Burnbanks. Cumb . . . 3G 103
Burnby. E Yor . . . 5C 100
Burncross. S Yor . . . 1H 85
Burneside. Cumb . . . 5G 103
Burness. Orkn . . . 3F 172
Burneston. N Yor . . . 1F 99
Burnett. Bath . . . 5B 34
Burnfoot. E Ayr . . . 4D 116
Burnfoot. Per . . . 3B 136
Burnfoot. Bord . . . 3H 119 (nr. Hawick)
Burnfoot. Bord . . . 3G 119 (nr. Roberton)
Burngreave. S Yor . . . 2A 86
Burnham. Buck . . . 2A 38
Burnham. N Lin . . . 3D 94
Burnham Deepdale. Norf . . . 1H 77
Burnham Green. Herts . . . 4C 52
Burnham Market. Norf . . . 1H 77
Burnham Norton. Norf . . . 1H 77
Burnham-on-Crouch. Essx . . . 1D 40
**Burnham-on-Sea**. Som . . . 2G 21
Burnham Overy Staithe. Norf . . . 1H 77
Burnham Overy Town. Norf . . . 1H 77
Burnham Thorpe. Norf . . . 1A 78
Burnhaven. Abers . . . 4H 161
Burnhead. Dum . . . 5A 118
Burnhervie. Abers . . . 2E 153
Burnhill Green. Staf . . . 5B 72
Burnhope. Dur . . . 5E 115
Burnhouse. N Ayr . . . 4E 127
Burniston. N Yor . . . 5H 107
Burnlee. W Yor . . . 4B 92
**Burnley**. Lanc . . . 1G 91
Burnmouth. Bord . . . 3F 131
Burn Naze. Lanc . . . 5C 96
Burn of Cambus. Stir . . . 3G 135
Burnopfield. Dur . . . 4E 115
Burnsall. N Yor . . . 3C 98
Burnside. Ang . . . 3E 145
Burnside. Ant . . . 8H 175
Burnside. Ant . . . 7J 175
Burnside. E Ayr . . . 3E 117
Burnside. Per . . . 3D 136
Burnside. Shet . . . 4D 173
Burnside. S Lan . . . 4H 127
Burnside. W Lot . . . 2D 129 (nr. Broxburn)
Burnside. W Lot . . . 2D 128 (nr. Winchburgh)
Burntcommon. Surr . . . 5B 38
Burntheath. Derbs . . . 2G 73
Burnt Heath. Essx . . . 3D 54
Burnt Hill. W Ber . . . 4D 36
Burnt Houses. Dur . . . 2E 105
Burntisland. Fife . . . 1F 129
Burnt Oak. G Lon . . . 1D 38
Burnton. E Ayr . . . 4D 117
Burntstalk. Norf . . . 2G 77
**Burntwood**. Staf . . . 5E 73
Burntwood Green. Staf . . . 5E 73
Burnt Yates. N Yor . . . 3E 99
Burnwynd. Edin . . . 3E 129
Burpham. Surr . . . 5B 38
Burpham. W Sus . . . 5B 26
Burradon. Nmbd . . . 4D 121
Burradon. Tyne . . . 2F 115
Burrafirth. Shet . . . 1H 173
Burragarth. Shet . . . 1G 173
Burras. Corn . . . 5A 6
Burraton. Corn . . . 3A 8
Burravoe. Shet . . . 3E 173 (nr. North Roe)
Burravoe. Shet . . . 5E 173 (on Mainland)
Burravoe. Shet . . . 4G 173 (on Yell)
Burray Village. Orkn . . . 8D 172
Burrells. Cumb . . . 3H 103
Burrelton. Per . . . 5A 144
Burren. New M . . . 7F 178
Burren Bridge. New M . . . 6H 179
Burridge. Devn . . . 2G 13
Burridge. Hants . . . 1D 16
Burrigill. High . . . 5E 169
Burrill. N Yor . . . 1E 99
Burringham. N Lin . . . 4B 94
Burrington. Devn . . . 1G 11
Burrington. Here . . . 3G 59
Burrington. N Som . . . 1H 21
Burrough End. Cambs . . . 5F 65
Burrough Green. Cambs . . . 5F 65
Burrough on the Hill. Leics . . . 4E 75
Burroughston. Orkn . . . 5E 172
Burrow. Devn . . . 4D 12
Burrow. Som . . . 2C 20
Burrowbridge. Som . . . 4G 21
Burrowhill. Surr . . . 4A 38
Burry. Swan . . . 3D 30
Burry Green. Swan . . . 3D 30
Burry Port. Carm . . . 5E 45
Burscough. Lanc . . . 3C 90
Burscough Bridge. Lanc . . . 3C 90
Bursea. E Yor . . . 1B 94
Burshill. E Yor . . . 5E 101
Bursledon. Hants . . . 2C 16
Burslem. Stoke . . . 1C 72
Burstall. Suff . . . 1D 54
Burstock. Dors . . . 2H 13
Burston. Devn . . . 2H 11
Burston. Norf . . . 2D 66
Burston. Staf . . . 2D 72
Burstow. Surr . . . 1E 27
Burstwick. E Yor . . . 2F 95
Burtersett. N Yor . . . 1A 98
Burtholme. Cumb . . . 3G 113
Burthorpe. Suff . . . 4G 65
Burthwaite. Cumb . . . 5F 113
Burtle. Som . . . 2H 21
Burtoft. Linc . . . 2B 76
Burton. Ches W . . . 4H 83 (nr. Kelsall)
Burton. Ches W . . . 3F 83 (nr. Neston)
Burton. Dors . . . 3G 15 (nr. Christchurch)
Burton. Dors . . . 3B 14 (nr. Dorchester)
Burton. Nmbd . . . 1F 121
Burton. Pemb . . . 4D 43
Burton. Som . . . 2E 21
Burton. Wilts . . . 4D 34 (nr. Chippenham)
Burton. Wilts . . . 3D 22 (nr. Warminster)
Burton. Wrex . . . 5F 83
Burton Agnes. E Yor . . . 3F 101
Burton Bradstock. Dors . . . 4H 13
Burton-by-Lincoln. Linc . . . 3G 87
Burton Coggles. Linc . . . 3G 75
Burton Constable. E Yor . . . 1E 95
Burton Corner. Linc . . . 1C 76
Burton End. Cambs . . . 1G 53
Burton End. Essx . . . 3F 53
Burton Fleming. E Yor . . . 2E 101
Burton Green. W Mid . . . 3G 61
Burton Green. Wrex . . . 5F 83
Burton Hastings. Warw . . . 2B 62
Burton-in-Kendal. Cumb . . . 2E 97

210 A-Z Great Britain Road Atlas

Burton in Lonsdale—Chapeltown

Burton in Lonsdale. *N Yor* 2F 97
Burton Joyce. *Notts* 1D 74
Burton Latimer. *Nptn* 3G 63
Burton Lazars. *Leics* 4E 75
Burton Leonard. *N Yor* 3F 99
Burton on the Wolds. *Leics* 3C 74
Burton Overy. *Leics* 1D 62
Burton Pedwardine. *Linc* 1A 76
Burton Pidsea. *E Yor* 1F 95
Burton Salmon. *N Yor* 2E 93
Burton's Green. *Essx* 3B 54
Burton Stather. *N Lin* 3B 94
Burton upon Stather. *N Lin* 3B 94
**Burton upon Trent**. *Staf* 3G 73
Burton Wolds. *Leics* 3D 74
Burtonwood. *Warr* 1H 83
Burwardsley. *Ches W* 5H 83
Burwarton. *Shrp* 2A 60
Burwash. *E Sus* 3A 28
Burwash Common. *E Sus* 3H 27
Burwash Weald. *E Sus* 3A 28
Burwell. *Cambs* 4E 65
Burwell. *Linc* 3C 88
Burwen. *IOA* 1D 80
Burwick. *Orkn* 9D 172
Bury. *Cambs* 2B 64
**Bury**. *G Man* 3G 91
Bury. *Som* 4C 20
Bury. *W Sus* 4B 26
Burybank. *Staf* 2C 72
Bury End. *Worc* 2F 49
Bury Green. *Herts* 3E 53
**Bury St Edmunds**. *Suff* 4H 65
Burythorpe. *N Yor* 3B 100
Busbridge. *Surr* 1A 26
Busby. *Per* 1C 136
Busby. *S Lan* 4G 127
Buscot. *Oxon* 2H 35
Bush. *Corn* 2C 10
Bush Bank. *Here* 5G 59
Bushbury. *W Mid* 5D 72
Bushby. *Leics* 5D 74
Bushey. *Dors* 4E 15
**Bushey**. *Herts* 1C 38
Bushey Heath. *Herts* 1C 38
Bush Green. *Norf* 1C 66
(nr. Attleborough)
Bush Green. *Norf* 2E 66
(nr. Harleston)
Bush Green. *Suff* 5B 66
Bushley. *Worc* 2D 49
Bushley Green. *Worc* 2D 48
Bushmead. *Bed* 4A 64
Bushmills. *Caus* 2F 174
Bushmoor. *Shrp* 2G 59
Bush, The. *M Ulst* 3C 178
Bushton. *Wilts* 4F 35
Bushy Common. *Norf* 4B 78
Busk. *Cumb* 5H 113
Buslingthorpe. *Linc* 2H 87
Bussage. *Glos* 5D 49
Bussex. *Som* 3G 21
Busta. *Shet* 5E 173
Butcher's Cross. *E Sus* 3G 27
Butcombe. *N Som* 5A 34
Bute Town. *Cphy* 5E 46
Butleigh. *Som* 3A 22
Butleigh Wootton. *Som* 3A 22
Butlers Marston. *Warw* 1B 50
Butley. *Suff* 5F 67
Butley High Corner. *Suff* 1G 55
Butlocks Heath. *Hants* 2C 16
Butterburn. *Cumb* 2H 113
Buttercrambe. *N Yor* 4B 100
Butterknowle. *Dur* 2E 105
Butterleigh. *Devn* 2C 12
Buttermere. *Cumb* 3C 102
Buttermere. *Wilts* 5B 36
Buttershaw. *W Yor* 2B 92
Butterstone. *Per* 4H 143
Butterton. *Staf* 5E 85
(nr. Leek)
Butterton. *Staf* 1C 72
(nr. Stoke-on-Trent)
Butterwick. *Dur* 2A 106
Butterwick. *Linc* 1C 76
Butterwick. *N Yor* 2B 100
(nr. Malton)
Butterwick. *N Yor* 2D 101
(nr. Weaverthorpe)
Butteryhaugh. *Nmbd* 5A 120
Butt Green. *Ches E* 5A 84
Buttington. *Powy* 5E 71
Buttonbridge. *Shrp* 3B 60
Buttonoak. *Shrp* 3B 60
Buttsash. *Hants* 2C 16
Butt's Green. *Essx* 5A 54
Butt Yeats. *Lanc* 3E 97
Buxhall. *Suff* 5C 66
Buxted. *E Sus* 3F 27
**Buxton**. *Derbs* 3E 85
Buxton. *Norf* 3E 79
Buxworth. *Derbs* 2E 85
**Bwcle**. *Flin* 4E 83
Bwlch. *Powy* 3E 47
Bwlchderwin. *Gwyn* 1D 68
Bwlchgwyn. *Wrex* 5E 83
Bwlch-Llan. *Cdgn* 5E 57
Bwlchnewydd. *Carm* 3D 44
Bwlchtocyn. *Gwyn* 3C 68
Bwlch-y-cibau. *Powy* 4D 70
Bwlchyddar. *Powy* 3D 70
Bwlch-y-fadfa. *Cdgn* 1E 45
Bwlch-y-ffridd. *Powy* 1C 58
Bwlch y Garreg. *Powy* 1C 58
Bwlch-y-groes. *Pemb* 1G 43
Bwlch-y-sarnau. *Powy* 3C 58
Bybrook. *Kent* 1E 28
Byermoor. *Tyne* 4E 115
Byers Garth. *Dur* 5G 115
Byers Green. *Dur* 1F 105
Byfield. *Nptn* 5C 62
**Byfleet**. *Surr* 4B 38
Byford. *Here* 1G 47
Bygrave. *Herts* 2C 52
Byker. *Tyne* 3F 115
Byland Abbey. *N Yor* 2H 99
Bylchau. *Cnwy* 4B 82
Byley. *Ches W* 4B 84
Bynea. *Carm* 3E 31
Byram. *N Yor* 2E 93
Byrness. *Nmbd* 4B 120
Bystock. *Devn* 4D 12
Bythorn. *Cambs* 3H 63
Byton. *Here* 4F 59
Bywell. *Nmbd* 3D 114
Byworth. *W Sus* 3A 26

## C

Cabharstadh. *W Isl* 6F 171
Cabourne. *Linc* 4E 95
Cabrach. *Arg* 3C 124
Cabrach. *Mor* 1A 152
Cabragh. *M Ulst* 3B 178
Cabus. *Lanc* 5D 97
Cadbury. *Devn* 2C 12
Cadder. *E Dun* 2H 127
Caddington. *C Beds* 4A 52
Caddonfoot. *Bord* 1G 119
Cadeby. *Leics* 5B 74
Cadeby. *S Yor* 4F 93
Cadeleigh. *Devn* 2C 12
Cade Street. *E Sus* 3H 27
Cadgwith. *Corn* 5E 5
Cadham. *Fife* 3E 137
Cadishead. *G Man* 1B 84
Cadle. *Swan* 3F 31
Cadley. *Lanc* 1D 90
Cadley. *Wilts* 1H 23
(nr. Ludgershall)
Cadley. *Wilts* 5H 35
(nr. Marlborough)
Cadmore End. *Buck* 2F 37
Cadnam. *Hants* 1A 16
Cadney. *N Lin* 4D 94
Cadole. *Flin* 4E 82
Cadoxton-juxta-Neath. *Neat* 2A 32
Cadwell. *Herts* 2B 52
Cadwst. *Den* 2C 70
Caeathro. *Gwyn* 4E 81
Caehopkin. *Powy* 4B 46
Caenby. *Linc* 2H 87
Caerau. *B'end* 2B 32
Caerau. *Card* 4E 33
Cae'r-bont. *Powy* 4B 46
Cae'r-bryn. *Carm* 4F 45
Caerdeon. *Gwyn* 4F 69
**Caerdydd**.
*Card* 4E 33 & **Cardiff** 193
Caerfarchell. *Pemb* 2B 42
**Caerffili**. *Cphy* 3E 33
**Caerfyrddin**. *Carm* 4E 45
Caergeiliog. *IOA* 3C 80
Caergwrle. *Flin* 5F 83
**Caergybi**. *IOA* 2B 80
Caerlaverock. *Per* 2A 136
Caerleon. *Newp* 2G 33
Caerlleon. *Carm* 2G 43
Caerllion. *Newp* 2G 33
**Caernarfon**. *Gwyn* 4D 81
**Caerphilly**. *Cphy* 3E 33
Caersws. *Powy* 1C 58
Caerwedros. *Cdgn* 5C 56
Caerwent. *Mon* 2H 33
Caerwys. *Flin* 3D 82
Caim. *IOA* 2F 81
Caio. *Carm* 2G 45
Cairinis. *W Isl* 2D 170
Cairisiadar. *W Isl* 4C 171
Cairminis. *W Isl* 9C 171
Cairnbaan. *Arg* 4F 133
Cairnbulg. *Abers* 2H 161
Cairncross. *Ang* 1D 145
Cairndow. *Arg* 2A 134
Cairness. *Abers* 2H 161
Cairneyhill. *Fife* 1D 128
Cairngarroch. *Dum* 5F 109
**Cairngorms**. *High* 3D 151
Cairnhill. *Abers* 5D 160
Cairnie. *Abers* 4B 160
Cairnorrie. *Abers* 4F 161
Cairnryan. *Dum* 3F 109
Cairston. *Orkn* 6B 172
Caister-on-Sea. *Norf* 4H 79
Caistor. *Linc* 4E 94
Caistor St Edmund. *Norf* 5E 79
Caistron. *Nmbd* 4D 121
Cakebole. *Worc* 3C 60
Calais Street. *Suff* 1C 54
Calanais. *W Isl* 4E 171
Calbost. *W Isl* 6G 171
Calbourne. *IOW* 4C 16
Calceby. *Linc* 3C 88
Calcot. *Glos* 4F 49
Calcot Row. *W Ber* 4E 37
Calcott. *Kent* 4F 41
Calcott. *Shrp* 4G 71
Caldback. *Shet* 1H 173
Caldbeck. *Cumb* 1E 102
Caldbergh. *N Yor* 1C 98
Caldecote. *Cambs* 5C 64
(nr. Cambridge)
Caldecote. *Cambs* 2A 64
(nr. Peterborough)
Caldecote. *Herts* 2C 52
Caldecote. *Nptn* 5D 62
Caldecote. *Warw* 1A 62
Caldecott. *Nptn* 4G 63
Caldecott. *Oxon* 2C 36
Caldecott. *Rut* 1F 63
Calderbank. *N Lan* 3A 128
Calder Bridge. *Cumb* 4B 102
Calderbrook. *G Man* 3H 91
Caldercruix. *N Lan* 3B 128
Calder Grove. *W Yor* 3D 92
Calder Mains. *High* 3C 168
Caldermill. *S Lan* 5H 127
Calder Vale. *Lanc* 5E 97
Calderwood. *S Lan* 4H 127
**Caldicot**. *Mon* 3H 33
Caldwell. *Derbs* 4G 73
Caldwell. *N Yor* 3E 105
Caldy. *Mers* 2E 83
Calebrack. *Cumb* 1E 103
Caledon. *M Ulst* 5B 178
Calf Heath. *Staf* 5D 72
Calford Green. *Suff* 1G 53
Calfsound. *Orkn* 4E 172
Calgary. *Arg* 3E 139
Califer. *Mor* 3E 159
California. *Cambs* 2E 65
California. *Falk* 2C 128
California. *Norf* 4H 79
California. *Suff* 1E 55
Calke. *Derbs* 3A 74
Callakille. *High* 3F 155
Callaly. *Nmbd* 4E 121
Callander. *Stir* 3F 135
Callaughton. *Shrp* 1A 60
Callendoun. *Arg* 1E 127
Callestick. *Corn* 3B 6
Calligarry. *High* 3E 147
Callington. *Corn* 2H 7
Callingwood. *Staf* 3F 73
Callow. *Here* 2H 47
Callowell. *Glos* 5D 48
Callow End. *Worc* 1D 48
Callow Hill. *Wilts* 3F 35
Callow Hill. *Worc* 3B 60
(nr. Bewdley)
Callow Hill. *Worc* 4E 61
(nr. Redditch)
Calmore. *Hants* 1B 16
Calmsden. *Glos* 5F 49
**Calne**. *Wilts* 4E 35
Calow. *Derbs* 3B 86
Calshot. *Hants* 2C 16
Calstock. *Corn* 2A 8
Calstone Wellington. *Wilts* 5F 35
Calthorpe. *Norf* 2D 78
Calthorpe Street. *Norf* 3G 79
Calthwaite. *Cumb* 5F 113
Calton. *N Yor* 4B 98
Calton. *Staf* 5F 85
Calveley. *Ches E* 5H 83
Calver. *Derbs* 3G 85
Calverhall. *Shrp* 2A 72
Calverleigh. *Devn* 1C 12
Calverley. *W Yor* 1C 92
Calvert. *Buck* 3E 51
Calverton. *Mil* 2F 51
Calverton. *Notts* 1D 74
Calvine. *Per* 2F 143
Calvo. *Cumb* 4C 112
Cam. *Glos* 2C 34
Camaghael. *High* 1F 141
Camas-luinie. *High* 1B 148
Camasnacroise. *High* 3C 140
Camastianavaig. *High* 5E 155
Camasunary. *High* 2D 146
Camault Muir. *High* 4H 157
Camb. *Shet* 2G 173
Camber. *E Sus* 4D 28
**Camberley**. *Surr* 5G 37
**Camberwell**. *G Lon* 3E 39
Camblesforth. *N Yor* 2G 93
Cambo. *Nmbd* 1D 114
Cambois. *Nmbd* 1G 115
**Camborne**. *Corn* 5A 6
Cambourne. *Cambs* 5C 64
**Cambridge**. *Cambs* 5D 64 & 193
Cambridge. *Glos* 5C 48
Cambrose. *Corn* 4A 6
Cambus. *Clac* 4A 136
Cambusbarron. *Stir* 4G 135
Cambuskenneth. *Stir* 4H 135
**Cambuslang**. *S Lan* 3H 127
Cambusnethan. *N Lan* 4B 128
Cambus o' May. *Abers* 4B 152
**Camden Town**. *G Lon* 2D 39
Cameley. *Bath* 1B 22
Camelford. *Corn* 4B 10
Camelon. *Falk* 1B 128
Camelsdale. *Surr* 3G 25
Camer's Green. *Worc* 2C 48
Camerton. *Bath* 1B 22
Camerton. *Cumb* 1B 102
Camerton. *E Yor* 2F 95
Camghouran. *Per* 3C 142
Camlough. *New M* 7E 178
Cammachmore. *Abers* 4G 153
Cammeringham. *Linc* 2G 87
Camore. *High* 4E 165
Campbelton. *N Ayr* 4C 126
Campbeltown. *Arg* 3B 122
Campbeltown Airport. *Arg* 3A 122
Cample. *Dum* 5A 118
Campmuir. *Per* 5B 144
Campsall. *S Yor* 3F 93
Campsea Ashe. *Suff* 5F 67
Camps End. *Cambs* 1G 53
Campsey. *Derr* 4A 174
Camp, The. *Glos* 5E 49
Campton. *C Beds* 2B 52
Camptoun. *E Lot* 2B 130
Camptown. *Bord* 3A 120
Camrose. *Pemb* 2D 42
Camserney. *Per* 4F 143
Camster. *High* 4E 169
Camus Croise. *High* 2E 147
Camuscross. *High* 2E 147
Camusdarach. *High* 4E 147
Camusnagaul. *High* 1E 141
(nr. Fort William)
Camusnagaul. *High* 5E 163
(nr. Little Loch Broom)
Camus Park. *Derr* 3F 176
Camusteel. *High* 4G 155
Camusterrach. *High* 4G 155
Camusvrachan. *Per* 4D 142
Canada. *Hants* 1A 16
Canadia. *E Sus* 4B 28
Canaston Bridge. *Pemb* 3E 43
Candlesby. *Linc* 4D 88
Candle Street. *Suff* 3C 66
Candy Mill. *S Lan* 5D 128
Cane End. *Oxon* 4E 37
Canewdon. *Essx* 1D 40
Canford Cliffs. *Pool* 4F 15
Canford Heath. *Pool* 3F 15
Canford Magna. *Pool* 3F 15
Cangate. *Norf* 4F 79
Canham's Green. *Suff* 4C 66
Canholes. *Derbs* 3E 85
Canisbay. *High* 1F 169
Canley. *W Mid* 3H 61
Cann. *Dors* 4D 22
Cann Common. *Dors* 4D 23
Cannich. *High* 5F 157
Cannington. *Som* 3F 21
**Cannock**. *Staf* 4D 73
Cannock Wood. *Staf* 4E 73
Canonbie. *Dum* 2E 113
Canon Bridge. *Here* 1H 47
Canon Frome. *Here* 1B 48
Canon Pyon. *Here* 1H 47
Canons Ashby. *Nptn* 5C 62
Canonstown. *Corn* 3C 4
**Canterbury**. *Kent* 5F 41 & 193
Cantley. *Norf* 5F 79
Cantley. *S Yor* 4G 93
Cantlop. *Shrp* 5H 71
Canton. *Card* 4E 33
Cantray. *High* 4B 158
Cantraybruich. *High* 4B 158
Cantraywood. *High* 4B 158
Cantsdam. *Fife* 4D 136
Cantsfield. *Lanc* 2F 97
**Canvey Island**. *Essx* 2B 40
Canwick. *Linc* 4G 87
Canworthy Water. *Corn* 3C 10
Caol. *High* 1F 141
Caolas. *Arg* 4B 138
Caolas. *W Isl* 9B 170
Caolas Liubharsaigh. *W Isl* 4D 170
Caolas Scalpaigh. *W Isl* 8E 171
Caolas Stocinis. *W Isl* 8D 171
Caol Ila. *Arg* 2C 124
Caol Loch Ailse. *High* 1F 147
Caol Reatha. *High* 1F 147
Capel. *Kent* 1H 27
Capel. *Surr* 1C 26
Capel Bangor. *Cdgn* 2F 57
Capel Betws Lleucu. *Cdgn* 5F 57
Capel Coch. *IOA* 2D 80
Capel Curig. *Cnwy* 5G 81
Capel Cynon. *Cdgn* 1D 45
Capel Dewi. *Carm* 3E 45
Capel Dewi. *Cdgn* 2F 57
(nr. Aberystwyth)
Capel Dewi. *Cdgn* 1E 45
(nr. Llandysul)
Capel Garmon. *Cnwy* 5H 81
Capel Green. *Suff* 1G 55
Capel Gwyn. *IOA* 3C 80
Capel Gwynfe. *Carm* 3H 45
Capel Hendre. *Carm* 4F 45
Capel Isaac. *Carm* 3F 45
Capel Iwan. *Carm* 1G 43
Capel-le-Ferne. *Kent* 2G 29
Capel Llanilltern. *Card* 4D 32
Capel Mawr. *IOA* 3D 80
Capel Newydd. *Pemb* 1G 43
Capel St Andrew. *Suff* 1G 55
Capel St Mary. *Suff* 2D 54
Capel Seion. *Carm* 4F 45
Capel Seion. *Cdgn* 3F 57
Capel Uchaf. *Gwyn* 1D 68
Capel-y-ffin. *Powy* 2F 47
Capenhurst. *Ches W* 3F 83
Capernwray. *Lanc* 2E 97
Capheaton. *Nmbd* 1D 114
Cappagh. *M Ulst* 3A 178
Cappercleuch. *Bord* 2E 119
Capplegill. *Dum* 4D 118
Capton. *Devn* 3E 9
Capton. *Som* 3D 20
Caputh. *Per* 5H 143
Caradon Town. *Corn* 5C 10
Carbis Bay. *Corn* 3C 4
Carbost. *High* 5C 154
(nr. Loch Harport)
Carbost. *High* 4D 154
(nr. Portree)
Carbrook. *S Yor* 2A 86
Carbrooke. *Norf* 5B 78
Carburton. *Notts* 3D 86
Carcluie. *S Ayr* 3C 116
Car Colston. *Notts* 1E 74
Carcroft. *S Yor* 4F 93
Cardenden. *Fife* 4E 136
Cardeston. *Shrp* 4F 71
Cardewlees. *Cumb* 4E 113
**Cardiff**. *Card* 4E 33 & 193
Cardiff Airport. *V Glam* 5D 32
Cardigan. *Cdgn* 1B 44
Cardinal's Green. *Cambs* 1G 53
Cardington. *Bed* 1A 52
Cardington. *Shrp* 1H 59
Cardinham. *Corn* 2F 7
Cardno. *Abers* 2G 161
Cardow. *Mor* 4F 159
Cardross. *Arg* 2E 127
Cardurnock. *Cumb* 4C 112
Careby. *Linc* 4H 75
Careston. *Ang* 2E 145
Carew. *Pemb* 4E 43
Carew Cheriton. *Pemb* 4E 43
Carew Newton. *Pemb* 4E 43
Carey. *Here* 2A 48
Carfin. *N Lan* 4A 128
Carfrae. *Bord* 4B 130
Cargan. *ME Ant* 5H 175
Cargate Green. *Norf* 4F 79
Cargenbridge. *Dum* 2G 111
Cargill. *Per* 5A 144
Cargo. *Cumb* 4E 113
Cargreen. *Corn* 2A 8
Carham. *Nmbd* 1C 120
Carhampton. *Som* 2D 20
Carharrack. *Corn* 4B 6
Carie. *Per* 3D 142
(nr. Loch Rannah)
Carie. *Per* 5D 142
(nr. Loch Tay)
Carisbrooke. *IOW* 4C 16
Cark. *Cumb* 2C 96
Carkeel. *Corn* 2A 8
Carlabhagh. *W Isl* 3E 171
Carland Cross. *Corn* 3C 6
Carlbury. *Darl* 3F 105
Carlby. *Linc* 4H 75
Carlecotes. *S Yor* 4B 92
Carleen. *Corn* 4D 4
Carlesmoor. *N Yor* 2D 98
Carleton. *Cumb* 4F 113
(nr. Carlisle)
Carleton. *Cumb* 4B 102
(nr. Egremont)
Carleton. *Cumb* 2G 103
(nr. Penrith)
Carleton. *Lanc* 5C 96
Carleton. *N Yor* 5B 98
Carleton. *W Yor* 2E 93
Carleton Forehoe. *Norf* 5C 78
Carleton Rode. *Norf* 1D 66
Carleton St Peter. *Norf* 5F 79
Carlidnack. *Corn* 4E 5
Carlingcott. *Bath* 1B 22
Carlin How. *Red C* 3E 107
**Carlisle**. *Cumb* 4F 113 & 193
Carloonan. *Arg* 2H 133
Carlops. *Bord* 4E 129
Carlton. *Bed* 5G 63
Carlton. *Cambs* 5F 65
Carlton. *Leics* 5A 74
Carlton. *N Yor* 1A 100
(nr. Helmsley)
Carlton. *N Yor* 1C 98
(nr. Middleham)
Carlton. *N Yor* 2G 93
(nr. Selby)
**Carlton**. *Notts* 1D 74
Carlton. *S Yor* 3D 92
Carlton. *Stoc T* 2A 106
Carlton. *Suff* 4F 67
Carlton. *W Yor* 2D 92
Carlton Colville. *Suff* 1H 67
Carlton Curlieu. *Leics* 1D 62
Carlton Husthwaite. *N Yor* 2G 99
Carlton in Cleveland. *N Yor* 4C 106
Carlton in Lindrick. *Notts* 2C 86
Carlton-le-Moorland. *Linc* 5G 87
Carlton Miniott. *N Yor* 1F 99
Carlton-on-Trent. *Notts* 4F 87
Carlton Scroop. *Linc* 1G 75
**Carluke**. *S Lan* 4B 128
Carlyon Bay. *Corn* 3E 7
**Carmarthen**. *Carm* 4E 45
Carmel. *Carm* 4F 45
Carmel. *Flin* 3D 82
Carmel. *Gwyn* 5D 81
Carmel. *IOA* 2C 80
Carmichael. *S Lan* 1B 118
Carmunnock. *Glas* 4H 127
Carmyle. *Glas* 3H 127
Carmyllie. *Ang* 4E 145
Carnaby. *E Yor* 3F 101
Carnach. *High* 1C 148
(nr. Lochcarron)
Carnach. *High* 4E 163
(nr. Ullapool)
Carnach. *Mor* 4E 159
Carnach. *W Isl* 8E 171
Carnachy. *High* 3H 167
Carnain. *Arg* 3B 124
Carnais. *W Isl* 4C 171
Carnan. *Arg* 4B 138
Carnan. *W Isl* 4C 170
Carnbee. *Fife* 3H 137
Carnbo. *Per* 3C 136
Carn Brea Village. *Corn* 4A 6
Carndu. *High* 1A 148
Carnduff. *Caus* 2G 175
Carne. *Corn* 5D 6
Carnell. *S Ayr* 1D 116
Carnforth. *Lanc* 2E 97
Carn-gorm. *High* 1B 148
Carnhedryn. *Pemb* 2C 42
Carnhell Green. *Corn* 3D 4
Carnie. *Abers* 3F 153
Carnkie. *Corn* 5B 6
(nr. Falmouth)
Carnkie. *Corn* 5A 6
(nr. Redruth)
Carnkief. *Corn* 3B 6
Carnlough. *ME Ant* 5J 175
Carnmoney. *Ant* 1H 179
Carno. *Powy* 1B 58
Carnock. *Fife* 1D 128
Carnon Downs. *Corn* 4B 6
**Carnoustie**. *Ang* 5E 145
Carnteel. *M Ulst* 4A 178
Carntyne. *Glas* 3H 127
Carnwath. *S Lan* 5C 128
Carnyorth. *Corn* 3A 4
Carol Green. *W Mid* 3G 61
Carpalla. *Corn* 3D 6
Carperby. *N Yor* 1C 98
Carradale. *Arg* 2C 122
Carragraich. *W Isl* 8D 171
Carrbridge. *High* 1D 150
Carr Cross. *Lanc* 3B 90
Carreglefn. *IOA* 2C 80
Carrhouse. *N Lin* 4A 94
Carrick Castle. *Arg* 4A 134
**Carrickfergus**. *ME Ant* 8L 175
Carrick Ho. *Orkn* 4E 172
Carrickmore. *Ferm* 2A 178
Carriden. *Falk* 1D 128
Carrington. *G Man* 1B 84
Carrington. *Linc* 5C 88
Carrington. *Midl* 3G 129
Carrog. *Cnwy* 1G 69
Carrog. *Den* 1D 70
Carron. *Falk* 1B 128
Carron. *Mor* 4G 159
Carronbridge. *Dum* 5A 118
Carronshore. *Falk* 1B 128
Carrowclare. *Caus* 4C 174
Carrowdore. *N Dwn* 2K 179
Carrow Hill. *Mon* 2H 33
Carr Shield. *Nmbd* 5B 114
Carrutherstown. *Dum* 2C 112
Carr Vale. *Derbs* 4B 86
Carrville. *Dur* 5G 115
Carryduff. *Lis* 3H 179
Carsaig. *Arg* 1C 132
Carscreugh. *Dum* 3H 109
Carsegowan. *Dum* 4B 110
Carse House. *Arg* 3F 125
Carseriggan. *Dum* 3A 110
Carsethorn. *Dum* 4A 112
**Carshalton**. *G Lon* 4D 39
Carsington. *Derbs* 5G 85
Carskiey. *Arg* 5A 122
Carsluith. *Dum* 4B 110
Carson Park. *New M* 4J 179
Carsphairn. *Dum* 5E 117
Carstairs. *S Lan* 5C 128
Carstairs Junction. *S Lan* 5C 128
Cartbridge. *Surr* 5B 38
Carterhaugh. *Ang* 4D 144
Carter's Clay. *Hants* 4B 24
**Carterton**. *Oxon* 5A 50
Carterway Heads. *Nmbd* 4D 114
Carthew. *Corn* 3E 6
Carthorpe. *N Yor* 1F 99
Cartington. *Nmbd* 4E 121
Cartland. *S Lan* 5B 128
Cartmel. *Cumb* 2C 96
Cartmel Fell. *Cumb* 1D 96
Cartworth. *W Yor* 4B 92
Carwath. *Cumb* 5E 112
Carway. *Carm* 5E 45
Carwinley. *Cumb* 2F 113
Cascob. *Powy* 4E 59
**Cas-gwent**. *Mon* 2A 34
Cash Feus. *Fife* 3E 136
Cashlie. *Per* 4B 142
Cashmoor. *Dors* 1E 15
Cas-Mael. *Pemb* 2E 43
**Casnewydd**.
*Newp* 3G 33 & **Newport** 200
Cassington. *Oxon* 4C 50
Cassop. *Dur* 1A 106
Castell. *Cnwy* 4G 81
Castell. *Den* 4D 82
Castell Hendre. *Pemb* 2E 43
**Castell-Nedd**. *Neat* 2A 32
Castell Newydd Emlyn.
*Carm* 1D 44
Castell-y-bwch. *Torf* 2F 33
Casterton. *Cumb* 2F 97
Castle. *Som* 2A 22
Castle Acre. *Norf* 4H 77
Castle Ashby. *Nptn* 5F 63
Castlebay. *W Isl* 9B 170
Castle Bolton. *N Yor* 5D 104
Castle Bromwich. *W Mid* 2F 61
Castle Bytham. *Linc* 4G 75
Castlebythe. *Pemb* 2E 43
Castle Caereinion. *Powy* 5D 70
Castle Camps. *Cambs* 1G 53
Castle Carrock. *Cumb* 4G 113
Castlecary. *N Lan* 2A 128
Castle Cary. *Som* 3B 22
Castlecaulfield. *M Ulst* 3B 178
Castle Combe. *Wilts* 4D 34
Castlecraig. *High* 2C 158
Castledawson. *M Ulst* 7F 174
Castlederg. *Derr* 4E 176
Castle Donington. *Leics* 3B 74
Castle Douglas. *Dum* 3E 111
Castle Eaton. *Swin* 2G 35
Castle Eden. *Dur* 1B 106
**Castleford**. *W Yor* 2E 93
Castle Frome. *Here* 1B 48
Castle Green. *Surr* 4A 38
Castle Green. *Warw* 3G 61
Castle Gresley. *Derbs* 4G 73
Castle Heaton. *Nmbd* 5F 131
Castle Hedingham. *Essx* 2A 54
Castle Hill. *Kent* 1A 28
Castlehill. *Per* 5B 144
Castlehill. *S Lan* 4B 128
Castle Hill. *Suff* 1E 55
Castlehill. *W Dun* 2E 127
Castle Kennedy. *Dum* 4G 109
Castle Lachlan. *Arg* 4H 133
Castlemartin. *Pemb* 5D 42
Castlemilk. *Glas* 4H 127
Castlemorris. *Pemb* 1D 42
Castlemorton. *Worc* 2C 48
Castle O'er. *Dum* 5E 119
Castle Park. *N Yor* 3F 107
Castlerigg. *Cumb* 2D 102
Castle Rising. *Norf* 3F 77
Castlerock. *Caus* 3D 174
Castleroe. *Caus* 4E 174
Castleside. *Dur* 5D 115
Castlethorpe. *Mil* 1F 51
Castleton. *Abers* 4F 151
Castleton. *Arg* 1G 125
Castleton. *Derbs* 2F 85
Castleton. *G Man* 3G 91
Castleton. *Mor* 1F 151
Castleton. *Newp* 3F 33
Castleton. *N Yor* 4D 107
Castleton. *Per* 2B 136
Castletown. *Cumb* 1G 103
Castletown. *Dors* 5B 14
Castletown. *High* 2D 169
Castletown. *IOM* 5B 108
Castletown. *Tyne* 4G 115
Castlewellan. *New M* 6H 179
Castley. *N Yor* 5E 99
Caston. *Norf* 1B 66
Castor. *Pet* 1A 64
Caswell. *Swan* 4E 31
Catacol. *N Ayr* 5H 125
Catbrook. *Mon* 5A 48
Catchems End. *Worc* 3B 60
Catchgate. *Dur* 4E 115
Catcleugh. *Nmbd* 4B 120
Catcliffe. *S Yor* 2B 86
Catcott. *Som* 3G 21
**Caterham**. *Surr* 5E 39
Catfield. *Norf* 3F 79
Catfield Common. *Norf* 3F 79
Catfirth. *Shet* 6F 173
**Catford**. *G Lon* 3E 39
Catforth. *Lanc* 1C 90
Cathcart. *Glas* 3G 127
Cathedine. *Powy* 3E 47
Catherine-de-Barnes. *W Mid* 2F 61
Catherington. *Hants* 1E 17
Catherston Leweston. *Dors* 3G 13
Catherton. *Shrp* 3A 60
Catisfield. *Hants* 2D 16
Catlodge. *High* 4A 150
Catlowdy. *Cumb* 2F 113
Catmore. *W Ber* 3C 36
Caton. *Devn* 5A 12
Caton. *Lanc* 3E 97
Catrine. *E Ayr* 2E 117
Cat's Ash. *Newp* 2G 33
Catsfield. *E Sus* 4B 28
Catsgore. *Som* 4A 22
Catshill. *Worc* 3D 60
Cattal. *N Yor* 4G 99
Cattawade. *Suff* 2E 54
Catterall. *Lanc* 5E 97
Catterick. *N Yor* 5F 105
Catterick Bridge. *N Yor* 5F 105
Catterick Garrison. *N Yor* 5E 105
Catterlen. *Cumb* 1F 103
Catterline. *Abers* 1H 145
Catterton. *N Yor* 5H 99
Catteshall. *Surr* 1A 26
Catthorpe. *Leics* 3C 62
Cattistock. *Dors* 3A 14
Catton. *Nmbd* 4B 114
Catton. *N Yor* 2F 99
Catwick. *E Yor* 5F 101
Catworth. *Cambs* 3H 63
Caudle Green. *Glos* 4E 49
Caulcott. *Oxon* 3D 50
Cauldhame. *Stir* 4F 135
Cauldmill. *Bord* 3H 119
Cauldon. *Staf* 1E 73
Cauldon Lowe. *Staf* 1E 73
Cauldwells. *Abers* 3E 161
Caulkerbush. *Dum* 4G 111
Caulside. *Dum* 1F 113
Caunsall. *Worc* 2C 60
Caunton. *Notts* 4E 87
Causewayend. *S Lan* 1C 118
Causewayhead. *Stir* 4H 135
Causey Park. *Nmbd* 5F 121
Caute. *Devn* 1E 11
Cautley. *Cumb* 5H 103
Cavendish. *Suff* 1B 54
Cavendish Bridge. *Leic* 3B 74
Cavenham. *Suff* 3G 65
Caversfield. *Oxon* 3D 50
Caversham. *Read* 4F 37
Caversham Heights. *Read* 4F 37
Caverswall. *Staf* 1D 72
Cawdor. *High* 4C 158
Cawkwell. *Linc* 2B 88
Cawood. *N Yor* 1F 93
Cawsand. *Corn* 3A 8
Cawston. *Norf* 3D 78
Cawston. *Warw* 3B 62
Cawthorne. *N Yor* 1B 100
Cawthorne. *S Yor* 4C 92
Cawthorpe. *Linc* 3H 75
Cawton. *N Yor* 2A 100
Caxton. *Cambs* 5C 64
Caynham. *Shrp* 3H 59
Caythorpe. *Linc* 1G 75
Caythorpe. *Notts* 1D 74
Cayton. *N Yor* 1E 101
Ceallan. *W Isl* 3D 170
Ceann a Bhàigh. *W Isl* 9C 171
(on Harris)
Ceann a Bhaigh. *W Isl* 2C 170
(on North Uist)
Ceann a Bhaigh. *W Isl* 8E 171
(on Scalpay)
Ceann a Bhaigh. *W Isl* 8D 171
(on South Harris)
Ceannacroc Lodge. *High* 2E 149
Ceann a Deas Loch Baghasdail.
*W Isl* 7C 170
Ceann an Leothaid. *High* 5E 147
Ceann a Tuath Loch Baghasdail.
*W Isl* 6C 170
Ceann Loch Ailleart. *High* 5F 147
Ceann Loch Muideirt. *High* 1B 140
Ceann-na-Cleithe. *W Isl* 8D 171
Ceann Shìphoirt. *W Isl* 6E 171
Ceann Tarabhaigh. *W Isl* 6E 171
Cearsiadar. *W Isl* 5F 171
Ceathramh Meadhanach.
*W Isl* 1D 170
Cefn Berain. *Cnwy* 4B 82
Cefn-brith. *Cnwy* 5B 82
Cefn-bryn-brain. *Carm* 4H 45
Cefn Bychan. *Cphy* 2F 33
Cefn-bychan. *Flin* 4D 82
Cefncaeau. *Carm* 3E 31
Cefn Canol. *Powy* 2E 71
Cefn Coch. *Powy* 5C 70
(nr. Llanfair Caereinion)
Cefn-coch. *Powy* 3D 70
(nr. Llanrhaeadr-ym-Mochnant)
Cefn-coed-y-cymmer.
*Mer T* 5D 46
Cefn Cribwr. *B'end* 3B 32
Cefn-ddwysarn. *Gwyn* 2B 70
Cefn Einion. *Shrp* 2E 59
Cefneithin. *Carm* 4F 45
Cefn Glas. *B'end* 3B 32
Cefngorwydd. *Powy* 1C 46
Cefn Llwyd. *Cdgn* 2F 57
Cefn-mawr. *Wrex* 1E 71
Cefn-y-bedd. *Flin* 5F 83
Cefn-y-coed. *Powy* 1D 58
Cefn-y-pant. *Carm* 2F 43
Cegidfa. *Powy* 4E 70
Ceinewydd. *Cdgn* 5C 56
Cellan. *Cdgn* 1G 45
Cellardyke. *Fife* 3H 137
Cellarhead. *Staf* 1D 72
Cemaes. *IOA* 1C 80
Cemmaes. *Powy* 5H 69
Cemmaes Road. *Powy* 5H 69
Cenarth. *Cdgn* 1C 44
Cenin. *Gwyn* 1D 68
Ceos. *W Isl* 5F 171
Ceres. *Fife* 2G 137
Ceri. *Powy* 2D 58
Cerist. *Powy* 2B 58
Cerne Abbas. *Dors* 2B 14
Cerney Wick. *Glos* 2F 35
Cerrigceinwen. *IOA* 3D 80
Cerrigydrudion. *Cnwy* 1B 70
Cess. *Norf* 4G 79
Cessford. *Bord* 2B 120
Ceunant. *Gwyn* 4E 81
Chaceley. *Glos* 2D 48
Chacewater. *Corn* 4B 6
Chackmore. *Buck* 2E 51
Chacombe. *Nptn* 1C 50
**Chadderton**. *G Man* 4H 91
Chaddesden. *Derb* 2A 74
Chaddesden Common. *Derb* 2A 74
Chaddesley Corbett. *Worc* 3C 60
Chaddlehanger. *Devn* 5E 11
Chaddleworth. *W Ber* 4C 36
Chadlington. *Oxon* 3B 50
Chadshunt. *Warw* 5H 61
Chadstone. *Nptn* 5F 63
Chad Valley. *W Mid* 2E 61
Chadwell. *Leics* 3E 75
Chadwell. *Shrp* 4B 72
Chadwell Heath. *G Lon* 2F 39
Chadwell St Mary. *Thur* 3H 39
Chadwick End. *W Mid* 3G 61
Chadwick Green. *Mers* 1H 83
Chaffcombe. *Som* 1G 13
Chafford Hundred. *Thur* 3H 39
Chagford. *Devn* 4H 11
Chailey. *E Sus* 4E 27
Chainbridge. *Cambs* 5D 76
Chain Bridge. *Linc* 1C 76
Chainhurst. *Kent* 1B 28
Chalbury. *Dors* 2F 15
Chalbury Common. *Dors* 2F 15
Chaldon. *Surr* 5E 39
Chaldon Herring. *Dors* 4C 14
Chale. *IOW* 5C 16
Chale Green. *IOW* 5C 16
Chalfont Common. *Buck* 1B 38
Chalfont St Giles. *Buck* 1A 38
**Chalfont St Peter**. *Buck* 2B 38
Chalford. *Glos* 5D 49
Chalgrove. *Oxon* 2E 37
Chalk. *Kent* 3A 40
Chalk End. *Essx* 4G 53
Chalk Hill. *Glos* 3G 49
Challaborough. *Devn* 4C 8
Challacombe. *Devn* 2G 19
Challister. *Shet* 5G 173
Challoch. *Dum* 3A 110
Challock. *Kent* 5E 40
Chalton. *C Beds* 5A 64
(nr. Bedford)
Chalton. *C Beds* 3A 52
(nr. Luton)
Chalton. *Hants* 1F 17
Chalvington. *E Sus* 5G 27
Champany. *Falk* 2D 128
Chance Inn. *Fife* 2F 137
Chancery. *Cdgn* 3E 57
Chandler's Cross. *Herts* 1B 38
Chandler's Cross. *Worc* 2C 48
Chandler's Ford. *Hants* 4C 24
Chanlockfoot. *Dum* 4G 117
Channel's End. *Bed* 5A 64
**Channel Tunnel**. *Kent* 2F 29
Channerwick. *Shet* 9F 173
Chantry. *Som* 2C 22
Chantry. *Suff* 1E 55
Chapel. *Cumb* 1D 102
Chapel. *Fife* 4E 137
Chapel Allerton. *Som* 1H 21
Chapel Allerton. *W Yor* 1C 92
Chapel Amble. *Corn* 1D 6
Chapel Brampton. *Nptn* 4E 63
Chapelbridge. *Cambs* 1B 64
Chapel Chorlton. *Staf* 2C 72
Chapel Cleeve. *Som* 2D 20
Chapel End. *C Beds* 1A 52
Chapel-en-le-Frith. *Derbs* 2E 85
Chapelfield. *Abers* 2G 145
Chapelgate. *Linc* 3D 76
Chapel Green. *Warw* 2G 61
(nr. Coventry)
Chapel Green. *Warw* 4B 62
(nr. Southam)
Chapel Haddlesey. *N Yor* 2F 93
Chapelhall. *N Lan* 3A 128
Chapel Hill. *Abers* 5H 161
Chapel Hill. *Linc* 5B 88
Chapel Hill. *Mon* 5A 48
Chapelhill. *Per* 1E 136
(nr. Glencarse)
Chapelhill. *Per* 5H 143
(nr. Harrietfield)
Chapelknowe. *Dum* 2E 112
Chapel Lawn. *Shrp* 3F 59
Chapel le Dale. *N Yor* 2G 97
Chapel Milton. *Derbs* 2E 85
Chapel of Garioch. *Abers* 1E 152
Chapel Row. *W Ber* 5D 36
Chapels. *Cumb* 1B 96
Chapel St Leonards. *Linc* 3E 89
Chapel Stile. *Cumb* 4E 102
Chapelthorpe. *W Yor* 3D 92
Chapelton. *Ang* 4F 145
Chapelton. *Devn* 4F 19
Chapelton. *High* 2D 150
(nr. Grantown-on-Spey)
Chapelton. *High* 3H 157
(nr. Inverness)
Chapelton. *S Lan* 5H 127
Chapeltown. *Bkbn* 3F 91
Chapel Town. *Corn* 3C 6
Chapeltown. *Mor* 1G 151
Chapeltown. *New M* 6K 179

Chapeltown—Colby


**Chapeltown**. S Yor 1A 86
Chapmanslade. Wilts 2D 22
Chapmans Well. Devn 3D 10
Chapmore End. Herts 4D 52
Chappel. Essx 3B 54
**Chard**. Som 2G 13
Chard Junction. Dors 2G 13
Chardstock. Devn 2G 13
Charfield. S Glo 2C 34
Charing. Kent 1D 28
Charing Heath. Kent 1D 28
Charing Hill. Kent 5D 40
Charingworth. Glos 2H 49
Charlbury. Oxon 4B 50
Charlcombe. Bath 5C 34
Charlcutt. Wilts 4E 35
Charlecote. Warw 5G 61
Charlemont. Arm 4C 178
Charles. Devn 3G 19
Charlesfield. Dum 3C 112
Charleshill. Surr 2G 25
Charleston. Ang 4C 144
Charleston. Ren 3F 127
Charlestown. Aber 3G 153
Charlestown. Abers 2H 161
Charlestown. Corn 3E 7
Charlestown. Dors 5B 14
Charlestown. Fife 1D 128
Charlestown. G Man 4G 91
Charlestown. High 1H 155 (nr. Gairloch)
Charlestown. High 4A 158 (nr. Inverness)
Charlestown. W Yor 2H 91
Charlestown of Aberlour. Mor 4G 159
Charles Tye. Suff 5C 66
Charlesworth. Derbs 1E 85
Charlton. G Lon 3F 39
Charlton. Hants 2B 24
Charlton. Herts 3B 52
Charlton. Nptn 2D 50
Charlton. Nmbd 1B 114
Charlton. Oxon 3C 36
Charlton. Som 1B 22 (nr. Radstock)
Charlton. Som 2B 22 (nr. Shepton Mallet)
Charlton. Som 4F 21 (nr. Taunton)
Charlton. Telf 4H 71
Charlton. W Sus 1G 17
Charlton. Wilts 3E 35 (nr. Malmesbury)
Charlton. Wilts 1G 23 (nr. Pewsey)
Charlton. Wilts 4E 23 (nr. Shaftesbury)
Charlton. Worc 1F 49 (nr. Evesham)
Charlton. Worc 3C 60 (nr. Stourport-on-Severn)
Charlton Abbots. Glos 3F 49
Charlton Adam. Som 4A 22
Charlton All Saints. Wilts 4G 23
Charlton Down. Dors 3B 14
Charlton Horethorne. Som 4B 22
**Charlton Kings**. Glos 3E 49
Charlton Mackrell. Som 4A 22
Charlton Marshall. Dors 2E 15
Charlton Musgrove. Som 4C 22
Charlton-on-Otmoor. Oxon 4D 50
Charlton on the Hill. Dors 2D 15
Charlwood. Hants 3E 25
Charlwood. Surr 1D 26
Charlynch. Som 3F 21
Charminster. Dors 3B 14
Charmouth. Dors 3G 13
Charndon. Buck 3E 51
Charney Bassett. Oxon 2B 36
Charnock Green. Lanc 3D 90
Charnock Richard. Lanc 3D 90
Charsfield. Suff 5E 67
Chart Corner. Kent 5B 40
Charter Alley. Hants 1D 24
Charterhouse. Som 1H 21
Charterville Allotments. Oxon 4B 50
Chartham. Kent 5F 41
Chartham Hatch. Kent 5F 41
Chartridge. Buck 5H 51
Chart Sutton. Kent 5B 40
Chart, The. Kent 5F 39
Charvil. Wok 4F 37
Charwelton. Nptn 5C 62
Chase Terrace. Staf 5E 73
Chasetown. Staf 5E 73
Chastleton. Oxon 3H 49
Chasty. Devn 2D 10
Chatburn. Lanc 5G 97
Chatcull. Staf 2B 72
**Chatham**. Medw 4B 40 & **Medway 197**
Chatham Green. Essx 4H 53
Chathill. Nmbd 2F 121
Chatley. Worc 4C 60
Chattenden. Medw 3B 40
Chatteris. Cambs 2C 64
Chattisham. Suff 1D 54
Chatton. Nmbd 2E 121
Chatwall. Shrp 1H 59
Chaulden. Herts 5A 52
Chaul End. C Beds 3A 52
Chawleigh. Devn 1H 11
Chawley. Oxon 5C 50
Chawston. Bed 5A 64
Chawton. Hants 3F 25
Chaxhill. Glos 4C 48
**Cheadle**. G Man 2C 84
**Cheadle**. Staf 1E 73
Cheadle Hulme. G Man 2C 84
Cheam. Surr 4D 38
Cheapside. Wind 4A 38
Chearsley. Buck 4F 51
Chebsey. Staf 3C 72
Checkendon. Oxon 3E 37
Checkley. Ches E 1B 72
Checkley. Here 2A 48
Checkley. Staf 2E 73
Chedburgh. Suff 5G 65
Cheddar. Som 1H 21
Cheddington. Buck 4H 51
Cheddleton. Staf 5D 84
Cheddon Fitzpaine. Som 4F 21
Chedglow. Wilts 2E 35
Chedgrave. Norf 1F 67
Chedington. Dors 2H 13
Chediston. Suff 3F 67
Chediston Green. Suff 3F 67
Chedworth. Glos 4F 49
Chedzoy. Som 3G 21
Cheeseman's Green. Kent 2E 29
Cheetham Hill. G Man 4G 91
Cheglinch. Devn 2F 19
Cheldon. Devn 1H 11
Chelford. Ches E 3C 84
Chellaston. Derb 2A 74
Chellington. Bed 5G 63
Chelmarsh. Shrp 2B 60
Chelmick. Shrp 1G 59
Chelmondiston. Suff 2F 55
Chelmorton. Derbs 4F 85
**Chelmsford**. Essx 5H 53
**Chelsea**. G Lon 3D 38
Chelsfield. G Lon 4F 39
Chelsham. Surr 5E 39
Chelston. Som 4E 21
Chelsworth. Suff 1C 54
**Cheltenham**. Glos 3E 49 & 193
Chelveston. Nptn 4G 63
Chelvey. N Som 5H 33
Chelwood. Bath 5B 34
Chelwood Common. E Sus 3F 27
Chelwood Gate. E Sus 3F 27
Chelworth. Wilts 2E 35
Chelworth Lower Green. Wilts 2F 35
Chelworth Upper Green. Wilts 2F 35
Chelynch. Som 2B 22
Cheney Longville. Shrp 2G 59
Chenies. Buck 1B 38
**Chepstow**. Mon 2A 34
Chequerfield. W Yor 2E 93
Chequers Corner. Norf 5D 77
Cherhill. Wilts 4F 35
Cherington. Glos 2E 35
Cherington. Warw 2A 50
Cheriton. Devn 2H 19
Cheriton. Hants 4D 24
Cheriton. Kent 2G 29
Cheriton. Pemb 5D 43
Cheriton. Swan 3D 30
Cheriton Bishop. Devn 3A 12
Cheriton Cross. Devn 3A 12
Cheriton Fitzpaine. Devn 2B 12
Cherrington. Telf 3A 72
Cherrybank. Per 1D 136
Cherry Burton. E Yor 5D 101
Cherry Green. Herts 3D 52
Cherry Hinton. Cambs 5D 65
Cherry Willingham. Linc 3H 87
**Chertsey**. Surr 4B 38
Cheselbourne. Dors 3C 14
**Chesham**. Buck 5H 51
Chesham. G Man 3G 91
Chesham Bois. Buck 1A 38
**Cheshunt**. Herts 5D 52
Cheslyn Hay. Staf 5D 73
Chessetts Wood. Warw 3F 61
Chessington. G Lon 4C 38
**Chester**. Ches W 4G 83 & 194
Chesterblade. Som 2B 22
**Chesterfield**. Derbs 3A 86
Chesterfield. Staf 5F 73
Chesterhope. Nmbd 1B 114
**Chester-le-Street**. Dur 4F 115
Chester Moor. Dur 5F 115
Chesters. Bord 3A 120
Chesterton. Cambs 4D 64 (nr. Cambridge)
Chesterton. Cambs 1A 64 (nr. Peterborough)
Chesterton. Glos 5F 49
Chesterton. Oxon 3D 50
Chesterton. Shrp 1B 60
Chesterton. Staf 1C 72
Chesterton Green. Warw 5H 61
Chesterwood. Nmbd 3B 114
Chestfield. Kent 4F 41
Cheston. Devn 3C 8
Cheswardine. Shrp 2B 72
Cheswell. Telf 4B 72
Cheswick. Nmbd 5G 131
Cheswick Green. W Mid 3F 61
Chetnole. Dors 2B 14
Chettiscombe. Devn 1C 12
Chettisham. Cambs 2E 65
Chettle. Dors 1E 15
Chetton. Shrp 1A 60
Chetwode. Buck 3E 51
Chetwynd Aston. Telf 4B 72
Cheveley. Cambs 4F 65
Chevening. Kent 5F 39
Chevington. Suff 5G 65
Chevithorne. Devn 1C 12
Chew Magna. Bath 5A 34
Chew Moor. G Man 4E 91
Chew Stoke. Bath 5A 34
Chewton Keynsham. Bath 5B 34
Chewton Mendip. Som 1A 22
Chichacott. Devn 3G 11
Chicheley. Mil 1H 51
**Chichester**. W Sus 2G 17
Chickerell. Dors 4B 14
Chickering. Suff 3E 66
Chicklade. Wilts 3E 23
Chicksands. C Beds 2B 52
Chickward. Here 5E 59
Chidden. Hants 1E 17
Chiddingfold. Surr 2A 26
Chiddingly. E Sus 4G 27
Chiddingstone. Kent 1G 27
Chiddingstone Causeway. Kent 1G 27
Chiddingstone Hoath. Kent 1F 27
Chideock. Dors 3H 13
Chidgley. Som 3D 20
Chidham. W Sus 2F 17
Chieveley. W Ber 4C 36
Chignal St James. Essx 5G 53
Chignal Smealy. Essx 4G 53
**Chigwell**. Essx 1F 39
Chigwell Row. Essx 1F 39
Chilbolton. Hants 2B 24
Chilcomb. Hants 4D 24
Chilcombe. Dors 3A 14
Chilcompton. Som 1B 22
Chilcote. Leics 4G 73
Childer Thornton. Ches W 3F 83
Child Okeford. Dors 1D 14
Childrey. Oxon 3B 36
Child's Ercall. Shrp 3A 72
Childswickham. Worc 2F 49
Childwall. Mers 2G 83
Childwick Green. Herts 4B 52
Chilfrome. Dors 3A 14
Chilgrove. W Sus 1G 17
Chilham. Kent 5E 41
Chilhampton. Wilts 3F 23
Chilla. Devn 2E 11
Chilland. Hants 3D 24
Chillaton. Devn 4E 11
Chillenden. Kent 5G 41
Chillerton. IOW 4C 16
Chillesford. Suff 5F 67
Chillingham. Nmbd 2E 121
Chillington. Devn 4D 9
Chillington. Som 1G 13
Chilmark. Wilts 3E 23
Chilmington Green. Kent 1D 28
Chilson. Oxon 4B 50
Chilsworthy. Corn 5E 11
Chilsworthy. Devn 2D 10
Chiltern Green. C Beds 4B 52
Chilthorne Domer. Som 1A 14
Chilton. Buck 4E 51
Chilton. Devn 2B 12
Chilton. Dur 2F 105
Chilton. Oxon 3C 36
Chilton Candover. Hants 2D 24
Chilton Cantelo. Som 4A 22
Chilton Foliat. Wilts 4B 36
Chilton Lane. Dur 1A 106
Chilton Polden. Som 3G 21
Chilton Street. Suff 1A 54
Chilton Trinity. Som 3F 21
Chilwell. Notts 2C 74
Chilworth. Hants 1C 16
Chilworth. Surr 1B 26
Chimney. Oxon 5B 50
Chimney Street. Suff 1H 53
Chineham. Hants 1E 25
**Chingford**. G Lon 1E 39
Chinley. Derbs 2E 85
Chinnor. Oxon 5F 51
Chipley. Som 4E 20
Chipnall. Shrp 2B 72
Chippenham. Cambs 4F 65
**Chippenham**. Wilts 4E 35
Chipperfield. Herts 5A 52
Chipping. Herts 2D 52
Chipping. Lanc 5F 97
Chipping Campden. Glos 2G 49
Chipping Hill. Essx 4B 54
Chipping Norton. Oxon 3B 50
Chipping Ongar. Essx 5F 53
**Chipping Sodbury**. S Glo 3C 34
Chipping Warden. Nptn 1C 50
Chipstable. Som 4D 20
Chipstead. Kent 5G 39
Chipstead. Surr 5D 38
Chirbury. Shrp 1E 59
Chirk. Wrex 2E 71
Chirmorie. S Ayr 2H 109
Chirnside. Bord 4E 131
Chirnsidebridge. Bord 4E 131
Chirton. Wilts 1F 23
Chisbridge Cross. Buck 3G 37
Chisbury. Wilts 5A 36
Chiselborough. Som 1H 13
Chiseldon. Swin 4G 35
Chiselhampton. Oxon 2D 36
Chiserley. W Yor 2A 92
**Chislehurst**. G Lon 3F 39
Chislet. Kent 4G 41
Chiswell. Dors 5B 14
Chiswell Green. Herts 5B 52
**Chiswick**. G Lon 3D 38
Chisworth. Derbs 1D 85
Chitcombe. E Sus 3C 28
Chithurst. W Sus 4G 25
Chittering. Cambs 4D 65
Chitterley. Devn 2C 12
Chitterne. Wilts 2E 23
Chittlehamholt. Devn 4G 19
Chittlehampton. Devn 4G 19
Chittoe. Wilts 5E 35
Chivelstone. Devn 5D 9
Chivenor. Devn 3F 19
Chobham. Surr 4A 38
Cholderton. Wilts 2H 23
Cholesbury. Buck 5H 51
Chollerford. Nmbd 2C 114
Chollerton. Nmbd 2C 114
Cholsey. Oxon 3D 36
Cholstrey. Here 5G 59
Chop Gate. N Yor 5C 106
Choppington. Nmbd 1F 115
Chopwell. Tyne 4E 115
Chorley. Ches E 5H 83
**Chorley**. Lanc 3D 90
Chorley. Shrp 2A 60
Chorley. Staf 4E 73
Chorleywood. Herts 1B 38
Chorlton. Ches E 5B 84
Chorlton-cum-Hardy. G Man 1C 84
Chorlton Lane. Ches W 1G 71
Choulton. Shrp 2F 59
Chrishall. Essx 2E 53
Christchurch. Cambs 1D 65
**Christchurch**. Dors 3G 15
Christchurch. Glos 4A 48
Christian Malford. Wilts 4E 35
Christleton. Ches W 4G 83
Christmas Common. Oxon 2F 37
Christon. N Som 1G 21
Christon Bank. Nmbd 2G 121
Christow. Devn 4B 12
Chryston. N Lan 2H 127
Chuck Hatch. E Sus 2F 27
Chudleigh. Devn 5B 12
Chudleigh Knighton. Devn 5B 12
Chulmleigh. Devn 1G 11
Chunal. Derbs 1E 85
Church. Lanc 2F 91
Churcham. Glos 4C 48
Church Aston. Telf 4B 72
Church Brampton. Nptn 4E 62
Church Brough. Cumb 3A 104
Church Broughton. Derbs 2G 73
Church Corner. Suff 2G 67
Church Crookham. Hants 1G 25
Churchdown. Glos 3D 49
Church Eaton. Staf 4C 72
Church End. Cambs 5D 65 (nr. Cambridge)
Church End. Cambs 2B 64 (nr. Sawtry)
Church End. Cambs 3C 64 (nr. Willingham)
Church End. Cambs 5C 76 (nr. Wisbech)
Church End. C Beds 3H 51 (nr. Dunstable)
Church End. C Beds 2B 52 (nr. Stotfold)
Church End. E Yor 4E 101
Church End. Essx 3H 53 (nr. Braintree)
Church End. Essx 3G 53 (nr. Great Dunmow)
Church End. Essx 1F 53 (nr. Saffron Walden)
Churchend. Essx 1E 40 (nr. Southend-on-Sea)
Church End. Glos 5C 48
Church End. Hants 1E 25
Church End. Linc 2B 76 (nr. Donington)
Church End. Linc 1D 88 (nr. North Somercotes)
Church End. Norf 4E 77
Church End. Warw 1G 61 (nr. Coleshill)
Church End. Warw 1G 61 (nr. Nuneaton)
Church End. Wilts 4F 35
Church Enstone. Oxon 3B 50
Church Fenton. N Yor 1F 93
Church Green. Devn 3E 13
Church Gresley. Derbs 4G 73
Church Hanborough. Oxon 4C 50
Church Hill. Ches W 4A 84
Church Hill. Worc 4E 61
Church Hougham. Kent 1G 29
Church Houses. N Yor 5D 106
Churchill. Devn 2G 13 (nr. Axminster)
Churchill. Devn 2F 19 (nr. Barnstaple)
Churchill. N Som 1H 21
Churchill. Oxon 3A 50
Churchill. Worc 3C 60 (nr. Kidderminster)
Churchill. Worc 5D 60 (nr. Worcester)
Churchinford. Som 1F 13
Church Knowle. Dors 4E 15
Church Laneham. Notts 3F 87
Church Langley. Essx 5E 53
Church Langton. Leics 1E 62
Church Lawford. Warw 3B 62
Church Lawton. Ches E 5C 84
Church Leigh. Staf 2E 73
Church Lench. Worc 5E 61
Church Mayfield. Staf 1F 73
Church Minshull. Ches E 4A 84
Church Norton. W Sus 3G 17
Churchover. Warw 2C 62
Church Preen. Shrp 1H 59
Church Pulverbatch. Shrp 5G 71
Churchstanton. Som 1E 13
Church Stoke. Powy 1E 59
Churchstow. Devn 4D 8
Church Stowe. Nptn 5D 62
Church Street. Kent 3B 40
Church Stretton. Shrp 1G 59
Churchtown. Cumb 5E 113
Churchtown. Derbs 4G 85
Churchtown. Devn 2G 19
Churchtown. IOM 2D 108
Churchtown. Lanc 5D 97
Church Town. Leics 4A 74
Churchtown. Mers 3B 90
Churchtown. New M 5K 179
Church Town. N Lin 4A 94
Churchtown. Shrp 2E 59
Church Village. Rhon 3D 32
Church Warsop. Notts 4C 86
Church Westcote. Glos 3H 49
Church Wilne. Derbs 2B 74
Churnsike Lodge. Nmbd 2H 113
Churston Ferrers. Torb 3F 9
Churt. Surr 3G 25
Churton. Ches W 5G 83
Churwell. W Yor 2C 92
Chute Standen. Wilts 1B 24
Chwilog. Gwyn 2D 68
Chwitffordd. Flin 3D 82
Chyandour. Corn 3B 4
Cilan Uchaf. Gwyn 3B 68
Cilcain. Flin 4D 82
Cilcennin. Cdgn 4E 57
Cilfrew. Neat 5A 46
Cilfynydd. Rhon 2D 32
Cilgerran. Pemb 1B 44
Cilgeti. Pemb 4F 43
Cilgwyn. Carm 3H 45
Cilgwyn. Pemb 1E 43
Ciliau Aeron. Cdgn 5D 57
Cill Amhlaidh. W Isl 4C 170
Cill Donnain. W Isl 6C 170
Cille a' Bhacstair. High 2C 154
Cille Bhrighde. W Isl 7C 170
Cille Pheadair. W Isl 7C 170
Cilmaengwyn. Neat 5H 45
Cilmeri. Powy 5C 58
Cilmery. Powy 5C 58
Cilrhedyn. Pemb 1G 43
Cilsan. Carm 3F 45
Ciltalgarth. Gwyn 1A 70
Ciltwrch. Powy 1E 47
Cilybebyll. Neat 5H 45
Cilycwm. Carm 1A 46
Cimla. Neat 2A 32
**Cinderford**. Glos 4B 48
Cinderhill. Derbs 1A 74
Cippenham. Slo 2A 38
Cippyn. Pemb 1B 44
Cirbhig. W Isl 3D 171
Circebost. W Isl 4D 171
**Cirencester**. Glos 5F 49
City. Powy 1E 58
City. V Glam 4C 32
City Centre. Stoke 1C 72 & **Stoke 202**
City Dulas. IOA 2D 80
City (London) Airport. G Lon 2F 39
City of Derry Airport. Derr 4B 174
**City of London**. G Lon 2E 39
City, The. Buck 2F 37
Civiltown. Arm 5F 178
Clabby. Ferm 4K 177
Clabhach. Arg 3C 138
Clachaig. Arg 1C 126
Clachaig. High 3F 141 (nr. Kinlochleven)
Clachaig. High 2E 151 (nr. Nethy Bridge)
Clachamish. High 3C 154
Clachan. Arg 4F 125 (on Kintyre)
Clachan. Arg 4C 140 (on Lismore)
Clachan. High 2H 167 (nr. Bettyhill)
Clachan. High 2D 155 (nr. Staffin)
Clachan. High 1D 154 (nr. Uig)
Clachan. High 5E 155 (on Raasay)
Clachan Farm. Arg 2A 134
Clachan na Luib. W Isl 2D 170
Clachan of Campsie. E Dun 2H 127
Clachan of Glendaruel. Arg 1A 126
Clachan-Seil. Arg 2E 133
Clachan Shannda. W Isl 1D 170
Clachan Strachur. Arg 3H 133
Clachbreck. Arg 2F 125
Clachnaharry. High 4A 158
Clachtoll. High 1E 163
Clackmannan. Clac 4B 136
**Clackmannanshire Bridge**. Falk 1C 128
Clackmarras. Mor 3G 159
**Clacton-on-Sea**. Essx 4E 55
Cladach a Chaolais. W Isl 2C 170
Cladach Chairinis. W Isl 3D 170
Cladach Chirceboist. W Isl 2C 170
Cladach Iolaraigh. W Isl 2C 170
Cladich. Arg 1H 133
Cladswell. Worc 5E 61
Clady. Derr 3E 176
Clady. M Ulst 6F 175
Claggan. High 1F 141 (nr. Fort William)
Claggan. High 3B 140 (nr. Lochaline)
Claigan. High 3B 154
Clandown. Bath 1B 22
Clanfield. Hants 1E 17
Clanfield. Oxon 5A 50
Clanville. Hants 2B 24
Clanville. Som 3B 22
Claonaig. Arg 4G 125
Clapgate. Dors 2F 15
Clapgate. Herts 3E 53
Clapham. Bed 5H 63
Clapham. Devn 4B 12
**Clapham**. G Lon 3D 39
Clapham. N Yor 3G 97
Clapham. W Sus 5B 26
Clap Hill. Kent 2E 29
Clappers. Bord 4F 131
Clappersgate. Cumb 4E 103
Clapphoull. Shet 9F 173
Clapton. Som 2H 13 (nr. Crewkerne)
Clapton. Som 1B 22 (nr. Radstock)
Clapton in Gordano. N Som 4H 33
Clapton-on-the-Hill. Glos 4G 49
Clapworthy. Devn 4G 19
Clara Vale. Tyne 3E 115
Clarbeston. Pemb 2E 43
Clarbeston Road. Pemb 2E 43
Clarborough. Notts 2E 87
Clare. Arm 5E 178
Clare. Suff 1A 54
Clarebrand. Dum 3E 111
Clarencefield. Dum 3B 112
Clarilaw. Bord 3H 119
Clark's Green. Surr 2C 26
Clark's Hill. Linc 3C 76
**Clarkston**. E Ren 4G 127
Clasheddy. High 2G 167
Clashindarroch. Abers 5B 160
Clashmore. High 5E 165 (nr. Dornoch)
Clashmore. High 1E 163 (nr. Stoer)
Clashnessie. High 5A 166
Clashnoir. Mor 1G 151
Clate. Shet 5G 173
Clathick. Per 1H 135
Clathy. Per 2B 136
Clatt. Abers 1C 152
Clatter. Powy 1B 58
Clatterford. IOW 4C 16
Clatworthy. Som 3D 20
Claudy. Derr 6B 174
Claughton. Lanc 3E 97 (nr. Caton)
Claughton. Lanc 5E 97 (nr. Garstang)
Claughton. Mers 2E 83
Claverdon. Warw 4F 61
Claverham. N Som 5H 33
Clavering. Essx 2E 53
Claverley. Shrp 1B 60
Claverton. Bath 5C 34
Clawdd-coch. V Glam 4D 32
Clawdd-newydd. Den 5C 82
Clawson Hill. Leics 3E 75
Clawton. Devn 3D 10
Claxby. Linc 3D 88 (nr. Alford)
Claxby. Linc 1A 88 (nr. Market Rasen)
Claxton. Norf 5F 79
Claxton. N Yor 3A 100
Claybrooke Magna. Leics 2B 62
Claybrooke Parva. Leics 2B 62
Clay Common. Suff 2G 67
Clay Coton. Nptn 3C 62
**Clay Cross**. Derbs 4A 86
Claydon. Oxon 5B 62
Claydon. Suff 5D 66
Clay End. Herts 3D 52
Claygate. Dum 2E 113
Claygate. Kent 1B 28
Claygate. Surr 4C 38
Claygate Cross. Kent 5H 39
Clayhall. Hants 3E 16
Clayhanger. Devn 4D 20
Clayhanger. W Mid 5E 73
Clayhidon. Devn 1E 13
Clay Hill. Bris 4B 34
Clayhill. E Sus 3C 28
Clayhill. Hants 2B 16
Clayhithe. Cambs 4E 65
Clayholes. Ang 5E 145
Clay Lake. Linc 3B 76
Clayock. High 3D 168
Claypits. Glos 5C 48
Claypole. Linc 1F 75
Claythorpe. Linc 3D 88
Clayton. G Man 1C 84
Clayton. S Yor 4E 93
Clayton. Staf 1C 72
Clayton. W Sus 4E 27
Clayton. W Yor 1B 92
Clayton Green. Lanc 2D 90
Clayton-le-Moors. Lanc 1F 91
Clayton-le-Woods. Lanc 2D 90
Clayton West. W Yor 3C 92
Clayworth. Notts 2E 87
Cleadale. High 5C 146
Cleadon. Tyne 3G 115
Clearbrook. Devn 2B 8
Clearwell. Glos 5A 48
Cleasby. N Yor 3F 105
Cleat. Orkn 3D 172 (nr. Braehead)
Cleat. Orkn 9D 172 (nr. St Margaret's Hope)
Cleatlam. Dur 3E 105
Cleator. Cumb 3B 102
Cleator Moor. Cumb 3B 102
**Cleckheaton**. W Yor 2B 92
Cleedownton. Shrp 2H 59
Cleehill. Shrp 3H 59
Cleekhimin. N Lan 4A 128
Clee St Margaret. Shrp 2H 59
Cleestanton. Shrp 3H 59
**Cleethorpes**. NE Lin 4G 95
Cleeton St Mary. Shrp 3A 60
Cleeve. N Som 5H 33
Cleeve. Oxon 3E 36
Cleeve Hill. Glos 3E 49
Cleeve Prior. Worc 1F 49
Clehonger. Here 2H 47
Cleigh. Arg 1F 133
Cleish. Per 4C 136
Cleland. N Lan 4B 128
Clench Common. Wilts 5G 35
Clenchwarton. Norf 3E 77
Clennell. Nmbd 4D 120
Clent. Worc 3D 60
Cleobury Mortimer. Shrp 3A 60
Cleobury North. Shrp 2A 60
Clephanton. High 3C 158
Clerkhill. High 2H 167
Clestrain. Orkn 7C 172
Clevancy. Wilts 4F 35
**Clevedon**. N Som 4H 33
Cleveley. Oxon 3B 50
**Cleveleys**. Lanc 5C 96
Clevelode. Worc 1D 48
Cleverton. Wilts 3E 35
Clewer. Som 1H 21
Cley next the Sea. Norf 1C 78
Cliaid. W Isl 8B 170
Cliasmol. W Isl 7C 171
Clibberswick. Shet 1H 173
Cliburn. Cumb 2G 103
Cliddesden. Hants 2E 25
Clieves Hills. Lanc 4B 90
Cliff. Warw 1G 61
Cliffburn. Ang 4F 145
Cliffe. Medw 3B 40
Cliffe. N Yor 3F 105 (nr. Darlington)
Cliffe. N Yor 1G 93 (nr. Selby)
Cliff End. E Sus 4C 28
Cliffe Woods. Medw 3B 40
Clifford. Here 1F 47
Clifford. W Yor 5G 99
Clifford Chambers. Warw 5F 61
Clifford's Mesne. Glos 3C 48
Cliffsend. Kent 4H 41
Clifton. Bris 4A 34
Clifton. C Beds 2B 52
Clifton. Cumb 2G 103
Clifton. Derbs 1F 73
Clifton. Devn 2G 19
Clifton. G Man 4F 91
Clifton. Lanc 1C 90
Clifton. Nmbd 1F 115
Clifton. N Yor 5D 98
Clifton. Nott 2C 74
Clifton. Oxon 2C 50
Clifton. S Yor 1C 86
Clifton. Stir 5H 141
Clifton. W Yor 2B 92
Clifton. Worc 1D 48
Clifton. York 4H 99
Clifton Campville. Staf 4G 73
Clifton Hampden. Oxon 2D 36
Clifton Hill. Worc 4B 60
Clifton Reynes. Mil 5G 63
Clifton upon Dunsmore. Warw 3C 62
Clifton upon Teme. Worc 4B 60
Cliftonville. Kent 3H 41
Cliftonville. Norf 2F 79
Climping. W Sus 5A 26
Climpy. S Lan 4C 128
Clink. Som 2C 22
Clint. N Yor 4E 99
Clint Green. Norf 4C 78
Clintmains. Bord 1A 120
Cliobh. W Isl 4C 171
Clipiau. Gwyn 4H 69
Clippesby. Norf 4G 79
Clippings Green. Norf 4C 78
Clipsham. Rut 4G 75
Clipston. Nptn 2E 62
Clipston. Notts 2D 74
Clipstone. Notts 4C 86
**Clitheroe**. Lanc 5G 97
Cliuthar. W Isl 8D 171
Clive. Shrp 3H 71
Clivocast. Shet 1G 173
Clixby. Linc 4D 94
Clocaenog. Den 5C 82
Clochan. Mor 2B 160
Clochforbie. Abers 3F 161
Clock Face. Mers 1H 83
Cloddiau. Powy 5E 70
Cloddymoss. Mor 2D 159
Clodock. Here 3G 47
Cloford. Som 2C 22
Clogh. ME Ant 5G 175
Clogher. M Ulst 4L 177
Cloghmills. Caus 5G 175
Clola. Abers 4H 161
Clonoe. M Ulst 3C 178
Clonvaraghan. New M 5H 179
Clophill. C Beds 2A 52
Clopton. Nptn 2H 63
Clopton Corner. Suff 5E 66
Clopton Green. Suff 5G 65
Closeburn. Dum 5A 118
Close Clark. IOM 4B 108
Closworth. Som 1A 14
Clothall. Herts 2C 52
Clotton. Ches W 4H 83
Clough. G Man 3H 91
Clough. New M 5J 179
Clough. W Yor 3A 92
Cloughey. N Dwn 4L 179
Clough Foot. W Yor 2H 91
Cloughton. N Yor 5H 107
Cloughton Newlands. N Yor 5H 107
Clousta. Shet 6E 173
Clouston. Orkn 6B 172
Clova. Abers 1B 152
Clova. Ang 1C 144
Clovelly. Devn 4D 18
Clovenfords. Bord 1G 119
Clovenstone. Abers 2E 153
Clovullin. High 2E 141
Clowne. Derbs 3B 86
Clows Top. Worc 3B 60
Cloy. Wrex 1F 71
Cloyfin. Caus 3E 174
Cluanie Inn. High 2C 148
Cluanie Lodge. High 2C 148
Cluddley. Telf 4A 72
Clun. Shrp 2F 59
Clunas. High 4C 158
Clunbury. Shrp 2F 59
Clunderwen. Pemb 3F 43
Clune. High 1B 150
Clunes. High 5E 148
Clungunford. Shrp 3F 59
Clunie. Per 4A 144
Clunton. Shrp 2F 59
Cluny. Fife 4E 137
Clutton. Bath 1B 22
Clutton. Ches W 5G 83
Clwt-y-bont. Gwyn 4E 81
Clwydfagwyr. Mer T 5D 46
Clydach. Mon 4F 47
**Clydach**. Swan 5G 45
Clydach Vale. Rhon 2C 32
**Clydebank**. W Dun 3G 127
Clydey. Pemb 1G 43
Clyffe Pypard. Wilts 4F 35
Clynder. Arg 1D 126
Clyne. Neat 5B 46
Clynelish. High 3F 165
Clynnog-fawr. Gwyn 1D 68
Clyro. Powy 1F 47
Clyst Honiton. Devn 3C 12
Clyst Hydon. Devn 2D 12
Clyst St George. Devn 4C 12
Clyst St Lawrence. Devn 2D 12
Clyst St Mary. Devn 3C 12
Clyth. High 5E 169
Cnip. W Isl 4C 171
Cnoc Amhlaigh. W Isl 4H 171
Cnwcau. Pemb 1C 44
Cnwch Coch. Cdgn 3F 57
Coad's Green. Corn 5C 10
Coagh. M Ulst 2C 178
Coal Aston. Derbs 3A 86
Coalbrookdale. Telf 5A 72
Coalbrookvale. Blae 5E 47
Coalburn. S Lan 1H 117
Coalburns. Tyne 3E 115
Coalcleugh. Nmbd 5B 114
Coaley. Glos 5C 48
Coalford. Abers 4F 153
Coalhall. E Ayr 3D 116
Coalhill. Essx 1B 40
Coalisland. M Ulst 3C 178
Coalpit Heath. S Glo 3B 34
Coal Pool. W Mid 5E 73
Coalport. Telf 5B 72
Coalsnaughton. Clac 4B 136
Coaltown of Balgonie. Fife 4F 137
Coaltown of Wemyss. Fife 4F 137
**Coalville**. Leics 4B 74
Coalway. Glos 4A 48
Coanwood. Nmbd 4H 113
Coat. Som 4H 21
**Coatbridge**. N Lan 3A 128
Coatdyke. N Lan 3A 128
Coate. Swin 3G 35
Coate. Wilts 5F 35
Coates. Cambs 1C 64
Coates. Glos 5E 49
Coates. Linc 2G 87
Coates. W Sus 4A 26
Coatham. Red C 2C 106
Coatham Mundeville. Darl 2F 105
Cobbaton. Devn 4G 19
Coberley. Glos 4E 49
Cobhall Common. Here 2H 47
Cobham. Kent 4A 40
**Cobham**. Surr 5C 38
Cobnash. Here 4G 59
Coburg. Devn 5B 12
Cockayne. N Yor 5D 106
Cockayne Hatley. C Beds 1C 52
Cock Bank. Wrex 1F 71
Cock Bridge. Abers 3G 151
Cockburnspath. Bord 2D 130
Cock Clarks. Essx 5B 54
Cockenzie and Port Seton. E Lot 2H 129
Cockerham. Lanc 4D 96
Cockermouth. Cumb 1C 102
Cockernhoe. Herts 3B 52
Cockfield. Dur 2E 105
Cockfield. Suff 5B 66
Cockfosters. G Lon 1D 39
Cock Gate. Here 4G 59
Cock Green. Essx 4G 53
Cocking. W Sus 1G 17
Cocking Causeway. W Sus 1G 17
Cockington. Torb 2E 9
Cocklake. Som 2H 21
Cocklaw. Abers 4H 161
Cocklaw. Nmbd 2C 114
Cockley Beck. Cumb 4D 102
Cockley Cley. Norf 5G 77
Cockmuir. Abers 3G 161
Cockpole Green. Wok 3F 37
Cockshutford. Shrp 2H 59
Cockshutt. Shrp 3G 71
Cockthorpe. Norf 1B 78
Cockwood. Devn 4C 12
Cockyard. Derbs 3E 85
Cockyard. Here 2H 47
Codda. Corn 5B 10
Coddenham. Suff 5D 66
Coddenham Green. Suff 5D 66
Coddington. Ches W 5G 83
Coddington. Here 1C 48
Coddington. Notts 5F 87
Codford. Wilts 3E 23
Codicote. Herts 4C 52
Codmore Hill. W Sus 3B 26
Codnor. Derbs 1B 74
Codrington. S Glo 4C 34
**Codsall**. Staf 5C 72
Codsall Wood. Staf 5C 72
**Coed Duon**. Cphy 2E 33
Coedely. Rhon 3D 32
Coedglasson. Powy 4C 58
Coedkernew. Newp 3F 33
Coed Morgan. Mon 4G 47
Coedpoeth. Wrex 5E 83
Coedway. Powy 4F 71
Coed-y-bryn. Cdgn 1D 44
Coed-y-paen. Mon 2G 33
Coed Ystumgwern. Gwyn 3E 69
Coelbren. Powy 4B 46
Coffinswell. Devn 2E 9
Cofton Hackett. Worc 3E 61
Cogan. V Glam 4E 33
Cogenhoe. Nptn 4F 63
Cogges. Oxon 5B 50
Coggeshall. Essx 3B 54
Coggeshall Hamlet. Essx 3B 54
Coggins Mill. E Sus 3G 27
Coignafearn Lodge. High 2A 150
Coig Peighinnean. W Isl 1H 171
Coig Peighinnean Bhuirgh. W Isl 2G 171
Coilleag. W Isl 7C 170
Coillemore. High 1A 158
Coillore. High 5C 154
Coire an Fhuarain. W Isl 4E 171
Coity. B'end 3C 32
Cokhay Green. Derbs 3G 73
Col. W Isl 3G 171
Colaboll. High 2C 164
Colan. Corn 2C 6
Colaton Raleigh. Devn 4D 12
Colbost. High 4B 154
Colburn. N Yor 5E 105
Colby. Cumb 2H 103
Colby. IOM 4B 108


212 A-Z Great Britain Road Atlas

Colby—Crossgates


Colby. *Norf* 2E **78**
**Colchester**. *Essx* 3D **54**
Cold Ash. *W Ber* 5D **36**
Cold Ashby. *Nptn* 3D **62**
Cold Ashton. *S Glo* 4C **34**
Cold Aston. *Glos* 4G **49**
Coldbackie. *High* 3G **167**
Cold Blow. *Pemb* 3F **43**
Cold Brayfield. *Mil* 5G **63**
Cold Cotes. *N Yor* 2G **97**
Coldean. *Brig* 5E **27**
Coldeast. *Devn* 5B **12**
Colden. *W Yor* 2H **91**
Colden Common. *Hants* 4C **24**
Coldfair Green. *Suff* 4G **67**
Coldham. *Cambs* 5D **76**
Coldham. *Staf* 5C **72**
Cold Hanworth. *Linc* 2H **87**
Coldharbour. *Corn* 4B **6**
Cold Harbour. *Dors* 3E **15**
Coldharbour. *Glos* 5A **48**
Coldharbour. *Kent* 5G **39**
Coldharbour. *Surr* 1C **26**
Cold Hatton. *Telf* 3A **72**
Cold Hatton Heath. *Telf* 3A **72**
Cold Hesledon. *Dur* 5H **115**
Cold Hiendley. *W Yor* 3D **92**
Cold Higham. *Nptn* 5D **62**
Coldingham. *Bord* 3F **131**
Cold Kirby. *N Yor* 1H **99**
Coldmeece. *Staf* 2C **72**
Cold Northcott. *Corn* 4C **10**
Cold Norton. *Essx* 5B **54**
Cold Overton. *Leics* 4F **75**
Coldrain. *Per* 3C **136**
Coldred. *Kent* 1G **29**
Coldridge. *Devn* 2G **11**
Cold Row. *Lanc* 5C **96**
Coldstream. *Bord* 5E **131**
Coldwaltham. *W Sus* 4B **26**
Coldwell. *Here* 2H **47**
Coldwells. *Abers* 5H **161**
Coldwells Croft. *Abers* 1C **152**
Cole. *Shet* 5E **173**
Cole. *Som* 3B **22**
Colebatch. *Shrp* 2F **59**
Colebrook. *Devn* 2D **12**
Colebrooke. *Devn* 3A **12**
Coleburn. *Mor* 3G **159**
Coleby. *Linc* 4G **87**
Coleby. *N Lin* 3B **94**
Cole End. *Warw* 2G **61**
Coleford. *Devn* 2A **12**
**Coleford**. *Glos* 4A **48**
Coleford. *Som* 2B **22**
Colegate End. *Norf* 2D **66**
Cole Green. *Herts* 4C **52**
Cole Henley. *Hants* 1C **24**
Colehill. *Dors* 2F **15**
Coleman Green. *Herts* 4B **52**
Coleman's Hatch. *E Sus* 2F **27**
Colemere. *Shrp* 2G **71**
Colemore. *Hants* 3F **25**
Colemore Green. *Shrp* 1B **60**
Coleorton. *Leics* 4B **74**
**Coleraine**. *Caus* 3E **174**
Colerne. *Wilts* 4D **34**
Colesbourne. *Glos* 4F **49**
Colesden. *Bed* 5A **64**
Coles Green. *Worc* 5B **60**
Coleshill. *Buck* 1A **38**
Coleshill. *Oxon* 2H **35**
Coleshill. *Warw* 2G **61**
Colestocks. *Devn* 2D **12**
Colethrop. *Glos* 4D **48**
Coley. *Bath* 1A **22**
Colgate. *W Sus* 2D **26**
Colinsburgh. *Fife* 3G **137**
Colinton. *Edin* 3F **129**
Colintraive. *Arg* 2B **126**
Colkirk. *Norf* 3B **78**
Collace. *Per* 5B **144**
Collam. *W Isl* 8D **171**
Collaton. *Devn* 5D **8**
Collaton St Mary. *Torb* 2E **9**
College of Roseisle. *Mor* 2F **159**
Collessie. *Fife* 2E **137**
Collier Row. *G Lon* 1F **39**
Colliers End. *Herts* 3D **52**
Collier Street. *Kent* 1B **28**
Colliery Row. *Tyne* 5G **115**
Collieston. *Abers* 1H **153**
Collin. *Dum* 2B **112**
Collingbourne Ducis. *Wilts* 1H **23**
Collingbourne Kingston. *Wilts* 1H **23**
Collingham. *Notts* 4F **87**
Collingham. *W Yor* 5F **99**
Collingtree. *Nptn* 5E **63**
Collins Green. *Warr* 1H **83**
Collins Green. *Worc* 5B **60**
Colliston. *Ang* 4F **145**
Colliton. *Devn* 2D **12**
Collydean. *Fife* 3E **137**
Collyweston. *Nptn* 5G **75**
Colmonell. *S Ayr* 1G **109**
Colmworth. *Bed* 5A **64**
Colnbrook. *Slo* 3B **38**
Colne. *Cambs* 3C **64**
**Colne**. *Lanc* 5A **98**
Colne Engaine. *Essx* 2B **54**
Colney. *Norf* 5D **78**
Colney Heath. *Herts* 5C **52**
Colney Street. *Herts* 5B **52**
Coln Rogers. *Glos* 5F **49**
Coln St Aldwyns. *Glos* 5G **49**
Coln St Dennis. *Glos* 4F **49**
Colpitts Grange. *Nmbd* 4C **114**
Colpy. *Abers* 5D **160**
Colscott. *Devn* 1D **10**
Colsterdale. *N Yor* 1D **98**
Colsterworth. *Linc* 3G **75**
Colston Bassett. *Notts* 2E **74**
Colstoun House. *E Lot* 2B **130**
Coltfield. *Mor* 2F **159**
Colthouse. *Cumb* 5E **103**
Coltishall. *Norf* 4E **79**
Coltness. *N Lan* 4B **128**
Colton. *Cumb* 1C **96**
Colton. *Norf* 5D **78**
Colton. *N Yor* 5H **99**
Colton. *Staf* 3E **73**
Colton. *W Yor* 1D **92**
Colt's Hill. *Kent* 1H **27**
Col Uarach. *W Isl* 4G **171**
Colvend. *Dum* 4F **111**
Colvister. *Shet* 2G **173**
Colwall. *Here* 1C **48**
Colwall Green. *Here* 1C **48**
Colwell. *Nmbd* 2C **114**
Colwich. *Staf* 3E **73**
Colwick. *Notts* 1D **74**
Colwinston. *V Glam* 4C **32**
Colworth. *W Sus* 5A **26**
**Colwyn Bay**. *Cnwy* 3A **82**
Colyford. *Devn* 3F **13**
Colyton. *Devn* 3F **13**
Combe. *Devn* 2D **8**
Combe. *Here* 4F **59**
Combe. *Oxon* 4C **50**
Combe. *W Ber* 5B **36**
Combe Almer. *Dors* 3E **15**
Combebow. *Devn* 4E **11**
Combe Down. *Bath* 5C **34**
Combe Fishacre. *Devn* 2E **9**
Combe Florey. *Som* 3E **21**
Combe Hay. *Bath* 5C **34**
Combeinteignhead. *Devn* 5C **12**
Combe Martin. *Devn* 2F **19**
Combe Moor. *Here* 4F **59**
Comber. *N Dwn* 3J **179**
Combe Raleigh. *Devn* 2E **13**
Comberbach. *Ches W* 3A **84**
Comberford. *Staf* 5F **73**
Comberton. *Cambs* 5C **64**
Comberton. *Here* 4G **59**
Combe St Nicholas. *Som* 1G **13**
Combpyne. *Devn* 3F **13**
Combridge. *Staf* 2E **73**
Combrook. *Warw* 5H **61**
Combs. *Derbs* 3E **85**
Combs. *Suff* 5C **66**
Combs Ford. *Suff* 5C **66**
Combwich. *Som* 2F **21**
Comers. *Abers* 3D **152**
Comhampton. *Worc* 4C **60**
Comins Coch. *Cdgn* 2F **57**
Comley. *Shrp* 1G **59**
Commercial End. *Cambs* 4E **65**
Commins. *Powy* 3D **70**
Commins Coch. *Powy* 5H **69**
Commondale. *N Yor* 3D **106**
Common End. *Cumb* 2B **102**
Common Hill. *Here* 2A **48**
Common Moor. *Corn* 2G **7**
Commonside. *Ches W* 3H **83**
Common Side. *Derbs* 3H **85**
(nr. Chesterfield)
Commonside. *Derbs* 1G **73**
(nr. Derby)
Common, The. *Wilts* 3H **23**
(nr. Salisbury)
Common, The. *Wilts* 3F **35**
(nr. Swindon)
Compstall. *G Man* 1D **84**
Compton. *Devn* 2E **9**
Compton. *Hants* 4C **24**
Compton. *Staf* 2C **60**
Compton. *Surr* 1A **26**
Compton. *W Ber* 4D **36**
Compton. *W Sus* 1F **17**
Compton. *Wilts* 1G **23**
Compton Abbas. *Dors* 1D **15**
Compton Abdale. *Glos* 4F **49**
Compton Bassett. *Wilts* 4F **35**
Compton Beauchamp. *Oxon* 3A **36**
Compton Bishop. *Som* 1G **21**
Compton Chamberlayne. *Wilts* 4F **23**
Compton Dando. *Bath* 5B **34**
Compton Dundon. *Som* 3H **21**
Compton Greenfield. *S Glo* 3A **34**
Compton Martin. *Bath* 1A **22**
Compton Pauncefoot. *Som* 4B **22**
Compton Valence. *Dors* 3A **14**
Comrie. *Fife* 1D **128**
Comrie. *Per* 1G **135**
Conaglen. *High* 2E **141**
Conchra. *Arg* 1B **126**
Conchra. *High* 1A **148**
Conder Green. *Lanc* 4D **96**
Conderton. *Worc* 2E **49**
Condicote. *Glos* 3G **49**
Condorrat. *N Lan* 2A **128**
Condover. *Shrp* 5G **71**
Coneyhurst. *W Sus* 3C **26**
Coneyisland. *New M* 6K **179**
Coneysthorpe. *N Yor* 2B **100**
Coneythorpe. *N Yor* 4F **99**
Coney Weston. *Suff* 3B **66**
Conford. *Hants* 3G **25**
Congdon's Shop. *Corn* 5C **10**
Congerstone. *Leics* 5A **74**
Congham. *Norf* 3G **77**
**Congleton**. *Ches E* 4C **84**
Congl-y-wal. *Gwyn* 1G **69**
Congresbury. *N Som* 5H **33**
Congreve. *Staf* 4D **72**
Conham. *S Glo* 4B **34**
Conicaval. *Mor* 3D **159**
Coningsby. *Linc* 5B **88**
Conington. *Cambs* 4C **64**
(nr. Fenstanton)
Conington. *Cambs* 2A **64**
(nr. Sawtry)
**Conisbrough**. *S Yor* 1C **86**
Conisby. *Arg* 3A **124**
Conisholme. *Linc* 1D **88**
Coniston. *Cumb* 5E **102**
Coniston. *E Yor* 1E **95**
Coniston Cold. *N Yor* 4B **98**
Conistone. *N Yor* 3B **98**
Conlig. *N Dwn* 2K **179**
**Connah's Quay**. *Flin* 3E **83**
Connel. *Arg* 5D **140**
Connel Park. *E Ayr* 3F **117**
Connista. *High* 1D **154**
Connor. *ME Ant* 7H **175**
Connor Downs. *Corn* 3C **4**
Conock. *Wilts* 1F **23**
Conon Bridge. *High* 3H **157**
Cononley. *N Yor* 5B **98**
Cononsyth. *Ang* 4E **145**
Conordan. *High* 5E **155**
Consall. *Staf* 1D **73**
**Consett**. *Dur* 4E **115**
Constable Burton. *N Yor* 5E **105**
Constantine. *Corn* 4E **5**
Constantine Bay. *Corn* 1C **6**
Contin. *High* 3G **157**
Contullich. *High* 1A **158**
Conwy. *Cnwy* 3G **81**
Conyer. *Kent* 4D **40**
Conyer's Green. *Suff* 4A **66**
Cooden. *E Sus* 5B **28**
Cooil. *IOM* 4C **108**
Cookbury. *Devn* 2E **11**
Cookbury Wick. *Devn* 2D **11**
Cookham. *Wind* 3G **37**
Cookham Dean. *Wind* 3G **37**
Cookham Rise. *Wind* 3G **37**
Cookhill. *Worc* 5E **61**
Cookley. *Suff* 3F **67**
Cookley. *Worc* 2C **60**
Cookley Green. *Oxon* 2E **37**
Cookney. *Abers* 4F **153**
Cooksbridge. *E Sus* 4F **27**
Cooksey Green. *Worc* 4D **60**
Cookshill. *Staf* 1D **72**
Cooksmill Green. *Essx* 5G **53**
**Cookstown**. *M Ulst* 2C **178**
Coolham. *W Sus* 3C **26**
Cooling. *Medw* 3B **40**
Cooling Street. *Medw* 3B **40**
Coombe. *Corn* 1C **10**
(nr. Bude)
Coombe. *Corn* 3D **6**
(nr. St Austell)
Coombe. *Corn* 4C **6**
(nr. Truro)
Coombe. *Devn* 3E **12**
(nr. Sidmouth)
Coombe. *Devn* 5C **12**
(nr. Teignmouth)
Coombe. *Glos* 2C **34**
Coombe. *Hants* 4E **25**
Coombe. *Wilts* 1G **23**
Coombe Bissett. *Wilts* 4G **23**
Coombe Hill. *Glos* 3D **49**
Coombe Keynes. *Dors* 4D **14**
Coombes. *W Sus* 5C **26**
Coopersale. *Essx* 5E **53**
Coopersale Street. *Essx* 5E **53**
Cooper's Corner. *Kent* 1F **27**
Cooper Street. *Kent* 5H **41**
Cootham. *W Sus* 4B **26**
Copalder Corner. *Cambs* 1C **64**
Copdock. *Suff* 1E **54**
Copford. *Essx* 3C **54**
Copford Green. *Essx* 3C **54**
Copgrove. *N Yor* 3F **99**
Copister. *Shet* 4F **173**
Cople. *Bed* 1B **52**
Copley. *Dur* 2D **105**
Coplow Dale. *Derbs* 3F **85**
Copmanthorpe. *York* 5H **99**
Copp. *Lanc* 1C **90**
Coppathorne. *Corn* 2C **10**
Coppenhall. *Ches E* 5B **84**
Coppenhall. *Staf* 4D **72**
Coppenhall Moss. *Ches E* 5B **84**
Copperhouse. *Corn* 3C **4**
Coppicegate. *Shrp* 2B **60**
Coppingford. *Cambs* 2A **64**
Copplestone. *Devn* 2A **12**
Coppull. *Lanc* 3D **90**
Coppull Moor. *Lanc* 3D **90**
Copsale. *W Sus* 3C **26**
Copshaw Holm. *Bord* 1F **113**
Copster Green. *Lanc* 1E **91**
Copston Magna. *Warw* 2B **62**
Copt Green. *Warw* 4F **61**
Copthall Green. *Essx* 5E **53**
Copt Heath. *W Mid* 3F **61**
Copt Hewick. *N Yor* 2F **99**
Copthill. *Dur* 5B **114**
Copthorne. *W Sus* 2E **27**
Coptiviney. *Shrp* 2G **71**
Copy's Green. *Norf* 2B **78**
Copythorne. *Hants* 1B **16**
Corbridge. *Nmbd* 3C **114**
**Corby**. *Nptn* 2F **63**
Corby Glen. *Linc* 3G **75**
Cordon. *N Ayr* 2E **123**
Coreley. *Shrp* 3A **60**
Corfe. *Som* 1F **13**
Corfe Castle. *Dors* 4E **15**
Corfe Mullen. *Dors* 3E **15**
Corfton. *Shrp* 2G **59**
Corgarff. *Abers* 3G **151**
Corhampton. *Hants* 4E **24**
Corkey. *Caus* 4G **175**
Corlae. *Dum* 5F **117**
Corlannau. *Neat* 2A **32**
Corley. *Warw* 2H **61**
Corley Ash. *Warw* 2G **61**
Corley Moor. *Warw* 2G **61**
Cormiston. *S Lan* 1C **118**
Cornaa. *IOM* 3D **108**
Cornaigbeg. *Arg* 4A **138**
Cornaigmore. *Arg* 2D **138**
(on Coll)
Cornaigmore. *Arg* 4A **138**
(on Tiree)
Corner Row. *Lanc* 1C **90**
Corney. *Cumb* 5C **102**
Cornforth. *Dur* 1A **106**
Cornhill. *Abers* 3C **160**
Cornhill. *High* 4C **164**
Cornhill-on-Tweed. *Nmbd* 1C **120**
Cornholme. *W Yor* 2H **91**
Cornish Hall End. *Essx* 2G **53**
Cornquoy. *Orkn* 7E **172**
Cornriggs. *Dur* 5B **114**
Cornsay. *Dur* 5E **115**
Cornsay Colliery. *Dur* 5E **115**
Corntown. *High* 3H **157**
Corntown. *V Glam* 4C **32**
Cornwell. *Oxon* 3A **50**
Cornwood. *Devn* 3C **8**
Cornworthy. *Devn* 3E **9**
Corpach. *High* 1E **141**
Corpusty. *Norf* 3D **78**
Corra. *Dum* 3F **111**
Corran. *High* 2E **141**
(nr. Arnisdale)
Corran. *High* 3A **148**
(nr. Fort William)
Corrany. *IOM* 3D **108**
Corribeg. *High* 1D **141**
Corrie. *N Ayr* 5B **126**
Corrie Common. *Dum* 1D **112**
Corriecravie. *N Ayr* 3D **122**
Corriekinloch. *High* 1A **164**
Corriemoillie. *High* 2F **157**
Corrievarkie Lodge. *Per* 1C **142**
Corrievorrie. *High* 1B **150**
Corrigall. *Orkn* 6C **172**
Corrimony. *High* 5F **157**
Corringham. *Linc* 1F **87**
**Corringham**. *Thur* 2B **40**
Corris. *Gwyn* 5G **69**
Corris Uchaf. *Gwyn* 5G **69**
Corrour Shooting Lodge. *High* 2B **142**
Corry. *High* 1E **147**
Corrybrough. *High* 1C **150**
Corrygills. *N Ayr* 2E **123**
Corry of Ardnagrask. *High* 4H **157**
Corsback. *High* 1E **169**
(nr. Dunnet)
Corsback. *High* 3E **169**
(nr. Halkirk)
Corscombe. *Dors* 2A **14**
Corse. *Abers* 4D **160**
Corse. *Glos* 3C **48**
Corsehill. *Abers* 3G **161**
Corse Lawn. *Worc* 2D **48**
Corse of Kinnoir. *Abers* 4C **160**
**Corsham**. *Wilts* 4D **34**
Corsley. *Wilts* 2D **22**
Corsley Heath. *Wilts* 2D **22**
Corsock. *Dum* 2E **111**
Corston. *Bath* 5B **34**
Corston. *Wilts* 3E **35**
Corstorphine. *Edin* 2F **129**
Cortachy. *Ang* 3C **144**
Corton. *Suff* 1H **67**
Corton. *Wilts* 2E **23**
Corton Denham. *Som* 4B **22**
Corwar House. *S Ayr* 1H **109**
Corwen. *Den* 1C **70**
Coryates. *Dors* 4B **14**
Coryton. *Devn* 4E **11**
Coryton. *Thur* 2B **40**
Cosby. *Leics* 1C **62**
Coscote. *Oxon* 3D **36**
Coseley. *W Mid* 1D **60**
Cosgrove. *Nptn* 1F **51**
Cosham. *Port* 2E **17**
Cosheston. *Pemb* 4E **43**
Coskills. *N Lin* 3D **94**
Cosmeston. *V Glam* 5E **33**
Cossall. *Notts* 1B **74**
Cossington. *Leics* 4D **74**
Cossington. *Som* 2G **21**
Costa. *Orkn* 5C **172**
Costessey. *Norf* 4D **78**
Costock. *Notts* 3C **74**
Coston. *Leics* 3F **75**
Coston. *Norf* 5C **78**
Cote. *Oxon* 5B **50**
Cotebrook. *Ches W* 4H **83**
Cotehill. *Cumb* 4F **113**
Cotes. *Cumb* 1D **97**
Cotes. *Leics* 3C **74**
Cotes. *Staf* 2C **72**
Cotesbach. *Leics* 2C **62**
Cotes Heath. *Staf* 2C **72**
Cotford St Luke. *Som* 4E **21**
Cotgrave. *Notts* 2D **74**
Cothal. *Abers* 2F **153**
Cotham. *Notts* 1E **75**
Cothelstone. *Som* 3E **21**
Cotheridge. *Worc* 5B **60**
Cotherstone. *Dur* 3D **104**
Cothill. *Oxon* 2C **36**
Cotland. *Mon* 5A **48**
Cotleigh. *Devn* 2F **13**
Cotmanhay. *Derbs* 1B **74**
Coton. *Cambs* 5D **64**
Coton. *Nptn* 3D **62**
Coton. *Staf* 3C **72**
(nr. Gnosall)
Coton. *Staf* 2D **73**
(nr. Stone)
Coton. *Staf* 5F **73**
(nr. Tamworth)
Coton Clanford. *Staf* 3C **72**
Coton Hayes. *Staf* 2D **73**
Coton Hill. *Shrp* 4G **71**
Coton in the Clay. *Staf* 3F **73**
Coton in the Elms. *Derbs* 4G **73**
Cotonwood. *Shrp* 2H **71**
Cotonwood. *Staf* 3C **72**
Cott. *Devn* 2D **9**
Cott. *Orkn* 5F **172**
Cottam. *E Yor* 3D **101**
Cottam. *Lanc* 1D **90**
Cottam. *Notts* 3F **87**
Cottartown. *High* 5E **159**
Cottarville. *Nptn* 4E **63**
Cottenham. *Cambs* 4D **64**
Cotterdale. *N Yor* 5B **104**
Cottered. *Herts* 3D **52**
Cotterstock. *Nptn* 1H **63**
Cottesbrooke. *Nptn* 3E **62**
Cottesmore. *Rut* 4G **75**
Cotteylands. *Devn* 1C **12**
Cottingham. *E Yor* 1D **94**
Cottingham. *Nptn* 1F **63**
Cottingley. *W Yor* 1B **92**
Cottisford. *Oxon* 2D **50**
Cotton. *Staf* 1E **73**
Cotton. *Suff* 4C **66**
Cotton End. *Bed* 1A **52**
Cottown. *Abers* 4F **161**
Cotts. *Devn* 2A **8**
Cotwalton. *Staf* 2D **72**
Couch's Mill. *Corn* 3F **7**
Coughton. *Here* 3A **48**
Coughton. *Warw* 4E **61**
Coulags. *High* 4B **156**
Coulby Newham. *Midd* 3C **106**
Coulderton. *Cumb* 4A **102**
Coulin Lodge. *High* 3C **156**
Coull. *Abers* 3C **152**
Coulport. *Arg* 1D **126**
**Coulsdon**. *G Lon* 5D **39**
Coulston. *Wilts* 1E **23**
Coulter. *S Lan* 1C **118**
Coultings. *Som* 2F **21**
Coulton. *N Yor* 2A **100**
Cound. *Shrp* 5H **71**
Coundon. *Dur* 2F **105**
Coundon Grange. *Dur* 2F **105**
Countersett. *N Yor* 1B **98**
Countess. *Wilts* 2G **23**
Countess Cross. *Essx* 2B **54**
Countesthorpe. *Leics* 1C **62**
Countisbury. *Devn* 2H **19**
Coupar Angus. *Per* 4B **144**
Coupe Green. *Lanc* 2D **90**
Coupland. *Cumb* 3A **104**
Coupland. *Nmbd* 1D **120**
Cour. *Arg* 5G **125**
Courance. *Dum* 5C **118**
Court-at-Street. *Kent* 2E **29**
Courteachan. *High* 4E **147**
Courteenhall. *Nptn* 5E **63**
Court Henry. *Carm* 3F **45**
Courtsend. *Essx* 1E **41**
Courtway. *Som* 3F **21**
Cousland. *Midl* 3G **129**
Cousley Wood. *E Sus* 2A **28**
Coustonn. *Arg* 2B **126**
Cove. *Arg* 1D **126**
Cove. *Devn* 1C **12**
Cove. *Hants* 1G **25**
Cove. *High* 4C **162**
Cove. *Bord* 2D **130**
Cove Bay. *Aber* 3G **153**
Covehithe. *Suff* 2H **67**
Coven. *Staf* 5D **72**
Coveney. *Cambs* 2D **65**
Covenham St Bartholomew. *Linc* 1C **88**
Covenham St Mary. *Linc* 1C **88**
Coven Heath. *Staf* 5D **72**
**Coventry**. *W Mid* 3H **61** & **194**
Coverack. *Corn* 5E **5**
Coverham. *N Yor* 1D **98**
Covesea. *Mor* 1F **159**
Covingham. *Swin* 3G **35**
Covington. *Cambs* 3H **63**
Covington. *S Lan* 1B **118**
Cowan Bridge. *Lanc* 2F **97**
Cowan Head. *Cumb* 5F **103**
Cowbar. *Red C* 3E **107**
Cowbeech. *E Sus* 4H **27**
Cowbit. *Linc* 4B **76**
Cowbridge. *V Glam* 4C **32**
Cowden. *Kent* 1F **27**
**Cowdenbeath**. *Fife* 4D **136**
Cowdenburn. *Bord* 4F **129**
Cowdenend. *Fife* 4D **136**
Cowers Lane. *Derbs* 1H **73**
**Cowes**. *IOW* 3C **16**
Cowesby. *N Yor* 1G **99**
Cowfold. *W Sus* 3D **26**
Cowfords. *Mor* 2H **159**
Cowgill. *Cumb* 1G **97**
Cowie. *Abers* 5F **153**
Cowie. *Stir* 1B **128**
Cowlam. *E Yor* 3D **100**
Cowley. *Devn* 3C **12**
Cowley. *Glos* 4E **49**
Cowley. *G Lon* 2B **38**
Cowley. *Oxon* 5D **50**
Cowley. *Staf* 4C **72**
Cowleymoor. *Devn* 1C **12**
Cowling. *Lanc* 3D **90**
Cowling. *N Yor* 1E **99**
(nr. Bedale)
Cowling. *N Yor* 5B **98**
(nr. Glusburn)
Cowlinge. *Suff* 5G **65**
Cowmes. *W Yor* 3B **92**
Cowpe. *Lanc* 2G **91**
Cowpen. *Nmbd* 1F **115**
Cowpen Bewley. *Stoc T* 2B **106**
Cowplain. *Hants* 1E **17**
Cowshill. *Dur* 5B **114**
Cowslip Green. *N Som* 5H **33**
Cowstrandburn. *Fife* 4C **136**
Cowthorpe. *N Yor* 4G **99**
Coxall. *Here* 3F **59**
Coxbank. *Ches E* 1A **72**
Coxbench. *Derbs* 1A **74**
Cox Common. *Suff* 2G **67**
Coxford. *Norf* 3H **77**
Coxgreen. *Staf* 2C **60**
Cox Green. *Surr* 2B **26**
Cox Green. *Tyne* 4G **115**
Coxheath. *Kent* 5B **40**
Coxhoe. *Dur* 1A **106**
Coxley. *Som* 2A **22**
Coxwold. *N Yor* 2H **99**
Coychurch. *B'end* 3C **32**
Coylton. *S Ayr* 3D **116**
Coylumbridge. *High* 2D **150**
Coynach. *Abers* 3B **152**
Coynachie. *Abers* 5B **160**
Coytrahen. *B'end* 3B **32**
Crabbs Cross. *Worc* 4E **61**
Crabgate. *Norf* 3C **78**
Crab Orchard. *Dors* 2F **15**
Crabtree. *W Sus* 3D **26**
Crabtree Green. *Wrex* 1F **71**
Crackaig. *High* 2G **165**
Crackenthorpe. *Cumb* 2H **103**
Crackington Haven. *Corn* 3B **10**
Crackley. *Staf* 5C **84**
Crackley. *Warw* 3G **61**
Crackleybank. *Shrp* 4B **72**
Crackpot. *N Yor* 5C **104**
Cracoe. *N Yor* 3B **98**
Craddock. *Devn* 1D **12**
Cradhlastadh. *W Isl* 4C **171**
Cradley. *Here* 1C **48**
Cradley. *W Mid* 2D **60**
Cradoc. *Powy* 2D **46**
Crafthole. *Corn* 3H **7**
Crafton. *Buck* 4G **51**
Cragabus. *Arg* 5B **124**
Crag Foot. *Lanc* 2D **97**
Craggan. *High* 1E **151**
Cragganmore. *Mor* 5F **159**
Cragganvallie. *High* 5H **157**
Craggie. *High* 2F **165**
Craggiemore. *High* 5B **158**
Cragg Vale. *W Yor* 2A **92**
Craghead. *Dur* 4F **115**
Crai. *Powy* 3B **46**
Craichie. *Ang* 4E **145**
Craig. *Arg* 5E **141**
Craig. *Dum* 2D **111**
Craig. *High* 4C **156**
(nr. Achnashellach)
Craig. *High* 2G **155**
(nr. Lower Diabaig)
Craig. *High* 5H **155**
(nr. Stromeferry)
Craiganour Lodge. *Per* 3D **142**
**Craigavon**. *Arm* 4E **178**
Craigbrack. *Arg* 4A **134**
Craig-Cefn-Parc. *Swan* 5G **45**
Craigdallie. *Per* 1E **137**
Craigdam. *Abers* 5F **161**
Craigdarragh. *Derr* 6B **174**
Craigdarroch. *E Ayr* 4F **117**
Craigdarroch. *High* 3G **157**
Craigdhu. *High* 4G **157**
Craigearn. *Abers* 2E **152**
Craigellachie. *Mor* 4G **159**
Craigend. *Per* 1D **136**
Craigendoran. *Arg* 1E **126**
Craigends. *Ren* 3F **127**
Craigenputtock. *Dum* 1E **111**
Craigens. *E Ayr* 3E **117**
Craighall. *Edin* 2E **129**
Craighead. *Fife* 2H **137**
Craighouse. *Arg* 3D **124**
Craigie. *Abers* 2G **153**
Craigie. *D'dee* 5D **144**
Craigie. *Per* 4A **144**
(nr. Blairgowrie)
Craigie. *Per* 1D **136**
(nr. Perth)
Craigie. *S Ayr* 1D **116**
Craigielaw. *E Lot* 2A **130**
Craiglemine. *Dum* 5B **110**
Craig-llwyn. *Shrp* 3E **71**
Craiglockhart. *Edin* 2F **129**
Craig Lodge. *Arg* 2B **126**
Craigmalloch. *E Ayr* 5D **117**
Craigmaud. *Abers* 3F **161**
Craigmill. *Stir* 4H **135**
Craigmillar. *Edin* 2F **129**
Craigmore. *Arg* 3C **126**
Craigmuie. *Dum* 1E **111**
Craignair. *Dum* 3F **111**
Craignant. *Shrp* 2E **71**
Craigneuk. *N Lan* 3A **128**
(nr. Airdrie)
Craigneuk. *N Lan* 4A **128**
(nr. Motherwell)
Craignure. *Arg* 5B **140**
Craigo. *Abers* 2F **145**
Craigrory. *High* 4A **158**
Craigrothie. *Fife* 2F **137**
Craigs. *Dum* 2D **112**
Craigshill. *W Lot* 3D **128**
Craigs, The. *High* 4B **164**
Craigton. *Aber* 3F **153**
Craigton. *Abers* 3E **152**
Craigton. *Ang* 5E **145**
(nr. Carnoustie)
Craigton. *Ang* 3C **144**
(nr. Kirriemuir)
Craigton. *High* 4A **158**
Craigtown. *High* 3A **168**
Craig-y-Duke. *Neat* 5H **45**
Craig-y-nos. *Powy* 4B **46**
Craik. *Bord* 4F **119**
Crail. *Fife* 3H **137**
Crailing. *Bord* 2A **120**
Crailinghall. *Bord* 2A **120**
Crakehill. *N Yor* 2G **99**
Crakemarsh. *Staf* 2E **73**
Crambe. *N Yor* 3B **100**
Crambeck. *N Yor* 3B **100**
**Cramlington**. *Nmbd* 2F **115**
Cramond. *Edin* 2E **129**
Cramond Bridge. *Edin* 2E **129**
Cranage. *Ches E* 4B **84**
Cranagh. *Derr* 7B **174**
Cranberry. *Staf* 2C **72**
Cranborne. *Dors* 1F **15**
Cranbourne. *Brac* 3A **38**
Cranbrook. *Devn* 3D **12**
Cranbrook. *Kent* 2B **28**
Cranbrook Common. *Kent* 2B **28**
Crane Moor. *S Yor* 4D **92**
Crane's Corner. *Norf* 4B **78**
Cranfield. *C Beds* 1H **51**
Cranford. *G Lon* 3C **38**
Cranford St Andrew. *Nptn* 3G **63**
Cranford St John. *Nptn* 3G **63**
Cranham. *Glos* 4D **49**
Cranham. *G Lon* 2G **39**
Crank. *Mers* 1H **83**
**Cranleigh**. *Surr* 2B **26**
Cranley. *Suff* 3D **66**
Cranloch. *Mor* 3G **159**
Cranmer Green. *Suff* 3C **66**
Cranmore. *IOW* 3C **16**
Cranmore. *Linc* 5A **76**
Crannich. *Arg* 4G **139**
Crannoch. *Mor* 3B **160**
Cranoe. *Leics* 1E **63**
Cransford. *Suff* 4F **67**
Cranshaws. *Bord* 3C **130**
Cranstal. *IOM* 1D **108**
Crantock. *Corn* 2B **6**
Cranwell. *Linc* 1H **75**
Cranwich. *Norf* 1G **65**
Cranworth. *Norf* 5B **78**
Craobh Haven. *Arg* 3E **133**
Craobhnaclag. *High* 4G **157**
Crapstone. *Devn* 2B **8**
Crarae. *Arg* 4G **133**
Crask. *High* 2H **167**
(nr. Bettyhill)
Crask. *High* 1C **164**
(nr. Lairg)
Crask of Aigas. *High* 4G **157**
Craster. *Nmbd* 3G **121**
Craswall. *Here* 2F **47**
Cratfield. *Suff* 3F **67**
Crathes. *Abers* 4E **153**
Crathie. *Abers* 4G **151**
Crathie. *High* 4H **149**
Crathorne. *N Yor* 4B **106**
Craven Arms. *Shrp* 2G **59**
Crawcrook. *Tyne* 3E **115**
Crawford. *Lanc* 4C **90**
Crawford. *S Lan* 2B **118**
Crawforddyke. *S Lan* 4B **128**
Crawfordjohn. *S Lan* 2A **118**
Crawfordsburn. *N Dwn* 1J **179**
Crawick. *Dum* 3G **117**
Crawley. *Devn* 2F **13**
Crawley. *Hants* 3C **24**
Crawley. *Oxon* 4B **50**
**Crawley**. *W Sus* 2D **26**
Crawley Down. *W Sus* 2E **27**
Crawley End. *Essx* 1E **53**
Crawley Side. *Dur* 5C **114**
Crawshawbooth. *Lanc* 2G **91**
Crawton. *Abers* 5F **153**
Cray. *N Yor* 2B **98**
Cray. *Per* 2A **144**
Crayford. *G Lon* 3G **39**
Crayke. *N Yor* 2H **99**
Craymere Beck. *Norf* 2C **78**
Crays Hill. *Essx* 1B **40**
Cray's Pond. *Oxon* 3E **37**
Crazies Hill. *Wok* 3F **37**
Creacombe. *Devn* 1B **12**
Creagan. *Arg* 4D **140**
Creag Aoil. *High* 1F **141**
Creag Ghoraidh. *W Isl* 4C **170**
Creaguaineach Lodge. *High* 2H **141**
Creamore Bank. *Shrp* 2H **71**
Creaton. *Nptn* 3E **62**
Creca. *Dum* 2D **112**
Credenhill. *Here* 1H **47**
Crediton. *Devn* 2B **12**
Creebridge. *Dum* 3B **110**
Creech. *Dors* 4E **15**
Creech Heathfield. *Som* 4F **21**
Creech St Michael. *Som* 4F **21**
Creed. *Corn* 4D **6**
Creekmoor. *Pool* 3E **15**
Creekmouth. *G Lon* 2F **39**
Creeting St Mary. *Suff* 5C **66**
Creeting St Peter. *Suff* 5C **66**
Creeton. *Linc* 3H **75**
Creetown. *Dum* 4B **110**
Creggan. *Ferm* 2A **178**
Creggan. *New M* 8D **178**
Creggans. *Arg* 3H **133**
Cregneash. *IOM* 5A **108**
Cregrina. *Powy* 5D **58**
Creich. *Arg* 2B **132**
Creich. *Fife* 1F **137**
Creighton. *Staf* 2E **73**
Creigiau. *Card* 3D **32**
Cremyll. *Corn* 3A **8**
Crendell. *Dors* 1F **15**
Crepkill. *High* 4D **154**
Cressage. *Shrp* 5H **71**
Cressbrook. *Derbs* 3F **85**
Cresselly. *Pemb* 4E **43**
Cressing. *Essx* 3A **54**
Cresswell. *Nmbd* 5G **121**
Cresswell. *Staf* 2D **73**
Cresswell Quay. *Pemb* 4E **43**
Creswell. *Derbs* 3C **86**
Creswell Green. *Staf* 4E **73**
Cretingham. *Suff* 4E **67**
**Crewe**. *Ches E* 5B **84**
Crewe-by-Farndon. *Ches W* 5G **83**
Crewgreen. *Powy* 4F **71**
Crewkerne. *Som* 2H **13**
Crews Hill. *G Lon* 5D **52**
Crewton. *Derb* 2A **74**
Crianlarich. *Stir* 1C **134**
Cribbs Causeway. *S Glo* 3A **34**
Cribyn. *Cdgn* 5E **57**
Criccieth. *Gwyn* 2D **69**
Crich. *Derbs* 5A **86**
Crichton. *Midl* 3G **129**
Crick. *Mon* 2H **33**
Crick. *Nptn* 3C **62**
Crickadarn. *Powy* 1D **46**
Cricket Hill. *Hants* 5G **37**
Cricket Malherbie. *Som* 1G **13**
Cricket St Thomas. *Som* 2G **13**
Crickham. *Som* 2H **21**
Crickheath. *Shrp* 3E **71**
Crickhowell. *Powy* 4F **47**
Cricklade. *Wilts* 2G **35**
Cricklewood. *G Lon* 2D **38**
Cridling Stubbs. *N Yor* 2F **93**
Crieff. *Per* 1A **136**
Criftins. *Shrp* 2F **71**
Criggion. *Powy* 4E **71**
Crigglestone. *W Yor* 3D **92**
Crimchard. *Som* 2G **13**
Crimdon Park. *Dur* 1B **106**
Crimond. *Abers* 3H **161**
Crimonmogate. *Abers* 3H **161**
Crimplesham. *Norf* 5F **77**
Crimscote. *Warw* 1H **49**
Crinan. *Arg* 4E **133**
Cringleford. *Norf* 5D **78**
Crinow. *Pemb* 3F **43**
Cripplesease. *Corn* 3C **4**
Cripplestyle. *Dors* 1F **15**
Cripp's Corner. *E Sus* 3B **28**
Croanford. *Corn* 5A **10**
Crockenhill. *Kent* 4G **39**
Crocker End. *Oxon* 3F **37**
Crockerhill. *Hants* 2D **16**
Crockernwell. *Devn* 3A **12**
Crocker's Ash. *Here* 4A **48**
Crockerton. *Wilts* 2D **22**
Crocketford. *Dum* 2F **111**
Crockey Hill. *York* 5A **100**
Crockham Hill. *Kent* 5F **39**
Crockhurst Street. *Kent* 1H **27**
Crockleford Heath. *Essx* 3D **54**
Croeserw. *Neat* 2B **32**
Croes-Goch. *Pemb* 1C **42**
Croes Hywel. *Mon* 4G **47**
Croes-lan. *Cdgn* 1D **45**
Croesor. *Gwyn* 1F **69**
**Croesoswallt**. *Shrp* 3E **71**
Croesyceiliog. *Carm* 4E **45**
Croesyceiliog. *Torf* 2G **33**
Croes-y-mwyalch. *Torf* 2G **33**
Croesywaun. *Gwyn* 5E **81**
Croford. *Som* 4E **20**
Croft. *Leics* 1C **62**
Croft. *Linc* 4E **89**
Croft. *Warr* 1A **84**
Croftamie. *Stir* 1F **127**
Croftfoot. *Glas* 3G **127**
Croftmill. *Per* 5F **143**
Crofton. *Cumb* 4E **112**
Crofton. *W Yor* 3D **93**
Crofton. *Wilts* 5A **36**
Croft-on-Tees. *N Yor* 4F **105**
Crofts. *Dum* 2E **111**
Crofts of Benachielt. *High* 5D **169**
Crofts of Dipple. *Mor* 3H **159**
Crofty. *Swan* 3E **31**
Croggan. *Arg* 1E **132**
Croglin. *Cumb* 5G **113**
Croich. *High* 4B **164**
Croick. *High* 3A **168**
Croig. *Arg* 3E **139**
Cromarty. *High* 2B **158**
Crombie. *Fife* 1D **128**
Cromdale. *High* 1E **151**
Cromer. *Herts* 3C **52**
Cromer. *Norf* 1E **78**
Cromford. *Derbs* 5G **85**
Cromhall. *S Glo* 2B **34**
Cromor. *W Isl* 5G **171**
Cromra. *High* 5H **149**
Cromwell. *Notts* 4E **87**
Cronberry. *E Ayr* 2F **117**
Crondall. *Hants* 2F **25**
Cronk, The. *IOM* 2C **108**
Cronk-y-Voddy. *IOM* 3C **108**
Cronton. *Mers* 2G **83**
Crook. *Cumb* 5F **103**
Crook. *Dur* 1E **105**
Crookdake. *Cumb* 5C **112**
Crooke. *G Man* 4D **90**
Crookedholm. *E Ayr* 1D **116**
Crooked Soley. *Wilts* 4B **36**
Crookes. *S Yor* 2H **85**
Crookgate Bank. *Dur* 4E **115**
Crookhall. *Dur* 4E **115**
Crookham. *Nmbd* 1D **120**
Crookham. *W Ber* 5D **36**
Crookham Village. *Hants* 1F **25**
Crooklands. *Cumb* 1E **97**
Crook of Devon. *Per* 3C **136**
Crookston. *Glas* 3G **127**
Cropredy. *Oxon* 1C **50**
Cropston. *Leics* 4C **74**
Cropthorne. *Worc* 1E **49**
Cropton. *N Yor* 1B **100**
Cropwell Bishop. *Notts* 2D **74**
Cropwell Butler. *Notts* 2D **74**
Cros. *W Isl* 1H **171**
Crosbie. *N Ayr* 4D **126**
Crosbost. *W Isl* 5F **171**
Crosby. *Cumb* 1B **102**
Crosby. *IOM* 4C **108**
**Crosby**. *Mers* 1F **83**
Crosby. *N Lin* 3B **94**
Crosby Court. *N Yor* 5A **106**
Crosby Garrett. *Cumb* 4A **104**
Crosby Ravensworth. *Cumb* 3H **103**
Crosby Villa. *Cumb* 1B **102**
Croscombe. *Som* 2A **22**
Crosland Moor. *W Yor* 3B **92**
Cross. *Som* 1H **21**
Crossaig. *Arg* 4G **125**
Crossapol. *Arg* 4A **138**
Cross Ash. *Mon* 4H **47**
Cross-at-Hand. *Kent* 1B **28**
Crossbush. *W Sus* 5B **26**
Crosscanonby. *Cumb* 1B **102**
Crossdale Street. *Norf* 2E **79**
Cross End. *Essx* 2B **54**
Crossens. *Mers* 2B **90**
Crossford. *Fife* 1D **128**
Crossford. *S Lan* 5B **128**
Cross Foxes. *Gwyn* 4G **69**
Crossgar. *New M* 4J **179**
Crossgate. *Orkn* 6D **172**
Crossgate. *Staf* 2D **72**
Crossgatehall. *E Lot* 3G **129**
Crossgates. *Fife* 1E **129**
Crossgates. *N Yor* 1E **101**
Crossgates. *Powy* 4C **58**

Cross Gates. W Yor 1D 92
Crossgill. Lanc 3E 97
Cross Green. Devn 4D 11
Cross Green. Staf 5D 72
Cross Green. Suff 5A 66
(nr. Cockfield)
Cross Green. Suff 5B 66
(nr. Hitcham)
Cross Hands. Carm 4F 45
(nr. Ammanford)
Crosshands. Carm 2F 43
(nr. Whitland)
Crosshands. E Ayr 1D 117
Cross Hill. Derbs 1B 74
Crosshill. E Ayr 2D 117
Crosshill. Fife 4D 136
Cross Hill. Glos 2A 34
Crosshill. S Ayr 4C 116
Crosshills. High 1A 158
Cross Hills. N Yor 5C 98
Cross Holme. N Yor 5C 106
Crosshouse. E Ayr 1C 116
Cross Houses. Shrp 5H 71
Crossings. Cumb 2G 113
Cross in Hand. E Sus 3G 27
Cross Inn. Cdgn 4E 57
(nr. Aberaeron)
Cross Inn. Cdgn 5C 56
(nr. New Quay)
Cross Inn. Rhon 3D 32
Crosskeys. Cphy 2F 33
Crosskirk. High 2C 168
Crosslands. Cumb 1C 96
Cross Lane Head. Shrp 1B 60
Cross Lanes. Corn 4D 5
Cross Lanes. Dur 3D 104
Cross Lanes. N Yor 3H 99
Crosslanes. Shrp 4F 71
Cross Lanes. Wrex 1F 71
Crosslee. Ren 3F 127
Crossmaglen. New M 8D 178
Crossmichael. Dum 3E 111
Crossmoor. Lanc 1C 90
Crossnacreevy. Lis 3H 179
Cross Oak. Powy 3E 46
Cross of Jackston. Abers 5E 161
Cross o' th' Hands. Derbs 1G 73
Crossroads. Abers 3G 153
(nr. Aberdeen)
Crossroads. Abers 4E 153
(nr. Banchory)
Crossroads. E Ayr 1D 116
Cross Side. Devn 4B 20
Cross Street. Suff 3D 66
Crosston. Ang 3E 145
Cross Town. Ches E 3B 84
Crossway. Mon 4H 47
Crossway. Powy 5C 58
Crossway Green. Mon 2A 34
Crossway Green. Worc 4C 60
Crossways. Dors 4C 14
Crosswell. Pemb 1F 43
Crosswood. Cdgn 3F 57
Crosthwaite. Cumb 5F 103
Croston. Lanc 3C 90
Crostwick. Norf 4E 79
Crostwight. Norf 3F 79
Crothair. W Isl 4D 171
Crouch. Kent 5H 39
Croucheston. Wilts 4F 23
Crouch Hill. Dors 1C 14
Croughton. Nptn 2D 50
Crovie. Abers 2F 161
Crow. Hants 2G 15
Crowan. Corn 3D 4
**Crowborough**. E Sus 2G 27
Crowcombe. Som 3E 21
Crowcroft. Worc 5B 60
Crowdecote. Derbs 4F 85
Crowden. Derbs 1E 85
Crowden. Devn 3E 11
Crowdhill. Hants 1C 16
Crowdon. N Yor 5G 107
Crow Edge. S Yor 4B 92
Crow End. Cambs 5C 64
Crowfield. Nptn 1E 50
Crowfield. Suff 5D 66
Crow Green. Essx 1G 39
Crow Hill. Here 3B 48
Crowhurst. E Sus 4B 28
Crowhurst. Surr 1E 27
Crowhurst Lane End. Surr 1E 27
Crowland. Linc 4B 76
Crowland. Suff 3C 66
Crowlas. Corn 3C 4
Crowle. N Lin 3A 94
Crowle. Worc 5D 60
Crowle Green. Worc 5D 60
Crowmarsh Gifford. Oxon 3E 36
Crown Corner. Suff 3E 67
Crownthorpe. Norf 5C 78
Crowntown. Corn 3D 4
Crows-an-wra. Corn 4A 4
Crowshill. Norf 5B 78
**Crowthorne**. Brac 5G 37
Crowton. Ches W 3H 83
Croxall. Staf 4F 73
Croxby. Linc 1A 88
Croxdale. Dur 1F 105
Croxden. Staf 2E 73
Croxley Green. Herts 1B 38
Croxton. Cambs 4B 64
Croxton. Norf 2B 78
(nr. Fakenham)
Croxton. Norf 2A 66
(nr. Thetford)
Croxton. N Lin 3D 94
Croxton. Staf 2B 72
Croxtonbank. Staf 2B 72
Croxton Green. Ches E 5H 83
Croxton Kerrial. Leics 3F 75
Croy. High 4B 158
Croy. N Lan 2A 128
Croyde. Devn 3E 19
Croydon. Cambs 1D 52
**Croydon**. G Lon 4E 39
Crubenbeg. High 4A 150
Crubenmore Lodge. High 4A 150
Cruckmeole. Shrp 5G 71
Cruckton. Shrp 4G 71
Cruden Bay. Abers 5H 161
Crudgington. Telf 4A 72
Crudie. Abers 3E 161
Crudwell. Wilts 2E 35
Cruft. Devn 3F 11
Crug. Powy 3D 58
Crughywel. Powy 4F 47
Crugmeer. Corn 1D 6
Crugybar. Carm 2G 45
Crug-y-byddar. Powy 2D 58
Crulabhig. W Isl 4D 171
Crumlin. Ant 2F 179
Crumlin. Cphy 2F 33
Crumpsall. G Man 4G 91
Crumpsbrook. Shrp 3A 60
Crundale. Kent 1E 29
Crundale. Pemb 3D 42
Cruwys Morchard. Devn 1B 12
Crux Easton. Hants 1C 24
Cruxton. Dors 3B 14
Crwbin. Carm 4E 45
Cryers Hill. Buck 2G 37
Crymych. Pemb 1F 43
Crynant. Neat 5A 46
Crystal Palace. G Lon 3E 39
Cuaich. High 5A 150
Cuaig. High 3G 155
Cuan. Arg 2E 133
Cubbington. Warw 4H 61
Cubert. Corn 3B 6
Cubley. S Yor 4C 92
Cubley Common. Derbs 2F 73
Cublington. Buck 3G 51
Cublington. Here 2G 47
Cuckfield. W Sus 3E 27
Cucklington. Som 4C 22
Cuckney. Notts 3C 86
Cuckron. Shet 6F 173
Cuddesdon. Oxon 5E 50
Cuddington. Buck 4F 51
Cuddington. Ches W 3A 84
Cuddington Heath. Ches W 1G 71
Cuddy Hill. Lanc 1C 90
Cudham. G Lon 5F 39
Cudlipptown. Devn 5F 11
Cudworth. Som 1G 13
**Cudworth**. S Yor 4D 93
Cudworth. Surr 1D 26
Cuerdley Cross. Warr 2H 83
Cuffley. Herts 5D 52
Cuidhir. W Isl 8B 170
Cuidhsiadar. W Isl 2H 171
Cuidhtinis. W Isl 9C 171
Culbo. High 2A 158
Culbokie. High 3A 158
Culburnie. High 4G 157
Culcabock. High 4A 158
Culcavy. Lis 3G 179
Culcharry. High 3C 158
Culcheth. Warr 1A 84
Culduie. High 4G 155
Culeave. High 4C 164
Culford. Suff 3H 65
Culgaith. Cumb 2H 103
Culham. Oxon 2D 36
Culkein. High 1E 163
Culkein Drumbeg. High 5B 166
Culkerton. Glos 2E 35
Cullaville. New M 8C 178
Cullen. Mor 2C 160
Cullercoats. Tyne 2G 115
Cullicudden. High 2A 158
Cullingworth. W Yor 1A 92
Cullipool. Arg 2E 133
Cullivoe. Shet 1G 173
Culloch. Per 2G 135
Culloden. High 4B 158
Cullompton. Devn 2D 12
Cullybackey. ME Ant 6G 175
Cullycapple. Caus 4E 174
Cullyhanna. New M 7D 178
Culm Davy. Devn 1E 13
Culmington. Shrp 2G 59
Culmore. Derr 4A 174
Culmstock. Devn 1E 12
Cul na Caepaich. High 5E 147
Culnacnoc. High 2E 155
Culnacraig. High 3E 163
Culnady. M Ulst 6E 174
Culrain. High 4C 164
Culross. Fife 1C 128
Culroy. S Ayr 3C 116
Culswick. Shet 7D 173
Cults. Aber 3F 153
Cults. Abers 5C 160
Cults. Fife 3F 137
Cultybraggan Camp. Per 1G 135
Culver. Devn 3B 12
Culverlane. Devn 2D 8
Culverstone Green. Kent 4H 39
Culverthorpe. Linc 1H 75
Culworth. Nptn 1D 50
Culzie Lodge. High 1H 157
Cumberlow Green. Herts 2D 52
**Cumbernauld**. N Lan 2A 128
Cumbernauld Village.
N Lan 2A 128
Cumberworth. Linc 3E 89
Cumdivock. Cumb 5E 113
Cuminestown. Abers 3F 161
Cumledge Mill. Bord 4D 130
Cumlewick. Shet 9F 173
Cummersdale. Cumb 4E 113
Cummertrees. Dum 3C 112
Cummingstown. Mor 2F 159
Cumnock. E Ayr 2E 117
Cumnor. Oxon 5C 50
Cumrew. Cumb 4G 113
Cumwhinton. Cumb 4F 113
Cumwhitton. Cumb 4G 113
Cundall. N Yor 2G 99
Cunninghamhead. N Ayr 5E 127
Cunning Park. S Ayr 3C 116
Cunningsburgh. Shet 9F 173
Cunnister. Shet 2G 173
Cupar. Fife 2F 137
Cupar Muir. Fife 2F 137
Cupernham. Hants 4B 24
Curbar. Derbs 3G 85
Curborough. Staf 4F 73
Curbridge. Hants 1D 16
Curbridge. Oxon 5B 50
Curdridge. Hants 1D 16
Curdworth. Warw 1F 61
Curland. Som 1F 13
Curland Common. Som 1F 13
Curran. M Ulst 7E 174
Curridge. W Ber 4C 36
Currie. Edin 3E 129
Curry Mallet. Som 4G 21
Curry Rivel. Som 4G 21
Curtisden Green. Kent 1B 28
Curtisknowle. Devn 3D 8
Cury. Corn 4D 5
Cusgarne. Corn 4B 6
Cushendall. Caus 4J 175
Cushendun. Caus 3J 175
Cusop. Here 1F 47
Cusworth. S Yor 4F 93
Cutcombe. Som 3C 20
Cuthill. E Lot 2G 129
Cutiau. Gwyn 4F 69
Cutlers Green. Essx 2F 53
Cutmadoc. Corn 2E 7
Cutnall Green. Worc 4C 60
Cutsdean. Glos 2F 49
Cutthorpe. Derbs 3H 85
Cuttiford's Door. Som 1G 13
Cuttivett. Corn 2H 7
Cutts. Shet 8E 173
Cuttybridge. Pemb 3D 42
Cuttyhill. Abers 3H 161
Cuxham. Oxon 2E 37
Cuxton. Medw 4B 40
Cuxwold. Linc 4E 95
Cwm. Blae 5E 47
Cwm. Den 3C 82
Cwm. Powy 1E 59
Cwmafan. Neat 2A 32
Cwmaman. Rhon 2C 32
Cwmann. Carm 1F 45
Cwmbach. Carm 2G 43
Cwmbach. Powy 2E 47
Cwmbach. Rhon 5D 46
Cwmbach Llechrhyd. Powy 5C 58
Cwmbelan. Powy 2B 58
**Cwmbran**. Torf 2F 33
Cwmbrwyno. Cdgn 2G 57
Cwm Capel. Carm 5E 45
Cwmcarn. Cphy 2F 33
Cwmcarvan. Mon 5H 47
Cwm-celyn. Blae 5F 47
Cwmcerdinen. Swan 5G 45
Cwm-Cewydd. Gwyn 4A 70
Cwm-cou. Cdgn 1C 44
Cwmcych. Carm 1G 43
Cwmdare. Rhon 5C 46
Cwmdu. Carm 2G 45
Cwmdu. Powy 3E 47
Cwmduad. Carm 2D 45
Cwm Dulais. Swan 5G 45
Cwmerfyn. Cdgn 2F 57
Cwmfelin. B'end 3B 32
Cwmfelin Boeth. Carm 3F 43
Cwmfelinfach. Cphy 2E 33
Cwmfelin Mynach. Carm 2G 43
Cwmffrwd. Carm 4E 45
Cwmgiedd. Powy 4A 46
Cwmgors. Neat 4H 45
Cwmgwili. Carm 4F 45
Cwmgwrach. Neat 5B 46
Cwmhiraeth. Carm 1H 43
Cwmifor. Carm 3G 45
Cwmisfael. Carm 4E 45
Cwm-Llinau. Powy 5H 69
Cwmllynfell. Neat 4H 45
Cwm-mawr. Carm 4F 45
Cwm-miles. Carm 2F 43
Cwmorgan. Carm 1G 43
Cwmparc. Rhon 2C 32
Cwm Penmachno. Cnwy 1G 69
Cwmpennar. Rhon 5D 46
Cwm Plysgog. Pemb 1B 44
Cwmrhos. Powy 3E 47
Cwmsychpant. Cdgn 1E 45
Cwmsyfiog. Cphy 5E 47
Cwmsymlog. Cdgn 2F 57
Cwmtillery. Blae 5F 47
Cwm-twrch Isaf. Powy 5A 46
Cwm-twrch Uchaf. Powy 4A 46
Cwmwysg. Powy 3B 46
Cwm-y-glo. Gwyn 4E 81
Cwmyoy. Mon 3G 47
Cwmystwyth. Cdgn 3G 57
Cwrt. Gwyn 5F 69
Cwrtnewydd. Cdgn 1E 45
Cwrt-y-Cadno. Carm 1G 45
Cydweli. Carm 5E 45
Cyffylliog. Den 5C 82
Cymau. Flin 5E 83
Cymer. Neat 2B 32
Cymmer. Neat 2B 32
Cymmer. Rhon 2D 32
Cyncoed. Card 3E 33
Cynghordy. Carm 2B 46
Cynheidre. Carm 5E 45
Cynonville. Neat 2B 32
Cynwyd. Den 1C 70
Cynwyl Elfed. Carm 3D 44
Cywarch. Gwyn 4A 70

## D

Dacre. Cumb 2F 103
Dacre. N Yor 3D 98
Dacre Banks. N Yor 3D 98
Daddry Shield. Dur 1B 104
Dadford. Buck 2E 51
Dadlington. Leics 1B 62
Dafen. Carm 5F 45
Daffy Green. Norf 5B 78
Dagdale. Staf 2E 73
**Dagenham**. G Lon 2F 39
Daggons. Dors 1G 15
Daglingworth. Glos 5E 49
Dagnall. Buck 4H 51
Dagtail End. Worc 4E 61
Dail. Arg 5E 141
Dail Beag. W Isl 3E 171
Dail bho Dheas. W Isl 1G 171
Dailly. S Ayr 4B 116
Dail Mor. W Isl 3E 171
Dairsie. Fife 2G 137
Daisy Bank. W Mid 1E 61
Daisy Hill. G Man 4E 91
Daisy Hill. W Yor 1B 92
Dalabrog. W Isl 6C 170
Dalavich. Arg 2G 133
Dalbeattie. Dum 3F 111
Dalblair. E Ayr 3F 117
Dalbury. Derbs 2G 73
Dalby. IOM 4B 108
Dalby Wolds. Leics 3D 74
Dalchalm. High 3G 165
Dalcharn. High 3G 167
Dalchork. High 2C 164
Dalchreichart. High 2E 149
Dalchruin. Per 2G 135
Dalcross. High 4B 158
Dalderby. Linc 4B 88
Dale. Cumb 5G 113
Dale. Pemb 4C 42
Dale Abbey. Derbs 2B 74
Dalebank. Derbs 4A 86
Dale Bottom. Cumb 2D 102
Dale Head. Cumb 3F 103
Dalehouse. N Yor 3E 107
Dalelia. High 2B 140
Dale of Walls. Shet 6C 173
Dalgarven. N Ayr 5D 126
**Dalgety Bay**. Fife 1E 129
Dalginross. Per 1G 135
Dalguise. Per 4G 143
Dalhalvaig. High 3A 168
Dalham. Suff 4G 65
Dalintart. Arg 1F 133
**Dalkeith**. Midl 3G 129
Dallas. Mor 3F 159
Dalleagles. E Ayr 3E 117
Dall House. Per 3C 142
Dallinghoo. Suff 5E 67
Dallington. E Sus 4A 28
Dallow. N Yor 2D 98
Dalmally. Arg 1A 134
Dalmarnock. Glas 3H 127
Dalmellington. E Ayr 4D 117
Dalmeny. Edin 2E 129
Dalmigavie. High 2B 150
Dalmilling. S Ayr 2C 116
Dalmore. High 2A 158
(nr. Alness)
Dalmore. High 3E 164
(nr. Rogart)
Dalmuir. W Dun 2F 127
Dalmunach. Mor 4G 159
Dalnabreck. High 2B 140
Dalnacardoch Lodge. Per 1E 142
Dalnamein Lodge. Per 2E 143
Dalnaspidal Lodge. Per 1D 142
Dalnatrat. High 3D 140
Dalnavie. High 1A 158
Dalnawillan Lodge. High 4C 168
Dalness. High 3F 141
Dalnessie. High 2D 164
Dalqueich. Per 3C 136
Dalquhairn. S Ayr 5C 116
Dalreavoch. High 3E 165
Dalreoch. Per 2C 136
Dalry. Edin 2F 129
Dalry. N Ayr 5D 126
Dalrymple. E Ayr 3C 116
Dalscote. Nptn 5D 62
Dalserf. S Lan 4B 128
Dalsmirren. Arg 4A 122
Dalston. Cumb 4E 113
Dalswinton. Dum 1G 111
Dalton. Dum 2C 112
Dalton. Lanc 4C 90
Dalton. Nmbd 4C 114
(nr. Hexham)
Dalton. Nmbd 2E 115
(nr. Ponteland)
Dalton. N Yor 4E 105
(nr. Richmond)
Dalton. N Yor 2G 99
(nr. Thirsk)
Dalton. S Lan 4H 127
Dalton. S Yor 1B 86
Dalton-in-Furness. Cumb 2B 96
Dalton-le-Dale. Dur 5H 115
Dalton Magna. S Yor 1B 86
Dalton-on-Tees. N Yor 4F 105
Dalton Piercy. Hart 1B 106
Daltot. Arg 1F 125
Dalvey. High 5F 159
Dalwhinnie. High 5A 150
Dalwood. Devn 2F 13
Damerham. Hants 1G 15
Damgate. Norf 5G 79
(nr. Acle)
Damgate. Norf 4G 79
(nr. Martham)
Dam Green. Norf 2C 66
Damhead. Mor 3E 159
Danaway. Kent 4C 40
Danbury. Essx 5A 54
Danby. N Yor 4E 107
Danby Botton. N Yor 4D 107
Danby Wiske. N Yor 5A 106
Danderhall. Midl 3G 129
Danebank. Ches E 2D 85
Danebridge. Ches E 4D 84
Dane End. Herts 3D 52
Danehill. E Sus 3F 27
Danesford. Shrp 1B 60
Daneshill. Hants 1E 25
Danesmoor. Derbs 4B 86
Danestone. Aber 2G 153
Dangerous Corner. Lanc 3D 90
Daniel's Water. Kent 1D 28
Dan's Castle. Dur 1E 105
Danzey Green. Warw 4F 61
Dapple Heath. Staf 3E 73
Daren. Powy 4F 47
Darenth. Kent 3G 39
Daresbury. Hal 2H 83
Darfield. S Yor 4E 93
Dargate. Kent 4E 41
Dargill. Per 2A 136
Darite. Corn 2G 7
Darkley. Arm 6C 178
Darlaston. W Mid 1D 61
Darley. N Yor 4E 98
Darley Abbey. Derb 2H 73
Darley Bridge. Derbs 4G 85
Darley Dale. Derbs 4G 85
Darley Head. N Yor 4D 98
Darlingscott. Warw 1H 49
**Darlington**. Darl 3F 105
Darliston. Shrp 2H 71
Darlton. Notts 3E 87
Darmsden. Suff 5C 66
Darnall. S Yor 2A 86
Darnford. Abers 4E 153
Darnford. Staf 5F 73
Darnhall. Ches W 4A 84
Darnick. Bord 1H 119
Darowen. Powy 5H 69
Darra. Abers 4E 161
Darracott. Devn 3E 19
Darragh Cross. New M 4J 179
Darras Hall. Nmbd 2E 115
Darrington. W Yor 2E 93
Darrow Green. Norf 2E 67
Darsham. Suff 4G 67
Dartfield. Abers 3H 161
**Dartford**. Kent 3G 39
**Dartford-Thurrock River Crossing**.
Kent 3G 39
Dartington. Devn 2D 9
Dartmeet. Devn 5G 11
**Dartmoor**. Devn 4F 11
Dartmouth. Devn 3E 9
**Darton**. S Yor 3D 92
Darvel. E Ayr 1E 117
**Darwen**. Bkbn 2E 91
Dassels. Herts 3D 53
Datchet. Wind 3A 38
Datchworth. Herts 4C 52
Datchworth Green. Herts 4C 52
Daubhill. G Man 4F 91
Dauntsey. Wilts 3E 35
Dauntsey Green. Wilts 3E 35
Dauntsey Lock. Wilts 3E 35
Dava. Mor 5E 159
Davenham. Ches W 3A 84
**Daventry**. Nptn 4C 62
Davidson's Mains. Edin 2F 129
Davidston. High 2B 158
Davidstow. Corn 4B 10
David's Well. Powy 3C 58
Davington. Dum 4E 119
Daviot. Abers 1E 153
Daviot. High 5B 158
Davyhulme. G Man 1B 84
Daw Cross. N Yor 4E 99
Dawdon. Dur 5H 115
Dawesgreen. Surr 1D 26
Dawley. Telf 5A 72
**Dawlish**. Devn 5C 12
Dawlish Warren. Devn 5C 12
Dawn. Cnwy 3A 82
Daws Heath. Essx 2C 40
Dawshill. Worc 5C 60
Daw's House. Corn 4D 10
Dawsmere. Linc 2D 76
Dayhills. Staf 2D 72
Dayhouse Bank. Worc 3D 60
Daylesford. Glos 3H 49
Daywall. Shrp 2E 71
Ddol. Flin 3D 82
Ddol Cownwy. Powy 4C 70
Deadman's Cross. C Beds 1B 52
Deadwater. Nmbd 5A 120
Deaf Hill. Dur 1A 106
**Deal**. Kent 5H 41
Dean. Cumb 2B 102
Dean. Devn 2G 19
(nr. Combe Martin)
Dean. Devn 2H 19
(nr. Lynton)
Dean. Dors 1E 15
Dean. Hants 1D 16
(nr. Bishop's Waltham)
Dean. Hants 3C 24
(nr. Winchester)
Dean. Oxon 3B 50
Dean. Som 2B 22
Dean Bank. Dur 1F 105
Deanburnhaugh. Bord 3F 119
Dean Cross. Devn 2F 19
Deane. Hants 1D 24
Deanich Lodge. High 5A 164
Deanland. Dors 1E 15
Deanlane End. W Sus 1F 17
Dean Park. Shrp 4A 60
Dean Prior. Devn 2D 8
Dean Row. Ches E 2C 84
Deans. W Lot 3D 128
Deanscales. Cumb 2B 102
Deanshanger. Nptn 1F 51
Deanston. Stir 3G 135
Dearham. Cumb 1B 102
**Dearne Valley**. S Yor 4D 93
Debach. Suff 5E 67
Debden. Essx 2F 53
Debden Green. Essx 1F 39
(nr. Loughton)
Debden Green. Essx 2F 53
(nr. Saffron Walden)
Debenham. Suff 4D 66
Dechmont. W Lot 2D 128
Deddington. Oxon 2C 50
Dedham. Essx 2D 54
Dedham Heath. Essx 2D 54
Deebank. Abers 4D 152
Deene. Nptn 1G 63
Deenethorpe. Nptn 1G 63
Deepcar. S Yor 1G 85
Deepcut. Surr 5A 38
Deepdale. Cumb 1G 97
Deepdale. N Lin 3D 94
Deepdale. N Yor 2A 98
Deeping Gate. Pet 5A 76
Deeping St James. Linc 4A 76
Deeping St Nicholas. Linc 4B 76
Deerhill. Mor 3B 160
Deerhurst. Glos 3D 48
Deerhurst Walton. Glos 3D 49
Deerness. Orkn 7E 172
Defford. Worc 1E 49
Defynnog. Powy 3C 46
Deganwy. Cnwy 3G 81
Deighton. N Yor 4A 106
Deighton. W Yor 3B 92
Deighton. York 5A 100
Deiniolen. Gwyn 4E 81
Delabole. Corn 4A 10
Delamere. Ches W 4H 83
Delfour. High 3C 150
Delliefure. High 5E 159
Dell, The. Suff 1G 67
Delly End. Oxon 4B 50
Delny. High 1B 158
Delph. G Man 4H 91
Delves. Dur 5E 115
Delves, The. W Mid 1E 61
Delvin End. Essx 2A 54
Dembleby. Linc 2H 75
Demelza. Corn 2D 6
Denaby Main. S Yor 1B 86
Denbeath. Fife 4F 137
Denbigh. Den 4C 82
Denbury. Devn 2E 9
Denby. Derbs 1A 74
Denby Common. Derbs 1B 74
Denby Dale. W Yor 4C 92
Denchworth. Oxon 2B 36
Dendron. Cumb 2B 96
Deneside. Dur 5H 115
Denford. Nptn 3G 63
Dengie. Essx 5C 54
Denham. Buck 2B 38
Denham. Suff 4G 65
(nr. Bury St Edmunds)
Denham. Suff 3D 66
(nr. Eye)
Denham Green. Buck 2B 38
Denham Street. Suff 3D 66
Denhead. Abers 5G 161
(nr. Ellon)
Denhead. Abers 3G 161
(nr. Strichen)
Denhead. Fife 2G 137
Denholm. Bord 3H 119
Denholme. W Yor 1A 92
Denholme Clough. W Yor 1A 92
Denholme Gate. W Yor 1A 92
Denio. Gwyn 2C 68
Denmead. Hants 1E 17
Dennington. Suff 4E 67
**Denny**. Falk 1B 128
Denny End. Cambs 4D 65
Dennyloanhead. Falk 1B 128
Den of Lindores. Fife 2E 137
Denshaw. G Man 3H 91
Denside. Abers 4F 153
Densole. Kent 1G 29
Denston. Suff 5G 65
Denstone. Staf 1F 73
Denstroude. Kent 4F 41
Dent. Cumb 1G 97
Den, The. N Ayr 4E 127
Denton. Cambs 2A 64
Denton. Darl 3F 105
Denton. E Sus 5F 27
**Denton**. G Man 1D 84
Denton. Kent 1G 29
Denton. Linc 2F 75
Denton. Norf 2E 67
Denton. Nptn 5F 63
Denton. N Yor 5D 98
Denton. Oxon 5D 50
Denver. Norf 5F 77
Denwick. Nmbd 3G 121
Deopham. Norf 5C 78
Deopham Green. Norf 1C 66
Depden. Suff 5G 65
Depden Green. Suff 5G 65
**Deptford**. G Lon 3E 39
Deptford. Wilts 3F 23
**Derby**. Derb 2A 74 & 194
Derbyhaven. IOM 5B 108
Derculich. Per 3F 143
**Dereham**. Norf 4B 78
Deri. Cphy 5E 47
Derril. Devn 2D 10
Derringstone. Kent 1G 29
Derrington. Shrp 1A 60
Derrington. Staf 3C 72
Derriton. Devn 2D 10
**Derry**. Derr 5A 174
Derryboye. New M 4J 179
Derrycrin. M Ulst 2D 178
Derrygonnelly. Ferm 7D 176
Derryguaig. Arg 5F 139
Derry Hill. Wilts 4E 35
Derrykeighan. Caus 3F 175
Derrylin. Ferm 7H 177
Derrymacash. Arm 3E 178
Derrythorpe. N Lin 4B 94
Derrytrasna. Arm 3D 178
Dersingham. Norf 2F 77
Dervaig. Arg 3F 139
Dervock. Caus 3F 175
Derwen. Den 5C 82
Derwen Gam. Cdgn 5D 56
Derwenlas. Powy 1G 57
Desborough. Nptn 2F 63
Desertmartin. M Ulst 7E 174
Desford. Leics 5B 74
Detchant. Nmbd 1E 121
Dethick. Derbs 5H 85
Detling. Kent 5B 40
Deuchar. Ang 2D 144
Deuddwr. Powy 4E 71
Devauden. Mon 2H 33
Devil's Bridge. Cdgn 3G 57
Devitts Green. Warw 1G 61
**Devizes**. Wilts 5F 35
Devonport. Plym 3A 8
Devonside. Clac 4B 136
Devoran. Corn 5B 6
Dewartown. Midl 3G 129
Dewlish. Dors 3C 14
Dewsall Court. Here 2H 47
**Dewsbury**. W Yor 2C 92
Dexbeer. Devn 2C 10
Dhoon. IOM 3D 108
Dhoor. IOM 2D 108
Dhowin. IOM 1D 108
Dial Green. W Sus 3A 26
Dial Post. W Sus 4C 26
Diamond, The. M Ulst 2D 178
Dibberford. Dors 2H 13
Dibden. Hants 2C 16
Dibden Purlieu. Hants 2C 16
Dickleburgh. Norf 2D 66
Didbrook. Glos 2F 49
**Didcot**. Oxon 2D 36
Diddington. Cambs 4A 64
Diddlebury. Shrp 2H 59
Didley. Here 2H 47
Didling. W Sus 1G 17
Didmarton. Glos 3D 34
Didsbury. G Man 1C 84
Didworthy. Devn 2C 8
Digby. Linc 5H 87
Digg. High 2D 154
Diggle. G Man 4A 92
Digmoor. Lanc 4C 90
Digswell. Herts 4C 52
Dihewyd. Cdgn 5D 57
Dilham. Norf 3F 79
Dilhorne. Staf 1D 72
Dillarburn. S Lan 5B 128
Dillington. Cambs 4A 64
Dilston. Nmbd 3C 114
Dilton Marsh. Wilts 2D 22
Dilwyn. Here 5G 59
Dimmer. Som 3B 22
Dimple. G Man 3F 91
Dinas. Carm 1G 43
Dinas. Gwyn 5D 81
(nr. Caernarfon)
Dinas. Gwyn 2B 68
(nr. Tudweiliog)
Dinas Cross. Pemb 1E 43
Dinas Dinlle. Gwyn 5D 80
Dinas Mawddwy. Gwyn 4A 70
Dinas Powys. V Glam 4E 33
Dinbych. Den 4C 82
Dinbych-y-Pysgod. Pemb 4F 43
Dinckley. Lanc 1E 91
Dinder. Som 2A 22
Dinedor. Here 2A 48
Dinedor Cross. Here 2A 48
Dingestow. Mon 4H 47
Dingle. Mers 2F 83
Dingleden. Kent 2C 28
Dingleton. Bord 1H 119
Dingley. Nptn 2E 63
Dingwall. High 3H 157
Dinmael. Cnwy 1C 70
Dinnet. Abers 4B 152
Dinnington. Som 1H 13
Dinnington. S Yor 2C 86
Dinnington. Tyne 2F 115
Dinorwig. Gwyn 4E 81
Dinton. Buck 4F 51
Dinton. Wilts 3F 23
Dinworthy. Devn 1D 10
Dipley. Hants 1F 25
Dippen. Arg 2B 122
Dippenhall. Surr 2G 25
Dippertown. Devn 4E 11
Dippin. N Ayr 3E 123
Dipple. S Ayr 4B 116
Diptford. Devn 3D 8
Dipton. Dur 4E 115
Dirleton. E Lot 1B 130
Dirt Pot. Nmbd 5B 114
Discoed. Powy 4E 59
Diseworth. Leics 3B 74
Dishes. Orkn 5F 172
Dishforth. N Yor 2F 99
Disley. Ches E 2D 85
Diss. Norf 3D 66
Disserth. Powy 5C 58
Distington. Cumb 2B 102
Ditchampton. Wilts 3F 23
Ditcheat. Som 3B 22
Ditchingham. Norf 1F 67
Ditchling. E Sus 4E 27
Ditteridge. Wilts 5D 34
Dittisham. Devn 3E 9
Ditton. Hal 2G 83
Ditton. Kent 5B 40
Ditton Green. Cambs 5F 65
Ditton Priors. Shrp 2A 60
Divach. High 1G 149
Dixonfield. High 2D 168
Dixton. Glos 2E 49
Dixton. Mon 4A 48
Dizzard. Corn 3B 10
Doagh. Ant 8J 175
Dobcross. G Man 4H 91
Dobs Hill. Flin 4F 83
Dobson's Bridge. Shrp 2G 71
Dobwalls. Corn 2G 7
Doccombe. Devn 4A 12
Dochgarroch. High 4A 158
Docking. Norf 2G 77
Docklow. Here 5H 59
Dockray. Cumb 2E 103
Doc Penfro. Pemb 4D 42 & 204
Dodbrooke. Devn 4D 8
Doddenham. Worc 5B 60
Doddinghurst. Essx 1G 39
Doddington. Cambs 1C 64
Doddington. Kent 5D 40
Doddington. Linc 3G 87
Doddington. Nmbd 1D 121
Doddington. Shrp 3A 60
Doddiscombsleigh. Devn 4B 12
Doddshill. Norf 2G 77
Dodford. Nptn 4D 62
Dodford. Worc 3D 60
Dodington. Som 2E 21
Dodington. S Glo 4C 34
Dodleston. Ches W 4F 83
Dods Leigh. Staf 2E 73
Dodworth. S Yor 4D 92
Doe Lea. Derbs 4B 86
Dogdyke. Linc 5B 88
Dogmersfield. Hants 1F 25
Dogsthorpe. Pet 5B 76
Dog Village. Devn 3C 12
Dolanog. Powy 4C 70
Dolau. Powy 4D 58
Dolau. Rhon 3D 32
Dolbenmaen. Gwyn 1E 69
Doley. Staf 3B 72
Dol-fâch. Powy 5B 70
(nr. Llanbrynmair)
Dolfach. Powy 3B 58
(nr. Llanidloes)
Dolfor. Powy 2D 58
Dolgarrog. Cnwy 4G 81
Dolgellau. Gwyn 4G 69
Dolgoch. Gwyn 5F 69
Dol-gran. Carm 2E 45
Dolhelfa. Powy 3B 58
Doll. High 3F 165
Dollar. Clac 4B 136
Dolley Green. Powy 4E 59
Dollingstown. Arm 4F 178
Dollwen. Cdgn 2F 57
Dolphin. Flin 3D 82
Dolphinholme. Lanc 4E 97
Dolphinton. S Lan 5E 129
Dolton. Devn 1F 11
Dolwen. Cnwy 3A 82
Dolwyddelan. Cnwy 5G 81
Dol-y-Bont. Cdgn 2F 57
Dolyhir. Powy 5E 59
Domgay. Powy 4E 71
Donagh. Ferm 7J 177
Donaghadee. N Dwn 2K 179
Donaghcloney. Arm 4F 178
Donaghmore. M Ulst 3B 178
**Doncaster**. S Yor 4F 93
Donhead St Andrew. Wilts 4E 23
Donhead St Mary. Wilts 4E 23
Doniford. Som 2D 20
Donington. Linc 2B 76
Donington. Shrp 5C 72
Donington Eaudike. Linc 2B 76
Donington le Heath. Leics 4B 74
Donington on Bain. Linc 2B 88
Donington South Ing. Linc 2B 76
Donisthorpe. Leics 4H 73
Donkey Street. Kent 2F 29
Donkey Town. Surr 4A 38
Donna Nook. Linc 1D 88
Donnington. Glos 3G 49
Donnington. Here 2C 48
Donnington. Shrp 5H 71
Donnington. Telf 4B 72
Donnington. W Ber 5C 36
Donnington. W Sus 2G 17
Donyatt. Som 1G 13
Doomsday Green. W Sus 3C 26
Doonfoot. S Ayr 3C 116
Doonholm. S Ayr 3C 116
Dorback Lodge. High 2E 151
**Dorchester**. Dors 3B 14
Dorchester on Thames.
Oxon 2D 36
Dordon. Warw 5G 73
Dore. S Yor 2H 85
Dores. High 5H 157
**Dorking**. Surr 1C 26
Dorking Tye. Suff 2C 54
Dormansland. Surr 1F 27
Dormans Park. Surr 1E 27
Dormanstown. Red C 2C 106
Dormington. Here 1A 48
Dormston. Worc 5D 61
Dorn. Glos 2H 49
Dorney. Buck 3A 38
Dornie. High 1A 148
Dornoch. High 5E 165
Dornock. Dum 3D 112
Dorrery. High 3C 168
Dorridge. W Mid 3F 61
Dorrington. Linc 5H 87
Dorrington. Shrp 5G 71
Dorsington. Warw 1G 49
Dorstone. Here 1G 47
Dorton. Buck 4E 51
Dosthill. Staf 5G 73
Dotham. IOA 3C 80
Dottery. Dors 3H 13
Doublebois. Corn 2F 7
Dougarie. N Ayr 2C 122
Doughton. Glos 2D 35
Douglas. IOM 4C 108
Douglas. S Lan 1H 117
Douglas Bridge. Derr 3F 176
Douglastown. Ang 4D 144
Douglas Water. S Lan 1A 118
Doulting. Som 2B 22
Dounby. Orkn 5B 172
Doune. High 2C 150
(nr. Kingussie)
Doune. High 3B 164
(nr. Lairg)
Doune. Stir 3G 135
Dounie. High 4C 164
(nr. Bonar Bridge)
Dounie. High 5D 164
(nr. Tain)
Dounreay. High 2B 168

Doura—Edenfield

Doura. N Ayr 5E 127
Dousland. Devn 2B 8
Dovaston. Shrp 3F 71
Dove Holes. Derbs 3E 85
Dovenby. Cumb 1B 102
**Dover**. Kent 1H 29 & 194
Dovercourt. Essx 2F 55
Doverdale. Worc 4C 60
Doveridge. Derbs 2F 73
Doversgreen. Surr 1D 26
Dowally. Per 4H 143
Dowbridge. Lanc 1C 90
Dowdeswell. Glos 4F 49
Dowlais. Mer T 5D 46
Dowland. Devn 1F 11
Dowlands. Devn 3F 13
Dowles. Worc 3B 60
Dowlesgreen. Wok 5G 37
Dowlish Wake. Som 1G 13
Downall Green. Mers 4D 90
Down Ampney. Glos 2G 35
Downderry. Corn 3H 7 (nr. Looe)
Downderry. Corn 3D 6 (nr. St Austell)
Downe. G Lon 4F 39
Downend. IOW 4D 16
Downend. S Glo 4B 34
Downend. W Ber 4C 36
Down Field. Cambs 3F 65
Downfield. D'dee 5C 144
Downgate. Corn 5D 10 (nr. Kelly Bray)
Downgate. Corn 5C 10 (nr. Upton Cross)
Downham. Essx 1B 40
Downham. Lanc 5G 97
Downham. Nmbd 1C 120
Downham Market. Norf 5F 77
Down Hatherley. Glos 3D 48
Downhead. Som 2B 22 (nr. Frome)
Downhead. Som 4A 22 (nr. Yeovil)
Downhill. Caus 3D 174
Downholland Cross. Lanc 4B 90
Downholme. N Yor 5E 105
Downies. Abers 4G 153
Downley. Buck 2G 37
**Downpatrick**. New M 5J 179
Down St Mary. Devn 2H 11
Downside. Som 1B 22 (nr. Chilcompton)
Downside. Som 2B 22 (nr. Shepton Mallet)
Downside. Surr 5C 38
Down, The. Shrp 1A 60
Down Thomas. Devn 3B 8
Downton. Hants 3A 16
Downton. Wilts 4G 23
Downton on the Rock. Here 3G 59
Dowsby. Linc 3A 76
Dowsdale. Linc 4B 76
Dowthwaitehead. Cumb 2E 103
Doxey. Staf 3D 72
Doxford. Nmbd 2F 121
Doynton. S Glo 4C 34
Drabblegate. Norf 3E 78
Draethen. Cphy 3F 33
Draffan. S Lan 5A 128
Dragonby. N Lin 3C 94
Dragon's Green. W Sus 3C 26
Drakelow. Worc 2C 60
Drakemyre. N Ayr 4D 126
Drakes Broughton. Worc 1E 49
Drakes Cross. Worc 3E 61
Drakewalls. Corn 5E 11
Draperstown. M Ulst 7D 174
Draughton. Nptn 3E 63
Draughton. N Yor 4C 98
Drax. N Yor 2G 93
Draycot. Oxon 5E 51
Draycote. Warw 3B 62
Draycot Foliat. Swin 4G 35
Draycott. Derbs 2B 74
Draycott. Glos 2G 49
Draycott. Shrp 1C 60
Draycott. Som 1H 21 (nr. Cheddar)
Draycott. Som 4A 22 (nr. Yeovil)
Draycott. Worc 1D 48
Draycott in the Clay. Staf 3F 73
Draycott in the Moors. Staf 1D 73
Drayford. Devn 1A 12
Drayton. Leics 1F 63
Drayton. Linc 2B 76
Drayton. Norf 4D 78
Drayton. Nptn 4C 62
Drayton. Oxon 2C 36 (nr. Abingdon)
Drayton. Oxon 1C 50 (nr. Banbury)
Drayton. Port 2E 17
Drayton. Som 4H 21
Drayton. Warw 5F 61
Drayton. Worc 3D 60
Drayton Bassett. Staf 5F 73
Drayton Beauchamp. Buck 4H 51
Drayton Parslow. Buck 3G 51
Drayton St Leonard. Oxon 2D 36
Drebley. N Yor 4C 98
Dreenhill. Pemb 3D 42
Drefach. Carm 4F 45 (nr. Meidrim)
Drefach. Carm 2D 44 (nr. Newcastle Emlyn)
Drefach. Carm 2G 43 (nr. Tumble)
Drefach. Cdgn 1E 45
Dreghorn. N Ayr 1C 116
Drellingore. Kent 1G 29
Drem. E Lot 2B 130
Dreumasdal. W Isl 5C 170
Drewsteignton. Devn 3H 11
Driby. Linc 3C 88
Driffield. E Yor 4E 101
Driffield. Glos 2F 35
Drift. Corn 4B 4
Drigg. Cumb 5B 102
Drighlington. W Yor 2C 92
Drimnin. High 3G 139
Drimpton. Dors 2H 13
Dringhoe. E Yor 4F 101
Drinisiadar. W Isl 8D 171
Drinkstone. Suff 4B 66
Drinkstone Green. Suff 4B 66
Drointon. Staf 3E 73
**Droitwich Spa**. Worc 4C 60
Droman. High 3B 166
Dromara. Lis 5G 179
Dromore. Arm 4G 179
Dromore. Ferm 6F 176
Dron. Per 2D 136
**Dronfield**. Derbs 3A 86
Dronfield Woodhouse. Derbs 3H 85
Drongan. E Ayr 3D 116
Dronley. Ang 5C 144
Droop. Dors 2C 14
Drope. V Glam 4E 32
Droxford. Hants 1E 16
**Droylsden**. G Man 1C 84
Druggers End. Worc 2C 48
Druid. Den 1C 70
Druid's Heath. W Mid 5E 73
Druidston. Pemb 3C 42
Druim. High 3D 158
Druimarbin. High 1E 141
Druim Fhearna. High 2E 147
Druimindarroch. High 5E 147
Druim Saighdinis. W Isl 2D 170
Drum. Per 3C 136
Drumaness. New M 5H 179
Drumaroad. New M 5H 179
Drumbeg. High 5B 166
Drumblade. Abers 4C 160
Drumbo. Lis 3H 179
Drumbuie. Dum 1C 110
Drumbuie. High 5G 155
Drumburgh. Cumb 4D 112
Drumburn. Dum 3A 112
Drumchapel. Glas 2G 127
Drumchardine. High 4H 157
Drumchork. High 5C 162
Drumclog. S Lan 1F 117
Drumeldrie. Fife 3G 137
Drumelzier. Bord 1D 118
Drumfearn. High 2E 147
Drumgask. High 4A 150
Drumgelloch. N Lan 3A 128
Drumgley. Ang 3D 144
Drumguish. High 4B 150
Drumin. Mor 5F 159
Drumindorsair. High 4G 157
Drumintee. New M 8E 178
Drumlamford House. S Ayr 2H 109
Drumlasie. Abers 3D 152
Drumlemble. Arg 4A 122
Drumlithie. Abers 5E 153
Drummoddie. Dum 5A 110
Drummond. High 2A 158
Drummore. Dum 5E 109
Drummuir. Mor 4A 160
Drumnacanvy. Arm 4E 178
Drumnadrochit. High 5H 157
Drumnagorrach. Mor 3C 160
Drumnakilly. Ferm 2L 177
Drumoak. Abers 4E 153
Drumquin. Ferm 5F 176
Drumraighland. Caus 4C 174
Drumrunie. High 3F 163
Drumry. W Dun 2G 127
Drums. Abers 1G 153
Drumsleet. Dum 2G 111
Drumsmittal. High 4A 158
Drums of Park. Abers 3C 160
Drumsturdy. Ang 5D 145
Drumsurn. Caus 5D 174
Drumtochty Castle. Abers 5D 152
Drumuie. High 4D 154
Drumuillie. High 1D 150
Drumvaich. Stir 3F 135
Drumwhindle. Abers 5G 161
Drunkendub. Ang 4F 145
Drury. Flin 4E 83
Drury Square. Norf 4B 78
Drybeck. Cumb 3H 103
Drybridge. Mor 2B 160
Drybridge. N Ayr 1C 116
Drybrook. Glos 4B 48
Drybrook. Here 4A 48
Dryburgh. Bord 1H 119
Dry Doddington. Linc 1F 75
Dry Drayton. Cambs 4C 64
Drym. Corn 3D 4
Drymen. Stir 1F 127
Drymuir. Abers 4G 161
Drynachan Lodge. High 5C 158
Drynie Park. High 3H 157
Drynoch. High 5D 154
Dry Sandford. Oxon 5C 50
Dryslwyn. Carm 3F 45
Dry Street. Essx 2A 40
Dryton. Shrp 5H 71
Dubford. Abers 2E 161
Dubiton. Abers 3D 160
Dubton. Ang 3E 145
Duchally. High 2A 164
Duck End. Essx 3G 53
Duckington. Ches W 5G 83
Ducklington. Oxon 5B 50
Duckmanton. Derbs 3B 86
Duck Street. Hants 2B 24
Dudbridge. Glos 5D 48
Duddenhoe End. Essx 2E 53
Duddingston. Edin 2F 129
Duddington. Nptn 5G 75
Duddleswell. E Sus 3F 27
Duddo. Nmbd 5F 131
Duddon. Ches W 4H 83
Duddon Bridge. Cumb 1A 96
Dudleston. Shrp 2F 71
Dudleston Heath. Shrp 2F 71
Dudley. Tyne 2F 115
**Dudley**. W Mid 2D 60
Dudston. Shrp 1E 59
Dudwells. Pemb 2D 42
Duffield. Derbs 1H 73
Duffryn. Neat 2B 32
Dufftown. Mor 4H 159
Duffus. Mor 2F 159
Dufton. Cumb 2H 103
Duggleby. N Yor 3C 100
Duirinish. High 5G 155
Duisdalemore. High 2E 147
Duisdeil Mòr. High 2E 147
Duisky. High 1E 141
Dukesfield. Nmbd 4C 114
Dukestown. Blae 5E 47
**Dukinfield**. G Man 1D 84
Dulas. IOA 2D 81
Dulcote. Som 2A 22
Dulford. Devn 2D 12
Dull. Per 4F 143
Dullatur. N Lan 2A 128
Dullingham. Cambs 5F 65
Dullingham Ley. Cambs 5F 65
Dulnain Bridge. High 1D 151
Duloe. Bed 4A 64
Duloe. Corn 3G 7
Dulverton. Som 4C 20
Dulwich. G Lon 3E 39
**Dumbarton**. W Dun 2F 127
Dumbleton. Glos 2F 49
Dumfin. Arg 1E 127
**Dumfries**. Dum 2A 112 & 194
Dumgoyne. Stir 1G 127
Dummer. Hants 2D 24
Dumpford. W Sus 4G 25
Dun. Ang 2F 145
Dunadry. Ant 1F 179
Dunaghy. Caus 4F 175
Dunagoil. Arg 4B 126
Dunalastair. Per 3E 142
Dunan. High 1D 147
Dunball. Som 2G 21
Dunbar. E Lot 2C 130
Dunbeath. High 5D 168
Dunbeg. Arg 5C 140
Dunblane. Stir 3G 135
Dunbog. Fife 2E 137
Dunbridge. Hants 4B 24
Duncanston. Abers 1C 152
Duncanston. High 3H 157
Dun Charlabhaigh. W Isl 3D 171
Dunchideock. Devn 4B 12
Dunchurch. Warw 3B 62
Duncote. Nptn 5D 62
Duncow. Dum 1A 112
Duncrievie. Per 3D 136
Duncton. W Sus 4A 26
**Dundee**. D'dee 5D 144 & 194
Dundee Airport. D'dee 1F 137
Dundon. Som 3H 21
**Dundonald**. Lis 2J 179
Dundonald. S Ayr 1C 116
Dundonnell. High 5E 163
Dundraw. Cumb 5D 112
Dundreggan. High 2F 149
Dundrennan. Dum 5E 111
Dundridge. Hants 1D 16
Dundrod. Lis 2G 179
Dundrum. New M 6J 179
Dundry. N Som 5A 34
Dunecht. Abers 3E 153
**Dunfermline**. Fife 1D 129
Dunford Bridge. S Yor 4B 92
**Dungannon**. M Ulst 3B 178
Dungate. Kent 5D 40
Dunge. Wilts 1D 23
Dungeness. Kent 4E 29
Dungiven. Caus 6C 174
Dungworth. S Yor 2G 85
Dunham-on-the-Hill. Ches W 3G 83
Dunham-on-Trent. Notts 3F 87
Dunhampton. Worc 4C 60
Dunham Town. G Man 2B 84
Dunham Woodhouses. G Man 2B 84
Dunholme. Linc 3H 87
Dunino. Fife 2H 137
Dunipace. Falk 1B 128
Dunira. Per 1G 135
Dunkeld. Per 4H 143
Dunkerton. Bath 1C 22
Dunkeswell. Devn 2E 13
Dunkeswick. N Yor 5F 99
Dunkirk. Kent 5E 41
Dunkirk. S Glo 3C 34
Dunkirk. Staf 5C 84
Dunkirk. Wilts 5E 35
Dunk's Green. Kent 5H 39
Dunlappie. Ang 2E 145
Dunley. Hants 1C 24
Dunley. Worc 4B 60
Dunlichity Lodge. High 5A 158
Dunlop. E Ayr 5F 127
Dunloy. Caus 5G 175
Dunmaglass Lodge. High 1H 149
Dunmore. Arg 3F 125
Dunmore. Falk 1B 128
Dunmore. High 4H 157
Dunmurry. Bel 3G 179
Dunnamanagh. Derr 6A 174
Dunnaval. New M 8G 179
Dunnet. High 1E 169
Dunnichen. Ang 4E 145
Dunning. Per 2C 136
Dunnington. E Yor 4F 101
Dunnington. Warw 5E 61
Dunnington. York 4A 100
Dunningwell. Cumb 1A 96
Dunnockshaw. Lanc 2G 91
**Dunoon**. Arg 2C 126
Dunphail. Mor 4E 159
Dunragit. Dum 4G 109
Dunrostan. Arg 1F 125
Duns. Bord 4D 130
Dunsby. Linc 3A 76
Dunscar. G Man 3F 91
Dunscore. Dum 1F 111
Dunscroft. S Yor 4G 93
Dunsdale. Red C 3D 106
Dunsden Green. Oxon 4F 37
Dunsfold. Surr 2B 26
Dunsford. Devn 4B 12
Dunshalt. Fife 2E 137
Dunshillock. Abers 4G 161
Dunsley. N Yor 3F 107
Dunsley. Staf 2C 60
Dunsmore. Buck 5G 51
Dunsop Bridge. Lanc 4F 97
**Dunstable**. C Beds 3A 52
Dunstal. Staf 3E 73
Dunstall. Staf 3F 73
Dunstall Green. Suff 4G 65
Dunstall Hill. W Mid 5D 72
Dunstan. Nmbd 3G 121
Dunster. Som 2C 20
Duns Tew. Oxon 3C 50
Dunston. Linc 4H 87
Dunston. Norf 5E 79
Dunston. Staf 4D 72
Dunston. Tyne 3F 115
Dunstone. Devn 3B 8
Dunston Heath. Staf 4D 72
Dunsville. S Yor 4G 93
Dunswell. E Yor 1D 94
Dunsyre. S Lan 5D 128
Dunterton. Devn 5D 11
Duntisbourne Abbots. Glos 5E 49
Duntisbourne Leer. Glos 5E 49
Duntisbourne Rouse. Glos 5E 49
Duntish. Dors 2B 14
Duntocher. W Dun 2F 127
Dunton. Buck 3G 51
Dunton. C Beds 1C 52
Dunton. Norf 2A 78
Dunton Bassett. Leics 1C 62
Dunton Green. Kent 5G 39
Dunton Patch. Norf 2A 78
Duntulm. High 1D 154
Dunure. S Ayr 3B 116
Dunvant. Swan 3E 31
Dunvegan. High 4B 154
Dunwich. Suff 3G 67
Dunwood. Staf 5D 84
Durdar. Cumb 4F 113
Durgates. E Sus 2H 27
**Durham**. Dur 5F 115 & 194
Durham Tees Valley Airport. Darl 3A 106
Durisdeer. Dum 4A 118
Durisdeermill. Dum 4A 118
Durkar. W Yor 3D 92
Durleigh. Som 3F 21
Durley. Hants 1D 16
Durley. Wilts 5H 35
Durley Street. Hants 1D 16
Durlow Common. Here 2B 48
Durnamuck. High 4E 163
Durness. High 2E 166
Durno. Abers 1E 152
Durns Town. Hants 3A 16
Duror. High 3D 141
Durran. Arg 3G 133
Durran. High 2D 169
Durrant Green. Kent 2C 28
Durrants. Hants 1F 17
Durrington. W Sus 5C 26
Durrington. Wilts 2G 23
**Dursley**. Glos 2C 34
Dursley Cross. Glos 4B 48
Durston. Som 4F 21
Durweston. Dors 2D 14
Dury. Shet 6F 173
Duston. Nptn 4E 63
Duthil. High 1D 150
Dutlas. Powy 3E 58
Duton Hill. Essx 3G 53
Dutson. Corn 4D 10
Dutton. Ches W 3H 83
Duxford. Cambs 1E 53
Duxford. Oxon 2B 36
Dwygyfylchi. Cnwy 3G 81
Dwyran. IOA 4D 80
Dyce. Aber 2F 153
Dyffryn. B'end 2B 32
Dyffryn. Carm 2H 43
Dyffryn. Pemb 1D 42
Dyffryn. V Glam 4D 32
Dyffryn Ardudwy. Gwyn 3E 69
Dyffryn Castell. Cdgn 2G 57
Dyffryn Ceidrych. Carm 3H 45
Dyffryn Cellwen. Neat 5B 46
Dyke. Linc 3A 76
Dyke. Mor 3D 159
Dykehead. Ang 2C 144
Dykehead. N Lan 3B 128
Dykehead. Stir 4E 135
Dykend. Ang 3B 144
Dykesfield. Cumb 4E 112
Dylife. Powy 1A 58
Dymchurch. Kent 3F 29
Dymock. Glos 2C 48
Dyrham. S Glo 4C 34
Dysart. Fife 4F 137
Dyserth. Den 3C 82

## E

Eachwick. Nmbd 2E 115
Eadar Dha Fhadhail. W Isl 4C 171
Eagland Hill. Lanc 5D 96
Eagle. Linc 4F 87
Eagle Barnsdale. Linc 4F 87
Eagle Moor. Linc 4F 87
**Eaglescliffe**. Stoc T 3B 106
Eaglesfield. Cumb 2B 102
Eaglesfield. Dum 2D 112
Eaglesham. E Ren 4G 127
Eaglethorpe. Nptn 1H 63
Eagley. G Man 3F 91
Eairy. IOM 4B 108
Eakley Lanes. Mil 5F 63
Eakring. Notts 4D 86
Ealand. N Lin 3A 94
**Ealing**. G Lon 2C 38
Eallabus. Arg 3B 124
Eals. Nmbd 4H 113
Eamont Bridge. Cumb 2G 103
Earby. Lanc 5B 98
Earcroft. Bkbn 2E 91
Eardington. Shrp 1B 60
Eardisland. Here 5G 59
Eardisley. Here 1G 47
Eardiston. Shrp 3F 71
Eardiston. Worc 4A 60
Earith. Cambs 3C 64
Earlais. High 2C 154
Earle. Nmbd 2D 121
Earlesfield. Linc 2G 75
Earlestown. Mers 1H 83
Earley. Wok 4F 37
Earlham. Norf 5D 78
Earlish. High 2C 154
Earls Barton. Nptn 4F 63
Earls Colne. Essx 3B 54
Earls Common. Worc 5D 60
Earl's Croome. Worc 1D 48
Earlsdon. W Mid 3H 61
Earlsferry. Fife 3G 137
Earlsford. Abers 5F 161
Earl's Green. Suff 4C 66
Earlsheaton. W Yor 2C 92
**Earl Shilton**. Leics 1B 62
Earl Soham. Suff 4E 67
Earl Sterndale. Derbs 4E 85
Earlston. E Ayr 1D 116
Earlston. Bord 1H 119
Earl Stonham. Suff 5D 66
Earlstoun. Dum 1D 110
Earlswood. Mon 2H 33
Earlswood. Warw 3F 61
Earlyvale. Bord 4F 129
Earnley. W Sus 3G 17
Earsairidh. W Isl 9C 170
Earsdon. Tyne 2G 115
Earsham. Norf 2F 67
Earsham Street. Suff 3E 67
Earswick. York 4A 100
Eartham. W Sus 5A 26
Earthcott Green. S Glo 3B 34
Easby. N Yor 4C 106 (nr. Great Ayton)
Easby. N Yor 4E 105 (nr. Richmond)
Easdale. Arg 2E 133
Easebourne. W Sus 4G 25
Easenhall. Warw 3B 62
Eashing. Surr 1A 26
Easington. Buck 4E 51
Easington. Dur 5H 115
Easington. E Yor 3G 95
Easington. Nmbd 1F 121
Easington. Oxon 2C 50 (nr. Banbury)
Easington. Oxon 2E 37 (nr. Watlington)
Easington. Red C 3E 107
Easington Colliery. Dur 5H 115
Easington Lane. Tyne 5G 115
Easingwold. N Yor 2H 99
Eassie. Ang 4C 144
Eassie and Nevay. Ang 4C 144
East Aberthaw. V Glam 5D 32
Eastacombe. Devn 4F 19
Eastacott. Devn 4G 19
East Allington. Devn 4D 8
East Anstey. Devn 4B 20
East Anton. Hants 2B 24
East Appleton. N Yor 5F 105
East Ardsley. W Yor 2D 92
East Ashley. Devn 1G 11
East Ashling. W Sus 2G 17
East Aston. Hants 2C 24
East Ayton. N Yor 1D 101
East Barkwith. Linc 2A 88
East Barnby. N Yor 3F 107
East Barnet. G Lon 1D 39
East Barns. E Lot 2D 130
East Barsham. Norf 2B 78
East Beach. W Sus 3G 17
East Beckham. Norf 2D 78
East Bedfont. G Lon 3B 38
East Bennan. N Ayr 3D 123
East Bergholt. Suff 2D 54
East Bierley. W Yor 2C 92
East Bilney. Norf 4B 78
East Blatchington. E Sus 5F 27
East Bloxworth. Dors 3D 15
East Boldre. Hants 2B 16
East Bolton. Nmbd 3F 121
Eastbourne. Darl 3F 105
**Eastbourne**. E Sus 5H 27 & 194
East Brent. Som 1G 21
East Bridge. Suff 4G 67
East Bridgford. Notts 1D 74
East Briscoe. Dur 3C 104
East Buckland. Devn 3G 19 (nr. Barnstaple)
East Buckland. Devn 4C 8 (nr. Thurlestone)
East Budleigh. Devn 4D 12
Eastburn. W Yor 5C 98
East Burnham. Buck 2A 38
East Burrafirth. Shet 6E 173
East Burton. Dors 4D 14
Eastbury. Herts 1B 38
Eastbury. W Ber 4B 36
East Butsfield. Dur 5E 115
East Butterleigh. Devn 2C 12
East Butterwick. N Lin 4B 94
Eastby. N Yor 4C 98
East Calder. W Lot 3D 129
East Carleton. Norf 5D 78
East Carlton. Nptn 2F 63
East Carlton. W Yor 5E 98
East Chaldon. Dors 4C 14
East Challow. Oxon 3B 36
East Charleton. Devn 4D 8
East Chelborough. Dors 2A 14
East Chiltington. E Sus 4E 27
East Chinnock. Som 1H 13
East Chisenbury. Wilts 1G 23
Eastchurch. Kent 3D 40
East Clandon. Surr 5B 38
East Claydon. Buck 3F 51
East Clevedon. N Som 4H 33
East Clyne. High 3F 165
East Clyth. High 5E 169
East Coker. Som 1A 14
Eastcombe. Glos 5D 49
East Combe. Som 3E 21
East Common. N Yor 1G 93
East Compton. Som 2B 22
East Cornworthy. Devn 3E 9
Eastcote. G Lon 2C 38
Eastcote. Nptn 5D 62
Eastcote. W Mid 3F 61
Eastcott. Corn 1C 10
Eastcott. Wilts 1F 23
East Cottingwith. E Yor 5B 100
Eastcourt. Wilts 5H 35 (nr. Pewsey)
Eastcourt. Wilts 2E 35 (nr. Tetbury)
East Cowes. IOW 3D 16
East Cowick. E Yor 2G 93
East Cowton. N Yor 4A 106
East Cramlington. Nmbd 2F 115
East Cranmore. Som 2B 22
East Creech. Dors 4E 15
East Croachy. High 1A 150
East Dean. E Sus 5G 27
East Dean. Glos 3B 48
East Dean. Hants 4A 24
East Dean. W Sus 4A 26
East Down. Devn 2G 19
East Drayton. Notts 3E 87
East Dundry. N Som 5A 34
East Ella. Hull 2D 94
East End. Cambs 3C 64
East End. Dors 3E 15
East End. E Yor 4F 101 (nr. Ulrome)
East End. E Yor 2F 95 (nr. Withernsea)
East End. Hants 3B 16 (nr. Lymington)
East End. Hants 5C 36 (nr. Newbury)
East End. Herts 3E 53
East End. Kent 3D 40 (nr. Minster)
East End. Kent 2C 28 (nr. Tenterden)
East End. N Som 4H 33
East End. Oxon 4B 50
East End. Som 1A 22
East End. Suff 2E 54
Easter Ardross. High 1A 158
Easter Balgedie. Per 3D 136
Easter Balmoral. Abers 4G 151
Easter Brae. High 2A 158
Easter Buckieburn. Stir 1A 128
Easter Compton. S Glo 3A 34
Easter Fearn. High 5D 164
Easter Galcantray. High 4C 158
Eastergate. W Sus 5A 26
Easterhouse. Glas 3H 127
Easter Howgate. Midl 3F 129
Easter Kinkell. High 3H 157
Easter Lednathie. Ang 2C 144
Easter Ogil. Ang 2D 144
Easter Ord. Abers 3F 153
Easter Quarff. Shet 8F 173
Easter Rhynd. Per 2D 136
Easter Skeld. Shet 7E 173
Easter Suddie. High 3A 158
Easterton. Wilts 1F 23
Eastertown. Som 1G 21
Easter Tulloch. Abers 1G 145
East Everleigh. Wilts 1H 23
East Farleigh. Kent 5B 40
East Farndon. Nptn 2E 62
East Ferry. Linc 1F 87
Eastfield. N Lan 3B 128 (nr. Caldercruix)
Eastfield. N Lan 3B 128 (nr. Harthill)
**Eastfield**. N Yor 1E 101
Eastfield. S Lan 3H 127
Eastfield Hall. Nmbd 4G 121
East Fortune. E Lot 2B 130
East Garforth. W Yor 1E 93
East Garston. W Ber 4B 36
Eastgate. Dur 1C 104
Eastgate. Norf 3D 78
East Ginge. Oxon 3C 36
East Gores. Essx 3B 54
East Goscote. Leics 4D 74
East Grafton. Wilts 5A 36
East Green. Suff 5F 65
East Grimstead. Wilts 4H 23
**East Grinstead**. W Sus 2E 27
East Guldeford. E Sus 3D 28
East Haddon. Nptn 4D 62
East Hagbourne. Oxon 3D 36
East Halton. N Lin 2E 95
**East Ham**. G Lon 2F 39
Eastham. Mers 2F 83
Eastham. Worc 4A 60
Eastham Ferry. Mers 2F 83
Easthampstead. Brac 5G 37
Easthampton. Here 4G 59
East Hanney. Oxon 2C 36
East Hanningfield. Essx 5A 54
East Hardwick. W Yor 3E 93
East Harling. Norf 2B 66
East Harlsey. N Yor 5B 106
East Harptree. Bath 1A 22
East Hartford. Nmbd 2F 115
East Harting. W Sus 1G 17
East Hatch. Wilts 4E 23
East Hatley. Cambs 5B 64
Easthaugh. Norf 4C 78
East Hauxwell. N Yor 5E 105
East Haven. Ang 5E 145
Eastheath. Wok 5G 37
East Heckington. Linc 1A 76
East Hedleyhope. Dur 5E 115
East Helmsdale. High 2H 165
East Hendred. Oxon 3C 36
East Heslerton. N Yor 2D 100
East Hoathly. E Sus 4G 27
East Holme. Dors 4D 15
Easthope. Shrp 1H 59
Easthorpe. Essx 3C 54
Easthorpe. Leics 2F 75
East Horrington. Som 2A 22
East Horsley. Surr 5B 38
East Horton. Nmbd 1E 121
Easthouses. Midl 3G 129
East Howe. Bour 3F 15
East Huntspill. Som 2G 21
East Hyde. C Beds 4B 52
East Ilsley. W Ber 3C 36
Eastington. Devn 2H 11
Eastington. Glos 4G 49 (nr. Northleach)
Eastington. Glos 5C 48 (nr. Stonehouse)
East Keal. Linc 4C 88
East Kennett. Wilts 5G 35
East Keswick. W Yor 5F 99
**East Kilbride**. S Lan 4H 127
East Kirkby. Linc 4C 88
East Knapton. N Yor 2C 100
East Knighton. Dors 4D 14
East Knowstone. Devn 4B 20
East Knoyle. Wilts 3D 23
East Kyloe. Nmbd 1E 121
East Lambrook. Som 1H 13
East Langdon. Kent 1H 29
East Langton. Leics 1E 63
East Langwell. High 3E 164
East Lavant. W Sus 2G 17
East Lavington. W Sus 4A 26
East Layton. N Yor 4E 105
Eastleach Martin. Glos 5H 49
Eastleach Turville. Glos 5G 49
East Leake. Notts 3C 74
East Learmouth. Nmbd 1C 120
Eastleigh. Devn 4E 19 (nr. Bideford)
East Leigh. Devn 2G 11 (nr. Crediton)
East Leigh. Devn 3C 8 (nr. Modbury)
**Eastleigh**. Hants 1C 16
East Lexham. Norf 4A 78
East Lilburn. Nmbd 2E 121
Eastling. Kent 5D 40
East Linton. E Lot 2B 130
East Liss. Hants 4F 25
East Lockinge. Oxon 3C 36
East Looe. Corn 3G 7
East Lound. N Lin 1E 87
East Lulworth. Dors 4D 14
East Lutton. N Yor 3D 100
East Lydford. Som 3A 22
East Lyng. Som 4G 21
East Mains. Abers 4D 152
East Malling. Kent 5B 40
East Marden. W Sus 1G 17
East Markham. Notts 3E 87
East Marton. N Yor 4B 98
East Meon. Hants 4E 25
East Mersea. Essx 4D 54
East Mey. High 1F 169
East Midlands Airport. Leics 3B 74 & 205
East Molesey. Surr 4C 38
Eastmoor. Norf 5G 77
East Morden. Dors 3E 15
East Morton. W Yor 5D 98
East Ness. N Yor 2A 100
East Newton. E Yor 1F 95
East Newton. N Yor 2A 100
Eastney. Port 3E 17
Eastnor. Here 2C 48
East Norton. Leics 5E 75
East Nynehead. Som 4E 21
East Oakley. Hants 1D 24
Eastoft. N Lin 3B 94
East Ogwell. Devn 5B 12
Easton. Cambs 3A 64
Easton. Cumb 4D 112 (nr. Burgh by Sands)
Easton. Cumb 2F 113 (nr. Longtown)
Easton. Devn 4H 11
Easton. Dors 5B 14
Easton. Hants 3D 24
Easton. Linc 3G 75
Easton. Norf 4D 78
Easton. Som 2A 22
Easton. Suff 5E 67
Easton. Wilts 4D 35
Easton Grey. Wilts 3D 35
Easton-in-Gordano. N Som 4A 34
Easton Maudit. Nptn 5F 63
Easton on the Hill. Nptn 5H 75
Easton Royal. Wilts 5H 35
East Orchard. Dors 1D 14
East Ord. Nmbd 4F 131
East Panson. Devn 3D 10
East Peckham. Kent 1A 28
East Pennard. Som 3A 22
East Perry. Cambs 4A 64
East Pitcorthie. Fife 3H 137
East Portlemouth. Devn 5D 8
East Prawle. Devn 5D 9
East Preston. W Sus 5B 26
East Putford. Devn 1D 10
East Quantoxhead. Som 2E 21
East Rainton. Tyne 5G 115
East Ravendale. NE Lin 1B 88
East Raynham. Norf 3A 78
Eastrea. Cambs 1B 64
East Rhidorroch Lodge. High 4G 163
Eastriggs. Dum 3D 112
East Rigton. W Yor 5F 99
Eastrington. E Yor 2A 94
East Rounton. N Yor 4B 106
East Row. N Yor 3F 107
East Rudham. Norf 3H 77
East Runton. Norf 1D 78
East Ruston. Norf 3F 79
Eastry. Kent 5H 41
East Saltoun. E Lot 3A 130
East Shaws. Dur 3D 105
East Shefford. W Ber 4B 36
Eastshore. Shet 10E 173
East Sleekburn. Nmbd 1F 115
East Somerton. Norf 4G 79
East Stockwith. Linc 1E 87
East Stoke. Dors 4D 14
East Stoke. Notts 1E 75
East Stoke. Som 1H 13
East Stour. Dors 4D 22
East Stourmouth. Kent 4G 41
East Stowford. Devn 4G 19
East Stratton. Hants 2D 24
East Studdal. Kent 1H 29
East Taphouse. Corn 2F 7
East-the-Water. Devn 4E 19
East Thirston. Nmbd 5F 121
East Tilbury. Thur 3A 40
East Tisted. Hants 3F 25
East Torrington. Linc 2A 88
East Tuddenham. Norf 4C 78
East Tytherley. Hants 4A 24
East Tytherton. Wilts 4E 35
East Village. Devn 2B 12
Eastville. Linc 5D 88
East Wall. Shrp 1H 59
East Walton. Norf 4G 77
East Week. Devn 3G 11
Eastwell. Leics 3E 75
East Wellow. Hants 4B 24
East Wemyss. Fife 4F 137
East Whitburn. W Lot 3C 128
Eastwick. Herts 4E 53
Eastwick. Shet 4E 173
East Williamston. Pemb 4E 43
East Winch. Norf 4F 77
East Winterslow. Wilts 3H 23
East Wittering. W Sus 3F 17
East Witton. N Yor 1D 98
**Eastwood**. Notts 1B 74
Eastwood. S'end 2C 40
East Woodburn. Nmbd 1C 114
Eastwood End. Cambs 1D 64
East Woodhay. Hants 5C 36
East Woodlands. Som 2C 22
East Worldham. Hants 3F 25
East Worlington. Devn 1A 12
East Wretham. Norf 1B 66
East Youlstone. Devn 1C 10
Eathorpe. Warw 4A 62
Eaton. Ches E 4C 84
Eaton. Ches W 4H 83
Eaton. Leics 3E 75
Eaton. Norf 2F 77 (nr. Heacham)
Eaton. Norf 5E 78 (nr. Norwich)
Eaton. Notts 3E 86
Eaton. Oxon 5C 50
Eaton. Shrp 2F 59 (nr. Bishop's Castle)
Eaton. Shrp 2H 59 (nr. Church Stretton)
Eaton Bishop. Here 2H 47
Eaton Bray. C Beds 3H 51
Eaton Constantine. Shrp 5H 71
Eaton Hastings. Oxon 2A 36
**Eaton Socon**. Cambs 5A 64
Eaton upon Tern. Shrp 3A 72
Eau Brink. Norf 4E 77
Eaves Green. W Mid 2G 61
Ebberley Hill. Devn 1F 11
Ebberston. N Yor 1C 100
Ebbesbourne Wake. Wilts 4E 23
Ebblake. Dors 2G 15
Ebbsfleet. Kent 3H 39
**Ebbw Vale**. Blae 5E 47
Ebchester. Dur 4E 115
Ebernoe. W Sus 3A 26
Ebford. Devn 4C 12
Ebley. Glos 5D 48
Ebnal. Ches W 1G 71
Ebrington. Glos 1G 49
Ecchinswell. Hants 1D 24
Ecclefechan. Dum 2C 112
**Eccles**. G Man 1B 84
Eccles. Kent 4B 40
Eccles. Bord 5D 130
Ecclesall. S Yor 2H 85
Ecclesfield. S Yor 1A 86
Eccles Green. Here 1G 47
Eccleshall. Staf 3C 72
Eccleshill. W Yor 1B 92
Ecclesmachan. W Lot 2D 128
Eccles on Sea. Norf 3G 79
Eccles Road. Norf 1C 66
Eccleston. Ches W 4G 83
Eccleston. Lanc 3D 90
Eccleston. Mers 1G 83
Eccup. W Yor 5E 99
Echt. Abers 3E 153
Eckford. Bord 2B 120
Eckington. Derbs 3B 86
Eckington. Worc 1E 49
Ecton. Nptn 4F 63
Edale. Derbs 2F 85
Eday Airport. Orkn 4E 172
Edburton. W Sus 4D 26
Edderside. Cumb 5C 112
Edderton. High 5E 164
Eddington. Kent 4F 41
Eddington. W Ber 5B 36
Eddleston. Bord 5F 129
Eddlewood. S Lan 4A 128
Eden. ME Ant 8L 175
Edenbridge. Kent 1F 27
Edendonich. Arg 1A 134
Edenfield. Lanc 3F 91

Edenhall—Flaunden

Edenhall. *Cumb* 1G 103
Edenham. *Linc* 3H 75
Edensor. *Derbs* 4G 85
Edentaggart. *Arg* 4C 134
Edenthorpe. *S Yor* 4G 93
Eden Vale. *Dur* 1B 106
Edern. *Gwyn* 2B 68
Ederney. *Ferm* 6E 176
Edgarley. *Som* 3A 22
Edgbaston. *W Mid* 2E 61
Edgcott. *Buck* 3E 51
Edgcott. *Som* 3B 20
Edge. *Glos* 5D 48
Edge. *Shrp* 5F 71
Edgebolton. *Shrp* 3H 71
Edge End. *Glos* 4A 48
Edgefield. *Norf* 2C 78
Edgefield Street. *Norf* 2C 78
Edge Green. *Ches W* 5G 83
Edgehead. *Midl* 3G 129
Edgeley. *Shrp* 1H 71
Edgeside. *Lanc* 2G 91
Edgeworth. *Glos* 5E 49
Edgiock. *Worc* 4E 61
Edgmond. *Telf* 4B 72
Edgmond Marsh. *Telf* 3B 72
Edgton. *Shrp* 2F 59
**Edgware**. *G Lon* 1C 38
Edgworth. *Bkbn* 3F 91
Edinbane. *High* 3C 154
**Edinburgh**. *Edin* 2F 129 & 195
Edinburgh Airport. *Edin* 2E 129
Edingale. *Staf* 4G 73
Edingley. *Notts* 5D 86
Edingthorpe. *Norf* 2F 79
Edington. *Som* 3G 21
Edington. *Wilts* 1E 23
Edingworth. *Som* 1G 21
Edistone. *Devn* 4C 18
Edithmead. *Som* 2G 21
Edith Weston. *Rut* 5G 75
Edlaston. *Derbs* 1F 73
Edlesborough. *Buck* 4H 51
Edlingham. *Nmbd* 4F 121
Edlington. *Linc* 3B 88
Edmondsham. *Dors* 1F 15
Edmondsley. *Dur* 5F 115
Edmondthorpe. *Leics* 4F 75
Edmonstone. *Orkn* 5E 172
Edmonton. *Corn* 1D 6
**Edmonton**. *G Lon* 1E 39
Edmundbyers. *Dur* 4D 114
Ednam. *Bord* 1B 120
Ednaston. *Derbs* 1G 73
Edney Common. *Essx* 5G 53
Edrom. *Bord* 4E 131
Edstaston. *Shrp* 2H 71
Edstone. *Warw* 4F 61
Edwalton. *Notts* 2C 74
Edwardstone. *Suff* 1C 54
Edwardsville. *Mer T* 2D 32
Edwinsford. *Carm* 2G 45
Edwinstowe. *Notts* 4D 86
Edworth. *C Beds* 1C 52
Edwyn Ralph. *Here* 5A 60
Edzell. *Ang* 2F 145
Efail-fach. *Neat* 2A 32
Efail Isaf. *Rhon* 3D 32
Efailnewydd. *Gwyn* 2C 68
Efail-rhyd. *Powy* 3D 70
Efailwen. *Carm* 2F 43
Efenechtyd. *Den* 5D 82
Effingham. *Surr* 5C 38
Effingham Common. *Surr* 5C 38
Effirth. *Shet* 6E 173
Efflinch. *Staf* 4F 73
Efford. *Devn* 2B 12
Efstigarth. *Shet* 2F 173
Egbury. *Hants* 1C 24
Egdon. *Worc* 5D 60
Egerton. *G Man* 3F 91
Egerton. *Kent* 1D 28
Egerton Forstal. *Kent* 1C 28
Eggborough. *N Yor* 2F 93
Eggbuckland. *Plym* 3A 8
Eggesford. *Devn* 1G 11
Eggington. *C Beds* 3H 51
Egginton. *Derbs* 3G 73
Egglescliffe. *Stoc T* 3B 106
Eggleston. *Dur* 2C 104
**Egham**. *Surr* 3B 38
Egham Hythe. *Surr* 3B 38
Egleton. *Rut* 5F 75
Eglingham. *Nmbd* 3F 121
Eglinton. *Derr* 4B 174
Eglish. *M Ulst* 4B 178
Egloshayle. *Corn* 5A 10
Egloskerry. *Corn* 4C 10
Eglwysbach. *Cnwy* 3H 81
Eglwys-Brewis. *V Glam* 5D 32
Eglwys Fach. *Cdgn* 1F 57
Eglwyswrw. *Pemb* 1F 43
Egmanton. *Notts* 4E 87
Egmere. *Norf* 2B 78
Egremont. *Cumb* 3B 102
Egremont. *Mers* 1F 83
Egton. *N Yor* 4F 107
Egton Bridge. *N Yor* 4F 107
Egypt. *Buck* 2A 38
Egypt. *Hants* 2C 24
Eight Ash Green. *Essx* 3C 54
Eight Mile Burn. *Midl* 4E 129
Eignaig. *High* 4B 140
Eilanreach. *High* 2G 147
Eildon. *Bord* 1H 119
Eileanach Lodge. *High* 2H 157
Eilean Fhlodaigh. *W Isl* 3D 170
Eilean Iarmain. *High* 2F 147
Einacleit. *W Isl* 5D 171
Eisgein. *W Isl* 6F 171
Eisingrug. *Gwyn* 2F 69
Elan Village. *Powy* 4B 58
Elberton. *S Glo* 3B 34
Elbridge. *W Sus* 5A 26
Elburton. *Plym* 3B 8
Elcho. *Per* 1D 136
Elcombe. *Swin* 3G 35
Elcot. *W Ber* 5B 36
Eldernell. *Cambs* 1C 64
Eldersfield. *Worc* 2D 48
Elderslie. *Ren* 3F 127
Elder Street. *Essx* 2F 53
Eldon. *Dur* 2F 105
Eldroth. *N Yor* 3G 97
Eldwick. *W Yor* 5D 98
Elfhowe. *Cumb* 5F 103
Elford. *Nmbd* 1F 121
Elford. *Staf* 4F 73
Elford Closes. *Cambs* 3D 65
**Elgin**. *Mor* 2G 159
Elgol. *High* 2D 146
Elham. *Kent* 1F 29
Elie. *Fife* 3G 137
Eling. *Hants* 1B 16
Eling. *W Ber* 4D 36
Elishaw. *Nmbd* 5C 120
Elizafield. *Dum* 2B 112
Elkesley. *Notts* 3D 86
Elkington. *Nptn* 3D 62
Elkins Green. *Essx* 5G 53
Elkstone. *Glos* 4E 49
Ellan. *High* 1C 150
**Elland**. *W Yor* 2B 92
Ellary. *Arg* 2F 125
Ellastone. *Staf* 1F 73
Ellbridge. *Corn* 2A 8
Ellel. *Lanc* 4D 97
Ellemford. *Bord* 3D 130
Ellenabeich. *Arg* 2E 133
Ellenborough. *Cumb* 1B 102
Ellenbrook. *Herts* 5C 52
Ellenhall. *Staf* 3C 72
Ellen's Green. *Surr* 2B 26
Ellerbeck. *N Yor* 5B 106
Ellerburn. *N Yor* 1C 100
Ellerby. *N Yor* 3E 107
Ellerdine. *Telf* 3A 72
Ellerdine Heath. *Telf* 3A 72
Ellerhayes. *Devn* 2C 12
Elleric. *Arg* 4E 141
Ellerker. *E Yor* 2C 94
Ellerton. *E Yor* 1H 93
Ellerton. *Shrp* 3B 72
Ellerton-on-Swale. *N Yor* 5F 105
Ellesborough. *Buck* 5G 51
Ellesmere. *Shrp* 2G 71
**Ellesmere Port**. *Ches W* 3G 83
Ellingham. *Hants* 2G 15
Ellingham. *Norf* 1F 67
Ellingham. *Nmbd* 2F 121
Ellingstring. *N Yor* 1D 98
Ellington. *Cambs* 3A 64
Ellington. *Nmbd* 5G 121
Ellington Thorpe. *Cambs* 3A 64
Elliot. *Ang* 5F 145
Ellisfield. *Hants* 2E 25
Ellishadder. *High* 2E 155
Ellistown. *Leics* 4B 74
Ellon. *Abers* 5G 161
Ellonby. *Cumb* 1F 103
Ellough. *Suff* 2G 67
Elloughton. *E Yor* 2C 94
Ellwood. *Glos* 5A 48
Elm. *Cambs* 5D 76
Elmbridge. *Glos* 4D 48
Elmbridge. *Worc* 4D 60
Elmdon. *Essx* 2E 53
Elmdon. *W Mid* 2F 61
Elmdon Heath. *W Mid* 2F 61
Elmesthorpe. *Leics* 1B 62
Elmfield. *IOW* 3E 16
Elm Hill. *Dors* 4D 22
Elmhurst. *Staf* 4F 73
Elmley Castle. *Worc* 1E 49
Elmley Lovett. *Worc* 4C 60
Elmore. *Glos* 4C 48
Elmore Back. *Glos* 4C 48
Elm Park. *G Lon* 2G 39
Elmscott. *Devn* 4C 18
Elmsett. *Suff* 1D 54
Elmstead. *Essx* 3D 54
Elmstead Heath. *Essx* 3D 54
Elmstead Market. *Essx* 3D 54
Elmsted. *Kent* 1F 29
Elmstone. *Kent* 4G 41
Elmstone Hardwicke. *Glos* 3E 49
Elmswell. *E Yor* 4D 101
Elmswell. *Suff* 4B 66
Elmton. *Derbs* 3C 86
Elphin. *High* 2G 163
Elphinstone. *E Lot* 2G 129
Elrick. *Abers* 3F 153
Elrick. *Mor* 1B 152
Elrig. *Dum* 5A 110
Elsdon. *Nmbd* 5D 120
Elsecar. *S Yor* 1A 86
Elsenham. *Essx* 3F 53
Elsfield. *Oxon* 4D 50
Elsham. *N Lin* 3D 94
Elsing. *Norf* 4C 78
Elslack. *N Yor* 5B 98
Elsrickle. *S Lan* 5D 128
Elstead. *Surr* 1A 26
Elsted. *W Sus* 1G 17
Elsted Marsh. *W Sus* 4G 25
Elsthorpe. *Linc* 3H 75
Elstob. *Dur* 2A 106
Elston. *Devn* 2A 12
Elston. *Lanc* 1E 90
Elston. *Notts* 1E 75
Elston. *Wilts* 2F 23
Elstone. *Devn* 1G 11
Elstow. *Bed* 1A 52
Elstree. *Herts* 1C 38
Elstronwick. *E Yor* 1F 95
Elswick. *Lanc* 1C 90
Elswick. *Tyne* 3F 115
Elsworth. *Cambs* 4C 64
Elterwater. *Cumb* 4E 103
**Eltham**. *G Lon* 3F 39
Eltisley. *Cambs* 5B 64
Elton. *Cambs* 1H 63
Elton. *Ches W* 3G 83
Elton. *Derbs* 4G 85
Elton. *Glos* 4C 48
Elton. *G Man* 3F 91
Elton. *Here* 3G 59
Elton. *Notts* 2E 75
Elton. *Stoc T* 3B 106
Elton Green. *Ches W* 3G 83
Eltringham. *Nmbd* 3D 115
Elvanfoot. *S Lan* 3B 118
Elvaston. *Derbs* 2B 74
Elveden. *Suff* 3H 65
Elvetham Heath. *Hants* 1F 25
Elvingston. *E Lot* 2A 130
Elvington. *Kent* 5G 41
Elvington. *York* 5B 100
Elwick. *Hart* 1B 106
Elwick. *Nmbd* 1F 121
Elworth. *Ches E* 4B 84
Elworth. *Dors* 4A 14
Elworthy. *Som* 3D 20
**Ely**. *Cambs* 2E 65
Ely. *Card* 4E 33
Emberton. *Mil* 1G 51
Embleton. *Cumb* 1C 102
Embleton. *Dur* 2B 106
Embleton. *Nmbd* 2G 121
Embo. *High* 4F 165
Emborough. *Som* 1B 22
Embo Street. *High* 4F 165
Embsay. *N Yor* 4C 98
Emery Down. *Hants* 2A 16
Emley. *W Yor* 3C 92
Emmbrook. *Wok* 5F 37
Emmer Green. *Read* 4F 37
Emmington. *Oxon* 5F 51
Emneth. *Norf* 5D 77
Emneth Hungate. *Norf* 5E 77
Empingham. *Rut* 5G 75
Empshott. *Hants* 3F 25
**Emsworth**. *Hants* 2F 17
Enborne. *W Ber* 5C 36
Enborne Row. *W Ber* 5C 36
Enchmarsh. *Shrp* 1H 59
Enderby. *Leics* 1C 62
Endmoor. *Cumb* 1E 97
Endon. *Staf* 5D 84
Endon Bank. *Staf* 5D 84
**Enfield**. *G Lon* 1E 39
Enfield Wash. *G Lon* 1E 39
Enford. *Wilts* 1G 23
Engine Common. *S Glo* 3B 34
Englefield. *W Ber* 4E 37
Englefield Green. *Surr* 3A 38
Englesea-brook. *Ches E* 5B 84
English Bicknor. *Glos* 4A 48
Englishcombe. *Bath* 5C 34
English Frankton. *Shrp* 3G 71
Enham Alamein. *Hants* 2B 24
Enmore. *Som* 3F 21
Ennerdale Bridge. *Cumb* 3B 102
Enniscaven. *Corn* 3D 6
**Enniskillen**. *Ferm* 8E 176
Enoch. *Dum* 4A 118
Enochdhu. *Per* 2H 143
Ensay. *Arg* 4E 139
Ensbury. *Bour* 3F 15
Ensdon. *Shrp* 4G 71
Ensis. *Devn* 4F 19
Enson. *Staf* 3D 72
Enstone. *Oxon* 3B 50
Enterkinfoot. *Dum* 4A 118
Enville. *Staf* 2C 60
Eolaigearraidh. *W Isl* 8C 170
Eorabus. *Arg* 1A 132
Eoropaidh. *W Isl* 1H 171
Epney. *Glos* 4C 48
Epperstone. *Notts* 1D 74
**Epping**. *Essx* 5E 53
Epping Green. *Essx* 5E 53
Epping Green. *Herts* 5C 52
Epping Upland. *Essx* 5E 53
Eppleby. *N Yor* 3E 105
Eppleworth. *E Yor* 1D 94
**Epsom**. *Surr* 4D 38
Epwell. *Oxon* 1B 50
Epworth. *N Lin* 4A 94
Epworth Turbary. *N Lin* 4A 94
Erbistock. *Wrex* 1F 71
Erbusaig. *High* 1F 147
Erchless Castle. *High* 4G 157
Erdington. *W Mid* 1F 61
Eredine. *Arg* 3G 133
Erganagh. *Derr* 4E 176
Eriboll. *High* 3E 167
Ericstane. *Dum* 3C 118
Eridge Green. *E Sus* 2G 27
Erines. *Arg* 2G 125
Eriswell. *Suff* 3G 65
**Erith**. *G Lon* 3G 39
Erlestoke. *Wilts* 1E 23
Ermine. *Linc* 3G 87
Ermington. *Devn* 3C 8
Ernesettle. *Plym* 3A 8
Erpingham. *Norf* 2D 78
Erriott Wood. *Kent* 5D 40
Errogie. *High* 1H 149
Errol. *Per* 1E 137
Errol Station. *Per* 1E 137
**Erskine**. *Ren* 2F 127
**Erskine Bridge**. *Ren* 2F 127
Ervie. *Dum* 3F 109
Erwarton. *Suff* 2F 55
Erwood. *Powy* 1D 46
Eryholme. *N Yor* 4A 106
Eryrys. *Den* 5E 82
Escalls. *Corn* 4A 4
Escomb. *Dur* 1E 105
Escrick. *N Yor* 5A 100
Esgair. *Carm* 3D 45
(nr. Carmarthen)
Esgair. *Carm* 3G 43
(nr. St Clears)
Esgairgeiliog. *Powy* 5G 69
Esh. *Dur* 5E 115
**Esher**. *Surr* 4C 38
Esholt. *W Yor* 5D 98
Eshott. *Nmbd* 5G 121
Eshton. *N Yor* 4B 98
Esh Winning. *Dur* 5E 115
Eskadale. *High* 5G 157
Eskbank. *Midl* 3G 129
Eskdale Green. *Cumb* 4C 102
Eskdalemuir. *Dum* 5E 119
Eskham. *Linc* 1C 88
Esknish. *Arg* 3B 124
Esk Valley. *N Yor* 4F 107
Eslington Hall. *Nmbd* 3E 121
Esprick. *Lanc* 1C 90
Essendine. *Rut* 4H 75
Essendon. *Herts* 5C 52
Essich. *High* 5A 158
Essington. *Staf* 5D 72
**Eston**. *Red C* 3C 106
Estover. *Plym* 3B 8
Eswick. *Shet* 6F 173
Etal. *Nmbd* 1D 120
Etchilhampton. *Wilts* 5F 35
Etchingham. *E Sus* 3B 28
Etchinghill. *Kent* 2F 29
Etchinghill. *Staf* 4E 73
Etherley Dene. *Dur* 2E 105
Ethie Haven. *Ang* 4F 145
Etling Green. *Norf* 4C 78
Etloe. *Glos* 5B 48
**Eton**. *Wind* 3A 38
Eton Wick. *Wind* 3A 38
Etteridge. *High* 4A 150
Ettersgill. *Dur* 2B 104
Ettiley Heath. *Ches E* 4B 84
Ettington. *Warw* 1A 50
Etton. *E Yor* 5D 101
Etton. *Pet* 5A 76
Ettrick. *Bord* 3E 119
Ettrickbridge. *Bord* 2F 119
Etwall. *Derbs* 2G 73
Eudon Burnell. *Shrp* 2B 60
Eudon George. *Shrp* 2A 60
Euston. *Suff* 3A 66
Euxton. *Lanc* 3D 90
Evanstown. *B'end* 3C 32
Evanton. *High* 2A 158
Evedon. *Linc* 1H 75
Evelix. *High* 4E 165
Evendine. *Here* 1C 48
Evenjobb. *Powy* 4E 59
Evenley. *Nptn* 2D 50
Evenlode. *Glos* 3H 49
Even Swindon. *Swin* 3G 35
Evenwood. *Dur* 2E 105
Evenwood Gate. *Dur* 2E 105
Everbay. *Orkn* 5F 172
Evercreech. *Som* 3B 22
Everdon. *Nptn* 5C 62
Everingham. *E Yor* 5C 100
Everleigh. *Wilts* 1H 23
Everley. *N Yor* 1D 100
Eversholt. *C Beds* 2H 51
Evershot. *Dors* 2A 14
Eversley. *Hants* 5F 37
Eversley Centre. *Hants* 5F 37
Eversley Cross. *Hants* 5F 37
Everthorpe. *E Yor* 1C 94
Everton. *C Beds* 5B 64
Everton. *Hants* 3A 16
Everton. *Mers* 1F 83
Everton. *Notts* 1D 86
Evertown. *Dum* 2E 113
Evesbatch. *Here* 1B 48
**Evesham**. *Worc* 1F 49
Evington. *Leic* 5D 74
Ewden Village. *S Yor* 1G 85
Ewdness. *Shrp* 1B 60
**Ewell**. *Surr* 4D 38
Ewell Minnis. *Kent* 1G 29
Ewelme. *Oxon* 2E 37
Ewen. *Glos* 2F 35
Ewenny. *V Glam* 4C 32
Ewerby. *Linc* 1A 76
Ewes. *Dum* 5F 119
Ewesley. *Nmbd* 5E 121
Ewhurst. *Surr* 1B 26
Ewhurst Green. *E Sus* 3B 28
Ewhurst Green. *Surr* 2B 26
Ewlo. *Flin* 4E 83
Ewloe. *Flin* 4E 83
Ewood Bridge. *Lanc* 2F 91
Eworthy. *Devn* 3E 11
Ewshot. *Hants* 1G 25
Ewyas Harold. *Here* 3G 47
Exbourne. *Devn* 2G 11
Exbury. *Hants* 2C 16
Exceat. *E Sus* 5G 27
Exebridge. *Som* 4C 20
Exelby. *N Yor* 1E 99
**Exeter**. *Devn* 3C 12 & 195
Exeter International Airport.
*Devn* 3D 12
Exford. *Som* 3B 20
Exfords Green. *Shrp* 5G 71
Exhall. *Warw* 5F 61
Exlade Street. *Oxon* 3E 37
Exminster. *Devn* 4C 12
**Exmoor**. *Som* 3B 20
**Exmouth**. *Devn* 4D 12
Exnaboe. *Shet* 10E 173
Exning. *Suff* 4F 65
Exton. *Devn* 4C 12
Exton. *Hants* 4E 24
Exton. *Rut* 4G 75
Exton. *Som* 3C 20
Exwick. *Devn* 3C 12
Eyam. *Derbs* 3G 85
Eydon. *Nptn* 5C 62
Eye. *Here* 4G 59
Eye. *Pet* 5B 76
Eye. *Suff* 3D 66
Eye Green. *Pet* 5B 76
Eyemouth. *Bord* 3F 131
Eyeworth. *C Beds* 1C 52
Eyhorne Street. *Kent* 5C 40
Eyke. *Suff* 5F 67
Eynesbury. *Cambs* 5A 64
Eynort. *High* 1B 146
Eynsford. *Kent* 4G 39
Eynsham. *Oxon* 5C 50
Eyre. *High* 3D 154
(on Isle of Skye)
Eyre. *High* 5E 155
(on Raasay)
Eythorne. *Kent* 1G 29
Eyton. *Here* 4G 59
Eyton. *Shrp* 2F 59
(nr. Bishop's Castle)
Eyton. *Shrp* 4F 71
(nr. Shrewsbury)
Eyton. *Wrex* 1F 71
Eyton on Severn. *Shrp* 5H 71
Eyton upon the Weald Moors.
*Telf* 4A 72

## F

Faccombe. *Hants* 1B 24
Faceby. *N Yor* 4B 106
Faddiley. *Ches E* 5H 83
Fadmoor. *N Yor* 1A 100
Fagwyr. *Swan* 5G 45
Faichem. *High* 3E 149
Faifley. *W Dun* 2G 127
Fail. *S Ayr* 2D 116
Failand. *N Som* 4A 34
Failford. *S Ayr* 2D 116
**Failsworth**. *G Man* 4H 91
Fairbourne. *Gwyn* 4F 69
Fairbourne Heath. *Kent* 5C 40
Fairburn. *N Yor* 2E 93
Fairfield. *Derbs* 3E 85
Fairfield. *Kent* 3D 28
Fairfield. *Worc* 3D 60
(nr. Bromsgrove)
Fairfield. *Worc* 1F 49
(nr. Evesham)
Fairford. *Glos* 5G 49
Fair Green. *Norf* 4F 77
Fair Hill. *Cumb* 1G 103
Fairhill. *S Lan* 4A 128
Fair Isle Airport. *Shet* 1B 172
Fairlands. *Surr* 5A 38
Fairlie. *N Ayr* 4D 126
Fairlight. *E Sus* 4C 28
Fairlight Cove. *E Sus* 4C 28
Fairmile. *Devn* 3D 12
Fairmile. *Surr* 4C 38
Fairmilehead. *Edin* 3F 129
Fair Oak. *Devn* 1D 12
Fair Oak. *Hants* 1C 16
(nr. Eastleigh)
Fair Oak. *Hants* 5D 36
(nr. Kingsclere)
Fairoak. *Staf* 2B 72
Fair Oak Green. *Hants* 5E 37
Fairseat. *Kent* 4H 39
Fairstead. *Essx* 4A 54
Fairstead. *Norf* 4F 77
Fairwarp. *E Sus* 3F 27
Fairwater. *Card* 4E 33
Fairy Cross. *Devn* 4E 19
Fakenham. *Norf* 3B 78
Fakenham Magna. *Suff* 3B 66
Fala. *Midl* 3H 129
Fala Dam. *Midl* 3H 129
Falcon. *Here* 2B 48
Faldingworth. *Linc* 2H 87
Falfield. *S Glo* 2B 34
Falkenham. *Suff* 2F 55
**Falkirk**. *Falk* 1B 128
Falkland. *Fife* 3E 137
Fallin. *Stir* 4H 135
Fallowfield. *G Man* 1C 84
Falmer. *E Sus* 5E 27
**Falmouth**. *Corn* 5C 6
Falsgrave. *N Yor* 1E 101
Falstone. *Nmbd* 1A 114
Fanagmore. *High* 4B 166
Fancott. *C Beds* 3A 52
Fanellan. *High* 4G 157
Fangdale Beck. *N Yor* 5C 106
Fangfoss. *E Yor* 4B 100
Fankerton. *Falk* 1A 128
Fanmore. *Arg* 4F 139
Fanner's Green. *Essx* 4G 53
Fannich Lodge. *High* 2E 156
Fans. *Bord* 5C 130
Farcet. *Cambs* 1B 64
Far Cotton. *Nptn* 5E 63
**Fareham**. *Hants* 2D 16
Farewell. *Staf* 4E 73
Far Forest. *Worc* 3B 60
Farforth. *Linc* 3C 88
Far Green. *Glos* 5C 48
Far Hoarcross. *Staf* 3F 73
Faringdon. *Oxon* 2A 36
Farington. *Lanc* 2D 90
Farlam. *Cumb* 4G 113
Farleigh. *N Som* 5H 33
Farleigh. *Surr* 4E 39
Farleigh Hungerford. *Som* 1D 22
Farleigh Wallop. *Hants* 2E 24
Farleigh Wick. *Wilts* 5D 34
Farlesthorpe. *Linc* 3D 88
Farleton. *Cumb* 1E 97
Farleton. *Lanc* 3E 97
Farley. *High* 4G 157
Farley. *Shrp* 5F 71
(nr. Shrewsbury)
Farley. *Shrp* 5A 72
(nr. Telford)
Farley. *Staf* 1E 73
Farley. *Wilts* 4H 23
Farley Green. *Suff* 5G 65
Farley Green. *Surr* 1B 26
Farley Hill. *Wok* 5F 37
Farley's End. *Glos* 4C 48
Farlington. *N Yor* 3A 100
Farlington. *Port* 2E 17
Farlow. *Shrp* 2A 60
Farmborough. *Bath* 5B 34
Farmcote. *Glos* 3F 49
Farmcote. *Shrp* 1B 60
Farmington. *Glos* 4G 49
Far Moor. *G Man* 4D 90
Farmoor. *Oxon* 5C 50
Farmtown. *Mor* 3C 160
Farnah Green. *Derbs* 1H 73
Farnborough. *G Lon* 4F 39
**Farnborough**. *Hants* 1G 25
Farnborough. *Warw* 1C 50
Farnborough. *W Ber* 3C 36
Farncombe. *Surr* 1A 26
Farndish. *Bed* 4G 63
Farndon. *Ches W* 5G 83
Farndon. *Notts* 5E 87
Farnell. *Ang* 3F 145
Farnham. *Dors* 1E 15
Farnham. *Essx* 3E 53
Farnham. *N Yor* 3F 99
Farnham. *Suff* 4F 67
**Farnham**. *Surr* 2G 25
Farnham Common. *Buck* 2A 38
Farnham Green. *Essx* 3E 53
Farnham Royal. *Buck* 2A 38
Farnhill. *N Yor* 5C 98
Farningham. *Kent* 4G 39
Farnley. *N Yor* 5E 98
Farnley Tyas. *W Yor* 3B 92
Farnsfield. *Notts* 5D 86
**Farnworth**. *G Man* 4F 91
Farnworth. *Hal* 2H 83
Far Oakridge. *Glos* 5E 49
Farr. *High* 2H 167
(nr. Bettyhill)
Farr. *High* 5A 158
(nr. Inverness)
Farr. *High* 3C 150
(nr. Kingussie)
Farraline. *High* 1H 149
Farringdon. *Devn* 3D 12
Farrington. *Dors* 1D 14
Farrington Gurney. *Bath* 1B 22
Far Sawrey. *Cumb* 5E 103
Farsley. *W Yor* 1C 92
Farthinghoe. *Nptn* 2D 50
Farthingstone. *Nptn* 5D 62
Farthorpe. *Linc* 3B 88
Fartown. *W Yor* 3B 92
Farway. *Devn* 3E 13
Fasag. *High* 3A 156
Fascadale. *High* 1G 139
Fasnacloich. *Arg* 4E 141
Fassfern. *High* 1E 141
Fatfield. *Tyne* 4G 115
Faugh. *Cumb* 4G 113
Fauld. *Staf* 3F 73
Fauldhouse. *W Lot* 3C 128
Faulkbourne. *Essx* 4A 54
Faulkland. *Som* 1C 22
Fauls. *Shrp* 2H 71
Faverdale. *Darl* 3F 105
**Faversham**. *Kent* 4E 40
Fawdington. *N Yor* 2G 99
Fawfieldhead. *Staf* 4E 85
Fawkham Green. *Kent* 4G 39
Fawler. *Oxon* 4B 50
Fawley. *Buck* 3F 37
**Fawley**. *Hants* 2C 16
Fawley. *W Ber* 3B 36
Fawley Chapel. *Here* 3A 48
Fawton. *Corn* 2F 7
Faxfleet. *E Yor* 2B 94
Faygate. *W Sus* 2D 26
Fazakerley. *Mers* 1F 83
Fazeley. *Staf* 5F 73
Feagour. *High* 4H 149
Fearann Dhomhnaill. *High* 3E 147
Fearby. *N Yor* 1D 98
Fearn. *High* 1C 158
Fearnan. *Per* 4E 142
Fearnbeg. *High* 3G 155
Fearnhead. *Warr* 1A 84
Fearnmore. *High* 2G 155
Featherstone. *Staf* 5D 72
**Featherstone**. *W Yor* 2E 93
Featherstone Castle.
*Nmbd* 3H 113
Feckenham. *Worc* 4E 61
Feeny. *Caus* 6C 174
Feering. *Essx* 3B 54
Feetham. *N Yor* 5C 104
Feizor. *N Yor* 3G 97
Felbridge. *Surr* 2E 27
Felbrigg. *Norf* 2E 78
Felcourt. *Surr* 1E 27
Felden. *Herts* 5A 52
Felhampton. *Shrp* 2G 59
Felindre. *Carm* 3F 45
(nr. Llandeilo)
Felindre. *Carm* 2G 45
(nr. Llandovery)
Felindre. *Carm* 2D 44
(nr. Newcastle Emlyn)
Felindre. *Powy* 2D 58
Felindre. *Swan* 5G 45
Felindre Farchog. *Pemb* 1F 43
Felinfach. *Cdgn* 5E 57
Felinfach. *Powy* 2D 46
Felinfoel. *Carm* 5F 45
Felingwmisaf. *Carm* 3F 45
Felingwmuchaf. *Carm* 3F 45
Felin Newydd. *Powy* 5C 70
(nr. Newtown)
Felin Newydd. *Powy* 3E 70
(nr. Oswestry)
Felin Wnda. *Cdgn* 1D 44
Felinwynt. *Cdgn* 5B 56
Felixkirk. *N Yor* 1G 99
**Felixstowe**. *Suff* 2F 55
Felixstowe Ferry. *Suff* 2G 55
Felkington. *Nmbd* 5F 131
Fell End. *Cumb* 5A 104
**Felling**. *Tyne* 3F 115
Fell Side. *Cumb* 1E 102
Felmersham. *Bed* 5G 63
Felmingham. *Norf* 3E 79
Felpham. *W Sus* 3H 17
Felsham. *Suff* 5B 66
Felsted. *Essx* 3G 53
**Feltham**. *G Lon* 3C 38
Felthamhill. *Surr* 3B 38
Felthorpe. *Norf* 4D 78
Felton. *Here* 1A 48
Felton. *N Som* 5A 34
Felton. *Nmbd* 4F 121
Felton Butler. *Shrp* 4F 71
Feltwell. *Norf* 1G 65
Fenay Bridge. *W Yor* 3B 92
Fence. *Lanc* 1G 91
Fence Houses. *Tyne* 4G 115
Fencott. *Oxon* 4D 50
Fen Ditton. *Cambs* 4D 65
Fen Drayton. *Cambs* 4C 64
Fen End. *Linc* 3B 76
Fen End. *W Mid* 3G 61
Fenham. *Nmbd* 5G 131
Fenham. *Tyne* 3F 115
Fenhouses. *Linc* 1B 76
Feniscowles. *Bkbn* 2E 91
Feniton. *Devn* 3D 12
Fenn Green. *Shrp* 2B 60
Fenn's Bank. *Wrex* 2H 71
Fenn Street. *Medw* 3B 40
Fenny Bentley. *Derbs* 5F 85
Fenny Bridges. *Devn* 3E 12
Fenny Compton. *Warw* 5B 62
Fenny Drayton. *Leics* 1H 61
Fenny Stratford. *Mil* 2G 51
Fenrother. *Nmbd* 5F 121
Fenstanton. *Cambs* 4C 64
Fen Street. *Norf* 1C 66
Fenton. *Cambs* 3C 64
Fenton. *Cumb* 4G 113
Fenton. *Linc* 5F 87
(nr. Caythorpe)
Fenton. *Linc* 3F 87
(nr. Saxilby)
Fenton. *Nmbd* 1D 120
Fenton. *Notts* 2E 87
Fenton. *Stoke* 1C 72
Fentonadle. *Corn* 5A 10
Fenton Barns. *E Lot* 1B 130
Fenwick. *E Ayr* 5F 127
Fenwick. *Nmbd* 5G 131
(nr. Berwick-upon-Tweed)
Fenwick. *Nmbd* 2D 114
(nr. Hexham)
Fenwick. *S Yor* 3F 93
Feochaig. *Arg* 4B 122
Feock. *Corn* 5C 6
Feolin Ferry. *Arg* 3C 124
Feorlan. *Arg* 5A 122
Ferindonald. *High* 3E 147
Feriniquarrie. *High* 3A 154
Fern. *Ang* 2D 145
**Ferndale**. *Rhon* 2C 32
**Ferndown**. *Dors* 2F 15
Ferness. *High* 4D 158
Fernham. *Oxon* 2A 36
Fernhill. *W Sus* 1E 27
Fernhill Heath. *Worc* 5C 60
Fernhurst. *W Sus* 4G 25
Fernieflatt. *Abers* 1H 145
Ferniegair. *S Lan* 4A 128
Fernilea. *High* 5C 154
Fernilee. *Derbs* 3E 85
Ferrensby. *N Yor* 3F 99
Ferriby Sluice. *N Lin* 2C 94
Ferring. *W Sus* 5B 26
Ferrybridge. *W Yor* 2E 93
Ferryden. *Ang* 3G 145
Ferryhill. *Aber* 3G 153
Ferry Hill. *Cambs* 2C 64
**Ferryhill**. *Dur* 1F 105
Ferryhill Station. *Dur* 1A 106
Ferryside. *Carm* 4D 44
Ferryton. *High* 2A 158
Fersfield. *Norf* 2C 66
Fersit. *High* 1A 142
Feshiebridge. *High* 3C 150
Fetcham. *Surr* 5C 38
Fetterangus. *Abers* 3G 161
Fettercairn. *Abers* 1F 145
Fewcott. *Oxon* 3D 50
Fewston. *N Yor* 4D 98
Ffairfach. *Carm* 3G 45
Ffair Rhos. *Cdgn* 4G 57
Ffaldybrenin. *Carm* 1G 45
Ffarmers. *Carm* 1G 45
Ffawyddog. *Powy* 4F 47
Ffodun. *Powy* 5E 71
Ffont-y-gari. *V Glam* 5D 32
Fforest. *Carm* 5F 45
Fforest-fach. *Swan* 3F 31
Fforest Goch. *Neat* 5H 45
Ffostrasol. *Cdgn* 1D 44
Ffos-y-ffin. *Cdgn* 4D 56
Ffrith. *Flin* 5E 83
Ffwl-y-mwn. *V Glam* 5D 32
Ffynnon-ddrain. *Carm* 3E 45
Ffynnongroyw. *Flin* 2D 82
Ffynnon Gynydd. *Powy* 1E 47
Ffynnon-oer. *Cdgn* 5E 57
Fiag Lodge. *High* 1B 164
Fidden. *Arg* 2B 132
Fiddington. *Glos* 2E 49
Fiddington. *Som* 2F 21
Fiddleford. *Dors* 1D 14
Fiddlers Hamlet. *Essx* 5E 53
Field. *Staf* 2E 73
Field Assarts. *Oxon* 4B 50
Field Broughton. *Cumb* 1C 96
Field Dalling. *Norf* 2C 78
Fieldhead. *Cumb* 1F 103
Field Head. *Leics* 5B 74
Fifehead Magdalen. *Dors* 4C 22
Fifehead Neville. *Dors* 1C 14
Fifehead St Quintin. *Dors* 1C 14
Fife Keith. *Mor* 3B 160
Fifield. *Oxon* 4H 49
Fifield. *Wilts* 1G 23
Fifield. *Wind* 3A 38
Fifield Bavant. *Wilts* 4F 23
Figheldean. *Wilts* 2G 23
Filby. *Norf* 4G 79
Filey. *N Yor* 1F 101
Filford. *Dors* 3H 13
Filgrave. *Mil* 1G 51
Filkins. *Oxon* 5H 49
Filleigh. *Devn* 1H 11
(nr. Crediton)
Filleigh. *Devn* 4G 19
(nr. South Molton)
Fillingham. *Linc* 2G 87
Fillongley. *Warw* 2G 61
Filton. *S Glo* 4B 34
Fimber. *E Yor* 3C 100
Finavon. *Ang* 3D 145
Fincham. *Norf* 5F 77
Finchampstead. *Wok* 5F 37
Fincharn. *Arg* 3G 133
Finchdean. *Hants* 1F 17
Finchingfield. *Essx* 2G 53
**Finchley**. *G Lon* 1D 38
Findern. *Derbs* 2H 73
Findhorn. *Mor* 2E 159
Findhorn Bridge. *High* 1C 150
Findochty. *Mor* 2B 160
Findo Gask. *Per* 1C 136
Findon. *Abers* 4G 153
Findon. *W Sus* 5C 26
Findon Mains. *High* 2A 158
Findon Valley. *W Sus* 5C 26
Finedon. *Nptn* 3G 63
Fingal Street. *Suff* 3E 66
Fingest. *Buck* 2F 37
Finghall. *N Yor* 1D 98
Fingland. *Cumb* 4D 112
Fingland. *Dum* 3G 117
Finglesham. *Kent* 5H 41
Fingringhoe. *Essx* 3D 54
Finiskaig. *High* 4A 148
Finmere. *Oxon* 2E 51
Finnart. *Per* 3C 142
Finningham. *Suff* 4C 66
Finningley. *S Yor* 1D 86
Finnygaud. *Abers* 3D 160
**Finsbury**. *G Lon* 2E 39
Finstall. *Worc* 4D 61
Finsthwaite. *Cumb* 1C 96
Finstock. *Oxon* 4B 50
Finstown. *Orkn* 6C 172
Fintona. *Ferm* 3K 177
Fintry. *Abers* 3E 161
Fintry. *D'dee* 5D 144
Fintry. *Stir* 1H 127
Finvoy. *Caus* 5F 175
Finwood. *Warw* 4F 61
Finzean. *Abers* 4D 152
Fionnphort. *Arg* 2B 132
Fionnsabhagh. *W Isl* 9C 171
Firbeck. *S Yor* 2C 86
Firby. *N Yor* 1E 99
(nr. Bedale)
Firby. *N Yor* 3B 100
(nr. Malton)
Firgrove. *G Man* 3H 91
Firle. *E Sus* 5F 27
Firsby. *Linc* 4D 88
Firsdown. *Wilts* 3H 23
First Coast. *High* 4D 162
Firth. *Shet* 4F 173
Fir Tree. *Dur* 1E 105
Fishbourne. *IOW* 3D 16
Fishbourne. *W Sus* 2G 17
Fishburn. *Dur* 1A 106
Fishcross. *Clac* 4A 136
Fisherford. *Abers* 5D 160
Fisherrow. *E Lot* 2G 129
Fisher's Pond. *Hants* 4C 24
Fisher's Row. *Lanc* 5D 96
Fisherstreet. *W Sus* 2A 26
Fisherton. *High* 3B 158
Fisherton. *S Ayr* 3B 116
Fisherton de la Mere. *Wilts* 3E 23
Fishguard. *Pemb* 1D 42
Fishlake. *S Yor* 3G 93
Fishley. *Norf* 4G 79
Fishnish. *Arg* 4A 140
Fishpond Bottom. *Dors* 3G 13
Fishponds. *Bris* 4B 34
Fishpool. *Glos* 3B 48
Fishpool. *G Man* 3G 91
Fishpools. *Powy* 4D 58
Fishtoft. *Linc* 1C 76
Fishtoft Drove. *Linc* 1C 76
Fishwick. *Bord* 4F 131
Fiskavaig. *High* 5C 154
Fiskerton. *Linc* 3H 87
Fiskerton. *Notts* 5E 87
Fitch. *Shet* 7E 173
Fitling. *E Yor* 1F 95
Fittleton. *Wilts* 2G 23
Fittleworth. *W Sus* 4B 26
Fitton End. *Cambs* 4D 76
Fitz. *Shrp* 4G 71
Fitzhead. *Som* 4E 20
Fitzwilliam. *W Yor* 3E 93
Fiunary. *High* 4A 140
Five Ash Down. *E Sus* 3F 27
Five Ashes. *E Sus* 3G 27
Five Bells. *Som* 2D 20
Five Bridges. *Here* 1B 48
Fivehead. *Som* 4G 21
Fivelanes. *Corn* 4C 10
Fivemiletown. *M Ulst* 5K 177
Five Oak Green. *Kent* 1H 27
Five Oaks. *W Sus* 3B 26
Five Roads. *Carm* 5E 45
Five Ways. *Warw* 3G 61
Flack's Green. *Essx* 4A 54
Flackwell Heath. *Buck* 3G 37
Fladbury. *Worc* 1E 49
Fladda. *Shet* 3E 173
Fladdabister. *Shet* 8F 173
Flagg. *Derbs* 4F 85
Flamborough. *E Yor* 2G 101
Flamstead. *Herts* 4A 52
Flansham. *W Sus* 5A 26
Flasby. *N Yor* 4B 98
Flash. *Staf* 4E 85
Flashader. *High* 3C 154
Flatt, The. *Cumb* 2G 113
Flaunden. *Herts* 5A 52

Flawborough—Glenfarquhar Lodge

Flawborough. Notts 1E 75
Flawith. N Yor 3G 99
Flax Bourton. N Som 5A 34
Flaxby. N Yor 4F 99
Flaxholme. Derbs 1H 73
Flaxley. Glos 4B 48
Flaxley Green. Staf 4E 73
Flaxpool. Som 3E 21
Flaxton. N Yor 3A 100
Fleck. Shet 10E 173
Fleckney. Leics 1D 62
Flecknoe. Warw 4C 62
Fledborough. Notts 3F 87
Fleet. Dors 4B 14
**Fleet**. Hants 1G 25
(nr. Farnborough)
Fleet. Hants 2F 17
(nr. South Hayling)
Fleet. Linc 3C 76
Fleet Hargate. Linc 3C 76
Fleetville. Herts 5B 52
**Fleetwood**. Lanc 5C 96
Fleggburgh. Norf 4G 79
Fleisirin. W Isl 4H 171
Flemingston. V Glam 5D 32
Flemington. S Lan 3H 127
(nr. Glasgow)
Flemington. S Lan 5A 128
(nr. Strathaven)
Flempton. Suff 4H 65
Fleoideabhagh. W Isl 9C 171
Fletcher's Green. Kent 1G 27
Fletchertown. Cumb 5D 112
Fletching. E Sus 3F 27
Fleuchary. High 4E 165
Flexbury. Corn 2C 10
Flexford. Surr 1A 26
Flimby. Cumb 1B 102
Flimwell. E Sus 2B 28
**Flint**. Flin 3E 83
Flintham. Notts 1E 75
Flint Mountain. Flin 3E 83
Flinton. E Yor 1F 95
Flintsham. Here 5F 59
Flishinghurst. Kent 2B 28
Flitcham. Norf 3G 77
Flitton. C Beds 2A 52
**Flitwick**. C Beds 2A 52
Flixborough. N Lin 3B 94
Flixton. G Man 1B 84
Flixton. N Yor 2E 101
Flixton. Suff 2F 67
Flockton. W Yor 3C 92
Flodden. Nmbd 1D 120
Flodigarry. High 1D 154
Flood's Ferry. Cambs 1C 64
Flookburgh. Cumb 2C 96
Flordon. Norf 1D 66
Flore. Nptn 4D 62
Flotterton. Nmbd 4E 121
Flowton. Suff 1D 54
Flushing. Abers 4H 161
Flushing. Corn 5C 6
Fluxton. Devn 3D 12
Flyford Flavell. Worc 5D 61
Fobbing. Thur 2B 40
Fochabers. Mor 3H 159
Fochriw. Cphy 5E 46
Fockerby. N Lin 3B 94
Fodderty. High 3H 157
Foddington. Som 4A 22
Foel. Powy 4B 70
Foffarty. Ang 4D 144
Foggathorpe. E Yor 1A 94
Fogo. Bord 5D 130
Fogorig. Bord 5D 130
Foindle. High 4B 166
Folda. Ang 2A 144
Fole. Staf 2E 73
Foleshill. W Mid 2A 62
Foley Park. Worc 3C 60
Folke. Dors 1B 14
**Folkestone**. Kent 2G 29 & 195
Folkingham. Linc 2H 75
Folkington. E Sus 5G 27
Folksworth. Cambs 2A 64
Folkton. N Yor 2E 101
Folla Rule. Abers 5E 161
Follifoot. N Yor 4F 99
Folly Cross. Devn 2E 11
Folly Gate. Devn 3F 11
Folly, The. Herts 4B 52
Fonmon. V Glam 5D 32
Fonthill Bishop. Wilts 3E 23
Fonthill Gifford. Wilts 3E 23
Fontmell Magna. Dors 1D 14
Fontwell. W Sus 5A 26
Font-y-gary. V Glam 5D 32
Foodieash. Fife 2F 137
Foolow. Derbs 3F 85
Footdee. Aber 3G 153
Footherley. Staf 5F 73
Foots Cray. G Lon 3F 39
Forbestown. Abers 2A 152
Force Forge. Cumb 5E 103
Force Mills. Cumb 5E 103
Forcett. N Yor 3E 105
Ford. Arg 3F 133
Ford. Buck 5F 51
Ford. Derbs 2B 86
Ford. Devn 4E 19
(nr. Bideford)
Ford. Devn 3C 8
(nr. Holbeton)
Ford. Devn 4D 9
(nr. Salcombe)
Ford. Glos 3F 49
Ford. Nmbd 1D 120
Ford. Plym 3A 8
Ford. Shrp 4G 71
Ford. Som 1A 22
(nr. Wells)
Ford. Som 4D 20
(nr. Wiveliscombe)
Ford. Staf 5E 85
Ford. W Sus 5B 26
Ford. Wilts 4D 34
(nr. Chippenham)
Ford. Wilts 3G 23
(nr. Salisbury)
Forda. Devn 3E 19
Ford Barton. Devn 1C 12
Fordcombe. Kent 1G 27
Fordell. Fife 1E 129
Forden. Powy 5E 71
Ford End. Essx 4G 53
Forder Green. Devn 2D 9
Ford Green. Lanc 5D 97
Fordham. Cambs 3F 65
Fordham. Essx 3C 54
Fordham. Norf 1F 65
Fordham Heath. Essx 3C 54
Ford Heath. Shrp 4G 71
Fordhouses. W Mid 5D 72
Fordie. Per 1G 135
Fordingbridge. Hants 1G 15
Fordington. Linc 3D 88
Fordon. E Yor 2E 101
Fordoun. Abers 1G 145
Ford Street. Essx 3C 54
Ford Street. Som 1E 13
Fordton. Devn 3B 12
Fordwells. Oxon 4B 50
Fordwich. Kent 5F 41
Fordyce. Abers 2C 160
Forebridge. Staf 3D 72
Foreglen. Caus 6C 174
Foremark. Derbs 3H 73
Forest. N Yor 4F 105
Forestburn Gate. Nmbd 5E 121
Foresterseat. Mor 3F 159
Forest Green. Glos 2D 34
Forest Green. Surr 1C 26
Forest Hall. Cumb 4G 103
Forest Head. Cumb 4G 113
Forest Hill. Oxon 5D 50
Forest-in-Teesdale. Dur 2B 104
Forest Lodge. Per 1G 143
Forest Mill. Clac 4B 136
Forest Row. E Sus 2F 27
Forestside. W Sus 1F 17
Forest Town. Notts 4C 86
**Forfar**. Ang 3D 144
Forgandenny. Per 2C 136
Forge. Powy 1G 57
Forge Side. Torf 5F 47
Forge, The. Here 5F 59
Forgewood. N Lan 4A 128
Forgie. Mor 3A 160
Forgue. Abers 4D 160
Forkill. New M 8E 178
**Formby**. Mers 4B 90
Forncett End. Norf 1D 66
Forncett St Mary. Norf 1D 66
Forncett St Peter. Norf 1D 66
Forneth. Per 4H 143
Fornham All Saints. Suff 4H 65
Fornham St Martin. Suff 4A 66
Forres. Mor 3E 159
Forrestfield. N Lan 3B 128
Forrest Lodge. Dum 1C 110
Forsbrook. Staf 1D 72
Forse. High 5E 169
Forsinard. High 4A 168
Forss. High 2C 168
Forstal, The. Kent 2E 29
Forston. Dors 3B 14
Fort Augustus. High 3F 149
Forteviot. Per 2C 136
Fort George. High 3B 158
Forth. S Lan 4C 128
Forthampton. Glos 2D 48
Forthay. Glos 2C 34
**Forth Road Bridge**. Fife 2E 129
Fortingall. Per 4E 143
Fort Matilda. Inv 2D 126
Forton. Hants 2C 24
Forton. Lanc 4D 97
Forton. Shrp 4G 71
Forton. Som 2G 13
Forton. Staf 3B 72
Forton Heath. Shrp 4G 71
Fortrie. Abers 4D 160
Fortrose. High 3B 158
Fortuneswell. Dors 5B 14
**Fort William**. High 1F 141
Forty Green. Buck 1A 38
Forty Hill. G Lon 1E 39
Forward Green. Suff 5C 66
Fosbury. Wilts 1B 24
Foscot. Oxon 3H 49
Fosdyke. Linc 2C 76
Foss. Per 3E 143
Fossebridge. Glos 4F 49
Foster Street. Essx 5E 53
Foston. Derbs 2F 73
Foston. Leics 1D 62
Foston. Linc 1F 75
Foston. N Yor 3A 100
Foston on the Wolds. E Yor 4F 101
Fotherby. Linc 1C 88
Fothergill. Cumb 1B 102
Fotheringhay. Nptn 1H 63
Foubister. Orkn 7E 172
Foula Airport. Shet 8A 173
Foul Anchor. Cambs 4D 76
Foulbridge. Cumb 5F 113
Foulden. Norf 1G 65
Foulden. Bord 4F 131
Foul Mile. E Sus 4H 27
Foulridge. Lanc 5A 98
Foulsham. Norf 3C 78
Fountainhall. Bord 5H 129
Four Alls, The. Shrp 2A 72
Four Ashes. Staf 5D 72
(nr. Cannock)
Four Ashes. Staf 2C 60
(nr. Kinver)
Four Ashes. Suff 3C 66
Four Crosses. Powy 5C 70
(nr. Llanerfyl)
Four Crosses. Powy 4E 71
(nr. Llanymynech)
Four Crosses. Staf 5D 72
Four Elms. Kent 1F 27
Four Forks. Som 3F 21
Four Gotes. Cambs 4D 76
Four Lane End. S Yor 4C 92
Four Lane Ends. Lanc 4E 97
Four Lanes. Corn 5A 6
Fourlanes End. Ches E 5C 84
Four Marks. Hants 3E 25
Four Mile Bridge. IOA 3B 80
Four Oaks. E Sus 3C 28
Four Oaks. Glos 3B 48
Four Oaks. W Mid 2G 61
Four Roads. Carm 5E 45
Four Roads. IOM 5B 108
Fourstones. Nmbd 3B 114
Four Throws. Kent 3B 28
Fovant. Wilts 4F 23
Foveran. Abers 1G 153
Fowey. Corn 3F 7
Fowlershill. Abers 2G 153
Fowley Common. Warr 1A 84
Fowlis. Ang 5C 144
Fowlis Wester. Per 1B 136
Fowlmere. Cambs 1E 53
Fownhope. Here 2A 48
Fox Corner. Surr 5A 38
Foxcote. Glos 4F 49
Foxcote. Som 1C 22
Foxdale. IOM 4B 108
Foxearth. Essx 1B 54
Foxfield. Cumb 1B 96
Foxham. Wilts 4E 35
Fox Hatch. Essx 1G 39
Foxhole. Corn 3D 6
Foxholes. N Yor 2E 101
Foxhunt Green. E Sus 4G 27
Fox Lane. Hants 1G 25
Foxley. Norf 3C 78
Foxley. Nptn 5D 62
Foxley. Wilts 3D 35
Foxlydiate. Worc 4E 61
Fox Street. Essx 3D 54
Foxt. Staf 1E 73
Foxton. Cambs 1E 53
Foxton. Dur 2A 106
Foxton. Leics 2D 62
Foxton. N Yor 5B 106
Foxup. N Yor 2A 98
Foxwist Green. Ches W 4A 84
Foxwood. Shrp 3A 60
Foy. Here 3A 48
Foyers. High 1G 149
Foynesfield. High 3C 158
Fraddam. Corn 3C 4
Fraddon. Corn 3D 6
Fradley. Staf 4F 73
Fradley South. Staf 4F 73
Fradswell. Staf 2D 73
Fraisthorpe. E Yor 3F 101
Framfield. E Sus 3F 27
Framingham Earl. Norf 5E 79
Framingham Pigot. Norf 5E 79
Framlingham. Suff 4E 67
Frampton. Dors 3B 14
Frampton. Linc 2C 76
Frampton Cotterell. S Glo 3B 34
Frampton Mansell. Glos 5E 49
Frampton on Severn. Glos 5C 48
Frampton West End. Linc 1B 76
Framsden. Suff 5D 66
Framwellgate Moor. Dur 5F 115
Franche. Worc 3C 60
Frandley. Ches W 3A 84
Frankby. Mers 2E 83
Frankfort. Norf 3F 79
Frankley. Worc 2D 61
Frank's Bridge. Powy 5D 58
Frankton. Warw 3B 62
Frankwell. Shrp 4G 71
Frant. E Sus 2G 27
**Fraserburgh**. Abers 2G 161
Frating Green. Essx 3D 54
Fratton. Port 2E 17
Freathy. Corn 3A 8
Freckenham. Suff 3F 65
Freckleton. Lanc 2C 90
Freeby. Leics 3F 75
Freefolk Priors. Hants 2C 24
Freehay. Staf 1E 73
Freeland. Oxon 4C 50
Freester. Shet 6F 173
Freethorpe. Norf 5G 79
Freiston. Linc 1C 76
Freiston Shore. Linc 1C 76
Fremington. Devn 3F 19
Fremington. N Yor 5D 104
Frenchay. S Glo 4B 34
Frenchbeer. Devn 4G 11
Frenich. Stir 3D 134
Frensham. Surr 2G 25
Frenze. Norf 2D 66
Fresgoe. High 2B 168
Freshfield. Mers 4A 90
Freshford. Bath 5C 34
Freshwater. IOW 4B 16
Freshwater Bay. IOW 4B 16
Freshwater East. Pemb 5E 43
Fressingfield. Suff 3E 67
Freston. Suff 2E 55
Freswick. High 2F 169
Fretherne. Glos 5C 48
Frettenham. Norf 4E 79
Freuchie. Fife 3E 137
Freystrop. Pemb 3D 42
Friar's Gate. E Sus 2F 27
Friar Waddon. Dors 4B 14
Friday Bridge. Cambs 5D 76
Friday Street. E Sus 5H 27
Friday Street. Surr 1C 26
Fridaythorpe. E Yor 4C 100
Friden. Derbs 4F 85
Friern Barnet. G Lon 1D 39
Friesthorpe. Linc 2H 87
Frieston. Linc 1G 75
Frieth. Buck 2F 37
Friezeland. Notts 5B 86
Frilford. Oxon 2C 36
Frilsham. W Ber 4D 36
**Frimley**. Surr 1G 25
Frimley Green. Surr 1G 25
Frindsbury. Medw 4B 40
Fring. Norf 2G 77
Fringford. Oxon 3E 50
Frinsted. Kent 5C 40
**Frinton-on-Sea**. Essx 4F 55
Friockheim. Ang 4E 145
Friog. Gwyn 4F 69
Frisby. Leics 5E 74
Frisby on the Wreake. Leics 4D 74
Friskney. Linc 5D 88
Friskney Eaudyke. Linc 5D 88
Friston. E Sus 5G 27
Friston. Suff 4G 67
Fritchley. Derbs 5A 86
Fritham. Hants 1H 15
Frith Bank. Linc 1C 76
Frith Common. Worc 4A 60
Frithelstock. Devn 1E 11
Frithelstock Stone. Devn 1E 11
Frithsden. Herts 5A 52
Frithville. Linc 5C 88
Frittenden. Kent 1C 28
Frittiscombe. Devn 4E 9
Fritton. Norf 5G 79
(nr. Great Yarmouth)
Fritton. Norf 1E 67
(nr. Long Stratton)
Fritwell. Oxon 3D 50
Frizinghall. W Yor 1B 92
Frizington. Cumb 3B 102
Frobost. W Isl 6C 170
Frocester. Glos 5C 48
Frochas. Powy 5D 70
Frodesley. Shrp 5H 71
Frodingham. N Lin 3C 94
Frodsham. Ches W 3H 83
Froggatt. Derbs 3G 85
Froghall. Staf 1E 73
Frogham. Hants 1G 15
Frogham. Kent 5G 41
Frogmore. Devn 4D 8
**Frogmore**. Hants 5G 37
Frogmore. Herts 5B 52
Frognall. Linc 4A 76
Frogshall. Norf 2E 79
Frogwell. Corn 2H 7
Frolesworth. Leics 1C 62
**Frome**. Som 2C 22
Fromefield. Som 2C 22
Frome St Quintin. Dors 2A 14
Fromes Hill. Here 1B 48
Fron. Gwyn 2C 68
Fron. Powy 4C 58
(nr. Llandrindod Wells)
Fron. Powy 1D 58
(nr. Newtown)
Fron. Powy 5E 71
(nr. Welshpool)
Froncysyllte. Wrex 1E 71
Frongoch. Gwyn 2B 70
Fron Isaf. Wrex 1E 71
Fronoleu. Gwyn 2G 69
Frosterley. Dur 1D 104
Frotoft. Orkn 5D 172
Froxfield. C Beds 2H 51
Froxfield. Wilts 5A 36
Froxfield Green. Hants 4F 25
Fryern Hill. Hants 4C 24
Fryerning. Essx 5G 53
Fryton. N Yor 2A 100
Fugglestone St Peter. Wilts 3G 23
Fulbeck. Linc 5G 87
Fulbourn. Cambs 5E 65
Fulbrook. Oxon 4A 50
Fulflood. Hants 3C 24
Fulford. Som 4F 21
Fulford. Staf 2D 72
Fulford. York 5A 100
**Fulham**. G Lon 3D 38
Fulking. W Sus 4D 26
Fuller's Moor. Ches W 5G 83
Fuller Street. Essx 4H 53
Fullerton. Hants 3B 24
Fulletby. Linc 3B 88
Full Sutton. E Yor 4B 100
Fullwood. E Ayr 4F 127
Fulmer. Buck 2A 38
Fulmodestone. Norf 2B 78
Fulnetby. Linc 3H 87
Fulney. Linc 3B 76
Fulstow. Linc 1C 88
Fulthorpe. Stoc T 2B 106
Fulwell. Tyne 4G 115
Fulwood. Lanc 1D 90
Fulwood. Notts 5B 86
Fulwood. Som 1F 13
Fulwood. S Yor 2G 85
Fundenhall. Norf 1D 66
Funtington. W Sus 2G 17
Funtley. Hants 2D 16
Funzie. Shet 2H 173
Furley. Devn 2F 13
Furnace. Arg 3H 133
Furnace. Carm 5F 45
Furnace. Cdgn 1F 57
Furner's Green. E Sus 3F 27
Furness Vale. Derbs 2E 85
Furneux Pelham. Herts 3E 53
Furzebrook. Dors 4E 15
Furzehill. Devn 2H 19
Furzehill. Dors 2F 15
Furzeley Corner. Hants 1E 17
Furzey Lodge. Hants 2B 16
Furzley. Hants 1A 16
Fyfield. Essx 5F 53
Fyfield. Glos 5H 49
Fyfield. Hants 2A 24
Fyfield. Oxon 2C 36
Fyfield. Wilts 5G 35
**Fylde, The**. Lanc 1B 90
Fylingthorpe. N Yor 4G 107
Fyning. W Sus 4G 25
Fyvie. Abers 5E 161

## G

Gabhsann bho Dheas.
W Isl 2G 171
Gabhsann bho Thuath.
W Isl 2G 171
Gabroc Hill. E Ayr 4F 127
Gadbrook. Surr 1D 26
Gaddesby. Leics 4D 74
Gadfa. IOA 2D 80
Gadgirth. S Ayr 2D 116
Gaer. Powy 3E 47
Gaerwen. IOA 3D 81
Gagingwell. Oxon 3C 50
Gaick Lodge. High 5B 150
Gailey. Staf 4D 72
Gainford. Dur 3E 105
**Gainsborough**. Linc 1F 87
Gainsborough. Suff 1E 55
Gainsford End. Essx 2H 53
Gairletter. Arg 1C 126
Gairloch. Abers 3E 153
Gairloch. High 1H 155
Gairlochy. High 5D 148
Gairney Bank. Per 4D 136
Gairnshiel Lodge. Abers 3G 151
Gaisgill. Cumb 4H 103
Gaitsgill. Cumb 5E 113
**Galashiels**. Bord 1G 119
Galgate. Lanc 4D 97
Galgorm. ME Ant 6G 175
Galhampton. Som 4B 22
Gallatown. Fife 4E 137
Galley Common. Warw 1H 61
Galleyend. Essx 5H 53
Galleywood. Essx 5H 53
Gallin. Per 4C 142
Gallowfauld. Ang 4D 144
Gallowhill. Per 5A 144
Gallowhill. Ren 3F 127
Gallowhills. Abers 3H 161
Gallows Green. Staf 1E 73
Gallows Green. Worc 4D 60
Gallowstree Common. Oxon 3E 37
Galltair. High 1G 147
Gallt Melyd. Den 2C 82
Galmington. Som 4F 21
Galmisdale. High 5C 146
Galmpton. Devn 4C 8
Galmpton. Torb 3E 9
Galmpton Warborough. Torb 3E 9
Galphay. N Yor 2E 99
Galston. E Ayr 1D 117
Galton. Dors 4C 14
Galtrigill. High 3A 154
Gamblesby. Cumb 1H 103
Gamblestown. Arm 4F 178
Gamelsby. Cumb 4D 112
Gamesley. Derbs 1E 85
Gamlingay. Cambs 5B 64
Gamlingay Cinques. Cambs 5B 64
Gamlingay Great Heath.
Cambs 5B 64
Gammaton. Devn 4E 19
Gammersgill. N Yor 1C 98
Gamston. Notts 2D 74
(nr. Nottingham)
Gamston. Notts 3E 86
(nr. Retford)
Ganarew. Here 4A 48
Ganavan. Arg 5C 140
Ganborough. Glos 3G 49
Gang. Corn 2H 7
Ganllwyd. Gwyn 3G 69
Gannochy. Ang 1E 145
Gannochy. Per 1D 136
Gansclet. High 4F 169
Ganstead. E Yor 1E 95
Ganthorpe. N Yor 2A 100
Ganton. N Yor 2D 101
Gants Hill. G Lon 2F 39
Gappah. Devn 5B 12
Garafad. High 2D 155
Garboldisham. Norf 2C 66
Garden City. Flin 4F 83
Gardeners Green. Wok 5G 37
Gardenstown. Abers 2F 161
Garden Village. S Yor 1G 85
Garden Village. Swan 3E 31
Garderhouse. Shet 7E 173
Gardham. E Yor 5D 100
Gardie. Shet 5C 173
(on Papa Stour)
Gardie. Shet 1H 173
(on Unst)
Gardie Ho. Shet 7F 173
Gare Hill. Som 2C 22
Garelochhead. Arg 4B 134
Garford. Oxon 2C 36
**Garforth**. W Yor 1E 93
Gargrave. N Yor 4B 98
Gargunnock. Stir 4G 135
Garleffin. S Ayr 1F 109
Garlieston. Dum 5B 110
Garlinge Green. Kent 5F 41
Garlogie. Abers 3E 153
Garmelow. Staf 3B 72
Garmond. Abers 3F 161
Garmondsway. Dur 1A 106
Garmony. Arg 4A 140
Garmouth. Mor 2H 159
Garmston. Shrp 5A 72
Garnant. Carm 4G 45
Garndiffaith. Torf 5F 47
Garndolbenmaen. Gwyn 1D 69
Garnett Bridge. Cumb 5G 103
Garnfadryn. Gwyn 2B 68
Garnkirk. N Lan 3H 127
Garnlydan. Blae 4E 47
Garnsgate. Linc 3D 76
Garnswllt. Swan 5G 45
Garn yr Erw. Torf 4F 47
Garrabost. W Isl 4H 171
Garrallan. E Ayr 3E 117
Garras. Corn 4E 5
Garreg. Gwyn 1F 69
Garrigill. Cumb 5A 114
Garrison. Ferm 7B 176
Garriston. N Yor 5E 105
Garrogie Lodge. High 2H 149
Garros. High 2D 155
Garrow. Per 4F 143
Garsdale. Cumb 1G 97
Garsdale Head. Cumb 5A 104
Garsdon. Wilts 3E 35
Garshall Green. Staf 2D 72
Garsington. Oxon 5D 50
Garstang. Lanc 5D 97
Garston. Mers 2G 83
Garswood. Mers 1H 83
Gartcosh. N Lan 3H 127
Garth. B'end 2B 32
Garth. Cdgn 2F 57
Garth. Gwyn 2E 69
Garth. IOM 4C 108
Garth. Powy 1C 46
(nr. Builth Wells)
Garth. Powy 3E 59
(nr. Knighton)
Garth. Shet 6D 173
(nr. Sandness)
Garth. Shet 6F 173
(nr. Skellister)
Garth. Wrex 1E 71
Garthamlock. Glas 3H 127
Garthbrengy. Powy 2D 46
Gartheli. Cdgn 5E 57
Garthmyl. Powy 1D 58
Garthorpe. Leics 3F 75
Garthorpe. N Lin 3B 94
Garth Owen. Powy 1D 58
Garth Place. Cphy 3E 33
Garth Row. Cumb 5G 103
Gartly. Abers 5C 160
Gartmore. Stir 4E 135
Gartness. N Lan 3A 128
Gartness. Stir 1G 127
Gartocharn. W Dun 1F 127
Garton. E Yor 1F 95
Garton-on-the-Wolds.
E Yor 4D 101
Gartsherrie. N Lan 3A 128
Gartymore. High 2H 165
Garvagh. Caus 5E 174
Garvaghy. Ferm 3L 177
Garvald. E Lot 2B 130
Garvamore. High 4H 149
Garvard. Arg 4A 132
Garvault. High 5H 167
Garve. High 2F 157
Garvestone. Norf 5C 78
Garvetagh. Derr 4E 176
Garvie. Arg 4H 133
Garvock. Abers 1G 145
Garvock. Inv 2D 126
Garway. Here 3H 47
Garway Common. Here 3H 47
Garway Hill. Here 3H 47
Garwick. Linc 1A 76
Gaskan. High 1C 140
Gasper. Wilts 3C 22
Gastard. Wilts 5D 35
Gasthorpe. Norf 2B 66
Gatcombe. IOW 4C 16
Gateacre. Mers 2G 83
Gatebeck. Cumb 1E 97
Gate Burton. Linc 2F 87
Gateforth. N Yor 2F 93
Gatehead. E Ayr 1C 116
Gate Helmsley. N Yor 4A 100
Gatehouse. Nmbd 1A 114
Gatehouse of Fleet. Dum 4D 110
Gatelawbridge. Dum 5B 118
Gateley. Norf 3B 78
Gatenby. N Yor 1F 99
Gatesgarth. Cumb 3C 102
**Gateshead**. Tyne 3F 115
Gatesheath. Ches W 4G 83
Gateside. Ang 4D 144
(nr. Forfar)
Gateside. Ang 4C 144
(nr. Kirriemuir)
Gateside. Fife 3D 136
Gateside. N Ayr 4E 127
Gathurst. G Man 4D 90
**Gatley**. G Man 2C 84
Gatton. Surr 5D 39
Gattonside. Bord 1H 119
Gatwick (London) Airport.
W Sus 1D 27 & 205
Gaufron. Powy 4B 58
Gaulby. Leics 5D 74
Gauldry. Fife 1F 137
Gaultree. Norf 5D 77
Gaunt's Common. Dors 2F 15
Gaunt's Earthcott. S Glo 3B 34
Gautby. Linc 3A 88
Gavinton. Bord 4D 130
Gawber. S Yor 4D 92
Gawcott. Buck 2E 51
Gawsworth. Ches E 4C 84
Gawthorpe. W Yor 2C 92
Gawthrop. Cumb 1F 97
Gawthwaite. Cumb 1B 96
Gay Bowers. Essx 5A 54
Gaydon. Warw 5A 62
Gayfield. Orkn 2D 172
Gayhurst. Mil 1G 51
Gayle. N Yor 1A 98
Gayles. N Yor 4E 105
Gay Street. W Sus 3B 26
Gayton. Mers 2E 83
Gayton. Norf 4G 77
Gayton. Nptn 5E 62
Gayton. Staf 3D 73
Gayton le Marsh. Linc 2D 88
Gayton le Wold. Linc 2B 88
Gayton Thorpe. Norf 4G 77
Gaywood. Norf 3F 77
Gazeley. Suff 4G 65
Geanies. High 1C 158
Gearraidh Bhailteas. W Isl 6C 170
Gearraidh Bhaird. W Isl 6F 171
Gearraidh ma Monadh.
W Isl 7C 170
Gearraidh na h-Aibhne.
W Isl 4E 171
Geary. High 2B 154
Geddes. High 3C 158
Gedding. Suff 5B 66
Geddington. Nptn 2F 63
Gedintailor. High 5E 155
Gedling. Notts 1D 74
Gedney. Linc 3D 76
Gedney Broadgate. Linc 3D 76
Gedney Drove End. Linc 3D 76
Gedney Dyke. Linc 3D 76
Gedney Hill. Linc 4C 76
Gee Cross. G Man 1D 84
Geeston. Rut 5G 75
Geilston. Arg 2E 127
Geirinis. W Isl 4C 170
Geise. High 2D 168
Geisiadar. W Isl 4D 171
Gelder Shiel. Abers 5G 151
Geldeston. Norf 1F 67
Gell. Cnwy 4A 82
Gelli. Pemb 3E 43
Gelli. Rhon 2C 32
Gellifor. Den 4D 82
**Gelligaer**. Cphy 2E 33
Gellilydan. Gwyn 2F 69
Gellinudd. Neat 5H 45
Gellyburn. Per 5H 143
Gellywen. Carm 2G 43
Gelston. Dum 4E 111
Gelston. Linc 1G 75
Gembling. E Yor 4F 101
Geneva. Cdgn 5D 56
Gentleshaw. Staf 4E 73
Geocrab. W Isl 8D 171
George Best Belfast City Airport.
Bel 2H 179
George Green. Buck 2A 38
Georgeham. Devn 3E 19
George Nympton. Devn 4H 19
Georgetown. Blae 5E 47
Georgetown. Ren 3F 127
Georth. Orkn 5C 172
Gerlan. Gwyn 4F 81
Germansweek. Devn 3E 11
Germoe. Corn 4C 4
Gerrans. Corn 5C 6
Gerrard's Bromley. Staf 2B 72
**Gerrards Cross**. Buck 2A 38
Gerston. High 3D 168
Gestingthorpe. Essx 2B 54
Gethsemane. Pemb 1A 44
Geuffordd. Powy 4E 70
Gibraltar. Buck 4F 51
Gibraltar. Linc 5E 89
Gibraltar. Suff 5D 66
Gibsmere. Notts 1E 74
Giddeahall. Wilts 4D 34
Gidea Park. G Lon 2G 39
Gidleigh. Devn 4G 11
**Giffnock**. E Ren 4G 127
Gifford. E Lot 3B 130
Giffordtown. Fife 2E 137
Giggetty. Staf 1C 60
Giggleswick. N Yor 3H 97
Gignog. Pemb 2C 42
Gilberdyke. E Yor 2B 94
Gilbert's End. Worc 1D 48
Gilbert's Green. Warw 3F 61
Gilchriston. E Lot 3A 130
Gilcrux. Cumb 1C 102
Gildersome. W Yor 2C 92
Gildingwells. S Yor 2C 86
Gilesgate Moor. Dur 5F 115
Gileston. V Glam 5D 32
Gilfach. Cphy 2E 33
Gilfach Goch. Rhon 3C 32
Gilfachreda. Cdgn 5D 56
Gilford. Arm 5E 178
Gilgarran. Cumb 2B 102
Gillamoor. N Yor 5D 107
Gillan. Corn 4E 5
Gillar's Green. Mers 1G 83
Gillen. High 3B 154
Gilling East. N Yor 2A 100
Gillingham. Dors 4D 22
**Gillingham**.
Medw 4B 40 & **Medway 197**
Gillingham. Norf 1G 67
Gilling West. N Yor 4E 105
Gillock. High 3E 169
Gillow Heath. Staf 5C 84
Gills. High 1F 169
Gill's Green. Kent 2B 28
Gilmanscleuch. Bord 2F 119
Gilmerton. Edin 3F 129
Gilmerton. Per 1A 136
Gilmonby. Dur 3C 104
Gilmorton. Leics 2C 62
Gilsland. Nmbd 3H 113
Gilsland Spa. Cumb 3H 113
Gilston. Midl 4H 129
Giltbrook. Notts 1B 74
Gilwern. Mon 4F 47
Gimingham. Norf 2E 79
Giosla. W Isl 5D 171
Gipping. Suff 4C 66
Gipsey Bridge. Linc 1B 76
Gipton. W Yor 1D 92
Girdle Toll. N Ayr 5E 127
Girlsta. Shet 6F 173
Girsby. N Yor 4A 106
Girthon. Dum 4D 110
Girton. Cambs 4D 64
Girton. Notts 4F 87
Girvan. S Ayr 5A 116
Gisburn. Lanc 5H 97
Gisleham. Suff 2H 67
Gislingham. Suff 3C 66
Gissing. Norf 2D 66
Gittisham. Devn 3E 13
Gladestry. Powy 5E 59
Gladsmuir. E Lot 2A 130
Glaichbea. High 5H 157
Glais. Swan 5H 45
Glaisdale. N Yor 4E 107
Glame. High 4E 155
Glamis. Ang 4C 144
Glanaman. Carm 4G 45
Glan-Conwy. Cnwy 5H 81
Glandford. Norf 1C 78
Glan Duar. Carm 1F 45
Glandwr. Blae 5F 47
Glandwr. Pemb 2F 43
Glan-Dwyfach. Gwyn 1D 69
Glandy Cross. Carm 2F 43
Glandyfi. Cdgn 1F 57
Glangrwyney. Powy 4F 47
Glanmule. Powy 1D 58
Glanrhyd. Gwyn 2B 68
Glanrhyd. Pemb 1B 44
(nr. Cardigan)
Glan-rhyd. Pemb 1F 43
(nr. Crymych)
Glan-rhyd. Powy 5A 46
Glanton. Nmbd 3E 121
Glanton Pyke. Nmbd 3E 121
Glanvilles Wootton. Dors 2B 14
Glan-y-don. Flin 3D 82
Glan-y-nant. Powy 2B 58
Glan-yr-afon. Gwyn 1C 70
Glan-yr-afon. IOA 2F 81
Glan-yr-afon. Powy 5C 70
Glan-y-wern. Gwyn 2F 69
Glapthorn. Nptn 1H 63
Glapwell. Derbs 4B 86
Glarryford. ME Ant 5G 175
Glas Aird. Arg 4A 132
Glas-allt Shiel. Abers 5G 151
Glasbury. Powy 2E 47
Glaschoil. High 5E 159
Glascoed. Den 3B 82
Glascoed. Mon 5G 47
Glascote. Staf 5G 73
Glascwm. Powy 5D 58
Glasfryn. Cnwy 5B 82
**Glasgow**. Glas 3G 127 & 195
Glasgow Airport.
Ren 3F 127 & 205
Glasgow Prestwick Airport.
S Ayr 2C 116
Glashvin. High 2D 154
Glasinfryn. Gwyn 4E 81
Glas na Cardaich. High 4E 147
Glasnacardoch. High 4E 147
Glasnakille. High 2D 146
Glaspwll. Powy 1G 57
Glassburn. High 5F 157
Glassenbury. Kent 2B 28
Glasserton. Dum 5B 110
Glassford. S Lan 5A 128
Glassgreen. Mor 2G 159
Glasshouse. Glos 3C 48
Glasshouses. N Yor 3D 98
Glasson. Cumb 3D 112
Glasson. Lanc 4D 96
Glassonby. Cumb 1G 103
Glasswater. New M 4J 179
Glasterlaw. Ang 3E 145
Glaston. Rut 5F 75
Glastonbury. Som 3H 21
Glatton. Cambs 2A 64
Glazebrook. Warr 1A 84
Glazebury. Warr 1A 84
Glazeley. Shrp 2B 60
Gleadless. S Yor 2A 86
Gleadsmoss. Ches E 4C 84
Gleann Dail bho Dheas.
W Isl 7C 170
Gleann Tholastaidh. W Isl 3H 171
Gleann Uige. High 1A 140
Gleaston. Cumb 2B 96
Glebe. Derr 3F 176
Glecknabae. Arg 3B 126
Gledrid. Shrp 2E 71
Gleiniant. Powy 1B 58
Glemsford. Suff 1B 54
Glen. Dum 4C 110
Glenancross. High 4E 147
Glenanne. Arm 6D 178
Glenariff. Caus 4J 175
Glenarm. ME Ant 5K 175
Glen Auldyn. IOM 2D 108
Glenavy. Lis 2F 179
Glenbarr. Arg 2A 122
Glenbeg. High 2G 139
Glen Bernisdale. High 4D 154
Glenbervie. Abers 5E 153
Glenboig. N Lan 3A 128
Glenborrodale. High 2A 140
Glenbranter. Arg 4A 134
Glenbreck. Bord 2C 118
Glenbrein Lodge. High 2G 149
Glenbrittle. High 1C 146
Glenbuchat Lodge. Abers 2H 151
Glenbuck. E Ayr 2G 117
Glenburn. Ren 3F 127
Glencalvie Lodge. High 5B 164
Glencaple. Dum 3A 112
Glencarron Lodge. High 3C 156
Glencarse. Per 1D 136
Glencassley Castle. High 3B 164
Glencat. Abers 4C 152
Glencoe. High 3F 141
Glen Cottage. High 5E 147
Glencraig. Fife 4D 136
Glendale. High 4A 154
Glendevon. Per 3B 136
Glendoebeg. High 3G 149
Glendoick. Per 1E 136
Glendoune. S Ayr 5A 116
Glenduckie. Fife 2E 137
Gleneagles. Per 3B 136
Glenegedale. Arg 4B 124
Glenegedale Lots. Arg 4B 124
Glenelg. High 2G 147
Glenernie. Mor 4E 159
Glenesslin. Dum 1F 111
Glenfarg. Per 2D 136
Glenfarquhar Lodge. Abers 5E 152

## Glenferness Mains—Hailey


Glenferness Mains. *High* 4D **158**
Glenfeshie Lodge. *High* 4C **150**
Glenfiddich Lodge. *Mor* 5H **159**
Glenfield. *Leics* 5C **74**
Glenfinnan. *High* 5B **148**
Glenfintaig Lodge. *High* 5E **148**
Glenfoot. *Per* 2D **136**
Glenfyne Lodge. *Arg* 2B **134**
Glengap. *Dum* 4D **110**
Glengarnock. *N Ayr* 4E **126**
Glengolly. *High* 2D **168**
Glengorm Castle. *Arg* 3F **139**
Glengormley. *Ant* 1H **179**
Glengrasco. *High* 4D **154**
Glenhead Farm. *Ang* 2B **144**
Glenholm. *Bord* 1D **118**
Glen House. *Bord* 1E **119**
Glenhurich. *High* 2C **140**
Glenkerry. *Bord* 3E **119**
Glenkiln. *Dum* 2F **111**
Glenkindie. *Abers* 2B **152**
Glenkinglass Lodge. *Arg* 5F **141**
Glenkirk. *Bord* 2C **118**
Glenlean. *Arg* 1B **126**
Glenlee. *Dum* 1D **110**
Glenleraig. *High* 5B **166**
Glenlichorn. *Per* 2G **135**
Glenlivet. *Mor* 1F **151**
Glenlochar. *Dum* 3E **111**
Glenlochsie Lodge. *Per* 1H **143**
Glenluce. *Dum* 4G **109**
Glenmarksie. *High* 3F **157**
Glenmassan. *Arg* 1C **126**
Glenmavis. *N Lan* 3A **128**
Glen Maye. *IOM* 4B **108**
Glenmazeran Lodge. *High* 1B **150**
Glenmidge. *Dum* 1F **111**
Glen Mona. *IOM* 3D **108**
Glenmore. *High* 2G **139**
(nr. Glenborrodale)
Glenmore. *High* 3D **151**
(nr. Kingussie)
Glenmore. *High* 4D **154**
(on Isle of Skye)
Glenmoy. *Ang* 2D **144**
Glennoe. *Arg* 5E **141**
Glen of Coachford. *Abers* 4B **160**
Glenogil. *Ang* 2D **144**
Glen Parva. *Leics* 1C **62**
Glenprosen Village. *Ang* 2C **144**
Glenree. *N Ayr* 3D **122**
Glenridding. *Cumb* 3E **103**
Glenrosa. *N Ayr* 2E **123**
**Glenrothes**. *Fife* 3E **137**
Glensanda. *High* 4C **140**
Glensaugh. *Abers* 1F **145**
Glenshero Lodge. *High* 4H **149**
Glensluain. *Arg* 4H **133**
Glenstockadale. *Dum* 3F **109**
Glenstriven. *Arg* 2B **126**
Glen Tanar House. *Abers* 4B **152**
Glentham. *Linc* 1H **87**
Glenton. *Abers* 1D **152**
Glentress. *Bord* 1E **119**
Glentromie Lodge. *High* 4B **150**
Glentrool Lodge. *Dum* 1B **110**
Glentrool Village. *Dum* 2A **110**
Glentruim House. *High* 4A **150**
Glentworth. *Linc* 2G **87**
Glenuig. *High* 1A **140**
Glen View. *New M* 6E **178**
Glen Village. *Falk* 2B **128**
Glen Vine. *IOM* 4C **108**
Glenwhilly. *Dum* 2G **109**
Glenzierfoot. *Dum* 2E **113**
Glespin. *S Lan* 2H **117**
Gletness. *Shet* 6F **173**
Glewstone. *Here* 3A **48**
Glib Cheois. *W Isl* 5F **171**
Glinton. *Pet* 5A **76**
Glooston. *Leics* 1E **63**
**Glossop**. *Derbs* 1E **85**
Gloster Hill. *Nmbd* 4G **121**
**Gloucester**. *Glos* 4D **48** & **195**
Gloucestershire Airport.
*Glos* 3D **49**
Gloup. *Shet* 1G **173**
Glusburn. *N Yor* 5C **98**
Glutt Lodge. *High* 5B **168**
Glutton Bridge. *Staf* 4E **85**
Gluvian. *Corn* 2D **6**
Glympton. *Oxon* 3C **50**
Glyn. *Cnwy* 3A **82**
Glynarthen. *Cdgn* 1D **44**
Glynbrochan. *Powy* 2B **58**
Glyn Ceiriog. *Wrex* 2E **70**
Glyncoch. *Rhon* 2D **32**
Glyncorrwg. *Neat* 2B **32**
Glynde. *E Sus* 5F **27**
Glyndebourne. *E Sus* 4F **27**
Glyndyfrdwy. *Den* 1D **70**
**Glyn Ebwy**. *Blae* 5E **47**
Glynllan. *B'end* 3C **32**
Glynn. *ME Ant* 7L **175**
Glyn-neath. *Neat* 5B **46**
Glynogwr. *B'end* 3C **32**
Glyntaff. *Rhon* 3D **32**
Glyntawe. *Powy* 4B **46**
Glynteg. *Carm* 2D **44**
Gnosall. *Staf* 3C **72**
Gnosall Heath. *Staf* 3C **72**
Goadby. *Leics* 1E **63**
Goadby Marwood. *Leics* 3E **75**
Goatacre. *Wilts* 4F **35**
Goathill. *Dors* 1B **14**
Goathland. *N Yor* 4F **107**
Goathurst. *Som* 3F **21**
Goathurst Common. *Kent* 5F **39**
Goat Lees. *Kent* 1E **28**
Gobernuisgach Lodge.
*High* 4E **167**
Gobernuisgeach. *High* 5B **168**
Gobhaig. *W Isl* 7C **171**
Gobowen. *Shrp* 2F **71**
**Godalming**. *Surr* 1A **26**
Goddard's Corner. *Suff* 4E **67**
Goddard's Green. *Kent* 2C **28**
(nr. Benenden)
Goddard's Green. *Kent* 2B **28**
(nr. Cranbrook)
Goddards' Green. *W Sus* 3D **27**
Godford Cross. *Devn* 2E **13**
Godleybrook. *Staf* 1D **73**
Godmanchester. *Cambs* 3B **64**
Godmanstone. *Dors* 3B **14**
Godmersham. *Kent* 5E **41**
Godolphin Cross. *Corn* 3D **4**
Godre'r-graig. *Neat* 5A **46**
Godshill. *Hants* 1G **15**
Godshill. *IOW* 4D **16**
Godstone. *Staf* 2E **73**
Godstone. *Surr* 5E **39**
Goetre. *Mon* 5G **47**
Goff's Oak. *Herts* 5D **52**
Gogar. *Edin* 2E **129**
Goginan. *Cdgn* 2F **57**
Golan. *Gwyn* 1E **69**
Golant. *Corn* 3F **7**
Golberdon. *Corn* 5D **10**
**Golborne**. *G Man* 1A **84**
Golcar. *W Yor* 3A **92**
Goldcliff. *Newp* 3G **33**
Golden Cross. *E Sus* 4G **27**
Golden Green. *Kent* 1H **27**
Golden Grove. *Carm* 4F **45**
Golden Grove. *N Yor* 4F **107**
Golden Hill. *Pemb* 2D **43**
Goldenhill. *Stoke* 5C **84**
Golden Pot. *Hants* 2F **25**
Golden Valley. *Glos* 3E **49**
Golders Green. *G Lon* 2D **38**
Goldhanger. *Essx* 5C **54**
Gold Hill. *Norf* 1E **65**
Golding. *Shrp* 5H **71**
Goldington. *Bed* 5H **63**
Goldsborough. *N Yor* 4F **99**
(nr. Harrogate)
Goldsborough. *N Yor* 3F **107**
(nr. Whitby)
Goldsithney. *Corn* 3C **4**
Goldstone. *Kent* 4G **41**
Goldstone. *Shrp* 3B **72**
Goldthorpe. *S Yor* 4E **93**
Goldworthy. *Devn* 4D **19**
Golfa. *Powy* 3D **70**
Gollanfield. *High* 3C **158**
Gollinglith Foot. *N Yor* 1D **98**
Golsoncott. *Som* 3D **20**
Golspie. *High* 4F **165**
Gomeldon. *Wilts* 3G **23**
Gomersal. *W Yor* 2C **92**
Gometra House. *Arg* 4E **139**
Gomshall. *Surr* 1B **26**
Gonalston. *Notts* 1D **74**
Gonerby Hill Foot. *Linc* 2G **75**
Gonfirth. *Shet* 5E **173**
Good Easter. *Essx* 4G **53**
Gooderstone. *Norf* 5G **77**
Goodleigh. *Devn* 3G **19**
Goodmanham. *E Yor* 5C **100**
Goodmayes. *G Lon* 2F **39**
Goodnestone. *Kent* 5G **41**
(nr. Aylesham)
Goodnestone. *Kent* 4E **41**
(nr. Faversham)
Goodrich. *Here* 4A **48**
Goodrington. *Torb* 3E **9**
Goodshaw. *Lanc* 2G **91**
Goodshaw Fold. *Lanc* 2G **91**
Goodstone. *Devn* 5A **12**
Goodwick. *Pemb* 1D **42**
Goodworth Clatford. *Hants* 2B **24**
**Goole**. *E Yor* 2H **93**
Goom's Hill. *Worc* 5E **61**
Goonabarn. *Corn* 3D **6**
Goonbell. *Corn* 4B **6**
Goonhavern. *Corn* 3B **6**
Goonlaze. *Corn* 5B **6**
Goonvrea. *Corn* 4B **6**
Goose Green. *Cumb* 1E **97**
Goose Green. *S Glo* 3C **34**
Gooseham. *Corn* 1C **10**
Goosewell. *Plym* 3B **8**
Goosey. *Oxon* 2B **36**
Goosnargh. *Lanc* 1D **90**
Goostrey. *Ches E* 3B **84**
Gorcott Hill. *Warw* 4E **61**
Gord. *Shet* 9F **173**
Gordon. *Bord* 5C **130**
Gordonbush. *High* 3F **165**
Gordonstown. *Abers* 3C **160**
(nr. Cornhill)
Gordonstown. *Abers* 5E **160**
(nr. Fyvie)
Gorebridge. *Midl* 3G **129**
Gorefield. *Cambs* 4D **76**
Gores. *Wilts* 1G **23**
Gorgie. *Edin* 2F **129**
Goring. *Oxon* 3E **36**
Goring-by-Sea. *W Sus* 5C **26**
Goring Heath. *Oxon* 4E **37**
Gorleston-on-Sea. *Norf* 5H **79**
Gornalwood. *W Mid* 1D **60**
Gorran Churchtown. *Corn* 4D **6**
Gorran Haven. *Corn* 4E **6**
Gorran High Lanes. *Corn* 4D **6**
Gors. *Cdgn* 3F **57**
Gorsedd. *Flin* 3D **82**
**Gorseinon**. *Swan* 3E **31**
Gorseness. *Orkn* 6D **172**
Gorseybank. *Derbs* 5G **85**
Gorsgoch. *Cdgn* 5D **57**
Gorslas. *Carm* 4F **45**
Gorsley. *Glos* 3B **48**
Gorsley Common. *Here* 3B **48**
Gorstan. *High* 2F **157**
Gorstella. *Ches W* 4F **83**
Gorsty Common. *Here* 2H **47**
Gorsty Hill. *Staf* 3F **73**
Gortantaoid. *Arg* 2B **124**
Gorteneorn. *High* 2A **140**
Gortenfern. *High* 2A **140**
Gortin. *Ferm* 8A **174**
Gortnahey. *Caus* 5C **174**
Gorton. *G Man* 1C **84**
Gosbeck. *Suff* 5D **66**
Gosberton. *Linc* 2B **76**
Gosberton Cheal. *Linc* 3B **76**
Gosberton Clough. *Linc* 3A **76**
Goseley Dale. *Derbs* 3H **73**
Gosfield. *Essx* 3A **54**
Gosford. *Oxon* 4D **50**
Gosforth. *Cumb* 4B **102**
**Gosforth**. *Tyne* 3F **115**
Gosmore. *Herts* 3B **52**
Gospel End. *Staf* 1C **60**
**Gosport**. *Hants* 3E **16**
Gossabrough. *Shet* 3G **173**
Gossington. *Glos* 5C **48**
Gossops Green. *W Sus* 2D **26**
Goswick. *Nmbd* 5G **131**
Gotham. *Notts* 2C **74**
Gotherington. *Glos* 3E **49**
Gott. *Arg* 4B **138**
Gott. *Shet* 7F **173**
Goudhurst. *Kent* 2B **28**
Goulceby. *Linc* 3B **88**
Gourdon. *Abers* 1H **145**
Gourock. *Inv* 2D **126**
Govan. *Glas* 3G **127**
Govanhill. *Glas* 3G **127**
Goverton. *Notts* 1E **74**
Goveton. *Devn* 4D **8**
Govilon. *Mon* 4F **47**
Gowanhill. *Abers* 2H **161**
Gowdall. *E Yor* 2G **93**
Gowdystown. *Arm* 4F **179**
Gowerton. *Swan* 3E **31**
Gowkhall. *Fife* 1D **128**
Gowthorpe. *E Yor* 4B **100**
Goxhill. *E Yor* 5F **101**
Goxhill. *N Lin* 2E **94**
Goxhill Haven. *N Lin* 2E **94**
Goytre. *Neat* 3A **32**
Grabhair. *W Isl* 6F **171**
Graby. *Linc* 3H **75**
Gracehill. *ME Ant* 6G **175**
Graffham. *W Sus* 4A **26**
Grafham. *Cambs* 4A **64**
Grafham. *Surr* 1B **26**
Grafton. *Here* 2H **47**
Grafton. *N Yor* 3G **99**
Grafton. *Oxon* 5A **50**
Grafton. *Shrp* 4G **71**
Grafton. *Worc* 2E **49**
(nr. Evesham)
Grafton. *Worc* 4H **59**
(nr. Leominster)
Grafton Flyford. *Worc* 5D **60**
Grafton Regis. *Nptn* 1F **51**
Grafton Underwood. *Nptn* 2G **63**
Grafty Green. *Kent* 1C **28**
Graianrhyd. *Den* 5E **82**
Graig. *Carm* 5E **45**
Graig. *Cnwy* 3H **81**
Graig. *Den* 3C **82**
Graig-fechan. *Den* 5D **82**
Graig Penllyn. *V Glam* 4C **32**
Grain. *Medw* 3C **40**
Grainsby. *Linc* 1B **88**
Grainthorpe. *Linc* 1C **88**
Grainthorpe Fen. *Linc* 1C **88**
Graiselound. *N Lin* 1E **87**
Gramasdail. *W Isl* 3D **170**
Grampound. *Corn* 4D **6**
Grampound Road. *Corn* 3D **6**
Granborough. *Buck* 3F **51**
Granby. *Notts* 2E **75**
Grandborough. *Warw* 4B **62**
Grandpont. *Oxon* 5D **50**
Grandtully. *Per* 3G **143**
Grange. *Cumb* 3D **102**
Grange. *E Ayr* 1D **116**
Grange. *Here* 3G **59**
Grange. *Mers* 2E **82**
Grange. *Per* 1E **137**
Grange Corner. *ME Ant* 7G **175**
Grange Crossroads. *Mor* 3B **160**
Grange Hill. *Essx* 1F **39**
Grangemill. *Derbs* 5G **85**
Grange Moor. *W Yor* 3C **92**
**Grangemouth**. *Falk* 1C **128**
Grange of Lindores. *Fife* 2E **137**
Grange-over-Sands. *Cumb* 2D **96**
Grangepans. *Falk* 1D **128**
Grange Park. *New M* 5J **179**
Grange, The. *N Yor* 5C **106**
Grangetown. *Card* 4E **33**
Grangetown. *Red C* 2C **106**
Grange Villa. *Dur* 4F **115**
Granish. *High* 2C **150**
Gransmoor. *E Yor* 4F **101**
Granston. *Pemb* 1C **42**
Grantchester. *Cambs* 5D **64**
**Grantham**. *Linc* 2G **75**
Grantley. *N Yor* 3E **99**
Grantlodge. *Abers* 2E **152**
Granton. *Edin* 2F **129**
Grantown-on-Spey. *High* 1E **151**
Grantshouse. *Bord* 3E **130**
Grappenhall. *Warr* 2A **84**
Grasby. *Linc* 4D **94**
Grasmere. *Cumb* 4E **103**
Grasscroft. *G Man* 4H **91**
Grassendale. *Mers* 2F **83**
Grassgarth. *Cumb* 5E **113**
Grassholme. *Dur* 2C **104**
Grassington. *N Yor* 3C **98**
Grassmoor. *Derbs* 4B **86**
Grassthorpe. *Notts* 4E **87**
Grateley. *Hants* 2A **24**
Gratton. *Devn* 1D **11**
Gratton. *Staf* 5D **84**
Gratwich. *Staf* 2E **73**
Graveley. *Cambs* 4B **64**
Graveley. *Herts* 3C **52**
Gravelhill. *Shrp* 4G **71**
Gravel Hole. *G Man* 4H **91**
Gravelly Hill. *W Mid* 1F **61**
Graven. *Shet* 4F **173**
Graveney. *Kent* 4E **41**
**Gravesend**. *Kent* 3H **39**
Grayingham. *Linc* 1G **87**
Grayrigg. *Cumb* 5G **103**
**Grays**. *Thur* 3H **39**
Grayshott. *Hants* 3G **25**
Grayson Green. *Cumb* 2A **102**
Grayswood. *Surr* 2A **26**
Graythorp. *Hart* 2C **106**
Grazeley. *Wok* 5E **37**
Grealin. *High* 2E **155**
Greasbrough. *S Yor* 1B **86**
**Greasby**. *Mers* 2E **83**
Great Abington. *Cambs* 1F **53**
Great Addington. *Nptn* 3G **63**
Great Alne. *Warw* 5F **61**
Great Altcar. *Lanc* 4B **90**
Great Amwell. *Herts* 4D **52**
Great Asby. *Cumb* 3H **103**
Great Ashfield. *Suff* 4B **66**
Great Ayton. *N Yor* 3C **106**
Great Baddow. *Essx* 5H **53**
Great Bardfield. *Essx* 2G **53**
Great Barford. *Bed* 5A **64**
Great Barr. *W Mid* 1E **61**
Great Barrington. *Glos* 4H **49**
Great Barrow. *Ches W* 4G **83**
Great Barton. *Suff* 4A **66**
Great Barugh. *N Yor* 2B **100**
Great Bavington. *Nmbd* 1C **114**
Great Bealings. *Suff* 1F **55**
Great Bedwyn. *Wilts* 5A **36**
Great Bentley. *Essx* 3E **54**
Great Billing. *Nptn* 4F **63**
Great Bircham. *Norf* 2G **77**
Great Blakenham. *Suff* 5D **66**
Great Blencow. *Cumb* 1F **103**
Great Bolas. *Telf* 3A **72**
Great Bookham. *Surr* 5C **38**
Great Bosullow. *Corn* 3B **4**
Great Bourton. *Oxon* 1C **50**
Great Bowden. *Leics* 2E **63**
Great Bradley. *Suff* 5F **65**
Great Braxted. *Essx* 4B **54**
Great Bricett. *Suff* 5C **66**
Great Brickhill. *Buck* 2H **51**
Great Bridgeford. *Staf* 3C **72**
Great Brington. *Nptn* 4D **62**
Great Bromley. *Essx* 3D **54**
Great Broughton. *Cumb* 1B **102**
Great Broughton. *N Yor* 4C **106**
Great Budworth. *Ches W* 3A **84**
Great Burdon. *Darl* 3A **106**
Great Burstead. *Essx* 1A **40**
Great Busby. *N Yor* 4C **106**
Great Canfield. *Essx* 4F **53**
Great Carlton. *Linc* 2D **88**
Great Casterton. *Rut* 5G **75**
Great Chalfield. *Wilts* 5D **34**
Great Chart. *Kent* 1D **28**
Great Chatwell. *Staf* 4B **72**
Great Chesterford. *Essx* 1F **53**
Great Cheverell. *Wilts* 1E **23**
Great Chilton. *Dur* 1F **105**
Great Chishill. *Cambs* 2E **53**
Great Clacton. *Essx* 4E **55**
Great Cliff. *W Yor* 3D **92**
Great Clifton. *Cumb* 2B **102**
Great Coates. *NE Lin* 3F **95**
Great Comberton. *Worc* 1E **49**
Great Corby. *Cumb* 4F **113**
Great Cornard. *Suff* 1B **54**
Great Cowden. *E Yor* 5G **101**
Great Coxwell. *Oxon* 2A **36**
Great Crakehall. *N Yor* 5F **105**
Great Cransley. *Nptn* 3F **63**
Great Cressingham. *Norf* 5A **78**
Great Crosby. *Mers* 4B **90**
Great Cubley. *Derbs* 2F **73**
Great Dalby. *Leics* 4E **75**
Great Doddington. *Nptn* 4F **63**
Great Doward. *Here* 4A **48**
Great Dunham. *Norf* 4A **78**
Great Dunmow. *Essx* 3G **53**
Great Durnford. *Wilts* 3G **23**
Great Easton. *Essx* 3G **53**
Great Easton. *Leics* 1F **63**
Great Eccleston. *Lanc* 5D **96**
Great Edstone. *N Yor* 1B **100**
Great Ellingham. *Norf* 1C **66**
Great Elm. *Som* 2C **22**
Great Eppleton. *Tyne* 5G **115**
Great Eversden. *Cambs* 5C **64**
Great Fencote. *N Yor* 5F **105**
Great Finborough. *Suff* 5C **66**
Greatford. *Linc* 4H **75**
Great Fransham. *Norf* 4A **78**
Great Gaddesden. *Herts* 4A **52**
Great Gate. *Staf* 1E **73**
Great Gidding. *Cambs* 2A **64**
Great Givendale. *E Yor* 4C **100**
Great Glemham. *Suff* 4F **67**
Great Glen. *Leics* 1D **62**
Great Gonerby. *Linc* 2F **75**
Great Gransden. *Cambs* 5B **64**
Great Green. *Norf* 2E **67**
Great Green. *Suff* 5B **66**
(nr. Lavenham)
Great Green. *Suff* 3D **66**
(nr. Palgrave)
Great Habton. *N Yor* 2B **100**
Great Hale. *Linc* 1A **76**
Great Hallingbury. *Essx* 4F **53**
Greatham. *Hants* 3F **25**
Greatham. *Hart* 2B **106**
Greatham. *W Sus* 4B **26**
Great Hampden. *Buck* 5G **51**
Great Harrowden. *Nptn* 3F **63**
**Great Harwood**. *Lanc* 1F **91**
Great Haseley. *Oxon* 5E **51**
Great Hatfield. *E Yor* 5F **101**
Great Haywood. *Staf* 3D **73**
Great Heath. *W Mid* 2H **61**
Great Heck. *N Yor* 2F **93**
Great Henny. *Essx* 2B **54**
Great Hinton. *Wilts* 1E **23**
Great Hockham. *Norf* 1B **66**
Great Holland. *Essx* 4F **55**
Great Horkesley. *Essx* 2C **54**
Great Hormead. *Herts* 2E **53**
Great Horton. *W Yor* 1B **92**
Great Horwood. *Buck* 2F **51**
Great Houghton. *Nptn* 5E **63**
Great Houghton. *S Yor* 4E **93**
Great Hucklow. *Derbs* 3F **85**
Great Kelk. *E Yor* 4F **101**
Great Kendale. *E Yor* 3E **101**
Great Kimble. *Buck* 5G **51**
Great Kingshill. *Buck* 2G **37**
Great Langdale. *Cumb* 4D **102**
Great Langton. *N Yor* 5F **105**
Great Leighs. *Essx* 4H **53**
Great Limber. *Linc* 4E **95**
Great Linford. *Mil* 1G **51**
Great Livermere. *Suff* 3A **66**
Great Longstone. *Derbs* 3G **85**
Great Lumley. *Dur* 5F **115**
Great Lyth. *Shrp* 5G **71**
**Great Malvern**. *Worc* 1C **48**
Great Maplestead. *Essx* 2B **54**
Great Marton. *Bkpl* 1B **90**
Great Massingham. *Norf* 3G **77**
Great Melton. *Norf* 5D **78**
Great Milton. *Oxon* 5E **51**
Great Missenden. *Buck* 5G **51**
Great Mitton. *Lanc* 1F **91**
Great Mongeham. *Kent* 5H **41**
Great Moulton. *Norf* 1D **66**
Great Munden. *Herts* 3D **52**
Great Musgrave. *Cumb* 3A **104**
Great Ness. *Shrp* 4F **71**
Great Notley. *Essx* 3H **53**
Great Oak. *Mon* 5G **47**
Great Oakley. *Essx* 3E **55**
Great Oakley. *Nptn* 2F **63**
Great Offley. *Herts* 3B **52**
Great Ormside. *Cumb* 3A **104**
Great Orton. *Cumb* 4E **113**
Great Ouseburn. *N Yor* 3G **99**
Great Oxendon. *Nptn* 2E **63**
Great Oxney Green. *Essx* 5G **53**
Great Parndon. *Essx* 5E **53**
Great Paxton. *Cambs* 4B **64**
Great Plumpton. *Lanc* 1B **90**
Great Plumstead. *Norf* 4F **79**
Great Ponton. *Linc* 2G **75**
Great Potheridge. *Devn* 1F **11**
Great Preston. *W Yor* 2E **93**
Great Raveley. *Cambs* 2B **64**
Great Rissington. *Glos* 4G **49**
Great Rollright. *Oxon* 2B **50**
Great Ryburgh. *Norf* 3B **78**
Great Ryle. *Nmbd* 3E **121**
Great Ryton. *Shrp* 5G **71**
Great Saling. *Essx* 3H **53**
Great Salkeld. *Cumb* 1G **103**
Great Sampford. *Essx* 2G **53**
**Great Sankey**. *Warr* 2H **83**
Great Saredon. *Staf* 5D **72**
Great Saxham. *Suff* 4G **65**
Great Shefford. *W Ber* 4B **36**
Great Shelford. *Cambs* 5D **64**
Great Shoddesden. *Hants* 2A **24**
Great Smeaton. *N Yor* 4A **106**
Great Snoring. *Norf* 2B **78**
Great Somerford. *Wilts* 3E **35**
Great Stainton. *Darl* 2A **106**
Great Stambridge. *Essx* 1C **40**
Great Staughton. *Cambs* 4A **64**
Great Steeping. *Linc* 4D **88**
Great Stonar. *Kent* 5H **41**
Greatstone-on-Sea. *Kent* 3E **29**
Great Strickland. *Cumb* 2G **103**
Great Stukeley. *Cambs* 3B **64**
Great Sturton. *Linc* 3B **88**
Great Sutton. *Ches W* 3F **83**
Great Sutton. *Shrp* 2H **59**
Great Swinburne. *Nmbd* 2C **114**
Great Tew. *Oxon* 3B **50**
Great Tey. *Essx* 3B **54**
Great Thirkleby. *N Yor* 2G **99**
Great Thorness. *IOW* 3C **16**
Great Thurlow. *Suff* 5F **65**
Great Torr. *Devn* 4C **8**
Great Torrington. *Devn* 1E **11**
Great Tosson. *Nmbd* 4E **121**
Great Totham North. *Essx* 4B **54**
Great Totham South. *Essx* 4B **54**
Great Tows. *Linc* 1B **88**
Great Urswick. *Cumb* 2B **96**
Great Wakering. *Essx* 2D **40**
Great Waldingfield. *Suff* 1C **54**
Great Walsingham. *Norf* 2B **78**
Great Waltham. *Essx* 4G **53**
Great Warley. *Essx* 1G **39**
Great Washbourne. *Glos* 2E **49**
Great Wenham. *Suff* 2D **54**
Great Whelnetham. *Suff* 5A **66**
Great Whittington. *Nmbd* 2D **114**
Great Wigborough. *Essx* 4C **54**
Great Wilbraham. *Cambs* 5E **65**
Great Wilne. *Derbs* 2B **74**
Great Wishford. *Wilts* 3F **23**
Great Witchingham. *Norf* 3D **78**
Great Witcombe. *Glos* 4E **49**
Great Witley. *Worc* 4B **60**
Great Wolford. *Warw* 2H **49**
Greatworth. *Nptn* 1D **50**
Great Wratting. *Suff* 1G **53**
Great Wymondley. *Herts* 3C **52**
**Great Wyrley**. *Staf* 5D **73**
Great Wytheford. *Shrp* 4H **71**
**Great Yarmouth**. *Norf* 5H **79**
Great Yeldham. *Essx* 2A **54**
Grebby. *Linc* 4D **88**
Greeba Castle. *IOM* 3C **108**
Greenbank. *Shet* 1G **173**
Greenbottom. *Corn* 4B **6**
Greenburn. *W Lot* 3C **128**
Greencastle. *Ferm* 1L **177**
Greencroft. *Dur* 4E **115**
Greendown. *Som* 1A **22**
Greendykes. *Nmbd* 2E **121**
Green End. *Bed* 1A **52**
(nr. Bedford)
Green End. *Bed* 4A **64**
(nr. St Neots)
Green End. *Herts* 2D **52**
(nr. Buntingford)
Green End. *Herts* 3D **52**
(nr. Stevenage)
Green End. *N Yor* 4F **107**
Green End. *Warw* 2G **61**
Greenfield. *Arg* 4B **134**
Greenfield. *C Beds* 2A **52**
Greenfield. *Flin* 3D **82**
Greenfield. *G Man* 4H **91**
Greenfield. *Oxon* 2F **37**
Greenfoot. *N Lan* 3A **128**
**Greenford**. *G Lon* 2C **38**
Greengairs. *N Lan* 2A **128**
Greengate. *Norf* 4C **78**
Greengill. *Cumb* 1C **102**
Greenhalgh. *Lanc* 1C **90**
Greenham. *Dors* 2H **13**
Greenham. *Som* 4D **20**
Greenham. *W Ber* 5C **36**
Green Hammerton. *N Yor* 4G **99**
Greenhaugh. *Nmbd* 1A **114**
Greenhead. *Nmbd* 3H **113**
Green Heath. *Staf* 4D **73**
Greenhill. *Dum* 2C **112**
Greenhill. *Falk* 2B **128**
Greenhill. *Kent* 4F **41**
Greenhill. *S Yor* 2H **85**
Greenhill. *Worc* 3C **60**
Greenhills. *N Ayr* 4E **127**
Greenhithe. *Kent* 3G **39**
Greenholm. *E Ayr* 1E **117**
Greenhow Hill. *N Yor* 3D **98**
Greenigoe. *Orkn* 7D **172**
Greenisland. *ME Ant* 8K **175**
Greenland. *High* 2E **169**
Greenland Mains. *High* 2E **169**
Greenlands. *Worc* 4E **61**
Green Lane. *Shrp* 3A **72**
Green Lane. *Warw* 4E **61**
Greenlaw. *Bord* 5D **130**
Greenlea. *Dum* 2B **112**
Greenloaning. *Per* 3H **135**
Greenmount. *G Man* 3F **91**
Greenmow. *Shet* 9F **173**
**Greenock**. *Inv* 2D **126**
Greenock Mains. *E Ayr* 2F **117**
Greenodd. *Cumb* 1C **96**
Green Ore. *Som* 1A **22**
Greenrow. *Cumb* 4C **112**
Greens. *Abers* 4F **161**
Greensgate. *Norf* 4D **78**
Greenside. *Tyne* 3E **115**
Greensidehill. *Nmbd* 3D **121**
Greens Norton. *Nptn* 1E **51**
Greenstead Green. *Essx* 3B **54**
Greensted Green. *Essx* 5F **53**
Green Street. *Herts* 1C **38**
Green Street. *Suff* 3D **66**
Green Street Green. *G Lon* 4F **39**
Green Street Green. *Kent* 3G **39**
Greenstreet Green. *Suff* 1D **54**
Green, The. *Cumb* 1A **96**
Green, The. *Wilts* 3D **22**
Green Tye. *Herts* 4E **53**
Greenwall. *Orkn* 7E **172**
Greenway. *Pemb* 1E **43**
Greenway. *V Glam* 4D **32**
Greenwell. *Cumb* 4G **113**
**Greenwich**. *G Lon* 3E **39**
Greet. *Glos* 2F **49**
Greete. *Shrp* 3H **59**
Greetham. *Linc* 3C **88**
Greetham. *Rut* 4G **75**
Greetland. *W Yor* 2A **92**
Gregson Lane. *Lanc* 2D **90**
Grein. *W Isl* 8B **170**
Greinetobht. *W Isl* 1D **170**
Greinton. *Som* 3H **21**
Gremista. *Shet* 7F **173**
Grenaby. *IOM* 4B **108**
Grendon. *Nptn* 4F **63**
Grendon. *Warw* 1G **61**
Grendon Common. *Warw* 1G **61**
Grendon Green. *Here* 5H **59**
Grendon Underwood. *Buck* 3E **51**
Grenofen. *Devn* 5E **11**
Grenoside. *S Yor* 1H **85**
Greosabhagh. *W Isl* 8D **171**
Gresford. *Wrex* 5F **83**
Gresham. *Norf* 2D **78**
Greshornish. *High* 3C **154**
Gressenhall. *Norf* 4B **78**
Gressingham. *Lanc* 3E **97**
Greta Bridge. *Dur* 3D **105**
Gretna. *Dum* 3E **112**
Gretna Green. *Dum* 3E **112**
Gretton. *Glos* 2F **49**
Gretton. *Nptn* 1G **63**
Gretton. *Shrp* 1H **59**
Grewelthorpe. *N Yor* 2E **99**
Greyabbey. *N Dwn* 3K **179**
Greygarth. *N Yor* 2D **98**
Grey Green. *N Lin* 4A **94**
Greylake. *Som* 3G **21**
Greysouthen. *Cumb* 2B **102**
Greysteel. *Caus* 4B **174**
Greystoke. *Cumb* 1F **103**
Greystoke Gill. *Cumb* 2F **103**
Greystone. *Ang* 4E **145**
Greystones. *S Yor* 2H **85**
Greywell. *Hants* 1F **25**
Griais. *W Isl* 3G **171**
Grianan. *W Isl* 4G **171**
Gribthorpe. *E Yor* 1A **94**
Gribun. *Arg* 5F **139**
Griff. *Warw* 2A **62**
Griffithstown. *Torf* 2F **33**
Griffydam. *Leics* 4B **74**
Griggs Green. *Hants* 3G **25**
Grimbister. *Orkn* 6C **172**
Grimeford Village. *Lanc* 3E **90**
Grimeston. *Orkn* 6C **172**
Grimethorpe. *S Yor* 4E **93**
Griminis. *W Isl* 3C **170**
(on Benbecula)
Griminis. *W Isl* 1C **170**
(on North Uist)
Grimister. *Shet* 2F **173**
Grimley. *Worc* 4C **60**
Grimness. *Orkn* 8D **172**
Grimoldby. *Linc* 2C **88**
Grimpo. *Shrp* 3F **71**
Grimsargh. *Lanc* 1D **90**
Grimsbury. *Oxon* 1C **50**
**Grimsby**. *NE Lin* 4F **95**
Grimscote. *Nptn* 5D **62**
Grimscott. *Corn* 2C **10**
Grimshaw. *Bkbn* 2F **91**
Grimshaw Green. *Lanc* 3C **90**
Grimsthorpe. *Linc* 3H **75**
Grimston. *E Yor* 1F **95**
Grimston. *Leics* 3D **74**
Grimston. *Norf* 3G **77**
Grimston. *York* 4A **100**
Grimstone. *Dors* 3B **14**
Grimstone End. *Suff* 4B **66**
Grinacombe Moor. *Devn* 3E **11**
Grindale. *E Yor* 2F **101**
Grindhill. *Devn* 3E **11**
Grindiscol. *Shet* 8F **173**
Grindle. *Shrp* 5B **72**
Grindleford. *Derbs* 3G **85**
Grindleton. *Lanc* 5G **97**
Grindley. *Staf* 3E **73**
Grindley Brook. *Shrp* 1H **71**
Grindlow. *Derbs* 3F **85**
Grindon. *Nmbd* 5F **131**
Grindon. *Staf* 5E **85**
Gringley on the Hill. *Notts* 1E **87**
Grinsdale. *Cumb* 4E **113**
Grinshill. *Shrp* 3H **71**
Grinton. *N Yor* 5D **104**
Griomsidar. *W Isl* 5G **171**
Grishipoll. *Arg* 3C **138**
Grisling Common. *E Sus* 3F **27**
Gristhorpe. *N Yor* 1E **101**
Griston. *Norf* 1B **66**
Gritley. *Orkn* 7E **172**
Grittenham. *Wilts* 3F **35**
Grittleton. *Wilts* 3D **34**
Grizebeck. *Cumb* 1B **96**
Grizedale. *Cumb* 5E **103**
Grobister. *Orkn* 5F **172**
Grobsness. *Shet* 5E **173**
Groby. *Leics* 5C **74**
Groes. *Cnwy* 4C **82**
Groes. *Neat* 3A **32**
Groes-faen. *Rhon* 3D **32**
Groesffordd. *Gwyn* 2B **68**
Groesffordd. *Powy* 3D **46**
Groeslon. *Gwyn* 5D **81**
Groes-lwyd. *Powy* 4E **70**
Groes-wen. *Cphy* 3E **33**
Grogport. *Arg* 5G **125**
Groigearraidh. *W Isl* 4C **170**
Gromford. *Suff* 5F **67**
Gronant. *Flin* 2C **82**
Groombridge. *E Sus* 2G **27**
Groomsport. *N Dwn* 1K **179**
Grosmont. *Mon* 3H **47**
Grosmont. *N Yor* 4F **107**
Grotton. *Suff* 1C **54**
Grove. *Dors* 5B **14**
Grove. *Kent* 4G **41**
Grove. *Notts* 3E **87**
Grove. *Oxon* 2B **36**
Grovehill. *E Yor* 1D **94**
Grove Park. *G Lon* 3F **39**
Grovesend. *Swan* 5F **45**
Grove, The. *Dum* 2A **112**
Grove, The. *Worc* 1D **48**
Grub Street. *Staf* 3B **72**
Grudie. *High* 2F **157**
Gruids. *High* 3C **164**
Gruinard House. *High* 4D **162**
Gruinart. *Arg* 3A **124**
Grulinbeg. *Arg* 3A **124**
Gruline. *Arg* 4G **139**
Grummore. *High* 5G **167**
Grundisburgh. *Suff* 5E **66**
Gruting. *Shet* 7D **173**
Grutness. *Shet* 10F **173**
Gualachulain. *High* 4F **141**
Gualin House. *High* 3D **166**
Guardbridge. *Fife* 2G **137**
Guarlford. *Worc* 1D **48**
Guay. *Per* 4H **143**
Gubblecote. *Herts* 4H **51**
Guestling Green. *E Sus* 4C **28**
Guestling Thorn. *E Sus* 4C **28**
Guestwick. *Norf* 3C **78**
Guestwick Green. *Norf* 3C **78**
Guide. *Bkbn* 2F **91**
Guide Post. *Nmbd* 1F **115**
Guilden Down. *Shrp* 2F **59**
Guilden Morden. *Cambs* 1C **52**
Guilden Sutton. *Ches W* 4G **83**
**Guildford**. *Surr* 1A **26** & **195**
Guildtown. *Per* 5A **144**
Guilsborough. *Nptn* 3D **62**
Guilsfield. *Powy* 4E **70**
Guineaford. *Devn* 3F **19**
**Guisborough**. *Red C* 3D **106**
Guiseley. *W Yor* 5D **98**
Guist. *Norf* 3B **78**
Guiting Power. *Glos* 3F **49**
Gulberwick. *Shet* 8F **173**
Gulladuff. *M Ulst* 7F **174**
Gullane. *E Lot* 1A **130**
Gulling Green. *Suff* 5H **65**
Gulval. *Corn* 3B **4**
Gulworthy. *Devn* 5E **11**
Gumfreston. *Pemb* 4F **43**
Gumley. *Leics* 1D **62**
Gunby. *E Yor* 1H **93**
Gunby. *Linc* 3G **75**
Gundleton. *Hants* 3E **24**
Gun Green. *Kent* 2B **28**
Gun Hill. *E Sus* 4G **27**
Gunn. *Devn* 3G **19**
Gunnerside. *N Yor* 5C **104**
Gunnerton. *Nmbd* 2C **114**
Gunness. *N Lin* 3B **94**
Gunnislake. *Corn* 5E **11**
Gunnista. *Shet* 7F **173**
Gunsgreenhill. *Bord* 3F **131**
Gunstone. *Staf* 5C **72**
Gunthorpe. *Norf* 2C **78**
Gunthorpe. *N Lin* 1F **87**
Gunthorpe. *Notts* 1D **74**
Gunthorpe. *Pet* 5A **76**
Gunville. *IOW* 4C **16**
Gupworthy. *Som* 3C **20**
Gurnard. *IOW* 3C **16**
Gurney Slade. *Som* 2B **22**
Gurnos. *Powy* 5A **46**
Gussage All Saints. *Dors* 1F **15**
Gussage St Andrew. *Dors* 1E **15**
Gussage St Michael. *Dors* 1E **15**
Guston. *Kent* 1H **29**
Gutcher. *Shet* 2G **173**
Guthram Gowt. *Linc* 3A **76**
Guthrie. *Ang* 3E **145**
Guyhirn. *Cambs* 5D **76**
Guyhirn Gull. *Cambs* 5C **76**
Guy's Head. *Linc* 3D **77**
Guy's Marsh. *Dors* 4D **22**
Guyzance. *Nmbd* 4G **121**
Gwaelod-y-garth. *Card* 3E **32**
Gwaenynog Bach. *Den* 4C **82**
Gwaenysgor. *Flin* 2C **82**
Gwalchmai. *IOA* 3C **80**
Gwastad. *Pemb* 2E **43**
Gwaun-Cae-Gurwen. *Neat* 4H **45**
Gwbert. *Cdgn* 1B **44**
Gweek. *Corn* 4E **5**
Gwehelog. *Mon* 5G **47**
Gwenddwr. *Powy* 1D **46**
Gwennap. *Corn* 4B **6**
Gwenter. *Corn* 5E **5**
Gwernaffield. *Flin* 4E **82**
Gwernesney. *Mon* 5H **47**
Gwernogle. *Carm* 2F **45**
Gwern-y-go. *Powy* 1E **58**
Gwernymynydd. *Flin* 4E **82**
Gwersyllt. *Wrex* 5F **83**
Gwespyr. *Flin* 2D **82**
Gwinear. *Corn* 3C **4**
Gwithian. *Corn* 2C **4**
Gwredog. *IOA* 2D **80**
Gwyddelwern. *Den* 1C **70**
Gwyddgrug. *Carm* 2E **45**
Gwynfryn. *Wrex* 5E **83**
Gwystre. *Powy* 4C **58**
Gwytherin. *Cnwy* 4A **82**
Gyfelia. *Wrex* 1F **71**
Gyffin. *Cnwy* 3G **81**


## H


Haa of Houlland. *Shet* 1G **173**
Habberley. *Shrp* 5G **71**
Habblesthorpe. *Notts* 2E **87**
Habergham. *Lanc* 1G **91**
Habin. *W Sus* 4G **25**
Habrough. *NE Lin* 3E **95**
Haceby. *Linc* 2H **75**
Hacheston. *Suff* 5F **67**
Hackenthorpe. *S Yor* 2B **86**
Hackford. *Norf* 5C **78**
Hackforth. *N Yor* 5F **105**
Hackland. *Orkn* 5C **172**
Hackleton. *Nptn* 5F **63**
Hackman's Gate. *Worc* 3C **60**
Hackness. *N Yor* 5G **107**
Hackness. *Orkn* 8C **172**
**Hackney**. *G Lon* 2E **39**
Hackthorn. *Linc* 2G **87**
Hackthorpe. *Cumb* 2G **103**
Haclait. *W Isl* 4D **170**
Haconby. *Linc* 3A **76**
Hadden. *Bord* 1B **120**
Haddenham. *Buck* 5F **51**
Haddenham. *Cambs* 3D **64**
Haddenham End Field.
*Cambs* 3D **64**
Haddington. *E Lot* 2B **130**
Haddington. *Linc* 4G **87**
Haddiscoe. *Norf* 1G **67**
Haddo. *Abers* 5F **161**
Haddon. *Cambs* 1A **64**
Hademore. *Staf* 5F **73**
Hadfield. *Derbs* 1E **85**
Hadham Cross. *Herts* 4E **53**
Hadham Ford. *Herts* 3E **53**
Hadleigh. *Essx* 2C **40**
Hadleigh. *Suff* 1D **54**
Hadleigh Heath. *Suff* 1C **54**
Hadley. *Telf* 4A **72**
Hadley. *Worc* 4C **60**
Hadley End. *Staf* 3F **73**
Hadley Wood. *G Lon* 1D **38**
Hadlow. *Kent* 1H **27**
Hadlow Down. *E Sus* 3G **27**
Hadnall. *Shrp* 3H **71**
Hadstock. *Essx* 1F **53**
Hadston. *Nmbd* 4G **121**
Hady. *Derbs* 3A **86**
Hadzor. *Worc* 4D **60**
Haffenden Quarter. *Kent* 1C **28**
Haggate. *Lanc* 1G **91**
Haggbeck. *Cumb* 2F **113**
Haggersta. *Shet* 7E **173**
Haggerston. *Nmbd* 5G **131**
Haggrister. *Shet* 4E **173**
Hagley. *Here* 1A **48**
Hagley. *Worc* 2D **60**
Hagnaby. *Linc* 4C **88**
Hagworthingham. *Linc* 4C **88**
Haigh. *G Man* 4E **90**
Haigh Moor. *W Yor* 2C **92**
Haighton Green. *Lanc* 1D **90**
Haile. *Cumb* 4B **102**
Hailes. *Glos* 2F **49**
Hailey. *Herts* 4D **52**
Hailey. *Oxon* 4B **50**

Hailsham—Hest Bank


**Hailsham.** E Sus 5G 27
Hail Weston. Cambs 4A 64
Hainault. G Lon 1F 39
Hainford. Norf 4E 78
Hainton. Linc 2A 88
Hainworth. W Yor 1A 92
Haisthorpe. E Yor 3F 101
Hakin. Pemb 4C 42
Halam. Notts 5D 86
Halbeath. Fife 1E 129
Halberton. Devn 1D 12
Halcro. High 2E 169
Hale. Cumb 2E 97
**Hale.** G Man 2B 84
Hale. Hal 2G 83
Hale. Hants 1G 15
Hale. Surr 2G 25
Hale Bank. Hal 2G 83
Halebarns. G Man 2B 84
Hales. Norf 1F 67
Hales. Staf 2B 72
Halesgate. Linc 3C 76
Hales Green. Derbs 1F 73
**Halesowen.** W Mid 2D 60
Hale Street. Kent 1A 28
Halesworth. Suff 3F 67
Halewood. Mers 2G 83
Halford. Shrp 2G 59
Halford. Warw 1A 50
Halfpenny. Cumb 1E 97
Halfpenny Furze. Carm 3G 43
Halfpenny Green. Staf 1C 60
Halfway. Carm 2G 45
Halfway. Powy 2B 46
Halfway. S Yor 2B 86
Halfway. W Ber 5C 36
Halfway House. Shrp 4F 71
Halfway Houses. Kent 3D 40
Halgabron. Corn 4A 10
**Halifax.** W Yor 2A 92
Halistra. High 3B 154
Halket. E Ayr 4F 127
Halkirk. High 3D 168
Halkyn. Flin 3E 82
Hall. E Ren 4F 127
Hallam Fields. Derbs 1B 74
Halland. E Sus 4G 27
Hallands, The. N Lin 2D 94
Hallaton. Leics 1E 63
Hallatrow. Bath 1B 22
Hallbank. Cumb 5H 103
Hallbankgate. Cumb 4G 113
Hall Dunnerdale. Cumb 5D 102
Hallen. S Glo 3A 34
Hall End. Bed 1A 52
Hallgarth. Dur 5G 115
Hall Green. Ches E 5C 84
Hall Green. Norf 2D 66
Hall Green. W Mid 2F 61
Hall Green. W Yor 3D 92
Hall Green. Wrex 1G 71
Halliburton. Bord 5C 130
Hallin. High 3B 154
Halling. Medw 4B 40
Hallington. Linc 2C 88
Hallington. Nmbd 2C 114
Halloughton. Notts 5D 86
Hallow. Worc 5C 60
Hallow Heath. Worc 5C 60
Hallowsgate. Ches W 4H 83
Hallsands. Devn 5E 9
Hall's Green. Herts 3C 52
Hallspill. Devn 4E 19
Hallthwaites. Cumb 1A 96
Hall Waberthwaite. Cumb 5C 102
Hallwood Green. Glos 2B 48
Hallworthy. Corn 4B 10
Hallyne. Bord 5E 129
Halmer End. Staf 1C 72
Halmond's Frome. Here 1B 48
Halmore. Glos 5B 48
Halnaker. W Sus 5A 26
Halsall. Lanc 3B 90
Halse. Nptn 1D 50
Halse. Som 4E 21
Halsetown. Corn 3C 4
Halsham. E Yor 2F 95
Halsinger. Devn 3F 19
**Halstead.** Essx 2B 54
Halstead. Kent 4F 39
Halstead. Leics 5E 75
Halstock. Dors 2A 14
Halsway. Som 3E 21
Haltcliff Bridge. Cumb 1E 103
Haltham. Linc 4B 88
Haltoft End. Linc 1C 76
Halton. Buck 5G 51
Halton. Hal 2H 83
Halton. Lanc 3E 97
Halton. Nmbd 3C 114
Halton. W Yor 1D 92
Halton. Wrex 2F 71
Halton East. N Yor 4C 98
Halton Fenside. Linc 4D 88
Halton Gill. N Yor 2A 98
Halton Holegate. Linc 4D 88
Halton Lea Gate. Nmbd 4H 113
Halton Moor. W Yor 1D 92
Halton Shields. Nmbd 3D 114
Halton West. N Yor 4H 97
Haltwhistle. Nmbd 3A 114
Halvergate. Norf 5G 79
Halwell. Devn 3D 9
Halwill. Devn 3E 11
Halwill Junction. Devn 3E 11
Ham. Devn 2F 13
Ham. Glos 2B 34
Ham. G Lon 3C 38
Ham. High 1E 169
Ham. Kent 5H 41
Ham. Plym 3A 8
Ham. Shet 8A 173
Ham. Som 1F 13
(nr. Ilminster)
Ham. Som 4F 21
(nr. Taunton)
Ham. Som 4E 21
(nr. Wellington)
Ham. Wilts 5B 36
Hambleden. Buck 3F 37
Hambledon. Hants 1E 17
Hambledon. Surr 2A 26
Hamble-le-Rice. Hants 2C 16
Hambleton. Lanc 5C 96
Hambleton. N Yor 1F 93
Hambridge. Som 4G 21
Hambrook. S Glo 4B 34
Hambrook. W Sus 2F 17
Ham Common. Dors 4D 22
Hameringham. Linc 4C 88
Hamerton. Cambs 3A 64
Ham Green. Here 1C 48
Ham Green. Kent 4C 40
Ham Green. N Som 4A 34
Ham Green. Worc 4E 61
Ham Hill. Kent 4A 40
Hamilton. Leics 5D 74
**Hamilton.** S Lan 4A 128
Hamiltonsbawn. Arm 5D 178
Hamister. Shet 5G 173
Hammer. W Sus 3G 25
**Hammersmith.** G Lon 3D 38
Hammerwich. Staf 5E 73
Hammerwood. E Sus 2F 27
Hammill. Kent 5G 41
Hammond Street. Herts 5D 52
Hammoon. Dors 1D 14
Hamnavoe. Shet 3D 173
(nr. Braehoulland)
Hamnavoe. Shet 8E 173
(nr. Burland)
Hamnavoe. Shet 4F 173
(nr. Lunna)
Hamnavoe. Shet 3F 173
(on Yell)
Hamp. Som 3G 21
Hampden Park. E Sus 5G 27
Hampen. Glos 4F 49
Hamperden End. Essx 2F 53
Hamperley. Shrp 2G 59
Hampnett. Glos 4F 49
Hampole. S Yor 3F 93
Hampreston. Dors 3F 15
**Hampstead.** G Lon 2D 38
Hampstead Norreys. W Ber 4D 36
Hampsthwaite. N Yor 4E 99
Hampton. Devn 3F 13
Hampton. G Lon 3C 38
Hampton. Kent 4F 41
Hampton. Shrp 2B 60
Hampton. Swin 2G 35
Hampton. Worc 1F 49
Hampton Bishop. Here 2A 48
Hampton Fields. Glos 2D 35
Hampton Hargate. Pet 1A 64
Hampton Heath. Ches W 1H 71
Hampton in Arden. W Mid 2G 61
Hampton Loade. Shrp 2B 60
Hampton Lovett. Worc 4C 60
Hampton Lucy. Warw 5G 61
Hampton Magna. Warw 4G 61
Hampton on the Hill. Warw 4G 61
Hampton Poyle. Oxon 4D 50
Hampton Wick. G Lon 4C 38
Hamptworth. Wilts 1H 15
Hamrow. Norf 3B 78
Hamsey. E Sus 4F 27
Hamsey Green. Surr 5E 39
Hamstall Ridware. Staf 4F 73
Hamstead. IOW 3C 16
Hamstead. W Mid 1E 61
Hamstead Marshall. W Ber 5C 36
Hamsterley. Dur 4E 115
(nr. Consett)
Hamsterley. Dur 1E 105
(nr. Wolsingham)
Hamsterley Mill. Dur 4E 115
Hamstreet. Kent 2E 28
Ham Street. Som 3A 22
Hamworthy. Pool 3E 15
Hanbury. Staf 3F 73
Hanbury. Worc 4D 60
Hanbury Woodend. Staf 3F 73
Hanby. Linc 2H 75
Hanchurch. Staf 1C 72
Hand and Pen. Devn 3D 12
Handbridge. Ches W 4G 83
Handcross. W Sus 2D 26
Handforth. Ches E 2C 84
Handley. Ches W 5G 83
Handley. Derbs 4A 86
Handsacre. Staf 4E 73
Handsworth. S Yor 2B 86
Handsworth. W Mid 1E 61
Handy Cross. Buck 2G 37
Hanford. Dors 1D 14
Hanford. Stoke 1C 72
Hangersley. Hants 2G 15
Hanging Houghton. Nptn 3E 63
Hanging Langford. Wilts 3F 23
Hangleton. Brig 5D 26
Hangleton. W Sus 5B 26
Hanham. S Glo 4B 34
Hanham Green. S Glo 4B 34
Hankelow. Ches E 1A 72
Hankerton. Wilts 2E 35
Hankham. E Sus 5H 27
**Hanley.** Stoke 1C 72 & **Stoke 202**
Hanley Castle. Worc 1D 48
Hanley Childe. Worc 4A 60
Hanley Swan. Worc 1D 48
Hanley William. Worc 4A 60
Hanlith. N Yor 3B 98
Hanmer. Wrex 2G 71
Hannaborough. Devn 2F 11
Hannaford. Devn 4G 19
Hannah. Linc 3E 89
Hannington. Hants 1D 24
Hannington. Nptn 3F 63
Hannington. Swin 2G 35
Hannington Wick. Swin 2G 35
Hanscombe End. C Beds 2B 52
Hanslope. Mil 1G 51
Hanthorpe. Linc 3H 75
Hanwell. G Lon 2C 38
Hanwell. Oxon 1C 50
Hanwood. Shrp 5G 71
Hanworth. G Lon 3C 38
Hanworth. Norf 2D 78
Happas. Ang 4D 144
Happendon. S Lan 1A 118
Happisburgh. Norf 2F 79
Happisburgh Common. Norf 3F 79
Hapsford. Ches W 3G 83
Hapton. Lanc 1F 91
Hapton. Norf 1D 66
Harberton. Devn 3D 9
Harbertonford. Devn 3D 9
Harbledown. Kent 5F 41
Harborne. W Mid 2E 61
Harborough Magna. Warw 3B 62
Harbottle. Nmbd 4D 120
Harbourneford. Devn 2D 8
Harbours Hill. Worc 4D 60
Harbridge. Hants 1G 15
Harbury. Warw 4A 62
Harby. Leics 2E 75
Harby. Notts 3F 87
Harcombe. Devn 3E 13
Harcombe Bottom. Devn 3G 13
Harcourt. Corn 5C 6
Harden. W Yor 1A 92
Hardenhuish. Wilts 4E 35
Hardgate. Abers 3E 153
Hardgate. Dum 3F 111
Hardham. W Sus 4B 26
Hardingham. Norf 5C 78
Hardingstone. Nptn 5E 63
Hardings Wood. Staf 5C 84
Hardington. Som 1C 22
Hardington Mandeville. Som 1A 14
Hardington Marsh. Som 2A 14
Hardington Moor. Som 1A 14
Hardley. Hants 2C 16
Hardley Street. Norf 5F 79
Hardmead. Mil 1H 51
Hardraw. N Yor 5B 104
Hardstoft. Derbs 4B 86
Hardway. Hants 2E 16
Hardway. Som 3C 22
Hardwick. Buck 4G 51
Hardwick. Cambs 5C 64
Hardwick. Norf 2E 66
Hardwick. Nptn 4F 63
Hardwick. Oxon 3D 50
(nr. Bicester)
Hardwick. Oxon 5B 50
(nr. Witney)
Hardwick. Shrp 1F 59
Hardwick. S Yor 2B 86
Hardwick. Stoc T 2B 106
Hardwick. W Mid 1E 61
Hardwicke. Glos 3E 49
(nr. Cheltenham)
Hardwicke. Glos 4C 48
(nr. Gloucester)
Hardwicke. Here 1F 47
Hardwick Village. Notts 3D 86
Hardy's Green. Essx 3C 54
Hare. Som 1F 13
Hareby. Linc 4C 88
Hareden. Lanc 4F 97
Harefield. G Lon 1B 38
Hare Green. Essx 3D 54
Hare Hatch. Wok 4G 37
Harehill. Derbs 2F 73
Harehills. W Yor 1D 92
Harehope. Nmbd 2E 121
Harelaw. Dum 2F 113
Harelaw. Dur 4E 115
Hareplain. Kent 2C 28
Haresceugh. Cumb 5H 113
Harescombe. Glos 4D 48
Haresfield. Glos 4D 48
Haresfinch. Mers 1H 83
Hareshaw. N Lan 3B 128
Hare Street. Essx 5E 53
Hare Street. Herts 3D 53
Harewood. W Yor 5F 99
Harewood End. Here 3A 48
Harford. Devn 3C 8
Hargate. Norf 1D 66
Hargatewall. Derbs 3F 85
Hargrave. Ches W 4G 83
Hargrave. Nptn 3H 63
Hargrave. Suff 5G 65
Harker. Cumb 3E 113
Harkland. Shet 3F 173
Harkstead. Suff 2E 55
Harlaston. Staf 4G 73
Harlaxton. Linc 2F 75
Harlech. Gwyn 2E 69
Harlequin. Notts 2D 74
Harlescott. Shrp 4H 71
Harleston. Devn 4D 9
Harleston. Norf 2E 67
Harleston. Suff 4C 66
Harlestone. Nptn 4E 62
Harley. Shrp 5H 71
Harley. S Yor 1A 86
Harling Road. Norf 2B 66
Harlington. C Beds 2A 52
Harlington. G Lon 3B 38
Harlington. S Yor 4E 93
Harlosh. High 4B 154
**Harlow.** Essx 4E 53
Harlow Hill. Nmbd 3D 115
Harlsey Castle. N Yor 5B 106
Harlthorpe. E Yor 1H 93
Harlton. Cambs 5C 64
Harlyn Bay. Corn 1C 6
Harman's Cross. Dors 4E 15
Harmby. N Yor 1D 98
Harmer Green. Herts 4C 52
Harmer Hill. Shrp 3G 71
Harmondsworth. G Lon 3B 38
Harmston. Linc 4G 87
Harnage. Shrp 5H 71
Harnham. Nmbd 1D 115
Harnham. Wilts 4G 23
Harnhill. Glos 5F 49
Harold Hill. G Lon 1G 39
Haroldston West. Pemb 3C 42
Haroldswick. Shet 1H 173
Harold Wood. G Lon 1G 39
Harome. N Yor 1A 100
**Harpenden.** Herts 4B 52
Harpford. Devn 3D 12
Harpham. E Yor 3E 101
Harpley. Norf 3G 77
Harpley. Worc 4A 60
Harpole. Nptn 4D 62
Harpsdale. High 3D 168
Harpsden. Oxon 3F 37
Harpswell. Linc 2G 87
Harpurhey. G Man 4G 91
Harpur Hill. Derbs 3E 85
Harraby. Cumb 4F 113
Harracott. Devn 4F 19
Harrapool. High 1E 147
Harrapul. High 1E 147
Harrietfield. Per 1B 136
Harrietsham. Kent 5C 40
Harrington. Cumb 2A 102
Harrington. Linc 3C 88
Harrington. Nptn 2E 63
Harringworth. Nptn 1G 63
Harriseahead. Staf 5C 84
Harriston. Cumb 5C 112
**Harrogate.** N Yor 4F 99 & 196
Harrold. Bed 5G 63
Harrop Dale. G Man 4A 92
**Harrow.** G Lon 2C 38
Harrowbarrow. Corn 2H 7
Harrowden. Bed 1A 52
Harrowgate Hill. Darl 3F 105
Harrow on the Hill. G Lon 2C 38
Harrow Weald. G Lon 1C 38
Harry Stoke. S Glo 4B 34
Harston. Cambs 5D 64
Harston. Leics 2F 75
Harswell. E Yor 5C 100
Hart. Hart 1B 106
Hartburn. Nmbd 1D 115
Hartburn. Stoc T 3B 106
Hartest. Suff 5H 65
Hartfield. E Sus 2F 27
Hartford. Cambs 3B 64
Hartford. Ches W 3A 84
Hartford. Som 4C 20
Hartford Bridge. Hants 1F 25
Hartford End. Essx 4G 53
Harthill. Ches W 5H 83
Harthill. N Lan 3C 128
Harthill. S Yor 2B 86
Hartington. Derbs 4F 85
Hartland. Devn 4C 18
Hartland Quay. Devn 4C 18
Hartle. Worc 3D 60
Hartlebury. Worc 3C 60
**Hartlepool.** Hart 1C 106
Hartley. Cumb 4A 104
Hartley. Kent 2B 28
(nr. Cranbrook)
Hartley. Kent 4H 39
(nr. Dartford)
Hartley. Nmbd 2G 115
Hartley Green. Staf 3D 73
Hartley Mauditt. Hants 3F 25
Hartley Wespall. Hants 1E 25
Hartley Wintney. Hants 1F 25
Hartlip. Kent 4C 40
Hartmount Holdings. High 1B 158
Hartoft End. N Yor 5E 107
Harton. N Yor 3B 100
Harton. Shrp 2G 59
Harton. Tyne 3G 115
Hartpury. Glos 3D 48
Hartshead. W Yor 2B 92
**Hartshill.** Warw 1H 61
Hartshorne. Derbs 3H 73
Hartsop. Cumb 3F 103
Hart Station. Hart 1B 106
Hartswell. Som 4D 20
Hartwell. Nptn 5E 63
Hartwood. Lanc 3D 90
Hartwood. N Lan 4B 128
Harvel. Kent 4A 40
Harvington. Worc 1F 49
(nr. Evesham)
Harvington. Worc 3C 60
(nr. Kidderminster)
Harwell. Oxon 3C 36
**Harwich.** Essx 2F 55 & 204
Harwood. Dur 1B 104
Harwood. G Man 3F 91
Harwood Dale. N Yor 5G 107
Harworth. Notts 1D 86
Hascombe. Surr 2A 26
Haselbech. Nptn 3E 62
Haselbury Plucknett. Som 1H 13
Haseley. Warw 4G 61
Hasfield. Glos 3D 48
Hasguard. Pemb 4C 42
Haskayne. Lanc 4B 90
Hasketon. Suff 5E 67
Hasland. Derbs 4A 86
**Haslemere.** Surr 2A 26
**Haslingden.** Lanc 2F 91
Haslingfield. Cambs 5D 64
Haslington. Ches E 5B 84
Hassall. Ches E 5B 84
Hassall Green. Ches E 5B 84
Hassell Street. Kent 1E 29
Hassendean. Bord 2H 119
Hassingham. Norf 5F 79
Hassness. Cumb 3C 102
Hassocks. W Sus 4E 27
Hassop. Derbs 3G 85
Haster. High 3F 169
Hasthorpe. Linc 4D 89
Hastigrow. High 2E 169
Hastingleigh. Kent 1E 29
**Hastings.** E Sus 5C 28
Hastingwood. Essx 5E 53
Hastoe. Herts 5H 51
Haston. Shrp 3H 71
Haswell. Dur 5G 115
Haswell Plough. Dur 5G 115
Hatch. C Beds 1B 52
Hatch Beauchamp. Som 4G 21
Hatch End. G Lon 1C 38
Hatch Green. Som 1G 13
Hatching Green. Herts 4B 52
Hatchmere. Ches W 3H 83
Hatch Warren. Hants 2E 24
Hatcliffe. NE Lin 4F 95
Hatfield. Here 5H 59
**Hatfield.** Herts 5C 52
**Hatfield.** S Yor 4G 93
Hatfield. Worc 5C 60
Hatfield Broad Oak. Essx 4F 53
Hatfield Garden Village. Herts 5C 52
Hatfield Heath. Essx 4F 53
Hatfield Hyde. Herts 4C 52
Hatfield Peverel. Essx 4A 54
Hatfield Woodhouse. S Yor 4G 93
Hatford. Oxon 2B 36
Hatherden. Hants 1B 24
Hatherleigh. Devn 2F 11
Hathern. Leics 3B 74
Hatherop. Glos 5G 49
Hathersage. Derbs 2G 85
Hathersage Booths. Derbs 2G 85
Hatherton. Ches E 1A 72
Hatherton. Staf 4D 72
Hatley St George. Cambs 5B 64
Hatt. Corn 2H 7
Hattersley. G Man 1D 85
Hattingley. Hants 3E 25
Hatton. Abers 5H 161
Hatton. Derbs 2G 73
Hatton. G Lon 3B 38
Hatton. Linc 3A 88
Hatton. Shrp 1G 59
Hatton. Warr 2A 84
Hatton. Warw 4G 61
Hattoncrook. Abers 1F 153
Hatton Heath. Ches W 4G 83
Hatton of Fintray. Abers 2F 153
Haugh. E Ayr 2D 117
Haugh. Linc 3D 88
Haugham. Linc 2C 88
Haugh Head. Nmbd 2E 121
Haughley. Suff 4C 66
Haughley Green. Suff 4C 66
Haugh of Ballechin. Per 3G 143
Haugh of Glass. Mor 5B 160
Haugh of Urr. Dum 3F 111
Haughton. Ches E 5H 83
Haughton. Notts 3D 86
Haughton. Shrp 1A 60
(nr. Bridgnorth)
Haughton. Shrp 3F 71
(nr. Oswestry)
Haughton. Shrp 5B 72
(nr. Shifnal)
Haughton. Shrp 4H 71
(nr. Shrewsbury)
Haughton. Staf 3C 72
Haughton Green. G Man 1D 84
Haughton le Skerne. Darl 3A 106
Haultwick. Herts 3D 52
Haunn. Arg 4E 139
Haunn. W Isl 7C 170
Haunton. Staf 4G 73
Hauxton. Cambs 5D 64
Havannah. Ches E 4C 84
**Havant.** Hants 2F 17
Haven. Here 5G 59
Haven Bank. Linc 5B 88
Havenstreet. IOW 3D 16
Haven, The. W Sus 2B 26
Havercroft. W Yor 3D 93
**Haverfordwest.** Pemb 3D 42
**Haverhill.** Suff 1G 53
Haverigg. Cumb 2A 96
Havering-Atte-Bower. G Lon 1G 39
Havering's Grove. Essx 1A 40
Haversham. Mil 1G 51
Haverthwaite. Cumb 1C 96
Haverton Hill. Stoc T 2B 106
Havyatt. Som 3A 22
**Hawarden.** Flin 4F 83
Hawbridge. Worc 1E 49
Hawcoat. Cumb 2B 96
Hawcross. Glos 2C 48
Hawen. Cdgn 1D 44
Hawes. N Yor 1A 98
Hawes Green. Norf 1E 67
**Hawick.** Bord 3H 119
Hawkchurch. Devn 2G 13
Hawkedon. Suff 5G 65
Hawkenbury. Kent 1C 28
Hawkeridge. Wilts 1D 22
Hawkerland. Devn 4D 12
Hawkesbury. S Glo 3C 34
Hawkesbury. Warw 2A 62
Hawkesbury Upton. S Glo 3C 34
Hawkes End. W Mid 2G 61
Hawk Green. G Man 2D 84
Hawkhurst. Kent 2B 28
Hawkhurst Common. E Sus 4G 27
Hawkinge. Kent 1G 29
Hawkley. Hants 4F 25
Hawkridge. Som 3B 20
Hawksdale. Cumb 5E 113
Hawkshaw. G Man 3F 91
Hawkshead. Cumb 5E 103
Hawkshead Hill. Cumb 5E 103
Hawkswick. N Yor 2B 98
Hawksworth. Notts 1E 75
Hawksworth. W Yor 5D 98
Hawkwell. Essx 1C 40
Hawley. Hants 1G 25
Hawley. Kent 3G 39
Hawling. Glos 3F 49
Hawnby. N Yor 1H 99
Haworth. W Yor 1A 92
Hawstead. Suff 5A 66
Hawthorn. Dur 5H 115
Hawthorn Hill. Brac 4G 37
Hawthorn Hill. Linc 5B 88
Hawthorpe. Linc 3H 75
Hawton. Notts 5E 87
**Haxby.** York 4A 100
Haxey. N Lin 1E 87
Haybridge. Shrp 3A 60
Haybridge. Som 2A 22
**Haydock.** Mers 1H 83
Haydon. Bath 1B 22
Haydon. Dors 1B 14
Haydon. Som 4F 21
Haydon Bridge. Nmbd 3B 114
Haydon Wick. Swin 3G 35
Haye. Corn 2H 7
Hayes. G Lon 4F 39
(nr. Bromley)
**Hayes.** G Lon 2B 38
(nr. Uxbridge)
Hayfield. Derbs 2E 85
Hay Green. Norf 4E 77
Hayhill. E Ayr 3D 116
Haylands. IOW 3D 16
Hayle. Corn 3C 4
Hayley Green. W Mid 2D 60
**Hayling Island.** Hants 3F 17
Hayne. Devn 2B 12
Haynes. C Beds 1A 52
Haynes West End. C Beds 1A 52
Hay-on-Wye. Powy 1F 47
Hayscastle. Pemb 2C 42
Hayscastle Cross. Pemb 2D 42
Hayshead. Ang 4F 145
Hay Street. Herts 3D 53
Hayton. Aber 3G 153
Hayton. Cumb 5C 112
(nr. Aspatria)
Hayton. Cumb 4G 113
(nr. Brampton)
Hayton. E Yor 5C 100
Hayton. Notts 2E 87
Hayton's Bent. Shrp 2H 59
Haytor Vale. Devn 5A 12
Haytown. Devn 1D 11
**Haywards Heath.** W Sus 3E 27
Haywood. S Lan 4C 128
Hazelbank. S Lan 5B 128
Hazelbury Bryan. Dors 2C 14
Hazeleigh. Essx 5B 54
Hazeley. Hants 1F 25
**Hazel Grove.** G Man 2D 84
Hazelhead. S Yor 4B 92
Hazelslade. Staf 4E 73
Hazel Street. Kent 2A 28
Hazelton Walls. Fife 1F 137
Hazelwood. Derbs 1H 73
Hazlemere. Buck 2G 37
Hazler. Shrp 1G 59
Hazlerigg. Tyne 2F 115
Hazles. Staf 1E 73
Hazleton. Glos 4F 49
Hazon. Nmbd 4F 121
Heacham. Norf 2F 77
Headbourne Worthy. Hants 3C 24
Headcorn. Kent 1C 28
Headingley. W Yor 1C 92
Headington. Oxon 5D 50
Headlam. Dur 3E 105
Headless Cross. Worc 4E 61
Headley. Hants 3G 25
(nr. Haslemere)
Headley. Hants 5D 36
(nr. Kingsclere)
Headley. Surr 5D 38
Headley Down. Hants 3G 25
Headley Heath. Worc 3E 61
Headley Park. Bris 5A 34
Head of Muir. Falk 1B 128
Headon. Notts 3E 87
Heads Nook. Cumb 4F 113
Heage. Derbs 5A 86
Healaugh. N Yor 5D 104
(nr. Grinton)
Healaugh. N Yor 5H 99
(nr. York)
Heald Green. G Man 2C 84
Heale. Devn 2G 19
Healey. G Man 3G 91
Healey. Nmbd 4D 114
Healey. N Yor 1D 98
Healeyfield. Dur 5D 114
Healing. NE Lin 3F 95
Heamoor. Corn 3B 4
Heanish. Arg 4B 138
**Heanor.** Derbs 1B 74
Heanton Punchardon. Devn 3F 19
Heapham. Linc 2F 87
Heartsease. Powy 4D 58
Heasley Mill. Devn 3H 19
Heaste. High 2E 147
Heath. Derbs 4B 86
Heath and Reach. C Beds 3H 51
Heath Common. W Sus 4C 26
Heathcote. Derbs 4F 85
Heath Cross. Devn 3H 11
Heathencote. Nptn 1F 51
Heath End. Derbs 3A 74
Heath End. Hants 5D 36
Heath End. W Mid 5E 73
Heather. Leics 4A 74
Heatherfield. High 4D 155
Heatherton. Derb 2H 73
Heathfield. Cambs 1E 53
Heathfield. Cumb 5C 112
Heathfield. Devn 5B 12
Heathfield. E Sus 3G 27
Heathfield. Ren 3E 126
Heathfield. Som 3E 21
(nr. Lydeard St Lawrence)
Heathfield. Som 4E 21
(nr. Norton Fitzwarren)
Heath Green. Worc 3E 61
Heathhall. Dum 2A 112
Heath Hayes. Staf 4E 73
Heath Hill. Shrp 4B 72
Heath House. Som 2H 21
Heathrow (London) Airport. G Lon 3B 38 & 205
Heathstock. Devn 2F 13
Heath, The. Norf 3E 79
(nr. Buxton)
Heath, The. Norf 3B 78
(nr. Fakenham)
Heath, The. Norf 3D 78
(nr. Hevingham)
Heath, The. Staf 2E 73
Heath, The. Suff 2E 55
Heathton. Shrp 1C 60
Heathtop. Derbs 2G 73
Heath Town. W Mid 1D 60
Heatley. Staf 3E 73
Heatley. Warr 2B 84
Heaton. Lanc 3D 96
Heaton. Staf 4D 84
Heaton. Tyne 3F 115
Heaton. W Yor 1B 92
Heaton Moor. G Man 1C 84
Heaton's Bridge. Lanc 3C 90
Heaverham. Kent 5G 39
Heavitree. Devn 3C 12
**Hebburn.** Tyne 3G 115
Hebden. N Yor 3C 98
Hebden Bridge. W Yor 2H 91
Hebden Green. Ches W 4A 84
Hebing End. Herts 3D 52
Hebron. Carm 2F 43
Hebron. Nmbd 1E 115
Heck. Dum 1B 112
Heckdyke. N Lin 1E 87
Heckfield. Hants 5F 37
Heckfield Green. Suff 3D 66
Heckfordbridge. Essx 3C 54
Heckington. Linc 1A 76
**Heckmondwike.** W Yor 2C 92
Heddington. Wilts 5E 35
Heddle. Orkn 6C 172
Heddon. Devn 4G 19
Heddon-on-the-Wall. Nmbd 3E 115
Hedenham. Norf 1F 67
**Hedge End.** Hants 1C 16
Hedgerley. Buck 2A 38
Hedging. Som 4G 21
Hedley on the Hill. Nmbd 4D 115
Hednesford. Staf 4E 73
Hedon. E Yor 2E 95
Hegdon Hill. Here 5H 59
Heglibister. Shet 6E 173
Heighington. Darl 2F 105
Heighington. Linc 4H 87
Heightington. Worc 3B 60
Heights of Brae. High 2H 157
Heights of Fodderty. High 2H 157
Heights of Kinlochewe. High 2C 156
Heiton. Bord 1B 120
Hele. Devn 2C 12
(nr. Exeter)
Hele. Devn 3D 10
(nr. Holsworthy)
Hele. Devn 2F 19
(nr. Ilfracombe)
Hele. Torb 2F 9
Helen's Bay. N Dwn 1J 179
**Helensburgh.** Arg 1D 126
Helford. Corn 4E 5
Helhoughton. Norf 3A 78
Helions Bumpstead. Essx 1G 53
Helland. Corn 5A 10
Helland. Som 4G 21
Hellandbridge. Corn 5A 10
Hellesdon. Norf 4E 78
Hellesveor. Corn 2C 4
Hellidon. Nptn 5C 62
Hellifield. N Yor 4A 98
Hellingly. E Sus 4G 27
Hellington. Norf 5F 79
Hellister. Shet 7E 173
Helmdon. Nptn 1D 50
Helmingham. Suff 5D 66
Helmington Row. Dur 1E 105
Helmsdale. High 2H 165
Helmshore. Lanc 2F 91
Helmsley. N Yor 1A 100
Helperby. N Yor 3G 99
Helperthorpe. N Yor 2D 100
Helpringham. Linc 1A 76
Helpston. Pet 5A 76
Helsby. Ches W 3G 83
Helsey. Linc 3E 89
Helston. Corn 4D 4
Helstone. Corn 4A 10
Helton. Cumb 2G 103
Helwith. N Yor 4D 105
Helwith Bridge. N Yor 3H 97
Helygain. Flin 3E 82
Hemblington. Norf 4F 79
**Hemel Hempstead.** Herts 5A 52
Hemerdon. Devn 3B 8
Hemingbrough. N Yor 1G 93
Hemingby. Linc 3B 88
Hemingfield. S Yor 4D 93
Hemingford Abbots. Cambs 3B 64
Hemingford Grey. Cambs 3B 64
Hemingstone. Suff 5D 66
Hemington. Leics 3B 74
Hemington. Nptn 2H 63
Hemington. Som 1C 22
Hemley. Suff 1F 55
Hemlington. Midd 3B 106
Hempholme. E Yor 4E 101
Hempnall. Norf 1E 67
Hempnall Green. Norf 1E 67
Hempriggs. High 4F 169
Hemp's Green. Essx 3C 54
Hempstead. Essx 2G 53
Hempstead. Medw 4B 40
Hempstead. Norf 2D 78
(nr. Holt)
Hempstead. Norf 3G 79
(nr. Stalham)
Hempsted. Glos 4D 48
Hempton. Norf 3B 78
Hempton. Oxon 2C 50
Hemsby. Norf 4G 79
Hemswell. Linc 1G 87
Hemswell Cliff. Linc 2G 87
Hemsworth. Dors 2E 15
**Hemsworth.** W Yor 3E 93
Hem, The. Shrp 5B 72
Hemyock. Devn 1E 13
Henallt. Carm 3E 45
Henbury. Bris 4A 34
Henbury. Ches E 3C 84
Hendomen. Powy 1E 58
**Hendon.** G Lon 2D 38
Hendon. Tyne 4H 115
Hendra. Corn 3D 6
Hendre. B'end 3C 32
Hendreforgan. Rhon 3C 32
Hendy. Carm 5F 45
Heneglwys. IOA 3D 80
Henfeddau Fawr. Pemb 1G 43
Henfield. S Glo 4B 34
Henfield. W Sus 4D 26
Henford. Devn 3D 10
Hengoed. Cphy 2E 33
Hengoed. Shrp 2E 71
Hengrave. Suff 4H 65
Henham. Essx 3F 53
Heniarth. Powy 5D 70
Henlade. Som 4F 21
Henley. Dors 2B 14
Henley. Shrp 2G 59
(nr. Church Stretton)
Henley. Shrp 3H 59
(nr. Ludlow)
Henley. Som 3H 21
Henley. Suff 5D 66
Henley. W Sus 4G 25
Henley Down. E Sus 4B 28
Henley-in-Arden. Warw 4F 61
**Henley-on-Thames.** Oxon 3F 37
Henley Street. Kent 4A 40
Henllan. Cdgn 1D 44
Henllan. Den 4C 82
Henllan. Mon 3F 47
Henllan Amgoed. Carm 3F 43
Henllys. Torf 2F 33
Henlow. C Beds 2B 52
Hennock. Devn 4B 12
Henny Street. Essx 2B 54
Henryd. Cnwy 3G 81
Henry's Moat. Pemb 2E 43
Hensall. N Yor 2F 93
Henshaw. Nmbd 3A 114
Hensingham. Cumb 3A 102
Henstead. Suff 2G 67
Hensting. Hants 4C 24
Henstridge. Som 1C 14
Henstridge Ash. Som 4C 22
Henstridge Bowden. Som 4B 22
Henstridge Marsh. Som 4C 22
Henton. Oxon 5F 51
Henton. Som 2H 21
Henwood. Corn 5C 10
Heogan. Shet 7F 173
Heolgerrig. Mer T 5D 46
Heol Senni. Powy 3C 46
Heol-y-Cyw. B'end 3C 32
Hepburn. Nmbd 2E 121
Hepple. Nmbd 4D 121
Hepscott. Nmbd 1F 115
Heptonstall. W Yor 2H 91
Hepworth. Suff 3B 66
Hepworth. W Yor 4B 92
Herbrandston. Pemb 4C 42
**Hereford.** Here 2A 48
Heribusta. High 1D 154
Heriot. Bord 4H 129
Hermiston. Edin 2E 129
Hermitage. Dors 2B 14
Hermitage. Bord 5H 119
Hermitage. W Ber 4D 36
Hermitage. W Sus 2F 17
Hermon. Carm 3G 45
(nr. Llandeilo)
Hermon. Carm 2D 44
(nr. Newcastle Emlyn)
Hermon. IOA 4C 80
Hermon. Pemb 1G 43
Herne. Kent 4F 41
**Herne Bay.** Kent 4F 41
Herne Common. Kent 4F 41
Herne Pound. Kent 5A 40
Herner. Devn 4F 19
Hernhill. Kent 4E 41
Herodsfoot. Corn 2G 7
Heronden. Kent 5G 41
Herongate. Essx 1H 39
Heronsford. S Ayr 1G 109
Heronsgate. Herts 1B 38
Heron's Ghyll. E Sus 3F 27
Herra. Shet 2H 173
Herriard. Hants 2E 25
Herringfleet. Suff 1G 67
Herringswell. Suff 4G 65
Herrington. Tyne 4G 115
Hersden. Kent 4G 41
Hersham. Corn 2C 10
Hersham. Surr 4C 38
Herstmonceux. E Sus 4H 27
Herston. Dors 5F 15
Herston. Orkn 8D 172
**Hertford.** Herts 4D 52
Hertford Heath. Herts 4D 52
Hertingfordbury. Herts 4D 52
Hesketh. Lanc 2C 90
Hesketh Bank. Lanc 2C 90
Hesketh Lane. Lanc 5F 97
Hesket Newmarket. Cumb 1E 103
Heskin Green. Lanc 3D 90
Hesleden. Dur 1B 106
Hesleyside. Nmbd 1B 114
Heslington. York 4A 100
Hessay. York 4H 99
Hessenford. Corn 3H 7
Hessett. Suff 4B 66
Hessilhead. N Ayr 4E 127
Hessle. E Yor 2D 94
Hestaford. Shet 6D 173
Hest Bank. Lanc 3D 96

Hulland Ward—Kingairloch


Hulland Ward. Derbs .1G 73
Hullavington. Wilts .3D 35
Hullbridge. Essx .1C 40
Hulme. G Man .1C 84
Hulme. Staf .1D 72
Hulme End. Staf .5F 85
Hulme Walfield. Ches E .4C 84
Hulverstone. IOW .4B 16
Hulver Street. Suff .2G 67
Humber. Devn .5C 12
Humber. Here .5H 59
**Humber Bridge**. N Lin .2D 94
Humberside Airport. N Lin .3D 94
Humberston. NE Lin .4G 95
Humberstone. Leic .5D 74
Humbie. E Lot .3A 130
Humbleton. E Yor .1F 95
Humbleton. Nmbd .2D 121
Humby. Linc .2H 75
Hume. Bord .5D 130
Humshaugh. Nmbd .2C 114
Huna. High .1F 169
Huncoat. Lanc .1F 91
Huncote. Leics .1C 62
Hundall. Derbs .3A 86
Hunderthwaite. Dur .2C 104
Hundleby. Linc .4C 88
Hundle Houses. Linc .5B 88
Hundleton. Pemb .4D 42
Hundon. Suff .1H 53
Hundred Acres. Hants .1D 16
Hundred House. Powy .5D 58
Hundred, The. Here .4H 59
Hungarton. Leics .5D 74
Hungerford. Hants .1G 15
Hungerford. Shrp .2H 59
Hungerford. Som .2D 20
Hungerford. W Ber .5B 36
Hungerford Newtown.
W Ber .4B 36
Hunger Hill. G Man .4E 91
Hungerton. Linc .2F 75
Hungladder. High .1C 154
Hungryhatton. Shrp .3A 72
Hunmanby. N Yor .2E 101
Hunmanby Sands. N Yor .2F 101
Hunningham. Warw .4A 62
Hunnington. Worc .2D 60
Hunny Hill. IOW .4C 16
Hunsdon. Herts .4E 53
Hunsdonbury. Herts .4E 53
Hunsingore. N Yor .4G 99
Hunslet. W Yor .1D 92
Hunslet Carr. W Yor .1D 92
Hunsonby. Cumb .1G 103
Hunspow. High .1E 169
Hunstanton. Norf .1F 77
Hunstanworth. Dur .5C 114
Hunston. Suff .4B 66
Hunston. W Sus .2G 17
Hunstrete. Bath .5B 34
Hunt End. Worc .4E 61
Hunterfield. Midl .3G 129
Hunters Forstal. Kent .4F 41
Hunter's Quay. Arg .2C 126
Huntham. Som .4G 21
Hunthill Lodge. Ang .1D 144
**Huntingdon**. Cambs .3B 64
Huntingfield. Suff .3F 67
Huntingford. Dors .4D 22
Huntington. Ches W .4G 83
Huntington. E Lot .2A 130
Huntington. Here .5E 59
Huntington. Staf .4D 72
Huntington. Telf .5A 72
Huntington. York .4A 100
Huntingtower. Per .1C 136
Huntley. Glos .4C 48
Huntley. Staf .1E 73
Huntly. Abers .5C 160
Huntlywood. Bord .5C 130
Hunton. Hants .3C 24
Hunton. Kent .1B 28
Hunton. N Yor .5E 105
Hunton Bridge. Herts .1B 38
Hunt's Corner. Norf .2C 66
Huntscott. Som .2C 20
Hunt's Cross. Mers .2G 83
Hunts Green. Warw .1F 61
Huntsham. Devn .4D 20
Huntshaw. Devn .4F 19
Huntspill. Som .2G 21
Huntstile. Som .3F 21
Huntworth. Som .3G 21
Hunwick. Dur .1E 105
Hunworth. Norf .2C 78
Hurcott. Som .1G 13
(nr. Ilminster)
Hurcott. Som .4A 22
(nr. Somerton)
Hurdcott. Wilts .3G 23
Hurdley. Powy .1E 59
Hurdsfield. Ches E .3D 84
Hurlet. Glas .3G 127
Hurley. Warw .1G 61
Hurley. Wind .3G 37
Hurlford. E Ayr .1D 116
Hurliness. Orkn .9B 172
Hurlston Green. Lanc .3C 90
Hurn. Dors .3G 15
Hursey. Dors .2H 13
Hursley. Hants .4C 24
Hurst. G Man .4H 91
Hurst. N Yor .4D 104
Hurst. Som .1H 13
Hurst. Wok .4F 37
Hurstbourne Priors. Hants .2C 24
Hurstbourne Tarrant. Hants .1B 24
Hurst Green. Ches E .1H 71
Hurst Green. E Sus .3B 28
Hurst Green. Essx .4D 54
Hurst Green. Lanc .1E 91
Hurst Green. Surr .5E 39
Hurstley. Here .1G 47
Hurstpierpoint. W Sus .4D 27
Hurstway Common. Here .1G 47
Hurst Wickham. W Sus .4D 27
Hurstwood. Lanc .1G 91
Hurtmore. Surr .1A 26
Hurworth-on-Tees. Darl .3A 106
Hurworth Place. Darl .4F 105
Hury. Dur .3C 104
Husbands Bosworth. Leics .2D 62
Husborne Crawley. C Beds .2H 51
Husthwaite. N Yor .2H 99
Hutcherleigh. Devn .3D 9
Hut Green. N Yor .2F 93
Huthwaite. Notts .5B 86
Huttoft. Linc .3E 89
Hutton. Cumb .2F 103
Hutton. E Yor .4E 101
Hutton. Essx .1H 39
Hutton. Lanc .2C 90
Hutton. N Som .1G 21
Hutton. Bord .4F 131
Hutton Bonville. N Yor .4A 106
Hutton Buscel. N Yor .1D 100
Hutton Conyers. N Yor .2F 99
Hutton Cranswick. E Yor .4E 101
Hutton End. Cumb .1F 103
Hutton Gate. Red C .3C 106
Hutton Henry. Dur .1B 106
Hutton-le-Hole. N Yor .5E 107
Hutton Magna. Dur .3E 105
Hutton Mulgrave. N Yor .4F 107
Hutton Roof. Cumb .2E 97
(nr. Kirkby Lonsdale)
Hutton Roof. Cumb .1E 103
(nr. Penrith)
Hutton Rudby. N Yor .4B 106
Huttons Ambo. N Yor .3B 100
Hutton Sessay. N Yor .2G 99
Hutton Village. Red C .3D 106
Hutton Wandesley. N Yor .4H 99
Huxham. Devn .3C 12
Huxham Green. Som .3A 22
Huxley. Ches W .4H 83
Huxter. Shet .6C 173
(on Mainland)
Huxter. Shet .5G 173
(on Whalsay)
**Huyton**. Mers .1G 83
**Hwlffordd**. Pemb .3D 42
Hycemoor. Cumb .1A 96
Hyde. Glos .5D 49
(nr. Stroud)
Hyde. Glos .3F 49
(nr. Winchcombe)
**Hyde**. G Man .1D 84
Hyde Heath. Buck .5H 51
Hyde Lea. Staf .4D 72
Hyde Park. S Yor .4F 93
Hydestile. Surr .1A 26
Hyndford Bridge. S Lan .5C 128
Hynish. Arg .5A 138
Hyssington. Powy .1F 59
**Hythe**. Hants .2C 16
**Hythe**. Kent .2F 29
Hythe End. Wind .3B 38
Hythie. Abers .3H 161
Hyton. Cumb .1A 96

## I

Ianstown. Mor .2B 160
Iarsiadar. W Isl .4D 171
Ibberton. Dors .2C 14
Ible. Derbs .5G 85
Ibrox. Glas .3G 127
Ibsley. Hants .2G 15
Ibstock. Leics .4B 74
Ibstone. Buck .2F 37
Ibthorpe. Hants .1B 24
Iburndale. N Yor .4F 107
Ibworth. Hants .1D 24
Icelton. N Som .5G 33
Ichrachan. Arg .5E 141
Ickburgh. Norf .1H 65
Ickenham. G Lon .2B 38
Ickenthwaite. Cumb .1C 96
Ickford. Buck .5E 51
Ickham. Kent .5G 41
Ickleford. Herts .2B 52
Icklesham. E Sus .4C 28
Ickleton. Cambs .1E 53
Icklingham. Suff .3G 65
Ickwell. C Beds .1B 52
Icomb. Glos .3H 49
Idbury. Oxon .4H 49
Iddesleigh. Devn .2F 11
Ide. Devn .3B 12
Ideford. Devn .5B 12
Ide Hill. Kent .5F 39
Iden. E Sus .3D 28
Iden Green. Kent .2C 28
(nr. Benenden)
Iden Green. Kent .2B 28
(nr. Goudhurst)
Idle. W Yor .1B 92
Idless. Corn .4C 6
Idlicote. Warw .1A 50
Idmiston. Wilts .3G 23
Idole. Carm .4E 45
Idridgehay. Derbs .1G 73
Idrigill. High .2C 154
Idstone. Oxon .3A 36
Iffley. Oxon .5D 50
Ifield. W Sus .2D 26
Ifieldwood. W Sus .2D 26
Ifold. W Sus .2B 26
Iford. E Sus .5F 27
Ifton Heath. Shrp .2F 71
Ightfield. Shrp .2H 71
Ightham. Kent .5G 39
Iken. Suff .5G 67
Ilam. Staf .5F 85
Ilchester. Som .4A 22
Ilderton. Nmbd .2E 121
**Ilford**. G Lon .2F 39
Ilford. Som .1G 13
**Ilfracombe**. Devn .2F 19
**Ilkeston**. Derbs .1B 74
Ilketshall St Andrew. Suff .2F 67
Ilketshall St Lawrence. Suff .2F 67
Ilketshall St Margaret. Suff .2F 67
**Ilkley**. W Yor .5D 98
Illand. Corn .5C 10
Illey. W Mid .2D 61
Illidge Green. Ches E .4B 84
Illington. Norf .2B 66
Illingworth. W Yor .2A 92
Illogan. Corn .4A 6
Illogan Highway. Corn .4A 6
Illston on the Hill. Leics .1E 62
Ilmer. Buck .5F 51
Ilmington. Warw .1H 49
Ilminster. Som .1G 13
Ilsington. Devn .5A 12
Ilsington. Dors .3C 14
Ilston. Swan .3E 31
Ilton. N Yor .2D 98
Ilton. Som .1G 13
Imachar. N Ayr .5G 125
Imber. Wilts .2E 23
**Immingham**. NE Lin .3E 95
Immingham Dock. NE Lin .3F 95
Impington. Cambs .4D 64
Ince. Ches W .3G 83
Ince Blundell. Mers .4B 90
**Ince-in-Makerfield**. G Man .4D 90
Inchbae Lodge. High .2G 157
Inchbare. Ang .2F 145
Inchberry. Mor .3H 159
Inchbraoch. Ang .3G 145
Inchbrook. Glos .5D 48
Incheril. High .2C 156
Inchinnan. Ren .3F 127
Inchlaggan. High .3D 148
Inchmichael. Per .1E 137
Inchnadamph. High .1G 163
Inchree. High .2E 141
Inchture. Per .1E 137
Inchyra. Per .1D 136
Indian Queens. Corn .3D 6
Ingatestone. Essx .1H 39
Ingbirchworth. S Yor .4C 92
Ingestre. Staf .3D 73
Ingham. Linc .2G 87
Ingham. Norf .3F 79
Ingham. Suff .3A 66
Ingham Corner. Norf .3F 79
Ingleborough. Norf .4D 76
Ingleby. Derbs .3H 73
Ingleby Arncliffe. N Yor .4B 106
Ingleby Barwick. Stoc T .3B 106
Ingleby Greenhow. N Yor .4C 106
Ingleigh Green. Devn .2G 11
Inglemire. Hull .1D 94
Inglesbatch. Bath .5C 34
Ingleton. Dur .2E 105
Ingleton. N Yor .2F 97
Inglewhite. Lanc .5E 97
Ingoe. Nmbd .2D 114
Ingol. Lanc .1D 90
Ingoldisthorpe. Norf .2F 77
Ingoldmells. Linc .4E 89
Ingoldsby. Linc .2H 75
Ingon. Warw .5G 61
Ingram. Nmbd .3E 121
Ingrave. Essx .1H 39
Ingrow. W Yor .1A 92
Ings. Cumb .5F 103
Ingst. S Glo .3A 34
Ingthorpe. Rut .5G 75
Ingworth. Norf .3D 78
Inishrush. M Ulst .6F 174
Inkberrow. Worc .5E 61
Inkford. Worc .3E 61
Inkpen. W Ber .5B 36
Inkstack. High .1E 169
Innellan. Arg .3C 126
Inner Hope. Devn .5C 8
Innerleith. Fife .2E 137
Innerleithen. Bord .1F 119
Innerleven. Fife .3F 137
Innermessan. Dum .3F 109
Innerwick. E Lot .2D 130
Innerwick. Per .4C 142
Innsworth. Glos .3D 48
Insch. Abers .1D 152
Insh. High .3C 150
Inshegra. High .3C 166
Inshore. High .1D 166
Inskip. Lanc .1C 90
Instow. Devn .3E 19
Intwood. Norf .5D 78
Inver. Abers .4G 151
Inver. High .5F 165
Inver. Per .4H 143
Inverailort. High .5F 147
Inverallgin. High .3H 155
Inverallochy. Abers .2H 161
Inveramsay. Abers .1E 153
Inveran. High .4C 164
Inveraray. Arg .3H 133
Inverarish. High .5E 155
Inverarity. Ang .4D 144
Inverarnan. Stir .2C 134
Inverarnie. High .5A 158
Inverbeg. Arg .4C 134
Inverbervie. Abers .1H 145
Inverboyndie. Abers .2D 160
Invercassley. High .3B 164
Invercharnan. High .4F 141
Inverchoran. High .3E 157
Invercreran. Arg .4E 141
Inverdruie. High .2D 150
Inverebrie. Abers .5G 161
Invereck. Arg .1C 126
Inveresk. E Lot .2G 129
Inveresragan. Arg .5D 141
Inverey. Abers .5E 151
Inverfarigaig. High .1H 149
Invergarry. High .3F 149
Invergeldie. Per .1G 135
Invergordon. High .2B 158
Invergowrie. Per .5C 144
Inverguseran. High .3F 147
Inverharroch. Mor .5A 160
Inverie. High .3F 147
Inverinan. Arg .2G 133
Inverinate. High .1B 148
Inverkeilor. Ang .4F 145
**Inverkeithing**. Fife .1E 129
Inverkeithny. Abers .4D 160
Inverkip. Inv .2D 126
Inverkirkaig. High .2E 163
Inverlael. High .5F 163
Inverliever Lodge. Arg .3F 133
Inverliver. Arg .5E 141
Inverlochlarig. Stir .2D 134
Inverlochy. High .1F 141
Inverlussa. Arg .1E 125
Inver Mallie. High .5D 148
Invermarkie. Abers .5B 160
Invermoriston. High .2G 149
Invernaver. High .2H 167
Inverneil House. Arg .1G 125
**Inverness**. High .4A 158 & 196
Inverness Airport. High .3B 158
Invernettie. Abers .4H 161
Inverpolly Lodge. High .2E 163
Inverquhomery. Abers .4H 161
Inverroy. High .5E 149
Inversanda. High .3D 140
Invershiel. High .2B 148
Invershin. High .4C 164
Invershore. High .5E 169
Inversnaid. Stir .3C 134
Inverugie. Abers .4H 161
Inveruglas. Arg .3C 134
**Inverurie**. Abers .1E 153
Invervar. Per .4D 142
Inverythan. Abers .4E 161
Inwardleigh. Devn .3F 11
Inworth. Essx .4B 54
Iochdar. W Isl .4C 170
Iping. W Sus .4G 25
Ipplepen. Devn .2E 9
Ipsden. Oxon .3E 37
Ipstones. Staf .1E 73
**Ipswich**. Suff .1E 55 & 196
Irby. Mers .2E 83
Irby in the Marsh. Linc .4D 88
Irby upon Humber. NE Lin .4E 95
Irchester. Nptn .4G 63
Ireby. Cumb .1D 102
Ireby. Lanc .2F 97
Ireland. Shet .9E 173
Ireleth. Cumb .2B 96
Ireshopeburn. Dur .1B 104
Ireton Wood. Derbs .1G 73
**Irlam**. G Man .1B 84
Irnham. Linc .3H 75
Iron Acton. S Glo .3B 34
Iron Bridge. Cambs .1D 65
Ironbridge. Telf .5A 72
Iron Cross. Warw .5E 61
Ironville. Derbs .5B 86
Irstead. Norf .3F 79
Irthington. Cumb .3F 113
Irthlingborough. Nptn .3G 63
Irton. N Yor .1E 101
**Irvine**. N Ayr .1C 116
Irvine Mains. N Ayr .1C 116
Irvinestown. Ferm .7E 176
Isabella Pit. Nmbd .1G 115
Isauld. High .2B 168
Isbister. Orkn .6C 172
Isbister. Shet .2E 173
(on Mainland)
Isbister. Shet .5G 173
(on Whalsay)
Isfield. E Sus .4F 27
Isham. Nptn .3F 63
Island Carr. N Lin .4C 94
Islay Airport. Arg .4B 124
Isle Abbotts. Som .4G 21
Isle Brewers. Som .4G 21
Isleham. Cambs .3F 65
Isle of Man Airport. IOM .5B 108
**Isle of Thanet**. Kent .4H 41
Isle of Whithorn. Dum .5B 110
**Isle of Wight**. IOW .4C 16
Isleornsay. High .2F 147
Islesburgh. Shet .5E 173
Isles of Scilly (St Mary's) Airport.
IOS .1B 4
Islesteps. Dum .2A 112
**Isleworth**. G Lon .3C 38
Isley Walton. Leics .3B 74
Islibhig. W Isl .5B 171
**Islington**. G Lon .2E 39
Islington. Telf .3B 72
Islip. Nptn .3G 63
Islip. Oxon .4D 50
Isombridge. Telf .4A 72
Istead Rise. Kent .4H 39
Itchen. Sotn .1C 16
Itchen Abbas. Hants .3D 24
Itchenor. W Sus .2F 17
Itchen Stoke. Hants .3D 24
Itchingfield. W Sus .3C 26
Itchington. S Glo .3B 34
Itlaw. Abers .3D 160
Itteringham. Norf .2D 78
Itteringham Common. Norf .3D 78
Itton. Devn .3G 11
Itton Common. Mon .2H 33
Ivegill. Cumb .5F 113
Ivelet. N Yor .5C 104
Iverchaolain. Arg .2B 126
Iver Heath. Buck .2B 38
Iveston. Dur .4E 115
Ivetsey Bank. Staf .4C 72
Ivinghoe. Buck .4H 51
Ivinghoe Aston. Buck .4H 51
Ivington. Here .5G 59
Ivington Green. Here .5G 59
Ivybridge. Devn .3C 8
Ivychurch. Kent .3E 29
Ivy Hatch. Kent .5G 39
Ivy Todd. Norf .5A 78
Iwade. Kent .4D 40
Iwerne Courtney. Dors .1D 14
Iwerne Minster. Dors .1D 14
Ixworth. Suff .3B 66
Ixworth Thorpe. Suff .3B 66

## J

Jackfield. Shrp .5A 72
Jack Hill. N Yor .4D 98
Jacksdale. Notts .5B 86
Jackton. S Lan .4G 127
Jacobstow. Corn .3B 10
Jacobstowe. Devn .2F 11
Jacobs Well. Surr .5A 38
Jameston. Pemb .5E 43
Jamestown. Dum .5F 119
Jamestown. Fife .1E 129
Jamestown. High .3G 157
Jamestown. W Dun .1E 127
Janetstown. High .2C 168
(nr. Thurso)
Janetstown. High .3F 169
(nr. Wick)
**Jarrow**. Tyne .3G 115
Jarvis Brook. E Sus .3G 27
Jasper's Green. Essx .3H 53
Jaywick. Essx .4E 55
Jedburgh. Bord .2A 120
Jeffreyston. Pemb .4E 43
Jemimaville. High .2B 158
Jenkins Park. High .3F 149
Jersey Marine. Neat .3G 31
Jesmond. Tyne .3F 115
Jevington. E Sus .5G 27
Jingle Street. Mon .4H 47
Jockey End. Herts .4A 52
Jodrell Bank. Ches E .3B 84
Johnby. Cumb .1F 103
John O'Gaunts. W Yor .2D 92
John o' Groats. High .1F 169
John's Cross. E Sus .3B 28
Johnshaven. Abers .2G 145
Johnson Street. Norf .4F 79
Johnston. Pemb .3D 42
**Johnstone**. Ren .3F 127
Johnstonebridge. Dum .5C 118
Johnstown. Carm .4E 45
Johnstown. Wrex .1F 71
Jonesborough. New M .8E 178
Joppa. Edin .2G 129
Joppa. S Ayr .3D 116
Jordan Green. Norf .3C 78
Jordans. Buck .1A 38
Jordanston. Pemb .1D 42
Jump. S Yor .4D 93
Jumpers Common. Dors .3G 15
Juniper. Nmbd .4C 114
Juniper Green. Edin .3E 129
Jurby East. IOM .2C 108
Jurby West. IOM .2C 108
Jury's Gap. E Sus .4D 28

## K

Kaber. Cumb .3A 104
Kaimend. S Lan .5C 128
Kaimes. Edin .3F 129
Kaimrig End. Bord .5D 129
Kames. Arg .2A 126
Kames. E Ayr .2F 117
Katesbridge. Arm .5G 179
Kea. Corn .4C 6
Keadby. N Lin .3B 94
Keady. Arm .6C 178
Keal Cotes. Linc .4C 88
Kearsley. G Man .4F 91
Kearsney. Kent .1G 29
Kearstwick. Cumb .1F 97
Kearton. N Yor .5C 104
Kearvaig. High .1C 166
Keasden. N Yor .3G 97
Keason. Corn .2H 7
Keckwick. Hal .2H 83
Keddington. Linc .2C 88
Keddington Corner. Linc .2C 88
Kedington. Suff .1H 53
Kedleston. Derbs .1H 73
Kedlock Feus. Fife .2F 137
Keekle. Cumb .3B 102
Keelby. Linc .3E 95
Keele. Staf .1C 72
Keeley Green. Bed .1A 52
Keeston. Pemb .3D 42
Keevil. Wilts .1E 23
Kegworth. Leics .3B 74
Kehelland. Corn .2D 4
Keig. Abers .2D 152
**Keighley**. W Yor .5C 98
Keilarsbrae. Clac .4A 136
Keillmore. Arg .1E 125
Keillor. Per .4B 144
Keillour. Per .1B 136
Keills. Arg .3C 124
Keiloch. Abers .4F 151
Keils. Arg .3D 124
Keinton Mandeville. Som .3A 22
Keir Mill. Dum .5A 118
Keirsleywell Row. Nmbd .4A 114
Keisby. Linc .3H 75
Keisley. Cumb .2A 104
Keiss. High .2F 169
**Keith**. Mor .3B 160
Keith Inch. Abers .4H 161
Kelbrook. Lanc .5B 98
Kelby. Linc .1H 75
Keld. Cumb .3G 103
Keld. N Yor .4B 104
Keldholme. N Yor .1B 100
Kelfield. N Lin .4B 94
Kelfield. N Yor .1F 93
Kelham. Notts .5E 87
Kellacott. Devn .4E 11
Kellan. Arg .4G 139
Kellas. Ang .5D 144
Kellas. Mor .3F 159
Kellaton. Devn .5E 9
Kelleth. Cumb .4H 103
Kelling. Norf .1C 78
Kellingley. N Yor .2F 93
Kellington. N Yor .2F 93
Kelloe. Dur .1A 106
Kelloholm. Dum .3G 117
Kells. Cumb .3A 102
Kells. ME Ant .7H 175
Kelly. Devn .4D 11
Kelly Bray. Corn .5D 10
Kelmarsh. Nptn .3E 63
Kelmscott. Oxon .2H 35
Kelsale. Suff .4F 67
Kelsall. Ches W .4H 83
Kelshall. Herts .2D 52
Kelsick. Cumb .4C 112
Kelso. Bord .1B 120
Kelstedge. Derbs .4H 85
Kelstern. Linc .1B 88
Kelsterton. Flin .3E 83
Kelston. Bath .5C 34
Keltneyburn. Per .4E 143
Kelton. Dum .2A 112
Kelton Hill. Dum .4E 111
Kelty. Fife .4D 136
Kelvedon. Essx .4B 54
Kelvedon Hatch. Essx .1G 39
Kelvinside. Glas .3G 127
Kelynack. Corn .3A 4
Kemback. Fife .2G 137
Kemberton. Shrp .5B 72
Kemble. Glos .2E 35
Kemerton. Worc .2E 49
Kemeys Commander. Mon .5G 47
Kemnay. Abers .2E 153
Kempe's Corner. Kent .1E 29
Kempley. Glos .3B 48
Kempley Green. Glos .3B 48
Kempsey. Worc .1D 48
Kempsford. Glos .2G 35
Kemps Green. Warw .3F 61
Kempshott. Hants .2E 24
**Kempston**. Bed .1A 52
Kempston Hardwick. Bed .1A 52
Kempton. Shrp .2F 59
Kemp Town. Brig .5E 27
Kemsing. Kent .5G 39
Kemsley. Kent .4D 40
Kenardington. Kent .2D 28
Kenchester. Here .1H 47
Kencot. Oxon .5A 50
**Kendal**. Cumb .5G 103
Kendleshire. S Glo .4B 34
Kendray. S Yor .4D 92
Kenfig. B'end .3B 32
Kenfig Hill. B'end .3B 32
Kengharair. Arg .4F 139
**Kenilworth**. Warw .3G 61
Kenknock. Stir .5B 142
Kenley. G Lon .5E 39
Kenley. Shrp .5H 71
Kenmore. High .3G 155
Kenmore. Per .4E 143
Kenn. Devn .4C 12
Kenn. N Som .5H 33
Kennacraig. Arg .3G 125
Kenneggy Downs. Corn .4C 4
Kennerleigh. Devn .2B 12
Kennet. Clac .4B 136
Kennethmont. Abers .1C 152
Kennett. Cambs .4G 65
Kennford. Devn .4C 12
Kenninghall. Norf .2C 66
Kennington. Kent .1E 28
Kennington. Oxon .5D 50
Kennoway. Fife .3F 137
Kennyhill. Suff .3F 65
Kennythorpe. N Yor .3B 100
Kenovay. Arg .4A 138
Kensaleyre. High .3D 154
**Kensington**. G Lon .3D 38
Kenstone. Shrp .3H 71
Kensworth. C Beds .4A 52
Kensworth Common.
C Beds .4A 52
Kentallen. High .3E 141
Kentchurch. Here .3H 47
Kentford. Suff .4G 65
Kentisbeare. Devn .2D 12
Kentisbury. Devn .2G 19
Kentisbury Ford. Devn .2G 19
Kentmere. Cumb .4F 103
Kenton. Devn .4C 12
Kenton. G Lon .2C 38
Kenton. Suff .4D 66
Kenton Bankfoot. Tyne .3F 115
Kentra. High .2A 140
Kentrigg. Cumb .5G 103
Kents Bank. Cumb .2C 96
Kent's Green. Glos .3C 48
Kent's Oak. Hants .4B 24
Kent Street. E Sus .4B 28
Kent Street. Kent .5A 40
Kent Street. W Sus .3D 26
Kenwick. Shrp .2G 71
Kenwyn. Corn .4C 6
Kenyon. Warr .1A 84
Keoldale. High .2D 166
Keppoch. High .1B 148
Kepwick. N Yor .5B 106
Keresley. W Mid .2H 61
Keresley Newland. Warw .2H 61
Keristal. IOM .4C 108
Kerne Bridge. Here .4A 48
Kerridge. Ches E .3D 84
Kerris. Corn .4B 4
Kerrow. High .5F 157
Kerry. Powy .2D 58
Kerrycroy. Arg .3C 126
Kerry's Gate. Here .2G 47
Kersall. Notts .4E 86
Kersbrook. Devn .4D 12
Kerse. Ren .4E 127
Kersey. Suff .1D 54
Kershopefoot. Cumb .1F 113
Kersoe. Worc .1E 49
Kerswell. Devn .2D 12
Kerswell Green. Worc .1D 48
Kesgrave. Suff .1F 55
Kesh. Ferm .6D 176
Kessingland. Suff .2H 67
Kessingland Beach. Suff .2H 67
Kestle. Corn .4D 6
Kestle Mill. Corn .3C 6
Keston. G Lon .4F 39
Keswick. Cumb .2D 102
Keswick. Norf .2F 79
(nr. North Walsham)
Keswick. Norf .5E 78
(nr. Norwich)
Ketsby. Linc .3C 88
**Kettering**. Nptn .3F 63
Ketteringham. Norf .5D 78
Kettins. Per .5B 144
Kettlebaston. Suff .5B 66
Kettlebridge. Fife .3F 137
Kettlebrook. Staf .5G 73
Kettleburgh. Suff .4E 67
Kettleholm. Dum .2C 112
Kettleness. N Yor .3F 107
Kettleshulme. Ches E .3D 85
Kettlesing. N Yor .4E 98
Kettlesing Bottom. N Yor .4E 99
Kettlestone. Norf .2B 78
Kettlethorpe. Linc .3F 87
Kettletoft. Orkn .4F 172
Kettlewell. N Yor .2B 98
Ketton. Rut .5G 75
Kew. G Lon .3C 38
Kewaigue. IOM .4C 108
Kewstoke. N Som .5G 33
Kexbrough. S Yor .4D 92
Kexby. Linc .2F 87
Kexby. York .4B 100
Keyford. Som .2C 22
Key Green. Ches E .4C 84
Key Green. N Yor .4F 107
Keyham. Leics .5D 74
Keyhaven. Hants .3B 16
Keyhead. Abers .3H 161
Keyingham. E Yor .2F 95
Keymer. W Sus .4E 27
**Keynsham**. Bath .5B 34
Keysoe. Bed .4H 63
Keysoe Row. Bed .4H 63
Key's Toft. Linc .5D 89
Keyston. Cambs .3H 63
Key Street. Kent .4C 40
Keyworth. Notts .2D 74
Kibblesworth. Tyne .4F 115
Kibworth Beauchamp. Leics .1D 62
Kibworth Harcourt. Leics .1D 62
Kidbrooke. G Lon .3F 39
Kidburngill. Cumb .2B 102
Kiddemore Green. Staf .5C 72
**Kidderminster**. Worc .3C 60
Kiddington. Oxon .3C 50
Kidd's Moor. Norf .5D 78
**Kidlington**. Oxon .4C 50
Kidmore End. Oxon .4E 37
Kidnal. Ches W .1G 71
**Kidsgrove**. Staf .5C 84
Kidstones. N Yor .1B 98
Kidwelly. Carm .5E 45
Kiel Crofts. Arg .5D 140
Kielder. Nmbd .5A 120
Kilbagie. Fife .4B 136
Kilbarchan. Ren .3F 127
Kilbeg. High .3E 147
Kilberry. Arg .3F 125
Kilbirnie. N Ayr .4E 126
Kilbride. Arg .1F 133
Kilbride. High .1D 147
Kilbucho Place. Bord .1C 118
Kilburn. Derbs .1A 74
Kilburn. G Lon .2D 38
Kilburn. N Yor .2H 99
Kilby. Leics .1D 62
Kilchattan. Arg .4A 132
Kilchattan Bay. Arg .4C 126
Kilchenzie. Arg .3A 122
Kilcheran. Arg .5C 140
Kilchiaran. Arg .3A 124
Kilchoan. High .4F 147
(nr. Inverie)
Kilchoan. High .2F 139
(nr. Tobermory)
Kilchoman. Arg .3A 124
Kilchrenan. Arg .1H 133
Kilclief. New M .5K 179
Kilconquhar. Fife .3G 137
Kilcoo. New M .6G 179
Kilcot. Glos .3B 48
Kilcoy. High .3H 157
Kilcreggan. Arg .1D 126
Kildale. N Yor .4D 106
Kildary. High .1B 158
Kildermorie Lodge. High .1H 157
Kildonan. Dum .4F 109
Kildonan. High .1G 165
(nr. Helmsdale)
Kildonan. High .3C 154
(on Isle of Skye)
Kildonan. N Ayr .3E 123
Kildonnan. High .5C 146
Kildrummy. Abers .2B 152
Kildwick. N Yor .5C 98
Kilfillan. Dum .4H 109
Kilfinan. Arg .2H 125
Kilfinnan. High .4E 149
Kilgetty. Pemb .4F 43
Kilgour. Fife .3E 136
Kilgrammie. S Ayr .4B 116
Kilham. E Yor .3E 101
Kilham. Nmbd .1C 120
Kilkeel. New M .8H 179
Kilkenneth. Arg .4A 138
Kilkhampton. Corn .1C 10
Killadeas. Ferm .7E 176
Killamarsh. Derbs .2B 86
Killandrist. Arg .4C 140
Killay. Swan .3F 31
Killean. Arg .5E 125
Killearn. Stir .1G 127
Killeen. M Ulst .3C 178
Killellan. Arg .4A 122
Killen. Derr .4E 176
Killen. High .3A 158
Killerby. Darl .3E 105
Killeter. Derr .4E 176
Killichonan. Per .3C 142
Killiechronan. Arg .4G 139
Killiecrankie. Per .2G 143
Killilan. High .5B 156
Killimster. High .3F 169
Killin. Stir .5C 142
Killinchy. N Dwn .3K 179
Killinghall. N Yor .4E 99
Killington. Cumb .1F 97
**Killingworth**. Tyne .2F 115
Killin Lodge. High .3H 149
Killinochonoch. Arg .4F 133
Killochyett. Bord .5A 130
Killough. New M .6K 179
Killowen. New M .8F 179
Killundine. High .4G 139
Killylea. Arm .5B 178
Killyleagh. New M .4K 179
Killyrammer. Caus .4F 175
Kilmacolm. Inv .3E 127
Kilmahog. Stir .3F 135
Kilmahumaig. Arg .4E 133
Kilmalieu. High .3C 140
Kilmaluag. High .1D 154
Kilmany. Fife .1F 137
Kilmarie. High .2D 146
**Kilmarnock**. E Ayr .1D 116 & 196
Kilmaron. Fife .2F 137
Kilmartin. Arg .4F 133
Kilmaurs. E Ayr .5F 127
Kilmelford. Arg .2F 133
Kilmeny. Arg .3B 124
Kilmersdon. Som .1B 22
Kilmeston. Hants .4D 24
Kilmichael Glassary. Arg .4F 133
Kilmichael of Inverlussa.
Arg .1F 125
Kilmington. Devn .3F 13
Kilmington. Wilts .3C 22
Kilmoluaig. Arg .4A 138
Kilmorack. High .4G 157
Kilmore. Arg .1F 133
Kilmore. Arm .4D 178
Kilmore. High .3E 147
Kilmore. New M .4J 179
Kilmory. Arg .2F 125
Kilmory. High .1G 139
(nr. Kilchoan)
Kilmory. High .3B 146
(on Rùm)
Kilmory. N Ayr .3D 122
Kilmory Lodge. Arg .3E 132
Kilmote. High .2G 165
Kilmuir. High .4B 154
(nr. Dunvegan)
Kilmuir. High .1B 158
(nr. Invergordon)
Kilmuir. High .4A 158
(nr. Inverness)
Kilmuir. High .1C 154
(nr. Uig)
Kilmun. Arg .1C 126
Kilnave. Arg .2A 124
Kilncadzow. S Lan .5B 128
Kilndown. Kent .2B 28
Kiln Green. Here .4B 48
Kiln Green. Wok .4G 37
Kilnhill. Cumb .1D 102
Kilnhurst. S Yor .1B 86
Kilninian. Arg .4E 139
Kilninver. Arg .1F 133
Kiln Pit Hill. Nmbd .4D 114
Kilnsea. E Yor .3H 95
Kilnsey. N Yor .3B 98
Kilnwick. E Yor .5D 101
Kiloran. Arg .4A 132
Kilpatrick. N Ayr .3D 122
Kilpeck. Here .2H 47
Kilpin. E Yor .2A 94
Kilpin Pike. E Yor .2A 94
Kilrea. Caus .5F 174
Kilrenny. Fife .3H 137
Kilsby. Nptn .3C 62
Kilspindie. Per .1E 136
**Kilsyth**. N Lan .2A 128
Kiltarlity. High .4H 157
Kilton. Som .2E 21
Kilton Thorpe. Red C .3D 107
Kilvaxter. High .2C 154
Kilve. Som .2E 21
Kilvington. Notts .1F 75
**Kilwinning**. N Ayr .5D 126
Kimberley. Norf .5C 78
**Kimberley**. Notts .1B 74
Kimblesworth. Dur .5F 115
Kimble Wick. Buck .5G 51
Kimbolton. Cambs .4H 63
Kimbolton. Here .4H 59
Kimcote. Leics .2C 62
Kimmeridge. Dors .5E 15
Kimmerston. Nmbd .1D 120
Kimpton. Hants .2A 24
Kimpton. Herts .4B 52
Kinallen. Arm .5G 179
Kinawley. Ferm .6H 177
Kinbeachie. High .2A 158
Kinbrace. High .5A 168
Kinbuck. Stir .3G 135
Kincaple. Fife .2G 137
Kincardine. Fife .1C 128
Kincardine. High .5D 164
**Kincardine Bridge**. Fife .1C 128
Kincardine O'Neil. Abers .4C 152
Kinchrackine. Arg .1A 134
Kincorth. Aber .3G 153
Kincraig. High .3C 150
Kincraigie. Per .4G 143
Kindallachan. Per .3G 143
Kineton. Glos .3F 49
Kineton. Warw .5H 61
Kinfauns. Per .1D 136
Kingairloch. High .3C 140

Kingarth—Ledmore

Kingarth. Arg 4B 126
Kingcoed. Mon 5H 47
King Edward. Abers 3E 160
Kingerby. Linc 1H 87
Kingham. Oxon 3A 50
Kingholm Quay. Dum 2A 112
Kinghorn. Fife 1F 129
Kingie. High 3D 148
Kinglassie. Fife 4E 137
Kingledores. Bord 2D 118
King o' Muirs. Clac 4A 136
Kingoodie. Per 1F 137
King's Acre. Here 1H 47
Kingsand. Corn 3A 8
Kingsash. Buck 5G 51
Kingsbarns. Fife 2H 137
Kingsbridge. Devn 4D 8
Kingsbridge. Som 3C 20
King's Bromley. Staf 4F 73
Kingsburgh. High 3C 154
Kingsbury. G Lon 2C 38
Kingsbury. Warw 1G 61
Kingsbury Episcopi. Som 4H 21
Kings Caple. Here 3A 48
Kingscavil. W Lot 2D 128
Kingsclere. Hants 1D 24
King's Cliffe. Nptn 1H 63
Kings Clipstone. Notts 4D 86
Kingscote. Glos 2D 34
Kingscott. Devn 1F 11
Kings Coughton. Warw 5E 61
Kingscross. N Ayr 3E 123
Kingsdon. Som 4A 22
Kingsdown. Kent 1H 29
Kingsdown. Swin 3G 35
Kingsdown. Wilts 5D 34
Kingseat. Fife 4D 136
Kingsey. Buck 5F 51
Kingsfold. Lanc 2D 90
Kingsfold. W Sus 2C 26
Kingsford. E Ayr 5F 127
Kingsford. Worc 2C 60
Kingsforth. N Lin 3D 94
Kingsgate. Kent 3H 41
King's Green. Glos 2C 48
Kingshall Street. Suff 4B 66
Kingsheanton. Devn 3F 19
King's Heath. W Mid 2E 61
Kings Hill. Kent 5A 40
Kingsholm. Glos 4D 48
Kingshouse. High 3G 141
Kingshouse. Stir 1E 135
Kingshurst. W Mid 2F 61
Kingskerswell. Devn 2E 9
Kingskettle. Fife 3F 137
Kingsland. Here 4G 59
Kingsland. IOA 2B 80
Kings Langley. Herts 5A 52
Kingsley. Ches W 3H 83
Kingsley. Hants 3F 25
Kingsley. Staf 1E 73
Kingsley Green. W Sus 3G 25
Kingsley Holt. Staf 1E 73
**King's Lynn**. Norf 3F 77
King's Meaburn. Cumb 2H 103
Kings Moss. Mers 4D 90
Kingsmuir. Ang 4D 145
Kingsmuir. Fife 3H 137
Kings Muir. Bord 1E 119
King's Newnham. Warw 3B 62
King's Newton. Derbs 3A 74
Kingsnorth. Kent 2E 28
Kingsnorth. Medw 3C 40
King's Norton. Leics 5D 74
Kings Norton. W Mid 3E 61
King's Nympton. Devn 1G 11
King's Pyon. Here 5G 59
Kings Ripton. Cambs 3B 64
King's Somborne. Hants 3B 24
King's Stag. Dors 1C 14
King's Stanley. Glos 5D 48
King's Sutton. Nptn 2C 50
Kingstanding. W Mid 1E 61
Kingsteignton. Devn 5B 12
Kingsteps. High 3D 158
King Sterndale. Derbs 3E 85
King's Thorn. Here 2A 48
Kingsthorpe. Nptn 4E 63
Kingston. Cambs 5C 64
Kingston. Devn 4C 8
Kingston. Dors 2C 14
(nr. Sturminster Newton)
Kingston. Dors 5E 15
(nr. Swanage)
Kingston. E Lot 1B 130
Kingston. Hants 2G 15
Kingston. IOW 4C 16
Kingston. Kent 5F 41
Kingston. Mor 2H 159
Kingston. W Sus 5B 26
Kingston Bagpuize. Oxon 2C 36
Kingston Blount. Oxon 2F 37
Kingston by Sea. W Sus 5D 26
Kingston Deverill. Wilts 3D 22
Kingstone. Here 2H 47
Kingstone. Som 1G 13
Kingstone. Staf 3E 73
Kingston Lisle. Oxon 3B 36
Kingston Maurward. Dors 3C 14
Kingston near Lewes. E Sus 5E 27
Kingston on Soar. Notts 3C 74
Kingston Russell. Dors 3A 14
Kingston St Mary. Som 4F 21
Kingston Seymour. N Som 5H 33
Kingston Stert. Oxon 5F 51
**Kingston upon Hull**. Hull 2E 94 & 196
**Kingston upon Thames**. G Lon 4C 38
King's Walden. Herts 3B 52
Kingswear. Devn 3E 9
Kingswells. Aber 3F 153
Kingswinford. W Mid 2C 60
Kingswood. Buck 4E 51
Kingswood. Glos 2C 34
Kingswood. Here 5E 59
Kingswood. Kent 5C 40
Kingswood. Per 5H 143
Kingswood. Powy 5E 71
Kingswood. Som 3E 20
**Kingswood**. S Glo 4B 34
Kingswood. Surr 5D 38
Kingswood. Warw 3F 61
Kingswood Common. Staf 5C 72
Kings Worthy. Hants 3C 24
Kingthorpe. Linc 3A 88
Kington. Here 5E 59
Kington. S Glo 2B 34
Kington. Worc 5D 61
Kington Langley. Wilts 4E 35
Kington Magna. Dors 4C 22
Kington St Michael. Wilts 4E 35
Kingussie. High 3B 150
Kingweston. Som 3A 22
Kinharrachie. Abers 5G 161
Kinhrive. High 1A 158
Kinkell Bridge. Per 2B 136
Kinknockie. Abers 4H 161
Kinkry Hill. Cumb 2G 113
Kinlet. Shrp 2B 60
Kinloch. High 5D 166
(nr. Loch More)
Kinloch. High 3A 140
(nr. Lochaline)
Kinloch. High 4B 146
(on Rùm)
Kinloch. Per 4A 144
Kinlochard. Stir 3D 134
Kinlochbervie. High 3C 166
Kinlocheil. High 1D 140
Kinlochewe. High 2C 156
Kinloch Hourn. High 3B 148
Kinloch Laggan. High 5H 149
Kinlochleven. High 2F 141
Kinloch Lodge. High 3F 167
Kinlochmoidart. High 1B 140
Kinlochmore. High 2F 141
Kinloch Rannoch. Per 3D 142
Kinlochspelve. Arg 1D 132
Kinloid. High 5E 147
Kinloss. Mor 2E 159
Kinmel Bay. Cnwy 2B 82
Kinmuck. Abers 2F 153
Kinnadie. Abers 4G 161
Kinnaird. Per 1E 137
Kinneff. Abers 1H 145
Kinnelhead. Dum 4C 118
Kinnell. Ang 3F 145
Kinnerley. Shrp 3F 71
Kinnernie. Abers 3E 152
Kinnersley. Here 1G 47
Kinnersley. Worc 1D 48
Kinnerton. Powy 4E 59
Kinnerton. Shrp 1F 59
Kinnesswood. Per 3D 136
Kinninvie. Dur 2D 104
Kinnordy. Ang 3C 144
Kinoulton. Notts 2D 74
Kinross. Per 3D 136
Kinrossie. Per 5A 144
Kinsbourne Green. Herts 4B 52
Kinsey Heath. Ches E 1A 72
Kinsham. Here 4F 59
Kinsham. Worc 2E 49
Kinsley. W Yor 3E 93
Kinson. Bour 3F 15
Kintbury. W Ber 5B 36
Kintessack. Mor 2E 159
Kintillo. Per 2D 136
Kinton. Here 3G 59
Kinton. Shrp 4F 71
Kintore. Abers 2E 153
Kintour. Arg 4C 124
Kintra. Arg 2B 132
Kintraw. Arg 3F 133
Kinveachy. High 2D 150
Kinver. Staf 2C 60
Kinwarton. Warw 5F 61
Kiplingcotes. E Yor 5D 100
Kippax. W Yor 1E 93
Kippen. Stir 4F 135
Kippford. Dum 4F 111
Kipping's Cross. Kent 1H 27
Kirbister. Orkn 7C 172
(nr. Hobbister)
Kirbister. Orkn 6B 172
(nr. Quholm)
Kirbuster. Orkn 5F 172
Kirby Bedon. Norf 5E 79
Kirby Bellars. Leics 4E 74
Kirby Cane. Norf 1F 67
Kirby Cross. Essx 3F 55
Kirby Fields. Leics 5C 74
Kirby Green. Norf 1F 67
Kirby Grindalythe. N Yor 3D 100
Kirby Hill. N Yor 4E 105
(nr. Richmond)
Kirby Hill. N Yor 3F 99
(nr. Ripon)
Kirby Knowle. N Yor 1G 99
Kirby-le-Soken. Essx 3F 55
Kirby Misperton. N Yor 2B 100
Kirby Muxloe. Leics 5C 74
Kirby Sigston. N Yor 5B 106
Kirby Underdale. E Yor 4C 100
Kirby Wiske. N Yor 1F 99
Kircubbin. N Dwn 3L 179
Kirdford. W Sus 3B 26
Kirk. High 3E 169
Kirkabister. Shet 8F 173
(on Bressay)
Kirkabister. Shet 6F 173
(on Mainland)
Kirkandrews. Dum 5D 110
Kirkandrews-on-Eden. Cumb 4E 113
Kirkapol. Arg 4B 138
Kirkbampton. Cumb 4E 112
Kirkbean. Dum 4A 112
Kirk Bramwith. S Yor 3G 93
Kirkbride. Cumb 4D 112
Kirkbridge. N Yor 5F 105
Kirkbuddo. Ang 4E 145
Kirkburn. E Yor 4D 101
Kirkburton. W Yor 3B 92
Kirkby. Linc 1H 87
**Kirkby**. Mers 1G 83
Kirkby. N Yor 4C 106
Kirkby Fenside. Linc 4C 88
Kirkby Fleetham. N Yor 5F 105
Kirkby Green. Linc 5H 87
**Kirkby-in-Ashfield**. Notts 5C 86
Kirkby-in-Furness. Cumb 1B 96
Kirkby la Thorpe. Linc 1A 76
Kirkby Lonsdale. Cumb 2F 97
Kirkby Malham. N Yor 3A 98
Kirkby Mallory. Leics 5B 74
Kirkby Malzeard. N Yor 2E 99
Kirkby Mills. N Yor 1B 100
Kirkbymoorside. N Yor 1A 100
Kirkby on Bain. Linc 4B 88
Kirkby Overblow. N Yor 5F 99
Kirkby Stephen. Cumb 4A 104
Kirkby Thore. Cumb 2H 103
Kirkby Underwood. Linc 3H 75
Kirkby Wharfe. N Yor 5H 99
**Kirkcaldy**. Fife 4E 137
Kirkcambeck. Cumb 3G 113
Kirkcolm. Dum 3F 109
Kirkconnel. Dum 3G 117
Kirkconnell. Dum 3A 112
Kirkcowan. Dum 3A 110
Kirkcudbright. Dum 4D 111
Kirkdale. Mers 1F 83
Kirk Deighton. N Yor 4F 99
Kirk Ella. E Yor 2D 94
Kirkfieldbank. S Lan 5B 128
Kirkforthar Feus. Fife 3E 137
Kirkgunzeon. Dum 3F 111
Kirk Hallam. Derbs 1B 74
Kirkham. Lanc 1C 90
Kirkham. N Yor 3B 100
Kirkhamgate. W Yor 2C 92
Kirk Hammerton. N Yor 4G 99
Kirkharle. Nmbd 1D 114
Kirkheaton. Nmbd 2D 114
Kirkheaton. W Yor 3B 92
Kirkhill. Ang 2F 145
Kirkhill. High 4H 157
Kirkhope. S Lan 4B 118
Kirkhouse. Bord 1F 119
Kirkibost. High 2D 146
Kirkinch. Ang 4C 144
Kirkinner. Dum 4B 110
**Kirkintilloch**. E Dun 2H 127
Kirk Ireton. Derbs 5G 85
Kirkland. Cumb 3B 102
(nr. Cleator Moor)
Kirkland. Cumb 1H 103
(nr. Penrith)
Kirkland. Cumb 5D 112
(nr. Wigton)
Kirkland. Dum 3G 117
(nr. Kirkconnel)
Kirkland. Dum 5H 117
(nr. Moniaive)
Kirkland Guards. Cumb 5C 112
Kirk Langley. Derbs 2G 73
Kirklauchline. Dum 4F 109
Kirkleatham. Red C 2C 106
Kirklevington. Stoc T 4B 106
Kirkley. Suff 1H 67
Kirklington. N Yor 1F 99
Kirklington. Notts 5D 86
Kirklinton. Cumb 3F 113
Kirkliston. Edin 2E 129
Kirkmabreck. Dum 4B 110
Kirkmaiden. Dum 5E 109
Kirk Merrington. Dur 1F 105
Kirk Michael. IOM 2C 108
Kirkmichael. Per 2H 143
Kirkmichael. S Ayr 4C 116
Kirkmuirhill. S Lan 5A 128
Kirknewton. Nmbd 1D 120
Kirknewton. W Lot 3E 129
Kirkney. Abers 5C 160
Kirk of Shotts. N Lan 3B 128
Kirkoswald. Cumb 5G 113
Kirkoswald. S Ayr 4B 116
Kirkpatrick. Dum 5B 118
Kirkpatrick Durham. Dum 2E 111
Kirkpatrick-Fleming. Dum 2D 112
**Kirk Sandall**. S Yor 4G 93
Kirksanton. Cumb 1A 96
Kirk Smeaton. N Yor 3F 93
Kirkstall. W Yor 1C 92
Kirkstile. Dum 5F 119
Kirkstyle. High 1F 169
Kirkthorpe. W Yor 2D 92
Kirkton. Abers 2D 152
(nr. Alford)
Kirkton. Abers 1D 152
(nr. Insch)
Kirkton. Abers 4F 161
(nr. Turriff)
Kirkton. Ang 5D 144
(nr. Dundee)
Kirkton. Ang 4D 144
(nr. Forfar)
Kirkton. Ang 5B 152
(nr. Tarfside)
Kirkton. Dum 1A 112
Kirkton. Fife 1F 137
Kirkton. High 4E 165
(nr. Golspie)
Kirkton. High 1G 147
(nr. Kyle of Lochalsh)
Kirkton. High 4B 156
(nr. Lochcarron)
Kirkton. Bord 3H 119
Kirkton. S Lan 2B 118
Kirktonhill. W Dun 2E 127
Kirkton Manor. Bord 1E 118
Kirkton of Airlie. Ang 3C 144
Kirkton of Auchterhouse. Ang 5C 144
Kirkton of Bourtie. Abers 1F 153
Kirkton of Collace. Per 5A 144
Kirkton of Craig. Ang 3G 145
Kirkton of Culsalmond. Abers 5D 160
Kirkton of Durris. Abers 4E 153
Kirkton of Glenbuchat. Abers 2A 152
Kirkton of Glenisla. Ang 2B 144
Kirkton of Kingoldrum. Ang 3C 144
Kirkton of Largo. Fife 3G 137
Kirkton of Lethendy. Per 4A 144
Kirkton of Logie Buchan. Abers 1G 153
Kirkton of Maryculter. Abers 4F 153
Kirkton of Menmuir. Ang 2E 145
Kirkton of Monikie. Ang 5E 145
Kirkton of Oyne. Abers 1D 152
Kirkton of Rayne. Abers 5D 160
Kirkton of Skene. Abers 3F 153
Kirktown. Abers 2G 161
(nr. Fraserburgh)
Kirktown. Abers 3H 161
(nr. Peterhead)
Kirktown of Alvah. Abers 2D 160
Kirktown of Auchterless. Abers 4E 160
Kirktown of Deskford. Mor 2C 160
Kirktown of Fetteresso. Abers 5F 153
Kirktown of Mortlach. Mor 5H 159
Kirktown of Slains. Abers 1H 153
Kirkurd. Bord 5E 129
Kirkwall. Orkn 6D 172
Kirkwall Airport. Orkn 7D 172
Kirkwhelpington. Nmbd 1C 114
Kirk Yetholm. Bord 2C 120
Kirmington. N Lin 3E 94
Kirmond le Mire. Linc 1A 88
Kirn. Arg 2C 126
Kirriemuir. Ang 3C 144
Kirstead Green. Norf 1E 67
Kirtlebridge. Dum 2D 112
Kirtleton. Dum 2D 112
Kirtling. Cambs 5F 65
Kirtling Green. Cambs 5F 65
Kirtlington. Oxon 4D 50
Kirtomy. High 2H 167
Kirton. Linc 2C 76
Kirton. Notts 4D 86
Kirton. Suff 2F 55
Kirton End. Linc 1B 76
Kirton Holme. Linc 1B 76
Kirton in Lindsey. N Lin 1G 87
Kishorn. High 4H 155
Kislingbury. Nptn 5D 62
Kites Hardwick. Warw 4B 62
Kittisford. Som 4D 20
Kittle. Swan 4E 31
Kittybrewster. Aber 3G 153
Kitwood. Hants 3E 25
Kivernoll. Here 2H 47
Kiveton Park. S Yor 2B 86
Knaith. Linc 2F 87
Knaith Park. Linc 2F 87
Knaphill. Surr 5A 38
Knapp. Hants 4C 24
Knapp. Per 5B 144
Knapp. Som 4G 21
Knapperfield. High 3E 169
Knapton. Norf 2F 79
Knapton. York 4H 99
Knapton Green. Here 5G 59
Knapwell. Cambs 4C 64
**Knaresborough**. N Yor 4F 99
Knarsdale. Nmbd 4H 113
Knatts Valley. Kent 4G 39
Knaven. Abers 4F 161
Knayton. N Yor 1G 99
Knebworth. Herts 3C 52
Knedlington. E Yor 2H 93
Kneesall. Notts 4E 86
Kneesworth. Cambs 1D 52
Kneeton. Notts 1E 74
Knelston. Swan 4D 30
Knenhall. Staf 2D 72
Knightacott. Devn 3G 19
Knightcote. Warw 5B 62
Knightcott. N Som 1G 21
Knightley. Staf 3C 72
Knightley Dale. Staf 3C 72
Knightlow Hill. Warw 3B 62
Knighton. Devn 4B 8
Knighton. Dors 1B 14
Knighton. Leic 5C 74
Knighton. Powy 3E 59
Knighton. Som 2E 21
Knighton. Staf 3B 72
(nr. Eccleshall)
Knighton. Staf 1B 72
(nr. Woore)
Knighton. Wilts 4A 36
Knighton. Worc 5E 61
Knighton Common. Worc 3A 60
Knight's End. Cambs 1D 64
Knightswood. Glas 3G 127
Knightwick. Worc 5B 60
Knill. Here 4E 59
Knipton. Leics 2F 75
Knitsley. Dur 5E 115
Kniveton. Derbs 5G 85
Knock. Arg 5G 139
Knock. Cumb 2H 103
Knock. Mor 3C 160
Knockally. High 5D 168
Knockan. Arg 1B 132
Knockan. High 2G 163
Knockandhu. Mor 1G 151
Knockando. Mor 4F 159
Knockarthur. High 3E 165
Knockbain. High 3A 158
Knockbreck. High 2B 154
Knockcloghrim. M Ulst 7E 174
Knockdee. High 2D 168
Knockdolian. S Ayr 1G 109
Knockdon. S Ayr 3C 116
Knockdown. Glos 3D 34
Knockenbaird. Abers 1D 152
Knockenkelly. N Ayr 3E 123
Knockentiber. E Ayr 1C 116
Knockfarrel. High 3H 157
Knockglass. High 2C 168
Knockholt. Kent 5F 39
Knockholt Pound. Kent 5F 39
Knockie Lodge. High 2G 149
Knockin. Shrp 3F 71
Knockinlaw. E Ayr 1D 116
Knockinnon. High 5D 169
Knocknacarry. Caus 3J 175
Knockrome. Arg 2D 124
Knocksharry. IOM 3B 108
Knockshinnoch. E Ayr 3D 116
Knockvennie. Dum 2E 111
Knockvologan. Arg 3B 132
Knodishall. Suff 4G 67
Knole. Som 4H 21
Knollbury. Mon 3H 33
Knolls Green. Ches E 3C 84
Knolton. Wrex 2F 71
Knook. Wilts 2E 23
Knossington. Leics 5F 75
Knott. High 3C 154
Knott End-on-Sea. Lanc 5C 96
Knotting. Bed 4H 63
Knotting Green. Bed 4H 63
**Knottingley**. W Yor 2E 93
Knotts. Cumb 2F 103
Knotty Ash. Mers 1G 83
Knotty Green. Buck 1A 38
Knowbury. Shrp 3H 59
Knowe. Dum 2A 110
Knowefield. Cumb 4F 113
Knowehead. Dum 5F 117
Knowes. E Lot 2C 130
Knowesgate. Nmbd 1C 114
Knoweside. S Ayr 3B 116
Knowes of Elrick. Abers 3D 160
Knowle. Bris 4B 34
Knowle. Devn 3E 19
(nr. Braunton)
Knowle. Devn 4D 12
(nr. Budleigh Salterton)
Knowle. Devn 2A 12
(nr. Crediton)
Knowle. Shrp 3H 59
**Knowle**. W Mid 3F 61
Knowle Green. Lanc 1E 91
Knowle St Giles. Som 1G 13
Knowlesands. Shrp 1B 60
Knowle Village. Hants 2D 16
Knowl Hill. Wind 4G 37
Knowlton. Kent 5G 41
Knowsley. Mers 1G 83
Knowstone. Devn 4B 20
Knucklas. Powy 3E 59
Knuston. Nptn 4G 63
**Knutsford**. Ches E 3B 84
Knypersley. Staf 5C 84
Krumlin. W Yor 3A 92
Kuggar. Corn 5E 5
Kyleakin. High 1F 147
Kyle of Lochalsh. High 1F 147
Kylerhea. High 1F 147
Kylesku. High 5C 166
Kyles Lodge. W Isl 9B 171
Kylesmorar. High 4G 147
Kylestrome. High 5C 166
Kymin. Mon 4A 48
Kynaston. Here 2B 48
Kynaston. Shrp 3F 71
Kynnersley. Telf 4A 72
Kyre Green. Worc 4A 60
Kyre Park. Worc 4A 60
Kyrewood. Worc 4A 60

## L

Labost. W Isl 3E 171
Lacasaidh. W Isl 5F 171
Lacasdail. W Isl 4G 171
Laceby. NE Lin 4F 95
Lacey Green. Buck 5G 51
Lach Dennis. Ches W 3B 84
Lache. Ches W 4F 83
Lack. Ferm 6E 176
Lackagh. Caus 5C 174
Lackford. Suff 3G 65
Lacock. Wilts 5E 35
Ladbroke. Warw 5B 62
Laddingford. Kent 1A 28
Lade Bank. Linc 5C 88
Ladock. Corn 3C 6
Lady. Orkn 3F 172
Ladybank. Fife 2F 137
Ladycross. Corn 4D 10
Lady Green. Mers 4B 90
Lady Hall. Cumb 1A 96
Ladykirk. Bord 5E 131
Ladysford. Abers 2G 161
Ladywood. W Mid 2E 61
Ladywood. Worc 4C 60
Laga. High 2A 140
Lagavulin. Arg 5C 124
Lagg. Arg 2D 125
Lagg. N Ayr 3D 122
Laggan. Arg 4A 124
Laggan. High 4E 149
(nr. Fort Augustus)
Laggan. High 4A 150
(nr. Newtonmore)
Laggan. Mor 5H 159
Lagganlia. High 3C 150
Lagganulva. Arg 4F 139
Laghey Corner. M Ulst 3C 178
Laglingarten. Arg 3A 134
Lagness. W Sus 2G 17
Laid. High 3E 166
Laide. High 4C 162
Laigh Fenwick. E Ayr 5F 127
Laindon. Essx 2A 40
Lairg. High 3C 164
Lairg Muir. High 3C 164
Laithes. Cumb 1F 103
Laithkirk. Dur 2C 104
Lake. Devn 3F 19
Lake. IOW 4D 16
Lake. Wilts 3G 23
**Lake District**. Cumb 3E 103
Lakenham. Norf 5E 79
Lakenheath. Suff 2G 65
Lakesend. Norf 1E 65
Lakeside. Cumb 1C 96
Laleham. Surr 4B 38
Laleston. B'end 3B 32
Lamancha. Bord 4F 129
Lamarsh. Essx 2B 54
Lamas. Norf 3E 79
Lamb Corner. Essx 2D 54
Lambden. Bord 5D 130
Lamberhead Green. G Man 4D 90
Lamberhurst. Kent 2A 28
Lamberhurst Quarter. Kent 2A 28
Lamberton. Bord 4F 131
**Lambeth**. G Lon 3E 39
Lambfell Moar. IOM 3B 108
Lambhill. Glas 3G 127
Lambley. Nmbd 4H 113
Lambley. Notts 1D 74
Lambourn. W Ber 4B 36
Lambourn End. Essx 1F 39
Lambourn Woodlands. W Ber 4B 36
Lambs Green. Dors 3E 15
Lambs Green. W Sus 2D 26
Lambston. Pemb 3D 42
Lamellion. Corn 2G 7
Lamerton. Devn 5E 11
Lamesley. Tyne 4F 115
Laminess. Orkn 4F 172
Lamington. High 1B 158
Lamington. S Lan 1B 118
Lamlash. N Ayr 2E 123
Lamonby. Cumb 1F 103
Lamorick. Corn 2E 7
Lamorna. Corn 4B 4
Lamorran. Corn 4C 6
Lampeter. Cdgn 1F 45
Lampeter Velfrey. Pemb 3F 43
Lamphey. Pemb 4E 43
Lamplugh. Cumb 2B 102
Lamport. Nptn 3E 63
Lamyatt. Som 3B 22
Lana. Devn 3D 10
(nr. Ashwater)
Lana. Devn 2D 10
(nr. Holsworthy)
Lanark. S Lan 5B 128
Lanarth. Corn 4E 5
**Lancaster**. Lanc 3D 97
Lanchester. Dur 5E 115
**Lancing**. W Sus 5C 26
Landbeach. Cambs 4D 65
Landcross. Devn 4E 19
Landerberry. Abers 3E 153
Landford. Wilts 1A 16
Land Gate. G Man 4D 90
Landhallow. High 5D 169
Landimore. Swan 3D 30
Landkey. Devn 3F 19
Landkey Newland. Devn 3F 19
Landore. Swan 3F 31
Landport. Port 2E 17
Landrake. Corn 2H 7
Landscove. Devn 2D 9
Land's End (St Just) Airport. Corn 4A 4
Landshipping. Pemb 3E 43
Landulph. Corn 2A 8
Landywood. Staf 5D 73
Lane. Corn 2C 6
Laneast. Corn 4C 10
Lane Bottom. Lanc 1G 91
Lane End. Buck 2G 37
Lane End. Hants 4D 24
Lane End. IOW 4E 17
Lane End. Wilts 2D 22
Lane Ends. Derbs 2G 73
Lane Ends. Dur 1E 105
Lane Ends. Lanc 4G 97
Laneham. Notts 3F 87
Lanehead. Dur 5B 114
(nr. Cowshill)
Lane Head. Dur 3E 105
(nr. Hutton Magna)
Lane Head. Dur 2D 105
(nr. Woodland)
Lane Head. G Man 1A 84
Lanehead. Nmbd 1A 114
Lane Head. W Yor 4B 92
Lane Heads. Lanc 1C 90
Lanercost. Cumb 3G 113
Laneshaw Bridge. Lanc 5B 98
Laney Green. Staf 5D 72
Langais. W Isl 2D 170
Langal. High 2B 140
Langar. Notts 2E 75
Langbank. Ren 2E 127
Langbar. N Yor 4C 98
Langburnshiels. Bord 4H 119
Langcliffe. N Yor 3H 97
Langdale End. N Yor 5G 107
Langdon. Corn 3C 10
Langdon Beck. Dur 1B 104
Langdon Cross. Corn 4D 10
Langdon Hills. Essx 2A 40
Langdown. Hants 2C 16
Langdyke. Fife 3F 137
Langenhoe. Essx 4D 54
Langford. C Beds 1B 52
Langford. Devn 2D 12
Langford. Essx 5B 54
Langford. Notts 5F 87
Langford. Oxon 5H 49
Langford. Som 4F 21
Langford Budville. Som 4E 20
Langham. Dors 4C 22
Langham. Essx 2D 54
Langham. Norf 1C 78
Langham. Rut 4F 75
Langham. Suff 4B 66
Langho. Lanc 1F 91
Langholm. Dum 1E 113
Langland. Swan 4F 31
Langleeford. Nmbd 2D 120
Langley. Ches E 3D 84
Langley. Derbs 1B 74
Langley. Essx 2E 53
Langley. Glos 3F 49
Langley. Hants 2C 16
Langley. Herts 3C 52
Langley. Kent 5C 40
Langley. Nmbd 3B 114
Langley. Slo 3B 38
Langley. Som 4D 20
Langley. Warw 4F 61
Langley. W Sus 4G 25
Langley Burrell. Wilts 4E 35
Langleybury. Herts 5A 52
Langley Common. Derbs 2G 73
Langley Green. Derbs 2G 73
Langley Green. Norf 5F 79
Langley Green. Warw 4F 61
Langley Green. W Sus 2D 26
Langley Heath. Kent 5C 40
Langley Marsh. Som 4D 20
Langley Moor. Dur 5F 115
Langley Park. Dur 5F 115
Langley Street. Norf 5F 79
Langney. E Sus 5H 27
Langold. Notts 2C 86
Langore. Corn 4C 10
Langport. Som 4H 21
Langrick. Linc 1B 76
Langridge. Bath 5C 34
Langridgeford. Devn 4F 19
Langrigg. Cumb 5C 112
Langrish. Hants 4F 25
Langsett. S Yor 4C 92
Langshaw. Bord 1H 119
Langstone. Hants 2F 17
Langthorne. N Yor 5F 105
Langthorpe. N Yor 3F 99
Langthwaite. N Yor 4D 104
Langtoft. E Yor 3E 101
Langtoft. Linc 4A 76
Langton. Dur 3E 105
Langton. Linc 4B 88
(nr. Horncastle)
Langton. Linc 3C 88
(nr. Spilsby)
Langton. N Yor 3B 100
Langton by Wragby. Linc 3A 88
Langton Green. Kent 2G 27
Langton Herring. Dors 4B 14
Langton Long Blandford. Dors 2D 15
Langton Matravers. Dors 5E 15
Langtree. Devn 1E 11
Langwathby. Cumb 1G 103
Langwith. Derbs 3C 86
Langworth. Linc 3H 87
Lanivet. Corn 2E 7
Lanjeth. Corn 3D 6
Lank. Corn 5A 10
Lanlivery. Corn 3E 7
Lanner. Corn 5B 6
Lanreath. Corn 3F 7
Lansallos. Corn 3F 7
Lansdown. Bath 5C 34
Lansdown. Glos 3E 49
Lanteglos Highway. Corn 3F 7
Lanton. Nmbd 1D 120
Lanton. Bord 2A 120
Lapford. Devn 2H 11
Lapford Cross. Devn 2H 11
Laphroaig. Arg 5B 124
Lapley. Staf 4C 72
Lapworth. Warw 3F 61
Larachbeg. High 4A 140
Larbert. Falk 1B 128
Larden Green. Ches E 5H 83
Larel. High 3D 169
Largie. Abers 5D 160
Largiemore. Arg 1H 125
Largoward. Fife 3G 137
**Largs**. N Ayr 4D 126
Largue. Abers 4D 160
Largybeg. N Ayr 3E 123
Largymeanoch. N Ayr 3E 123
Largymore. N Ayr 3E 123
Larkfield. Inv 2D 126
Larkfield. Kent 5B 40
Larkhall. Bath 5C 34
**Larkhall**. S Lan 4A 128
Larkhill. Wilts 2G 23
Larling. Norf 2B 66
**Larne**. ME Ant 6L 175
Larport. Here 2A 48
Lartington. Dur 3D 104
Lary. Abers 3H 151
Lasham. Hants 2E 25
Lashenden. Kent 1C 28
Lasswade. Midl 3G 129
Lastingham. N Yor 5E 107
Latchford. Herts 3D 53
Latchford. Oxon 5E 51
Latchingdon. Essx 5B 54
Latchley. Corn 5E 11
Latchmere Green. Hants 1E 25
Lathbury. Mil 1G 51
Latheron. High 5D 169
Latheronwheel. High 5D 169
Lathom. Lanc 4C 90
Lathones. Fife 3G 137
Latimer. Buck 1B 38
Latteridge. S Glo 3B 34
Lattiford. Som 4B 22
Latton. Wilts 2F 35
Laudale House. High 3B 140
Lauder. Bord 5B 130
Laugharne. Carm 3H 43
Laughterton. Linc 3F 87
Laughton. E Sus 4G 27
Laughton. Leics 2D 62
Laughton. Linc 1F 87
(nr. Gainsborough)
Laughton. Linc 2H 75
(nr. Grantham)
Laughton Common. S Yor 2C 86
Laughton en le Morthen. S Yor 2C 86
Launcells. Corn 2C 10
Launceston. Corn 4D 10
Launcherley. Som 2A 22
Launton. Oxon 3E 50
Laurelvale. Arm 5E 178
Laurencekirk. Abers 1G 145
Laurieston. Dum 3D 111
Laurieston. Falk 2C 128
Lavendon. Mil 5G 63
Lavenham. Suff 1C 54
Laverhay. Dum 5D 118
Laversdale. Cumb 3F 113
Laverstock. Wilts 3G 23
Laverstoke. Hants 2C 24
Laverton. Glos 2F 49
Laverton. N Yor 2E 99
Laverton. Som 1C 22
Lavister. Wrex 5F 83
Law. S Lan 4B 128
Lawers. Per 5D 142
Lawford. Essx 2D 54
Lawhitton. Corn 4D 10
Lawkland. N Yor 3G 97
Lawley. Telf 5A 72
Lawnhead. Staf 3C 72
Lawrencetown. Arm 5E 178
Lawrenny. Pemb 4E 43
Lawshall. Suff 5A 66
Lawton. Here 5G 59
Laxey. IOM 3D 108
Laxfield. Suff 3E 67
Laxfirth. Shet 6F 173
Laxo. Shet 5F 173
Laxton. E Yor 2A 94
Laxton. Nptn 1G 63
Laxton. Notts 4E 87
Laycock. W Yor 5C 98
Layer Breton. Essx 4C 54
Layer-de-la-Haye. Essx 3C 54
Layer Marney. Essx 4C 54
Laymore. Dors 2G 13
Laysters Pole. Here 4H 59
Layter's Green. Buck 1A 38
Laytham. E Yor 1H 93
Lazenby. Red C 3C 106
Lazonby. Cumb 1G 103
Lea. Derbs 5H 85
Lea. Here 3B 48
Lea. Linc 2F 87
Lea. Shrp 2F 59
(nr. Bishop's Castle)
Lea. Shrp 5G 71
(nr. Shrewsbury)
Lea. Wilts 3E 35
Leabrooks. Derbs 5B 86
Leac a Li. W Isl 8D 171
Leachd. Arg 4H 133
Leachkin. High 4A 158
Leachpool. Pemb 3D 42
Leadburn. Midl 4F 129
Leadenham. Linc 5G 87
Leaden Roding. Essx 4F 53
Leaderfoot. Bord 1H 119
Leadgate. Cumb 5A 114
Leadgate. Dur 4E 115
Leadgate. Nmbd 4E 115
Leadhills. S Lan 3A 118
Leadingcross Green. Kent 5C 40
Lea End. Worc 3E 61
Leafield. Oxon 4B 50
Leagrave. Lutn 3A 52
Lea Hall. W Mid 2F 61
Lea Heath. Staf 3E 73
Leake. N Yor 5B 106
Leake Common Side. Linc 5C 88
Leake Fold Hill. Linc 5D 88
Leake Hurn's End. Linc 1D 76
Lealholm. N Yor 4E 107
Lealt. Arg 4D 132
Lealt. High 2E 155
Leam. Derbs 3G 85
Lea Marston. Warw 1G 61
Leamington Hastings. Warw 4B 62
**Leamington Spa, Royal**. Warw 4H 61
Leamonsley. Staf 5F 73
Leamside. Dur 5G 115
Leargybreck. Arg 2D 124
Lease Rigg. N Yor 4F 107
Leasgill. Cumb 1D 97
Leasingham. Linc 1H 75
Leasingthorne. Dur 1F 105
Leasowe. Mers 1E 83
**Leatherhead**. Surr 5C 38
Leathley. N Yor 5E 99
Leaths. Dum 3E 111
Leaton. Shrp 4G 71
Leaton. Telf 4A 72
Lea Town. Lanc 1C 90
Leaveland. Kent 5E 40
Leavenheath. Suff 2C 54
Leavening. N Yor 3B 100
Leaves Green. G Lon 4F 39
Lea Yeat. Cumb 1G 97
Leazes. Dur 4E 115
Lebberston. N Yor 1E 101
Lechlade on Thames. Glos 2H 35
Leck. Lanc 2F 97
Leckford. Hants 3B 24
Leckfurin. High 3H 167
Leckgruinart. Arg 3A 124
Leckhampstead. Buck 2F 51
Leckhampstead. W Ber 4C 36
Leckhampton. Glos 4E 49
Leckmelm. High 4F 163
Leckwith. V Glam 4E 33
Leconfield. E Yor 5E 101
Ledaig. Arg 5D 140
Ledburn. Buck 3H 51
Ledbury. Here 2C 48
Ledgemoor. Here 5G 59
Ledgowan. High 3D 156
Ledicot. Here 4G 59
Ledmore. High 2G 163

Lednabirichen—Llangwyllog


Lednabirichen. High 4E 165
Lednagullin. High 2A 168
Ledsham. Ches W 3F 83
Ledsham. W Yor 2E 93
Ledston. W Yor 2E 93
Ledstone. Devn 4D 8
Ledwell. Oxon 3C 50
Lee. Devn 2E 19
(nr. Ilfracombe)
Lee. Devn 4B 20
(nr. South Molton)
Lee. G Lon 3E 39
Lee. Hants 1B 16
Lee. Lanc 4E 97
Lee. Shrp 2G 71
Leeans. Shet 7E 173
Leebotten. Shet 9F 173
Leebotwood. Shrp 1G 59
Lee Brockhurst. Shrp 3H 71
Leece. Cumb 3B 96
Leechpool. Mon 3A 34
Lee Clump. Buck 5H 51
Leeds. Kent 5C 40
Leeds. W Yor 1C 92 & 196
Leeds Bradford Airport.
W Yor 5E 99
Leedstown. Corn 3D 4
Leegomery. Telf 4A 72
Lee Head. Derbs 1E 85
Leek. Staf 5D 85
Leekbrook. Staf 5D 85
Leek Wootton. Warw 4G 61
Lee Mill. Devn 3B 8
Leeming. N Yor 1E 99
Leeming Bar. N Yor 5F 105
Lee Moor. Devn 2B 8
Lee Moor. W Yor 2D 92
Lee-on-the-Solent. Hants 2D 16
Lees. Derbs 2G 73
Lees. G Man 4H 91
Lees. W Yor 1A 92
Lees, The. Kent 5E 40
Leeswood. Flin 4E 83
Lee, The. Buck 5H 51
Leetown. Per 1E 136
Leftwich. Ches W 3A 84
Legbourne. Linc 2C 88
Legburthwaite. Cumb 3E 102
Legerwood. Bord 5B 130
Legsby. Linc 2A 88
Leicester. Leic 5C 74 & 196
Leicester Forest East. Leics 5C 74
Leigh. Dors 2B 14
Leigh. G Man 4E 91
Leigh. Kent 1G 27
Leigh. Shrp 5F 71
Leigh. Surr 1D 26
Leigh. Wilts 2F 35
Leigh. Worc 5B 60
Leigham. Plym 3B 8
Leigh Beck. Essx 2C 40
Leigh Common. Som 4C 22
Leigh Delamere. Wilts 4D 35
Leigh Green. Kent 2D 28
Leighland Chapel. Som 3D 20
Leigh-on-Sea. S'end 2C 40
Leigh Park. Hants 2F 17
Leigh Sinton. Worc 5B 60
Leighterton. Glos 2D 34
Leigh, The. Glos 3D 48
Leighton. N Yor 2D 98
Leighton. Powy 5E 71
Leighton. Shrp 5A 72
Leighton. Som 2C 22
Leighton Bromswold.
Cambs 3A 64
Leighton Buzzard. C Beds 3H 51
Leigh-upon-Mendip. Som 2B 22
Leinthall Earls. Here 4G 59
Leinthall Starkes. Here 4G 59
Leintwardine. Here 3G 59
Leire. Leics 1C 62
Leirinmore. High 2E 166
Leishmore. High 4G 157
Leiston. Suff 4G 67
Leitfie. Per 4B 144
Leith. Edin 2F 129
Leitholm. Bord 5D 130
Leitrim. New M 6H 179
Lelant. Corn 3C 4
Lelant Downs. Corn 3C 4
Lelley. E Yor 1F 95
Lem Hill. Worc 3B 60
Lemington. Tyne 3E 115
Lempitlaw. Bord 1B 120
Lemsford. Herts 4C 52
Lenacre. Cumb 1F 97
Lenchie. Abers 5C 160
Lenchwick. Worc 1F 49
Lendalfoot. S Ayr 1G 109
Lendrick. Stir 3E 135
Lenham. Kent 5C 40
Lenham Heath. Kent 1D 28
Lenimore. N Ayr 5G 125
Lennel. Bord 5E 131
Lennoxtown. E Dun 2H 127
Lenton. Linc 2H 75
Lentran. High 4H 157
Lenwade. Norf 4C 78
Lenzie. E Dun 2H 127
Leochel Cushnie. Abers 2C 152
Leogh. Shet 1B 172
Leominster. Here 5G 59
Leonard Stanley. Glos 5D 48
Lepe. Hants 3C 16
Lephenstrath. Arg 5A 122
Lephin. High 4A 154
Lephinchapel. Arg 4G 133
Lephinmore. Arg 4G 133
Leppington. N Yor 3B 100
Lepton. W Yor 3C 92
Lerryn. Corn 3F 7
Lerwick. Shet 7F 173
Lerwick (Tingwall) Airport.
Shet 7F 173
Lesbury. Nmbd 3G 121
Leslie. Abers 1C 152
Leslie. Fife 3E 137
Lesmahagow. S Lan 1H 117
Lesnewth. Corn 3B 10
Lessingham. Norf 3F 79
Lessonhall. Cumb 4D 112
Leswalt. Dum 3F 109
Letchmore Heath. Herts 1C 38
Letchworth Garden City.
Herts 2C 52
Letcombe Bassett. Oxon 3B 36
Letcombe Regis. Oxon 3B 36
Letham. Ang 4E 145
Letham. Falk 1B 128
Letham. Fife 2F 137
Lethanhill. E Ayr 3D 116
Lethenty. Abers 4F 161
Letheringham. Suff 5E 67
Letheringsett. Norf 2C 78
Lettaford. Devn 4H 11
Lettan. Orkn 3G 172
Letter. Abers 2E 153
Letterewe. High 1B 156
Letterfearn. High 1A 148
Lettermore. Arg 4F 139
Letters. High 5F 163
Lettershendoney. Derr 5B 174
Letterston. Pemb 2D 42
Letton. Here 1G 47
(nr. Kington)
Letton. Here 3F 59
(nr. Leintwardine)
Letty Green. Herts 4C 52
Letwell. S Yor 2C 86
Leuchars. Fife 1G 137
Leumrabhagh. W Isl 6F 171
Leusdon. Devn 5H 11
Levaneap. Shet 5F 173
Levedale. Staf 4C 72
Leven. E Yor 5F 101
Leven. Fife 3F 137
Levencorroch. N Ayr 3E 123
Levenhall. E Lot 2G 129
Levens. Cumb 1D 97
Levens Green. Herts 3D 52
Levenshulme. G Man 1C 84
Levenwick. Shet 9F 173
Leverburgh. W Isl 9C 171
Leverington. Cambs 4D 76
Leverton. Linc 1C 76
Leverton. W Ber 4B 36
Leverton Lucasgate. Linc 1D 76
Leverton Outgate. Linc 1D 76
Levington. Suff 2F 55
Levisham. N Yor 5F 107
Levishie. High 2G 149
Lew. Oxon 5B 50
Lewaigue. IOM 2D 108
Lewannick. Corn 4C 10
Lewdown. Devn 4E 11
Lewes. E Sus 4F 27
Leweston. Pemb 2D 42
Lewisham. G Lon 3E 39
Lewiston. High 1H 149
Lewistown. B'end 3C 32
Lewknor. Oxon 2F 37
Leworthy. Devn 3G 19
(nr. Barnstaple)
Leworthy. Devn 2D 10
(nr. Holsworthy)
Lewson Street. Kent 4D 40
Lewthorn Cross. Devn 5A 12
Lewtrenchard. Devn 4E 11
Ley. Corn 2F 7
Leybourne. Kent 5A 40
Leyburn. N Yor 5E 105
Leycett. Staf 1B 72
Leyfields. Staf 5G 73
Ley Green. Herts 3B 52
Ley Hill. Buck 5H 51
Leyland. Lanc 2D 90
Leylodge. Abers 2E 153
Leymoor. W Yor 3B 92
Leys. Per 5B 144
Leysdown-on-Sea. Kent 3E 41
Leysmill. Ang 4F 145
Leyton. G Lon 2E 39
Leytonstone. G Lon 2F 39
Lezant. Corn 5D 10
Leziate. Norf 4F 77
Lhanbryde. Mor 2G 159
Lhen, The. IOM 1C 108
Liatrie. High 5E 157
Libanus. Powy 3C 46
Libberton. S Lan 5C 128
Libbery. Worc 5D 60
Liberton. Edin 3F 129
Liceasto. W Isl 8D 171
Lichfield. Staf 5F 73
Lickey. Worc 3D 61
Lickey End. Worc 3D 60
Lickfold. W Sus 3A 26
Liddaton. Devn 4E 11
Liddington. Swin 3H 35
Liddle. Orkn 9D 172
Lidgate. Suff 5G 65
Lidgett. Notts 4D 86
Lidham Hill. E Sus 4C 28
Lidlington. C Beds 2H 51
Lidsey. W Sus 5A 26
Lidstone. Oxon 3B 50
Lienassie. High 1B 148
Liff. Ang 5C 144
Lifford. W Mid 2E 61
Lifton. Devn 4D 11
Liftondown. Devn 4D 10
Lighthorne. Warw 5H 61
Light Oaks. Stoke 5D 84
Lightwater. Surr 4A 38
Lightwood. Staf 1E 73
Lightwood. Stoke 1D 72
Lightwood Green. Ches E 1A 72
Lightwood Green. Wrex 1F 71
Lilbourne. Nptn 3C 62
Lilburn Tower. Nmbd 2E 121
Lillesdon. Som 4G 21
Lilleshall. Telf 4B 72
Lilley. Herts 3B 52
Lilliesleaf. Bord 2H 119
Lillingstone Dayrell. Buck 2F 51
Lillingstone Lovell. Buck 1F 51
Lillington. Dors 1B 14
Lilstock. Som 2E 21
Lilybank. Inv 2E 126
Lilyhurst. Shrp 4B 72
Limavady. Caus 4C 174
Limbrick. Lanc 3E 90
Limbury. Lutn 3A 52
Limekilnburn. S Lan 4A 128
Limekilns. Fife 1D 129
Limerigg. Falk 2B 128
Limestone Brae. Nmbd 5A 114
Lime Street. Worc 2D 48
Limington. Som 4A 22
Limpenhoe. Norf 5F 79
Limpley Stoke. Wilts 5C 34
Limpsfield. Surr 5F 39
Limpsfield Chart. Surr 5F 39
Linburn. W Lot 3E 129
Linby. Notts 5C 86
Linchmere. W Sus 3G 25
Lincluden. Dum 2A 112
Lincoln. Linc 3G 87 & 197
Lincomb. Worc 4C 60
Lindale. Cumb 1D 96
Lindal in Furness. Cumb 2B 96
Lindean. Bord 1G 119
Linden. Glos 4D 48
Lindfield. W Sus 3E 27
Lindford. Hants 3G 25
Lindores. Fife 2E 137
Lindridge. Worc 4A 60
Lindsell. Essx 3G 53
Lindsey. Suff 1C 54
Lindsey Tye. Suff 1C 54
Linford. Hants 2G 15
Linford. Thur 3A 40
Lingague. IOM 4B 108
Lingdale. Red C 3D 106
Lingen. Here 4F 59
Lingfield. Surr 1E 27
Lingreabhagh. W Isl 9C 171
Lingwood. Norf 5F 79
Lingy Close. Cumb 4E 113
Linicro. High 2C 154
Linkend. Worc 2D 48
Linkenholt. Hants 1B 24
Linkinhorne. Corn 5D 10
Linklater. Orkn 9D 172
Linksness. Orkn 6E 172
Linktown. Fife 4E 137
Linkwood. Mor 2G 159
Linley. Shrp 1F 59
(nr. Bishop's Castle)
Linley. Shrp 1A 60
(nr. Bridgnorth)
Linley Green. Here 5A 60
Linlithgow. W Lot 2C 128
Linlithgow Bridge. Falk 2C 128
Linneraineach. High 3F 163
Linshiels. Nmbd 4C 120
Linsiadar. W Isl 4E 171
Linsidemore. High 4C 164
Linslade. C Beds 3H 51
Linstead Parva. Suff 3F 67
Linstock. Cumb 4F 113
Linthwaite. W Yor 3B 92
Lintlaw. Bord 4E 131
Lintmill. Mor 2C 160
Linton. Cambs 1F 53
Linton. Derbs 4G 73
Linton. Here 3B 48
Linton. Kent 1B 28
Linton. N Yor 3B 98
Linton. Bord 2B 120
Linton. W Yor 5F 99
Linton Colliery. Nmbd 5G 121
Linton Hill. Here 3B 48
Linton-on-Ouse. N Yor 3G 99
Lintzford. Tyne 4E 115
Lintzgarth. Dur 5C 114
Linwood. Hants 2G 15
Linwood. Linc 2A 88
Linwood. Ren 3F 127
Lionacleit. W Isl 4C 170
Lionacro. High 2C 154
Lionacuidhe. W Isl 4C 170
Lional. W Isl 1H 171
Liphook. Hants 3G 25
Lipley. Shrp 2B 72
Lipyeate. Som 1B 22
Liquo. N Lan 4B 128
Lisbane. N Dwn 3J 179
Lisbellaw. Ferm 8F 176
Lisburn. Lis 3G 179
Liscard. Mers 1F 83
Liscolman. Caus 3F 175
Liscombe. Som 3B 20
Lishahawley. Derr 4A 174
Liskeard. Corn 2G 7
Lislea. New M 7E 178
Lisle Court. Hants 3B 16
Lisnarick. Ferm 7D 176
Lisnaskea. Ferm 6J 177
Liss. Hants 4F 25
Lissett. E Yor 4F 101
Liss Forest. Hants 4F 25
Lissington. Linc 2A 88
Liston. Essx 1B 54
Listooder. New M 4J 179
Lisvane. Card 3E 33
Liswerry. Newp 3G 33
Litcham. Norf 4A 78
Litchard. B'end 3C 32
Litchborough. Nptn 5D 62
Litchfield. Hants 1C 24
Litherland. Mers 1F 83
Litlington. Cambs 1D 52
Litlington. E Sus 5G 27
Littemill. Nmbd 3G 121
Litterty. Abers 3E 161
Little Abington. Cambs 1F 53
Little Addington. Nptn 3G 63
Little Airmyn. N Yor 2H 93
Little Alne. Warw 4F 61
Little Ardo. Abers 5F 161
Little Asby. Cumb 4H 103
Little Aston. Staf 5E 73
Little Atherfield. IOW 4C 16
Little Ayton. N Yor 3C 106
Little Baddow. Essx 5A 54
Little Badminton. S Glo 3D 34
Little Ballinluig. Per 3G 143
Little Bampton. Cumb 4D 112
Little Bardfield. Essx 2G 53
Little Barford. Bed 5A 64
Little Barningham. Norf 2D 78
Little Barrington. Glos 4H 49
Little Barrow. Ches W 4G 83
Little Barugh. N Yor 2B 100
Little Bavington. Nmbd 2C 114
Little Bealings. Suff 1F 55
Littlebeck. Cumb 3H 103
Little Bedwyn. Wilts 5A 36
Little Bentley. Essx 3E 54
Little Berkhamsted. Herts 5C 52
Little Billing. Nptn 4F 63
Little Billington. C Beds 3H 51
Little Birch. Here 2A 48
Little Bispham. Bkpl 5C 96
Little Blakenham. Suff 1E 54
Little Blencow. Cumb 1F 103
Little Bognor. W Sus 3B 26
Little Bolas. Shrp 3A 72
Little Bollington. Ches E 2B 84
Little Bookham. Surr 5C 38
Littleborough. Devn 1B 12
Littleborough. G Man 3H 91
Littleborough. Notts 2F 87
Littlebourne. Kent 5G 41
Little Bourton. Oxon 1C 50
Little Bowden. Leics 2E 63
Little Bradley. Suff 5F 65
Little Brampton. Shrp 2F 59
Little Brechin. Ang 2E 145
Littlebredy. Dors 4A 14
Little Brickhill. Mil 2H 51
Little Bridgeford. Staf 3C 72
Little Brington. Nptn 4D 62
Little Bromley. Essx 3D 54
Little Broughton. Cumb 1B 102
Little Budworth. Ches W 4H 83
Little Burstead. Essx 1A 40
Little Burton. E Yor 5F 101
Littlebury. Essx 2F 53
Littlebury Green. Essx 2E 53
Little Bytham. Linc 4H 75
Little Canfield. Essx 3F 53
Little Canford. Dors 3F 15
Little Carlton. Linc 2C 88
Little Carlton. Notts 5E 87
Little Casterton. Rut 5H 75
Little Catwick. E Yor 5F 101
Little Catworth. Cambs 3A 64
Little Cawthorpe. Linc 2C 88
Little Chalfont. Buck 1A 38
Little Chart. Kent 1D 28
Little Chesterford. Essx 1F 53
Little Cheverell. Wilts 1E 23
Little Chishill. Cambs 2E 53
Little Clacton. Essx 4E 55
Little Clanfield. Oxon 5A 50
Little Clifton. Cumb 2B 102
Little Coates. NE Lin 4F 95
Little Comberton. Worc 1E 49
Little Common. E Sus 5B 28
Little Compton. Warw 2A 50
Little Cornard. Suff 2B 54
Littlecote. Buck 3G 51
Littlecott. Wilts 1G 23
Little Cowarne. Here 5A 60
Little Coxwell. Oxon 2A 36
Little Crakehall. N Yor 5F 105
Little Crawley. Mil 1H 51
Little Creich. High 5D 164
Little Cressingham. Norf 5A 78
Little Crosby. Mers 4B 90
Little Crosthwaite. Cumb 2D 102
Little Cubley. Derbs 2F 73
Little Dalby. Leics 4E 75
Little Dawley. Telf 5A 72
Littledean. Glos 4B 48
Little Dens. Abers 4H 161
Little Dewchurch. Here 2A 48
Little Ditton. Cambs 5F 65
Little Down. Hants 1B 24
Little Downham. Cambs 2E 65
Little Drayton. Shrp 2A 72
Little Driffield. E Yor 4E 101
Little Dunham. Norf 4A 78
Little Dunkeld. Per 4H 143
Little Dunmow. Essx 3G 53
Little Easton. Essx 3G 53
Little Eaton. Derbs 1A 74
Little Eccleston. Lanc 5D 96
Little Ellingham. Norf 1C 66
Little Elm. Som 2C 22
Little End. Essx 5F 53
Little Everdon. Nptn 5C 62
Little Eversden. Cambs 5C 64
Little Faringdon. Oxon 5H 49
Little Fencote. N Yor 5F 105
Little Fenton. N Yor 1F 93
Littleferry. High 4F 165
Little Fransham. Norf 4B 78
Little Gaddesden. Herts 4H 51
Little Garway. Here 3H 47
Little Gidding. Cambs 2A 64
Little Glemham. Suff 5F 67
Little Glenshee. Per 5G 143
Little Gransden. Cambs 5B 64
Little Green. Suff 3C 66
Little Green. Wrex 1G 71
Little Grimsby. Linc 1C 88
Little Habton. N Yor 2B 100
Little Hadham. Herts 3E 53
Little Hale. Linc 1A 76
Little Hallingbury. Essx 4E 53
Littleham. Devn 4E 19
(nr. Bideford)
Littleham. Devn 4D 12
(nr. Exmouth)
Little Hampden. Buck 5G 51
Littlehampton. W Sus 5B 26
Little Haresfield. Glos 5D 48
Little Harrowden. Nptn 3F 63
Little Haseley. Oxon 5E 51
Little Hatfield. E Yor 5F 101
Little Hautbois. Norf 3E 79
Little Haven. Pemb 3C 42
Little Hay. Staf 5F 73
Little Hayfield. Derbs 2E 85
Little Haywood. Staf 3E 73
Little Heath. W Mid 2H 61
Little Heck. N Yor 2F 93
Littlehempston. Devn 2E 9
Little Herbert's. Glos 4E 49
Little Hereford. Here 4H 59
Little Horkesley. Essx 2C 54
Little Hormead. Herts 3D 53
Little Horsted. E Sus 4F 27
Little Horton. W Yor 1B 92
Little Horwood. Buck 2F 51
Little Houghton. Nptn 5F 63
Littlehoughton. Nmbd 3G 121
Little Houghton. S Yor 4E 93
Little Hucklow. Derbs 3F 85
Little Hulton. G Man 4F 91
Little Irchester. Nptn 4G 63
Little Kelk. E Yor 3E 101
Little Kimble. Buck 5G 51
Little Kineton. Warw 5H 61
Little Kingshill. Buck 2G 37
Little Langdale. Cumb 4E 102
Little Langford. Wilts 3F 23
Little Laver. Essx 5F 53
Little Lawford. Warw 3B 62
Little Leigh. Ches W 3A 84
Little Leighs. Essx 4H 53
Little Leven. E Yor 5E 101
Little Lever. G Man 4F 91
Little Linford. Mil 1G 51
Little London. Buck 4E 51
Little London. E Sus 4G 27
Little London. Hants 2B 24
(nr. Andover)
Little London. Hants 1E 24
(nr. Basingstoke)
Little London. Linc 3D 76
(nr. Long Sutton)
Little London. Linc 3B 76
(nr. Spalding)
Little London. Norf 2E 79
(nr. North Walsham)
Little London. Norf 1G 65
(nr. Northwold)
Little London. Norf 2D 78
(nr. Saxthorpe)
Little London. Norf 1F 65
(nr. Southery)
Little London. Powy 2C 58
Little Longstone. Derbs 3F 85
Little Malvern. Worc 1C 48
Little Maplestead. Essx 2B 54
Little Marcle. Here 2B 48
Little Marlow. Buck 3G 37
Little Massingham. Norf 3G 77
Little Melton. Norf 5D 78
Littlemill. Abers 4H 151
Littlemill. E Ayr 3D 116
Littlemill. High 4D 158
Little Mill. Mon 5G 47
Little Milton. Oxon 5E 50
Little Missenden. Buck 1A 38
Littlemoor. Derbs 4A 86
Littlemoor. Dors 4B 14
Littlemore. Oxon 5D 50
Little Mountain. Flin 4E 83
Little Musgrave. Cumb 3A 104
Little Ness. Shrp 4G 71
Little Neston. Ches W 3E 83
Little Newcastle. Pemb 2D 43
Little Newsham. Dur 3E 105
Little Oakley. Essx 3F 55
Little Oakley. Nptn 2F 63
Little Onn. Staf 4C 72
Little Ormside. Cumb 3A 104
Little Orton. Cumb 4E 113
Little Orton. Leics 5H 73
Little Ouse. Norf 2F 65
Little Ouseburn. N Yor 3G 99
Littleover. Derb 2H 73
Little Packington. Warw 2G 61
Little Paxton. Cambs 4A 64
Little Petherick. Corn 1D 6
Little Plumpton. Lanc 1B 90
Little Plumstead. Norf 4F 79
Little Ponton. Linc 2G 75
Littleport. Cambs 2E 65
Little Posbrook. Hants 2D 16
Little Potheridge. Devn 1F 11
Little Preston. Nptn 5C 62
Little Raveley. Cambs 3B 64
Little Reynoldston. Swan 4D 31
Little Ribston. N Yor 4F 99
Little Rissington. Glos 4G 49
Little Rogart. High 3E 165
Little Rollright. Oxon 2A 50
Little Ryburgh. Norf 3B 78
Little Ryle. Nmbd 3E 121
Little Ryton. Shrp 5G 71
Little Salkeld. Cumb 1G 103
Little Sampford. Essx 2G 53
Little Sandhurst. Brac 5G 37
Little Saredon. Staf 5D 72
Little Saxham. Suff 4G 65
Little Scatwell. High 3F 157
Little Shelford. Cambs 5D 64
Little Shoddesden. Hants 2A 24
Little Singleton. Lanc 1B 90
Little Smeaton. N Yor 3F 93
Little Snoring. Norf 2B 78
Little Sodbury. S Glo 3C 34
Little Somborne. Hants 3B 24
Little Somerford. Wilts 3E 35
Little Soudley. Shrp 3B 72
Little Stainforth. N Yor 3H 97
Little Stainton. Darl 3A 106
Little Stanney. Ches W 3G 83
Little Staughton. Bed 4A 64
Little Steeping. Linc 4D 88
Littlester. Shet 3G 173
Little Stoke. Staf 2D 72
Littlestone-on-Sea. Kent 3E 29
Little Stonham. Suff 4D 66
Little Stretton. Leics 5D 74
Little Stretton. Shrp 1G 59
Little Strickland. Cumb 3G 103
Little Stukeley. Cambs 3B 64
Little Sugnall. Staf 2C 72
Little Sutton. Ches W 3F 83
Little Sutton. Linc 3D 76
Little Swinburne. Nmbd 2C 114
Little Tew. Oxon 3B 50
Little Tey. Essx 3B 54
Little Thetford. Cambs 3E 65
Little Thirkleby. N Yor 2G 99
Little Thornage. Norf 2C 78
Little Thornton. Lanc 5C 96
Littlethorpe. Leics 1C 62
Littlethorpe. N Yor 3F 99
Little Thorpe. W Yor 2B 92
Little Thurlow. Suff 5F 65
Little Thurrock. Thur 3H 39
Littleton. Ches W 4G 83
Littleton. Hants 3C 24
Littleton. Som 3H 21
Littleton. Surr 1A 26
(nr. Guildford)
Littleton. Surr 4B 38
(nr. Staines)
Littleton Drew. Wilts 3D 34
Littleton Pannell. Wilts 1F 23
Littleton-upon-Severn.
S Glo 3A 34
Little Torboll. High 4E 165
Little Torrington. Devn 1E 11
Little Totham. Essx 4B 54
Little Town. Cumb 3D 102
Littletown. Dur 5G 115
Littletown. High 5E 165
Little Town. Lanc 1E 91
Little Twycross. Leics 5H 73
Little Urswick. Cumb 2B 96
Little Wakering. Essx 2D 40
Little Walden. Essx 1F 53
Little Waldingfield. Suff 1C 54
Little Walsingham. Norf 2B 78
Little Waltham. Essx 4H 53
Little Warley. Essx 1H 39
Little Weighton. E Yor 1C 94
Little Wenham. Suff 2D 54
Little Wenlock. Telf 5A 72
Little Whelnetham. Suff 4A 66
Little Whittingham Green.
Suff 3E 67
Littlewick Green. Wind 4G 37
Little Wilbraham. Cambs 5E 65
Littlewindsor. Dors 2H 13
Little Wisbeach. Linc 2A 76
Little Witcombe. Glos 4E 49
Little Witley. Worc 4B 60
Little Wittenham. Oxon 2D 36
Little Wolford. Warw 2A 50
Littleworth. Bed 1A 52
Littleworth. Glos 2G 49
Littleworth. Oxon 2B 36
Littleworth. Staf 4E 73
(nr. Cannock)
Littleworth. Staf 3B 72
(nr. Eccleshall)
Littleworth. Staf 3D 72
(nr. Stafford)
Littleworth. W Sus 3C 26
Littleworth. Worc 4D 61
(nr. Redditch)
Littleworth. Worc 5C 60
(nr. Worcester)
Little Wratting. Suff 1G 53
Little Wymondley. Herts 3C 52
Little Wyrley. Staf 5E 73
Little Yeldham. Essx 2A 54
Littley Green. Essx 4G 53
Litton. Derbs 3F 85
Litton. N Yor 2B 98
Litton. Som 1A 22
Litton Cheney. Dors 3A 14
Liurbost. W Isl 5F 171
Liverpool. Mers 1F 83 & 197
Liverpool John Lennon Airport.
Mers 2G 83
Liversedge. W Yor 2B 92
Liverton. Devn 5B 12
Liverton. Red C 3E 107
Liverton Mines. Red C 3E 107
Livingston. W Lot 3D 128
Livingston Village. W Lot 3D 128
Lixwm. Flin 3D 82
Lizard. Corn 5E 5
Llaingoch. IOA 2B 80
Llaithddu. Powy 2C 58
Llampha. V Glam 4C 32
Llan. Powy 5A 70
Llanaber. Gwyn 4F 69
Llanaelhaearn. Gwyn 1C 68
Llanaeron. Cdgn 4D 57
Llanafan. Cdgn 3F 57
Llanafan-fawr. Powy 5B 58
Llanafan-fechan. Powy 5B 58
Llanallgo. IOA 2D 81
Llanandras. Powy 4F 59
Llananno. Powy 3C 58
Llanarmon. Gwyn 2D 68
Llanarmon Dyffryn Ceiriog.
Wrex 2D 70
Llanarmon-yn-Ial. Den 5D 82
Llanarth. Cdgn 5D 56
Llanarth. Mon 4G 47
Llanarthne. Carm 3F 45
Llanasa. Flin 2D 82
Llanbabo. IOA 2C 80
Llanbadarn Fawr. Cdgn 2F 57
Llanbadarn Fynydd. Powy 3D 58
Llanbadarn-y-garreg. Powy 1E 46
Llanbadoc. Mon 5G 47
Llanbadrig. IOA 1C 80
Llanbeder. Newp 2G 33
Llanbedr. Gwyn 3E 69
Llanbedr. Powy 3F 47
(nr. Crickhowell)
Llanbedr. Powy 1E 47
(nr. Hay-on-Wye)
Llanbedr-Dyffryn-Clwyd.
Den 5D 82
Llanbedrgoch. IOA 2E 81
Llanbedrog. Gwyn 2C 68
Llanbedr Pont Steffan. Cdgn 1F 45
Llanbedr-y-cennin. Cnwy 4G 81
Llanberis. Gwyn 4E 81
Llanbethery. V Glam 5D 32
Llanbister. Powy 3D 58
Llanblethian. V Glam 4C 32
Llanboidy. Carm 2G 43
Llanbradach. Cphy 2E 33
Llanbrynmair. Powy 5A 70
Llanbydderi. V Glam 5D 32
Llancadle. V Glam 5D 32
Llancarfan. V Glam 4D 32
Llancatal. V Glam 5D 32
Llancayo. Mon 5G 47
Llancloudy. Here 3H 47
Llancoch. Powy 3E 58
Llancynfelyn. Cdgn 1F 57
Llandaff. Card 4E 33
Llandanwg. Gwyn 3E 69
Llandarcy. Neat 3G 31
Llandawke. Carm 3G 43
Llanddaniel Fab. IOA 3D 81
Llanddarog. Carm 4F 45
Llanddeiniol. Cdgn 3E 57
Llanddeiniolen. Gwyn 4E 81
Llandderfel. Gwyn 2B 70
Llanddeusant. Carm 3A 46
Llanddeusant. IOA 2C 80
Llanddew. Powy 2D 46
Llanddewi. Swan 4D 30
Llanddewi Brefi. Cdgn 5F 57
Llanddewi'r Cwm. Powy 1D 46
Llanddewi Rhydderch. Mon 4G 47
Llanddewi Velfrey. Pemb 3F 43
Llanddewi Ystradenni.
Powy 4D 58
Llanddoged. Cnwy 4H 81
Llanddona. IOA 3E 81
Llanddowror. Carm 3G 43
Llanddulas. Cnwy 3B 82
Llanddwywe. Gwyn 3E 69
Llanddyfnan. IOA 3E 81
Llandecwyn. Gwyn 2F 69
Llandefaelog Fach. Powy 2D 46
Llandefaelog-tre'r-graig.
Powy 2E 47
Llandefalle. Powy 2E 46
Llandegfan. IOA 3E 81
Llandegla. Den 5D 82
Llandegley. Powy 4D 58
Llandegveth. Mon 2G 33
Llandeilo. Carm 3G 45
Llandeilo Graban. Powy 1D 46
Llandeilo'r Fan. Powy 2B 46
Llandeloy. Pemb 2C 42
Llandenny. Mon 5H 47
Llandevaud. Newp 2H 33
Llandevenny. Mon 3H 33
Llandilo. Pemb 2F 43
Llandinabo. Here 3A 48
Llandinam. Powy 2C 58
Llandissilio. Pemb 2F 43
Llandogo. Mon 5A 48
Llandough. V Glam 4C 32
(nr. Cowbridge)
Llandough. V Glam 4E 33
(nr. Penarth)
Llandovery. Carm 2A 46
Llandow. V Glam 4C 32
Llandre. Cdgn 2F 57
Llandrillo. Den 2C 70
Llandrillo-yn-Rhos. Cnwy 2H 81
Llandrindod. Powy 4C 58
Llandrindod Wells. Powy 4C 58
Llandrinio. Powy 4E 71
Llandudno. Cnwy 2G 81
Llandudno Junction. Cnwy 3G 81
Llandudoch. Pemb 1B 44
Llandw. V Glam 4C 32
Llandwrog. Gwyn 5D 80
Llandybie. Carm 4G 45
Llandyfaelog. Carm 4E 45
Llandyfan. Carm 4G 45
Llandyfriog. Cdgn 1D 44
Llandyfrydog. IOA 2D 80
Llandygai. Gwyn 3F 81
Llandygwydd. Cdgn 1C 44
Llandynan. Den 1D 70
Llandyrnog. Den 4D 82
Llandysilio. Powy 4E 71
Llandyssil. Powy 1D 58
Llandysul. Cdgn 1E 45
Llanedeyrn. Card 3F 33
Llaneglwys. Powy 2D 46
Llanegryn. Gwyn 5F 69
Llanegwad. Carm 3F 45
Llaneilian. IOA 1D 80
Llanelian-yn-Rhos. Cnwy 3A 82
Llanelidan. Den 5D 82
Llanelieu. Powy 2E 47
Llanellen. Mon 4G 47
Llanelli. Carm 3E 31
Llanelltyd. Gwyn 4G 69
Llanelly. Mon 4F 47
Llanelly Hill. Mon 4F 47
Llanelwedd. Powy 5C 58
Llan-Elwy. Den 3C 82
Llanenddwyn. Gwyn 3E 69
Llanengan. Gwyn 3B 68
Llanerch. Powy 1F 59
Llanerchymedd. IOA 2D 80
Llanerfyl. Powy 5C 70
Llaneuddog. IOA 2D 80
Llanfachraeth. IOA 2C 80
Llanfachreth. Gwyn 3G 69
Llanfaelog. IOA 3C 80
Llanfaelrhys. Gwyn 3B 68
Llanfaenor. Mon 4H 47
Llanfaes. IOA 3F 81
Llanfaes. Powy 3D 46
Llanfaethlu. IOA 2C 80
Llanfaglan. Gwyn 4D 80
Llanfair. Gwyn 3E 69
Llanfair. Here 1F 47
Llanfair Caereinion. Powy 5D 70
Llanfair Clydogau. Cdgn 5F 57
Llanfair Dyffryn Clwyd. Den 5D 82
Llanfairfechan. Cnwy 3F 81
Llanfair-Nant-Gwyn. Pemb 1F 43
Llanfair Pwllgwyngyll. IOA 3E 81
Llanfair Talhaiarn. Cnwy 3B 82
Llanfair Waterdine. Shrp 3E 59
Llanfair-ym-Muallt. Powy 5C 58
Llanfairyneubwll. IOA 3C 80
Llanfairynghornwy. IOA 1C 80
Llanfallteg. Carm 3F 43
Llanfallteg West. Carm 3F 43
Llanfaredd. Powy 5C 58
Llanfarian. Cdgn 3E 57
Llanfechain. Powy 3D 70
Llanfechell. IOA 1C 80
Llanfendigaid. Gwyn 5E 69
Llanferres. Den 4D 82
Llan Ffestiniog. Gwyn 1G 69
Llanfflewyn. IOA 2C 80
Llanfihangel-ar-Arth. Carm 2E 45
Llanfihangel Glyn Myfyr.
Cnwy 1B 70
Llanfihangel Nant Bran.
Powy 2C 46
Llanfihangel-Nant-Melan.
Powy 5D 58
Llanfihangel near Rogiet.
Mon 3H 33
Llanfihangel Rhydithon.
Powy 4D 58
Llanfihangel Tal-y-llyn.
Powy 3E 46
Llanfihangel-uwch-Gwili.
Carm 3E 45
Llanfihangel-y-Creuddyn.
Cdgn 3F 57
Llanfihangel-yng-Ngwynfa.
Powy 4C 70
Llanfihangel yn Nhowyn.
IOA 3C 80
Llanfihangel-y-pennant.
Gwyn 1E 69
(nr. Golan)
Llanfihangel-y-pennant.
Gwyn 5F 69
(nr. Tywyn)
Llanfihangel-y-traethau.
Gwyn 2E 69
Llanfilo. Powy 2E 46
Llanfleiddan. V Glam 4C 32
Llanfoist. Mon 4F 47
Llanfor. Gwyn 2B 70
Llanfrechfa. Torf 2G 33
Llanfrothen. Gwyn 1F 69
Llanfrynach. Powy 3D 46
Llanfwrog. Den 5D 82
Llanfwrog. IOA 2C 80
Llanfyllin. Powy 4D 70
Llanfynydd. Carm 3F 45
Llanfynydd. Flin 5E 83
Llanfyrnach. Pemb 1G 43
Llangadfan. Powy 4C 70
Llangadog. Carm 3H 45
(nr. Llandovery)
Llangadog. Carm 5E 45
(nr. Llanelli)
Llangadwaladr. IOA 4C 80
Llangadwaladr. Powy 2D 70
Llangaffo. IOA 4D 80
Llangain. Carm 4D 45
Llangammarch Wells. Powy 1C 46
Llangan. V Glam 4C 32
Llangarron. Here 3A 48
Llangasty-Talyllyn. Powy 3E 47
Llangathen. Carm 3F 45
Llangattock. Powy 4F 47
Llangattock Lingoed. Mon 3G 47
Llangattock-Vibon-Avel.
Mon 4H 47
Llangedwyn. Powy 3D 70
Llangefni. IOA 3D 80
Llangeinor. B'end 3C 32
Llangeitho. Cdgn 5F 57
Llangeler. Carm 2D 44
Llangelynin. Gwyn 5E 69
Llangendeirne. Carm 4E 45
Llangennech. Carm 5F 45
Llangennith. Swan 3D 30
Llangenny. Powy 4F 47
Llangernyw. Cnwy 4A 82
Llangian. Gwyn 3B 68
Llangiwg. Neat 5H 45
Llangloffan. Pemb 1D 42
Llanglydwen. Carm 2F 43
Llangoed. IOA 3F 81
Llangoedmor. Cdgn 1B 44
Llangollen. Den 1E 70
Llangolman. Pemb 2F 43
Llangorse. Powy 3E 47
Llangorwen. Cdgn 2F 57
Llangovan. Mon 5H 47
Llangower. Gwyn 2B 70
Llangranog. Cdgn 5C 56
Llangristiolus. IOA 3D 80
Llangrove. Here 4A 48
Llangua. Mon 3G 47
Llangunllo. Powy 3E 58
Llangunnor. Carm 3E 45
Llangurig. Powy 3B 58
Llangwm. Cnwy 1B 70
Llangwm. Mon 5H 47
Llangwm. Pemb 4D 43
Llangwm-isaf. Mon 5H 47
Llangwnnadl. Gwyn 2B 68
Llangwyfan. Den 4D 82
Llangwyfan-isaf. IOA 4C 80
Llangwyllog. IOA 3D 80

Llangwyryfon—Magheramason

Llangwyryfon. Cdgn 3F 57
Llangybi. Cdgn 5F 57
Llangybi. Gwyn 1D 68
Llangybi. Mon 2G 33
Llangyfelach. Swan 3F 31
Llangynhafal. Den 4D 82
Llangynidr. Powy 4E 47
Llangynin. Carm 3G 43
Llangynog. Carm 3H 43
Llangynog. Powy 3C 70
Llangynwyd. B'end 3B 32
Llanhamlach. Powy 3D 46
Llanharan. Rhon 3D 32
Llanharry. Rhon 3D 32
Llanhennock. Mon 2G 33
Llanhilleth. Blae 5F 47
Llanidloes. Powy 2B 58
Llaniestyn. Gwyn 2B 68
Llanigon. Powy 1F 47
Llanilar. Cdgn 3F 57
Llanilid. Rhon 3C 32
**Llanilltud Fawr**. V Glam 5C 32
Llanishen. Card 3E 33
Llanishen. Mon 5H 47
Llanllawddog. Carm 3E 45
Llanllechid. Gwyn 4F 81
Llanllowell. Mon 2G 33
Llanllugan. Powy 5C 70
Llanllwch. Carm 4D 45
Llanllwchaiarn. Powy 1D 58
Llanllwni. Carm 2E 45
Llanllyfni. Gwyn 5D 80
Llanmadoc. Swan 3D 30
Llanmaes. V Glam 5C 32
Llanmartin. Newp 3G 33
Llanmerwig. Powy 1D 58
Llanmihangel. V Glam 4C 32
Llan-mill. Pemb 3F 43
Llanmiloe. Carm 4G 43
Llanmorlais. Swan 3E 31
Llannefydd. Cnwy 3B 82
Llannon. Carm 5F 45
Llan-non. Cdgn 4E 57
Llannor. Gwyn 2C 68
Llanover. Mon 5G 47
Llanpumsaint. Carm 3E 45
Llanrhaeadr. Den 4C 82
Llanrhaeadr-ym-Mochnant. Powy 3D 70
Llanrhian. Pemb 1C 42
Llanrhidian. Swan 3D 31
Llanrhos. Cnwy 2G 81
Llanrhyddlad. IOA 2C 80
Llanrhystud. Cdgn 4E 57
Llanrothal. Here 4H 47
Llanrug. Gwyn 4E 81
Llanrumney. Card 3F 33
Llanrwst. Cnwy 4G 81
Llansadurnen. Carm 3G 43
Llansadwrn. Carm 2G 45
Llansadwrn. IOA 3E 81
Llansaint. Carm 5D 45
Llansamlet. Swan 3F 31
Llansanffraid Glan Conwy. Cnwy 3H 81
Llansannan. Cnwy 4B 82
Llansannor. V Glam 4C 32
Llansantffraed. Cdgn 4E 57
Llansantffraed. Powy 3E 46
Llansantffraed Cwmdeuddwr. Powy 4B 58
Llansantffraed-in-Elwel. Powy 5C 58
Llansantffraid-ym-Mechain. Powy 3E 70
Llansawel. Carm 2G 45
Llansawel. Neat 3G 31
Llansilin. Powy 3E 70
Llansoy. Mon 5H 47
Llanspyddid. Powy 3D 46
Llanstadwell. Pemb 4D 42
Llansteffan. Carm 4D 44
Llanstephan. Powy 1E 46
Llantarnam. Torf 2G 33
Llanteg. Pemb 3F 43
Llanthony. Mon 3F 47
Llantilio Crossenny. Mon 4G 47
Llantilio Pertholey. Mon 4G 47
Llantood. Pemb 1B 44
Llantrisant. Mon 2G 33
Llantrisant. Rhon 3D 32
Llantrithyd. V Glam 4D 32
Llantwit Fardre. Rhon 3D 32
**Llantwit Major**. V Glam 5C 32
Llanuwchllyn. Gwyn 2A 70
Llanvaches. Newp 2H 33
Llanvair Discoed. Mon 2H 33
Llanvapley. Mon 4G 47
Llanvetherine. Mon 4G 47
Llanveynoe. Here 2G 47
Llanvihangel Crucorney. Mon 3G 47
Llanvihangel Gobion. Mon 5G 47
Llanvihangel Ystern-Llewern. Mon 4H 47
Llanwarne. Here 3A 48
Llanwddyn. Powy 4C 70
Llanwenarth. Mon 4F 47
Llanwenog. Cdgn 1E 45
Llanwern. Newp 3G 33
Llanwinio. Carm 2G 43
Llanwnda. Gwyn 5D 80
Llanwnda. Pemb 1D 42
Llanwnnen. Cdgn 1F 45
Llanwnog. Powy 1C 58
Llanwrda. Carm 2H 45
Llanwrin. Powy 5G 69
Llanwrthwl. Powy 4B 58
Llanwrtud. Powy 1B 46
Llanwrtyd. Powy 1B 46
Llanwrtyd Wells. Powy 1B 46
Llanwyddelan. Powy 5C 70
Llanyblodwel. Shrp 3E 71
Llanybri. Carm 3H 43
Llanybydder. Carm 1F 45
Llanycefn. Pemb 2E 43
Llanychaer. Pemb 1D 43
Llanycil. Gwyn 2B 70
Llanymawddwy. Gwyn 4B 70
Llanymddyfri. Carm 2A 46
Llanymynech. Shrp 3E 71
Llanynghenedl. IOA 2C 80
Llanynys. Den 4D 82
Llan-y-pwll. Wrex 5F 83
Llanyrafon. Torf 2G 33
Llanyre. Powy 4C 58
Llanystumdwy. Gwyn 2D 68
Llanywern. Powy 3E 46
Llawhaden. Pemb 3E 43
Llawndy. Flin 2D 82
Llawnt. Shrp 2E 71
Llawr Dref. Gwyn 3B 68
Llawryglyn. Powy 1B 58
Llay. Wrex 5F 83
Llechfaen. Powy 3D 46
Llechryd. Cphy 5E 46
Llechryd. Cdgn 1C 44
Llechrydau. Wrex 2E 71
Lledrod. Cdgn 3F 57
Llethrid. Swan 3E 31
Llidiad-Nenog. Carm 2F 45
Llidiardau. Gwyn 2A 70
Llidiart y Parc. Den 1D 70
Llithfaen. Gwyn 1C 68
Lloc. Flin 3D 82
Llong. Flin 4E 83
Llowes. Powy 1E 47
Lloyney. Powy 3E 59
Llundain-fach. Cdgn 5E 57
Llwydcoed. Rhon 5C 46
Llwyncelyn. Cdgn 5D 56
Llwyncelyn. Swan 5G 45
Llwyndafydd. Cdgn 5C 56
Llwynderw. Powy 5E 70
Llwyn-du. Mon 4F 47
Llwyngwril. Gwyn 5E 69
Llwynhendy. Carm 3E 31
Llwynmawr. Wrex 2E 71
Llwyn-on Village. Mer T 4D 46
Llwyn-têg. Carm 5F 45
Llwyn-y-brain. Carm 3F 43
Llwynygog. Powy 1A 58
Llwyn-y-groes. Cdgn 5E 57
Llwynypia. Rhon 2C 32
Llynclys. Shrp 3E 71
Llynfaes. IOA 3D 80
Llysfaen. Cnwy 3A 82
Llyswen. Powy 2E 47
Llysworney. V Glam 4C 32
Llys-y-fran. Pemb 2E 43
Llywel. Powy 2B 46
Llywernog. Cdgn 2G 57
Loan. Falk 2C 128
Loanend. Nmbd 4F 131
Loanhead. Midl 3F 129
Loaningfoot. Dum 4A 112
Loanreoch. High 1A 158
Loans. S Ayr 1C 116
Loansdean. Nmbd 1E 115
Lobb. Devn 3E 19
Lobhillcross. Devn 4E 11
Lochaber. Mor 3E 159
Loch a Charnain. W Isl 4D 170
Loch a Ghainmhich. W Isl 5E 171
Lochailort. High 5F 147
Lochaline. High 4A 140
Lochans. Dum 4F 109
Locharbriggs. Dum 1A 112
Lochardil. High 4A 158
Lochassynt Lodge. High 1F 163
Lochavich. Arg 2G 133
Lochawe. Arg 1A 134
Loch Baghasdail. W Isl 7C 170
Lochboisdale. W Isl 7C 170
Lochbuie. Arg 1D 132
Lochcarron. High 5A 156
Loch Choire Lodge. High 5G 167
Lochdochart House. Stir 1D 134
Lochdon. Arg 5B 140
Lochearnhead. Stir 1E 135
Lochee. D'dee 5C 144
Lochend. High 5H 157 (nr. Inverness)
Lochend. High 2E 169 (nr. Thurso)
Locherben. Dum 5B 118
Loch Euphort. W Isl 2D 170
Lochfoot. Dum 2F 111
Lochgair. Arg 4G 133
Lochgarthside. High 2H 149
Lochgelly. Fife 4D 136
Lochgilphead. Arg 1G 125
Lochgoilhead. Arg 3A 134
Loch Head. Dum 5A 110
Lochhill. Mor 2G 159
Lochindorb Lodge. High 5D 158
Lochinver. High 1E 163
Lochlane. Per 1H 135
**Loch Lomond**. Arg 3C 134
Loch Loyal Lodge. High 4G 167
Lochluichart. High 2F 157
Lochmaben. Dum 1B 112
Lochmaddy. W Isl 2E 170
Loch nam Madadh. W Isl 2E 170
Lochore. Fife 4D 136
Lochportain. W Isl 1E 170
Lochranza. N Ayr 4H 125
Loch Sgioport. W Isl 5D 170
Lochside. Abers 2G 145
Lochside. High 5A 168 (nr. Achentoul)
Lochside. High 3C 158 (nr. Nairn)
Lochslin. High 5F 165
Lochstack Lodge. High 4C 166
Lochton. Abers 4E 153
Lochty. Fife 3H 137
Lochuisge. High 3B 140
Lochussie. High 3G 157
Lochwinnoch. Ren 4E 127
Lochyside. High 1F 141
Lockengate. Corn 2E 7
Lockerbie. Dum 1C 112
Lockeridge. Wilts 5G 35
Lockerley. Hants 4A 24
Lockhills. Cumb 5G 113
Locking. N Som 1G 21
Lockington. E Yor 5D 101
Lockington. Leics 3B 74
Lockleywood. Shrp 3A 72
Locksgreen. IOW 3C 16
**Locks Heath**. Hants 2D 16
Lockton. N Yor 5F 107
Loddington. Leics 5E 75
Loddington. Nptn 3F 63
Loddiswell. Devn 4D 8
Loddon. Norf 1F 67
Lode. Cambs 4E 65
Loders. Dors 3H 13
Lodsworth. W Sus 3A 26
Lofthouse. N Yor 2D 98
Lofthouse. W Yor 2D 92
Lofthouse Gate. W Yor 2D 92
Loftus. Red C 3E 107
Logan. E Ayr 2E 117
Loganlea. W Lot 3C 128
Logaston. Here 5F 59
Loggerheads. Staf 2B 72
Loggie. High 4F 163
Logie. Ang 2F 145
Logie. Fife 1G 137
Logie. Mor 3E 159
Logie Coldstone. Abers 3B 152
Logie Pert. Ang 2F 145
Logierait. Per 3G 143
Login. Carm 2F 43
Lolworth. Cambs 4C 64
Lonbain. High 3F 155
Londesborough. E Yor 5C 100
**London**. G Lon 2E 39 & 198-199
London Apprentice. Corn 3E 6
London Ashford (Lydd) Airport. Kent 3E 29
London City Airport. G Lon 2F 39
London Colney. Herts 5B 52
**Londonderry**. Derr 5A 174
Londonderry. N Yor 1F 99
London Gatwick Airport. W Sus 1D 26 & 205
London Heathrow Airport. G Lon 3B 38 & 205
London Luton Airport. Lutn 3B 52 & 205
London Southend Airport. Essx 2C 40
London Stansted Airport. Essx 3F 53 & 205
Londonthorpe. Linc 2G 75
Londubh. High 5C 162
Lone. High 4D 166
Lonemore. High 5E 165 (nr. Dornoch)
Lonemore. High 1G 155 (nr. Gairloch)
Long Ashton. N Som 4A 34
Long Bank. Worc 3B 60
Longbar. N Ayr 4E 127
Long Bennington. Linc 1F 75
**Longbenton**. Tyne 3F 115
Longborough. Glos 3G 49
Long Bredy. Dors 3A 14
Longbridge. Warw 4G 61
Longbridge. W Mid 3E 61
Longbridge Deverill. Wilts 2D 22
Long Buckby. Nptn 4D 62
Long Buckby Wharf. Nptn 4D 62
Longburgh. Cumb 4E 112
Longburton. Dors 1B 14
Long Clawson. Leics 3E 74
Longcliffe. Derbs 5G 85
Long Common. Hants 1D 16
Long Compton. Staf 3C 72
Long Compton. Warw 2A 50
Longcot. Oxon 2A 36
Long Crendon. Buck 5E 51
Long Crichel. Dors 1E 15
Longcroft. Cumb 4D 112
Longcroft. Falk 2A 128
Longcross. Surr 4A 38
Longdale. Cumb 4H 103
Longdales. Cumb 5G 113
Longden. Shrp 5G 71
Longden Common. Shrp 5G 71
Long Ditton. Surr 4C 38
Longdon. Staf 4E 73
Longdon. Worc 2D 48
Longdon Green. Staf 4E 73
Longdon on Tern. Telf 4A 72
Longdown. Devn 3B 12
Longdowns. Corn 5B 6
Long Drax. N Yor 2G 93
Long Duckmanton. Derbs 3B 86
**Long Eaton**. Derbs 2B 74
Longfield. Kent 4H 39
Longfield. Shet 10E 173
Longfield Hill. Kent 4H 39
Longford. Derbs 2G 73
Longford. Glos 3D 48
Longford. G Lon 3B 38
Longford. Shrp 2A 72
Longford. Telf 4B 72
Longford. W Mid 2A 62
Longforgan. Per 5C 144
Longformacus. Bord 4C 130
Longframlington. Nmbd 4F 121
Long Gardens. Essx 2B 54
Long Green. Ches W 3G 83
Long Green. Worc 2D 48
Longham. Dors 3F 15
Longham. Norf 4B 78
Long Hanborough. Oxon 4C 50
Longhedge. Wilts 2D 22
Longhill. Abers 3H 161
Longhirst. Nmbd 1F 115
Longhope. Glos 4B 48
Longhope. Orkn 8C 172
Longhorsley. Nmbd 5F 121
Longhoughton. Nmbd 3G 121
Long Itchington. Warw 4B 62
Longlands. Cumb 1D 102
Longlane. Derbs 2G 73
Long Lane. Telf 4A 72
Longlane. W Ber 4C 36
Long Lawford. Warw 3B 62
Long Lease. N Yor 4G 107
Longley Green. Worc 5B 60
Long Load. Som 4H 21
Longmanhill. Abers 2E 161
Long Marston. Herts 4G 51
Long Marston. N Yor 4H 99
Long Marston. Warw 1G 49
Long Marton. Cumb 2H 103
Long Meadow. Cambs 4E 65
Long Meadowend. Shrp 2G 59
Long Melford. Suff 1B 54
Longmoor Camp. Hants 3F 25
Longmorn. Mor 3G 159
Longmoss. Ches E 3C 84
Long Newnton. Glos 2E 35
Longnewton. Bord 2H 119
Long Newton. Stoc T 3A 106
Longney. Glos 4C 48
Longniddry. E Lot 2H 129
Longnor. Shrp 5G 71
Longnor. Staf 4E 85 (nr. Leek)
Longnor. Staf 4C 72 (nr. Stafford)
Longparish. Hants 2C 24
Longpark. Cumb 3F 113
Long Preston. N Yor 4H 97
Longridge. Lanc 1E 90
Longridge. Staf 4D 72
Longridge. W Lot 3C 128
Longriggend. N Lan 2B 128
Long Riston. E Yor 5F 101
Longrock. Corn 3C 4
Longsdon. Staf 5D 84
Longshaw. G Man 4D 90
Longshaw. Staf 1E 73
Longside. Abers 4H 161
Longslow. Shrp 2A 72
Longstanton. Cambs 4C 64
Longstock. Hants 3B 24
Longstowe. Cambs 5C 64
Long Stratton. Norf 1D 66
Long Street. Mil 1F 51
Longstreet. Wilts 1G 23
Long Sutton. Hants 2F 25
Long Sutton. Linc 3D 76
Long Sutton. Som 4H 21
Longthorpe. Pet 1A 64
Long Thurlow. Suff 4C 66
Longthwaite. Cumb 2F 103
**Longton**. Lanc 2C 90
Longton. Stoke 1D 72
Longtown. Cumb 3E 113
Longtown. Here 3G 47
Longville in the Dale. Shrp 1H 59
Long Whatton. Leics 3B 74
Longwick. Buck 5F 51
Long Wittenham. Oxon 2D 36
Longwitton. Nmbd 1D 115
Longworth. Oxon 2B 36
Longyester. E Lot 3B 130
Lonmore. High 4B 154
Looe. Corn 3G 7
Loose. Kent 5B 40
Loosegate. Linc 3C 76
Loosley Row. Buck 5G 51
Lopcombe Corner. Wilts 3A 24
Lopen. Som 1H 13
Loppington. Shrp 3G 71
Lorbottle. Nmbd 4E 121
Lordington. W Sus 2F 17
Loscoe. Derbs 1B 74
Loscombe. Dors 3A 14
Losgaintir. W Isl 8C 171
Lossiemouth. Mor 2G 159
Lossit. Arg 4A 124
Lostock Gralam. Ches W 3A 84
Lostock Green. Ches W 3A 84
Lostock Hall. Lanc 2D 90
Lostock Junction. G Man 4E 91
Lostwithiel. Corn 3F 7
Lothbeg. High 2G 165
Lothersdale. N Yor 5B 98
Lothianbridge. Midl 3G 129
Lothianburn. Edin 3F 129
Lothmore. High 2G 165
Lottisham. Som 3A 22
Loudwater. Buck 1A 38
**Loughborough**. Leics 4C 74
Loughbrickland. Arm 5F 178
Loughgall. Arm 4D 178
Loughguile. Caus 4G 175
Loughinisland. New M 5J 179
Loughmacrory. Ferm 2L 177
Loughor. Swan 3E 31
Loughries. N Dwn 2K 179
**Loughton**. Essx 1F 39
Loughton. Mil 2G 51
Loughton. Shrp 2A 60
Lound. Linc 4H 75
Lound. Notts 2D 86
Lound. Suff 1H 67
Lount. Leics 4A 74
Loup, The. M Ulst 1D 178
**Louth**. Linc 2C 88
Love Clough. Lanc 2G 91
Lovedean. Hants 1E 17
Lover. Wilts 4H 23
Loversall. S Yor 1C 86
Loves Green. Essx 5G 53
Loveston. Pemb 4E 43
Lovington. Som 3A 22
Low Ackworth. W Yor 3E 93
Low Angerton. Nmbd 1D 115
Low Ardwell. Dum 5F 109
Low Ballochdowan. S Ayr 2F 109
Lowbands. Glos 2C 48
Low Barlings. Linc 3H 87
Low Bell End. N Yor 5E 107
Low Bentham. N Yor 3F 97
Low Borrowbridge. Cumb 4H 103
Low Bradfield. S Yor 1G 85
Low Bradley. N Yor 5C 98
Low Braithwaite. Cumb 5F 113
Low Brunton. Nmbd 2C 114
Low Burnham. N Lin 4A 94
Lowca. Cumb 2A 102
Low Catton. E Yor 4B 100
Low Coniscliffe. Darl 3F 105
Low Coylton. S Ayr 3D 116
Low Crosby. Cumb 4F 113
Low Dalby. N Yor 1C 100
Lowdham. Notts 1D 74
Low Dinsdale. Darl 3A 106
Lowe. Shrp 2H 71
Low Ellington. N Yor 1E 98
Lower Amble. Corn 1D 6
Lower Ansty. Dors 2C 14
Lower Arboll. High 5F 165
Lower Arncott. Oxon 4E 50
Lower Ashton. Devn 4B 12
Lower Assendon. Oxon 3F 37
Lower Auchenreath. Mor 2A 160
Lower Badcall. High 4B 166
Lower Ballam. Lanc 1B 90
Lower Ballinderry. Lis 3F 178
Lower Basildon. W Ber 4E 36
Lower Beeding. W Sus 3D 26
Lower Benefield. Nptn 2G 63
Lower Bentley. Worc 4D 61
Lower Beobridge. Shrp 1B 60
Lower Bockhampton. Dors 3C 14
Lower Boddington. Nptn 5B 62
Lower Bordean. Hants 4E 25
Lower Brailes. Warw 2B 50
Lower Breakish. High 1E 147
Lower Broadheath. Worc 5C 60
Lower Brynamman. Neat 4H 45
Lower Bullingham. Here 2A 48
Lower Bullington. Hants 2C 24
Lower Burgate. Hants 1G 15
Lower Cam. Glos 5C 48
Lower Catesby. Nptn 5C 62
Lower Chapel. Powy 2D 46
Lower Cheriton. Devn 2E 12
Lower Chicksgrove. Wilts 3E 23
Lower Chute. Wilts 1B 24
Lower Clopton. Warw 5F 61
Lower Common. Hants 2E 25
Lower Crossings. Derbs 2E 85
Lower Cumberworth. W Yor 4C 92
Lower Darwen. Bkbn 2E 91
Lower Dean. Bed 4H 63
Lower Dean. Devn 2D 8
Lower Diabaig. High 2G 155
Lower Dicker. E Sus 4G 27
Lower Dounreay. High 2B 168
Lower Down. Shrp 2F 59
Lower Dunsforth. N Yor 3G 99
Lower East Carleton. Norf 5D 78
Lower Egleton. Here 1B 48
Lower Ellastone. Staf 1F 73
Lower End. Nptn 4F 63
Lower Everleigh. Wilts 1G 23
Lower Eype. Dors 3H 13
Lower Failand. N Som 4A 34
Lower Faintree. Shrp 2A 60
Lower Farringdon. Hants 3F 25
Lower Foxdale. IOM 4B 108
Lower Frankton. Shrp 2F 71
Lower Froyle. Hants 2F 25
Lower Gabwell. Devn 2F 9
Lower Gledfield. High 4C 164
Lower Godney. Som 2H 21
Lower Gravenhurst. C Beds 2B 52
Lower Green. Essx 2E 53
Lower Green. Norf 2B 78
Lower Green. W Ber 5B 36
Lower Halstow. Kent 4C 40
Lower Hardres. Kent 5F 41
Lower Hardwick. Here 5G 59
Lower Hartshay. Derbs 5A 86
Lower Hawthwaite. Cumb 1B 96
Lower Haysden. Kent 1G 27
Lower Hayton. Shrp 2H 59
Lower Hergest. Here 5E 59
Lower Heyford. Oxon 3C 50
Lower Heysham. Lanc 3D 96
Lower Higham. Kent 3B 40
Lower Holbrook. Suff 2E 55
Lower Holditch. Dors 2G 13
Lower Hordley. Shrp 3F 71
Lower Horncroft. W Sus 4B 26
Lower Horsebridge. E Sus 4G 27
Lower Kilcott. Glos 3C 34
Lower Killeyan. Arg 5A 124
Lower Kingcombe. Dors 3A 14
Lower Kingswood. Surr 5D 38
Lower Kinnerton. Ches W 4F 83
Lower Langford. N Som 5H 33
Lower Largo. Fife 3G 137
Lower Layham. Suff 1D 54
Lower Ledwyche. Shrp 3H 59
Lower Leigh. Staf 2E 73
Lower Lemington. Glos 2H 49
Lower Lenie. High 1H 149
Lower Ley. Glos 4C 48
Lower Llanfadog. Powy 4B 58
Lower Lode. Glos 2D 49
Lower Lovacott. Devn 4F 19
Lower Loxhore. Devn 3G 19
Lower Loxley. Staf 2E 73
Lower Lydbrook. Glos 4A 48
Lower Lye. Here 4G 59
Lower Machen. Newp 3F 33
Lower Maes-coed. Here 2G 47
Lower Meend. Glos 5A 48
Lower Midway. Derbs 3H 73
Lower Milovaig. High 3A 154
Lower Moor. Worc 1E 49
Lower Morton. S Glo 2B 34
Lower Mountain. Flin 5F 83
Lower Nazeing. Essx 5D 53
Lower Netchwood. Shrp 1A 60
Lower Nyland. Dors 4C 22
Lower Oakfield. Fife 4D 136
Lower Oddington. Glos 3H 49
Lower Ollach. High 5E 155
Lower Penarth. V Glam 5E 33
Lower Penn. Staf 1C 60
Lower Pennington. Hants 3B 16
Lower Peover. Ches W 3B 84
Lower Pilsley. Derbs 4B 86
Lower Pitkerrie. High 1C 158
Lower Place. G Man 3H 91
Lower Quinton. Warw 1G 49
Lower Rainham. Medw 4C 40
Lower Raydon. Suff 2D 54
Lower Seagry. Wilts 3E 35
Lower Shelton. C Beds 1H 51
Lower Shiplake. Oxon 4F 37
Lower Shuckburgh. Warw 4B 62
Lower Sketty. Swan 3F 31
Lower Slade. Devn 2F 19
Lower Slaughter. Glos 3G 49
Lower Soudley. Glos 4B 48
Lower Stanton St Quintin. Wilts 3E 35
Lower Stoke. Medw 3C 40
Lower Stondon. C Beds 2B 52
Lower Stonnall. Staf 5E 73
Lower Stow Bedon. Norf 1B 66
Lower Street. Norf 2E 79
Lower Strensham. Worc 1E 49
Lower Sundon. C Beds 3A 52
Lower Swanwick. Hants 2C 16
Lower Swell. Glos 3G 49
Lower Tale. Devn 2D 12
Lower Tean. Staf 2E 73
Lower Thurlton. Norf 1G 67
Lower Thurnham. Lanc 4D 96
Lower Thurvaston. Derbs 2G 73
Lowertown. Corn 4D 4
Lower Town. Here 1B 48
Lower Town. IOS 1B 4
Lowertown. Orkn 8D 172
Lower Town. Pemb 1D 42
Lower Tysoe. Warw 1B 50
Lower Upham. Hants 1D 16
Lower Upnor. Medw 3B 40
Lower Vexford. Som 3E 20
Lower Walton. Warr 2A 84
Lower Wear. Devn 4C 12
Lower Weare. Som 1H 21
Lower Welson. Here 5E 59
Lower Whatcombe. Dors 2D 14
Lower Whitley. Ches W 3A 84
Lower Wield. Hants 2E 25
Lower Withington. Ches E 4C 84
Lower Woodend. Buck 3G 37
Lower Woodford. Wilts 3G 23
Lower Wraxall. Dors 2A 14
Lower Wych. Ches W 1G 71
Lower Wyche. Worc 1C 48
Lowesby. Leics 5E 74
**Lowestoft**. Suff 1H 67
Loweswater. Cumb 2C 102
Low Etherley. Dur 2E 105
Lowfield Heath. W Sus 1D 26
Lowford. Hants 1C 16
Low Fulney. Linc 3B 76
Low Gate. Nmbd 3C 114
Lowgill. Cumb 5H 103
Lowgill. Lanc 3F 97
Low Grantley. N Yor 2E 99
Low Green. N Yor 4E 98
Low Habberley. Worc 3C 60
Low Ham. Som 4H 21
Low Hameringham. Linc 4C 88
Low Hawsker. N Yor 4G 107
Low Hesket. Cumb 5F 113
Low Hesleyhurst. Nmbd 5E 121
Lowick. Cumb 1B 96
Lowick. Nptn 2G 63
Lowick. Nmbd 1E 121
Lowick Bridge. Cumb 1B 96
Lowick Green. Cumb 1B 96
Low Knipe. Cumb 2G 103
Low Leighton. Derbs 2E 85
Low Lorton. Cumb 2C 102
Low Marishes. N Yor 2C 100
Low Marnham. Notts 4F 87
Low Mill. N Yor 5D 106
Low Moor. Lanc 5G 97
Low Moor. W Yor 2B 92
Low Moorsley. Tyne 5G 115
Low Newton-by-the-Sea. Nmbd 2G 121
Lownie Moor. Ang 4D 145
Lowood. Bord 1H 119
Low Row. Cumb 3G 113 (nr. Brampton)
Low Row. Cumb 5C 112 (nr. Wigton)
Low Row. N Yor 5C 104
Lowsonford. Warw 4F 61
Low Street. Norf 5C 78
Lowther. Cumb 2G 103
Lowthorpe. E Yor 3E 101
Lowton. Devn 2G 11
Lowton. G Man 1A 84
Lowton. Som 1E 13
Lowton Common. G Man 1A 84
Low Torry. Fife 1D 128
Low Toynton. Linc 3B 88
Low Valleyfield. Fife 1C 128
Low Westwood. Dur 4E 115
Low Whinnow. Cumb 4E 112
Low Wood. Cumb 1C 96
Low Worsall. N Yor 4A 106
Low Wray. Cumb 4E 103
Loxbeare. Devn 1C 12
Loxhill. Surr 2B 26
Loxhore. Devn 3G 19
Loxley. S Yor 2H 85
Loxley. Warw 5G 61
Loxley Green. Staf 2E 73
Loxton. N Som 1G 21
Loxwood. W Sus 2B 26
Lubcroy. High 3A 164
Lubenham. Leics 2E 62
Lubinvullin. High 2F 167
Luccombe. Som 2C 20
Luccombe Village. IOW 4D 16
Lucker. Nmbd 1F 121
Luckett. Corn 5D 11
Luckington. Wilts 3D 34
Lucklawhill. Fife 1G 137
Luckwell Bridge. Som 3C 20
Lucton. Here 4G 59
Ludag. W Isl 7C 170
Ludborough. Linc 1B 88
Ludchurch. Pemb 3F 43
Luddenden. W Yor 2A 92
Luddenden Foot. W Yor 2A 92
Luddenham. Kent 4D 40
Ludderburn. Cumb 5F 103
Luddesdown. Kent 4A 40
Luddington. N Lin 3B 94
Luddington. Warw 5F 61
Luddington in the Brook. Nptn 2A 64
Ludford. Linc 2A 88
Ludford. Shrp 3H 59
Ludgershall. Buck 4E 51
Ludgershall. Wilts 1A 24
Ludgvan. Corn 3C 4
Ludham. Norf 4F 79
Ludlow. Shrp 3H 59
Ludstone. Shrp 1C 60
Ludwell. Wilts 4E 23
Ludworth. Dur 5G 115
Luffenhall. Herts 3C 52
Luffincott. Devn 3D 10
Lugar. E Ayr 2E 117
Luggate Burn. E Lot 2C 130
Lugg Green. Here 4G 59
Luggiebank. N Lan 2A 128
Lugton. E Ayr 4F 127
Lugwardine. Here 1A 48
Luib. High 1D 146
Luib. Stir 1D 135
Lulham. Here 1H 47
Lullington. Derbs 4G 73
Lullington. E Sus 5G 27
Lullington. Som 1C 22
Lulsgate Bottom. N Som 5A 34
Lulsley. Worc 5B 60
Lulworth Camp. Dors 4D 14
Lumb. Lanc 2G 91
Lumby. N Yor 1E 93
Lumphanan. Abers 3C 152
Lumphinnans. Fife 4D 136
Lumsdaine. Bord 3E 131
Lumsden. Abers 1B 152
Lunan. Ang 3F 145
Lunanhead. Ang 3D 145
Luncarty. Per 1C 136
Lund. E Yor 5D 100
Lund. N Yor 1G 93
Lundie. Ang 5B 144
Lundin Links. Fife 3G 137
Lundy Green. Norf 1E 67
Lunna. Shet 5F 173
Lunning. Shet 5G 173
Lunnon. Swan 4E 31
Lunsford. Kent 5A 40
Lunsford's Cross. E Sus 4B 28
Lunt. Mers 4B 90
Luppitt. Devn 2E 13
Lupridge. Devn 3D 8
Lupset. W Yor 3D 92
Lupton. Cumb 1E 97
**Lurgan**. Arm 4E 178
Lurganare. New M 6E 178
Lurgashall. W Sus 3A 26
Lurley. Devn 1C 12
Lusby. Linc 4C 88
Luscombe. Devn 3D 9
Luson. Devn 4C 8
Luss. Arg 4C 134
Lussagiven. Arg 1E 125
Lusta. High 3B 154
Lustleigh. Devn 4A 12
Luston. Here 4G 59
Luthermuir. Abers 2F 145
Luthrie. Fife 2F 137
Lutley. Staf 2C 60
Luton. Devn 2D 12 (nr. Honiton)
Luton. Devn 5C 12 (nr. Teignmouth)
**Luton**. Lutn 3A 52
Luton (London) Airport. Lutn 3B 52 & 205
Lutterworth. Leics 2C 62
Lutton. Devn 3B 8 (nr. Ivybridge)
Lutton. Devn 2C 8 (nr. South Brent)
Lutton. Linc 3D 76
Lutton. Nptn 2A 64
Lutton Gowts. Linc 3D 76
Lutworthy. Devn 1A 12
Luxborough. Som 3C 20
Luxley. Glos 3B 48
Luxulyan. Corn 3E 7
Lybster. High 5E 169
Lydbury North. Shrp 2F 59
Lydcott. Devn 3G 19
Lydd. Kent 3E 29
Lydden. Kent 1G 29 (nr. Dover)
Lydden. Kent 4H 41 (nr. Margate)
Lyddington. Rut 1F 63
Lydd (London Ashford) Airport. Kent 3E 29
Lydd-on-Sea. Kent 3E 29
Lydeard St Lawrence. Som 3E 21
Lyde Green. Hants 1F 25
Lydford. Devn 4F 11
Lydford Fair Place. Som 3A 22
Lydgate. G Man 4H 91
Lydgate. W Yor 2H 91
Lydham. Shrp 1F 59
Lydiard Millicent. Wilts 3F 35
Lydiate. Mers 4B 90
Lydiate Ash. Worc 3D 61
Lydlinch. Dors 1C 14
Lydmarsh. Som 2G 13
Lydney. Glos 5B 48
Lydstep. Pemb 5E 43
Lye. W Mid 2D 60
Lye Green. Buck 5H 51
Lye Green. E Sus 2G 27
Lye Head. Worc 3B 60
Lye, The. Shrp 1A 60
Lyford. Oxon 2B 36
Lyham. Nmbd 1E 121
Lylestone. N Ayr 5E 127
Lymbridge Green. Kent 1F 29
Lyme Regis. Dors 3G 13
Lyminge. Kent 1F 29
**Lymington**. Hants 3B 16
Lyminster. W Sus 5B 26
**Lymm**. Warr 2A 84
Lymore. Hants 3A 16
Lympne. Kent 2F 29
Lympsham. Som 1G 21
Lympstone. Devn 4C 12
Lynaberack Lodge. High 4B 150
Lynbridge. Devn 2H 19
Lynch. Som 2C 20
Lynchat. High 3B 150
Lynch Green. Norf 5D 78
Lyndhurst. Hants 2B 16
Lyndon. Rut 5G 75
Lyne. Bord 5F 129
Lyne. Surr 4B 38
Lyneal. Shrp 2G 71
Lyne Down. Here 2B 48
Lyneham. Oxon 3A 50
Lyneham. Wilts 4F 35
Lyneholmeford. Cumb 2G 113
Lynemouth. Nmbd 5G 121
Lyne of Gorthleck. High 1H 149
Lyne of Skene. Abers 2E 153
Lynesack. Dur 2D 105
Lyness. Orkn 8C 172
Lyng. Norf 4C 78
Lyngate. Norf 2E 79 (nr. North Walsham)
Lyngate. Norf 3F 79 (nr. Worstead)
Lynmouth. Devn 2H 19
Lynn. Staf 5E 73
Lynn. Telf 4B 72
Lynsted. Kent 4D 40
Lynstone. Corn 2C 10
Lynton. Devn 2H 19
Lynwilg. High 2C 150
Lyon's Gate. Dors 2B 14
Lyonshall. Here 5F 59
Lytchett Matravers. Dors 3E 15
Lytchett Minster. Dors 3E 15
Lyth. High 2E 169
Lytham. Lanc 2B 90
**Lytham St Anne's**. Lanc 2B 90
Lythe. N Yor 3F 107
Lythes. Orkn 9D 172
Lythmore. High 2C 168

## M

Mabe Burnthouse. Corn 5B 6
Mabie. Dum 2A 112
Mablethorpe. Linc 2E 89
Macbiehill. Bord 4E 129
**Macclesfield**. Ches E 3D 84
Macclesfield Forest. Ches E 3D 84
Macduff. Abers 2E 160
Machan. S Lan 4A 128
Macharioch. Arg 5B 122
Machen. Cphy 3F 33
Machrie. N Ayr 2C 122
Machrihanish. Arg 3A 122
Machroes. Gwyn 3C 68
Machynlleth. Powy 5G 69
Mackerye End. Herts 4B 52
Mackworth. Derb 2H 73
Macmerry. E Lot 2H 129
Macosquin. Caus 4E 174
Madderty. Per 1B 136
Maddington. Wilts 2F 23
Maddiston. Falk 2C 128
Madehurst. W Sus 4A 26
Madeley. Staf 1B 72
Madeley. Telf 5A 72
Madeley Heath. Staf 1B 72
Madeley Heath. Worc 3D 60
Madford. Devn 1E 13
Madingley. Cambs 4C 64
Madley. Here 2H 47
Madresfield. Worc 1D 48
Madron. Corn 3B 4
Maenaddwyn. IOA 2D 80
Maenclochog. Pemb 2E 43
Maendy. V Glam 4D 32
Maenporth. Corn 4E 5
Maentwrog. Gwyn 1F 69
Maen-y-groes. Cdgn 5C 56
Maer. Staf 2B 72
Maerdy. Carm 3G 45
Maerdy. Cnwy 1C 70
Maerdy. Rhon 2C 32
Maesbrook. Shrp 3F 71
Maesbury. Shrp 3F 71
Maesbury Marsh. Shrp 3F 71
Maes-glas. Flin 3D 82
Maesgwyn-Isaf. Powy 4D 70
Maeshafn. Den 4E 82
Maes Llyn. Cdgn 1D 44
Maesmynis. Powy 1D 46
**Maesteg**. B'end 2B 32
Maestir. Cdgn 1F 45
Maesybont. Carm 4F 45
Maesycrugiau. Carm 1E 45
Maesycwmmer. Cphy 2E 33
Maesyrhandir. Powy 1C 58
Magdalen Laver. Essx 5F 53
Maggieknockater. Mor 4H 159
Maghaberry. Lis 3F 179
Magham Down. E Sus 4H 27
Maghera. M Ulst 6E 174
Maghera. New M 6H 179
Magherafelt. M Ulst 7E 174
Magheralin. Arm 4F 178
Magheramason. Derr 1F 176

Milton—Newchapel

Milton. *High* 4H 157 (nr. Inverness)
Milton. *High* 3F 169 (nr. Wick)
Milton. *Mor* 2C 160 (nr. Cullen)
Milton. *Mor* 2F 151 (nr. Tomintoul)
Milton. *N Som* 5G 33
Milton. *Notts* 3E 86
Milton. *Oxon* 2C 50 (nr. Bloxham)
Milton. *Oxon* 2C 36 (nr. Didcot)
Milton. *Pemb* 4E 43
Milton. *Port* 3E 17
Milton. *Som* 4H 21
Milton. *S Ayr* 2D 116
Milton. *Stir* 3E 135 (nr. Aberfoyle)
Milton. *Stir* 4D 134 (nr. Drymen)
Milton. *Stoke* 5D 84
Milton. *W Dun* 2F 127
Milton Abbas. *Dors* 2D 14
Milton Abbot. *Devn* 5E 11
Milton Auchlossan. *Abers* 3C 152
Milton Bridge. *Midl* 3F 129
Milton Bryan. *C Beds* 2H 51
Milton Clevedon. *Som* 3B 22
Milton Coldwells. *Abers* 5G 161
Milton Combe. *Devn* 2A 8
Milton Common. *Oxon* 5E 51
Milton Damerel. *Devn* 1D 11
Miltonduff. *Mor* 2F 159
Milton End. *Glos* 5G 49
Milton Ernest. *Bed* 5H 63
Milton Green. *Ches W* 5G 83
Milton Hill. *Devn* 5C 12
Milton Hill. *Oxon* 2C 36
**Milton Keynes**. *Mil* 2G 51 & 200
Milton Keynes Village. *Mil* 2G 51
Milton Lilbourne. *Wilts* 5G 35
Milton Malsor. *Nptn* 5E 63
Milton Morenish. *Per* 5D 142
Milton of Auchinhove. *Abers* 3C 152
Milton of Balgonie. *Fife* 3F 137
Milton of Barras. *Abers* 1H 145
Milton of Campsie. *E Dun* 2H 127
Milton of Cultoquhey. *Per* 1A 136
Milton of Cushnie. *Abers* 2C 152
Milton of Finavon. *Ang* 3D 145
Milton of Gollanfield. *High* 3B 158
Milton of Lesmore. *Abers* 1B 152
Milton of Leys. *High* 4A 158
Milton of Tullich. *Abers* 4A 152
Milton on Stour. *Dors* 4C 22
Milton Regis. *Kent* 4C 40
Milton Street. *E Sus* 5G 27
Milton-under-Wychwood. *Oxon* 4A 50
Milverton. *Som* 4E 20
Milverton. *Warw* 4H 61
Milwich. *Staf* 2D 72
Mimbridge. *Surr* 4A 38
Minard. *Arg* 4G 133
Minchington. *Dors* 1E 15
Minchinhampton. *Glos* 5D 48
Mindrum. *Nmbd* 1C 120
Minehead. *Som* 2C 20
Minera. *Wrex* 5E 83
Minerstown. *New M* 6J 179
Minety. *Wilts* 2F 35
Minffordd. *Gwyn* 2E 69
Mingarrypark. *High* 2A 140
Mingary. *High* 2G 139
Mingearraidh. *W Isl* 6C 170
Miningsby. *Linc* 4C 88
Minions. *Corn* 5C 10
Minishant. *S Ayr* 3C 116
Minllyn. *Gwyn* 4A 70
Minnigaff. *Dum* 3B 110
Minorca. *IOM* 3D 108
Minskip. *N Yor* 3F 99
Minstead. *Hants* 1A 16
Minsted. *W Sus* 4G 25
Minster. *Kent* 4H 41 (nr. Ramsgate)
**Minster**. *Kent* 3D 40 (nr. Sheerness)
Minsteracres. *Nmbd* 4D 114
Minsterley. *Shrp* 5F 71
Minster Lovell. *Oxon* 4B 50
Minsterworth. *Glos* 4C 48
Minterne Magna. *Dors* 2B 14
Minterne Parva. *Dors* 2B 14
Minting. *Linc* 3A 88
Mintlaw. *Abers* 4H 161
Minto. *Bord* 2H 119
Minton. *Shrp* 1G 59
Minwear. *Pemb* 3E 43
Minworth. *W Mid* 1F 61
Miodar. *Arg* 4B 138
Mirbister. *Orkn* 5C 172
Mirehouse. *Cumb* 3A 102
Mireland. *High* 2F 169
**Mirfield**. *W Yor* 3C 92
Miserden. *Glos* 5E 49
Miskin. *Rhon* 3D 32
Misson. *Notts* 1D 86
Misterton. *Leics* 2C 62
Misterton. *Notts* 1E 87
Misterton. *Som* 2H 13
Mistley. *Essx* 2E 54
Mistley Heath. *Essx* 2E 55
**Mitcham**. *G Lon* 4D 39
Mitcheldean. *Glos* 4B 48
Mitchell. *Corn* 3C 6
Mitchel Troy. *Mon* 4H 47
Mitcheltroy Common. *Mon* 5H 47
Mitford. *Nmbd* 1E 115
Mithian. *Corn* 3B 6
Mitton. *Staf* 4C 72
Mixbury. *Oxon* 2E 50
Mixenden. *W Yor* 2A 92
Mixon. *Staf* 5E 85
Moaness. *Orkn* 7B 172
Moarfield. *Shet* 1G 173
Moat. *Cumb* 2F 113
Moats Tye. *Suff* 5C 66
Mobberley. *Ches E* 3B 84
Mobberley. *Staf* 1E 73
Moccas. *Here* 1G 47
Mochdre. *Cnwy* 3H 81
Mochdre. *Powy* 2C 58
Mochrum. *Dum* 5A 110
Mockbeggar. *Hants* 2G 15
Mockerkin. *Cumb* 2B 102
Modbury. *Devn* 3C 8
Moddershall. *Staf* 2D 72
Modsarie. *High* 2G 167
Moelfre. *Cnwy* 3B 82
Moelfre. *IOA* 2E 81
Moelfre. *Powy* 3D 70
Moffat. *Dum* 4C 118
Moggerhanger. *C Beds* 1B 52
Mogworthy. *Devn* 1B 12
Moira. *Leics* 4H 73
Moira. *Lis* 3F 178
Molash. *Kent* 5E 41
Mol-chlach. *High* 2C 146
Mold. *Flin* 4E 83
Molehill Green. *Essx* 3F 53
Molescroft. *E Yor* 5E 101
Molesden. *Nmbd* 1E 115
Molesworth. *Cambs* 3H 63
Moll. *High* 1D 146
Molland. *Devn* 4B 20
Mollington. *Ches W* 3F 83
Mollington. *Oxon* 1C 50
Mollinsburn. *N Lan* 2A 128
Monachty. *Cdgn* 4E 57
Monachyle. *Stir* 2D 135
Monar Lodge. *High* 4E 156
Monaughty. *Powy* 4E 59
Monea. *Ferm* 7D 176
Monewden. *Suff* 5E 67
Moneydie. *Per* 1C 136
Moneyglass. *Ant* 7G 175
Moneymore. *M Ulst* 1C 178
Moneyneany. *M Ulst* 7D 174
Moneyreagh. *Lis* 3J 179
Moneyrow Green. *Wind* 4G 37
Moneyslane. *Arm* 6G 179
Moniaive. *Dum* 5G 117
Monifieth. *Ang* 5E 145
Monikie. *Ang* 5E 145
Monimail. *Fife* 2E 137
Monington. *Pemb* 1B 44
Monk Bretton. *S Yor* 4D 92
Monken Hadley. *G Lon* 1D 38
Monk Fryston. *N Yor* 2F 93
Monk Hesleden. *Dur* 1B 106
Monkhide. *Here* 1B 48
Monkhill. *Cumb* 4E 113
Monkhopton. *Shrp* 1A 60
Monkland. *Here* 5G 59
Monkleigh. *Devn* 4E 19
Monknash. *V Glam* 4C 32
Monkokehampton. *Devn* 2F 11
Monkseaton. *Tyne* 2G 115
Monks Eleigh. *Suff* 1C 54
Monk's Gate. *W Sus* 3D 26
Monk's Heath. *Ches E* 3C 84
Monk Sherborne. *Hants* 1E 24
Monkshill. *Abers* 4E 161
Monksilver. *Som* 3D 20
Monks Kirby. *Warw* 2B 62
Monk Soham. *Suff* 4E 66
Monk Soham Green. *Suff* 4E 66
Monkspath. *W Mid* 3F 61
Monks Risborough. *Buck* 5G 51
Monksthorpe. *Linc* 4D 88
Monkstown. *Ant* 1H 179
Monk Street. *Essx* 3G 53
Monkswood. *Mon* 5G 47
Monkton. *Devn* 2E 13
Monkton. *Kent* 4G 41
Monkton. *Pemb* 4D 42
Monkton. *S Ayr* 2C 116
Monkton Combe. *Bath* 5C 34
Monkton Deverill. *Wilts* 3D 22
Monkton Farleigh. *Wilts* 5D 34
Monkton Heathfield. *Som* 4F 21
Monktonhill. *S Ayr* 2C 116
Monkton Up Wimborne. *Dors* 1F 15
Monkton Wyld. *Dors* 3G 13
Monkwearmouth. *Tyne* 4G 115
Monkwood. *Dors* 3H 13
Monkwood. *Hants* 3E 25
Monmarsh. *Here* 1A 48
Monmouth. *Mon* 4A 48
Monnington on Wye. *Here* 1G 47
Monreith. *Dum* 5A 110
Montacute. *Som* 1H 13
Monteith. *Arm* 5F 179
Montford. *Arg* 3C 126
Montford. *Shrp* 4G 71
Montford Bridge. *Shrp* 4G 71
Montgarrie. *Abers* 2C 152
Montgarswood. *E Ayr* 2E 117
Montgomery. *Powy* 1E 58
Montgreenan. *N Ayr* 5E 127
Montrave. *Fife* 3F 137
**Montrose**. *Ang* 3G 145
Monxton. *Hants* 2B 24
Monyash. *Derbs* 4F 85
Monymusk. *Abers* 2D 152
Monzie. *Per* 1A 136
Moodiesburn. *N Lan* 2H 127
Moon's Green. *Kent* 3C 28
Moonzie. *Fife* 2F 137
Moor. *Som* 1H 13
Moor Allerton. *W Yor* 1C 92
Moorbath. *Dors* 3H 13
Moorbrae. *Shet* 3F 173
Moorby. *Linc* 4B 88
Moorcot. *Here* 5F 59
Moor Crichel. *Dors* 2E 15
Moor Cross. *Devn* 3C 8
Moordown. *Bour* 3F 15
Moore. *Hal* 2H 83
Moorend. *Dum* 2D 112
Moor End. *E Yor* 1B 94
Moorend. *Glos* 5C 48 (nr. Dursley)
Moorend. *Glos* 4D 48 (nr. Gloucester)
Moorends. *S Yor* 3G 93
Moorfields. *ME Ant* 7H 175
Moorgate. *S Yor* 1B 86
Moorgreen. *Hants* 1C 16
Moorgreen. *Notts* 1B 74
Moor Green. *Wilts* 5D 34
Moorhaigh. *Notts* 4C 86
Moorhall. *Derbs* 3H 85
Moorhampton. *Here* 1G 47
Moorhouse. *Cumb* 4E 113 (nr. Carlisle)
Moorhouse. *Cumb* 4D 112 (nr. Wigton)
Moorhouse. *Notts* 4E 87
Moorhouse. *Surr* 5F 39
Moorhouses. *Linc* 5B 88
Moorland. *Som* 3G 21
Moorlinch. *Som* 3H 21
Moor Monkton. *N Yor* 4H 99
Moor of Granary. *Mor* 3E 159
Moor Row. *Cumb* 3B 102 (nr. Whitehaven)
Moor Row. *Cumb* 5D 112 (nr. Wigton)
Moorsholm. *Red C* 3D 107
Moorside. *Dors* 1C 14
Moorside. *G Man* 4H 91
Moor, The. *Kent* 3B 28
Moortown. *Devn* 3D 10
Moortown. *Hants* 2G 15
Moortown. *IOW* 4C 16
Moortown. *Linc* 1H 87
Moortown. *M Ulst* 2D 178
Moortown. *Telf* 4A 72
Moortown. *W Yor* 1D 92
Morangie. *High* 5E 165
Morar. *High* 4E 147
Morborne. *Cambs* 1A 64
Morchard Bishop. *Devn* 2A 12
Morcombelake. *Dors* 3H 13
Morcott. *Rut* 5G 75
Morda. *Shrp* 3E 71
**Morden**. *G Lon* 4D 38
Mordiford. *Here* 2A 48
Mordon. *Dur* 2A 106
More. *Shrp* 1F 59
Morebath. *Devn* 4C 20
Morebattle. *Bord* 2B 120
**Morecambe**. *Lanc* 3D 96
Morefield. *High* 4F 163
Moreleigh. *Devn* 3D 8
Morenish. *Per* 5C 142
Moresby Parks. *Cumb* 3A 102
Morestead. *Hants* 4D 24
Moreton. *Dors* 4D 14
Moreton. *Essx* 5F 53
Moreton. *Here* 4H 59
**Moreton**. *Mers* 1E 83
Moreton. *Oxon* 5E 51
Moreton. *Staf* 4B 72
Moreton Corbet. *Shrp* 3H 71
Moretonhampstead. *Devn* 4A 12
Moreton-in-Marsh. *Glos* 2H 49
Moreton Jeffries. *Here* 1B 48
Moreton Morrell. *Warw* 5H 61
Moreton on Lugg. *Here* 1A 48
Moreton Pinkney. *Nptn* 1D 50
Moreton Say. *Shrp* 2A 72
Moreton Valence. *Glos* 5C 48
Morfa. *Cdgn* 5C 56
Morfa Bach. *Carm* 4D 44
Morfa Bychan. *Gwyn* 2E 69
Morfa Glas. *Neat* 5B 46
Morfa Nefyn. *Gwyn* 1B 68
Morganstown. *Card* 3E 33
Morgan's Vale. *Wilts* 4G 23
Morham. *E Lot* 2B 130
Moriah. *Cdgn* 3F 57
Morland. *Cumb* 2G 103
Morley. *Ches E* 2C 84
Morley. *Derbs* 1A 74
Morley. *Dur* 2E 105
**Morley**. *W Yor* 2C 92
Morley St Botolph. *Norf* 1C 66
Morningside. *Edin* 2F 129
Morningside. *N Lan* 4B 128
Morningthorpe. *Norf* 1E 66
**Morpeth**. *Nmbd* 1F 115
Morrey. *Staf* 4F 73
Morridge Side. *Staf* 5E 85
Morridge Top. *Staf* 4E 85
Morrington. *Dum* 1F 111
Morris Green. *Essx* 2H 53
Morriston. *Swan* 3F 31
Morston. *Norf* 1C 78
Mortehoe. *Devn* 2E 19
Morthen. *S Yor* 2B 86
Mortimer. *W Ber* 5E 37
Mortimer's Cross. *Here* 4G 59
Mortimer West End. *Hants* 5E 37
Mortomley. *S Yor* 1H 85
Morton. *Cumb* 1F 103 (nr. Calthwaite)
Morton. *Cumb* 4E 113 (nr. Carlisle)
Morton. *Derbs* 4B 86
Morton. *Linc* 3H 75 (nr. Bourne)
Morton. *Linc* 1F 87 (nr. Gainsborough)
Morton. *Linc* 4F 87 (nr. Lincoln)
Morton. *Norf* 4D 78
Morton. *Notts* 5E 87
Morton. *Shrp* 3E 71
Morton. *S Glo* 2B 34
Morton Bagot. *Warw* 4F 61
Morton Mill. *Shrp* 3H 71
Morton-on-Swale. *N Yor* 5A 106
Morton Tinmouth. *Dur* 2E 105
Morvah. *Corn* 3B 4
Morval. *Corn* 3G 7
Morvich. *High* 3E 165 (nr. Golspie)
Morvich. *High* 1B 148 (nr. Shiel Bridge)
Morvil. *Pemb* 1E 43
Morville. *Shrp* 1A 60
Morwenstow. *Corn* 1C 10
Morwick. *Nmbd* 4G 121
**Mosborough**. *S Yor* 2B 86
Moscow. *E Ayr* 5F 127
Mose. *Shrp* 1B 60
Mosedale. *Cumb* 1E 103
Moseley. *W Mid* 2E 61 (nr. Birmingham)
Moseley. *W Mid* 5D 72 (nr. Wolverhampton)
Moseley. *Worc* 5C 60
Moss. *Arg* 4A 138
Moss. *High* 2A 140
Moss. *S Yor* 3F 93
Moss. *Wrex* 5F 83
Mossatt. *Abers* 2B 152
Moss Bank. *Mers* 1H 83
Mossbank. *Shet* 4F 173
Mossblown. *S Ayr* 2D 116
Mossbrow. *G Man* 2B 84
Mossburnford. *Bord* 3A 120
Mossdale. *Dum* 2D 110
Mossedge. *Cumb* 3F 113
Mossend. *N Lan* 3A 128
Mossgate. *Staf* 2D 72
Moss Lane. *Ches E* 3D 84
Mossley. *Ant* 1H 179
Mossley. *Ches E* 4C 84
**Mossley**. *G Man* 4H 91
Mossley Hill. *Mers* 2F 83
Moss of Barmuckity. *Mor* 2G 159
Mosspark. *Glas* 3G 127
Mosspaul. *Bord* 5G 119
Moss-Side. *Caus* 3G 175
Moss Side. *Cumb* 4C 112
Moss Side. *G Man* 1C 84
Moss-side. *High* 3C 158
Moss Side. *Lanc* 1B 90 (nr. Blackpool)
Moss Side. *Lanc* 2D 90 (nr. Preston)
Moss Side. *Mers* 4B 90
Moss-side of Cairness. *Abers* 2H 161
Mosstodloch. *Mor* 2H 159
Mosswood. *Nmbd* 4D 114
Mossy Lea. *Lanc* 3D 90
Mosterton. *Dors* 2H 13
Moston. *Shrp* 3H 71
Moston Green. *Ches E* 4B 84
Mostyn. *Flin* 2D 82
Mostyn Quay. *Flin* 2D 82
Motcombe. *Dors* 4D 22
Mothecombe. *Devn* 4C 8
Motherby. *Cumb* 2F 103
**Motherwell**. *N Lan* 4A 128
Mottingham. *G Lon* 3F 39
Mottisfont. *Hants* 4B 24
Mottistone. *IOW* 4C 16
**Mottram in Longdendale**. *G Man* 1D 85
Mottram St Andrew. *Ches E* 3C 84
Mott's Mill. *E Sus* 2G 27
Mouldsworth. *Ches W* 3H 83
Moulin. *Per* 3G 143
Moulsecoomb. *Brig* 5E 27
Moulsford. *Oxon* 3D 36
Moulsoe. *Mil* 1H 51
Moulton. *Ches W* 4A 84
Moulton. *Linc* 3C 76
Moulton. *Nptn* 4E 63
Moulton. *N Yor* 4F 105
Moulton. *Suff* 4F 65
Moulton. *V Glam* 4D 32
Moulton Chapel. *Linc* 4B 76
Moulton Eaugate. *Linc* 4C 76
Moulton St Mary. *Norf* 5F 79
Moulton Seas End. *Linc* 3C 76
Mount. *Corn* 2F 7 (nr. Bodmin)
Mount. *Corn* 3B 6 (nr. Newquay)
**Mountain Ash**. *Rhon* 2D 32
Mountain Cross. *Bord* 5E 129
Mountain Street. *Kent* 5E 41
Mountain Water. *Pemb* 2D 42
Mount Ambrose. *Corn* 4B 6
Mountbenger. *Bord* 2F 119
Mountblow. *W Dun* 2F 127
Mount Bures. *Essx* 2C 54
Mountfield. *E Sus* 3B 28
Mountfield. *Ferm* 2L 177
Mountgerald. *High* 2H 157
Mount Hawke. *Corn* 4B 6
Mount High. *High* 2A 158
Mountjoy. *Corn* 2C 6
Mountjoy. *Ferm* 2K 177
Mount Lothian. *Midl* 4F 129
Mountnessing. *Essx* 1H 39
Mountnorris. *Arm* 6D 178
Mounton. *Mon* 2A 34
Mount Pleasant. *Buck* 2E 51
Mount Pleasant. *Ches E* 5C 84
Mount Pleasant. *Derbs* 1H 73 (nr. Derby)
Mount Pleasant. *Derbs* 4G 73 (nr. Swadlincote)
Mount Pleasant. *E Sus* 4F 27
Mount Pleasant. *Hants* 3A 16
Mount Pleasant. *Norf* 1B 66
Mount Skippett. *Oxon* 4B 50
Mountsorrel. *Leics* 4C 74
Mount Stuart. *Arg* 4C 126
Mousehole. *Corn* 4B 4
Mouswald. *Dum* 2B 112
Mow Cop. *Ches E* 5C 84
Mowden. *Darl* 3F 105
Mowhaugh. *Bord* 2C 120
Mowmacre Hill. *Leic* 5C 74
Mowsley. *Leics* 2D 62
Moy. *High* 5B 158
Moy. *M Ulst* 4C 178
Moygashel. *M Ulst* 3C 178
Moylgrove. *Pemb* 1B 44
Moy Lodge. *High* 5G 149
Muasdale. *Arg* 5E 125
Muchalls. *Abers* 4G 153
Much Birch. *Here* 2A 48
Much Cowarne. *Here* 1B 48
Much Dewchurch. *Here* 2H 47
Muchelney. *Som* 4H 21
Muchelney Ham. *Som* 4H 21
Much Hadham. *Herts* 4E 53
Much Hoole. *Lanc* 2C 90
Muchlarnick. *Corn* 3G 7
Much Marcle. *Here* 2B 48
Muchrachd. *High* 5E 157
Much Wenlock. *Shrp* 5A 72
Mucking. *Thur* 2A 40
Muckle Breck. *Shet* 5G 173
Muckleford. *Dors* 3B 14
Mucklestone. *Staf* 2B 72
Muckleton. *Norf* 2H 77
Muckleton. *Shrp* 3H 71
Muckley. *Shrp* 1A 60
Muckley Corner. *Staf* 5E 73
Muckton. *Linc* 2C 88
Mudale. *High* 5F 167
Muddiford. *Devn* 3F 19
Mudeford. *Dors* 3G 15
Mudford. *Som* 1A 14
Mudgley. *Som* 2H 21
Mugdock. *Stir* 2G 127
Mugeary. *High* 5D 154
Muggington. *Derbs* 1G 73
Muggintonlane End. *Derbs* 1G 73
Muggleswick. *Dur* 4D 114
Mugswell. *Surr* 5D 38
Muie. *High* 3D 164
Muirden. *Abers* 3E 160
Muirdrum. *Ang* 5E 145
Muiredge. *Per* 1E 137
Muirend. *Glas* 3G 127
Muirhead. *Ang* 5C 144
Muirhead. *Fife* 3E 137
Muirhead. *N Lan* 3H 127
Muirhouses. *Falk* 1D 128
Muirkirk. *E Ayr* 2F 117
Muir of Alford. *Abers* 2C 152
Muir of Fairburn. *High* 3G 157
Muir of Fowlis. *Abers* 2C 152
Muir of Miltonduff. *Mor* 3F 159
Muir of Ord. *High* 3H 157
Muir of Tarradale. *High* 3H 157
Muirshearlich. *High* 5D 148
Muirtack. *Abers* 5G 161
Muirton. *High* 2B 158
Muirton. *Per* 1D 136
Muirton of Ardblair. *Per* 4A 144
Muirtown. *Per* 2B 136
Muiryfold. *Abers* 3E 161
Muker. *N Yor* 5C 104
Mulbarton. *Norf* 5D 78
Mulben. *Mor* 3A 160
Mulindry. *Arg* 4B 124
Mulla. *Shet* 5F 173
Mullach Charlabhaigh. *W Isl* 3E 171
Mullacott. *Devn* 2F 19
Mullaghbane. *New M* 8D 178
Mullaghboy. *ME Ant* 6L 175
Mullaghglass. *New M* 7E 178
Mullion. *Corn* 5D 5
Mullion Cove. *Corn* 5D 4
Mumbles. *Swan* 4F 31
Mumby. *Linc* 3E 89
Munderfield Row. *Here* 5A 60
Munderfield Stocks. *Here* 5A 60
Mundesley. *Norf* 2F 79
Mundford. *Norf* 1H 65
Mundham. *Norf* 1F 67
Mundon. *Essx* 5B 54
Munerigie. *High* 3E 149
Muness. *Shet* 1H 173
Mungasdale. *High* 4D 162
Mungrisdale. *Cumb* 1E 103
Munlochy. *High* 3A 158
Munsley. *Here* 1B 48
Munslow. *Shrp* 2H 59
Murchington. *Devn* 4G 11
Murcot. *Worc* 1F 49
Murcott. *Oxon* 4D 50
Murdishaw. *Hal* 2H 83
Murieston. *W Lot* 3D 128
Murkle. *High* 2D 168
Murlaggan. *High* 4C 148
Murra. *Orkn* 7B 172
Murrayfield. *Edin* 2F 129
Murray, The. *S Lan* 4H 127
Murrell Green. *Hants* 1F 25
Murroes. *Ang* 5D 144
Murrow. *Cambs* 5C 76
Mursley. *Buck* 3G 51
Murthly. *Per* 5H 143
Murton. *Cumb* 2A 104
Murton. *Dur* 5G 115
Murton. *Nmbd* 5F 131
Murton. *Swan* 4E 31
Murton. *York* 4A 100
Musbury. *Devn* 3F 13
Muscoates. *N Yor* 1A 100
Muscott. *Nptn* 4D 62
**Musselburgh**. *E Lot* 2G 129
Muston. *Leics* 2F 75
Muston. *N Yor* 2E 101
Mustow Green. *Worc* 3C 60
Muswell Hill. *G Lon* 2D 39
Mutehill. *Dum* 5D 111
Mutford. *Suff* 2G 67
Muthill. *Per* 2A 136
Mutterton. *Devn* 2D 12
Muxton. *Telf* 4B 72
Mwmbwls. *Swan* 4F 31
Mybster. *High* 3D 168
Myddfai. *Carm* 2A 46
Myddle. *Shrp* 3G 71
Mydroilyn. *Cdgn* 5D 56
Myerscough. *Lanc* 1C 90
Mylor Bridge. *Corn* 5C 6
Mylor Churchtown. *Corn* 5C 6
Mynachlog-ddu. *Pemb* 1F 43
Mynydd-bach. *Mon* 2H 33
Mynydd Isa. *Flin* 4E 83
Mynyddislwyn. *Cphy* 2E 33
Mynydd Llandegai. *Gwyn* 4F 81
Mynydd Mechell. *IOA* 1C 80
Mynydd-y-briw. *Powy* 3D 70
Mynyddygarreg. *Carm* 5E 45
Mynytho. *Gwyn* 2C 68
Myrebird. *Abers* 4E 153
Myrelandhorn. *High* 3E 169
Mytchett. *Surr* 1G 25
Mythe, The. *Glos* 2D 49
Mytholmroyd. *W Yor* 2A 92
Myton-on-Swale. *N Yor* 3G 99
Mytton. *Shrp* 4G 71

## N

Naast. *High* 5C 162
Na Buirgh. *W Isl* 8C 171
Naburn. *York* 5H 99
Nab Wood. *W Yor* 1B 92
Nackington. *Kent* 5F 41
Nacton. *Suff* 1F 55
Nafferton. *E Yor* 4E 101
Na Gearrannan. *W Isl* 3D 171
Nailbridge. *Glos* 4B 48
Nailsbourne. *Som* 4F 21
**Nailsea**. *N Som* 4H 33
Nailstone. *Leics* 5B 74
Nailsworth. *Glos* 2D 34
Nairn. *High* 3C 158
Nalderswood. *Surr* 1D 26
Nancegollan. *Corn* 3D 4
Nancledra. *Corn* 3B 4
Nangreaves. *G Man* 3G 91
Nanhyfer. *Pemb* 1E 43
Nannerch. *Flin* 4D 82
Nanpantan. *Leics* 4C 74
Nanpean. *Corn* 3D 6
Nanstallon. *Corn* 2E 7
Nant-ddu. *Powy* 4D 46
Nanternis. *Cdgn* 5C 56
Nantgaredig. *Carm* 3E 45
Nantgarw. *Rhon* 3E 33
Nant Glas. *Powy* 4B 58
Nantglyn. *Den* 4C 82
Nantgwyn. *Powy* 3B 58
Nantlle. *Gwyn* 5E 81
Nantmawr. *Shrp* 3E 71
Nantmel. *Powy* 4C 58
Nantmor. *Gwyn* 1F 69
Nant Peris. *Gwyn* 5F 81
**Nantwich**. *Ches E* 5A 84
Nant-y-bai. *Carm* 1A 46
Nant-y-bwch. *Blae* 4E 47
Nant-y-Derry. *Mon* 5G 47
Nant-y-dugoed. *Powy* 4B 70
Nant-y-felin. *Cnwy* 3F 81
Nantyffyllon. *B'end* 2B 32
Nantyglo. *Blae* 4E 47
Nant-y-meichiaid. *Powy* 4D 70
Nant-y-moel. *B'end* 2C 32
Nant-y-pandy. *Cnwy* 3F 81
Naphill. *Buck* 2G 37
Nappa. *N Yor* 4A 98
Napton on the Hill. *Warw* 4B 62
Narberth. *Pemb* 3F 43
Narberth Bridge. *Pemb* 3F 43
Narborough. *Leics* 1C 62
Narborough. *Norf* 4G 77
Narkurs. *Corn* 3H 7
Narth, The. *Mon* 5A 48
Narthwaite. *Cumb* 5A 104
Nasareth. *Gwyn* 5D 80
Naseby. *Nptn* 3D 62
Nash. *Buck* 2F 51
Nash. *Here* 4F 59
Nash. *Kent* 5G 41
Nash. *Newp* 3G 33
Nash. *Shrp* 3A 60
Nash Lee. *Buck* 5G 51
Nassington. *Nptn* 1H 63
Nasty. *Herts* 3D 52
Natcott. *Devn* 4C 18
Nateby. *Cumb* 4A 104
Nateby. *Lanc* 5D 96
Nately Scures. *Hants* 1F 25
Natland. *Cumb* 1E 97
Naughton. *Suff* 1D 54
Naunton. *Glos* 3G 49
Naunton. *Worc* 2D 49
Naunton Beauchamp. *Worc* 5D 60
Navenby. *Linc* 5G 87
Navestock. *Essx* 1G 39
Navestock Side. *Essx* 1G 39
Navidale. *High* 2H 165
Nawton. *N Yor* 1A 100
Nayland. *Suff* 2C 54
Nazeing. *Essx* 5E 53
Neacroft. *Hants* 3G 15
Nealhouse. *Cumb* 4E 113
Neal's Green. *Warw* 2H 61
Near Sawrey. *Cumb* 5E 103
Neasden. *G Lon* 2D 38
Neasham. *Darl* 3A 106
**Neath**. *Neat* 2A 32
Neath Abbey. *Neat* 3G 31
Neatishead. *Norf* 3F 79
Neaton. *Norf* 5B 78
Nebo. *Cdgn* 4E 57
Nebo. *Cnwy* 5H 81
Nebo. *Gwyn* 5D 81
Nebo. *IOA* 1D 80
Necton. *Norf* 5A 78
Nedd. *High* 5B 166
Nedderton. *Nmbd* 1F 115
Nedging. *Suff* 1D 54
Nedging Tye. *Suff* 1D 54
Needham. *Norf* 2E 67
Needham Market. *Suff* 5C 66
Needham Street. *Suff* 4G 65
Needingworth. *Cambs* 3C 64
Needwood. *Staf* 3F 73
Neen Savage. *Shrp* 3A 60
Neen Sollars. *Shrp* 3A 60
Neenton. *Shrp* 2A 60
Nefyn. *Gwyn* 1C 68
Neilston. *E Ren* 4F 127
Neithrop. *Oxon* 1C 50
Nelly Andrews Green. *Powy* 5E 71
Nelson. *Cphy* 2E 32
**Nelson**. *Lanc* 1G 91
Nelson Village. *Nmbd* 2F 115
Nemphlar. *S Lan* 5B 128
Nempnett Thrubwell. *Bath* 5A 34
Nene Terrace. *Linc* 5B 76
Nenthall. *Cumb* 5A 114
Nenthead. *Cumb* 5A 114
Nenthorn. *Bord* 1A 120
Nercwys. *Flin* 4E 83
Neribus. *Arg* 4A 124
Nerston. *S Lan* 4H 127
Nesbit. *Nmbd* 1D 121
Nesfield. *N Yor* 5C 98
Ness. *Ches W* 3F 83
Nesscliffe. *Shrp* 4F 71
Ness of Tenston. *Orkn* 6B 172
**Neston**. *Ches W* 3E 83
Neston. *Wilts* 5D 34
Nethanfoot. *S Lan* 5B 128
Nether Alderley. *Ches E* 3C 84
Netheravon. *Wilts* 2G 23
Nether Blainslie. *Bord* 5B 130
Netherbrae. *Abers* 3E 161
Netherbrough. *Orkn* 6C 172
Nether Broughton. *Leics* 3D 74
Netherburn. *S Lan* 5B 128
Nether Burrow. *Lanc* 2F 97
Netherbury. *Dors* 3H 13
Netherby. *Cumb* 2E 113
Nether Careston. *Ang* 3E 145
Nether Cerne. *Dors* 3B 14
Nether Compton. *Dors* 1A 14
Nethercote. *Glos* 3G 49
Nethercote. *Warw* 4C 62
Nethercott. *Devn* 3E 19
Nethercott. *Oxon* 3C 50
Nether Dallachy. *Mor* 2A 160
Nether Durdie. *Per* 1E 136
Nether End. *Derbs* 3G 85
Netherend. *Glos* 5A 48
Nether Exe. *Devn* 2C 12
Netherfield. *E Sus* 4B 28
Netherfield. *Notts* 1D 74
Nethergate. *Norf* 3C 78
Netherhampton. *Wilts* 4G 23
Nether Handley. *Derbs* 3B 86
Nether Haugh. *S Yor* 1B 86
Nether Heage. *Derbs* 5A 86
Nether Heyford. *Nptn* 5D 62
Netherhouses. *Cumb* 1B 96
Nether Howcleugh. *S Lan* 3C 118
Nether Kellet. *Lanc* 3E 97
Nether Kinmundy. *Abers* 4H 161
Netherland Green. *Staf* 2F 73
Nether Langwith. *Notts* 3C 86
Netherlaw. *Dum* 5E 111
Netherley. *Abers* 4F 153
Nethermill. *Dum* 1B 112
Nethermills. *Mor* 3C 160
Nether Moor. *Derbs* 4A 86
Nether Padley. *Derbs* 3G 85
Netherplace. *E Ren* 4G 127
Nether Poppleton. *York* 4H 99
Netherseal. *Derbs* 4G 73
Nether Silton. *N Yor* 5B 106
Nether Stowey. *Som* 3E 21
Nether Street. *Essx* 4F 53
Netherstreet. *Wilts* 5E 35
Netherthird. *E Ayr* 3E 117
Netherthong. *W Yor* 4B 92
Netherton. *Ang* 3E 145
Netherton. *Cumb* 1B 102
Netherton. *Devn* 5B 12
Netherton. *Hants* 1B 24
Netherton. *Here* 3A 48
Netherton. *Mers* 1F 83
Netherton. *N Lan* 4A 128
Netherton. *Nmbd* 4D 121
Netherton. *Per* 3A 144
Netherton. *Shrp* 2B 60
Netherton. *Stir* 2G 127
Netherton. *W Mid* 2D 60
Netherton. *W Yor* 3C 92 (nr. Horbury)
Netherton. *W Yor* 3B 92 (nr. Huddersfield)
Netherton. *Worc* 1E 49
Nethertown. *Cumb* 4A 102
Nethertown. *High* 1F 169
Nethertown. *Staf* 4F 73
Nether Urquhart. *Fife* 3D 136
Nether Wallop. *Hants* 3B 24
Nether Wasdale. *Cumb* 4C 102
Nether Welton. *Cumb* 5E 113
Nether Westcote. *Glos* 3H 49
Nether Whitacre. *Warw* 1G 61
Nether Winchendon. *Buck* 4F 51
Netherwitton. *Nmbd* 5F 121
Nether Worton. *Oxon* 2C 50
Nethy Bridge. *High* 1E 151
Netley. *Shrp* 5G 71
Netley Abbey. *Hants* 2C 16
Netley Marsh. *Hants* 1B 16
Nettlebed. *Oxon* 3F 37
Nettlebridge. *Som* 2B 22
Nettlecombe. *Dors* 3A 14
Nettlecombe. *IOW* 5D 16
Nettleden. *Herts* 4A 52
Nettleham. *Linc* 3H 87
Nettlestead. *Kent* 5A 40
Nettlestead Green. *Kent* 5A 40
Nettlestone. *IOW* 3E 16
Nettlesworth. *Dur* 5F 115
Nettleton. *Linc* 4E 94
Nettleton. *Wilts* 4D 34
Netton. *Devn* 4B 8
Netton. *Wilts* 3G 23
Neuadd. *Powy* 5C 70
Neuk, The. *Abers* 4E 153
Nevendon. *Essx* 1B 40
Nevern. *Pemb* 1E 43
New Abbey. *Dum* 3A 112
New Aberdour. *Abers* 2F 161
**New Addington**. *G Lon* 4E 39
Newall. *W Yor* 5E 98
New Alresford. *Hants* 3D 24
New Alyth. *Per* 4B 144
Newark. *Orkn* 3G 172
Newark. *Pet* 5B 76
**Newark-on-Trent**. *Notts* 5E 87
New Arley. *Warw* 2G 61
Newarthill. *N Lan* 4A 128
New Ash Green. *Kent* 4H 39
New Balderton. *Notts* 5F 87
New Barn. *Kent* 4H 39
New Barnetby. *N Lin* 3D 94
Newbattle. *Midl* 3G 129
New Bewick. *Nmbd* 2E 121
Newbie. *Dum* 3C 112
Newbiggin. *Cumb* 2H 103 (nr. Appleby)
Newbiggin. *Cumb* 3B 96 (nr. Barrow-in-Furness)
Newbiggin. *Cumb* 5G 113 (nr. Cumrew)
Newbiggin. *Cumb* 2F 103 (nr. Penrith)
Newbiggin. *Cumb* 5B 102 (nr. Seascale)
Newbiggin. *Dur* 5E 115 (nr. Consett)
Newbiggin. *Dur* 2C 104 (nr. Holwick)
Newbiggin. *Nmbd* 5C 114
Newbiggin. *N Yor* 5C 104 (nr. Askrigg)
Newbiggin. *N Yor* 1F 101 (nr. Filey)
Newbiggin. *N Yor* 1B 98 (nr. Thoralby)
Newbiggin-by-the-Sea. *Nmbd* 1G 115
Newbigging. *Ang* 5D 145 (nr. Monikie)
Newbigging. *Ang* 4B 144 (nr. Newtyle)
Newbigging. *Ang* 5D 144 (nr. Tealing)
Newbigging. *Edin* 2E 129
Newbigging. *S Lan* 5D 128
Newbiggin-on-Lune. *Cumb* 4A 104
Newbold. *Derbs* 3A 86
Newbold. *Leics* 4B 74
Newbold on Avon. *Warw* 3B 62
Newbold on Stour. *Warw* 1H 49
Newbold Pacey. *Warw* 5G 61
Newbold Verdon. *Leics* 5B 74
New Bolingbroke. *Linc* 5C 88
Newborough. *IOA* 4D 80
Newborough. *Pet* 5B 76
Newborough. *Staf* 3F 73
Newbottle. *Nptn* 2D 50
Newbottle. *Tyne* 4G 115
New Boultham. *Linc* 3G 87
Newbourne. *Suff* 1F 55
New Brancepeth. *Dur* 5F 115
Newbridge. *Cphy* 2F 33
Newbridge. *Cdgn* 5E 57
Newbridge. *Corn* 3B 4
New Bridge. *Dum* 2G 111
Newbridge. *Edin* 2E 129
Newbridge. *Hants* 1A 16
Newbridge. *IOW* 4C 16
Newbridge. *N Yor* 1C 100
Newbridge. *Pemb* 1D 42
Newbridge. *Wrex* 1E 71
Newbridge Green. *Worc* 2D 48
Newbridge-on-Usk. *Mon* 2G 33
Newbridge on Wye. *Powy* 5C 58
New Brighton. *Flin* 4E 83
New Brighton. *Hants* 2F 17
New Brighton. *Mers* 1F 83
New Brinsley. *Notts* 5B 86
Newbrough. *Nmbd* 3B 114
New Broughton. *Wrex* 5F 83
New Buckenham. *Norf* 1C 66
New Buildings. *Derr* 5A 174
Newbuildings. *Devn* 2A 12
Newburgh. *Abers* 1G 153
Newburgh. *Fife* 2E 137
Newburgh. *Lanc* 3C 90
**Newburn**. *Tyne* 3E 115
**Newbury**. *W Ber* 5C 36
Newbury. *Wilts* 2D 22
Newby. *Cumb* 2G 103
Newby. *N Yor* 2G 97 (nr. Ingleton)
Newby. *N Yor* 1E 101 (nr. Scarborough)
Newby. *N Yor* 3C 106 (nr. Stokesley)
Newby Bridge. *Cumb* 1C 96
Newby Cote. *N Yor* 2G 97
Newby East. *Cumb* 4F 113
Newby Head. *Cumb* 2G 103
New Byth. *Abers* 3F 161
Newby West. *Cumb* 4E 113
Newby Wiske. *N Yor* 1F 99
Newcastle. *B'end* 3B 32
Newcastle. *Mon* 4H 47
Newcastle. *New M* 6H 179
Newcastle. *N Dwn* 4L 179
Newcastle. *Shrp* 2E 59
Newcastle Emlyn. *Carm* 1D 44
Newcastle International Airport. *Tyne* 2E 115
Newcastleton. *Bord* 1F 113
**Newcastle-under-Lyme**. *Staf* 1C 72
**Newcastle upon Tyne**. *Tyne* 3F 115 & 197
Newchapel. *Pemb* 1G 43

Odsey—Pen-y-cae


Odsey. Cambs 2C 52
Odstock. Wilts 4G 23
Odstone. Leics 5A 74
Offchurch. Warw 4A 62
Offenham. Worc 1F 49
Offenham Cross. Worc 1F 49
Offerton. G Man 2D 84
Offerton. Tyne 4G 115
Offham. E Sus 4E 27
Offham. Kent 5A 40
Offham. W Sus 5B 26
Offleyhay. Staf 3C 72
Offley Hoo. Herts 3B 52
Offleymarsh. Staf 3B 72
Offord Cluny. Cambs 4B 64
Offord D'Arcy. Cambs 4B 64
Offton. Suff 1D 54
Offwell. Devn 3E 13
Ogbourne Maizey. Wilts 4G 35
Ogbourne St Andrew. Wilts 4G 35
Ogbourne St George. Wilts 4H 35
Ogden. G Man 3H 91
Ogle. Nmbd 2E 115
Ogmore. V Glam 4B 32
Ogmore-by-Sea. V Glam 4B 32
Ogmore Vale. B'end 2C 32
Okeford Fitzpaine. Dors 1D 14
Okehampton. Devn 3F 11
Okehampton Camp. Devn 3F 11
Okraquoy. Shet 8F 173
Okus. Swin 3G 35
Old. Nptn 3E 63
Old Aberdeen. Aber 3G 153
Old Alresford. Hants 3D 24
Oldany. High 5B 166
Old Arley. Warw 1G 61
Old Basford. Nott 1C 74
Old Basing. Hants 1E 25
Oldberrow. Warw 4F 61
Old Bewick. Nmbd 2E 121
Old Bexley. G Lon 3F 39
Old Blair. Per 2F 143
Old Bolingbroke. Linc 4C 88
Oldborough. Devn 2A 12
Old Brampton. Derbs 3H 85
Old Bridge of Tilt. Per 2F 143
Old Bridge of Urr. Dum 3E 111
Old Brumby. N Lin 4B 94
Old Buckenham. Norf 1C 66
Old Burghclere. Hants 1C 24
Oldbury. Shrp 1B 60
Oldbury. Warw 1H 61
**Oldbury**. W Mid 2D 61
Oldbury-on-Severn. S Glo 2B 34
Oldbury on the Hill. Glos 3D 34
Old Byland. N Yor 1H 99
Old Cassop. Dur 1A 106
Oldcastle. Mon 3G 47
Oldcastle Heath. Ches W 1G 71
Old Catton. Norf 4E 79
Old Clee. NE Lin 4F 95
Old Cleeve. Som 2D 20
Old Colwyn. Cnwy 3A 82
Oldcotes. Notts 2C 86
Old Coulsdon. G Lon 5E 39
Old Dailly. S Ayr 5B 116
Old Dalby. Leics 3D 74
Old Dam. Derbs 3F 85
Old Deer. Abers 4G 161
Old Dilton. Wilts 2D 22
Old Down. S Glo 3B 34
Oldeamere. Cambs 1C 64
Old Edlington. S Yor 1C 86
Old Eldon. Dur 2F 105
Old Ellerby. E Yor 1E 95
Old Fallings. W Mid 5D 72
Oldfallow. Staf 4D 73
Old Felixstowe. Suff 2G 55
Oldfield. Shrp 2A 60
Oldfield. Worc 4C 60
Old Fletton. Pet 1A 64
Oldford. Som 1C 22
Old Forge. Here 4A 48
Old Glossop. Derbs 1E 85
Old Goole. E Yor 2H 93
Old Gore. Here 3B 48
Old Graitney. Dum 3E 112
Old Grimsby. IOS 1A 4
Oldhall. High 3E 169
Old Hall Street. Norf 2F 79
**Oldham**. G Man 4H 91
Oldhamstocks. E Lot 2D 130
Old Heathfield. E Sus 3G 27
Old Hill. W Mid 2D 60
Old Hunstanton. Norf 1F 77
Oldhurst. Cambs 3B 64
Old Hutton. Cumb 1E 97
Old Kea. Corn 4C 6
Old Kilpatrick. W Dun 2F 127
Old Kinnernie. Abers 3E 152
Old Knebworth. Herts 3C 52
Oldland. S Glo 4B 34
Old Laxey. IOM 3D 108
Old Leake. Linc 5D 88
Old Lenton. Nott 2C 74
Old Llanberis. Gwyn 5F 81
Old Malton. N Yor 2B 100
Oldmeldrum. Abers 1F 153
Old Micklefield. W Yor 1E 93
Old Mill. Corn 5D 10
Oldmixon. N Som 1G 21
Old Monkland. N Lan 3A 128
Old Newton. Suff 4C 66
Old Park. Telf 5A 72
Old Pentland. Midl 3F 129
Old Philpstoun. W Lot 2D 128
Old Quarrington. Dur 1A 106
Old Radnor. Powy 5E 59
Old Rayne. Abers 1D 152
Oldridge. Devn 3B 12
Old Romney. Kent 3E 29
Old Scone. Per 1D 136
Oldshore Beg. High 3B 166
Oldshoremore. High 3C 166
Old Snydale. W Yor 2E 93
Old Sodbury. S Glo 3C 34
Old Somerby. Linc 2G 75
Old Spital. Dur 3C 104
Oldstead. N Yor 1H 99
Old Stratford. Nptn 1F 51
Old Swan. Mers 1F 83
Old Swarland. Nmbd 4F 121
Old Tebay. Cumb 4H 103
Old Town. Cumb 5F 113
Old Town. E Sus 5G 27
Oldtown. High 5C 164
Old Town. IOS 1B 4
Old Town. Nmbd 5C 120
Old Trafford. G Man 1C 84
Old Tupton. Derbs 4A 86
Oldwall. Cumb 3F 113
Oldwalls. Swan 3D 31
Old Warden. C Beds 1B 52
Oldways End. Som 4B 20
Old Westhall. Abers 1D 152
Old Weston. Cambs 3H 63
Oldwhat. Abers 3F 161
Old Windsor. Wind 3A 38
Old Wives Lees. Kent 5E 41
Old Woking. Surr 5B 38
Oldwood Common. Worc 4H 59
Old Woodstock. Oxon 4C 50
Olgrinmore. High 3C 168
Oliver's Battery. Hants 4C 24
Ollaberry. Shet 3E 173
Ollerton. Ches E 3B 84
Ollerton. Notts 4D 86
Ollerton. Shrp 3A 72
Olmarch. Cdgn 5F 57
Olmstead Green. Cambs 1G 53
Olney. Mil 5F 63
Olrig. High 2D 169
Olton. W Mid 2F 61
Olveston. S Glo 3B 34
**Omagh**. Ferm 2K 177
Ombersley. Worc 4C 60
Ompton. Notts 4D 86
Omunsgarth. Shet 7E 173
Onchan. IOM 4D 108
Onecote. Staf 5E 85
Onehouse. Suff 5C 66
Onen. Mon 4H 47
Ongar Hill. Norf 3E 77
Ongar Street. Here 4F 59
Onibury. Shrp 3G 59
Onich. High 2E 141
Onllwyn. Neat 4B 46
Onneley. Staf 1B 72
Onslow Green. Essx 4G 53
Onslow Village. Surr 1A 26
Onthank. E Ayr 1D 116
Openwoodgate. Derbs 1A 74
Opinan. High 1G 155
(nr. Gairloch)
Opinan. High 4C 162
(nr. Laide)
Orasaigh. W Isl 6F 171
Orbost. High 4B 154
Orby. Linc 4D 89
Orchard Hill. Devn 4E 19
Orchard Portman. Som 4F 21
Orcheston. Wilts 2F 23
Orcop. Here 3H 47
Orcop Hill. Here 3H 47
Ord. High 2E 147
Ordale. Shet 1H 173
Ordhead. Abers 2D 152
Ordie. Abers 3B 152
Ordiquish. Mor 3H 159
Ordley. Nmbd 4C 114
Ordsall. Notts 3E 86
Ore. E Sus 4C 28
Oreton. Shrp 2A 60
Orford. Suff 1H 55
Orford. Warr 1A 84
Organford. Dors 3E 15
Orgil. Orkn 7B 172
Orgreave. Staf 4F 73
Oridge Street. Glos 3C 48
Orlestone. Kent 2D 28
Orleton. Here 4G 59
Orleton. Worc 4A 60
Orleton Common. Here 4G 59
Orlingbury. Nptn 3F 63
Ormacleit. W Isl 5C 170
Ormathwaite. Cumb 2D 102
Ormesby. Midd 3C 106
Ormesby St Margaret. Norf 4G 79
Ormesby St Michael. Norf 4G 79
Ormiscaig. High 4C 162
Ormiston. E Lot 3H 129
Ormsaigbeg. High 2F 139
Ormsaigmore. High 2F 139
Ormsary. Arg 2F 125
Ormsgill. Cumb 2A 96
**Ormskirk**. Lanc 4C 90
Orphir. Orkn 7C 172
**Orpington**. G Lon 4F 39
**Orrell**. G Man 4D 90
Orrell. Mers 1F 83
Orrisdale. IOM 2C 108
Orsett. Thur 2H 39
Orslow. Staf 4C 72
Orston. Notts 1E 75
Orthwaite. Cumb 1D 102
Orton. Cumb 4H 103
Orton. Mor 3H 159
Orton. Nptn 3F 63
Orton. Staf 1C 60
Orton Longueville. Pet 1A 64
Orton-on-the-Hill. Leics 5H 73
Orton Waterville. Pet 1A 64
Orton Wistow. Pet 1A 64
Orwell. Cambs 5C 64
Osbaldeston. Lanc 1E 91
Osbaldwick. York 4A 100
Osbaston. Leics 5B 74
Osbaston. Shrp 3F 71
Osbournby. Linc 2H 75
Osclay. High 5E 169
Oscroft. Ches W 4H 83
Ose. High 4C 154
Osgathorpe. Leics 4B 74
Osgodby. Linc 1H 87
Osgodby. N Yor 1E 101
(nr. Scarborough)
Osgodby. N Yor 1G 93
(nr. Selby)
Oskaig. High 5E 155
Oskamull. Arg 5F 139
Osleston. Derbs 2G 73
Osmaston. Derb 2A 74
Osmaston. Derbs 1G 73
Osmington. Dors 4C 14
Osmington Mills. Dors 4C 14
Osmondthorpe. W Yor 1D 92
Osmondwall. Orkn 9C 172
Osmotherley. N Yor 5B 106
Osnaburgh. Fife 2G 137
Ospisdale. High 5E 164
Ospringe. Kent 4E 40
**Ossett**. W Yor 2C 92
Ossington. Notts 4E 87
Ostend. Essx 1D 40
Ostend. Norf 2F 79
Osterley. G Lon 3C 38
Oswaldkirk. N Yor 2A 100
**Oswaldtwistle**. Lanc 2F 91
**Oswestry**. Shrp 3E 71
Otby. Linc 1A 88
Otford. Kent 5G 39
Otham. Kent 5B 40
Otherton. Staf 4D 72
Othery. Som 3G 21
Otley. Suff 5E 66
**Otley**. W Yor 5E 98
Otterbourne. Hants 4C 24
Otterburn. Nmbd 5C 120
Otterburn. N Yor 4A 98
Otterburn Camp. Nmbd 5C 120
Otterburn Hall. Nmbd 5C 120
Otter Ferry. Arg 1H 125
Otterford. Som 1F 13
Otterham. Corn 3B 10
Otterhampton. Som 2F 21
Otterham Quay. Kent 4C 40
Ottershaw. Surr 4B 38
Otterspool. Mers 2F 83
Otterswick. Shet 3G 173
Otterton. Devn 4D 12
Otterwood. Hants 2C 16
Ottery St Mary. Devn 3D 12
Ottinge. Kent 1F 29
Ottringham. E Yor 2F 95
Oughterby. Cumb 4D 112
Oughtershaw. N Yor 1A 98
Oughterside. Cumb 5C 112
Oughtibridge. S Yor 1H 85
Oughtrington. Warr 2A 84
Oulston. N Yor 2H 99
Oulton. Cumb 4D 112
Oulton. Norf 3D 78
Oulton. Staf 3B 72
(nr. Gnosall Heath)
Oulton. Staf 2D 72
(nr. Stone)
Oulton. Suff 1H 67
Oulton. W Yor 2D 92
Oulton Broad. Suff 1H 67
Oulton Street. Norf 3D 78
Oundle. Nptn 2H 63
Ousby. Cumb 1H 103
Ousdale. High 2H 165
Ousden. Suff 5G 65
Ousefleet. E Yor 2B 94
Ouston. Dur 4F 115
Ouston. Nmbd 4A 114
(nr. Bearsbridge)
Ouston. Nmbd 2D 114
(nr. Stamfordham)
Outer Hope. Devn 4C 8
Outertown. Orkn 6B 172
Outgate. Cumb 5E 103
Outhgill. Cumb 4A 104
Outlands. Staf 2B 72
Outlane. W Yor 3A 92
Out Newton. E Yor 2G 95
Out Rawcliffe. Lanc 5D 96
Outwell. Norf 5E 77
Outwick. Hants 1G 15
Outwood. Surr 1E 27
Outwood. W Yor 2D 92
Outwood. Worc 3D 60
Outwoods. Leics 4B 74
Outwoods. Staf 4B 72
Ouzlewell Green. W Yor 2D 92
Ovenden. W Yor 2A 92
Over. Cambs 3C 64
Over. Ches W 4A 84
Over. Glos 4D 48
Over. S Glo 3A 34
Overbister. Orkn 3F 172
Over Burrows. Derbs 2G 73
Overbury. Worc 2E 49
Overcombe. Dors 4B 14
Over Compton. Dors 1A 14
Over End. Cambs 1H 63
Over Finlarg. Ang 4D 144
Overgreen. Derbs 3H 85
Over Green. W Mid 1F 61
Over Haddon. Derbs 4G 85
Over Hulton. G Man 4E 91
Over Kellet. Lanc 2E 97
Over Kiddington. Oxon 3C 50
Overleigh. Som 3H 21
Overley. Staf 4F 73
Over Monnow. Mon 4A 48
Over Norton. Oxon 3B 50
Over Peover. Ches E 3B 84
Overpool. Ches W 3F 83
Overscaig. High 1B 164
Overseal. Derbs 4G 73
Over Silton. N Yor 5B 106
Oversland. Kent 5E 41
Overstone. Nptn 4F 63
Over Stowey. Som 3E 21
Overstrand. Norf 1E 79
Over Stratton. Som 1H 13
Over Street. Wilts 3F 23
Overthorpe. Nptn 1C 50
Overton. Aber 2F 153
Overton. Ches W 3H 83
Overton. Hants 2D 24
Overton. High 5E 169
Overton. Lanc 4D 96
Overton. N Yor 4H 99
Overton. Shrp 2A 60
(nr. Bridgnorth)
Overton. Shrp 3H 59
(nr. Ludlow)
Overton. Swan 4D 30
Overton. W Yor 3C 92
Overton. Wrex 1F 71
Overtown. Lanc 2F 97
Overtown. N Lan 4B 128
Overtown. Swin 4G 35
Over Wallop. Hants 3A 24
Over Whitacre. Warw 1G 61
Over Worton. Oxon 3C 50
Oving. Buck 3F 51
Oving. W Sus 5A 26
Ovingdean. Brig 5E 27
Ovingham. Nmbd 3D 115
Ovington. Dur 3E 105
Ovington. Essx 1A 54
Ovington. Hants 3D 24
Ovington. Norf 5B 78
Ovington. Nmbd 3D 114
Owen's Bank. Staf 3G 73
Ower. Hants 2C 16
(nr. Holbury)
Ower. Hants 1B 16
(nr. Totton)
Owermoigne. Dors 4C 14
Owlbury. Shrp 1F 59
Owler Bar. Derbs 3G 85
Owlerton. S Yor 1H 85
Owlsmoor. Brac 5G 37
Owlswick. Buck 5F 51
Owmby. Linc 4D 94
Owmby-by-Spital. Linc 2H 87
Ownham. W Ber 4C 36
Owrytn. Wrex 1F 71
Owslebury. Hants 4D 24
Owston. Leics 5E 75
Owston. S Yor 3F 93
Owston Ferry. N Lin 4B 94
Owstwick. E Yor 1F 95
Owthorne. E Yor 2G 95
Owthorpe. Notts 2D 74
Owton Manor. Hart 2B 106
Oxborough. Norf 5G 77
Oxbridge. Dors 3H 13
Oxcombe. Linc 3C 88
Oxen End. Essx 3G 53
Oxenhall. Glos 3C 48
Oxenholme. Cumb 5G 103
Oxenhope. W Yor 1A 92
Oxen Park. Cumb 1C 96
Oxenpill. Som 2H 21
Oxenton. Glos 2E 49
Oxenwood. Wilts 1B 24
**Oxford**. Oxon 5D 50 & 200
Oxgangs. Edin 3F 129
Oxhey. Herts 1C 38
Oxhill. Warw 1B 50
Oxley. W Mid 5D 72
Oxley Green. Essx 4C 54
Oxley's Green. E Sus 3A 28
Oxlode. Cambs 2D 65
Oxnam. Bord 3B 120
Oxshott. Surr 4C 38
Oxspring. S Yor 4C 92
**Oxted**. Surr 5E 39
Oxton. Mers 2F 83
Oxton. N Yor 5H 99
Oxton. Notts 5D 86
Oxton. Bord 4A 130
Oxwich. Swan 4D 31
Oxwich Green. Swan 4D 31
Oxwick. Norf 3B 78
Oykel Bridge. High 3A 164
Oyne. Abers 1D 152
Oystermouth. Swan 4F 31
Ozleworth. Glos 2C 34


## P


Pabail Iarach. W Isl 4H 171
Pabail Uarach. W Isl 4H 171
Pachesham Park. Surr 5C 38
Packers Hill. Dors 1C 14
Packington. Leics 4A 74
Packmoor. Stoke 5C 84
Packmores. Warw 4G 61
Packwood. W Mid 3F 61
Packwood Gullet. W Mid 3F 61
Padanaram. Ang 3D 144
Padbury. Buck 2F 51
**Paddington**. G Lon 2D 38
Paddington. Warr 2A 84
Paddlesworth. Kent 2F 29
Paddock. Kent 5D 40
Paddockhole. Dum 1D 112
Paddock Wood. Kent 1A 28
Paddolgreen. Shrp 2H 71
Padeswood. Flin 4E 83
**Padiham**. Lanc 1F 91
Padside. N Yor 4D 98
Padson. Devn 3F 11
Padstow. Corn 1D 6
Padworth. W Ber 5E 36
Page Bank. Dur 1F 105
Pagham. W Sus 3G 17
Paglesham Churchend. Essx 1D 40
Paglesham Eastend. Essx 1D 40
Paibeil. W Isl 2C 170
(on North Uist)
Paibeil. W Isl 8C 171
(on Taransay)
Paiblesgearraidh. W Isl 2C 170
**Paignton**. Torb 2E 9
Pailton. Warw 2B 62
Paine's Corner. E Sus 3H 27
Painleyhill. Staf 2E 73
Painscastle. Powy 1E 47
Painshawfield. Nmbd 3D 114
Painsthorpe. E Yor 4C 100
Painswick. Glos 5D 48
Painter's Forstal. Kent 5D 40
Painthorpe. W Yor 3D 92
Pairc Shiaboist. W Isl 3E 171
**Paisley**. Ren 3F 127
Pakefield. Suff 1H 67
Pakenham. Suff 4B 66
Pale. Gwyn 2B 70
Palehouse Common. E Sus 4F 27
Palestine. Hants 2A 24
Paley Street. Wind 4G 37
Palgowan. Dum 1A 110
Palgrave. Suff 3D 66
Pallington. Dors 3C 14
Palmarsh. Kent 2F 29
Palmer Moor. Derbs 2F 73
Palmers Cross. W Mid 5C 72
Palmerstown. V Glam 5E 33
Palnackie. Dum 4F 111
Palnure. Dum 3B 110
Palterton. Derbs 4B 86
Pamber End. Hants 1E 24
Pamber Green. Hants 1E 24
Pamber Heath. Hants 5E 36
Pamington. Glos 2E 49
Pamphill. Dors 2E 15
Pampisford. Cambs 1E 53
Panborough. Som 2H 21
Panbride. Ang 5E 145
Pancrasweek. Devn 2C 10
Pandy. Gwyn 2A 70
(nr. Bala)
Pandy. Gwyn 5F 69
(nr. Tywyn)
Pandy. Mon 3G 47
Pandy. Powy 5B 70
Pandy. Wrex 2D 70
Pandy Tudur. Cnwy 4A 82
Panfield. Essx 3H 53
Pangbourne. W Ber 4E 37
Pannal. N Yor 4F 99
Pannal Ash. N Yor 4E 99
Pannanich. Abers 4A 152
Pant. Shrp 3E 71
Pant. Wrex 1E 71
Pantasaph. Flin 3D 82
Pant Glas. Gwyn 1D 68
Pant-glas. Shrp 2E 71
Pantgwyn. Carm 3F 45
Pantgwyn. Cdgn 1C 44
Pant-lasau. Swan 5G 45
Panton. Linc 3A 88
Pant-pastynog. Den 4C 82
Pantperthog. Gwyn 5G 69
Pant-teg. Carm 3E 45
Pant-y-Caws. Carm 2F 43
Pant-y-dwr. Powy 3B 58
Pant-y-ffridd. Powy 5D 70
Pantyffynnon. Carm 4G 45
Pantygasseg. Torf 5F 47
Pant-y-llyn. Carm 4G 45
Pant-yr-awel. B'end 3C 32
Pant y Wacco. Flin 3D 82
Panxworth. Norf 4F 79
Papa Stour Airport. Shet 6C 173
Papa Westray Airport. Orkn 2D 172
Papcastle. Cumb 1C 102
Papigoe. High 3F 169
Papil. Shet 8E 173
Papple. E Lot 2B 130
Papplewick. Notts 5C 86
Papworth Everard. Cambs 4B 64
Papworth St Agnes. Cambs 4B 64
Par. Corn 3E 7
Paramour Street. Kent 4G 41
Parbold. Lanc 3C 90
Parbrook. Som 3A 22
Parbrook. W Sus 3B 26
Parc. Gwyn 2A 70
Parcllyn. Cdgn 5B 56
Parc-Seymour. Newp 2H 33
Pardown. Hants 2D 24
Pardshaw. Cumb 2B 102
Parham. Suff 4F 67
Park. Abers 4E 153
Park. Arg 4D 140
Park. Derr 6B 174
Park. Dum 5B 118
Park Bottom. Corn 4A 6
Parkburn. Abers 5E 161
Park Corner. E Sus 2G 27
Park Corner. Oxon 3E 37
Parkend. Glos 5B 48
Park End. Nmbd 2B 114
Parkeston. Essx 2F 55
Parkfield. Corn 2H 7
Parkgate. Ant 8J 175
Parkgate. Ches W 3E 83
Parkgate. Cumb 5D 112
Parkgate. Dum 1B 112
Park Gate. Hants 2D 16
Parkgate. Surr 1D 26
Park Gate. Worc 3D 60
Parkhall. W Dun 2F 127
Parkham. Devn 4D 19
Parkham Ash. Devn 4D 18
Parkhead. Cumb 5E 113
Parkhead. Glas 3H 127
Park Hill. Mers 4C 90
Parkhouse. Mon 5A 48
Parkhurst. IOW 3C 16
Park Lane. G Man 4F 91
Park Lane. Staf 5C 72
Parkmill. Swan 4E 31
Park Mill. W Yor 3C 92
Parkneuk. Abers 1G 145
Parkside. N Lan 4B 128
Parkstone. Pool 3F 15
Park Street. Herts 5B 52
Park Street. W Sus 2C 26
Park Town. Oxon 5D 50
Park Village. Nmbd 3H 113
Parkway. Here 2C 48
Parley Cross. Dors 3F 15
Parmoor. Buck 3F 37
Parr. Mers 1H 83
Parracombe. Devn 2G 19
Parrog. Pemb 1E 43
Parsonage Green. Essx 4H 53
Parsonby. Cumb 1C 102
Parson Cross. S Yor 1H 85
Parson Drove. Cambs 5C 76
Partick. Glas 3G 127
Partington. G Man 1B 84
Partney. Linc 4D 88
Parton. Cumb 2A 102
(nr. Whitehaven)
Parton. Cumb 4D 112
(nr. Wigton)
Parton. Dum 2D 111
Partridge Green. W Sus 4C 26
Parwich. Derbs 5F 85
Passenham. Nptn 2F 51
Passfield. Hants 3G 25
Passingford Bridge. Essx 1G 39
Paston. Norf 2F 79
Pasturefields. Staf 3D 73
Patchacott. Devn 3E 11
Patcham. Brig 5E 27
Patchetts Green. Herts 1C 38
Patching. W Sus 5B 26
Patchole. Devn 2G 19
Patchway. S Glo 3B 34
Pateley Bridge. N Yor 3D 98
Pathe. Som 3G 21
Pathfinder Village. Devn 3B 12
Pathhead. Abers 2G 145
Pathhead. E Ayr 3F 117
Pathhead. Fife 4E 137
Pathhead. Midl 3G 129
Pathlow. Warw 5F 61
Path of Condie. Per 2C 136
Pathstruie. Per 2C 136
Patmore Heath. Herts 3E 53
Patna. E Ayr 3D 116
Patney. Wilts 1F 23
Patrick. IOM 3B 108
Patrick Brompton. N Yor 5F 105
Patrington. E Yor 2G 95
Patrington Haven. E Yor 2G 95
Patrixbourne. Kent 5F 41
Patterdale. Cumb 3E 103
Pattiesmuir. Fife 1D 129
Pattingham. Staf 1C 60
Pattishall. Nptn 5D 62
Pattiswick. Essx 3B 54
Patton Bridge. Cumb 5G 103
Paul. Corn 4B 4
Paulerspury. Nptn 1F 51
Paull. E Yor 2E 95
Paulton. Bath 1B 22
Pauperhaugh. Nmbd 5F 121
Pave Lane. Telf 4B 72
Pavenham. Bed 5G 63
Pawlett. Som 2F 21
Pawston. Nmbd 1C 120
Paxford. Glos 2G 49
Paxton. Bord 4F 131
Payhembury. Devn 2D 12
Paythorne. Lanc 4H 97
Payton. Som 4E 20
**Peacehaven**. E Sus 5F 27
Peak Dale. Derbs 3E 85
**Peak District**. Derbs 2F 85
Peak Forest. Derbs 3F 85
Peak Hill. Linc 4B 76
Peakirk. Pet 5A 76
Pearsie. Ang 3C 144
Peasedown St John. Bath 1C 22
Peaseland Green. Norf 4C 78
Peasemore. W Ber 4C 36
Peasenhall. Suff 4F 67
Pease Pottage. W Sus 2D 26
Peaslake. Surr 1B 26
Peasley Cross. Mers 1H 83
Peasmarsh. E Sus 3C 28
Peasmarsh. Som 1G 13
Peasmarsh. Surr 1A 26
Peaston. E Lot 3H 129
Peastonbank. E Lot 3H 129
Peathill. Abers 2G 161
Peat Inn. Fife 3G 137
Peatling Magna. Leics 1C 62
Peatling Parva. Leics 2C 62
Peaton. Arg 1D 126
Peaton. Shrp 2H 59
Peats Corner. Suff 4D 66
Pebmarsh. Essx 2B 54
Pebworth. Worc 1G 49
Pecket Well. W Yor 2H 91
Peckforton. Ches E 5H 83
Peckham Bush. Kent 5A 40
Peckleton. Leics 5B 74
Pedair-ffordd. Powy 3D 70
Pedham. Norf 4F 79
Pedlinge. Kent 2F 29
Pedmore. W Mid 2D 60
Pedwell. Som 3H 21
Peebles. Bord 5F 129
Peel. IOM 3B 108
Peel. Bord 1G 119
Peel Common. Hants 2D 16
Peening Quarter. Kent 3C 28
Peggs Green. Leics 4B 74
Pegsdon. C Beds 2B 52
Pegswood. Nmbd 1F 115
Peinchorran. High 5E 155
Peinlich. High 3D 154
Pelaw. Tyne 3F 115
Pelcomb Bridge. Pemb 3D 42
Pelcomb Cross. Pemb 3D 42
Peldon. Essx 4C 54
**Pelsall**. W Mid 5E 73
Pelton. Dur 4F 115
Pelutho. Cumb 5C 112
Pelynt. Corn 3G 7
Pemberton. Carm 5F 45
Pembrey. Carm 5E 45
Pembridge. Here 5F 59
Pembroke. Pemb 4D 43
Pembroke Dock. Pemb 4D 42 & 204
Pembroke Ferry. Pemb 4D 42
Pembury. Kent 1H 27
Penallt. Mon 4A 48
Penally. Pemb 5F 43
Penalt. Here 3A 48
Penalum. Pemb 5F 43
Penare. Corn 4D 6
**Penarth**. V Glam 4E 33
Penbeagle. Corn 3C 4
Penberth. Corn 4B 4
Pen-bont Rhydybeddau. Cdgn 2F 57
Penbryn. Cdgn 5B 56
Pencader. Carm 2E 45
Pen-cae. Cdgn 5D 56
Pencaenewydd. Gwyn 1D 68
Pencaerau. Neat 3G 31
Pencaitland. E Lot 3H 129
Pencarnisiog. IOA 3C 80
Pencarreg. Carm 1F 45
Pencarrow. Corn 4B 10
Pencelli. Powy 3D 46
Pen-clawdd. Swan 3E 31
Pencoed. B'end 3C 32
Pencombe. Here 5H 59
Pencraig. Here 3A 48
Pencraig. Powy 3C 70
Pendeen. Corn 3A 4
Pendeford. W Mid 5C 72
Penderyn. Rhon 5C 46
Pendine. Carm 4G 43
**Pendlebury**. G Man 4F 91
Pendleton. G Man 1C 84
Pendleton. Lanc 1F 91
Pendock. Worc 2C 48
Pendoggett. Corn 5A 10
Pendomer. Som 1A 14
Pendoylan. V Glam 4D 32
Pendre. B'end 3C 32
Penegoes. Powy 5G 69
Penelewey. Corn 4C 6
Penffordd. Pemb 2E 43
Penffordd-Lâs. Powy 1A 58
Penfro. Pemb 4D 43
Pengam. Cphy 2E 33
Pengam. Card 4F 33
**Penge**. G Lon 4E 39
Pengelly. Corn 4A 10
Pengenffordd. Powy 2E 47
Pengersick. Corn 4C 4
Pengorffwysfa. IOA 1D 80
Pengover Green. Corn 2G 7
Pengwern. Den 3C 82
Penhale. Corn 5D 5
(nr. Mullion)
Penhale. Corn 3D 6
(nr. St Austell)
Penhale Camp. Corn 3B 6
Penhallow. Corn 3B 6
Penhalvean. Corn 5B 6
Penhelig. Gwyn 1F 57
Penhill. Swin 3G 35
Penhow. Newp 2H 33
Penhurst. E Sus 4A 28
Peniarth. Gwyn 5F 69
**Penicuik**. Midl 3F 129
Peniel. Carm 3E 45
Penifiler. High 4D 155
Peninver. Arg 3B 122
Penisa'r Waun. Gwyn 4E 81
Penistone. S Yor 4C 92
Penketh. Warr 2H 83
Penkill. S Ayr 5B 116
Penkridge. Staf 4D 72
Penley. Wrex 2G 71
Penllech. Gwyn 2B 68
Penllergaer. Swan 3F 31
Pen-llyn. IOA 2C 80
Penmachno. Cnwy 5G 81
Penmaen. Swan 4E 31
Penmaenmawr. Cnwy 3G 81
Penmaenpool. Gwyn 4F 69
Penmaen Rhos. Cnwy 3A 82
Pen-marc. V Glam 5D 32
Penmark. V Glam 5D 32
Penmarth. Corn 5B 6
Penmon. IOA 2F 81
Penmorfa. Gwyn 1E 69
Penmynydd. IOA 3E 81
Penn. Buck 1A 38
Penn. Dors 3G 13
Penn. W Mid 1C 60
Pennal. Gwyn 5G 69
Pennan. Abers 2F 161
Pennant. Cdgn 4E 57
Pennant. Den 2C 70
Pennant. Gwyn 3B 70
Pennant. Powy 1A 58
Pennant Melangell. Powy 3C 70
Pennar. Pemb 4D 42
Pennard. Swan 4E 31
Pennerley. Shrp 1F 59
Pennington. Cumb 2B 96
Pennington. G Man 1A 84
Pennington. Hants 3B 16
Pennorth. Powy 3E 46
Penn Street. Buck 1A 38
Pennsylvania. Devn 3C 12
Pennsylvania. S Glo 4C 34
Penny Bridge. Cumb 1C 96
Pennycross. Plym 3A 8
Pennygate. Norf 3F 79
Pennyghael. Arg 1C 132
Penny Hill. Linc 3C 76
Pennylands. Lanc 4C 90
Pennymoor. Devn 1B 12
Pennyvenie. E Ayr 4D 117
Pennywell. Tyne 4G 115
Penparc. Cdgn 1C 44
Penparcau. Cdgn 2E 57
Pen-pedair-heol. Cphy 2E 33
Penperlleni. Mon 5G 47
Penpillick. Corn 3E 7
Penpol. Corn 5C 6
Penpoll. Corn 3F 7
Penponds. Corn 3D 4
Penpont. Corn 5A 10
Penpont. Dum 5H 117
Penpont. Powy 3C 46
Penprysg. B'end 3C 32
Penquit. Devn 3C 8
Penrherber. Carm 1G 43
Penrhiw. Pemb 1C 44
Penrhiwceiber. Rhon 2D 32
Pen-Rhiw-fawr. Neat 4H 45
Penrhiw-llan. Cdgn 1D 44
Penrhiw-pal. Cdgn 1D 44
Penrhos. Gwyn 2C 68
Penrhos. Here 5F 59
Penrhos. IOA 2B 80
Penrhos. Mon 4H 47
Penrhos. Powy 4B 46
Penrhos Garnedd. Gwyn 3E 81
Penrhyn. IOA 1C 80
Penrhyn Bay. Cnwy 2H 81
Penrhyn-coch. Cdgn 2F 57
Penrhyndeudraeth. Gwyn 2F 69
Penrhyn-side. Cnwy 2H 81
Penrice. Swan 4D 31
**Penrith**. Cumb 2G 103
Penrose. Corn 1C 6
Penruddock. Cumb 2F 103
Penryn. Corn 5B 6
Pen-sarn. Carm 4E 45
Pen-sarn. Gwyn 3E 69
Pensax. Worc 4B 60
Pensby. Mers 2E 83
Penselwood. Som 3C 22
Pensford. Bath 5B 34
Pensham. Worc 1E 49
Penshaw. Tyne 4G 115
Penshurst. Kent 1G 27
Pensilva. Corn 2G 7
Pensnett. W Mid 2D 60
Penston. E Lot 2H 129
Penstone. Devn 2A 12
Pentewan. Corn 4E 6
Pentir. Gwyn 4E 81
Pentire. Corn 2B 6
Pentlepoir. Pemb 4F 43
Pentlow. Essx 1B 54
Pentney. Norf 4G 77
Penton Mewsey. Hants 2B 24
Pentraeth. IOA 3E 81
Pentre. Powy 1E 59
(nr. Church Stoke)
Pentre. Powy 2D 58
(nr. Kerry)
Pentre. Powy 2C 58
(nr. Mochdre)
Pentre. Rhon 2C 32
Pentre. Shrp 4F 71
Pentre. Wrex 2D 70
(nr. Llanfyllin)
Pentre. Wrex 1E 71
(nr. Rhosllanerchrugog)
Pentrebach. Carm 2B 46
Pentre-bach. Cdgn 1F 45
Pentrebach. Mer T 5D 46
Pentre-bach. Powy 2C 46
Pentrebach. Swan 5G 45
Pentre Berw. IOA 3D 80
Pentre-bont. Cnwy 5G 81
Pentrecagal. Carm 1D 44
Pentre-celyn. Den 5D 82
Pentre-clawdd. Shrp 2E 71
Pentreclwydau. Neat 5B 46
Pentre-cwrt. Carm 2D 45
Pentre Dolau Honddu. Powy 1C 46
Pentre-dwr. Swan 3F 31
Pentrefelin. Carm 3F 45
Pentrefelin. Cdgn 1G 45
Pentrefelin. Cnwy 3H 81
Pentrefelin. Gwyn 2E 69
Pentrefoelas. Cnwy 5A 82
Pentre Galar. Pemb 1F 43
Pentregat. Cdgn 5C 56
Pentre Gwenlais. Carm 4G 45
Pentre Gwynfryn. Gwyn 3E 69
Pentre Halkyn. Flin 3E 82
Pentre Hodre. Shrp 3F 59
Pentre-Llanrhaeadr. Den 4C 82
Pentre Llifior. Powy 1D 58
Pentrellwyn. IOA 2E 81
Pentre-llwyn-llwyd. Powy 5B 58
Pentre-llyn-cymmer. Cnwy 5B 82
Pentre Meyrick. V Glam 4C 32
Pentre-piod. Gwyn 2A 70
Pentre-poeth. Newp 3F 33
Pentre'r beirdd. Powy 4D 70
Pentre'r-felin. Powy 2C 46
Pentre-tafarn-y-fedw. Cnwy 4H 81
Pentre-ty-gwyn. Carm 2B 46
Pentre-uchaf. Gwyn 2C 68
Pentrich. Derbs 5A 86
Pentridge. Dors 1F 15
Pen-twyn. Cphy 5F 47
(nr. Oakdale)
Pentwyn. Cphy 5E 46
(nr. Rhymney)
Pentwyn. Card 3F 33
Pentyrch. Card 3E 32
Pentywyn. Carm 4G 43
Penuwch. Cdgn 4E 57
Penwithick. Corn 3E 7
Penwyllt. Powy 4B 46
Penybanc. Carm 4G 45
(nr. Ammanford)
Pen-y-banc. Carm 3G 45
(nr. Llandeilo)
Pen-y-bont. Carm 2H 43
Penybont. Powy 4D 58
(nr. Llandrindod Wells)
Pen-y-bont. Powy 3E 70
(nr. Llanfyllin)
**Pen-y-Bont Ar Ogwr**. B'end 3C 32
Penybontfawr. Powy 3C 70
Penybryn. Cphy 2E 33
Pen-y-bryn. Pemb 1B 44
Pen-y-bryn. Wrex 1E 71
Pen-y-cae. Powy 4B 46

Penycae—Ragnall

Penycae. *Wrex* 1E 71
Pen-y-cae mawr. *Mon* 2H 33
Penycaerau. *Gwyn* 3A 68
Pen-y-cefn. *Flin* 3D 82
Pen-y-clawdd. *Mon* 5H 47
Pen-y-coedcae. *Rhon* 3D 32
Penycwm. *Pemb* 2C 42
Pen-y-Darren. *Mer T* 5D 46
Pen-y-fai. *B'end* 3B 32
Penyffordd. *Flin* 4F 83 (nr. Mold)
Pen-y-ffordd. *Flin* 2D 82 (nr. Prestatyn)
Penyffridd. *Gwyn* 5E 81
Pen-y-garn. *Cdgn* 2F 57
Pen-y-garnedd. *IOA* 3E 81
Penygarnedd. *Powy* 3D 70
Pen-y-graig. *Gwyn* 2B 68
Penygraig. *Rhon* 2C 32
Penygraigwen. *IOA* 2D 80
Pen-y-groes. *Carm* 4F 45
Penygroes. *Gwyn* 5D 80
Penygroes. *Pemb* 1F 43
Pen-y-Mynydd. *Carm* 5E 45
Penymynydd. *Flin* 4F 83
Penyrheol. *Cphy* 3E 33
Pen-yr-heol. *Mon* 4H 47
Penyrheol. *Swan* 3E 31
Penysarn. *IOA* 1D 80
Pen-y-stryt. *Den* 5D 82
Penywaun. *Rhon* 5C 46
**Penzance**. *Corn* 3B 4
Peopleton. *Worc* 5D 60
Peover Heath. *Ches E* 3B 84
Peper Harow. *Surr* 1A 26
Peplow. *Shrp* 3A 72
Pepper Arden. *N Yor* 4F 105
Perceton. *N Ayr* 5E 127
Percyhorner. *Abers* 2G 161
Perham Down. *Wilts* 2A 24
Periton. *Som* 2C 20
Perkinsville. *Dur* 4F 115
Perlethorpe. *Notts* 3D 86
Perranarworthal. *Corn* 5B 6
Perranporth. *Corn* 3B 6
Perranuthnoe. *Corn* 4C 4
Perranwell. *Corn* 5B 6
Perranzabuloe. *Corn* 3B 6
Perrott's Brook. *Glos* 5F 49
Perry. *W Mid* 1E 61
Perry Barr. *W Mid* 1E 61
Perry Crofts. *Staf* 5G 73
Perry Green. *Essx* 3B 54
Perry Green. *Herts* 4E 53
Perry Green. *Wilts* 3E 35
Perry Street. *Kent* 3H 39
Perry Street. *Som* 2G 13
Perrywood. *Kent* 5E 41
Pershall. *Staf* 3C 72
Pershore. *Worc* 1E 49
Pertenhall. *Bed* 4H 63
**Perth**. *Per* 1D 136 & 201
Perthy. *Shrp* 2F 71
Perton. *Staf* 1C 60
Pertwood. *Wilts* 3D 23
**Peterborough**. *Pet* 1A 64 & 201
Peterburn. *High* 5B 162
Peterchurch. *Here* 2G 47
Peterculter. *Aber* 3F 153
**Peterhead**. *Abers* 4H 161
**Peterlee**. *Dur* 5H 115
**Petersfield**. *Hants* 4F 25
Petersfinger. *Wilts* 4G 23
Peters Green. *Herts* 4B 52
Peters Marland. *Devn* 1E 11
Peterstone Wentlooge. *Newp* 3F 33
Peterston-super-Ely. *V Glam* 4D 32
Peterstow. *Here* 3A 48
Peters Village. *Kent* 4B 40
Peter Tavy. *Devn* 5F 11
Petertown. *Orkn* 7C 172
Petham. *Kent* 5F 41
Petherwin Gate. *Corn* 4C 10
Petrockstowe. *Devn* 2F 11
Petsoe End. *Mil* 1G 51
Pett. *E Sus* 4C 28
Pettaugh. *Suff* 5D 66
Pett Bottom. *Kent* 5F 41
Petteridge. *Kent* 1A 28
Pettinain. *S Lan* 5C 128
Pettistree. *Suff* 5E 67
Petton. *Devn* 4D 20
Petton. *Shrp* 3G 71
Petts Wood. *G Lon* 4F 39
Pettycur. *Fife* 1F 129
Pettywell. *Norf* 3C 78
Petworth. *W Sus* 3A 26
Pevensey. *E Sus* 5H 27
Pevensey Bay. *E Sus* 5A 28
Pewsey. *Wilts* 5G 35
Pheasants Hill. *Buck* 3F 37
Philadelphia. *Tyne* 4G 115
Philham. *Devn* 4C 18
Philiphaugh. *Bord* 2G 119
Phillack. *Corn* 3C 4
Philleigh. *Corn* 5C 6
Philpstoun. *W Lot* 2D 128
Phocle Green. *Here* 3B 48
Phoenix Green. *Hants* 1F 25
Pibsbury. *Som* 4H 21
Pibwrlwyd. *Carm* 4E 45
Pica. *Cumb* 2B 102
Piccadilly. *Warw* 1G 61
Piccadilly Corner. *Norf* 2E 67
Piccotts End. *Herts* 5A 52
Pickering. *N Yor* 1B 100
Picket Piece. *Hants* 2B 24
Picket Post. *Hants* 2G 15
Pickford. *W Mid* 2G 61
Pickhill. *N Yor* 1F 99
Picklenash. *Glos* 3C 48
Picklescott. *Shrp* 1G 59
Pickletillem. *Fife* 1G 137
Pickmere. *Ches E* 3A 84
Pickstock. *Telf* 3B 72
Pickwell. *Devn* 2E 19
Pickwell. *Leics* 4E 75
Pickworth. *Linc* 2H 75
Pickworth. *Rut* 4G 75
Picton. *Ches W* 3G 83
Picton. *Flin* 2D 82
Picton. *N Yor* 4B 106
Pict's Hill. *Som* 4H 21
Piddinghoe. *E Sus* 5F 27
Piddington. *Buck* 2G 37
Piddington. *Nptn* 5F 63
Piddington. *Oxon* 4E 51
Piddlehinton. *Dors* 3C 14
Piddletrenthide. *Dors* 2C 14
Pidley. *Cambs* 3C 64
Pidney. *Dors* 2C 14
Pie Corner. *Here* 4A 60
Piercebridge. *Darl* 3F 105
Pierowall. *Orkn* 3D 172
Pigdon. *Nmbd* 1E 115
Pightley. *Som* 3F 21
Pikehall. *Derbs* 5F 85
Pikeshill. *Hants* 2A 16
Pilford. *Dors* 2F 15
Pilgrims Hatch. *Essx* 1G 39
Pilham. *Linc* 1F 87
Pill. *N Som* 4A 34
Pillaton. *Corn* 2H 7
Pillaton. *Staf* 4D 72
Pillerton Hersey. *Warw* 1B 50
Pillerton Priors. *Warw* 1A 50
Pilleth. *Powy* 4E 59
Pilley. *Hants* 3B 16
Pilley. *S Yor* 4D 92
Pillgwenlly. *Newp* 3G 33
Pilling. *Lanc* 5D 96
Pilling Lane. *Lanc* 5C 96
Pillowell. *Glos* 5B 48
Pill, The. *Mon* 3H 33
Pillwell. *Dors* 1C 14
Pilning. *S Glo* 3A 34
Pilsbury. *Derbs* 4F 85
Pilsdon. *Dors* 3H 13
Pilsgate. *Pet* 5H 75
Pilsley. *Derbs* 3G 85 (nr. Bakewell)
Pilsley. *Derbs* 4B 86 (nr. Clay Cross)
Pilson Green. *Norf* 4F 79
Piltdown. *E Sus* 3F 27
Pilton. *Edin* 2F 129
Pilton. *Nptn* 2H 63
Pilton. *Rut* 5G 75
Pilton. *Som* 2A 22
Pilton Green. *Swan* 4D 30
Pimperne. *Dors* 2E 15
Pinchbeck. *Linc* 3B 76
Pinchbeck Bars. *Linc* 3A 76
Pinchbeck West. *Linc* 3B 76
Pinfold. *Lanc* 3B 90
Pinford End. *Suff* 5H 65
Pinged. *Carm* 5E 45
Pinhoe. *Devn* 3C 12
Pinkerton. *E Lot* 2D 130
Pinkneys Green. *Wind* 3G 37
Pinley. *W Mid* 3A 62
Pinley Green. *Warw* 4G 61
Pinmill. *Suff* 2F 55
Pinmore. *S Ayr* 5B 116
**Pinner**. *G Lon* 2C 38
Pins Green. *Worc* 1C 48
Pinsley Green. *Ches E* 1H 71
Pinvin. *Worc* 1E 49
Pinwherry. *S Ayr* 1G 109
Pinxton. *Derbs* 5B 86
Pipe and Lyde. *Here* 1A 48
Pipe Aston. *Here* 3G 59
Pipe Gate. *Shrp* 1B 72
Pipehill. *Staf* 5E 73
Piperhill. *High* 3C 158
Pipe Ridware. *Staf* 4E 73
Pipers Pool. *Corn* 4C 10
Pipewell. *Nptn* 2F 63
Pippacott. *Devn* 3F 19
Pipton. *Powy* 2E 47
Pirbright. *Surr* 5A 38
Pirnmill. *N Ayr* 5G 125
Pirton. *Herts* 2B 52
Pirton. *Worc* 1D 49
Pisgah. *Stir* 3G 135
Pishill. *Oxon* 3F 37
Pistyll. *Gwyn* 1C 68
Pitagowan. *Per* 2F 143
Pitcairn. *Per* 3F 143
Pitcairngreen. *Per* 1C 136
Pitcalnie. *High* 1C 158
Pitcaple. *Abers* 1E 152
Pitchcombe. *Glos* 5D 48
Pitchcott. *Buck* 3F 51
Pitchford. *Shrp* 5H 71
Pitch Green. *Buck* 5F 51
Pitch Place. *Surr* 5A 38
Pitcombe. *Som* 3B 22
Pitcox. *E Lot* 2C 130
Pitcur. *Per* 5B 144
Pitfichie. *Abers* 2D 152
Pitgrudy. *High* 4E 165
Pitkennedy. *Ang* 3E 145
Pitlessie. *Fife* 3F 137
Pitlochry. *Per* 3G 143
Pitmachie. *Abers* 1D 152
Pitmaduthy. *High* 1B 158
Pitmedden. *Abers* 1F 153
Pitminster. *Som* 1F 13
Pitnacree. *Per* 3G 143
Pitney. *Som* 4H 21
Pitroddie. *Per* 1E 136
Pitscottie. *Fife* 2G 137
Pitsea. *Essx* 2B 40
Pitsford. *Nptn* 4E 63
Pitsford Hill. *Som* 3E 20
Pitsmoor. *S Yor* 2A 86
Pitstone. *Buck* 4H 51
Pitt. *Hants* 4C 24
Pitt Court. *Glos* 2C 34
Pittentrail. *High* 3E 164
Pittenweem. *Fife* 3H 137
Pittington. *Dur* 5G 115
Pitton. *Swan* 4D 30
Pitton. *Wilts* 3H 23
Pittswood. *Kent* 1H 27
Pittulie. *Abers* 2G 161
Pittville. *Glos* 3E 49
Pitversie. *Per* 2D 136
Pityme. *Corn* 1D 6
Pity Me. *Dur* 5F 115
Pixey Green. *Suff* 3E 67
Pixley. *Here* 2B 48
Place Newton. *N Yor* 2C 100
Plaidy. *Abers* 3E 161
Plaidy. *Corn* 3G 7
Plain Dealings. *Pemb* 3E 43
Plains. *N Lan* 3A 128
Plainsfield. *Som* 3E 21
Plaish. *Shrp* 1H 59
Plaistow. *Here* 2B 48
Plaistow. *W Sus* 2B 26
Plaitford. *Wilts* 1A 16
Plastow Green. *Hants* 5D 36
Plas yn Cefn. *Den* 3C 82
Platt Bridge. *G Man* 4E 90
Platt Lane. *Shrp* 2H 71
Platts Common. *S Yor* 4D 92
Platt's Heath. *Kent* 5C 40
Platt, The. *E Sus* 2G 27
Plawsworth. *Dur* 5F 115
Plaxtol. *Kent* 5H 39
Playden. *E Sus* 3D 28
Playford. *Suff* 1F 55
Play Hatch. *Oxon* 4F 37
Playing Place. *Corn* 4C 6
Playley Green. *Glos* 2C 48
Plealey. *Shrp* 5G 71
Plean. *Stir* 1B 128
Pleasington. *Bkbn* 2E 91
Pleasley. *Derbs* 4C 86
Pledgdon Green. *Essx* 3F 53
Plenmeller. *Nmbd* 3A 114
Pleshey. *Essx* 4G 53
Plockton. *High* 5H 155
Plocrapol. *W Isl* 8D 171
Ploughfield. *Here* 1G 47
Plowden. *Shrp* 2F 59
Ploxgreen. *Shrp* 5F 71
Pluckley. *Kent* 1D 28
Plucks Gutter. *Kent* 4G 41
Plumbland. *Cumb* 1C 102
Plumbridge. *Derr* 7A 174
Plumgarths. *Cumb* 5F 103
Plumley. *Ches E* 3B 84
Plummers Plain. *W Sus* 3D 26
Plumpton. *Cumb* 1F 103
Plumpton. *E Sus* 4E 27
Plumpton. *Nptn* 1D 50
Plumpton Foot. *Cumb* 1F 103
Plumpton Green. *E Sus* 4E 27
Plumpton Head. *Cumb* 1G 103
Plumstead. *G Lon* 3F 39
Plumstead. *Norf* 2D 78
Plumtree. *Notts* 2D 74
Plumtree Park. *Notts* 2D 74
Plungar. *Leics* 2E 75
Plush. *Dors* 2C 14
Plushabridge. *Corn* 5D 10
Plwmp. *Cdgn* 5C 56
**Plymouth**. *Plym* 3A 8 & 201
Plympton. *Plym* 3B 8
Plymstock. *Plym* 3B 8
Plymtree. *Devn* 2D 12
Pockley. *N Yor* 1A 100
Pocklington. *E Yor* 5C 100
Pode Hole. *Linc* 3B 76
Podimore. *Som* 4A 22
Podington. *Bed* 4G 63
Podmore. *Staf* 2B 72
Poffley End. *Oxon* 4B 50
Point Clear. *Essx* 4D 54
Pointon. *Linc* 2A 76
Pokesdown. *Bour* 3G 15
Polbae. *Dum* 2H 109
Polbain. *High* 3E 163
Polbathic. *Corn* 3H 7
Polbeth. *W Lot* 3D 128
Polbrock. *Corn* 2E 6
Polchar. *High* 3C 150
Polebrook. *Nptn* 2H 63
Pole Elm. *Worc* 1D 48
Polegate. *E Sus* 5G 27
Pole Moor. *W Yor* 3A 92
Poles. *High* 4E 165
Polesworth. *Warw* 5G 73
Polglass. *High* 3E 163
Polgooth. *Corn* 3D 6
Poling. *W Sus* 5B 26
Poling Corner. *W Sus* 5B 26
Polio. *High* 1B 158
Polkerris. *Corn* 3E 7
Polla. *High* 3D 166
Pollard Street. *Norf* 2F 79
Pollicott. *Buck* 4F 51
Pollington. *E Yor* 3G 93
Polloch. *High* 2B 140
Pollok. *Glas* 3G 127
Pollokshaws. *Glas* 3G 127
Pollokshields. *Glas* 3G 127
Polmaily. *High* 5G 157
Polmassick. *Corn* 4D 6
**Polmont**. *Falk* 2C 128
Polnessan. *E Ayr* 3D 116
Polnish. *High* 5F 147
Polperro. *Corn* 3G 7
Polruan. *Corn* 3F 7
Polscoe. *Corn* 2F 7
Polsham. *Som* 2A 22
Polskeoch. *Dum* 4F 117
Polstead. *Suff* 2C 54
Polstead Heath. *Suff* 1C 54
Poltesco. *Corn* 5E 5
Poltimore. *Devn* 3C 12
Polton. *Midl* 3F 129
Polwarth. *Bord* 4D 130
Polyphant. *Corn* 4C 10
Polzeath. *Corn* 1D 6
Pomeroy. *M Ulst* 2A 178
Ponde. *Powy* 2E 46
Pondersbridge. *Cambs* 1B 64
Ponders End. *G Lon* 1E 39
Pond Street. *Essx* 2E 53
Pondtail. *Hants* 1G 25
Ponsanooth. *Corn* 5B 6
Ponsongath. *Corn* 5E 5
Ponsworthy. *Devn* 5H 11
Pontamman. *Carm* 4G 45
Pontantwn. *Carm* 4E 45
**Pontardawe**. *Neat* 5H 45
Pontarddulais. *Swan* 5F 45
Pontarfynach. *Cdgn* 3G 57
Pont-ar-gothi. *Carm* 3F 45
Pont ar Hydfer. *Powy* 3B 46
Pontarllechau. *Carm* 3H 45
Pontarsais. *Carm* 3E 45
Pontblyddyn. *Flin* 4E 83
Pontbren Llwyd. *Rhon* 5C 46
Pont-Cyfyng. *Cnwy* 5G 81
Pontdolgoch. *Powy* 1C 58
**Pontefract**. *W Yor* 2E 93
**Ponteland**. *Nmbd* 2E 115
Ponterwyd. *Cdgn* 2G 57
Pontesbury. *Shrp* 5G 71
Pontesford. *Shrp* 5G 71
Pontfadog. *Wrex* 2E 71
Pontfaen. *Pemb* 1E 43
Pont-faen. *Powy* 2C 46
Pont-Faen. *Shrp* 2E 71
Pontgarreg. *Cdgn* 5C 56
Pont-Henri. *Carm* 5E 45
Ponthir. *Torf* 2G 33
Ponthirwaun. *Cdgn* 1C 44
Pont-iets. *Carm* 5E 45
Pontllanfraith. *Cphy* 2E 33
Pontlliw. *Swan* 5G 45
Pont Llogel. *Powy* 4C 70
Pontllyfni. *Gwyn* 5D 80
Pontlottyn. *Cphy* 5E 46
Pontneddfechan. *Neat* 5C 46
Pont-newydd. *Carm* 5E 45
Pont-newydd. *Flin* 4D 82
Pontnewydd. *Torf* 2F 33
Ponton. *Shet* 6E 173
Pont Pen-y-benglog. *Gwyn* 4F 81
Pontrhydfendigaid. *Cdgn* 4G 57
Pont Rhyd-y-cyff. *B'end* 3B 32
Pontrhydyfen. *Neat* 2A 32
Pont-rhyd-y-groes. *Cdgn* 3G 57
Pontrhydyrun. *Torf* 2F 33
Pont-Rhythallt. *Gwyn* 4E 81
Pontrilas. *Here* 3G 47
Pontrilas Road. *Here* 3G 47
Pontrobert. *Powy* 4D 70
Pont-rug. *Gwyn* 4E 81
Ponts Green. *E Sus* 4A 28
Pontshill. *Here* 3B 48
Pont-Sian. *Cdgn* 1E 45
Pontsticill. *Mer T* 4D 46
Pont-Walby. *Neat* 5B 46
Pontwelly. *Carm* 2E 45
Pontwgan. *Cnwy* 3G 81
Pontyates. *Carm* 5E 45
Pontyberem. *Carm* 4F 45
Pontybodkin. *Flin* 5E 83
Pontyclun. *Rhon* 3D 32
Pontycymer. *B'end* 2C 32
Pontyglazier. *Pemb* 1F 43
Pontygwaith. *Rhon* 2D 32
Pont-y-pant. *Cnwy* 5G 81
**Pontypool**. *Torf* 2F 33
**Pontypridd**. *Rhon* 3D 32
**Pontypwl**. *Torf* 2F 33
Pontywaun. *Cphy* 2F 33
Pooksgreen. *Hants* 1B 16
Pool. *Corn* 4A 6
Pool. *W Yor* 5E 99
Poole. *N Yor* 2E 93
**Poole**. *Pool* 3F 15 & 204
Poole. *Som* 4E 21
Poole Keynes. *Glos* 2E 35
Poolend. *Staf* 5D 84
Poolewe. *High* 5C 162
Pooley Bridge. *Cumb* 2F 103
Poolfold. *Staf* 5C 84
Pool Head. *Here* 5H 59
Pool Hey. *Lanc* 3B 90
Poolhill. *Glos* 3C 48
Poolmill. *Here* 3A 48
Pool o' Muckhart. *Clac* 3C 136
Pool Quay. *Powy* 4E 71
Poolsbrook. *Derbs* 3B 86
Pool Street. *Essx* 2A 54
Pootings. *Kent* 1F 27
Pope Hill. *Pemb* 3D 42
Pope's Hill. *Glos* 4B 48
Popeswood. *Brac* 5G 37
Popham. *Hants* 2D 24
**Poplar**. *G Lon* 2E 39
Popley. *Hants* 1E 25
Porchfield. *IOW* 3C 16
Porin. *High* 3F 157
Poringland. *Norf* 5E 79
Porkellis. *Corn* 5A 6
Porlock. *Som* 2B 20
Porlock Weir. *Som* 2B 20
Portachoillan. *Arg* 4F 125
Port Adhair Bheinn na Faoghla. *W Isl* 3C 170
Port Adhair Thirlodh. *Arg* 4B 138
**Portadown**. *Arm* 4E 178
Portaferry. *N Dwn* 4K 179
Port Ann. *Arg* 1H 125
Port Appin. *Arg* 4D 140
Port Asgaig. *Arg* 3C 124
Port Askaig. *Arg* 3C 124
Portavadie. *Arg* 3H 125
Portavogie. *N Dwn* 3L 179
Portballintrae. *Caus* 2F 174
Port Bannatyne. *Arg* 3B 126
Portbury. *N Som* 4A 34
Port Carlisle. *Cumb* 3D 112
Port Charlotte. *Arg* 4A 124
Portchester. *Hants* 2E 16
Port Clarence. *Stoc T* 2B 106
Port Driseach. *Arg* 2A 126
Port Dundas. *Glas* 3G 127
Port Ellen. *Arg* 5B 124
Port Elphinstone. *Abers* 1E 153
Portencalzie. *Dum* 2F 109
Portencross. *N Ayr* 5C 126
Port Erin. *IOM* 5A 108
Port Erroll. *Abers* 5H 161
Porter's Fen Corner. *Norf* 5E 77
Portesham. *Dors* 4B 14
Portessie. *Mor* 2B 160
Port e Vullen. *IOM* 2D 108
Port-Eynon. *Swan* 4D 30
Portfield. *Som* 4H 21
Portfield Gate. *Pemb* 3D 42
Portgate. *Devn* 4E 11
Port Gaverne. *Corn* 4A 10
**Port Glasgow**. *Inv* 2E 127
Portglenone. *ME Ant* 6F 175
Portgordon. *Mor* 2A 160
Portgower. *High* 2H 165
Porth. *Corn* 2C 6
Porth. *Rhon* 2D 32
Porthaethwy. *IOA* 3E 81
Porthallow. *Corn* 3G 7 (nr. Looe)
Porthallow. *Corn* 4E 5 (nr. St Keverne)
**Porthcawl**. *B'end* 4B 32
Porthceri. *V Glam* 5D 32
Porthcothan. *Corn* 1C 6
Porthcurno. *Corn* 4A 4
Port Henderson. *High* 1G 155
Porthgain. *Pemb* 1C 42
Porthgwarra. *Corn* 4A 4
Porthill. *Shrp* 4G 71
Porthkerry. *V Glam* 5D 32
Porthleven. *Corn* 4D 4
Porthllechog. *IOA* 1D 80
Porthmadog. *Gwyn* 2E 69
Porthmeor. *Corn* 3B 4
Porth Navas. *Corn* 4E 5
Portholland. *Corn* 4D 6
Porthoustock. *Corn* 4F 5
Porthtowan. *Corn* 4A 6
Porth Tywyn. *Carm* 5E 45
Porth-y-felin. *IOA* 2B 80
Porthyrhyd. *Carm* 4F 45 (nr. Carmarthen)
Porthyrhyd. *Carm* 2H 45 (nr. Llandovery)
Porth-y-waen. *Shrp* 3E 71
Portincaple. *Arg* 4B 134
Portington. *E Yor* 1A 94
Portinnisherrich. *Arg* 2G 133
Portinscale. *Cumb* 2D 102
Port Isaac. *Corn* 1D 6
**Portishead**. *N Som* 4H 33
Portknockie. *Mor* 2B 160
Port Lamont. *Arg* 2B 126
Portlethen. *Abers* 4G 153
Portlethen Village. *Abers* 4G 153
Portling. *Dum* 4F 111
Port Lion. *Pemb* 4D 43
Portloe. *Corn* 5D 6
Port Logan. *Dum* 5F 109
Portmahomack. *High* 5G 165
Portmead. *Swan* 3F 31
Portmeirion. *Gwyn* 2E 69
Portmellon. *Corn* 4E 6
Port Mholair. *W Isl* 4H 171
Port Mor. *High* 1F 139
Portmore. *Hants* 3B 16
Port Mulgrave. *N Yor* 3E 107
Portnacroish. *Arg* 4D 140
Portnahaven. *Arg* 4A 124
Portnalong. *High* 5C 154
Portnaluchaig. *High* 5E 147
Portnancon. *High* 2E 167
Port Nan Giuran. *W Isl* 4H 171
Port nan Long. *W Isl* 1D 170
Port Nis. *W Isl* 1H 171
Portobello. *Edin* 2G 129
Portobello. *W Yor* 3D 92
Port of Menteith. *Stir* 3E 135
Porton. *Wilts* 3G 23
Portormin. *High* 5D 168
Portpatrick. *Dum* 4F 109
Port Quin. *Corn* 1D 6
Port Ramsay. *Arg* 4C 140
Portreath. *Corn* 4A 6
Portree. *High* 4D 155
Port Righ. *High* 4D 155
Portrush. *Caus* 3E 174
Port St Mary. *IOM* 5B 108
Portscatho. *Corn* 5C 6
Portsea. *Port* 2E 17
Port Seton. *E Lot* 2H 129
Portskerra. *High* 2A 168
Portskewett. *Mon* 3A 34
**Portslade-by-Sea**. *Brig* 5D 26
**Portsmouth**. *Port* 2E 17 & 201
Portsmouth. *W Yor* 2H 91
Port Soderick. *IOM* 4C 108
Port Solent. *Port* 2E 17
Portsonachan. *Arg* 1H 133
Portsoy. *Abers* 2C 160
Portstewart. *Caus* 3E 174
Port Sunlight. *Mers* 2F 83
Portswood. *Sotn* 1C 16
**Port Talbot**. *Neat* 3A 32
Porttannachy. *Mor* 2A 160
Port Tennant. *Swan* 3F 31
Portuairk. *High* 2F 139
Portway. *Here* 1H 47
Portway. *Worc* 3E 61
Port Wemyss. *Arg* 4A 124
Port William. *Dum* 5A 110
Portwrinkle. *Corn* 3H 7
Poslingford. *Suff* 1A 54
Postbridge. *Devn* 5G 11
Postcombe. *Oxon* 2F 37
Post Green. *Dors* 3E 15
Postling. *Kent* 2F 29
Postlip. *Glos* 3F 49
Post-Mawr. *Cdgn* 5D 56
Postwick. *Norf* 5E 79
Potarch. *Abers* 4D 152
Potsgrove. *C Beds* 3H 51
Potten End. *Herts* 5A 52
Potter Brompton. *N Yor* 2D 101
Pottergate Street. *Norf* 1D 66
Potterhanworth. *Linc* 4H 87
Potterhanworth Booths. *Linc* 4H 87
Potter Heigham. *Norf* 4G 79
Potter Hill. *Leics* 3E 75
**Potteries, The**. *Stoke* 1C 72
Potterne. *Wilts* 1E 23
Potterne Wick. *Wilts* 1F 23
Potternewton. *W Yor* 1D 92
**Potters Bar**. *Herts* 5C 52
Potters Brook. *Lanc* 4D 97
Potter's Cross. *Staf* 2C 60
Potters Crouch. *Herts* 5B 52
Potter Somersal. *Derbs* 2F 73
Potterspury. *Nptn* 1F 51
Potter Street. *Essx* 5E 53
Potterton. *Abers* 2G 153
Potthorpe. *Norf* 3B 78
Pottle Street. *Wilts* 2D 22
Potto. *N Yor* 4B 106
Potton. *C Beds* 1C 52
Pott Row. *Norf* 3G 77
Pott Shrigley. *Ches E* 3D 84
Poughill. *Corn* 2C 10
Poughill. *Devn* 2B 12
Poulner. *Hants* 2G 15
Poulshot. *Wilts* 1E 23
Poulton. *Glos* 5G 49
**Poulton-le-Fylde**. *Lanc* 1B 90
Pound Bank. *Worc* 3B 60
Poundbury. *Dors* 3B 14
Poundfield. *E Sus* 2G 27
Poundgate. *E Sus* 3F 27
Pound Green. *E Sus* 3G 27
Pound Green. *Suff* 5G 65
Pound Hill. *W Sus* 2D 27
Poundland. *S Ayr* 1G 109
Poundon. *Buck* 3E 51
Poundsgate. *Devn* 5H 11
Poundstock. *Corn* 3C 10
Pound Street. *Hants* 5C 36
Pounsley. *E Sus* 3G 27
Powburn. *Nmbd* 3E 121
Powderham. *Devn* 4C 12
Powerstock. *Dors* 3A 14
Powfoot. *Dum* 3C 112
Powick. *Worc* 5C 60
Powmill. *Per* 4C 136
Poxwell. *Dors* 4C 14
Poyle. *Slo* 3B 38
Poynings. *W Sus* 4D 26
Poyntington. *Dors* 4B 22
**Poynton**. *Ches E* 2D 84
Poynton. *Telf* 4H 71
Poynton Green. *Telf* 4H 71
Poyntz Pass. *Arm* 6E 178
Poystreet Green. *Suff* 5B 66
Praa Sands. *Corn* 4C 4
Pratt's Bottom. *G Lon* 4F 39
Praze-an-Beeble. *Corn* 3D 4
Prees. *Shrp* 2H 71
Preesall. *Lanc* 5C 96
Preesall Park. *Lanc* 5C 96
Prees Green. *Shrp* 2H 71
Prees Higher Heath. *Shrp* 2H 71
Prendergast. *Pemb* 3D 42
Prendwick. *Nmbd* 3E 121
Pren-gwyn. *Cdgn* 1E 45
Prenteg. *Gwyn* 1E 69
Prenton. *Mers* 2F 83
**Prescot**. *Mers* 1G 83
Prescott. *Devn* 1D 12
Prescott. *Shrp* 3G 71
Preshute. *Wilts* 5G 35
Pressen. *Nmbd* 1C 120
**Prestatyn**. *Den* 2C 82
Prestbury. *Ches E* 3D 84
Prestbury. *Glos* 3E 49
Presteigne. *Powy* 4F 59
Presthope. *Shrp* 1H 59
Prestleigh. *Som* 2B 22
Preston. *Brig* 5E 27
Preston. *Devn* 5B 12
Preston. *Dors* 4C 14
Preston. *E Lot* 2B 130 (nr. East Linton)
Preston. *E Lot* 2G 129 (nr. Prestonpans)
Preston. *E Yor* 1E 95
Preston. *Glos* 5F 49
Preston. *Herts* 3B 52
Preston. *Kent* 4G 41 (nr. Canterbury)
Preston. *Kent* 4E 41 (nr. Faversham)
**Preston**. *Lanc* 2D 90 & 201
Preston. *Nmbd* 2F 121
Preston. *Rut* 5F 75
Preston. *Bord* 4D 130
Preston. *Shrp* 4H 71
Preston. *Suff* 5B 66
Preston. *Wilts* 4A 36 (nr. Aldbourne)
Preston. *Wilts* 4F 35 (nr. Lyneham)
Preston Bagot. *Warw* 4F 61
Preston Bissett. *Buck* 3E 51
Preston Bowyer. *Som* 4E 21
Preston Brockhurst. *Shrp* 3H 71
Preston Brook. *Hal* 2H 83
Preston Candover. *Hants* 2E 24
Preston Capes. *Nptn* 5C 62
Preston Cross. *Glos* 2B 48
Preston Gubbals. *Shrp* 4G 71
Preston-le-Skerne. *Dur* 2A 106
Preston Marsh. *Here* 1A 48
Prestonmill. *Dum* 4A 112
Preston on Stour. *Warw* 1H 49
Preston on the Hill. *Hal* 2H 83
Preston on Wye. *Here* 1G 47
Prestonpans. *E Lot* 2G 129
Preston Plucknett. *Som* 1A 14
Preston-under-Scar. *N Yor* 5D 104
Preston upon the Weald Moors. *Telf* 4A 72
Preston Wynne. *Here* 1A 48
**Prestwich**. *G Man* 4G 91
Prestwick. *Nmbd* 2E 115
**Prestwick**. *S Ayr* 2C 116
Prestwold. *Leics* 3C 74
Prestwood. *Buck* 5G 51
Prestwood. *Staf* 1F 73
Price Town. *B'end* 2C 32
Prickwillow. *Cambs* 2E 65
Priddy. *Som* 1A 22
Priestcliffe. *Derbs* 3F 85
Priesthill. *Glas* 3G 127
Priest Hutton. *Lanc* 2E 97
Priestland. *E Ayr* 1E 117
Priest Weston. *Shrp* 1E 59
Priestwood. *Brac* 4G 37
Priestwood. *Kent* 4A 40
Primethorpe. *Leics* 1C 62
Primrose Green. *Norf* 4C 78
Primrose Hill. *Glos* 5B 48
Primrose Hill. *Lanc* 4B 90
Primrose Valley. *N Yor* 2F 101
Primsidemill. *Bord* 2C 120
Princes Gate. *Pemb* 3F 43
Princes Risborough. *Buck* 5G 51
Princethorpe. *Warw* 3B 62
Princetown. *Devn* 5F 11
Prinsted. *W Sus* 2F 17
Prion. *Den* 4C 82
Prior Muir. *Fife* 2H 137
Prior's Frome. *Here* 2A 48
Priors Halton. *Shrp* 3G 59
Priors Hardwick. *Warw* 5B 62
Priorslee. *Telf* 4B 72
Priors Marston. *Warw* 5B 62
Prior's Norton. *Glos* 3D 48
Priory, The. *W Ber* 5B 36
Priory Wood. *Here* 1F 47
Priston. *Bath* 5B 34
Pristow Green. *Norf* 2D 66
Prittlewell. *S'end* 2C 40
Privett. *Hants* 4E 25
Prixford. *Devn* 3F 19
Probus. *Corn* 4C 6
Prospect. *Cumb* 5C 112
Prospect Village. *Staf* 4E 73
Provanmill. *Glas* 3H 127
**Prudhoe**. *Nmbd* 3D 115
Publow. *Bath* 5B 34
Puckeridge. *Herts* 3D 53
Puckington. *Som* 1G 13
Pucklechurch. *S Glo* 4B 34
Puckrup. *Glos* 2D 49
Puddinglake. *Ches W* 4B 84
Puddington. *Ches W* 3F 83
Puddington. *Devn* 1B 12
Puddlebrook. *Glos* 4B 48
Puddledock. *Norf* 1C 66
Puddletown. *Dors* 3C 14
Pudleston. *Here* 5H 59
**Pudsey**. *W Yor* 1C 92
Pulborough. *W Sus* 4B 26
Puleston. *Telf* 3B 72
Pulford. *Ches W* 5F 83
Pulham. *Dors* 2C 14
Pulham Market. *Norf* 2D 66
Pulham St Mary. *Norf* 2E 66
Pulley. *Shrp* 5G 71
Pulloxhill. *C Beds* 2A 52
Pulpit Hill. *Arg* 1F 133
Pulverbatch. *Shrp* 5G 71
Pumpherston. *W Lot* 3D 128
Pumsaint. *Carm* 1G 45
Puncheston. *Pemb* 2E 43
Puncknowle. *Dors* 4A 14
Punnett's Town. *E Sus* 3H 27
Purbrook. *Hants* 2E 17
Purfleet. *Thur* 3G 39
Puriton. *Som* 2G 21
Purleigh. *Essx* 5B 54
**Purley**. *G Lon* 4E 39
Purley on Thames. *W Ber* 4E 37
Purlogue. *Shrp* 3E 59
Purl's Bridge. *Cambs* 2D 65
Purse Caundle. *Dors* 1B 14
Purslow. *Shrp* 2F 59
Purston Jaglin. *W Yor* 3E 93
Purtington. *Som* 2G 13
Purton. *Glos* 5B 48 (nr. Lydney)
Purton. *Glos* 5B 48 (nr. Sharpness)
Purton. *Wilts* 3F 35
Purton Stoke. *Wilts* 2F 35
Pury End. *Nptn* 1F 51
Pusey. *Oxon* 2B 36
Putley. *Here* 2B 48
**Putney**. *G Lon* 3D 38
Putsborough. *Devn* 2E 19
Puttenham. *Herts* 4G 51
Puttenham. *Surr* 1A 26
Puttock End. *Essx* 1B 54
Puttock's End. *Essx* 4F 53
Puxey. *Dors* 1C 14
Puxton. *N Som* 5H 33
Pwll. *Carm* 5E 45
Pwll. *Powy* 5D 70
Pwllcrochan. *Pemb* 4D 42
Pwll-glas. *Den* 5D 82
Pwllgloyw. *Powy* 2D 46
Pwllheli. *Gwyn* 2C 68
Pwllmeyric. *Mon* 2A 34
Pwlltrap. *Carm* 3G 43
Pwll-y-glaw. *Neat* 2A 32
Pyecombe. *W Sus* 4D 27
Pye Corner. *Herts* 4E 53
Pye Corner. *Newp* 3G 33
Pye Green. *Staf* 4D 73
Pyewipe. *NE Lin* 3F 95
**Pyle**. *B'end* 3B 32
Pyle. *IOW* 5C 16
Pyle Hill. *Surr* 5A 38
Pylle. *Som* 3B 22
Pymoor. *Cambs* 2D 65
Pymore. *Dors* 3H 13
Pyrford. *Surr* 5B 38
Pyrford Village. *Surr* 5B 38
Pyrton. *Oxon* 2E 37
Pytchley. *Nptn* 3F 63
Pyworthy. *Devn* 2D 10

## Q

Quabbs. *Shrp* 2E 58
Quadring. *Linc* 2B 76
Quadring Eaudike. *Linc* 2B 76
Quainton. *Buck* 3F 51
Quaking Houses. *Dur* 4E 115
Quarley. *Hants* 2A 24
Quarndon. *Derbs* 1H 73
Quarrendon. *Buck* 4G 51
Quarrier's Village. *Inv* 3E 127
Quarrington. *Linc* 1H 75
Quarrington Hill. *Dur* 1A 106
Quarry Bank. *W Mid* 2D 60
Quarry, The. *Glos* 2C 34
Quarrywood. *Mor* 2F 159
Quartalehouse. *Abers* 4G 161
Quarter. *N Ayr* 3C 126
Quarter. *S Lan* 4A 128
Quatford. *Shrp* 1B 60
Quatt. *Shrp* 2B 60
Quebec. *Dur* 5E 115
Quedgeley. *Glos* 4D 48
Queen Adelaide. *Cambs* 2E 65
Queenborough. *Kent* 3D 40
Queen Camel. *Som* 4A 22
Queen Charlton. *Bath* 5B 34
Queen Dart. *Devn* 1B 12
Queenhill. *Worc* 2D 48
Queen Oak. *Dors* 3C 22
Queensbury. *W Yor* 1B 92
Queensferry. *Flin* 4F 83
Queenstown. *Bkpl* 1B 90
Queen Street. *Kent* 1A 28
Queenzieburn. *N Lan* 2H 127
Quemerford. *Wilts* 5F 35
Quendale. *Shet* 10E 173
Quendon. *Essx* 2F 53
Queniborough. *Leics* 4D 74
Quenington. *Glos* 5G 49
Quernmore. *Lanc* 3E 97
Quethiock. *Corn* 2H 7
Quholm. *Orkn* 6B 172
Quick's Green. *W Ber* 4D 36
Quidenham. *Norf* 2C 66
Quidhampton. *Hants* 1D 24
Quidhampton. *Wilts* 3G 23
Quilquox. *Abers* 5G 161
Quina Brook. *Shrp* 2H 71
Quindry. *Orkn* 8D 172
Quine's Hill. *IOM* 4C 108
Quinton. *Nptn* 5E 63
Quinton. *W Mid* 2D 61
Quintrell Downs. *Corn* 2C 6
Quixhill. *Staf* 1F 73
Quoditch. *Devn* 3E 11
Quorn. *Leics* 4C 74
Quorndon. *Leics* 4C 74
Quothquan. *S Lan* 1B 118
Quoyloo. *Orkn* 5B 172
Quoyness. *Orkn* 7B 172
Quoys. *Shet* 5F 173 (on Mainland)
Quoys. *Shet* 1H 173 (on Unst)

## R

Rableyheath. *Herts* 4C 52
Raby. *Cumb* 4C 112
Raby. *Mers* 3F 83
Rachan Mill. *Bord* 1D 118
Rachub. *Gwyn* 4F 81
Rack End. *Oxon* 5C 50
Rackenford. *Devn* 1B 12
Rackham. *W Sus* 4B 26
Rackheath. *Norf* 4E 79
Racks. *Dum* 2B 112
Rackwick. *Orkn* 8B 172 (on Hoy)
Rackwick. *Orkn* 3D 172 (on Westray)
Radbourne. *Derbs* 2G 73
**Radcliffe**. *G Man* 4F 91
Radcliffe. *Nmbd* 4G 121
Radcliffe on Trent. *Notts* 2D 74
Radclive. *Buck* 2E 51
Radernie. *Fife* 3G 137
Radfall. *Kent* 4F 41
Radford. *Bath* 1B 22
Radford. *Nott* 1C 74
Radford. *Oxon* 3C 50
Radford. *W Mid* 2H 61
Radford. *Worc* 5E 61
Radford Semele. *Warw* 4H 61
Radipole. *Dors* 4B 14
Radlett. *Herts* 1C 38
Radley. *Oxon* 2D 36
Radnage. *Buck* 2F 37
**Radstock**. *Bath* 1B 22
Radstone. *Nptn* 1D 50
Radway. *Warw* 1B 50
Radway Green. *Ches E* 5B 84
Radwell. *Bed* 5H 63
Radwell. *Herts* 2C 52
Radwinter. *Essx* 2G 53
Radyr. *Card* 3E 33
RAF Coltishall. *Norf* 3E 79
Rafford. *Mor* 3E 159
Raffrey. *New M* 4J 179
Ragdale. *Leics* 4D 74
Ragdon. *Shrp* 1G 59
Ragged Appleshaw. *Hants* 2B 24
Raggra. *High* 4F 169
Raglan. *Mon* 5H 47
Ragnall. *Notts* 3F 87

Ryall—Shepway


Ryall. *Dors* 3H 13
Ryall. *Worc* 1D 48
Ryarsh. *Kent* 5A 40
Rychraggan. *High* 5G 157
Rydal. *Cumb* 4E 103
**Ryde**. *IOW* 3D 16
Rye. *E Sus* 3D 28
Ryecroft Gate. *Staf* 4D 84
Ryeford. *Here* 3B 48
Rye Foreign. *E Sus* 3D 28
Rye Harbour. *E Sus* 4D 28
Ryehill. *E Yor* 2F 95
Rye Street. *Worc* 2C 48
Ryhall. *Rut* 4H 75
Ryhill. *W Yor* 3D 93
Ryhope. *Tyne* 4H 115
Ryhope Colliery. *Tyne* 4H 115
Rylands. *Notts* 2C 74
Rylstone. *N Yor* 4B 98
Ryme Intrinseca. *Dors* 1A 14
Ryther. *N Yor* 1F 93
Ryton. *Glos* 2C 48
Ryton. *N Yor* 2B 100
Ryton. *Shrp* 5B 72
**Ryton**. *Tyne* 3E 115
Ryton. *Warw* 2B 62
Ryton-on-Dunsmore. *Warw* 3A 62
Ryton Woodside. *Tyne* 3E 115


## S


Saasaig. *High* 3E 147
Sabden. *Lanc* 1F 91
Sacombe. *Herts* 4D 52
Sacriston. *Dur* 5F 115
Sadberge. *Darl* 3A 106
Saddell. *Arg* 2B 122
Saddington. *Leics* 1D 62
Saddle Bow. *Norf* 4F 77
Saddlescombe. *W Sus* 4D 26
**Saddleworth**. *G Man* 4H 91
Sadgill. *Cumb* 4F 103
**Saffron Walden**. *Essx* 2F 53
Sageston. *Pemb* 4E 43
Saham Hills. *Norf* 5B 78
Saham Toney. *Norf* 5A 78
Saighdinis. *W Isl* 2D 170
Saighton. *Ches W* 4G 83
Sain Dunwyd. *V Glam* 5C 32
Sain Hilari. *V Glam* 4D 32
St Abbs. *Bord* 3F 131
St Agnes. *Corn* 3B 6
**St Albans**. *Herts* 5B 52
St Allen. *Corn* 3C 6
**St Andrews**. *Fife* 2H 137
St Andrews Major. *V Glam* 4E 33
St Anne's. *Lanc* 2B 90
St Ann's. *Dum* 5C 118
St Ann's Chapel. *Corn* 5E 11
St Ann's Chapel. *Devn* 4C 8
St Anthony. *Corn* 5C 6
St Anthony-in-Meneage. *Corn* 4E 5
St Arvans. *Mon* 2A 34
**St Asaph**. *Den* 3C 82
St Athan. *V Glam* 5D 32
Sain Tathan. *V Glam* 5D 32
**St Austell**. *Corn* 3E 6
St Bartholomew's Hill. *Wilts* 4E 23
St Bees. *Cumb* 3A 102
St Blazey. *Corn* 3E 7
St Blazey Gate. *Corn* 3E 7
St Boswells. *Bord* 1A 120
St Breock. *Corn* 1D 6
St Breward. *Corn* 5A 10
St Briavels. *Glos* 5A 48
St Brides. *Pemb* 3B 42
St Brides Major. *V Glam* 4B 32
St Bride's Netherwent. *Mon* 3H 33
St Bride's-super-Ely. *V Glam* 4D 32
St Brides Wentlooge. *Newp* 3F 33
St Budeaux. *Plym* 3A 8
Saintbury. *Glos* 2G 49
St Buryan. *Corn* 4B 4
St Catherine. *Bath* 4C 34
St Catherines. *Arg* 3A 134
St Clears. *Carm* 3G 43
St Cleer. *Corn* 2G 7
St Clement. *Corn* 4C 6
St Clether. *Corn* 4C 10
St Colmac. *Arg* 3B 126
St Columb Major. *Corn* 2D 6
St Columb Minor. *Corn* 2C 6
St Columb Road. *Corn* 3D 6
St Combs. *Abers* 2H 161
St Cross. *Hants* 4C 24
St Cross South Elmham. *Suff* 2E 67
St Cyrus. *Abers* 2G 145
**St Davids**. *Pemb* 2B 42
St David's. *Per* 1B 136
St Day. *Corn* 4B 6
St Dennis. *Corn* 3D 6
St Dogmaels. *Pemb* 1B 44
St Dominick. *Corn* 2H 7
St Donat's. *V Glam* 5C 32
St Edith's Marsh. *Wilts* 5E 35
St Endellion. *Corn* 1D 6
St Enoder. *Corn* 3C 6
St Erme. *Corn* 4C 6
St Erney. *Corn* 3H 7
St Erth. *Corn* 3C 4
St Erth Praze. *Corn* 3C 4
St Ervan. *Corn* 1C 6
St Eval. *Corn* 2C 6
St Ewe. *Corn* 4D 6
St Fagans. *Card* 4E 32
St Fergus. *Abers* 3H 161
Saintfield. *New M* 4J 179
St Fillans. *Per* 1F 135
St Florence. *Pemb* 4E 43
St Gennys. *Corn* 3B 10
St George. *Cnwy* 3B 82
St George's. *N Som* 5G 33
St Georges. *V Glam* 4D 32
St George's Hill. *Surr* 4B 38
St Germans. *Corn* 3H 7
St Giles in the Wood. *Devn* 1F 11
St Giles on the Heath. *Devn* 3D 10
St Giles's Hill. *Hants* 4C 24
St Gluvias. *Corn* 5B 6
St Harmon. *Powy* 3B 58
St Helena. *Warw* 5G 73
St Helen Auckland. *Dur* 2E 105
St Helens. *Cumb* 1B 102
St Helen's. *E Sus* 4C 28
St Helens. *IOW* 4E 17
**St Helens**. *Mers* 1H 83
St Hilary. *Corn* 3C 4
St Hilary. *V Glam* 4D 32
Saint Hill. *Devn* 2D 12
Saint Hill. *W Sus* 2E 27
St Illtyd. *Blae* 5F 47
St Ippolyts. *Herts* 3B 52
St Ishmael. *Carm* 5D 44
St Ishmael's. *Pemb* 4C 42
St Issey. *Corn* 1D 6
St Ive. *Corn* 2H 7
**St Ives**. *Cambs* 3C 64
**St Ives**. *Corn* 2C 4
St Ives. *Dors* 2G 15
St James' End. *Nptn* 4E 63
St James South Elmham. *Suff* 2F 67
St Jidgey. *Corn* 2D 6
St John. *Corn* 3A 8
St John's. *IOM* 3B 108
St John's. *Worc* 5C 60
St John's Chapel. *Devn* 4F 19
St John's Chapel. *Dur* 1B 104
St John's Fen End. *Norf* 4E 77
St John's Town of Dalry. *Dum* 1D 110
St Judes. *IOM* 2C 108
St Just. *Corn* 3A 4
St Just in Roseland. *Corn* 5C 6
St Katherines. *Abers* 5E 161
St Keverne. *Corn* 4E 5
St Kew. *Corn* 5A 10
St Kew Highway. *Corn* 5A 10
St Keyne. *Corn* 2G 7
St Lawrence. *Corn* 2E 7
St Lawrence. *Essx* 5C 54
St Lawrence. *IOW* 5D 16
St Leonards. *Buck* 5H 51
St Leonards. *Dors* 2G 15
St Leonards. *E Sus* 5B 28
St Levan. *Corn* 4A 4
St Lythans. *V Glam* 4E 32
St Mabyn. *Corn* 5A 10
St Madoes. *Per* 1D 136
St Margarets. *Here* 2G 47
St Margaret's. *Herts* 4A 52 (nr. Hemel Hempstead)
St Margarets. *Herts* 4D 53 (nr. Hoddesdon)
St Margaret's. *Wilts* 5H 35
St Margaret's at Cliffe. *Kent* 1H 29
St Margaret's Hope. *Orkn* 8D 172
St Margaret South Elmham. *Suff* 2F 67
St Mark's. *IOM* 4B 108
St Martin. *Corn* 4E 5 (nr. Helston)
St Martin. *Corn* 3G 7 (nr. Looe)
St Martins. *Per* 5A 144
St Martin's. *Shrp* 2F 71
St Mary Bourne. *Hants* 1C 24
St Marychurch. *Torb* 2F 9
St Mary Church. *V Glam* 4D 32
St Mary Cray. *G Lon* 4F 39
St Mary Hill. *V Glam* 4C 32
St Mary Hoo. *Medw* 3C 40
St Mary in the Marsh. *Kent* 3E 29
St Mary's. *Orkn* 7D 172
St Mary's Bay. *Kent* 3E 29
St Marys Platt. *Kent* 5H 39
St Maughan's Green. *Mon* 4H 47
St Mawes. *Corn* 5C 6
St Mawgan. *Corn* 2C 6
St Mellion. *Corn* 2H 7
St Mellons. *Card* 3F 33
St Merryn. *Corn* 1C 6
St Mewan. *Corn* 3D 6
St Michael Caerhays. *Corn* 4D 6
St Michael Penkevil. *Corn* 4C 6
St Michaels. *Kent* 2C 28
St Michaels. *Torb* 3E 9
St Michaels. *Worc* 4H 59
St Michael's on Wyre. *Lanc* 5D 96
St Michael South Elmham. *Suff* 2F 67
St Minver. *Corn* 1D 6
St Monans. *Fife* 3H 137
St Neot. *Corn* 2F 7
**St Neots**. *Cambs* 4A 64
St Newlyn East. *Corn* 3C 6
St Nicholas. *Pemb* 1C 42
St Nicholas. *V Glam* 4D 32
St Nicholas at Wade. *Kent* 4G 41
St Nicholas South Elmham. *Suff* 2F 67
St Ninians. *Stir* 4G 135
St Olaves. *Norf* 1G 67
St Osyth. *Essx* 4E 54
St Osyth Heath. *Essx* 4E 55
St Owen's Cross. *Here* 3A 48
St Paul's Cray. *G Lon* 4F 39
St Paul's Walden. *Herts* 3B 52
St Peter's. *Kent* 4H 41
St Peter The Great. *Worc* 5C 60
St Petrox. *Pemb* 5D 42
St Pinnock. *Corn* 2G 7
St Quivox. *S Ayr* 2C 116
St Ruan. *Corn* 5E 5
St Stephen. *Corn* 3D 6
St Stephens. *Corn* 4D 10 (nr. Launceston)
St Stephens. *Corn* 3A 8 (nr. Saltash)
St Teath. *Corn* 4A 10
St Thomas. *Devn* 3C 12
St Thomas. *Swan* 3F 31
St Tudy. *Corn* 5A 10
St Twynnells. *Pemb* 5D 42
St Veep. *Corn* 3F 7
St Vigeans. *Ang* 4F 145
St Wenn. *Corn* 2D 6
St Weonards. *Here* 3H 47
St Winnolls. *Corn* 3H 7
St Winnow. *Corn* 3F 7
Salcombe. *Devn* 5D 8
Salcombe Regis. *Devn* 4E 13
Salcott. *Essx* 4C 54
**Sale**. *G Man* 1B 84
Saleby. *Linc* 3D 88
Sale Green. *Worc* 5D 60
Salehurst. *E Sus* 3B 28
Salem. *Carm* 3G 45
Salem. *Cdgn* 2F 57
Salen. *Arg* 4G 139
Salen. *High* 2A 140
Salesbury. *Lanc* 1E 91
Saleway. *Worc* 5D 60
Salford. *C Beds* 2H 51
**Salford**. *G Man* 1C 84 & **Manchester** 197
Salford. *Oxon* 3A 50
Salford Priors. *Warw* 5E 61
Salfords. *Surr* 1D 27
Salhouse. *Norf* 4F 79
Saligo. *Arg* 3A 124
Saline. *Fife* 4C 136
**Salisbury**. *Wilts* 3G 23 & 201
Salkeld Dykes. *Cumb* 1G 103
Sallachan. *High* 2D 141
Sallachy. *High* 3C 164 (nr. Lairg)
Sallachy. *High* 5B 156 (nr. Stromeferry)
Salle. *Norf* 3D 78
Salmonby. *Linc* 3C 88
Salmond's Muir. *Ang* 5E 145
Salperton. *Glos* 3F 49
Salph End. *Bed* 5H 63
Salsburgh. *N Lan* 3B 128
Salt. *Staf* 3D 72
Salta. *Cumb* 5B 112
Saltaire. *W Yor* 1B 92
**Saltash**. *Corn* 3A 8
Saltburn. *High* 2B 158
Saltburn-by-the-Sea. *Red C* 2D 106
Saltby. *Leics* 3F 75
Saltcoats. *Cumb* 5B 102
**Saltcoats**. *N Ayr* 5D 126
**Saltdean**. *Brig* 5E 27
Salt End. *E Yor* 2E 95
Salter. *Lanc* 3F 97
Salterforth. *Lanc* 5A 98
Salters Lode. *Norf* 5E 77
Salterswall. *Ches W* 4A 84
Salterton. *Wilts* 3G 23
Saltfleet. *Linc* 1D 88
Saltfleetby All Saints. *Linc* 1D 88
Saltfleetby St Clements. *Linc* 1D 88
Saltfleetby St Peter. *Linc* 2D 88
Saltford. *Bath* 5B 34
Salthouse. *Norf* 1C 78
Saltmarshe. *E Yor* 2A 94
Saltness. *Orkn* 9B 172
Saltness. *Shet* 7D 173
Saltney. *Flin* 4F 83
Salton. *N Yor* 2B 100
Saltrens. *Devn* 4E 19
Saltwick. *Nmbd* 2E 115
Saltwood. *Kent* 2F 29
Salum. *Arg* 4B 138
Salwarpe. *Worc* 4C 60
Salwayash. *Dors* 3H 13
Samalaman. *High* 1A 140
Sambourne. *Warw* 4E 61
Sambourne. *Wilts* 2D 22
Sambrook. *Telf* 3B 72
Samhia. *W Isl* 2C 170
Samlesbury. *Lanc* 1D 90
Samlesbury Bottoms. *Lanc* 2E 90
Sampford Arundel. *Som* 1E 12
Sampford Brett. *Som* 2D 20
Sampford Courtenay. *Devn* 2G 11
Sampford Peverell. *Devn* 1D 12
Sampford Spiney. *Devn* 5F 11
Samsonslane. *Orkn* 5F 172
Samuelston. *E Lot* 2A 130
Sanaigmore. *Arg* 2A 124
Sancreed. *Corn* 4B 4
Sancton. *E Yor* 1C 94
Sand. *High* 4D 162
Sand. *Shet* 7E 173
Sand. *Som* 2H 21
Sandaig. *Arg* 4A 138
Sandaig. *High* 3F 147
Sandale. *Cumb* 5D 112
Sandal Magna. *W Yor* 3D 92
Sandavore. *High* 5C 146
Sanday Airport. *Orkn* 3F 172
**Sandbach**. *Ches E* 4B 84
Sandbank. *Arg* 1C 126
Sandbanks. *Pool* 4F 15
Sandend. *Abers* 2C 160
Sanderstead. *G Lon* 4E 39
Sandfields. *Neat* 3G 31
Sandford. *Cumb* 3A 104
Sandford. *Devn* 2B 12
Sandford. *Dors* 4E 15
Sandford. *Hants* 2G 15
Sandford. *IOW* 4D 16
Sandford. *N Som* 1H 21
Sandford. *Shrp* 3F 71 (nr. Oswestry)
Sandford. *Shrp* 2H 71 (nr. Whitchurch)
Sandford. *S Lan* 5A 128
Sandfordhill. *Abers* 4H 161
Sandford-on-Thames. *Oxon* 5D 50
Sandford Orcas. *Dors* 4B 22
Sandford St Martin. *Oxon* 3C 50
Sandgate. *Kent* 2F 29
Sandgreen. *Dum* 4C 110
Sandhaven. *Abers* 2G 161
Sandhead. *Dum* 4F 109
Sandhill. *Cambs* 2E 65
Sandhills. *Dors* 1B 14
Sandhills. *Oxon* 5D 50
Sandhills. *Surr* 2A 26
Sandhoe. *Nmbd* 3C 114
Sand Hole. *E Yor* 1B 94
Sandholes. *M Ulst* 2B 178
Sandholme. *E Yor* 1B 94
Sandholme. *Linc* 2C 76
**Sandhurst**. *Brac* 5G 37
Sandhurst. *Glos* 3D 48
Sandhurst. *Kent* 3B 28
Sandhurst Cross. *Kent* 3B 28
Sandhutton. *N Yor* 1F 99 (nr. Thirsk)
Sand Hutton. *N Yor* 4A 100 (nr. York)
Sandiacre. *Derbs* 2B 74
Sandilands. *Linc* 2E 89
Sandiway. *Ches W* 3A 84
Sandleheath. *Hants* 1G 15
Sandling. *Kent* 5B 40
Sandlow Green. *Ches E* 4B 84
Sandness. *Shet* 6C 173
Sandon. *Essx* 5H 53
Sandon. *Herts* 2D 52
Sandon. *Staf* 3D 72
Sandonbank. *Staf* 3D 72
**Sandown**. *IOW* 4D 16
Sandplace. *Corn* 3G 7
Sandridge. *Herts* 4B 52
Sandringham. *Norf* 3F 77
Sandsend. *N Yor* 3F 107
Sandside. *Cumb* 2C 96
Sandsound. *Shet* 7E 173
Sands, The. *Surr* 2G 25
Sandtoft. *N Lin* 4H 93
Sandvoe. *Shet* 2E 173
Sandway. *Kent* 5C 40
Sandwich. *Kent* 5H 41
Sandwick. *Cumb* 3F 103
Sandwick. *Orkn* 6B 172 (on Mainland)
Sandwick. *Orkn* 9D 172 (on South Ronaldsay)
Sandwick. *Shet* 9F 173 (on Mainland)
Sandwick. *Shet* 5G 173 (on Whalsay)
Sandwith. *Cumb* 3A 102
Sandy. *Carm* 5E 45
Sandy. *C Beds* 1B 52
Sandy Bank. *Linc* 5B 88
Sandycroft. *Flin* 4F 83
Sandy Cross. *Here* 5A 60
Sandygate. *Devn* 5B 12
Sandygate. *IOM* 2C 108
Sandy Haven. *Pemb* 4C 42
Sandyhills. *Dum* 4F 111
Sandylands. *Lanc* 3D 96
Sandylane. *Swan* 4E 31
Sandy Lane. *Wilts* 5E 35
Sandystones. *Bord* 2H 119
Sandyway. *Here* 3H 47
Sangobeg. *High* 2E 167
Sangomore. *High* 2E 166
Sankyn's Green. *Worc* 4B 60
Sanna. *High* 2F 139
Sanndabhaig. *W Isl* 4G 171 (on Isle of Lewis)
Sanndabhaig. *W Isl* 4D 170 (on South Uist)
Sannox. *N Ayr* 5B 126
Sanquhar. *Dum* 3G 117
Santon. *Cumb* 4B 102
Santon Bridge. *Cumb* 4C 102
Santon Downham. *Suff* 2H 65
Sapcote. *Leics* 1B 62
Sapey Common. *Here* 4B 60
Sapiston. *Suff* 3B 66
Sapley. *Cambs* 3B 64
Sapperton. *Derbs* 2F 73
Sapperton. *Glos* 5E 49
Sapperton. *Linc* 2H 75
Saracen's Head. *Linc* 3C 76
Sarclet. *High* 4F 169
Sardis. *Carm* 5F 45
Sardis. *Pemb* 4D 42 (nr. Milford Haven)
Sardis. *Pemb* 4F 43 (nr. Tenby)
Sarisbury Green. *Hants* 2D 16
Sarn. *B'end* 3C 32
Sarn. *Powy* 1E 58
Sarnau. *Carm* 3E 45
Sarnau. *Cdgn* 5C 56
Sarnau. *Gwyn* 2B 70
Sarnau. *Powy* 2D 46 (nr. Brecon)
Sarnau. *Powy* 4E 71 (nr. Welshpool)
Sarn Bach. *Gwyn* 3C 68
Sarnesfield. *Here* 5F 59
Sarn Meyllteyrn. *Gwyn* 2B 68
Saron. *Carm* 4G 45 (nr. Ammanford)
Saron. *Carm* 2D 45 (nr. Newcastle Emlyn)
Saron. *Gwyn* 4E 81 (nr. Bethel)
Saron. *Gwyn* 5D 80 (nr. Bontnewydd)
Sarratt. *Herts* 1B 38
Sarre. *Kent* 4G 41
Sarsden. *Oxon* 3A 50
Satley. *Dur* 5E 115
Satron. *N Yor* 5C 104
Satterleigh. *Devn* 4G 19
Satterthwaite. *Cumb* 5E 103
Satwell. *Oxon* 3F 37
Sauchen. *Abers* 2D 152
Saucher. *Per* 5A 144
Saughall. *Ches W* 3F 83
Saughtree. *Bord* 5H 119
Saul. *Glos* 5C 48
Saul. *New M* 5K 179
Saundby. *Notts* 2E 87
Saundersfoot. *Pemb* 4F 43
Saunderton. *Buck* 5F 51
Saunderton Lee. *Buck* 2G 37
Saunton. *Devn* 3E 19
Sausthorpe. *Linc* 4C 88
Saval. *High* 3C 164
Saverley Green. *Staf* 2D 72
Sawbridge. *Warw* 4C 62
**Sawbridgeworth**. *Herts* 4E 53
Sawdon. *N Yor* 1D 100
Sawley. *Derbs* 2B 74
Sawley. *Lanc* 5G 97
Sawley. *N Yor* 3E 99
Sawston. *Cambs* 1E 53
Sawtry. *Cambs* 2A 64
Saxby. *Leics* 3F 75
Saxby. *Linc* 2H 87
Saxby All Saints. *N Lin* 3C 94
Saxelby. *Leics* 3D 74
Saxelbye. *Leics* 3D 74
Saxham Street. *Suff* 4C 66
Saxilby. *Linc* 3F 87
Saxlingham. *Norf* 2C 78
Saxlingham Green. *Norf* 1E 67
Saxlingham Nethergate. *Norf* 1E 67
Saxlingham Thorpe. *Norf* 1E 66
Saxmundham. *Suff* 4F 67
Saxondale. *Notts* 1D 74
Saxon Street. *Cambs* 5F 65
Saxtead. *Suff* 4E 67
Saxtead Green. *Suff* 4E 67
Saxthorpe. *Norf* 2D 78
Saxton. *N Yor* 1E 93
Sayers Common. *W Sus* 4D 26
Scackleton. *N Yor* 2A 100
Scadabhagh. *W Isl* 8D 171
Scaddy. *New M* 5J 179
Scaftworth. *Notts* 1D 86
Scagglethorpe. *N Yor* 2C 100
Scaitcliffe. *Lanc* 2F 91
Scaladal. *W Isl* 6D 171
Scalasaig. *Arg* 4A 132
Scalby. *E Yor* 2B 94
Scalby. *N Yor* 5H 107
Scalby Mills. *N Yor* 5H 107
Scaldwell. *Nptn* 3E 63
Scaleby. *Cumb* 3F 113
Scaleby Hill. *Cumb* 3F 113
Scale Houses. *Cumb* 5G 113
Scales. *Cumb* 2B 96 (nr. Barrow-in-Furness)
Scales. *Cumb* 2E 103 (nr. Keswick)
Scalford. *Leics* 3E 75
Scaling. *Red C* 3E 107
Scaling Dam. *Red C* 3E 107
Scalloway. *Shet* 8F 173
Scalpaigh. *W Isl* 8E 171
Scalpay House. *High* 1E 147
Scamblesby. *Linc* 3B 88
Scamodale. *High* 1C 140
Scampston. *N Yor* 2C 100
Scampton. *Linc* 3G 87
Scaniport. *High* 5A 158
Scapa. *Orkn* 7D 172
Scapegoat Hill. *W Yor* 3A 92
Scar. *Orkn* 3F 172
Scarasta. *W Isl* 8C 171
**Scarborough**. *N Yor* 1E 101
Scarcliffe. *Derbs* 4B 86
Scarcroft. *W Yor* 5F 99
Scardroy. *High* 3E 156
Scarfskerry. *High* 1E 169
Scargill. *Dur* 3D 104
Scarinish. *Arg* 4B 138
Scarisbrick. *Lanc* 3B 90
Scarning. *Norf* 4B 78
Scarrington. *Notts* 1E 75
Scarth Hill. *Lanc* 4C 90
Scartho. *NE Lin* 4F 95
Scarva. *Arm* 5E 178
Scarvister. *Shet* 7E 173
Scatness. *Shet* 10E 173
Scatwell. *High* 3F 157
Scaur. *Dum* 4F 111
Scawby. *N Lin* 4C 94
Scawby Brook. *N Lin* 4C 94
Scawsby. *S Yor* 4F 93
Scawton. *N Yor* 1H 99
Scaynes Hill. *W Sus* 3E 27
Scethrog. *Powy* 3E 46
Scholar Green. *Ches E* 5C 84
Scholes. *G Man* 4D 90
Scholes. *W Yor* 2B 92 (nr. Bradford)
Scholes. *W Yor* 4B 92 (nr. Holmfirth)
Scholes. *W Yor* 1D 93 (nr. Leeds)
Scholey Hill. *W Yor* 2D 93
School Aycliffe. *Dur* 2F 105
School Green. *Ches W* 4A 84
School Green. *Essx* 2H 53
Scissett. *W Yor* 3C 92
Scleddau. *Pemb* 1D 42
Scofton. *Notts* 2D 86
Scole. *Norf* 3D 66
Scollogstown. *New M* 6J 179
Scolpaig. *W Isl* 1C 170
Scolton. *Pemb* 2D 43
Scone. *Per* 1D 136
Sconser. *High* 5E 155
Scoonie. *Fife* 3F 137
Scopwick. *Linc* 5H 87
Scoraig. *High* 4E 163
Scorborough. *E Yor* 5E 101
Scorrier. *Corn* 4B 6
Scorriton. *Devn* 2D 8
Scorton. *Lanc* 5E 97
Scorton. *N Yor* 4F 105
Sco Ruston. *Norf* 3E 79
Scotbheinn. *W Isl* 3D 170
Scotby. *Cumb* 4F 113
**Scotch Corner**. *N Yor* 4F 105
Scotch Street. *Arm* 4D 178
Scotforth. *Lanc* 3D 97
Scot Hay. *Staf* 1C 72
Scothern. *Linc* 3H 87
Scotland End. *Oxon* 2B 50
Scotlandwell. *Per* 3D 136
Scot Lane End. *G Man* 4E 91
Scotsburn. *High* 1B 158
Scotsburn. *Mor* 2G 159
Scotsdike. *Cumb* 2E 113
Scot's Gap. *Nmbd* 1D 114
Scotstoun. *Glas* 3G 127
Scotstown. *High* 2C 140
Scotswood. *Tyne* 3F 115
Scottas. *High* 3F 147
Scotter. *Linc* 4B 94
Scotterthorpe. *Linc* 4B 94
Scottlethorpe. *Linc* 3H 75
Scotton. *Linc* 1F 87
Scotton. *N Yor* 5E 105 (nr. Catterick Garrison)
Scotton. *N Yor* 4F 99 (nr. Harrogate)
Scottow. *Norf* 3E 79
Scoulton. *Norf* 5B 78
Scounslow Green. *Staf* 3E 73
Scourie. *High* 4B 166
Scourie More. *High* 4B 166
Scousburgh. *Shet* 10E 173
Scout Green. *Cumb* 4G 103
Scouthead. *G Man* 4H 91
Scrabster. *High* 1C 168
Scrafield. *Linc* 4C 88
Scrainwood. *Nmbd* 4D 121
Scrane End. *Linc* 1C 76
Scraptoft. *Leics* 5D 74
Scratby. *Norf* 4H 79
Scrayingham. *N Yor* 3B 100
Scredington. *Linc* 1H 75
Scremby. *Linc* 4D 88
Scremerston. *Nmbd* 5G 131
Screveton. *Notts* 1E 75
Scrivelsby. *Linc* 4B 88
Scriven. *N Yor* 4F 99
Scronkey. *Lanc* 5D 96
Scrooby. *Notts* 1D 86
Scropton. *Derbs* 2F 73
Scrub Hill. *Linc* 5B 88
Scruton. *N Yor* 5F 105
Scuggate. *Cumb* 2F 113
Sculamus. *High* 1E 147
Sculcoates. *Hull* 1D 94
Sculthorpe. *Norf* 2B 78
**Scunthorpe**. *N Lin* 3B 94
Scurlage. *Swan* 4D 30
Sea. *Som* 1G 13
Seaborough. *Dors* 2H 13
Seabridge. *Staf* 1C 72
Seabrook. *Kent* 2F 29
Seaburn. *Tyne* 3H 115
Seacombe. *Mers* 1F 83
Seacroft. *Linc* 4E 89
Seacroft. *W Yor* 1D 92
Seadyke. *Linc* 2C 76
Seafield. *High* 5G 165
Seafield. *Midl* 3F 129
Seafield. *S Ayr* 2C 116
Seafield. *W Lot* 3D 128
**Seaford**. *E Sus* 5F 27
Seaforde. *New M* 5J 179
Seaforth. *Mers* 1F 83
Seagrave. *Leics* 4D 74
**Seaham**. *Dur* 5H 115
Seahouses. *Nmbd* 1G 121
Seal. *Kent* 5G 39
Sealand. *Flin* 4F 83
Seale. *Surr* 2G 25
Seamer. *N Yor* 1E 101 (nr. Scarborough)
Seamer. *N Yor* 3B 106 (nr. Stokesley)
Seamill. *N Ayr* 5D 126
Sea Mills. *Bris* 4A 34
Sea Palling. *Norf* 3G 79
Seapatrick. *Arm* 5F 178
Searby. *Linc* 4D 94
Seasalter. *Kent* 4E 41
Seascale. *Cumb* 4B 102
Seaside. *Per* 1E 137
Seater. *High* 1F 169
Seathorne. *Linc* 4E 89
Seathwaite. *Cumb* 3D 102 (nr. Buttermere)
Seathwaite. *Cumb* 5D 102 (nr. Ulpha)
Seatle. *Cumb* 1C 96
Seatoller. *Cumb* 3D 102
Seaton. *Corn* 3H 7
Seaton. *Cumb* 1B 102
Seaton. *Devn* 3F 13
Seaton. *Dur* 4G 115
Seaton. *E Yor* 5F 101
Seaton. *Nmbd* 2G 115
Seaton. *Rut* 1G 63
Seaton Burn. *Tyne* 2F 115
Seaton Carew. *Hart* 2C 106
Seaton Delaval. *Nmbd* 2G 115
Seaton Junction. *Devn* 3F 13
Seaton Ross. *E Yor* 5B 100
Seaton Sluice. *Nmbd* 2G 115
Seatown. *Abers* 2C 160
Seatown. *Dors* 3H 13
Seatown. *Mor* 2C 160 (nr. Cullen)
Seatown. *Mor* 1G 159 (nr. Lossiemouth)
Seave Green. *N Yor* 4C 106
Seaview. *IOW* 3E 17
Seaville. *Cumb* 4C 112
Seavington St Mary. *Som* 1H 13
Seavington St Michael. *Som* 1H 13
Seawick. *Essx* 4E 55
Sebastopol. *Torf* 2F 33
Sebergham. *Cumb* 5E 113
Seckington. *Warw* 5G 73
Second Coast. *High* 4D 162
Sedbergh. *Cumb* 5H 103
Sedbury. *Glos* 2A 34
Sedbusk. *N Yor* 5B 104
Sedgeberrow. *Worc* 2F 49
Sedgebrook. *Linc* 2F 75
Sedgefield. *Dur* 2A 106
Sedgeford. *Norf* 2G 77
Sedgehill. *Wilts* 4D 22
Sedgley. *W Mid* 1D 60
Sedgwick. *Cumb* 1E 97
Sedlescombe. *E Sus* 4B 28
Seend. *Wilts* 5E 35
Seend Cleeve. *Wilts* 5E 35
Seer Green. *Buck* 1A 38
Seething. *Norf* 1F 67
Sefster. *Shet* 6E 173
Sefton. *Mers* 4B 90
Sefton Park. *Mers* 2F 83
Segensworth. *Hants* 2D 16
Seggat. *Abers* 4E 161
Seghill. *Nmbd* 2F 115
Seifton. *Shrp* 2G 59
Seighford. *Staf* 3C 72
Seilebost. *W Isl* 8C 171
Seisdon. *Staf* 1C 60
Seisiadar. *W Isl* 4H 171
Selattyn. *Shrp* 2E 71
Selborne. *Hants* 3F 25
**Selby**. *N Yor* 1G 93
Selham. *W Sus* 3A 26
Selkirk. *Bord* 2G 119
Sellack. *Here* 3A 48
Sellafirth. *Shet* 2G 173
Sellick's Green. *Som* 1F 13
Sellindge. *Kent* 2F 29
Selling. *Kent* 5E 41
Sells Green. *Wilts* 5E 35
Selly Oak. *W Mid* 2E 61
Selmeston. *E Sus* 5G 27
Selsdon. *G Lon* 4E 39
Selsey. *W Sus* 3G 17
Selsfield Common. *W Sus* 2E 27
Selside. *Cumb* 5G 103
Selside. *N Yor* 2G 97
Selsley. *Glos* 5D 48
Selsted. *Kent* 1G 29
Selston. *Notts* 5B 86
Selworthy. *Som* 2C 20
Semblister. *Shet* 6E 173
Semer. *Suff* 1D 54
Semington. *Wilts* 5D 35
Semley. *Wilts* 4D 23
Sempringham. *Linc* 2A 76
Send. *Surr* 5B 38
Send Marsh. *Surr* 5B 38
Senghenydd. *Cphy* 2E 32
Sennen. *Corn* 4A 4
Sennen Cove. *Corn* 4A 4
Sennybridge. *Powy* 3C 46
Serlby. *Notts* 2D 86
Seskinore. *Ferm* 3K 177
Sessay. *N Yor* 2G 99
Setchey. *Norf* 4F 77
Setley. *Hants* 2B 16
Setter. *Shet* 3F 173
Settiscarth. *Orkn* 6C 172
Settle. *N Yor* 3H 97
Settrington. *N Yor* 2C 100
Seven Ash. *Som* 3E 21
Sevenhampton. *Glos* 3F 49
Sevenhampton. *Swin* 2H 35
**Sevenoaks**. *Kent* 5G 39
Sevenoaks Weald. *Kent* 5G 39
Seven Sisters. *Neat* 5B 46
Seven Springs. *Glos* 4E 49
Severn Beach. *S Glo* 3A 34
Severn Stoke. *Worc* 1D 48
Sevington. *Kent* 1E 29
Sewards End. *Essx* 2F 53
Sewardstone. *Essx* 1E 39
Sewell. *C Beds* 3H 51
Sewerby. *E Yor* 3G 101
Seworgan. *Corn* 5B 6
Sewstern. *Leics* 3F 75
Sgallairidh. *W Isl* 9B 170
Sgarasta Mhor. *W Isl* 8C 171
Sgiogarstaigh. *W Isl* 1H 171
Sgreadan. *Arg* 4A 132
Shabbington. *Buck* 5E 51
Shackerley. *Shrp* 5C 72
Shackerstone. *Leics* 5A 74
Shackleford. *Surr* 1A 26
Shadforth. *Dur* 5G 115
Shadingfield. *Suff* 2G 67
Shadoxhurst. *Kent* 2D 28
Shadsworth. *Bkbn* 2F 91
Shadwell. *Norf* 2B 66
Shadwell. *W Yor* 1D 92
Shaftesbury. *Dors* 4D 22
Shafton. *S Yor* 3D 93
Shafton Two Gates. *S Yor* 3D 93
Shaggs. *Dors* 4D 14
Shakesfield. *Glos* 2B 48
Shalbourne. *Wilts* 5B 36
Shalcombe. *IOW* 4B 16
Shalden. *Hants* 2E 25
Shaldon. *Devn* 5C 12
Shalfleet. *IOW* 4C 16
Shalford. *Essx* 3H 53
Shalford. *Surr* 1B 26
Shalford Green. *Essx* 3H 53
Shallowford. *Devn* 2H 19
Shallowford. *Staf* 3C 72
Shalmsford Street. *Kent* 5E 41
Shalstone. *Buck* 2E 51
Shamley Green. *Surr* 1B 26
Shandon. *Arg* 1D 126
Shandwick. *High* 1C 158
Shangton. *Leics* 1E 62
Shankhouse. *Nmbd* 2F 115
**Shanklin**. *IOW* 4D 16
Shannochie. *N Ayr* 3D 123
Shap. *Cumb* 3G 103
Shapwick. *Dors* 2E 15
Shapwick. *Som* 3H 21
Sharcott. *Wilts* 1G 23
Shardlow. *Derbs* 2B 74
Shareshill. *Staf* 5D 72
Sharlston. *W Yor* 3D 93
Sharlston Common. *W Yor* 3D 93
Sharnal Street. *Medw* 3B 40
Sharnbrook. *Bed* 5G 63
Sharneyford. *Lanc* 2G 91
Sharnford. *Leics* 1B 62
Sharnhill Green. *Dors* 2C 14
Sharoe Green. *Lanc* 1D 90
Sharow. *N Yor* 2F 99
Sharpenhoe. *C Beds* 2A 52
Sharperton. *Nmbd* 4D 120
Sharpness. *Glos* 5B 48
Sharp Street. *Norf* 3F 79
Sharpthorne. *W Sus* 2E 27
Sharrington. *Norf* 2C 78
Shatterford. *Worc* 2B 60
Shatton. *Derbs* 2F 85
Shaugh Prior. *Devn* 2B 8
Shavington. *Ches E* 5B 84
**Shaw**. *G Man* 4H 91
Shaw. *W Ber* 5C 36
Shaw. *Wilts* 5D 35
Shawbirch. *Telf* 4A 72
Shawbury. *Shrp* 3H 71
Shawell. *Leics* 2C 62
Shawford. *Hants* 4C 24
Shawforth. *Lanc* 2G 91
Shaw Green. *Lanc* 3D 90
Shawhead. *Dum* 2F 111
Shaw Mills. *N Yor* 3E 99
Shawwood. *E Ayr* 2E 117
Shearington. *Dum* 3B 112
Shearsby. *Leics* 1D 62
Shearston. *Som* 3F 21
Shebbear. *Devn* 2E 11
Shebdon. *Staf* 3B 72
Shebster. *High* 2C 168
Sheddocksley. *Aber* 3F 153
Shedfield. *Hants* 1D 16
Shedog. *N Ayr* 2D 122
Sheen. *Staf* 4F 85
Sheepbridge. *Derbs* 3A 86
Sheep Hill. *Dur* 4E 115
Sheepscar. *W Yor* 1D 92
Sheepscombe. *Glos* 4D 49
Sheepstor. *Devn* 2B 8
Sheepwash. *Devn* 2E 11
Sheepwash. *Nmbd* 1F 115
Sheepway. *N Som* 4H 33
Sheepy Magna. *Leics* 5H 73
Sheepy Parva. *Leics* 5H 73
Sheering. *Essx* 4F 53
**Sheerness**. *Kent* 3D 40
Sheerwater. *Surr* 4B 38
Sheet. *Hants* 4F 25
**Sheffield**. *S Yor* 2A 86 & 202
Sheffield Bottom. *W Ber* 5E 37
Sheffield Green. *E Sus* 3F 27
Shefford. *C Beds* 2B 52
Shefford Woodlands. *W Ber* 4B 36
Sheigra. *High* 2B 166
Sheinton. *Shrp* 5A 72
Shelderton. *Shrp* 3G 59
Sheldon. *Derbs* 4F 85
Sheldon. *Devn* 2E 12
Sheldon. *W Mid* 2F 61
Sheldwich. *Kent* 5E 40
Sheldwich Lees. *Kent* 5E 40
Shelf. *W Yor* 2B 92
Shelfanger. *Norf* 2D 66
Shelfield. *Warw* 4F 61
Shelfield. *W Mid* 5E 73
Shelford. *Notts* 1D 74
Shelford. *Warw* 2B 62
Shell. *Worc* 5D 60
Shelley. *Suff* 2D 54
Shelley. *W Yor* 3C 92
Shell Green. *Hal* 2H 83
Shellingford. *Oxon* 2B 36
Shellow Bowells. *Essx* 5G 53
Shelsley Beauchamp. *Worc* 4B 60
Shelsley Walsh. *Worc* 4B 60
Shelthorpe. *Leics* 4C 74
Shelton. *Bed* 4H 63
Shelton. *Norf* 1E 67
Shelton. *Notts* 1E 75
Shelton. *Shrp* 4G 71
Shelton Green. *Norf* 1E 67
Shelton Lock. *Derb* 2A 74
Shelve. *Shrp* 1F 59
Shelwick. *Here* 1A 48
Shelwick Green. *Here* 1A 48
Shenfield. *Essx* 1H 39
Shenington. *Oxon* 1B 50
Shenley. *Herts* 5B 52
Shenley Brook End. *Mil* 2G 51
Shenleybury. *Herts* 5B 52
Shenley Church End. *Mil* 2G 51
Shenmore. *Here* 2G 47
Shennanton. *Dum* 3A 110
Shenstone. *Staf* 5F 73
Shenstone. *Worc* 3C 60
Shenstone Woodend. *Staf* 5F 73
Shenton. *Leics* 5A 74
Shenval. *Mor* 1G 151
Shepeau Stow. *Linc* 4C 76
Shephall. *Herts* 3C 52
Shepherd's Bush. *G Lon* 2D 38
Shepherd's Gate. *Norf* 4E 77
Shepherd's Green. *Oxon* 3F 37
Shepherd's Port. *Norf* 2F 77
Shepherdswell. *Kent* 1G 29
Shepley. *W Yor* 4B 92
Sheppardstown. *High* 4D 169
Shepperdine. *S Glo* 2B 34
Shepperton. *Surr* 4B 38
Shepreth. *Cambs* 1D 53
**Shepshed**. *Leics* 4B 74
Shepton Beauchamp. *Som* 1H 13
Shepton Mallet. *Som* 2B 22
Shepton Montague. *Som* 3B 22
Shepway. *Kent* 5B 40

Spurstow—Swannington


Spurstow. Ches E 5H 83
Squires Gate. Lanc 1B 90
Sraid Ruadh. Arg 4A 138
Srannda. W Isl 9C 171
Sron an t-Sithein. High 2C 140
Sronphadruig Lodge. Per 1E 142
Sruth Mor. W Isl 2E 170
Stableford. Shrp 1B 60
Stackhouse. N Yor 3H 97
Stackpole. Pemb 5D 43
Stackpole Elidor. Pemb 5D 43
Stacksford. Norf 1C 66
Stacksteads. Lanc 2G 91
Staddiscombe. Plym 3B 8
Staddlethorpe. E Yor 2B 94
Staddon. Devn 2D 10
Stadhampton. Oxon 2E 36
Stadhlaigearraidh. W Isl 5C 170
Stafainn. High 2D 155
Staffield. Cumb 5G 113
Staffin. High 2D 155
**Stafford**. Staf 3D 72
Stafford Park. Telf 5B 72
Stagden Cross. Essx 4G 53
Stagsden. Bed 1H 51
Stag's Head. Devn 4G 19
Stainburn. Cumb 2B 102
Stainburn. N Yor 5E 99
Stainby. Linc 3G 75
Staincliffe. W Yor 2C 92
Staincross. S Yor 3D 92
Staindrop. Dur 2E 105
**Staines-upon-Thames**. Surr 3B 38
Stainfield. Linc 3H 75 (nr. Bourne)
Stainfield. Linc 3A 88 (nr. Lincoln)
Stainforth. N Yor 3H 97
Stainforth. S Yor 3G 93
Staining. Lanc 1B 90
Stainland. W Yor 3A 92
Stainsacre. N Yor 4G 107
Stainton. Cumb 4E 113 (nr. Carlisle)
Stainton. Cumb 1E 97 (nr. Kendal)
Stainton. Cumb 2F 103 (nr. Penrith)
Stainton. Dur 3D 104
Stainton. Midd 3B 106
Stainton. N Yor 5E 105
Stainton. S Yor 1C 86
Stainton by Langworth. Linc 3H 87
Staintondale. N Yor 5G 107
Stainton le Vale. Linc 1A 88
Stainton with Adgarley. Cumb 2B 96
Stair. Cumb 2D 102
Stair. E Ayr 2D 116
Stairhaven. Dum 4H 109
Staithes. N Yor 3E 107
Stakeford. Nmbd 1F 115
Stake Pool. Lanc 5D 96
Stakes. Hants 2E 17
Stalbridge. Dors 1C 14
Stalbridge Weston. Dors 1C 14
Stalham. Norf 3F 79
Stalham Green. Norf 3F 79
Stalisfield Green. Kent 5D 40
Stallen. Dors 1B 14
Stallingborough. NE Lin 3F 95
Stalling Busk. N Yor 1B 98
Stallington. Staf 2D 72
Stalmine. Lanc 5C 96
**Stalybridge**. G Man 1D 84
Stambourne. Essx 2H 53
**Stamford**. Linc 5H 75
Stamford. Nmbd 3G 121
Stamford Bridge. Ches W 4G 83
Stamford Bridge. E Yor 4B 100
Stamfordham. Nmbd 2D 115
Stamperland. E Ren 4G 127
Stanah. Lanc 5C 96
Stanborough. Herts 4C 52
Stanbridge. C Beds 3H 51
Stanbridge. Dors 2F 15
Stanbury. W Yor 1A 92
Stand. N Lan 3A 128
Standburn. Falk 2C 128
Standeford. Staf 5D 72
Standen. Kent 1C 28
Standen Street. Kent 2C 28
Standerwick. Som 1D 22
Standford. Hants 3G 25
Standford Bridge. Telf 3B 72
Standingstone. Cumb 5D 112
Standish. Glos 5D 48
**Standish**. G Man 3D 90
Standish Lower Ground. G Man 4D 90
Standlake. Oxon 5B 50
Standon. Hants 4C 24
Standon. Herts 3D 53
Standon. Staf 2C 72
Standon Green End. Herts 4D 52
Stane. N Lan 4B 128
Stanecastle. N Ayr 1C 116
Stanfield. Norf 3B 78
Stanfield. Suff 5G 65
Stanford. C Beds 1B 52
Stanford. Kent 2F 29
Stanford Bishop. Here 5A 60
Stanford Bridge. Worc 4B 60
Stanford Dingley. W Ber 4D 36
Stanford in the Vale. Oxon 2B 36
**Stanford-le-Hope**. Thur 2A 40
Stanford on Avon. Nptn 3C 62
Stanford on Soar. Notts 3C 74
Stanford on Teme. Worc 4B 60
Stanford Rivers. Essx 5F 53
Stanfree. Derbs 3B 86
Stanghow. Red C 3D 107
Stanground. Pet 1B 64
Stanhoe. Norf 2H 77
Stanhope. Dur 1C 104
Stanhope. Bord 2D 118
Stanion. Nptn 2G 63
Stanley. Derbs 1B 74
**Stanley**. Dur 4E 115
Stanley. Per 5A 144
Stanley. Shrp 2B 60
Stanley. Staf 5D 84
**Stanley**. W Yor 2D 92
Stanley Common. Derbs 1B 74
Stanley Crook. Dur 1E 105
Stanley Hill. Here 1B 48
Stanlow. Ches W 3G 83
Stanmer. Brig 5E 27
**Stanmore**. G Lon 1C 38
Stanmore. Hants 4C 24
Stanmore. W Ber 4C 36
Stannersburn. Nmbd 1A 114
Stanningfield. Suff 5A 66
Stannington. Nmbd 2F 115
Stannington. S Yor 2H 85
Stansbatch. Here 4F 59
Stanshope. Staf 5F 85
Stanstead. Suff 1B 54
Stanstead Abbotts. Herts 4D 53
Stansted. Kent 4H 39
Stansted (London) Airport. Essx 3F 53 & 205
Stansted Mountfitchet. Essx 3F 53
Stanthorne. Ches W 4A 84
Stanton. Derbs 4G 73
Stanton. Glos 2F 49
Stanton. Nmbd 5F 121
Stanton. Staf 1F 73
Stanton. Suff 3B 66
Stanton by Bridge. Derbs 3A 74
Stanton-by-Dale. Derbs 2B 74
Stanton Chare. Suff 3B 66
Stanton Drew. Bath 5A 34
Stanton Fitzwarren. Swin 2G 35
Stanton Harcourt. Oxon 5C 50
Stanton Hill. Notts 4B 86
Stanton in Peak. Derbs 4G 85
Stanton Lacy. Shrp 3G 59
Stanton Long. Shrp 1H 59
Stanton-on-the-Wolds. Notts 2D 74
Stanton Prior. Bath 5B 34
Stanton St Bernard. Wilts 5F 35
Stanton St John. Oxon 5D 50
Stanton St Quintin. Wilts 4E 35
Stanton Street. Suff 4B 66
Stanton under Bardon. Leics 4B 74
Stanton upon Hine Heath. Shrp 3H 71
Stanton Wick. Bath 5B 34
Stanwardine in the Fields. Shrp 3G 71
Stanwardine in the Wood. Shrp 3G 71
Stanway. Essx 3C 54
Stanway. Glos 2F 49
Stanwell. Surr 3B 38
Stanwell Green. Suff 3D 66
Stanwell Moor. Surr 3B 38
Stanwick. Nptn 3G 63
Stanydale. Shet 6D 173
Staoinebrig. W Isl 5C 170
Stape. N Yor 5E 107
Stapehill. Dors 2F 15
Stapeley. Ches E 1A 72
Stapenhill. Staf 3G 73
Staple. Kent 5G 41
Staple Cross. Devn 4D 20
Staplecross. E Sus 3B 28
Staplefield. W Sus 3D 27
Staple Fitzpaine. Som 1F 13
Stapleford. Cambs 5D 64
Stapleford. Herts 4D 52
Stapleford. Leics 4F 75
Stapleford. Linc 5F 87
**Stapleford**. Notts 2B 74
Stapleford. Wilts 3F 23
Stapleford Abbotts. Essx 1G 39
Stapleford Tawney. Essx 1G 39
Staplegrove. Som 4F 21
Staplehay. Som 4F 21
Staple Hill. S Glo 4B 34
Staplehurst. Kent 1B 28
Staplers. IOW 4D 16
Stapleton. Bris 4B 34
Stapleton. Cumb 2G 113
Stapleton. Here 4F 59
Stapleton. Leics 1B 62
Stapleton. N Yor 3F 105
Stapleton. Shrp 5G 71
Stapleton. Som 4H 21
Stapley. Som 1E 13
Staploe. Bed 4A 64
Staplow. Here 1B 48
Star. Fife 3F 137
Star. Pemb 1G 43
Starbeck. N Yor 4F 99
Starbotton. N Yor 2B 98
Starcross. Devn 4C 12
Stareton. Warw 3H 61
Starkholmes. Derbs 5H 85
Starling. G Man 3F 91
Starling's Green. Essx 2E 53
Starston. Norf 2E 67
Start. Devn 4E 9
Startforth. Dur 3D 104
Start Hill. Essx 3F 53
Startley. Wilts 3E 35
Stathe. Som 4G 21
Stathern. Leics 2E 75
Station Town. Dur 1B 106
Staughton Green. Cambs 4A 64
Staughton Highway. Cambs 4A 64
Staunton. Glos 3C 48 (nr. Cheltenham)
Staunton. Glos 4A 48 (nr. Monmouth)
Staunton in the Vale. Notts 1F 75
Staunton on Arrow. Here 4F 59
Staunton on Wye. Here 1G 47
Staveley. Cumb 5F 103
**Staveley**. Derbs 3B 86
Staveley. N Yor 3F 99
Staveley-in-Cartmel. Cumb 1C 96
Staverton. Devn 2D 9
Staverton. Glos 3D 49
Staverton. Nptn 4C 62
Staverton. Wilts 5D 34
Stawell. Som 3G 21
Stawley. Som 4D 20
Staxigoe. High 3F 169
Staxton. N Yor 2E 101
Staylittle. Powy 1A 58
Staynall. Lanc 5C 96
Staythorpe. Notts 5E 87
Stean. N Yor 2C 98
Stearsby. N Yor 2A 100
Steart. Som 2F 21
Stebbing. Essx 3G 53
Stebbing Green. Essx 3G 53
Stedham. W Sus 4G 25
Steel. Nmbd 4C 114
Steel Cross. E Sus 2G 27
Steelend. Fife 4C 136
Steele Road. Bord 5H 119
Steel Heath. Shrp 2H 71
Steen's Bridge. Here 5H 59
Steep. Hants 4F 25
Steep Lane. W Yor 2A 92
Steeple. Dors 4E 15
Steeple. Essx 5C 54
Steeple Ashton. Wilts 1E 23
Steeple Aston. Oxon 3C 50
Steeple Barton. Oxon 3C 50
Steeple Bumpstead. Essx 1G 53
Steeple Claydon. Buck 3E 51
Steeple Gidding. Cambs 2A 64
Steeple Langford. Wilts 3F 23
Steeple Morden. Cambs 1C 52
Steeton. W Yor 5C 98
Stein. High 3B 154
Steinmanhill. Abers 4E 161
Stelling Minnis. Kent 1F 29
Stembridge. Som 4H 21
Stemster. High 2D 169 (nr. Halkirk)
Stemster. High 2C 168 (nr. Westfield)
Stenalees. Corn 3E 6
Stenhill. Devn 1D 12
Stenhouse. Edin 2F 129
**Stenhousemuir**. Falk 1B 128
Stenigot. Linc 2B 88
Stenscholl. High 2D 155
Stenso. Orkn 5C 172
Stenson. Derbs 3H 73
Stenson Fields. Derbs 2H 73
Stenton. E Lot 2C 130
Stenwith. Linc 2F 75
Steòrnabhagh. W Isl 4G 171
Stepaside. Pemb 4F 43
Stepford. Dum 1F 111
**Stepney**. G Lon 2E 39
Steppingley. C Beds 2A 52
Stepps. N Lan 3H 127
Sterndale Moor. Derbs 4F 85
Sternfield. Suff 4F 67
Stert. Wilts 1F 23
Stetchworth. Cambs 5F 65
**Stevenage**. Herts 3C 52
**Stevenston**. N Ayr 5D 126
Stevenstone. Devn 1F 11
Steventon. Hants 2D 24
Steventon. Oxon 2C 36
Steventon End. Essx 1F 53
Stevington. Bed 5G 63
Stewartby. Bed 1A 52
Stewarton. Arg 4A 122
Stewarton. E Ayr 5F 127
Stewartstown. M Ulst 2C 178
Stewkley. Buck 3G 51
Stewkley Dean. Buck 3G 51
Stewley. Som 1G 13
Stewton. Linc 2C 88
Steyning. W Sus 4C 26
Steynton. Pemb 4D 42
Stibb. Corn 1C 10
Stibbard. Norf 3B 78
Stibb Cross. Devn 1E 11
Stibb Green. Wilts 5H 35
Stibbington. Cambs 1H 63
Stichill. Bord 1B 120
Sticker. Corn 3D 6
Stickford. Linc 4C 88
Sticklepath. Devn 3G 11
Sticklinch. Som 3A 22
Stickling Green. Essx 2E 53
Stickney. Linc 5C 88
Stiffkey. Norf 1B 78
Stifford's Bridge. Here 1C 48
Stileway. Som 2H 21
Stillingfleet. N Yor 5H 99
Stillington. N Yor 3H 99
Stillington. Stoc T 2A 106
Stilton. Cambs 2A 64
Stinchcombe. Glos 2C 34
Stinsford. Dors 3C 14
Stiperstones. Shrp 5F 71
Stirchley. Telf 5B 72
Stirchley. W Mid 2E 61
Stirling. Abers 4H 161
**Stirling**. Stir 4G 135 & 202
Stirton. N Yor 4B 98
Stisted. Essx 3A 54
Stitchcombe. Wilts 5H 35
Stithians. Corn 5B 6
Stittenham. High 1A 158
Stivichall. W Mid 3H 61
Stixwould. Linc 4A 88
Stoak. Ches W 3G 83
Stobo. Bord 1D 118
Stobo Castle. Bord 1D 118
Stoborough. Dors 4E 15
Stoborough Green. Dors 4E 15
Stobs Castle. Bord 4H 119
Stobswood. Nmbd 5G 121
Stock. Essx 1A 40
Stockbridge. Hants 3B 24
Stockbridge. W Yor 5C 98
Stockbury. Kent 4C 40
Stockcross. W Ber 5C 36
Stockdalewath. Cumb 5E 113
Stocker's Head. Kent 5D 40
Stockerston. Leics 1F 63
Stock Green. Worc 5D 61
Stocking. Here 2B 48
Stockingford. Warw 1H 61
Stocking Green. Essx 2F 53
Stocking Pelham. Herts 3E 53
Stockland. Devn 2F 13
Stockland Bristol. Som 2F 21
Stockleigh English. Devn 2B 12
Stockleigh Pomeroy. Devn 2B 12
Stockley. Wilts 5F 35
Stocklinch. Som 1G 13
**Stockport**. G Man 2C 84
**Stocksbridge**. S Yor 1G 85
Stocksfield. Nmbd 3D 114
Stocks, The. Kent 3D 28
Stockstreet. Essx 3B 54
Stockton. Here 4H 59
Stockton. Norf 1F 67
Stockton. Shrp 1B 60 (nr. Bridgnorth)
Stockton. Shrp 5E 71 (nr. Chirbury)
Stockton. Telf 4B 72
Stockton. Warw 4B 62
Stockton. Wilts 3E 23
Stockton Brook. Staf 5D 84
Stockton Cross. Here 4H 59
Stockton Heath. Warr 2A 84
**Stockton-on-Tees**. Stoc T 3B 106
Stockton on Teme. Worc 4B 60
Stockton-on-the-Forest. York 4A 100
Stockwell Heath. Staf 3E 73
Stockwood. Bris 5B 34
Stock Wood. Worc 5E 61
Stodmarsh. Kent 4G 41
Stody. Norf 2C 78
Stoer. High 1E 163
Stoford. Som 1A 14
Stoford. Wilts 3F 23
Stogumber. Som 3D 20
Stogursey. Som 2F 21
Stoke. Devn 4C 18
Stoke. Hants 1C 24 (nr. Andover)
Stoke. Hants 2F 17 (nr. South Hayling)
Stoke. Medw 3C 40
Stoke. W Mid 3A 62
Stoke Abbott. Dors 2H 13
Stoke Albany. Nptn 2F 63
Stoke Ash. Suff 3D 66
Stoke Bardolph. Notts 1D 74
Stoke Bliss. Worc 4A 60
Stoke Bruerne. Nptn 1F 51
Stoke by Clare. Suff 1H 53
Stoke-by-Nayland. Suff 2C 54
Stoke Canon. Devn 3C 12
Stoke Charity. Hants 3C 24
Stoke Climsland. Corn 5D 10
Stoke Cross. Here 5A 60
Stoke D'Abernon. Surr 5C 38
Stoke Doyle. Nptn 2H 63
Stoke Dry. Rut 1F 63
Stoke Edith. Here 1B 48
Stoke Farthing. Wilts 4F 23
Stoke Ferry. Norf 5G 77
Stoke Fleming. Devn 4E 9
Stokeford. Dors 4D 14
Stoke Gabriel. Devn 3E 9
Stoke Gifford. S Glo 4B 34
Stoke Golding. Leics 1A 62
Stoke Goldington. Mil 1G 51
Stokeham. Notts 3E 87
Stoke Hammond. Buck 3G 51
Stoke Heath. Shrp 3A 72
Stoke Holy Cross. Norf 5E 79
Stokeinteignhead. Devn 5C 12
Stoke Lacy. Here 1B 48
Stoke Lyne. Oxon 3D 50
Stoke Mandeville. Buck 4G 51
Stokenchurch. Buck 2F 37
**Stoke Newington**. G Lon 2E 39
Stokenham. Devn 4E 9
Stoke on Tern. Shrp 3A 72
**Stoke-on-Trent**. Stoke 1C 72 & 202
Stoke Orchard. Glos 3E 49
Stoke Pero. Som 2B 20
Stoke Poges. Buck 2A 38
Stoke Prior. Here 5H 59
Stoke Prior. Worc 4D 60
Stoke Rivers. Devn 3G 19
Stoke Rochford. Linc 3G 75
Stoke Row. Oxon 3E 37
Stoke St Gregory. Som 4G 21
Stoke St Mary. Som 4F 21
Stoke St Michael. Som 2B 22
Stoke St Milborough. Shrp 2H 59
Stokesay. Shrp 2G 59
Stokesby. Norf 4G 79
Stokesley. N Yor 4C 106
Stoke sub Hamdon. Som 1H 13
Stoke Talmage. Oxon 2E 37
Stoke Town. Stoke 1C 72 & 202
Stoke Trister. Som 4C 22
Stoke Wake. Dors 2C 14
Stolford. Som 2F 21
Stondon Massey. Essx 5F 53
Stone. Buck 4F 51
Stone. Glos 2B 34
Stone. Kent 3G 39
Stone. Som 3A 22
**Stone**. Staf 2D 72
Stone. Worc 3C 60
Stonea. Cambs 1D 64
Stoneacton. Shrp 1H 59
Stone Allerton. Som 1H 21
Ston Easton. Som 1B 22
Stonebridge. N Som 1G 21
Stonebridge. Surr 1C 26
Stone Bridge Corner. Pet 5B 76
Stonebroom. Derbs 5B 86
Stonebyres Holdings. S Lan 5B 128
Stone Chair. W Yor 2B 92
Stone Cross. E Sus 5H 27
Stone Cross. Kent 2G 27
Stone-edge Batch. N Som 4H 33
Stoneferry. Hull 1D 94
Stonefield. Arg 5D 140
Stonefield. S Lan 4H 127
Stonegate. E Sus 3A 28
Stonegate. N Yor 4E 107
Stonegrave. N Yor 2A 100
Stonehall. Worc 1D 49
Stonehaugh. Nmbd 2A 114
**Stonehaven**. Abers 5F 153
Stone Heath. Staf 2D 72
Stone Hill. Kent 2E 29
Stone House. Cumb 1G 97
Stonehouse. Glos 5D 48
Stonehouse. Nmbd 4H 113
Stonehouse. S Lan 5A 128
Stone in Oxney. Kent 3D 28
Stoneleigh. Warw 3H 61
Stoneley Green. Ches E 5A 84
Stonely. Cambs 4A 64
Stonepits. Worc 5E 61
Stoner Hill. Hants 4F 25
Stonesby. Leics 3F 75
Stonesfield. Oxon 4B 50
Stones Green. Essx 3E 55
Stone Street. Kent 5G 39
Stone Street. Suff 2C 54 (nr. Boxford)
Stone Street. Suff 2F 67 (nr. Halesworth)
Stonethwaite. Cumb 3D 102
Stoneyburn. W Lot 3C 128
Stoney Cross. Hants 1A 16
Stoneyford. Devn 2D 12
Stoneygate. Leic 5D 74
Stoneyhills. Essx 1D 40
Stoneykirk. Dum 4F 109
Stoney Middleton. Derbs 3G 85
Stoney Stanton. Leics 1B 62
Stoney Stoke. Som 3C 22
Stoney Stratton. Som 3B 22
Stoney Stretton. Shrp 5F 71
Stoneywood. Aber 2F 153
Stonham Aspal. Suff 5D 66
Stonnall. Staf 5E 73
Stonor. Oxon 3F 37
Stonton Wyville. Leics 1E 63
Stonybreck. Shet 1B 172
Stony Cross. Devn 4F 19
Stony Cross. Here 1C 48 (nr. Great Malvern)
Stony Cross. Here 4H 59 (nr. Leominster)
Stonyford. Lis 2G 179
Stony Houghton. Derbs 4B 86
Stony Stratford. Mil 1F 51
Stoodleigh. Devn 3G 19 (nr. Barnstaple)
Stoodleigh. Devn 1C 12 (nr. Tiverton)
Stopham. W Sus 4B 26
Stopsley. Lutn 3B 52
Stoptide. Corn 1D 6
Storeton. Mers 2F 83
Stormontfield. Per 1D 136
Stornoway. W Isl 4G 171
Stornoway Airport. W Isl 4G 171
Storridge. Here 1C 48
Storrington. W Sus 4B 26
Storrs. Cumb 5E 103
Storth. Cumb 1D 97
Storwood. E Yor 5B 100
Stotfield. Mor 1G 159
Stotfold. C Beds 2C 52
Stottesdon. Shrp 2A 60
Stoughton. Leics 5D 74
Stoughton. Surr 5A 38
Stoughton. W Sus 1G 17
Stoul. High 4F 147
Stoulton. Worc 1E 49
**Stourbridge**. W Mid 2C 60
Stourpaine. Dors 2D 14
**Stourport-on-Severn**. Worc 3C 60
Stour Provost. Dors 4C 22
Stour Row. Dors 4D 22
Stourton. Staf 2C 60
Stourton. Warw 2A 50
Stourton. W Yor 1D 92
Stourton. Wilts 3C 22
Stourton Caundle. Dors 1C 14
Stove. Orkn 4F 172
Stove. Shet 9F 173
Stoven. Suff 2G 67
Stow. Linc 2H 75 (nr. Billingborough)
Stow. Linc 2F 87 (nr. Gainsborough)
Stow. Bord 5A 130
Stow Bardolph. Norf 5F 77
Stow Bedon. Norf 1B 66
Stowbridge. Norf 5F 77
Stow cum Quy. Cambs 4E 65
Stowe. Glos 5A 48
Stowe. Shrp 3F 59
Stowe. Staf 4F 73
Stowe-by-Chartley. Staf 3E 73
Stowell. Som 4B 22
Stowey. Bath 1A 22
Stowford. Devn 2G 19 (nr. Combe Martin)
Stowford. Devn 4D 12 (nr. Exmouth)
Stowford. Devn 4E 11 (nr. Tavistock)
Stowlangtoft. Suff 4B 66
Stow Longa. Cambs 3A 64
Stow Maries. Essx 1C 40
**Stowmarket**. Suff 5C 66
Stow-on-the-Wold. Glos 3G 49
Stowting. Kent 1F 29
Stowupland. Suff 5C 66
Straad. Arg 3B 126
**Strabane**. Derr 3F 176
Strachan. Abers 4D 152
Stradbroke. Suff 3E 67
Stradishall. Suff 5G 65
Stradsett. Norf 5F 77
Stragglethorpe. Linc 5G 87
Stragglethorpe. Notts 2D 74
Straid. Ant 7K 175
Straid. ME Ant 7G 175
Straid. S Ayr 5A 116
Straight Soley. Wilts 4B 36
Straiton. Edin 3F 129
Straiton. S Ayr 4C 116
Straloch. Per 2H 143
Stramshall. Staf 2E 73
Strang. IOM 4C 108
Strangford. Here 3A 48
Strangford. New M 5K 179
Stranocum. Caus 3G 175
**Stranraer**. Dum 3F 109
Strata Florida. Cdgn 4G 57
Stratfield Mortimer. W Ber 5E 37
Stratfield Saye. Hants 5E 37
Stratfield Turgis. Hants 1E 25
Stratford. Glos 2D 49
**Stratford**. G Lon 2E 39
Stratford St Andrew. Suff 4F 67
Stratford St Mary. Suff 2D 54
Stratford sub Castle. Wilts 3G 23
Stratford Tony. Wilts 4F 23
**Stratford-upon-Avon**. Warw 5G 61 & 202
Strath. High 1G 155 (nr. Gairloch)
Strath. High 3E 169 (nr. Wick)
Strathan. High 4B 148 (nr. Fort William)
Strathan. High 1E 163 (nr. Lochinver)
Strathan. High 2F 167 (nr. Tongue)
Strathan Skerray. High 2G 167
Strathaven. S Lan 5A 128
Strathblane. Stir 2G 127
Strathcanaird. High 3F 163
Strathcarron. High 4B 156
Strathcoil. Arg 5A 140
Strathdon. Abers 2A 152
Strathkinness. Fife 2G 137
Strathmashie House. High 4H 149
Strathmiglo. Fife 2E 136
Strathmore Lodge. High 4D 168
Strathpeffer. High 3G 157
Strathrannoch. High 1F 157
Strathtay. Per 3G 143
Strathvaich Lodge. High 1F 157
Strathwhillan. N Ayr 2E 123
Strathy. High 1A 158 (nr. Invergordon)
Strathy. High 2A 168 (nr. Melvich)
Strathyre. Stir 2E 135
Stratton. Corn 2C 10
Stratton. Dors 3B 14
Stratton. Glos 5F 49
Stratton Audley. Oxon 3E 50
Stratton-on-the-Fosse. Som 1B 22
Stratton St Margaret. Swin 3G 35
Stratton St Michael. Norf 1E 66
Stratton Strawless. Norf 3E 78
Stravithie. Fife 2H 137
Straw. M Ulst 7D 174
Stream. Som 3D 20
Streat. E Sus 4E 27
**Streatham**. G Lon 3E 39
Streatley. C Beds 3A 52
Streatley. W Ber 3D 36
Street. Corn 3C 10
Street. Lanc 4E 97
Street. N Yor 4E 107
Street. Som 2G 13 (nr. Chard)
**Street**. Som 3H 21 (nr. Glastonbury)
Street Ash. Som 1F 13
Street Dinas. Shrp 2F 71
Street End. Kent 5F 41
Street End. W Sus 3G 17
Streetgate. Tyne 4F 115
Streethay. Staf 4F 73
Streethouse. W Yor 2D 93
Streetlam. N Yor 5A 106
Street Lane. Derbs 1A 74
Streetly. W Mid 1E 61
Streetly End. Cambs 1G 53
Street on the Fosse. Som 3B 22
Strefford. Shrp 2G 59
Strelley. Notts 1C 74
Strensall. York 3A 100
Strensall Camp. York 4A 100
Stretcholt. Som 2F 21
Strete. Devn 4E 9
**Stretford**. G Man 1C 84
Stretford. Here 5H 59
Strethall. Essx 2E 53
Stretham. Cambs 3E 65
Stretton. Ches W 5G 83
Stretton. Derbs 4A 86
Stretton. Rut 4G 75
Stretton. Staf 4C 72 (nr. Brewood)
Stretton. Staf 3G 73 (nr. Burton upon Trent)
Stretton. Warr 2A 84
Stretton en le Field. Leics 4H 73
Stretton Grandison. Here 1B 48
Stretton Heath. Shrp 4F 71
Stretton-on-Dunsmore. Warw 3B 62
Stretton-on-Fosse. Warw 2H 49
Stretton Sugwas. Here 1H 47
Stretton under Fosse. Warw 2B 62
Stretton Westwood. Shrp 1H 59
Strichen. Abers 3G 161
Strines. G Man 2D 84
Stringston. Som 2E 21
Strixton. Nptn 4G 63
Stroanfreggan. Dum 5F 117
Stroat. Glos 2A 34
Stromeferry. High 5A 156
Stromemore. High 5A 156
Stromness. Orkn 7B 172
Stronachie. Per 3C 136
Stronachlachar. Stir 2D 134
Stronchreggan. High 1E 141
Strone. Arg 1C 126
Strone. High 1H 149 (nr. Drumnadrochit)
Strone. High 3B 150 (nr. Kingussie)
Stronenaba. High 5E 148
Stronganess. Shet 1G 173
Stronmilchan. Arg 1A 134
Stronsay Airport. Orkn 5F 172
Strontian. High 2C 140
Strood. Kent 2C 28
**Strood**. Medw 4B 40
Strood Green. Surr 1D 26
Strood Green. W Sus 3B 26 (nr. Billingshurst)
Strood Green. W Sus 2C 26 (nr. Horsham)
Strothers Dale. Nmbd 4C 114
**Stroud**. Glos 5D 48
Stroud. Hants 4F 25
Stroud Green. Essx 1C 40
Stroxton. Linc 2G 75
Struan. High 5C 154
Struan. Per 2F 143
Struanmore. High 5C 154
Strubby. Linc 2D 88
Strugg's Hill. Linc 2B 76
Strumpshaw. Norf 5F 79
Strutherhill. S Lan 4A 128
Struy. High 5G 157
Stryd. IOA 2B 80
Stryt-issa. Wrex 1E 71
Stuartfield. Abers 4G 161
**Stubbington**. Hants 2D 16
Stubbins. Lanc 3F 91
Stubble Green. Cumb 5B 102
Stubb's Cross. Kent 2D 28
Stubbs Green. Norf 1F 67
Stubhampton. Dors 1E 15
Stubton. Linc 1F 75
Stubwood. Staf 2E 73
Stuckton. Hants 1G 15
Studham. C Beds 4A 52
Studland. Dors 4F 15
Studley. Warw 4E 61
Studley. Wilts 4E 35
Studley Roger. N Yor 2E 99
Stuntney. Cambs 3E 65
Stunts Green. E Sus 4H 27
Sturbridge. Staf 2C 72
Sturgate. Linc 2F 87
Sturmer. Essx 1G 53
Sturminster Marshall. Dors 2E 15
Sturminster Newton. Dors 1C 14
Sturry. Kent 4F 41
Sturton. N Lin 4C 94
Sturton by Stow. Linc 2F 87
Sturton le Steeple. Notts 2E 87
Stuston. Suff 3D 66
Stutton. N Yor 5G 99
Stutton. Suff 2E 55
Styal. Ches E 2C 84
Stydd. Lanc 1E 91
Styrrup. Notts 1D 86
Suainebost. W Isl 1H 171
Suardail. W Isl 4G 171
Succoth. Abers 5B 160
Succoth. Arg 3B 134
Suckley. Worc 5B 60
Suckley Knowl. Worc 5B 60
Sudborough. Nptn 2G 63
Sudbourne. Suff 5G 67
Sudbrook. Linc 1G 75
Sudbrook. Mon 3A 34
Sudbrooke. Linc 3H 87
Sudbury. Derbs 2F 73
**Sudbury**. Suff 1B 54
Sudgrove. Glos 5E 49
Suffield. Norf 2E 79
Suffield. N Yor 5G 107
Sugnall. Staf 2B 72
Sugwas Pool. Here 1H 47
Suisnish. High 5E 155
Sulaisiadar. W Isl 4H 171
Sùlaisiadar Mòr. High 4D 155
Sulby. IOM 2C 108
Sulgrave. Nptn 1D 50
Sulham. W Ber 4E 37
Sulhamstead. W Ber 5E 37
Sullington. W Sus 4B 26
Sullom. Shet 4E 173
Sully. V Glam 5E 33
Sumburgh. Shet 10F 173
Sumburgh Airport. Shet 10E 173
Summer Bridge. N Yor 3E 98
Summercourt. Corn 3C 6
Summergangs. Hull 1E 94
Summerhill. Aber 3G 153
Summerhill. Pemb 4F 43
Summer Hill. W Mid 1D 60
Summerhouse. Darl 3F 105
Summersdale. W Sus 2G 17
Summerseat. G Man 3F 91
Summit. G Man 3H 91
**Sunbury**. Surr 4C 38
Sunderland. Cumb 1C 102
Sunderland. Lanc 4D 96
**Sunderland**. Tyne 4G 115 & 202
Sunderland Bridge. Dur 1F 105
Sundon Park. Lutn 3A 52
Sundridge. Kent 5F 39
Sunk Island. E Yor 3F 95
Sunningdale. Wind 4A 38
Sunninghill. Wind 4A 38
Sunningwell. Oxon 5C 50
Sunniside. Dur 1E 105
Sunniside. Tyne 4F 115
Sunny Bank. Cumb 5D 102
Sunny Hill. Derb 2H 73
Sunnyhurst. Bkbn 2E 91
Sunnylaw. Stir 4G 135
Sunnymead. Oxon 5D 50
Sunnyside. S Yor 1B 86
Sunnyside. W Sus 2E 27
Sunton. Wilts 1H 23
**Surbiton**. G Lon 4C 38
Surby. IOM 4B 108
Surfleet. Linc 3B 76
Surfleet Seas End. Linc 3B 76
Surlingham. Norf 5F 79
Surrex. Essx 3B 54
Sustead. Norf 2D 78
Susworth. Linc 4B 94
Sutcombe. Devn 1D 10
Suton. Norf 1C 66
Sutors of Cromarty. High 2C 158
Sutterby. Linc 3C 88
Sutterton. Linc 2B 76
Sutterton Dowdyke. Linc 2B 76
Sutton. Buck 3B 38
Sutton. Cambs 3D 64
Sutton. C Beds 1C 52
Sutton. E Sus 5F 27
**Sutton**. G Lon 4D 38
Sutton. Kent 1H 29
Sutton. Norf 3F 79
Sutton. Notts 2E 75
Sutton. Oxon 5C 50
Sutton. Pemb 3D 42
Sutton. Pet 1H 63
Sutton. Shrp 2B 60 (nr. Bridgnorth)
Sutton. Shrp 2A 72 (nr. Market Drayton)
Sutton. Shrp 3F 71 (nr. Oswestry)
Sutton. Shrp 4H 71 (nr. Shrewsbury)
Sutton. Som 3B 22
Sutton. S Yor 3F 93
Sutton. Staf 3B 72
Sutton. Suff 1G 55
Sutton. W Sus 4A 26
Sutton. Worc 4A 60
Sutton Abinger. Surr 1C 26
Sutton at Hone. Kent 3G 39
Sutton Bassett. Nptn 1E 63
Sutton Benger. Wilts 4E 35
Sutton Bingham. Som 1A 14
Sutton Bonington. Notts 3C 74
Sutton Bridge. Linc 3D 76
Sutton Cheney. Leics 5B 74
**Sutton Coldfield, Royal**. W Mid 1F 61
Sutton Corner. Linc 3D 76
Sutton Courtenay. Oxon 2D 36
Sutton Crosses. Linc 3D 76
Sutton cum Lound. Notts 2D 86
Sutton Gault. Cambs 3D 64
Sutton Grange. N Yor 2E 99
Sutton Green. Surr 5B 38
Sutton Howgrave. N Yor 2F 99
**Sutton in Ashfield**. Notts 5B 86
Sutton-in-Craven. N Yor 5C 98
Sutton Ings. Hull 1E 94
Sutton in the Elms. Leics 1C 62
Sutton Lane Ends. Ches E 3D 84
Sutton Leach. Mers 1H 83
Sutton Maddock. Shrp 5B 72
Sutton Mallet. Som 3G 21
Sutton Mandeville. Wilts 4E 23
Sutton Montis. Som 4B 22
Sutton on Hull. Hull 1E 94
Sutton on Sea. Linc 2E 89
Sutton-on-the-Forest. N Yor 3H 99
Sutton on the Hill. Derbs 2G 73
Sutton on Trent. Notts 4E 87
Sutton Poyntz. Dors 4C 14
Sutton St Edmund. Linc 4C 76
Sutton St Edmund's Common. Linc 5C 76
Sutton St James. Linc 4C 76
Sutton St Michael. Here 1A 48
Sutton St Nicholas. Here 1A 48
Sutton Scarsdale. Derbs 4B 86
Sutton Scotney. Hants 3C 24
Sutton-under-Brailes. Warw 2B 50
Sutton-under-Whitestonecliffe. N Yor 1G 99
Sutton upon Derwent. E Yor 5B 100
Sutton Valence. Kent 1C 28
Sutton Veny. Wilts 2E 23
Sutton Waldron. Dors 1D 14
Sutton Weaver. Ches W 3H 83
Swaby. Linc 3C 88
**Swadlincote**. Derbs 4G 73
Swaffham. Norf 5H 77
Swaffham Bulbeck. Cambs 4E 65
Swaffham Prior. Cambs 4E 65
Swafield. Norf 2E 79
Swainby. N Yor 4B 106
Swainshill. Here 1H 47
Swainsthorpe. Norf 5E 78
Swainswick. Bath 5C 34
Swalcliffe. Oxon 2B 50
Swalecliffe. Kent 4F 41
Swallow. Linc 4E 95
Swallow Beck. Linc 4G 87
Swallowcliffe. Wilts 4E 23
Swallowfield. Wok 5F 37
Swallownest. S Yor 2B 86
Swampton. Hants 1C 24
**Swanage**. Dors 5F 15
Swanbister. Orkn 7C 172
Swanbourne. Buck 3G 51
Swanbridge. V Glam 5E 33
Swan Green. Ches W 3B 84
Swanland. E Yor 2C 94
**Swanley**. Kent 4G 39
Swanmore. Hants 1D 16
Swannington. Leics 4B 74

Torphichen—Upton St Leonards


Torphichen. *W Lot* 2C **128**
Torphins. *Abers* 3D **152**
Torpoint. *Corn* 3A **8**
**Torquay**. *Torb* 2F **9**
Torr. *Devn* 3B **8**
Torra. *Arg* 4B **124**
Torran. *High* 4E **155**
Torrance. *E Dun* 2H **127**
Torrans. *Arg* 1B **132**
Torranyard. *E Ayr* 5E **127**
Torre. *Som* 3D **20**
Torre. *Torb* 2F **9**
Torridon. *High* 3B **156**
Torrin. *High* 1D **147**
Torrisdale. *Arg* 2B **122**
Torrisdale. *High* 2G **167**
Torrish. *High* 2G **165**
Torrisholme. *Lanc* 3D **96**
Torroble. *High* 3C **164**
Torroy. *High* 4C **164**
Torry. *Aber* 3G **153**
Torryburn. *Fife* 1D **128**
Torthorwald. *Dum* 2B **112**
Tortington. *W Sus* 5B **26**
Tortworth. *S Glo* 2C **34**
Torvaig. *High* 4D **155**
Torver. *Cumb* 5D **102**
Torwood. *Falk* 1B **128**
Torworth. *Notts* 2D **86**
Toscaig. *High* 5G **155**
Toseland. *Cambs* 4B **64**
Tosside. *Lanc* 4G **97**
Tostock. *Suff* 4B **66**
Totaig. *High* 3A **154**
Totardor. *High* 5C **154**
Tote. *High* 4D **154**
Totegan. *High* 2A **168**
Tothill. *Linc* 2D **88**
Totland. *IOW* 4B **16**
Totley. *S Yor* 3H **85**
Totnell. *Dors* 2B **14**
Totnes. *Devn* 2E **9**
Toton. *Notts* 2B **74**
Totronald. *Arg* 3C **138**
Totscore. *High* 2C **154**
**Tottenham**. *G Lon* 1E **39**
Tottenhill. *Norf* 4F **77**
Tottenhill Row. *Norf* 4F **77**
Totteridge. *G Lon* 1D **38**
Totternhoe. *C Beds* 3H **51**
Tottington. *G Man* 3F **91**
**Totton**. *Hants* 1B **16**
Touchen-end. *Wind* 4G **37**
Toulvaddie. *High* 5F **165**
Towans, The. *Corn* 3C **4**
Toward. *Arg* 3C **126**
Towcester. *Nptn* 1E **51**
Towednack. *Corn* 3B **4**
Tower End. *Norf* 4F **77**
Tower Hill. *Mers* 4C **90**
Tower Hill. *W Sus* 3C **26**
Towersey. *Oxon* 5F **51**
Towie. *Abers* 2B **152**
Towiemore. *Mor* 4A **160**
Tow Law. *Dur* 1E **105**
Town End. *Cambs* 1D **64**
Town End. *Cumb* 4F **103** (nr. Ambleside)
Town End. *Cumb* 2H **103** (nr. Kirkby Thore)
Town End. *Cumb* 1D **96** (nr. Lindale)
Town End. *Cumb* 1C **96** (nr. Newby Bridge)
Town End. *Mers* 2G **83**
Townend. *W Dun* 2F **127**
Townfield. *Dur* 5C **114**
Towngate. *Cumb* 5G **113**
Towngate. *Linc* 4A **76**
Town Green. *Lanc* 4C **90**
Town Head. *Cumb* 4E **103** (nr. Grasmere)
Town Head. *Cumb* 3H **103** (nr. Great Asby)
Townhead. *Cumb* 1G **103** (nr. Lazonby)
Townhead. *Cumb* 1B **102** (nr. Maryport)
Townhead. *Cumb* 1H **103** (nr. Ousby)
Townhead. *Dum* 5D **111**
Townhead of Greenlaw. *Dum* 3E **111**
Townhill. *Fife* 1E **129**
Townhill. *Swan* 3F **31**
Townjoy. *M Ulst* 3D **178**
Town Kelloe. *Dur* 1A **106**
Town Littleworth. *E Sus* 4F **27**
Town Row. *E Sus* 2G **27**
Towns End. *Hants* 1D **24**
Townsend. *Herts* 5B **52**
Townshend. *Corn* 3C **4**
Town Street. *Suff* 2G **65**
Town, The. *IOS* 1A **4**
Town Yetholm. *Bord* 2C **120**
Towthorpe. *E Yor* 3D **100**
Towthorpe. *York* 4A **100**
Towton. *N Yor* 1E **93**
Towyn. *Cnwy* 3B **82**
Toxteth. *Mers* 2F **83**
Toynton All Saints. *Linc* 4C **88**
Toynton Fen Side. *Linc* 4C **88**
Toynton St Peter. *Linc* 4D **88**
Toy's Hill. *Kent* 5F **39**
Trabboch. *E Ayr* 2D **116**
Traboe. *Corn* 4E **5**
Tradespark. *High* 3C **158**
Tradespark. *Orkn* 7D **172**
Trafford Park. *G Man* 1B **84**
Trallong. *Powy* 3C **46**
Tranent. *E Lot* 2H **129**
Tranmere. *Mers* 2F **83**
Trantlebeg. *High* 3A **168**
Trantlemore. *High* 3A **168**
Tranwell. *Nmbd* 1E **115**
Trapp. *Carm* 4G **45**
Traquair. *Bord* 1F **119**
Trash Green. *W Ber* 5E **37**
Trawden. *Lanc* 1H **91**
Trawscoed. *Powy* 2D **46**
Trawsfynydd. *Gwyn* 2G **69**
Trawsgoed. *Cdgn* 3F **57**
Treaddow. *Here* 3A **48**
Trealaw. *Rhon* 2D **32**
Treales. *Lanc* 1C **90**
Trearddur. *IOA* 3B **80**
Treaslane. *High* 3C **154**
Treator. *Corn* 1D **6**
Trebanog. *Rhon* 2D **32**
Trebanos. *Neat* 5H **45**
Trebarber. *Corn* 2C **6**
Trebartha. *Corn* 5C **10**
Trebarwith. *Corn* 4A **10**
Trebetherick. *Corn* 1D **6**
Treborough. *Som* 3D **20**
Trebudannon. *Corn* 2C **6**
Trebullett. *Corn* 5D **10**
Treburley. *Corn* 5D **10**
Treburrick. *Corn* 1C **6**
Trebyan. *Corn* 2E **7**
Trecastle. *Powy* 3B **46**
Trecenydd. *Cphy* 3E **33**
Trecott. *Devn* 2G **11**
Trecwn. *Pemb* 1D **42**
Trecynon. *Rhon* 5C **46**
Tredaule. *Corn* 4C **10**
Tredavoe. *Corn* 4B **4**
**Tredegar**. *Blae* 5E **47**
Trederwen. *Powy* 4E **71**
Tredington. *Glos* 3E **49**
Tredington. *Warw* 1A **50**
Tredinnick. *Corn* 2F **7** (nr. Bodmin)
Tredinnick. *Corn* 3G **7** (nr. Looe)
Tredinnick. *Corn* 1D **6** (nr. Padstow)
Tredogan. *V Glam* 5D **32**
Tredomen. *Powy* 2E **46**
Tredunnock. *Mon* 2G **33**
Tredustan. *Powy* 2E **47**
Treen. *Corn* 4A **4** (nr. Land's End)
Treen. *Corn* 3B **4** (nr. St Ives)
Treeton. *S Yor* 2B **86**
Trefaldwyn. *Powy* 1E **58**
Trefasser. *Pemb* 1C **42**
Trefdraeth. *IOA* 3D **80**
Trefdraeth. *Pemb* 1E **43**
Trefecca. *Powy* 2E **47**
Trefechan. *Mer T* 5D **46**
Trefeglwys. *Powy* 1B **58**
Trefenter. *Cdgn* 4F **57**
Treffgarne. *Pemb* 2D **42**
Treffynnon. *Flin* 3D **82**
Treffynnon. *Pemb* 2C **42**
Trefil. *Blae* 4E **46**
Trefilan. *Cdgn* 5E **57**
Trefin. *Pemb* 1C **42**
Treflach. *Shrp* 3E **71**
Trefnant. *Den* 3C **82**
Trefonen. *Shrp* 3E **71**
Trefor. *Gwyn* 1C **68**
Trefor. *IOA* 2C **80**
Treforest. *Rhon* 3D **32**
Trefrew. *Corn* 4B **10**
Trefriw. *Cnwy* 4G **81**
Tref-y-Clawdd. *Powy* 3E **59**
Trefynwy. *Mon* 4A **48**
Tregada. *Corn* 4D **10**
Tregadillett. *Corn* 4C **10**
Tregare. *Mon* 4H **47**
Tregarne. *Corn* 4E **5**
Tregaron. *Cdgn* 5F **57**
Tregarth. *Gwyn* 4F **81**
Tregear. *Corn* 3C **6**
Tregeare. *Corn* 4C **10**
Tregeiriog. *Wrex* 2D **70**
Tregele. *IOA* 1C **80**
Tregeseal. *Corn* 3A **4**
Tregiskey. *Corn* 4E **6**
Tregole. *Corn* 3B **10**
Tregolwyn. *V Glam* 4C **32**
Tregonetha. *Corn* 2D **6**
Tregonhawke. *Corn* 3A **8**
Tregony. *Corn* 4D **6**
Tregoodwell. *Corn* 4B **10**
Tregorrick. *Corn* 3E **6**
Tregoss. *Corn* 2D **6**
Tregowris. *Corn* 4E **5**
Tregoyd. *Powy* 2E **47**
Tregrehan Mills. *Corn* 3E **7**
Tre-groes. *Cdgn* 1E **45**
Tregullon. *Corn* 2E **7**
Tregurrian. *Corn* 2C **6**
Tregynon. *Powy* 1C **58**
Trehafod. *Rhon* 2D **32**
Trehan. *Corn* 3A **8**
**Treharris**. *Mer T* 2D **32**
Treherbert. *Rhon* 2C **32**
Trehunist. *Corn* 2H **7**
Trekenner. *Corn* 5D **10**
Trekenning. *Corn* 2D **6**
Treknow. *Corn* 4A **10**
Trelales. *B'end* 3B **32**
Trelan. *Corn* 5E **5**
Trelash. *Corn* 3B **10**
Trelassick. *Corn* 3C **6**
Trelawnyd. *Flin* 3C **82**
Trelech. *Carm* 1G **43**
Treleddyd-fawr. *Pemb* 2B **42**
Trelewis. *Mer T* 2E **32**
Treligga. *Corn* 4A **10**
Trelights. *Corn* 1D **6**
Trelill. *Corn* 5A **10**
Trelissick. *Corn* 5C **6**
Trellech. *Mon* 5A **48**
Trelleck Grange. *Mon* 5H **47**
Trelogan. *Flin* 2D **82**
Trelystan. *Powy* 5E **71**
Tremadog. *Gwyn* 1E **69**
Tremail. *Corn* 4B **10**
Tremain. *Cdgn* 1C **44**
Tremaine. *Corn* 4C **10**
Tremar. *Corn* 2G **7**
Trematon. *Corn* 3H **7**
Tremeirchion. *Den* 3C **82**
Tremore. *Corn* 2E **6**
Tremorfa. *Card* 4F **33**
Trenance. *Corn* 2C **6** (nr. Newquay)
Trenance. *Corn* 1D **6** (nr. Padstow)
Trenarren. *Corn* 4E **7**
Trench. *Telf* 4A **72**
Trencreek. *Corn* 2C **6**
Trendeal. *Corn* 3C **6**
Trenear. *Corn* 5A **6**
Treneglos. *Corn* 4C **10**
Trenewan. *Corn* 3F **7**
Trengune. *Corn* 3B **10**
Trent. *Dors* 1A **14**
Trentham. *Stoke* 1C **72**
Trentishoe. *Devn* 2G **19**
Trentlock. *Derbs* 2B **74**
Treoes. *V Glam* 4C **32**
Treorchy. *Rhon* 2C **32**
Treorci. *Rhon* 2C **32**
Tre'r-ddol. *Cdgn* 1F **57**
Tre'r llai. *Powy* 5E **71**
Trerulefoot. *Corn* 3H **7**
Tresaith. *Cdgn* 5B **56**
Trescott. *Staf* 1C **60**
Trescowe. *Corn* 3C **4**
Tresham. *Glos* 2C **34**
Tresigin. *V Glam* 4C **32**
Tresillian. *Corn* 4C **6**
Tresimwn. *V Glam* 4D **32**
Tresinney. *Corn* 4B **10**
Treskillard. *Corn* 5A **6**
Treskinnick Cross. *Corn* 3C **10**
Tresmeer. *Corn* 4C **10**
Tresparrett. *Corn* 3B **10**
Tresparrett Posts. *Corn* 3B **10**
Tressady. *High* 3D **164**
Tressait. *Per* 2F **143**
Tresta. *Shet* 2H **173** (on Fetlar)
Tresta. *Shet* 6E **173** (on Mainland)
Treswell. *Notts* 3E **87**
Treswithian. *Corn* 3D **4**
Tre Taliesin. *Cdgn* 1F **57**
Trethomas. *Cphy* 3E **33**
Trethosa. *Corn* 3D **6**
Trethurgy. *Corn* 3E **7**
Tretio. *Pemb* 2B **42**
Tretire. *Here* 3A **48**
Tretower. *Powy* 3E **47**
Treuddyn. *Flin* 5E **83**
Trevadlock. *Corn* 5C **10**
Trevalga. *Corn* 4A **10**
Trevalyn. *Wrex* 5F **83**
Trevance. *Corn* 1D **6**
Trevanger. *Corn* 1D **6**
Trevanson. *Corn* 1D **6**
Trevarrack. *Corn* 3B **4**
Trevarren. *Corn* 2D **6**
Trevarrian. *Corn* 2C **6**
Trevarrick. *Corn* 4D **6**
Trevaughan. *Carm* 3E **45** (nr. Carmarthen)
Trevaughan. *Carm* 3F **43** (nr. Whitland)
Treveighan. *Corn* 5A **10**
Trevellas. *Corn* 3B **6**
Trevelmond. *Corn* 2G **7**
Treverva. *Corn* 5B **6**
Trevescan. *Corn* 4A **4**
Trevethin. *Torf* 5F **47**
Trevia. *Corn* 4A **10**
Trevigro. *Corn* 2H **7**
Trevilley. *Corn* 4A **4**
Treviscoe. *Corn* 3D **6**
Trevivian. *Corn* 4B **10**
Trevone. *Corn* 1C **6**
Trevor. *Wrex* 1E **71**
Trevor Uchaf. *Den* 1E **71**
Trew. *Corn* 4D **4**
Trewalder. *Corn* 4A **10**
Trewarlett. *Corn* 4D **10**
Trewarmett. *Corn* 4A **10**
Trewassa. *Corn* 4B **10**
Treween. *Corn* 4C **10**
Trewellard. *Corn* 3A **4**
Trewen. *Corn* 4C **10**
Trewennack. *Corn* 4D **5**
Trewern. *Powy* 4E **71**
Trewetha. *Corn* 5A **10**
Trewidland. *Corn* 3G **7**
Trewint. *Corn* 3B **10**
Trewithian. *Corn* 5C **6**
Trewoofe. *Corn* 4B **4**
Trewoon. *Corn* 3D **6**
Treworthal. *Corn* 5C **6**
Trewyddel. *Pemb* 1B **44**
Treyarnon. *Corn* 1C **6**
Treyford. *W Sus* 1G **17**
Triangle. *Staf* 5E **73**
Triangle. *W Yor* 2A **92**
Trickett's Cross. *Dors* 2F **15**
Trillick. *Ferm* 7F **176**
Trimdon. *Dur* 1A **106**
Trimdon Colliery. *Dur* 1A **106**
Trimdon Grange. *Dur* 1A **106**
Trimingham. *Norf* 2E **79**
Trimley Lower Street. *Suff* 2F **55**
Trimley St Martin. *Suff* 2F **55**
Trimley St Mary. *Suff* 2F **55**
Trimpley. *Worc* 3B **60**
Trimsaran. *Carm* 5E **45**
Trimstone. *Devn* 2F **19**
Trinafour. *Per* 2E **143**
Trinant. *Cphy* 2F **33**
**Tring**. *Herts* 4H **51**
Trinity. *Ang* 2F **145**
Trinity. *Edin* 2F **129**
Trisant. *Cdgn* 3G **57**
Triscombe. *Som* 3E **21**
Trislaig. *High* 1E **141**
Trispen. *Corn* 3C **6**
Tritlington. *Nmbd* 5G **121**
Trochry. *Per* 4G **143**
Troedrhiwdalar. *Powy* 5B **58**
Troedrhiwfuwch. *Cphy* 5E **47**
Troedrhiw-gwair. *Blae* 5E **47**
Troedyraur. *Cdgn* 1D **44**
Troedyrhiw. *Mer T* 5D **46**
Trondavoe. *Shet* 4E **173**
Troon. *Corn* 5A **6**
**Troon**. *S Ayr* 1C **116**
Troqueer. *Dum* 2A **112**
Troston. *Suff* 3A **66**
Trottiscliffe. *Kent* 4H **39**
Trotton. *W Sus* 4G **25**
Troutbeck. *Cumb* 4F **103** (nr. Ambleside)
Troutbeck. *Cumb* 2E **103** (nr. Penrith)
Troutbeck Bridge. *Cumb* 4F **103**
Troway. *Derbs* 3A **86**
**Trowbridge**. *Wilts* 1D **22**
Trowell. *Notts* 2B **74**
Trowle Common. *Wilts* 1D **22**
Trowley Bottom. *Herts* 4A **52**
Trowse Newton. *Norf* 5E **79**
Trudoxhill. *Som* 2C **22**
Trull. *Som* 4F **21**
Trumaisgearraidh. *W Isl* 1D **170**
Trumpan. *High* 2B **154**
Trumpet. *Here* 2B **48**
Trumpington. *Cambs* 5D **64**
Trumps Green. *Surr* 4A **38**
Trunch. *Norf* 2E **79**
Trunnah. *Lanc* 5C **96**
**Truro**. *Corn* 4C **6**
Trusham. *Devn* 4B **12**
Trusley. *Derbs* 2G **73**
Trusthorpe. *Linc* 2E **89**
Tryfil. *IOA* 2D **80**
Trysull. *Staf* 1C **60**
Tubney. *Oxon* 2C **36**
Tuckenhay. *Devn* 3E **9**
Tuckhill. *Shrp* 2B **60**
Tuckingmill. *Corn* 4A **6**
Tuckton. *Bour* 3G **15**
Tuddenham. *Suff* 3G **65**
Tuddenham St Martin. *Suff* 1E **55**
Tudeley. *Kent* 1H **27**
Tudhoe. *Dur* 1F **105**
Tudhoe Grange. *Dur* 1F **105**
Tudorville. *Here* 3A **48**
Tudweiliog. *Gwyn* 2B **68**
Tuesley. *Surr* 1A **26**
Tufton. *Hants* 2C **24**
Tufton. *Pemb* 2E **43**
Tugby. *Leics* 5E **75**
Tugford. *Shrp* 2H **59**
Tughall. *Nmbd* 2G **121**
Tulchan. *Per* 1B **136**
Tullibardine. *Per* 2B **136**
Tullibody. *Clac* 4A **136**
Tullich. *Arg* 2H **133**
Tullich. *High* 4B **156** (nr. Lochcarron)
Tullich. *High* 1C **158** (nr. Tain)
Tullich. *Mor* 4H **159**
Tullich Muir. *High* 1B **158**
Tulliemet. *Per* 3G **143**
Tulloch. *Abers* 5F **161**
Tulloch. *High* 4D **164** (nr. Bonar Bridge)
Tulloch. *High* 5F **149** (nr. Fort William)
Tulloch. *High* 2D **151** (nr. Grantown-on-Spey)
Tulloch. *Per* 1C **136**
Tullochgorm. *Arg* 4G **133**
Tullybeagles Lodge. *Per* 5H **143**
Tullyhogue. *M Ulst* 2C **178**
Tullymurdoch. *Per* 3B **144**
Tullynessle. *Abers* 2C **152**
Tumble. *Carm* 4F **45**
Tumbler's Green. *Essx* 3B **54**
Tumby. *Linc* 4B **88**
Tumby Woodside. *Linc* 5B **88**
Tummel Bridge. *Per* 3E **143**
**Tunbridge Wells, Royal**. *Kent* 2G **27**
Tunga. *W Isl* 4G **171**
Tungate. *Norf* 3E **79**
Tunley. *Bath* 1B **22**
Tunstall. *E Yor* 1G **95**
Tunstall. *Kent* 4C **40**
Tunstall. *Lanc* 2F **97**
Tunstall. *Norf* 5G **79**
Tunstall. *N Yor* 5F **105**
Tunstall. *Staf* 3B **72**
Tunstall. *Stoke* 5C **84**
Tunstall. *Suff* 5F **67**
Tunstall. *Tyne* 4G **115**
Tunstead. *Derbs* 3F **85**
Tunstead. *Norf* 3E **79**
Tunstead Milton. *Derbs* 2E **85**
Tunworth. *Hants* 2E **25**
Tupsley. *Here* 1A **48**
Tupton. *Derbs* 4A **86**
Turfholm. *S Lan* 1H **117**
Turfmoor. *Devn* 2F **13**
Turgis Green. *Hants* 1E **25**
Turkdean. *Glos* 4G **49**
Turkey Island. *Hants* 1D **16**
Tur Langton. *Leics* 1E **62**
Turleigh. *Wilts* 5D **34**
Turlin Moor. *Pool* 3E **15**
Turnastone. *Here* 2G **47**
Turnberry. *S Ayr* 4B **116**
Turnchapel. *Plym* 3A **8**
Turnditch. *Derbs* 1G **73**
Turners Hill. *W Sus* 2E **27**
Turners Puddle. *Dors* 3D **14**
Turnford. *Herts* 5D **52**
Turnhouse. *Edin* 2E **129**
Turnworth. *Dors* 2D **14**
Turriff. *Abers* 4E **161**
Tursdale. *Dur* 1A **106**
Turton Bottoms. *Bkbn* 3F **91**
Turtory. *Mor* 4C **160**
Turves Green. *W Mid* 3E **61**
Turvey. *Bed* 5G **63**
Turville. *Buck* 2F **37**
Turville Heath. *Buck* 2F **37**
Turweston. *Buck* 2E **50**
Tushielaw. *Bord* 3F **119**
Tutbury. *Staf* 3G **73**
Tutnall. *Worc* 3D **61**
Tutshill. *Glos* 2A **34**
Tuttington. *Norf* 3E **79**
Tutts Clump. *W Ber* 4D **36**
Tutwell. *Corn* 5D **11**
Tuxford. *Notts* 3E **87**
Twatt. *Orkn* 5B **172**
Twatt. *Shet* 6E **173**
Twechar. *E Dun* 2H **127**
Tweedale. *Telf* 5B **72**
Tweedbank. *Bord* 1H **119**
Tweedmouth. *Nmbd* 4F **131**
Tweedsmuir. *Bord* 2C **118**
Twelveheads. *Corn* 4B **6**
Twemlow Green. *Ches E* 4B **84**
Twenty. *Linc* 3A **76**
Twerton. *Bath* 5C **34**
**Twickenham**. *G Lon* 3C **38**
Twigworth. *Glos* 3D **48**
Twineham. *W Sus* 4D **26**
Twinhoe. *Bath* 1C **22**
Twinstead. *Essx* 2B **54**
Twinstead Green. *Essx* 2B **54**
Twiss Green. *Warr* 1A **84**
Twiston. *Lanc* 5H **97**
Twitchen. *Devn* 3A **20**
Twitchen. *Shrp* 3F **59**
Two Bridges. *Devn* 5G **11**
Two Bridges. *Glos* 5B **48**
Two Dales. *Derbs* 4G **85**
Two Gates. *Staf* 5G **73**
Two Mile Oak. *Devn* 2E **9**
Twycross. *Leics* 5H **73**
Twyford. *Buck* 3E **51**
Twyford. *Derbs* 3H **73**
Twyford. *Dors* 1D **14**
Twyford. *Hants* 4C **24**
Twyford. *Leics* 4E **75**
Twyford. *Norf* 3C **78**
Twyford. *Wok* 4F **37**
Twyford Common. *Here* 2A **48**
Twynholm. *Dum* 4D **110**
Twyning. *Glos* 2D **49**
Twyning Green. *Glos* 2E **49**
Twynllanan. *Carm* 3A **46**
Twyn-y-Sheriff. *Mon* 5H **47**
Twywell. *Nptn* 3G **63**
Tyberton. *Here* 2G **47**
Tyburn. *W Mid* 1F **61**
Tyby. *Norf* 3C **78**
Tycroes. *Carm* 4G **45**
Tycrwyn. *Powy* 4D **70**
**Tyddewi**. *Pemb* 2B **42**
Tydd Gote. *Linc* 4D **76**
Tydd St Giles. *Cambs* 4D **76**
Tydd St Mary. *Linc* 4D **76**
Tye. *Hants* 2F **17**
Tye Green. *Essx* 3F **53** (nr. Bishop's Stortford)
Tye Green. *Essx* 3A **54** (nr. Braintree)
Tye Green. *Essx* 2F **53** (nr. Saffron Walden)
Tyersal. *W Yor* 1B **92**
Ty Issa. *Powy* 2D **70**
**Tyldesley**. *G Man* 4E **91**
Tyler Hill. *Kent* 4F **41**
Tylers Green. *Buck* 2G **37**
Tyler's Green. *Essx* 5F **53**
Tylorstown. *Rhon* 2D **32**
Tylwch. *Powy* 2B **58**
Tynan. *Arm* 5B **178**
Ty-nant. *Cnwy* 1B **70**
Tyndrum. *Stir* 5H **141**
Tyneham. *Dors* 4D **15**
Tynehead. *Midl* 4G **129**
**Tynemouth**. *Tyne* 3G **115**
**Tyneside**. *Tyne* 3F **115**
**Tyne Tunnel**. *Tyne* 3G **115**
Tynewydd. *Rhon* 2C **32**
Tyninghame. *E Lot* 2C **130**
Tynron. *Dum* 5H **117**
Ty'n-y-bryn. *Rhon* 3D **32**
Tyn-y-celyn. *Wrex* 2D **70**
Tyn-y-cwm. *Swan* 5G **45**
Tyn-y-ffridd. *Powy* 2D **70**
Tynygongl. *IOA* 2E **81**
Tynygraig. *Cdgn* 4F **57**
Ty'n-y-groes. *Cnwy* 3G **81**
Ty'n-yr-eithin. *Cdgn* 4F **57**
Tyn-y-rhyd. *Powy* 4C **70**
Tyn-y-wern. *Powy* 3C **70**
Tyrie. *Abers* 2G **161**
Tyringham. *Mil* 1G **51**
Tythecott. *Devn* 1E **11**
Tythegston. *B'end* 4B **32**
Tytherington. *Ches E* 3D **84**
Tytherington. *Som* 2C **22**
Tytherington. *S Glo* 3B **34**
Tytherington. *Wilts* 2E **23**
Tytherleigh. *Devn* 2G **13**
Tywardreath. *Corn* 3E **7**
Tywardreath Highway. *Corn* 3E **7**
Tywyn. *Cnwy* 3G **81**
Tywyn. *Gwyn* 5E **69**


## U


Uachdar. *W Isl* 3D **170**
Uags. *High* 5G **155**
Ubbeston Green. *Suff* 3F **67**
Ubley. *Bath* 1A **22**
Uckerby. *N Yor* 4F **105**
**Uckfield**. *E Sus* 3F **27**
Uckinghall. *Worc* 2D **48**
Uckington. *Glos* 3E **49**
Uckington. *Shrp* 5H **71**
Uddingston. *S Lan* 3H **127**
Uddington. *S Lan* 1A **118**
Udimore. *E Sus* 4C **28**
Udny Green. *Abers* 1F **153**
Udny Station. *Abers* 1G **153**
Udston. *S Lan* 4H **127**
Udstonhead. *S Lan* 5A **128**
Uffcott. *Wilts* 4G **35**
Uffculme. *Devn* 1D **12**
Uffington. *Linc* 5H **75**
Uffington. *Oxon* 3B **36**
Uffington. *Shrp* 4H **71**
Ufford. *Pet* 5H **75**
Ufford. *Suff* 5E **67**
Ufton. *Warw* 4A **62**
Ufton Nervet. *W Ber* 5E **37**
Ugadale. *Arg* 3B **122**
Ugborough. *Devn* 3C **8**
Ugford. *Wilts* 3F **23**
Uggeshall. *Suff* 2G **67**
Ugglebarnby. *N Yor* 4F **107**
Ugley. *Essx* 3F **53**
Ugley Green. *Essx* 3F **53**
Ugthorpe. *N Yor* 3E **107**
Uidh. *W Isl* 9B **170**
Uig. *Arg* 3C **138**
Uig. *High* 2C **154** (nr. Balgown)
Uig. *High* 3A **154** (nr. Dunvegan)
Uigshader. *High* 4D **154**
Uisken. *Arg* 2A **132**
Ulbster. *High* 4F **169**
Ulcat Row. *Cumb* 2F **103**
Ulceby. *Linc* 3D **88**
Ulceby. *N Lin* 3E **94**
Ulceby Skitter. *N Lin* 3E **94**
Ulcombe. *Kent* 1C **28**
Uldale. *Cumb* 1D **102**
Uley. *Glos* 2C **34**
Ulgham. *Nmbd* 5G **121**
Ullapool. *High* 4F **163**
Ullenhall. *Warw* 4F **61**
Ulleskelf. *N Yor* 1F **93**
Ullesthorpe. *Leics* 2C **62**
Ulley. *S Yor* 2B **86**
Ullingswick. *Here* 5H **59**
Ullinish. *High* 5C **154**
Ullock. *Cumb* 2B **102**
Ulpha. *Cumb* 5C **102**
Ulrome. *E Yor* 4F **101**
Ulsta. *Shet* 3F **173**
Ulting. *Essx* 5B **54**
Ulva House. *Arg* 5F **139**
**Ulverston**. *Cumb* 2B **96**
Ulwell. *Dors* 4F **15**
Umberleigh. *Devn* 4G **19**
Unapool. *High* 5C **166**
Underbarrow. *Cumb* 5F **103**
Undercliffe. *W Yor* 1B **92**
Underdale. *Shrp* 4H **71**
Underhoull. *Shet* 1G **173**
Underriver. *Kent* 5G **39**
Under Tofts. *S Yor* 2H **85**
Underton. *Shrp* 1A **60**
Underwood. *Newp* 3G **33**
Underwood. *Notts* 5B **86**
Underwood. *Plym* 3B **8**
Undley. *Suff* 2F **65**
Undy. *Mon* 3H **33**
Union Mills. *IOM* 4C **108**
Union Street. *E Sus* 2B **28**
Unstone. *Derbs* 3A **86**
Unstone Green. *Derbs* 3A **86**
Unthank. *Cumb* 5E **113** (nr. Carlisle)
Unthank. *Cumb* 5H **113** (nr. Gamblesby)
Unthank. *Cumb* 1F **103** (nr. Penrith)
Unthank End. *Cumb* 1F **103**
Upavon. *Wilts* 1G **23**
Up Cerne. *Dors* 2B **14**
Upchurch. *Kent* 4C **40**
Upcott. *Devn* 2F **11**
Upcott. *Here* 5F **59**
Upend. *Cambs* 5F **65**
Up Exe. *Devn* 2C **12**
Upgate. *Norf* 4D **78**
Upgate Street. *Norf* 1C **66**
Uphall. *Dors* 2A **14**
Uphall. *W Lot* 2D **128**
Uphall Station. *W Lot* 2D **128**
Upham. *Devn* 2B **12**
Upham. *Hants* 4D **24**
Uphampton. *Here* 4F **59**
Uphampton. *Worc* 4C **60**
Up Hatherley. *Glos* 3E **49**
Uphill. *N Som* 1G **21**
Up Holland. *Lanc* 4D **90**
Uplawmoor. *E Ren* 4F **127**
Upleadon. *Glos* 3C **48**
Upleatham. *Red C* 3D **106**
Uplees. *Kent* 4D **40**
Uploders. *Dors* 3A **14**
Uplowman. *Devn* 1D **12**
Uplyme. *Devn* 3G **13**
Up Marden. *W Sus* 1F **17**
**Upminster**. *G Lon* 2G **39**
Up Nately. *Hants* 1E **25**
Upottery. *Devn* 2F **13**
Uppat. *High* 3F **165**
Upper Affcot. *Shrp* 2G **59**
Upper Arley. *Worc* 2B **60**
Upper Armley. *W Yor* 1C **92**
Upper Arncott. *Oxon* 4E **50**
Upper Astrop. *Nptn* 2D **50**
Upper Badcall. *High* 4B **166**
Upper Ballinderry. *Lis* 3F **179**
Upper Bangor. *Gwyn* 3E **81**
Upper Basildon. *W Ber* 4D **36**
Upper Batley. *W Yor* 2C **92**
Upper Beeding. *W Sus* 4C **26**
Upper Benefield. *Nptn* 2G **63**
Upper Bentley. *Worc* 4D **61**
Upper Bighouse. *High* 3A **168**
Upper Boddam. *Abers* 5D **160**
Upper Boddington. *Nptn* 5B **62**
Upper Bogside. *Mor* 3G **159**
Upper Booth. *Derbs* 2F **85**
Upper Borth. *Cdgn* 2F **57**
Upper Boyndlie. *Abers* 2G **161**
Upper Brailes. *Warw* 1B **50**
Upper Breinton. *Here* 1H **47**
Upper Broughton. *Notts* 3D **74**
Upper Brynamman. *Carm* 4H **45**
Upper Bucklebury. *W Ber* 5D **36**
Upper Bullington. *Hants* 2C **24**
Upper Burgate. *Hants* 1G **15**
Upper Caldecote. *C Beds* 1B **52**
Upper Canterton. *Hants* 1A **16**
Upper Catesby. *Nptn* 5C **62**
Upper Chapel. *Powy* 1D **46**
Upper Cheddon. *Som* 4F **21**
Upper Chicksgrove. *Wilts* 4E **23**
Upper Church Village. *Rhon* 3D **32**
Upper Chute. *Wilts* 1A **24**
Upper Clatford. *Hants* 2B **24**
Upper Coberley. *Glos* 4E **49**
Upper Coedcae. *Torf* 5F **47**
Upper Cound. *Shrp* 5H **71**
Upper Cudworth. *S Yor* 4D **93**
Upper Cumberworth. *W Yor* 4C **92**
Upper Cuttlehill. *Abers* 4B **160**
Upper Cwmbran. *Torf* 2F **33**
Upper Dallachy. *Mor* 2A **160**
Upper Dean. *Bed* 4H **63**
Upper Denby. *W Yor* 4C **92**
Upper Derraid. *High* 5E **159**
Upper Diabaig. *High* 2H **155**
Upper Dicker. *E Sus* 5G **27**
Upper Dinchope. *Shrp* 2G **59**
Upper Dochcarty. *High* 2H **157**
Upper Dounreay. *High* 2B **168**
Upper Dovercourt. *Essx* 2F **55**
Upper Dunsforth. *N Yor* 3G **99**
Upper Dunsley. *Herts* 4H **51**
Upper Eastern Green. *W Mid* 2G **61**
Upper Elkstone. *Staf* 5E **85**
Upper Ellastone. *Staf* 1F **73**
Upper End. *Derbs* 3E **85**
Upper Enham. *Hants* 2B **24**
Upper Farmcote. *Shrp* 1B **60**
Upper Farringdon. *Hants* 3F **25**
Upper Framilode. *Glos* 4C **48**
Upper Froyle. *Hants* 2F **25**
Upper Gills. *High* 1F **169**
Upper Glenfintaig. *High* 5E **149**
Upper Godney. *Som* 2H **21**
Upper Gravenhurst. *C Beds* 2B **52**
Upper Green. *Essx* 2E **53**
Upper Green. *W Ber* 5B **36**
Upper Green. *W Yor* 2C **92**
Upper Grove Common. *Here* 3A **48**
Upper Hackney. *Derbs* 4G **85**
Upper Hale. *Surr* 2G **25**
Upper Halliford. *Surr* 4B **38**
Upper Halling. *Medw* 4A **40**
Upper Hambleton. *Rut* 5G **75**
Upper Hardres Court. *Kent* 5F **41**
Upper Hardwick. *Here* 5G **59**
Upper Hartfield. *E Sus* 2F **27**
Upper Haugh. *S Yor* 1B **86**
Upper Hayton. *Shrp* 2H **59**
Upper Heath. *Shrp* 2H **59**
Upper Hellesdon. *Norf* 4E **78**
Upper Helmsley. *N Yor* 4A **100**
Upper Hengoed. *Shrp* 2E **71**
Upper Hergest. *Here* 5E **59**
Upper Heyford. *Nptn* 5D **62**
Upper Heyford. *Oxon* 3C **50**
Upper Hill. *Here* 5G **59**
Upper Hindhope. *Bord* 4B **120**
Upper Hopton. *W Yor* 3B **92**
Upper Howsell. *Worc* 1C **48**
Upper Hulme. *Staf* 4E **85**
Upper Inglesham. *Swin* 2H **35**
Upper Kilcott. *Glos* 3C **34**
Upper Killay. *Swan* 3E **31**
Upper Kirkton. *Abers* 5E **161**
Upper Kirkton. *N Ayr* 4C **126**
Upper Knockando. *Mor* 4F **159**
Upper Knockchoilum. *High* 2G **149**
Upper Lambourn. *W Ber* 3B **36**
Upperlands. *M Ulst* 6E **174**
Upper Langford. *N Som* 1H **21**
Upper Langwith. *Derbs* 4C **86**
Upper Largo. *Fife* 3G **137**
Upper Latheron. *High* 5D **169**
Upper Layham. *Suff* 1D **54**
Upper Leigh. *Staf* 2E **73**
Upper Lenie. *High* 1H **149**
Upper Lochton. *Abers* 4D **152**
Upper Longdon. *Staf* 4E **73**
Upper Longwood. *Shrp* 5A **72**
Upper Lybster. *High* 5E **169**
Upper Lydbrook. *Glos* 4B **48**
Upper Lye. *Here* 4F **59**
Upper Maes-coed. *Here* 2G **47**
Upper Midway. *Derbs* 3G **73**
Uppermill. *G Man* 4H **91**
Upper Millichope. *Shrp* 2H **59**
Upper Milovaig. *High* 4A **154**
Upper Minety. *Wilts* 2F **35**
Upper Mitton. *Worc* 3C **60**
Upper Nash. *Pemb* 4E **43**
Upper Neepaback. *Shet* 3G **173**
Upper Netchwood. *Shrp* 1A **60**
Upper Nobut. *Staf* 2E **73**
Upper North Dean. *Buck* 2G **37**
Upper Norwood. *W Sus* 4A **26**
Upper Nyland. *Dors* 4C **22**
Upper Oddington. *Glos* 3H **49**
Upper Ollach. *High* 5E **155**
Upper Outwoods. *Staf* 3G **73**
Upper Padley. *Derbs* 3G **85**
Upper Pennington. *Hants* 3B **16**
Upper Poppleton. *York* 4H **99**
Upper Quinton. *Warw* 1G **49**
Upper Rissington. *Glos* 4H **49**
Upper Rochford. *Worc* 4A **60**
Upper Rusko. *Dum* 3C **110**
Upper Sandaig. *High* 2F **147**
Upper Sanday. *Orkn* 7E **172**
Upper Sapey. *Here* 4A **60**
Upper Seagry. *Wilts* 3E **35**
Upper Shelton. *C Beds* 1H **51**
Upper Sheringham. *Norf* 1D **78**
Upper Skelmorlie. *N Ayr* 3C **126**
Upper Slaughter. *Glos* 3G **49**
Upper Sonachan. *Arg* 1H **133**
Upper Soudley. *Glos* 4B **48**
Upper Staploe. *Bed* 5A **64**
Upper Stoke. *Norf* 5E **79**
Upper Stondon. *C Beds* 2B **52**
Upper Stowe. *Nptn* 5D **62**
Upper Street. *Hants* 1G **15**
Upper Street. *Norf* 4F **79** (nr. Horning)
Upper Street. *Norf* 4F **79** (nr. Hoveton)
Upper Street. *Suff* 2E **55**
Upper Strensham. *Worc* 2E **49**
Upper Studley. *Wilts* 1D **22**
Upper Sundon. *C Beds* 3A **52**
Upper Swell. *Glos* 3G **49**
Upper Tankersley. *S Yor* 1H **85**
Upper Tean. *Staf* 2E **73**
Upperthong. *W Yor* 4B **92**
Upperthorpe. *N Lin* 4A **94**
Upper Thurnham. *Lanc* 4D **96**
Upper Tillyrie. *Per* 3D **136**
Upperton. *W Sus* 3A **26**
Upper Tooting. *G Lon* 3D **39**
Uppertown. *Derbs* 4H **85** (nr. Ashover)
Upper Town. *Derbs* 5G **85** (nr. Bonsall)
Upper Town. *Derbs* 5G **85** (nr. Hognaston)
Upper Town. *Here* 1A **48**
Uppertown. *High* 1F **169**
Upper Town. *N Som* 5A **34**
Uppertown. *Nmbd* 2B **114**
Uppertown. *Orkn* 8D **172**
Upper Tysoe. *Warw* 1B **50**
Upper Upham. *Wilts* 4H **35**
Upper Upnor. *Medw* 3B **40**
Upper Urquhart. *Fife* 3D **136**
Upper Wardington. *Oxon* 1C **50**
Upper Weald. *Mil* 2F **51**
Upper Weedon. *Nptn* 5D **62**
Upper Wellingham. *E Sus* 4F **27**
Upper Whiston. *S Yor* 2B **86**
Upper Wield. *Hants* 3E **25**
Upper Winchendon. *Buck* 4F **51**
Upperwood. *Derbs* 5G **85**
Upper Woodford. *Wilts* 3G **23**
Upper Wootton. *Hants* 1D **24**
Upper Wraxall. *Wilts* 4D **34**
Upper Wyche. *Here* 1C **48**
Uppincott. *Devn* 2B **12**
Uppingham. *Rut* 1F **63**
Uppington. *Shrp* 5A **72**
Upsall. *N Yor* 1G **99**
Upsettlington. *Bord* 5E **131**
Upshire. *Essx* 5E **53**
Up Somborne. *Hants* 3B **24**
Upstreet. *Kent* 4G **41**
Up Sydling. *Dors* 2B **14**
Upthorpe. *Suff* 3B **66**
Upton. *Buck* 4F **51**
Upton. *Cambs* 3A **64**
Upton. *Ches W* 4G **83**
Upton. *Corn* 2C **10** (nr. Bude)
Upton. *Corn* 5C **10** (nr. Liskeard)
Upton. *Cumb* 1E **102**
Upton. *Devn* 2D **12** (nr. Honiton)
Upton. *Devn* 4D **8** (nr. Kingsbridge)
Upton. *Dors* 3E **15** (nr. Poole)
Upton. *Dors* 4C **14** (nr. Weymouth)
Upton. *E Yor* 4F **101**
Upton. *Hants* 1B **24** (nr. Andover)
Upton. *Hants* 1B **16** (nr. Southampton)
Upton. *IOW* 3D **16**
Upton. *Leics* 1A **62**
Upton. *Linc* 2F **87**
Upton. *Mers* 2E **83**
Upton. *Norf* 4F **79**
Upton. *Nptn* 4E **62**
Upton. *Notts* 3E **87** (nr. Retford)
Upton. *Notts* 5E **87** (nr. Southwell)
Upton. *Oxon* 3D **36**
Upton. *Pemb* 4E **43**
Upton. *Pet* 5A **76**
Upton. *Slo* 3A **38**
Upton. *Som* 4H **21** (nr. Somerton)
Upton. *Som* 4C **20** (nr. Wiveliscombe)
Upton. *Warw* 5F **61**
Upton. *W Yor* 3E **93**
Upton. *Wilts* 3D **22**
Upton Bishop. *Here* 3B **48**
Upton Cheyney. *S Glo* 5B **34**
Upton Cressett. *Shrp* 1A **60**
Upton Crews. *Here* 3B **48**
Upton Cross. *Corn* 5C **10**
Upton End. *C Beds* 2B **52**
Upton Grey. *Hants* 2E **25**
Upton Heath. *Ches W* 4G **83**
Upton Hellions. *Devn* 2B **12**
Upton Lovell. *Wilts* 2E **23**
Upton Magna. *Shrp* 4H **71**
Upton Noble. *Som* 3C **22**
Upton Pyne. *Devn* 3C **12**
Upton St Leonards. *Glos* 4D **48**

West Littleton—Womenswold

West Littleton. *S Glo* 4C **34**
West Looe. *Corn* 3G **7**
West Lulworth. *Dors* 4D **14**
West Lutton. *N Yor* 3D **100**
West Lydford. *Som* 3A **22**
West Lyng. *Som* 4G **21**
West Lynn. *Norf* 4F **77**
West Mains. *Per* 2B **136**
West Malling. *Kent* 5A **40**
West Malvern. *Worc* 1C **48**
Westmancote. *Worc* 2E **49**
West Marden. *W Sus* 1F **17**
West Markham. *Notts* 3E **86**
Westmarsh. *Kent* 4G **41**
West Marsh. *NE Lin* 4F **95**
West Marton. *N Yor* 4A **98**
West Meon. *Hants* 4E **25**
West Mersea. *Essx* 4D **54**
Westmeston. *E Sus* 4E **27**
Westmill. *Herts* 3D **52** (nr. Buntingford)
Westmill. *Herts* 2B **52** (nr. Hitchin)
West Milton. *Dors* 3A **14**
**Westminster**. *G Lon* 3D **39**
West Molesey. *Surr* 4C **38**
West Monkton. *Som* 4F **21**
Westmoor End. *Cumb* 1B **102**
West Moors. *Dors* 2F **15**
West Morden. *Dors* 3E **15**
West Muir. *Ang* 2E **145** (nr. Brechin)
Westmuir. *Ang* 3C **144** (nr. Forfar)
West Murkle. *High* 2D **168**
West Ness. *N Yor* 2A **100**
Westness. *Orkn* 5C **172**
Westnewton. *Cumb* 5C **112**
West Newton. *E Yor* 1E **95**
West Newton. *Norf* 3F **77**
Westnewton. *Nmbd* 1D **120**
West Newton. *Som* 4F **21**
West Norwood. *G Lon* 3E **39**
Westoe. *Tyne* 3G **115**
West Ogwell. *Devn* 2E **9**
Weston. *Bath* 5C **34**
Weston. *Ches E* 5B **84** (nr. Crewe)
Weston. *Ches E* 3C **84** (nr. Macclesfield)
Weston. *Devn* 2E **13** (nr. Honiton)
Weston. *Devn* 4E **13** (nr. Sidmouth)
Weston. *Dors* 5B **14** (nr. Weymouth)
Weston. *Dors* 2A **14** (nr. Yeovil)
Weston. *Hal* 2H **83**
Weston. *Hants* 4F **25**
Weston. *Here* 5F **59**
Weston. *Herts* 2C **52**
Weston. *Linc* 3B **76**
Weston. *Nptn* 1D **50**
Weston. *Notts* 4E **87**
Weston. *Shrp* 1H **59** (nr. Bridgnorth)
Weston. *Shrp* 3F **59** (nr. Knighton)
Weston. *Shrp* 3H **71** (nr. Wem)
Weston. *S Lan* 5D **128**
Weston. *Staf* 3D **73**
Weston. *Suff* 2G **67**
Weston. *W Ber* 4B **36**
Weston Bampfylde. *Som* 4B **22**
Weston Beggard. *Here* 1A **48**
Westonbirt. *Glos* 3D **34**
Weston by Welland. *Nptn* 1E **63**
Weston Colville. *Cambs* 5F **65**
Westoncommon. *Shrp* 3G **71**
Weston Coyney. *Stoke* 1D **72**
Weston Ditch. *Suff* 3F **65**
Weston Favell. *Nptn* 4E **63**
Weston Green. *Cambs* 5F **65**
Weston Green. *Norf* 4D **78**
Weston Heath. *Shrp* 4B **72**
Weston Hills. *Linc* 4B **76**
Weston in Arden. *Warw* 2A **62**
Westoning. *C Beds* 2A **52**
Weston in Gordano. *N Som* 4H **33**
Weston Jones. *Staf* 3B **72**
Weston Longville. *Norf* 4D **78**
Weston Lullingfields. *Shrp* 3G **71**
Weston-on-Avon. *Warw* 5F **61**
Weston-on-the-Green. *Oxon* 4D **50**
Weston-on-Trent. *Derbs* 3B **74**
Weston Patrick. *Hants* 2E **25**
Weston Rhyn. *Shrp* 2E **71**
Weston-sub-Edge. *Glos* 1G **49**
**Weston-super-Mare**. *N Som* 5G **33**
Weston Town. *Som* 2C **22**
Weston Turville. *Buck* 4G **51**
Weston under Lizard. *Staf* 4C **72**
Weston under Penyard. *Here* 3B **48**
Weston under Wetherley. *Warw* 4A **62**
Weston Underwood. *Derbs* 1G **73**
Weston Underwood. *Mil* 5F **63**
Westonzoyland. *Som* 3G **21**
West Orchard. *Dors* 1D **14**
West Overton. *Wilts* 5G **35**
Westow. *N Yor* 3B **100**
Westown. *Per* 1E **137**
West Panson. *Devn* 3D **10**
West Park. *Hart* 1B **106**
West Parley. *Dors* 3F **15**
West Peckham. *Kent* 5H **39**
West Pelton. *Dur* 4F **115**
West Pennard. *Som* 3A **22**
West Pentire. *Corn* 2B **6**
West Perry. *Cambs* 4A **64**
West Pitcorthie. *Fife* 3H **137**
West Plean. *Stir* 1B **128**
West Poringland. *Norf* 5E **79**
West Porlock. *Som* 2B **20**
Westport. *Som* 1G **13**
West Putford. *Devn* 1D **10**
West Quantoxhead. *Som* 2E **20**
Westra. *V Glam* 4E **33**
West Rainton. *Dur* 5G **115**
West Rasen. *Linc* 2H **87**
West Ravendale. *NE Lin* 1B **88**
Westray Airport. *Orkn* 2D **172**
West Raynham. *Norf* 3A **78**
Westrigg. *W Lot* 3C **128**
West Rounton. *N Yor* 4B **106**
West Row. *Suff* 3F **65**
West Rudham. *Norf* 3H **77**
West Runton. *Norf* 1D **78**
Westruther. *Bord* 4C **130**
Westry. *Cambs* 1C **64**
West Saltoun. *E Lot* 3A **130**
West Sandford. *Devn* 2B **12**
West Sandwick. *Shet* 3F **173**
West Scrafton. *N Yor* 1C **98**
Westside. *Orkn* 5C **172**
West Sleekburn. *Nmbd* 1F **115**
West Somerton. *Norf* 4G **79**
West Stafford. *Dors* 4C **14**
West Stockwith. *Notts* 1E **87**
West Stoke. *W Sus* 2G **17**
West Stonesdale. *N Yor* 4B **104**
West Stoughton. *Som* 2H **21**
West Stour. *Dors* 4C **22**
West Stourmouth. *Kent* 4G **41**
West Stow. *Suff* 3H **65**
West Stowell. *Wilts* 5G **35**
West Strathan. *High* 2F **167**
West Stratton. *Hants* 2D **24**
West Street. *Kent* 5D **40**
West Tanfield. *N Yor* 2E **99**
West Taphouse. *Corn* 2F **7**
West Tarbert. *Arg* 3G **125**
West Thirston. *Nmbd* 4F **121**
West Thorney. *W Sus* 2F **17**
West Thurrock. *Thur* 3G **39**
West Tilbury. *Thur* 3A **40**
West Tisted. *Hants* 4E **25**
West Tofts. *Norf* 1H **65**
West Torrington. *Linc* 2A **88**
West Town. *Bath* 5A **34**
West Town. *Hants* 3F **17**
West Town. *N Som* 5H **33**
West Tytherley. *Hants* 4A **24**
West Tytherton. *Wilts* 4E **35**
West View. *Hart* 1B **106**
Westville. *Notts* 1C **74**
West Walton. *Norf* 4D **76**
Westward. *Cumb* 5D **112**
Westward Ho!. *Devn* 4E **19**
Westwell. *Kent* 1D **28**
Westwell. *Oxon* 5H **49**
Westwell Leacon. *Kent* 1D **28**
West Wellow. *Hants* 1A **16**
West Wemyss. *Fife* 4F **137**
Westwick. *Cambs* 4D **64**
Westwick. *Dur* 3D **104**
Westwick. *Norf* 3E **79**
West Wick. *N Som* 5G **33**
West Wickham. *Cambs* 1G **53**
West Wickham. *G Lon* 4E **39**
West Williamston. *Pemb* 4E **43**
West Willoughby. *Linc* 1G **75**
West Winch. *Norf* 4F **77**
West Winterslow. *Wilts* 3H **23**
West Wittering. *W Sus* 3F **17**
West Witton. *N Yor* 1C **98**
Westwood. *Devn* 3D **12**
Westwood. *Kent* 4H **41**
Westwood. *Pet* 5A **76**
Westwood. *S Lan* 4H **127**
Westwood. *Wilts* 1D **22**
West Woodburn. *Nmbd* 1B **114**
West Woodhay. *W Ber* 5B **36**
West Woodlands. *Som* 2C **22**
West Woodside. *Cumb* 5E **112**
Westwoodside. *N Lin* 1E **87**
West Worldham. *Hants* 3F **25**
West Worlington. *Devn* 1A **12**
West Worthing. *W Sus* 5C **26**
West Wratting. *Cambs* 5F **65**
West Wycombe. *Buck* 2G **37**
West Wylam. *Nmbd* 3E **115**
West Yatton. *Wilts* 4D **34**
West Yell. *Shet* 3F **173**
West Youlstone. *Corn* 1C **10**
Wetheral. *Cumb* 4F **113**
Wetherby. *W Yor* 5G **99**
Wetherden. *Suff* 4C **66**
Wetheringsett. *Suff* 4D **66**
Wethersfield. *Essx* 2H **53**
Wethersta. *Shet* 5E **173**
Wetherup Street. *Suff* 4D **66**
Wetley Rocks. *Staf* 1D **72**
Wettenhall. *Ches E* 4A **84**
Wetton. *Staf* 5F **85**
Wetwang. *E Yor* 4D **100**
Wetwood. *Staf* 2B **72**
Wexcombe. *Wilts* 1A **24**
Wexham Street. *Buck* 2A **38**
Weybourne. *Norf* 1D **78**
Weybourne. *Surr* 2G **25**
Weybread. *Suff* 2E **67**
**Weybridge**. *Surr* 4B **38**
Weycroft. *Devn* 3G **13**
Weydale. *High* 2D **168**
Weyhill. *Hants* 2B **24**
**Weymouth**. *Dors* 5B **14** & **204**
Weythel. *Powy* 5E **59**
Whaddon. *Buck* 2G **51**
Whaddon. *Cambs* 1D **52**
Whaddon. *Glos* 4D **48**
Whaddon. *Wilts* 4G **23**
Whale. *Cumb* 2G **103**
Whaley. *Derbs* 3C **86**
Whaley Bridge. *Derbs* 2E **85**
Whaley Thorns. *Derbs* 3C **86**
Whalley. *Lanc* 1F **91**
Whalton. *Nmbd* 1E **115**
Whaplode. *Linc* 3C **76**
Whaplode Drove. *Linc* 4C **76**
Whaplode St Catherine. *Linc* 3C **76**
Wharfe. *N Yor* 3G **97**
Wharles. *Lanc* 1C **90**
Wharley End. *C Beds* 1H **51**
Wharncliffe Side. *S Yor* 1G **85**
Wharram-le-Street. *N Yor* 3C **100**
Wharton. *Ches W* 4A **84**
Wharton. *Here* 5H **59**
Whashton. *N Yor* 4E **105**
Whasset. *Cumb* 1E **97**
Whatcote. *Warw* 1B **50**
Whateley. *Warw* 1G **61**
Whatfield. *Suff* 1D **54**
Whatley. *Som* 2G **13** (nr. Chard)
Whatley. *Som* 2C **22** (nr. Frome)
Whatlington. *E Sus* 4B **28**
Whatmore. *Shrp* 3A **60**
Whatstandwell. *Derbs* 5H **85**
Whatton. *Notts* 2E **75**
Whauphill. *Dum* 5B **110**
Whaw. *N Yor* 4C **104**
Wheatacre. *Norf* 1G **67**
Wheatcroft. *Derbs* 5A **86**
Wheathampstead. *Herts* 4B **52**
Wheathill. *Shrp* 2A **60**
Wheatley. *Devn* 3B **12**
Wheatley. *Hants* 2F **25**
Wheatley. *Oxon* 5E **50**
Wheatley. *S Yor* 4F **93**
Wheatley. *W Yor* 2A **92**
Wheatley Hill. *Dur* 1A **106**
Wheatley Lane. *Lanc* 1G **91**
Wheatley Park. *S Yor* 4F **93**
Wheaton Aston. *Staf* 4C **72**
Wheatstone Park. *Staf* 5C **72**
Wheddon Cross. *Som* 3C **20**
Wheelerstreet. *Surr* 1A **26**
Wheelock. *Ches E* 5B **84**
Wheelock Heath. *Ches E* 5B **84**
Wheelton. *Lanc* 2E **90**
Wheldrake. *York* 5A **100**
Whelford. *Glos* 2G **35**
Whelpley Hill. *Buck* 5H **51**
Whelpo. *Cumb* 1E **102**
Whelston. *Flin* 3E **82**
Whenby. *N Yor* 3A **100**
Whepstead. *Suff* 5H **65**
Wherstead. *Suff* 1E **55**
Wherwell. *Hants* 2B **24**
Wheston. *Derbs* 3F **85**
Whetsted. *Kent* 1A **28**
Whetstone. *G Lon* 1D **38**
Whetstone. *Leics* 1C **62**
Whicham. *Cumb* 1A **96**
Whichford. *Warw* 2B **50**
**Whickham**. *Tyne* 3F **115**
Whiddon. *Devn* 2E **11**
Whiddon Down. *Devn* 3G **11**
Whigstreet. *Ang* 4D **145**
Whilton. *Nptn* 4D **62**
Whimble. *Devn* 2D **10**
Whimple. *Devn* 3D **12**
Whimpwell Green. *Norf* 3F **79**
Whinburgh. *Norf* 5C **78**
Whin Lane End. *Lanc* 5C **96**
Whinney Hill. *Stoc T* 3A **106**
Whinnyfold. *Abers* 5H **161**
Whippingham. *IOW* 3D **16**
Whipsnade. *C Beds* 4A **52**
Whipton. *Devn* 3C **12**
Whirlow. *S Yor* 2H **85**
Whisby. *Linc* 4G **87**
Whissendine. *Rut* 4F **75**
Whissonsett. *Norf* 3B **78**
Whisterfield. *Ches E* 3C **84**
Whistley Green. *Wok* 4F **37**
Whiston. *Mers* 1G **83**
Whiston. *Nptn* 4F **63**
Whiston. *S Yor* 1B **86**
Whiston. *Staf* 1E **73** (nr. Cheadle)
Whiston. *Staf* 4C **72** (nr. Penkridge)
Whiston Cross. *Shrp* 5B **72**
Whiston Eaves. *Staf* 1E **73**
Whitacre Heath. *Warw* 1G **61**
Whitbeck. *Cumb* 1A **96**
Whitbourne. *Here* 5B **60**
Whitburn. *Tyne* 3H **115**
**Whitburn**. *W Lot* 3C **128**
Whitburn Colliery. *Tyne* 3H **115**
Whitby. *Ches W* 3F **83**
**Whitby**. *N Yor* 3F **107**
Whitbyheath. *Ches W* 3F **83**
Whitchester. *Bord* 4D **130**
Whitchurch. *Bath* 5B **34**
Whitchurch. *Buck* 3F **51**
Whitchurch. *Card* 4E **33**
Whitchurch. *Devn* 5E **11**
Whitchurch. *Hants* 2C **24**
Whitchurch. *Here* 4A **48**
Whitchurch. *Pemb* 2B **42**
Whitchurch. *Shrp* 1H **71**
Whitchurch Canonicorum. *Dors* 3G **13**
Whitchurch Hill. *Oxon* 4E **37**
Whitchurch-on-Thames. *Oxon* 4E **37**
Whitcombe. *Dors* 4C **14**
Whitcot. *Shrp* 1F **59**
Whitcott Keysett. *Shrp* 2E **59**
Whiteabbey. *Ant* 1H **179**
Whiteash Green. *Essx* 2A **54**
Whitebog. *High* 2B **158**
Whitebridge. *High* 2G **149**
Whitebrook. *Mon* 5A **48**
Whitecairns. *Abers* 2G **153**
Whitechapel. *Lanc* 5E **97**
Whitechurch. *Pemb* 1F **43**
White Colne. *Essx* 3B **54**
White Coppice. *Lanc* 3E **90**
White Corries. *High* 3G **141**
Whitecraig. *E Lot* 2G **129**
Whitecroft. *Glos* 5B **48**
White Cross. *Corn* 4D **5** (nr. Mullion)
Whitecross. *Corn* 1D **6** (nr. Wadebridge)
Whitecross. *Falk* 2C **128**
Whitecross. *New M* 6D **178**
White End. *Worc* 2C **48**
Whiteface. *High* 5E **164**
Whitefarland. *N Ayr* 5G **125**
Whitefaulds. *S Ayr* 4B **116**
Whitefield. *Dors* 3E **15**
**Whitefield**. *G Man* 4G **91**
Whitefield. *Som* 4D **20**
Whiteford. *Abers* 1E **152**
Whitegate. *Ches W* 4A **84**
Whitehall. *Devn* 1E **13**
Whitehall. *Hants* 1F **25**
Whitehall. *Orkn* 5F **172**
Whitehall. *W Sus* 3C **26**
**Whitehaven**. *Cumb* 3A **102**
Whitehaven. *Shrp* 3E **71**
Whitehead. *ME Ant* 7L **175**
Whitehill. *Hants* 3F **25**
Whitehill. *N Ayr* 4D **126**
Whitehills. *Abers* 2D **160**
Whitehills. *Ang* 3D **144**
White Horse Common. *Norf* 3F **79**
Whitehough. *Derbs* 2E **85**
Whitehouse. *Abers* 2D **152**
Whitehouse. *Arg* 3G **125**
Whiteinch. *Glas* 3G **127**
Whitekirk. *E Lot* 1B **130**
White Kirkley. *Dur* 1D **104**
White Lackington. *Dors* 3C **14**
Whitelackington. *Som* 1G **13**
White Ladies Aston. *Worc* 5D **60**
White Lee. *W Yor* 2C **92**
Whiteley. *Hants* 2D **16**
Whiteley Bank. *IOW* 4D **16**
Whiteley Village. *Surr* 4B **38**
Whitemans Green. *W Sus* 3E **27**
White Mill. *Carm* 3E **45**
Whitemire. *Mor* 3D **159**
Whitemoor. *Corn* 3D **6**
Whitenap. *Hants* 4B **24**
Whiteness. *Shet* 7F **173**
White Notley. *Essx* 4A **54**
Whiteoak Green. *Oxon* 4B **50**
Whiteparish. *Wilts* 4H **23**
White Pit. *Linc* 3C **88**
Whiterashes. *Abers* 1F **153**
Whiterock. *N Dwn* 3K **179**
White Rocks. *Here* 3H **47**
White Roding. *Essx* 4F **53**
Whiterow. *High* 4F **169**
Whiterow. *Mor* 3E **159**
Whiteshill. *Glos* 5D **48**
Whiteside. *Nmbd* 3A **114**
Whiteside. *W Lot* 3C **128**
Whitesmith. *E Sus* 4G **27**
Whitestaunton. *Som* 1F **13**
Whitestone. *Abers* 4D **152**
Whitestone. *Devn* 3B **12**
White Stone. *Here* 1A **48**
Whitestones. *Abers* 3F **161**
Whitestreet Green. *Suff* 2C **54**
Whitewall Corner. *N Yor* 2B **100**
White Waltham. *Wind* 4G **37**
Whiteway. *Glos* 4E **49**
Whitewell. *Lanc* 5F **97**
Whitewell Bottom. *Lanc* 2G **91**
Whiteworks. *Devn* 5G **11**
Whitewreath. *Mor* 3G **159**
Whitfield. *D'dee* 5D **144**
Whitfield. *Kent* 1H **29**
Whitfield. *Nptn* 2E **50**
Whitfield. *Nmbd* 4A **114**
Whitfield. *S Glo* 2B **34**
Whitford. *Devn* 3F **13**
Whitford. *Flin* 3D **82**
Whitgift. *E Yor* 2B **94**
Whitgreave. *Staf* 3C **72**
Whithorn. *Dum* 5B **110**
Whiting Bay. *N Ayr* 3E **123**
Whitkirk. *W Yor* 1D **92**
Whitland. *Carm* 3G **43**
Whitleigh. *Plym* 3A **8**
Whitletts. *S Ayr* 2C **116**
Whitley. *N Yor* 2F **93**
Whitley. *Wilts* 5D **35**
**Whitley Bay**. *Tyne* 2G **115**
Whitley Chapel. *Nmbd* 4C **114**
Whitley Heath. *Staf* 3C **72**
Whitley Lower. *W Yor* 3C **92**
Whitley Thorpe. *N Yor* 2F **93**
Whitlock's End. *W Mid* 3F **61**
Whitminster. *Glos* 5C **48**
Whitmore. *Dors* 2F **15**
Whitmore. *Staf* 1C **72**
Whitnage. *Devn* 1D **12**
Whitnash. *Warw* 4H **61**
Whitney. *Here* 1F **47**
Whitrigg. *Cumb* 4D **112** (nr. Kirkbride)
Whitrigg. *Cumb* 1D **102** (nr. Torpenhow)
Whitsbury. *Hants* 1G **15**
Whitsome. *Bord* 4E **131**
Whitson. *Newp* 3G **33**
**Whitstable**. *Kent* 4F **41**
Whitstone. *Corn* 3C **10**
Whittingham. *Nmbd* 3E **121**
Whittingslow. *Shrp* 2G **59**
Whittington. *Derbs* 3B **86**
Whittington. *Glos* 3F **49**
Whittington. *Lanc* 2F **97**
Whittington. *Norf* 1G **65**
Whittington. *Shrp* 2F **71**
Whittington. *Staf* 2C **60** (nr. Kinver)
Whittington. *Staf* 5F **73** (nr. Lichfield)
Whittington. *Warw* 1G **61**
Whittington. *Worc* 5C **60**
Whittington Barracks. *Staf* 5F **73**
Whittlebury. *Nptn* 1E **51**
Whittleford. *Warw* 1H **61**
Whittle-le-Woods. *Lanc* 2D **90**
**Whittlesey**. *Cambs* 1B **64**
Whittlesford. *Cambs* 1E **53**
Whittlestone Head. *Bkbn* 3F **91**
Whitton. *N Lin* 2C **94**
Whitton. *Nmbd* 4E **121**
Whitton. *Powy* 4E **59**
Whitton. *Bord* 2B **120**
Whitton. *Shrp* 3H **59**
Whitton. *Stoc T* 2A **106**
Whittonditch. *Wilts* 4A **36**
Whittonstall. *Nmbd* 4D **114**
Whitway. *Hants* 1C **24**
Whitwell. *Derbs* 3C **86**
Whitwell. *Herts* 3B **52**
Whitwell. *IOW* 5D **16**
Whitwell. *N Yor* 5F **105**
Whitwell. *Rut* 5G **75**
Whitwell-on-the-Hill. *N Yor* 3B **100**
Whitwick. *Leics* 4B **74**
Whitwood. *W Yor* 2E **93**
Whitworth. *Lanc* 3G **91**
Whixall. *Shrp* 2H **71**
Whixley. *N Yor* 4G **99**
Whoberley. *W Mid* 3H **61**
Whorlton. *Dur* 3E **105**
Whorlton. *N Yor* 4B **106**
Whygate. *Nmbd* 2A **114**
Whyle. *Here* 4H **59**
Whyteleafe. *Surr* 5E **39**
Wibdon. *Glos* 2A **34**
Wibtoft. *Warw* 2B **62**
Wichenford. *Worc* 4B **60**
Wichling. *Kent* 5D **40**
Wick. *Bour* 3G **15**
Wick. *Devn* 2E **13**
Wick. *High* 3F **169**
Wick. *Shet* 8F **173** (on Mainland)
Wick. *Shet* 1G **173** (on Unst)
Wick. *Som* 2F **21** (nr. Bridgwater)
Wick. *Som* 1G **21** (nr. Burnham-on-Sea)
Wick. *Som* 4H **21** (nr. Somerton)
Wick. *S Glo* 4C **34**
Wick. *V Glam* 4C **32**
Wick. *W Sus* 5B **26**
Wick. *Wilts* 4G **23**
Wick. *Worc* 1E **49**
Wick Airport. *High* 3F **169**
Wicken. *Cambs* 3E **65**
Wicken. *Nptn* 2F **51**
Wicken Bonhunt. *Essx* 2E **53**
Wickenby. *Linc* 2H **87**
Wicken Green Village. *Norf* 2H **77**
Wickersley. *S Yor* 1B **86**
Wicker Street Green. *Suff* 1C **54**
**Wickford**. *Essx* 1B **40**
Wickham. *Hants* 1D **16**
Wickham. *W Ber* 4B **36**
Wickham Bishops. *Essx* 4B **54**
Wickhambreaux. *Kent* 5G **41**
Wickhambrook. *Suff* 5G **65**
Wickhamford. *Worc* 1F **49**
Wickham Green. *Suff* 4C **66**
Wickham Heath. *W Ber* 5C **36**
Wickham Market. *Suff* 5F **67**
Wickhampton. *Norf* 5G **79**
Wickham St Paul. *Essx* 2B **54**
Wickham Skeith. *Suff* 4C **66**
Wickham Street. *Suff* 4C **66**
Wick Hill. *Wok* 5F **37**
Wicklewood. *Norf* 5C **78**
Wickmere. *Norf* 2D **78**
Wick St Lawrence. *N Som* 5G **33**
Wickwar. *S Glo* 3C **34**
Widdington. *Essx* 2F **53**
Widdrington. *Nmbd* 5G **121**
Widdrington Station. *Nmbd* 5G **121**
Widecombe in the Moor. *Devn* 5H **11**
Widegates. *Corn* 3G **7**
Widemouth Bay. *Corn* 2C **10**
Wide Open. *Tyne* 2F **115**
Widewall. *Orkn* 8D **172**
Widford. *Essx* 5G **53**
Widford. *Herts* 4E **53**
Widham. *Wilts* 3F **35**
Widmer End. *Buck* 2G **37**
Widmerpool. *Notts* 3D **74**
**Widnes**. *Hal* 2H **83**
Widworthy. *Devn* 3F **13**
**Wigan**. *G Man* 4D **90**
Wigbeth. *Dors* 2F **15**
Wigborough. *Som* 1H **13**
Wiggaton. *Devn* 3E **12**
Wiggenhall St Germans. *Norf* 4E **77**
Wiggenhall St Mary Magdalen. *Norf* 4E **77**
Wiggenhall St Mary the Virgin. *Norf* 4E **77**
Wiggenhall St Peter. *Norf* 4F **77**
Wiggens Green. *Essx* 1G **53**
Wigginton. *Herts* 4H **51**
Wigginton. *Oxon* 2B **50**
Wigginton. *Staf* 5G **73**
Wigginton. *York* 4H **99**
Wigglesworth. *N Yor* 4H **97**
Wiggonby. *Cumb* 4D **112**
Wiggonholt. *W Sus* 4B **26**
Wighill. *N Yor* 5G **99**
Wighton. *Norf* 2B **78**
Wightwick. *W Mid* 1C **60**
Wigley. *Hants* 1B **16**
Wigmore. *Here* 4G **59**
Wigmore. *Medw* 4B **40**
Wigsley. *Notts* 3F **87**
Wigsthorpe. *Nptn* 2H **63**
**Wigston**. *Leics* 1D **62**
Wigtoft. *Linc* 2B **76**
Wigton. *Cumb* 5D **112**
Wigtown. *Dum* 4B **110**
Wike. *W Yor* 5F **99**
Wilbarston. *Nptn* 2F **63**
Wilberfoss. *E Yor* 4B **100**
Wilburton. *Cambs* 3D **65**
Wilby. *Norf* 2C **66**
Wilby. *Nptn* 4F **63**
Wilby. *Suff* 3E **67**
Wilcot. *Wilts* 5G **35**
Wilcott. *Shrp* 4F **71**
Wilcove. *Corn* 3A **8**
Wildboarclough. *Ches E* 4D **85**
Wilden. *Bed* 5H **63**
Wilden. *Worc* 3C **60**
Wildern. *Hants* 1C **16**
Wilderspool. *Warr* 2A **84**
Wilde Street. *Suff* 3G **65**
Wildhern. *Hants* 1B **24**
Wildmanbridge. *S Lan* 4B **128**
Wildmoor. *Worc* 3D **60**
Wildsworth. *Linc* 1F **87**
Wildwood. *Staf* 3D **72**
Wilford. *Nott* 2C **74**
Wilkesley. *Ches E* 1A **72**
Wilkhaven. *High* 5G **165**
Wilkieston. *W Lot* 3E **129**
Wilksby. *Linc* 4B **88**
Willand. *Devn* 1D **12**
Willaston. *Ches E* 5A **84**
Willaston. *Ches W* 3F **83**
Willaston. *IOM* 4C **108**
Willen. *Mil* 1G **51**
Willenhall. *W Mid* 3A **62** (nr. Coventry)
Willenhall. *W Mid* 1D **60** (nr. Wolverhampton)
Willerby. *E Yor* 1D **94**
Willerby. *N Yor* 2E **101**
Willersey. *Glos* 2G **49**
Willersley. *Here* 1G **47**
Willesborough. *Kent* 1E **28**
Willesborough Lees. *Kent* 1E **29**
**Willesden**. *G Lon* 2D **38**
Willesley. *Wilts* 3D **34**
Willett. *Som* 3E **20**
Willey. *Shrp* 1A **60**
Willey. *Warw* 2B **62**
Willey Green. *Surr* 5A **38**
Williamscot. *Oxon* 1C **50**
Williamsetter. *Shet* 9E **173**
Willian. *Herts* 2C **52**
Willingale. *Essx* 5F **53**
Willingdon. *E Sus* 5G **27**
Willingham. *Cambs* 3D **64**
Willingham by Stow. *Linc* 2F **87**
Willingham Green. *Cambs* 5F **65**
Willington. *Bed* 1B **52**
Willington. *Derbs* 3G **73**
Willington. *Dur* 1E **105**
Willington. *Tyne* 3G **115**
Willington. *Warw* 2A **50**
Willington Corner. *Ches W* 4H **83**
Willisham Tye. *Suff* 5C **66**
Willitoft. *E Yor* 1H **93**
Williton. *Som* 2D **20**
Willoughbridge. *Staf* 1B **72**
Willoughby. *Linc* 3D **88**
Willoughby. *Warw* 4C **62**
Willoughby-on-the-Wolds. *Notts* 3D **74**
Willoughby Waterleys. *Leics* 1C **62**
Willoughton. *Linc* 1G **87**
Willow Green. *Worc* 5B **60**
Willows Green. *Essx* 4H **53**
Willsbridge. *S Glo* 4B **34**
Willslock. *Staf* 2E **73**
Wilmcote. *Warw* 5F **61**
Wilmington. *Bath* 5B **34**
Wilmington. *Devn* 3F **13**
Wilmington. *E Sus* 5G **27**
Wilmington. *Kent* 3G **39**
**Wilmslow**. *Ches E* 2C **84**
Wilnecote. *Staf* 5G **73**
Wilney Green. *Norf* 2C **66**
Wilpshire. *Lanc* 1E **91**
Wilsden. *W Yor* 1A **92**
Wilsford. *Linc* 1H **75**
Wilsford. *Wilts* 3G **23** (nr. Amesbury)
Wilsford. *Wilts* 1F **23** (nr. Devizes)
Wilsill. *N Yor* 3D **98**
Wilsley Green. *Kent* 2B **28**
Wilson. *Here* 3A **48**
Wilson. *Leics* 3B **74**
Wilsontown. *S Lan* 4C **128**
Wilstead. *Bed* 1A **52**
Wilsthorpe. *E Yor* 3F **101**
Wilsthorpe. *Linc* 4H **75**
Wilstone. *Herts* 4H **51**
Wilton. *Cumb* 3B **102**
Wilton. *N Yor* 1C **100**
Wilton. *Red C* 3C **106**
Wilton. *Bord* 3H **119**
Wilton. *Wilts* 5A **36** (nr. Marlborough)
Wilton. *Wilts* 3F **23** (nr. Salisbury)
Wimbish. *Essx* 2F **53**
Wimbish Green. *Essx* 2G **53**
Wimblebury. *Staf* 4E **73**
**Wimbledon**. *G Lon* 3D **38**
Wimblington. *Cambs* 1D **64**
Wimboldsley. *Ches W* 4A **84**
**Wimborne Minster**. *Dors* 2F **15**
Wimborne St Giles. *Dors* 1F **15**
Wimbotsham. *Norf* 5F **77**
Wimpole. *Cambs* 1D **52**
Wimpstone. *Warw* 1H **49**
Wincanton. *Som* 4C **22**
Winceby. *Linc* 4C **88**
Wincham. *Ches W* 3A **84**
Winchburgh. *W Lot* 2D **129**
Winchcombe. *Glos* 3F **49**
Winchelsea. *E Sus* 4D **28**
Winchelsea Beach. *E Sus* 4D **28**
**Winchester**. *Hants* 4C **24** & **203**
Winchet Hill. *Kent* 1B **28**
Winchfield. *Hants* 1F **25**
Winchmore Hill. *Buck* 1A **38**
Winchmore Hill. *G Lon* 1E **39**
Wincle. *Ches E* 4D **84**
Windermere. *Cumb* 5F **103**
Winderton. *Warw* 1B **50**
Windhill. *High* 4H **157**
Windle Hill. *Ches W* 3F **83**
Windlesham. *Surr* 4A **38**
Windley. *Derbs* 1H **73**
Windmill. *Derbs* 3F **85**
Windmill Hill. *E Sus* 4H **27**
Windmill Hill. *Som* 1G **13**
Windrush. *Glos* 4G **49**
**Windsor**. *Wind* 3A **38** & **203**
Windsor Green. *Suff* 5A **66**
Windyedge. *Abers* 4F **153**
Windygates. *Fife* 3F **137**
Windyharbour. *Ches E* 3C **84**
Windyknowe. *W Lot* 3C **128**
Wineham. *W Sus* 3D **26**
Winestead. *E Yor* 2G **95**
Winfarthing. *Norf* 2D **66**
Winford. *IOW* 4D **16**
Winford. *N Som* 5A **34**
Winforton. *Here* 1F **47**
Winfrith Newburgh. *Dors* 4D **14**
Wing. *Buck* 3G **51**
Wing. *Rut* 5F **75**
Wingate. *Dur* 1B **106**
Wingates. *G Man* 4E **91**
Wingates. *Nmbd* 5F **121**
Wingerworth. *Derbs* 4A **86**
Wingfield. *C Beds* 3A **52**
Wingfield. *Suff* 3E **67**
Wingfield. *Wilts* 1D **22**
Wingfield Park. *Derbs* 5A **86**
Wingham. *Kent* 5G **41**
Wingmore. *Kent* 1F **29**
Wingrave. *Buck* 4G **51**
Winkburn. *Notts* 5E **86**
Winkfield. *Brac* 3A **38**
Winkfield Row. *Brac* 4G **37**
Winkhill. *Staf* 5E **85**
Winklebury. *Hants* 1E **24**
Winkleigh. *Devn* 2G **11**
Winksley. *N Yor* 2E **99**
Winkton. *Dors* 3G **15**
Winlaton. *Tyne* 3E **115**
Winlaton Mill. *Tyne* 3E **115**
Winless. *High* 3F **169**
Winmarleigh. *Lanc* 5D **96**
Winnal Common. *Here* 2H **47**
Winnard's Perch. *Corn* 2D **6**
Winnersh. *Wok* 4F **37**
Winnington. *Ches W* 3A **84**
Winnington. *Staf* 2B **72**
Winnothdale. *Staf* 1E **73**
Winscales. *Cumb* 2B **102**
Winscombe. *N Som* 1H **21**
**Winsford**. *Ches W* 4A **84**
Winsford. *Som* 3C **20**
Winsham. *Devn* 3E **19**
Winsham. *Som* 2G **13**
Winshill. *Staf* 3G **73**
Winsh-wen. *Swan* 3F **31**
Winskill. *Cumb* 1G **103**
Winslade. *Hants* 2E **25**
Winsley. *Wilts* 5D **34**
Winslow. *Buck* 3F **51**
Winson. *Glos* 5F **49**
Winson Green. *W Mid* 2E **61**
Winsor. *Hants* 1B **16**
Winster. *Cumb* 5F **103**
Winster. *Derbs* 4G **85**
Winston. *Dur* 3E **105**
Winston. *Suff* 4D **66**
Winstone. *Glos* 5E **49**
Winswell. *Devn* 1E **11**
Winterborne Clenston. *Dors* 2D **14**
Winterborne Herringston. *Dors* 4B **14**
Winterborne Houghton. *Dors* 2D **14**
Winterborne Kingston. *Dors* 3D **14**
Winterborne Monkton. *Dors* 4B **14**
Winterborne St Martin. *Dors* 4B **14**
Winterborne Stickland. *Dors* 2D **14**
Winterborne Whitechurch. *Dors* 2D **14**
Winterborne Zelston. *Dors* 3D **15**
Winterbourne. *S Glo* 3B **34**
Winterbourne. *W Ber* 4C **36**
Winterbourne Abbas. *Dors* 3B **14**
Winterbourne Bassett. *Wilts* 4G **35**
Winterbourne Dauntsey. *Wilts* 3G **23**
Winterbourne Earls. *Wilts* 3G **23**
Winterbourne Gunner. *Wilts* 3G **23**
Winterbourne Monkton. *Wilts* 4G **35**
Winterbourne Steepleton. *Dors* 4B **14**
Winterbourne Stoke. *Wilts* 2F **23**
Winterbrook. *Oxon* 3E **36**
Winterburn. *N Yor* 4B **98**
Winter Gardens. *Essx* 2B **40**
Winterhay Green. *Som* 1G **13**
Winteringham. *N Lin* 2C **94**
Winterley. *Ches E* 5B **84**
Wintersett. *W Yor* 3D **93**
Winterton. *N Lin* 3C **94**
Winterton-on-Sea. *Norf* 4G **79**
Winthorpe. *Linc* 4E **89**
Winthorpe. *Notts* 5F **87**
Winton. *Bour* 3F **15**
Winton. *Cumb* 3A **104**
Winton. *E Sus* 5G **27**
Wintringham. *N Yor* 2C **100**
Winwick. *Cambs* 2A **64**
Winwick. *Nptn* 3D **62**
Winwick. *Warr* 1A **84**
Wirksworth. *Derbs* 5G **85**
Wirswall. *Ches E* 1H **71**
**Wisbech**. *Cambs* 4D **76**
Wisbech St Mary. *Cambs* 5D **76**
Wisborough Green. *W Sus* 3B **26**
Wiseton. *Notts* 2E **86**
**Wishaw**. *N Lan* 4A **128**
Wishaw. *Warw* 1F **61**
Wisley. *Surr* 5B **38**
Wispington. *Linc* 3B **88**
Wissenden. *Kent* 1D **28**
Wissett. *Suff* 3F **67**
Wistanstow. *Shrp* 2G **59**
Wistanswick. *Shrp* 3A **72**
Wistaston. *Ches E* 5A **84**
Wiston. *Pemb* 3E **43**
Wiston. *S Lan* 1B **118**
Wiston. *W Sus* 4C **26**
Wistow. *Cambs* 2B **64**
Wistow. *N Yor* 1F **93**
Wiswell. *Lanc* 1F **91**
Witcham. *Cambs* 2D **64**
Witchampton. *Dors* 2E **15**
Witchford. *Cambs* 3E **65**
**Witham**. *Essx* 4B **54**
Witham Friary. *Som* 2C **22**
Witham on the Hill. *Linc* 4H **75**
Witham St Hughs. *Linc* 4F **87**
Withcall. *Linc* 2B **88**
Witherenden Hill. *E Sus* 3H **27**
Withergate. *Norf* 3E **79**
Witheridge. *Devn* 1B **12**
Witheridge Hill. *Oxon* 3E **37**
Witherley. *Leics* 1H **61**
Withermarsh Green. *Suff* 2D **54**
Withern. *Linc* 2D **88**
Withernsea. *E Yor* 2G **95**
Withernwick. *E Yor* 5F **101**
Withersdale Street. *Suff* 2E **67**
Withersfield. *Suff* 1G **53**
Witherslack. *Cumb* 1D **96**
Withiel. *Corn* 2D **6**
Withiel Florey. *Som* 3C **20**
Withington. *Glos* 4F **49**
Withington. *G Man* 1C **84**
Withington. *Here* 1A **48**
Withington. *Shrp* 4H **71**
Withington. *Staf* 2E **73**
Withington Green. *Ches E* 3C **84**
Withington Marsh. *Here* 1A **48**
Withleigh. *Devn* 1C **12**
Withnell. *Lanc* 2E **91**
Withnell Fold. *Lanc* 2E **90**
Withybrook. *Warw* 2B **62**
Withycombe. *Som* 2D **20**
Withycombe Raleigh. *Devn* 4D **12**
Withyham. *E Sus* 2F **27**
Withypool. *Som* 3B **20**
Witley. *Surr* 1A **26**
Witnesham. *Suff* 5D **66**
**Witney**. *Oxon* 4B **50**
Wittering. *Pet* 5H **75**
Wittersham. *Kent* 3C **28**
Witton. *Norf* 5F **79**
Witton. *Worc* 4C **60**
Witton Bridge. *Norf* 2F **79**
Witton Gilbert. *Dur* 5F **115**
Witton-le-Wear. *Dur* 1E **105**
Witton Park. *Dur* 1E **105**
Wiveliscombe. *Som* 4D **20**
Wivelrod. *Hants* 3E **25**
Wivelsfield. *E Sus* 3E **27**
Wivelsfield Green. *E Sus* 4E **27**
Wivenhoe. *Essx* 3D **54**
Wiveton. *Norf* 1C **78**
Wix. *Essx* 3E **55**
Wixford. *Warw* 5E **61**
Wixhill. *Shrp* 3H **71**
Wixoe. *Suff* 1H **53**
Woburn. *C Beds* 2H **51**
Woburn Sands. *Mil* 2H **51**
**Woking**. *Surr* 5B **38**
**Wokingham**. *Wok* 5G **37**
Wolborough. *Devn* 5B **12**
Woldingham. *Surr* 5E **39**
Wold Newton. *E Yor* 2E **101**
Wold Newton. *NE Lin* 1B **88**
Wolferlow. *Here* 4A **60**
Wolferton. *Norf* 3F **77**
Wolfhill. *Per* 5A **144**
Wolf's Castle. *Pemb* 2D **42**
Wolfsdale. *Pemb* 2D **42**
Wolgarston. *Staf* 4D **72**
Wollaston. *Nptn* 4G **63**
Wollaston. *Shrp* 4F **71**
Wollaston. *W Mid* 2C **60**
Wollaton. *Nott* 1C **74**
Wollerton. *Shrp* 2A **72**
Wollescote. *W Mid* 2D **60**
Wolseley Bridge. *Staf* 3E **73**
Wolsingham. *Dur* 1D **105**
Wolstanton. *Staf* 1C **72**
Wolston. *Warw* 3B **62**
Wolsty. *Cumb* 4C **112**
Wolterton. *Norf* 2D **78**
Wolvercote. *Oxon* 5C **50**
**Wolverhampton**. *W Mid* 1D **60** & **203**
Wolverley. *Shrp* 2G **71**
Wolverley. *Worc* 3C **60**
Wolverton. *Hants* 1D **24**
Wolverton. *Mil* 1G **51**
Wolverton. *Warw* 4G **61**
Wolverton. *Wilts* 3C **22**
Wolverton Common. *Hants* 1D **24**
Wolvesnewton. *Mon* 2H **33**
Wolvey. *Warw* 2B **62**
Wolvey Heath. *Warw* 2B **62**
Wolviston. *Stoc T* 2B **106**
Womaston. *Powy* 4E **59**
Wombleton. *N Yor* 1A **100**
**Wombourne**. *Staf* 1C **60**
**Wombwell**. *S Yor* 4D **93**
Womenswold. *Kent* 5G **41**

# INDEX TO SELECTED PLACES OF INTEREST

(1) A strict alphabetical order is used e.g. Benmore Botanic Gdn. follows Ben Macdui but precedes Ben Nevis.

(2) Entries shown without a main map index reference have the name of the appropriate Town Plan and its page number;
e.g. Ashmolean Mus. of Art & Archaeology (OX1 2PH) . . . . **Oxford 200**
The Town Plan title is not given when this is included in the name of the Place of Interest.

(3) Entries in italics are not named on the map but are shown with a symbol only.
Where this occurs and enclosed in (brackets) are not shown on the map.
Where this occurs the nearest town or village may also be given, unless that name is already included in the name of the Place of Interest.

## SAT NAV POSTCODES

Postcodes (in brackets) are included as a navigation aid to assist Sat Nav users and are supplied on this basis. It should be noted that postcodes have been selected by their proximity to the Place of Interest and that they may not form part of the actual postal address. Drivers should follow the Tourist Brown Signs when available.

## ABBREVIATIONS USED IN THIS INDEX

Garden : Gdn.  Museum : Mus.
Gardens : Gdns.  National : Nat
Park : Pk.

Copyright of Geographers' A-Z Map Company Ltd.

The representation on the maps of a road, track or footpath is no evidence of the existence of a right of way.

No reproduction by any method whatsoever of any part of this publication is permitted without the prior consent of the copyright owners.

Limited Interchange Motorway Junctions are shown on the mapping pages by red junction indicators 2

## M1

| Junction | | |
|---|---|---|
| 2 | Northbound<br>Southbound | No exit, access from A1 only<br>No access, exit to A1 only |
| 4 | Northbound<br>Southbound | No exit, access from A41 only<br>No access, exit to A41 only |
| 6a | Northbound<br>Southbound | No exit, access from M25 only<br>No access, exit to M25 only |
| 17 | Northbound<br>Southbound | No access, exit to M45 only<br>No exit, access from M45 only |
| 19 | Northbound<br>Southbound | Exit to M6 only, access from A14 only<br>Access from M6 only, exit to A14 only |
| 21a | Northbound<br>Southbound | No access, exit to A46 only<br>No exit, access from A46 only |
| 24a | Northbound<br>Southbound | Access from A50 only<br>Exit to A50 only |
| 35a | Northbound<br>Southbound | No access, exit to A616 only<br>No exit, access from A616 only |
| 43 | Northbound<br>Southbound | Exit to M621 only<br>Access from M621 only |
| 48 | Eastbound<br>Westbound | Exit to A1(M) northbound only<br>Access from A1(M) southbound only |

## M2

| Junction | | |
|---|---|---|
| 1 | Eastbound<br>Westbound | Access from A2 eastbound only<br>Exit to A2 westbound only |

## M3

| Junction | | |
|---|---|---|
| 8 | Eastbound<br>Westbound | No exit, access from A303 only<br>No access, exit to A303 only |
| 10 | Northbound<br>Southbound | No access from A31<br>No exit to A31 |
| 13 | Southbound | No access from A335 to M3 leading to M27 Eastbound |

## M4

| Junction | | |
|---|---|---|
| 1 | Eastbound<br>Westbound | Exit to A4 eastbound only<br>Access from A4 westbound only |
| 21 | Eastbound<br>Westbound | No exit to M48<br>No access from M48 |
| 23 | Eastbound<br>Westbound | No access from M48<br>No exit to M48 |
| 25 | Eastbound<br>Westbound | No exit<br>No access |
| 25a | Eastbound<br>Westbound | No exit<br>No access |
| 29 | Eastbound<br>Westbound | No exit, access from A48(M) only<br>No access, exit to A48(M) only |
| 38 | Westbound | No access, exit to A48 only |
| 39 | Eastbound<br>Westbound | No access or exit<br>No exit, access from A48 only |
| 42 | Eastbound<br>Westbound | No access from A48<br>No exit to A48 |

## M5

| Junction | | |
|---|---|---|
| 10 | Northbound<br>Southbound | No exit, access from A4019 only<br>No access, exit to A4019 only |
| 11a | Southbound | No exit to A417 westbound |
| 18a | Northbound<br>Southbound | No access from M49<br>No exit to M49 |

## M6

| Junction | | |
|---|---|---|
| 3a | Eastbound<br>Westbound | No exit to M6 Toll<br>No access from M6 Toll |
| 4 | Northbound<br><br>Southbound | No exit to M42 northbound<br>No access from M42 southbound<br>No exit to M42<br>No access from M42 southbound |
| 4a | Northbound<br>Southbound | No exit, access from M42 southbound only<br>No access, exit to M42 only |
| 5 | Northbound<br>Southbound | No access, exit to A452 only<br>No exit, access from A452 only |
| 10a | Northbound<br>Southbound | No access, exit to M54 only<br>No exit, access from M54 only |
| 11a | Northbound<br>Southbound | No exit to M6 Toll<br>No access from M6 Toll |
| 20 | Northbound<br>Southbound | No exit to M56 eastbound<br>No access from M56 westbound |
| 24 | Northbound<br>Southbound | No exit, access from A58 only<br>No access, exit to A58 only |
| 25 | Northbound<br>Southbound | No access, exit to A49 only<br>No exit, access from A49 only |
| 30 | Northbound<br>Southbound | No exit, access from M61 northbound only<br>No access, exit to M61 southbound only |
| 31a | Northbound<br>Southbound | No access, exit to B6242 only<br>No exit, access from B6242 only |
| 45 | Northbound<br>Southbound | No access onto A74(M)<br>No exit from A74(M) |

## M6 Toll

| Junction | | |
|---|---|---|
| T1 | Northbound<br>Southbound | No exit<br>No access |
| T2 | Northbound<br>Southbound | No access or exit<br>No access |
| T5 | Northbound<br>Southbound | No exit<br>No access |
| T7 | Northbound<br>Southbound | No access from A5<br>No exit |
| T8 | Northbound<br>Southbound | No exit to A460 northbound<br>No exit |

## M8

| Junction | | |
|---|---|---|
| 6 | Eastbound<br>Westbound | No exit, access only<br>No access, exit only |
| 6 | Eastbound<br>Westbound | No exit, access only<br>No access, exit only |
| 6a | Eastbound<br>Westbound | No access, exit only<br>No exit, access only |
| 7 | Eastbound<br>Westbound | No access, exit only<br>No exit, access only |
| 7a | Eastbound<br><br>Westbound | No exit, access from A725 Northbound only<br>No access, exit to A725 Southbound only |
| 8 | Eastbound<br>Westbound | No exit to M73 northbound<br>No access from M73 southbound |
| 9 | Eastbound<br>Westbound | No access, exit only<br>No exit, access only |
| 13 | Eastbound<br>Westbound | No access from M80 southbound<br>No exit to M80 northbound |
| 14 | Eastbound<br>Westbound | No access, exit only<br>No exit, access only |
| 16 | Eastbound<br>Westbound | No exit, access only<br>No access, exit only |
| 17 | Eastbound<br>Westbound | No exit, access from A82 only<br>No access, exit to A82 only |
| 18 | Westbound | No exit, access only |
| 19 | Eastbound<br>Westbound | No exit to A814 eastbound<br>No access from A814 westbound |
| 20 | Eastbound<br>Westbound | No exit, access only<br>No access, exit only |
| 21 | Eastbound<br>Westbound | No access, exit only<br>No exit, access only |
| 22 | Eastbound<br>Westbound | No exit, access from M77 only<br>No access, exit to M77 only |
| 23 | Eastbound<br>Westbound | No exit, access from B768 only<br>No access, exit to B768 only |
| 25 | Eastbound &<br>Westbound | Access from A739 southbound only<br>Exit to A739 northbound only |
| 25a | Eastbound<br>Westbound | Access only<br>Exit only |
| 28 | Eastbound<br>Westbound | No exit, access from airport only<br>No access, exit to airport only |

## M9

| Junction | | |
|---|---|---|
| 2 | Northbound<br>Southbound | No exit, access from B8046 only<br>No access, exit to B8046 only |
| 3 | Northbound<br>Southbound | No access, exit to A803 only<br>No exit, access from A803 only |
| 6 | Northbound<br>Southbound | No exit, access only<br>No access, exit to A905 only |
| 8 | Northbound<br>Southbound | No access, exit to M876 only<br>No exit, access from M876 only |

## M11

| Junction | | |
|---|---|---|
| 4 | Northbound<br>Southbound | No exit, access from A406 eastbound only<br>No access, exit to A406 westbound only |
| 5 | Northbound<br>Southbound | No access, exit to A1168 only<br>No exit, access from A1168 only |
| 8a | Northbound<br>Southbound | No access, exit only<br>No exit, access only |
| 9 | Northbound<br>Southbound | No access, exit only<br>No exit, access only |
| 13 | Northbound<br>Southbound | No access, exit only<br>No exit, access only |
| 14 | Northbound<br><br>Southbound | No access from A428 eastbound<br>No exit to A428 westbound<br>No exit, access from A428 eastbound only |

## M20

| Junction | | |
|---|---|---|
| 2 | Eastbound<br><br>Westbound | No access, exit to A20 only<br>(access via M26 Junction 2a)<br>No exit, access only (exit via M26 Jun.2a) |
| 3 | Eastbound<br>Westbound | No exit, access from M26 eastbound only<br>No access, exit to M26 westbound only |
| 11a | Eastbound<br>Westbound | No access from Channel Tunnel<br>No exit to Channel Tunnel |

## M23

| Junction | | |
|---|---|---|
| 7 | Northbound<br>Southbound | No exit to A23 southbound<br>No access from A23 northbound |

## M25

| Junction | | |
|---|---|---|
| 5 | Clockwise<br>Anti-clockwise | No exit to M26 eastbound<br>No access from M26 westbound |
| Spur to A21 | Northbound<br>Southbound | No exit to M26 eastbound<br>No access from M26 westbound |
| 19 | Clockwise<br>Anti-clockwise | No access, exit only<br>No exit, access only |
| 21 | Clockwise &<br>Anti-clockwise | No exit to M1 southbound<br>No access from M1 northbound |
| 31 | Northbound<br>Southbound | No access, exit only (access via Jun.30)<br>No exit, access only (exit via Jun.30) |

## M26

**Junction with M25** (M25 Jun.5)

| | | |
|---|---|---|
| Eastbound | No access from M25 clockwise or spur from A21 northbound |
| Westbound | No exit to M25 anti-clockwise or spur to A21 southbound |

**Junction with M20** (M20 Jun.3)

| | |
|---|---|
| Eastbound | No exit to M20 westbound |
| Westbound | No access from M20 eastbound |

## M27

| Junction | | |
|---|---|---|
| 4 | Eastbound &<br>Westbound | No exit to A33 southbound (Southampton)<br>No access from A33 northbound |
| 10 | Eastbound<br>Westbound | No exit, access from A32 only<br>No access, exit to A32 only |

## M40

| Junction | | |
|---|---|---|
| 3 | North-Westbound<br>South-Eastbound | No access, exit to A40 only<br>No exit, access from A40 only |
| 7 | N.W bound<br>S.E bound | No exit, access only<br>No exit, access only |
| 13 | N.W bound<br>S.E bound | No access, exit only<br>No exit, access only |
| 14 | N.W bound<br>S.E bound | No exit, access only<br>No access, exit only |
| 16 | N.W bound<br>S.E bound | No exit, access only<br>No access, exit only |

## M42

| Junction | | |
|---|---|---|
| 1 | Eastbound<br>Westbound | No exit<br>No access |
| 7 | Northbound<br>Southbound | No access, exit to M6 only<br>No exit, access from M6 northbound only |
| 8 | Northbound<br>Southbound | No exit, access from M6 southbound only<br>Exit to M6 nothbound only<br>Access from M6 southbound only |

## M45

**Junction with M1** (M1 Jun.17)

| | |
|---|---|
| Eastbound | No exit to M1 northbound |
| Westbound | No access from M1 southbound |

**Junction with A45 east of Dunchurch**

| | |
|---|---|
| Eastbound | No access, exit to A45 only |
| Westbound | No exit, access from A45 northbound only |

## M48

**Junction with M4** (M4 Jun.21)

| | |
|---|---|
| Eastbound | No exit to M4 westbound |
| Westbound | No access from M4 eastbound |

**Junction with M4** (M4 Jun.23)

| | |
|---|---|
| Eastbound | No access from M4 westbound |
| Westbound | No exit to M4 eastbound |

## M53

| Junction | | |
|---|---|---|
| 11 | Northbound &<br>Southbound | No access from M56 eastbound,<br>no exit to M56 westbound |

## M56

| Junction | | |
|---|---|---|
| 1 | Eastbound<br><br>S.E bound<br>Westbound | No exit to M60 N.W bound<br>No exit to A34 southbound<br>No access from A34 northbound<br>No access from M60 |
| 2 | Eastbound<br>Westbound | No exit, access from A560 only<br>No access, exit to A560 only |
| 3 | Eastbound<br>Westbound | No access, exit only<br>No exit, access only |
| 4 | Eastbound<br>Westbound | No exit, access only<br>No access, exit only |
| 7 | Westbound | No access, exit only |
| 8 | Eastbound<br>Westbound | No access or exit<br>No exit, access from A556 only |
| 9 | Eastbound<br>Westbound | No access from M6 northbound<br>No exit to M60 southbound |
| 10a | Northbound<br>Southbound | No exit, access only<br>No access, exit only |
| 15 | Eastbound<br>Westbound | No exit to M53<br>No access from M53 |

## M57

| Junction | | |
|---|---|---|
| 3 | Northbound<br>Southbound | No exit, access only<br>No access, exit only |
| 5 | Northbound<br>Southbound | No exit, access from A580 westbound only<br>No access, exit to A580 eastbound only |

## M58

| Junction | | |
|---|---|---|
| 1 | Eastbound<br>Westbound | No exit, access from A506 only<br>No access, exit to A506 only |

## M60

| Junction | | |
|---|---|---|
| 2 | N.E bound<br>S.W bound | No access, exit to A560 only<br>No exit, access from A560 only |
| 3 | Eastbound<br>Westbound | No access from A34 southbound<br>No exit to A34 northbound |
| 4 | Eastbound<br><br>Westbound | No exit to M56 S.W bound<br>No exit to A34 northbound<br>No access from A34 southbound<br>No access from M56 eastbound |
| 5 | N.W bound<br>S.E bound | No access from or exit to A5103 southbound<br>No access from or exit to A5103 northbound |
| 14 | Eastbound<br><br>Westbound | No exit to A580<br>No access from A580 westbound<br>No exit to A580 eastbound<br>No access from A580 |
| 16 | Eastbound<br>Westbound | No exit, access from A666 only<br>No access, exit to A666 only |
| 20 | Eastbound<br>Westbound | No access from A664<br>No exit to A664 |
| 22 | Westbound | No access from A62 |
| 25 | S.W bound | No access from A560 / A6017 |
| 26 | N.E bound | No access or exit |
| 27 | N.E bound<br>S.W bound | No access, exit only<br>No exit, access only |

## M61

| Junction | | |
|---|---|---|
| 2&3 | N.W bound<br>S.E bound | No access from A580 eastbound<br>No exit to A580 westbound |

**Junction with M6** (M6 Jun.30)

| | |
|---|---|
| N.W bound | No exit to M6 southbound |
| S.E bound | No access from M6 northbound |

## M62

| Junction | | |
|---|---|---|
| 23 | Eastbound<br>Westbound | No access, exit to A640 only<br>No exit, access from A640 only |

## M65

| Junction | | |
|---|---|---|
| 9 | N.E bound<br>S.W bound | No access, exit to A679 only<br>No exit, access from A679 only |
| 11 | N.E bound<br>S.W bound | No exit, access only<br>No access, exit only |

## M66

| Junction | | |
|---|---|---|
| 1 | Northbound<br>Southbound | No access, exit to A56 only<br>No exit, access from A56 only |

## M67

| Junction | | |
|---|---|---|
| 1 | Eastbound<br>Westbound | Access from A57 eastbound only<br>Exit to A57 westbound only |
| 1a | Eastbound<br>Westbound | No access, exit to A6017 only<br>No exit, access from A6017 only |
| 2 | Eastbound<br>Westbound | No exit, access from A57 only<br>No access, exit to A57 only |

## M69

| Junction | | |
|---|---|---|
| 2 | N.E bound<br>S.W bound | No exit, access from B4669 only<br>No access, exit to B4669 only |

## M73

| Junction | | |
|---|---|---|
| 1 | Southbound | No exit to A721 eastbound |
| 2 | Northbound<br><br>Southbound | No access from M8 eastbound<br>No exit to A89 eastbound<br>No exit to M8 westbound<br>No access from A89 westbound |
| 3 | Northbound<br>Southbound | No exit to A80 S.W bound<br>No access from A80 N.E bound |

## M74

| Junction | | |
|---|---|---|
| 1 | Eastbound<br>Westbound | No access from M8 Westbound<br>No exit to M8 Westbound |
| 3 | Eastbound<br>Westbound | No exit<br>No access |
| 7 | Northbound<br>Southbound | No exit, access from A72 only<br>No access, exit to A72 only |
| 9 | Northbound<br>Southbound | No access or exit<br>No access, exit to B7078 only |
| 10 | Southbound | No exit, access from B7078 only |
| 11 | Northbound<br>Southbound | No exit, access from B7078 only<br>No access, exit to B7078 only |
| 12 | Northbound<br>Southbound | No access, exit to A70 only<br>No exit, access from A70 only |

## M77

**Junction with M8** (M8 Jun.22)

| | |
|---|---|
| Northbound | No exit to M8 westbound |
| Southbound | No access from M8 eastbound |

| Junction | | |
|---|---|---|
| 4 | Northbound<br>Southbound | No exit<br>No access |
| 6 | Northbound<br>Southbound | No exit to A77<br>No access from A77 |
| 7 | Northbound | No access from A77<br>No exit to A77 |

## M80

| Junction | | |
|---|---|---|
| 1 | Northbound<br>Southbound | No access from M8 westbound<br>No exit to M8 eastbound |
| 4a | Northbound<br>Southbound | No access<br>No exit |
| 6a | Northbound<br>Southbound | No exit<br>No access |
| 8 | Northbound<br>Southbound | No access from M876<br>No exit to M876 |

## M90

| Junction | | |
|---|---|---|
| 1 | Northbound<br>Southbound | No exit<br>No Access from A90 |
| 2a | Northbound<br>Southbound | No access, exit to A92 only<br>No exit, access from A92 only |
| 7 | Northbound<br>Southbound | No exit, access from A91 only<br>No access, exit to A91 only |
| 8 | Northbound<br>Southbound | No access, exit to A91 only<br>No exit, access from A91 only |
| 10 | Northbound<br><br>Southbound | No access from A912<br>Exit to A912 northbound only<br>No exit to A912<br>Access from A912 southbound only |

## M180

| Junction | | |
|---|---|---|
| 1 | Eastbound<br>Westbound | No access, exit only<br>No exit, access from A18 only |

## M606

| Junction | | |
|---|---|---|
| 2 | Northbound | No access, exit only |

## M621

| Junction | | |
|---|---|---|
| 2a | Eastbound<br>Westbound | No exit, access only<br>No access, exit only |
| 4 | Southbound | No exit |
| 5 | Northbound<br>Southbound | No access, exit to A61 only<br>No exit, access from A61 only |
| 6 | Northbound<br>Southbound | No exit, access only<br>No access, exit only |
| 7 | Eastbound<br>Westbound | No access, exit only<br>No exit, access only |
| 8 | Northbound<br>Southbound | No access, exit only<br>No exit, access only |

## M876

**Junction with M80** (M80 Jun.5)

| | |
|---|---|
| N.E bound | No access from M80 southbound |
| S.W bound | No exit to M80 northbound |

**Junction with M9** (M9 Jun.8)

| | |
|---|---|
| N.E bound | No exit to M9 northbound |
| S.W bound | No access from M9 southbound |

## A1(M)

**Hertfordshire Section**

| Junction | | |
|---|---|---|
| 2 | Northbound<br>Southbound | No access, exit only<br>No exit, access from A1001 only |
| 3 | Southbound | No access, exit only |
| 5 | Northbound<br>Southbound | No exit, access only<br>No access or exit |

**Cambridgeshire Section**

| Junction | | |
|---|---|---|
| 14 | Northbound<br>Southbound | No exit, access only<br>No access, exit only |

**Leeds Section**

| Junction | | |
|---|---|---|
| 40 | Southbound | Exit to A1 southbound only |
| 43 | Northbound<br>Southbound | Access from M1 eastbound only<br>Exit to M1 westbound only |

**Durham Section**

| Junction | | |
|---|---|---|
| 57 | Northbound<br>Southbound | No access, exit to A66(M) only<br>No exit, access from A66(M) |
| 65 | Northbound<br><br>Southbound | Exit to A1 N.W bound and to A194(M) only<br>Access from A1 S.E bound and from A194(M) only |

## A3(M)

| Junction | | |
|---|---|---|
| 4 | Northbound<br>Southbound | No access, exit only<br>No exit, access only |

## Aston Expressway A38(M)

**Junction with Victoria Road, Aston**

| | |
|---|---|
| Northbound | No exit, access only |
| Southbound | No access, exit only |

## A48(M)

**Junction with M4** (M4 Jun.29)

| | |
|---|---|
| N.E bound | Exit to M4 eastbound only |
| S.W bound | Access from M4 westbound only |

| Junction | | |
|---|---|---|
| 29a | N.E bound<br>S.W bound | Access from A48 eastbound only<br>Exit to A48 westbound only |

## Mancunian Way A57(M)

**Junction with A34 Brook Street, Manchester**

| | |
|---|---|
| Eastbound | No access, exit to A34 Brook Street, southbound only |
| Westbound | No exit, access only |

## Leeds Inner Ring Road A58(M)

**Junction with Park Lane / Westgate**

| | |
|---|---|
| Southbound | No access, exit only |

## Leeds Inner Ring Road A64(M) (continuation of A58(M))

**Junction with A58 Clay Pit Lane**

| | |
|---|---|
| Eastbound | No access |
| Westbound | No exit |

## A66(M)

**Junction with A1(M)** (A1(M) Jun.57)

| | |
|---|---|
| N.E bound | Access from A1(M) northbound only |
| S.W bound | Exit to A1(M) southbound only |

## A74(M)

| Junction | | |
|---|---|---|
| 18 | Northbound<br>Southbound | No access<br>No exit |

## Newcastle Central Motorway A167(M)

**Junction with Camden Street**

| | |
|---|---|
| Northbound | No exit, access only |
| Southbound | No access or exit |

## A194(M)

**Junction with A1(M)** (A1(M) Jun.65) **and A1 Gateshead Western By-Pass**

| | |
|---|---|
| Northbound | Access from A1(M) only |
| Southbound | Exit to A1(M) only |

# Northern Ireland

## M1

| Junction | | |
|---|---|---|
| 3 | Northbound<br>Southbound | No exit, access only<br>No access, exit only |
| 7 | Westbound | No access, exit only |

## M2

| Junction | | |
|---|---|---|
| 2 | Eastbound<br>Westbound | No access to M5 northbound<br>No exit to M5 southbound |

## M5

| Junction | | |
|---|---|---|
| 2 | Northbound<br>Southbound | No access from M2 eastbound<br>No exit to M2 westbound |

# Did you know what else we do?

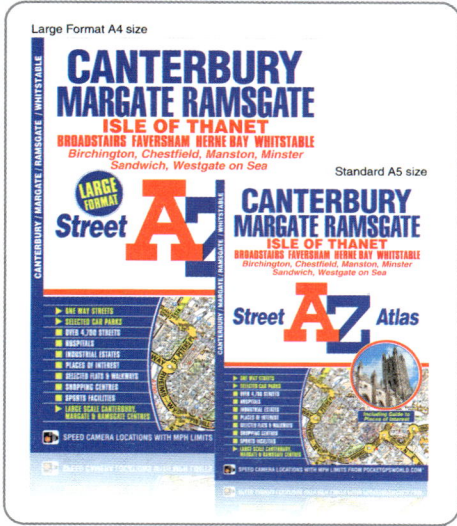

## Large Format Atlases

**Would you benefit from an A-Z large print map?**

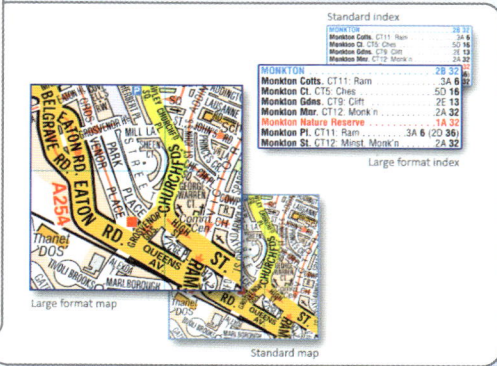

## Gifts

**A growing range of gift ideas**

## Historical Maps

**Mapping from the past**

## Digital Mapping Data

**Base mapping digital tiles for GIS applications**

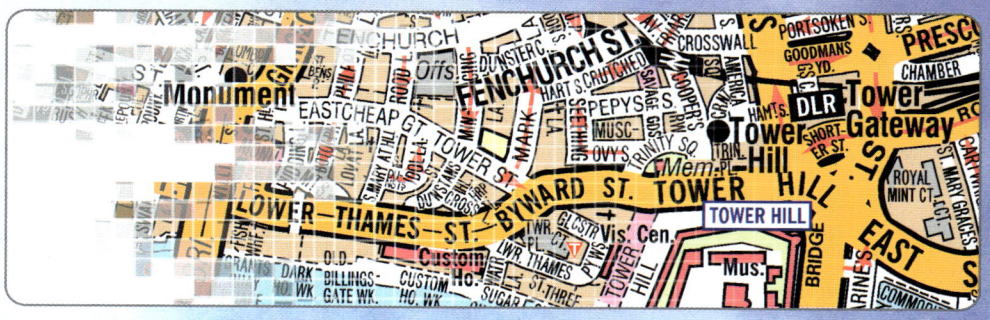

## Home Decor

**Maps on canvas and wallpaper to decorate your home or office**

## Print on demand maps

**A bespoke A-Z map service**
Enabling customers to order and print area specific current and historic map products on demand